American Economic Policy in the 1990s

American Economic Policy in the 1990s

Editors:

Jeffrey Frankel

Peter Orszag

MIT Press
Cambridge, Massachusetts

This book was set in Palatino on 3B2 by Asco Typesetters, Hong Kong, and was printed and bound in the United States of America.

Library of Congress Cataloging-in-Publication Data

American economic policy in the 1990s / editors, Jeffrey Frankel, Peter Orszag.
    p. cm.
Includes bibliographical references and index.
ISBN 0-262-06230-5
1. United States—Economic policy—1993–2001. 2. United States—Economic conditions—1981–2001. I. Frankel, Jeffrey A. II. Orszag, Peter R.
HC106.82.A456 2002
338.973′009′049—dc21

2002019898

Contents

Preface and
Acknowledgments

The genesis of this project was a conversation between Ira Jackson and Jeff Frankel in the courtyard of the Kennedy School of Government at Harvard University in mid-2000. Jackson, having recently assumed the directorship of the Center for Business and Government, was looking for innovative ways to promote the study of economic policy, while bridging the gap between the government and the rest of society. Frankel, having recently returned to academia from a stint in the White House, believed that much that is of scholarly interest could be learned by interacting with high-level policy-makers—not while they were in office and could not speak freely, but soon after they left office. The outcome was the idea of a retrospective on economic policy in the just-completed decade, which would enlist both policy-makers and top-level academic economists.

We are indebted to Ira for his unwavering support for this project. Early enthusiasm for the idea was also expressed by a number of former officials in the Bill Clinton administration, particularly Robert Rubin, and some former members of earlier administrations, particularly Martin Feldstein. Peter Orszag was speedily signed on as coeditor for the project. And the conference was held June 27–30, 2001, at the Kennedy School.

The topic of intellectual property gained new importance in the 1990s, as several chapters in this volume show. Sometimes innovators don't file patents, and the rest of us benefit. Two examples are relevant. First, 20 years ago, Ira Jackson was instrumental in the invention of the Forum, the atrium that is the architectural heart of the Kennedy School, which is used for public events and has been widely copied elsewhere. Several of the sessions of the June 2001 conference took place in the Forum. Second, Martin Feldstein invented the "wise man" style of research conference, the most notable example of which was a meeting of policy-makers and economists ten years ago that produced the volume *American Economic Policy in the 1980s* (University of Chicago Press, 1994). Our conference was closely modeled on this earlier project, and we would like to acknowledge our intellectual debt to Feldstein. The one note-worthy respect in which the ground rules for our project differed from his was that our participants could take policy positions: they could pass judgment on decisions made in the 1990s or make recommendations for the future—provided only that their discussion of the issues was fair and balanced.

We would like to thank the authors and other participants, all very busy people, for putting up with a very rigorous timetable, which allowed the con-ference and publication of this volume to take place while the 1990s were still fresh in everyone's mind.

For financial support, we are indebted not only to the Center for Business and Government, but also to the Robert Wood Johnson Foundation and the Fannie Mae Foundation. We would like to acknowledge the hard work of CBG staff members Cathey Park, Amy Christofer, and Shannon Quinn, and the executive director, Dow Davis. Carol Knell worked especially hard getting the manuscript in shape for publication, for which we are grateful. Special thanks are also due to a number of graduate students for acting as rapporteurs for the discussion: Joseph E. Aldy, Joseph Booth, Sheila Cavanagh, Yu-Chin Chen, Andrew R. Feldman, David M. Linsenmeier, Fiona Paua, and Ayako Saiki. They contributed importantly to the volume and should say so on their curricula vitae.

Perhaps somewhere on the list of many people who helped make this con-ference and volume a success are the names of those who, 10 years from now, will decide to record the history of American economic policy in the new decade.

Introduction

Decades seem to take on characteristics. The 1970s make us think of oil shocks and Watergate, and the 1980s of supply-side economics and the end of the cold war. How will historians—or economic historians, at any rate—remember the 1990s?

It is not too soon to predict. The New Economy and Greenspan. The Internet, dot coms, and IPOs. The cell phone and the Palm Pilot. Policy-wonk slogans, some carefully planned and some unplanned: "The Economy, Stupid"; "The era of big government is over"; and "Save Social Security First." The Contract with America and the Gingrich revolution. NAFTA and the "giant sucking sound." The Asian crisis. Tobacco litigation and the Microsoft trial.

The two Clinton terms occupied most of the 1990s. Unquestionably, history will remember this period as a time of economic accomplishment. Between 1993 and 2000 the United States exhibited the best economic performance of the past three decades. In 2000 the U.S. economic expansion surpassed in length the expansion of the 1960s, and thus became the longest on record. During Clinton's second term, real economic growth averaged 4.5 percent per year, and unemployment fell to 4 percent, the level that had been specified as the goal of national policy by the Humphrey-Hawkins legislation three decades earlier. During the early 1990s economists would have considered these outcomes wildly unattainable.

Strong growth and low unemployment were particularly remarkable because they were accompanied by structural budget surpluses and low inflation. Long expansions have historically been fueled in large part by expansionary fiscal or monetary policies, with the result that, by their six-year mark, debt ratios and inflation rates had risen to high levels, sowing the seeds of a subsequent contraction. Furthermore, productivity growth typically slows as an expansion matures. The 1990s American boom, to the contrary, was led by private-sector spending and private-sector employment. And for the first time in three decades, productivity growth rose substantially in the late 1990s, despite the length of the expansion at that point. The cause of this acceleration in productivity is still the subject of debate. (Section III of this introduction briefly catalogs the factors that are likely to have contributed to the strong performance of the U.S. economy during the 1990s.)

To be sure, some observers found cause for concern in various aspects of economic performance during the 1990s. Personal bankruptcies climbed, the personal saving rate plummeted (as measured in the national income statistics), the trade deficit expanded dramatically, and the stock market may well have become substantially overvalued. Overall, however, U.S. economic performance during the 1990s was outstanding.

The reader may wonder whether the subject of this book is the years 1991–2000 or the Clinton administration per se (1993–2000). The answer is that it examines both. The period 1990–2000 approximates a complete business cycle. The economy was close to potential in early 1990, before Iraq invaded Kuwait. The recession of 1990–91 and the continued high unemployment rates over the two years after the recession had technically ended—which initially tarred the expansion with the label "jobless recovery"—are widely thought to have cost George Bush the 1992 election. The years 1990–92 thus set the stage for the years 1993–2000. This generalization is true in macroeconomic terms, as well as in many of the specific areas of policy addressed by chapters of this book. By the year 2000, the economy had returned to approximately the same point in the business cycle it had occupied in 1990.[1] Incidentally, the pattern of recession in the early years of the decade, followed by steady growth in the remainder, repeated the pattern of the 1960s, 1970s, and 1980s.

I   The Goal of the Book

The goal of *American Economic Policy in the 1990s* is to provide a preliminary history of U.S. economic policy-making during the decade. If it is true, as often said, that journalists have already written the first draft of history, then this volume provides the second draft.

The book is divided into 14 chapters in addition to this introduction. Each of the chapters examines a different area of economic policy. In each area, questions to be addressed include the following:

· What were the alternative options under consideration?

· What were their pros and cons?

---

1. Unemployment reached 4.0 percent in 2000. (In three months of that year it dipped to 3.9 percent.) Unemployment began to rise in the following year. The Business Cycle Dating Committee of the National Bureau of Economic Research has found that the ten-year expansion ended in March 2001.

• What decision was made?

• Why was that decision made? What were the relevant economic arguments, and what was the political economy? Who were the political interest groups and other major players, and how did they interact?

• Were other options missing?

• Can one make a judgment on whether the decision was the right one, or how the policy could have been implemented differently?

• Are there lessons for the future?

One might think that many observers—journalists, op-ed writers, social scientists, historians, and others—would address these same questions. In fact, the questions are rarely posed or answered. For example, American political journalists, in their desire to be immune from charges of political bias, often prefer to avoid such questions (at least in print) because answering them requires value judgments. Op-ed writers, in part because of space constraints inconsistent with a complete analysis of the issues, typically build a case that on the surface makes the decision-makers look foolish but that does not fully address one side of the trade-off or another. Social scientists often employ models that abstract from the detail that determines real-life decisions, and that are thus unable to help policy-makers with the actual decisions they face.[2] And some historians now appear to believe that the actions of policy-makers do not merit proportionately more attention, per capita, than the actions of the populace at large.

This volume is thus a unique attempt to answer the questions posed in the preceding bullet points. We address the questions in an environment that seems likely to obtain insightful answers: with the direct involvement of those who made the policy decisions, as well as knowledgeable outsiders. A majority of the contributors to this volume were direct players in the 1990s; the rest are there largely to keep the first group honest—as critics or holders of similar positions in earlier administrations, or as disinterested arbiters and analysts. One way to view the volume is thus a "debriefing" of those who made the history, with knowledgeable outsiders involved to ensure the accuracy of the debriefing.

---

2. Most of the questions faced by policy-makers involve marginal changes from the political status quo. Yet much of the outside academic research upon which policy-makers could potentially draw is not particularly helpful in evaluating such questions. As Herbert Stein once wrote, a presidential economic advisor "must arrive at conclusions relevant to his local and temporal limits, and he gets little help in that from the body of economics in the journal mill. Generally, he must 'roll his own' conclusions from his observations and experience."

II Clintonomics

Arguably, the Clinton administration had an overarching vision. It sought to adopt some of the promarket orientation associated with the ascendancy of the Republicans in the 1980s and marry it with traditional Democratic values such as concern for the environment and a more progressive income distribution. This combination made sense from an economic viewpoint. Standard textbook economics says that environmental externalities, anticompetitive practices, and other market failures or social goals require government involvement, while everything else should be left to the market.[3] Yet it produced tension within the administration and with traditional Democratic constituencies. The "softhearted" and "hardheaded" components of the strategy were often in conflict, as evidenced by the debate over welfare reform, corporate responsibility, trade and the environment, and deficit reduction as an alternative to aggressive public investments.

The 1993 budget package offers perhaps the most vivid example of the underlying vision of—but also the tensions inherent in—the Clintonomics approach. The 1993 budget agreement was politically difficult. Democrats feared that it might cost them their positions in Congress, a fear that eventually turned out to be accurate in some cases. By the end of the 1990s, however, Democrats had largely embraced what one pundit called the "progressive fiscal conservatism" of the 1993 package. Such progressive fiscal conservatism combines modest attempts at redistribution (the progressive component) and budget discipline (the fiscal conservative component). Thus the 1993 package included significant spending reductions and tax increases. But it concentrated the tax increases on upper-income taxpayers, while substantially expanding the Earned Income Tax Credit, Head Start, and other government programs aimed at lower earners.

The experience of the 1990s eventually convinced even many liberal-leaning policy-makers that the progressive fiscal conservatism at the heart of Clintonomics offered an auspicious alternative to more traditional Democratic fiscal policies, which had emphasized government spending and public investment rather than fiscal discipline and private investment. One explanation for the shift may be that fiscal discipline had traditionally been presented as offering long-term benefits in exchange for short-term costs, a calculus that is not appealing in a political context. But as Douglas W. Elmendorf, Jeffrey B. Liebman, and David W. Wilcox describe in their chapter on fiscal policy and Social Security (Chapter 2), fiscal discipline in the 1990s appeared to promote

---

3. The weights to be placed on these goals, of course, must be determined by society, not by economists.

strong economic performance *even in the short run*. The short-run stimulative effect of long-run deficit reduction packages with accommodating monetary policy brought potential benefits for lower-income workers and others dispro-portionately affected by cyclical fluctuations in the economy. It thus relieved some of the tension inherent in progressive fiscal conservatism. Since economic benefits of long-term fiscal discipline appeared to manifest themselves even in the short run, sound economic strategy was also a viable political strategy. (President Clinton urged supporters to "vote Democratic so that they could live like Republicans.")

Despite the conflicts in Clintonomics, or perhaps partly as a reflection of them, the combination of fiscal discipline and progressive policies made sense from a political viewpoint. If Democratic leaders in the 1970s and 1980s had often lost office by deviating too far to the "left" of the median American voter, and if Republican leaders since 1996 have often lost political support by devi-ating too far to the "right," Bill Clinton's policies were more in tune with the preferences of the median voter. This positioning undoubtedly contributed to his generally high popularity ratings and electoral success.

Indeed, critics of President Clinton often argued that he was *too* much in tune with the median voter—that he allowed polls and public opinion to determine policy positions. But it would not be right to say that he never took positions that differed from what he thought the public wanted. The Mexican bailout of January 1995 provides perhaps the most vivid example. Chapter 4, by J. Brad-ford DeLong and Barry Eichengreen, argues that management of this and sub-sequent financial crises in emerging markets turned out, quite unexpectedly, to be the second most important accomplishment of the administration, after elimination of the budget deficit. But it was not popular.

Critics of Clintonomics also argued that it was consumed with "nano"-level, or small-bore, policies, such as targeted tax cuts or minor changes to existing programs. The emphasis on small-bore policies reflected several fundamental forces.

First, the defining events in the administration's first two years were the enactment of the 1993 budget agreement and the failure to enact the admin-istration's Health Security Act. The fiscal discipline created by the 1990 budget agreement and extended by the 1993 budget deal substantially reduced the scope for policy-makers to create or expand programs in a dramatic fashion. As a result, the natural tendency of policy-makers to "do" something, or at least to be viewed as doing something, was subsequently channeled into small-bore activities. The policies of the later years are therefore partly a reflection of the successful macro policy of 1990 and 1993. Furthermore, the budget agreements also created pressure for emphasizing targeted tax cuts rather than spending programs within the sphere of small-bore policies. As explained by Eugene Steuerle in his treatment of tax policy in the 1990s (Chapter 3), the budget agreements of 1990, 1993, and 1997 imposed tight limits on discretionary spending, but allowed tax cuts as long as they were coupled with "offsets" (reductions in entitlement spending or increases in other taxes). The budget rules, combined with the political economy favoring tax cuts rather than spending, biased policy-makers toward narrowly targeted tax cuts. Targeted tax credits were thus used in areas such as higher education (the Hope scholarship and the lifelong learning credit) and environmental research and development efforts (the proposed tax credit for high-mileage vehicles) that would traditionally have been addressed through spending programs.

The second reason for the emphasis on small-bore issues was that, as explained in Chapter 12 by David Cutler and Jonathan Gruber, the failure of the Health Security Act in 1994 convinced policy-makers in the Clinton administration that it was wiser to attempt small changes than large ones, since the larger ones were unlikely to be passed. Within health care, the upshot was a focus on providing health insurance coverage to women and children first. This approach (which Cutler and Gruber label the *Titanic* strategy) continued a trend that preceded the Clinton administration: throughout the mid- and late 1980s, policy-makers had successively loosened access to the Medicaid program for poor children and mothers.

The basic continuity of policy across administrations extends into many other areas. Often a new president, notwithstanding attacks on his predecessor during the election campaign, discovers not long after taking office that there turn out to have been good reasons for the way some things were done. Robert Z. Lawrence, for example, discusses such continuity in the context of international trade in Chapter 5.

Third, the Republican takeover of Congress in 1994, the so-called Gingrich revolution, affected administration strategy. In the face of Republican opposition to major Democratic initiatives, the administration was forced to adopt more modest goals in many areas. The major domestic exception was welfare reform, which is discussed in Chapter 11 by Rebecca M. Blank and David T. Ellwood. Welfare reform was opposed by many traditional Democrats and may therefore support the general point that the political split between the executive and legislative branches precluded dramatic policy shifts toward "Democratic" policies; given Republican control of Congress, enactment of significant changes seemed possible only when the executive branch was willing to adopt a "Republican" policy. Some Republicans complained that Clinton was co-opting their issues. But it is hard to see why a move toward the position held by the median voters is inherently suspect; it could be viewed as democracy at its best.

This volume focuses primarily on the executive branch. As most of the chapters make clear, however, the executive branch does not exist in a vacuum. The constraints imposed by, and policies favored by, Congress strongly condition executive-branch policy-making.

Fourth, small-bore initiatives often represented sound political strategy in the context of larger budget and programmatic reductions. For example, as Joseph P. Newhouse describes in Chapter 13, on Medicare during the 1990s, it was estimated that the Balanced Budget Agreement of 1997 would reduce Medicare spending by $385 billion over 10 years. Yet it also included small expansions in certain benefits—such as coverage for prostate cancer screening, annual rather than biannual mammograms, and annual pap smears—that helped to generate support for the overall package. The administration's presentations tended to emphasize the expansions almost as much as the overall reductions, despite the dramatically different scales of the two policies. Whether the small-bore policies were necessary in order to make the overall package politically acceptable, and therefore whether the small-bore policies played a critical economic as well as political role, is an important question. In some cases, the complexity created by the small-bore policies was arguably the cost necessary for enacting a broader set of economically beneficial policies.

Finally, it is important to emphasize that many individual policy questions properly merit at most a small-scale government response. The cumulative effect of even small-bore policies can be significant. In information technology, for example, Pamela Samuelson and Hal R. Varian in Chapter 6 emphasize the array of initiatives that the Clinton administration adopted. The cumulative effect of those initiatives represented sound policy with regard to the Internet and other technological developments. More aggressive government intervention would have undesirably encumbered the IT revolution. In other areas, similarly, relatively small annual expansions in programs cumulated to a significant increase over the eight years of the administration. For example, as Alan B. Krueger and Cecelia E. Rouse describe in their treatment of labor and education policies (Chapter 10), funding for Head Start more than doubled in constant dollars between 1992 and 2000, while enrollment rose by 38 percent.

Leaving aside the question of the Clinton administration's focus on small-bore policies, some analysts argue that the administration could not take credit for the success of the U.S. economy during the 1990s because that success was due to factors other than the administration's own policies. We turn now to the various factors affecting U.S. performance during the 1990s.

III   Explaining U.S. Economic Performance in the 1990s

What are the reasons for the outstanding U.S. economic performance of the 1990s? A variety of short-term, medium-term, and long-term factors played a role. The short-term factors were luck, the medium-term factors were skill, and the long-term factors were ongoing favorable structural trends in the U.S. economy. Here we elaborate briefly on each.

Short-Term Factors: Temporary Good Luck on Prices

In the 1990s relative prices for computers and health care fell significantly. (Chapter 12, by Cutler and Gruber, examines the role of the move toward managed care.) Until 1999, world prices for oil also remained low (as Paul L. Joskow's Chapter 8, on energy, discusses). And U.S. import prices were low generally, due both to the appreciation of the dollar in the second half of the 1990s and to deflation in some partner countries, particularly in East Asia. All these factors put downward pressure on inflation and thus prevented overheating despite rapid growth in the economy. Measured consumer price inflation was also temporarily restrained by revisions to the price index. Thoughtful observers knew these trends were unlikely to continue for long, and indeed some of the trends did come to an end at the close of the decade. But even if one adjusted the inflation rate for such short-term factors, the record of price stability at a time of high employment and growth was still impressive.

Medium-Term Factors: Good Macroeconomic Policy

The skillful exercise of macroeconomic policy, both fiscal and monetary, contributed significantly to the strong economic performance of the 1990s. Three key fiscal policy turning points included the 1990 budget agreement, the 1993 budget agreement, and the 1998–2000 preservation of the emerging unified budget surpluses for debt reduction. The 1990 budget agreement represented an important step toward fiscal discipline, and it included marginal tax rate increases that imposed substantial political costs on President George Bush. In 1993 the Clinton administration built upon and strengthened the 1990 deficit reduction effort by further raising taxes on the highest-income taxpayers and reducing spending relative to the budget baseline. These efforts, along with strong growth in income and therefore tax revenue, replaced intractable budget deficits with substantial surpluses by the end of the decade. In the last years of the decade, the principal fiscal accomplishment of policy-makers was what they didn't do—dissipate the accruing surpluses in the form of substantial tax cuts or program expansions—rather than what they did do.

Whatever the explanation, the federal government's movement from deficit to surplus accounted for all of the improvement in net national saving between 1993 and 2000. This additional saving restrained long-term interest rates, thereby boosting private-sector domestic investment. As noted previously and discussed further in Chapter 2 by Elmendorf, Liebman, and Wilcox, the experience of the 1990s highlights the economic stimulus that can be provided by a long-run path of deficit reduction accompanied by monetary ease—a phenomenon that had been discounted by many macroeconomists before the 1990s.

Fiscal responsibility ultimately proved to be more politically popular than could have been expected from President Bush's experience in 1990. The surprising popularity that Ross Perot achieved in 1992 with the budget issue pointed the way. The public had apparently learned from the experience of the 1980s to be skeptical of politicians selling snake-oil tax cuts. A decade ago it looked as if the country might be doomed to a procyclical fiscal policy of pursuing fiscal expansion when times were good and finding discipline only in time of recession, the point in the business cycle when raising taxes was least appropriate. The Clinton administration's clever "Save Social Security First" strategy in 1998 underscored the political viability of fiscal discipline even in an expansion, transforming what had previously appeared to be politically unattractive—the preservation of the unified budget surplus for debt reduction—into a politically successful strategy.

True, the long-term fiscal positions of Social Security and, especially, Medicare were not fully addressed, as discussed in Chapter 2 by Elmendorf, Liebman, and Wilcox on fiscal policy and Social Security, and in Chapter 13 by Newhouse on Medicare. Furthermore, the new Bush administration succeeded in passing a significant tax cut in 2001, even though polls indicated that many Americans would rather spend the money on paying off the debt and putting Social Security and Medicare on a sound footing than on a tax cut. Moreover, after September 11, 2001, it became clear how rapidly budget prospects can shift. Where both parties had pledged a short time before to preserve budget balance without drawing on the Social Security surplus, after the terrorist attacks Washington discovered that it was likely to spend the entire surplus, Social Security and all, for at least several years and perhaps for much longer. The problems of long-term fiscal solvency and the retirement of the baby-boom generation faded from the public debate. Nevertheless, the large surpluses of the late 1990s remain as historical evidence that fiscal responsibility is feasible and is not inherently incompatible with a Democratic presidency.

We turn now from fiscal policy to monetary policy. The Clinton administration made two contributions to monetary policy. First, the elimination of the budget deficit allowed the Fed to lower interest rates. Second, the Clinton administration's monetary policy otherwise was simple to state: leave it to the Fed. Adhering to this hands-off policy is more difficult than it sounds. The political temptation is always strong to nudge the central bank toward an easier monetary policy: even if the monetary authorities don't respond, the complaints give the administration someone to blame in the future if the economy slows down. In addition, officials are naturally tempted to respond to press inquiries with statements that, while not intended to be critical, or even substantive, are nevertheless inevitably interpreted as second-guessing the Fed. With remarkably few exceptions, the administration adhered to its self-imposed rule of silence.

The lack of administration interference worked well because the Fed was skillful. Even if, in retrospect, the tightening of 1999–2000 may have gone one step too far, Chairman Alan Greenspan's record overall during the decade was quite impressive. As N. Gregory Mankiw shows in Chapter 1, the truly remarkable feature of the 1990s was not just its low inflation, but its low and steady inflation. At least some of the credit for this stability must belong to Greenspan, despite Mankiw's argument that most of the Greenspan performance can be explained by a simple econometric rule. Like Paul Volcker before him, Greenspan followed a tight monetary policy early in his term, established a reputation for discipline, and was thereby able to take a more moderate stance during the remainder of his term. His forbearance during 1995–1998, even as growth and employment exceeded levels previously considered inflationary, was a gamble; but it turned out to be a wise gamble and an important component of the expansion's longevity.

Perhaps the simplest overall conclusion one can draw from the 1990s is that the U.S. economy runs well given a little luck and the avoidance of major macroeconomic policy mistakes.

Long-Term Factors

Many of the most fundamental factors in explaining U.S. economic performance during the 1990s stretch back over two decades or more:

• *Deregulation.* The U.S. economy has long been less regulated than most other industrialized economies. But the past 25 years have witnessed important further steps away from deregulation. The deregulation trend began during the Jimmy Carter administration, in trucking, airlines, natural gas, and banking.

During the Ronald Reagan administration, deregulation was extended to the telecommunications sector. More recently, further deregulation has occurred in the electricity market, and market-friendly environmental regulation, such as in the sulfur dioxide permit program, has been expanded. (Chapter 8, by Joskow, and Chapter 9, by Robert W. Hahn and Robert N. Stavins, cover, respectively, energy and environmental regulation.) Some of these deregulation efforts have faced bumps in the road, particularly banking and electricity. Nevertheless, the overall effect of deregulation has been to make the U.S. economy more efficient in the long run. The fundamental continuity of policy across administrations in these areas also highlights a theme mentioned earlier: despite the drama of changes in administrations, policy does not shift nearly as much as one would imagine.

• *Globalization.* With important exceptions, the United States has had a basic free-trade orientation since World War II. The ratio of trade to GDP has more than tripled since the middle of the 20th century and now stands at 26 percent (imports plus exports, including services, which have increased especially rapidly). Economic theory tells us that trade improves economic performance. This statement is true both of old trade theory (classical "comparative advantage") and of new trade theory (which allows for changing technology, increasing returns to scale, and imperfect competition). Perhaps more convincingly, the statistical evidence also tells us that openness contributes to growth. Exports grew rapidly, a major selling point for free-trade policy. Even the increases in imports and in the trade deficit during the 1990s, though politically unpopular, were a useful safety valve during the strongest phase of the U.S. expansion. They released pressure from rapidly growing domestic demand, pressure that would otherwise have shown up as higher inflation and interest rates. In Chapter 5, Lawrence examines trade policy in the 1990s in detail.

• *Innovation.* The third category of favorable long-run structural factors is innovation. Innovation can be further divided into three types: technology, competition and flexibility in goods and labor markets, and the public sector. Technological innovation, especially information technology, received much attention during the 1990s and is discussed further in Chapter 6 by Samuelson and Varian. Although the IT revolution was not the sole reason for strong U.S. economic performance in the 1990s, it certainly was a positive factor. The second type of innovation involves competitive markets. The United States has always had relatively competitive goods and labor markets, compared with Europe for example. But the last two decades have seen a further movement in this direction, including the initially unpopular corporate restructuring of the 1980s and the initially popular dot-com start-up firms of the 1990s. Antitrust enforcement became more active during the Clinton administration, as Robert E. Litan and Carl Shapiro show in Chapter 7. The final category is innovation in the public sector. Public-sector reforms include reinventing government and defense reconversion, which have allowed previously low-productivity resources to be shifted to more productive uses, and welfare reform (which is discussed further by Blank and Ellwood in Chapter 11).

Apportioning Credit

Short-term luck on the supply side, medium-term skill in macroeconomic policy management, and long-term favorable structural trends that were called by some a "new economy"—this is a long list of factors. After compiling the list, is it possible to apportion the credit among the various factors? In particular, many observers and pundits are interested in how much credit for the strong economic performance of the 1990s should be given to the Clinton administration's policies. Unfortunately, providing a specific answer to this question is not possible, at least not in this book.

On the one hand, we often speak as if the perceived performance of the economy during a given period shows directly the virtues of the president and his team during that period. On the other hand, observers often note that the course of the economy in fact reflects exogenous factors to a greater extent than it reflects the actual personal strengths and weaknesses of the man who was president, with the implication that the contribution of the latter should be dismissed. It should be evident that the president in fact generally deserves a share of credit for what happens on his watch that is neither zero nor 100 percent. But the question is still more complicated.

A metaphor may offer insight. Imagine the president as the captain of a large ship. Whether the passengers in the hold experience rough seas or a calm ride depends on factors such as the weather and the construction of the ship to a greater extent than the skills of the captain. Nevertheless, helmsmen can be skilled or incompetent, and the difference affects the ride.

Disentangling causality, credit, and blame for either a smooth sail or a rough one is exceedingly complex. Things can go wrong through no fault of the leadership, or they can go right for the wrong reason. If an unpredictable squall arises on a particular navigational route, it does not mean that the captain erred in choosing that route over another. Conversely, smooth sailing does not mean that he picked the best route. Thus it is not meaningful to parcel out fractions of the total credit for the economy's good economic performance in the 1990s to Bill Clinton, Alan Greenspan, information technology, or other forces.

An example illustrates the problems in distributing credit for what happened (or did not happen). The White House sent Zhu Rongji away in the spring of 1999 without an agreement on Chinese accession to the World Trade Organization (WTO), even though China had made many important concessions (relative to what other developing countries have agreed to when joining the WTO, and to what had been expected). Was this a mistake on the part of the White House? It seemed like a mistake over the subsequent months, as the U.S. business community reacted adversely, Zhu and other reformers were undercut politically in China, and the accidental bombing of the Chinese embassy in Belgrade further worsened U.S.-China relations. In judging the wisdom of the spring 1999 decision, however, the key question is, Did the decision reflect a sensible balancing of the pros and cons at the time, given the information that was available? Such an evaluation would have to include the political constraints on the White House, which are often conveniently forgotten in discussions of this type. For example, the White House had to consider the reactions an agreement on Chinese accession would elicit from senators opposed to such an agreement, and the reaction (or absence thereof) from businessmen favoring it. It would have been of little use to sign a good agreement that could not have been ratified by the Senate. Complaints from the business community about the lack of an agreement were in the end important in persuading Congress to vote for it. These voices might not have been heard had the opposite desision been made.

Too often, we evaluate the captain's performance only by conducting polls among the passengers in the hold. It is indeed worth knowing whether the passengers feel they are experiencing a smooth ride. But journalists, academics, and other opinion leaders have the ability to go on deck and observe for themselves what sort of job the captain is doing. It is their responsibility to do so, and they owe it to the passengers to report on what they see. In undertaking such evaluations, five different levels of performance are relevant:

• *Personal characteristics.* How do the president's talents compare to others who have held the office or could have held the office? Relevant criteria include stamina, capacity to absorb and synthesize information, ability to make decisions, speaking facility, ability to communicate warmth and inspire confidence in common people, honesty, skill at picking good staff, and so on. In the specific case of economic policy, another relevant attribute is whether the president is economically literate and numerate.

• *Process.* How well does the president's administration function? When it is reported in the press that the president has done something, often it is in fact not he but his representatives who have done it. Of course it is appropriate to hold him, as a manager, responsible. But analytically we must realize that other random factors begin to enter at this second stage. To take but one example, if many of the president's nominees have not been confirmed by the Senate, nor even considered by the Senate, the president may not be wholly to blame if the policy process then does not run smoothly. In Chapter 14, Jonathan Orszag, Peter Orszag, and Laura Tyson examine the process of economic policy-making during the Clinton administration.

• *Quality of policies implemented*. How good are the spending programs, tax policies, regulatory decisions, international negotiations, and so forth that are implemented? In the face of congressional opposition, it may be foolish to blame the White House for a budget or a trade measure if it is clear that it did its best to argue for some other better decision but was stopped by Congress.

• *Outcomes*. What are the actual results in the economy? What are the rates of growth, unemployment, and inflation? How strong is the budget position? The government may function well, and the policies chosen may be good, but exogenous shocks, like the oil price increases of the 1970s or some favorable developments in the 1990s, may be beyond its control.

• *Perceptions*. What are the public's *perceptions* of the president's performance? Although economists are primarily interested in actual outcomes, much of the rest of society is interested in this final level. What are the president's popularity ratings, what do polls say about aspects of his performance, what are the editorial writers and other opinion leaders saying, how well do he and his party do at the next elections, and what is the judgment of history?

To be sure, causality runs in all directions among these five levels of evaluation. For example, confidence about the direction in which the country is headed is often reflected in consumer confidence and stock market prices, which in turn can affect consumption, investment, and overall growth. But the central point is that, even though only the first level concerns the intrinsic abilities of the president, additional exogenous random factors can enter at each stage as we move down the chain to lower levels. As a result, judging a president solely by perceived (or even actual) outcomes is difficult: we can't trace our way back up the chain from the perceived or actual outcomes to the president's own characteristics.

Thus it is not the task of this book to evaluate the quality of presidential leadership in the 1990s. Rather the point is primarily to examine in detail the many policy decisions that were made—the third stage listed. This examination will shed light on the links back to the first and second levels, as well as forward to the fourth and fifth levels. But it does not answer, nor even attempt to answer, the question of what specific share of the credit for good economic performance during this period should be given to the Clinton administration.

IV A Note of Warning

We close this Introduction with a note of caution: future endeavors of this type may be undermined by the rules and practices governing disclosure of internal information. Advocating transparency has become akin to advocating motherhood and apple pie. For example, it is an important part of reforms urged on governments in developing countries, as well as on the International Monetary Fund itself, in the aftermath of the international currency crises of 1997–98. But there can be such a thing as too much transparency. To take an example, sunshine laws essentially forbid a group of governors of the Federal Reserve Board from informally discussing monetary policy with each other outside official meetings. What is gained by this prohibition?

Our experience in the Clinton administration suggests that despite the general benefits of disclosure in promoting good government, the formal disclosure rules have become counterproductive. In particular, the Freedom of Information Act (FOIA) and the rules governing congressional subpoena powers sometimes discourage executive-branch policy-makers from writing things down. The reason is that such written material is too often subject to congressional inquiry, discovered through the FOIA process, or otherwise proven to be politically problematic.

The intent of these rules is to expose the decision-making process to scrutiny. Such scrutiny is generally beneficial. But the ultimate effect of the rules may be to expose decisions to *less* scrutiny, because of the response of policy-makers to the incentives posed by the rules. It is not only the policy-making process that suffers as a result; historians will also find it much more difficult to discern what actually happened, and why, without the benefit of an accurate paper trail. Furthermore, compliance with the current system consumes an inordinate amount of policy-makers' time.

The balance between public disclosure and internal candor thus, in our opinion, tipped too far toward the former in the United States in the 1990s. For example, top administration economists spent substantial amounts of time combing through files in response to congressional subpoenas, looking for internal background memoranda on climate change. Such internal memoranda, which explored potential policy options and evaluated the pros and cons of different approaches, were essential to an honest internal policy process. But some were also politically sensitive. The benefits of transparency in such cases are not entirely clear: what specific public benefit (as opposed to political benefit to the administration's opponents) arises from publicly releasing internal analyses of potential administration policies by the Council of Economic Advisers, including policies not chosen by the administration? How should one weigh any such benefits against the costs of the associated incentive to avoid writing things down?

In our view, it would be beneficial to provide more protection for pre-decision internal analyses. Put simply, the administration should be expected to provide rigorous analysis of the option it finally chooses, but it should be able to protect—temporarily—materials regarding the options not chosen as well as internal views of the pros and cons regarding the chosen option. For such politically sensitive internal analyses, disclosure could be undertaken after some suitable period of time had elapsed, thereby limiting the potential political costs but still imposing discipline on policy-makers (who know that their internal analyses may eventually see the light of day).[4] This model would mimic the policy of the Federal Reserve Board, which releases the minutes of its confidential meetings only after some delay.

This volume benefited from the policy-making paper trail on numerous issues. The danger is that future volumes of this type may not benefit from such access if disclosure rules discourage policy-makers from committing their thoughts and opinions to paper. The ultimate cost will then be borne not by future administrations but rather by those seeking lessons to be learned but finding only incomplete or inaccurate histories.

---

4. Similar reforms could be applied to the Federal Advisory Committee Act (FACA), which imposes strict disclosure rules on the use of outside experts. The all-too-frequent result of FACA restrictions is that the government agency forgoes the use of outsiders or acquires their views in a haphazard and informal manner. Rather than making advice-giving more transparent, the unintended result of FACA is sometimes that no advice at all is proffered—or that it is imported in less visible ways. Delayed disclosure may be beneficial in the FACA context also.

I Macroeconomics

1   Monetary Policy

U.S. Monetary Policy During the 1990s

N. Gregory Mankiw

PANELISTS: *Alan Blinder, William Poole, and Alice M. Rivlin*

I'm baffled. I find it hard to believe. . . . What I'm puzzled about is whether, and if so how, they suddenly learned how to regulate the economy. Does Alan Greenspan have an insight into movements in the economy and the shocks that other people don't have?

Milton Friedman, May 2000

No aspect of U.S. policy in the 1990s is more widely hailed as a success than monetary policy. Fed Chairman Alan Greenspan is often viewed as a miracle worker. Many Americans share the admiration that Senator John McCain expressed during his presidential bid. When the senator was asked about Greenspan's conduct of monetary policy, McCain said that if anything were to happen to the Fed chairman, as president he would take the strategy followed in the movie *Weekend at Bernie's*: he would prop up the chairman's body, give him some sunglasses, and keep him on the job as long as possible.

Greenspan's tenure at the Fed has had its share of historic events, impinging on (as well as being affected by) the stance of monetary policy. On October 19, 1987, two months after Greenspan took office, the stock market fell 22 percent—a one-day plunge larger than anything seen before or since. The Fed

The author is grateful to Ricardo Reis for research assistance and to Laurence Ball, Jeffrey Frankel, Seamus Smyth, and David Wilcox for comments.

reacted by flooding the economy with liquidity, lowering interest rates and averting a recession. But soon inflation became the more pressing concern, and the Fed started raising interest rates. The federal funds rate rose from 6.7 percent in November 1987 to 9.8 percent in May 1989. This Fed tightening, together with other factors, pushed the economy into a recession the following year. More than any other single event, the recession set the stage for the economic policies of the 1990s: it helped Bill Clinton, a little-known governor from Arkansas, defeat George Bush, an incumbent president who, only a short time earlier, had enjoyed overwhelming popularity following the Gulf War.

The Clinton years brought their own challenges to monetary policy-makers. International financial crises in Mexico in 1994–95 and in Asia in 1997–98, as well as the infamous failure of the hedge fund Long-Term Capital Management in 1998, put the world financial system in jeopardy and the Fed at center stage. At the same time, the push for fiscal discipline, which turned the U.S. government budget from deficit to surplus, made the Fed's job easier. So did the acceleration of productivity growth, which most analysts attribute to the advances in information technology associated with the so-called new economy. Another (perhaps related) development was a gradual decline in the U.S. unemployment rate, without the inflationary pressures that normally accompany such a change. Explaining this happy but surprising shift, as well as deciding how to respond to it, remains a topic of debate among students and practitioners of monetary policy.

The purpose of this paper is to look back at these events. My goal is not to tell the story of U.S. monetary policy during the 1990s: Bob Woodward's widely read book *Maestro* already does that. Instead, I offer an analytic review of monetary policy during this period, which should complement more narrative treatments of the topic.

I proceed as follows. Section 1.1 compares the macroeconomic performance of the 1990s to other recent decades. Section 1.2 considers whether some of the good performance of the 1990s can be attributed to good luck rather than good policy. Section 1.3 examines how policy was different from earlier decades. Section 1.4 considers the legacy that the monetary policy of the 1990s leaves for the future. Section 1.5 summarizes the conclusions from this experience.

1.1   The Macroeconomic Performance of the 1990s

I begin by comparing the performance of the economy during the 1990s with other recent decades. I concentrate on three standard time series: inflation, unemployment, and real growth. Economists, policy-makers, and pundits watch these measures of the economy's performance more than any others. They do so for good reason: If a nation enjoys low and stable inflation, low and stable unemployment, and high and stable growth, the fundamentals are in place to permit prosperity for most of its citizens.

1.1.1 The Level and Stability of Inflation

Inflation is the first piece of data to look at, in part because a central banker's first job is to keep inflation in check. There is no doubt that central bankers also influence unemployment and real growth and that they do (and should) keep an eye on these variables as well. But according to standard theories of monetary policy, central-bank actions have only a transitory effect on unemployment and real growth. By contrast, the effects of monetary policy on inflation continue in the long run—and indeed are strongest in the long run. So, if monetary policy-makers take a long view of their actions, inflation is their first order of concern.

Table 1.1 shows the performance of inflation during the 1990s and the preceding four decades. The first row shows average inflation for each of the decades. The second row shows the standard deviation, which is a common measure of volatility.

As judged by the average inflation rate, the 1990s were not exceptional. Inflation was lower in the 1950s and 1960s than it was in the 1990s. For those with shorter memories, however, the 1990s can be viewed as a low-inflation decade. There was substantially less inflation in the 1990s than there was in the 1980s and especially the 1970s.

This decline in inflation is largely the result of the tough disinflationary policies that Paul Volcker put into place in the early 1980s: inflation fell from

Table 1.1
The Inflation Experience, Decade by Decade

	1950s	1960s	1970s	1980s	1990s
Average inflation	2.07	2.33	7.09	5.66	3.00
Standard deviation of inflation	2.44	1.48	2.72	3.53	1.12
Maximum inflation	9.36	6.20	13.29	14.76	6.29
Date of maximum inflation	Feb 50	Dec 69	Dec 79	Mar 80	Oct 90

Source: Department of Labor and author's calculations.

Note: In this and subsequent tables, the decade of the 1950s refers to the period from the first month (or quarter) of 1950 to last month (or quarter) of 1959, and so on. Inflation is the rate of change in the Consumer Price Index over the previous 12 months.

a peak of 14.8 percent in March 1980 to 3.6 percent three years later. As is almost always the case, this large and persistent decline in inflation was associated with temporarily declining production and rising unemployment. By most measures, the recession of the early 1980s was the most severe economic downturn since the Great Depression of the 1930s.

The 1990s look more exceptional once we look at the standard deviation of inflation. The second row of Table 1.1 shows that inflation was far more stable during the 1990s than during any other recent decade. The differences are substantial in magnitude. Inflation was only one-third as volatile during the 1990s as it was during the 1980s. It was 24 percent less volatile during the 1990s than it was during the 1960s, the second-best decade as ranked by inflation volatility. There is no doubt that by historical standards the 1990s were a decade of remarkably stable inflation.

Another way to look at the data is to examine how bad inflation was at its worst. The third line of Table 1.1 shows the highest annual inflation rate recorded over the 120 months of each decade. By this measure, inflation was lowest in the 1960s and 1990s. But there is an important difference between these two periods. In the 1960s, the highest inflation rate occurred at the end of the decade, representing the beginning of a problem that would persist into the 1970s. By contrast, in the 1990s, inflation peaked at the beginning of the decade and thereafter became tame. After January 1992, inflation remained in a remarkably narrow range from 1.34 percent to 3.32 percent.

1.1.2 Judging the Inflation Experience

These comparisons of inflation over the past five decades bring up a classic question of economic theory: What costs does inflation impose on a society? Or, to focus the issue for the purposes at hand, is it more important for the central bank to produce low inflation or stable inflation? If low average inflation is the goal, then the monetary policy-makers of the 1990s can be given only an average grade. But if stable inflation is the goal, then they go to the top of the class.

Textbook discussions of the costs of inflation emphasize both the level and stability of inflation. A high level of inflation is costly for several reasons: (1) Because inflation raises the costs of holding money, it diverts people's time and attention toward conserving their money holdings and away from more productive uses. (2) Inflation induces firms to incur more "menu costs"—the costs associated with changing prices and distributing the new prices to salesmen and customers. (3) Because price adjustment is staggered, inflation induces spurious volatility in the prices of some firms relative to others, which impedes the price system's ability to allocate resources efficiently. (4) Because the tax laws are not indexed, inflation raises the effective tax on capital income and thereby discourages capital accumulation and economic growth. (5) Inflation makes economic calculation more difficult, because the currency is less reliable as a yardstick for measuring value.

All five of these costs indicate that low average inflation is desirable, but they suggest that the stability of inflation matters as well. Standard theory implies that these costs of inflation are "convex," meaning that the cost of incremental inflation rises with inflation itself. In other words, an increase in inflation from 4 to 6 percent is worse than an increase from 2 to 4 percent. If this observation is true, then these five benefits to low inflation also argue for stable inflation. The cost of steady 4 percent inflation is less than the average cost of inflation that fluctuates back and forth between 2 and 6 percent.

In addition to these five costs, there is another cost associated directly with inflation volatility: (6) Because an unexpected change in the price level redistributes real wealth between debtors and creditors, highly volatile inflation creates unnecessary risk for all parties. As people try to avoid these risks, long-term contracts using money as the unit of account become less tenable.

Although these six costs of inflation are widely accepted among economists, there is debate about whether the costs are large or small in total, and which are larger than others. Moreover, there is little direct evidence of convexity in the costs of inflation. As a result, it is hard to compare quantitatively the benefits of low inflation with the benefits of stable inflation. The more weight is given to inflation stability as a policy objective, the more exceptional the monetary policy of the 1990s appears.

1.1.3   Two Arguments in Favor of Inflation

Some economists argue that there are some benefits to inflation, at least if the inflation is only moderate. These arguments are worth noting, in part because they are associated with some prominent policy-makers of the 1990s.

In particular, long before he was U.S. Treasury secretary, Lawrence Summers (1991) wrote, "the optimal inflation rate is surely positive, perhaps as high or 2 or 3 percent." Although Summers has never had direct control over monetary policy, Fed policy-makers are well aware of the views of prominent Treasury officials. Moreover, nations that have adopted a policy of inflation targeting (which were numerous during the 1990s) have typically chosen a positive number, rather than zero, for their target. In this environment, claims that the Fed is aiming for "price stability" should perhaps not be taken too literally. The 3 percent inflation experienced during the 1990s may be close to the target policy-makers had in mind.

1.1.3.1 The Possibility of Negative Real Interest Rates

One argument for a target rate of inflation greater than zero is that it permits real interest rates (that is, interest rates corrected for inflation) to become negative. Because individuals can always hold cash rather than bonds, it is impossible for nominal interest rates to fall below zero. Under zero inflation, real interest rates also can never become negative. But if inflation is, say, 3 percent, then the central bank can lower the nominal rate toward zero and send the real interest toward negative 3 percent. The ability to produce negative real interest rates gives the central bank more latitude to stimulate the economy in a recession.

Some economists point to Japan in the 1990s as an example of why some inflation is desirable. With inflation at about zero and nominal interest rates at zero, the Bank of Japan appears to have had little room to stimulate the economy. Japan is said to have been stuck in a "liquidity trap" when monetary policy loses its effectiveness. If Japan had inherited a tradition of more inflation, the argument goes, then when the bank lowered nominal rates to zero, real rates would have become negative. A negative real rate would have stimulated spending and helped pull the economy out of its lingering recession.

This line of reasoning is controversial. Some economists dispute the claim that Japan was stuck in a liquidity trap. They argue that more aggressive Japanese monetary expansion would have lowered real rates by raising inflation expectations or that it would have stimulated exports by causing the yen to depreciate in foreign exchange markets.

Nonetheless, this argument for positive inflation may well have influenced U.S. monetary policy during the 1990s. Lawrence Summers endorsed this argument at the beginning of the decade. Moreover, the Japanese experience in the aftermath of its stock market and real estate bubble was a warning flag of what might happen in the United States if the booming stock market were ever to suffer a similar collapse. The 3 percent inflation rate gave Fed policy-makers the option to stimulate spending with negative real interest rates, had the need ever arisen.

1.1.3.2 Greasing the Wheels of Labor Markets

A second argument for moderate inflation starts with the observation that cuts in nominal wages are rare. For some reason, firms are reluctant to cut their workers' nominal wages, and workers are reluctant to accept such cuts. A 2 percent wage cut in a zero-inflation world is, in real terms, the same as a 3 percent raise with 5 percent inflation, but workers do not always see it that way. The 2 percent wage cut may seem like an insult, whereas the 3 percent raise is, after all, still a raise. Empirical studies confirm that nominal wages rarely fall.

This fact suggests that inflation may make labor markets work better. Here's the argument. The supply and demand for different kinds of labor is always changing. Sometimes an increase in supply or decrease in demand leads to a fall in the equilibrium real wage for a group of workers. If nominal wages can't be cut, then the only way to cut real wages is to allow inflation to do the job. Without inflation, the real wage will be stuck above the equilibrium level, resulting in higher unemployment.

For this reason, some economists argue that inflation "greases the wheels" of labor markets. Only a little inflation is needed: An inflation rate of 2 percent lets real wages fall by 2 percent per year, or 20 percent per decade, without cuts in nominal wages. Such automatic reductions in real wages are impossible with zero inflation.

There is reason to suspect that this argument for positive inflation also influenced U.S. monetary policy in the 1990s. Once again, Lawrence Summers endorsed this view at the beginning of the decade when he proposed a target rate of inflation of 2 to 3 percent. Subsequently, the case was advanced by a Brookings research team that included George Akerlof, husband to Janet Yellen, a Clinton appointee to the Federal Reserve.[1] These facts suggest that some U.S. monetary policy-makers during the 1990s may have been skeptical about the desirability of pushing inflation all the way down to zero. The 3 percent inflation realized during this period may have been exactly what they were aiming for.

1.1.4   Real Economic Performance: Unemployment and Growth

The other key aspect of macroeconomic performance beyond inflation is the real economy, which is most often monitored by unemployment and growth in real GDP. Keep in mind that monetary policy is not the most important determinant of these economic variables. Indeed, according to standard theory, the Fed has no ability at all to influence unemployment and real growth in the long run.

What determines the long-run rates of unemployment and real growth? Unemployment is determined by labor market features, institutions, and policies, such as the demographic structure of the workforce, the bargaining power of unions, minimum-wage laws, unemployment-insurance policies, and the

---

1. See Akerlof, Dickens, and Perry (1996).

Table 1.2
Unemployment and Real Economic Growth, Decade by Decade

	1950s	1960s	1970s	1980s	1990s
Unemployment					
Average	4.51	4.78	6.22	7.27	5.76
Standard deviation	1.29	1.07	1.16	1.48	1.05
Real GDP Growth					
Average	4.18	4.43	3.28	3.02	3.03
Standard deviation	3.89	2.13	2.80	2.68	1.56

Source: Department of Labor, Department of Commerce, and author's calculations.

Note: Unemployment is the monthly, seasonally adjusted percentage of the labor force without a job. Real GDP growth is the growth rate of inflation-adjusted gross domestic product from four quarters earlier.

mechanisms available for matching workers and jobs. These factors also influence real economic growth (because lower unemployment means higher production), but the primary determinant of real economic growth in the long run is the rate of technological progress. Notice that when discussing the long-run forces setting unemployment and real growth, monetary policy is far in the background.

Yet monetary policy influences unemployment and growth in the short run. What the "short run" means is a subject of some dispute, but most economists agree that the central-bank actions influence these variables over a period of at least two or three years. Therefore, the central bank can potentially help stabilize the economy. (And if policy is badly run, it can destabilize it—the Great Depression of the 1930s being a prominent example.) In the jargon of economics, monetary policy is neutral in the long run, but not in the short run. The practical implications of this textbook theory are the following: The average levels of unemployment and growth over long periods are beyond the central bank's powers, but the volatility of these series from year to year is something it can influence.

Table 1.2 presents summary statistics on unemployment and real growth for each of the last five decades of the 20th century. It presents both the average level over the decade and the standard deviation as a measure of volatility.

As the table shows, the average level of unemployment during the 1990s was lower than it was during the previous two decades (although still higher than during the 1950s and 1960s). There is no consensus among economists on the reasons for this decline in the normal level of unemployment. It could, for instance, be related to the aging of the workforce, as the baby boom reaches middle age. Older workers tend to have more stable jobs than younger workers, so it is natural to expect declining unemployment as the workforce ages. Alternatively, as I discuss later, the decline in normal unemployment during the 1990s could be related to the acceleration in productivity growth resulting from advances in information technology. But whatever the cause for the long-run decline in unemployment, few economists would credit monetary policy.

Data on real economic growth show that average growth during the 1990s was similar to that experienced during the 1980s and substantially lower than that experienced during the 1950s and 1960s. This fact might seem surprising in light of the great hoopla surrounding the so-called new economy. The explanation is that the acceleration of economic growth occurred in the middle of the decade. Once the rapid growth in the second half of the decade is averaged with the recession and slow growth in the first half, overall growth during the 1990s is no longer impressive.

What's important for evaluating monetary policy, however, are not the averages in Table 1.2 but the standard deviations. Here the numbers tell a striking story: Unemployment and economic growth were more stable during the 1990s than during any recent decade. The change in the volatility of GDP growth is large. The economy's production was 27 percent less volatile during the 1990s than it was during the 1960s, the second most stable decade.

These statistics suggest amazing success by monetary policy-makers during the 1990s. As we saw earlier, the economy enjoyed low volatility in inflation. One might wonder whether this success came at a cost. That is, did the Fed achieve stable inflation by giving less weight to the goals of stable employment and growth? The answer appears to be no: the economy became more stable in every dimension.

Of course, improvement in economic stabilization does not necessarily mean that policy-makers are doing a better job. Perhaps they were just lucky.

1.2 The Role of Luck

The Fed's job is to respond to shocks to the economy in order to stabilize output, employment, and inflation. Standard analyses of economic fluctuations divide shocks into two types. Demand shocks are those that alter the overall demand for goods and services. Supply shocks are those that alter the prices at which firms are willing and able to supply goods and services.

Demand shocks are the easier type for the Fed to handle because, like monetary policy, they push output, employment, and inflation in the same direction. A stock market crash, for instance, reduces aggregate demand, putting downward pressure on output, employment, and inflation. The standard response is

Table 1.3
Food and Energy Price Shocks, Decade by Decade

	1960s	1970s	1980s	1990s
Average shock	−0.12	0.61	−0.51	−0.22
Standard deviation of shocks	0.45	1.41	0.97	0.50
Worst shock	1.34	4.65	2.26	1.02
Date of worst shock	Feb '66	Feb '74	Mar '80	Oct '90

Source: Department of Labor and author's calculations.

Note: The shock here is measured as the CPI inflation rate over 12 months minus the core CPI inflation rate over the same period. The core CPI is the index excluding food and energy.

for the Fed to lower interest rates by increasing the money supply. If well timed, such an action can restore aggregate demand and offset the effects of the shock on both inflation and the real economy.

Supply shocks pose a more difficult problem. An increase in the world price of oil, for instance, raises firms' costs and the prices they charge. These increases tend to raise inflation and, for given aggregate demand, push the economy toward recession. The Fed then has a choice between contracting policy to fight inflation and expanding policy to fight recession. In the face of supply shocks, the Fed cannot stabilize inflation and the real economy simultaneously. Supply shocks force upon the Fed a trade-off between inflation stability and employment stability.

Yet during the 1990s the U.S. economy enjoyed stability of both kinds. One possible reason is dumb luck. Perhaps the economy just did not experience the supply shocks that caused so much turmoil in earlier decades.

1.2.1 Food and Energy Price Shocks

The most significant supply shocks in recent U.S. history are the food and energy shocks of the 1970s. These shocks are often blamed as one proximate cause of the rise in inflation that occurred during this decade not only in the United States but also around the world. So a natural place to start looking for supply shocks is in the prices of food and energy.[2]

Table 1.3 shows some summary statistics on these shocks. They are measured here as CPI inflation minus core inflation, where core inflation is based on the Consumer Price Index excluding food and energy. This measure is positive when food and energy prices are rising relative to other prices in the economy.

---

2. Blinder (1979) offers a classic analysis of the stagflation of the 1970s, emphasizing the role of supply shocks related to food and energy.

The first two rows of the table show the average shock and the standard deviation of the shocks in each decade. The 1990s were a lucky time. The low standard deviation shows that large supply shocks were not common. Moreover, the negative value for the average shock indicates that good shocks were more common than bad shocks.

The third row of the table shows the worst shock that the Fed had to deal with during each decade. Not surprisingly, the worst shock in the entire period was in the 1970s: because of adverse shocks to food and energy, CPI inflation rose 4.65 percentage points more than core inflation during the 12 months ending February 1974. By contrast, the worst shock of the 1990s was less than one-fourth as large. This shock occurred in 1990 as a result of the Gulf War. For the rest of the decade, there was no adverse food and energy shock as large as a full percentage point.

Given these data, it is hard to escape the conclusion that the macroeconomic success of the 1990s was in part due to luck. Food and energy prices were unusually well behaved, and the economy reaped the benefit of this stability.

1.2.2   Productivity

Another potential source of supply shocks is the rate of technological advance. This is a natural hypothesis to explain the good macroeconomic performance of the 1990s. During these years there was much discussion of the "new economy" and the increasing role of information technology.

Table 1.4 shows data on the productivity growth in the nonfarm business sector. The pickup in productivity growth is evident in these data. It is even clearer if the 1990s are split in half: productivity growth was higher in the second half of the decade than in the first. While the productivity speedup is a fortuitous development, its importance should not be overstated. Compared to the data from the 1950s and 1960s, the average rate of productivity growth during the 1990s is not unusual.

Table 1.4
Productivity Growth, Decade by Decade

	1950s	1960s	1970s	1980s	1990s
Average productivity growth	2.80	2.84	2.05	1.48	2.07
Standard deviation of productivity growth	4.29	4.20	4.30	2.91	2.62

Source: Department of Commerce and author's calculations.

Note: Productivity growth is the quarterly change in output per hour in the nonfarm business sector, expressed at an annual rate.

What is more anomalous is the low volatility of productivity growth, as shown in the second row of the table. To the extent that productivity reflects technological progress, the 1990s were a decade of smooth advances in technology. It is possible that this fact might explain the low volatility in other macroeconomic variables. Yet it is also possible that the tame business cycle led to low volatility in productivity, rather than the other way around.

The productivity data suggest an intriguing observation: The 1990s were in many ways the opposite of the 1970s. The 1970s saw a large increase in the price of a major intermediate good—oil. At the same time, productivity growth decelerated, while unemployment and inflation rose. The 1990s saw a large decrease in the price of a major intermediate good—computer chips. At the same time, productivity growth accelerated, while unemployment and inflation fell.

Economists do not fully understand the links among productivity, unemployment, and inflation, but one hypothesis may help explain the 1990s. If workers' wage demands lag behind news about productivity, accelerating productivity may tend to lower the natural rate of unemployment until workers' aspirations catch up. If the central bank is unaware of the falling natural rate of unemployment, it may leave more slack in the economy than it realizes, putting downward pressure on inflation. Thus, even if the average rate of productivity growth was not exceptional during the 1990s, the surprising acceleration from the poor productivity growth of the 1970s and 1980s may have acted like a lucky shock to aggregate supply.[3]

1.2.3   The Stock Market

It would be an oversight in any discussion of luck in the 1990s to neglect the stock market. For investors in the stock market, this decade was extraordinarily lucky.

Table 1.5 shows the average return and the standard deviation of returns for each of the past five decades. It also shows the ratio of the average return to the standard deviation, which is commonly used as a measure of how much reward an investor gets for taking on risk. The table shows that the 1990s were exceptional. Returns were high, and volatility was low. There was never a better time to be in the market.

To a large extent, the performance of the stock market is just a reflection of the macroeconomic events we have already seen in other statistics. Low volatility in the stock market reflects low volatility in the overall economy. The high return reflects the surprising acceleration in productivity growth, which helped

---

3. Some of these ideas are explored in a recent paper by Laurence Ball and Robert Moffitt (2001).

Table 1.5
Stock Market Returns, Decade by Decade

	1950s	1960s	1970s	1980s	1990s
Average return	21.46	9.55	6.05	18.58	18.83
Standard deviation of return	15.88	12.30	16.36	17.09	12.04
Ratio of average return to standard deviation	1.35	0.78	0.37	1.09	1.56

Source: Standard & Poors and author's calculations.

Note: Calculations are based on monthly data on total returns on the S&P 500 index over the previous 12 months.

fuel growth in corporate profits. If the stock market is merely a mirror being held up to the economy, then it has little independent role in the conduct or analysis of monetary policy.

There are, however, two reasons why the stock market may have a role to play. The first is that the stock market may be an indicator of things to come. According to the "efficient markets" theory, stock-market investors are rationally looking ahead to future economic conditions and constantly processing all relevant information. Thus, news about the economy might show up first in the stock market. The 1990s are a case in point. The bull market preceded the acceleration in productivity growth by several years, suggesting the possibility that Wall Street knew about the "new economy" long before it showed up in standard macroeconomic statistics.

A second reason why the stock market may be relevant to monetary policy is that it can be a driving force of the business cycle. John Maynard Keynes suggested that movements in the market are driven by the "animal spirits" of investors. Alan Greenspan reprised this idea during the 1990s when he questioned whether investors were suffering from "irrational exuberance." Such exuberance could push stock prices higher than their fundamental value and make households feel richer than they truly are.

Under either theory, monetary policy-makers might react to a rise in the stock market by setting interest rates higher than they otherwise would. This is the other side of the coin to the Fed's policy in October 1987, when it responded to a stock market crash by increasing liquidity and cutting interest rates. Regardless of whether the movements in the stock market are rational, they alter the aggregate demand for goods and services, and as a result they are of interest to monetary policy-makers. Indeed, the decline in the personal saving rate during the 1990s was mostly due to the booming stock market, for the "wealth effect" was a potent stimulus to consumer spending.

Of course, saying that monetary policy might react to the stock market is different from saying that it did. As I will discuss in the next section, there is scant evidence that the booming stock market of the 1990s played a large, independent role in monetary policy during this period.

1.3 The Role of Policy

Let's now turn to looking directly at policy to see how, if at all, it was different in the 1990s than in earlier decades. I look at two standard gauges of monetary policy—the money supply and interest rates.

Before doing so, let's clear up a potential confusion. Although a central bank can control both the money supply and the level of interest rates, it would be wrong to view these two variables as distinct policy instruments. The reason is that the central bank influences interest rates by adjusting the money supply. In essence, interest rates are the price of money. The central bank affects the price of money by controlling the quantity of money.

As a first approximation, the central bank's only policy lever is the supply of high-powered money (currency plus bank reserves), which it controls through open-market operations and, to a lesser extent, lending at its discount window. It can use this single lever to target a broad monetary aggregate, such as M1 or M2, an interest rate, an exchange rate, or the price of bananas. But once it chooses one intermediate target, the game is over: the central bank has used up its power over economic conditions.

1.3.1 The Demise of Monetary Aggregates

There once was a time when critics of Fed policy thought the key to good monetary policy was stable growth in the money supply. If the Fed would only keep M1 or M2 growing at a low, stable rate, the argument went, the economy would avoid high inflations, painful deflations, and the major booms and busts of the business cycle. Milton Friedman was the most prominent proponent of this so-called "monetarist" view.

It is easy to see how such a viewpoint arose. The two most painful macroeconomic events of the 20th century were the Great Depression of the 1930s and the Great Inflation of the 1970s. Both calamities would likely have been avoided if the Fed had been following the Friedman prescription of low, stable money growth.

In the early 1930s, high-powered money continued to grow at a moderate rate, but the collapse of the banking system caused broader measures of the money supply to plunge. Worries about bank solvency caused households to hold more money in the form of currency rather than demand deposits and banks to hold more deposits in the form of reserves rather than bank loans.

Both actions reduced the amount of bank lending; the creation of inside money by the banking system went in reverse. As measured by currency plus demand deposits, the quantity of money fell by 25 percent from 1929 to 1933. If the Fed had been committed to stable growth in the broader monetary aggregates, it would have pursued a more expansionary policy than it did, and the Great Depression would have been less severe.

Generals are said to often make the mistake of fighting the last war, and the same may be true of central bankers. Perhaps because of the memory of its insufficient expansion during the 1930s, the Fed was too expansionary during the 1970s. The proximate cause of the Great Inflation was not monetary policy: the fiscal expansion resulting from the Vietnam War in the late 1960s and the OPEC oil shocks of 1973–74 and 1979–81 deserve much of the blame. But monetary policy accommodated these shocks to a degree that ensured persistent high inflation. The money supply grew rapidly throughout the 1970s, and inflation reached some of its highest levels on record. How best to handle supply shocks is a topic about which economists disagree. But there is no doubt that if the Fed had kept money growth to a slower rate during the 1970s, it would have better contained the inflationary pressures.

With these two formative episodes as the historical background, one might have expected subsequent improvements in monetary policy to be associated with increased concern at the Fed to maintain low, stable money growth. Indeed, increased reliance on target ranges for the monetary aggregates was allegedly part of Paul Volcker's 1979 change in the direction of monetary policy, which helped set the stage for the 1990s.[4] If the improved macroeconomic performance of the 1990s went hand in hand with greater stability in the money supply, monetarists could have claimed intellectual victory.

Alas, it was not to be. Table 1.6 shows the average growth rate and the standard deviation of the growth rate for M1 and M2, the two most commonly used measures of the money supply. (I omit the 1950s here because the Fed's consistent data on monetary aggregates start in 1959.) One clear fact is that the 1990s saw slower money growth than the 1970s and 1980s. The basic lesson of the quantity theory of money—that slower money growth and lower inflation go hand in hand—receives ample support from this decade.

Yet the data give no support for the monetarist view that stability in the monetary aggregates is a prerequisite for economic stability. The standard deviation of M2 growth was not unusually low during the 1990s, and the standard deviation of M1 growth was the highest of the past four decades. In other

---

4. I say "allegedly" because it is not obvious whether Volcker's professed interest in the monetary aggregates was genuine or just a political feint to distract attention from the very high interest rates he needed to disinflate.

Table 1.6
Growth in the Money Supply, Decade by Decade

	1960s	1970s	1980s	1990s
M1				
Average	3.69	6.35	7.78	3.63
Standard deviation	2.15	1.61	4.10	5.42
M2				
Average	7.05	9.49	7.97	4.04
Standard deviation	1.63	3.22	2.29	2.39

Source: Federal Reserve and author's calculations.
Note: Calculations are with monthly data. The growth rate is calculated from 12 months earlier.

words, while the nation was enjoying macroeconomic tranquillity, the money supply was exhibiting high volatility.

From the standpoint of economic theory, this result is not a puzzle. The money supply is one determinant of the overall demand for goods and services in the economy, but there are many others, such as consumer confidence, investor psychology, and the health of the banking system. The view that monetary stability is the only ingredient needed for economic stability is based on a narrow view of what causes the ups and downs of the business cycle. In the end, it's a view that is hard to reconcile with the data.

This lesson was not lost on monetary policy-makers during the 1990s. In February 1993, Fed chairman Alan Greenspan announced that the Fed would pay less attention to the monetary aggregates than it had in the past. The aggregates, he said, "do not appear to be giving reliable indications of economic developments and price pressures."[5] It's easy to see why he might have reached this conclusion when he did. Over the previous 12 months, M1 had grown at an extremely high 12 percent rate, while M2 had grown at an extremely low 0.5 percent rate. Depending on how much weight was given to each of these two measures, monetary policy was either very loose, very tight, or somewhere in between.

Henceforth, the Fed would conduct policy by setting a target for the federal funds rate, the short-term interest rate at which banks make loans to one another. It would adjust the target interest rate in response to changing economic conditions, but it would permit the money supply to do whatever necessary to keep the interest rate on target. If the subsequent performance of the economy is any guide, this policy of ignoring data on the monetary aggregates has proven a remarkably effective operating procedure.

---

5. "Greenspan Upbeat on U.S. Economy," *Financial Times*, February 20, 1993.

1.3.2   Interest Rate Policy: The End of the Inflation Spiral

Choosing the short-term interest rate as an intermediate target for Fed policy is only the first step in conducting monetary policy. The next, more difficult step is to decide what the target rate should be and how the target should respond to changing economic conditions.

There is a long tradition of concern among economists that a central bank's reliance on interest-rate targets could prove inflationary. The argument runs as follows. Imagine that some event—an accidental overheating of the economy, an adverse supply shock, or a sudden scare about impending inflation—starts to drive up expectations of inflation. If the central bank is targeting the nominal interest rate, the rise in expected inflation means an automatic fall in the real interest rate. The fall in the real interest rate stimulates the aggregate demand for goods and services, which in turn puts upward pressure on prices. The rise in prices confirms and reinforces the inflationary expectations that began the process. Thus, expected inflation begets actual inflation, which in turn begets even higher expected inflation. The central bank, committed to its interest-rate target, ends up increasing the money supply at an ever more rapid rate. Inflation spirals out of control.

Fortunately, there is a simple way to avoid this problem: A central bank should raise its interest-rate target in response to any inflationary pressure by enough to choke off that pressure. How much is enough? Economic theory suggests a natural benchmark: if the central bank responds to a one-percentage-point increase in inflation by raising the nominal interest rate by more than one percentage point, then the real interest rate will rise, cooling off the economy. In other words, it is not sufficient that the central bank raise nominal interest rates in response to higher inflation; it is crucial that the response be greater than one-for-one.

These theoretical insights go a long way to explaining the success of monetary policy in the 1990s, as well as its failures in previous decades. The first line of Table 1.7 shows how much the federal funds rate typically responds to changes in core inflation. These numbers are based on a simple statistical analysis of the data on interest rates, unemployment, and inflation (described in the note to the table).

The key result in this table is that the responsiveness of interest rates to inflation has been rising over time. In earlier decades, the response was less than one-for-one. In the 1960s, for instance, when inflation rose by 1 percentage point, the federal funds rate rose by only 0.69 of a percentage point. The theory of spiraling inflation may be the right explanation for the Great Inflation of the

Table 1.7
The Federal Funds Rate, Decade by Decade

	1960s	1970s	1980s	1990s
The typical response of the federal funds rate to a one-percentage-point increase in core inflation	0.69	0.85	0.88	1.39
Standard deviation of the federal funds rate	1.78	2.54	3.38	1.39

Source: Federal Reserve, Department of Labor, and author's calculations.

Note: These numbers are computed using 120 months of data for each decade. The first line is derived from an ordinary least-squares regression of the federal funds rate on a constant, the unemployment rate, and the core inflation rate over the previous 12 months; the table reports the coefficient on core inflation.

1970s. In other words, this episode was the result of the inadequate response of interest-rate policy to the inflationary pressures arising first from the Vietnam war and later from the OPEC oil shocks.

The situation was just the opposite during the 1990s. Each rise in the inflation rate was met by an even larger rise in the nominal interest rate. When inflation rose by 1 percentage point, the federal funds rate typically rose by 1.39 percentage points. This substantial response prevented any incipient inflation from getting out of control.

Although the 1990s saw high responsiveness of interest rates to inflation, it was not a decade of volatile interest rates. The second line in Table 1.7 shows that the federal funds rate, in fact, exhibited low volatility by historical standards. High responsiveness and low volatility may seem a paradoxical combination, but they are easy to reconcile: the more the Fed responds to inflationary pressures when they arise, the less of a problem inflation becomes, and the less it has to respond to later.

Overall, the U.S. experience with monetary policy during the 1990s teaches a simple lesson. To maintain stable inflation and stable interest rates in the long run, a central bank should raise interest rates substantially in the short run in response to any inflationary threat.[6]

1.3.3 A Simple Way to Set Interest Rates Like a Pro

Consider the following simple formula for setting the federal funds rate:

Federal funds rate $= 8.5 + 1.4 \times$ (Core inflation $-$ Unemployment)

---

6. My discussion of interest rates in this section and the next one builds on John Taylor's seminal work on monetary policy rules. See, for instance, Taylor (1999).

Here "core inflation" is the CPI inflation rate over the previous 12 months excluding food and energy, and "unemployment" is the seasonally adjusted unemployment rate. For example, if core inflation is at 3 percent and unemployment is at 5 percent, the federal funds rate should be set at 5.7 percent. The parameters in this formula were chosen to offer the best fit for data from the 1990s.

1.3.3.1 The Case for the Interest-Rate Formula

The logic behind such an interest-rate formula is straightforward. The Fed raises interest rates in response to higher inflation to cool the economy. As we just discussed, the response is more than one-for-one to avoid spiraling inflation. In addition, the Fed responds to high unemployment by cutting interest rates to stimulate aggregate demand.

There are two reasons why the Fed might want to respond to unemployment. First, employment stability may be a goal in itself. At times, legislation has been proposed that would give the Fed single-minded concern about price stability. But the Fed's actual congressional mandate has always been much broader.

Second, unemployment is a leading indicator of future inflation. Low unemployment tends to put upward pressure on wages, which in turn raises production costs and the prices of goods and services. Although some observers have suggested that the combination of low unemployment and low inflation in the late 1990s casts doubt on the "Phillips curve" trade-off between these variables, careful statistical analyses suggest that unemployment and related variables are among the most useful data for forecasting inflation.[7] Other things equal, a Fed that wants to keep inflation in check will respond to low unemployment by raising interest rates.

1.3.3.2 What the Formula Says about Monetary Policy During the 1990s

Figure 1.1 shows the federal funds rate predicted by this simple interest-rate formula and the actual federal funds beginning from 1958. Comparing these two series leads to several conclusions about the conduct of monetary policy.

The first, important observation is that during the 1990s, the two series in Figure 1.1 move closely together. According to a standard measure of goodness of fit (the R^2 statistic), the formula explains 85 percent of movements in the federal funds rate during this time. This tight fit has profound implications for understanding monetary policy. It means that the interest-rate policy during

---

7. See Stock and Watson (1999).

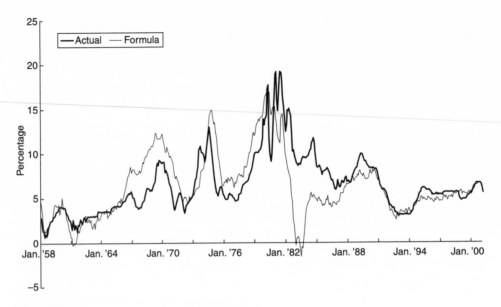

Figure 1.1
Federal Funds Rate: Actual and Hypothetical Formula

the 1990s can be viewed as largely a response to the contemporaneous levels of inflation and unemployment.[8]

A corollary to this conclusion is that the many other issues that dominated public debate over monetary policy during the 1990s must be of secondary importance. The media spent much time discussing the Fed chairman's broad interests, including the stance of fiscal policy, the "irrational exuberance" of the stock market, the productivity gains of the "new economy," the financial crises in Mexico and Asia, and sundry obscure economic data. Apparently, these did not exert a great influence over interest rates. If they had, the formula would not be able to track actual interest rates so well.

A second important observation is that the two series in Figure 1.1 move at about the same time. There was much discussion during the 1990s of the need for the Fed to be preemptive, to respond to economic pressures before they showed up in inflation and unemployment. Being preemptive makes sense, if forecasting is good enough to make the task feasible, because monetary policy influences the economy with a lag typically estimated to be 6 to 12 months. But the strong contemporaneous correlation in Figure 1.1, along with the absence of

---

8. The Greenspan Fed deviated from this formula during the late 1980s, when interest rates rose substantially more than the formula recommended. Arguably, the formula did the better job, and the actual policy was the mistake leading to the 1990–91 recession.

any tendency for the actual interest rate to move before the formula indicates, suggests that policy was not in fact preemptive at all.

1.3.3.3 What the 1990s Teach Us about Earlier Monetary Policy

Figure 1.1 can also be used to make some judgments about monetary policy of the past. We can view the interest-rate formula as a rough approximation to the Greenspan Fed. By comparing the two series, we can see how the Greenspan Fed might have responded to the economic circumstances facing monetary policy-makers of the past.

One conclusion is that the Greenspan Fed of the 1990s would likely have averted the Great Inflation of the 1970s. From the late 1960s to the early 1970s, the formula interest rate in Figure 1.1 is consistently several percentage points above the actual interest rate. The same is true, to a lesser extent, in the late 1970s. This finding is consistent with the result presented in Table 1.7: Fed policy-makers of the 1990s responded more to rising inflation than did their predecessors.

A second conclusion from Figure 1.1 is that the Greenspan Fed would have been much more expansionary in the early 1980s. As the economy experienced the deepest recession since the Great Depression, the Fed would have cut interest rates much more aggressively. (Taken literally, the interest-rate formula says interest rates should have become negative, which is of course impossible.) The disinflation would have been less rapid, but some of the very high unemployment would have been averted.

1.3.4 The Role of the White House

So far, this paper has said little about the Clinton administration. In some ways, this absence is to be expected: Monetary policy is made by the Federal Reserve, which is independent of the executive branch. But the administration did influence monetary policy in several important ways.

The most obvious is the reappointment of Alan Greenspan. In retrospect, this decision may seem like a no-brainer, but at the time it was less obvious. When Greenspan came up for reappointment during Clinton's first term, his reputation was not as solid as it would become: Some observers (including some members of the administration of the elder George Bush) blamed Greenspan for the recession of 1990–91. Moreover, Greenspan was a conservative Republican. It would have been natural for Clinton to want to put a more Democratic stamp on the nation's central bank. That he chose not to do so is notable. To the extent that Greenspan's Fed has been a success, the Clinton administration deserves some of the credit.

The Clinton administration also influenced monetary policy with its other appointments to the Board of Governors. These included Alan Blinder, Ned Gramlich, Laurence Meyer, Alice Rivlin, and Janet Yellen. Compared to the typical appointment to the Fed by other presidents, the Clinton appointees were more prominent within the community of academic economists. Some observers may applaud Clinton for drawing top talent into public service (while others may decry the brain drain from academia). Whether this had any effect on policy is hard to say.

In addition to appointments, the administration also made a significant policy decision: Throughout its eight years, it avoided making public comments about Federal Reserve policy. Given the great influence the Fed has on the economy and the great influence the economy has on presidential popularity, presidents and their subordinates usually have a tough time remaining silent about monetary policy. Yet the Clinton administration avoided this temptation.

A large academic literature indicates that more-independent central banks produce lower and more stable inflation without greater volatility in output or employment. One contributor to this literature was Lawrence Summers, who would later spend eight years as a high Treasury official in the Clinton administration, culminating in the position of Treasury secretary.[9] Thus it is hardly an accident that the Clinton administration was unusually respectful of the Fed's independence. What effect this attitude had on policy is hard to gauge. Perhaps the administration's restraint made it easier for the Fed to raise interest rates when needed without instigating political opposition. It may also have made it easier for the Fed to cut interest rates when needed without sacrificing credibility in the fight against inflation. In this way, the administration's respect for Fed independence may have contributed to the increased responsiveness of interest rates to inflation. If so, the White House again deserves some credit for the Fed's success.

1.4 Is There a Greenspan Legacy?

In May 1964 the *Journal of Finance* published a short paper by a young economist named Alan Greenspan. It was called "Liquidity as a Determinant of Industrial Prices and Interest Rates." Greenspan began his summary of the paper as follows: "I have endeavored to integrate several theoretical approaches to the forecasting of prices, with special emphasis on its relation to interest rates."

---

9. See Alesina and Summers (1993). Campillo and Miron (1997) offer a contrary view.

The paper was a sign of things to come in several ways. First, and most obviously, it showed Greenspan's early interest in liquidity, inflation, and interest rates—topics that are the essence of monetary policy. Second, the paper demonstrated his interest in looking intensely at the data to try to divine upcoming macroeconomic events. According to all staff reports, this has also been a hallmark of his time at the Fed.

Third, the desire to integrate various points of view shows a lack of dogma and nimbleness of mind. Without doubt, these traits have served Greenspan well in his role as Fed chairman. They have made it easier to get along with both Republican and Democratic administrations and to forge a consensus among open-market committee members with their differing theoretical perspectives. They have also made it easier for him to respond to economic circumstances that are changing, unpredictable, and sometimes inexplicable even after the fact.

But there may also be a fourth, less favorable way in which Greenspan's paper presaged the author's later career: It left no legacy. According to the online Social Science Citation Index, the paper was cited in the subsequent literature exactly zero times. This observation raises the question of whether the monetary policy of the 1990s faces a similar fate. Will Greenspan's tenure as Fed chairman leave a legacy for future monetary policy-makers, or will the successful policy of the Greenspan era leave office with the man himself?

Imagine that Greenspan's successor decides to continue the monetary policy of the Greenspan era. How would he do it? The policy has never been fully explained. Quite the contrary: the Fed chairman is famous for being opaque. If a successor tries to emulate the Greenspan Fed, he won't have any idea how. The only consistent policy seems to be: study all the data carefully, and then set interest rates at the right level. Beyond that, there are no clearly stated guidelines.

There is a great irony here. Conservative economists like Milton Friedman have long argued that discretionary monetary policy leads to trouble. They claim that it is too uncertain, too political, and too inflationary. They conclude that monetary policy-makers need to be bound by some sort of monetary-policy rule. This argument is the economic counterpart to John Adams' famous aphorism that "we are a nation of laws, not of men."

These views, together with the great inflation of the 1970s, have influenced central banks around the world. Although no country has yet replaced its central bankers with computers programmed to an automatic monetary rule, as the most extreme critics suggest, there has been movement away from giving central bankers unconstrained discretion. During the 1990s, many nations adopted some form of inflation targeting. In essence, inflation targeting is a commitment to keep inflation at some level or within some narrow range. It can be viewed as a kind of soft rule, or perhaps a way of constraining discretion.[10]

Despite this environment, as well as the fact that a prominent conservative headed the U.S. central bank, the Fed during the 1990s avoided any type of commitment to a policy rule. Conservative economists are skeptical about policies that rely heavily on the judgments of any one man. But that is how monetary policy was made over this decade, and it was hailed as a success by liberals and conservatives alike.

As a practical matter, Fed policy of the 1990s might well be described as "covert inflation targeting" at a rate of about 3 percent. That is, if the Fed had adopted an explicit inflation target at the beginning of the 1990s, the rest of the decade might not have been any different. The virtue of eschewing such a policy framework is that it kept options open—as unconstrained discretion always does. The downside is that it makes it harder for subsequent Fed chairmen to build on the legacy of the 1990s, because it is hard to know what that legacy is.

1.5 The Lessons of the 1990s

This paper has covered a lot of ground. So I finish by summarizing four key lessons for students of monetary policy.

1. The macroeconomic performance of the 1990s was exceptional. Although the average levels of inflation, unemployment, and real growth were similar to those that were experienced in some previous decades, the stability of these measures is unparalleled in U.S. economic history.

2. A large share of the impressive performance of the 1990s was due to good luck. The economy experienced no severe shocks to food or energy prices during this period. Accelerating productivity growth resulting from advances in information technology may also have helped lower unemployment and inflation.

3. Compared to previous eras, monetary policy during the 1990s adjusted interest rates more aggressively in response to changes in core inflation. This approach prevented spiraling inflation. Increased stability in monetary aggregates played no role in the improved macroeconomic performance of this era.

4. The low inflation and economic stability of the 1990s shows that discretionary monetary policy can work well. Yet it leaves only a limited legacy for

---

10. See Bernanke and Mishkin (1997) for a discussion of inflation targeting.

future policy-makers. U.S. monetary policy-makers during the 1990s may well have been engaged in "covert inflation targeting" at a rate of about 3 percent, but they never made that policy explicit.

References

Akerlof, George A., William T. Dickens, and George L. Perry. 1996. "The Macroeconomics of Low Inflation." *Brookings Papers on Economic Activity*, 1:1–76.

Alesina, Alberto, and Lawrence H. Summers. 1993. "Central Bank Independence and Macroeconomic Performance: Some Comparative Evidence." *Journal of Money, Credit, and Banking*, 25 (May): 151–162.

Ball, Laurence, and Robert Moffitt. 2001. "Productivity Growth and the Phillips Curve," Johns Hopkins University.

Bernanke, Ben S., and Frederic S. Mishkin. 1997. "Inflation Targeting: A New Framework for Monetary Policy?" *Journal of Economic Perspective*, 11 (Spring): 97–116.

Blinder, Alan S. 1979. *Economic Policy and the Great Stagflation*. New York: Academic Press.

Campillo, Marta, and Jeffrey A. Miron. 1997. "Why Does Inflation Differ Across Countries?" In Christina D. Romer and David H. Romer, eds., *Reducing Inflation: Motivation and Strategy*, 335–362. Chicago: University of Chicago Press.

Friedman, Milton. 2001. An Interview. *Macroeconomic Dynamics*, 5:101–131.

Greenspan, Alan. 1964. "Liquidity as a Determinant of Industrial Prices and Interest Rates." *Journal of Finance*, 19, no. 2 (May): 159–169.

Stock, James H., and Mark W. Watson. 1999. "Forecasting Inflation." *Journal of Monetary Economics*, 44, no. 2 (October): 293–335.

Summers, Lawrence. 1991. "How Should Long-Term Monetary Policy Be Determined?" *Journal of Money, Credit, and Banking*, 23, no. 3, part 2 (August): 625–631.

Taylor, John B. 1999. "A Historical Analysis of Monetary Policy Rules." In John B. Taylor, ed., *Monetary Policy Rules*. Chicago: University of Chicago Press.

Comments

Alan Blinder

Opening

While the session has a broader title, I will follow Gregory Mankiw's nice background paper in restricting my remarks to monetary policy. I want to briefly review the stellar record of the 1990s, suggest that there really is a Greenspan legacy, and close with a few remarks on the role of Bill Clinton. I should add that Janet Yellen and I have written a short book on the macroeconomic history of the United States.[1] While these remarks are my own, the thoughts are hers as well.

The Greenspan Record

Alan Greenspan, of course, had a great rookie season in 1987—earning well-deserved kudos for his handling of the stock market crash and its aftermath. Some economists—such as Gregory, but *not* me—would argue that he then went too far in raising interest rates in 1988–89, thereby bringing on the recession that brought on Bill Clinton. And many—now *including* me—would argue that he was too slow to cut interest rates in 1990 and 1991. At that point, one might have rated him a B+ or A− central banker. But since then, it is hard to find fault with the Greenspan record, which is simply off the charts.

Gregory's means and variances by decade do not quite "speak for themselves." To put some meat on these bones, let me briefly review the four main episodes of monetary policy during the Clinton presidency. When the story opens in January 1993, the real federal funds rate is roughly zero, indicating the extraordinarily expansionary monetary stance that the Greenspan Fed finally attained in mid-1992.

---

1. Alan S. Blinder and Janet L. Yellen, *The Fabulous Decade: Macroeconomic Lessons from the 1990s.* New York: Century Foundation Press, 2001.

I call the first episode *pedal to the metal*, and it illustrates that doing nothing can sometimes be a remarkably effective and even bold policy. The Fed held the real funds rate at about zero until February 1994—a period of more than 18 months.[2] That constituted an extremely large dose of extremely easy money— more than enough to make most traditional central bankers' knuckles turn white. Indeed, the transcripts of FOMC meetings in late 1993 and early 1994 reveal that Greenspan was restraining several members of the committee who wanted to raise rates sooner and faster.

The second praiseworthy episode is the vaunted *soft landing* in 1994–95. The Fed raised interest rates by 300 basis points between February 1994 and February 1995. But, unlike its own past history and the history of many central banks, it did not take the tightening cycle too far and cause a recession. I was vice chairman of the Fed during this period, and I can tell you that several of the calls were neither obvious nor easy. Hawkish sentiment and inflation phobia were running high—both in the financial markets and in the FOMC—and there were some truly contentious FOMC meetings. But the Fed stopped in time and then backed off its peak rates (starting in July 1995), thereby guiding the economy to what then appeared to be a tolerable estimate of the NAIRU.

Episode three begins in early 1996 and stretches into mid-1999, with a notable interruption in 1998 to deal with the world financial crisis. I call this the period of *forbearance* because, once again, the Fed did essentially nothing— despite the fact that the economy grew surprisingly rapidly and the unemployment rate fell and fell and fell. Yes, there was plenty of good luck during this period—indeed, more than Gregory mentions. But Gregory fails to appreciate how difficult it is for a central banker to hold his fire in the face of such provocations! I believe that few if any previous Fed chairmen or heads of other central banks would have let the punch bowl sit there so long while the party raged on. And we know that superdove Greenspan was holding the FOMC hawks at bay through much of this period. To me, it was his finest hour.

The fourth episode is still in progress, and therefore too early to appraise—or even to name! The policy of forbearance ended in June 1999 and the Fed raised interest rates 175 basis points between then and May 2000. At the time of this writing, it is anybody's guess whether this tightening will produce a second soft landing (which would set a new Olympic record) or a recession.

---

2. Since inflation was stable at about 3 percent, that meant holding the nominal federal funds rate constant at 3 percent.

Is There a Greenspan Legacy?

Gregory is dubious, and his point about the purely discretionary and sometimes opaque "Greenspan standard" is surely correct. But let me mention three
legacies that I think will prove to be of enduring importance.

First, Alan Greenspan has demonstrated that what we once called fine-tuning
is indeed possible—if not in theory, then at least in practice. As a Princeton
undergraduate in the optimistic 1960s, I was taught that intelligent and nimble
applications of fiscal and monetary policy could stabilize the economy. When
Gregory was a Princeton student in the unhappy late 1970s, he was taught (by
people like me!) that fine-tuning was impossible—which continues to be the
conventional wisdom. But Greenspan has proven this conventional wisdom
wrong. Yes, he was lucky. But he was also skillful, making a series of excellent
judgments that were not always obvious. What Greenspan has accomplished
probably eclipses Walter Heller's fondest dreams.

Second, I believe the Greenspan Fed has dramatically demonstrated the benefits of giving your central bank a dual mandate—to pursue both price stability
and high levels of employment. Just ask yourself what might have happened in
the United States in the 1990s if, say, the old Bundesbank or the new ECB had
made our monetary policy? Gregory observes that a certain Taylor rule characterizes the decisions of the Greenspan Fed quite well. It does. But remember:
That equation is a statistical average of episodes in which the Fed was concentrating on reducing unemployment and others in which it was concentrating on
fighting inflation. A comparison of today's monetary policy here and in Euro-
land is again instructive. In the United States, headline inflation has roughly
doubled and the unemployment rate is still near a generational low. Yet the
Fed has been aggressively cutting interest rates. In Europe, the macroeconomy
is deteriorating, but the ECB is hamstrung by its inflation-only mandate. You
choose.

Third, while it is true that Greenspan is far from an open book, it is also
true—though barely noticed—that he has moved a long way along the road to
transparency. As late as 1993, the FOMC did not even announce its decisions
when they were made; they left it to market insiders to figure out. Greenspan
even defended this indefensible practice. Then he changed it. The Fed's myste-
rious (and unannounced) "bias" has given way to a much clearer (and publicly
announced) "balance of risk" sentence that accompanies each FOMC decision.
You no longer hear Greenspan priding himself on "mumbling with great inco-
herence" (his own self-description) or telling senators that, if they thought they
understood what he meant, he must have misspoken. Those days are gone—
forever, I believe.

The Contribution of Bill Clinton

Finally, a few points on the contributions of President Clinton to the successful monetary policy of the 1990s are in order. Gregory mentions two of them.

First, excluding myself but including Alice Rivlin, his appointments to the Fed were truly excellent—and quite nonpolitical. Most important, of course, were his decisions to reappoint Greenspan as chairman in both 1996 and 2000. But his overall list compares favorably to that of any president, I believe.

Second, and not to be underestimated, was Clinton's religious adherence to a hands-off-the-Fed policy. This is not a natural position for the leader of the free world, and few, if any, of our past presidents have managed to do it. I vividly recall the day in Little Rock in January 1993 when I told President-elect Clinton that, where the economy was concerned, he had just been elected to the *second* most important position in the country—the first was already filled by Alan Greenspan. You could see him frown a bit. But Clinton listened to his economic advisers—most of whom are present at this conference—and never jawboned the Fed. This extreme respect for the central bank's independence made the Fed's job easier, I believe. It never had to dig in its heels to prove its manhood.

Third, and finally, we should not forget the deficit reduction package of 1993. For years, the budget deficit was a source of conflict between the president and the central bank. In the Reagan-Volcker years, it led to a ruinous policy mix of loose fiscal policy and excruciatingly tight money. Bill Clinton helped reverse that, and the Clinton-Greenspan mix of tight budgets and easier money contributed to the investment boom. According to Bob Woodward, Greenspan told Clinton in January 2000 that "I couldn't have done it without what you did on deficit reduction. If you had not turned the fiscal situation around, we couldn't have had the kind of monetary policy we've had."[3] While we should perhaps apply a politeness discount to these words, we should not ignore them. Greenspan was in a position to know.

---

3. Bob Woodward, *Maestro: Greenspan's Fed and the American Boom.* New York: Simon and Schuster, 2000, page 221.

Comments

William Poole

I'm in the vulnerable position, of course, of speaking about my boss. Beyond that risk, there are always two risks in talking about a legacy for someone who is still in office. Obviously, historians don't like to do that. Perhaps economists take risks that historians do not. But the Greenspan era is not over. And the evaluation of this era is going to depend on some of the data yet to come. So I'll just note that fact at the outset of my discussion.

I also want to issue the standard Fed disclaimer. I'm speaking for myself and not representing official Federal Reserve policy.

My remarks will overlap to some extent with what Alan Blinder just said. I do want to focus on the legacy issue because I think that issue is particularly interesting. I'll concentrate on three particular elements of the legacy issue. One element is attitudes toward inflation; a second, disclosure; and the third, the conduct of monetary policy. I'll finish by offering a couple of comments about Gregory Mankiw's assertions on luck.

In terms of attitudes toward inflation and performance in creating low and steady inflation, I think we really need to talk about the Volcker-Greenspan years and the legacy that comes from their period in office. They have clearly shown that bringing down inflation and keeping it down can be done. And this experience shows that the economy works better at low inflation. These outcomes may seem obvious now, in 2001. But there was certainly an awful lot of discussion in the 1970s about the enormous costs of bringing down inflation. Some argued that the real issue was steady inflation, not high inflation. The argument was that high inflation really didn't matter if inflation was steady. But we now have convincing evidence that the economy really does work better at low inflation. So, a part of the Volcker-Greenspan legacy is an understanding that we don't have to put up with an economy that is operating in an environment such as we had in the 1970s.

Moreover, the courage and skill of both Volcker and Greenspan in pursuing a strategy of low inflation when it was certainly not so easy will make it more likely that the Fed will pursue sound policy in difficult and uncomfortable circumstances—that is, the task will be easier for future Fed leadership. Once you have a record of success, it's easier to build on that record and to continue to pursue such policies.

The experience of the 1990s certainly shows that sustained low inflation is not inconsistent with high economic growth and high employment. Now, we may say it is obvious that such an outcome was possible. And there were certainly a lot of economists who insisted that low inflation is good for growth and employment. But that view was by no means generally accepted by all economists, and certainly not necessarily accepted among the broader general public.

Second on my list of important legacies is disclosure. I think that we underestimate the importance of the FOMC decision in February 1994 to release its policy decision immediately following the FOMC meeting. That decision, of course, wiped out a substantial chunk of capital from those Fed watchers who no longer had that aspect of their job to perform. But thinking more broadly, it used to be that the Fed tried to signal its intentions through discount rate changes. Sometimes the Fed matched discount rate changes with changes in the Fed funds target and sometimes not, intending to send a signal of some sort. In fact, it's a lot easier to make announcements through the use of English and press statements than it is through these obtuse policy maneuvers, which left the market trying to decipher the entrails of the various policy actions. I think that moving toward greater disclosure and clearer Fed communication with the market has been a very productive thing to do.

Moreover, I really do have the sense that the press commentary about Fed policy and the general public understanding of monetary policy have quite dramatically improved in recent years. Disclosure has contributed to the improved understanding. Certainly Greenspan's high public visibility contributes to that too, as does the general success of monetary policy. Improved public understanding of what the Fed is doing is a healthy development.

I'll now talk about the conduct of monetary policy. I'll start by quoting a sentence in Gregory's paper. He says, "Imagine that Greenspan's successor decides to continue the monetary policy of the Greenspan era. How would he do it? The policy has never been fully explained." I understand Gregory's point but there's a lot more to be said on this subject.

First of all, amplifying a point Alan Blinder made, without any doubt Greenspan has demonstrated that it is possible for the Federal Reserve to manage policy quite actively. Although we may disagree on exactly what the nature of "fine-tuning" is and how to characterize it, I agree that Greenspan has managed policy actively. And doing so has produced a better outcome than would have been likely under a constant-money-growth rule. Further, the outcome has been better than *any* rule that anyone has yet constructed. The Taylor rule is useful, but when you look carefully, particularly episode by episode, I think that the actual Fed policy actions have beaten the Taylor rule or any other rule. This observation means that macroeconomists have a big agenda because we ought to be working on formalizing what the Fed does so that we may pass the regularities of successful policy along to another generation. Greenspan's success with active policy management sets up a research agenda, but the fact that he hasn't come up with an analysis of the policy regularities underlying his success does not detract at all from his accomplishment.

Second, I think that one of the characteristics of the Taylor rule which Mankiw rightly emphasizes is that in the 1990s the Fed's target rate for the Fed funds rate moved aggressively relative to the inflation rate. In the Taylor rule, the funds rate responds more than one-for-one to the inflation rate. That is an important characteristic of successful policy and is part of the legacy of this era. We understand better than before that the Fed does need to move aggressively to keep inflation under control, and that understanding is well incorporated in current policy practice. But more than that, I think that particular episodes where the Fed has moved aggressively—1994 is the best example—demonstrate the value of moving vigorously *before* there is any noticeable inflation to move against. There was a lot of squawking in 1994 because people kept saying, "Where is the inflation?" "Why does the Fed have to move?"

The fact that we came out of the 1994 episode so favorably also establishes part of the legacy for a future policy that is preemptive—that prevents inflation from getting started in the first place. There are other episodes that teach the same lesson.

I agree with what Alan Blinder said about the relationship between the Federal Reserve and the administration. A low-decibel relationship between the administration and the Fed is very helpful for achieving a good monetary policy, and the standard set during the Clinton years sets a fine precedent for the future. In fact, the Greenspan era has produced a double piece of evidence on that issue because the relationship with the first Bush administration was not so constructive in that regard.

I would also emphasize the importance of a high degree of credibility. Credibility buys a lot. One of the reasons why the Greenspan Fed has been able to move so vigorously at certain times is that, certainly by now, and not many years into his tenure, there was never any doubt about his commitment to low inflation or about his nerve and skill to actually adjust policy to yield low inflation. It's quite interesting to look at measures of inflation expectations and to see how little they have moved even though there have been some pretty significant changes from time to time in the headline CPI. Longer-term inflation expectations have held just about rock solid. The market's view reflects an understanding of a Federal Reserve commitment. The Fed does enjoy a high degree of credibility; otherwise, inflation expectations would not behave that way.

Let me finish with a couple of comments about luck. The Greenspan years were not without shocks. It's outside the 1990s, of course, but the 1987 stock market crash was a huge shock—a very large surprise. The crash was a shock for which our knowledge and precedents from the past of exactly what to do were not all that well worked out. I think most of us thought about the stock market crash of 1929 as an event that could never recur. And yet it did happen again in 1987, and the Greenspan Fed was successful in dealing with it. The Gulf War was a significant shock. In 1997 and 1998 we saw the Asian financial crisis, the Russian default, the near collapse of Long-Term Capital Management, and associated disruptions in the U.S. financial markets. The Fed dealt pretty successfully with those problems.

I believe that the Fed's clear commitment to low inflation reduces the number and severity of shocks and makes it easier to deal with those that do occur. The issues of luck and credibility are intertwined. Good policy contributes to good luck. Anyone who has been in office, I think, knows that once things start to go wrong, then often there are other things that go wrong as well. Once you start to get a string of bad luck, perhaps because of some of the ways the political process works, then things tend to become unstuck more generally. So part of what Mankiw views as good luck is in fact a consequence of good policy. I really believe that. If any of you have ever been involved in competitive sailing, you know that the people who win races always seem to be on the right side of the lucky wind shifts. Somehow they are able to sniff out the wind. And in fact it's not just luck that things go so very well.

Comments

Alice M. Rivlin

I enjoyed Gregory Mankiw's excellent paper and agreed with much of it. In particular, I strongly concur that the superb performance of the United States economy in the 1990s cannot be attributed primarily to monetary policy. Mankiw refers to the role of "luck," meaning primarily the absence of the demand and supply shocks that beset other recent decades, especially the 1970s.

I prefer to emphasize a longer list of favorable economic factors that came together in the 1990s:

• Being at a point in the technology cycle when an extraordinary volume of innovation was ready for implementation.

• Having an extremely competitive economy, as a result of American firms' responses to globalization plus several decades of increasingly procompetitive policies, such as freer trade and deregulation.

• Smoothly functioning capital markets, including a well-developed venture capital market.

• Strong fiscal policy dedicated to reducing the federal budget deficit and ultimately, to reducing the national debt.

These factors are not exactly "luck," but they combined powerfully to make monetary policy easier.

Mankiw's assignment was to focus on "the 1990s," so he understandably used decades as units of analysis. For some purposes this approach works well. Indeed, the striking decline in the volatility of almost all the macroeconomic indicators he examines distinguishes the 1990s clearly from other decades.

With respect to productivity, however, the decade is not a suitable time unit. Clearly, something bad happened to productivity growth after 1973 and lasted more than 20 years. Something good happened after 1994 and lasted, at least, through 2000. (As others have pointed out, 2000 belongs in the 1990s.) My brief career as a central banker occurred during this remarkable spurt of productivity growth.

During my tenure at the Federal Reserve (mid-1996 to mid-1999), the Federal Open Market Committee (FOMC) was focused on three big monetary policy dilemmas:

• How to understand the strong productivity growth—was it a temporary fluke or a more sustained shift to a higher potential growth path?

• How to react to the world financial crisis—should we keep our eyes on the domestic economy or try to be the central bank of the world?

• What, if anything, to do about the stock market—should we only worry about the market's impact on the macro economy or try to prevent a bubble that might later burst?

Mankiw suggests that the Federal Reserve policy in the 1990s reflected a covert inflation target of 3 percent. I think that means that he believes the Fed consciously followed a policy rule designed to keep inflation at or below 3 percent, but did not make the rule public. I do not believe the FOMC consciously pursued a specific inflation target during my tenure, but perhaps someone forgot to tell me.

In evaluating the Federal Reserve policy actions, it is important to remember that, despite the impression created by the press and books such as Bob Woodward's *Maestro*, Alan Greenspan does not make monetary policy all by himself. He chairs a committee. The FOMC is a large, unwieldy committee— all 19 members participate actively, although only 12 vote at any one time— and members often have quite diverse views about the objectives of monetary policy.

In a committee situation, most chairmen find it easier to get agreement on policy than on the objectives of policy, and the FOMC is no exception. Greenspan is a strong chairman, but he devotes his leadership skill to forging consensus views on policy, and he does not waste time trying to get agreement on policy rules.

During the period I was at the Fed, I remember only one serious discussion about inflation targeting. It was a seminar-type session of the FOMC, instigated by Janet Yellen, probably in the summer of 1996. We had a stimulating discussion that touched on many of the issues treated in Gregory Mankiw's paper, including the question of whether or not moderate rates of inflation actually do some good. But we did not reach a consensus on the need for an inflation target, much less on what the target should be if we were to have one. There were proponents of zero inflation, proponents of 2 or 3 percent, proponents of ranges, and advocates, including myself, of not having an inflation target at all.

Personally, I think an inflation target for the Federal Reserve is a bad idea, whose time has passed. Inflation targets may be useful for small open economies or developing countries in danger of hyperinflation, but not for big industrial economies such as our own. Keeping inflation under control should not be the only objective of the central bank. The ultimate objective is a higher standard of living for average people. Hence, the central bank ought to be trying to keep the economy on the highest sustainable growth path. Inflation matters only if it is high enough to threaten the sustainability of growth.

Mankiw reminds us more than once in his paper that monetary theory tells us that monetary policy does not affect growth in the long run. That is certainly the received wisdom, but it may not be entirely true. A central bank that is willing, as the Fed was from 1996 to 1999 (Blinder's "forbearance period"), to run the inflation risk of extremely tight labor markets, may be able to raise potential growth for the long run. Extremely tight labor markets provide powerful incentives for workers to get more training, for companies to use their workforce more productively, and for investing in laborsaving technology. In any case, central bank decisions about interest rates are always made in the short run, when the trade-offs between more growth and less inflation always appear to be real.

When the central bank is performing a balancing act with respect to growth and inflation, an explicit inflation target can reduce its flexibility, as the current situation of the European Central Bank (ECB) amply illustrates. At a moment when both European and world growth are slowing and a bit of easing from the ECB would help to reinforce the easing policy of the Fed, the ECB is stuck with a 0 to 2 percent inflation target, stated in terms of a headline consumer price index buffeted by energy prices.

Nor is inflation targeting useful when the central bank faces a stagnant economy, such as the one facing the Bank of Japan, with falling prices and interest rates in the zero range. The central bank can say that inflation has fallen below its target range, and that it is trying to generate more inflation, but that is a tough case to make to the public. The real objective of the central bank is not more rapid price increase, but faster growth, and it would seem more honest to say so.

I believe that FOMC members ought to keep stressing to the public that their goal is to maximize sustainable growth—to keep the economy as close as possible to its potential growth rate. The problem is that it is so hard to know what potential growth is. During 1996–99, we were guessing. We were increasingly sure that potential growth was shifting up, but we did not know by how much; nor did we know how long the new trend rate would last. We were also guessing about inflation. Was the inflation rate falling for temporary reasons that might easily reverse? When might these positive forces, such as the high dollar and subdued medical cost growth, turn around? These are interesting questions, but they do not make it easy to set monetary policy.

In the history of monetary policy in the 1990s, I believe one episode deserves special attention—namely, the monetary easing in the fall of 1998. That was the moment when the Federal Reserve found itself not just the central bank of the world's largest economy, but close to being the central bank of the world. The world financial crisis, which had begun the year before in Thailand, had spread from Asia to Russia to Long-Term Credit Management (LTCM), and it was threatening to engulf Brazil. Investors were pulling back everywhere. Risk aversion was rampant. No one seemed to want to own anything riskier than U.S. Treasuries. There was no cogent domestic reason for cutting interest rates—the U.S. economy was growing rapidly—and the U.S. short-term interest rate hardly seemed an ideal instrument for dealing with a world financial crisis. But it was the only instrument we had available, so we used it. We cut the Fed funds rate three times, largely in an effort to reassure world financial markets that the Fed was on the case and doing what it could to get things back to normal. It worked—or something worked—and the threatened next round of financial market instability did not occur.

Finally, there was the stock market. The rising tide of equity prices—out of line with earnings—was worrisome. Clearly, there was irrational exuberance, as Alan Greenspan put it. It might well be a bubble, and, if so, it might burst. The situation was nervous-making. The United States did not have general asset price inflation, as the Japanese and others had faced in the past, but we clearly had equity price inflation, especially in the high-flying technology sector.

The problem was that we did not have a specific instrument for restraining stock prices without punishing the rest of the economy, and we did not have a cogent case for slowing the whole economy down. So, we worried, but we did not do anything.

We worried mostly about whether the wealth effect was overstimulating consumption. However, there were plenty of other reasons for consumer spending being high—high employment, rising incomes, strong confidence—and it was not clear that the wealth effect was dominant. In retrospect, I think we focused too much on possible equity price effects on consumption and not enough on investment effects. We thought that investment had to be good—good for productivity, and hence for future growth—and did not worry enough about the possibility that all that cheap equity was creating excess capacity. But hindsight is easier than foresight!

Alan Blinder, in response to Gregory Mankiw's presentation, pointed out that in practice, inflation targeting is not a rule in the sense of Friedman, which would require a machine, not a "king." Under inflation targeting, one still needs to decide what to do at each particular instance. *Mankiw* agreed and termed this a form of "constrained discretion" as described by Bernanke and Mishkin, a halfway house between complete discretion and a rigid rule.

William Poole felt that it is misleading to look at the entire Greenspan tenure as one unbroken block. We should recognize that there is a natural cycle for anyone coming into a new position. The earlier Greenspan years, for example, had a much stronger focus on building credibility. *Jeffrey Frankel's* view is that the same was true of Paul Volcker in the first few years of his tenure, and of the entire European Central Bank now.

Ben Friedman opened up the general discussion with three additional comments about the 1990s. First, he asserted that part of the legacy of the 1990s is not just a commitment to low inflation, but a noncommitment to zero inflation. With new evidence that 2.5 or 3 percent inflation can also be stable, Friedman was glad to see the "mania" for zero inflation gone in the 1990s. The second change is the acceptance and willingness to focus on core inflation. One used to hear that it was not legitimate to dismiss prices that were rapidly rising, even if they were oil or food prices. Now it is accepted. It would be interesting to consider whether the 1970s might have worked out better had the focus been put on core rather than "headline" inflation. Finally, he saw as another legacy Greenspan's demonstrated willingness to use monetary policy to address the needs of the real economy. Suggesting that actions of the Federal Reserve are still far from transparent, Friedman nevertheless praised the Fed's apparent willingness to let the growth rate of the economy rise and unemployment fall without intervening.

Alice Rivlin concurred that she didn't perceive the Fed as being reluctant to express its concern about the real economy, and said that the FOMC statements reflect this point of view fully. She then gave *Alan Blinder* credit for pushing for more transparency in explaining the Fed's actions to the public while he was there.

Mankiw agreed that the Fed is aiming for price stability defined as an inflation rate of 3 percent, not zero. He cited a paper by Lawrence Summers a decade ago arguing for an optimal inflation rate between 2 and 3 percent, and marveled that it is indeed what we have today. As for caring about the real economy, he pointed out that it is not inconsistent with using inflation targeting as a rule. As many studies have shown, real economic activities are some of the most important variables for forecasting inflation.

Martin Baily first raised some concerns about the interpretation of the finding of a Taylor rule with an 85 percent R^2 in *Mankiw's* paper. He questioned the use of the unemployment rate, a lagging indicator, as something that the Federal Reserve would use as a target, and asked James Stock to comment on whether unemployment is indeed a good forecaster for inflation. In addition, he pointed out that the core Personal Consumption Expenditure (PCE) deflator would have been a more appropriate inflation variable to look at, rather than the Consumer Price Index (CPI). In terms of successful monetary policy-making, he praised Greenspan for his willingness and ability to read and interpret large amounts of data, and to detect early signs of turning points in the economy.

William Poole agreed that Greenspan has an uncanny ability to read and interpret data within a real, coherent framework. As for the issue of core versus headline inflation, and particularly the energy component, he pointed out the additional advantage we have today of a well-developed futures market with long maturities. This makes the situation very different from the 1970s when such information was not available to assess market sentiments. With the use of core inflation and the help of futures price information, it is much easier for the Fed to distinguish transitory versus permanent disturbances.

Alan Blinder commented on the 85 percent R^2 result and the feasibility of adopting a Taylor-rule approach in practice. He stated that at any FOMC meeting, the staff would present the committee with many different versions of the Taylor rule, using different specific definitions of the variables. Each version would have an R^2 of at least 85 percent, and yet the equations would generate an interest rate range of 100 to 150 basis points. This range of variation was much greater than the range of variation in which the FOMC was considering setting interest rates.

On why the economy did so well in the 1990s, *Mankiw* put the answers into three categories. One is luck. We had good shocks, and these are definitely part of the explanation. Second, the Fed reacted more aggressively to offset inflationary pressure, as demonstrated in the data by the substantially larger coefficient measuring the reaction of interest rates. The last part is what one may call the "Magic of Greenspan," actions independent of inflation and unemployment signals. *Mankiw* attributed this to the leftover 15 percent residual in the equation. He argued that the combination of luck and aggressive response is a much larger part of the story than the publicly perceived Greenspan miracle. And had better data been used instead, as suggested by Baily, the R^2 would presumably have been higher than 85 percent, and thus the residual would have been even less of a "miracle."

James Stock clarified the issue of an unemployment-based Taylor rule. The equation is usually specified with an output gap rather than an unemployment gap. He pointed out that during the last half of the 1990s the unemployment rate had gone down significantly. As the Taylor rule is designed to look for deviations of the interest rate from some long-term natural rate of interest that shifts up if productivity shifts up, this downward trend of the unemployment rate, as a target, would pick up the upward trend in productivity. This interpretation may be one explanation of why Mankiw's model fits well. While it may be coincidental or reflect some deeper relationship, one should not just dismiss it as spurious.

In response to *Rivlin's* remark on whether the Fed should have responded to the investment effect of the stock market boom, *Hal Varian* pointed out that the stock market boom was mostly a NASDAQ boom, by which he meant a high-tech boom, with little movement in the rest of the S&P. The Fed would not have any policy tools to deflate the NASDAQ without deflating the S&P.

Alice Rivlin concurred with this view and said that even to the extent that the boom was in the broader market, the Fed could not have deflated it without hurting the rest of the economy. She suggested that perhaps the Fed could have considered raising the margin requirement rate.

Bill Niskanen stated that the most important macro lesson from the last two decades is that there is no long-term Phillips curve, with the implication that a monetary policy rule needs to be consistent with a low expected core inflation rate. Between 1992 and the first quarter of 1998, he contended, the Fed followed a very tight McCallum rule, where domestic final sales never deviated from the equation more than 0.3 percent on a quarterly basis. The subsequent two years were characterized by domestic demand growing at roughly 8 percent per annum, presumably in response to the international financial crises. Now we are in the middle of correcting that surge. He urged the profession to reflect on these experiences of the 1990s to assess what the appropriate monetary rule should be, as it is a lesson yet to be learned.

William Poole was in general agreement, and offered additional insights on the making of monetary policy. He pointed out that the detail of statistical record shows numerous instances of the market interest rates moving well in advance of the federal funds rate. Most recently, for example, the long-term rates peaked in May 2000 and went down long before the Federal Reserve adjusted the federal funds rate. Subsequently, the long rates stayed relatively constant in 2001 despite the enormous decline in federal funds rate. Poole attributed this constancy to the credibility the Fed has achieved over the years, allowing it to sit back and rely more heavily on the stabilizing mechanism of the market itself. *Mankiw* agreed with Poole's observation. When the Fed was credibly committed to adjusting the short rate aggressively in response to inflationary pressure, then the need to be preemptive would disappear, as the long rates would be preemptive for it.

Rivlin felt that following a strict monetary rule is a very academic exercise. The Fed would not benefit from setting a specific inflation target. She believed giving sensible people with good working knowledge of the economy the discretion to run the Fed is more effective.

Robert Lawrence observed that while much has been made of the discipline the Clinton administration exercised in not commenting on monetary policy, and appropriately so, the Federal Reserve does not seem to have the same inhibition in commenting on other public policies. He asked for panelists' views on this practice.

Rivlin expressed concern about the impact of Greenspan's comments on the Bush tax bill. She said she thought even Greenspan was surprised by the public reaction it generated, as he had intended simply to reassert his view as a conservative economist in favor of lowering taxes and having a small government, rather than to endorse any particular tax plan.

Niskanen pointed out, however, that Greenspan had raised a new point, in addition to the small-government point, which is that he did not want to use Fanny Mae bonds to conduct monetary policy. So, Greenspan was worried about prematurely paying off all of the explicit government debt and depriving the Fed of a market in which to operate. *Rivlin* said she was less worried than Chairman Greenspan about the consequences of running out of federal debt.

Alan Blinder pointed out that these comments are specific to the leader of the Fed, but not to all members of the FOMC. He felt that while Greenspan has somehow acquired the license to be a "guru" on all policies, this license would not necessarily get transferred to the next leader of the Fed. Blinder perceived such behavior as hazardous. If the Fed can poach on other people's turf, then other people can poach on the Fed's.

Poole stated that his own policy is to not comment at all, even on the practices of other central banks in the world. However, in Greenspan's defense, he was not the first chairman to comment on fiscal policy.

Eugene Steuerle suggested that besides the interaction between monetary and fiscal policies, the interaction between monetary and tax policies can also have significant impact on investment decisions and the state of the economy. In periods of high inflation and high tax rates, confusions in accounting are likely to result in erroneous investment decisions. For example, with an inflation rate of 10 percent and a tax rate of 50 percent, the interest rate needs to rise by up to 20 percentage points to achieve a positive real after-tax interest rate. If it does not, Steuerle argued, investment could go into semi-unproductive channels. With the inflation rate declining and moderate taxes since the 1980s, investment decisions have improved, as the accounting system matures and the before- and after-tax returns converge.

Mankiw agreed regarding this cost of inflation. He then suggested that, although in a hyperinflationary environment monetary and fiscal policies do closely interact, their linkage might be overstated in a moderate-inflation, moderate-deficit country such as the United States. Agreeing with William Poole's view that the Greenspan policy is a continuation of Volcker's, Mankiw pointed to successful use of monetary policy to reduce inflation despite the large budget deficit in the early 1980s, and now the budget surplus.

Rivlin asked about the recessionary period in the early 1980s. *Mankiw* responded that while there is no doubt that monetary policy had caused the recession, fiscal policy didn't make it any easier or harder to reduce inflation. The recession would have occurred with or without the fiscal policy.

Blinder did not think there was one Volcker-Greenspan policy, as the two faced fundamentally different challenges. Paul Volcker came in with the mandate to squelch high inflation, while during Greenspan's tenure there was essentially no net change in the inflation rate. So Greenspan's legacy is indeed his incredible ability to fine-tune the economy, a very different task from Volcker's.

David Wilcox argued that an unfavorable versus favorable monetary and fiscal policy mix is essential for explaining the macroeconomic differences between the 1980s and the 1990s. He suggested that while Volcker was confronted with high interest rates, low capital formation, and low productivity growth, Greenspan had the benefit of a favorable mix, with interest rates at their appropriate level, lots of capital formation, and accelerated productivity growth.

Mankiw clarified his view that while he does not think monetary policy can completely ignore fiscal conditions, monetary policy-making is not fundamentally different under a 2 percent budget deficit or 2 percent surplus. He also reemphasized accelerated productivity growth as part of Greenspan's good luck. He attributed this growth to the budget surplus and a technological take-off, having little to do with deliberate policy, either monetary or fiscal.

Fiscal Policy and Social Security Policy During the 1990s

Douglas W. Elmendorf, Jeffrey B. Liebman, and David W. Wilcox

PANELISTS: *Martin Feldstein, Rudolph G. Penner, and Robert Rubin*

2.1 Introduction

The 1990s witnessed two fundamental changes in U.S. fiscal policy: a dramatic improvement in the current and projected budget balance and a shift to a new political consensus in favor of balancing the budget excluding Social Security rather than the unified budget. In contrast, the 1990s did not witness significant changes in Social Security policy, although alternative visions of Social Security reform received tremendous analytic and popular attention. This paper reviews the course of fiscal policy and Social Security policy during the 1990s, including the economic and political forces that changed fiscal policy and left Social Security policy largely unchanged.

In January 1990 the Congressional Budget Office (CBO) projected that the unified budget deficit would exceed $100 billion during the fiscal year then under way and would remain at about that level for the following five years. Two years later, the CBO projected that the budget deficit would hit $350

We thank Al Davis, Peter Diamond, Edward Gramlich, Peter Orszag, Gene Sperling, and Lawrence Summers for comments on an earlier draft. The views expressed in this paper are those of the authors and are not necessarily shared by any of the institutions with which they are affiliated.

billion in fiscal year 1992, fall by half over the following four years, and then turn up again to pass $400 billion in 2002.[1] Yet, by January 2001 the budget had recorded its third consecutive unified surplus, and the CBO projected that, under unchanged law, unified surpluses would total more than $5.5 trillion over the next decade. This dramatic shift in the budget outlook stemmed both from favorable developments in the economic environment and from deliberate policy actions that reduced budget deficits and later did not spend down the surpluses.

The second respect in which the fiscal landscape was transformed during the 1990s was in the presumed standard for determining whether the federal government was living within its means. Until the past few years, debate and decision-making about the federal budget almost invariably were conducted in terms of the unified budget, and the fiscal objective was generally assumed—either implicitly or explicitly—to be balance in the unified budget. But in the summer of 1999, buoyed by the progress of the preceding several years, the political consensus shifted suddenly and dramatically to the objective of balancing the budget excluding the current operations of the Social Security system, while aiming to put Social Security into 75-year actuarial balance. This change has had important implications for the political conversation about the budget. For example, in early 2001, Congress debated the disposition of roughly $3.1 trillion in projected on-budget surpluses over the next ten years rather than $5.6 trillion in unified surpluses. The disposition of roughly $2.5 trillion in projected Social Security surpluses essentially was not disputed; virtually everyone assumed that they would be used to pay down debt held by the public.

Changes of comparable magnitude did not occur in Social Security policy during the 1990s, although significant reforms of the program were debated at great length. It has been clear for some time that the aging of the U.S. population will eventually require significant changes in Social Security revenues or benefits. The reforms enacted in 1977 and 1983 set payroll tax revenues above contemporaneous outlays, so that future benefits could be partly prefunded through an accumulation of assets in the Social Security trust fund. The 1994–96 Advisory Council on Social Security presented three reform plans that placed important emphasis on additional prefunding. Each involved some form of investment in equities—either centrally, through the trust fund, or in a decentralized manner, through individual accounts. Late in the decade, with the emergence of on-budget surpluses, the possibility of general revenue contributions to the Social Security system came under serious consideration. In

---

1. The CBO was too pessimistic about FY1992: the unified deficit that year came in at $290 billion.

the end, President Bill Clinton decided to pursue Social Security reform based on general revenue contributions to the trust fund and centralized investment in equities rather than creating individual accounts, but his proposal was not adopted.

The remainder of the paper explores these themes more closely. The second section summarizes the changing budget outlook, and the subsequent sections proceed chronologically through a decade of fiscal policy and Social Security policy.

2.2 Budget Outcomes and Projections

Figures 2.1 and 2.2 plot the unified federal budget surplus and federal debt held by the public, both expressed as a share of GDP, since the end of World War II. The improvement in federal finances during the 1990s is striking. Early in the decade, federal budget deficits exceeded 4 percent of GDP, and the debt held by the public reached nearly 50 percent of GDP for the first time since the 1950s. By the end of the decade, the budget had recorded its third consecutive unified surplus for the first time since 1947–49, as well as the largest surplus relative to GDP since 1948; debt held by the public had dropped below 35 percent of GDP.

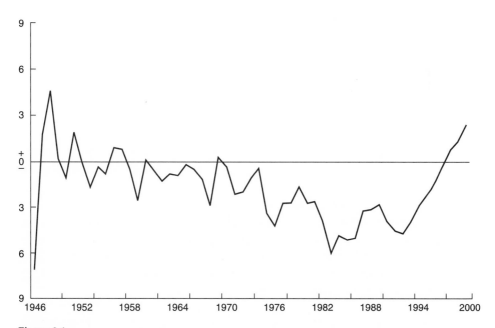

Figure 2.1
Federal Budget Surplus: 1946–2000 (percentage of GDP)

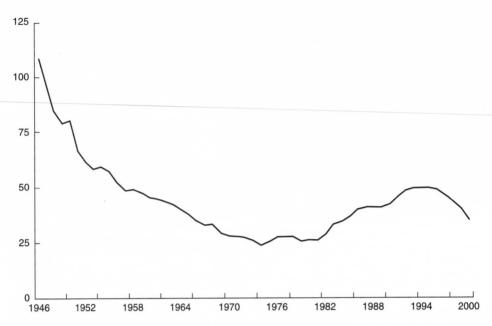

Figure 2.2
Debt Held by the Public: 1946–2000 (percentage of GDP)

2.2.1 Improved Budget Picture

Table 2.1 presents key budget data from the past 15 years. The table shows that the remarkable improvement in the unified budget balance during the 1990s resulted from a significant increase in revenue and a nearly equal decrease in noninterest outlays, both as shares of GDP, together with the resulting impact on interest payments. Tax revenue increased as a share of GDP in part because of tax policy but also because of changing economic conditions; we return to both these topics later. Noninterest spending declined as a share of GDP in large part because defense spending fell in nominal dollars and thus dropped sharply relative to GDP.

The federal budget outlook beyond the 1990s also improved sharply during the decade. The CBO's first ten-year projection, published in January 1992, showed large and rising budget deficits in the first years of the 21st century assuming that the law on the books in 1992 was maintained. Further, the CBO's first 75-year budget projection, released in May 1996, showed public debt exceeding GDP by 2020. In contrast, the CBO's ten-year projection in January 2001 showed large and rising budget *surpluses* during the next decade; it also showed the public debt being eliminated (on a net basis) in fiscal year 2009.

Table 2.1
The Turnaround in the Federal Budget (share of GDP; fiscal years)

Year	Unified Budget Balance	Receipts	Non-interest Outlays	Debt Held by Public	Individual Income Taxes	Defense Spending	Entitlement Spending
1986	−5.0	17.5	19.4	39.6	7.9	6.2	10.5
1987	−3.2	18.4	18.6	40.6	8.4	6.1	10.2
1988	−3.1	18.1	18.2	40.9	8.0	5.8	10.1
1989	−2.8	18.3	18.1	40.5	8.2	5.6	10.2
1990	−3.9	18.0	18.6	42.0	8.1	5.2	10.9
1991	−4.5	17.8	19.0	45.4	7.9	5.4	11.8
1992	−4.7	17.5	19.0	48.2	7.7	4.9	11.5
1993	−3.9	17.6	18.5	49.5	7.8	4.5	11.2
1994	−2.9	18.1	18.1	49.4	7.8	4.1	11.3
1995	−2.2	18.5	17.5	49.2	8.1	3.7	11.2
1996	−1.4	18.9	17.2	48.5	8.5	3.5	11.1
1997	−0.3	19.3	16.5	46.0	9.0	3.3	10.9
1998	0.8	19.9	16.3	42.9	9.6	3.1	10.8
1999	1.4	20.0	16.1	39.7	9.6	3.0	10.7
2000	2.4	20.6	15.9	34.7	10.2	3.0	10.5

Source: CBO (2001).

Moreover, the 75-year projections released in October 2000 showed net public indebtedness below *zero* through 2050. The CBO summarizes its very long-run projections in terms of an estimated "fiscal gap," which is the immediate, permanent tax increase or spending decrease needed to keep public debt below its contemporaneous size relative to GDP for the 75 years following the date of the projection. In May 1996 this gap was 5.4 percent of GDP; by October 2000 the gap had shrunk to 0.8 percent of GDP.

To be sure, some analysts believe that the assumptions underlying these projections are too optimistic. Auerbach and Gale (2000) argue that, over the next decade, discretionary spending is not likely to fall further as a share of GDP and that the number of people affected by the alternative minimum tax (AMT) will not be allowed to increase by a factor of 10; both these assumptions are implicit in the CBO projections. The CBO itself notes that the fiscal gap could be substantially larger under alternative assumptions about health care costs and long-term productivity growth. That said, for the purpose of assessing the extent of fiscal improvement over the last several years, the relevant question is whether the assumptions underlying the projections have become more optimistic in the last few years, and if so, by how much. Although it is difficult to

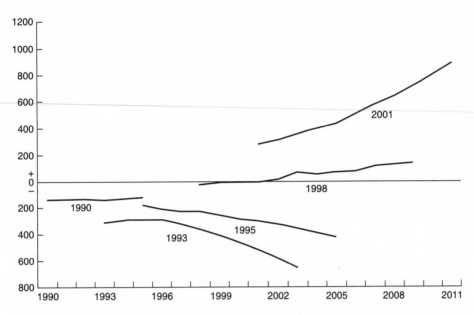

Figure 2.3
CBO Budget Surplus Projections (billions of dollars, projections as of January of year shown)

judge, we believe that the change in the projections likely provides a reasonable measure of the progress that has been made.[2]

2.2.2 Sources of Improvement

We explore the timing and sources of the budget improvement in several ways. Figure 2.3 shows the CBO's surplus and deficit projections in January of 1990, 1993, 1995, 1998, and 2001. As can be seen, the budget picture deteriorated between 1990 and 1993, but improved steadily thereafter.

This improvement stems from a variety of positive developments. The CBO parses the revisions to its projections into the contributions of legislative factors (i.e., policy changes), economic factors (i.e., changes in aggregate economic conditions such as productivity growth and inflation), and technical factors (essentially a residual category showing the total budget change that cannot be attributed to the first two categories). The most important technical factor in

---

2. Between January 1998 and January 2001, the CBO increased its estimate of productivity growth during the 10-year budget window by nearly one full percentage point. However, the latest long-run outlook from the CBO also includes a substantial increase in the projected rate of health spending growth.

the late 1990s was a surge in tax revenue relative to GDP beyond the increase that would be expected given our progressive tax code. The CBO (2000) attributed this surge to a combination of factors: an increase in corporate profits and workers' wages and salaries relative to GDP, an increase in the share of income received by people in the highest tax brackets, and a surge in capital gains from the booming stock market. Indeed, individual income taxes rose from 8.1 percent of GDP in 1995 to 10.2 percent in 2000, even though no significant tax increases were enacted between those years. Another important technical factor during the late 1990s was a sharp deceleration in federal health spending beyond that which was predicted based on changes in Medicare policy.

We present our summary of the CBO's revisions in Table 2.2. We total the revisions between each pair of projection dates shown in Figure 2.3. Each column pertains to a fixed budget window. For example, column 1 shows the cumulative revisions between 1990 and 1993 in surplus projections for fiscal years 1991 through 1995, the five-year budget window for which projections were released in January 1990. For the other pairs of years, the revisions apply to the ten-year budget window following the first year in that pair; for example, the revisions between 1998 and 2001 apply to fiscal years 1999 through 2008. In order to decompose the revisions into policy, economic, and technical factors, we cumulate the decompositions presented in each of the CBO projections published between the two end points, typically three projections per year.

Table 2.2
Sources of Improvement in the CBO's Budget Projections

Source of Revision	Revision to Projected 5-Year Surplus	Revision to Projected 10-Year Surpluses		
	From Jan. 1990 to Jan. 1993	From Jan. 1993 to Jan. 1995	From Jan. 1995 to Jan. 1998	From Jan. 1998 to Jan. 2001
Total	−$782 billion (100%)	$1603 billion (100%)	$3107 billion (100%)	$3196 billion (100%)
Policy	460 (59%)	1570 (98%)	501 (16%)	−1606 (50%)
Economic	−330 (42%)	−39 (2%)	1272 (41%)	2669 (84%)
Technical	−337 (43%)	44 (3%)	1247 (40%)	2126 (67%)
Other	−575 (74%)	28 (2%)	87 (3%)	7 (0%)

Notes: Revisions are from January to January of the years shown. Decomposition is by the CBO, cumulated by the authors across projection updates. Percentages apply to the total revision during the period indicated without regard to sign.

Before discussing our results, we note four ways in which these calculations likely understate the role of policy actions during the 1990s. First, the most significant policy actions were taken early in the decade when the nominal amounts of revenues and outlays were smaller and the budget window was shorter; this fact tends to downplay the true importance of these actions compared with the favorable developments later in the decade. Second, because the CBO does not retrospectively reestimate policy effects, it may have underestimated the role of some specific policy changes in the 1990s. For example, the increase in the top income tax rate in 1993 may have raised more revenue than expected because the CBO considerably underestimated the share of income that would be received by people in the highest tax brackets.[3] And health spending slowed much more sharply after the 1997 reforms than anticipated, perhaps because the reforms had more bite than the CBO realized. Third, the policy actions presumably played a role in improving economic conditions and thereby contributed to the positive economic and technical factors. Fourth, the relative *lack* of policy actions in the face of large and growing surpluses in the late 1990s could be viewed as an active contribution of policy, because the political system had previously aimed simply to balance the unified budget. We return to the third and fourth issues later.[4]

Table 2.2 presents the results, which we summarize here and discuss in greater detail in our chronology of the decade. During the early 1990s, budget projections deteriorated as the substantial deficit-reduction actions in the Omnibus Budget Reconciliation Act of 1990 (OBRA90) were more than offset by weaker-than-expected economic growth, higher-than-expected federal spending on health programs, and the ballooning cost of dealing with failing thrift institutions. However, the projections in early 1993 represented the nadir. The passage of the Omnibus Budget Reconciliation Act of 1993 (OBRA93) reduced projected budget deficits substantially, and—in contrast with OBRA90—had the good fortune to be followed by several years in which economic and technical factors had little net effect on the budget outlook rather than causing it to deteriorate substantially.[5] Even so, in January 1995 the CBO was still project-

---

3. Of course, people who faced higher tax rates after 1993 might have reported even higher income in the absence of the policy change. Feldstein (discussion in this chapter) elaborates on this point.

4. It is worth emphasizing that the CBO's "no-policy change" baseline projections assume that discretionary spending grows with inflation and therefore shrinks over time relative to GDP. Under a baseline that assumed that discretionary spending would remain constant relative to GDP, the policy category would receive credit for the fact that discretionary spending declined relative to GDP over this decade.

5. According to the CBO, OBRA93 reduced projected budget deficits by more than $400 billion over five years and by more than $1,500 billion over ten years. The former figure was central in the political discourse of the time, but the latter figure is consistent with the current focus on ten-year budget windows and therefore is shown in our table.

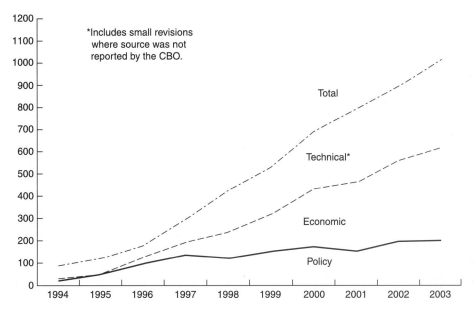

Figure 2.4
Revisions to CBO Surplus Projections Between 1993 and 2001 (billions of dollars)

ing rising deficits under current law. Three years later, the outlook was much better: the beneficial effects of the Balanced Budget Act of 1997 (BBA97) and other policies, coupled with very large gains in both economic and technical factors, produced a forecast of imminent surpluses. By January 2001 the budget picture had again improved dramatically, owing to positive economic and technical revisions of an astounding magnitude. Policy actions in the late 1990s were scored as reducing projected surpluses; the most prominent of these actions was the sharp increase in late 2000 in the discretionary spending caps. However, the CBO tally does not incorporate the effects of President Clinton's "Save Social Security First" strategy (discussed later) which arguably allowed hundreds of billions and perhaps trillions of dollars of surpluses to flow through to pay down debt, rather than being used for additional spending or tax cuts.

A final perspective on the improving fiscal situation during the 1990s is provided by Figure 2.4. This figure decomposes the difference between the CBO's January 1993 projection and the actual outcome (or the 2001 projection for the years beyond 2000). Thus, whereas Table 2.2 cumulated revisions between several pairs of projection dates, Figure 2.4 shows cumulative revisions relative to a single projection date, 1993. During the years around the turn of the century, policy changes contributed about one-quarter of the total improvement, with the rest nearly evenly split between economic and technical factors. Over the entire period between 1994 and 2000, actual outcomes were roughly $2.6 trillion better than the CBO's 1993 projection—and policy changes accounted for one-third of this improvement. Moreover, as discussed earlier, this estimate should be seen as a lower bound on the true contribution of policy, in part because it omits all contributions from potential surplus-dissipating actions not taken.

In sum, the remarkable improvement in the budget outlook during the 1990s can be attributed in substantial part to policy actions taken and avoided. But it also occurred in important measure because of an economic boom that surpassed expectations, higher tax revenue than would have been anticipated given overall economic conditions, and slower-than-expected growth in health costs. We turn now to a chronological review of developments in budget and Social Security policy during the decade.

2.3   Budget Deficit Reduction: 1990 Through 1997

In 1985 rising concern about large federal budget deficits led to passage of the Gramm-Rudman-Hollings deficit-reduction law, which set explicit annual deficit targets that declined to zero over several years. When the target proved too difficult to meet in 1987, the targets were raised. Thus, when the 1990s began, the size of federal deficits—and the apparent inability of the political process to reduce them—were central features of the political landscape.

2.3.1   OBRA90

In the spring and summer of 1990, President George Bush and the Congress debated and negotiated alternative routes to deficit reduction. These initial discussions were inconclusive, despite the president's expressed willingness to increase taxes as part of a broader budget package (which ran counter to the views expressed by many Republicans). However, the Iraqi invasion of Kuwait and deteriorating economic conditions seemed to provide additional impetus to the desire to "put our fiscal house in order," and President Bush and the congressional leadership announced a budget agreement on October 1. Yet, the House of Representatives voted down the plan by a wide margin four days later, again throwing the budget picture into disarray. Indeed, this initial failure of the long-term budget deal created a short-term problem as well: a temporary appropriations bill lapsed, shutting down most of the government for a long weekend. In late October, Treasury Secretary Nicholas Brady stated that President Bush was open to a rate increase on upper-income taxpayers.

Several days later, Congress approved an altered plan for deficit reduction as OBRA90.

According to the CBO's projections, OBRA90 reduced the deficit by nearly $500 billion over five years compared with then-current law. This accomplishment had an important effect on the fiscal outcomes of the 1990s and on the fiscal situation faced by the incoming Clinton administration several years later. In two key respects, the plan represented an approach to deficit reduction that differed significantly from that used in the late 1980s and that became a model for fiscal constraints in the 1990s. First, the plan included a set of specific actions to reduce the deficit, rather than a set of deficit targets. Therefore, this new approach did not require incremental fiscal stringency in response to a slowing economy, which was important because it preserved the functioning of the automatic stabilizers, and because it avoided forcing Congress to tighten the budget precisely when doing so would be most politically painful.

Second, the plan introduced a new set of budget enforcement rules designed to deter legislative actions that would worsen the deficit. One rule was a "pay-as-you-go," or "paygo," constraint on taxes and entitlement spending: any tax cut and any increase in entitlement spending would need to be offset by an equal amount of tax increase or entitlement spending reduction. Another aspect of the enforcement system was "caps," or limits, on discretionary spending over the following several years. The caps were set so that they increased by less than expected inflation, thereby squeezing down real discretionary spending over time. Because discretionary spending is ultimately determined in annual appropriations bills, this approach allowed policy-makers to defer some difficult deficit-reduction decisions; nevertheless, the caps were adhered to for a time, and in combination with the prevailing determination to shore up the nation's fiscal foundations, likely contributed to the improvement in the budget situation.

2.3.2   OBRA93

During his campaign for the presidency, Bill Clinton argued that America needed to tackle both the budget deficit and the "public investment deficit." His economic plan *Putting People First* explained:

Our strategy puts people first by investing more than $50 billion each year over the next four years to put America back to work—the most dramatic economic growth program since the Second World War. Our strategy recognizes that the only way to lay the foundation for renewed American prosperity is to spur both public and private investment. To reclaim our future, we must strive to close both the budget deficit and the investment gap.... To pay for these investments and reduce our national debt, we will save nearly $300 billion by cutting spending, closing tax loopholes, and requiring the very wealthy to pay their fair share of taxes. Our plan will cut the deficit in half within four years and assure that it continues to fall each year after that. (*Clinton and Gore*, 1992, p. 7)

This plan ultimately evolved into OBRA93.

2.3.2.1   The First Clinton Budget

In February 1993 the Clinton administration put forward its first budget document, *A Vision of Change for America*. President Clinton enunciated his economic strategy this way:

My plan has three key elements: economic stimulus to create jobs now while laying the foundation for long-term economic growth; long-term public investments to increase the productivity of our people and businesses; and a serious, fair, and balanced deficit-reduction plan to stop the government from draining the private investments that generate jobs and increase incomes. (*Vision of Change*, cover letter)

The administration described its budget over five years as follows: First, the budget included $328 billion of revenue increases, $329 billion of noninterest spending cuts, and $46 billion of reduced debt service, for "gross deficit reduction" of $704 billion. The tax increases included a new top income tax bracket, removal of the wage cap for Medicare taxes, and a broad-based energy tax based on the energy content (measured in Btu's) of fuel consumed. The spending reductions included cuts in Medicare provider reimbursements, defense spending, and a range of nondefense discretionary spending, along with an extension of the discretionary spending caps and paygo rules of OBRA90. Second, the budget proposal included $144 billion of additional "investment outlays," which we discuss shortly. Third, the plan had $77 billion of "tax incentives," including a significant expansion of the Earned Income Tax Credit. Last, the plan had about $15 billion of "stimulus outlays." Overall, therefore, the plan was projected to provide nearly $500 billion of net deficit reduction.[6]

Woodward (1994) and Reich (1997) provide accounts of the behind-the-scenes development of the Clinton budget. Both sources emphasize the ongoing conflict between the desire for deficit reduction and the desire to provide both short-term economic stimulus and long-term public investments. We turn to these issues now.

2.3.2.2   Deficit Reduction and Economic Stimulus

Traditional economic analysis of deficit reduction implies that reducing government spending or increasing taxes depresses economic activity in the short run but by raising saving and investment boosts productivity and the overall

---

6. In fact, about half of the stimulus outlays were scheduled to occur during fiscal year 1993, which was already under way and which preceded the five-year budget window.

productive capacity of the economy down the road. However, an alternative view of the short-run effect of deficit reduction was developed in the 1980s by Blanchard (1984) and Branson (1985) among others. The idea is straightforward: an expectation of lower future deficits reduces *future short-term* interest rates, and these lower future short-term rates generate lower *current long-term* interest rates. Lower long-term interest rates could stimulate business investment and other interest-sensitive spending immediately, offsetting at least some part of the direct contractionary effect of deficit reduction. The net effect on short-run output depends in part on the size of the reduction in the current deficit compared with the expected reduction in the future deficit. Indeed, the 1984 *Economic Report of the President* (pp. 40–41) invoked this line of reasoning a decade earlier in arguing that a credible phased-in deficit reduction plan would not hamper economic growth even in the short run. This argument is basically the standard "crowding out" view of fiscal policy run in reverse: greater fiscal restraint should lower interest rates and thereby "crowd in" private activity. The novel twist is that the stimulus from the lower interest rates might be elicited even before the contractionary impact of actual cuts in spending or increases in taxes had been felt.

Yet as of 1993 this theory was largely untested, and President Clinton received differing advice about its likely importance. Some members of the economic team believed that long-term interest rates were unusually high because of expectations about the federal deficit, and that altering those expectations would bring down long-term rates and thereby stimulate economic growth. Others argued, however, that reducing the deficit would likely slow the economy and "cost jobs" in the short run, although it would increase private investment and productivity over time. While these advisers acknowledged the possibility that a decline in long-term interest rates would cushion the economy from some of the direct contractionary effect of deficit reduction, they tended to view a full offset as a long shot. The uncertainty about the short-run effect of deficit reduction continued throughout the year. A July 15 memo to the president from the Council of Economic Advisers reportedly noted that the economy was weaker than had been anticipated and that the budget plan then working its way through Congress was more contractionary in direct terms than the president's original proposal. Nonetheless, the administration retained its public commitment to deficit reduction.

2.3.2.3 Public Investments
A key element of President Clinton's campaign platform was targeted increases in public spending. The detailed description of the economic plan referred to a significant increase in annual infrastructure investment, the

creation of a civilian research and development agency to encourage conversion of a "defense-based economy to a peacetime one," a nationwide network of community development banks, additional police officers, "empowering those on welfare by providing education, training, and child care," fully funding the Head Start and Women, Infants, and Children (WIC) programs, a Youth Opportunity Corps, greater availability of subsidized college loans, and guaranteed health benefits for all Americans. Indeed, the first Clinton budget stated: "Deficit reduction at the expense of public investment has been and will continue to be self-defeating. The Clinton plan is explicitly and emphatically aimed at reducing the deficit while increasing much-needed public investment" (page 10).

Nevertheless, increasing these outlays was clearly at odds with the objective of reducing the budget deficit, and the deterioration in deficit projections in late 1992 heightened this conflict. While the president's economic team was united in believing that both public investments and deficit reduction were important, different members of the team put different weights on the two objectives. Moreover, the president's political advisers were said to be generally quite critical of the focus on deficit reduction, viewing the proposed outlays as the objectives over which they had fought the election.

In the end, the additional outlays proposed during the campaign were whittled down very substantially. The president was reported to be torn— determined to rectify a perceived deficit in public investment in both physical and human capital, but also believing that the best way to gain the ability to address that agenda was to first get control of the fiscal situation. And Robert Rubin (then director of the National Economic Council and later Treasury secretary) said near the end of the administration that President Clinton had understood the potential stimulative effects of lower budget deficits and lower interest rates: "Clinton said, 'I have a jobs program, and my jobs program is deficit reduction'" (*New York Times*, Dec. 25, 2000). Ultimately, the president's budget included only part of the new outlays proposed during the campaign, and only a fraction of that amount was contained in the final legislation. In particular, while new funding was provided for the Earned Income Tax Credit, Head Start, and WIC, the proposed infrastructure spending was largely abandoned.

2.3.2.4 Passage of OBRA93

President Clinton presented his budget in mid-February. Several days later, Alan Greenspan testified before the Senate Banking Committee, commenting that "the president is to be commended for placing on the table for debate" a "serious" and "plausible" economic plan. Newspaper stories interpreted

Greenspan's remarks as essentially endorsing Clinton's overall strategy while staying removed from the specifics.

About one month later, the House of Representatives approved a budget resolution based on the framework of the administration's deficit-reduction plan, though as noted previously the resolution included only a fraction of the public investments that Clinton had proposed. Separately, the House then passed the stimulus package as well. The Senate followed by passing a budget resolution that was similar to the House's, but balked at the stimulus package. After an extended filibuster, Clinton announced in mid-April that he would withdraw the stimulus package.[7] Shortly thereafter, the proposed Btu tax also ran into heavy resistance, especially in the critical Senate Finance Committee. In early June, Treasury Secretary Lloyd Bentsen said publicly that there would not be a so-called Btu tax.

The House and Senate passed separate budget plans by very narrow margins in May and June, but the outcome of the conference process was still very uncertain. Finally, in August, the House approved a deficit-reduction plan by a 218-to-216 vote, with all Republican members voting against and nearly all Democrats voting in favor. The next day, the Senate passed the bill, on a vote of 50–50, again with all Republicans voting against, and with Vice President Al Gore casting the tie-breaking vote in favor of passage. President Clinton signed this bill into law as OBRA93.

2.3.3 What Did Deficit Reduction Ultimately Accomplish?

Throughout the debate on OBRA93, sharply differing views were expressed about the economic implications of the package. A number of the harshest critics prophesied that a recession would surely result if the budget framework were enacted. As it turned out, economic growth accelerated in 1994, and the second half of the 1990s witnessed an extraordinary economic boom. What role did deficit reduction play in this success story? That is inherently a difficult question to answer, but we believe that the fiscal discipline launched by OBRA90 and OBRA93 made an important contribution to the 1990s economic expansion.[8]

Most notably, the expansion was characterized by a remarkable surge in investment, especially in business equipment and software. Between 1990 and 2000, outlays in this category increased at an average annual rate of more than

---

7. A $4 billion bill extending unemployment compensation, which had been part of the stimulus package, was passed separately.

8. See Blinder and Yellen (2001) and Rubin (discussion in this chapter) for endorsements of this view.

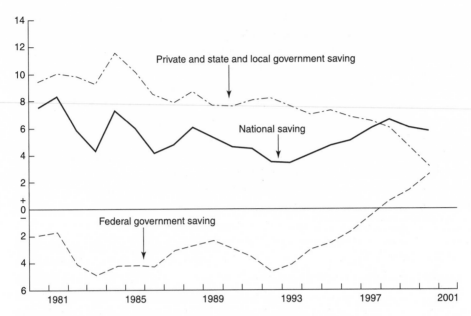

Figure 2.5
Net National Saving and its Components (percentage of GDP)

10 percent in real terms. Several factors likely contributed to this explosion, including strong output growth, robust profits, and rapid technological progress. But investment was also supported by the sharp reduction in federal government deficits that left more resources available for private use. Indeed, we think it likely that both technical advances and greater national saving were necessary for the investment boom that the country enjoyed, and that neither alone would have been sufficient.

Figure 2.5 shows net national saving (that is, total saving less capital depreciation) and its components as shares of GDP during the past 20 years. The turnaround in the federal budget caused saving to be about 7 percent of GDP higher than it would have been if deficits had remained at their 1992 level. Between 1992 and 1997, a decline in saving by households, businesses, and state and local governments offset some of the rise in federal saving, but national saving still increased by almost 3 percent of GDP. After 1997 a sharp drop in nonfederal saving more than offset the continued increase in federal saving, and national saving declined. Although a Ricardian might view the decline in private saving as a response to the additional federal saving, the consensus view attributes that decline primarily to the dramatic runup in stock prices.

An alternative indication of the effect of deficit reduction can be gleaned from the path of interest rates over the course of 1993. Interest rates reflect the balance of supply and demand in the market for loanable funds. A reasonable presumption is that the private demand for funds was, if anything, increasing over the course of 1993 as the economic recovery gathered strength. Even so, market interest rates declined during 1993, suggesting that the net supply of funds (after federal government demands had been satisfied) must have been seen as increasing. This response would be consistent with the hypothesis that the market interpreted OBRA93 as reducing the pressure that the government would be putting on credit markets. Moreover, the day-to-day timing of the decline in interest rates aligns well with news about the prospects for passage of OBRA93 (see the discussion in the 1994 *Economic Report of the President*).

The significant increase in the nation's capital stock generated by the investment boom of the 1990s benefited the economy in several ways. First, it helped to raise productivity: labor productivity increased nearly twice as fast between 1995 and 2000 as between 1975 and 1995. Second, it helped contain inflation: the rate of change in the price index for personal consumption expenditures excluding food and energy drifted downward through most of the decade, even as the strength of the economic expansion increased.

The improvement in the federal budget balance did *not* end the large deficits in international trade that the United States began to run during the 1980s. At that time, popular discourse linked the burgeoning budget and trade deficits together as the "twin deficits," and not without reason: as a matter of arithmetic, domestic investment must be financed either by domestic saving or foreign saving. Therefore, assuming no change in domestic investment, a decline in domestic saving resulting from a larger government deficit must be offset by a greater inflow of foreign saving. But foreigners direct their saving to this country by exporting more goods and services to us than we send to them—in other words, by causing us to run a larger trade deficit. Thus, the popular moniker of "twin deficits" was valid as far as it went, but it failed to account for changes in domestic investment. And, as we have noted, one of the most dramatic developments in the 1990s was a surge in domestic investment, to such an extent as to overwhelm the increase in domestic saving and require an increase in the supply of funds from abroad.

2.3.4   *The Republican-Controlled Congress*

The most prominent federal policy issue between the fall of 1993 and the fall of 1994 was the Clinton administration's proposal for national health care reform. This proposal is discussed at length by Cutler and Gruber (Chapter 12 of this volume). Here we simply note that one concern about the administration plan—both inside and outside the administration—was its likely effect on the budget deficit. Indeed, when the CBO released its analysis of the administration proposal, it estimated that the proposal would, on balance, increase the deficit. No comprehensive health care reform plan passed the Congress in 1994.

Then, in the 1994 election, Republicans won majorities in both the Senate and the House of Representatives. The Republican leadership said that it had a mandate for a multipart platform known as the "Contract with America." Planks in this platform called for large tax cuts, line-item veto power for the president, a constitutional amendment requiring a balanced federal budget, and the elimination of the budget deficit by 2002.

In 1995, congressional Republicans tried to implement these policies. The House approved a balanced-budget amendment in January—by nearly a three-to-one margin—but the Senate rejected the amendment in March, as support fell just short of the two-thirds majority needed. The House and Senate also approved line-item veto legislation that would have given presidents the ability to reject individual items in spending bills without vetoing entire bills. Although Clinton signed the legislation into law, the Supreme Court struck down the law as an unconstitutional delegation of congressional authority to the executive branch. Both houses of Congress also passed bills cutting spending by $16 billion in the fiscal year then under way. And both houses passed budget resolutions in May laying out broad frameworks for balancing the budget by 2002.

The Clinton administration responded to the Contract with America in part by trying to occupy the political center. Thus, the administration's budget included small middle-class tax cuts as well as various spending cuts that, taken together, provided a small net reduction in projected budget deficits. President Clinton attacked the balanced budget amendment and charged that the Republicans' proposed "deep cuts in federal spending amount to war on children" (*New York Times*, Feb. 25, 1995, p. 1). He cast his first veto as president to reject the legislated cuts in current-year spending, although he later approved a revised package of cuts totaling the same amount. Then, in June, Clinton outlined a plan to balance the budget by 2005. By achieving balance more gradually than the Republicans, using the more optimistic projections of the Office of Management and Budget rather than the CBO, and including smaller tax cuts than the Republicans, the administration reduced the scale of the required spending reductions. In particular, the administration emphasized that the Republican plan would have entailed much larger cuts in Medicare and Medicaid than the administration's plan.

As budget negotiations stretched into the fall, congressional Republicans tried to force the administration to accept their budget framework using two different strategies. One strategy was based on appropriations bills, and it resulted in two government shutdowns. By mid-November, only three of the 13 appropriations bills for the fiscal year already under way had been passed. The continuing resolution (CR) that was funding the agencies not covered by those three bills was expiring, and the Republicans refused to pass a further CR without concessions on the overall budget plan that the administration refused to make. All "nonessential" workers in those agencies were then furloughed for six days, until President Clinton accepted the Republicans' goal of balancing the budget in seven years and the Congress approved another CR. Yet negotiations broke down again by mid-December, and most of the federal government was shuttered for another three weeks. Eventually, the Republicans abandoned this strategy in January 1996.

The congressional Republicans' second strategy, pursued simultaneously with the appropriations battle, was based on the statutory limit on federal debt. The government was on track to exceed the debt limit by November; doing so would have caused the government to default for the first time in history, because it would have been unable to borrow sufficient funds to meet its obligations. The administration defeated this strategy by taking a variety of complex steps to keep the officially measured debt below the statutory limit while still carrying on the government's activities. In mid-November, Treasury Secretary Rubin ordered the suspension of new investments for the federal employees' defined-contribution retirement plan and the early redemption of some bonds held by the civil service defined-benefit retirement fund. In mid-February, with the impasse over the debt limit still continuing, Rubin suspended investment of Treasury's Exchange Stabilization Fund, redeemed additional securities prior to maturity from the civil service retirement fund, and authorized a set of asset exchanges among a government trust fund, a government corporation, and the Treasury. Some members of Congress criticized these actions, and Representative Gerald Solomon called for Rubin's impeachment. In the end, default was avoided, the debt limit was finally increased in March 1996, and the assets of these various funds were restored to what they would have been in the absence of these maneuvers.

By April 1996, President Clinton and Congress essentially agreed to disagree: they passed a modest budget package that funded the government at close to current-law levels and made small changes in tax policy. Many observers believed that President Clinton had won the battle over the shutdown and had staked out the political center as a fiscally disciplined moderate.

2.3.5 BBA97

According to projections available in early 1997, deficits under then-current law would persist and eventually increase again, despite the sharp improvement in the fiscal outlook during the preceding several years. In February 1997 the administration put forward a budget designed to achieve balance in five years. Negotiations between the administration and Congress stalled until mid-March, when House Speaker Newt Gingrich expressed his willingness to scale back Republican tax-cut plans. Budget talks resumed in early April, and a deal had nearly been reached on an overall budget framework by May 1. Then the CBO told the administration and congressional leadership that it was reducing its projection of budget deficits over the following five years by $225 billion. Taking advantage of that last-minute windfall, negotiators announced the outline of an agreement the next day. Filling in the details of that outline proved to be a contentious undertaking. After two weeks of haggling, a complete budget deal was announced on May 15. But passing the specific bills needed to implement that deal involved further sparring and, eventually, compromise. At the end of July, the Taxpayer Relief and Balanced Budget Acts of 1997 passed by wide margins in both the House and Senate, and were signed into law by President Clinton in early August.

The CBO estimated that this legislation would produce much less deficit reduction than OBRA90 or OBRA93, but would lead to a balanced unified budget in 2002. Outlays were trimmed by nearly $200 billion over the following five years, including a reduction in payments to Medicare providers and a modification and extension of the discretionary spending caps. But taxes were cut by about $80 billion over the five-year period, including several new tax credits favored by the administration and a cut in the capital gains tax rate favored by Republicans. In retrospect, this law may have trimmed outlays by more than the CBO anticipated, because Medicare spending fell well below CBO projections in subsequent years.[9]

2.4 Entitlement Reform and Saving Social Security First

Throughout the 1990s, many institutions, analysts, and commissions sounded the alarm about longer-term fiscal issues. The annual reports of the Social Security and Medicare Trustees projected that both systems were significantly out of actuarial balance and would eventually require reform; new long-run

---

9. More than half of the five-year reduction in outlays was scheduled to occur in FY2002, the target date for deficit elimination. Moreover, the net tax cut in FY2002 was only about half of the net tax cut in either FY2001 or FY2003, owing to shifts in the timing of tax obligations.

budget models from OMB and CBO predicted exploding levels of debt after 2010; and generational accounts calculated both inside and outside the government showed large tax burdens on future generations. For example, the Social Security Trustees projected in 1997 (Board of Trustees, 1997) that Social Security outlays would rise from 11 percent of payroll in 1997 to 20 percent of payroll in 2075, requiring a 50 percent increase in the payroll tax if no other changes were made. At the same time, the CBO projected that total government expenditures would exceed revenues by as much as 17 percent of GDP in 2030 and that public debt would reach 100 percent of GDP in 2030.[10] Generational accounts published in the 1993 federal budget suggested that lifetime net tax rates would have to rise from 34 percent to 71 percent to sustain then-current fiscal policies.[11]

The primary causes of these projected long-term imbalances were—and continue to be—rising medical costs and the aging of the population. Declining fertility and rising life expectancy imply that the ratio of workers to beneficiaries will fall from 3:1 to 2:1 between 2000 and 2030 (Board of Trustees, 2001). Because longevity gains and low fertility rates are expected to persist, this is not simply a temporary phenomenon associated with the retirement of the baby boom generation, but rather the leading edge of a new plateau. Moreover, spending on medical care is projected to rise faster than GDP for decades to come as a result of both population aging and the adoption of new medical technology.

2.4.1 Entitlement Commissions

Three important commissions on entitlement reform during the 1990s considered changes in Social Security: the Bipartisan Commission on Entitlement and Tax Reform cochaired by Senators Bob Kerrey and John Danforth, the 1994–96 Advisory Council on Social Security chaired by Edward Gramlich, and the 1997–98 National Commission on Retirement Policy cochaired by Senators John Breaux and Judd Gregg and Congressmen Jim Kolbe and Charles Stenholm.

---

10. CBO (1997) presents deficit projections for 2030 that range from 8 percent to 17 percent of GDP. The lower estimate assumes that discretionary spending grows at the rate of inflation, and therefore shrinks substantially as a share of GDP, and that there is no economic feedback between the budget deficit and other economic variables. The higher estimate assumes that discretionary spending remains constant as a share of GDP, and that—by soaking up national saving that otherwise would have been available for investment in productive plant and equipment—the deficit reduces economic growth.

11. See Auerbach, Gokhale, and Kotlikoff (1994) for a description of these estimates.

2.4.1.1 Kerrey-Danforth

In order to secure Senator Kerrey's decisive vote for the 1993 budget agreement, President Clinton agreed to create a commission on entitlement reform and appoint the senator as chairman. The commission set for itself the goal of developing a package of revenue and spending measures that would bring Social Security into long-run balance and hold the unified budget deficit at its 1995 level relative to GDP in the long run. In December 1994 the commission issued a staff report summarizing entitlement and tax reform options. The Social Security options included raising the age of eligibility for full benefits, reducing cost-of-living adjustments and spouses' benefits, subjecting more benefits to taxation, and diverting a portion of the Social Security payroll tax into mandatory private retirement accounts. Not all of these options would have been required to bring the system into balance, but they are representative of the approaches that were generally under consideration at the time. The Medicare options included imposing a new monthly premium for beneficiaries and increasing the deductible from $100 to as much as $1,200. The options on the revenue side included eliminating deductions for state and local taxes and for charitable contributions.

A majority of commission members voted against the proposals ultimately put forth by Senators Kerrey and Danforth (Bipartisan Commission, 1995), and congressional leaders and administration officials distanced themselves from the commission's findings. For example, incoming House Speaker Newt Gingrich responded to the proposals by saying, "I think Social Security is off the table for the foreseeable future. We have so many other more pressing and more immediate problems and we ought to focus on the ones that are immediate, not the ones that are 20 years out" (*Washington Post*, Dec. 12, 1994, p. A8). White House Chief of Staff Leon Panetta stated that the administration was opposed to any proposal for reducing Social Security spending (*Washington Post*, Dec. 15, 1995, p. A18). Nonetheless, Senator Kerrey and commission member Senator Alan Simpson went on to introduce Social Security reform legislation based on the commission's work.[12] The Kerrey-Simpson bills gradually raised the early retirement age from 62 to 65 and the age of eligibility for full benefits to 70, reduced cost of living adjustments for Social Security, and shrank benefits for spouses. The legislation also permitted 25 percent of the Social Security trust fund to be invested in private-sector stocks and bonds, and gave workers the option of diverting 2 percentage points of their payroll tax payments to individual investment accounts in exchange for lower Social Security benefits.

---

12. Senator Danforth retired from the Senate at the end of 1994.

2.4.1.2 Social Security Advisory Council

Secretary of Health and Human Services Donna Shalala appointed the second major commission, the 1994–96 Advisory Council on Social Security, in response to a legal requirement that an advisory council be empaneled every four years to review the Trustees' estimates and comment on relevant policy issues.[13] This particular advisory council was given an unusually broad mandate and charged with reviewing Social Security's long-run financing, the equity and adequacy of benefits, and the relative roles of the public and private sectors in the provision of retirement income. The 13-member committee was chaired by Edward Gramlich and followed the traditional practice of including three representatives from organized labor, three representatives from the employer community, and other experts. The council intended to complete its work by the end of 1995, but the breadth of its mandate and the contentious nature of its discussions led it to delay its final report until January 1997.[14]

The members of the advisory council came to consensus on three key issues.[15] First, there should be substantially more advance funding of Social Security's long-term obligations in order to boost national saving. Second, equity investments should play an important part in Social Security reform. And third, reform should not only meet the traditional goal of bringing the system into 75-year balance, but also leave the ratio of the trust fund to annual benefits stable at the end of the 75-year period. However, council members disagreed quite strongly about the way in which these changes should be implemented, splitting into three factions with different recommended solutions for Social Security's long-run financing problem.

Six of the 13 council members, led by former Social Security Commissioner Robert Ball, favored a plan that aimed to preserve the present Social Security benefit structure as much as possible. The key feature of this plan was investing 40 percent of the Social Security trust fund in equities instead of the special Treasury bonds traditionally held by the trust fund. Because equities are projected to earn a higher expected return than bonds, this change in the trust

---

13. By tradition, the quadrennial advisory councils in turn sponsored technical review panels that examined the assumptions and methods underlying the Trustees' estimates of actuarial imbalance. The 1994 legislation making Social Security an independent agency eliminated the quadrennial advisory councils and replaced them with a more permanent advisory board.

14. Schieber and Shoven (1999) provide a fascinating account of these discussions.

15. In addition to the issues we highlight, the advisory council also reached a consensus on restructuring Social Security family benefits, extending mandatory coverage to all state and local government workers, extending the period over which the average of lifetime earnings is computed, accelerating the increase in the age of eligibility for full retirement benefits, and revising the income taxation of Social Security benefits. See Advisory Council (1997) for details.

fund's portfolio would be scored as achieving 75-year solvency with relatively small changes in revenues and benefits.[16] To prevent the system from ultimately drifting out of balance, the plan also proposed raising the payroll tax by 1.6 percentage points beginning in 2045.

Two members, led by council chairman Gramlich, proposed adding individual accounts on top of the existing Social Security system. In contrast with the Kerrey-Simpson individual account proposal, this plan maintained the entire 12.4 percent payroll tax for the traditional defined-benefit program, with the result that its benefit cuts did not have to be as deep. The individual accounts were to be funded by mandatory additional contributions of 1.6 percent of covered payroll, which it was hoped would represent additional national saving. Individuals would choose how to allocate their account balances among a limited number of equity and bond index funds.[17]

Five council members, led by Sylvester Schieber and Carolyn Weaver, proposed much larger individual accounts. They suggested that 5 percentage points of the payroll tax be diverted to individual accounts; another 5 percentage points would provide a flat benefit to all retirees at about two-thirds of the poverty line; and the remaining 2.4 percentage points would be used to continue survivor's and disability insurance. Additional tax revenue equal to 1.5 percent of payroll for the next 75 years would be needed to fund the transition to this system.

The Gramlich commission struggled to reach consensus around a single plan, but eventually published a final report that reflected these three starkly different visions of Social Security reform. Ironically, the commission may have been considerably more valuable for not having reached consensus, because its analysis of these three alternatives served as a valuable launching pad for future analysis, including the work of Clinton administration staff.[18] It is also worth noting that, despite the divisions on the commission, the majority of members supported some sort of individual accounts as part of Social Security. Thus, the idea of individual accounts had, in a few short years, made a remarkable tran-

---

16. In the final report, the supporters of this plan did not actually recommend equity investments. Instead, they wrote that the plan "envisions, after a period of study and evaluation, the possibility of large-scale investment of [Social Security trust fund] monies in the equity market in order to help bring the program into balance." There was no recommendation for eliminating the actuarial imbalance if equity investments were not ultimately pursued.

17. Gramlich (1998) explains the reasoning behind this plan.

18. Another reason why the report was so valuable was that it incorporated a great deal of analytical material developed under the direction of Harry Ballantyne and Steve Goss, chief actuary and deputy chief actuary, respectively, at the Social Security Administration, as well as by the members of the technical review panels.

sition from the white papers of libertarian think tanks to the mainstream policy debate.

2.4.1.3 Breaux-Gregg-Kolbe-Stenholm

Unlike the first two commissions, the Center for Strategic and International Studies' National Commission on Retirement Policy was not government sponsored, although its cochairs Senators Breaux and Gregg and Congressmen Kolbe and Stenholm were committed to introducing the commission's ultimate recommendations in legislation. The group was launched in January 1997 and released its proposal in May 1998. It recommended diverting 2 percentage points of the payroll tax to create individual accounts. To rectify the imbalance in the traditional system (made even deeper by the carve-out of tax revenue), the plan raised both the normal and early retirement ages, assumed that further cost-reducing changes would be made to the Consumer Price Index, and reduced benefit levels by altering the formula that translates lifetime earnings into benefits. In order to shield low-income households from some of the benefit cuts, the plan introduced a new minimum benefit for workers with at least 20 years of earnings. This benefit increased from 60 percent to 100 percent of the poverty line as a worker's years of earnings increased from 20 to 40, so a household headed by a worker with 40 years of earnings would never fall below the poverty line.

Despite the persistent belief during this period that current fiscal policy was not sustainable in the long run, none of these proposals came close to being enacted. Quite understandably, the need to reform a system that was projected to remain solvent for at least another 30 years took second place on the political agenda to the urgency of addressing the near-term fiscal deficits.[19]

2.4.2 Social Security

Within the White House, serious consideration of tackling long-run entitlement issues began in the middle of 1997. During the preparations for his second inaugural address, President Clinton had told his advisers that he wanted to make strengthening Social Security one of his top goals for his second term. In addition, Congress was insisting on creating a Medicare commission as part of

---

19. The other important piece of Social Security legislation during this period was introduced by Senator Daniel P. Moynihan. It proposed to cut the payroll tax and give workers the option of using the tax savings to fund an individual account, in which case their contribution would be matched by the employer share as well. The plan also included various benefit cuts and, in the long run, increased the payroll tax to 13.4 percent of payroll.

the 1997 budget agreement, and the administration needed to decide how to respond. Most important, the administration realized that its next budget projections would include substantial unified surpluses between 2002 and 2007. Because these surpluses would fall within the ten-year budget window, the administration would need to propose a policy for allocating them.

This imminent end to the era of deficits was viewed by the administration as creating both opportunities and dangers. On one hand, the availability of surpluses gave the administration the freedom to contemplate new ambitious goals. On the other hand, President Clinton had successfully headed off Republican calls for deep tax cuts during the previous five years by calling for fiscal responsibility and deficit reduction. In an era of surpluses, it was harder to see what strategy would be more popular than Republican tax cuts, which were viewed by the administration as likely to have adverse distributional consequences and to reduce national saving at a time when the country should be saving more to prepare for the retirement of the baby-boom generation.

2.4.2.1 Political Pressures

The administration's economic team met throughout the summer and fall of 1997 to consider tax reform options, strategies for the new surplus era, and entitlement reform. Although these meetings initially were conducted on separate tracks, it was realized eventually that these topics were closely related, and the three topics were merged into a single set of "special issues" meetings that focused on ways to use the projected surpluses.

At an early point in this process, the president's health advisers argued that fundamental Medicare reform should not be pursued aggressively. These advisers believed that the combination of population aging and rising health costs per beneficiary made Medicare's long-term financing problems too large to resolve at that time. They also felt that the 1997 budget agreement already embodied many of the steps that the administration was ready to embrace with respect to Medicare reform.

Fundamental tax reform was also viewed as having substantial political and economic risks. First, if the president opened the door to a major tax bill, the administration might well lose control of the process to Congress. Then, a flat-tax plan with significant revenue loss (and therefore a negative effect on national saving) and adverse distributional consequences could have become the focus of the debate. Second, any reform that simplified the tax code or encouraged saving to a significant degree would likely create millions of losers as well as millions of winners, even with the commitment of substantial surplus funds. Last, no particular tax reform proposal ever gathered momentum among the economic team.

In contrast, there was considerable enthusiasm among the economic team for undertaking Social Security reform. This enthusiasm stemmed in part from the plausible reform alternatives laid out by the Gramlich commission and in part from the Rooseveltian legacy for the president that would come from putting Social Security on secure ground for the coming century. But the president's advisers also believed that proposing to use the surpluses for Social Security reform was more likely than the other alternatives to block both tax cuts and new spending. Thus reforming Social Security could do double duty: helping to solidify the improving budget outlook—President Clinton's most important economic accomplishment—by permitting the projected surpluses to feed through to national saving, and facilitating the rejuvenation of the nation's most important social program. Indeed, the economic team believed that even in the likely event that the reform effort failed, the debate over Social Security reform would be healthy in and of itself, and could go a long way toward maintaining fiscal discipline.

The administration's economic team was also aware of a significant group within the Democratic Party that downplayed the need for Social Security reform, partly in order to prevent radical change in the program. This group emphasized that, under the Social Security Trustees' low-cost assumptions, the system remains solvent throughout the 75-year projection period. Given this possibility that the existing system might be viable, why open the Pandora's box of "reforming" the crown jewel of American social programs? The administration's economists gave less weight to this argument for two reasons. First, the low-cost projections assume that a large number of factors such as fertility growth, mortality rates, immigration, and economic growth all turn out much better than expected—an outcome which presumably has very low probability. Second, recent research by academic demographers (for example, Lee and Tuljapurkar, 1998) suggests that longevity will likely increase more rapidly than projected by the Social Security Trustees, a trend that would raise the costs of the program. Thus the distribution of possible outcomes seemed weighted toward a worse, not a better, financial situation than projected by the trustees.

In a similar way, some observers noted that the Social Security Trustees' assumption of 1.6 percent annual GDP growth in the long run was far below the 3.1 percent annual average growth experienced in the last 30 years, and argued accordingly that the Trustees were being much too pessimistic about growth.[20] This argument missed the point that the growth of the labor force is projected to slow from its current pace of about 1 percent per year to approximately zero when the baby-boom generation begins retiring in earnest. GDP growth can

---

20. The numbers in this paragraph are taken from the 2001 Board of Trustees' Report.

be decomposed into the sum of the growth of the labor force (the number of workers) and the growth of productivity (output per worker). The Social Security trustees are assuming that productivity growth in the long run will roughly match its 1.5 percent annual historical average. With the growth of the labor force dropping to about zero, productivity growth would have to roughly double from its historical average rate in order for GDP growth to be maintained at its historical average pace. Moreover, faster economic growth has limited ability to improve Social Security's finances in the long run because a retiree's initial level of Social Security benefits is indexed to aggregate wage growth during his or her working years. It is only because benefits after retirement are indexed to inflation rather than wages that economic growth improves the actuarial standing of the system.

2.4.2.2 National Saving

The goal of increasing national saving was central to the administration's thinking about Social Security reform. Conventional wisdom indicates that the nation should save more now in preparation for the retirement of the baby boom generation. With lower fertility and rising longevity, the output generated by each worker will need to support the consumption of a larger number of workers and retirees in the future than it does today. The nation can smooth consumption in the face of this rising dependency burden by setting aside a larger share of current output as saving, thereby increasing the future capital stock and making future workers more productive.

Despite this rationale, the economic case for increasing national saving is less clear-cut than one might think. The fundamental issue is whether current generations should consume less in order to increase the well-being of future generations. In the absence of population aging, determining the optimal amount of saving involves balancing two considerations. On one hand, because future generations will benefit from gains in productivity over time, they are likely to be substantially better off than current generations. On the other hand, because forgone consumption compounds at the marginal product of capital, it is relatively inexpensive for current generations to provide additional resources for future generations.

Population aging introduces three additional considerations into the analysis. First, the increase in the dependency ratio caused by population aging will reduce the standard of living of future generations relative to what it would be without population aging, suggesting that additional resources should be transferred to future generations and therefore that additional saving would be desirable. Second, the slowdown in population growth will increase the capital-labor ratio, and therefore depress the return on capital; the lower return on capital suggests that less saving would be desirable (Cutler, Poterba, Sheiner, and Summers, 1990). Elmendorf and Sheiner (2000) use simulations to quantify these effects and conclude that the United States probably should not undertake substantial additional saving in response to the anticipated demographic shock. A third consideration is that tax rates would have to rise significantly over time to fund current-law benefits on a pay-as-you-go basis. For example, current projections imply that the Social Security payroll tax rate would have to rise from its current level of 12.4 percent to about 18 percent by 2070, an increase of roughly half. Since deadweight loss rises with the square of the tax rate, economic efficiency would be increased by raising taxes on current workers in order to decrease required future tax rates.

Quite aside from issues of population aging, many economists believe that a number of factors are causing U.S. national saving to be too low. For example, households may be shortsighted in their preparation for retirement, government policies may discourage saving by imposing a tax on capital income (interest, dividends, and capital gains), pay-as-you-go retirement programs like Social Security may crowd out private saving, and positive externalities from capital accumulation may drive the social return to saving above the private return. A Social Security reform that increased national saving could therefore raise social welfare even if population aging per se does not justify higher saving.

It is very difficult to predict the impact of a given Social Security reform plan on national saving. For example, if budget policy is made with the aim of balancing the unified budget, any increase in Social Security surpluses will result simply in additional spending or tax cuts in the non–Social Security part of the budget. Similarly, households may respond to Social Security reform by changing their own saving in ways that offset additional saving generated directly by the reform plan. Elmendorf and Liebman (2000) estimate the effect on national saving of seven different approaches to Social Security reform and show that the effects of alternative reforms depend critically on how households and the rest of the federal budget respond to reform.

2.4.3 Saving Social Security First

Before the January 1998 State of the Union address, the administration's economic team presented President Clinton with three options for pursuing Social Security reform. The first was to make a surprise announcement of a complete reform plan in the State of the Union address. The second was to name a commission to produce a reform plan in a short time, with the aim of engaging the Republican leadership in high-level negotiations in the spring of 1998. The third was to launch a year of public education, with the aim of releasing a proposal after the fall 1998 congressional elections, possibly in the 1999 State of the Union address.

As work progressed, the discussion ultimately focused on two possibilities. One was to allocate a specific percentage of the surplus to the Social Security trust fund and announce the date to which trust fund solvency would be extended by this action; the other was to reserve the entire surplus pending Social Security reform. The administration viewed the first proposal as a more dramatic announcement and an approach that would free up the remainder of the surplus for other priorities. But reserving all of the surplus was seen as a simpler and more sustainable message than announcing that some seemingly arbitrary fraction should be reserved. Moreover, it avoided the risk that a specific proposal to allocate surpluses to the trust fund would serve simply as a lightning rod for criticism and end up reducing the chance of achieving reform.

The administration ultimately adopted the second option, a strategy that became known as Save Social Security First. In the State of the Union address, President Clinton announced that his budget would reserve all of the projected unified budget surpluses pending Social Security reform. This strategy did not mean that the entire surplus would necessarily be used for reform, but rather that the president would not support other uses of the surplus—either for tax cuts or spending increases—until reform was accomplished and it became clear how much of the surplus was needed to finance that reform. Thus the policy was intended both to preserve the projected surpluses in case they were needed to finance the transition to a more fully funded Social Security system and to provide the reward of being able to use the remaining surpluses for tax cuts or more spending as an incentive to Congress for tackling Social Security reform.

President Clinton also launched a year-long national dialogue, including bipartisan forums designed to educate the public that would culminate in a December 1998 White House conference. At the first of these forums, in Kansas City, the president presented five principles that he said should guide Social Security reform: (1) strengthen and protect Social Security for the 21st century; (2) maintain universality and fairness; (3) provide a benefit people can count on; (4) preserve financial security for low-income and disabled beneficiaries; and (5) maintain fiscal discipline. The principles were designed to rule out proposals for radical privatization, including opt-out plans,[21] and proposals that would adversely affect low-income beneficiaries. The president also made

---

21. "Opt-out" plans—in which individuals could choose whether to remain in a scaled-back version of the current system or to allocate instead a share of their payroll tax to individual accounts—were considered particularly risky because high-income individuals might disproportionately opt out of the current system, turning it into a welfare program and depriving it of universal political support.

clear that all reform options other than an increase in the payroll tax rate should be on the table. Throughout the year, President Clinton accepted the advice of his economic team and did not rule out an eventual increase in the normal retirement age. Moreover, the president consistently maintained that individual reform elements should not be judged in the abstract, but rather as components of complete plans, and that those plans should be evaluated against the principles he laid out in Kansas City. He thought that by providing cover for those who were willing to make politically unpopular proposals for Social Security reform, he could increase the chance that reform would ultimately be accomplished.

2.5 Social Security Reform Options

After the 1998 State of the Union address, the administration launched a systematic process to develop a Social Security reform plan. A working group jointly chaired by National Economic Council Director Gene Sperling and Deputy Treasury Secretary Lawrence Summers met once or twice nearly every week to develop and analyze reform options. These working group meetings culminated in meetings with the economic team principals roughly once every three weeks, and in intermittent meetings with the president that increased in frequency in advance of key decisions.

In order to be prepared for the debate that was expected to arise, the working group studied a wide range of reform options—including many that the administration opposed. To be clear, the president never determined whether there was any plan built around individual accounts that he could have supported. To our knowledge, he never gave any of his advisers a brief for negotiations with Congress, and the administration certainly was never on the verge of striking a deal. The president's advisers rejected all plans for individual accounts that would have diverted resources away from the traditional defined-benefit program—so-called carve-out plans. Whether a so-called add-on plan could have garnered the support of the president is impossible to know. It was clear that any such plan would have put strict limits on the extent to which an individual's overall benefit might be at risk from poor investment results, in line with one of the president's principles for Social Security reform. Similarly, the administration would have put considerable emphasis on the redistribution accomplished under a proposed reform plan—again in line with one of the president's principles—and might well have insisted that a reformed system be more progressive than the current one.

The working group studied analytic issues that cut across various reform options. Most of the analysis focused on two broad topics: mechanisms for using the projected budget surpluses to pre-fund Social Security benefits, and mechanisms for investing those pre-funded amounts in private financial assets. Much of the effort ultimately was directed toward devising ways of bridging the gap between defenders of the current defined-benefit system and advocates of individual accounts, including hybrid plans that included features of both approaches.

Relatively little time was spent analyzing traditional reform options such as raising the retirement age, adjusting the indexation of benefits, or changing the tax status of benefits. This lack of attention largely reflected the familiarity of these options, owing in part to the analysis conducted by the Gramlich commission. What was new in the current situation was the availability of additional resources, in the form of emerging surpluses, that might be used to reduce the pain of putting the system on a sound footing. Moreover, it did not make much sense to focus on specific revenue raisers and benefit cuts until the president had settled on a particular approach to reform. Last, the administration believed that the specific painful elements of a Social Security deal would need to be introduced at the last minute as part of bipartisan negotiations with Congress. The administration's view was that any specific painful options put forward before a complete deal was reached would be attacked, and responsible policies would be taken off the table prematurely.

2.5.1 Using Projected Budget Surpluses as Part of Social Security Reform

There were two principal challenges in using near-term budget surpluses to help pay long-term Social Security benefits. The first challenge was to set aside the money today in a way that would actually boost the resources available to future generations, rather than being dissipated down the road by future presidents and Congresses. The second challenge was to ensure that the incremental future resources would actually be used to finance retirement benefits.

Maintaining budget surpluses—and thus paying down public debt—was seen as the most direct way to boost national saving, but by itself this approach had several shortcomings. First, it was not clear how to give Social Security a claim on the additional future resources that would be made available by paying down the debt. Second, this strategy would pay off the entire public debt long before Social Security was fully pre-funded, raising the question of how the ensuing "national asset" should be invested. Third, it was difficult to see how this strategy could be locked in for any length of time: if future presidents and Congresses decided to use the surpluses for tax cuts or new spending, then these resources would not be available as planned.

These concerns led the administration working group to devise a set of reform plans that involved transferring some portion of the unified budget surplus to the Social Security trust fund. Mechanically, these plans transferred funds from the non–Social Security part of the federal government to Social Security. If written into law, these transfers would have given Social Security a legal entitlement to future resources, and would have ensured that any later diversion of the surpluses to other purposes would have had an adverse implication for the Social Security trust fund. The transfers were also designed to take projected surpluses "off the table," so that they could not be allocated to tax cuts or new spending, but would be used to reduce the public debt.

One important disadvantage of these plans was their vulnerability to the charge of "double counting" the Social Security surplus. Much of the projected unified budget surpluses originated in Social Security and therefore were already credited to the Social Security trust fund under current law. Thus, according to the critics, transferring unified surpluses to Social Security caused the same dollars of revenue in effect to be counted twice to the benefit of Social Security. Yet the status quo involved precisely the same approach to budgeting: as long as the budget process was focused on balancing the unified budget, dollars that were credited to the Social Security trust fund were still perceived to be available for new spending or tax cuts. The administration's economic team believed that a dollar of the unified budget surplus could therefore legitimately be transferred to Social Security and credited to the trust fund, provided that the transfer would take the dollar off the table and prevent it from being used for other purposes. In that case, the transfer would result in an extra dollar's worth of public debt being paid down relative to the status quo, and therefore in an extra dollar of government saving.

Nevertheless, the administration was well aware that this approach "had bad optics," and internally a number of economists argued vigorously against adopting a plan that would be subject to this criticism.[22] However, the obvious alternative of taking Social Security out of the budget and transferring only non–Social Security surpluses to the trust fund was not a strong alternative at this point because the non–Social Security part of the budget remained in deficit. Thus this approach would have imposed too much fiscal stringency and would have required the administration to give up talking about its proudest economic accomplishment, the unified budget surplus, and instead report an on-budget deficit.

Another disadvantage of this approach was the need for novel budget accounting in order to truly take the surpluses "off the table."[23] Under conventional budget scoring, a dollar transferred from the non–Social Security part

---

22. In the Clinton White House, "had bad optics" meant simply "did not look good."
23. See Penner (1998) for a discussion of budget scoring issues that arise in Social Security reform plans.

of the budget to Social Security would not reduce the unified budget—so the amount of surplus apparently available for tax cuts or new spending would not actually be reduced. Therefore, the administration proposed a new scoring rule in which every dollar transferred from the non–Social Security budget to the Social Security trust fund would result in a one-dollar reduction in the *reported* unified surplus. There was considerable internal debate over whether such a scoring rule would be sustainable, or whether some future president or Congress would revert to conventional scoring methods and erase the incremental government saving that would be achieved under this type of approach.

2.5.2 Investments in Private Financial Assets

Beginning with the Gramlich commission, nearly all Social Security reform proposals involved some investments in private financial assets. Yet this consensus left a wide gap between those favoring individual accounts and those favoring collective investing through the Social Security trust fund. During the late 1990s, Henry Aaron, Peter Diamond, Robert Reischauer, and others emphasized the high administrative costs and portfolio risks associated with individual accounts, and they devised mechanisms to protect collective investment systems from political interference (Aaron and Reischauer, 1998; Diamond, 1996, 1997, 2000). On the other side, Martin Feldstein, Andrew Samwick, and others argued that individual accounts need not involve high costs or risks, and were the most effective way of pre-funding Social Security benefits (Feldstein and Samwick, 1997, 1998). The analysis conducted within the administration built upon this academic work and extended it significantly along four dimensions: administrative feasibility and costs, portfolio risk, political interference in markets and corporate governance, and redistribution.

2.5.2.1 Administrative Feasibility and Costs

Peter Diamond had shown that administering individual accounts had been very expensive in Chile and the United Kingdom, and argued that costs might also be high in the United States. In particular, he pointed out that an annual administrative cost of 100 basis points—similar to many U.S. mutual funds today—would reduce the retirement income available to an individual with 40 years of work history by roughly 20 percent. In order to ensure that the economic team's advice to the president would be accurate and did not promise something that could not be achieved, Lawrence Summers insisted that the working group determine whether setting up an individual accounts system was even remotely feasible, what kind of service it could provide, and at what cost.

The information technology staff at the Treasury Department and the Social Security Administration were given the task of determining exactly how information and dollars would flow from workers' earnings statements to private investment managers. Extremely detailed estimates were produced of how much additional manpower would be necessary for such a system to function. For example, one option was for workers to indicate their choices of private sector fund managers on their 1040 tax forms. The working group went so far as to determine how many digits would be needed for each fund's ID number and therefore how many key strokes would be required to enter all of the ID numbers each year. Separate estimates of cost and necessary manpower were produced depending on whether the processing would occur by May of each year (sharply increasing IRS workload during its peak period) or by early August (which was much cheaper).

Two principal considerations were how long it would take to get a system up and running and whether the system could provide service similar to what many workers now experience in the 401(k) plans offered by their employers. On the first issue, it was considered important from a political standpoint that the system be up and running before President Clinton left office in early 2001. However, the information technology teams throughout the government were busy with Y2K preparations, so it did not seem possible that substantial resources could be devoted to setting up individual accounts until after those preparations were completed. At one point in mid-1998, consideration was given to starting the process of setting up the administrative structure for individual accounts right away, a year before there was any chance of a plan being enacted by Congress, so as to shave a year off the time between enactment and the existence of the accounts.

On the issue of service quality, a major concern of the working group was whether contributions could be made to individual accounts in a timely manner. Employers do not report their workers' annual earnings until the first quarter of the following year; it then takes the IRS several months to process and reconcile these earnings records, so it is typically August before a mostly complete set of earnings records for the previous year is available. The working group thought that it would be unappealing for account contributions to be made as much as 18 months after the earnings on which they were based. Options were developed for making estimated contributions to accounts based on workers' previous years' earnings, or for investing all of the funds in a default portfolio and then allocating them to individual accounts (including the within-year returns) when the information on individual earnings became available.

Yet the working group remained very concerned that any feasible, inexpensive individual account system would be perceived as providing inferior service compared with employer-run accounts. Because the cost of a system of individual accounts depends mainly on the number of accounts, rather than the amount invested in them, the existence in a public system of millions of very small accounts could generate administrative costs that were much larger on a "load" basis than for employer-run systems. Minimizing those costs would generally require a reduction in service and flexibility relative to those private systems. Thus, Lawrence Summers was fond of saying that we had to guard against the risk of setting up the Post Office when people were used to dealing with Federal Express.

The working group concluded that managing a system of individual accounts would be feasible but that the government would have to play a major role in the system and only bare-bones accounts could be administered at a reasonable cost. In particular, the government would have to collect the revenue and set up a clearinghouse to direct deposits to the private-sector fund managers selected by each worker. Other options such as having workers send contributions directly to fund managers or mandating that employers administer the accounts would be prohibitively expensive. One way to reduce costs was to allow people no investment choice until their accounts reached a minimum size (perhaps $5,000); until then the funds would be invested collectively. Moreover, the range of investment choices would need to be sharply limited, to perhaps a dozen firms offering broad-based index funds. Account statements would be mailed at most once a year, and phone inquiries would not be toll free. Borrowing against account balances would be prohibited, partly to preserve the balances exclusively for retirement use and partly because loan administration has proved very costly in the private sector.

The working group's best estimate was that such a system could be run at an annual cost of $20 to $30 per account, while accounts with service similar to that in current 401(k)s (though not including loans) would be two or three times as expensive. With roughly 180 million accounts, total annual costs could exceed $5 billion a year in today's dollars (more than half as large as the current budget of the IRS and therefore more than half the cost of administering the entire federal tax code) and tens of thousands of new government workers would be needed to answer phone inquiries and process worker choices of fund managers. Thus, even though administering an individual account system was thought to be feasible, administrative costs remained a significant downside to that approach. The group also believed that it was important that costs be spread across all accounts in proportion to their assets; otherwise a very substantial share of the investment returns of lower-income people with small account balances would be consumed by the administrative costs.

2.5.2.2 Portfolio Risk

Social Security reform plans that involve investment in equities could introduce two sorts of portfolio risk. First, aggregate stock-market fluctuations could leave different cohorts with higher-than-expected or lower-than-expected retirement income. Second, retirement income could differ among members of the same cohort if individuals were allowed to make their own investment choices. The extent of these risks varies considerably across different reform plans. On the one hand, collective investment by the trust fund would produce no variation in benefits among members of the same generation, and—to the extent that there is some mean reversion in equity prices—could smooth some of the risk across generations as well. On the other hand, individual accounts with relatively unrestricted IRA-style investment options could result in substantial numbers of ill-informed investors making very different investment choices. As a result, two individuals born in the same year and with identical earnings histories might retire with very different benefits because they assumed different idiosyncratic risks or because aggregate stock-market fluctuations had affected them differently.

The economic team emphasized to President Clinton the portfolio risks under different reform proposals and the reasons to be cautious about equity investments. For example, the S&P 500 did not regain its 1968 value in real terms until 1983 (even including reinvested dividends), and Japan's Nikkei index had fallen by 60 percent since 1989. Moreover, a persuasive explanation for why the return on stocks in the 20th century was so much higher than the return on bonds has never been given, raising concerns about whether this gap will persist in the future. Robert Rubin was particularly concerned about adding portfolio risk to the Social Security system, and he argued that it would be a mistake to have Social Security benefits depend on equity returns whether it was the trust fund or individuals doing the investing. He worried that the stock-market boom of the 1990s had erased people's memories of earlier periods such as the 1970s during which stock prices did not rise at all, and reminded the economic team of the *Business Week* cover story from 1979: "The Death of Equities?"

On balance, however, the economic team did not think that market risk was a sufficiently important concern to rule out plans that involved equities, for several reasons. First, steps would have been taken to closely circumscribe the exposure of benefits to equity risk. If collective investment were undertaken, only a limited fraction of the trust fund would have been eligible for investment in equities. If individual accounts were part of the picture, they would have been small add-on accounts with limited investment options.

Second, in the United States, even large stock market declines have ultimately been more than made up for in subsequent rebounds. For example, the S&P 500 lost 85 percent of its value between September 1929 and June 1932, but had returned to its 1929 level by the end of 1936. Nevertheless, there was some concern that there might not be sufficient political patience to remain invested in equities after a large market downturn.

Third, although valuations were then very high relative to historic levels, a correction during the next decade or so would be relatively unimportant for retirement benefits, since total equity holdings would not yet have grown very much.

Fourth, under the reform plans the administration was considering, the existing Social Security payroll tax would still be allocated entirely to the purchase of Treasury securities by the trust fund. Only general revenue contributions to the system would be invested in equities. Thus, even in the unimaginable circumstance in which all of the stock investments became worthless (in which case, the solvency of Social Security would probably not be first on the list of the country's problems!), Social Security would be no worse off than under current law.

Fifth, the current Social Security system already involves substantial risks, including the political risk that benefit rules will change, the demographic risk that forecasts of mortality and fertility will be wrong, and the economic risk that productivity growth will be higher or lower than currently projected. Introducing equities would add a new form of risk, and might increase the total amount of risk, but it would not be converting a currently riskless system into a risky one. Nonetheless, the economic team viewed market risk as a significant drawback of plans that involved equities, and this drawback would need to be balanced against any potential benefits of such an approach.

The administration working group also analyzed policy options that could reduce the risk faced by holders of individual accounts. One problem was that individuals might shift out of equities after a market decline, missing the recovery in equity prices. Another problem was that individuals who retired shortly after a substantial market drop—and annuitized their account balances based on those lower equity prices—might believe it was unfair that workers who had retired only shortly before were receiving much larger annuity payments. Indeed, this perceived unfairness might be acute even if the later retirees received higher annuities by investing in equities throughout their working lives than if they had invested entirely in government bonds. This issue could be addressed, at least in part, by mandating gradual annuitization or investment in variable-rate annuities, which would reduce the dependence of retirement income on equity prices at a moment in time. Another way to reduce risk would be a guarantee that each worker would do at least as well as if he or she had invested in government bonds. Yet, this approach presented the danger that guarantees would induce people to take too much risk in their portfolios or would simply represent a large contingent liability for the government.[24]

2.5.2.3 Political Interference in Markets and Corporate Governance

Although the administration working group thought that centralized investment in equities had important advantages, the group also recognized that such investment had significant potential disadvantages. Chief among these was that government ownership of private financial assets raised difficult issues of corporate governance and potential political interference in capital markets.

Under the Social Security reform proposals of Robert Ball and Henry Aaron and Robert Reischauer, as much as 50 percent of the Social Security trust fund would be invested in equities. This holding would represent a large share of the U.S. stock market—somewhere between 15 percent and 30 percent in 2030, depending on the relative growth rates of GDP and the stock market. Even with a smaller part of the trust fund invested in equities, the government could still end up as the largest shareholder of many companies. If political considerations influenced the investment decisions of the trust fund, the efficiency of capital markets in allocating resources could be degraded. Certainly, the track record of state and local governments in the United States as well as foreign governments around the world was sufficient to give one pause on this issue. It is not difficult to compile a sobering list of examples in which political intrusion had materially reduced investment returns and arguably reduced the efficiency of various economies. Moreover, government ownership of equities might discourage the government from pursuing other policies that could lower equity prices. If the government were a major stockholder in Corporation XYZ, would the Justice Department shy away from pursuing a meritorious antitrust case against XYZ? Or would the Environmental Protection Agency or Occupational Safety and Health Administration refrain from enforcing their regulations against XYZ?

A related problem is how the government would exercise its rights as a shareholder to choose corporations' managers and participate in business decisions. Simply abstaining from voting might not be an adequate strategy, since it could effectively turn minority shareholders into majority shareholders who would not necessarily look out for the interests of the other shareholders. In

---

24. Indeed, research by Kent Smetters (2001) suggested that the contingent liability implicit in such a guarantee might be essentially as large as the unfunded liability in the current system.

addition, voting rights may represent an important source of value in owning equity; would the government be fulfilling its fiduciary responsibilities if it simply ignored that source of value altogether?

Some members of the economic team believed that these problems were not insurmountable. They argued that investments could be handled by an independent board modeled after the Federal Reserve Board, with members chosen from the private sector and charged with acting in the sole interest of trust fund beneficiaries. Investments could be limited to "widely used index funds," in order to inhibit investments in funds that excluded particular firms engaged in some specified out-of-favor activity. The private fund managers could be chosen in a competitive process, instructed to vote proxies on behalf of the trust fund's beneficiaries, and required to commingle the public money with the assets of their private clients. Even still, future Congresses could alter such safeguards at any time, so developing a culture of noninterference would be very important.

The working group also came to appreciate that many of these same issues would arise, to at least some degree, under a system of individual accounts, especially to the extent that investment choices were tightly constrained. Indeed, most legislation proposing individual accounts would put strict limits on investment choices; it was not hard to believe that political interference might well affect the choices offered.[25] At the same time, individuals may be more vigilant in policing deviations from return-maximizing investment policies for accounts that they own personally rather than accounts that are held by the government—and Congress may therefore be more constrained in deviating from performance-maximizing choices with regard to such accounts. For example, the Thrift Savings Plan is a defined-contribution plan for federal employees that has existed for years without political interference.

2.5.2.4 Redistribution

A central principle for the administration was that Social Security reform should not reduce the extent of redistribution in Social Security from high-income households to low-income households. In particular, the administration believed that reform should help the demographic groups that are most dependent on Social Security for staying out of poverty, such as elderly women who are widowed, divorced, or never married. Indeed, Gene Sperling argued

25. For example, the Archer-Shaw proposal discussed later required all individual accounts to be invested in index funds with 60 percent equities and 40 percent bonds. The Breaux-Gregg-Kolbe-Stenholm plan limited investments to a small number of options similar to those in the federal Thrift Savings Plan.

that any negotiations with congressional Republicans about individual account plans should be limited to only those plans that would result in a more progressive system overall than current-law Social Security.

The most frequently proposed way of funding individual accounts was to make contributions proportional to an individual's earnings, such as 2 percent of earnings. Because this approach would provide no redistribution to lower-income workers, the administration working group studied other options for funding individual accounts.[26] One approach was to use the projected budget surpluses to fund equal-dollar contributions to each worker's account. Contributions of $300 per worker had roughly the same aggregate cost as contributions of 1 percent of payroll, so contributions of $600 would be a highly progressive alternative to contributions of 2 percent of earnings.[27] Contributions equal to $300 plus one percent of earnings would come very close to replicating the redistribution in the current Social Security system.[28] In April 1998, Newt Gingrich proposed using the surplus to give every American a tax cut in the form of an equal-dollar contribution to a "Social Security Plus" individual saving account; thus there was some hope that a plan along these lines could receive bipartisan support.[29]

An alternative to funding individual accounts in a redistributive manner would be to make the traditional system more redistributive at the same time that nonredistributive individual accounts were introduced. This approach was used in the Breaux-Gregg-Kolbe-Stenholm plan. The administration's economic team had serious concerns about this approach because it would lower even further the return received by higher income people in the traditional system, and thus run the risk of eroding support for a universal program.

The working group also gave a great deal of attention to ways of reducing poverty among elderly women. Elderly women who are divorced, widowed, or never married now have poverty rates around 20 percent, roughly twice the population-wide average. An interagency process developed a set of options

---

26. With mandatory annuitization at a single price, "2 percent accounts" would appear to redistribute from poor to rich, because the rich tend to live longer. However, the overall distributional impact of such a plan depends on the source of the contributions. If the funding is generated from a progressive source like the personal income tax, then even accounts funded proportionally to earnings can be progressive.

27. Contributions would likely be limited to workers with at least a threshold amount of earnings in the year (perhaps the amount that would qualify a worker for four quarters of Social Security coverage, currently around $3,000).

28. See Feldstein and Liebman (2002) and Liebman (2002) for further discussion.

29. Of course, there are many other redistributive formulas that could be used. For example, contributions could equal 10 percent of the first few thousand dollars of earnings, 5 percent of the next few thousand dollars, and a smaller percentage of additional earnings.

for addressing this problem and produced a report that was issued in conjunction with a presidential event on the importance of Social Security to women.[30] The options included increasing Supplemental Security Income (SSI) benefits; providing Social Security earnings credits for years spent out of the labor force raising children; and offering a new widow benefit equal to 75 percent of the benefit received by the married couple before the deceased spouse passed away (capped at the benefit received by a worker with average earnings).[31] These options were seen both as good policy and as a way to sweeten a Social Security reform package, particularly one with individual accounts, for congressional Democrats. Although these proposals were never formally advanced by President Clinton, versions of them were put forth later by Vice President Gore during his presidential campaign.

Another important concern was to make sure that Social Security reform did not reduce the income of Social Security disability beneficiaries. Because the formulas for retirement benefits and disability benefits are linked, cuts to retirement benefits would generally reduce disability benefits as well. Yet many disabled beneficiaries would not have had a chance to accumulate significant individual account balances by the time they become disabled, so they could not compensate for cuts to the traditional benefit using the proceeds of their individual accounts in the same way that retirees could. Therefore, the working group believed that any cuts to traditional retirement benefits should not pass through to disability benefits; all of the reform plans constructed by the group were scored under this assumption.

2.5.3 Potential Compromise Reform Proposals

The administration working group believed that there was more potential for substantive consensus on Social Security reform than the heated rhetoric on the topic suggested. Clearly, the political challenge of achieving reform was immense, and the substantive gap among competing proposals remained wide. Nonetheless, the administration believed that the concept of using the proceeds of fiscal discipline to help address the nation's long-run fiscal challenges—and therefore to justify general revenue transfers to the Social Security trust fund—had the potential for bipartisan support. And on two of the most disputed

---

30. *Women and Retirement Security*, available at www.ssa.gov/policy/pubs/womenrs.html.
31. Providing earnings credits for time spent out of the labor force raising children implicitly values that time the same regardless of a woman's earnings level. In contrast, the more traditional proposal to provide "drop-out" years in the Social Security benefit formula implicitly values the time of high-earning women more highly than the time of low-earning women. Thus the new option was essentially a more progressive version of the traditional proposal.

issues—whether investments in private securities should be handled collectively or individually, and whether individual accounts should be created as part of Social Security—there was nearly a continuum of options, and proposals from the left and the right seemed to be moving toward each other.

On the first issue, proponents of individual accounts had originally argued that investment options should be completely unrestricted. For example, Martin Feldstein had initially proposed that individual accounts be funded through a tax credit and invested in any of the assets that are eligible for use in an IRA. Yet, in response to concerns about administrative costs and naive investors, the main Republican legislative proposals ended up restricting investment choices to a few broad index funds. Similarly, early plans for private investments by the Social Security trust fund envisioned the government investing directly through a single large fund. But as concerns about government interference in markets were raised, proposals tended to set up independent investment boards and to spread the investments across a number of private managers. Thus, by late 1998, alternative investment mechanisms appeared to be converging to some degree.

A similar convergence may have been occurring on whether individual accounts should be part of Social Security. Some Democrats argued that individual accounts had the potential to create wealth for all Americans, provide choice for individuals, and allow for some bequests.[32] Other Democrats were willing to consider supplementing Social Security benefits with government-subsidized accounts targeted at low-income households. At the same time, some Republicans who had initially favored diverting a portion of the existing Social Security payroll tax to individual accounts—and then cutting the traditional benefit substantially—turned to proposals in which general revenue was used to fund individual accounts.[33] Indeed, there was a growing understanding that reshuffling the revenue stream already dedicated to paying retirement benefits would not help close the underlying financing gap, and that additional resources would be needed. Moreover, some of the Republican proposals involved redistributive funding of individual accounts. Thus, by late 1998, there appeared to be the possibility for convergence around using non–Social Security funds to make redistributive contributions to individual accounts, contributions that might or might not bear any direct mechanical relationship to the traditional Social Security system.

---

32. Clearly, an individual account system that allowed for bequests would have lower average retirement benefits than a system that used the account balances of deceased workers to supplement the retirement benefits of survivors—unless additional resources were contributed to the system.
33. In some of these plans, part of the Social Security payroll tax was diverted to individual accounts, while general revenue was directed to the trust fund to make up for the diverted monies.

Three main types of Social Security reform plans occupied the "policy space" defined by this possible convergence of views. The first and simplest were add-on individual accounts like those proposed by Edward Gramlich. Under this approach, the entire existing Social Security payroll tax would continue to be used exclusively for funding traditional Social Security benefits, and benefit cuts and revenue raisers would be used to bring the system into financial balance. At the same time, general revenue would be contributed to individual accounts to compensate for the reduction in the traditional benefit.[34]

The second type of eligible plan was a so-called clawback plan, initially developed by Martin Feldstein and Andrew Samwick. Under this approach, general revenue from the budget surplus would be contributed to individual accounts, and a significant share of the account balances (possibly in excess of 75 percent) would be "clawed back" when workers reached retirement in order to finance traditional Social Security benefits; individuals would receive the remaining account balances directly.[35] House Ways and Means Committee Chairman Bill Archer and his colleague Clay Shaw introduced a plan of this form.

The third type of possible consensus plan was a "hybrid" plan that included both trust fund investments in equities and the establishment of small individual accounts. Some analysts saw these plans as "splitting the difference" between the two sides in the political debate. In addition, this approach offered an interesting opportunity for addressing concerns about government interference in markets: trust fund investments could simply mirror the investment choices that individuals made in their own accounts. This could be done through a single fund that matched the aggregation of individuals' choices, or it could be done through individual "mirror accounts" in the name of each worker that were invested on behalf of the trust fund. However, some analysts argued that the smaller individual accounts in hybrid plans made little sense, because the fixed costs of administering the accounts would consume an excessive fraction of the investment returns.

An important concern of the economic team was that a reform plan involving modest individual accounts in the beginning might be a "slippery slope" toward total privatization. Yet there was considerable disagreement about what sort of reform presented the greatest such risk. Some members of the team

---

34. It would also be possible to fund add-on accounts by requiring workers to make mandatory contributions to these accounts above and beyond their current payroll taxes. This approach was taken in the Gramlich plan.

35. The clawback can also be specified as a reduction in Social Security benefits equal to some fraction of account withdrawals. For example, a worker might lose 75 cents of his or her traditional benefit for each dollar of retirement income from an individual account.

argued that a clawback approach would best preserve the existing system, since nearly all of the retirement benefits would continue to be paid out through the traditional defined-benefit formula. From that perspective, a clawback plan could be viewed as a backdoor way for the Social Security trust fund to invest in equities while leaving the investment decisions to individuals rather than the government. Other members of the economic team argued that the clawback approach tied Social Security benefits too closely to individual accounts, and that it would not be politically feasible to tax such a large portion of the accounts at retirement. Under this view, clawback plans were simply a way of building up sufficient assets to make total privatization possible (and likely) at a later date.

More generally, the working group recognized that the details of reform proposals would have a tremendous impact on their economic and social consequences—and thus on the acceptability of those proposals to the administration. Thus, an "individual accounts" proposal that was funded out of the existing payroll tax in a nonprogressive manner with unrestricted investment options and high administrative costs represented a completely different view of the future than a proposal with a similar label but different funding source and account design.

2.5.4   The 1999 State of the Union Social Security Proposal

Throughout 1998 the administration working group studied the analytic issues underlying Social Security reform and constructed specific illustrative reform plans. Briefings for President Clinton covered not only the substantive issues detailed in the preceding pages, but also political strategies for achieving bipartisan agreement on reform. Options that were given some very preliminary thought included the "Andrews Air Force Base approach," echoing the negotiations over the 1990 budget deal, in which White House officials and the congressional leadership were sequestered in nonstop negotiations at the base just outside Washington, DC; the "spontaneous" emergence of a bipartisan piece of legislation from a moderate Democrat on the Senate Finance Committee, as had almost worked on tobacco legislation; and the formation of a commission made up of key members of Congress and administration officials.

The administration also spent 1998 pursuing an active "external" strategy on Social Security reform. This effort included briefings for members of Congress, public education efforts surrounding the three national Social Security forums, and preparation for the December White House conference. Congressional distrust of the administration's work on Social Security reform ran very deep, in part because of the potentially momentous importance of the issue. Some

Democrats doubted whether the administration had a bedrock commitment to preserving Social Security in its current form to the greatest extent possible. Congressional Republicans were even less trusting of the administration, and they sought assurances that President Clinton was serious about achieving bipartisan reform and not simply trying to trick Republicans into taking an unpopular position on the issue that Democrats could then use to retake control of Congress. Indeed, when Archer and Shaw introduced a specific reform plan, some of their Republican colleagues complained that they had fallen into the Clinton administration's trap.

In the end, President Clinton decided to pursue Social Security reform based on bolstering the Social Security trust fund rather than on creating individual accounts. The president proposed transferring general revenue into the trust fund and investing a portion of the transferred amounts in equities. The equity investments would be restricted to never exceed 5 percent of the total U.S. stock market. This decision may have been influenced by the changing political dynamic in late 1998, as the possibility that the president would be impeached came clearly into view. Whether the president would have pursued a different approach in the absence of impeachment will never be known.

The other key decision that was made in the run-up to the 1999 State of the Union address was whether to stick with a unified budget framework or to switch to a budget framework that allocated only the non–Social Security surplus. The central advantage of the unified budget framework was that there would be sufficient funds available not only to shore up Social Security but also to extend Medicare solvency, provide for additional discretionary spending, and establish progressive individual savings accounts outside of Social Security. A key disadvantage was that transferring a portion of the unified budget surplus to Social Security might be seen as "double counting." In contrast, the on-budget approach would avoid the double-counting critique, but there would not be sufficient resources available for all of the non–Social Security initiatives. Moreover, it would be necessary to project on-budget deficits for some of the individual years in the ten-year budget window. Ultimately, the president decided to stick with the unified budget approach to budgeting that had been the norm since the Lyndon B. Johnson administration.

2.6 Budget Surpluses: 1998 Through 2000

During the final years of the Clinton administration, attention focused on the rapidly rising budget surpluses and their appropriate disposition. We review the economics and politics of that budget debate in this section.

2.6.1 The 1999 State of the Union Budget Framework

In his 1999 State of the Union address, President Clinton built on the earlier strategy to "Save Social Security First" by proposing a specific budget framework for Social Security reform and long-term fiscal discipline. This framework proposed an allocation of *unified* budget surpluses. In contrast with prevailing practice, this allocation extended over the unusually long time frame of 15 years because there were insufficient resources in the first 10 years to accomplish all of the president's objectives. In line with the earlier strategy, all the proposed uses of the surpluses were conditioned on reforming Social Security.

The proposed allocation of the unified surpluses was as follows: First, 62 percent of the surpluses were allocated to Social Security and 15 percent to Medicare. Transfers in these amounts would be made to the respective trust funds, and the associated budget resources would be viewed as fully "used" and hence not available for other purposes. Because the monies were not needed by these programs to pay current benefits, they would be used predominantly to pay down the publicly held debt of the federal government, with a limited amount of the revenue transferred to Social Security used to purchase equities. The plan was projected to extend the solvency of the Social Security trust fund to 2055 and the Medicare Part A trust fund to 2020.

Another 12 percent of the surpluses were allocated to create new Universal Savings Accounts (USAs). As the administration described in more detail later in the spring, the accounts would involve an automatic contribution by the government for all workers earning less than a specified amount, as well as a matching contribution also available to workers with income below a certain threshold. A primary motivation for these accounts was to serve as a bridge between the proponents and opponents of introducing individual accounts into the Social Security system. On one hand, USAs gave the administration a means of promoting wealth creation on a broad scale, and they signaled the president's willingness to discuss the appropriate role of individual accounts in the U.S. retirement system. On the other hand, the administration emphasized that the accounts would have been entirely separate from Social Security— funded from revenue outside the existing payroll tax, and having no implication for an account holder's traditional Social Security benefits. Indeed, to reinforce the separateness of USAs from Social Security, and to ensure that USAs were not seen as undermining the existing private pension system, the administration proposed that contributions to 401(k) plans would qualify for government matching. As it turned out, however, USAs never received serious legislative consideration.

The budget framework also allowed for additional tax cuts for child care, long-term care, school construction, and investment in economically depressed areas, but the cost of these proposals was financed entirely by other revenue-raising provisions such as curtailing tax subsidies and closing some tax shelters and other loopholes. The final 11 percent of the surpluses were allocated to military readiness and other spending.

Federal Reserve Chairman Alan Greenspan testified before Congress on the day after the State of the Union address. His prepared remarks concerned macroeconomic conditions and therefore did not mention the president's proposals of the previous evening. However, in the question-and-answer session, he provided crucial support for transfers to the Social Security trust fund while reiterating his strong opposition to government investment in private markets:

[Greenspan] endorsed President Clinton's proposal to let federal budget surpluses accumulate by locking up most of the money in the Social Security and Medicare trust funds. But he attacked Mr. Clinton's plan to invest as much as 15 percent of the Social Security trust fund in the stock market, arguing that it would be "virtually impossible" to insulate investment managers from political influence. (*Wall Street Journal*, January 21, 1999, p. A3)

Much of the media coverage focused on Greenspan's opposition to government ownership of private equities. Even so, these testimonies helped the administration build credibility within the Beltway for the plan's central device for preserving a large fraction of the unified surpluses.

The proposed budget framework was also criticized on the grounds that it "double-counted" the projected Social Security surpluses. As we discussed earlier, the unified surplus equals the "off-budget" surplus (overwhelmingly the Social Security surplus) plus the "on-budget" surplus (essentially, the surplus on the non–Social Security portion of the government's operations). The critics argued that the administration's plan for allocating unified surpluses was transferring to Social Security some budgetary resources that had originated in the Social Security system, and therefore had already been credited to the Social Security trust fund once. Consider, for example, the hypothetical case in which *all* the unified surpluses originated in Social Security. In that case, a $1 surplus in the Social Security system would have increased the trust fund balance by $1.62—$1 as under current law, and an additional 62 cents from the proposed transfers. The administration responded that the budget debate in preceding decades had been a debate about the unified budget, with an implicit—though often unspoken—objective of balancing the unified budget. By contrast, the administration now aimed to leave a unified surplus. If one accepted the administration's assertion that "business as usual" would have left no unified surpluses, then the State of the Union plan generated incremental government saving, and the budget framework simply proposed to allocate this incremental saving to Social Security.

Republicans responded to the president's proposals by pledging to create a "lockbox" to ensure that the Social Security surplus would be used to pay down debt. In addition, they proposed to allocate the on-budget surplus primarily to a 10 percent across-the-board tax cut and increases in defense spending.

2.6.2   Balancing the Budget Excluding Social Security

Against a backdrop of the double-counting allegation and continued dramatic improvement in budget projections, the administration significantly revamped its budget framework for the Mid-Session Review (MSR) released in June 1999. The new framework proposed to balance the budget in each year *exclusive of the operations of the Social Security system*. The MSR projected that the on-budget account would run a surplus of $5 billion in fiscal year 2000 if no policy changes were enacted; as it turned out, the on-budget account finished fiscal year *1999* with a surplus of less than $1 billion, the first surplus by that measure in 40 years, and followed that with a surplus of more than $86 billion in fiscal year 2000.

2.6.2.1   The Logic

Social Security had been taken officially "off budget" in 1983, and this action was reaffirmed in the budget legislation of 1985 and 1990 (Koitz, 1998). But none of this legislative action was sufficient to redirect policy attention to the on-budget balance. The key objective of the administration and others who favored the MSR approach to budgeting was to refocus the political conversation on the disposition of the on-budget surpluses, and thereby establish the presumption that the Social Security surpluses would result in unified surpluses of at least the same size on average, and thus be used to pay down public debt. While the new framework clearly had political value to the administration in potentially blocking Republican tax-cut proposals, it was also motivated by economic policy considerations.

The administration's economic team viewed the MSR approach as significantly improving the legitimacy of the Social Security trust fund as a mechanism for pre-funding the government's future retirement-related obligations. Under the old approach, in which the implicit fiscal objective was to balance the unified budget, an incipient Social Security surplus would tend to elicit either tax cuts or new spending. Depending on the size of this offset, the net result could be little or no government contribution to national saving, even though the balance in the Social Security trust fund would have increased. Thus, in the preceding 15 years, Social Security surpluses probably raised government saving by much less than 100 percent of the accumulation in the trust fund. In essence, the nation had been doing less to prepare itself for the retirement of the baby-boom generation than one would have thought by looking at the rising trust fund balance.

In contrast, the new approach implies that Social Security trust fund accumulations would be backed, dollar-for-dollar, by government contributions to national saving. By itself, the new approach leaves open the question of *how much* pre-funding of future Social Security obligations should be undertaken, but it provides much more assurance that the government is doing as much pre-funding as it appears to be doing.[36] By bringing trust fund accumulations and increments to government saving into alignment, the new framework took an important step toward "truth in government." Put differently, this approach takes the "double-counting" critique completely off the table, because Social Security surpluses unambiguously would be "used" once and only once (to pay down the debt held by the public).

The new framework also provided an organized context for executing general revenue transfers into the Social Security trust fund. Such transfers would be scored as an "expense" of the on-budget account; if the accepted goal is to balance the on-budget account, then this expense would reduce the resources available for other uses. As a result, all accumulations in the trust fund would be matched, dollar for dollar, by an incremental increase in government saving. In this budget framework, general revenue transfers to Social Security are not simply a paper transaction, but generate true economic pre-funding of future obligations. The administration proposed sufficient transfers in the 1999 MSR to extend the solvency of the Social Security trust fund to 2053. To motivate a specific amount of those transfers, they were set equal to the interest savings that would result from using the Social Security surpluses to pay down public debt rather than cut taxes or raise spending. The transfers would have begun in 2011 based on debt reduction in the preceding decade.

The MSR plan did not fully resolve the difficulties with general revenue transfers, because it left Medicare as part of the on-budget account while proposing to transfer general revenue into the Hospital Insurance (Medicare Part

---

36. One view is that the objective of balancing the on-budget account should be complemented with the objective of putting the Social Security system into some form of long-term actuarial balance. Determining how to satisfy that second leg of the overall fiscal objective would supply the answer as to *how much* pre-funding we should be undertaking.

A) trust fund. Under traditional budget scoring rules, the net effect of these transfers on the on-budget surplus would have been zero, because the transfers would have appeared as both an outlay and a receipt. To deal with this problem, the administration adopted the obvious modification to the usual accounting rules—treating the transfers as a "full use" of those monies, and therefore as reducing the amount of on-budget surpluses available for other uses. The proposed transfers were projected to extend the solvency of the Medicare trust fund to 2027, by far the longest solvency horizon in the history of the program. However, no action was taken by Congress to implement either the Social Security or Medicare transfers.

2.6.2.2   The Lockbox

Because the details of national saving and budget accounting are not viewed as attractive material for political messages, the new approach was proposed to be implemented through creation of a Social Security "lockbox." The lockbox was designed to create a mental picture of a strong safe that would contain not only the current-law Social Security surpluses but also the proposed general revenue transfers. By placing these funds in a "lockbox," the administration meant to increase the public's assurance that those monies would be saved—which in this instance meant that they would be used to pay down debt held by the public. The substance of the lockbox consisted of a set of procedural hurdles that Congress (and especially the Senate) would have to overcome before the government could run a deficit in the on-budget account.

That said, the most important guarantor of the new framework is something more amorphous—specifically, the terms of the political debate. So long as the political debate focuses on the disposition of the on-budget surpluses, the procedural hurdles underlying the lockbox probably will not come under serious challenge. But if the consensus changes, Congress will find ways around those hurdles. Thus far, the political consensus appears to be holding, and it remains politically dangerous to "dip into the Social Security surpluses." However, it is far from certain that this consensus will continue to hold if the on-budget account returns to deficit.

A critical factor that smoothed the way to shifting the focus of the budget debate was the ongoing improvement in the fiscal situation. After the budget stringency that had been required to balance the budget on a unified basis, there would have been little appetite for balancing the on-budget account if doing so would have entailed substantial additional pain. That said, it would be a mistake to underestimate the discipline that was required to achieve the higher standard. At every step of the way, the opportunity cost in terms of forgone tax cuts and additional spending was keenly felt.

Congressional Republicans generally embraced the shift in budget objective toward balancing the on-budget account, but they rejected President Clinton's proposed disposition of the projected on-budget surpluses. In the MSR plan, the president allocated these resources to transfers to Social Security and Medicare, new spending (especially a Medicare drug benefit), and a limited set of tax cuts. The framework also incorporated a comprehensive reform of Medicare, which is discussed in greater detail by Newhouse (Chapter 13). All told, the debt held by the public would have been paid off, on a net basis, by 2015 under the president's plan. In contrast, congressional Republicans continued to place much greater emphasis on tax reduction—at one point proposing that the entire projected on-budget surplus be devoted to a tax cut and providing no new resources for either Social Security or Medicare.

2.6.3 Fiscal Policy in 2000

During its last year the Clinton administration framed its fiscal policy around the goal of eliminating the debt held by the public. Treasury Secretary Summers explained the logic of this objective in a May speech. First, Summers argued, paying down the debt "will maximize investment at a time when the reward for investing is especially great." Summers piggybacked on the observation of Alan Greenspan that the return to investment appeared to be historically high, and therefore that the opportunity cost of failing to invest also was historically high.

Second, paying down the debt "will help to increase supply in our economy, rather than demand." The economy was then operating beyond its normal productive capacity, and even the administration's own economic projection showed a gradual upward drift in the unemployment rate over the succeeding few years. Against that backdrop, many analysts believed that fiscal policy should aim to increase aggregate supply by adding to the available pool of capital, rather than fueling aggregate demand.

Third, a failure to pay down debt "is likely to exacerbate the U.S. trade deficit." The size of the trade deficit may just have reflected the relative economic strength of the United States and its major trading partners. But it was one of the few economic imbalances at the time, and the moment seemed inopportune for a more expansionary fiscal policy that might appreciate the dollar, reduce foreign demand for our goods and services, and increase our demand for theirs.

Fourth, Summers said, a failure to pay down debt "will reduce our capacity to meet the demographic challenges ahead." Summers strongly endorsed the view that the most important preparation the federal government could make for the retirement of the baby-boom generation was to improve its fiscal position, thereby increasing national saving and expanding the productive capacity of the economy. And finally, "the current strength of our economy and budget, combined with the enormous uncertainty attached to budget projections, make this a time when we should be prudent in our commitments." Summers argued implicitly that it was preferable to be too cautious rather than too aggressive in extrapolating recent economic performance.

In line with this view, the administration's budget framework released in early 2000 was aimed at preserving fiscal discipline. The projected Social Security surpluses were again protected in a "lockbox," and the administration again proposed that general revenue be transferred to the Social Security trust fund and added to the "lockbox." These transfers would begin in 2011 based on the interest savings from debt reduction between 2000 and 2010. Roughly $300 billion in general revenue would be transferred to the Medicare trust fund over 10 years and used for debt reduction. The remaining on-budget surplus was divided into nearly $200 billion of additional spending for a prescription drug benefit for Medicare beneficiaries and health insurance coverage for low-income Americans, and more than $250 billion of tax cuts focused on retirement saving, marriage penalty relief, educational opportunities, community revitalization, affordable health care, and tax simplification.

In June the administration announced another upward revision to the baseline budget surpluses over the next 10 years, this time in the amount of $1.3 trillion. The Mid-Session Review proposed the next step toward shoring up the conceptual foundations of the budget by taking Medicare out of the budget in the same way that Social Security was out of the budget. Accordingly, the MSR allocated baseline surpluses over the following 10 years *excluding both Social Security and Medicare*. The administration maintained its policies on Medicare reform, health coverage, and targeted tax cuts, and set aside $500 billion as a "reserve for America's future." Even if all of these funds were used for spending increases or tax reductions, the debt held by the public was still projected to be paid off, on a net basis, by 2012.

The Congress did not adopt the central features of this budget framework. Neither Social Security nor Medicare reforms were enacted.[37] Although no

---

37. Notable changes to the Social Security earnings test did occur during this decade. The earnings test reduces or eliminates benefit payments to beneficiaries with income from work that exceeds a threshold amount. These beneficiaries subsequently receive higher benefits to compensate them for the withheld benefits. Legislation in 1996 significantly raised the level of earnings that would trigger benefit reductions. Legislation in 2000 eliminated the earnings test altogether for beneficiaries who are at or above the normal retirement age (currently 65 years and two months and scheduled to increase to 67 by 2022). See Gruber and Orszag (2000) for an overview of the impact of the earnings test on labor supply and benefit receipt.

fewer than five "lockbox" bills to set aside both the Social Security and Medicare surpluses passed the Republican-controlled House between 1999 and 2001, none were passed by the Senate and therefore no legislation taking Medicare out of the budget (which would have given it the same treatment as Social Security) was ever enacted.

Just working out the annual appropriations bills proved an especially arduous undertaking: a succession of continuing resolutions kept the government functioning after the beginning of the new fiscal year on October 1, and the final bills were not approved until December 15. President Clinton announced the administration's final set of budget projections in late December. Based on these projections, the debt held by the public could be eliminated on a net basis by 2010.

2.6.4   A National Asset

Toward the end of the Clinton administration, the possibility of eliminating the debt held by the public became increasingly realistic. The arithmetic associated with this possibility is straightforward: if the on-budget account is kept in balance over the next 10 to 15 years, the Social Security surpluses will be enough to pay down the entire pubic debt. Beyond that point, the continued Social Security surpluses that are now projected would transform the federal government from a net debtor to the rest of the economy into a net creditor. In other words, the government might become a net holder of private assets.[38] The Clinton administration recognized this possibility, but did not wrestle with the associated policy issues at any great length.

Indeed, under current projections, the accumulation of assets is likely to begin even sooner than the basic math suggests. First, part of the debt held by the public is in forms that would be difficult or unpopular to retire. For example, there are roughly $200 billion in outstanding savings bonds, and this program—which provides a convenient savings vehicle especially for low- and moderate-income households—seems unlikely to be terminated in the name of increasing national saving. Second, part of the debt is scheduled to mature well after the debt would be eliminated on a net basis. Some portion could be bought back before its scheduled maturity date, but at some unknown point,

---

38. In some very limited respects, the federal government already holds private assets. For example, the Treasury maintains cash balances in commercial banks, the Thrift Saving Plan holds equities on behalf of its individual beneficiaries, and the Pension Benefit Guarantee Corporation holds private assets in part as legacies from retirement plans that have been turned over to it. However, these current holdings are dwarfed in size by the investments that might be conducted on behalf of the Social Security trust fund or the central government.

the holders of this long-term debt might demand an increasing premium in order to give it up.[39] In sum, the debt elimination date is only about a decade away, assuming that Social Security surpluses materialize as projected and continue to be used to pay down debt.

Accumulation of private financial assets by the federal government raises all the same issues regarding corporate governance and potential political interference in capital markets that arise when considering whether to invest part of the Social Security trust fund in private assets. Indeed, some have argued that the dangers are even greater in this situation, since the Social Security trust fund is at least somewhat removed from the political process and is intimately linked with a popular cause and powerful lobby. In general, the same potential solutions to these problems pertain. The federal government could attempt to set up a neutral, nondistortionary method of investing the surplus monies in the private market, running all the risks that would be inherent in that approach. Alternatively, the Social Security trust fund could invest in private securities, thereby commensurately increasing the amount of government debt in private hands. Still another possibility is that individual accounts might be used to preserve some of the saving inherent in the projected surpluses, while reducing (though not avoiding altogether) the governance and political interference concerns associated with centralized investment. Finally, increases in spending or larger tax cuts obviously could eliminate unwanted asset accumulation, though at the sacrifice of some or all of the potential government contribution to national saving. Such a return to balancing the unified budget instead of the budget excluding Social Security would also break the link between government saving and the accumulation in the Social Security trust fund, impairing the validity of that fund as a signal of the preparation that the nation is undertaking for the retirement of the baby-boom generation.

The current long-term outlook for fiscal policy also raises questions with regard to the social value of Treasury debt. In particular, a number of commentators have pointed out that the existence of a deep and liquid market for Treasury securities has provided significant benefits to U.S. capital markets. For example, Treasury securities have served as pricing benchmarks for other debt instruments, meaning that prices and yields on corporate and other securities are often quoted relative to Treasury securities rather than in absolute terms. In addition, Treasury securities have been seen as convenient vehicles for hedging interest-rate risk.

---

39. The extent of this problem depends on the Treasury Department's debt issuance policy from here forward. Already, there has been considerable speculation in the financial press that Treasury's 30-year bonds will be discontinued because new bonds of that maturity would extend so far beyond the currently projected debt-elimination date.

Yet it is not evident whether these functions require the existence of Treasury debt per se or simply the existence of some debt market that is very deep and very liquid. Indeed, as market participants have come to recognize the possibility of at least a substantial paydown of Treasury debt (even if not total elimination), there has been substantial market innovation. Alternative instruments are now vying for the role that has been played by Treasury securities; where this process will lead is unclear, especially because the market may dictate that there is room for only one successor rather than many.[40] Thus the current situation leaves open the question of whether a large market for Treasury securities provides some benefit for the economy that (1) cannot be provided by any private issuer, (2) can be provided more efficiently by the federal government, or (3) represents a valuable monopoly franchise that should be provided by the federal government so that taxpayers can reap the financial rewards rather than private monopolists. Quantifying the benefits of a deep and liquid Treasury market is very difficult. Moreover, those benefits must be weighed against the costs of either less saving or the holding of private assets by the government. Indeed, if the social value of government debt is great enough, it could even be optimal for the government to gross up its balance sheet by issuing extra debt and purchasing private assets simply to maintain a viable debt market.

2.7 Conclusion

The 1990s were marked by an unexpected turnaround in the U.S. fiscal situation as a seemingly intractable budget deficit problem gave way to large budget surpluses.[41] A potent symbol of the improvement in the fiscal situation over the decade was the announcement on May 13, 2000, that the "debt clock" in New York's Times Square would be dismantled in September 2000, essentially for lack of interest.[42] The tax increases and spending discipline imposed by the 1990, 1993, and 1997 budget deals played a significant part in this improvement in the budget picture, as did the restraint of Congress and the president from enacting tax cuts or spending increases that would have dissipated the incipient surpluses. But good luck in the form of a strong economy also was important. And the impact of the initial policy decisions on the subsequent economic performance should not be discounted.

---

40. If there were more than one potential successor to Treasury debt, the market might eventually "tip" to one or the other in order to gain the extra efficiency associated with maximum depth and liquidity in a single market.

41. Larry Lindsey is the only person we are aware of who predicted this transformation. His 1990 book *The Growth Experiment* contains a chapter titled "The Great Surplus of '99."

42. See http://www.cnn.com/2000/US/09/07/debt.clock/.

Although the Clinton administration's fiscal policy helped bring the budget deficit under control and reduce the ratio of debt to GDP from 50 percent to 35 percent, the administration was only partially able to lock in fiscal discipline for the future. The consensus that emerged in 1999 to pay down debt with the Social Security surplus will, assuming the consensus holds, ensure that the debt-to-GDP ratio continues to fall steadily for the next decade. But the administration's attempts to preserve the budget surpluses to help solve the entitlement problem ended in failure as it took the subsequent administration less than six months to dissipate much of the surpluses by passing a large consumption-oriented tax cut. Given the magnitude of the long-run fiscal imbalance and of the budget surpluses that could potentially have been allocated to address this problem, a significant opportunity to pre-fund future retirement and health benefits was missed.

References

Advisory Council on Social Security, 1994–96. 1997. *Report of the 1994–96 Advisory Council on Social Security*. Washington, DC.

Aaron, Henry J., and Robert D. Reischauer. 1998. *Countdown to Reform: The Great Social Security Debate*. New York: Century Foundation Press.

Auerbach, Alan J., and William G. Gale. 2000. "Perspectives on the Budget Surplus." NBER Working Paper 7837, Cambridge, MA: National Bureau of Economic Research (August).

Auerbach, Alan, Jagadeesh Gokhale, and Lawrence Kotlikoff. 1994. "Generational Accounting: A Meaningful Way to Evaluate Fiscal Policy." *Journal of Economic Perspectives*, 8(1): 73–94.

Bipartisan Commission on Entitlement and Tax Reform. 1995. *Final Report to the President*. Washington, DC, January.

Blanchard, Olivier J. 1984. "Current and Anticipated Deficits, Interest Rates, and Economic Activity." *European Economic Review* 25: 7–27.

Blinder, Alan S., and Janet L. Yellen. 2001."The Fabulous Decade: A Macroeconomic History of the 1990s." Paper prepared for Russell Sage Foundation/Century Foundation Project on Sustainable Employment.

Board of Trustees of the Federal Old-Age and Survivors and Disability Insurance Trust Funds. 1997. *The 1997 Annual Report of the Board of Trustees of the Federal Old-Age and Survivors Insurance and Disability Insurance Trust Funds*. Washington, DC: Social Security Administration.

———. 2001. *The 2001 Annual Report of the Board of Trustees of the Federal Old-Age and Survivors Insurance and Disability Insurance Trust Funds*. Washington, DC: Social Security Administration.

Branson, William. 1985. "Causes of Appreciation and Volatility of the Dollar." In *The U.S. Dollar— Recent Developments, Outlook, and Policy Options*. Federal Reserve Bank of Kansas City Annual Conference, pp. 33–63.

Clinton, Bill, and Al Gore. 1992. *Putting People First*. New York: Times Books.

Congressional Budget Office. Various years. *The Economic and Budget Outlook*.

———. Various years. *The Economic and Budget Outlook: An Update*.

———. Various years. *An Analysis of the President's Budgetary Proposals*.

———. 1997. *Long-Term Budgetary Pressures and Policy Options*. Washington, DC, March.

———. 2000. *The Long-Term Budget Outlook*. Washington, DC, October.

Cutler, David M., James M. Poterba, Louise M. Sheiner, and Lawrence H. Summers. 1990. "An Aging Society: Opportunity or Challenge?" *Brookings Papers on Economic Activity* 1:1–56.

Diamond, Peter A. 1996. "Proposals to Restructure Social Security." *Journal of Economic Perspectives*, 10(3): 67–88.

———. 1997. "Macroeconomics of Social Security Reform." *Brookings Papers on Economic Activity*, 2:1–87.

———. 2000. "Administrative Costs and Equilibrium Charges with Individual Accounts." In John B. Shoven, ed., *Administrative Aspects of Investment-Based Social Security Reform*. Chicago: University of Chicago Press, pp. 137–162.

Economic Report of the President. 1984. Washington, DC.

Economic Report of the President. 1994. Washington, DC.

Elmendorf, Douglas W., and Jeffrey B. Liebman. 2000. "Social Security Reform and National Saving in an Era of Budget Surpluses." *Brookings Papers on Economic Activity* 2:1–71.

Elmendorf, Douglas W., and Louise M. Sheiner. 2000. "Should America Save for Its Old Age? Fiscal Policy, Population Aging, and National Saving." *Journal of Economic Perspectives*, 14(3): 57–74.

Feldstein, Martin, and Jeffrey B. Liebman. 2002. "The Distributional Effects of An Investment-Based Social Security System." NBER Working Paper 7492. Forthcoming in Martin Feldstein and Jeffrey Liebman, eds., *The Distributional Aspects of Social Security and Social Security Reform*. Chicago: University of Chicago Press.

Feldstein, Martin, and Andrew A. Samwick. 1997. "The Economics of Prefunding Social Security and Medicare Benefits." *NBER Macroeconomics Annual, 1997*, 115–147. Cambridge, MA: MIT Press.

Feldstein, Martin, and Andrew A. Samwick. 1998. "Potential Effects of Two Percent Personal Retirement Accounts." *Tax Notes*, 79, no. 5 (May 4): 615–620.

Gramlich, Edward. 1998. *Is It Time to Reform Social Security?* Ann Arbor: University of Michigan Press.

Gruber, Jonathan, and Peter Orszag. 2000. "Does the Social Security Earnings Test Affect Labor Supply and Benefits Receipt?" NBER Working Paper 7923.

Koitz, David Stuart. 1998. *Social Security and the Federal Budget: What Does Social Security's Being "Off Budget" Mean?* Report for Congress 98–422. Washington, DC: Congressional Research Service.

Lee, Ronald, and Shripad Tuljapurkar. 1998. "Uncertain Demographic Futures and Social Security Finances." *American Economic Review*, 88(2): 237–241.

Liebman, Jeffrey B. 2002. "Redistribution in the Current U.S. Social Security System." NBER Working Paper 8625. Forthcoming in Martin Feldstein and Jeffrey Liebman, eds., *The Distributional Aspects of Social Security and Social Security Reform*. Chicago: University of Chicago Press.

Lindsey, Lawrence B. 1990. *The Growth Experiment*. New York: Basic Books.

Penner, Rudolph G. 1998. "Trust Fund Accounting and the Scoring Rules for Proposed Reforms of the Social Security System." In *Social Security Reform: Economic and Budget Concepts, Enforcement, and Scorekeeping Perspectives*. Washington, DC: Committee for a Responsible Federal Budget.

Reich, Robert B. 1997. *Locked in the Cabinet*. New York: Alfred A. Knopf.

Schieber, Sylvester J., and John B. Shoven. 1999. *The Real Deal: The History and Future of Social Security*. New Haven, CT: Yale University Press.

Smetters, Kent. 2001. "The Effect of Pay-When-Needed Benefit Guarantees on the Impact of Social Security Privatization." In John Campbell and Martin Feldstein, eds., *Risk Aspects of Investment-Based Social Security Reform*. Chicago: University of Chicago Press, pp. 91–105.

Vision of Change for America, A. 1993. Washington, DC: Office of Management and Budget.

Woodward, Bob. 1994. *The Agenda*. New York: Simon and Schuster.

Comments

Martin Feldstein

I believe that President Clinton made a very positive contribution to the development of Social Security reform even though he failed to achieve any Social Security legislation. In contrast, his tax policy had a quite negative effect as a result of one of the few significant pieces of legislation that he did succeed in enacting. I will begin by discussing Social Security and then turn to fiscal policy.

Social Security Reform

President Clinton performed a great service by alerting the American public that Social Security faces a long-run financing problem that is the inevitable result of the aging of the population, by establishing the goal of "saving Social Security" without increasing the payroll tax rate, and by proposing a role for equity investments in achieving that goal. The several policy options that he considered were all based on the correct idea that increasing national saving now, with the accumulated assets devoted to future pension benefits, would permit lower taxes later; in the language of economics, such a policy provides a favorable trade-off although not an intergenerational Pareto improvement.

The Clinton speeches and the official national education campaign that he launched moved the discussion of investment-based Social Security reform away from an ideological debate about the merits of government versus private systems to the more technical issues of how to design a mixed system that includes both pay-as-you go benefits and investment-based defined contribution annuities.[1]

---

1. In such a mixed system, retirees receive a combination of the traditional tax financed pay-as-you-go benefits and the annuities that result from accumulating assets in personal retirement accounts. Andrew Samwick and I calculated that personal retirement account contributions of 2 percent of covered earnings would produce an annuity which, in combination with the benefits that can be financed in each future year with the existing 12.4 percent pay-as-you-go tax, could equal or exceed

The specific Clinton administration proposals used the same key building blocks as the plans that were being developed by congressional Republicans including Bill Archer, Phil Gramm, Newt Gingrich, John Kasich, Clay Shaw, and others. These building blocks included individual accounts, a freeze on the current payroll tax rate, maintenance of the same future expected benefits, and the use of equity investments. Although the way in which these building blocks were used differed between Republicans and the president—for example, making the individual accounts part of Social Security or supplemental to Social Security—the common building blocks provided a clear basis for a compromise in which Democrats and Republicans could both claim that the resulting plan reflected their own principles.[2,3]

It is a great pity that this initiative failed. Such a Social Security reform would have been an extremely useful contribution to the long-term fiscal health of the nation and would have been a major political legacy for an administration that is short on bragging rights.

The failure to reach an agreement did not reflect irreconcilable differences between the president and the congressional Republicans. Instead, according to knowledgeable Clinton administration officials, after the House Democrats provided the votes to prevent President Clinton's impeachment, the president

---

in each future year the benefits projected in current law. Thus total benefits could be maintained by shifting to a mixed system with the existing payroll tax and a 2 percent personal retirement account contribution rather than continuing a pure pay-as-you-go system financed with a payroll tax of about 19 percent. This calculation assumed a 5.5 percent real rate of return on the stock-bond portfolio, about 1.5 percent less than the 50-year average return through 1995 on a portfolio of 60 percent stocks and 40 percent corporate bonds. The 1.5 percent difference provides an allowance for administrative costs and a margin for risk. See M. Feldstein and A. Samwick, "Potential Effects of Two Percent Personal Retirement Accounts," in *Tax Notes*, 79, no. 5 (May 4, 1998), pp. 615–620. An updated version based on more recent actuarial assumptions is available as "New Estimates of the Potential Effects of Two Percent Personal Retirement Accounts," NBER Working Paper 6540.

2. I developed this idea in "Common Ground on Social Security," *New York Times*, Mar. 31, 1999.

3. One of the key issues in designing a mixed system is the risk inherent in investing personal retirement account assets in a portfolio of stocks and bonds. One option is to guarantee that the combination of the two types of benefits is at least as large as the benefits projected in current law. This can be done by allowing the retiree to keep the full investment-based annuity but reducing the traditional pay-as-you-go benefit by a fraction of the annuity that the individual receives, a method that is unfortunately described as a "clawback." An equivalent alternative that avoids this appearance is to supplement the annuity with a conditional pay-as-you-go benefit that compensates for poor overall stock and bond market performance during the individual's working and retirement life. Elena Ranguelova and I examined a variety of approaches to risk in several papers, including "Individual Risk and Intergenerational Risk Sharing in an Investment-Based Social Security Program," NBER Working Paper No. 6839, a portion of which appears in "Individual Risk in an Investment-Based Social Security System," *American Economic Review*, forthcoming (available as NBER Working Paper 8074). An NBER project on this subject resulted in the volume *Risks Aspects of Investment-Based Social Security Reform*, ed. John Campbell and Martin Feldstein (Chicago: University of Chicago Press, 2001).

acceded to their wish to drop Social Security reform so that they could use it as a negative issue in the upcoming congressional elections.

But despite his failure to enact any Social Security legislation, President Clinton did change the debate,[4] making it easier for George W. Bush to advocate a mixed Social Security program with investment-based personal retirement accounts during his presidential campaign. Bill Clinton had turned off the power on the "third rail of politics" that had previously prevented rational political discussion of Social Security reform.

Nevertheless, the partisan attacks on the Bush proposal during the presidential campaign now threaten to offset the fact that such a plan has much in common with what President Clinton and his team had developed. I hope that, after the bipartisan Social Security Commission reports in late 2001, congressional Democrats will focus on the Clinton administration's contribution to these ideas rather than on the negative rhetoric of the election campaign.

In thinking about the Clinton and Bush proposals, it is interesting to ask why we in the Reagan administration did not offer a similar proposal in the early 1980s when a Social Security financing crisis occurred.[5] The Social Security trust fund was then about to hit zero, and annual payroll tax revenue was not enough to finance benefit outlays. The Greenspan commission proposed and Congress enacted a combination of higher payroll taxes and cuts in the benefits of higher income retirees (by subjecting benefits above a relatively high income exclusion to the personal income tax and injecting that extra tax revenue into the trust fund). Congress also voted to increase the normal retirement age from 65 to 67, but only after a delay of two decades. But there was no serious consideration of an investment-based solution.

President Reagan was very unhappy with the commission's recommendations but was persuaded by political advisers that any proposed general reduction of benefits (through reduced inflation indexing or changes in the benefit formula) would be unsuccessful in Congress and would be a long-term burden on future Republican candidates. The result was an immediate rise in taxes with the prospect of further tax rate increases in the more distant future.

---

4. The earlier Clinton proposal for health care financing reform and the ensuing public and congressional discussions also changed the future policy debate, although in a quite different way, by ending any serious political interest for at least a very long time in such ideas as national limits on private health spending, mandatory employer premium payments that imply very high costs for each additional insured individual, and phase-out rules for subsidized insurance that raise implicit marginal tax rates dramatically. It was a health policy and an associated implicit tax policy that deserved to fail.

5. For some earlier thoughts on these events, see my introductory chapter in M. Feldstein, *American Economic Policy in the 1980s* (Chicago: University of Chicago Press, 1993), pp. 1–80.

I recall a meeting in 1982 at which President Reagan asked if there could be some alternative to tax increases or benefit cuts, some more fundamental reform of Social Security that would avoid the ever increasing tax burden that was already projected at that time. We had nothing to recommend.

Why didn't we propose investment-based accounts? There were two reasons. First, because the trust fund was empty and the overall budget was in substantial deficit, starting to fund investment-based accounts would have required a tax increase or an even larger overall budget deficit. What makes the current (and recent past) situation a unique opportunity for investment-based Social Security reform is that the trust fund now has substantial accounting reserves, the payroll tax revenues are much more than the amount needed to pay current benefits, and the overall budget is in surplus.[6] Ironically, the Reagan Social Security reforms produced the current large Social Security surpluses, and the Reagan tax policies stimulated the growth and current tax revenues that together with general spending restraint in the 1990s provided the potential financing for the Clinton (and now Bush) investment-based Social Security options.

The second and more fundamental reason that we didn't propose an investment-based plan is that we did not understand that the tax increase needed to start such a plan is very small. We were put off by the common argument that the transition to an investment-based system (even a partially investment-based mixed system) would require the transition generation of employees to "pay double," that is, to pay for the pay-as-you-go benefits of the current retirees and for their own account accumulation. It was only many years later, after research that I did with Andrew Samwick, that I realized that even a complete transition to an investment-based system can be done with annual additional contributions of less than 1 percent of GDP.[7] Unfortunately, we will never know how President Reagan would have responded if he had been given such an option.

---

6. I made this case in 1997 when the possibility of future budget surpluses began to emerge; see M. Feldstein, "Don't Waste the Budget Surplus," *Wall Street Journal*, Nov. 4, 1997.

7. See Martin Feldstein and Andrew Samwick, "The Transition Path in Privatizing Social Security," in M. Feldstein, *Privatizing Social Security* (Chicago: University of Chicago Press, 1998), and "The Economics of Prefunding Social Security and Medicare Benefits" in *NBER Macroeconomic Annual 1997*. These papers describe a gradual transition to a system that is completely investment based. A more realistic mixed system that retains a pay-as-you-go system financed by the current 12.4 percent payroll tax and supplements it with an investment-based component is discussed in M. Feldstein and A. Samwick, "Potential Effects of Two Percent Personal Retirement Accounts," in *Tax Notes*, 79, no. 5 (May 4, 1998), pp. 615–620. An updated version based on more recent actuarial assumptions is available as "New Estimates of the Potential Effects of Two Percent Personal Retirement Accounts," NBER Working Paper 6540.

Fiscal Policy

I can speak more briefly about the fiscal policy of the Clinton years because not
very much happened. The key fiscal action was the 1993 tax increase in which
the top marginal statutory personal tax rate rose from 31 percent to 42 percent
(including the effect of eliminating the ceiling on income subject to the 2.4 percent Medicare payroll tax) and the alternative minimum tax (AMT) expanded.
Both changes were in principle aimed at collecting more revenue and doing so
from high-income taxpayers. There was no fundamental improvement of the
tax system comparable to the Tax Reform Act of 1986 which redefined taxable
income, changed the tax rules relating to business investment, and slashed
personal tax rates.

The primary fiscal development during the Clinton years was the shift from
a sizable budget deficit to large budget surpluses as tax revenue rose rapidly.
Although it is tempting to think of these budget surpluses as a deliberate policy
of national debt reduction, I think the reality is simply that Republicans in
Congress blocked spending increases that would have dissipated these increased tax funds while President Clinton blocked Republican initiatives to cut
taxes.[8]

The extra tax revenue that contributed to the budget surpluses was not the
result of the Clinton tax rate increases. The Congressional Budget Office estimates imply that only about one-fourth of the increased tax revenue was due to
the Clinton statutory tax changes, with the rest coming from economic growth
and increases in taxable incomes at each level of GDP. But even this one-fourth
estimate is misleading because it assumes that the higher marginal tax rates
had no adverse effect on taxable income. Common sense and past experience
show that the opposite is true. High marginal tax rates reduce taxable income
by reducing labor supply, shifting income into nontaxable forms, and encouraging increased tax deductions.[9] Taking these behavioral responses into account would substantially reduce the estimate of the revenue increase due to
the Clinton statutory rate changes and might even show that the increase in the
high marginal tax rate actually lowered tax receipts, leaving the changes in the
AMT as the only statutory source of additional revenue.[10] The real source of

8. In addition, Medicare payments to providers were substantially reduced as part of a policy of
protecting the Medicare Trust Fund.
9. Several studies have shown the substantial cumulative size of this effect. See, for example, Martin
Feldstein, "The Effect of Marginal Tax Rates on Taxable Income: A Panel Study of the 1986 Tax
Reform Act," *Journal of Political Economy*, 103:3 (June 1995), pp. 551–572, and John Gruber
and Emannuel Saez, "The Elasticity of Taxable Income: Evidence and Implications," NBER working
paper 7512, forthcoming in the *Journal of Public Economics*.
10. See M. Feldstein, "Clinton's Revenue Mirage," *Wall Street Journal*, Apr. 6, 1993.

the extra revenue that was the primary source for eliminating the budget deficits was the increase in economic growth driven by the new technology that raised taxable personal incomes, corporate profits, and capital gains.

The fiscal legacy of the Clinton policies was therefore neither a significant increase in revenue nor a reform of the tax system. Rather it was an increase in marginal tax rates that substantially exacerbated the inefficiency—that is, the deadweight loss—of the income tax system.

Comments

Rudolph G. Penner

What a contrast between the fiscal situation in 1990 and that in 1999! In January 1990, the Congressional Budget Office (CBO) projected a baseline deficit for fiscal 1990 equal to 2.5 percent of the GDP with modest progress to 1.6 percent projected for 1995. That was too optimistic. In January 1999, CBO projected a baseline surplus of 1.2 percent of GDP for that fiscal year rising to 2.2 percent by 2004. That was too pessimistic.[1] By January 2001, the baseline surplus projection for 2004 had been increased to 3.3 percent, and 2.4 percent remains after the tax cut. The news has been so good that forecasting adjustments to surplus projections over the last two years have more than paid for the recent tax cut. The nation has not experienced a fiscal situation this healthy for more than 70 years.

In 1990, President Bush and Congress agreed to the largest deficit reduction package relative to GDP enacted since 1982. Its tax increases probably cost the elder Bush his presidency. Clinton engineered another large deficit reduction package in 1993. But by 1999, fiscal discipline was deemed unnecessary. It became clear that fiscal plenty and restrained spending were now incompatible. Nondefense discretionary spending that had grown at a real annual rate of only 1.2 percent between 1990 and 1998 grew 3.1 percent in 1999 and 4.6 percent in 2000. Defense also grew substantially in 2000 after a long decline beginning in 1990 with the end of the cold war.

In 1990 we also saw the enactment of the Budget Enforcement Act (BEA) that imposed caps on discretionary spending and prevented tax and entitlement policy from increasing deficits by insisting that tax cuts and entitlement increases be paid for. Those rules were very valuable in ending deficits. By 1999 it was clear that the BEA was unraveling, and even worse, the disciplining rules enacted as part of the 1974 Budget Act were also coming unglued.

---

1. Although the 1999 estimate of the 2004 surplus may have been too pessimistic given the policies then in effect, the policy changes provoked by the September 11 emergency have now caused a significant deterioration in the budget outlook.

The spending caps had always contained the loophole that emergency spending was exempt, but not counting Desert Storm, emergency spending averaged only $5 billion per year in the period 1991 through 1998. In 1999 emergencies totaled $34.4 billion. In 2000 emergencies were cheaper, but the English language suffered a setback when we declared the census to be an emergency even though we had known it was coming since 1789.

The 1974 Budget Act provided for a budget resolution that was to set targets for spending, revenues, and the budget balance. That is the only place where Congress adds up these budget aggregates. It proved impossible to pass a resolution for fiscal 1999, and in 2000 the surplus fell $61 billion short of the target for policy reasons—the largest miss relative to GDP by far since the early 1980s. At a most superficial level, you might say the budget resolution limited our recent tax cut in that it budgeted a $1.35 trillion revenue loss over 10 years and the tax cut was designed to fit within this budget. The only problem is that the design of the tax cut is implausible with its many phase-ins and sunsets.

It is not clear whether disciplining budget rules can be resurrected or even whether such rules are appropriate in an era of surpluses. The only disciplining force in budgeting remaining since the late 1990s is the notion that the Social Security and Medicare surpluses should be used to retire debt rather than to finance a deficit in the rest of the government. The background paper basically likes the rule, although it expresses uneasiness about some of its features. I am even more uneasy.

My uneasiness would rise if the rule is made very rigid and enforced with automatic spending cuts as in some proposals of the late 1990s for so-called lockbox legislation. A very rigid rule is not very practical. CBO's average forecasting error relative to GDP would change the 2002 baseline surplus by about $120 billion. There is no way Congress could change policies sufficiently, using either automatic or discretionary mechanisms, to compensate for a negative change of this magnitude. The rule has held so far only because forecasts have recently become ever more optimistic. Once forecasts move in a pessimistic direction the rule will be destroyed just as Gramm-Rudman rules were destroyed by unanticipated economic events. Even if the rule could be enforced, you would not want to do so in most cases, because it would intensify the magnitude of the business cycle.

The rule's best rationalization reflects the desire to convert a limited amount of funding of Social Security and Medicare into national saving, but the fact that there is no meaningful target for trust fund surpluses means that if the lockbox is taken literally, a decline in the surpluses, say, for demographic reasons, leads to the peculiar result that less national debt will be retired just when more debt redemption may be desirable.

Most disturbing is the rhetoric surrounding the rule. The rhetoric implies that if the rule is violated, the probability of honoring future Social Security and Medicare promises will go down significantly. The rhetoric speaks of raiding the trust funds or worse, stealing from them. This is mischievous and could frighten near retirees, because it is inevitable that the rule will be broken sometime. Moreover, whether we follow the rule or simply balance the unified budget has no perceptible effect on the share of future GDP promised to Social Security and Medicare in the long run. The likely contribution to the nation's capital stock is just not that large given the huge capital wealth of this nation. The only observable effect is to save an amount of interest that is small relative to increases in the cost of future promises.[2]

The most interesting thing about the rule, given current budget projections, is that it implies that the entire redeemable public debt will be paid off by the end of the decade. But you may not be ecstatic about this result if you believe that government debt serves a useful purpose as a unique investment vehicle for Americans and foreigners, and you want to avoid using other mechanisms for running monetary policy, and you further believe that it would be dangerous for the U.S. government to avoid retiring debt by buying private assets with its surpluses. If all this is true, we should purposely be reducing the budget surplus much faster than we have with our recent paltry tax cut. Being completely arbitrary, if I was to say that a ratio of debt to GDP of 20 percent was just the right ratio—the previous postwar record low was 24 percent in 1974—it can be noted that we shall be getting close to 20 percent by the end of fiscal 2004. That's the budget that will be debated in the spring and summer of 2003. Noting also that maintaining a debt ratio of 20 percent involves running a unified budget deficit of about 1 percent of GDP, it is clear that moving there over two years from the 2002 surplus of about 2 percent of GDP would be a significant and perhaps dangerous expansionary shock. It is this arithmetic that worries Alan Greenspan.

We should already be debating the issue of how much debt we want, if any, or if we want to divert some of the surplus into individual accounts. Some indications of a debt shortage are already upon us in that the spread over the last year between various measures of corporate bond rates and 30-year Treasuries have not been as high since 30-year Treasuries were invented and are much higher than at other times of economic stress.

Turning to Social Security, there were no significant policy changes in the 1990s, but the politics changed radically. Someone turned off the power to the

---

2. Rudolph G. Penner, Sandeep Solanki, Eric Toder, and Michael Weisner, *Saving the Surplus to Save Social Security: What Does It Mean?*, Retirement Project Brief No. 7, Urban Institute, Washington, DC, August 1999.

third rail of politics. Politicians who previously only discussed the issue in the privacy of their own homes began to debate reform openly. Presidential candidate Bush suffered no grievous harm from openly advocating reform. Numerous legislative initiatives have been introduced by Senators Gregg, Breaux, Moynihan, and Kerrey and Representatives Kolbe, Stenholm, Smith, Porter, Shaw, Archer, and others. Although some have been viciously demagogued on the issue in their home districts, no one introducing reforms, to my knowledge, has failed to be reelected if he or she tried.

However, the reformers still constitute a small minority of Congress, and it was discouraging to read that the Republican leadership tried to prevent President Bush from appointing his Commission on Strengthening Social Security. On the other side, Republicans watched the recent special election in Tidewater Virginia intently as the Republican candidate for Congress was associated with a Bush-type Social Security reform by some very nasty TV ads. (It is not clear that he actually supported a Bush-type reform.) He prevailed 52–48 in a formerly Democratic district. I hope that result gives other Republicans some courage.

Comments

Robert Rubin

Before getting to the specifics of our panel's topic, let me make a general comment that in my view, at least, is essential in thinking about the Clinton years. From the very beginning of this administration, the president had a comprehensive and consistent concept of his economic strategy, and he followed that strategy consistently throughout the administration. During the $6\frac{1}{2}$ years that I was in this administration, the president faced many difficult and controversial topics, and there was often a lot of speculation as to where he would come out on these issues. I used to say in response that on the big issues I had no doubt as to where he would come out. And that was because his decisions were not ad hoc responses to circumstances or to different sources of advice, but rather grounded in his consistent strategy.

In contrast, he was often seen as wavering and as responding to influences of the moment. I once mentioned that perception to him, and he said that he had given a great deal of thought to that contrast, and he had concluded that he often discussed his thinking in public, together with his weighing and balancing of competing considerations, and what people wanted instead was a man on a white horse with a simple answer. In fact, one of the difficulties the administration had in conveying to the American people the president's economic strategy was precisely that it was not simple but broad based and had an intellectual complication commensurate with the complexity of the world which it addressed. That complexity, in my view, was a virtue with respect to setting policy, but clearly was a problem with respect to communication. Thus, for example, in the trade arena, the president consistently supported trade liberalization measures, but he also recognized the dislocations that change—whether from trade or technology—could bring, and he acknowledged those dislocations and advocated a parallel agenda of education, health care insurance, and the like to deal with those dislocations.

I lived on a daily basis through the development of the globalization of capital markets and integration of trade and capital flows across national boundaries. President Clinton had an exceedingly good understanding of the new landscape of the global economy, and that understanding of the greatly altered landscape created by globalization, spread of market-based economics, the new technologies, the growth in developing countries, and so much else informed the president's strategy and decisions.

Turning now to the subject of our panel's discussion, I thought that the paper by Douglas Elmendorf, Jeffrey Leibman, and David Wilcox captured the actions and debate in the administration around fiscal and Social Security problems very well, with a couple of limited exceptions.

In my view, the single most important moment in this administration's life with respect to the economic issues was the transition meeting on January 7, 1993, which has been much reported but not always with great accuracy.

The new economic team had put together a set of options with respect to fiscal policy, viewed as the central decision that the president needed to make. When we arrived for the six-hour meeting in Little Rock, one of his political advisers told me that we could not possibly expect the president to make a decision on substantial deficit reduction at this first meeting, especially since that meant sacrificing or deferring so much else that he wanted to do.

As I recollect, very early in the meeting, the president-elect looked at us and said that deficit reduction was the threshold issue, that the economy, in his judgment, could not be put on a track of sustained recovery without deficit reduction, that he was elected to restore economic health, and that he was going to put in place a significant deficit reduction program even though it meant considerable curtailment of other programs he advocated. It is also important to remember that all of this took place after a late December 1992 substantial increase in the projected deficit by the outgoing administration.

The discussion was then conducted in the context of that remark, and the debate centered around varying possibilities with respect to how powerful a substantial deficit reduction program should be, but all against the backdrop there would be a deficit reduction program. Laura Tyson, Alan Blinder, and Lawrence Summers made a key presentation discussing the trade-off between the contractionary impact of deficit reduction and the potential expansionary impact of the lower interest rates that would hopefully flow from deficit reduction. Only later did we realize that even more important would be the effect on confidence. That discussion, as well as many subsequent discussions and decisions over the ensuing months, was conducted predominately in the context of the effects on the bond market, though the effect on the Federal Reserve Board also entered into the discussion. That statement is contrary to one reported view, which is totally at odds with all this evidence of these many months of meetings and is, in my view, simply wrong, that there had been a deal between the president and the chairman of the Federal Reserve Board.

I remember the economic malaise of the early 1990s very well, and one of the central features was loss of confidence in our country—both here and abroad—that in some fair measure was created by our fiscal mess, in part because our fiscal position was taken to symbolize a larger inability on the part of our country to manage its economic life effectively and with discipline. The consequence of the deficit reduction program of 1993, once the market actually believed that it was real, was not only lower interest rates, but also—in my view, probably much more importantly—a great increase in confidence both here and abroad, both for the intangible symbolic reasons I just mentioned and because the restoration of fiscal discipline reduced or eliminated the possibility that continued fiscal morass would eventually lead either to an effort to inflate our way out of debt problems or to higher taxes to pay debt service. And that increase in confidence affected business decisions about investment, expansion, and hiring, as well as consumer decisions, and produced a greater flow of foreign capital into our savings deficient nation to finance investment here, thus lowering our cost of capital. I have no doubt that the 1993 program and the eight years of a policy of fiscal discipline were key and indispensable in a virtuous cycle of deficit reduction promoting growth which further reduced the deficit, which then in turn further increased growth, and so on back and forth, and that this policy was thus key and indispensable in generating the economic and fiscal developments of the Clinton years. It may well be that the tools of economic analysis won't capture this, for three reasons: (1) the beneficial effect on interest rates was real but masked because demand for funds was increasing during an economic recovery; (2) more importantly, the increase in confidence and the effects of increased confidence are hard to capture but were key to this whole period; and (3) the mutual feedback between fiscal policy and economic growth may make meaningful deconstruction difficult or impossible. The fact is that there was a remarkable eight years that coincided with a dramatic shift in fiscal policy, and from the very beginning of the new policy, the many critics of the policy predicted large increases in unemployment, even recession, and reduced tax revenues. Instead, the opposite occurred. This created eight years of frustration for the critics, who then strenuously worked throughout this period to find ways that would deny credit to the policies they had so vigorously criticized or even reviled for the prosperity that they had predicted would not happen. And that process is still going on.

Throughout the eight years of the Clinton administration, there was great tension between the administration's espousal of fiscal discipline and the espousal by the Republicans in Congress of lower taxes, and that tension produced many of most important political conflicts of this period—for example, the struggle over the 1993 deficit reduction program, the 1995 government shutdown and the difficulties over the debt ceiling, the 1996 presidential campaign, and the 1998 decision (so very well described in the paper) by the administration to save Social Security first. I think a lasting legacy of this administration will be the successful experiment of promoting economic recovery and sustained growth through fiscal discipline rather than through fiscal expansion, and, as discussed in the paper, the redefinition at the end of the administration of budget balance to focus on the non–Social Security budget—or perhaps even the nonentitlement budget—as opposed to the unified budget. I do believe that the tax cut enacted in 2001 by the new administration—based on ten-year projections universally acknowledged as unreliable and numbers on discretionary spending and extension of expiring tax benefits that neutral budget experts view as unrealistically low, and involving a much higher running rate in later years and substantial additional debt service cost—creates a high likelihood of deficits on the nonentitlement side of the budget and was most unwise.

Let me now use my remaining few minutes to comment on a few separate items I wish to discuss.

I entered the administration knowing virtually nothing about the exceedingly complex rules and practices with respect to the federal budget, but developed a fascination with the budget. My own experience left me with a view that there is relatively little understanding of federal budget matters, not only in the public, but even among many members of Congress, and that there is also relatively little appetite for accepting the real trade-offs, including present constraint for future good, that are involved in fiscal matters or Social Security. Both make meaningful public debate and optimal decision-making in the political system far more difficult.

At the beginning of the Social Security discussion in 1997, I had the feeling that there might be some chance to seriously consider—and then accept or reject—some real changes in the Social Security system, for example, perhaps some change in the retirement age effective many years in the future or realistic adjustments to the CPI. However, once a greatly increased surplus was projected, that created the far easier path for Social Security reform of focusing on using the surpluses for funding. The other political easy path was to substitute equities for debt, and then take credit for greatly increased expected rates of return. While higher expected returns might accurately reflect history, this is a far more complex subject than a simple extrapolation from the past would suggest, and the risks in equities and the vast range of possible outcomes for the market overall or for individual portfolios, though considered in the debate, were not appropriately weighed in the decision-making, in my view, by many of those involved. Clearly the discussion of equities was heavily influenced by

the atmosphere of rapidly increasing equity prices during that period. Moreover, having spent close to 28 years on Wall Street, I think that many people
are not equipped, in terms of understanding securities valuation and in terms
of discipline and thoughtfulness, to invest effectively in equity markets for the
long term. In addition, if there were to be untoward results in equity markets
over a substantial period, or if there were periods during which large numbers
of people were adversely affected in their individual portfolios, there is a substantial probability that the political pressure to make good on those losses
from the federal budget would be enormous, and doing so would increase the
cost of funding future retirement. Once these politically easier paths became
apparent, the politics of reform of the program itself went from difficult to impossible. Unlike a report I saw in today's press, carve-out private accounts,
after careful examination, were rejected on the merits, and were not supported
by any senior members of the president's economic team, as opposed to accounts outside of Social Security, which had strong support.

One matter not touched on in the paper, except slightly, was the intense
focus the administration had on allocating resources within the context of
deficit reduction. As the paper said, in 1993, even though the budget was
directed predominately toward deficit reduction, the earned income tax credit
was greatly increased, and throughout the $6\frac{1}{2}$ years that I was there, there was
always a strong effort to increase the portion of the budget used for the public
investment areas that the president advocated so strongly.

For me, perhaps the moment of greatest surprise during my entire $6\frac{1}{2}$ years
in government was the assertion by some in Congress—even a few on Wall
Street—that default by the federal government through refusal to raise the
debt ceiling was a price worth paying to pressure the president into signing the
congressional majorities' budget proposal in 1995. I believe that default by this
country, as a political act, could have done untold damage, by undermining
the concept of the sanctity of debt obligations in the global financial system. We
avoided this result though unprecedented use of various mechanisms over a
period of seven to eight months. Fortunately, as time went on, the concept of
default lost its political appeal, and thus this problem was solved. I don't believe that the future Congress will be tempted to resort to this mechanism,
though I do believe that the debt ceiling should be eliminated.

Let me end with two points. First, while budget rules can be useful, there are
many ways to evade them through various mechanisms or the assumptions
being used. Thus, I believe the real key—as the paper suggests—is the political
environment and attitude with respect to fiscal discipline. Second, market reaction to economic policy—whatever it may be—is critical, and in 1993 one of
our great concerns was whether the markets would believe in the validity of

our deficit reduction program, given the markets' well-grounded skepticism about the political system's willingness to deal with the deficit. In that instance, the program gained market credibility very quickly. I believed then, and still believe, that the key reason was that our assumptions and numbers were real. Another reason was the inclusion of a small energy tax, because that was taken as evidence of seriousness of purpose and thus had disproportionate symbolic purpose.

Let me conclude that in my view, because of the great economic changes at world in the 1990s and because the Clinton administration was intently focused on implementing a strategy geared to that greatly changed environment, what this administration thought and did—whether you agree or disagree with that—is worth intensive focus, in providing input to future policy-making. Thus I think this conference is a very useful undertaking, to try to create a record of what happened and why, while it is still relatively fresh in people's minds. I would guess that five or ten years from now, with the distance of time, another level of analysis and judgment will be possible about the experience of this period, and I think the record created so soon after the fact can be very useful for those efforts. I greatly appreciate being invited to join with you in this undertaking. Thank you.

Robert Rubin responded to *Martin Feldstein* by making two points. First, in response to Feldstein's argument that the strong economic performance of the 1990s was due to the Reagan tax cuts, Rubin noted that such an argument had roughly the same plausibility as attributing the performance to Herbert Hoover's policies. Second, based on his experience in the private sector, Rubin doubted that changing marginal tax rates by roughly 10 percentage points has a significant effect on how people decide between leisure and work.

Although he gave President Clinton credit for his efforts to educate the public about the Social Security issue in 1998, *Rudolph Penner* criticized the Clinton administration for subsequently producing budget proposals "devoted more to confusing people about Social Security than educating."

Feldstein then declared himself an optimist on the prospects for Social Security reform, and predicted that the United States would move to a system that relied in part on investments, and thereby avoid both future reductions in support to retirees and increases in taxes on workers. He noted that many countries have moved to such mixed systems. Feldstein responded to *Rubin* by noting that empirical evidence suggested that changes in tax rates, even small ones, can lead to significant changes in behavior. Feldstein added that he doubted that the increase in tax rates in 1993 per se actually produced additional revenue. Additional tax revenue reflected economic growth, greater stock market gains, and tougher alternative minimum tax rules. Rather, he argued, the stalemate between the president and the Republican majority in Congress blocked both spending increases and tax cuts, and that was a primary reason for the surplus.

A member of the audience asked if, under an individual account system, workers would be protected from losses in the stock market. *Feldstein* responded that the Bush administration had not resolved the details of its proposal, but that his own preference was for a mixed system in which the pay-as-you-go component continued to finance at least two-thirds of benefits, limiting the exposure of individuals to risk. Furthermore, he argued, some sort of guarantee could be created to soften the impact of poor market performance. *Peter Diamond* added that if equity investment were pursued through the Social Security trust fund rather than through individual accounts, equity market fluctuations would affect the trust fund, rather than individuals' accounts, reducing the risk to an individual.

Another member of the audience asked about the potential for individuals to receive a current lump sum in place of their future Social Security benefit stream and invest that lump sum in the market. *Rubin* suggested that only wealthier individuals should even contemplate such a risk. *Diamond* noted that the question called to mind an oddity in the political economy of the individual accounts debate: those most strongly urging individual accounts tend to be wealthy, for whom the option of investing some portion of their Social Security contributions in the stock market should be relatively unimportant because they already hold significant wealth in the stock market.

Eugene Steuerle criticized the idea of setting a deficit target in terms of the so-called on-budget, or unified budget excluding Social Security. He described this focus as an odd one for government saving, since it resembles neither a private pension rule (which relates saving today to projected future needs) nor a defined contribution rule (which typically defines saving today as a specific percentage of income), and asserted that Social Security would be better served by one of the latter two rules.

David Wilcox responded, saying that a balanced budget excluding Social Security was not the only target. That target made sense in combination with the additional goal of maintaining a 75-year actuarial balance for Social Security itself. Together, Wilcox suggested, the two provide a sensible rule. *Feldstein* suggested that the rule might not be sufficient to keep the political process from spending Social Security surpluses. He added that an advantage of individual accounts was to shift future surpluses out of the hands of government, preventing them from being spent. *Penner* noted that a real test of the existing rule would come if budget projections became more pessimistic. *Diamond* added that the Social Security surpluses in the wake of the 1983 reform probably added to national savings. While the rest of the budget was heavily in deficit, that deficit was probably not made larger by the full amount of the Social Security surpluses, if at all.

Gene Sperling remarked that, while the administration was ultimately not able to pass Social Security reform legislation, it did create a political competition in which both parties tried to appear more responsible vis-à-vis the Social Security surplus and debt reduction. This competition fundamentally changed fiscal policy by freezing both tax cuts and spending increases. Sperling then asked *Feldstein* if the recent dissipation of the general surplus to fund the Bush tax cut made Social Security reform more difficult. *Feldstein* agreed that reform would be more difficult without non–Social Security revenue, although he noted that we would have to wait and see what the Bush administration proposed.

Another member of the audience noted that both deficit reduction and advances in information technology had contributed to the Clinton-era growth and asked the panel to assess their relative contributions. *Rubin* responded that it was difficult to separate the various contributions, since without the boost to confidence provided by the deficit reduction package, the investment boom would not have occurred. He noted that Japan and Europe both had access to the same technology as U.S. firms, but did not share the same strong productivity growth as occurred in the United States in the 1990s. He also suggested that the flexibility of the U.S. economy and a cultural willingness to take risks allowed the United States to capture the benefits of innovation in a way that Japan and Europe did not.

3 Tax Policy

Tax Policy from 1990 to 2001

Eugene Steuerle

PANELISTS: *Henry J. Aaron, Leonard Burman, and William A. Niskanen*

3.1 Introduction and Summary

An examination of tax policy in the decade of the 1990s (1991–2000) would not be complete without inclusion of two bookends—the laws enacted in 1990 and 2001. A cynic might suggest that the counting of 12 years as a decade merely reflects the type of math used during the period to fit tax bills within budgetary constraints. With or without the bookends, the period will go down in history as a period of very active but hardly revolutionary tax policy. Like many decades before it, much of what "happened" to taxpayers was driven by budgetary considerations and by broader economic activity—increases in wage levels, stock market growth, increasing cross-border activity—as they interacted with the tax system.

Tax policy is so broad that summarizing it must necessarily shortchange important parts. Tax policy today involves far more than issues of how to collect revenues fairly and efficiently: it has evolved into a major tool for both macro or fiscal policy and, more than ever, expenditure and social policy. This chapter will emphasize the following themes:

• Another set of battles between what I will label as the progressives and the supply-siders came more or less to a draw—leaving the United States with a moderately progressive tax system that interferes only moderately in a fairly competitive private market. The labels are perhaps a bit unfair: at its best, the debate is over the classic trade-off between progressivity and economic efficiency, although the two need not always be antagonistic. At least as far as individual income tax rates are concerned, the top federal rate bounced around between 28 percent and nearly 41 percent—with a reduction to 35 percent legislated in 2001. The major exception was for those who accrue their income: their lumpy capital gains and estate taxes were significantly reduced. If one looks to average tax rates, federal revenues as a percent of GDP on net increased a little, but stayed close to their post–World War II range. However, other factors—such as large capital gains realizations, a more unequal distribution of income, and continual state and local tax growth—boosted average total federal, state, and local tax rates to an all-time high. For a taxpayer with about average or median income, however, the effective average tax rate changed little over the period.

· Traditional tax policy principles in many ways took it on the chin, especially when it came to taxation of the individual. Little concern was paid to the equal treatment of equals (equal taxation of those with equal ability to pay), efficiency (neutrality among different sources of income and different types of consumption), and, especially, simplification. New tax breaks proliferated, and individual tax expenditures grew. A large increase in the number of taxpayers subject to the alternative minimum tax (AMT) is only one among many new complications, and taxpayers must often solve simultaneous-equation problems to figure out their taxes. Some coping is achieved through efforts at IRS reorganization and through vast expansion of computer and World Wide Web capabilities.

· Social policy and children's policy increasingly became implemented through the tax system. There is an increasing emphasis on work-related policies rather than pure welfare, and the IRS in many ways has the best reporting system on wages. Social tax policy brings to light once again the arbitrariness of attempting to deal with tax and expenditure (especially transfer) issues separately.

· With respect to business taxation, the 1990s saw the compromise of 1986 hold up—limited corporate tax breaks in exchange for a lower rate of tax in the mid-30s range. Lower rates of inflation also resulted in modestly lower effective tax rates on capital income. Cross-border transactions and business tax shelters continue to play havoc with income and sales tax systems, although it is not clear whether those tails will eventually wag the dog. Meanwhile, new savings incentives proliferated but with little hope of solving the major problem that the majority of households go into retirement with very little in the way of pensions.

· The name of the game at the federal level more and more has been to "spend" anything one can as far into the future as one can—before somebody else gets to make the choice. This is likely the primary source of inefficiency in the tax and budget process. The 2001 tax legislation set a new record with a 10-year implementation period for tax changes. If one looks at the current-law tax system, average tax rates will fall a little over time. If one looks at the current-law expenditure system, average tax rates are scheduled to increase dramatically mainly because entitlement expenditures under current law have huge built-in growth. Thus, at the start of the 21st century, the future of taxation (and the budget itself) may be largely driven by conflict set up for future legislators to deal with the choices of legislators who will be dead or retired by that time.

We will return to these themes after providing a brief historical review, first of how the tax changes examined here fit more broadly into post–World War II tax policy, and second, of the changes in the 1990s themselves.

3.2   The 1990–2001 Period in the Context of Post–World War II Tax Policy

The 1990–2001 period can be understood only by putting it in the context of changes occurring over a longer time span. In many ways the period fits well into a long post–World War II adjustment phase. The following summary is hardly a complete description of the changes of this longer period, but it does reflect the more continuous nature of tax policy developments.

3.2.1   The 1950s—Codification of the Modern Income Tax System

The movement into and out of the Korean conflict highlighted the beginning of this decade. After World War II, taxes were reduced only moderately, relative to the wartime increases. Paying off the national debt and then sustaining a strong military were the greater priorities of the period. But after the Korean conflict, average tax rates never fell nor rose very much relative to GDP—a story that remains true today. Tax policy during this decade is highlighted by the adoption of the Internal Revenue Code of 1954—a true attempt at the codification or recodification of many practices, regulations, and laws that had evolved previously. Meanwhile, Social Security tax rate (and benefit) increases reflected the first full acceptance of that system by both political parties.

3.2.2   The 1960s—Macroeconomic Issues to the Fore

It was during the 1960s that the use of tax policy was asserted most forcefully for other than tax policy reasons. Although they had been advocated by Keynes in the 1930s, the 1960s really represents the first time that revenue reductions were sought mainly for nontax reasons (e.g., temporary deficits would spur demand, a lower cost of capital would spur new investments). U.S.-style Keynesian fiscal policy—the use of the tax system to make macroeconomic adjustments—centered largely on rate cuts and investment credits. The Kennedy round of tax cuts was at the time largely considered a success, although in truth almost any deficit was temporary in nature whether the Keynesians were right or not about feedback effects on the economy. That is, relative to the 1990s, most expenditures were discretionary in nature. Since taxes would grow whether the economy grew slow or fast, they would soon overtake any fixed level of discretionary spending that would grow only if new legislation were enacted. (By the 1990s, most expenditures were not discretionary and had large, fixed, built-in growth.) Some traditional tax reform was proposed as part of the Kennedy round of tax cuts, but it was quickly abandoned when the administration was given a choice as to whether to promote more traditional equity and efficiency goals or its promises of tax cuts. Countercyclical policy was harder to maintain when it came to raising, rather than lowering, taxes. A late Vietnam surcharge, which hit 10 percent of current income taxes for only one year, was actually sold as part of a long-term tax cut that would remain after the surcharges were gone.

3.2.3 The 1970s—Coping with Stagflation

Just as Keynesian policy became more accepted by political leaders of all stripes (including President Richard Nixon), escalating inflation combined with stagnation in economic growth. Opportunities for tax arbitrage arose from the combination of taxes and inflation, leading increasingly to investment in unproductive assets.[1] Tax policy adjustments were varied. Tax cuts were offered in ever greater profusion, and further accelerated allowances were made for depreciation purposes. But other tax policy measures were more random and sometimes contradictory: the energy crises led to attempts to tax "windfall profits" in energy and to subsidize other energy production, at least temporarily; capital gains tax changes were first proposed as increases, then enacted as decreases. Overall, tax cuts couldn't keep up with tax increases that resulted from inflation. In fact, the most significant tax changes of the decade were not legislated directly: the very high increase in marginal tax rates on upper-middle classes, together with the large percentage increases in local real estate tax as tax arbitrage opportunities, led to large increases in real estate values offset by declines in stock values.

---

1. See Steuerle (1985) for an explanation of how inflation and accounting systems—including the tax system—can create stagnation.

3.2.4   The 1980s—Tax Reform and Lower Rates[2]

The tax revolt against higher real estate and income taxes (largely a result of 1970s inflation) played itself out at the state level mostly in the late 1970s, and at the federal level in 1981. The 1981 act lowered tax rates by 23 percent and accelerated depreciation allowances even more than they had formerly been accelerated (on top of an investment credit that was in reality the primary tax incentive for physical investment). Then, in the years from 1982 to 1987— including the Tax Reform Act of 1986—the income tax went through more base broadening and traditional tax reform than at any other time in its history. The acceptance of business tax reform with lower rates and less investment incentives in many ways reflected the movement from an economy focused on physical capital to one where human capital, technology, and information were more dominant. By one measure, over $200 billion of tax expenditures were exchanged for lower rates in the 1986 act alone. Almost all significant tax changes after 1981 were for the purpose of revenue raising.

3.2.5   The 1990s—Backseat to Budget and Expenditure Policy

In many ways, the period from 1990 to 2001 is the hardest of all to characterize. Many of the battles of the previous decades—over rates, progressivity, capital gains taxation, the use of the tax code for macroeconomic and nonrevenue purposes—are reengaged but with much more voter apathy or, perhaps, weariness. Budget measures of deficits (and which deficit to count) largely determine or limit the size of tax changes sought. The period is bracketed by tax increases (deficit-reduction efforts) at the beginning and tax cuts (surplus-reducing efforts) at the end. While one could argue that budgetary considerations also dominated 1980s tax policy, actions were channeled in that decade by strong demands to keep rates low and to broaden the tax base. By the late 1980s, however, concern over the tax base waned. In the early 1990s, tax increases fell primarily upon the top earners in the income distribution. The counter-counterrevolution in 2001, in turn, broadly reduced tax rates on all earners, with individual rate reductions directly occupying 60 percent to 90 percent of the bill. At the same time, social spending and expenditure policy become increasingly implemented through the tax code, as best symbolized by the proliferation in refundable credits for households with children in 1990, 1993, and 2001.

---

2. For a history of tax policy in the 1980s, see Steuerle (1991).

3.3   From Revenue Raising to Tax Cutting: A Brief Account of Significant Legislation in the 1990–2001 Period

The 1990–2001 time frame can be divided into its early revenue-raising (in particular, 1990 and 1993) and late revenue-cutting portions, with a period in between of relative legislative stalemate while deficits continued to fall. This generalization ignores the many pieces of tax legislation that occurred during the period—with IRS restructuring as part of 1998 legislation perhaps the most worthy of note. (For more details on the major tax acts of this period, see Table A.3.1.)

3.3.1   Tax Increases: The Budget Acts of 1990 and 1993

The largest revenue increases in the 1990s occurred in the budget acts of 1990 and 1993. These two acts, enacted successively under a Republican and a Democratic president, had a great deal in common:

• *A rise in the top rate.* The Tax Reform Act of 1986 had reduced the top rate of tax to 28 percent for those with very high incomes, although it had created a 33 percent rate at modestly high income levels (a so-called bubble). The Omnibus Budget Reconciliation Act of 1990 raised the top statutory rate from 28 percent to 31 percent and increased the individual alternative minimum tax from 21 to 24 percent, while creating two new substitute "bubbles" in the form of a phase-out of the value of the personal exemption (acronym, PEPS) and a phaseout of some itemized deductions (called Pease after then-Congressman Donald Pease of Ohio). The 1993 act, in turn, raised the top rate from 31 percent to 39.6 percent and created a new 36 percent tax bracket as well.

• *An expansion of the Medicare tax base.* In 1990, the Medicare or Hospital Insurance (HI) tax base was raised to $125,000, well above that applying to Old Age, Survivors, and Disability Insurance (OASDI). In 1993 the cap on earnings subject to Medicare was removed altogether.

• *Expansion of the Earned Income Tax Credit (EITC).* In 1990 a vigorous debate took place over whether minimum wages should be increased. The Bush administration instead supported increases in the EITC as a more targeted means of providing support for low-income families, believing that most of any minimum-wage increase would go to secondary workers, part-time workers, and other persons generally not viewed as lower income. The 1990 legislation would be the first time that the EITC subsidy rate would go above any combined Social Security and income tax rate—thus insuring a net subsidy. The 1993 act, in turn, increased the EITC again (though not by as much as the 1990 legislation)—

primarily by raising the benefit for larger families. In 1993 the push for an EITC expansion came from two sources: the emphasis on progressivity in general in the tax bill, and an argument that the act of working should reward families with a standard of living above poverty (although the EITC would not get a family there alone). The 1990 and 1993 acts were the third and fourth major acts dealing with the EITC.[3] Almost without notice, the EITC would become the dominant means-tested income transfer program in the nation.

• *Other common features.* Both the 1990 and 1993 legislation included an increase in the motor fuels tax. Despite knowledge that the alternative minimum tax could not stand forever under its current unindexed structure, both acts also raised the rate of tax under the AMT.

• *Miscellaneous other changes.*[4] The 1990 legislation also enacted a luxury tax on automobiles, yachts, airplanes, and furs. Most of it was later repealed. The 1993 act increased the amount of Social Security benefits potentially subject to income taxation (above a given income level) from 50 percent to 85 percent.

Numerous other provisions were part of these acts, affecting the taxation of energy, revenue-raising bonds, health insurance deductions for the self-employed, extension of expiring provisions such as credits for corporate research and development, low-income housing, and much else.

3.3.2 Tax Cuts: The Taxpayer "Relief" Acts of 1997 and 2001

Just like the tax increases in the earlier period, later tax cuts were to have a good deal in common. The parallel is not complete. The two big budget acts of the earlier period were roughly the same size (actually, the first President Bush's deficit reduction, as a percent of GDP, was larger than that of President Clinton). However, the 1997 tax cuts were part of legislation that claimed to further reduce the deficit, whereas the 2001 legislation was aimed almost entirely at reducing taxes.

Common features were as follows:

• *Estate and gift tax reduction.* Under the 1997 legislation, a unified credit under the estate and gift tax was gradually increased so that it would exempt up to $1

---

3. First passed in 1975, the EITC had been expanded significantly and its parameters indexed in the Tax Reform Act of 1986. Equal to 11 percent of wages up to a maximum credit of $550 in 1986, the succession of the 1986, 1990, and 1993 acts boosted its phase-in rate to 40 cents of tax benefit for each additional dollar earned, on about the first $10,000 of income in 2000, producing a maximum benefit of about $4,000 for households with two or more children.

4. Note, by the way, that the budget acts were also similar on the expenditure side—in particular, in the attempt to cut back on Medicare costs by limiting prices in various ways.

million per person from tax by 2006, versus $600,000 in 1998. The 2001 legislation, in contrast, would eventually lead to repeal of the estate tax in 2011, with its effective exemption level raised to $3 million per person before then and the top rate of tax gradually reduced from 55 percent to 35 percent (before final repeal in 2011). Repeal would involve a newly reinstated gift tax and carryover of basis of assets for heirs, effectively subjecting them to capital gains taxes on the unrealized capital gains passed on by decedents.

• *Establishment and expansion of new child credit.* The 1997 legislation established a new credit of $500 per child per year. In 2001 this amount would be gradually raised to $1,000, and, moreover, some portions of it would be refundable for taxpayers with incomes as low as $10,000, who would owe no income tax.

• *Individual Retirement Account (IRA) and pension modifications.* The 1997 legislation made a number of modifications to individual retirement accounts, the most significant of which was the establishment of a "Roth IRA," under which nondeductible contributions would be allowed to accounts for which income tax on earnings would never be owed. The 2001 legislation significantly raised maximum contribution limits for IRAs and 401(k) plans and made dozens of other changes, making it easier to deposit more money into tax-deferred retirement accounts.

• *Education credits and deductions.* President Clinton pushed hard to establish a new scholarship credit for higher education (the "HOPE" and "Lifetime Learning" credits). In 2001 additional deductions were allowed for deposits to education savings accounts.

3.3.2.1   The Emphasis on Individual Rate Reduction in 2001

Before proceeding, it must be noted that *all the new tax rates and rate repeals contained in the 2001 tax bill are scheduled to sunset by 2011*—meaning that old-law tax rates and regulations will enter back into force that January, unless the current legislation is extended or otherwise amended. Moreover, the bill has numerous delayed phase-ins and temporary provisions. The analysis that follows, however, treats the various components as if they are fully phased in. Obviously, future legislation—whether to extend, remove, or reform features of the 2001 tax act—will determine the final outcome.

Although we have drawn some analogies between the 2001 legislation and that of 1997, the 2001 legislation emphasized tax rates and can more appropriately be labeled an heir of earlier legislation in 1981. When fully effective after almost a decade of phase-in, the top tax rate would be reduced from 39.6 percent to 35 percent, and the two bubbles (PEPs and Pease) would in one case be eliminated. The 1981 legislation also emphasized marriage penalty relief, mainly by allocating income among moderate- and middle-income couples so that no matter how it was split in reality, one would be as well off or better off married than filing as single individuals. (This relief did not extend fully to high- or low-income individuals, although, in both cases, there was usually some relief.)

Individual rate reduction by itself would comprise about three-fifths of the total revenue cost for the next 10 years (estimated, with some budget games-manship, at $1.35 trillion over roughly a 10-year time span). If one considers marriage penalty relief primarily as rate reduction for married couples, estate and gift tax changes as rates reductions for the wealthy, and child credit changes mainly as reductions in the bottom rate of tax, then rate reduction comprised almost 90 percent of the bill. Unlike 1981, however, there were few proposed changes in business taxation—again maintaining the 1986 compromise

3.3.3 IRS Restructuring

At least one other set of actions during this period deserves mention—the attempt to restructure IRS. Changes surrounding IRS administration had been occurring for some time: large increases in staff during the 1980s in an attempt to go after noncompliance, then large decreases in staff in the 1990s in an attempt to cut back on the size of government as measured by the number of people it hires (as opposed to the number with whom it contracts). Computer operations had lagged for decades with inability to hire top-notch people, partly because computers and software had become outdated. Demands on the system proliferated—the movement toward continual legislation and the large increase in special provisions in recent years only adding to the problem.

By the late 1990s, complaints rose to a high enough level that Congress at-tempted its first major restructuring in decades. It added moderately to IRS resources once again, but as the overall budget was moving toward balance it deemphasized tax collection and reemphasized taxpayer service. (In some peri-ods of high deficits, Congress seriously considered moving almost all taxpayer service money into compliance efforts.) The net result was the first hiring of a business and operations commissioner (as opposed to a tax expert), a signifi-cant buying spree for software and computers and information technology, a large decline in direct audit efforts,[5] the creation of a semiautonomous National Taxpayer Advocate (superseding the Taxpayer Ombudsman) who can inde-pendently make recommendations to Congress, the creation of a new board, a

---

5. A report by the General Accounting Office notes that the IRS attributed declining audit rates to a commensurate decline in the agency's audit staff (more than half), the imposition of additional duties on existing auditors such as assisting taxpayers with compliance, and increased audit administration requirements generally. See GAO (2001).

raised legal standing for taxpayers in court, and a restructuring of the agency's major divisions.

3.4   Tax Rates and Progressivity

Having completed this necessarily terse history of the 1990–2001 period, we now examine in more depth the themes summarized at the beginning of this study. By far the most vigorous battle over taxation centered on tax rates and, in particular, on the tax rates to be imposed on those with the highest incomes. A continued increase in income disparity from the late 1970s up to and including much of this period was one source of the controversy. From one perspective, this more uneven distribution was justification for more progression in tax rates. From a supply-side viewpoint, however, the highest tax rates in a progressive system were more likely to be marginal than inframarginal and therefore to affect decision-making. Moreover, economic theory suggests that distortions in behavior rise with the square of the tax rate. Of course, in parallel with the debate over tax rates is the debate over the size of government. Some believe that higher taxes almost inevitably will be spent inefficiently, so that government spending should be constrained by keeping rates low. Others believe that societal demands for different types of public goods required higher taxes.

The economic literature during this period put renewed emphasis on examining just how much people were able to offset tax rate increases with portfolio and other behavioral change. While an interesting literature, I view its results as inconclusive because crude proxies must be used to try to measure avoidance activities (see, among others, Slemrod, 2000; Feenberg and Poterba, 2000; Feldstein, 1995; Auten and Carroll, 1994; and Slemrod, 1994).

The next few figures show that from a broad historical perspective, the battle over the taxes in the period wasn't too far from a draw. The rate at the highest income levels was raised from 28 percent to 39.6 percent, then scheduled to be reduced gradually to 35 percent in the 2001 legislation (see Figure 3.1). The drop in rates near the top would also eventually include removal of implicit tax rates from PEPS and Pease. Interestingly, a clean 35 percent top rate (without hidden rates) was suggested in the 1984 Treasury study which I coordinated and which led to the Tax Reform Act of 1986.

A separate view of marginal rates can be seen in Figure 3.2. For the vast majority of taxpayers, marginal rates did not change over the period 1990 to 1998 (the last year for which numbers were available). That is, most taxpayers remained in a 15 percent tax bracket. However, the 1993 legislation clearly did increase marginal rates at the very top, as already noted—largely by removing

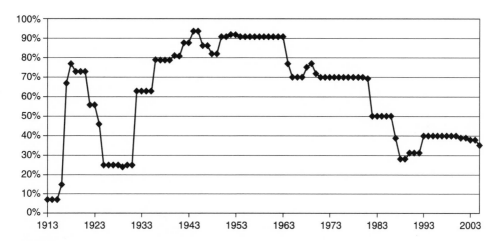

Figure 3.1
Highest Tax Rates, 1913–2005. (*Sources:* Eugene Steuerle, Urban Institute Press; Joseph Pechman, Federal Tax Policy; Joint Committee on Taxation.)

Note: This figure contains a number of simplifications and ignores a number of factors, such as a maximum tax on earned income of 50 percent when the top rate was 70 percent and the current increase in rates due to income-related reductions in the value of itemized deductions. Perhaps most importantly, it ignores the large increase in the percentage of returns that were subject to this top rate.

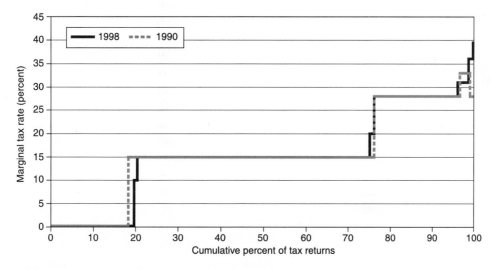

Figure 3.2
Cumulative Percent of Federal Income Tax Returns Taxed at or below Each Successive Marginal Rate. (*Source:* Department of the Treasury, Internal Revenue Service, *SOI Bulletin*, Statistics of Income Division, Summer 1994 and Spring 2001.)

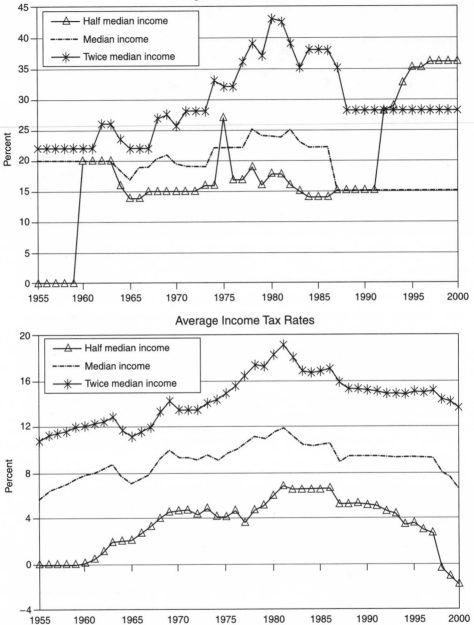

Figure 3.3
Federal Income Tax Rates for a Family of Four at Various Income Levels, 1955–2000. (*Source:* Tax Facts, Allen Lerman, Department of the Treasury, Office of Tax Analysis, January 15, 1998.)

Note: Median income is for a four-person family. All income is assumed to be earned by one spouse. Itemized deductions are assumed to equal 23 percent of income through 1986 and 18 percent of income thereafter. Median incomes are from the U.S. Census Bureau, "Current Population Reports, Series P-60," various issues. Average and marginal tax rates are from Department of Treasury calculations.

a bubble in rates whereby the highest income taxpayers had paid a 28 percent rate, but those just below them in the income scale paid a 33 percent rate. Also note that these calculations do not take account of phaseouts of benefits, as from the earned income tax credit or the phaseout of personal exemptions.

Still another way of looking at these marginal rates is shown at the top of Figure 3.3. This analysis, performed periodically by Allen Lerman of Treasury, shows that at median and twice median income, marginal tax rates were fairly constant over the 1990s. The real action is taking place at one-half the median income, where taxpayers are facing the phaseout of the earned income tax credit. Partly due to the EITC, the Joint Committee on Taxation warns that about one-quarter of all taxpayers have an effective marginal tax rate different from the statutory rate. At least 22 provisions, however, are involved (Joint Committee on Taxation, Mar. 7, 2001).

If we turn to average tax rates, Figure 3.3 shows that rates tended to drop at twice median, median, and half median income—and are scheduled to drop a bit more under the 2001 legislation. Indeed, average income tax rates for those at half median income turn negative—an issue we will turn to in more detail later. However, during this period incomes became much more uneven. That distributional effect, combined with the higher tax rates on high-income individuals, led overall to an increase in average tax rates. This can be seen in Figure 3.4 when viewing total individual income tax receipts. Note also that the average rate rises both for total federal receipts and for total federal, state, and local receipts.

Despite all the battles over federal individual income taxes, state and local revenue had grown to 9.4 percent of GDP in 2000 from 5.7 percent in 1950 and 9.1 percent in 1990 (see Figure 3.4). During the last decade, the growth in state individual income taxes offset declines in other sources, as many states saw average individual rates rise as a result of both real and inflationary income growth (many state income taxes are not indexed for inflation). The federal system itself has been moving more toward balance of power between national and state governments ever since the end of World War II, and the 1990s seem to be no exception.

As noted in the historical section, much of what happened legislatively at the federal level—in particular, in 1993 and 2001—was determined by budgetary deficits and surpluses. Nonetheless, in terms of overall revenue, even the largest changes in 1990, 1993, and 2001 were moderate in size, despite political rhetoric to the contrary. None, when fully implemented, was scheduled to be greater than 1.5 percent of gross domestic product. A major nonevent of the period was that Social Security tax rates did *not* increase—the first decade during which no increase has occurred since the system was founded in the late 1930s.

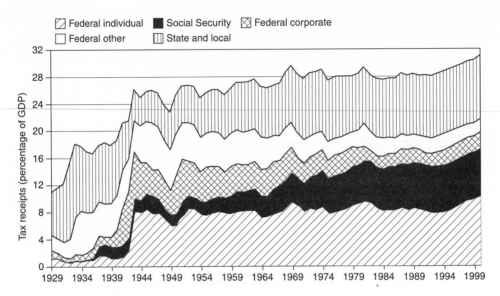

Figure 3.4
Tax Receipts as a Percentage of GDP, 1929–2000. (*Source:* Bureau of Economic Analysis, National Income and Product Accounts, Annual Tables 1.1, 3.2, 3.3, 3.6.)

Finally, Figure 3.5 shows effective total and individual tax rates for a variety of years in and surrounding this period. As can be seen, effective tax rates in almost all income classes stay fairly constant. There is a slight drop for the top 1 percent and for the bottom quintile, whose individual rates turn negative because of the earned income tax credit. The numbers do not reflect actions in 2001, which, if fully implemented, would lower rates in all classes. Nor does the calculation include the federal estate tax changes that may occur over the 2001–2010 period.

My own conclusion is that in this period of relative peace, the United States has managed to maintain a moderately progressive tax system while imposing only moderate distortions on initiative, invention, hard work, entrepreneurship, and the other qualities that tend to produce growth. I do not mean to imply that there are not serious problems—some of which I will discuss later—but relative to most other nations the complicated, inconsistent, often inequitable, and inefficient U.S. system still seems to achieve a rough balance between the goals of progressivity and growth.

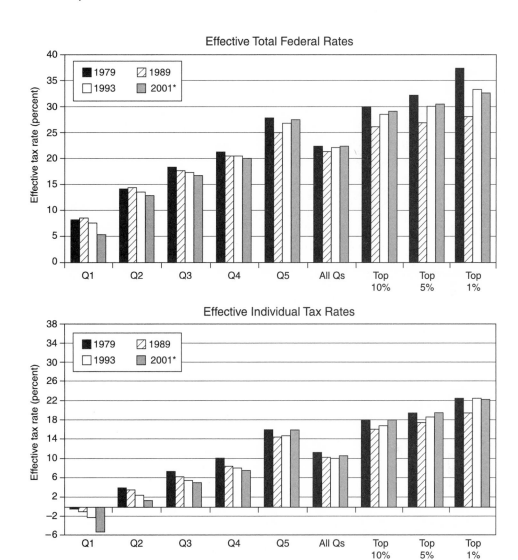

Figure 3.5
Effective Tax Rates for All Households by Income Class and Select Year. (*Source:* CBO, "Historical Effective Tax Rates, 1979–97 (Preliminary Edition)." Table G-1a, May 2001.)

* April 2001 tax law applied to 1997 income distribution; does not include effects of new EGTRRA 2001 rates, most of which are scheduled to take effect after 2001.

3.5   Traditional Tax Policy Concerns and the New Tax Expenditure Debate

In the period from 1990 to 2001, more social and individual expenditures than ever have moved into the tax code, and they have been done in ways that often promoted the inequitable treatment of equals, distortions in choice of investment and consumption, and high administrative and enforcement costs either for the taxpayer or the IRS. One way to try to follow what goes on is through the list of tax expenditures—an incomplete but nonetheless useful list of potentially special exceptions in the tax code.[6]

The tax expenditure debate itself is hardly new—the term itself having been given most prominence by Stanley Surrey.[7] But in its early incarnations and from the 1960s through mid-1980s, the tax expenditure debate was largely over business and investment expenditures. One major attack on these expenditures, for instance, was that they were not progressive and tended to favor businesses and higher income taxpayers. (Whether this argument is correct depends upon what one thinks would have happened otherwise to tax rates, but certainly many tax expenditures were not available to moderate- and middle-income taxpayers.)

Tax reform in 1986 successfully exchanged many tax expenditures for lower rates, but mainly with respect to business incentives. Base broadening, nonetheless, would be quite modest at middle-income ranges, and the EITC was expanded at low-income levels. Since 1986, the window has opened to even more types of tax expenditure options. Today the tax expenditure budget largely involves middle-class entitlements for individuals through the tax system (see Figure 3.6).

Two developments have added to this momentum. First, tighter budgetary limits were placed on discretionary spending than on spending in the tax system, which could be integrated with other tax changes. Second, despite the movement of tax expenditures toward the middle class, "conservatives" still hold onto a belief that tax expenditures are reductions in tax and ways of giving money back to people even while "liberals" have come to realize that they can achieve certain social objectives more easily if enacted as a tax cut. President Clinton was often able to exploit this difference by countering broad-scale tax-cutting efforts with proposals for tax cuts "targeted" more at particular needs and individuals.

In addition to its effect on complexity, these developments have led to a lack of adequate analysis of policy in general. The IRS for the most part does

---

6. I use the term "potentially" because some items should not be on the list and other excluded items should be. But my purpose here is not to examine how this list may be improved.
7. See, for instance, Surrey and McDaniel (1985).

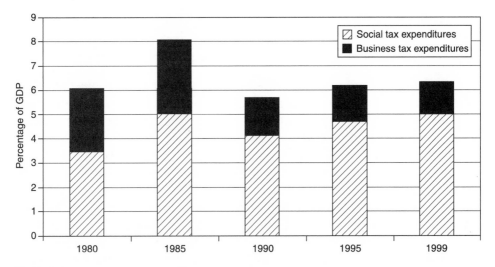

Figure 3.6
Trends in Tax Expenditures, 1980–1999 (expressed as a percentage of GDP). (*Source:* Eric Toder, "The Changing Composition of Tax Incentives, 1980–99," Urban Institute, March 1999, Chart 1.)

not evaluate policies under its control, at least as separate items. Treasury does some analysis but mainly for internal purposes, while congressional agencies randomly look at a few items. Neither government nor foundations subsidize much tax policy research, and, when they do, they often want certain results in advance. These developments have led to a lack of systematic treatment of most tax programs, whether they involve subsidies for charitable contributions, education, health, pensions, the poor, enterprise zones, commerce, housing, political campaigns, or anything else. An unevaluated program is often inefficient, whether or not the subsidy for the particular activity is appropriate.

A partial response to the proliferation of tax programs—perhaps even a development that has made it possible—has been changes in tax administration. The advance of computer tax software not only accommodated increased levels of complication, but also may eventually affect just what types of tax systems are developed in the future. Meanwhile, Congress pushed a new modernization program on the IRS. Here, too, much is centered on the computer, but along the way audit rates have dropped,[8] weakening the IRS's ability to deal with self-reported income and deduction items for which there are no corroborating reports (1099s or W-2s). Meanwhile, paper filing is gradually being replaced,

---

8. The General Accounting Office reports that audit rates have declined 70 percent for all income classes over the period 1996–2000. See GAO (2001).

with more than 29 million electronic returns filed in 1999, including about 6 million by phone.

Joel Slemrod of the University of Michigan estimates that the resources spent on income tax filing are equal to about $130 billion a year, or about 10 percent of the total income from tax collections.[9] These are probably the best estimates available, although they are not adjusted for recent changes. Nor do they fully account for the cost of filing to the taxpayer: by estimating the cost at the wage level of the taxpayer, they do not account for the negative value that the taxpayer also puts on wasting her time and on meeting many of these filing requirements.

Complexity certainly is not endemic to the 1990s; it has been a complaint for a long time. Nonetheless, it is fair to say that concern over adding to it has been given very little heed in this period. Some complexities—such as higher rates of AMT taxation that policy-makers knew were neither sustainable nor fair and the multiple layers and rates of capital gains taxation (Burman, 1999)— are symbolic of the era.

Complexity is occasionally reversed. In this case, however, reversal probably requires primary focus on complexity and the leadership of a president. Historically politicians have given simplification little weight in the political process relative to such goals as tax relief, revenue raising, and progressivity. However, so much increased complexity is now scheduled in the AMT that a counter-reaction could set in, and it could be the horse on which broader simplification rides.[10] It may be hard to sell AMT simplification (mainly for upper-middle and upper-income taxpayers) by itself, but it will be even harder to ignore the perverse effect of this tax on a growing number of taxpayers. Hence, a package of simplification for all income classes may be the only way out of the dilemma.

3.6   The Social Agenda and Subsidies for Low-Income Households with Children

With the movement away from welfare in the form of cash payments have come expansions in both the earned income tax credit and, in 1997 and 2001, the child credit. These expansions of the tax breaks for families with children along with the contractions in welfare have tended to favor those who work

---

9. Communication with author.

10. Overall, the 2001 legislation, by reducing statutory tax rates but not AMT tax rates, actually increased by millions the number of people who will be subject to the AMT in the next 10 years. According to the Joint Committee on Taxation, 1.4 million taxpayers are affected by the AMT in 2001, but the number rises to 5.3 million by 2004 and 35.5 million by 2010 (even under pre-2001 law, the corresponding numbers would have been 5.4 million and 17.5 million, respectively).

relative to those who do not. From a social policy perspective, many analysts believe this is a worthwhile trade-off. Certainly, it has encouraged more work among those lower-income individuals who formerly were not in the workforce, but the economic literature is more mixed on whether credits like the earned income tax credit increase work overall (Blank and Haskins, 2001). Part of the dilemma in any estimating process, of course, is determining the alternative or counterfactual: whether one counts the EITC as a pure add-on to the current system or a replacement for something like AFDC.

Refundable "tax" credits are counted in the budget as direct expenditures even though they are administered by the tax authorities. The budgetary objection to hiding subsidies in the tax system, therefore, is not as applicable as with other tax expenditures where positive subsidies get counted as zero expenditures and negative taxes. Rather, the broader issue here is how should we integrate tax and transfer systems, especially as we move people from (1) welfare to (2) work with tax benefit supports to (3) net taxpayers. The compromise we seem to have reached at this stage in our history is that cash benefits (whether in the tax code or elsewhere) are not available to the nondisabled who do not work, but they will be made available to those who perform some minimum amount of work.

Still, the tax rate system has evolved so that very high marginal tax rates now affect nonworkers less and moderate income taxpayers much more than previously. One study shows that a person who has moved out of welfare, defined as Temporary Assistance to Needy Families (TANF), still faces penalties from the EITC, Food Stamps, and Medicaid (not to mention housing, child care, and other subsidies) that are substantial. For instance, if a head of household with two children and earning minimum wage for full-time work were to marry someone making $8 an hour, their combined income would fall by 22 percent, or $7,570, because of marriage.[11] The issue of high tax rates for low- to moderate-income households is a fairly new phenomenon in our tax/transfer system and one not yet addressed in any rigorous fashion.

The debates surrounding the EITC and child credits in tax legislation from 1990 to 2001 in many ways highlight the fundamental failure of analysis aimed solely at the tax or transfer systems. Even public finance textbooks are notorious for their separation of these issues along lines similar to those creating division of legislation. However, once transfers are recognized as negative taxes, taxes recognized as negative transfers, hidden tax rates recognized in expenditure programs, and hidden expenditures recognized in tax programs, the absurdity of this separation becomes ever more apparent.

---

11. See Steuerle (2001).

In 2001 these problems played themselves out in debates over how to change the child credit to affect the marginal tax rates, as well as marriage penalties (see Ellwood and Liebman, 2001; Sawhill, 2001; and Sammartino, Steuerle, and Carasso, 2001). Politically, it also played out in the debate over what to do about nontaxpayers. With significant expansion of low-income relief in recent years, the income tax has now been converted into one where more than one-third of the income distribution pays no net income tax. This fact makes it difficult to allocate some "share" of a tax cut to them without adding on some "refundable" credit so that they garner actual benefits. But since refundable credits are recognized as expenditures from a budget standpoint, what is really going on is an indirect attempt to increase expenditures for lower-income individuals.

The compromise in the 2001 legislation was to allow some refundability starting at $10,000—almost precisely the level of income where the EITC was fully phased in. The administration itself had proposed increases in child credits and a new 10 percent tax bracket so that positive income tax rates would not be faced generally below about $32,000. At this point the EITC would have fully phased out (i.e., its 21 percent phaseout rate would not then combine with the lowest tax rate in the income tax rate schedule). In general, the 2001 legislation did tend to lower marginal tax rates and reduce marriage penalties for many low-income individuals, although they were raised for some others, and the tax problems arising from most other transfer programs were not taken into account.

In general, I would rate the movement toward work support as a positive development, as well as later efforts (e.g., through a partially refundable child credit) to lower marginal tax rates and marriage penalties for low- and moderate-income workers. Still, these tax rates and penalties remain high because of the failure to adequately integrate thinking about tax and transfer systems. One wonders how much longer public finance issues will be separated into tax and expenditure components. Tax expenditures and expenditure taxes (tax rates hidden in phaseouts of expenditure programs) abound. When looking at how a government composed largely of social programs treats people, it is simply not possible to measure progressivity, equity, efficiency, or marginal tax rates by looking at just one side of the ledger at a time. (Perhaps we never should have done so.)

3.7   The Taxation of Business and Saving

In many ways, there is much less of a story to tell with respect to business taxation throughout the 1990 to 2001 period. Legislative action was limited. The corporate tax rate was raised one percentage point and the depreciation lives of structures extended in 1993, and in various years research and development tax credits kept getting renewed. Federal corporate taxes as a percent of GDP rose from 2.04 percent to 2.45 percent from 1990 to 2000, but the rise was less than the increase in financial profits. In many ways, the compromise of 1986 crudely held through this period: no large-scale tax breaks were added, and corporate rates were changed only slightly.

The reduction in the inflation rate effectively lowered tax rates more than any statutory change and more than offset a one-percentage-point increase in the statutory corporate rate and an increase in tax lives for structures in 1993 legislation. Lower inflation enhances the value of future depreciation allowances because they are stated in nominal, not real, dollars. Gravelle (2001), for instance, finds that the effective tax rate on equipment fell from 32 percent to 27 percent between 1986 law and 1993 law when inflation is only 2 percent (the effective rates are about the same under 1986 law and 1993 law at a 5 percent inflation rate). For structures and office buildings, she finds almost no difference between 1986 law and 1993 law at a 2 percent inflation rate.

New tensions over the taxation of capital income certainly were created, but they will have to be played out in the future:

• First, a large-scale debate arose over so-called corporate and business tax shelters. However, the meaning of the term has always been vague. In general, accountants and lawyers have become extraordinarily good at arbitraging almost any differential—tax rates among countries, deductions allowed in one jurisdiction but not in another, exemption of some income in the government and nonprofit sectors but not in the business sector, limitations on losses in one company but not another, and so on. They also have become better at marketing these as packages and techniques in ways hard for the IRS to detect. Suffice it to say at the time of this writing that no conclusion has been reached either with respect to the size of these shelter activities or a solution. Nonetheless, even the anecdotal evidence from specific examples indicates that the amounts involved are fairly large.

• A second dynamic of business taxation—affecting both interstate and international transactions—is the increased difficulty of determining the nexus of taxation on a geographical basis. E-commerce brings this problem to light: think of a product with inputs from Ireland using invention from France, assembled and shipped from Colorado, with e-mail sales staff located in the Caribbean, and lawyers everywhere. Make it a product mainly with intellectual content (e.g., a piece of software or a music CD), and the problem is even more complicated.[12] Interestingly, the reaction of some countries like Germany has been to move away from a system of taxation integrated across corporate and individual lines. Instead, to capture some tax on activities, the notion has arisen that it is necessary to have both a residence-based tax on income received and a source-based tax on income produced. In many ways, this is a movement back toward an unintegrated system of taxation such as exists in the United States.

During the 1990s there were also a large number of new saving incentives adopted, as well as increases in the amount of deposits that could be made under existing vehicles such as IRA accounts. These provisions were often not coordinated, and the number of saving options available to individuals has become very large and very hard to understand. Different contribution limits, withdrawal rules, discrimination rules, exemption from Social Security tax rules, and so on apply to a wide variety of pension incentives. Moreover, the taxpayer is now asked to make a choice between an up-front deduction in an individual retirement account [and, assuming implementation of the 2001 legislation, in 401(k) accounts] and a lifetime of exemption of earnings from taxation.

While some view these provisions as moves toward a consumption tax, they are exceedingly complex and sometimes are even more generous than consumption tax treatment. Moreover, they have not yet been coordinated in a way that would enhance retirement policy. For whatever reason, the system still fails to cover well the majority of households—usually those with the greatest needs and lowest incomes in retirement. Allowance of withdrawals for education, housing, and other purposes may also lead to a weakening of retirement policy, although the jury is still out, since these options may enhance accumulations of capital in nonpension form by time of retirement.

3.8   Spend It Before Somebody Else Does: The New Dynamics of Tax and Expenditure Entitlement Policy

The period from 1990 to 2001 involved significant efforts to put in place what I have labeled tax entitlements, in no small part in competition with direct expenditure entitlements. Perhaps the two most symbolic elements of this dynamic on the tax side have been the establishment of Roth IRAs and Roth

---

12. The 1990s have seen several efforts to prevent taxation of products sold over the Internet, but this is really the tip of the iceberg. In many states, for instance, it has already become difficult to tax interstate catalog and similar sales even when the Internet is not used. Moreover, most states still have sales taxes mainly on goods, but not on many services such as health, legal, and other growing sectors of the economy.

401(k)s, and 10-year periods to phase in tax cuts. As best as I can tell, never before has so much been promised in the way of future changes in taxes for so many years into the future. Indeed, Roth IRAs set up today promise the taxpayer tax relief for a lifetime.

The name of the game in Washington today is to spend money before the other person does. And the money to be spent is not merely what is currently available, but what economic growth would provide in the future. Thus, Social Security, Medicare, and Medicaid are assumed to absorb almost all revenue growth for the next 100 years and more, while those who would lower taxes have decided that they want to get in this game also.[13] It's like a husband who contracts to spend future wage growth that he and his wife expect over coming decades, so the wife decides she must spend it, too, and then they fight over who is fiscally imprudent.

While I cannot prove it, I believe that this is the most glaring economic inefficiency of federal tax, spending, and budget policy. Making choices today for an uncertain future by its very nature must be extraordinarily inefficient because it attempts to ascertain future needs of the population before the time has come. It limits options. It's equivalent to determining the consumption of our children for decades to come because they are adolescents whom we will never trust. Now certainly, some of these choices will be offset by future changes in the law, but that is not a sufficient response. Some promises are hard to renege on, and this type of process in any case creates an unlevel playing field. Tax entitlements and regular expenditure entitlements require a supermajority (e.g., a majority of both houses of Congress and the support of the president) to be slowed down; discretionary spending requires a similar majority simply to attain any level of spending. In no small part, then, the future of the tax system depends upon setting up a budget process that deals with these larger issues.

3.9 Conclusion

The period from 1990 to 2001 was a period of extraordinary activity. The tax code became the primary ground upon which budgetary action would take place—whether the goal was deficit cuts, tax rate cuts, or new subsidies and expenditures. Literally trillions of dollars were shuffled around through tax policy during this decade.

In very rough terms, the tax system was not much different by the end of the period in its overall progressivity or average tax rate for the population, with

---

13. To be fair in the comparison, the built-in growth in regular entitlements is much larger than growth in tax entitlements or scheduled reductions in tax rates.

the exception of the very highest wealth class and the lowest income quintile. Traditional principles of equal treatment of equals, efficiency, and simplicity were often ignored, since tax policy was largely determined by budgetary, spending, and other concerns. Complexity at all levels—for example, high- and middle-income taxpayers subject to the AMT and low-income taxpayers with multiple tax benefits to calculate—was perhaps the worst part of the aftermath. When tax and spending policy are considered together, nonetheless, the movement away from welfare and toward work subsidies should be considered a positive development, although very high tax rates from a variety of spending programs (including the EITC) remain a source of concern. Business taxation was not changed dramatically, although issues arising there could change that story in the future. Savings policies were disjointed and did not succeed in increasing personal saving, particularly among those who need it most. With tax changes now enacted for years into the future, tax policy has come to match more and more the game that is played on the direct entitlement part of the budget. While budget policy clearly reduced deficits and went toward surplus, the net result is still a budget projected to remain in long-term imbalance at both the start and end of the period. Perhaps more importantly, this process continues to restrict considerably options over how to meet the needs of tomorrow.

References

Aaron, Henry J., and William G. Gale. 1996. *Economic Effects of Fundamental Tax Reform*. Washington, DC: Brookings Institution.

Auten, Gerald, and Robert Carroll. 1994. "Behavior of the Affluent and the 1986 Tax Reform Act." *National Tax Association: Proceedings of the Eighty-Sixth Annual Conference*, 70–76.

———. 1997. "The Effect of Income Taxes on Household Behavior."

Bakija, Jon, and C. Eugene Steuerle. 1991. "Individual Income Taxation Since 1948." *National Tax Journal*, 44, no. 4, part 2 (December).

Blank, Rebecca, and Ron Haskins, eds. 2001. *The New World of Welfare: Shaping a Post-TANF Agenda for Policy*, Washington, DC: Brookings Institution Press.

Budget of the United States Government, Analytical Perspectives, Fiscal Year 2002.

Bureau of Economic Analysis, U.S. Department of Commerce. *The National Income and Product Accounts*, Tables 1.1, 3.2, 3.3, 3.6. www.bea.gov.

Burman, Leonard E. 1999. *The Labyrinth of Capital Gains Tax Policy: A Guide for the Perplexed*. Washington, DC: Brookings Institution Press.

Congressional Budget Office. 1994. "An Economic Analysis of the Revenue Provisions of OBRA-93," January.

———. 2000. "An Economic Analysis of the Taxpayer Relief Act of 1997," April.

————. 2001. "Effective Tax Rates, 1979–97 (Preliminary Edition)," May.

Ellwood, David T., and Jeffrey B. Liebman. 2001. "Confronting the Middle Class Parent Penalty Created by Existing Child Benefits in the U.S. Tax Code," Policy brief presented at *Integrating Tax Benefits for Families: A Cross Disciplinary Approach*. Conference at the Urban Institute, May 4.

Feenberg, Daniel, and James Poterba. 2000. "The Income and Tax Share of Very High Income Households, 1960–95." NBER Working Paper No. W7525. February.

Feldstein, Martin. 1995. "The Effect of Marginal Tax Rates on Taxable Income: A Panel Study of the 1986 Tax Reform Act," *Journal of Political Economy*, 103 (June): 551–572.

Feldstein, Martin, and Daniel Feenberg. 1993. "Higher Tax Rates with Little Revenue Gain: An Empirical Analysis of the Clinton Tax Plan," *Tax Notes*, March 22.

Fox, John O. 2001. *If Americans Really Understood the Income Tax: Uncovering Our Most Expensive Ignorance*. Boulder, CO: Westview Press.

Fullerton, Don. 1994. "Inputs to Tax Policy Making: The Supply Side, the Deficit, and the Level Playing Field." In Martin Feldstein, ed., *American Economic Policy in the 1980s*. Chicago: National Bureau of Economic Research, University of Chicago Press.

General Accounting Office. 2001. "IRS Audit Rates: Rate for Individual Taxpayers Has Declined but Effect on Compliance Is Unknown," GAO-01-484, April 25.

Gravelle, Jane G. Forthcoming. "Whither Tax Depreciation." *National Tax Journal*.

Joint Committee on Taxation. 1996. "General Explanation of Tax Legislation Enacted in the 104th Congress." Washington, DC: U.S. Government Printing Office, Dec. 18.

————. 1997. "General Explanation of Tax Legislation Enacted in 1997." Washington, DC: U.S. Government Printing Office, Dec. 17.

————. 1998. "General Explanation of Tax Legislation Enacted in 1998." Washington, DC: U.S. Government Printing Office, Nov. 24.

————. 2001. "Overview of Present Law and Economic Analysis Relating to Marginal Tax Rates and the President's Individual Income Tax Rate Proposals." Public Hearing before the Senate Committee on Finance, Mar. 7.

————. 2001. "Estimated Budget Effects of the Conference Agreement for H.R. 1836 [1], Fiscal Years 2001–2011," May 26.

Office of Tax Analysis. 1998. *Tax Facts*. U.S. Department of the Treasury, January.

Sammartino, Frank, C. Eugene Steuerle, and Adam Carasso. 2001. "Options for Revising the Child Credit." Urban Institute, May 4.

Sawhill, Isabel, and Adam Thomas. 2001. "A Hand Up for the Bottom Third: Toward a New Agenda for Low-Income Working Families." Washington, DC: Brookings Institution, May.

Slemrod, Joel, ed. 2000. *Does Atlas Shrug? The Economic Consequences of Taxing the Rich*. Cambridge, MA: Harvard University Press.

————. 1994. "On the High-Income Laffer Curve." *Tax Progressivity and Income Inequality*, 177–210. Cambridge: Cambridge University Press.

Steuerle, C. Eugene. 1985. *Taxes, Loans, and Inflation*. Washington, DC: Brookings Institution.

————. 1991. *The Tax Decade: How Taxes Came to Dominate the Public Agenda*. Washington, DC: Urban Institute Press.

————. 2001. "Valuing Marital Commitment in Our Transfer and Tax Systems," Statement Before the Subcommittee on Human Resources, Committee on Ways and Means, U.S. House of Representatives, May 21.

Surrey, Stanley S., and Paul R. McDaniel. 1985. *Tax Expenditures*. Cambridge, MA: Harvard University Press.

Toder, Eric. 1999. "The Changing Composition of Tax Incentives, 1980–99." Urban Institute, March.

U.S. Congress, 103rd Session. 1993. "The Revenue Reconciliation Act of 1993: Conference Bill and Statement of Conference Managers (H. Rept. 103–213) for the Revenue Provisions of Title XIII of the Omnibus Budget Reconciliation Act of 1993 (H.R. 2264)." New York: Research Institute of America.

Table A.3.1
Summary of Major Enacted Tax Legislation, 1990–2001

Omnibus Budget Reconciliation Act of 1990

Excise tax increases. Imposed a 30% excise tax on the amount of price over $30,000 for autos, $100,000 for boats, $250,000 for airplanes, and $10,000 for furs. Increased motor fuels taxes by 5 cents per gallon. Increased taxes on tobacco and alcoholic beverages: by 8 cents per pack of cigarettes, by $1.00 per "proof gallon" of liquor; by 16 cents per six-pack of beer; and by 18 cents per bottle of table wine. Extended airport and airway trust fund taxes and increased them by 25%. Permanently extended 3% excise tax on telephone service.

Individual income tax rate increases. Increased top statutory tax rate from 28% to 31%, and increased the individual alternative minimum tax rate from 21% to 24%. Capped the capital gains rate at 28%. Limited value of high-income itemized deductions: reduced by 3% times the extent to which AGI exceeds $100,000. Modified the "bubble": temporarily created the personal exemption phaseout applicable to the range of taxable income between $150,000 and $275,000.

Payroll tax rate increases. Raised the cap on taxable wages for Hospital Insurance (Medicare) from $53,400 to $125,000. Extended social security taxes to state and local employees without other pension coverage. Imposed a supplemental 0.2% unemployment insurance surtax.

Earned income tax credit (EITC) expansion and other low-income credits. Adjusted EITC benefit levels and phase-in and phaseout rates for family size. Created a low-income credit for the premium costs of health insurance that includes coverage for children.

Income tax base erosion. Extended expiring provisions: tax credits for research and exploration, low-income housing, business energy, targeted jobs, and orphan drugs; tax exemptions for mortgage revenues and issue bonds; exclusions for employer-provided legal and educational assistance; and 25% health insurance deduction for the self-employed. Extended and created new energy producer tax benefits: extended nonconventional fuels credit and tax incentives for ethanol production; created a new credit for enhanced oil recovery costs; amended percentage depletion; reduced alternative minimum tax preference treatment of energy items. Created a small-business-oriented credit for accommodations for disabled persons. Modified estate "freeze" rules. Eliminated appreciation of certain donated property as a minimum tax preference item.

Miscellaneous revenue raisers. Permitted transfers from "overfunded" pension plans for retiree health; added chemicals subject to ozone-depleting chemicals tax; reimposed Leaking Underground Storage Tank Trust Fund tax; reduced loss deductions by property and casualty insurance companies; improved IRS ability to obtain information from foreign corporations; increased harbor maintenance tax; reduced business income tax loopholes.

Tax Extension Act of 1991

Tax provision extensions. Provided a six-month extension for a number of tax provisions and credits facing expiration. These categories included research tax credits; exclusions for employer-provided educational assistance; targeted jobs credits; alternative energy credits; itemized deduction for health insurance costs; drug clinical testing credits; issuance authority for mortgage revenue bonds, certificates, and manufacturing/farm facility construction; credit for charitable contributions of appreciated tangible property.

Energy Security Bill of 1992

Energy and conservation-related tax provisions. Exclusions for employer-provided transportation; energy conservation subsidies for public utilities; credits for electric vehicles and for energy produced from renewable resources; repeal of minimum tax preferences for depletion and intangible drilling costs of independent oil and gas producers and royalty owners; permanent extension of alternative energy investment credit.

Table A.3.1 (continued)

Omnibus Budget Reconciliation Act of 1993

Individual income tax rate increases. Imposed new tax rates of 36% and 39.6%. Increased tax rates and exemption amounts under the AMT. Permanently extended the itemized deduction limitation and the personal exemption phaseout legislated in OBRA 1990.

Corporate tax rate increases. Increased corporate tax rate to 35% on income above $10 million.

Hospital Insurance wage base cap repeal. Repeals the cap on the HI tax base—set at $135,000 in 1993—so that the HI tax applies to all income.

Social Security benefit taxation expansion. Expanded the taxable portion of Social Security benefits from 50% to 85%, when modified AGI goes above $44,000 for joint returns and $34,000 for single returns.

Motor fuels tax increase. Increased fuel taxes by 4.3 cents per gallon (plus extended the current motor fuels tax of 2.5 cents per gallon).

Business meals and entertainment deduction reduction.

EITC expansion. Extended EITC to single workers with no children earning $9,000 or less.

Taxpayer Bill of Rights 2 of 1996

Taxpayer Advocate. Establishes position of Taxpayer Advocate within the IRS, replacing Taxpayer Ombudsman. The advocate is appointed by the commissioner. The advocate has four responsibilities: (1) assist taxpayers in resolving problems with the IRS, (2) identify problem areas where taxpayers have difficulty dealing with the IRS, (3) propose administrative changes within IRS that might mitigate these problem areas, and (4) identify potential legislative changes that might mitigate these problem areas.

Installment agreement modification. Where the IRS enters into a paid installment agreement with taxpayers to facilitate the collection of taxes, it must notify said taxpayers within 30 days if such agreement is modified or terminated for any reason other than that the collection of the tax is determined to be in jeopardy Additionally, the IRS must establish procedures for independent administrative review of installment agreements that are modified or terminated.

Interest and penalties abatement. IRS is directed to abate interest penalties against the taxpayer caused by any unreasonable error or delay on the part of IRS management.

Other provisions. Reexamination of joint and several liability for spouses filing joint returns; flexibility in moderating collection activities according to level of compliance; and a number of other provisions that boost taxpayers' standing relative to the IRS in legal disputes.

Revenue Provisions of the Small Business Job Protection Act of 1996

Small business expensing increase. Increases the $17,500 of qualified property allowed to be expensed to $25,000.

Social Security tax credit. Credit applicable to Social Security taxes paid with respect to employee cash tips.

Pension simplification provisions. Included here are provisions allowing contributions to a spousal IRA for a nonworking spouse (thus doubling potential maximum contributions from $2,000 to $4,000 for eligible participants), simplifying distributions from small business pension plans, tightening of nondiscrimination provisions, eliminating special aggregation rules applying to self-employed individual plans, and reform of miscellaneous pension rules governing state and local, special job-status, or professional individuals.

Table A.3.1 (continued)

Revenue Provisions of the Health Insurance and Portability Act of 1996

Medical savings accounts. Offers these IRA-like vehicles for the tax-advantaged accumulation of assets against possible medical expenses for employees covered under an employer-sponsored high-deductible plan (e.g., at least a $1,500 deductible) of a small employer and self-employed individuals, regardless of the size of the entity for which they perform work. Individual contributions to an MSA are deductible (within limits) in determining AGI (i.e., "above the line"); additionally, employer contributions are excludible from gross income.

Health expense deduction increases for self-employed.

Treatment of long-term care services and accelerated death benefits.

Income tax exemption for state-sponsored health organizations covering high-risk individuals.

IRA withdrawals for health care expenses. Makes such withdrawals penalty free.

Group health plan requirements. Application and enforcement of plan provisions to ensure genuine portability regarding preexisting conditions and health status. Levies an excise tax on sponsoring employers or, in the case of multiemployer plans, the plan itself.

Taxpayer Relief Act of 1997

Child tax credit. Introduced a child credit of $500 per child per year.

Education tax credit. Introduced the HOPE and Lifetime Learning nonrefundable education credits. The Hope credit is the maximum of taxable income or $1,500 per student for at most the first two years of school. The Lifetime Learning credit is the maximum of 20% of taxable income or $1,000 per taxpayer return (rather than per student), with no limit on the number of years claimed.

Estate and gift tax reductions. Boosts the present-law unified credit beginning in 1998 from $600,000 per person to $1 million by 2006. Also indexes other estate and gift tax parameters, such as the $10,000 annual gift exclusion, to inflation after 1998.

Capital gains rates reduction. Reduced capital gains tax rates from 28% and 15% to 20% and 10%, respectively.

IRA modification. Extends AGI phaseouts for deductible IRAs, allows tax-free withdrawals for first-time home purchases, creates new Roth IRAs and education IRAs.

Alternative minimum tax reductions. Repeals the AMT for small businesses (those averaging less than $7.5 million in gross receipts in the prior three years), modifies the depreciation adjustment used in the AMT calculation, and repeals the AMT installment method adjustment for farmers.

Excise taxes. Phased-in 30 cents per pack increase in the cigarette tax. Extended air transportation excise taxes.

Surface Transportation Revenue Act of 1998

Motor fuels tax extension. Simply extends current taxes on varieties of motor fuels through 2003: 18.3 cents per gallon on gasoline, 24.3 cents per gallon on diesel and kerosene, 13.6 cents per gallon on propane, and 11.9 cents per gallon on liquefied natural gas, among others.

Internal Revenue Service Restructuring Act of 1998

Mission statement revision. The IRS was directed to revise its mission statement to provide greater emphasis on serving the public and meeting the needs of taxpayers. This included replacing the three-tier geographic organization with a structure that features operating units geared around different types of taxpayers and their specialized needs. Additionally, created an independent appeals function within the IRS.

IRS Oversight Board. Oversees the administration, management, and conduct of the IRS, ensuring that the organization and operations of the IRS allow it to properly carry out its mission.

Table A.3.1 (continued)

Appointment and duties of IRS commissioner and other appointed personnel. The Oversight Board recommends candidates, who should have a strong management background, to the president, for appointment to a statutory five-year term (instead of a nonspecific term), with the advice and consent of the Senate. The belief is that a statutory term will enhance continuity of management at IRS. The president is not obliged to select any candidate so recommended and can remove the commissioner at will. The board may also recommend the commissioner's removal, subject to the president's discretion.

Taxpayer advocate role revision. Because of the broad powers granted the National Taxpayer Advocate in the 1996 legislation that created the position, Congress felt the need to have the position appointed by the secretary of the treasury, limit the advocate's former and future involvement with the IRS, and provide clearer definitions and limits on the scope of taxpayer assistance orders that the advocate can issue on behalf of certain taxpayers.

The Tax Relief Extension Act of 1999

Extends the tax applicability of a host of nonrefundable credits. Extends the provision that allows nonrefundable credits (the dependent care credit, the credit for the elderly and disabled, the adoption credit, the child tax credit, the HOPE Scholarship, etc.) to offset the individual's regular tax liability in full—as opposed to only the amount by which the regular tax exceeds the tentative minimum tax—to taxable years beginning in 1999. For taxable years beginning in 2000 and 2001, the personal nonrefundable credits may offset both the regular tax and the minimum tax.

The Community Renewal Tax Relief Act of 2000

The provision authorizes the designation of 40 "renewal communities" within which special tax incentives will be available. Applicable tax incentives include a zero capital gains rate; employment credit; commercial revitalization deduction; additional "section 179" expensing; extension of work opportunity credit.

Extends past empowerment zone tax incentives. Applies to empowerment zone tax incentives created in the 1993 OBRA and 1997 Taxpayer Relief Act.

The Economic Growth and Tax Relief Reconciliation Act of 2001

Individual income tax rate reductions. When fully phased in by 2006, levies a new 10% rate on the first $12,000 of income for a married couple ($10,000 for a single head of household and $6,000 for an individual); the 15% rate begins thereafter; it further reduces the 28% rate to 25%, the 31% rate to 28%, the 36% rate to 33%, and the 39.6% rate to 35%. Also repeals the phaseout of the itemized deduction and personal exemption. Makes the 10% bracket retroactive to January 1, 2001, to result in refund checks of up to $300 for individuals and $600 for couples 4–5 months hence.

Child tax credit increase. Doubles the $500 per child tax credit to $1,000 and makes it refundable for persons earning above $10,000 to the extent that their Social Security taxes exceed their income tax liability.

Marriage penalty abatement. Lowers marriage penalties for couples by making the standard deduction and 15% bracket twice as large as for a single taxpayer.

Child and dependent care tax credit increases. Provides a credit of 25% on expenditures for employer-provided child care and increases the dependent care and adoption credits.

Estate and gift tax reduction and elimination. Gradually reduces the estate and gift tax rate from 55% to 45% by 2007; raises the per-spouse exemption from $1 million in 2002 to $3.5 million in 2009. Eliminates the estate tax portion entirely in 2010 in lieu of a capital gains tax assessed on $1.3 million of individual income, but disregarding $3.3 million in transfers to a surviving spouse. Retains the gift tax after 2010 with a $1 million lifetime exclusion and a tax rate no higher than the top rate on individual income.

Table A.3.1 (continued)

Retirement savings contribution ceiling increases. Increases IRA annual contribution limits from $2,000 to $5,000 and 401(k) limits from $10,000 to $15,000, but allows individuals 50 and older to make larger, catch-up contributions; permits Roth 401(k)s beginning in 2006; and establishes a temporary credit for retirement savings for households earning $50,000 or less.

Education credit and deduction expansions. Allows $4,000 maximum deduction of college tuition expenses; allows tax-free distributions from prepaid college tuition plans, allows private institutions to offer these, and allows taxpayers to simultaneously claim HOPE or Lifetime Learning credits in some instances; eliminates the 60-month limit on student loan interest deduction and raises eligibility to $65,000 from $55,000 for singles and $130,000 from $75,000 for couples; increases contribution limits for education IRAs to $2,000 from $500, extends applicability to private elementary and secondary institutions, and allows participating taxpayers to simultaneously claim HOPE and/or Lifetime Learning credits.

Sources: Various documents from the Joint Committee on Taxation and the Congressional Budget Office (see References); Steuerle, 1991.

Comments

Henry J. Aaron

Eugene Steuerle provides an admirable review of developments in tax policy over a 12-year "decade" that begins with the Bush I deficit reduction agreement of 1990 and ends with the Bush II surplus termination tax bill of 2001. He looks back at tax developments in the previous decades and forward to distant budget events well beyond the lives of most living Americans. His tone, for the most part, is notably detached. Base and rate changes have come and gone, he notes. The net result is a draw, at least since the tax reform plan of 1984 on which he did such distinguished work. He characterizes the 1990s as a period of active but hardly revolutionary legislation. He becomes indignant only about the effects of tax and transfer policy on budget prospects in the far distant future. These elicit wry and humorous criticism of congressional and presidential willingness to bind the hands of future Congresses and presidents.

I have no sharp disagreements with his presentation, but I do believe that certain topics merit more emphasis than he gives them. I also think that his concern about the distant future is somewhat misplaced. He should, I believe, be more indignant and worried about deceptive practices affecting current tax policy and far less worried about the distant future.

I will use my time to make three points:

• Tax legislation has become an instrument for debasing the currency of honest political debate.

• Long-term projections get way too much attention.

• The retrogression from reforms of the Tax Reform Act of 1986 is larger than Steuerle acknowledges.

The views expressed are those of the author and do not necessarily represent those of the staff, officers, or trustees of the Brookings Institution.

Budget Accounting

The most recent debate over tax policy signals new lows for budgetary duplicity. A few excellent editorials and op-ed columns have pointed out various absurdities. The largest is the failure to adjust the alternative minimum tax (AMT). The AMT will deny all or some of the promised tax cuts to roughly 20 million filers by 2012. The pattern of denial is capricious and senseless. But the cost of updating the minimum tax is large. So, the authors of the 2001 tax bill left out AMT reform to make more room for larger cuts, safe in the knowledge that later Congresses would find it impossible not to fix the AMT. Even more absurd, if possible, is the termination of all tax cuts after nine years. Like the undead in some B-flick out of Hollywood, the estate and gift tax rises from the grave in the tenth year after having been interred in the ninth. In this Nightmare out of Capitol Hill, the supposedly reduced income tax rates likewise spring back to life in 2011. Other provisions, in contrast, are phased in gradually to hold down the 10-year revenue loss.

All this was done to comply in a formal sense with a total 10-year revenue reduction target of $1.35 trillion. If one disregards these false repeals and delayed phase-ins and allows for added interest costs generated by the tax cut, the revenue loss in the first 10 years is $2.3 trillion, not a "mere" $1.35 trillion. In the next 10 years, the cost more than triples to $4.5 trillion. Were any of us to read about such practices in some $500-per-capita-income country, we would cluck condescendingly on how governmental fecklessness keeps people mired in poverty. We have seen budgetary game-playing before. But in 2001, Congress and the president seem to have jointly retired the trophy.

Well, maybe not. If budgetary hell, like Dante's, has seven levels, we may have several layers yet to go. Consider, for example, the opportunity for imaginative accounting as part of Social Security reform. The Social Security deficit equals about 2 percent of payroll over the next 75 years. If an additional 2 percentage points of payroll tax is diverted to individual accounts, the deficit rises to 4 percent of payroll. If benefits for older workers and retirees and all disability and survivor benefits are excluded from benefit cuts, as President Bush has pledged, the remaining benefits would have to be cut about 44 percent on the average over the next 75 years. No plausible buildup in individual accounts could replace more than about half of that reduction.

The key to a politically acceptable reform is the use of general revenues to forestall large benefit cuts, either by funding individual accounts or subsidizing Social Security. But the general revenues necessary to ease such a transition were just spent on tax cuts.

So, what is a poor Social Security reformer to do? The responsible answer would be to suspend many of the tax cuts and use the savings either to close the deficit in Social Security or fund individual accounts. One could, for example, stop short of completely repealing the estate and gift tax by increasing the exemption and, as Peter Diamond has suggested, earmark the remaining revenue to the Social Security fund. One could reduce the ultimate rate reductions and deposit some of the revenue, either in Social Security reserves or individual accounts, according to one's pension policy tastes. In either case, the diversion of revenues from tax cuts into accumulation of reserves (public or private) would raise national saving and contribute to meeting the long-run burden of an increased elderly population.

What one fears, however, is another budgetary shell game. The instrument in this case would be "bridge loans" from the Social Security system. According to current budget rules, the Social Security trust fund could lend money for the creation of individual accounts. As long as it is assumed that these loans will be repaid within 75 years, these loans would not be treated as a net cost to the *off-budget* Social Security system. Nor, because they would come from the off-budget Social Security account, would they be recorded as an *on-budget* expenditure. Of course, one would need to assume that the return on the individual accounts would be sufficient to support such repayments as well as the buildup in individual accounts. But mechanically projecting the historical equity premium of about 5 percentage points is child's play, despite the strong evidence of stock market overvaluation presented by Robert Shiller and John Campbell. Doing so is a marvelous example of what David Cutler once called "Lotus policy analysis"—stick the number of your choice in a spreadsheet, and let the computer produce irrefutable proof by repeated compounding.

Through bridge-loan alchemy, one can create individual accounts that seem to have substance but in truth add nothing to national saving or to the nation's capacity to care for a growing elderly population. Six months ago, I would have dismissed such deceptions as too absurd for the public to swallow, but after the nonsense that marked the tax cut debate, who knows?

Thirty-five years ago, a presidential commission on budget concepts proposed reforms to improve budget accounting. It is time now to convene another presidential commission with a similar charge. Among the issues such a body should consider are how to prevent the duplicity that marked the recent tax cut debate. To be sure, no formal arrangement can ever be immune to manipulation. But the current system is getting out of hand. If we could adopt new safeguards, it might take a while for Congress and the president to discover new ways to circumvent the limits. One might be a bar on using all budget surpluses projected beyond three or four years, as Robert Reischauer has urged. In addition, such a commission could determine whether the recent ad hoc shift from the unified budget to the "on-budget" accounts (the unified budget less Social Security) should be formalized. If it does endorse this shift, it could consider whether the annual budget debate should also exclude government employee pension programs and Medicare. All of these programs represent long-term commitments on which private sector agents make long-term plans. None of them should be subject to annual buffeting. All are currently running surpluses that should be used to augment national saving.

Long-Term Projections

Steuerle reserves his most scathing label ("the most glaring economic ineffi- ciency in the federal tax system") and his liveliest prose ("determining the consumption of children ... we will never trust") for the creation of what he calls tax and transfer entitlements. I believe that his indictment confuses genu- ine abuses with perfectly respectable public policy. Steuerle tars with the same brush the ten-year phase-ins and phaseouts for tax policy, Roth IRAs and 401(k)s, Social Security, Medicare, and Medicaid.

Let's start with Roth-type savings vehicles. They require workers to pay taxes on deposits to savings accounts but exempt all withdrawals from tax (other than possible penalties for early withdrawals). Such tax policy is not more in- efficient or dishonest than ordinary IRAs or 401(k)s, just as a wage tax is not inherently more inefficient or dishonest than a consumption tax.[1] In the case of the Roth savings vehicles and the wage tax, one pays tax up front and never faces tax again. In the case of ordinary IRAs and 401(k)s and consumption taxes, one pays tax only later on, when the funds are withdrawn or used. Behavioral economics suggests that the response of savers to these mathematically equiva- lent approaches may differ. Hence, one may be preferable to the other on policy grounds. The real problem is that under the five- or 10-year budget accounting windows the timing of tax payments has been used to manipulate legislation for entirely artificial reasons. The problem is the budget rules, not the policy.

The issues concerning Medicaid, Social Security, and Medicare are quite dif- ferent from these tax issues and different from each other. Both Social Security and Medicare Hospital Insurance are currently running large surpluses. Both are projected to continue running surpluses for many years—more than two dec- ades in the case of Social Security and 15 years for Medicare. But both also face projected long-term deficits fueled by demographic shifts and, in the case of

---

1. Different economic effects may arise when converting from an income tax to a wage tax from those arising when converting from an income tax to a consumption tax. The differences arise because different transition rules may produce different effects.

Medicare, by health technology. These deficits merit early attention, and they are likely to get it. For that reason, it is simply wrong in my view to suggest that either program has tied the hands of future Congresses or presidents. Congress has twice in the past quarter century enacted significant reductions in Social Security benefits, once in 1977 and again in 1983. Were it to enact modifications no larger than those recommended by the Greenspan commission in 1983 and enacted by Congress, the projected long-term deficit would almost vanish. In 1997, Congress enacted changes in Medicare that were far from fundamental, but they were followed by reductions in the projected long-term deficit in the Health Insurance Trust Fund by two-thirds.

Let me be clear.... There are good reasons for debating the design of both Social Security and Medicare. But there is not much basis for bewailing constraints under which these programs place future Congresses or presidents. To be sure, opponents of change can filibuster in the Senate. To change these programs or other entrenched legislation is difficult. It should be. People have made plans, and institutions have been built around existing legislation. But when action is required, Social Security *has* been cut, investment tax credits *have* been repealed, capital gains tax rates *have* been raised as well as lowered. Although faith in democracy may be unfashionable, the record is clear—when the democratic will of the people is strong, action follows. With respect to Medicaid, there is no real obstacle in Washington to benefit cuts, as states remain free to choose different benefit levels. One need look no farther than the dramatic drop in rolls in the past five years.

What then is the source of Steuerle's misplaced angst that we have removed the fiscal choices of future Americans? It is, I think, a tendency to reify mechanical projections. In the bad old days, we used projections of an unindexed tax system and an unindexed Social Security system. We collectively wrung our hands over fiscal drag. We fretted over the tendency of taxes to claim ever larger hunks of our incomes. The Social Security actuaries annually reported on the enormous surpluses that would accrue even as the population aged.

Yet these problems never arose. Elected officials managed to widen tax brackets, raise exemptions, and increase standard deductions. They thereby held the income tax to a virtually unchanging proportion of personal income. Somehow Congress managed to raise Social Security benefits so that the real purchasing power of benefits remained constant.

Now we have indexed both taxes and transfers. Indexation automatically accomplishes what Congress once did manually. But tax shares have not fallen and Social Security replacement rates have not risen since adjustments became automatic. Projected revenues and benefit costs are massively sensitive over just a few years to seemingly modest policy changes or to normal economic fluctuations. When we see problems in the distant future, we should prepare gradually to meet them. But we should do so in a way that takes account of the likelihood that current projections will be wrong—*very* wrong. And we would be foolish to bewail an imagined incapacity to deal with distant imbalances based on extrapolation of arbitrary assumptions.

The Demise of an Important Reform

I believe that Steuerle's comments on the trend in tax burdens is misleading in a key respect. He mentions the reduction in capital gains tax rates, but does not, in my view, attach sufficient weight to the mischief of that policy shift in undoing the very important reforms contained in the Tax Reform Act of 1986.

He describes the history of tax rates on ordinary income clearly and accurately. The maximum tax rate on ordinary income after the Tax Reform Act of 1986 was 33 percent (a statutory rate of 28 percent, plus a 5 percentage point bubble). If the 2001 tax legislation is fully implemented, the maximum rate on ordinary income will be 35 percent, hardly a major change. Tax rates at the bottom of the income distribution, in contrast, have been dramatically reduced and are now negative for many households. The trend reflects liberalization of the earned income tax credit, introduction of the child credit (which the 2001 legislation makes partially refundable), and the addition of the 10 percent tax bracket. Indeed tax rates for all quintiles except the top quintile are lower in 2001 than those in effect following the Tax Reform Act of 1986.

Yet this rate shift has almost nothing to do with the sharp increase in the proportion of taxes collected from the richest 1 percent and 5 percent of taxpayers. This shift reflects the massive increases in incomes accruing to the wealthy. Incomes of the richest 1 percent of taxpayers rose 70.5 percent between 1987 and 1997. Over the same period incomes of the four lowest quintiles rose no more than 8.8 percent. Rather than slowing in the late 1990s, the drift to increased inequality accelerated. The richest 1 percent of filers enjoying an income rise of 33.6 percent in just the two years from 1995 to 1997.[2] To this pretax good fortune one must add the blessings of the dramatically reduced rates on long-term capital gains, more than half of which accrue to the wealthiest 1 percent of filers. In addition, the reductions in capital gains rates significantly increase the incentive to convert ordinary income into capital gains, a clear loss for simplicity and economic efficiency. The virtual elimination of the tax rate differential between ordinary income and capital gains was a keystone of the Tax Reform Act of 1986. That aspect of the reform has been thoroughly and completely gutted.

---

2. Congressional Budget Office, *Historical Effective Tax Rates, 1979–1997*, May 2001, Table G1-c, p. 74.

Comments

Leonard Burman

Gene Steuerle has done a fine job of documenting what happened in tax policy in the 1990s. Gene is ideally suited to the task, having literally written the book on tax policy in the 1980s—*The Tax Decade*. This first installment on the sequel is particularly appropriate and revealing.

I agree with Gene's analysis, but I'd like to emphasize a few points and elaborate on several others. I will start by talking a bit about the big picture—in particular, the new budget paradigm that distorted tax and budget policy in the 1990s. I will then summarize some of the good and bad things that came out of tax policy in the 1990s. Finally, I will reflect a little bit on the process.

The Importance of Budget Rules

Gene talked about the effect of budget rules in tax policy. I think that may be one of the most important features of tax policy in the 1990s. The budget rules were designed to constrain spending, and the overall budget caps clearly helped accomplish that purpose.

But they also altered the terms of trade between direct expenditures and tax expenditures. They required legislators to pay for a spending increase (above legislated discretionary caps) by cutting other spending. New tax expenditures, however, could be paid for either by a cut in spending or by an increase in other taxes. The result was that, on the margin, new spending was easier to accomplish on the tax side of the ledger than on the expenditure side.[1]

I received helpful comments from Melissa Herrick Burman, Bill Gale, Karl Scholz, and Eric Toder. Views expressed are mine alone and should not be attributed to the Urban Institute, its trustees, or its funders.
1. The White House seemed to believe that tax expenditures were much easier to accomplish than direct expenditures, but that perception may have been incorrect. Most of the revenue offsets proposed by the Clinton administration were extremely unpopular in Congress, and that fact limited the political feasibility of the tax cut proposals they would have paid for.

Consequently, new programs were more likely to be designed as inefficient tax expenditures than as direct expenditures, even if the spending program would be more effective and efficient. Much of the debate in the Clinton administration surrounded that trade-off.

That process had a perverse effect on public policy. If one assumes that the budget caps were effective, then the overall size of the government budget was fixed. Moreover, the amount of discretionary spending was also fixed (assuming that the discretionary caps were binding—a safe assumption). The only variable was the amount of tax expenditures, which were permitted to be financed by offsetting taxes. Thus, for any given size of government, a larger share of spending had to be done through inefficient tax expenditures rather than through more efficient direct expenditures. In this model, the rules that distinguish tax expenditures from direct expenditures reduce the efficiency of government without affecting its size or the overall tax burden.

If the budget constraint were not fixed, limiting marginal policies to ones that don't work might reduce the odds that those policies would be enacted. Conceivably, that could reduce the overall budget. Under the further assumption that, unconstrained, government would be too large, that trade-off might be efficient in a second-best sense.

I am reminded of an argument made by Michael Best and William Connolly (1976)—two socialist political scientists—in *The Politicized Economy*. They complained that our two-party system would never work effectively because Republicans hate government and Democrats love any new government program. So they compromise on programs that don't work. That makes the Republicans happy because it validates their view that government doesn't work. And it makes the Democrats happy because they can claim credit for all the new programs.

Arguably, Republicans offered Democrats a larger public sector so long as all the growth was on the tax side of the budget. That is, they compromised on programs that don't work very well.

Good and Bad Features of Tax Policy in the 1990s

Fiscal discipline was, I believe, the great accomplishment of the 1990s. It clearly was both a result of tax policy and also a major factor in the development of tax policy.

In the beginning of the decade, deficits were large and growing. By 1993 debt reached 50 percent of GDP. Because of the 1990 and 1993 tax increases, spending restraint, and the longest economic expansion in history, we managed to eliminate the deficits and also produce a humorous debate about the risk of surpluses that no one could have imagined ten years ago (Burman, 1999).

President Clinton deserves a lot of credit for that accomplishment. He stood up to people in his own party who wanted to increase spending and to Republicans (and some Democrats) who wanted to cut taxes when he committed to balance the budget. Of course, that commitment was not new. Ronald Reagan had made a similar pledge. What was new was the resolve to make the tough choices necessary to actually improve the budget situation, and then to close the deal when favorable budget projections showed that surpluses were actually in sight (Waldman, 2001).

By the time I got to Treasury in 1998, surpluses were a reality, and it seemed certain that nothing could prevent a large tax cut. President Clinton and his economic team, however, managed to maintain the political momentum for fiscal discipline by inventing and endlessly repeating the mantra "Save Social Security First." Orszag, Orszag, and Tyson (Chapter 14 of this volume) point out that the Social Security plan probably did not advance the prospects for meaningful reform, but it did fundamentally alter the tax and budget debate. Members of both parties eventually agreed that the portion of the surplus attributable to Social Security should be considered off limits both for new spending and tax cuts. That made it possible for President Clinton to sustain a veto of several significant (and sometimes politically popular) tax cuts in the last two years of the administration and to deter other tax cut proposals.

In addition, some worthwhile tax policies were enacted in the 1990s. Most notably in my view, taxes were cut substantially for low-income families. The earned income tax credit was expanded twice—in 1990 and 1993. The child credit, enacted in 1997, also helped millions of lower-middle-income families.

The Clinton administration also made some proposals that would have been very positive had they been enacted. When I was at Treasury (from 1998 to 2000), we proposed real relief from the alternative minimum tax (AMT) that effectively would have kept children from being treated like tax shelters for purposes of the AMT. It would have cut the number of people on the AMT in half.[2] By comparison, the tax bill that was just enacted would effect a tiny and temporary reduction in the number of people on the AMT. Moreover, it sunsets after 2004. By the end of the decade, the Joint Committee on Taxation projects that the number of people on the AMT will double. That increase is a serious problem.

But the tax system also changed in many ways for the worse. First of all, we continued the pattern of frequent tax changes. Major tax bills were enacted

2. The AMT relief proposal was the result of years of lobbying by senior tax policy staff in the Clinton administration. We were all convinced that the AMT was complicated, distortionary, unfair, and a potentially huge political liability. Because it seemed like a distant problem, it took seven years to win approval to put forward a proposal to the president, but he immediately embraced it.

in 1990, 1993 and 1997. Martin Feldstein (1976) pointed out that frequent tax changes are costly because they make it hard for businesses to plan, and the transition from one set of rules to another is costly. Tax changes also affect individuals. Politicians' compulsion to do something all the time—and especially right after presidential elections—means it's very hard for taxpayers to actually keep track of what the tax system is at any point in time.

Unfortunately, the situation does not look any more sanguine for this decade. The bill that was just enacted basically legislates a major tax change every year for the next nine years. And then it's repealed. It's safe to predict that taxpayer confusion will be the norm for some time.

In the 1990s, there was a proliferation of hidden taxes. Although they weren't invented in the last decade, the technology clearly advanced. Most notably, the phaseout of itemized deductions, enacted in 1990, adds over one percentage point to effective tax rates for most taxpayers with incomes over $100,000. The phaseout of personal exemptions, enacted the same year, adds a surtax based on family size.[3] These are hidden taxes that almost nobody understands.

There was a strange migration of education policy from the spending side of the budget to the tax side. And there were dozens of proposals for new tax expenditures. Most weren't enacted, but unfortunately those proposals are going to remain a threat to sensible tax policy for a long time. Indeed, President Bush embraced several in his budget and energy proposals.

Nonetheless, I don't share Henry Aaron's total dismay about the unraveling of the Tax Reform Act of 1986 (TRA). At the end of the decade we had lower tax rates than we did before TRA. And much of the base broadening enacted in 1986 survived the 1990s. But we definitely were moving in the wrong direction.

The deal in 1986 was broad base and low rates, but rates increased and new loopholes were created in the 1990s. As Steuerle noted, the new loopholes were mostly on the individual side of the budget, which is important. In contrast, the loopholes in the 1980s, which were eliminated by the TRA, were mostly on the business side.

The narrow base and high rates that we were trending toward is probably the worst alternative from a tax policy perspective. For example, if we had a broad base with high rates, there wouldn't be many opportunities for tax shelters, even though people would want to engage in them. We would raise a lot of revenue. As a result, the additional government savings could undo some of the damage done by having high tax rates on individuals. Although a narrow base with low rates wouldn't raise much revenue, there wouldn't be much incentive to engage in tax shelters and avoidance if rates are low. But a narrow

---

3. The 2001 tax bill will phase out both of these hidden taxes between 2005 and 2009.

tax base with high tax rates, as Steuerle points out, violates every principle of tax policy. It creates all sorts of inequities. Probably more important, it makes people feel that the tax system is unfair and that they are not getting their fair share of tax breaks. It's inefficient and it's complicated.

From my perspective, one of the worst things that comes from the proliferation of targeted tax incentives is that they create a huge constituency for tax complexity. The next tax reform will be a lot harder to attain than the last one. We can't replace a lot of targeted tax preferences with lower tax rates without raising taxes on some people.[4] And many who benefit from a special provision oppose reform in that area even though they'd like to reform other people's tax breaks.

Politicians certainly treat this perception as a constraint. The most recent tax bill illustrates the case. Congress had an opportunity to eliminate one of the most complex provisions affecting lower income people: FRED. FRED refers to Full Refundability for Excess Dependents. (It is actually partially refundable.) Under FRED, a family with three or more children could get a refundable child credit to the extent that the employee share of Social Security taxes plus individual income taxes exceeded its earned income tax credit up to the amount of the full child credit. It was very complicated. Not many people benefited from it, but it did have a cute nickname.

Largely because of very effective analysis and lobbying by people at this conference, including Robert Greenstein, Jeffrey Liebman, and Eugene Steuerle, the Senate added a new, much more generous, provision for refundability of the child tax credit to the 2001 tax bill. When it is fully phased in, the child credit will be refundable up to 15 percent of earnings above $10,000. Although it's not totally transparent, it's a lot simpler than FRED. It was obviously time to pull the plug on FRED. The new refundable credit would cut taxes for more than 90 percent of those who currently benefit from FRED—and for millions more who don't. It would make the tax system fairer and simpler.

But repealing FRED would violate the rule that nobody can pay higher taxes. A very small number of people would be worse off under the new credit. To avoid this outcome, Congress agreed to let taxpayers calculate their refundable credit under the new rules and compare that credit to the amount that they could claim under the old rules (FRED) and take the larger credit. In other words, they get the complexity of FRED *plus* the complexity of the new proposal. We now

---

4. Of course, economists know that corporate taxes also fall on people, so eliminating corporate loopholes effectively raises taxes on shareholders, workers, or consumers. However, the success of the TRA suggests that politicians and their constituents had not grasped that particular economics lesson. Indeed, a pivotal factor in the success of the TRA was the support of influential CEOs who were happy to trade higher taxes on their corporations for lower personal taxes for themselves (Birnbaum and Murray, 1988).

have not only an alternative minimum tax, but also an alternative refundable child credit. This is supposed to be something that people with a high school education or less could figure out.

At the same time that targeted tax incentives make reform less likely, they also make it much more important. People come to view the tax system as hopelessly complex and unfair, a perception that has bad effects. It undermines support for fair progressive taxation. And it even undermines the new tax incentives themselves because people can't respond to an incentive that they don't understand.

The Tax Policy Process in the Clinton Administration

I'm going to talk a little bit about the process. I saw the process more than the results because no significant tax legislation was enacted while I was at Treasury. The interesting thing about the process was that it was at least a pretty good caricature of enlightened economic decision-making. Public finance principles say that you shouldn't alter market prices unless there is a market failure. Many of the discussions that we had within the administration were about whether externalities or other market failures existed that could justify a new tax incentive.

Unfortunately, that approach didn't help quite as much as one might imagine, because advocates of tax incentives were incredibly innovative in finding market failures. But some really dumb proposals—such as the tax credit for corporate responsibility alluded to in Orszag, Orszag, and Tyson (Chapter 14)—were ultimately rejected because they could not meet minimal standards of public finance.

Another thing that was interesting and novel about this last decade was that Lawrence Summers, an economist, was the Treasury's lead on tax policy for the last half of the Clinton administration. Having an economist in such a position was an unusual and historic event. And it indicated economics was on the table as part of tax policy-making.

The National Economic Council (NEC) process, as described in Orszag et al., was another innovation aimed at improving economic policy-making. The NEC process was good in the sense that it greatly facilitated communication and co-ordination. Lone rangers were not generally running off doing their own thing. The NEC also did a great service by effectively selling the policies that we put together. That would have been hard for people at Treasury to do in a lot of cases. But the NEC played a much more active role at the end of the Clinton administration than simply a neutral honest broker. It was clearly a leader in initiating ideas for new tax incentives, many of which would not have made the tax system better were they enacted.

There was a political perception that there had to be a tangible policy response to every problem that faced the nation.[5] Every summer Gene Sperling and the NEC staff would make a list of ideas that could address these problems. Proposals were grouped into broad theme areas such as education, economic development, housing, health care, worker training, bridging the digital divide, encouraging philanthropy, energy, and climate change. (Lawrence Summers added one on vaccines.) And program agencies would add numerous additional ideas.

The NEC was incredibly effective at creating ideas that sounded like they might work. But the problem was that the new tax incentives would have added great complexity to a system that people already don't understand. Even though most of the really bad ideas were ultimately rejected as a result of the NEC process (informed by terrific staff work by the nonpartisan staff in the Treasury's Office of Tax Policy), the constant flow of complicated proposals tied up Treasury staff and got in the way of necessary improvements to the models used for revenue estimating and distributional analysis, basic research that might have informed future policy development, and regulations to implement tax laws already passed.

There also was a sense that we had to have rapid reactions to issues that are on the table. I think tax policy is an extraordinarily poor instrument for rapid reaction to short-term policy problems.

And then there were some policy accomplishments that wouldn't be worth winning. For example, after lengthy negotiations with auto manufacturers, the White House's Council on Environmental Quality proposed a tax credit for highly fuel efficient "hybrid" vehicles. A hybrid automobile stores much of the energy typically lost in braking in a battery, which is then used to boost the car back to cruising speed after a stop. If widely adopted, such cars would clearly improve the environment and reduce greenhouse gas emissions. The problem was that American auto manufacturers would not be able to produce hybrid vehicles until at least 2003, while Honda and Toyota were ready to bring theirs to market in 2000. The U.S. car manufacturers did not want to subsidize Japanese companies, so they insisted that the credit be delayed until 2003. Had the credit been enacted, it would have given American consumers an incentive *not* to purchase the most fuel-efficient cars in the market.

---

5. Ironically, this process may have accelerated at the end of the Clinton administration. Waldman (2000) observes that the administration felt intense pressure to show that it was continuing to function during the Lewinsky scandal and impeachment. Many of the budget proposals that came out of the NEC process ultimately became the subject of a Saturday morning radio address or a speech by the president.

On balance, things did not turn out so badly, in large part because of Gene Sperling and the NEC. On the really big issue of fiscal responsibility, the administration was focused and effective. Balancing the budget was a huge policy triumph. Moreover, the administration's commitment to fiscal discipline combined with the difficulty of coming up with politically acceptable revenue offsets prevented most of the tax proposals (good and bad) from becoming law.

Unfortunately, the surpluses that came from that fiscal discipline mean that the current administration is not operating under the same constraints.

References

Best, Michael H., and William E. Connolly. 1976. *The Politicized Economy*. Lexington, MA: Heath.

Birnbaum, Jeffrey H., and Alan S. Murray. 1988. *Showdown at Gucci Gulch: Lawmakers, Lobbyists, and the Unlikely Triumph of Tax Reform*. New York: Vintage Books.

Burman, Leonard E. 1999. "Surplus Tax Policy?" *National Tax Journal*, 52, no. 3 (September): 405–411.

Feldstein, Martin. 1976. "On the Theory of Tax Reform." *Journal of Public Economics*, 77–104.

Waldman, Michael. 2000. *POTUS Speaks: Finding the Words That Defined the Clinton Presidency*. New York: Simon and Schuster.

Comments

William A. Niskanen

Eugene Steuerle's summary and analysis of federal tax policy in the 1990s effectively covers all of the major issues except one—the relation between taxes and spending. He acknowledges, "Of course, in parallel with the debate over tax rates is the debate over the size of government." And he observes, "Some believe that higher taxes almost inevitably will be spent inefficiently, so that government spending should be constrained by keeping rates low. Others believe that societal demands for different types of public goods required higher taxes." But that is all; he does not present any evidence of the actual relation between taxes and spending during this period or the implications of this relation.

As Steuerle observes, both the right and the left appear to believe that an increase in federal tax receipts would increase federal spending. The actual relation between spending and taxes during both the 1980s and 1990s, however, was quite different. Figure 3.7 presents federal spending and tax receipts as a percent of GDP by calendar year from 1981 through 2000. As this figure illustrates, most of the changes in the relative level of federal spending were coincident with changes in the federal tax burden in the *opposite* direction. Figure 3.8, which presents the same data as a scatter diagram, makes this point more dramatically; for 20 years, there has been a strong *negative* relation between the relative level of federal spending and tax receipts. Over the past 20 years, the increase in federal tax receipts from 17.6 percent to 20.7 percent of GDP was associated with a *reduction* in federal spending from 22.6 percent to 18.2 percent of GDP.

What is going on? The most direct interpretation of Figure 3.8 is that it represents a demand curve, with federal spending a negative function of the tax price. But what else happened during this period that may be a better explanation of this simple negative relation between federal spending and taxes?

A reexamination of the time pattern in Figure 3.7 suggests one answer: an increase in the unemployment rate increased federal spending and reduced federal revenues; for this reason, an estimate of the relation between federal taxes

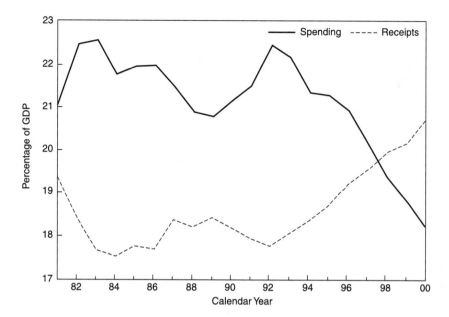

Figure 3.7
Federal Expenditures and Receipts

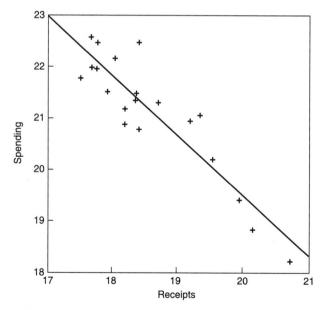

Figure 3.8
Relation of Spending and Receipts (percent of GDP)

and spending should control for the unemployment rate. A second plausible answer is that the increasing focus of fiscal policy on reducing the deficit led to a combination of measures that reduced the growth of federal spending and increased taxes; for this reason, an estimate of the relation between taxes and spending should also control for the fiscal balance in the prior year. A third important fiscal change during this period was the increase in the relative level of federal expenditures for national defense and net interest outlays through 1985 and the subsequent general decline of these fixed costs; for this reason, an estimate of the relation between taxes and spending should also control for the relative level of expenditures for national defense and net interest outlays. During the conference, one participant offered a fourth alternative interpretation: the income elasticity of demand for federal spending may be less than one; but this interpretation seems inconsistent with the substantial growth of the federal spending share of GDP over a longer period.

The relation between federal spending and taxes during this period is best summarized by the following least-squares regression:

$$S = 27.75 + .49U - .52R + .66AR(1) + u$$
$$\quad (3.48) \quad (.10) \quad (.16) \quad (.18)$$

$$R^2 = .93 \quad S.E.R = .30 \quad D.W. = 1.63$$

where S is total current federal expenditures as a percent of GDP, U is the unemployment rate of civilian workers, R is total current federal receipts as a percent of GDP, $AR(1)$ is an adjustment for autocorrelation, and the numbers in parentheses are the standard errors.

Two other variables were also tested and found to have had *no* significant effect on relative federal spending: the relative level of the budget surplus or deficit in the prior year and the relative level of federal expenditures for national defense and net interest outlays. A recognition that the unemployment rate and federal receipts may be endogenous also led me to reestimate this equation using a two-stage regression; the results are nearly identical.

The major lessons from this regression are that (1) almost all of the variation in federal spending as a percent of GDP during this period is explained by only two conditions; (2) for a given level of federal tax receipts, federal spending increased by about one-half percent of GDP for each one percentage point increase in the unemployment rate; (3) for a given unemployment rate, federal spending *declined* by about one-half percent of GDP for each one percentage point increase in the relative level of federal tax receipts; and (4) the balance of spending and receipts in the prior year and the relative level of spending for national defense and net interest payments had *no* significant effect on federal spending during this period.

This note is offered more as a puzzle than as a conclusive challenge to the conventional wisdom on these fiscal issues. For this reason, the following observations are offered more as implications to be considered than as conclusions:

1. Both the right and the left may not be correct in their shared belief that an increase in relative federal tax receipts is likely to lead to an increase in relative federal spending.

2. At least in the short run, the budget surplus or deficit has no apparent effect on the relative level of federal spending.

3. Total federal spending in a mature welfare state may be independent of spending for national defense and net interest payments.

4. And politicians of both parties may have a special incentive to approve a tax reduction if they expect to control the allocation of the resulting additional spending. The Reagan tax cut, for example, may have reduced the perceived price of the Reagan defense buildup. In contrast, the Bush I and Clinton tax increases may have reduced the political support for Clinton's major health care proposal. Finally, with no further reduction in the unemployment rate in prospect, the recent Bush II tax reduction may *increase* the relative level of future federal spending.

The long-term implications of this relation are more disturbing. In the absence of effective constitutional constraints, the politics of fiscal policy for both parties may lead to an ultimately unsustainable combination of spending increases and tax reductions. As an economist with a commitment to fiscal responsibility, I am concerned that tax cuts, within the relevant range, may increase federal spending. As a libertarian with a commitment to limited constitutional government, I am concerned that a tax increase may be the most effective policy to reduce the relative size of government. On these issues, I would be pleased to be proven wrong.

Peter Orszag noted that given political economy constraints, there was some optimal level of complexity in the tax system, and that the optimal level was unlikely to be zero. The political bias against spending programs, along with the potential inefficiencies in spending programs as well as tax programs, according to Orszag, means that some important public objectives would not be pursued if tax policy were devoted solely to achieving a broad base and low tax rate. Orszag then asked whether new computer software that helped individuals complete their tax forms could increase the optimal level of complexity by making tax preparation easier.

Leonard Burman agreed that one cannot rule out all tax expenditures simply because they have an efficiency cost. (Direct expenditure programs are not perfect either, he noted.) However, he said, there should be a "high hurdle" when adding complexity. This means that additional complexity should be created only when something important is achieved in return. He noted that the Treasury Department's *Green Book* (which describes the administration's tax proposals) in 2001 was about 250 pages long, suggesting a substantial degree of complexity in the proposals.

On the issue of computer software for tax preparation, *Burman* said that software might reduce the problem of the complexity of taxes for some, but he noted that low-income Americans are much less likely to have access to this technology. Even if everyone had access to the software, he said, it is not clear that tax incentives should be implemented if people do not understand how those incentives actually affect them, as could happen if taxpayers merely punch numbers into a computer and get back the amount they owe. *Orszag* thought that popular software already ensures, through alerts and help menus, that taxpayers are at least partially aware of the incentives provided by the tax code for various activities.

Martin Feldstein asked *Gene Sperling* whether Republicans were to blame for the Clinton administration's apparent use of tax expenditures rather than direct expenditures. That is, Republicans accused Democrats of being the party of taxing and spending, so the Clinton administration responded by finding a way to achieve implicit spending objectives while ostensibly reducing taxes.

Sperling responded that he largely agreed with that statement. He argued that while academic and policy analysts debated the relative benefits of tax expenditures and direct expenditures, the political reality was much different. In higher education policy, for example, any proposed increases in spending would simply not have been passed by the Republican Congress. Given this constraint, along with a desire to promote higher education, the policy-relevant question was how to design the best possible tax cut. The tax cut for higher education was targeted to middle-income families, he noted. He also mentioned several cases in which the administration fought for the refundability of tax credits, which was crucial in order to ensure that a tax-based approach to policy-making was consistent with a more progressive distribution of resources. He said he was unapologetically happy that the administration was able to enact the so-called FRED provisions within the child tax credit (which allows partial refundability of the credit for families with three or more children) because it "paved the ground for doing even more."

Sperling concluded by noting that it was unclear whether small steps toward simplification, as opposed to dramatic simplification, would be particularly beneficial to the American public. He argued that because of the EITC and the number of people using EZ forms, the American public is not demanding marginal simplification measures. Without evidence that individuals face a great burden in filling out their taxes, he concluded that the advocates of tax simplification are left mainly with efficiency arguments.

Rebecca Blank said that the discussion of tax expenditures versus direct expenditures reminded her of the voluminous economic literature on in-kind welfare programs as opposed to simple cash transfer programs. She noted that one reason for favoring in-kind programs was for political reasons—just as there were political reasons to favor tax expenditures. Another reason related to the question, Whose utility do you want to maximize? For example, she said, one might care about making certain groups better off (such as low-income families). But one might also care a great deal about the preferences and tastes of the average taxpayer, she explained. From that perspective, having tightly constrained programs that select a targeted group of recipients and provide limited transfers under specific conditions may make sense. She concluded that tax expenditures, like in-kind programs, may be better from a social perspective even though in some perfect economic world they were less efficient.

Henry Aaron responded that there was no doubt that taxpayers' preferences were involved in choosing tax policy, just as they were in choosing the optimal transfer program. He noted that most Americans were not income egalitarians, but commodity egalitarians. In other words, they care less about income distribution and more about whether their fellow citizens receive food, housing, and schooling. That was the primary motivation for in-kind transfers, he said, and it could also explain the structure of certain targeted tax incentives.

Burman said that the most important aspect of the tax system was that it raise revenue in a fair way. His concern, he explained, was that the addition of so many special tax preferences caused people to have the sense that the system is unfair. He argued that it would be easier to judge the system's fairness if one could simply look at the rate schedule and possibly a handful of special incentives that one qualified for. Given dozens of special incentives, however, such judgments were more difficult. In the case of higher education, he noted, there were at least seven different tax incentives that overlapped, making it very difficult for anyone, especially those without higher education, to figure out which one to take.

On the issue of tax complexity, *William Niskanen* said that while he favored a simple tax system, the experience following the 1986 tax reform suggested that this type of reform was not politically sustainable without a change in congressional voting rules on taxes. Congress began to raise rates almost immediately after the 1986 reform was passed. (With a broad base, he noted, an increase in tax rates generated more revenue than it did before the base broadening.) He therefore suggested that tax reform be accompanied by new voting rules—either by a constitutional reform to lock in tax rates or by a requirement of a supermajority vote on tax increases.

Gene Steuerle concluded by arguing that tax complexity raised an equity issue in addition to its efficiency costs. With complex tax provisions, Steuerle argued, taxes are unequally distributed across people with equal needs—violating a fundamental principle of equal justice. Furthermore, complexity also leads to bad government: incomprehensible policies—whether on the tax or expenditure side—should be avoided. He concluded that complexity does not necessarily deserve the "prime seat" at the policy table, but rather *a* seat.

4   International Finance and Crises in Emerging Markets

Between Meltdown and Moral Hazard: The International Monetary and Financial Policies of the Clinton Administration[1]

J. Bradford DeLong and Barry Eichengreen

PANELISTS: *Stanley Fischer, Lawrence Summers, and Allan H. Meltzer*

4.1   Introduction

There was no reason at the outset for thinking that international monetary and financial questions would feature so prominently in the activities of the Clinton administration. They had absorbed far less time and attention during the presidency of George Herbert Walker Bush than the budget deficit, the trade deficit, the 1990–91 recession, and any number of other strictly economic problems.[2] International monetary and financial issues were hardly mentioned in a campaign whose final months coincided with an episode of serious currency-market instability in Europe. Yet the Mexican rescue, the Asian crisis, and reform of the international financial system turned out to be major preoccupations of the new president and his advisers.

It has been suggested that there is a regular cycle in the term of a political leader in countries like the United States.[3] First is the naive phase in which

---

1. Sam Saddigh and Salah Mattoo provided valuable research assistance. We thank, without implicating, Caroline Atkinson, Fred Bergsten, Stanley Fischer, Jeffrey Frankel, Jeff Frieden, Timothy Geithner, Peter Kenen, David Lipton, Sherman Robinson, Dani Rodrik, Jeffrey Shafer, Larry Summers, Dan Tarullo, Ted Truman, and Janet Yellen.
2. Not to mention Operation Desert Storm, German reunification, and the collapse of the Soviet Union.
3. See Bergsten (1986) and Frankel (1994).

international monetary and financial concerns (and perhaps also trade) are essentially ignored because the leader has typically won his office by courting exclusively domestic constituencies and is not fully aware of the connections between domestic and international issues (including the constraints imposed on his domestic ambitions by international factors). There then follows the more mature phase, as the leader becomes more aware of international economic relations and international diplomacy offers a useful diversion of popular attention from domestic conflicts. In the case of the Clinton administration, although the president and his staff wanted to focus on health care, welfare, public investment, education, and the information superhighway, in its first two years the Clinton White House failed to win the support of a divided Senate for major domestic initiatives other than the 1993 Clinton-Mitchell-Foley deficit-reduction package. And following the loss of Democratic control of the Congress in 1994, all ambitious domestic initiatives were obviously dead in the water. If this fact didn't exactly create a political vacuum and a demand for newspaper headlines that could only be filled by international events, it at least facilitated the efforts of Treasury and other economic agencies to bring these issues to the attention of the president and his core political advisors.

But there were also fundamental structural reasons for this shift within the administration, notably the growing importance of international financial markets. Portfolio capital flows to emerging-market countries had begun growing explosively, reflecting the effects of the Brady Plan restructurings in clearing away problem debts and the progress of economic reform in Latin America, at about the same time the Democratic candidates started spending significant amounts of time and money in New Hampshire (see Figure 4.1). The information and communications revolution that would become the subject of so much attention and hubris was already quietly under way; among its effects was to greatly reduce the cost, and thereby stimulate the volume, of foreign-exchange trading and cross-border financial flows generally.[4]

Moreover, domestic deregulation in many countries had already made it more difficult to halt capital flows at the border by opening up new channels for response and evasion by financial institutions. And the recognition in the 1980s that capital controls were better at redistributing wealth to friends of the ruling party than at allocating scarce foreign currency to the most developmentally

---

4. The Bank for International Settlements, in its triannual survey of the level of foreign exchange turnover, estimated that the volume of foreign exchange trading worldwide rose by 42 percent between 1989 and 1992, by a further 48 percent between 1992 and 1995, and by a slower but still substantial 25 percent between 1995 and 1998.

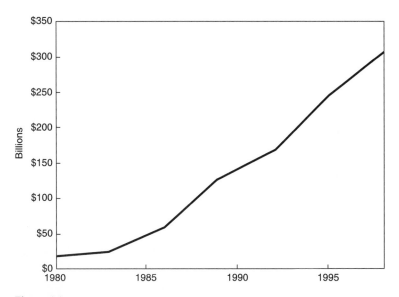

Figure 4.1
Daily Turnover in U.S. Foreign Exchange Markets. (*Source:* Federal Reserve Bank of New York, Bank for International Settlements, Jeffrey Frankel. Datafile: http://www.j-bradford-delong.net/ Econ_Articles/CIEP/CIEP_data/forex_trading.xls.)

productive uses had undermined support for their utilization. Reflecting both the fact and the ethos of financial liberalization, controls on capital flows in both advanced-industrial and developing countries were already on their way out.[5] As video terminals displaying real-time financial information began popping up on the desks of senior political staff all over Washington, international financial problems acquired a potential political salience that they had not possessed in many years.

In this paper we analyze how it was that this potential for salience became actual, review the efforts of the Clinton administration to grapple with the monetary and financial consequences, and assess the results of its policies. It is often said that this was an administration that thrived on or even was defined by crises. It is thus no surprise that our analysis of its international monetary and financial policies should focus on the Mexican peso crisis, the Asian financial

---

5. Naturally, this shift first became evident in the advanced-industrial countries. There, the turning point was the Single European Act of 1986, which required its signatories to dismantle their remaining capital controls in order to forge a single financial market, something they did in the run-up to 1992. In developing countries, the prevalence of capital controls, multiple exchange rates, and export surrender requirements reached a local maximum in 1991 before declining sharply and monotonically thereafter. See Eichengreen, Mussa, et al. (1998), Figure 7.

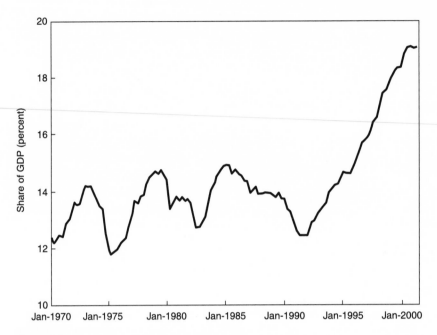

Figure 4.2
Fixed Private Domestic Investment as a Share of Real GDP, 1970–2000. (*Source:* Federal Reserve Bank of St. Louis via http://www.economagic.com/. Datafile: http://www.j-bradford-delong.net/ Econ_Articles/CIEP/CIEP_data/inv_share_real*.xls.)

crisis, and the crisis of confidence and legitimacy of the international monetary and financial system.[6]

There was also a broader context, however, for the decisions taken in response to these events. That context was an economic and political strategy that emphasized private investment as the engine for U.S. economic growth (see Figure 4.2). Both components of this term, "private" and "investment," had implications for the administration's international economic strategy. From the point of view of investment, it was important that international events not pressure the Federal Reserve to raise interest rates, since such increases would have curtailed capital formation and vitiated the effects of the administration's signature achievement: deficit reduction. A strong dollar—or rather a dollar that was not expected to weaken—was a key component of a policy that aimed at keeping the Fed comfortable with low interest rates. In addition, it was important to create a demand for the goods and services generated by this additional

6. Space constraints require us to be selective about the issues we consider. Thus we do not consider a variety of additional topics and episodes ranging from support for Russian reform at the start of the decade to the Turkish crisis at its end.

productive capacity. To the extent that this demand resided abroad, administration officials saw it as important that the process of increasing international integration, of both trade and finance, move forward for the interest of economic development in emerging markets and therefore in support of U.S. economic growth.[7]

This was all part of a "New Democratic" agenda that placed more faith in and emphasis on the private sector—on market forces—than had been true of previous 20th-century Democratic administrations. In an era of financial liberalization, this in turn meant relying on financial markets. Symbolic of this commitment was the president's reliance on Robert Rubin, an individual possessing long experience in those markets, first as head of his National Economic Council (NEC) and then as his Treasury secretary. Rubin's experience in the markets informed the administration's support for financial and capital account liberalization, as well as domestic financial liberalization, which extended to emerging markets as well as the United States.

Indisputably, the policy of moving forward with the liberalization of domestic and international financial transactions, even though corporate governance and prudential supervision remained underdeveloped in many of the emerging markets participating in this trend, comprised part of the setting for the financial crises that so disrupted the 1990s. Though the United States was not solely responsible for the adoption of these policies, which also reflected the operation of the deeper forces described earlier, the administration at least acquiesced to their pursuit. At the same time, Rubin's long experience in the markets had rendered him somewhat skeptical of their efficiency. In his view, markets reach for yield and are prone to excess (Rubin, in press), tendencies that render periodic crises all but inevitable.[8] This view that markets provided the best approach to economic development, but that they still succumb to crises from time to time, informed the Clinton Treasury's approach to crisis management and shaped its efforts to strengthen the international financial architecture.

Before proceeding, it behooves us to make a few comments on methodology. The literature on the political economy of policy-making is organized around the tripartite distinction between ideas, institutions, and interests. It asks whether policy choices are shaped mainly by intellectual outlook and ideological predisposition, by institutional and bureaucratic constraints, or by the lobbying efforts of special interest groups. Given the difficulty of measuring the influence,

---

7. "Open markets work. Open societies are resilient and just. And together they offer the best hope for lifting people's lives," as Secretary of State Madeline Albright put it during the Asian crisis. *South China Morning Post* (29 July 1998), http://special.scmp.com/AsianCrisis/.

8. This is very similar to the view of Alan Greenspan, another individual whose views strongly informed and shaped the economic policies of the 1990s (as described by Gregory Mankiw in Chapter 1 of this volume).

quantifying the importance, and testing the significance of these factors, scholars generally attribute some role to each. For better or for worse, our analysis is subject to these same limitations and, predictably, adopts this same synthetic posture. But, relative to other historical analyses of the same events (once they come to exist), we place disproportionate emphasis on the first two of the three *i*'s (ideas and institutions). Try as we may, we find it hard to frame our discussion of the international monetary and financial policies of the Clinton administration as a response to special interest politics—to tell the story of exchange-rate politics in terms of lobbying by export- and import-competing interests or the story of bailouts as a response to the pressure applied by self-interested investment and commercial banks. On many of the policy issues under review here, otherwise cohesive lobbies were divided. And the technical nature of financial issues—in contrast to trade, for example—provided those responsible for policy with a degree of natural insulation.[9]

It is tempting to dismiss our emphasis on the role of ideas as the predictable preoccupation of academics who habitually exaggerate the importance of the scribbling of defunct economists.[10] That said, the Clinton administration was distinctive for the participation, at the highest levels, of academics who had helped to shape the scholarly literature and were in turn receptive to the arguments of the academic community. This was an administration and an issue area where ideas mattered more than most.

But the overarching theme of our paper, if it has one, is the role of institutional constraints in shaping the Clinton administration's international monetary and financial policies. In any administration the Treasury Department, as the listening post for Wall Street and the agency vested with responsibility for U.S. exchange-rate policy, will play a prominent role in the formulation of international monetary and financial policies. It will possess both agenda-setting and veto powers. But what was distinctive about the Clinton administration

9. To be sure, that insulation was less than complete. An example is administration initiatives to see that the private sector was "bailed in" rather than "bailed out" when officials came to the rescue of crisis countries. Evaluating the influence of "Wall Street" on the administration's stance on this question is difficult. On the one hand, Treasury was constantly at odds (one insider characterizes it as "at war") with the Institute of International Finance (IIF), the organization that spoke for the banks. Treasury viewed the IIF's analyses as underdeveloped and obstructionist. On the other hand, Treasury backed away from its initial enthusiasm for mandating changes in contractual arrangements in favor of the voluntary approach preferred by the IIF, and in the end there was a strong similarity between Treasury's views and those of the various IIF working group reports. Whether this reflected common intellectual influences or the pressure applied to the official sector by financial interests is hard for outsiders to say. We describe the evolution of this policy in more detail in Section 4.5.

10. As Keynes went on to say in the same famous passage we paraphrase, "I am sure that the power of vested interests is vastly exaggerated compared with the gradual encroachment of ideas."

was Treasury's disproportionate influence. In part this reflected the growing importance of market sentiment in an era of financial liberalization. No policy was workable that would not be favorably received by the markets; consequently, a Treasury Department attuned to market sentiment, led by much of the period by a secretary with long experience in the markets, had more agenda-setting and veto power than most. In addition, analytical capacity, when it came to international monetary matters, was heavily concentrated at 1500 Pennsylvania Avenue. The White House lacked the staff and rival departments lacked the expertise to develop ideas sufficiently to argue them persuasively.[11] Treasury could thus exercise its veto simply by demanding a full-blown, coherent proposal, knowing that one would not be forthcoming. Among other things, our story thus illustrates how policy is affected when an administration allows one agency to become so disproportionately powerful.

4.2   The Strong Dollar Policy

When President-elect Clinton assembled a star-studded cast of experts in Little Rock during the interregnum between the election and the inauguration, he did not question them about the problem of managing capital flows and averting threats to international financial stability.[12] His concerns, indicative of the times, were rather with the trade and budget deficits, and his predispositions, unsurprisingly for a Democrat, were activist. One prominent academic well known to this audience won no points with the president-elect when he responded to a question about what should be done about the trade deficit by saying, in essence,

---

11. How this situation came about is properly regarded as the subject of another paper. But we cannot resist a few words. In part, the creation of the National Economic Council defined the natural counterweight to Treasury within the executive branch, but one that, as it happened, was grossly understaffed, particularly on the international financial side. The NEC's occasional Treasury detailees provided no solution to this problem given their knowledge that they would not get good assignments back at the Treasury if they were too tough on their home agency during their detail to the White House. And rivalry between the NEC and the Council of Economic Advisers prevented the latter from providing the needed input. Treasury, for its part, had little interest in addressing this problem. While Treasury staff had a high regard for NEC staff, they also knew that the Clinton NEC staff were more interested in the substance of policy than the typical staffer belonging to the White House Office of Policy Development. Treasury staff feared what would happen under some future administration if the White House staff's voice in international economic policy was amplified. They had only to look to the relationship between the State Department and the National Security Council. The half-century-long bureaucratic war between State and the NSC had led to some notable foreign policy disasters as underbriefed NSC staff shut State Department expertise out of the policy-planning process. Consider for example the U.S. tilt toward the genocidal dictator Yahya Khan when he decided to kill everyone with a college education in what was then East Pakistan, or the transfer of weapons to Iran in the 1980s.

12. Although there was one prominent exchange over the dollar, as we will describe later.

"nothing." Clinton's eventual choice to head the Council of Economic Advisers, Laura Tyson of the University of California, Berkeley, arrived in Washington with a reputation for advocating the aggressive use of trade policy to pry open foreign markets with the goal of bringing down the trade deficit.

There were impediments, of course, to the aggressive use of trade policy.[13] The United States had already concluded a major free-trade agreement with Canada. It had its GATT commitments. The promise of closer trade relations was an obvious way of supporting economic liberalization and democratization in Latin America and the former Soviet bloc. Candidate Clinton had already opted to support NAFTA and the Uruguay Round during the 1992 campaign out of a conviction that the economy had to move forward and not backward (where "forward" in part meant embracing globalization) and in order to define himself as a New Democrat (thereby distinguishing his views from those of the then-prevailing congressional Democratic position). The traditional constituency for protection, the import-competing manufacturing belt, figured less importantly in the U.S. economy and therefore in the political debate than it had a decade before, while U.S. exporters of goods and services, financial services in particular, had gained additional voice and were unlikely to look sympathetically on the use of trade-unfriendly measures. Although the administration made use of antidumping measures, both those to which it was entitled under the General Agreement on Tariffs and Trade and unilateral measures such as Super 301 (Section 301 of the 1988 Omnibus Trade and Competitiveness Act), its commitment to free trade was never in doubt.[14]

The one instrument obviously available for addressing the trade deficit and the concerns of import-competing producers was the level of the dollar. There were several reasons for thinking that the new administration might try to talk or push down the dollar. This had been the observed behavior, or at least the imputed temptation, of previous incoming Democratic presidents: Franklin D. Roosevelt had depreciated the dollar to deal with the macroeconomic problems he inherited, and it was widely (but mistakenly) thought that John F. Kennedy would do the same when he took office in 1961. Treasury secretaries hailing from Texas (James Baker and John Connolly), closer to the country's commodity-producing heartland than its financial center, had a record of favoring a weak dollar; thus Clinton's selection of Lloyd Bentsen as his Treasury secretary was taken in some circles as a signal of the administration's prospective approach to the exchange rate.

---

13. Trade policy is properly the subject of Chapter 5 in this volume, by Robert Lawrence. We touch on it here because it provides part of the context for the subject of this section, namely, the evolution of the strong dollar policy.

14. The incidence of antidumping actions fluctuated with the level of the dollar, falling between 1992 and 1995, along with the currency, and rising thereafter (Knetter and Prusa, 2000).

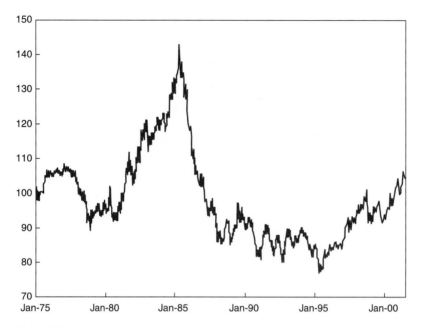

Figure 4.3
Value of the Dollar Against Major Currencies, 1975–2000. (*Source:* Federal Reserve Board. Datafile:
http://www.j-bradford-delong.net/Econ_Articles/CIEP/CIEP_data/weekly_major_curr.xls.)

Nor can it be argued that anything that could remotely be called a strong dollar policy was in place in the early Clinton years. The dollar declined from Y125 when Clinton took office to Y80 two years later, an exceptionally sharp swing in a short period even by the standards of the 1970s and 1980s (see Figure 4.3).[15] The "economic populists" in the White House (George Stephanopoulos, for example) saw a weaker dollar as useful for enhancing U.S. international competitiveness. Secretary Bentsen saw it as potentially helpful for solving the trade-deficit problem.[16] U.S. Trade Representative Mickey Kantor saw a weaker dollar as giving him leverage in trade negotiations, since he could argue that it was Japan's "unfair advantage" due to barriers to imports of automobiles and parts that was responsible for the weak currency that found disfavor among foreign governments.

15. While the dollar strengthened against the Mexican peso and the Canadian dollar, moderating the decline in the (trade-weighted) effective exchange rate, it was the yen-dollar rate that drew the attention of financial market participants and the concern of policy-makers.
16. Bentsen's reputation for favoring a weaker dollar resulted from an offhand response to a reporter's question about whether he would like to see the dollar fall, to which he responded that he wouldn't mind seeing the yen rise. Seeing how such comments could be interpreted, Bentsen then shifted course and made every effort to cultivate the image of a strong money man. But the damage was done.

That said, there were several causes for concern over the weakness of the dollar. The currency's decline hurt rather than helped with the trade deficit in the short run because of the J-curve effect (that is, the tendency for import prices to rise before import volumes began to fall). Its slide threatened to fan inflation. Fears of inflation and about the sustainability of the external deficit combined to raise the specter of higher interest rates, which unsettled the financial markets.[17] The dollar's continued decline created financial volatility and increased the cost of credit by inflicting losses on financial firms (hedge funds, among others) that had shorted the yen and deutsche mark in late 1993 and early 1994.[18]

At a deeper level, the strong dollar policy was part and parcel with the administration's overall fiscal and monetary strategy. Clinton had fought the election on the basis of a middle-class tax cut and additional public spending on infrastructure and skill formation, but his administration inherited an exploding budget deficit that left little room for such initiatives. The only hope was that deficit reduction would bring down interest rates and create an environment conducive to faster economic growth and therefore to the shared prosperity that the candidate had promised the middle and working classes. As a result of a series of internal struggles (colorfully recounted by Woodward, 1994, and Reich, 1997), the decision was made to eschew substantial new spending programs and middle-class tax cuts and to focus instead on fiscal consolidation in order to create a financial environment conducive to investment and growth.

How was the level of the dollar related to this choice? Reducing the interest rates on which investment depended was the key to stimulating faster growth.[19] The Federal Open Market Committee, it was hoped, would see fiscal consolidation as implying a reduction in inflationary pressure and respond by cutting rates. Its members were most likely to do so if the financial markets perceived things the same way—that is, if bond prices responded positively.

From this perspective, a weak exchange rate was a danger. In a world of international mobile capital, U.S. interest rates would inevitably exceed foreign interest rates to the extent that the dollar was expected to fall (by virtue of the arbitrage condition known as interest parity). Moreover, since expectations of higher import prices were something to which the Federal Reserve looked

---

17. See, for example, "Weaker Greenback Campaign Heats Up," *Capital Markets Report*, Dow Jones News Service, Dec. 10, 1996.

18. See International Monetary Fund (1994).

19. Within two years of the president's inauguration, the Council of Economic Advisers was highlighting the close connection between investment and productivity growth, thus suggesting that the lower interest rates needed to boost investment were the key to faster growth (Council of Economic Advisers, 1995, pp. 27–28). Lower interest rates also had the ancillary advantage of addressing the problem of chronic budget deficits by reducing debt-servicing costs.

when forecasting inflation, the prospect of a falling dollar fanned fears among financial-market participants of rising Federal Reserve discount rates.

For these and other reasons, the belief that the administration might push the dollar down, perhaps in response to pressures emanating from domestic auto and steel producers, had to be vanquished in order to reap the full benefits of deficit reduction and to implement its investment-led growth strategy.

The president himself appears to have instinctually understood the connections between the stability of the dollar and his administration's fiscal-cum-growth strategy, as the press noted when covering the Economic Summit held in Little Rock during the interregnum.[20] Undersecretary Summers saw the linkage between exchange-rate policy and interest-rate policy from his arrival at Treasury and was the main opponent in these early days of arguments in favor of pushing down the dollar.[21] Deputy Secretary Roger Altman gave these arguments a name—the strong dollar policy—at a meeting in Summers' office in the summer of 1994. The relative strength of the Treasury Department vis-à-vis Commerce and others within the Clinton administration also played a role, as the standard arguments put forth in every administration by Treasury staff and principals had greater weight in the 1990s.

Bold public advocacy of a strong dollar policy was inaugurated by the transition from Secretary Bentsen to Secretary Rubin at Treasury at the beginning of 1995.[22] Rubin, while head of the NEC, had been central to the campaign for

---

20. "A strong dollar and a relatively conservative fiscal policy seem likely to form a central part of the Clinton administration's strategy for improving long-term economic performance," the *Financial Times* led its story covering the economic conference on December 16, 1992. "'I'm for a strong dollar,' declared President-elect Bill Clinton during a debate about exchange rate policy at the economic conference.... Mr. Clinton, however, added the proviso that the dollar could be strong in the long term only if supported by 'the underlying competitive reality of our economy.' ... Mr. Clinton's remarks on the dollar were a response to Professor Rudi Dornbusch of the Massachusetts Institute of Technology, who urged a substantial devaluation of the dollar against Asian currencies over the next three years. Mr. Dornbusch said financial markets were likely to anticipate a stronger dollar as the US economy recovered but that 'we cannot afford that.'"

21. Summers reportedly clashed with U.S. Trade Representative Kantor and Commerce Secretary Ronald Brown in a closed-door meeting, after they had mused publicly that a weaker exchange rate might not be so bad (*Business Week*, Mar. 20, 1995, p. 45). Summers publicly stated as early as August 1993 that a strong yen (a more convenient name to attach to the phenomenon, in the tradition of Bentsen, than a weak dollar) was not in the interest of the U.S. economy. All this makes it peculiar that Summers' commitment to the policy was questioned when he succeeded Rubin as Treasury secretary in 1999.

22. Bentsen had asserted in a July 1994 speech in New York that the administration favored "a stronger dollar," but any impact on the markets was offset by the president's statement at the G-7 summit in Naples a few days later that "it is important not to overreact" to the currency's weakness. Combined with Bentsen's jawboning of the Fed not to raise interest rates, the impression, according to financial commentary, was that the administration still favored a weaker dollar. See *Wall Street Journal Europe* (July 12, 1994), p. 10; *Economist* (July 16, 1994), p. 74.

lower interest rates as a way of energizing U.S. economic growth, and Summers' analytical arguments against pushing down the dollar coincided with Rubin's instincts honed by years of experience in financial markets and with the views of Treasury staff. In his confirmation hearings before the Senate Finance Committee, Rubin stated that a strong dollar was in the best interest of the U.S. economy and warned that the exchange rate should not be used as an instrument of U.S. trade policy.

The new approach acquired prominence as a result of three events in the spring of 1995. First, there was the prime-time news conference on April 19 during which Clinton stated that the United States "wants a strong dollar" and that it "has an interest over the long run in a strong currency." Second, there was the extraordinary statement on April 25 by G-7 finance ministers, meeting under Rubin's chairmanship, who overcame their normal reticence about addressing such delicate matters and declared that a reversal of the decline of the dollar against the yen was now desirable. Finally there was prominent intervention in the foreign exchange market by the United States and Japan, with the cooperation of Germany and other G-7 countries, to support the currency, starting in March and April of 1995 (accompanied by comments by Rubin that the intervention reflects "a shared commitment to a stronger dollar" and a common view that a stronger dollar "is in the most general interest of the economies of the world").[23]

By August the dollar had reversed course.[24] The Federal Reserve began lowering interest rates in a trend that similarly dates from the summer of that year.[25] That the administration preferred a strong dollar became the regular mantra of officials, and discipline was imposed to ensure that pronouncements about the currency would be made by the Treasury alone. Still, it took a surprising amount of time for the existence of a new policy to be recognized. Figure 4.4, which shows the number of LexisNexis hits on "strong dollar" and "strong dollar policy," suggests that while this realization first dawned in 1996 (leading the National Association of Manufacturers and U.S. auto producers to complain that currency appreciation was hurting their exports), it took hold only two years later.

Expectations of a stable or strengthening dollar were key to the Clinton administration's entire macroeconomic strategy. The rising dollar helped to keep

---

23. *Wall Street Journal*, Apr. 6, 1995, p. C11. The published history of U.S. intervention suggests that the United States was buying dollars already in 1993, although the prominence of the spring 1995 interventions was what drew so much attention to the policy.

24. It then moved up to nearly Y120 (a 42-month high) by the time of the November 1996 election.

25. The strong dollar and the anti-inflation effects of its appreciation were only one factor behind the adjustment of monetary policy; more important surely were signs of distress in financial markets and worries about an economic downturn.

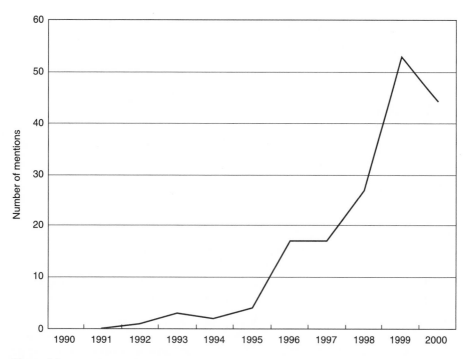

Figure 4.4
References in "Major Newspapers" to Strong Dollar Policy. (*Source:* LexisNexis database.)

inflation subdued. By encouraging the Fed to maintain low interest rates, it helped create a favorable climate for the investment that fueled a decade of rapid growth. This explains how the administration was able to sustain a posture of benign neglect toward the trade deficit through its two terms: if the deficit reflected a high level of productive investment rather than simply a low level of saving, then it was not a problem—the rapid productivity growth and economic growth generally financed by foreign capital inflows, which were the flip side of the trade deficit, would enable those foreign obligations to be easily financed. If the trade deficit cum capital inflow reflected the attractiveness of investing in the United States, then there was little reason to worry.[26]

If there was a downside to the strategy, it was the competitive pressure that was felt by emerging markets that pegged to the dollar, de facto or de jure. As the dollar rose against the yen, Asian countries that pegged to the U.S. currency

---

26. This was the so-called Lawson doctrine—that a current account deficit was not a problem if it reflected the attractiveness of investment, an argument associated with one-time British Chancellor of the Exchequer Nigel Lawson. It will rear its head again in our discussion of the Mexican and Thai current account deficits.

found their exports priced out of third markets, notably Japan's, and their profit margins squeezed.[27] But, in fact, the first instance of this phenomenon was in Mexico in the first half of 1994, when a modest rise in the dollar brought to the fore that country's competitiveness problems.

4.3 The Mexican Rescue

The context for the Mexican crisis was the successful conclusion of the North American Free Trade Agreement (NAFTA), negotiated and signed by the Salinas and Bush administrations in 1992 and amended and implemented by the Salinas and Clinton administrations in 1993. NAFTA offered Mexico two major benefits. It guaranteed that U.S. protectionism would not disrupt Mexican growth.[28] And, by tying reform to an international agreement, it reduced the odds that Mexico would abandon efforts to restructure its economy.

But there was also a third, unintended benefit. The violence of the political fight over NAFTA, and thus the status of the agreement as one of the Clinton administration's two significant accomplishments of 1993, meant that the administration had a considerable investment in NAFTA's success and thus in Mexico's. Winning approval for NAFTA was supposed to be easy—resistance was supposed to be minimal and pro forma—yet somehow opposition caught fire.[29] The political fight to ratify the agreement was bitter and close. In the aftermath of the ratification vote, the White House found that it had acquired a strong political interest in seeing that the policy was a success.

The start of 1994 saw a rise in political risk. The January 1994 uprising in Chiapas, scattered incidents of terrorism in Mexico City, the forthcoming Mexican presidential election in August, and rumblings that the cadres of the then-ruling Institutional Revolutionary Party (PRI) were unhappy with the dismantlement of Mexico's corporatist system and sought a reversal of reform caused observers to wonder whether Mexico's economic future was as bright as commonly suggested. GDP growth in 1993 turned out to be a deeply dis-

---

27. This is not a criticism of the U.S. policy or its architects, since they were not responsible for the decision by other governments to peg their currencies to the dollar, although some have argued that the United States might have done more to alert other countries to the potential adverse consequences.

28. Ironically, NAFTA did not offer any significant increase in access to the U.S. market, since the U.S. market was already almost completely open to imports from Mexico.

29. Raising the minimum wage, restricting the use of replacement workers, health care reform, better ways to look for jobs, and programs to subsidize education and training each promised to do more to boost the standard of living of union members than whatever minimal Stolper-Samuelson-driven reduction in U.S. working-class wages would follow from additional competition from Mexican workers. In any case, objections missed the essential point that Mexico was dismantling far higher barriers against U.S. goods than vice versa.

appointing 0.4 percent. Still, there were few signs of significant capital flight in early 1994, although the peso did weaken by about 8 percent in the first two months of the year. When Secretary Bentsen visited Mexico City in mid-February, he gave no public indication of concern, telling reporters that Mexico's economic policies had "become an example for all of Latin America."[30] Mexico's economic fundamentals—a balanced federal budget, a successful privatization campaign, and financial liberalization among them—were strong enough to similarly elicit a strong endorsement of the country's economic management by the IMF in the spring. In neither case were the principals being more optimistic than their staffs: both Treasury and IMF staff were optimistic about the sustainability of Mexican economic reform and economic growth.

March saw the assassination of the PRI's designated presidential candidate, Luis Donaldo Colosio. The announcement of a special $6 billion foreign currency swap agreement with the U.S. Treasury and the Fed and the rapid naming of Ernesto Zedillo to replace Colosio limited the market impact.[31] The American financial press still wrote that political risk was limited: "modernization in Mexico has developed its own momentum," Zedillo "shares the reformist vision," and the PRI would not "reverse ... [its] commitment to a more open social and economic structure."[32] But following a poor showing by Zedillo in a nationally televised campaign debate, the Bank of Mexico, notwithstanding the statutory independence it had gained on April 1, stepped up the rate of credit creation in order to "pump up the economy and ensure a PRI victory."[33] As the peso drifted toward the lower edge of its trading band, the bank was forced to undo its previous expansionary initiative, boosting short-term interest rates to 18 percent in order to prevent the currency from falling further.

Already in 1993 the Congressional Budget Office had issued a warning about the Mexican economy.[34] The Federal Reserve Board was monitoring conditions

---

30. *Washington Post*, Feb. 13, 1995, p. A1.

31. This bilateral arrangement employed the model of the U.S. portion of a multilateral contingency facility established the previous November to deal with trouble if the NAFTA vote had gone wrong. Treasury and Fed officials had also begun to discuss the need for a standing consultative mechanism to anticipate exchange-rate problems within the North American free-trade area already in late 1993, allowing them to launch the North American Framework Agreement and North American Financial Group with Canada in April 1994. Another multilateral contingency arrangement was put in place in July and August in anticipation of possible post-election troubles (but never activated, as we will describe later).

32. David Asman, "Zedillo Follows Salinas Model for Mexico," *Wall Street Journal*, Mar. 30, 1994. In contrast, a classified estimate by the National Intelligence Council, circulated in midsummer, gauged the probability of a smooth election and orderly transition as less than 50 percent.

33. *Washington Post*, Feb. 13, 1995, p. A1. Allan Meltzer, in testimony to the Senate Committee on Banking, Housing and Urban Affairs (Mar. 9, 1995), traced the roots of this monetary expansion back to 1993 (U.S. Senate Banking Committee, 1995, p. 220).

34. See CBO (1993).

south of the border and warned incoming administration officials that they were likely to face a crisis on their watch.[35] Now prominent economists such as Rudiger Dornbusch, Alejandro Werner, Guillermo Calvo, Leo Leiderman, and Carmen Reinhart chimed in.[36] They warned that while the Mexican government was doing most things right—the budget deficit had been wound down, businesses were being privatized, and tariffs were being reduced—growth remained disappointingly slow. Dornbusch and Werner blamed the nearly fixed peso-dollar exchange rate, coupled with persistent inflation, which had saddled the country with a currency overvalued in real terms. Their remedy was to devalue the peso by 20 percent and then to allow it to drift down even more, to the extent that Mexican inflation continued to exceed U.S. inflation. The counterargument was that the slowly crawling band within which the peso was allowed to fluctuate was critical for the success of Mexico's disinflation program. To suddenly abandon the nominal exchange rate anchor, even with good reason, might revive doubts about policy credibility and rekindle inflationary expectations.

Dornbusch and Werner presented their arguments to heavily attended seminars at the Federal Reserve Board and elsewhere around town in the spring, summer, and fall of 1994. The reaction in administration circles was "Perhaps." An internal June 1994 Federal Reserve Board staff memorandum concluded that a peso devaluation of around 20 percent was "quite likely within the next several years—but is not ... necessarily imminent."[37] Although Mexican inflation was outrunning U.S. inflation, so too might productivity growth, assuming that the government followed through on reform.[38] This possibility held out the promise of lower inflation in the future. That no acceleration in productivity growth was evident yet was not necessarily disturbing, since such things took time. The fundamental value of the peso was that at which Mexico's trade deficit was equal to desired long-term net investment in Mexico. To the extent that markets were expecting reform to continue and productivity to pick up, desired long-term net investment in Mexico might be large, and the true fundamental value of the peso might be high. It followed that there was no necessary reason

---

35. The reader may wonder how we have access to so much inside information about the Mexican crisis. Much of this information was unearthed and published in the course of the subsequent congressional investigation.

36. In Dornbusch and Werner (1994) and Calvo, Leiderman, and Reinhart (1994).

37. *Wall Street Journal*, July 6, 1995, p. A1.

38. The skeptics of Dornbusch and Werner's thesis also argued that fast productivity growth in Mexico might also help to reconcile relatively fast inflation there with the pegged rate of the peso through the operation of the Balassa-Samuelson effect (which predicts that the price of nontradables, and therefore the overall inflation rate, will rise faster in more rapidly growing countries, even in equilibrium). The problem was that, by most measures, the rate of increase of traded-goods prices in Mexico was also running well in excess of comparable U.S. rates.

to worry about the country's considerable current account deficit, which reached 8 percent of GDP in 1994, to the extent that this gap reflected an excess of investment over savings, reflecting in turn the attractions of investment in a country with considerable upside productivity potential.[39]

To be sure, if the current account reflected booming consumption as much as investment, and if the productivity payoff of the latter was still uncertain, there was more reason for concern.[40] But "uncertain" is the operative word; in the absence of stronger evidence it was not prudent for Treasury to urge a risky devaluation on a foreign sovereign, especially one so dependent on market confidence. Treasury issued warnings of "greater urgency as the year progressed," Undersecretary Summers later told a Senate panel.[41] But warnings were, understandably, not demands. The "policies that Mexico pursued ... were Mexico's," as Summers put it in his testimony.

And even if Dornbusch and Werner were right, it was not clear in the spring and summer of 1994 that dire consequences would follow. The peso might have to be devalued by 20 percent, but there the story would end. Currency crises with devastating consequences for economies only happen—or so economists thought back then—when governments have allowed their macroeconomic policies to run out of control and lack the political wherewithal to change them fast enough when the speculative attack begins. The Mexican budget was not in significant deficit. (There were deficits hiding in the accounts of the development banks, but this fact was not known at the time.) The central bank was not frantically printing money.

With benefit of hindsight, we now know that this model neglected a key point: that financial sources of vulnerability can be every bit as important as

---

39. The version of the Lawson doctrine was emphasized by Mexican Finance Minister Pedro Aspe in his discussions with U.S. officials (*Wall Street Journal*, July 6, 1995, p. A1).

40. The validity of the general point, whether or not it applied to Mexico, is evident in the fact that current account deficits have only a weak ability to predict currency crises (Edwards, 2001). From this point of view it is not surprising that alarm over the size of Mexico's external deficit was less than universal. One wonders whether U.S. officials, encouraged to dismiss the dangers of their own deficit by the Lawson doctrine, were led by analogical reasoning to underestimate the risks implicit in the Mexican deficit.

41. In particular, Summers discussed his concerns over the magnitude of the current account with Aspe's deputy, Guillermo Ortiz. Secretary Bentsen raised the issue with a number of Mexican officials (*Wall Street Journal*, July 6, 1995, p. A1). "Senator, there were many conversations between Treasury officials and Mexican officials, Treasury officials at all levels and their counterparts in the Mexican government, and between U.S. central bank officials and the Mexican central bank," Summers later told Senator D'Amato in testimony before the Senate Banking Committee. "Those conversations by the fall emphasized that Mexico's policy path was in our judgment unsustainable; that unless they were prepared to take some other substantial policy action, that it would be necessary for them to devalue, but that it was possible that with other substantial policy action, a devaluation might not be necessary" (Federal News Service, Mar. 10, 1995, p. 4).

macroeconomic ones in a world where domestic and international financial markets have been liberalized. Part of the Mexican government's strategy for coping with investor jitters had been to replace conventional short-term borrowing with the famous *tesobonos*, short-term securities whose principal was indexed to the dollar, as a means of retaining the funds of investors who feared devaluation.[42]

Effectively, this was a double-or-nothing bet. While the policy succeeded in attracting and retaining some $23 billion of financing, it meant that if devaluation did come it would be an order of magnitude more dangerous and destructive. In particular, it would greatly increase the burden of dollar-denominated public debt. Even if the public finances were otherwise sound, the fact that so much of the debt was dollar linked meant that they would not remain sound if the currency crashed.[43]

That this risk was inadequately appreciated is no surprise. In 1994 observers inside the U.S. government dismissed the possibility of a major financial crisis in Mexico by pointing to evidence from the recent record that major crises happened only when governments ran huge persistent deficits and pursued unsustainable policies. No one was preoccupied by the risk of issuing *tesobonos*, since everyone's worst-case scenario was a peso devaluation of 20 percent, nowhere near large enough for the balance-sheet effects to be seriously destabilizing.[44]

Only in the aftermath of the devaluation did it become clear that because Mexico had floated so much short-term debt, a major crisis could materialize out of thin air, and because so much of that short-term debt was dollar linked, the macroeconomic fallout could be severe. Thus large-scale foreign-currency borrowing robs exchange rate depreciation of its usefulness as a stabilization device. A standard reaction when a country suddenly finds that foreign demand for its current-account goods and services exports has fallen, or that foreign demand for its capital-account exports—for investments located on its territory—has fallen, is to allow the exchange rate to depreciate. When demand for a private business's products falls, one natural response is for the business to cut its prices. When demand for a country's products—and that is what

---

42. The Mexican government acted on the advice of the Weston Group, a New York–based group of financiers that specialized in peso investments.

43. This is an example of the logic behind so-called second-generation models of balance-of-payments crises, whose relevance to the case at hand was not fully appreciated before the fact.

44. There had been discussion of Mexico's *tesobono* innovation at Treasury and the Federal Reserve Board already in July, but that discussion turned on how to interpret the willingness of investors to buy these assets (and what this said about exchange-rate expectations), more than whether the existence of these assets implied a more serious crisis in the event of a devaluation. As late as December 16 (four days prior to the devaluation), a group of nearly 50 U.S. intelligence analysts, Wall Street financiers, and academic experts who gathered at the State Department "for an unusual, closed-door discussion of the Mexican economy" concluded that the negative fallout would be minimal (*Washington Post*, Feb. 13, 1995, p. A1).

exports plus capital inflow are, demand for a country's products—falls, the natural response is for a country to cut its prices. And the easiest, simplest, and most straightforward way to accomplish this is through an exchange-rate depreciation. But this is not the case if the country's banks and corporations have borrowed abroad in hard currencies. Then a depreciation writes up the home-currency value of their debts, erodes their entrepreneurial net worth, and sets in motion the debt-deflation process.

In a sense, then, the basic ingredients of the Asian crisis that erupted in 1997 were already evident in Mexico in 1994. In particular, how the current-account deficit was financed later became a central consideration for those attempting to forecast crises in emerging markets. The year 1994 was the first time this variable appeared on official radar screens. Thus it is not surprising that many of the reforms of the international financial system proposed by the Clinton administration following the outbreak of the Asian crisis were already tabled in the wake of the Mexican crisis some three years earlier.[45] What is disappointing, in retrospect, is that more was not done after the Mexican crisis to implement those recommendations quickly and head off future crises of a very similar sort.

But this was not the view in the middle of 1994. Rather, the assumption was that while a modest exchange-rate depreciation might be a political embarrassment, it hardly heralded an economic disaster. The problem was that among those ending up with red faces might be administration officials, since a visible change in the exchange rate would give additional ammunition to the opponents of NAFTA, who already argued that low Mexican wages meant unfair competition for American workers. Thus it is hardly surprising that the administration did not place more pressure on the outgoing Salinas government to devalue.[46] Treasury did suggest that Mexico might wish to widen the band for the peso and allow the currency to fluctuate more widely in order to allow the loss of competitiveness to be made up. In other words, it might contemplate a "limited devaluation." But it was not clear that this could be done without disturbing investor confidence, since Mexico's entire disinflation strategy was anchored by the exchange rate peg. It was not clear that there existed such a thing as a "limited devaluation," in other words, in the 1990s world of high capital mobility. Not surprisingly, Treasury's prodding produced no concrete result. In a sense, Mexico was the first example of another problem that would become chronic as the 1990s progressed: the dangers of not having an exit strategy from an ostensibly temporary currency peg.

---

45. As described in Section 4.5.

46. In addition there was the fact that the White House was sponsoring Salinas to head the newly created World Trade Organization and that an embarrassing devaluation might be seen as raising questions about his economic competence (although this probably did more to discourage Salinas from contemplating adjustment than the Treasury from pushing for it).

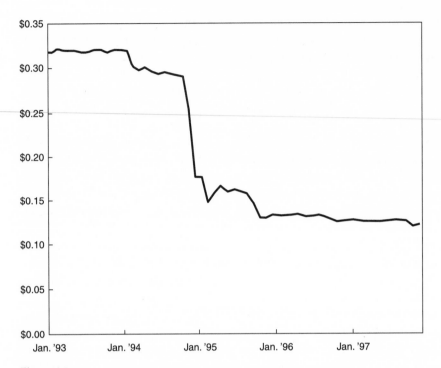

Figure 4.5
Value of the Mexican Peso, 1993–97. (*Source:* Federal Reserve Bank of St. Louis. Datafile: http://
www.j-bradford-delong.net/Econ_Articles/CIEP/CIEP_data/peso*.xls.)

The summer of 1994 saw the beginnings of capital flight as nervous investors
contemplated the aftermath of the August election. By the beginning of August,
capital flight had reached perhaps $150 million a week, depressing the exchange
rate to 3.4 pesos per U.S. dollar. The fear was that Zedillo might win the election in dirty and unconvincing fashion, and that such a win would be followed
by chaos. But as the election results came in and pointed to a solid and reasonably fair win, administration officials breathed a sigh of relief. The peso rose 4
percent from the bottom of its trading band in the wake of the election. Forecasters raised their estimates of Mexican growth in 1994 to 3 percent (and of
future economic growth to 4 percent), and the stock market jumped.[47] The Bank
of Mexico signaled that short-term interest rates would decline, as observers
awaited the arrival of "the famous investments from the NAFTA that never
came because of Chiapas and the Colosio assassination."[48]

---

47. Mexican export and GDP growth continued to be strong throughout the fall.
48. Craig Torres, "Mexico Could Post Its Strongest Growth in Five Years," *Wall Street Journal*, Aug.
25, 1994.

Then the situation deteriorated again. The assassination of senior PRI member Jose F. Ruiz Massieu in October seemed to demonstrate that Mexico still had a problem of political stability, and financial capital started hemorrhaging out of the country. This response came as a surprise to official Washington, which had expected capital inflows to resume following the election.[49] Slowly the view that "limited adjustment" of the exchange rate was necessary gained adherents in Washington, along with the realization that simply urging the Mexican government to undertake it would not accomplish the task. Rather, the United States had to make clear its unwillingness to help sustain an unsustainable currency peg. In November, Undersecretary Summers memoed his Treasury colleagues that Mexico should not be allowed to borrow from the United States to support an overvalued peso. Chairman Greenspan's staff reportedly reached the same conclusion.[50]

When the Federal Reserve raised interest rates by more than expected in November, the issue came to a head. The peso came under pressure, leading to a weekend of consultation between U.S. and Mexican officials. Bentsen told Pedro Aspe, the finance minister, that as far as he could see Mexico had no choice but to adjust the exchange rate. Aspe rejected the advice, and Bentsen wished him "good luck."[51]

All this is consistent with the belief that the Mexican government unwisely put off the inevitable day of reckoning—that it compounded the problem by waiting too long. From nearly $30 billion before the assassination of Colosio, foreign exchange reserves had fallen to barely $5 billion when the decision was taken to abandon the pegged rate against the U.S. dollar in December. At each stage the Mexican government, preoccupied with the election campaign, bet that the loss of reserves was temporary—that it reflected a passing disturbance to market conditions rather than a permanent change in investor sentiment. But up until late summer it was hard to say with any conviction that the Salinas

---

49. The unexpected nature of this event was one reason for the deer-frozen-in-the-headlights posture of the U.S. government in October and November. "As an official who participated in interagency meetings in Washington throughout this period recalled, 'I don't remember ... any economic bells ringing'" (*Washington Post*, Feb. 13, 1995, p. A1). In addition, the administration was preoccupied by preparations for the lame-duck session of Congress at which approval of the Uruguay Round negotiation would be obtained. Zedillo met with Secretary of State Warren Christopher during a November 1994 visit to Washington, and Treasury Secretary Bentsen met with Zedillo in Mexico City after the election, but there was reportedly no State Department–Treasury Department joint meeting on Mexico until after the peso devaluation in December (ibid.).

50. *Wall Street Journal*, July 6, 1995, p. A1.

51. *Washington Post*, Mar. 3, 1995, p. A29. The role of a firm exchange-rate anchor in Mexico's stabilization and adjustment program was personally associated with Aspe, who threatened to resign whenever the possibility of devaluation was raised in the interregnum between the election and the inauguration of the new government.

government was wrong. While inflows of foreign portfolio investment had stopped in the wake of political assassinations and the Chiapas rebellion, they had also stopped when the U.S. Congress looked ready to reject NAFTA, only to resume after the NAFTA implementation votes.

Could the administration have done more to force the issue? Did it compound the problem by issuing repeated public expressions of support and providing contingency finance in advance of the 1994 presidential election? Given the historical association of peso crises with Mexican elections, to make no financial contingency plans in 1994 would have been reckless, to say the least. Morever, the conditions attached to the multilateral contingent credit line would have required Aspe to reconsider Mexico's exchange-rate policy in the event that the finance was drawn (which it was not) and pressure on the peso failed to dissipate. It was the existence of this arrangement that provided a context in which U.S. officials could consult with their Mexican counterparts during the interregnum between the election and inauguration of the new government. But Mexico was a sovereign state; the United States could not force it to devalue. Nor was it appropriate for the U.S. government to attempt to compel it to do so. Public pressure would have destabilized the markets and been viewed as interfering first with the election and then with the transition. Bentsen's wishing Aspe "good luck" is about as blunt as such messages can get.

In December, after a year of political assassinations, a not-very-clean presidential election, and the appearance of an armed guerrilla movement in Chiapas, Mexico ran to the edge of its foreign-exchange reserves. It was public knowledge that inflows of foreign portfolio capital had not resumed. Expectations of inflows gave way to expectations of outflows. In a pattern that would be repeated in the Asian crisis two years later, each investor feared that other investors would pull their money out, leaving the last investor standing to lose the greatest amount, through either near-hyperinflation (as the Mexican government frantically printed pesos to cover its peso-denominated debts), the imposition of capital controls (which would trap foreign money in the country for an indefinite period of time), or formal default (in a repeat of 1980s-style dealings with commercial banks).

A government possessing only $5 billion in reserves to offset $23 billion of *tesebono* liabilities had no good choices. If it pushed interest rates sky-high in an effort to keep capital in the country, the extraordinary cost of money would strangle investment and employment, and would repel inward foreign investment. If, finding itself unable to borrow, it began printing money at a rapid rate, hyperinflation would do the same. And if it defaulted, the hope of U.S. finance for Mexican economic development would be dashed.

None of this was preordained, of course. If investors had not interpreted the decision of Zedillo's newly appointed finance minister, Jaime Serra, to devalue the peso as a repudiation of Aspe's promise that the peso band was inviolate (and if Aspe had not repeated that promise in such unconditional terms in a series of private meetings that closely preceded the change of government), then the reaction might not have been so violent. If investors had been willing to roll over the country's short-term debts, contractionary policies and a moderate devaluation to reduce imports and encourage exports would have sufficed to cover the Mexican government's foreign liabilities when they came due. Although a moderate devaluation coupled with contractionary policies might cause a recession, that recession would be shorter and shallower than what faced Mexico in the absence of funds to roll over its short-term debts.

Thus the peso support package: the United States, the International Monetary Fund, and other sundry and assorted contributors cobbled together some $40 billion in dollar-denominated assets. Initially the White House sought to get Congress to approve $50 billion in loan guarantees. The White House knew that this request was risky; President Clinton was told that his reelection prospects could be effectively destroyed by this one issue if Mexico failed to pay the money back. Nothing, more than the decision to nonetheless go ahead, could have made the commitment to globalization and openness more clear. The congressional leadership, Newt Gingrich and Bob Dole, were willing to give the president rope; initially they agreed to support the loan-guarantee request. The willingness of the executive and legislative branches to work together to minimize the impact of the peso crisis was unsurprising; after all, economic engagement with Mexico was the policy of both the Democratic executive and the Republican legislative majority. Moral suasion was mobilized: Chairman Greenspan telephoned Rush Limbaugh at his studio to lobby for the package (which he characterized as the "least worst of the various alternatives that confront us").

But the Treasury's state-by-state analysis of how a Mexican meltdown would affect U.S. employment was apparently not brought to the attention of congressional staffers. And the congressional leadership badly overestimated its ability to overcome the reservations of a rank and file that thus failed to see the impact on their individual districts. Soon congressional leaders as highly placed as Speaker Gingrich's lieutenant, Majority Leader Dick Armey, began demanding that the administration gather 100 House Democratic votes for the package as a precondition for Republican support. Perennial presidential candidate Patrick Buchanan called the support package a gift to Wall Street, "not free-market economics [but] Goldman-Sachsanomics." Ralph Nader urged Congress to vote down the support package and to instead demand that Mexico raise real wages. *Wall Street Journal* columnists demanded that support be provided only if Mexico first returned the peso to its pre-December nominal parity. Isolationist Republicans and protectionist Democrats claimed that NAFTA had caused the crisis and vowed to fight the package. Almost alone on the other side of the debate was the newly elected governor of Texas, George W. Bush, who trumpeted his firm support for the rescue on the grounds that a collapse of confidence in Mexico would be "unbelievably disastrous."[52]

Congress's failure to quickly pass the package meant that discussions of U.S. financial assistance did more to roil than calm the markets. Barely a month into 1995, the congressional leadership had abandoned any attempt to pass loan guarantees. Treasury staff developed a plan to take large-scale recourse to the Exchange Stabilization Fund (ESF), and Gingrich et al., chastened by their failure to pass the loan guarantees, responded with an unconditionally supportive letter.

The original legislation governing use of the ESF had assumed that it would be used for short-term exchange market interventions to stabilize the value of the dollar against other major international currencies, not that it might be used by the executive branch to stabilize the peso.[53] But the statute was revised in the 1970s to provide that the ESF should be used in a manner consistent with U.S. exchange obligations under the amended IMF Articles of Agreement. Indeed, it had been used before, repeatedly, for just this purpose, to help stabilize the currencies of foreign countries, including prominently the United Kingdom in 1976 and, revealingly, Mexico in 1982. But the scale on which it was to be utilized in 1995 was unprecedented (both in terms of amount and duration of the exposure), prompting Treasury to solicit and obtain the written approval of the congressional leadership before the fact. In authorizing that the ESF be used on this scale, Congress effectively abdicated to the White House a substantial measure of its institutional power over international economic policy. The vitriolic hearings over the Mexican rescue and over the administration's use of the ESF that followed in 1995 were to some degree the congressional rank and file's effort to undo the consequences.

In this way the program to support the peso was put in place. The IMF Executive Board, under strong pressure from Managing Director Michel Camdessus, ponied up a large contribution over the objections of some European directors. As we noted at the beginning of this section, there was virtually no chance that the Clinton administration would not respond rapidly and aggressively to a Mexican financial crisis. The centrality of the debate over NAFTA in its first year, followed by the legislative disaster of its second, meant that NAFTA had become, by default, one of the administration's two signature accomplishments. The national security team supported an aggressive U.S. response for its own

---

52. *Economist*, Feb. 4, 1995, p. 24.
53. See Schwartz (1997).

reasons; national security adviser Tony Lake was among those who argued that the crisis could threaten political stability in Mexico and that political disorder might mean a wave of illegal immigration into the United States.[54] From this standpoint, it could be argued that the loan was a good investment.

The same argument could be made from a narrowly economic point of view. The Mexican government was already following sustainable macroeconomic policies—if it could only find the money to repay its *tesobonos* without having to resort to the printing press. In a matter of months or, at worst, years, New York investors would calm down and recognize that there was more than a measure of truth in the optimism toward investing in Mexico that had prevailed in 1993. And then the loan could be paid back, with interest.

This is more or less what came to pass once the *tesobono* problem was cleared from the boards. The restoration of external balance was all but immediate as the heavily depreciated peso boosted exports and made imports unaffordable to Mexicans. The volume of exports rose by fully 30 percent in 1995, while imports fell by more than 8 percent. The swing in net exports between 1994 and 1995 was nearly $30 billion, allowing Mexico to register a $7 billion trade surplus in 1995.

The restoration of internal balance took longer. Real GDP fell by nearly 10 percent in the year from 1994–Q3. Monetary and fiscal policies did little to support domestic absorption and therefore Mexican GDP. This result raises the question of why the Zedillo government insisted on such a rapid adjustment. After all, one purpose of a support program is to allow macroeconomic adjustment to take place in a kinder, gentler fashion (with more monetary and fiscal support for domestic demand) and to give time for expenditure switching to take place. In large part the Zedillo government responded in this way because of pressure from the United States. The chair of the Senate Banking Committee, Alfonse D'Amato, spent much of 1995 hunting for the head of the person responsible for the "Mexican disaster."[55] D'Amato believed that he had a winning case no matter what explanations Treasury officials offered: either the U.S. government had failed to foresee the Mexican crisis, in which case Treasury officials were incompetent; or they had foreseen it but failed to warn investors, in which case they had effectively stolen money from his constituents to prop

---

54. *Washington Post*, Feb. 13, 1995, p. A1.

55. See, for example, Federal News Service (1995). From another perspective, D'Amato's lead role in the critique of policy toward Mexico was distinctly odd. He was the junior senator from New York. Whatever you thought of U.S. loans to the Mexican government, they were used to pay debts owed to D'Amato's constituents. To protest that U.S. money should not be used to make sure that New York companies were repaid was a strange move for a senator from New York. Indeed, D'Amato had initially backed the original loan guarantee program.

up the PRI. Pressure from the Senate Finance Committee and the fear that still-outstanding U.S. government money would become an issue in the 1996 presidential campaign led the United States to take part of the peso support package out of Mexico in 1996.[56]

How successful on balance was the U.S.-led rescue of Mexico? A fully adequate answer requires a paper of its own. While the 1995 recession was deep, the recovery that commenced in 1996 was rapid and sustained. Contrary to worries that Mexico, let off easy with help from its big brother to the north, would soon be back for another infusion of official finance, the country did not appeal again to the United States for assistance. It did not backtrack on reform. The neoliberal model of market opening and reform was not discredited; rather, it continued to spread to other parts of Latin America.[57]

But did countries elsewhere in the world grow overconfident that they too would receive exceptional support if they encountered financial difficulties? Did investors come to anticipate the extension of official finance for crisis countries and act on this expectation? The assessment of the Mexican rescue is more negative if it created moral hazard, bred contagion, and set the stage for the Asian crisis. The quantitative evidence is inconclusive, not surprisingly; isolating deviations from the efficient prices and quantities that would obtain in the absence of expectations of official intervention requires a consensus model of asset price determination, something that we do not have.[58] At some level, it is

---

56. As a domestic political strategy this was very desirable: the fact that the United States had made a handsome profit silenced Congressional criticism.

57. But Mexico's financial system continues in disarray. And Mexican income inequality appears to have taken an upward leap as a consequence of the 1994–95 crisis.

58. Thus the attempts of Zhang (1999) and Spadafora (2000) to identify the effects of moral hazard by estimating an ad hoc model of emerging-market bond spreads, and looking for a pattern of outliers (that is, spreads narrower than predicted) following the Mexican crisis, is no more convincing than that ad hoc model. It is not surprising in this light that these authors reach diametrically opposing conclusions. Lane and Phillips (2000) review approaches to identifying moral hazard in international financial markets. While arguing that "It is inherently plausible that financing from the IMF generates some element of moral hazard" (p. 1), they find that the evidence is inconclusive, although they are able to decisively reject the limiting hypothesis "that investors perceive a full guarantee from the Fund" (p. 28). And, even if there exists evidence that the potential availability of Treasury and IMF money to fight international financial crises eased the minds of investors, inducing them to lend and invest more than would otherwise have been the case, this is not necessarily a bad thing to guard against. As DeLong, Shleifer, Summers, and Waldmann (1990) pointed out, a well-functioning financial market is one that takes appropriate account of "fundamental" risk. The risk that investors will panic is not a fundamental in the relevant sense. A financial market that discounts prices because of this possibility is not setting prices equal to social marginal value. In this case the level of international lending and borrowing, absent official intervention, will be inefficiently low. Of course, a pattern of overly frequent, unconditional intervention can tip the balance the other way, but excessive lending at inefficiently tight spreads is not the only possible outcome.

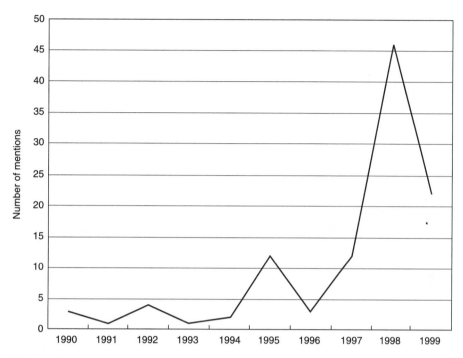

Figure 4.6
References in Major Newspapers to Moral Hazard. (*Source:* LexisNexis database.)

hard to believe that investors were wholly unaffected.[59] But there is little sign
that the Mexican rescue, by itself, constituted in investors' minds a pattern of
support. The phrase "moral hazard" appeared in the newspapers in 1995, in the
wake of the Mexican rescue, only one-fourth as often as it would appear in
1998, following Asia (see Figure 4.6). The idea of a "moral-hazard play"—that
G-10 governments and multilaterals were prepared to eliminate the downside
risk of investing in countries like Brazil that were too important systemically
and like Russia that were too nuclear to be allowed to fail—became current
only in the wake of the Asian loans that followed Mexico by two to three years.
There were concerns about moral hazard in 1995, in other words, but it would
take the Asian crisis (and the Russian crisis after it) to give them resonance.

---

59. On the other hand, there is the argument that the backlash against the Mexican rescue on
Capitol Hill gave investors reason to doubt that the experience would be repeated (Willett, 1999).
And administration officials could and did argue that Mexico was more a liquidity than a solvency
crisis. Help was justified on efficiency grounds by the predominance of the liquidity element,
where successor countries whose crises had deeper structural roots (and investors in those countries) should not expect comparable help. Of course, whether investors could draw these subtle
distinctions is an empirical question.

4.4 Responding to the Asian Crisis

Coming in the wake of Mexico, Thailand's crisis was less of a surprise. Indeed, the kingdom's problems bore an eerie resemblance to those of its Latin predecessor. A large current-account deficit was raising questions about competitiveness. There were worries that monetary policy was too expansionary to remain consistent with the exchange-rate peg maintained by the central bank. The baht, according to some estimates, was overvalued by the now customary 20 percent.[60]

To be sure, Thailand, like Mexico before it, was not running a large budget deficit; the problem did not obviously lie in the profligacy of the government.[61] As in Mexico, the authorities defended themselves by arguing that the strength of the baht and the magnitude of the current account deficit reflected the country's admirably high level of investment. But there were signs that companies were taking on excessive debt burdens: by 1996 companies in Thailand, excluding banks, were spending the equivalent of 18 percent of GDP on interest.

And, even more than in Mexico, there were reasons to doubt the productivity of much of that investment. Valuations on the Bangkok stock exchange had been trending downward since 1996. The inefficiency of infrastructure investment and the frothiness of the real estate market were notorious. Many construction loans had already gone bad, undermining the solvency of banks and finance companies and implying a significant fiscal obligation for the authorities (the government having already announced that it would not allow depositors to suffer when financial institutions that had gone bad were closed down). Nonperforming loans were perhaps $20 billion by the start of 1997. By the start of 1997 there were whispers that the cost of bailing out insolvent financial institutions could be as high as 6 percent of GDP.

The IMF had been warning for more than a year that the situation in Thailand was unsustainable. Its managing director, Michel Camdessus, had visited Thailand four times between July 1996 and July 1997, exhorting the government to "get rid of this very dangerous peg to the dollar." The existence of these

---

60. This is the retrospective estimate of Chinn (1998). "Customary" refers to the precedent of Mexico in 1994.

61. It can be argued that the overheated state of the Thai economy implied the need for a substantial surplus, not just a balanced budget, a point with which, with benefit of hindsight, we would agree. But the issue here is whether fiscal variables were "flashing red" and sending out early warning signals of an impending crisis. The answer, clearly, is no. Those who insist that fiscal policy, while not the problem, could nonetheless have been part of the solution must be able to argue that higher taxes and lower public spending would have significantly narrowed the current account deficit (where the "twin deficits" literature suggests that the link here is tenuous) and could have raised the average quality of investment.

problems was familiar to the Federal Reserve and the U.S. Treasury: Treasury officials, from Rubin on down, were vocal in insisting on the need to clean up the financial sector and adjust the exchange rate. What came as a surprise was not that Thailand had a crisis and experienced macroeconomic distress but the severity of the fallout and the speed and scope of its spread.

Under most circumstances this tinderbox would have ignited even earlier than it did. It was clear that the banks were bust, rendering the Thai authorities reluctant to use higher interest rates to defend the currency (given the additional pain that this action would inflict on the already suffering banking system).[62] That the conflagration only erupted in July 1997 can perhaps be explained by the ease with which emerging markets generally, and not merely Thailand, could finance their external deficits, given the conditions prevailing on global financial markets (and the perception that they were "miracle economies").

An astonishing $240 billion in private capital had flowed out of the industrial core into the developing periphery in 1996. More than a quarter went to the fast-growing economies of East Asia. All signs at the start of 1997 were that this flow would continue and, if anything, increase. Japanese banks in particular were pouring in money through the Bangkok International Banking Facility (BIBF), something to which the Japanese Ministry of Finance paid no mind (despite warnings from the Fed and the U.S. Treasury).[63] That said, there were already some who had begun to worry that the miracle was oversold and that financing was too easy to get.[64] Moral hazard emanating from the Mexican rescue could conceivably have supported this financial flow, but more plausible in our view is that investors found investing in the East Asian miracle irresistible, wanted a piece of the action, and were confident that they could get out in time if, in Thailand or elsewhere, something finally went wrong.

Some critics of the markets go a step further and argue that the origin of the Asian crisis lay in the major money centers, that the East Asian economies were fundamentally sound, and that the true source of crisis was an investor panic. We are more inclined to the position staked out by Summers (1999a): while there would have been no crisis of this magnitude in the absence of investor panic, an investor panic would not have produced a crisis of this magnitude in the absence of serious problems of nonperforming loans, inadequate and weak financial regulation, and currency and maturity mismatches, all of

---

62. As in fact turned out to be the case. While the Thai authorities raised interest rates when the crisis broke out, they lowered them "prematurely" (in the words of Boorman et al., 2000) in early August and again in mid-September, arguably undermining the confidence of investors in their commitment to defense of the exchange rate.

63. We will return to the political economy of the BIBF later.

64. See, for example, Krugman (1994).

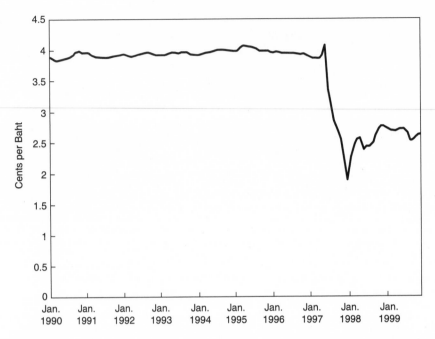

Figure 4.7
Value of the Thai Baht, 1990–99. (*Source:* Federal Reserve Bank of St. Louis via http://www.
economagic.com/. Datafile: http://www.j-bradford-delong.net/Econ_Articles/CIEP/CIEP_data/
baht*.xls.)

which had major implications for future (quasi) fiscal deficits and hence for
sustainable monetary policies. Both the fundamental financial problems of
the East Asian economies and an investor panic were needed for the situation
to develop as it did, and it was their interaction that was key. The buildup
of short-term, foreign-currency-denominated debt left East Asia's economies
vulnerable to a sudden collapse of confidence. Depreciating currencies and
falling asset prices exacerbated the strains on private-sector balance sheets and
unleashed a vicious spiral.

In May the Bank of Thailand successfully fought off a speculative attack,
using Singapore's support to engineer a bear squeeze. The attack convinced
the government that reform could not be further delayed. In June it initiated
steps to restructure the financial system, closing down 16 insolvent finance companies. But this action was too little, too late, what with capital and reserves
continuing to hemorrhage out. On July 2, 1997, the central bank scrapped the
fixed exchange rate and watched the baht fall by one-sixth on that day alone (see
Figure 4.7). The bank raised short-term interest rates that day by two percentage
points, to 12.5 percent annualized, to prevent a larger, potentially destabilizing

fall. Observers feared that if the exchange rate weakened further, many Thai companies with dollar-denominated debts would see their profits vanish under the impact of higher repayment costs. The consensus estimate of Thai companies' short-term dollar-denominated debt was that $50 billion was maturing within the year, a sum more than half again as large as the perhaps $30 billion of Thai foreign exchange reserves. And no one knew how much of this dollar-denominated debt was unhedged.

Yet there was little sense at the very start of July that the Thai situation was as serious as Mexico's had been or that the crisis would spread to other East Asian economies. The government in Bangkok had already taken steps to begin to liquidate insolvent financial institutions and strengthen the financial system—steps that the Mexican government had failed to take. The Bank of Thailand had engaged intervention on the forward foreign-exchange market, the losses from which would absorb a significant portion of its reserves, but its losses were not known to the market, since the IMF's efforts to enhance transparency had not extended to the off-balance-sheet liabilities of central banks.[65] The dollar value of the Thai stock market fell on July 2, but by "only" 9 percent, a little more than half as much as the currency.

Suddenly everything changed. On July 6 the Philippine finance minister was quoted by the *Straits Times* as saying that his country's peso "might devalue." Five days later the Philippines, another country with chronic competitiveness problems, had abandoned its fixed exchange rate, following Thailand down.[66] While this action helped the Philippines avoid a more serious crisis, it raised further questions about the stability of other currencies. On July 8 the Malaysian ringgit came under heavy speculative pressure. On July 11 Indonesia announced that it was widening its exchange-rate band and then stopped defending the rate. On July 13 Korea's eighth-largest chaebol, Kia, and its creditor banks announced an urgent restructuring designed to avoid bankruptcy (following other failures by smaller chaebol earlier in the year). And on July 14, Malaysia stopped supporting the ringgit. Now the crisis was in full swing. Before the end of July the East Asian economies had opened discussions with

---

65. Whether such a requirement is feasible remains an open question. To the extent that financial market rocket scientists and their customers are always one step ahead of the markets, concocting new instruments ostensibly exempt from existing disclosure mandates, the IMF has increasingly focused on codes of transparency for central banks to induce voluntary disclosure and measures to strengthen corporate governance as a way of promoting disclosure by private-sector entities. We will return to this topic later.

66. The Philippines' blessing, as it were, was that no one had mistaken it for an Asian "tiger" or a "miracle" economy. It had not imported capital on the same scale as Thailand. It had not experienced the same construction and real estate boom, and the problems in its banking system, while chronic, were in some sense less acute. But the Philippines exported many of the same products as Thailand (textiles and apparel, for example), and hence had good reason to follow the baht.

the IMF for support, and Malaysian Prime Minister Mahathir Muhammed had launched his denunciations of international currency speculators and of foreign-exchange markets in general.

Both the Fed and the Treasury saw Thailand as a problem best handled by the IMF in light of the surprisingly bitter and long-lingering controversy over the Mexican rescue and the fact that Thailand was hardly in America's backyard. August saw the IMF assemble and approve its $17 billion support package, which included parallel bilateral financing, Japan making the major contribution.[67] The United States did not contribute (although it supported the idea of parallel financing). Treasury was fettered by Senator D'Amato's rider to the appropriations bill constraining the use of the ESF, which did not expire until September 30 (the end of the fiscal year).[68] U.S. inability or unwillingness to participate (the decision was interpreted variously) created considerable enmity in Asia.

Any potentially favorable impact on market confidence was immediately destroyed by the revelation that the Bank of Thailand had $23 billion of outstanding forward dollar sales (and now associated losses) that it had to cover. This fact had been uncovered by the IMF mission and was known to the executive board (and hence the U.S. government). Treasury and the Federal Reserve pushed the IMF and the Thais to reveal the position on the grounds that anything known to the board was bound to leak.[69]

As the shock waves radiated outward, Indonesia abandoned its support of the rupiah. By the end of September the Korean chaebol Jinro and Kia had gone bankrupt, adding the third-largest economy in the hemisphere to the list of the vulnerable. By late November, Thailand would have returned to the IMF for a second package (the terms and targets of the first one having been rendered irrelevant by the collapse of the currency).

During the fall of 1997 proposals for an Asia-only $100 billion bailout fund were shot down by the U.S. and European governments.[70] Treasury and the Fed worried that a large, freestanding source of funds would undermine the role of the IMF and its conditionality by providing generous finance on lax terms. They doubted that a different mix of adjustment and financing, which the existence of a large, freestanding regional fund implied, was more appropriate for Asia than for the rest of the world. And, in practice, this large, freestanding

---

67. Japan contributed $4.3 billion through a pari pasu arrangement. In addition, there were contributions from the World Bank, the Asian Development Bank, Australia, China, Hong Kong, Singapore, and other Asian countries.

68. We will provide more discussion of this topic later.

69. In addition, making public the fact that the Thai reserve position was even weaker than it seemed provided additional political justification for the large (505 percent of quota) IMF package.

70. In addition, China opposed the fund, both for its strategic implications and out of doubts that softer or unconditional money would be helpful for crisis prevention and resolution.

source of funds would have been dominated by Japan's Ministry of Finance and the Bank of Japan.[71] Looking at the course of the Japanese economy from 1989 to 1997, it was impossible to have any confidence in the ability of those institutions to handle a domestic, let alone an international, financial crisis.

That U.S. opposition to the Asia-fund idea, on the grounds that national influence would undermine the role of the IMF, provoked such a hostile reaction in Japan and other parts of Asia is hardly surprising when one observes how profoundly U.S. influence shaped the actions of that institution. Just saying "no, no, no" was thus not a feasible political position for the United States. The U.S. administration's counterproposal was the Manila Framework Agreement, launched at a meeting in the Philippines in mid-November. This led to agreement at the Asia Pacific Economic Cooperation summit in Vancouver to strengthen mutual surveillance within the region, and to create an Asia fund with no dedicated staff, with no specific funding level, and, critically, with the proviso that funds could be lent only with IMF supervision.

Returning to the crisis itself, what is particularly striking is the failure of all concerned—in government, in the markets, in the multilaterals—to anticipate how widely, quickly, and powerfully instability would spread. Almost no one warned that Indonesia, for example, was at risk of suffering a crisis like Thailand or Mexico.[72] The country's current account deficit was less than one-third as large a share of GDP as Thailand's. Indonesia had never pegged its exchange rate, and the band within which it allowed its exchange rate to fluctuate was relatively wide (and was widened further after the Thai devaluation). Yet Indonesia also suffered from politically directed lending through state banks, tangled corporate control, a lack of easily accessible information about corporate finances, insider lending, and poor banking supervision. Most important, however, was the magnitude of unhedged foreign hard-currency borrowing. Thus, once the rupiah began to lose value, Indonesia's situation deteriorated very rapidly. Debt owed to foreign banks relative to Indonesian GDP quadrupled as the rupiah fell, reaching a peak of perhaps $1\frac{1}{2}$ times a year's GDP.

In October the Indonesian government announced that it was seeking IMF assistance, and by the end of the month a $40 billion support program had been unveiled. Having recognized that the crisis could spread from region to region like weeds from one backyard to another (and no longer constrained by the rider to the Treasury appropriation that complicated the use of the ESF), this time the administration committed (still in the face of congressional opposition)

---

71. Although the latter was not a big fan of the idea, fearing that it would end up having to pay for the initiative.

72. This despite the fact that G-10 deputies, together with representatives of the emerging markets and multilaterals, had emphasized the role of weak institutions and flawed structural policies in the Draghi Report issued in April of that same year (discussed later).

to making available a contingent line of credit worth about $3 billion in the event that the IMF rescue package proved inadequate to stabilize the economy.

However, the Indonesian government's willingness to carry out the actions needed to obtain continued IMF funding was unclear. In the late fall of 1997 it did close a few—but not all—potentially insolvent banks (controversially, in that there was no deposit insurance and the risk of depositor panic was great), including at least one bank owned by the Suharto family. But when Suharto's commitments to restrain government spending on infrastructure projects ran up against his eldest daughter's interests, family won. Thus it remained uncertain whether the Indonesian government truly was willing to take the policy steps that the IMF hoped would reassure foreign investors. And between the second quarter of 1997 and the second quarter of 1998, Indonesian real GDP fell by 16.5 percent.

Malaysia decided to go its own way, rejecting the conditions sought by the IMF. Mahathir Muhammed would claim that the financial crisis was a Western conspiracy to impoverish emerging Asian economies, and that the Malaysian economy was fundamentally sound. Yet in the summer of 1997 Malaysia's domestic bank lending was equal to more than $1\frac{2}{3}$ times a year's GDP, and many feared that much of this lending had gone into unproductive investments. The twin Petronas Towers in Kuala Lampur—the tallest office building in the world and the set for the Sean Connery movie *Entrapment*—became a symbol of the claim that Malaysia too had suffered from an investment bubble in the mid-1990s.

One reason Mahathir was so desperate to keep the IMF at bay was his fear that the Fund would demand, as part of structural reform to promote economic efficiency, the end to the distortions and subsidies that give economic preference to those descended from Malaysia's indigenous population as opposed to those descended from Chinese immigrants. Since these policy measures were at the core of Mahathir's political support, he may have seen his political career at an end should a structural adjustment mission land at Kuala Lampur. Eventually Mahathir would opt for capital outflow controls rather than IMF-style programs to contain the crisis.[73]

The fourth of the severely afflicted fast-growing East Asian economies was South Korea, whose problems were exacerbated by politically driven lending. For decades the government had directed its banks to lend to favored sectors of the economy, encouraging heavy corporate borrowing and high debt-equity ratios. Even as of the end of 1996, the 25 largest chaebol had a debt-equity ratio of more than four to one. Eight chaebol went bankrupt in 1997, leaving the

---

73. According to Kaplan and Rodrik (2001), it is not clear that Malaysia lost much in terms of speed of recovery from its heterodox policies. Their methodology is controversial; others would point to other explanations for the relatively mild nature of Malaysia's crisis (such as its low level of international debt).

banks with a large but uncertain exposure to bad loans. And the country's banks and operating companies had unknown but staggering unhedged dollar-denominated debts. The country was thought to have $65 billion of short-term foreign debt, but we now know that the true figure was at least twice that large.

It is striking, then, that everyone was in denial on Korea until early November, when the crisis spilled over from the rest of Asia. In response, Korea and the Fund agreed on a support program of $57 billion, the largest IMF-led program ever.[74] But even this supersized package proved too small. The failure of the Korean package to staunch the bleeding was particularly alarming: not only was Korea one of the 12 largest economies in the world, but the inability of multilateral finance to stabilize conditions cast doubt on the viability of the entire IMF-U.S. led rescue strategy, leading for the first time to dire predictions in December of the possible meltdown of the global financial system.

Korea epitomized the "bailout problem"—that for every dollar of official money that was pumped in, the banks could take a dollar of their money out. Not only did this debilitate efforts to end the liquidity crisis, but it had adverse political consequences (congressional critics complained of "welfare for bankers") and heightened concerns about moral hazard (insofar as international banks that had taken on risky loans were now able to "get off scot-free"). But exhorting the banks to keep their money in the country was ineffectual in a situation beset by collective action problems. Not only might individual banks decline to participate in concerted action, but so might individual governments. Thus, as late as mid-December, Japan, preoccupied by the health of its own financial system, was urging that country's banks to pull out of Korea. Only when Korea was pushed to the brink of default, on—to pick a date—Christmas eve, did the IMF, in concert with G-7 governments, get the banks to first roll over their maturing short-term claims, by offering to accelerate the second line of defense conditional on a successful effort by a critical mass of Korea's foreign bank creditors to extend the maturity of their exposure to the Korean banking system and then to convert these and other short-term obligations into (highly remunerative) long-term bonds.[75]

---

74. The IMF contribution alone came to 2000 percent of quota, far exceeding the conventional ratios of 100 percent of quota in a year and 300 percent of quota over the lifetime of a program.

75. Treasury and the Federal Reserve Board encouraged William McDonough, chairman of the Federal Reserve Bank of New York, to convene a meeting of the six largest U.S. banks to impress on them the urgency of doing so, which he did on December 22 (Callaghy, 2000). The Bank of England did the same for the U.K. banks, on December 24, while the German Finance Ministry did so on December 29. William Rhodes, vice-chairman of Citicorp, worked on behalf of the U.S. banks to open channels to the Japanese banks and to impress upon them the importance of participating in the rollover. He and his colleagues contacted each of the top 10 Japanese banks and the Japanese vice-minister of finance, Eisuke Sakakibara. As a result of these initiatives the Japanese were represented at the next meeting in New York, on December 29, by officials from Bank of Tokyo Mitsubishi (*Euromoney*, March 1998).

Ex post evaluations criticize officials for not having moved faster to bail in the banks. It is argued that if the same steps that were taken at the end of December had in fact been taken in November, perhaps following the Manila meeting at which the country's difficulties became known, then the first IMF package would have had a better chance of working. Preventing so much bank money from bleeding out would have avoided so demoralizing the markets. But whether the same steps would have been feasible earlier is questionable. For much of the period, Korea was still in the heat of a contested election (which took place in the third week of December). Despite the IMF's efforts to get all the candidates to endorse its program, it was uncertain whether the winner would follow through with the prescribed reforms. There was the danger that attempting to arrange a concerted rollover might so alarm the markets as to spread the crisis to Brazil and back to Russia. It may have been necessary to allow the least patient (Japanese) banks to exit before it was possible to obtain the cooperation of the others. Above all, it is doubtful that the banks—or, for that matter, the Japanese government—would have agreed to act in the collective interest before there was evidence of how truly dire the circumstances were. A few foreign banks had in fact tried on their own to orchestrate a stay/maturity extension package a week or so before Christmas, but their head offices had refused to go along.

The winter and spring of 1998 saw the IMF programs begin to work, as the Thai and Korean governments began to change their economic policies in accord with IMF conditions. Indonesia was a harder case. The draft budget unveiled by President Suharto in early January substantially exceeded the IMF's targets. Suharto gave way, following meetings in Jakarta in mid-January with IMF First Deputy Managing Director Stanley Fischer and Summers, who had become Deputy Treasury Secretary, and phone calls from President Clinton, among others. Suharto signed a revised letter of intent on January 15. The event was memorialized by the notorious photograph showing IMF Managing Director Michel Camdessus, his arms folded, standing behind the Indonesian president (though the IMF claims that film clips show that Camdessus in fact struck this pose for only a few moments).

President Suharto promised to axe infrastructure projects dear to his eldest daughter, to phase out tax breaks and loan subsidies to the Indonesian auto companies controlled by his youngest son, and to eliminate his family's private monopolies. But he continued to look for running room: promoting the regulation- and government-investment-minded Bucharuddin Jusuf Habibie, and announcing plans to establish a currency board that many observers saw as a scam to enable Suharto and his family to repay their dollar-denominated debts at an artificially high exchange rate before the currency board's collapse.

Nevertheless, even in Indonesia the direction of policy began to shift in the way advocated by the IMF.

Were these policy shifts a good idea? As the critics of IMF intervention had pointed out repeatedly already in 1997, the Asian crisis was very different from the crises that the Fund was used to handling. Asian countries had high savings rates. Asian governments had run budget surpluses. Asian central banks had inflation under control. Hence, the standard conditions attached to IMF lending —raise taxes and cut government spending to shift the budget toward surplus and reassure observers that the government would not resort to the printing press to finance its expenditures, curb demand in order to compress imports and generate a trade surplus, establish a monetary regime that would create confidence that inflation would remain under control—were of questionable relevance, except possibly in Thailand.

Is there any validity to the even stronger indictment of these policies—that they were not only of questionable relevance but in fact damaging and coun-terproductive? Much ink has been spilled over these questions. There is now widespread consensus, with which we would concur, that the initial demands for fiscal cuts on the part of the crisis countries were excessive; by further compressing demand in an already depressed environment, they made post-crisis recessions worse.[76] There was no need for sharp fiscal consolidation in the interest of either confidence or fiscal sustainability in countries that had not entered their crises with large budget deficits or exploding debts. Here, it can be argued, the IMF's principal shareholder did not do enough at the outset to rein in Fund staff's ingrained habit of associating crises with fiscal excesses.

On monetary policy, in contrast, there is no such consensus.[77] The critics, from Stiglitz to Sachs, argued that sharp hikes in interest rates were more destabilizing than stabilizing for countries with high debt gearing and weak financial systems. The official position, of the U.S. Treasury as well as the Fund, was that avoiding sharp hikes in interest rates was even worse, since failure to tighten would signal a lack of commitment to defending the exchange rate and provide no pecuniary incentive for investors to keep their money in the coun-try, causing the currency to crash and bringing down with it banks and firms with foreign-currency-denominated liabilities.[78]

Clearly, this was a Hobson's choice. Governments finding themselves in this situation have no good options (as Mexico had learned in 1995). The IMF's

---

76. Note, for example, the obervation of IMF First Managing Director Stanley Fischer (2001a), "that the Fund on occasion makes mistakes; of course, we recognized that formally in the Asian crisis with fiscal policy, which was excessively tight for a few months at the beginning" (p. 5).

77. See, inter alia, Furman and Stiglitz (1998), Kraay (1998), and Tanner (1999).

78. There was no enthusiasm in Treasury for squaring this circle by encouraging the crisis countries to impose capital and exchange controls, for reasons that we will detail in the following section.

gamble was that high interest rates would restore confidence quickly, stabilizing the currency and enabling the cost of credit to be brought down to customary levels before widespread bankruptcy ensued. In addition, IMF-led financial support clearly allowed governments to have higher exchange rates (and thus lower hard-currency debt burdens) and lower interest rates (and thus higher domestic investment) than otherwise, giving time to put in place financial-sector reforms and industrial-sector restructurings while awaiting the return of investor confidence.

If the fundamental imbalances underlying old-style crises were the result of bad macroeconomic policy decisions, the fundamental imbalances underlying new-style crises were more likely to be the result of bad structural policy decisions: unproductive public investments, unconditional guarantees for banks and firms, and financial policies that conduced to excessively high debt-equity ratios.[79] Awareness of this fact led IMF conditionality to take a new and unprecedented turn, in the direction of structural reform, with the active support of the Clinton administration.[80] Not surprisingly, financial reforms—closing bad banks, recapitalizing the survivors, and strengthening prudential supervision—were key elements of the IMF's crisis programs in Asia. But these bad private-sector decisions reflected more than simply the weakness of prudential supervision and regulation. They reflected a pattern of close ties between govern-

---

79. The major macroeconomic policy failure, in our view, was to continue pegging exchange rates to the dollar too firmly for too long, providing implicit insurance against currency risk to the private sector and thereby encouraging accumulation of the unhedged exposures that so aggravated the crisis when it finally came (and inadvertently aggravating problems of competitiveness in a period when the dollar was appreciating against the yen). At a deeper level, however, the distinction between macroeconomic and structural policies is harder to sustain. Pegging was a corollary of the Asian development strategy of government-led investment, relying on the banks as the instrument of industrial policy. It can be implicated under this heading for having encouraged the extension to the financial sector of implicit guarantees that encouraged lending (by, inter alia, foreigners) without due regard to the underlying risks. But this discussion takes us beyond the parameters of the present paper.

80. Although the number of structural conditions attached to IMF programs peaked in 1997, the increase in such measures was not specific to Asia or to its crisis. The number of structural conditions per program more than doubled between the late 1980s and early 1990s and doubled again between the first and second half of the most recent decade (Goldstein, 2000). Explanations for the trend include the priority that came to be attached to restoring growth in highly indebted countries in the 1980s (complaints that the Fund placed too much weight on stabilization and therefore was too tolerant of recession led to this emphasis on growth, which in turn required structural reform) and the emphasis on structural transformation and institution building in formerly centrally planned economies in the 1990s. While these experiences help to explain why the Fund became accustomed to giving growth-related advice and applying structural conditions, they do not justify its preoccupation with micro- and sectoral reforms in East Asia, a region with an admirable record of growth and no history of deep structural problems. They do not explain why the conditions attached to the Fund's 1997 and 1998 programs with Indonesia, South Korea, and Thailand were so numerous and detailed.

ment and powerful corporations, typically family led, in countries otherwise as different as Indonesia and South Korea. It was not just the ready availability of finance from poorly regulated banks but also the expectation that the borrowers themselves would be bailed out rather than closed down when things went wrong that weakened market discipline and encouraged lax investment decision-making. This was the "crony capitalism hypothesis" that led the IMF by November to festoon its Asian programs with a host of structural conditions.

Like interest rate policy, the efficacy of this new structural policy was questioned: it was not clear that conditions which pointed to weaknesses in a country's economic system did more to undermine than to restore confidence.[81] To a considerable extent the skeptical view has prevailed. Goldstein (2000), in his definitive analysis of the issue, concludes that as far as structural reforms were concerned, the IMF had "bitten off more . . . than either it or its member countries can chew." By 1999 the Clinton administration was advocating a somewhat streamlined and simplified loan conditionality that focused more narrowly on macroeconomic and financial problems.[82]

As late as the summer of 1998 it was not clear that the crisis had been surmounted. The U.S. Treasury was relieved that the IMF-led programs had avoided a potentially catastrophic default in Korea and led to a substantial strengthening of the Thai stock market and currency, and that the crisis had not spread beyond East Asia. Trade balances had turned around, and interest rates and exchange rates had stabilized. But there were still no signs of improvement in Indonesia, where it was not at all clear that a stabilization program would be implemented.

Moreover, even though forecasters were anticipating a rapid turnaround in East Asian current accounts in 1998, they pushed expectations of a resumption of rapid economic growth back to the start of 1999. Disappointing export growth, especially exports to Japan, were at the heart of beliefs that recovery would not come as rapidly as had been expected. The weakness of the yen and worries that the Chinese renmenbi might be devalued (voiced by administration officials at a Manila Framework Group meeting in Tokyo in June) reinforced these fears. Poor export performance was assisted by the fact that the magnitude of dollar-denominated liabilities and nonperforming loans had turned out to be larger than even the most pessimistic estimates as of mid-1997. In Indonesia real GDP was expected to shrink by as much as 10 percent (a forecast that turned out to be too optimistic). In Thailand real GDP was expected to fall by as much as 6 percent (a forecast that turned out to be too pessimistic). In Korea

---

81. If it is believed that these weaknesses were generally known, of course, then the argument that it is dangerous to address them on confidence grounds dissolves.
82. As we will analyze at more length in the next section.

the economy was expected to shrink by as much as 4 percent. And in Malaysia growth in 1998 was expected to be zero.

As news continued to be mixed in the spring and summer of 1998, policy-makers at the IMF, in the U.S. Treasury, and elsewhere took the fact that the news was not worse as evidence of the positive impact of their policies. There had been no meltdown. A slide into the depths of a great depression like that which started in 1931 with the collapse of Austria's Credit Anstalt did not occur in the spring and summer of 1998, notwithstanding the warnings of the Cassandras (Krugman, 1999). But the slowness of Asia's recovery was worri-some. Swift recovery from the Mexican crisis had come because the main des-tination for Mexican exports—the United States—was growing rapidly, while recovery from the East Asian crisis was likely to be slow because the main focus of East Asian exports—Japan—was stagnating and unprepared to do anything to solve its problem.

The success of East Asia's recovery therefore required that the Federal Re-serve risk some possible rise in inflation in the United States. Fed staff con-tinued to oppose further easing, until Russia's default and the subsequent flight to quality shocked them out of their complacency. By the end of August, Fed Chairman Greenspan had accepted the need for further loosening and was actively raising Secretary Rubin's level of worry over the risk that the crisis could spill over into U.S. capital markets. Substantial easing of monetary policy in the industrial core, led by the Fed, then followed.

But continued stagnation in Asia combined with Russia's default to produce a large rise in yield spreads throughout the world. It was this sharp rise in spreads that was the proximate cause of the financial distress of Long-Term Capital Management. Quickly confidence in Brazil and its peg began to dete-riorate, raising fears of another round of contagion. The financial press wrote of a "financial firestorm" that had generated the "most baffling currency cris[i]s since the system of fixed exchange rates crumbled a quarter of a century ago."[83] President Clinton spoke in September of the gravest financial crisis of the post-war era. Doubts mounted about whether the IMF had the resources needed to contain its spread.

Fortunately, before long, looser credit conditions began to work, and the in-nate productive potential of the Asian economies began to reassert itself. By the end of 1998 there were clear signs of recovery in Korea and Thailand, countries that had basically followed IMF prescriptions, curbing domestic demand, re-structuring their financial systems (even if more slowly, hesitantly, and incom-pletely than the IMF had wished), and keeping interest rates high enough to

---

83. Davis, Friedland, and Moffett (1998).

avoid the extremes of depreciation. But there were also clear signs of recovery in Malaysia, which had followed its own very different course. Only Indonesia, where the East Asian financial crisis had segued into the Suharto succession crisis, remained in severe distress. By early 1999—save for Indonesia—the Asian financial crisis was over.

The last of the major international financial crises confronting the Clinton administration—Brazil in late 1998 and early 1999—unfolded differently. Superficially the circumstances were similar. The currency was overvalued, again by a familiar 20 percent. The current account was in deficit; reserves were running down. Treasury officials were less than happy about having to support another unsustainable peg, but in the fall of 1998 fears of contagion to other emerging markets and even the United States led them to conclude that there was no alternative, especially in light of the losses suffered by commercial banks, investment banks, and other institutional investors as a result of the combination of Russia and LTCM. They doubted, in other words, whether the system could "take another hit." And, though they would have preferred seeing Brazil move to a more flexible exchange rate earlier, as in the case of Mexico four years previously, U.S. officials lacked the power to compel this change.

The U.S.- and IMF-led response was cut from the same cloth as its predecessors: a large IMF loan (600 percent of quota) with numerous conditions (but no unconditional demand that the country alter its currency peg) and a nearly matching amount from the United States, Japan, the World Bank, and the Interamerican Development Bank, in November 1998. As in these other cases, official finance put off the day of reckoning but did not avoid the denouement. Unlike Mexico and Asia, however, Brazil's abandonment of its peg and forced shift to floating in January 1999 did not precipitate a major output decline; contrary to the consensus forecast of a serious slump, real GDP declined only modestly before recovering robustly in the second half of the year. It did not spread contagion to other emerging markets. It did not infect the United States.

Had the Clinton administration and its collaborators on 19th Street finally learned the secret of how to manage an exit from an unsustainable peg? The strong family resemblance of the Brazilian package to its Asian and Mexican predecessors casts doubt on this Whig interpretation of recent financial history. It is sometimes said that the very fact that the banks could see the crisis coming encouraged them to hedge their exposures, a response which limited the adverse financial fallout after the fact. But it had also been possible to foresee the Mexican and Thai crises, and foresight did not avert the adverse financial consequences, thereby casting doubt on this interpretation.

It is suggested that previous crises had taught the Brazilian government the importance of building credibility with the markets and of replacing its peg with a clear and coherent monetary-policy operating strategy; hence it installed Arminio Fraga and inflation targeting. But why Brazil should have been faster to learn these lessons than other countries is far from clear.

Brazil was less dependent on trade than either Mexico or the East Asians, with the result that a misaligned exchange rate posed less of a threat to its economy. But while Brazil may have been less open to trade, it was highly open to finance, and it was the financial fallout that proved surprisingly mild.

Finally, it is argued that the combination of the Asian crisis, Russia's default, and the flight to quality following the near-collapse of LTCM led to a sharp reduction in leverage in international financial markets, which reduced the scope for contagion. But while this can help explain the limited spread of the Brazilian crisis, it does not help us to understand why the macroeconomic consequences in Brazil itself were so mild, in international comparative terms. The very different aftermath of Brazil's crisis remains one of those late-20th-century mysteries to be unraveled by future historians.

4.5 Strengthening the International Financial Architecture

This sequence of events ignited a debate, which still simmers, about how to better prevent and manage financial crises. Treasury was quick off the mark with speeches by Secretary Rubin at Georgetown and Brookings in February 1998 on the need to "strengthen … the architecture of the international financial system."[84] Of course, Rubin's speech was not the administration's first foray into this area. Although the Mexican rescue had not provoked an equally contentious debate, it had created concerns, both inside and outside the administration, about moral hazard. And it raised red flags about inadequate transparency and weak financial systems. In response, the international policy community, with impetus from the Clinton Treasury, started down the path it has been following ever since.

Mexico's crisis had highlighted problems of inadequate monetary and fiscal transparency. Data on the Bank of Mexico's reserves had come to the market late (in 1994 as much as six months late), and deficits had been hidden in the accounts of the development banks (as noted earlier). The market reaction was abrupt and violent, the conclusion followed, because deterioration of underlying conditions had been hidden, rendering the devaluation of the peso an unpleasant surprise. This was an argument for encouraging countries to release such information in a more timely fashion so that investors would curtail the provision of credit more gradually and ratchet up the pressure for corrective action without precipitating a crisis.

---

84. See Rubin (1998a).

Moreover, the magnitude of the assistance extended to Mexico was unprecedented, reflecting the increased scope for funds to flow over the capital account, in turn forcing the administration to resort to the Exchange Stabilization Fund on a large scale to obtain the necessary finance. In response, Congress convened hearings, and Representative Bernie Sanders of Vermont succeeded in introducing a bill that would have made it more difficult for the Treasury to again draw on the ESF for Mexico-style operations.[85] In addition, D'Amato succeeded in adding a rider to the appropriations bill for fiscal year 1998 that limited the use of the ESF for international rescues. (The rider required that the president certify that any use of the ESF would not cost the United States money—that repayment was guaranteed. In addition, it required that, except in an emergency, the president obtain congressional approval for any loan of more than $1 billion for more than six months. These conditions effectively prevented the use of the ESF in 1997 during the first, Thai, stage of the crisis, as we explained earlier.)[86] If rescue operations were to be repeated, therefore, their financial basis had to be regularized. And doing so required international agreement.

America's G-7 partners had been ambivalent, to put it mildly, about the Mexican rescue. The crisis had not erupted in their backyards. Their investors had not held large numbers of *tesobonos*. European governments and central banks had always interpreted the lender-of-last-resort doctrine conservatively and taken the moral-hazard critique seriously. For all these reasons, it was not clear that they would support future Mexico-style rescue operations.

The first time these issues were formally addressed was the G-7 summit in Halifax in June 1995, at the conclusion of which the heads of state released an unusually detailed analytical document (G-7, 1995). This document reflected each of the lessons drawn by the Clinton administration from the crisis. Reflecting the belief that many of Mexico's monetary, fiscal, and financial problems had been hidden, it recommended greater transparency and requested that the IMF should sharpen its surveillance, issue franker assessments of country conditions, and establish templates for data dissemination. This last request led to the creation of the IMF's Special Data Dissemination Standard in March 1996.[87]

The premise was that market discipline could be relied on to rein in financial excesses before they got out of hand. Countries would not again be allowed to

---

85. Though Sanders' bill never became law, as an indication of congressional sentiment it surely added to the reluctance of the administration to again resort to the ESF.

86. The rider expired after September 30, 1997, the end of the fiscal year (as already noted), and was not renewed subsequently.

87. It is important to recall, in other words, that this standard was not simply a child of the Asian crisis. Subscription to the SDDS remains voluntary (that is, IMF members are not obliged to subscribe).

get into a Mexican-style bind where they found themselves with $23 billion of short-term foreign-currency liabilities but only $5 billion of reserves, since the markets would curtail the provision of short-term credit before things got out of hand, and the government would feel the pressure sooner to undertake the necessary adjustments. With benefit of hindsight we can say that the emphasis placed by the Treasury's "financial architects" on the risks of inadequate financial transparency and excessive reliance on short-term foreign debt were right on the mark; these were the problems that would return, with a vengeance, in Thailand, South Korea, and Indonesia two years later.

But, aided by 20–20 hindsight, we would argue that too much was asked of transparency and market discipline. Investors' attention span is limited, causing the application of market discipline to be uneven.[88] Market discipline does not function well in an environment where other distortions—implicit guarantees for banks and corporations, for example—are pervasive.

In addition, efforts to encourage transparency were uneven. Some would say there was something of a double standard: in the same way that the administration lectured Russia about democracy but hesitated to do the same to Saudi Arabia, it lectured Latin America about transparency but was reluctant to do so in Asia. There was a sense, shared in Europe and Japan, that Asian culture was different and that Anglo-Saxon-style transparency was too much to ask. Thus, efforts to encourage greater transparency did not prevent Asian governments from pursuing policies (like the Bangkok International Banking Facility and the Korean government's decision to free bank-to-bank borrowing before permitting foreigners access to Korean stock and bond markets) that greatly heightened their susceptibility to capital-flow reversals.[89]

To allow the IMF to respond more adequately to capital account crises, the administration called for the G-10 (together with other countries not previously involved) to double the credits they made available to the Fund through the General Agreements to Borrow and the newly created New Agreements to Borrow.[90] This call was embraced by the G-7 at its June 1995 Halifax Summit, and adopted by the IMF executive board in a decision taken in January 1997,

---

88. Indeed, the example of Long-Term Capital Management suggests that the application of market discipline is uneven even where the stakes are large, distortions are absent, and the way that the institutions work is well known. See Lowenstein (2000).

89. As more than one very senior U.S. Treasury official has pointed out, crises had a much higher chance of striking countries that had significant nonneutralities in favor of hot-money capital flows.

90. The NAB did not replace the existing GAB, but it became the first and principal recourse in the event that the institution needed supplementary recourses. The new name and separate arrangement were needed because the expanded arrangement was to include additional countries. As formulated, it involved 25 members and institutions. The original proposal at the Halifax summit to double the size of the GAB had not envisaged a separate arrangement because it had not anticipated the need to draw additional finance from new members.

although it took until 1998 and the lesson of the Asian crisis for Congress to agree to fund the NAB and therefore for the new arrangement to become operational. While the Europeans continued to warn of moral hazard, they concluded that it was better that such rescue operations as were mounted should be arranged through the IMF where they could have a say.

The G-7 also asked G-10 finance ministers and central bank governors to review procedures for crisis resolution. The result was the Rey Report (G-10, 1996), which addressed concerns that large-scale rescue packages were an engine of moral hazard and discussed the feasibility of alternatives ranging from limited changes in contractual provisions to the creation of ambitious new institutions (such as an international bankruptcy court for sovereign debts).[91] The report concluded that moral hazard was best addressed by modest changes in the institutional framework. While there could be occasions when officials, rather than extending emergency financing, might want to allow the country and its creditors to restructure their debts, the feasibility of this approach should not be taken for granted. It was something that needed to be facilitated by institutional changes such as IMF lending into arrears (to provide the crisis country the equivalent of "debtor-in-possession financing") and the introduction of collective action clauses into bond indentures (as a way of preventing restructuring from being blocked by opportunistic creditors), a contractual innovation that governments might have to actively encourage.[92]

The Rey report was the product of a G-10 process; some of its limitations reflected the fact that the emerging markets were not directly involved. This observation led to a second exercise: the Draghi report, composed by a working party made up of G-10 deputies together with representatives of emerging markets (Argentina, Indonesia, Korea, Thailand—it is not as if officials missed the obvious suspects—along with Hong Kong, Mexico, Poland, and Singapore), and the multilaterals. Jeffrey Shafer and Timothy Geithner spoke for the U.S. Treasury, Edwin Truman for the Federal Reserve Board. Its report, issued in May 1997 (Working Party, 1997), was remarkable for its prescience. Not only did it flag the usual macroeconomic sources of vulnerability, including debt management as well as monetary and fiscal policies, but it gave equal weight to "sector-specific sources of vulnerability" (corporate governance, and market

---

91. Treasury had wanted to say no to the sherpa proposal in 1995 that eventually resulted in the Rey Report, not knowing what recommendations such a high-profile international committee, which clearly possessed the expertise to articulate full-blown, coherent proposals, might table. On this occasion it was led to reverse its position by White House staff.

92. The IMF board agreed that its long-standing policy of lending into sovereign arrears on short-term loans from banks should be applied also to bonded debt. However, no official steps were taken to sharpen the incentives for the adoption of collective action clauses. We will return to this point later.

infrastructure and discipline, supervision and regulation—what the subsequent literature would refer to as weak institutions and flawed structural policies).

Particular emphasis was placed on the prerequisites for a robust financial system, not only the macroeconomic requirements but also the legal and juridical framework, accounting and other information systems, stakeholder rights, and limits on the extent of the safety net. Someone clearly saw the Asian crisis coming, although it is not clear that they saw it coming in Asia.[93] If there is a criticism of this document, it is that it placed more emphasis on the identification of problems than their solution and on the design of optimal policies than on the capacity to administer them. And it lacked a sense of urgency; there was no sense that the relevant reforms had to be implemented in short order if a major regional crisis was to be headed off.

Be that as it may, the point is that the main issues raised by the Asian crisis were on the table before that crisis struck. The Clinton Treasury was a prime mover behind the push for greater transparency, for larger IMF facilities, and for examining the causes and resolution of sovereign liquidity crises. While rejecting ambitious schemes for an international bankruptcy procedure on grounds of political feasibility and worries that doing so would simply substitute one source of moral hazard for another, it acknowledged the need for modest institutional changes that would permit market-based restructuring as an alternative to large-scale financial rescues of crisis countries.[94]

But if the Tequila crisis highlighted the need for institutional changes to cope with the rapid growth of capital flows, it did not lead the administration to rethink its core strategy of encouraging the deeper integration of countries into global financial markets as a way of promoting reform and faster growth. How much responsibility the Clinton administration deserves for this push for capital account liberalization is a contentious issue.[95] As already noted, the initial impetus came from elsewhere. Rubin and Summers themselves had always had relatively nuanced views of the merits of capital account liberalization; as noted earlier, neither was an unmitigated believer in the wisdom and efficiency of the markets. But the administration clearly could have done more to prevent the train from careening down the tracks. Much later, Rubin, then a former secretary, acknowledged in an interview, "With the benefit of hindsight I would say that we should have put more of an emphasis earlier on getting the rest of it right" (*New York Times*, Dec. 12, 2000, p. 1), where in referring to "the rest of it" he meant "making sure countries had a regulatory structure and an under-

---

93. As noted previously, the exercise did not enable officials to foresee the crisis in Indonesia, the paradigmatic case of a country with weak institutions and flawed structural policies.
94. See Summers (1996).
95. As our readers, who disagree among themselves, have reminded us.

standing of what could befall them if the world picked up its money and moved it elsewhere."

The administration's support for capital account liberalization flowed naturally from its belief in free and open markets. It reflected the experience and predisposition of a Treasury secretary with extensive experience in the markets. As Rubin put it in a speech timed to coincide with the spring 1999 Bank-Fund meetings, "Our approach ... has been informed by the fundamental belief that a market-based system provides the best prospect for creating jobs, spurring economic activity, and raising living standards in the United States and around the world."[96] It was a function of the belief that controls on capital flows created opportunities for corruption. It reflected the view that domestic financial liberalization had profoundly important benefits, but also the side effect of rendering capital controls that much more difficult and distortionary to administer and operate. Finally, it followed from the administration's commitment to trade liberalization, insofar as trade in merchandise was increasingly superseded by trade in services.[97]

This approach reached its pinnacle (some would say its nadir) with efforts to secure an amendment to the IMF Articles of Agreement to oblige the members to establish the convertibility of their currencies on capital account.[98] Although

---

96. Rubin (1999), p. 1. Or, as he put it on another occasion, "Any discussion of changes to the global financial system should be, from my perspective, grounded in a fundamental belief that a market-based global economic system, based on the relatively free flow of goods, services and capital between nations around the world, will best promote global economic well being in the decades ahead" (Rubin, 1998b, p. 2).

97. Politically, Treasury could not be significantly less aggressive in attempting to secure national treatment for American banks than the U.S. Trade Representative (USTR) was in pursuing market access for other U.S. exporters. This fact led to a curious role reversal during the WTO financial services negotiations, with the USTR, hoping to secure a deal, arguing that the United States had gone as far as it should in pushing developing countries to allow commercial banks and insurance firms to enter their markets, while the Treasury continued to insist that more was necessary and desirable. Throughout, Treasury sought to draw a distinction between opening the capital account to financial flows and cross-border business and extending the right of establishment and national treatment to foreign financial firms in domestic markets. Summers, in a speech delivered soon after the outbreak of the Asian crisis, insisted that capital account liberalization "is logically separable from the degree of domestic market access enjoyed by foreign financial institutions" but then went on to acknowledge that in practice the two tend to be linked (Summers, 1997, p. 3). A notorious example of linkage is Thailand, where the government opened the Bangkok International Banking Facility and then announced that it would give the broadest licenses to those who brought in the most money. With benefit of hindsight, it can be argued that more attention should have been paid to such dangers.

98. In the language of the declaration of the Interim Committee of the IMF, the amendment would have made the liberalization of capital movements "one of the purposes" of the Fund. By analogy to the provision in the Articles of Agreement obliging members to establish the convertibility of their currencies on current account, governments would still have been able to delay this step for a transitional period, during which supportive measures were put in place. Still, the amendment would have ratcheted up the pressure for them to move in this direction.

this initiative did not originate in Washington (it emanated from the British and French treasuries, as we understand it, and was enthusiastically received by Camdessus's IMF at both staff and management levels), neither did the administration oppose it. The administration owed one to the IMF managing director after Mexico: its life had been made much easier by Camdessus's willingness to turn on a dime and instantly contribute the lion's share of money for the peso support package in spite of the opposition of the British and German executive directors. And in the aftermath of the peso crisis, which reflected imprudent debt management by an emerging market country, Treasury saw merit in extending multilateral surveillance to the process of capital account liberalization.

With benefit of hindsight we can say that this initiative was at best poorly timed and at worst fundamentally misconceived. If there is one lesson of the Asian crisis, it is that premature capital account liberalization, initiated before prudential supervision is upgraded, corporate governance is strengthened, and government guarantees for domestic financial intermediaries are removed, creates conditions that can be described as an accident waiting to happen. However carefully the amendment to the articles might have been scripted, and however long actual implementation of capital-account liberalization was to be delayed—viewed as an ultimate goal rather than a current policy—nevertheless the pressure to adopt it sent the wrong signal. Even though the administration supported broad deference to supervisory concerns as a legitimate constraint on capital account liberalization, Camdessus's speeches on the amendment and the priority to be attached to the objective were less nuanced; and given the influence of the United States in the Fund and the fact of close Treasury-IMF links, there was the perception, right or wrong, that the United States was a wholehearted supporter of this push.

The rebuttal is that the problem was not with the policy but with its implementation in Asia: the Koreans opened their capital account exactly backward (freeing their banks to borrow offshore before liberalizing inward direct foreign investment and foreign access to domestic bond and equity markets), and the Thais subsidized short-term bank-to-bank borrowing by establishing the notorious Bangkok International Banking Facility. But this argument ignores the limited administrative capacity and politicization of policy that were facts of economic life in much of Asia and that should have more profoundly shaped the Washington consensus.

Learning from the experience, the administration drew back from this position following the Hong Kong Bank-Fund meetings, adopting a more careful and nuanced position emphasizing the benefits of "properly sequenced and supported" capital account liberalization. It became "quietly sympathetic" to the use of Chilean-style taxes designed to limit short-term interbank borrowing.[99] By the winter of 1997–98 the amendment to the articles was off the table, as policy-makers became preoccupied by the Asian crisis.

The recognition that a backlash was brewing against financial globalization and the need to head off radical proposals for reform were what prompted Secretary Rubin to deliver his high-profile speeches on the subject of architecture in advance of the spring 1998 meetings of the Fund and the Bank.[100] Rubin laid out the three-pronged approach to strengthening the international financial system that was to characterize Treasury's efforts in this area for the remainder of the administration: initiatives to enhance disclosure and transparency, initiatives to strengthen national financial sectors, and mechanisms to ensure that the market more fully bore the consequences of its credit and investment decisions (that rather than investors being "bailed out," they were "bailed in").

While these recommendations echoed the conclusions of the Halifax and Lyon summits, they also transcended them. On data and disclosure Rubin pointed to the problems, raised by the Asian crisis, of obtaining a complete picture of the forward and derivative liabilities of central banks and the foreign currency liabilities of commercial banks and corporations. He called for promoting "new, more flexible forms of debt agreements and indentures" to provide a framework for direct negotiations between debtors and creditors.[101] And he proposed the development of "a more complete range of global standards" to guide governments' efforts to strengthen their domestic financial systems.[102]

---

99. In the words of a *Wall Street Journal* report (Apr. 5, 1999, p. A22). Others of us would instead say "at least acquiescent," and distinguish Treasury's tolerance for Chilean-style measures where they already existed from its reluctance to actively urge their more widespread adoption. The new approach is encapsulated in the report of G-7 finance ministers to the June 1999 Cologne summit, which concluded that "the use of controls on capital inflows may be justified for a transitional period as countries strengthen the institutional and regulatory environment in their domestic financial systems. Where financial sectors and supervisory regimes are weak, safeguards may be appropriate to limit foreign currency exposure of the banking system" (G-7, 1999, p. 10).

100. Indeed, discussions had begun, within Treasury and between the Treasury, Fed, and White House (represented by the CEA), on the need for fundamental measures to strengthen the international financial system (a "Halifax II") almost immediately following the outbreak of the crisis.

101. While not mentioning collective action clauses by name. Actually, the Brookings speech as printed referred to direct negotiations between "creditors and investors" where it presumably meant "debtors and investors."

102. The push for standards was not exclusively a U.S. initiative; the U.K. Treasury and Bank of England played prominent roles in the formulation of this approach. To be sure, this standards-centered approach had other precedents, notably the Standard for Capital Adequacy for International Banks promulgated by the Basle Committee of Banking Supervisors. This too had been a U.S. initiative. (We understand it as a U.S. response to the debt crisis of the 1980s, and specifically to Paul Volcker's concern that this crisis had revealed the tendency for international competition to exert competitive pressures that undermined the capital adequacy of international banks.)

This was a more completely articulated agenda for strengthening the international financial architecture than potential rivals could claim. Camdessus was immediately receptive to the argument for encouraging transparency and promulgating international standards as a way of structuring international efforts to strengthen emerging economies' financial systems. He saw standards and codes as a vehicle for exerting pressure on member countries to upgrade their national financial policies and practices while at the same time providing an objective basis for IMF surveillance and conditionality and freeing the institution from criticism that its interventions were arbitrary and capricious. Camdessus and his staff recognized that, by placing the Fund at the center of these efforts to strengthen financial systems, it might be possible to further expand the mission of the institution.[103]

The G-22, an outgrowth of the so-called Willard Group (an earlier effort by the administration to bring together the developed and developing countries around a single set of policy recommendations), quickly issued reports on transparency and disclosure, on strengthening national financial systems, and on private sector burden sharing, all of which were in line with Treasury thinking.[104] To the extent that the recommendations differed from those of the Rey Report two years earlier, they reflected the Treasury's increased insistence on "voluntary" solutions, which represented a backing away from Rey.[105]

It was in the area of crisis resolution that the administration was least successful in clearing a path. Its role was largely one of vetoing schemes, which it viewed as counterproductive or worse, to contain and resolve crises by giving national governments or multilaterals the power to override the markets. Ad-

---

103. To be sure, the Fund had already crafted a "Framework for Financial Stability" that essentially described standards for the supervision and regulation of banks and securities markets. The Fund had also developed a code for fiscal transparency, also in response to impetus from the U.K. Treasury. But there was considerable resistance in its higher echelons to widening the focus of surveillance from the Fund's core competencies of monetary, fiscal, and exchange-rate policies, resistance that was only overcome in the wake of Rubin's architecture speeches. Compare, for example, the absence of any reference to standards in Camdessus's February 1998 speech to the Bretton Woods Committee (Camdessus, 1998a) with the emphasis placed on this initiative in his May speech to the Royal Institute (Camdessus, 1998b).

104. See G-22 (1998a, 1998b, 1998c). President Clinton's offer to organize the G-22 meeting originated with a proposal that Prime Minister Goh of Singapore made while the two were playing golf before the November 1997 APEC meeting in Vancouver. In a repeat of the pattern when it had been proposed to create the Rey Committee in 1995 (discussed earlier), Treasury opposed the idea, until it was reformulated by the White House. The G-22 was later expanded into the G-33 (adding the remainder of the G-10) before being slimmed down into the present G-20, which held its first ministerial meeting in December 1999.

105. One participant in G-22 report drafting tells us that it was a struggle to keep "voluntary" out of every paragraph—it kept coming back in, in the handwriting of high Treasury officials.

ministration officials torpedoed France's proposal in 1998 for a "financial safe-guard clause" (analogous to the safeguard clauses that exist in international trade) under whose umbrella countries might impose temporary capital con-trols. They resisted Canadian and British calls for an international standstill mechanism for sovereign debts. If debt standstills and restructurings were to emerge as an alternative to large-scale financial rescues, they insisted, their fea-sibility would have to be demonstrated by the markets.

But administration officials did not offer specific suggestions for institu-tional changes to facilitate this process. For the proposed changes suggested by others—mandating the addition of collective action clauses to loan contracts, or establishing standing committees of creditors, for example—they showed little enthusiasm. For example, they rejected measures to mandate the adop-tion of collective action clauses as a means to this end. In 1996, Deputy Secre-tary Summers had described the case for collective action clauses as "obvious" (Summers, 1996, p. 6), and it was anticipated that the United States would support some kind of official action to encourage their adoption. It quickly be-came apparent, however, that financial-market participants, represented in this instance by the Institute of International Finance, strongly opposed legislation and regulations that might require them to modify their contracts. The extent to which this private-sector pressure influenced U.S. policy is unclear. Rubin's experience with the markets encouraged in him the belief that, if changes in contractual arrangements were desirable, they would come of their own voli-tion; this may have been all that was at play.

Be that as it may, by 1998 the administration had distanced itself from the idea of providing official incentives for the more widespread adoption of these provisions, and argued in international forums that the official sector had no business mandating the provisions of private loan contracts. The G-22 Working Group on International Financial Crises (G-22, 1998c), led by U.S. Under-secretary David Lipton, recommended only that governments engage in "edu-cational efforts" in the major financial centers and that they "examine" the use of such clauses; it did not suggest that the IMF should key its lending rates and disbursements on their willingness to do so.

Was there any positive result in terms of creating an alternative to large-scale financial rescues as a way of addressing crisis problems? The scholarly answer would be that it is still too early to tell. When the IMF lends there is now a presumption that it will ask for a commitment from investors not to withdraw funds as quickly as the official sector pumps them in. But whether or not the markets can manage the process of debt restructuring smoothly enough to avert serious output losses and relieve the IMF of pressure to intervene still remains unclear.[106] Institutional innovations like exit consents (pioneered in the case of Ecuador) provide some grounds for thinking that the markets are up to the challenge. Be that as it may, the transition from the Clinton administration to the Bush administration may increase the likelihood that we will have an experiment to see how this works.[107] But if the process is difficult and proves highly disruptive to the markets, the pressure for IMF intervention in the event of future crises will only intensify again, reviving the case for institutional changes to facilitate an alternative.

The exchange-rate issue played surprisingly little role in these early architecture debates. To be sure, the issue came up in every official postmortem of the crises, but it hardly occupied a place of prominence, and official pronouncements remained weak soup. This lack of emphasis seems curious with hindsight, given the undeniable association of crises with currency pegs starting with Europe in 1992 and proceeding through Mexico in 1994 before arriving in Asia in 1997 and Brazil in 1998. Every major financial crisis since Mexico's in some way involved a fixed or pegged exchange-rate regime, as even the IMF was eventually forced to acknowledge.[108]

From this perspective, it is striking that only in April 1999 did a G-7 leader, Rubin, state outright that the IMF should no longer support shaky currency pegs and that emerging markets should move away from such arrangements in favor of hard pegs or, in most cases, more flexible rates. His deputy, Summers, had been pushing this "corner solutions" argument for some time.[109] The argument resonated with Rubin's experience in the markets, which informed his view that currency pegs were fragile and accident-prone. Indeed, the advocacy by the Rubin-Summers Treasury of the corner-solutions view (that only hard pegs and relatively free floats are viable in a world of high capital mobility) was stronger and less conditional than many others in the administration found to their liking (though right on the mark, in our view).

---

106. We are not arguing that it is desirable to eliminate all output losses following crises—any more than it is desirable to eliminate all crises. Dooley (2000) develops the argument that output costs of misbehavior are necessary in order for lending to occur in the first place but exaggerates the implications, in our view. If one believes, as we do, that the IMF feels compelled to lend because these output losses are judged excessive by that institution's principal shareholders and that the moral hazard that flows from those loans is a source of inefficiency, then institutional reform that reduces those output losses and therefore the moral hazard created by a pattern of IMF lending is a step in the right, efficiency-enhancing, direction.

107. Early experience with Turkey to the contrary notwithstanding.

108. In contrast, countries without pegged rates—South Africa and Mexico in 1998, for example—while not immune from international capital market disturbances, suffered to a much lesser degree than countries with pegs (Fischer, 2001c).

109. For example, in a speech to the Interamerican Development Bank meetings the month before (Rubin, 1999, p. 4).

This was a coherent intellectual position, but the United States was not able to assemble the coalition needed to operationalize it. The Europeans, given their history and their plan to create a monetary union, were not sympathetic to the case for floating rates; they had blocked frank discussion of the issue in the deliberations leading up to the Rey Report and again at the time of the G-22 report on managing financial crises. Asian governments, for their part, were reluctant to entrust their currency values to the market and resisted calls for greater exchange-rate flexibility. The IMF, being an institution of many members (and headed by a managing director who continued, even in the face of the crisis, to favor a return to fixed rates), continued to offer weak advice to the effect that "no one size fits all" and "what matters above all is consistency between exchange rate and other policies."[110] The U.S. Treasury was unable to overcome this hesitancy and division.

Here, moreover, the failure to develop alternative mechanisms of crisis resolution came home to haunt the administration. For countries with balance-sheet mismatches, abandoning a currency peg could create serious financial difficulties and even widespread bankruptcies, as the case of Indonesia had shown. The cost of servicing dollar- and yen-denominated loans would soar if the exchange rate fell by a significant amount, leaving firms, many of whose earnings were in local currency, no way of keeping current on their debts. Widespread bankruptcy was the unavoidable result.[111] Absent mechanisms for more speedily resolving these problems, this was not an option that anyone was prepared to contemplate. Not surprisingly, when push came to shove, as in Brazil in 1998 and Turkey in 1999, the Fund, backed by its principal shareholders, continued to intervene in support of governments' efforts to maintain those pegs. And knowing that they still stood to receive international support, governments were understandably slow to move to greater flexibility. Notwithstanding this reluctance, there has been slow but steady movement in the direction of greater exchange rate flexibility in the developing world, something that has clearly reduced the risk of further financial crises.[112] But that movement has tended to be involuntary—the result of a crisis (as in Turkey and Argentina) rather than a preemptive step to avert one.

The final item on the architecture agenda was IMF reform. A first issue was the structure of conditionality. The Fund had been attaching additional

---

110. Fischer (2001a) may indicate some change of opinion on this subject among the senior management of the institution, as may the appointment of a new managing director (although only time will tell). More generally, the implications of subsequent changes in the IMF management team for views on this subject remain to be seen.

111. As described in more detail in Section 4.4.

112. See Fischer (2001b).

structural conditions to its loans since at least the mid-1980s (the time of the Baker Plan). In Asia in 1997, these conditions were intended to precipitate "a vast change in domestic business practices, corporate culture, and government behavior."[113] The 1997 Indonesian program typified both the aspiration and the excesses: the conditions of the IMF program dealt with, among other things, reforestation, the national car program, local content programs for motor vehicles, the compulsory 2 percent after-tax charitable contribution, restrictive market agreements for cement and paper, the forced planting of sugarcane, the introduction of a microcredit scheme for small businesses, and the elimination of the Clove Marketing Board. While the "Christmas-tree" nature of this program was a product of the IMF bureaucracy and of Indonesian technocrats, who viewed it as an opportunity to push through much-needed domestic reform in the shelter of an IMF package but failed to deliver their principal, we are not aware of strong Treasury warnings of the dangers.

Treasury was sensitive to the danger that any evidence that Fund conditionality was being used to advance the country's own agenda (which in this case might have included opening up sheltered markets to international competition and giving U.S. commercial and investment banks improved market access) would undermine the legitimacy of IMF conditionality and the credibility of U.S. policy advice. It therefore resisted USTR pressure to use the crisis as an opportunity to gain specific concessions on market access for U.S. banks and corporations. Indeed, it is hard to find structural conditions in the fund's programs that worked to the particular advantage of U.S. banks and firms.

On the intrinsic merits of structural conditionality, Treasury was torn. On the one hand, its own approach to prudential supervision and regulation emphasized the need for competition, transparency, and arms-length dealing, and it instinctively wished to export these features of U.S. market structure and organization to emerging markets with the help of the IMF. It saw the crisis, and the resort of the Asian tigers to the Fund, as an opportunity to apply pressure and to reinforce domestic support for fundamental opening and reform—to encourage these countries to break with crony capitalism, which may have been an appropriate arrangement for getting industrialization off the ground but was no longer a viable basis for growth in an increasingly advanced, competitive, financially deregulated and technologically dynamic region. It saw the crisis, and the IMF programs crafted in response, as a window of opportunity to encourage much-needed domestic reforms and to support reform-minded elements in various Asian countries. On the other hand, U.S. officials could not fail to appreciate the danger of a backlash—that intrusive conditionality might fuel

---

113. Camdessus (1998a), p. 3.

popular resentment of the Fund, as well as of the country that was its principal shareholder.

Whether this emphasis on structural conditions was counterproductive, as authors like Feldstein (1998) insist, only time will tell. We are of the view that whether it is wise for the United States or the IMF to explore with national leaders which things they would like to be pushed can only be decided on a case-by-case basis; blanket rules for what should be in or out of IMF programs are unlikely to be feasible or desirable. If, as a result of the Asian crisis and the response, countries like Korea are really breaking with crony capitalism, creating capital markets, and opening up (as some would have it), then the case for at least limited structural conditionality will look strong. Whatever the answer turns out to be, the administration itself concluded that the expansion of structural conditionality had gone too far and came out in late 1999 in favor of a simplified and streamlined process (Summers, 1999b).[114]

Russia's default and the near-collapse of the Greenwich, Connecticut–based hedge fund, Long-Term Capital Management, by impressing upon the G-7 that financial fragility was not just an emerging-market problem, lent additional urgency to the architecture debate. Once more the administration sought to set the international agenda. Clinton, in his speech at the Council on Foreign Relations on September 28, 1998, warned that failure to act could "put our own prosperity at risk."[115] The main substantive innovation he suggested was the idea of a new facility to provide emergency financing for countries pursuing strong policies but nonetheless vulnerable to financial problems occurring elsewhere in the world.

Reflecting the perceived severity of the threat posed by the crisis, the concept was quickly endorsed by the G-7 in the extraordinary out-of-cycle declaration of October 1998 (G-7, 1998), and that endorsement led to creation of the IMF's new Contingent Credit Line (CCL) in 1999. The CCL was a quick-disbursing facility intended to prevent collateral damage to innocent bystanders in the event of crises. Limiting access to countries with strong policies addressed the moral hazard concern, while prequalifying them for assistance promised to shorten the delay between requests for assistance and their disbursal.

---

114. Although it never went so far as being recommended by such critics as Feldstein (1998) and Meltzer et al. (2000). Some would suggest that it staked out this position in order to anticipate and preempt a conclusion of the Meltzer commission and thus to head off some of its more radical recommendations.

115. In retrospect, this rhetoric can be criticized as alarmist. But its purpose was to ratchet up the pressure on Congress to vote a quota increase for the IMF, thereby increasing the resources available to the institution; in effect, it warned the politicians on Capitol Hill that they would be held responsible for the crisis if they did proceed accordingly.

Unfortunately, the new facility delivered less than hoped. Rather than seeing the CCL as an additional line of defense against market turbulence, emerging-market governments feared that it would be seen as evidence that they were worried about crisis problems. And because strong policies could weaken, access to the CCL was never automatic; even countries that prequalified were subject to a further review by the IMF board upon their request to actually draw. For both reasons, the CCL had no obvious advantage over a normal IMF program. At the time of writing, no country has applied for one.[116]

The Asian crisis, like the Mexican crisis before it, underscored the extent to which the growth of market liquidity had outpaced the growth of IMF resources. This created an obvious argument for a quota increase. Given Republican control of Congress and the firestorm of criticism surrounding the expansion of IMF financial activities, the administration's success in pushing through a quota increase in late 1998 was nothing short of miraculous.[117] Officials testified at least 11 times on the Hill on IMF funding, more than three times as often as on domestic issues such as tobacco legislation and reform of the Internal Revenue Service. Their efforts were helped along by press coverage of Russia's default and the collapse of LTCM as threatening a global meltdown; Congress clearly didn't want to run the risk of being held responsible.[118]

The price was agreement to the demand to establish a bipartisan commission (ultimately chaired by Allan Meltzer) to recommend reforms of the international financial institutions.[119] The Meltzer commission came back with a recommendation that IMF assistance be extended only to countries with strong policies and at risk of destabilization through no fault of their own,[120] that such loans should be contingent on prior actions rather than conditions regarding

---

116. Although rumor has it that this situation may have changed by the time our audience receives this chapter. The IMF subsequently attempted to make the CCL more attractive by simplifying access at the point of disbursal and by reducing the associated interest charges. Defenders of the CCL have argued that its mere existence may have played a role in preventing Brazil's end-1998 crisis from spreading to other countries, but we know of no evidence to this effect.

117. This increase raised the Fund's lending capacity from about $130 billion to some $195 billion (not counting the expansion of the General Arrangements to Borrow into the New Arrangements to Borrow, something that had been proposed by the administration following the Mexican crisis and that was acted upon by Congress in 1998). The U.S. contribution was $14.5 billion for the quota increase and $3.4 billion for the New Arrangements to Borrow.

118. As noted earlier, the president ratcheted up the pressure that Congress felt in his Council on Foreign Relations speech, where he characterized its failure to vote the quota increase as "irresponsible."

119. In addition, the IMF Authorization and Appropriations Act of 1998 required an annual report and testimony by the secretary of the Treasury on the IMF and required that the GAO prepare an annual report on IMF programs and policies.

120. Which would seem to exclude Mexico, Thailand, Indonesia, and Korea, for in all these cases weaknesses in government policy played some role in setting the stage for the crisis.

subsequent policies, and that the terms and conditions of IMF loans should be tightened to discourage countries from taking excessive resource to the Fund.[121] The Treasury's response challenged the realism of a policy of benign neglect of crises in countries whose policies were less than impeccably strong, questioned the feasibility of prequalifying countries for assistance, and rejected the notion that policy conditionality could be eliminated.[122] Treasury was in a position to dismiss some of the more extreme recommendations of the commission because it had already conceded the moderate ones, like the desirability of higher interest rates and shorter terms to maturity on IMF loans (notably in a speech by Secretary Summers to the London Business School in December 1999).[123]

The final issue under this subheading, governance of the international monetary and financial system, was a delicate one, given not only the need to give emerging markets greater voice in order to enhance the legitimacy of the process (and give them "ownership" of the reform agenda) but also the fact that changes in IMF governance might jeopardize the "U.S. veto" (the fact that important decisions require agreement by countries accounting for at least 85 percent of IMF quotas and that the United States possesses more than 15 percent of those quota rights). Predictably, it was easier to make changes outside the IMF where financial commitments were not involved.[124] The impetus the Clinton administration provided for the creation of the Willard Group and the G-22 responded to a real need to create a talk shop for high-level officials and their deputies that was not limited to the advanced-industrial countries, but it also limited the pressure for a fundamental reform of IMF quotas. In addition, the administration—and the Fund itself—emphasized the need for more transparency in IMF decision-making and documentation as a way of holding the fund more accountable to its ultimate constituents. It made progress in this direction despite the hesitations of a number of European and emerging-market members.

---

121. See International Financial Institution Advisory Commission (2000).

122. See U.S. Treasury (2000).

123. See Summers (1999b). The United States tabled proposals for raising interest charges on Fund borrowing and reducing the term of loans at the time of the IMF's spring meetings in 2000, most of which were then adopted. Space limitations prevent us from discussing the efficacy of these changes in any detail. One question is whether higher interest rates and shorter terms to maturity are efficiency enhancing. Here, reasonable people (like the two present authors) can disagree; one's answer depends on whether one thinks that the main problem with the status quo ante was moral hazard (in which case higher interest rates and shorter terms may be desirable) or that governments are often too focused on how to pay back their loans to the IMF in the next 24 months (in which case they are not). A prior question is whether modest changes in the term and cost of borrowing will significantly affect the behavior of crisis countries desperate for external finance.

124. Thus the United States sought in 1999 to build support for a realignment of the constituency system, reducing the number of Europe-led constituencies in order to free up seats for Asian, African, and Latin American countries, but without success.

To what extent, in summary, did the Clinton administration guide the course of the architecture debate? Our assessment is "very considerably."[125] The presumption of the benefits of international financial liberalization that infused the Rubin-Summers Treasury remained a given, notwithstanding the reservations of foreign governments and the fact of emerging-market crises. The enhanced transparency and international financial standards advocated by the administration (with the strong support of the British) became the centerpieces of efforts to upgrade financial policies and financial systems. The administration played an important role in encouraging the IMF to upgrade its surveillance of financial markets.[126] It provided the impetus for creating the Group of 22, which developed into the Group of 20. It proposed the establishment of a "Market Conditions Advisory Group" composed of private-sector experts, which was the seed from which sprang the Capital Markets Consultative Group in which the Fund now takes such pride. Its recommendations had flaws and were not always clearly successful or even adopted. (Witness the Contingent Credit Line and the continued muddle with the Europeans and Japanese over exchange-rate arrangements.) Nor were its damage-control efforts always successful. But it possessed the loudest and most articulate voice.

These initiatives all had the strong support of the U.S. financial community. In contrast, where the administration had less support from its financial constituency, such as in developing new approaches to crisis resolution, it was less successful in setting the agenda for reform. By moving away from its early advocacy of institutional changes to facilitate orderly debt workouts, partly in response, it would appear, to opposition from U.S. financial interests, and by adopting a more ad hoc approach to involving the private sector in the resolution of crises, it heightened uncertainty about the process of crisis resolution and reinforced worries about the moral hazard caused by a pattern of financial rescues, problems that linger to this day.

4.6   Conclusion

International economic problems and policies occupied the Clinton White House and Treasury to a greater extent than anyone had anticipated in 1992. In part this emphasis reflected the failure of the president and his staff to develop domestic initiatives other than deficit reduction that could command the sup-

---

125. Coeure and Pisani-Ferry (2000, p. 34) agree: they write, "Over the last three years, the discussions on reforming the international financial architecture have been by and large an exercise in American leadership."
126. Thus, it lobbied for the creation of a Capital Markets Department in the fund that would take the monitoring of market conditions and gathering of market intelligence as its mandate.

port of swing votes in the Senate. More fundamentally it reflected far-reaching changes in the world economy. Falling transport costs raised the benefits of international trade for developed and developing countries and not least for the United States. Financial liberalization and the information revolution combined to accelerate the process of capital market integration, creating new opportunities for those on both sides of the international investment equation but at the same time heightening the economic and financial risks.

From a domestic point of view, the administration's monetary and financial policy was extraordinarily successful. Deficit reduction created space for monetary ease, which in turn supported the investment-led recovery that ended a two-decade-long productivity slowdown and powered one of the longest, strongest expansions in history.[127] Moreover, these events played a positive role in the rest of the world. European policy-makers spent much of the 1990s preparing for monetary union and grappling with the chronic fiscal problems that were the principal obstacle to achieving it. They had little room in which to adjust aggregate demand in the interest of global growth and stability. Japanese policy-makers spent the decade trying to minimize the embarrassment of executives and organizations who had made bad choices in the bubble economy years; they paid little attention to managing aggregate demand even to support their own growth. Only U.S. policy-makers worried about global demand and sought to do something about it. In this context, they deserve more credit than blame for their willingness to risk the growth of the U.S. trade deficit and allow the United States to be the importer of last resort.

Others would describe the Clinton administration as blindsided by a series of international monetary and financial problems that it should have seen coming. These crises came as a surprise because economists' models and half a century of historical experience both suggested that crises arise when it becomes impossible to sustain unsustainable policies. The symptoms of such unsustainability

---

127. The story by which the 1990 Bush-Mitchell-Foley and 1993 Clinton-Mitchell-Foley deficit-reduction packages broke the back of the Reagan deficits, allowed the Federal Reserve to reduce interest rates, and thus boosted the share of investment spending in GDP in the United States in the 1990s is well known. The links between the investment boom and the rapid pace of productivity growth achieved in the United States in the 1990s are probable, but less certain. A large component of rapid productivity growth came from the technological revolutions in data processing and data communications. But such productivity growth does not fall from the air. It is built from the ground up as businesses slowly and methodically install and learn how to use the capital goods that embody the new revolutionary technologies. Budget deficits that raise interest rates discourage this process of investment and increase the gap between the standard-installed and the innovative best-practice levels of technology. It is not clear how long the acceleration in United States productivity growth was delayed by the Reagan deficits in the 1980s. It is clear, however, that productivity growth in the 1990s would have been significantly slower had the U.S. federal budget deficit remained high. Here the Clinton administration pursued good policies, and also got lucky as the economic payoff to deficit reduction turned out to be much larger than anyone had imagined.

(large budget deficits, rapid inflation) are common knowledge, as is the medicine appropriate for treating them (monetary and fiscal retrenchment).

But while the Thai, Russian, and, arguably, the Mexican and Brazilian crises fit this mold, many of the other crises of the 1990s did not. In particular, the Asian crisis of 1997–98 hit countries that were in broad macroeconomic balance and had been following broadly sustainable policies. Those crises had structural roots. Lending by Asian banks was often guided as much by political as economic criteria. Countries in the region had weak systems of corporate government and opaque forms of financial organization that made it hard for outsiders to influence and even determine what was going on. And even where macroeconomic imbalances were present, structural problems accentuated their effects: in Mexico, for example, there was an overhang of dollar-denominated and dollar-indexed debt coupled with fears of political instability that rendered policy commitments (including the exchange-rate commitment) fragile.

Still, in each of these cases, the afflicted countries' sins against the gods of macroeconomics seemed minor compared to the punishment, which was harsh and swift. These aspects of the crisis problem were all corollaries of the liberalization of domestic and international financial markets, a policy to which U.S. support actively contributed with what in retrospect can be criticized as a bit of excessive zest.

Because these crises followed a new pattern, they surprised policy-makers. The response therefore had to be assembled on the run. Unsurprisingly, it can be and has been criticized: too much reliance on the standard monetary and fiscal instruments in addressing crises whose roots were not fundamentally monetary or fiscal, too much well-meant but ill-timed advice on how affected countries should reform their economies. At the same time, the IMF and the U.S. Treasury did make substantial loans to crisis-affected countries, these loans greatly eased the process of adjustment and recovery, and only one country (Indonesia) suffered more than a short interruption to its growth.[128] Successful international monetary and financial policies thereby supported the processes of growth and development that pulled more than 4 billion people past the takeoff stage and onto the escalator that leads to modern industrial and postindustrial living standards. In this view, the fundamentally sound international monetary and financial policies of the United States helped to sustain growth and development worldwide. Compared to the problems of the dollar cycle and the Latin

---

128. It can be argued that deep political problems in Indonesia rendered the patient immune to the conventional economic treatment (and even rendered the tender ministrations of the international money doctors counterproductive). It seems probable that most of Indonesia's current economic problems are the result of the Suharto succession crisis, in other words, and thus are analytically distinct from the East Asian crisis—even if the second did trigger the first.

American debt crisis in the 1980s, or of the oil shocks and the breakdown of the Bretton Woods System in the 1970s, the 1990s have to count as a pretty good decade.

Still, workers in Mexico, Korea, and Indonesia paid a price. It can be argued that the price was to a considerable extent avoidable because the crises in which it was incurred were not in fact very new—that they really should not have come as such a surprise. During the crises of the 1990s, observers rediscovered the dangers of fickle animal spirits destabilizing capital flows, of the vulnerability of investment to crony capitalism, of how poor banking-sector regulation can generate an international financial crisis, and of how the existence of resources to provide support and rescue funds in a crisis could lead the private sector to hold imprudent portfolios that increased the risk to the system. But these were issues that had been familiar from 19th-century experience with financial globalization; they had been raised by John Maynard Keynes and Harry Dexter White in the negotiations that culminated in the Bretton Woods Agreement of 1944.

It is not as though those responsible for the international monetary and financial policies of the Clinton administration were blind to these risks. U.S. Treasury Secretary Robert Rubin had spent his career at Goldman Sachs making money from the failure of the market to accurately value securities; he was no naive believer in the efficiency and rationality of the markets. When still in academia, U.S. Treasury Secretary Lawrence Summers had long been an intellectual opponent of casual reliance on the efficient-markets hypothesis.

So what explains their failure to warn more loudly of the risks of international financial liberalization? More than anything, the explanation lies in their belief that, if markets were not perfect, the alternatives were worse. There was a hope that by forcing the pace of financial liberalization, countries might be compelled to more quickly upgrade their domestic regulations and institutions. Conversely, encouraging them to open only after the requisite domestic reforms were well advanced applied no pressure for reform; it was a road map to a destination that might never be reached. The strategy was risky, as the series of financial crises that punctuated the decade of the 1990s so graphically revealed. But the extent of fundamental reform in much of Asia and Latin America, and the speed with which growth resumed following crisis in many of the affected countries, suggests that this may have been a gamble worth taking.

References

Bergsten, C. Fred. 1986. "America's Unilateralism." In C. Fred Bergsten, E. Davignon, and I. Miyazaki, *Conditions for Partnership in International Economic Management*, Report no. 32. New York: Trilateral Commission.

Boorman, Jack, Timothy Lane, Marianne Schulze-Ghattas, Ales Bulir, Atish Ghosh, Javier Hamann, Alexandros Mourmouras, and Steven Phillips. 2000. "Managing Financial Crises: The Experience in East Asia." IMF Working Paper No. WP/00/107 (June).

Callaghy, Thomas. 2000. "The Vagaries of Debt: Indonesia and Korea." In Gregory Noble and John Ravenhill, eds., *The Asian Financial Crisis and the Architecture of Global Finance*, 213–234. Cambridge: Cambridge University Press.

Camdessus, Michel. 1998a. "The Role of the IMF: Past, Present and Future." Remarks at the Annual Meeting of the Bretton Woods Committee, February 13.

———. 1998b. "Toward a New Financial Architecture for a Globalized World." Address to the Royal Institute of International Affairs, May 8.

Chinn, Menzie. 1998. "Before the Fall: Were the East Asian Currencies Overvalued?" NBER Working Paper 6491, April.

Clinton, W. J. 1998. "Address to the Council on Foreign Relations," September 28. www.whitehouse.gov.

Congressional Budget Office. 1993. *An Analysis of the Economic and Budgetary Impact of NAFTA*. Washington, DC: GPO.

Council of Economic Advisers. 1995. *Economic Report of the President, 1995*. Washington, DC: GPO, February.

Coeure, Benoit, and Jean Pisani-Ferry. 2000. "Events, Ideas and Actions: An Intellectual and Institutional Retrospective on the Reform of the International Financial Architecture." Conseil D'Analyse Economique Working Paper No. 04-2000, July.

Davis, Bob, Jonathan Friedland, and Matt Moffett. 1998. "Epidemic? As Currency Crisis Spreads, Need of a Cure Grows More Pressing." *Wall Street Journal*, Aug. 24, 1998.

DeLong, J. Bradford, Andrei Shleifer, Lawrence H. Summers, and Robert J. Waldmann. 1990. "Noise Trader Risk in Financial Markets." *Journal of Political Economy*, 98:703–738.

Dooley, Michael. 2000. "Can Output Losses Following International Financial Crises Be Avoided?" NBER Working Paper no. 7531, February.

Dornbusch, Rudiger. 2001. "A Primer on Emerging Market Crises." Unpublished manuscript. www.mit.edu.

Edwards, Sebastian. 2001. "Does the Current Account Matter?" NBER Working Paper No. 8275, May.

Eichengreen, Barry, and Michael Mussa, with Giovanni Dell'Ariccia, Enrica Detragiache, Gian Maria Milesi-Ferretti, and Andrew Tweedie. 1998. *Capital Account Liberalization: Theoretical and Practical Aspects*. Occasional Paper No. 172. Washington, DC: IMF, September.

Federal News Service. 1995. "Hearing Before the Senate Banking Committee: Mexico and the Exchange Stabilization Fund, July 14, 1995.

Feldstein, Martin. 1998. "Refocusing the IMF." *Foreign Affairs*, 77:20–33.

Fischer, Stanley. 2001a. "Transcript of a Press Conference," May 8. www.imf.org/external.

———. 2001b. "Exchange Rate Regimes: Is the Bipolar View Correct?" Distinguished Lecture on Economics in Government, Delivered at the Meetings of the American Economic Association, New Orleans, January 9. Forthcoming in the *Journal of Economic Perspectives*.

———. 2001c. "Asia and the IMF." Remarks at the Institute of Policy Studies, Singapore, June 1. www.imf.org.external.

Frankel, Jeffrey A. 1994. "Exchange Rate Policy." In Martin Feldstein, ed., *American Economic Policy in the 1980s*, 293–341. Chicago: University of Chicago Press.

Furman, Jason, and Joseph Stiglitz. 1998. "Economic Crises: Evidence and Insight from East Asia." *Brookings Papers on Economic Activity*, 2:1–135.

Goldstein, Morris. 2000. "IMF Structural Programs." In Martin Feldstein, ed., *Economic and Financial Crises in Emerging Market Economies*. Chicago: University of Chicago Press.

Greenspan, Alan. 1999. "Efforts to Improve the 'Architecture' of the International Financial System." Testimony Before the Committee on Banking and Financial Services, U.S. House of Representatives, May 20. http://www.bog.frb.fed.us.

G-7 Finance Ministers. 1999. "Strengthening the International Financial Architecture." Report of G7 Finance Ministers to the Cologne Economic Summit, June 18–20. http://www.ustreas.gov.

G-7 Heads. 1995. "Examination of the International Financial Institutions." Information of the Halifax Summit, June.

———. 1998. "Declaration of G-7 Finance Ministers and Central Bank Governors," October 30. http://www.imf.org/external/np/g7/103098dc.htm.

G-10. 1996. *The Resolution of Sovereign Liquidity Crises*. Basle: BIS, May.

G-22. 1998a. *Report of the Working Group on Transparency and Accountability*. Washington, DC: G-22.

———. 1998b. *Report of the Working Group on Strengthening Financial Systems*. Washington, DC: G-22.

———. 1998c. *Report of the Working Group on International Financial Crises*. Washington, DC: G-22.

Institute of International Finance. 1999. "Report of the Working Group on Financial Crises in Emerging Markets." Washington, DC: Institute of International Finance.

International Financial Institution Advisory Commission. 2000. *Report*. Washington, DC: IFIAC.

International Monetary Fund. 1994. *International Capital Markets Report*. Washington, DC: IMF, October.

Kaplan, Ethan, and Dani Rodrik. 2001. "Did the Malaysian Capital Controls Work?" NBER Working Paper No. 8182, January.

Knetter, Michael M., and Thomas J. Prusa. 2000. "Macroeconomic Factors and Antidumping Filings: Evidence from Four Countries." NBER Working Paper No. 8010, November.

Kraay, Aart. 1998. "Do High Interest Rates Defend Currencies During Speculative Attacks?" Unpublished manuscript, World Bank.

Krugman, Paul. 1994. "The Myth of Asia's Miracle." *Foreign Affairs*, 73:62–78.

———. 1999. *The Return of Depression Economics*. New York: Norton.

Lane, Timothy, and Steven Phillips. 2000. "Does IMF Financing Result in Moral Hazard?" IMF Working Paper No. 00/168, October.

Lowenstein, Roger. 2000. *When Genius Failed: The Rise and Fall of Long-Term Capital Management*. New York: Random House.

Meltzer, Allan, et al. 2000. *Report*. Washington, DC: International Financial Institutional Advisory Commission.

Nurkse, Ragnar. 1944. *International Currency Experience*. Geneva: League of Nations.

Reich, Robert B. 1997. *Locked in the Cabinet*. New York: Alfred A. Knopf.

Rubin, Robert. 1998a. "Strengthening the Architecture of the International Financial System." Speech delivered at the Brookings Institution, April 14. http://www.brook.edu/comm/transcripts/rubin/htm.

———. 1998b. "Remarks to the Dow Jones/Wall Street Journal Annual Conference on the Americas," October 1. http://ibreaudigilib.usia.gov/aug99/usiaweb/regional/ea/asiafin/rubin101/htm

———. 1999. "Remarks on Reform of the International Financial Architecture." *Treasury News*, RR-3093, April 21.

———. In press. "Comment on 'Industrial Country Policies.'" In Martin Feldstein, ed., *Economic and Financial Crises in Emerging Market Economies*. Chicago: University of Chicago Press.

Schwartz, Anna J. 1997. "From Obscurity to Notoriety: A Biography of the Exchange Stabilization Fund." *Journal of Money, Credit, and Banking*, 29, no. 2 (May): 135–153.

Spadafora, Francesco. 2000. "The Pricing of Syndicated Bank Loans to Emerging Markets: Some Further Results." Unpublished manuscript, Bank of Italy.

Summers, Lawrence H. 1996. "Introduction." In Peter B. Kenen, ed., *From Halifax to Lyons: What Has Been Done about Crisis Management?* Essays in International Finance 200, International Finance Section, Department of Economics, Princeton University, pp. 1–6.

———. 1997. "Building a Global Financial System for the 21st Century." Speech to the Congressional Economic Leadership Institute, August 12. http://www.celi.org/summers.htm.

———. 1999a. "Reflections on Managing Global Integration." *Journal of Economic Perspectives*, 13:3–18.

———. 1999b. "The Right Kind of IMF for a Stable Global Financial System." Remarks to the London Business School, December 14.

Tanner, Evan. 1999. "Exchange Market Pressure and Monetary Policy: Asia and Latin America in the 1990s." IMF Working Paper WP/99/114.

U.S. Senate Banking Committee. 1995. *The Mexican Peso Crisis*. Hearings Before the Committee on Banking, Housing, and Urban Affairs, S. Hrg. 104–164. Washington, DC: GPO.

U.S. Treasury. 2000. Response to the Report of the International Financial Institution Advisory Commission. Washington, DC: GPO.

Willett, Thomas D. 1999. "Did the Mexican Bailout Really Cause the Asian Crisis?" Claremont Policy Briefs, Issue No. 99–01.

Woodward, Bob. 1994. *The Agenda: Inside the Clinton White House*. New York: Simon & Schuster.

Working Party on Financial Stability in Emerging Market Economies. 1997. "Financial Stability in Emerging Market Economies." Basle: Group of Ten, April. www.bis.org.

Zhang, Xiaoming. 1999. "Testing for 'Moral Hazard' in Emerging Markets Lending." Research Paper No. 99-1. Washington, DC: Institute of International Finance, August.

Comments

Stanley Fischer

In 1990 it was possible to believe that the leadership of the international economic system was moving away from the United States, toward Japan and Europe. A decade later there was no question that the United States had for good or ill maintained and strengthened its position.

I believe it was mainly for the good.

In describing the development and exercise of that leadership, I will focus on two closely related topics: the financial crises in Mexico, Asia, and Russia; and the reform of the international monetary system.

The Financial Crises

Despite some early wrestling over the question of the value of the yen in its first two years, the Clinton administration first became deeply involved in issues of the international financial system during the Mexican crisis in 1994–95. The IMF, the U.S. Treasury, and the international community all learned important lessons from that experience.

At the fund, having been surprised by the crisis, we learned that we had to operate on a real-time basis in our surveillance of economies and markets. In 1994 there were no Reuters or Bloomberg screens in the fund. Some argued that we should take the long-term perspective, and not focus too much on day-to-day market movements. Possibly that was true before the emerging market countries emerged into the international capital markets. But the Mexican experience— labeled by then Managing Director Michel Camdessus as the first international financial crisis of the 21st century—drove home how essential it is to pay very close attention both to capital account developments and to market developments. The fund now monitors market and market-related political developments continuously, through staff access to financial news services, and with seven to eight news summaries a day circulated by e-mail. In the summer of 2001 our new International Capital Markets department started operating. It is dedicated to further improving surveillance of the international capital markets, to improving our understanding of those markets, and to helping our members take advantage of them (and deal with the risks they bring).

The United States learned lessons too. NAFTA had just been set up, and Mexico had recently joined the OECD. There was a view in the Treasury that such a country does not go to the IMF for assistance. In addition, the United States did not share whatever advanced information it had about the developing crisis in Mexico with the IMF, and for about two weeks after the December 20 devaluation, the Treasury tried to handle the problem on its own—though to be sure, the Mexican authorities did visit the fund soon after the devaluation to explain the policies they would follow. Eventually, the Mexicans decided to ask for IMF support for the program. The lesson here is clear: when a country gets into trouble, trying to help it fix its problems bilaterally is much more difficult than trying to do so in the context of a multilateral organization, to which the country itself belongs, and in which it has certain membership rights.

Over the course of its existence, the Clinton administration progressively moved away from attempts to handle problems bilaterally, toward involving the IMF much more quickly. And as the IMF reformed itself, it was quickly involved in crises in any event. Such rapid response was good for the system and good for the administration. Of course, these changes didn't mean the Treasury didn't try to micromanage crises—or that doing so wasn't frequently a mistake.

A second lesson emerged when the $40 billion package of financial support for Mexico proposed by the administration fell apart at the end of January 1998. The administration turned to the IMF to provide about half the financial package. The lesson: the IMF was set up in part as an international mechanism to lend to countries in financial trouble, with international burden sharing in the provision of loans (and they are of course loans, not grants) determined by the size of IMF quotas. It is an effective and fair way of dealing with financial crises, and it should be used for that purpose.

The administration's support for the IMF was expressed in concrete form in 1998, when a quota increase became necessary. The congressional battle over the quota increase (like the battles over the funding of IDA, the World Bank's concessional window, and the funding of the United Nations) was difficult and intense, but the administration was able to deliver. Equally important to the IMF and particularly its staff was the unambiguous support for the institution expressed by Secretary Rubin during the times when the fund was under most intense attack during the global crisis.

The international community learned lessons from the Mexican crisis too. The most important was the need for transparency, especially as regards economic data. The IMF and investors simply did not know what was happening to Mexico's reserves in the lead-up to the crisis. There was a massive effort immediately after the crisis had stabilized to improve public data provision by member countries. The result of this effort took the form of the so-called Special Data Dissemination Standard (SDDS), to which nearly 50 countries now subscribe. The reserves template in the SDDS requires detailed information on reserves to be made available monthly, with a maximum one-month lag. If the reserves template had been in operation before 1994, several of the later crises could not have happened in the way they did, for public availability of data on reserves would have forced changes in central bank policy much earlier.

The Asian crisis is too big a topic to take up comprehensively in these comments, but let me mention a few issues relevant to U.S. policy. The first is the Thai package. Thailand was the first Asian country to get into trouble. The IMF provided a loan to Thailand, and so did a group of bilateral creditors, with Japan as the single largest contributor. The United States decided to stay out of that arrangement, possibly because of the domestic heat it had taken over its loans to Mexico. The Thais still remember that the United States did not participate in the bilateral financing package. This nonparticipation was a diplomatic mistake, which the United States was wise not to repeat in Indonesia and Korea.

Another important issue at the time was the proposal to create an Asian Monetary Fund (AMF). This was an attempt, led by Japan, to set up a regional monetary organization that would help countries in trouble in a kinder, gentler way than the IMF, the United States, or the Europeans would do. The IMF and the United States opposed the creation of the AMF. I believe the AMF would have failed if it had been set up then, because the notion that there was some easy way of resolving these crises was false. All it would have meant is that a lot more money would have been lost before the problems confronting the affected economies were dealt with. However, active consideration is now being given to gradual regional monetary integration in Asia—and this is an issue that future administrations will have to consider how to deal with.

Eichengreen and DeLong do not discuss Russia much. But there is an important question here: whether the United States (more generally, the G-7) and the IMF continued assisting Russia for too long?

There is room to quibble about whether assistance to Russia should have stopped three months earlier or six months earlier than it did. But the aid effort to Russia—relying largely on IMF and other IFI funding, as well as bilateral contributions from Germany and others—was fundamentally successful. The main evidence for that view is that there is now absolutely no disagreement in Russia on the right economic path to take. Everything that we in the IMF were trying to support in the way of macroeconomic stability and the direction of structural reforms is now conventional wisdom in Russia. No doubt the path of reform will not be smooth and there will still be setbacks along the way, but the goal and the route are clear to Russians.

The International Financial System

Now let me turn to the U.S. role in the reform of the international financial system. DeLong and Eichengreen describe this as a three-pronged approach: first, increasing transparency and disclosure of information to markets; second, strengthening the financial assistance available to countries in trouble; and third, exerting a greater effort to make the private sector bear some of the costs of these crises. The last is the most difficult of these prongs to make stick, and more work remains to be done to ensure that private-sector involvement operates effectively. But overall, this approach to improving the international financial architecture is proving successful.

I would add to the list the emphasis on the strengthening of financial systems. This is a particularly important area, in which there has been much progress—and the effort is continuing. There are also areas on the margin where more could have been done: for instance, in requiring greater provision of information by hedge funds.

U.S. leadership in the reform of the international financial system often took the form of institutional innovation. Within the IMF, the United States took the lead in promoting changes in our lending facilities. These included the introduction of the Systemic Transformation Facility in 1993, designed to help start transition economies on the road to reform. In 1995 the fund adopted a policy to offer support for currency stabilization funds within standby or extended arrangements, to help countries support fixed exchange-rate pegs as a way of getting out of high inflations. The Supplemental Reserve Facility (SRF) was introduced in 1997, moving the fund more in the direction of a classic lender of last resort, by increasing the amounts that could be lent without invoking the exceptional circumstances clause, and by raising fees and shortening repayment periods. The impetus for these changes came from the U.S. Treasury, and they were very important.

The United States was also strongly behind the most recent innovation, the Contingent Credit Line (CCL) facility. CCLs are a way of providing precautionary lending, helping countries strengthen their policies by making a line of credit available to them to help withstand the effect of crises elsewhere. Prequalification for loans was favored by the Meltzer commission, and it is an important direction for the fund to move for some of its lending. We should soon have our first taker for that facility.

Having helped introduce these new lending facilities, the administration, together with its European allies, also pushed hard for a simplification of the fund's array of lending vehicles. So we abolished a few outdated ones—including the CSF introduced in 1994—and that made sense too.

Other innovations included setting up new groupings. The G-20 brings 20 of the main industrial and developing countries into a group whose precise purpose is not yet clear. Another newly created institution was the Financial Stability Forum, where the lead was taken by the Europeans. This proliferation of institutions has not been entirely helpful. There are too many meetings, too many overlapping groups, and too many working groups, which must surely take officials away from their regular work. Some rationalization of these groupings would be welcome. Such a rationalization could also involve making the meetings of the International Monetary and Finance Committee (IMFC) less formal and more useful to the participants, as well as possibly changing the composition of the IMFC.

The administration's views on capital mobility did not change much during its period in office. Throughout, it maintained its support for countries keeping the capital account open, as well as for moving gradually, as the financial system and macroeconomic framework strengthened, to liberalize capital movements. Initially it supported amending the IMF's Articles of Agreement to make promotion of capital account liberalization a goal of the fund, but in the face of congressional opposition, it later withdrew its support. That decision was a pity, for giving the IMF the goal of promoting *orderly* capital account liberalization would make it more likely that future liberalizations will be well done—and some of the crises of the past were due to badly done liberalization.

My final comment is to note how the administration's views on exchange-rate regimes evolved over time. Like the IMF, but much more so, its view shifted from support for pegs, at least as a tool for disinflation, to a strong preference for flexible exchange rates. At the same time, the administration recognized that once a country is in a pegged-rate regime, forcing it out is very difficult.

Comments

Lawrence Summers

Before I turn to the topic of this session, the Clinton administration's approach to global financial markets, I want to say a few words about two other enduring international economic legacies of the administration: its sound macroeconomic management and its recognition of the benefits of global economic integration.

Macroeconomic Management

The first legacy of the Clinton administration is the idea that you can be progressive and yet stand for macroeconomic and financial rectitude. This legacy was, in turn, built upon three pillars of our policy:

• A commitment to deficit reduction, since running the federal government's budget in a prudent way would carry the major economic benefits of higher investments and growth.

• Respect for the independence of the Federal Reserve, since bashing the Fed was a fool's game. The Fed wouldn't listen (so short-term interest rates wouldn't change), but the market would listen (so long-term interest rates would go up).

• Recognition that a strong dollar was in the nation's interest, since artificially seeking to depress a currency for competitive advantage is a short-sighted strategy. Seeking to depress the value of a domestic currency doesn't increase competitiveness in the long run, but does cause a lack of confidence in financial markets and ultimately undermines the discipline needed to increase productivity.

Those three ideas—that surpluses were good, that administrations were better off ignoring the Fed, and that a strong currency was a good idea—were hypotheses supported by some, but certainly not all, economists in 1993. Eight years later, there is a much clearer track record in support of each of them. And if one listens to economic debates in Europe or in emerging markets, they reflect those three ideas to a much greater extent than would have been the case 10 years ago.

The first international economic legacy of the Clinton administration was thus the example it set for other nations in terms of economic policy management. Finance ministers all over the world now state that a strong currency, whatever their currency is, is in their nation's interest. There is also much more respect for the independence of central banks and much greater commitment to maintaining a budget surplus.

Recognition of the Benefits of Global Economic Integration

The second legacy of the Clinton administration involves recognition of the benefits from the economic integration of high-income countries and low-income countries. That idea found its expression in much of the president's rhetoric. But it found its expression in more than just rhetoric. Witness NAFTA, the Uruguay Round, and the emphasis on the desirability of free trade in the Americas.

It also found its expression in the aggressive response to financial crises when they arose in emerging markets. And it found its expression in the political groupings that the administration supported, including the president's participation in APEC meetings, as well as the formulation first of the G-20 and then the G-30 groups to bring larger numbers of countries into the financial dialogue. The administration recognized that an important part of the new interaction in the world was going to be between industrial economies and emerging economies, something that becomes increasingly important as the populations of the industrial economies age. The world's population growth and no small part of its economic growth will take place in the developing world in the future.

The idea that economic policy is centrally about integration with developing countries is not something one thought of when discussing trade and financial policy in the 1980s and the early 1990s. And a strong involvement of the United States with the developing world will be one of the important legacies of this administration.

Was it a successful legacy? In important respects, it was. If one looks at emerging markets, one has to be struck that over the last decade, Mexico has moved from South America to North America—with enormous benefits to American security—in no small part, I believe, because of NAFTA and the financial rescue for Mexico. Similarly, the inclusion of China in the world trading system will have a favorable impact on geopolitics for a long time to come. So will the recognition that global disease and poverty ultimately have moral consequences and, potentially, more profound direct consequences for us. These are all themes that are very large in the debate and were not large in the debate 10 years ago.

Approach to Global Financial Markets

The third legacy of the Clinton administration is its approach to the global capital markets. It is a serious mistake to frame this issue as it is usually framed, in terms of how many crises there were and the responses to those crises.

A proper history of aviation would recognize that crashes occur, that those crashes are a very bad thing, that it is very important to minimize crashes, but that the right test was how much transportation took place how effectively and with what risks. Counting the number of crashes—by which criterion the invention of the jet airplane would have been a failure for its first 15 years—is not the correct way to evaluate the success of aviation or of economic policy.

During the past decade, we went from a world in which a small minority of countries were able to access capital from a limited number of institutions to a world in which a large number of countries were able to access capital from a large set of institutions. As a consequence, this was a decade when, if you weight by population, the developing world performed better relative to the industrial world than during any previous decade in history. And that process of convergence, which carries with it potentially great benefits both for us and for developing countries, took place on a large scale.

It is a central task of the major creditor countries to create a world economic system in which the flow of capital from industrial to developing countries is strong and sustainable. From that point of view, the efforts of the Clinton administration did not focus on wholesale liberalization of financial markets in developing countries. That was never, contrary to many assertions, a central objective of policy. But it is important to recognize that there were important benefits to participation by foreign financial institutions in developing countries.

We must also realize that financial crises involve an important bank-run element: Instead of watching the underlying economics in the situation, investors start watching all the other investors and deciding who is going to get out first. Such situations arise from time to time, and it is very important that an aggressive response to them be mounted quickly, based on a combination of policy changes (to ensure that the fundamentals are sound) and the provision of finance on a sufficient scale (to allow a restoration of confidence). As a measure of relative efficacy of mounting an aggressive kind of response to these crises, it is instructive to contrast the lost decade in Latin America following the financial crisis that began in 1982, with the very rapid recovery of Mexico after its financial crisis in 1994 and with the rapid recovery in those countries that were prepared to take the necessary steps—Brazil, South Korea, and Thailand—that took place after the Asian financial crisis.

It is sometimes suggested that these policies are misbegotten because the availability of emergency finance somehow encourages unsound lending to the developing world. In my judgment, there is little evidence of substantial capital flows that were premised on the idea that finance would be provided in the moment of emergency, with the possible exception of Russia in 1998.

It is very important to distinguish, as people rarely do, between the classic U.S. example of the S&L crisis—in which funds are provided in cash to people who have invested in defunct institutions—and the situation in the international financial system, in which loans are made available, now at premium interest rates, with the assurance of repayment and in which the cost to the provider is zero. Indeed, the present value of many international loans may actually be negative, as it proved to be with the United States' rescue of Mexico. The U.S. Treasury made a profit.

Conclusion

That these policies were pursued is a tribute to the political courage of the president who pursued them. There was no strong constituency in his political party for the deficit reduction strategy, the strong currency strategy, or the idea of respecting the independence of the Federal Reserve. There is no strong internal political constituency in the United States for doing anything with the developing world.

And these financial rescues were mounted at enormous political risk. When we presented to the president the Mexican rescue program, which we were recommending that he adopt, we explained that it would cost $25 billion. We were corrected by one of his political advisers, who said that we must mean $25 million. And we said no, we actually meant $25 billion. The political class became a little quiet at that point, and then a senior official said: Mr. President, if this money goes to Mexico and it doesn't come back, it is likely to cost you the next election. And these people are telling you that it may not come back. And the president took that in. And he took in the report that they'd done a poll on our proposal, showing that 80 percent of the respondents were against it (a statistic which might lead you to the fallacy of thinking that 20 percent were in favor, but 14 percent were undecided). And the president, to his very great credit, responded by saying that we were there to do what we thought was the best thing, and that if we lost the election, we lost the election. But he couldn't sleep at night if he wasn't prepared to take something like this on. And in a matter of about a half an hour he made what was for him, politically, an enormously risky decision.

No president can afford to be courageous on every question that he faces. And certainly, President Clinton wasn't courageous on every question he faced. But on these crucial issues of defining America's international role, he was very much committed to an expansive, inclusive, internationalist vision, even at very great costs. And perhaps that idea will be the most enduring legacy of his administration.

Comments

Allan H. Meltzer

My comments focus on four major areas of international economic policy in the Clinton years. Bear in mind that actual policy actions represent a mixture of what is economically desirable and what is politically feasible. One way to judge economic policies is the degree to which they sacrifice economic efficiency and welfare for short-term political advantage. Another standard by which we should judge policy decisions and actions is the degree to which the policy benefits the present at the expense of the future or the reverse. And all administrations must choose where they will devote time, energy, and political capital. We can judge their priorities both to praise good choices and criticize what they neglected.

At a deeper level, we should inquire whether an administration's actions served to strengthen democratic government, the rule of law, and the protection of personal and property rights. Policy actions are often a response to events, rather than a deliberate choice of a policy path. The Clinton administration responded to crises in Mexico, Asia, Russia, and elsewhere. Crisis response often is the occasion for actions that stretch the meaning and intent of laws. This generalization was certainly true in the 1990s.

Trade Policy

The Clinton administration had two different trade policies. One sought to open markets. It produced ratification of the Uruguay Round of trade liberalization and the approval of the North American Free Trade Agreement (NAFTA). Purists may criticize NAFTA for the trade diversion that it created or the administration for emphasizing, incorrectly, job creation instead of productivity and welfare enhancement. These objections pale beside the accomplishment. President Clinton and his administration put much energy and political capital into getting ratification. This was a real achievement, against strong opposition, much of it coming from the administration's core constituencies, the labor unions and the environmental activists. The administration later followed these achievements by working effectively to win congressional support for admission of China to the World Trade Organization, again working for long-term benefits, providing a public good, and sacrificing the interests of its own constituents.

The other side of the ledger shows two major failures. First is the failure to get new negotiating authority (called fast track) to work out an agreement with Latin Americans or another round of global market opening. To an outsider, the administration seemed unwilling to mount an effort comparable to the effort it had used for NAFTA or China. Freer trade creates a global public good. The United States failed to lead the region and the world toward greater openness. This was a failure of Clinton policy, a choice of narrow, short-term political advantage over long-term benefit to us and others.

The president compounded this failure in Seattle by scuttling his administration's initiative for a new round of negotiations. This time President Clinton pandered to the labor union activists and the crowds in the street by supporting labor and environmental provisions that were unacceptable to most developing countries. This action sacrificed the economic development of emerging market countries through trade for electoral support of domestic antitrade groups. It sacrificed extensions of the rule of law for domestic political advantage.

The Strong Dollar Policy

Rhetoric aside, it is hard to know what this policy is. Economists understand that changes in the nominal exchange rate—the rate that is quoted in the market—have little lasting importance. The only ways to weaken the dollar in more than a temporary way are to either inflate faster than our trading partners or slow productivity growth relative to growth abroad, say, by taxing capital or investment heavily.

The dollar strengthened after the middle 1990s in large measure because U.S. productivity growth increased. With higher productivity growth, relative to Japan, Europe, and many other parts of the world, capital flowed here from abroad. The capital inflow is the way foreigners share in the higher profits and expected future profits that new technology is expected to bring. Because the increased productivity growth reflected, in part, new techniques, new processes, and new products, foreign companies invested directly, usually by buying U.S. companies. Other foreign firms bought hotels, retailers, theaters, and other domestic firms that profited from the spending boom. And foreign investors bought shares in U.S. companies.

The strong dollar resulted from the individual decisions of individuals and firms abroad, not from the administration's dollar policy. There was a surge of foreign investment toward the United States. The appreciation of the dollar was not policy induced.

What can we say about the rhetoric? What does it mean to say we have "a strong dollar policy"? Perhaps it means that administration officials did not criticize the Federal Reserve publicly or insist on lower interest rates and more inflation than Federal Reserve actions produced. This restraint is commendable and a great improvement over the rhetoric of its predecessors in the Bush administration. It is praiseworthy. But we should not confuse rhetoric with substantive policy.

The exchange rate is a price. With a floating exchange rate, that price adjusts to current and anticipated future economic conditions here and abroad. A floating exchange rate is a policy. Given the floating exchange rate, it is hard to know what a strong dollar policy is.

Financial Crises and International Financial Institutions

The size and frequency of international financial crises increased dramatically in the 1980s and 1990s. Latin America, Mexico, Asia, Russia, Brazil, and most recently, Argentina and Turkey drew hundreds of billions of dollars in rescue packages. Two nearly universal features of these rescues should be noted. The first is moral hazard: lenders suffered few losses, while the citizens of the affected countries suffered often-devastating losses of real income. Second, the International Monetary Fund (IMF) often pressured by the Clinton administration, insisted on a lengthy list of conditions because, as former Secretary Summers has said many times, crises provide excellent opportunities for insisting on reforms. The current IMF management has now recognized that most of these reforms had no bearing on a country's liquidity, solvency, or macroeconomic stability. This was a command and control system with a vengeance.

The command and control system had many flaws; two are major flaws. First, it subverted democratic processes. Although I deplore the methods chosen by the street demonstrators, many of their criticisms of the command and control system are correct. Second, for better or worse, the command and control system is ineffective. While there are difficulties in all studies of the effect of IMF conditionality, most find no significant effect on real income. The safest conclusion at this stage is that any positive effect is small. Certainly, no strong, positive effect leaps out of the data, whether the research is done within or outside the IMF.

Recently, the World Bank has advanced roughly $20 billion to $30 billion a year for poverty relief and economic development. The largest part, about 70 percent, goes to middle-income countries that can borrow in the international capital markets. For example, China receives $60 billion annually in private investment and loans from the capital market. It pays an interest rate only slightly higher than the rate at which the World Bank lends. Why should the World Bank lend to China? Would not the benefit be much greater if the bank financed effective programs in poor countries? As Jeff Sachs has emphasized, elimination of tropical diseases and improvements in tropical agriculture and forestry are examples of programs that could benefit many people in very poor countries.

In 1999, Congress voted to establish a commission to consider reform of the principal international financial institutions. The Clinton administration vigorously opposed establishment of the commission. It agreed, finally, as the price of getting congressional approval of $18 billion in additional funding for the IMF.

The international financial institutions have important roles to play. The *Report of the International Financial Institution Advisory Commission* called on the IMF to supply three valuable public goods: first, improvement in global financial stability and reduction in the magnitude and frequency of financial crises; second, improvement in the quantity and quality of information available in the market and in the timeliness of that information; and, third, provision of the services of a quasi-lender of last resort during financial panics.

The commission's most important reforms proposed an incentive system for the failed system based on command and control at the IMF and proposed far-reaching reforms of the World Bank and other development banks. These reforms would increase efficiency and effectiveness of multilateral development finance by making grants instead of loans to raise the quality of life in the poorest countries of the world, by providing incentives for initiating and sustaining the structural reforms necessary for permanently raising living standards, and by financing regional and global public goods.

To this observer, admittedly an interested observer, the Treasury's response can only be characterized as hostile. The administration made prodigious efforts, including telephone calls from President Clinton and Secretary Summers, to members of the commission urging them to oppose the report. These efforts failed to prevent a bipartisan vote in favor of the report. Later, the Treasury rejected every major recommendation in the report when it submitted the comments required by Congress. This hostility seems strange and counterproductive in view of the more cordial reception of the proposals at the IMF and the later endorsement by Secretary Summers of the proposal for grants.

I can only speculate on the reasons. There is, first, IMBIBU—it must be invented by us. Second is a commitment to command and control practices, a belief that we can impose policies on countries in times of crisis. The commission rejected this approach as flawed and unproductive. It subverts democratic processes abroad, encourages resentment and street demonstrations, and undermines institutions like the IMF, the WTO, and the development banks that, if restructured, would remain as important providers of public goods.

In the 1994–95 Mexican crisis, the Clinton administration, with the connivance of Congress, used the Exchange Stabilization Fund (ESF) to lend money to Mexico. This action was extralegal. The ESF, created to support the dollar, was used as a ready slush fund to avoid the budget process after Congress showed little inclination to approve a large loan to Mexico. Actions of this kind subvert the budget process and undermine the rule of law.

The Clinton administration developed a modern version of the medieval morality play. When the play's action reached a point at which it became impossible to bring the pieces together, it was time for the deus ex machina. A god descended in a basket and resolved all conflicts. In the Clinton years, the Treasury and the IMF rode in the basket. The deus ex machina was cash to prevent default by the debtor. Few lenders lost money. Often they earned substantial fees for restructuring the debt. Risk and return were separated. Moral hazard, excessive reliance on short-term capital to finance long-term development, and weak financial systems that relied on short-term capital increased the risk of crises and instability.

Japan

Japan's problems are mainly homemade. Mainly, but not entirely. The U.S. Treasury had a role, too. It recommended publicly—and, I am told, privately—that Japan should rely on fiscal stimulus and avoid sufficient monetary stimulus to depreciate the yen/dollar exchange rate. In the Japanese system, fiscal stimulus meant increased government spending, and spend it did. Japan has little to show for its massive fiscal spending except some social capital, much of it with low productivity, and the largest ratio of public debt to GDP of any developed country. Unemployment in Japan is now higher than in the United States for the first time in 50 years. Deflation persists.

In 1998 monetary stimulus showed signs of depreciating the exchange rate. The yen/dollar exchange rate depreciated to 145 in June from about 100 a few months earlier. Then Deputy Secretary Summers came to Tokyo and ended that policy. The yen soon appreciated to 105, a massive and foolish change in an economy with falling prices and rising unemployment.

The policy was mistaken and wrong, and it failed. The major mistake was a failure to recognize that the yen was overvalued. If Japan could not depreciate its nominal exchange rate, prices had to fall until Japan had a real exchange rate that was consistent with steady growth and stable prices. This process took time and is still continuing. Where was the strong dollar policy?

This failure was extremely costly to Japan, to Asia, and to us. A stronger, more rapidly growing Japanese economy would certainly have mitigated, and possibly prevented, the Asian financial crisis. Japan would serve as a source of demand for Asian exports now, when U.S. demand has slowed.

A lesser Asian crisis would have avoided the unsustainable U.S. current account deficit. The Federal Reserve would not have found it necessary to use heavy monetary stimulus in 1998 and 1999, running the risk of higher inflation to prevent the Asian crisis from spreading and deepening. Our expansion permitted many Asian countries to export their way out of the crisis, but the stimulus also helped to produce soaring stock prices and their aftermath.

Do not misinterpret what I have said. Under the circumstances, the administration and Federal Reserve program was the right policy in the Asian crisis and its aftermath. The world economy would be much worse if the United States failed to expand. But the expansion might have been unnecessary and would certainly have been smaller if the Japanese economy had not followed the Clinton administration's advice or if the advice had had a more long-run orientation, and less of a short-term U.S. domestic political orientation.

The Clinton administration talked endlessly about its prudent fiscal policy and the budget surplus they left behind. They don't mention that they also left a large current account deficit that cannot be sustained permanently. We have not seen the end of that story. We can hope the ending will come slowly so that the story ends happily. But, we do not know that it will, and we cannot draw a final conclusion about the record of the 1990s until we do.

Summary of Discussion

Lawrence Summers challenged *Allan Meltzer* to produce any serious legal opinion to support the contention that the Mexican action had been illegal. The wisdom of the action could be debated, according to Summers, but not the legality. Summers also argued that no U.S. policy-maker had ever counseled against easier money in Japan. The specific intervention that Meltzer criticized had been undertaken with considerable reluctance and only in response to the pleading of Japanese and other Asian authorities.

On conditionality, *Summers* argued that the quotation attributed to him was not something he had ever said in that context. Rather, Summers emphasized that when a country is experiencing large and continuing capital outflows, it is imprudent to lend money to that country without requiring a change in fundamental conditions. Thus the rationale for conditionality is simply that it is unwise to lend money into a situation that has proven to fail. To be sure, the specific parameters of conditionality programs are something that reasonable people can debate. But Summers pointed to two specific cases of successful conditionality: Mexico, in which the move to fiscal consolidation and tighter money (which would not have happened without conditionality) helped to resolve the financial crisis, and Korea, in which conditionality reduced the government's proclivity to provide excessive guarantees.

Finally, *Summers* echoed *Barry Eichengreen's* point that North American and global views regarding the benefits associated with exchange-rate stability differed significantly. For that reason, he argued that *Fischer's* portrayal of a joint evolution of doctrine between the United States and the IMF on exchange rates was somewhat misleading. The United States was ahead of the IMF in becoming increasingly concerned about attempts by the European Union to peg exchange rates. To this day, reflecting the global constitution of its membership, the IMF is reluctant to counsel against almost any exchange-rate scheme that its member countries judge to be ideal.

Meltzer argued that the policy Adam Lerrick and he proposed in the *Financial Times* would involve zero costs except for the time of someone like Stanley Fischer and his staff. In response to *Summers*, Meltzer noted that, having served as an adviser to the Bank of Japan for 15 years, he has a close association with people working in the bank. He argued that it was commonly stated in Japan that during the Clinton years it was not possible to devalue the yen substantially because of opposition from the U.S. Treasury. Meltzer argued that perceptions clearly differed about this issue, as they do about many other policy issues.

In response to a question about money laundering, *Summers* argued that the ongoing multilateral processes created during the Clinton years achieved modest successes by inducing a variety of Caribbean havens to tighten their statutes and controls. But, he added, there was much left to be done. He was therefore troubled by the Bush administration's reluctance to address money laundering seriously, and in particular he was concerned about the administration's effort to scuttle the OECD's very important work in the area.

In response to a question about hedge funds in the Asian crisis, *Eichengreen* noted that he had been tasked with studying precisely that issue when he arrived at the IMF. He then circled the world talking to hedge fund managers, government officials, central bankers, and others. The basic result of the study was that only in Thailand, where these highly leveraged institutions had large positions in 1997, could the crisis be linked to hedge fund activities. But even there, there was little that was special about their actions and investments: What a hedge fund can do, in some sense, an investment bank and commercial bank can do better because they have more capital at their disposal. His conclusion was that it wasn't productive to single out the hedge funds or their managers.

A member of the audience asked how the panelists would change the institutional structure within the executive branch to handle crises. *Summers* responded that the Clinton administration's National Economic Council played a very constructive role in bringing different agencies together to address questions of this kind. He argued that it was difficult to manage a technical area like financial policy because policy-makers had to balance political constraints and the technical prospects of success, and the latter consideration required that decisions be concentrated in a significant way among those who have expertise in the relevant economic and financial issues. He concluded that the National Economic Council and the coordination it provides was probably a constructive way of organizing a government response to these types of issues.

Meltzer added that every administration finds the means of organizing its policy process in a manner compatible with the president's operating style. He argued that there is no single administrative structure that is going to be good for all times.

In response to a question about monitoring compliance with IMF packages in Pakistan, *Fischer* noted that Pakistan has had loans from the IMF in the past, and it also gets loans from the World Bank. What has happened frequently is that the international financial institutions lend in tranches, so that the country does something and then gets some money, the country does some more, and gets more money, and so on. But as an outsider, the IMF and World Bank cannot sit there and determine everything that a country does. Conditionality is limited. The issue in Pakistan was therefore not a lack of monitoring; it was a lack of ability to control what was done, and also a lack of control by the government. On taxation, *Fischer* argued that the major problem in Pakistan was that many people don't pay taxes. He noted that when he listens to the sins of the IMF, he often wonders why people don't ask what their own government should be doing.

Summers agreed with *Fischer*, but also pointed out that the U.S. Treasury pushed for more external auditing of central banks. He added that, if, five years from now, the IMF has 40 fewer economists and 40 more forensic accountants looking for various kinds of corruption and diversion, it may be able to do its job better.

II

Microeconomics

5   Trade Policy

International Trade Policy in the 1990s

Robert Z. Lawrence

PANELISTS: *Charlene Barshefsky,*
Jagdish Bhagwati, and Lael Brainard

In the 1990s the U.S. economy was both more prosperous and more open than at any time in its history.[1] Its performance was particularly striking because it came after almost two decades with low productivity growth, scant progress in reducing poverty, stagnant wages, and rising inequality.[2] The strong U.S. performance in the 1990s was driven by innovation in information technologies. Americans not only invested heavily in equipment, but they also reorganized the economy to use technology more effectively. Indeed the performance marked such a change from previous trends that many came to speak of a "new economy."

Globalization has played an important role in this new economy.[3] It has provided the capital that allowed the United States to maintain investment in excess of domestic saving. It provided the large export markets that allowed U.S. innovators to achieve scale economies that are crucial in financing R&D

I thank Kim Elliot, Jeff Frankel, Rachel McCulloch, Dan Tarullo, and my discussants at the conference for their helpful comments. I should disclose that I was a member of the administration in its final two years, although the opinions expressed reflect my own views.
1. See U.S. Council of Economic Advisers (2000), pp. 202–204.
2. In 1999 the poverty rate fell to 11.8 percent, its lowest level since 1993, and wage gains between 1993 and 2000 in the lowest quintile matched those in the highest (U.S. Council of Economic Advisers, 2000).
3. For a discussion of the links between recent U.S. economic performance and globalization, see U.S. Council of Economic Advisers (2001), chapter 4.

activities with large up-front costs. It provided the competitive pressures that have stimulated innovation and adoption of new technologies. It provided access to imported components and equipment at lower prices and in greater variety, allowing U.S. firms to attain optimal levels of cost and quality.[4] And finally, it provided the access and conditions to operate abroad that allow U.S. firms to produce using global supply chains, carrying out stages of production in locations to which they are best suited.

Declining transportation costs and innovation in communications technology and international finance helped drive globalization, to be sure; but it also reflected the impact of policies followed by the Clinton administration and its predecessors in opening markets at home and abroad. Indeed, trade policy was a key element of the Clinton economic strategic triad, which comprised opening foreign markets, achieving fiscal discipline, and investing in people and technologies. On the basis of the economic performance in the 1990s, these policies appear to have succeeded.

However, trade policy is about politics as much as it is about economics. Congressional prerogatives, public opinion, and interest group pressures all play important roles. Article I of the U.S. Constitution gives Congress the final say in trade agreements, and Congress guards this power jealously. The relationship between the president and Congress is frequently strained over trade policy, and the delegation of authority to the president by Congress is filled with tension.[5] This relationship has critically important implications for the way the United States negotiates and the way it behaves.[6] Trade policy in the United States should not, therefore, be described as if it reflected the unilateral choices made by the president, whatever his preferences. Ultimately, in appraising the performance of trade policy, we need to understand the politics of trade and the constraints it places on the president.

The politics of trade policy in the 1990s presents an entirely different story from the economics. In its first two years the administration was able to implement what one writer accurately described as "a more ambitious record of trade liberalization than any president since at least Harry S. Truman."[7] The record included NAFTA and the Uruguay Round, a New Economic Framework with Japan, a decision to emphasize trade over human rights with China, and

---

4. In 2000 imported computers accounted for over 60 percent of the value of new U.S. computer purchases, nearly twice the level in 1987 (U.S. Council of Economic Advisers, 2001).

5. In the 1988 Omnibus Trade Act, for example, considerable efforts were made via the new Super-301 provision to force the president to become more aggressive with respect to trading partners such as Japan; see Destler (1995), pp. 92–98.

6. The U.S. trade representative (USTR), for example, is as much the president's special representative to Congress as she is his representative to the rest of the world.

7. Ronald Brownstein, *Los Angeles Times*, Dec. 5, 1994, Part A, p. 5.

declarations to (1) achieve free trade and investment in the Asia-Pacific Economic Cooperation Group (APEC) region by 2020 and (2) negotiate an agreement for free trade in the Americas by 2005. Both domestic and international political conditions for trade liberalization appeared favorable. The administration was able to negotiate successfully abroad and to obtain congressional support at home. Given the weak economy, the history of wage stagnation and inequality, and the high degree of economic insecurity at the time, these were remarkable accomplishments.

After this flourish, the period of consolidation that took place over the next two years might have been expected, but paradoxically, as the economic performance improved, the political environment deteriorated. To be sure, between 1997 and 1999, three multilateral single-sector agreements were concluded.[8] But there were also several initiatives that ended with remarkable failures: abandonment of the Multilateral Agreement on Investment, inability to obtain fast-track negotiating authority (in 1997 and 1998), failure to obtain agreements on sectoral liberalization at APEC, and the debacle at the Seattle ministerial meeting in 1999. By contrast, 2000 was a year with solid accomplishment highlighted by successful negotiations with China over its entry into the WTO and the vote to provide permanent normal trade relations, passage of free trade agreements with Africa and the Caribbean, negotiation of an agreement with Jordan, and initiation of talks with Singapore and Chile. Nonetheless, a serious set of conflicts with Europe remained unresolved, and the prospects for a new trade round remained uncertain. More fundamentally, conflicts over the appropriate relationship among labor and environmental standards and trade agreements remained unresolved, and the prospects of obtaining fast-track authority were unclear.

Trade policy in the Clinton years thus featured a basic paradox: the economic accomplishments were impressive, but the political consensus in support of trade agreements in the United States was severely eroded. In the final section of this chapter I will discuss how these results came about, by considering the domestic political impact of the trend toward deeper international integration. Trade agreements and rules no longer focus narrowly on border barriers. As their scope has increased, they have become a battleground for domestic political conflicts, thereby greatly adding to the complexity of conducting U.S. trade policy. Before presenting this discussion, however, the story of trade policy in the 1990s must be told. Section 5.1 describes the initial circumstances facing the administration at home and abroad and considers the strategic options that

---

8. The Information Technology Agreement, the Agreement on Basic Telecommunication, and the Agreement on Financial Services.

were available to it; section 5.2 provides an account of the major trade policy developments; section 5.3 then evaluates the performance in terms of its economic and political achievements; and section 5.4 concludes with some reflections on policy.

5.1 The Clinton Approach to Trade

Several key elements are important in establishing the context for U.S. trade policy in the early 1990s. The first was the weakness of the economy. In his final years in office, George Bush had the misfortune to preside over a stagnant economy. In 1990 the U.S. economy had experienced a recession, and in 1991 and 1992 its recovery had been sluggish with unemployment remaining high. In addition, the economy had experienced slow productivity growth for almost two decades and, since the 1980s, growing inequality and slow wage growth.[9] The weak economy gave William Clinton the opportunity to unseat an incumbent president. It also presented him with his most important challenge, exemplified by the unofficial slogan first coined by his campaign adviser: "It's the Economy, Stupid."

But the task was complicated further by a second factor. The U.S. economy had become globalized. It was increasingly dependent on foreign markets, foreign capital, and foreign technology.[10] Some saw this globalization of the economy as threatening, because America was widely viewed as in decline.[11] Some fatalistically explained this decline as inevitable. The U.S. lead was bound to erode because it is easier to copy than to innovate. But others placed the blame more squarely on U.S. trade policies. America had subordinated trade policy to foreign policy. Driven by geostrategic concerns motivated by the cold war, the United States had opened its markets, but foreign countries had not reciprocated. The claim was that since foreign governments supported their firms with industrial policies while the United States had a laissez-faire approach, the result was disastrous.[12] Foreigners were enjoying increasing shares of the leading edge industries, and America was being deindustrialized. U.S. trade relations with Japan exemplified these conflicts. Japan had enjoyed access to U.S. markets, but barriers both visible and invisible inhibited access at home.

---

9. Real compensation per hour had increased just 0.7 percent annually on average between 1973 and 1990 (U.S. Council of Economic Advisers, 2000, p. 26).

10. Between 1970 and 1990 the share of trade in goods and services as a percent of GDP increased from 12 to 20 percent. In the 1980s the United States had become a major recipient of foreign direct investment. The United States had also experienced record trade and current-account deficits in the 1980s.

11. See, for example, Kennedy (1987).

12. See Prestowitz (1988), for example.

For much of the postwar period, the United States had sought economic liberalization around the world, partly out of a desire to contain Soviet expansion. The U.S. strategy had succeeded, particularly with respect to liberalization in Europe and Japan, but many developing countries had retained high protective trade barriers. The triumph of capitalism over socialism dramatically changed the picture. Much of the world was suddenly embracing freer markets and more-open trade. The economies in transition were seeking to become capitalist. Developing countries were now abandoning import-substitution policies, unilaterally lowering trade barriers, and seeking foreign investment. Suddenly the environment for trade agreements had become far more favorable. The United States now felt pressures to put its money where its mouth was and deliver what it had long argued for. President Carlos Salinas de Gortari of Mexico was just the first of a long line of leaders now seeking freer trade with the United States.

A third key factor was the political situation. Many blue-collar workers had not done well in the U.S. economy in the 1980s, and this fact had placed particular pressures on their political representatives.[13] Despite its free trade ideology, the Reagan administration had succumbed on numerous occasions to protectionist pressures, with quotas on imports of steel and machine tools providing important examples.[14] In 1988 the Omnibus Trade Act had embodied congressional frustrations in new Super 301 legislation, which was designed to pressure the president to be more aggressive with U.S. trading partners. In 1991, when George Bush sought fast-track authority for NAFTA, only a third of the Democrats, the majority party in Congress, were willing to give it to him. The Republican Party provided solid support, but for a Democratic president, trade agreements had costs.

Given these conditions, in principle, the incoming president in 1993 needed to make four basic strategic choices. Would he seek further trade liberalization? If so, with which countries should agreements be sought? Which issues should agreements cover? And how should they be enforced? Let us briefly review some of the considerations behind each of these choices.

5.1.1 More Free Trade?

Free traders argue that trade barriers are inefficient. They raise costs to consumers and deny the economy the benefits that come from specialization.

---

13. See Scheve and Slaughter (2001) for an analysis that demonstrates the erosion in support for free trade among less-skilled U.S. workers.
14. For an analysis see the excellent piece by Richardson (1994) in the Feldstein predecessor to this volume.

Accordingly, these barriers should be eliminated. Some argue this elimination of barriers should be done unilaterally. But for a large country, like the United States, it makes more sense to use its bargaining power to use reductions in barriers at home to improve access to markets abroad. Thus the United States almost always reduces its domestic barriers in negotiations.

There are cases justified by solid economic theory in which trade protection could actually increase national welfare.[15] One key problem with these strategic trade arguments is that they are difficult to implement in practice. Political pressures in the United States, where Congress has power over trade, would make it very difficult to confine protection to those sectors or activities which have "strategic" merit. In addition, were the United States to move in this direction, it would inevitably set off foreign retaliation that would nullify its strategic economic advantages and undermine its international political relationships.

5.1.2   Multilateral or Multitrack?

Until the early 1980s, the United States relied almost exclusively on multilateral trade liberalization through the GATT.[16] To be sure, it engaged bilaterally with Japan, Europe, and other trading partners, but unlike the European Union, the United States had not sought regional agreements, partly because of its role as leader of the free world, partly because of unfortunate experiences in the 1930s of being discriminated against. But in the 1980s, when the multilateral negotiations were stalled, the United States decided to go "regional." It concluded an agreement with Israel and followed it with the U.S.-Canada FTA. George Bush had provided further movement in this direction by negotiating NAFTA and launching the Enterprise for the America's Initiative, which was intended to promote western hemisphere free trade.

Economists have long felt ambivalent about regional—or, more accurately, preferential—trade agreements because they may divert as well as create trade.[17] The NAFTA, for example, could enhance U.S. welfare if Americans now buy products from Mexico that Mexico makes more cheaply than the United States. But the NAFTA could also reduce U.S. welfare if Americans now buy a product from Mexico that we used to buy from Korea. Korea may produce at lower cost, but cannot sell because it is encumbered with tariffs. Because of

---

15. One example is the so-called optimal tariff in which a country improves its terms of trade by reducing its purchases from the rest of the world. Others involve the use of so-called strategic trade policies in which rents are shifted to domestic producers. For a more complete discussion, see Lawrence and Schultze (1990), pp. 15–18.

16. The U.S.-Canada auto pact was an exception.

17. Preferential free trade arrangements are second-best when compared with complete multilateral free trade. But so too are *partial* multilateral free trade agreements.

this possibility, some economists have advised the United States against undertaking such agreements.[18] But this advice ignores the fact that with free trade areas countries remain free to lower their barriers to third countries and offset the diversion.[19]

The real issue, however, concerns the dynamic implications of these arrangements. As Jagdish Bhagwati has asked so memorably, "Are they building blocks or stumbling blocks?" Do the preferential agreements represent a stepping-stone to full-blown multilateral free trade, or will they prevent its occurrence?

5.1.3 Coverage

Should trade agreements deal only with border barriers, or should they also cover other domestic barriers? Should they be confined to trade or deal with policies such as competition, intellectual property protection, labor standards, human rights, and the environment?

Over the postwar period, there was a fundamental shift in the scope of trade policies. Initially negotiations had been concentrated on lowering trade barriers at the border (elimination of quotas and reductions in tariffs). Over time, however, it became apparent that there were other obstacles to trade. Thus rules covering standards, customs valuations and practices, and government procurement became part of trade agreements. But the process of deepening had not stopped there. Trade agreements had begun to cover what had formerly been considered matters of purely domestic concern, such as intellectual property rights, competition, and other regulatory policies.[20] Some agreements have included provisions relating to labor and environment.

One force for this deeper integration is functional. As trade liberalization is extended to include services and foreign investment, many domestic policies become relevant to foreign firms. Foreign investors establishing a plant have to be concerned about regulations, taxes, rules on expropriation, standards, intellectual property, and so on. A second force for deeper integration is political. As international competition intensifies, the major political groups in our societies—business, labor, and environmentalists—feel foreigners have an unfair advantage and therefore seek "a level playing field."

---

18. See Bhagwati and Panagariya (1996).

19. This statement would not hold for customs unions unless they agreed to reduce the common external tariff.

20. Deeper integration could be seen in multilateral talks on question of trade-related intellectual property (TRIPs) and trade-related investment measures (TRIMs), in regional agreements (most notably EC92), and in bilateral negotiations between the United States and Japan under the Structural Impediments Initiative in the late 1980s.

Deeper integration is a double-edged sword.[21] It can enhance the benefits from global integration by reducing obstacles and enhancing market contestability. But it also represents an increasing intrusion on national sovereignty. Likewise, trade policies could help improve the environment and advance labor rights, but there are dangers that such policies could be inappropriate for some countries and that they could be used as a pretext for protectionism. Bringing more issues into trade negotiations could help build political support, but it could also undermine the negotiations if the issues are controversial and difficult to negotiate.

The shift toward deeper integration has also raised important new conceptual problems for trade policy. In essence, how far should the international harmonization of policies proceed, and to what degree should such harmonization occur within trade agreements? Border barriers and their effects are relatively well understood, but agreements bringing areas such as intellectual property and regulatory standards into the trading system raise new challenges.[22]

5.1.4 Enforcement

Many international agreements depend on the good intentions of the signatories to carry them out, but often such agreements have little credibility. Agreements that are binding and entail sanctions are more credible, but a key issue is how disputes should be resolved. The General Agreement on Tariffs and Trade (GATT) in principle allowed sanctions, but it had a weak dispute-settlement system in which the defendant could block hearings and punishment. Partly in response, the United States had implemented legislation called Section 301 in which the United States investigated foreign barriers to U.S. exports and was prepared, unilaterally, to impose sanctions in the event foreigners refused to remove such barriers. The United States claimed this right, not only when such barriers represented violations of agreements but also when they were deemed unreasonable.

5.1.5 Compete and Not Retreat

How did the Clinton administration decide to answer these questions? The short answer is that it chose freer trade, pursued by a multitrack approach in order to conclude agreements that would include a wide array of policies and be enforced through sanctions. A more complete answer will emerge in the

---

21. For a more complete discussion, see Birdsall and Lawrence (1999).
22. See again Birdsall and Lawrence (1999).

detailed account of the policies in section 5.2. But a sense of the approach could already be gleaned from Clinton's first major speech on trade policy as president given at American University in February 1993. The basic principle was to "compete and not retreat," a posture driven by the view that "open and competitive markets will enrich us as a nation." The United States would adopt an aggressive approach aimed at opening foreign markets for U.S. exporters and firms through negotiating multilaterally, plurilaterally, and bilaterally. It would "continue to welcome foreign products and services but insist that our products and services be able to enter their markets on equal terms." This insistence would be achieved through tough efforts to pursue disputes. Economic policy would be elevated to a position of parity with national security policy through the creation of a National Economic Council. In his campaign for president, Clinton had sought to give labor and environment greater prominence in trade agreements. In particular, he had withheld his support for NAFTA until side agreements on labor and the environment could be negotiated. His approach would therefore seek deeper integration.

The key message was that the United States was neither becoming protectionist nor withdrawing from its role of leadership. Indeed, the president was signaling strongly that he was committed to free trade agreements. Although a majority of his party might oppose them, he would pursue every avenue he could to extend and enforce them.

5.2   Trade Policy in the 1990s: The Major Developments

Given this choice of a multitrack strategy, it makes sense to present this selective account of the major trade policy developments in the 1990s by differentiating actions according to whether they occurred in initiatives that were multilateral, regional, bilateral, or unilateral.

5.2.1   Multilateral Initiatives

Multilateral initiatives at the GATT, and its successor the WTO, played an important role in U.S. trade policy in the 1990s. Major agreements the United States was able to support included the Uruguay Round, the Information Technology Agreement, the Financial Services Agreement, and the Basic Telecommunications Agreement. The new, more effective, dispute-settlement system established at the WTO enhanced the international rule of law. It allowed the United States to reduce its use of unilateral measures to enforce trade agreements and provided America's trading partners with a rules-based recourse to challenge U.S. actions.

In the second half of the 1990s, however, there were also noteworthy failures in the multilateral arena: The United States was unable to introduce labor standards into the multilateral trading system at the Singapore ministerial meeting in 1996; the negotiations on a multilateral agreement on investment at the OECD were suspended in 1998; the Seattle ministerial meeting failed to launch a new round in late 1999; and even though the United States succeeded in WTO cases against the European Union on beef and bananas, it was unable to enforce compliance. This section discusses some of these events in greater detail.

5.2.1.1 Uruguay Round

Much of the work for completing the Uruguay Round had already been accomplished by the time the Clinton administration assumed office in 1993. However, controversial issues, concerning farm subsidies, the treatment of the film industry, and the rules governing dumping, remained unresolved. Negotiations over details continued. In December 1993 the administration decided it had received its best offers on these issues, and the agreement was concluded.[23] The agreement represented an important accomplishment. It (1) extended the trading rules to sectors such as agricultural products and services; (2) provided for new international disciplines on nontariff barriers such as trade-related investment measures, voluntary export restraints, technical barriers to trade, sanitary and phytosanitary measures, rules of origin, and government procurement, many of which had been the source of obstacles for U.S. exports in the past; (3) tried to clarify the rules for unfair trade that deal with subsidies and dumping; (4) contained an international agreement on intellectual property rights (TRIPs) that provided U.S. high-tech producers with rights they had hitherto not enjoyed; (5) tightened the disciplines of the international system by establishing the new World Trade Organization in the place of GATT and a new and more binding system for settling international disputes; and (6) provided for the eventual elimination of the network of quotas—the Multifiber Agreement—that protected the textile industries in developed countries, while retaining tariff protection for U.S. textile and apparel workers. Particularly noteworthy was the fact that the agreement was "a single undertaking" with all GATT members accepting all obligations.

---

23. After holding out for many years, eventually the United States and the Cairns group of farm-product exporting nations settled for modest limits on European subsidies and commitments by Korea and Japan to import small amounts of rice, in return for bringing agriculture as a whole under GATT disciplines and converting all agricultural quotas into tariffs. In the final hours of the negotiation, U.S. Trade Representative Mickey Kantor also agreed not to push to have films included in the agreement. He was insistent, however, on achieving modifications of the text on antidumping that tended to increase the ease with which petitioners could obtain relief.

The Uruguay Round had ended without full agreement in key service sectors such as telecommunications, financial services, and maritime transportation. In addition, the General Agreement on Trade in Services (GATS) remains full of exceptions. The trading system, therefore, remained far from the goal of free trade in services. There was also considerable scope for further liberalization in agriculture and civil aircraft.

After the final details of the text were signed at a meeting in Marrakesh in April 1994, and after the midterm elections in November, the agreement was eventually ratified, with both parties supporting the bill by margins of two to one.[24]

The United States also participated in the negotiations under the WTO Committee on Trade in Financial Services. An interim Agreement on Financial Services had been concluded in 1995, without U.S. commitments, although the United States had been extended MFN privileges on an interim basis. The negotiating group on basic telecommunications began deliberations in May 1994 and concluded in April 1996, also as part of the extended negotiations on service sectors following the conclusion of the Uruguay Round.[25]

The United States sought to obtain foreign commitments to market access and national treatment and foreign adoption of procompetitive principles. However, after the United States indicated that the offers were not sufficiently trade liberalizing, participants extended the negotiations further, and they were eventually concluded in February 1997 after 46 trading partners improved their offers and 21 countries submitted new offers. Scheduled to come into effect in January 1998, "the accord was signed by 69 countries, covering 91 percent of $600 billion in annual global telecommunications revenues.[26]

At the ministerial meeting of the WTO held in Singapore in 1996, the United States sought commitments to further liberalize trade in information technology products, basic telecommunications, and financial services. On the first issue it was particularly successful, when ministers from 28 current and prospective members issued a declaration, known as the Information Technology

24. However, the ratification vote occurred only after (a) the adoption of several measures in the implementing legislation that in part tilted the antidumping rules further in favor of petitioners (see Destler, 1995, pp. 240–244); (b) a failed effort by Mickey Kantor to obtain fast-track negotiating authority that included "labor standards" and "trade and the environment" as principal trade negotiating objectives; and (c) the introduction of a provision, introduced by Senator Robert Dole, to establish a commission that would review WTO dispute-settlement reports and could propose withdrawal of the United States from the WTO if deemed necessary.

25. Participants provided schedules for liberalization in voice telephony; local, long-distance, and international telephone service; data transmission services; cellular and other mobile service; private leased circuit services; and satellite services (U.S. International Trade Commision, 1997, p. 37).

26. This paragraph is drawn from U.S. International Trade Commission (1997), p. 39.

Agreement (ITA), that would lead to the elimination of tariffs in certain information technology products and, with sufficient participation, was set to enter into force on July 1, 1997.

At Singapore the United States sought to advance the observance of internationally recognized labor standards and increased recognition of multilateral environmental agreements (MEAs) by the WTO. Both efforts were unsuccessful. The U.S. attempts at establishing a working party on labor standards failed. In the final declaration, although members "renewed their commitment to the observance of internationally recognized core labor standards," they noted that "the International Labor Organization (ILO) is the competent body to set and deal with these standards."[27]

At Singapore the Committee on Trade and the Environment (CTE), which had been established at Marrakesh in 1994, issued a report that encouraged multilateral solutions to transboundary problems but that was cautious about whether the WTO rules should be formally amended to take MEAs into account.[28] The United States registered disappointment that the CTE was unwilling to state that WTO rules should not hinder the ability of MEAs to achieve their environmental objectives. The United States was also unable to obtain the CTE's endorsement for environmental reviews of trade agreements.

5.2.1.2   Foreign Investment

At a meeting of the trade ministers of the United States, the European Union, Japan, and Canada in Los Angeles in 1994, U.S. Trade Representative (USTR) Mickey Kantor called for the launch of negotiations in the OECD for a "multilateral agreement on investment," or MAI. The aim was to create a set of rules that would liberalize foreign investment and ultimately replace the patchwork bilateral treaties (BITs) that governed foreign direct investment. "The United States emphasized that only a "state-of-the-art" MAI meeting or exceeding the standards of these BITs would be of interest."[29] By producing a "world-class" set of rules at the OECD, the (mainly) developed countries could develop a pro-

---

27. The United States also had "sought a non-negotiating and non-prejudicial dialogue in the WTO on how observance of core labor standards and trade liberalization can be mutually supportive." However, as the U.S. International Trade Commission noted, "these ideas generally met with lukewarm support—or outright opposition—from other developed countries and virtually uniform opposition from developing countries" (U.S. International Trade Commission, 1997, p. 24).

28. U.S. International Trade Commission (1997), p. 18.

29. U.S. Trade Representative (1996), p. 71. The United States sought an agreement that would go beyond existing OECD obligations and provide foreign investors with (a) the better of national or MFN treatment, (b) freedom from performance requirements, (c) freedom to make investment-related transfers of profits, royalties, and fees, (d) international law standards for expropriation, and (e) access to binding arbitration (U.S. Trade Representative, 1996, p. 71).

totype that could subsequently be introduced into the WTO. In May 1995 the OECD ministers agreed to launch the negotiations.

The proposed MAI generated considerable opposition in the United States and other countries.[30] Public Citizen, the organization headed by Ralph Nader, which leaked an early draft of the agreement, called the MAI "a license to loot." The opponents were concerned that governments would promote the interests of multinational corporations at the expense of other interests. They were particularly concerned about the constraints such an agreement would place on domestic policy. This was a problem that had already become apparent as a result of experience with Chapter 11 of the NAFTA, which provided foreign investors with very broad rights to compensation from expropriation. The negotiations became a target for hundreds of grassroots environmental, consumer, labor, and development organizations. The nongovernmental organizations (NGOs) were particularly effective in using the Internet to galvanize opposition to the MAI.

Aside from these pressures, negotiators also faced substantive difficulties in crafting an agreement. Most developed countries were already open to foreign investors. Thus the restrictions that remained reflected concerns and interests that they were unwilling to forgo. In October 1998 participants suspended the MAI negotiations following the withdrawal of France, according to the USTR, "in light of significant differences of view in the nature and extent of acceptable exceptions to the agreement, and the need for further consideration of concerns raised by environment and labor interests."[31]

Regardless of the degree to which the NGOs were responsible for killing the talks, the fight invigorated and empowered many of these organizations to continue their campaign against the perceived injustices of international trade and investment systems. This success would lead them to mobilize for Seattle with greater enthusiasm and the U.S. administration to view an agreement on investment in the WTO with considerable ambivalence.

5.2.1.3 Seattle
In May 1998 at Geneva the WTO held its second ministerial meeting, which was attended by President Clinton. The United States was successful at this meeting in launching an initiative that would keep cyberspace duty free, but the most significant decision made at the meeting was to launch a new trade round at the next ministerial gathering, which was to be held in Seattle in late 1999. One goal was to give President Clinton a platform where he could

---

30. See Graham (2000) for more discussion of this issue.
31. U.S. Trade Representative (1999), p. 152.

discuss trade policy with the American public. It was already agreed that the new round would include ongoing work in liberalizing agriculture and services, but much remained to be resolved. Indeed, it turned out that too much remained to be resolved, and the meeting ended in failure.

In retrospect, the efforts to launch a new round at Seattle seemed doomed from the start. The United States had considerable demands: these included no restrictions on trade in e-commerce, considerable liberalization in services and agriculture (in particular, the elimination of export subsidies), measures to make the WTO more transparent, and a working group in the WTO on the issue of core labor standards. At the same time, the United States appeared unwilling to give up anything, indeed even unwilling to place what others wanted on the table. In particular, it would entertain no discussion of the antidumping rules and was unsupportive of bringing competition policy and investment rules into the negotiations. The United States wanted the talks to have a narrow focus so that the negotiations would end within three years.

The Europeans, by contrast, sought a broad negotiation that would include competition policy and investment, and they were less willing to agree to focus as heavily on agriculture. Japan, likewise, was reluctant to liberalize agriculture, and it emphasized reform of the antidumping rules—the very issue the United States refused to discuss. The developing countries wanted accelerated liberalization in agriculture and textiles, but many also wished to backtrack from agreements they had signed on trade-related intellectual property (TRIPs) and trade-related investment measures (TRIMs), arguing that they lacked enforcement capacity.

In the end, therefore, there was little common ground. Among the numerous areas of disagreement, the question of labor standards stood out. Developing countries would not agree to even the very modest U.S. proposal for "a study group on trade and labor." They were particularly fearful that such standards could eventually become a pretext for protectionism. Their suspicions were particularly aroused by President Clinton, who told the *Seattle-Post Intelligencer* on the eve of the meeting, that "ultimately I would favor a system in which sanctions would come for violating" such provisions.

While the Seattle delegates were failing to reach agreement inside its meeting rooms, pandemonium raged outside the halls, as large, vocal, and sometimes violent groups of protesters gathered to voice their opposition to globalization in general and trade agreements and the WTO in particular. The opponents represented a wide range of views. Some sought the elimination of the WTO; others sought radical reform; some claimed to be concerned about reducing poverty in developing countries; others were against economic growth. It was clear, though, that a large number of organizations, opposed to globalization for a variety of reasons, had become increasingly effective at organizing protests.

The administration would probably have been able to make concessions on issues such as investment and competition policies. It would also have had to be realistic on the issue of workers' rights. But it faced powerful, perhaps fatal, political obstacles that prevented it from being more forthcoming on the antidumping rules. These rules enjoyed strong support from both business and labor. For the unions, in particular, the antidumping rules had just proved their worth, as the only effective means available for responding to the steel import surge in 1998 (see discussion in section 5.2.2.3). The administration was unable to win even the smallest of fig-leaf concessions on bringing labor standards into the WTO. It had further enraged its labor supporters by concluding an agreement with China that promised a destructive conflict within the Democratic Party during an election year. Any weakness on dumping could fatally impair its ability on the Hill to win permanent normal trade relations for China.

Nonetheless, it was unfortunate that the United States was forced to take this position, which severely undermined its leadership role. Certainly, it was unreasonable for the United States to be unwilling even to *contemplate* modification of these rules. While there is a strong case for rules that define fair trade and prevent predatory behavior, these particular rules, and the manner in which they are applied, are highly questionable. The U.S. strategy of seeking a narrow agenda limited only to the areas in which it had an interest played into the hands of those who were already mistrustful of U.S. dominance.

5.2.1.4 Dispute Settlement

The United States was a particularly active participant in the new WTO dispute-settlement process. In 1995 alone, the United States launched complaints relating to EU import restrictions on beef and bananas, Japanese taxes on distilled spirits and failure to protect rights in sound recordings, Australian import restrictions on salmon, and Korean regulations and testing/inspection requirements for agricultural imports.[32] The United States was also able to settle cases against the European Union on access issues in grain markets and Korea on exports of beef. The United States was also the defendant in a case brought by Venezuela and Brazil relating to its environmental regulations on gasoline.

Several cases brought to the WTO in the mid-1990s were important, not simply because of the specific complaints they dealt with, but also because of the systemic issues they raised. These related to questions of health and

---

32. See U.S. Trade Representative (1998).

environmental regulation, competition policy, and compliance with dispute settlement rulings.

Beef   The U.S. dispute with the European Union over hormone-fed beef had a long history. It was a leading-edge case exploring the tension between regulatory autonomy—the right of the European Union to implement whatever food safety regulations it chose—and the need for regulations that were nondiscriminatory and based on science.[33] The Uruguay Round Agreement on Sanitary and Phytosanitary Standards (SPS) had recognized the right of members to take measures necessary to protect health and life within their territories, but held they could do so only if such measures were not arbitrary or unjustifiably discriminatory. In addition, the SPS agreement stated that the international standards for food safety would be those established by the International Codex Alimentarius Commission.

In 1995 the Codex had, by a vote of 33 to 29 (with seven abstentions), accepted standards that permit the use of growth-promoting hormones. In April 1996, joined by Australia, New Zealand, and Canada, the United States filed a formal complaint at the WTO accusing the European Union of blocking U.S. exports. The case was significant in that the European Union was not accused of discriminatory behavior but rather of having adopted regulations that were not based on adequate analysis. In August 1997 the panel found the European Union in violation of its international obligations. The European Union lost its appeal, and, since it refused to comply, the United States imposed sanctions in 1999. By that time, with the outbreak of the deadly brain disease nvJCD (mad cow) in Britain, several other food scares, an outbreak of hoof and mouth disease, and growing concerns about the use of genetically modified organisms in food, the food safety issue had become extremely prominent in Europe. Although the United States was successful from a legal standpoint, the prospects of Europe allowing in U.S. hormone-fed beef remained dim.

Gasoline   The United States was also the defendant in a case brought by Venezuela and Brazil on standards for reformulated and conventional gasoline under the Clean Air Act. The complainants claimed the EPA rules subjected imported gasoline to standards that were more stringent than those on domestic gasoline. The WTO panel and subsequent appeal body ruled against the United States. The ruling did not reject the ability of the United States to undertake

---

33. Although its own scientists had issued reports finding that the use of hormones to stimulate beef growth was safe, in 1989 the Europeans had decided to ban all nontherapeutic use of hormones in cattle. In the late 1980s, therefore, the United States had brought a 301 case against Europe that had eventually resulted in the imposition of retaliatory sanctions. This account is based on Deveraux (2001b).

measures necessary to protect the environment under Article 20 of the GATT. However, it did find that the United States had failed to provide imports equal competitive opportunities.[34] The United States eventually brought its rules into compliance. The case was later used by free trade opponents to bolster their claims that WTO rules unduly constrained U.S. environmental regulations.

Shrimp and Turtles Similarly, in October 1996, India, Malaysia, Pakistan, and Thailand filed a WTO complaint against the United States because the United States had embargoed imports of shrimp and shrimp products, some of which had been caught without using devices that excluded sea turtles. The appellate body of the WTO ruled that the U.S. ban on shrimp imports could be provisionally exempted from GATT rules because it met the Article 20(g) provision allowing trade restrictions to protect exhaustible natural resources. However, it found that the United States had implemented the law in a discriminatory manner.

Film In May 1995 the Kodak company had filed a 301 action against Japan claiming its sales had been impeded in Japan by the anticompetitive actions taken by the Japanese authorities. A year later the USTR chose to pursue the case at the WTO. The claim was that Japan had "nullified and impaired" trade concessions it had granted the United States by permitting anticompetitive practices and by failing to implement a transparent regulatory system. The panel issued a report in December 1997 that ruled against the U.S. government on all substantive allegations. The case was significant because it established that, as they stood, the WTO rules were not well suited to deal with problems relating to weak national enforcement of competition policy. International rules would have to be explicitly negotiated and specified if the WTO were to encompass competition policy considerations.

Bananas The United States brought a case on behalf of its major banana distributor Chiquita claiming that the European Union had established a discriminatory import regime that had violated the rules of both goods (the GATT) and services (the GATS). The United States, joined by Ecuador, was successful in this case, and later when Europe failed to bring its import system into compliance, was permitted to invoke trade sanctions. The case was finally settled in early 2001.[35]

In the late 1980s the United States had angered many of its trading partners by undertaking unilateral actions under its Section 301 provisions that aimed

---

34. U.S. Trade Representative (1996), p. 57.
35. For a more complete description, see Rosegrant (1999).

at "unreasonable and unjustifiable" foreign barriers to U.S. exports. The United States had often claimed that the weakness of the GATT dispute settlement mechanism necessitated these actions.[36] The tougher, more binding WTO dispute settlement was the response. The ability to use this mechanism has, indeed, allowed (and induced) the Clinton administration to curtail unilateral U.S. actions. Though the United States has not eliminated 301 (or Super 301), it has, wherever possible, resolved 301 issues through the multilateral dispute mechanism. The new dispute system has also provided numerous U.S. trading partners with an effective means of challenging and altering U.S. practices.[37] Nonetheless, there continue to be frustrations over the difficulties of forcing compliance, as exemplified by efforts in the U.S. Congress to introduce a so-called carousel system that would rotate the sectors being sanctioned with the aim of inflicting more political pain. There is also controversy over particular panel findings.

5.2.2 Regional Initiatives

The Clinton administration followed in the steps of its Republican predecessors by using a variety of regional trade initiatives to complement its participation in the multilateral trading system. The initial focus was on North America, with the NAFTA, which was implemented in 1994. In addition, throughout the decade, the United States participated actively in APEC, as well as in the preparatory work for a free trade agreement for the western hemisphere. The United States participated in a transatlantic partnership with Europe and implemented new free trade initiatives for sub-Saharan Africa and the Caribbean. Negotiations for a U.S.-Jordan free trade agreement were concluded, and negotiations for free trade agreements with Singapore and Chile were launched.

5.2.2.1 NAFTA

The Bush administration concluded its negotiations for the North American Free Trade Agreement in August 1992. The agreement was a remarkable accomplishment because its implementation would result in free trade and free investment between a developing country and two industrialized counterparts. The NAFTA built on the Canada-U.S. FTA but was more extensive in several noteworthy respects: it included the protection of intellectual property rights,

---

36. See Bhagwati and Patrick (1990).
37. In 1998 the European Union challenged the Foreign Sales Corporation provisions of U.S. tax law, on the grounds that these constituted prohibited export subsidies. In February 2000 the appelate body concurred with the European Union contention that the FSC violated WTO rules. The United States responded in 2000 with legislation in an effort to come into compliance.

contained rules against distortions on investment, and went further in liberalizing services, including transportation. Most tariff and nontariff barriers were to be eliminated within 10 years and all were to be removed within 15 years. Remarkably, the NAFTA will establish free trade in agricultural products between the United States and Mexico. The agreement also eliminated all tariff and nontariff barriers in textiles and apparel. From a free trade perspective, it is flawed by the highly restrictive North American rules of origin that products (particularly textiles, clothing, autos, and auto parts) are required to meet to be eligible for duty-free access.

While the NAFTA was a remarkable achievement, the agreement came under fire for inadequately protecting the environment and workers' rights. This was a crucial weakness from the standpoint of the Democratic majorities in both houses of Congress. As a candidate, Bill Clinton had at first been neutral on NAFTA. In October 1992, in the heat of the campaign, he endorsed the NAFTA text, but also announced his intention to seek supplemental agreements that would deal with environmental protection, labor, and mechanisms to restrain unexpected import surges. Despite their presidential candidate's position, many Democrats continued to oppose NAFTA throughout the 1992 campaign. It was clear, therefore, in early 1993, that the administration faced an uphill ratification battle in which the side agreements might play an important part. They also provided the president with a mechanism to indicate his support simultaneously for free trade and for environmental and labor rights.

Prior to the NAFTA, as Mayer notes, environmental organizations in the United States had no history of involvement with trade negotiations.[38] When the NAFTA negotiations were announced, however, they were galvanized on the issue as an opportunity to focus attention on the impact of trade agreements on environmental regulations and on the environmental problems in the Mexican free trade zones known as maquiladoras. As vividly described by Mayer, the environmental organizations were split on NAFTA. Some were against,[39] but several middle-of-the-road organizations prepared to support it,[40] provided that the environmental provisions were acceptable. Accordingly the administration worked with these groups and by August 1993 obtained side agreements that several of them endorsed.

One controversial issue when it comes to issues of international labor and environmental standards is whose standards should apply. This is particularly difficult when nations are at different levels of development. The NAFTA side

---

38. Mayer (1998), p. 74.
39. Most notably, Sierra Club, Greenpeace, and Friends of the Earth (Mayer, 1998, p. 186).
40. World Wildlife Fund, Audubon Society, Natural Resources Defense Council, Environmental Defense Fund, and National Wildlife Federation (ibid).

agreements reflected an innovative principle in which the emphasis was placed on implementation. The basic principle was to have international oversight of national laws. The United States and Mexico agreed that in extreme cases failure to implement domestic laws could be met by sanctions authorized by an international dispute panel. Canada agreed to make international decisions on its laws enforceable in Canadian courts.[41]

The debate over NAFTA was highly contentious. The economic questions were heavily focused on employment issues. Proponents argued that it would generate additional employment opportunities, opponents contending it would cost large numbers of jobs. While Ross Perot claimed NAFTA would generate "a giant sucking sound," those using conventional economic studies agreed that the number of jobs involved was on the order of 250,000 to 500,000—very small numbers in a labor market with employment of 120 million. However, NAFTA also focused attention on the environment, drugs, immigration, human rights, and sovereignty. In most of these areas, as with employment, the marginal role of the NAFTA was probably small, but these issues were far more salient politically. Concerns about these issues brought about an alignment of strange bedfellows stretching from Patrick Buchanan and Ross Perot on the right to the AFL-CIO and Ralph Nader on the left.[42]

The administration made huge efforts to gather support for NAFTA. A war room, under the leadership of William Daley, was established at the White House to monitor the campaign. Vice President Gore played a critical role in debating Ross Perot on CNN. The president and cabinet officials strongly lobbied members of Congress, cutting numerous deals to obtain support. Eventually, the NAFTA was supported by 102 Democrats and 132 Republicans in the House of Representatives. Conspicuously, however, the House leaders Richard Gephardt and David Bonior remained opposed, despite the efforts that had been made to reflect their views in the side agreements.

It had taken a great deal of political courage for President Clinton to defy a majority in his party and many on his White House staff to lead the fight for the NAFTA at a time of high unemployment. Its passage was unquestionably a major accomplishment. Shortly after the NAFTA was implemented, Mexico

---

41. Sanctions were generally tougher in the environment side agreements than in the labor side agreements. In part, according to Mayer (1998, p. 198), because the CTM union in Mexico feared competition from other unions and in part because unions in the United States were less influential than environmentalists because even the toughest side agreement would not have induced them to support NAFTA.

42. "NAFTA is about more than trade," wrote Patrick Buchanan. "NAFTA is the chosen field upon which the defiant forces of a new patriotism have elected to fight America's foreign policy elite for control of the national destiny" (p. 387).

experienced a financial crisis. Despite the recession that followed, Mexico continued to meet its commitments—proving that the NAFTA had indeed locked in its economic reforms. The immediate decline in the U.S. trade balance with Mexico that reflected the Mexican slump was used by opponents to suggest that the NAFTA had failed. However, over the following six years, U.S.-Mexico trade enjoyed explosive growth.

5.2.2.2   Beyond NAFTA

As discussed earlier, there is a debate among economists as to whether regional arrangements are more likely to be "building blocks or stumbling blocks" in the movement toward full multilateral liberalization.[43] Some argue that members of such an arrangement who benefit from preferential treatment will resist further extensions. Others point out, however, that those who are excluded will have an incentive to seek membership. Some call this latter force the domino effect.[44] The European experience certainly supports the notion of ever-expanding membership. After all, the European Union started with just the three members of Benelux and today has 15 full members and a large additional number about to join.

The United States is a global trader. As soon as it negotiates agreements with some of its trading partners, the United States inevitably feels pressures from others to extend them similar benefits. President Bush, Sr., felt compelled to announce his Enterprise for the Americas Initiative, which called for a free trade area in the western hemisphere, at the same time as he announced his negotiations with Mexico. Similarly, during his second presidential campaign, he announced that he was prepared to negotiate free trade agreements with other nations outside the hemisphere. Having successfully achieved the passage of the NAFTA and concluded the Uruguay Round, the Clinton administration might have shifted its policy back toward a more exclusive reliance on multilateral approaches to liberalization. However, it chose to continue with the multitrack approach by emphasizing two overlapping agreements involving nations from the Asia-Pacific area and the western hemisphere.

APEC   In November 1994 the president participated in the APEC summit in Bogor, Indonesia, where the 18 nations of the Asia-Pacific Economic Cooperation Group committed themselves to achieve free trade and investment in the region by the year 2020. (Industrialized countries would proceed more rapidly and achieve such measures by 2010.)

---

43. For a more complete discussion, see Lawrence (1995) and Frankel (1997).
44. On the domino theory of regionalism, see Baldwin (1996).

The APEC meeting in Indonesia clearly revealed both the strengths and the weaknesses of the APEC organization. The strength lies in the ability of APEC to bring together a large number of extremely diverse economies and to obtain agreement among them. These nations range from large and developed countries such as the United States and Japan to small countries such as Brunei and developing countries such as Mexico and the Philippines. The weakness lies in the problems of forging an agreement that is acceptable, credible, and binding given the diversity and scope of the membership.

Clearly the Bogor Declaration helped several nations meet short-term political goals. In particular, many Asian countries had been concerned about being shut out of the NAFTA market, but since both Canada and Mexico were part of APEC, an APEC free trade area would prevent this outcome. Similarly, some Asian nations were concerned that the United States could lose interest in the Pacific region; again APEC's initiatives helped keep the United States involved. Several nations, including the United States, Australia, and New Zealand, were concerned that an exclusionary East Asian Economic Caucus could develop. Again the APEC arrangement and the agreement by Malaysia to host a future meeting helped allay these concerns.

But over the long run, important differences remained to be resolved before the APEC commitments could be considered to be credible. First, several APEC members were clearly uncomfortable participating in a regional arrangement that might undermine their strong multilateral trading relationships. Accordingly, APEC strongly endorsed the concept of "open regionalism." However, the precise meaning of this term remained vague. In particular, did it simply imply that other nations could join APEC, or that even large countries such as the United States would unconditionally extend their APEC liberalization measures to all their trading partners? For the United States to win support for meaningful liberalization benefits from Congress, it would inevitably have to indicate that other APEC members had reciprocated in a legally binding way. However, other APEC members rejected the notion of legally binding commitments as incompatible with "the Asian way." Likewise, the fact that the precise meaning of "free trade" was not defined raised important questions that future negotiations will have to deal with. Indeed, several participants, most notably Japan, clearly went along with the Bogor agreement in order to be team players rather than out of conviction.

Western Hemisphere   On December 9, 1994, just one month after the Bogor meeting, a hemispheric summit was held in Miami at which 34 leaders from throughout the Americas committed themselves to create a Free Trade Area of the Americas (FTAA) by 2005. In addition, President Clinton announced that the United States, together with its NAFTA partners Mexico and Canada, would initiate negotiations with Chile on accession to NAFTA.

The nations of Latin America had moved extensively to liberalize their markets. As was the case with the NAFTA for Mexico, participating in an international free trade agreement with the United States made their reforms more credible and permanent. For the United States, NAFTA extensions would help cement economic and foreign policy relations with important neighboring nations that were extending hands of friendship.

Europe The free trade initiatives that were launched in Bogor and Miami naturally raised the question of whether a similar initiative should be implemented between the United States and Europe. A free trade area between the world's two largest trading economies would be attractive, but it could also represent a threat to the multilateral system. If the United States and the European Union took care of their problems bilaterally, their trading partners would feel threatened and excluded. In addition, a formal free trade agreement would have to include agriculture, which would be extremely difficult for Europe because of its powerful farm lobbies. Moreover, the major problems facing U.S.-EU trade and investment were not those of border barriers such as tariffs. Instead they related more to the obstacles presented by different regulatory systems and rules.

At the U.S.-EU summit in Madrid in 1995, President Clinton and European leaders launched an initiative to deepen the U.S.-EU relationship known as the New Transatlantic Agenda. The trade component of this initiative, the Transatlantic Marketplace, reflected commitments by the parties to work together multilaterally to eliminate tariffs on information technology and intellectual property rights, and (at the OECD) to conclude a multilateral agreement on investment (MAI). Other actions planned included efforts to achieve mutual recognition agreements (MRAs), which would reduce regulatory burdens entailed by standards conformity assessment.[45] These MRAs were in fact implemented in 1998.

Implementing the Declarations In the aftermath of the Summit of the Americas in Miami, negotiators from the NAFTA countries and Chile met in a series of meetings to prepare the basis for Chile's accession to the NAFTA. In the fall of 1995, however, "the government of Chile determined it was inappropriate

---

45. An important companion to this Transatlantic Marketplace initiative was the Transatlantic Business Dialogue. Launched in Seville in November 1995, this forum of leading American and European business leaders provided private-sector recommendations on how their governments could reduce barriers to U.S.-European trade and investment. Subsequently, other dialogues were launched among labor, environmental, and consumer representatives.

to continue negotiations until the U.S. Congress had provided the President 'fast track' authority to negotiate trade agreements."[46] Talks were therefore suspended and only resumed in late 2000, by which time Chile had been persuaded that the absence of such authority did not preclude negotiations.

Work proceeded on the FTAA for the following six years. After the Miami summit, 12 working groups laid the groundwork for eventual negotiations by compiling inventories of hemisphere practices, identifying areas of commonality and differences, and providing recommendations on how to proceed. In April 1998 a second summit of the Americas was held in Santiago, Chile, at which formal negotiations were launched. Substantive talks began in ten areas.[47] A draft text for the agreement, with many bracketed sections, was completed just prior to the third summit which was held in Quebec in 2001.

It could be argued that the APEC initiative was on track in the summits that followed in 1995 in Osaka, Japan, and in 1996 at Subic, Philippines, at which countries presented and then developed both individual and collective action plans for implementing the Bogor declaration. Moreover, at Subic the APEC members provided valuable impetus and endorsement for the Information Technology Agreement that was then agreed to by the full membership of the WTO at the ministerial meeting held in Singapore in December 1996. The APEC members also made considerable progress in their collective action plans in the nuts-and-bolts work of trade facilitation, streamlining and modernizing customs procedures, improving access for business travel, and providing technical assistance and training to less developed members. But APEC members also worked on an initiative to liberalize priority sectors that proved to be much less successful.

When APEC met in Vancouver in November 1997, nine sectors were selected for immediate work, with implementation of liberalization to begin in 1999.[48,49] APEC members succeeded in reaching an agreement providing mutual recognition of standards-conformity-assessment procedures in telecommunications equipment in June 1998. But Japan (which refused to open fish and forest products), Korea, and China were cool to the idea of sectoral liberalization, and in

---

46. United States Trade Representative, 1995 Regional Trade Agreements Report on Web. http://www.ustr.gov/html/1996_tpa_regional_2.html.

47. These were market access, investment, services, government procurement, dispute settlement, agriculture, intellectual property rights, subsidies, antidumping and countervailing duties, and competition policy.

48. These were environmental goods and services, energy equipment and services, fish and fish products, toys, forest products, gems and jewelry, medical equipment and instruments, chemicals, and telecommunications.

49. Work was also scheduled to begin in six other sectors: rubber, civil aircraft, automotive, fertilizer, oilseeds, and food.

1998, in Kuala Lumpur, the ministers terminated the effort to open up additional sectors and called for the priority sectors to be liberalized in the WTO. Instead, the momentum for APEC liberalization had clearly stalled.

At Auckland, in 1999, members again placed their hopes on the WTO, calling for a new three-year round of WTO negotiations, which would include accelerated tariff liberalization sectors that they had identified in 1997–98. But three months later, APEC members were part of the failure to launch such a round in Seattle. The summit in Brunei in 2000 similarly accomplished little in this regard beyond a vague endorsement of resuming WTO negotiations, but no concrete efforts to deal with problems that had surfaced at Seattle.[50]

All told, the APEC free trade initiative cannot be considered a great success. APEC may have served some important political goals, and it may also have helped to improve cooperation, but it has yet to prove its worth as a vehicle for trade liberalization. APEC is so large and diverse that the preferences an APEC FTA would afford its members are unlikely to be particularly valuable or attractive. It is unclear, therefore, what could be accomplished at APEC that could not be done with more inclusiveness at the WTO.

Africa In June 1997, President Clinton unveiled his "Partnership for Economic Growth and Opportunity in Africa" initiative. Its primary goals included increasing U.S.-Africa trade and investment flows, supporting economic reform and growth in sub-Saharan Africa, and furthering Africa's successful integration into the global community of trading nations. The president also announced his support for a bipartisan congressional initiative: the Africa Growth and Opportunity Act (AGOA). These initiatives promised aggressive African reformers expanded GSP access, debt reduction, financial support for regional activities, and the eventual establishment of free trade agreements.[51] However, the bill was stalled in Congress and was only passed in 2000. A bill providing benefits to the Caribbean Basin nations was passed at the same time. In both cases, passage rested on including sufficiently tight restrictions on rules of origin for textile products to encourage foreign clothing producers to use American cloth.

5.2.2.3 Other Free Trade Initiatives

In 2000 the United States completed negotiations on a free trade agreement with Jordan. This agreement represented yet another example of the "domino" effect, since Jordanians viewed such an agreement as important in their competition with Israel (which already had an FTA with the United States) as a

---

50. See Bergsten (2001).
51. U.S. Trade Representative (1998), p. 234.

location for international investment. The agreement was part of a broader U.S. strategy of encouraging free trade in the Middle East as a complement to the peace process. The agreement was also noteworthy because its text explicitly included provisions on the enforcement of labor and environmental standards. The countries also reaffirmed their belief that it is inappropriate to lower standards to encourage trade, and agreed in principle to strive to improve their labor and environmental standards. Each side agreed to enforce its own existing labor and environmental laws and to settle disagreements on enforcement of these laws through a dispute-settlement process.[52] In 2000 the United States also initiated negotiations for an FTA with Singapore and resumed negotiations with Chile when it reversed its position requiring fast track as a condition for negotiating.

U.S.-Japan   By the early 1990s, Japan had emerged as America's most important international economic competitor and the focus of concerns about whether the U.S. version of capitalism was fundamentally flawed. Many argued that Japan's superior performance resulted from the close links between its government and its firms, its closely knit corporate groups, and its superior management practices.[53] There was a popular view that the United States should emulate these practices.

The concerns about United States competitiveness were heightened by the problems faced by foreigners when selling and investing in Japan. These problems were highlighted by (1) many anecdotes relating to allegedly exclusionary practices by Japanese officials and firms; (2) a wide variety of indicators that suggested that foreign participation in the Japanese economy was unusually low; and (3) the large bilateral trade deficit between the United States and Japan. While academic economists continued to debate the reasons why Japan's behavior was unusual, both the U.S. government and the private sector strongly supported policy action to improve foreign access to the Japanese market.[54]

The primary policy debate concerned the manner in which Japan was to be pried open. Some argued the focus should be on eliminating regulatory practices that discriminated against foreigners. Others objected, however, that simply changing the rules would not necessarily guarantee results. Given their close relationships ("invisible handshakes") and protectionist history, Japanese firms would continue to discriminate against foreign firms and products even when these were cheaper or superior. Likewise, Japanese officials would

---

52. USTR Fact Sheet on the U.S.-Jordanian FTA.
53. Prestowitz (1988).
54. For examples of the academic debate, see Lawrence (1993) and Saxonhouse (1993).

engage in protectionist actions even when the rules were no longer discriminatory. Accordingly, many, particularly in the business community, advised the USTR that the Japanese government should be required to guarantee that foreigners gained a minimum share of the market.

Since the early 1970s, U.S. efforts at opening Japan had generally emphasized changing the rules.[55] In the mid-1980s, however, the United States and Japan had negotiated the Semiconductor Trade Agreement, which contained a "confidential" side-letter that mentioned a goal of 20 percent for foreign semiconductors in the Japanese market.[56] This was a remarkable commitment, since in 1986 the share was just 9.0 percent. Initially, the response was sluggish. However, in the late 1980s, foreign semiconductor sales in Japan began to rise sharply, and by 1991, when the agreement was renewed for five more years, the share had increased to almost 30 percent.[57,58]

By the early 1990s, for many Americans, the wisdom of a results-oriented approach had been proven by the semiconductor experience, although analysts continue to debate the role of the agreement in obtaining this outcome. Many Japanese officials, however, came to the opposite conclusion. They felt it had been a great mistake for the government to agree to control private-sector outcomes. Japanese officials had intended the quantitative aspects of the Semiconductor Agreement to remain private. It was an embarrassment to have the government publicly concur with the notion that the Japanese system was amenable to government manipulation.[59] Many economists, too, remained skeptical of this approach.[60] Their fundamental concern was that a managed trade approach to deal with "Japan, Inc." would actually strengthen the relationships between the government and business and reinforce the cartelization of the economy rather than weaken it. Setting targets could lead to fixing markets rather than freeing them.

---

55. In the SII talks they had sought to make Japan more open through measures to relax restrictions on large-scale retail stores and tougher antitrust policies. In other talks, some of which were part of the Super 301 measures implemented in 1988, they had focused on sectoral barriers such as government procurement of satellites and supercomputers and technical barriers in forest products.

56. The Japanese government stated that it "understood, welcomed, and would make efforts to assist foreign companies in reaching their goal of a 20 percent market share within five years" (Tyson, 1992).

57. Flamm (1996), p. 436.

58. A second example using quantitative targets occurred in 1992, when on his visit to Japan, President Bush had managed to obtained a voluntary plan of action in which Japanese auto companies agreed to a goal of increasing purchases of auto parts by $10 billion between 1990 and 1995 (Dryden, 1995, p. 375).

59. According to Lincoln it might also require the government to be more effective in other market-opening exercises (Lincoln, 1999, p. 124).

60. See the chapter by Tyson and discussion by Dixit in Lawrence and Schultze (1990).

The Clinton administration was intent on raising the profile of economic issues in the U.S.-Japan relationship and on implementing a tougher market-opening approach that would emphasize results. In July 1993, President Clinton and Prime Minister Kiichi Miyazawa signed a so-called Framework Agreement. The agreement called for biannual economic meetings. It sought a significant reduction in Japan's current-account surplus and called for negotiations to "deal with structural and sectoral issues in order substantially to increase access and sales of competitive foreign goods and services." Attention was to be given to issues such as intellectual property, distribution, deregulation, transparent government procedures, and inward direct investment, but there were also to be sector-specific agreements. There was an increased emphasis on obtaining sizable, measurable results.[61] "The two governments will assess the implementation of measures and policies taken in each sectoral and structural area . . . based upon sets of objective criteria, either qualitative or quantitative or both as appropriate."[62] Note, however, that there was no mention of specific numerical targets or quotas.

Progress toward implementing the agreement was slow. At the February 1994 summit, Prime Minister Morihiro Hosokawa and Clinton could not produce any agreements. However, spurred in part by the administration's announcement of its intention to invoke Super 301, numerous agreements were eventually reached in 1994. They included intellectual property, government procurement of medical equipment, government procurement of telecommunications equipment, and financial services (aside from insurance).

By 1995 the major remaining bilateral problem in U.S.-Japan relations was in autos. U.S. concerns related to the paucity of dealers in Japan that carried foreign autos, as well as the small shares of foreign auto parts in new cars (in both Japan and transplants) and aftermarket sales. With the talks bogged down, on the basis of a 301 action the administration on May 10, 1995, announced the imposition of punitive 100 percent tariffs on 13 luxury Japanese imports, with collection of duties postponed for a month. The United States also sent a letter of intent to file a case at the WTO within 45 days. Japan responded with a case of its own, alleging that the United States had violated its WTO commitments by this unilateral and discriminatory action.

These pressures were effective in bringing about an agreement on June 28, just hours before the U.S. government would have begun to collect the tariffs. The agreement dealt with changes in Japanese regulations and clarified the abil-

---

61. In autos, for example, the agreement was to achieve "significantly expanded sales opportunities to result in a significant expansion of purchases of foreign parts by Japanese firms in Japan and through their transplants" (Lincoln, 1999, p. 127).
62. Lincoln (1999), p. 127.

ity of existing Japanese dealers to carry additional lines of foreign cars. It also contained language on using objective indicators for the follow-up evaluation by the two governments.

Conspicuously, however, the governments gave very different and separate interpretations about what had been agreed. The United States provided numerical forecasts of the impact the agreement was expected to have on increasing purchases of U.S.-made auto parts and the number of Japanese dealers who would carry U.S. cars. But the Japanese made clear they had not participated in making these estimates. There seemed to be more disagreement than agreement.

It is important to understand the economic context in which these initiatives were occurring. In particular, the Japanese economy was reeling in the aftermath of the bubble economy of the late 1980s that had burst in 1990. By 1993 the economy was stagnant. The strong yen was providing an incentive for greater imports, but it actually made government officials more resistant to change. Japanese were unwilling participants in these talks.

Results-oriented policies proved almost impossible to define and implement. Treading the fine line between "managed trade with specific numerical targets" and "objective indicators or benchmarks" was extremely difficult. There were differences within the administration itself over what it really wanted that added to the confusion. In any case, the demands for objective indicators backfired politically, because they allowed the Japanese to seize the moral high ground. In fact, Japan had, and continues to have, serious structural problems, and the case for genuine deregulation in Japan had never been stronger, but it was not a popular strategy in a period of stagnation.

Rather than depart radically from its predecessors, in the end the combination of the difficulties of defining a results-oriented strategy and Japanese resistance forced the Clinton administration to follow a course that was quite similar. The data suggest too, that, as in the past, the agreements did have an impact in some sectors, although, as in the past, it was not an impact that convinced skeptics that Japan was no longer an unusually closed market. Over the following few years, imports in sectors in which agreements had been concluded rose considerably faster than imports in general.[63]

After the auto dispute in 1995, U.S. trade relations with Japan become less visible, and the focus shifted to the security relationship and the major macroeconomic problems faced by Japan. Japan's economic problems and the resurgence of the United States made the concerns about competitiveness less salient. In addition, the emergence of China shifted the focus of U.S. attention. There were additional negotiations in sectors such as insurance, telecommunications,

---

63. See Lincoln (1999).

civil aviation, and harbor services.[64] The United States successfully launched cases at the WTO in liquor taxes and copyright and unsuccessfully pursued a case on photographic film and paper. There was also an Enhanced Initiative on Deregulation and Competition Policy, which produced reports and agreements designed to address the regulatory obstacles that impede market access in key sectors of the economy. For the Clinton administration the era of major high-profile negotiations over trade barriers was over.

U.S.-China   Even in the aftermath of the Tienanmen Square incident, President Bush had refused to link human rights with most-favored-nation status.[65] In 1992 he twice vetoed a conditional MFN bill linking trade with human rights.[66] As a candidate, Bill Clinton was harshly critical of this Bush policy of engagement with China. During his acceptance speech at the Democratic convention, Clinton said that the United States needed a government that "does not coddle tyrants from Baghdad to Beijing." Clinton also noted in an interview that "there is no more striking example of Mr. Bush's indifference toward democracy than his policy toward China."[67]

When he became president, Clinton followed through with his vision, issuing an executive order in May 1993 that made the renewal of China's MFN trade status in 1994 conditional on improvements in human rights and other areas. However, it proved easier to make threats about imposing economic sanctions than to follow through on them. The president's order was extremely unpopular with the business community. The result was the formation of a coalition known as "the new China lobby" described by I. M. Destler as "perhaps the most formidable protrade coalition ever sustained by U.S. business on its own initiative."[68]

The efforts to change Chinese behavior were singularly unsuccessful. In the months following the executive order, the Chinese made a point of defying U.S. conditions by publicly arresting well-known political dissidents.[69] In March 1994, Secretary of State Warren Christopher went to China to press the link-

---

64. In 1996, conspicuously, a new plurilateral agreement on semiconductors eliminated numerical indicators.

65. The Bush administration was prepared to take actions on trade questions. It initiated Section 301 actions against China on its trade barriers. It had also named China as a "priority foreign country" under Special 301 for purportedly failing to provide adequate protection to patents, trademarks, copyrights, and trade secrets. In both instances, threats to invoke sanctions had eventually ended in settlements.

66. In August 1992 the United States and China signed a memorandum of understanding (MOU) to ensure that China would not export products made with prison labor to the United States. (Imports of goods produced with forced labor are prohibited under U.S. law.)

67. These quotes are drawn from Deveraux (2001a).

68. Destler (1995), p. 234.

69. Deveraux (2001a).

age policy, but he was roundly rebuffed by Chinese officials. A few days later, upon his return, the secretary met an equally critical reception at a meeting of the Council of Foreign Relations in Washington, DC.[70] Eventually, when the annual vote for extending MFN status to China came due in June 1994, the administration faced the hard choice of either violating the spirit of the order or imposing costly economic sanctions. The president decided that engagement was ultimately a more effective policy than denial of MFN and stated that he was moving to "delink human rights from the annual extension of Most Favored Nation trading statues for China."[71]

It was striking that while it appeared impervious to administration pressures on the broad question of human rights, China was later to prove more susceptible to pressures on the question of intellectual property rights. Apparently, while demands that China alter its human rights practices were seen as a fundamental threat to its regime, the demand for intellectual property enforcement was seen as a more limited request that could be complied with. In June 1994, USTR once again designated China as a Special 301 "priority foreign country" because of the lack of progress in enforcing IPR. After negotiation in which the United States threatened to impose sanctions, China and the United States reached an agreement on IPR enforcement on February 26, 1995.[72]

The TRIPs is an integral part of the WTO rules to which all parties both developed and developing are expected to adhere. Thus an important element in China's compliance with the U.S. initiatives on intellectual property in the 1990s was its desire to win WTO membership. China had requested the restoration of its status as a full contracting party to the GATT in 1986, but had been unable to enter because of controversies associated with the obligations it would have to assume. In particular, China sought to join as a developing country, a status which would grant it certain exemptions and longer transition periods for meeting WTO obligations. While many other developed nations were willing to allow China to join under such conditions, the United States refused to concur. The U.S. administration insisted that China could join only on "commercially meaningful terms."[73] In 1995 the USTR laid out a "road map" which set forth the conditions that the United States required. The demands were extensive and entailed not simply major reductions in tariff and nontariff barriers, but also market access for service industries and major liberalization of the mechanisms by which the Chinese conducted international trade. It became

---

70. Destler (1995).
71. Destler and Balint (2000), p. 235.
72. In May 1996 the USTR again put the Chinese on notice for failing to enforce IPR by designating China as a Special 301 "priority foreign country." Ultimately, after the closure of 70 factories that were mass-producing "pirated" U.S. products, USTR Charlene Barshefsky announced that the United States was satisfied that China was taking steps to fulfill the 1995 IPR agreement.
73. Deveraux (2001a), p. 5.

clear to the Chinese that WTO entry on these terms would require a commitment to major domestic reforms.

The Clinton administration took the view that China was already a large trading nation and, given its rate of growth over the 1980s and 1990s, was likely to become even larger. Allowing China to enter the WTO but not to play by all of its rules could seriously undermine the system. Moreover, China's entry gave the United States a one-time opportunity to try to ensure that in the future the Chinese market would not present the problems for the United States that Japan had. From one vantage point these U.S. demands were unreasonable. Surely China is a developing country. But the U.S. demands also provided China with a unique opportunity to galvanize domestic reform. Indeed, by acceding to the WTO under these terms, the Chinese leadership could signal to both domestic and international audiences that China was irrevocably committed to a genuine rules-based market system. Before 1997 the leadership was not prepared to do so. But in 1997 the Communist Party announced a set of policies that established the legitimacy of private enterprise in China and indicated the intention to compel state-owned enterprises to operate as profit-making firms.

In 1998, U.S.-China negotiations became more intense, but agreement could not be reached by the time of President Clinton's state visit to China in June. However, it was agreed that Premier Zhu Rongi would visit the United States in the spring of 1999. When he did visit, the agreement was almost completed, but the administration backed away partly because the agreement was not viewed as satisfactory in some areas (textiles, brokerage firms, and auto financing) but primarily because of domestic political difficulties. The deal was unpopular on the left, with labor and human rights groups, and on the right, with those concerned with national security.[74]

Despite the political damage his visit had inflicted on Zhu Rongi, and despite the souring of relations after the calamitous accidental bombing of the Chinese embassy in Belgrade, agreement was reached in November 1999.[75] The agreement was remarkably comprehensive and rigorous. It covered tariff and nontariff barriers to exports of industrial goods, agricultural products, and services. China agreed to apply specific rules to address import surges, antidumping, and subsidies. It agreed in addition to constraints relating to export performance requirements, local content, offsets, and technology transfers. Many of the commitments would come into effect when China completed its accession. Almost all were to be phased in within five years.

---

74. News had just broken that a nuclear weapons scientist, Wen Ho Lee, had been arrested and accused of espionage at Los Alamos National Laboratories.

75. Ambassador Barshefsky, accompanied by Gene Sperling, head of the National Economic Council, partly as a display of President Clinton's political commitment, had spent almost a week in Beijing completing the deal.

China would not have granted these benefits to the United States without the elimination of the annual vote on extending it permanent normal trading relations (PNTR). Accordingly, the United States was obligated to secure PNTR for China on the basis of the agreement. The administration made the passage of PNTR its chief trade objective for 2000, and its extensive campaign succeeded, despite the fact that in the House of Representatives only 73 out of 211 Democrats supported it.[76]

When China will be able to join the WTO and whether it will fully meet its obligations remains to be seen. But the prospect of entry has already had a powerful impact in accelerating the pace of reform in China. Enterprises throughout China have undertaken changes to prepare their own strategies for meeting the international competition they are anticipating China's entry will bring. Likewise, the obligation, contained in GATT Article 10, that members implement trade policy in "a transparent and impartial manner" has provided support for those seeking Chinese government reform.

Helms-Burton   The United States has had an embargo on most trade with Cuba since 1962. On March 12, 1996, President Clinton signed into law the Cuban Liberty and Democratic Solidarity (Libertad) Act of 1996 (also known as the Helms-Burton Act) in the aftermath of the downing of two unarmed U.S. civilian aircraft over international waters. Among its numerous measures, this act created a private right of action that allowed U.S. nationals whose property was confiscated by the Cuban government to sue Cuban governmental entities or foreign investors who use or profit in any way from these properties.[77] This provision was scheduled to become effective August 1, 1996. However, the act allowed the president to suspend the right to file suit if he determines that such action is in the national interest and would expedite a transition to democracy in Cuba.

Several trading partners objected to the United States seeking to extend its rules to apply beyond its borders (i.e., extraterritoriality). In response, the president suspended the act for six months in July 1996 in an effort to achieve a common approach with United States allies and trading partners. Both Canada and the European Union issued laws refusing to aid in collecting judgments against their firms, and the European Union brought the issue to a WTO dispute-settlement panel. After another six-month suspension, in April 1997 the United

---

76. Many in Congress were concerned that PNTR would reduce the attention that had been paid to Chinese human rights violations as a result of the annual MFN votes. Under the leadership of Representative Sandy Levin, bipartisan support was provided to establish a commission, modeled on the Helsinki Commission, to monitor human rights. The commission allowed swing voters to support the vote.

77. U.S. International Trade Commission (1997), p. 160.

States and European Union reached a settlement in which they agreed to work cooperatively to develop binding disciplines on dealings in property confiscated in Cuba, and the European Union suspended the panel but retained the right to reinstate it. The episode was a prime example of the ability of the U.S. congress, independently, to take measures that create political problems for U.S. trade relationships—a theme to which I will return in later discussion.

Softwood Lumber   On May 29, 1996, the United States and Canada entered into a five-year agreement intended to prevent material injury to U.S. producers resulting from imports from Canada. The agreement established annual allocations and fees for lumber exports of the Canadian provinces of British Columbia, Quebec, Alberta, and Ontario. The agreement reflected U.S. concerns over Canadian practices that promoted domestic lumber production by (1) providing private firms with the right to harvest trees in government-owned forests with stumpage fees that were extremely low and (2) banning the export of logs. The settlement had been reached in part because of a case that had eventually gone to a NAFTA dispute panel.

Steel   The steel industry has a long history of seeking trade protection. Other presidents of both parties have succumbed to these pressures. But despite being faced by a crisis with two episodes, the Clinton administration was unusual in providing the industry with only the relief provided for by the trade rules. In 1998 the United States experienced a surge in steel imports, primarily because of the collapse in world steel demand occasioned by the Asian crisis. Steel imports from Japan, Korea, Russia, and other nations increased by more than 9 million metric tons—33 percent above their 1997 levels—raising import penetration from 24 to 30 percent.[78] Steel prices declined precipitously, and steel employment fell by 10,000. In response there were calls for protection and for the passage of a quota, supported by the United Steel Workers, which would protect the industry. There were also calls on the administration to support an easing of the conditions under which industries could obtain safeguard relief.

In January 1999 the White House announced a steel action program. The plan called for enhanced monitoring of steel imports and trade trends, the early release of steel import statistics, and examination of subsidies and market-distorting trade barriers. The administration rejected the proposals for quotas and did not support a relaxation of the safeguard standards.[79] Instead it

---

78. Lindsey, Grisworld, et al. (1999).
79. The administration negotiated a comprehensive agreement with Russia (not a WTO member) that placed quotas on all steel imports.

relied on vigorous enforcement of the antidumping laws[80] and tough bilateral consultations with steel exporters from Japan, Korea, and the States of the former Soviet Union.[81] On March 17, 1999, the U.S. House of Representatives voted 289 to 141 to impose steel quotas, but the bill was defeated in the Senate.[82]

Steel imports fell in 1999, and capacity utilization rates recovered to their previous highs. In May 2000, however, domestic demand for steel in the United States slackened, and by late 2000 the U.S. economy had slowed down with dire consequences for an industry that had been weakened by the earlier crisis. The industry sought relief, requesting that the administration initiate a 201 action or launch an investigation on national security grounds. In both cases the administration took no action. The administration's willingness to withstand pleas from the steel industry was underscored when, in striking contrast, in early 2001 the Bush administration succumbed to these requests and agreed to initiate a 201 action.

5.3 Appraising the Arguments

Several charges have been levied against U.S. trade policy in the 1990s. Let us first consider arguments that are made by free trade critics, next examine those made by people favoring protection and those seeking tougher labor and environmental standards,[83] and then appraise the record in economic and political terms.

5.3.1 Multilateral Free Traders

Proponents of multilateral free trade views argue that the United States has erred in following a multitrack approach to trade liberalization. Instead of seeking more free trade agreements, once the Uruguay Round had been completed the United States should have confined itself to the pursuit of multilateral liberalization at the WTO and WTO mechanisms to settle disputes.

---

80. In 1999 the Commerce Department completed 34 antidumping and countervailing duty cases and began another 24 cases. Investigations of hot-rolled steel from Japan and Russia and several other cases were expedited.

81. The USTR initiated "high-level dialogues" with Korea and Japan (which involved essentially jawboning these countries to reduce steel exports to the United States).

82. In 1999 the president also signed into law the Steel Loan Guarantee Program, which would guarantee loans for companies most severely impacted by the crisis.

83. Prominent among these are economists associated with the American Enterprise Institute (Krueger, 1995; Bhagwati, 2000) and the Cato Institute. See http://www.freetrade.org/.

The last point is readily dealt with. In fact, since the Uruguay Round was concluded with a more effective dispute-resolution mechanism, charges of U.S. unilateralism have had much less merit. Indeed, U.S. trade sanctions against WTO members were only undertaken in response to findings by a WTO panel.[84]

What about regional FTAs? Multilateral free trade critics oppose free trade agreements because they favor insiders and may be less efficient than multilateral free trade. In economic jargon they are "second best" compared to multilateral free trade, which is "first best." But multilateral free trade is currently not the relevant option; so the real debate is whether it is best to advance toward fully free trade exclusively by partial multilateral liberalization (which is also "second best") or by complementing multilateral efforts with additional preferential agreements. The experience of both the United States and the European Union suggests that these approaches can be complementary. In addition, they indicate that more extensive liberalization can occur regionally. (Note the NAFTA's rules on services and investment and deeper integration in the European Union.) To be sure, complex protectionist rules of origin are a problem with free trade agreements, but that is a reason to make them simple rather than to avoid concluding such arrangements.[85,86] Multilateral free traders also ignore the role that can be played by credible regional arrangements in locking in domestic economic reforms. This is particularly the case, as with NAFTA, when the agreements go beyond what has been achieved in multilateral agreements. For example, the NAFTA allowed Mexico to signal its commitments to free foreign direct investment in a manner not possible through WTO membership.

Free trade critics also claim that the United States has been hypocritical in seeking liberalization abroad, but refusing to talk about its own protectionist measures—in particular, the antidumping laws—at home. The United States has also failed to take adequate account of the needs of developing countries by not liberalizing sufficiently.

On these points the critics make valid arguments, but they underestimate or ignore the political difficulties involved for any president who implements their recommendations. Undoubtedly, the United States would have been a more credible leader internationally if it had been prepared to remove all trade barriers to goods from the least developed countries, undertake major tariff reduc-

---

84. Though it did come dangerously close to imposing unilateral sanctions in the U.S.-Japan auto dispute.

85. See Lawrence (1996a) for a more complete discussion.

86. Likewise trade diversion may be a problem, but with free trade agreements, countries can always lower their external barriers.

tions in textiles and agriculture (particularly sugar), and indicate a willingness to negotiate changes in the antidumping rules.[87] But all these measures faced fierce resistance in Congress. The antidumping rules, in particular, have many ardent supporters in Congress.[88] This is the case even though, as measures supposedly designed to prevent predatory behavior, they are poorly crafted and widely abused.[89] The textile and apparel industries, facing the elimination of all quota protection from the Multifiber Arrangement (MFA) in 2005, are extremely resistant to additional liberalization, and again U.S. sugar growers enjoy congressional support for an uneconomic system that keeps domestic sugar prices far above those in world market. Ultimately these particular issues come back to politics. But without making progress on these questions, the U.S. ability to act as a credible global leader will remain weak.

5.3.2 Opponents of Free Trade Agreements

Some groups are even more critical of U.S. trade policies in the 1990s. They divide into two camps. One group is protectionist and seeks repeal or rejection of trade agreements. Their reasons include the following: (1) High-wage U.S. workers cannot compete with low-wage foreign labor; (2) trade agreements impinge excessively on U.S. sovereignty; and (3) these agreements harm developing countries.[90]

The protectionists ignore the degree to which the United States has prospered in the 1990s. They fail to understand that international competition reflects relative costs, and countries with high wages compete by offsetting higher wages with higher productivity.[91] These critics also generally exaggerate the extent to which trade agreements constrain domestic U.S. regulatory action.[92] As the numerous WTO cases described earlier have made clear, the major focus of the trade rules is not on preventing regulations that are necessary to preserve the environment and maintain public health and safety both domestically and

---

87. The administration was able, with considerable effort, to eventually achieve passage of the Africa Growth and Opportunity Act, but even this achieved rather modest liberalization in which tariff reductions were accompanied by strict quotas: Even after eight years, African imports cannot exceed 3.5 percent of all U.S. textile imports.

88. As David Sanger notes, "Just prior to the Seattle meeting, more than 300 members of Congress wrote the president a letter warning that they would work to defeat any deal that threatened America's ability to apply its dumping laws unilaterally" (2001, p. 73).

89. For a more complete discussion of the antidumping rules, see Lawrence (1999).

90. Free trade critics include Patrick Buchanan on the right and Ralph Nader on the left.

91. To be sure, they cannot compete in all industries, so they must specialize.

92. For a more complete discussion, see Burtless, Lawrence, et al. (1998), pp. 110–126. Although critics have a point in their concerns about the impact of NAFTA Chapter 11, see Graham (2000), pp. 37–40.

internationally but rather those that *discriminate* against foreigners.[93] Finally, the fact that developing countries have sought WTO membership in such large numbers is surely testimony that they do not believe it is harmful to their development.

A second group of critics, "standards setters," accept that globalization is inevitable but are concerned that without agreements, there will be a race to the bottom as standards are weakened to attract foreign investment and improve competitiveness.[94] They argue that they would support trade agreements provided that these reinforce labor and environmental standards. They point out that the trade regime has responded to corporate need by implementing the TRIPs and call for similar treatment for blue (collar) and green concerns. On these questions, however, the free traders and standards setters part company.[95] The view of the free traders is that unless they are international in scope, environmental issues should be dealt with at the national level. Likewise, most aspects of labor standards should be matters for national governments to decide. To the degree that there are international aspects of these issues, they should be dealt with in institutions specifically set up for this purpose: the International Labor Organization for labor standards and the secretariats of international environmental agreements. The WTO does not have the competence or the mandate to deal with these questions. There is a danger that such rules could become a pretext for protection. Moreover, the more forceful the WTO is on these issues, the more threatening it will become to national sovereignty.

5.3.3 A Third Way?

President Clinton clearly agreed with free traders on the potential benefits that trade could bring (1) in stimulating economic growth, both in the United States and the rest of the world, and (2) in promoting world peace. He disagreed with those who would rely only an multilateral approaches, and he sought freer trade wherever he could get it. He supported NAFTA, concluded the Uruguay Round, and participated in APEC and the FTAA; he also sought a new multilateral round, MFN and PNTR with China, and, even in the waning hours of his administration, free trade agreements with Jordan, Chile, and Singapore.[96]

---

93. These points are emphasized in the Venezuelan case on clean air and the shrimp-turtle decision. The beef hormone case was not about discriminatory treatment but rather the use of regulations that are not based on science or appropriate analysis.

94. For an excellent discussion of race to the bottom, see Wilson (1996).

95. Some free traders argue that the TRIPs should not have been part of the WTO rules.

96. The idea that he deliberately sought to prevent the launching of a new round at Seattle could not be further from the truth (Bhagwati, 1999).

Clinton also believed that the United States needed to be more assertive in furthering its economic interests. Hence the establishment of the National Economic Council, the aggressive campaign from the Commerce Department to promote exports in his first term, the U.S.-Japan framework talks, and the willingness to remove export barriers through bringing disputes to the WTO.

But Clinton also understood that trade has the potential to create losers and require adjustments that are painful. Ultimately, therefore, political support for free trade can be tenuous. In his view, trade protection is not the correct response to this dilemma. Instead, it requires domestic policies that help people deal with economic change and a trading system that commands political support because it is perceived as fair and because its benefits are widespread. Clinton therefore supported measures such as the NAFTA Trade Adjustment Assistance Program, and he agreed with those in his party who believed that measures to promote core labor standards and environmentally sound policies would help achieve that support.[97] Moreover, he believed that these standards could be achieved without raising trade barriers and inhibiting the growth of developing countries—both in the context of trade agreements and through strengthening other international institutions and agreements. Clinton's desire to put "a human face" on the global economy was the subject of numerous speeches in his last few years in office. Long before that, however, his decision to negotiate side agreements to the NAFTA that covered labor and the environment exemplified his desire to achieve a third way in trade rules.

Implementing this approach proved difficult politically.[98] Bringing labor and the environment into trade helps gain political support from unions and greens—but does not necessarily win their votes. At the same time, however, it leads to less support both at home, from Republicans and business groups, and abroad, from many in developing countries who fear that ultimately these standards could compromise legitimate diversity and lead to disguised protectionism. The side agreements to NAFTA were successful in bringing support from some environmental groups, but they failed to move Richard Gephardt, the majority leader who led the fight against it. The fast-track formulation crafted by Mickey Kantor in 1994, which sought to give labor standards a more prominent role, helped bring Democratic support, but it alienated Republicans. The fast-track formulation crafted by Charlene Barshefsky in 1997 was more acceptable to Republicans, but it alienated Democrats as, not surprisingly, did the formulation crafted by the House Republicans in 1998.

---

97. Clinton also argued in his speech at the WTO ministerial in Geneva, "We must do more to ensure that spirited economic competition among nations never becomes a race to the bottom—in environmental protections, consumer protections, or labor standards. We should be leveling up, not leveling down" (Waldman, 2000, p. 231).
98. See Elliot (2001).

5.4 Appraising the Record

Was trade policy in the 1990s a success? We will examine three issues: economic outcomes, political outcomes, and the negotiating record.

5.4.1 Economic Outcomes

Judging whether trade policy was a success in terms of economic outcomes, the answer is surely that it was. Trade and investment became increasingly important to the U.S. economy in part because U.S. trade policy succeeded in opening markets at home and abroad. U.S. trade with Mexico enjoyed explosive growth, in part because of NAFTA. The United States resisted pressures to act extra-legally using quotas or voluntary restraint arrangements. U.S. industries were granted additional protection on occasion, but only through WTO-legal mechanisms that entailed the use of antidumping, safeguard, and countervailing duty provisions.

U.S. trade policies also played an important role in creating an environment in which the U.S. and other economies could benefit from technology and innovation.[99] The Uruguay Round strengthened intellectual property rights (TRIPs), improved market access in goods and services, and enhanced the role of standards based on risk analysis and sound science—an important rule for biotech.[100] The United States also played a major role in the WTO agreements to liberalize basic telecommunications and financial services, remove tariffs on information technology products, and establish open commerce in cyberspace by keeping the Internet a duty-free zone. Bilateral sectoral negotiations with Japan emphasized sectors such as semiconductors, financial services, telecommunications, and cellular telephones.[101] The United States was also able to facilitate trade in electronics, instruments, and pharmaceuticals through mutual-recognition agreements on conformity assessment with Europe and in APEC. U.S. trade policy also kept the U.S. market open to foreign goods and investment.

5.4.1.1 America Can Compete

For anyone who followed the debates in the 1980s, the major surprise in trade policy in the 1990s was the minor role played in trade policy by concerns about

99. For an excellent discussion of future challenges for high-tech trade, see Barshefsky (2001).
100. The United States had also emphasized intellectual property protection through its use of the Special 301 law in the 1988 trade act. While the TRIPs encourages more innovation, it could also discourage use. Thus its overall impact is more controversial.
101. In 1996 the semiconductor agreement with Japan was broadened to include Europe, Taiwan, and South Korea and to cover issues such as R&D, market access, and private sector cooperation with government (Barshefsky, 2001, p. 138).

U.S. competitiveness. In the 1980s many argued that the United States, with its open market and lack of assistance to domestic firms, simply could not compete with other industrial countries that had more closed markets and more interventionist economic strategies. Of particular worry were the implications of these practices for U.S. leadership in high-technology industries. Japan and the newly industrializing Asian economies (NIEs) in particular had been the focus of these fears.

Economic theorists had questioned the credibility of these views by demonstrating how (under appropriate assumptions) governments could implement strategic trade policies that would shift rents (higher than normal profits and wages) in favor of their nationals.[102] But during the 1990s the United States had restored its global leadership in the industries of the future, the Japanese economy had collapsed, and the newly industrial countries in Asia experienced deep crises. In its first few years, the Clinton administration was concerned about preventing U.S. decline; by the end of the administration, the concern was sustaining growth in the rest of the world. To be sure, several U.S. industries, notably steel and apparel, experienced difficulties in competing internationally, but their problems were generally viewed as sector-specific rather than indicative of an endemic weakness. U.S. capitalism had turned out to be not only viable, but also remarkably successful in simultaneously generating rapid productivity growth and low unemployment.[103] There remained little talk of America needing a new "industrial policy."

While the administration had not sought to protect U.S. firms at home, it was more ambivalent about the use of managed trade abroad. It tried, in its first few years, to craft a tougher approach to market entry in Japan that could be based on "objective indicators." But over time, partly because the approach was intrinsically problematic, and partly because Japan's stagnation made its market less enticing, the policy shifted back to the more traditional approaches to deal with sector-specific and generic structural problems.

5.4.1.2 Jobs

Economists may point to the benefits of open trade in improving living standards, but the most salient political trade concern is employment. The major fear about NAFTA was that it would destroy jobs and lead to mass unemployment. It is certainly true that some workers have been displaced as a result of NAFTA, but others have been provided with job opportunities. It is hard to quantify the net impact of NAFTA from the data, since other developments—most notably the Mexican financial crisis—have occurred in the interim. Nonetheless, after NAFTA was implemented in early 1994, U.S. employment creation was robust.

---

102. For an elaboration, see Lawrence and Schultze (1990).
103. For the case that the U.S. system has been successful, see Freeman (2000).

Between 1993 and 1997, for example, total U.S. payroll employment increase by 10.3 million, and manufacturing payrolls were up by 600,000.[104] The flaw in the claim of a mechanical relationship between the trade deficit and overall employment was also clearly exposed in the late 1990s as the economy simultaneously achieved full employment and a large trade deficit.[105]

5.4.1.3 Wages

A second area of controversy has been the impact of trade on U.S. wage inequality. The United States did experience rising wage inequality between 1980 and 1993. Generally explanations have been split between two schools, one emphasizing the role of trade and a second the role of skill-biased technical change.[106] The remarkable feature of the U.S. economy in the second half of the 1990s, however, was that real-wage gains in the lowest deciles matched those in the highest.[107] Indeed, between 1994 and 1999 the broadest measure of inequality in the United States, the Gini coefficient, was basically unchanged.[108] These developments were particularly noteworthy, since over this period (1) the economy became more open than it had ever been before,[109] (2) the trade deficit increased dramatically, (3) relative prices of manufactured goods from developing countries declined, and (4) the pace of technological change as measured by productivity growth accelerated. The alleged drivers of earlier inequality became more powerful, yet inequality did not increase. Why?

An important missing element in the earlier explanations was the aggregate state of the labor market.[110] Unemployment rates of less skilled and disadvantaged Americans are often twice those of workers who are well educated. In the 1980s the (annual) unemployment rate did not fall below 5.3 percent, and for much of the decade it was above 7 percent. As the U.S. economy moved closer to full employment in the 1990s, however, with the unemployment rate more than a percentage point lower, workers at the bottom experienced increasing

---

104. U.S. Council of Economic Advisers (2000), pp. 358–359.

105. The United States has experienced a large and growing trade deficit over the course of the 1990s that has been the subject of some concern and debate. While this is an important issue, the deficit is essentially a reflection of aggregate U.S. spending patterns rather than its competitiveness or its trade policy.

106. For a survey of the debate and evidence, see Lawrence (1996b).

107. Mishel, Bernstein, and Schmitt (2001), Table 2.18.

108. U.S. Council of Economic Advisers (2001).

109. U.S. Council of Economic Advisers (2000), chap. 6 and p. 31.

110. Tighter labor markets have relatively more powerful effects on the demand for less-skilled workers. According to the Bureau of Labor Statistics, between January 1993 and December 2000 the unemployment rate of workers who are over 25 with less than a high school degree fell by 4.8 percentage points (from 11.1 to 6.3 percent). By contrast, over the same period, the unemployment rate for workers with a high school degree fell by 3.2 percentage points (from 6.6 to 3.4 percent), and the rate for those with a college degree fell by just 1.5 percentage points (from 3.1 to 1.6 percent).

wages and employment opportunities. Ironically, it was precisely the alleged drivers of inequality—rapid productivity growth (due to technological change) and openness to trade (and excess capacity abroad)—that helped the U.S. economy to operate and sustain a high-employment economy without inflation and improve wages and employment for less-skilled workers.[111]

5.4.2 Political Outcomes

Yet the paradox of U.S. trade policy was that, despite this economic success, the ability to advance trade agreements was reduced in the second half of the 1990s.[112] This trend is apparent in congressional voting behavior. The study by Baldwin and Magee (2000) found that a district's unemployment rate played a greater role later in the decade. They conclude, "The main reason for the defeat of the 1998 Fast Track bill was that legislators were more willing in the late 1990s than in the early 1990s to vote against trade-liberalizing measures on income distribution grounds."[113] This conclusion is, again, paradoxical because unemployment rates were much lower in 1998 than in 1993.

One plausible hypothesis is that U.S. public opinion increasingly shifted against free trade over the decade, but perhaps surprisingly, this does not seem to be the case.[114] Scheve and Slaughter (2001) have studied public opinion of trade liberalization. They do find that "a wide range of public opinion surveys report that a plurality or a majority of U.S. citizens oppose policies to further liberalize trade, immigration and FDI."[115] Moreover, preferences are aligned with education, with more educated citizens favoring trade.[116] But they observe that "public opinion is not markedly more skeptical about globalization in the 1990s than in the late 1970s and 1980s."[117] This comment suggests that what has

---

111. The earlier shocks due to technology and trade could have dissipated over time. The decline in relative wages of less-skilled workers could have induced "unskill-biased" technical change. The economy could also have become more specialized, producing products that were not directly competitive with those produced by developing countries and thus less subject to downward wage pressures.

112. To be sure, PNTR for China was passed in 2000, but as Wall Street columnist Albert Hunt observed, "More remarkable than the passage, however, was how tough it was to approve a measure so demonstrably beneficial. Americans are currently enjoying the best economy ever. If it's a struggle to pass free-trade bills in this environment, what would it be like in less bullish times?" (quoted by Scheve and Slaughter, 2001, p. 5).

113. Baldwin and Magee (2000), p. 42.

114. Scheve and Slaughter (2001).

115. "The probability that an American supports trade protection falls by 30 percentage points when that American increases his or her schooling from 11 years to 16 years" (p. 9).

116. Shaffer (2000).

117. Scheve and Slaughter report that survey responses prior to the 1970s were less protectionist than those in 1970s.

happened recently is that these antitrade sentiments have been more effectively mobilized and translated into political action. Why?

One reason is money. Business groups found it less necessary to give money to the Democrats when they were no longer in the majority. As a result, Democrats became more dependent on labor support, which was against freer trade agreements. Baldwin and Magee find that "13 Democratic votes [against fast track in 1998] can be explained by the increased dependence of Democrats on labor PAC contributions relative to business contributions."[118] A second reason is that the antitrade organizations have become more effective. The experience of the NAFTA brought a variety of antitrade groups together and induced many environmental organizations to become involved in the trade debate. The MAI experience taught groups how to use the Internet effectively.[119] Seattle demonstrated their ability to organize and further emboldened trade opponents. A third reason is that the political alignment of a Democratic president and Republican congressional majorities created an environment in which bipartisan cooperation on trade was extremely difficult.[120] Fast-track authority, in particular, requires congressional trust in the president. Republicans were reluctant to provide this trust unless they could tightly restrict his negotiating scope. A fourth reason is that the U.S. economy became more globalized, so that trade concerns became relatively more important. But probably the most important reason was that, as the focus of trade policy broadened to include issues of deeper integration, debates about trade agreements became a major locus of domestic political conflict. While the broad public has long been opposed to free trade, more educated opinion leaders and the media tend to support it. As trade issues became entangled with other concerns, support in some sectors wavered.

5.4.2.1 The Rise of Trade and . . .

Though the record on traditional trade-policy issues of competitiveness, employment, and labor were strong, during the 1990s the focus of trade policy shifted from disagreements over the economic merits of free trade to disagreements over the role of trade in enforcing other goals.

---

118. Baldwin and Magee (2000), p. 38.

119. At the same time, the lessons of China PNTR are also important, demonstrating that opposition forces are not invincible. There was actually learning on both sides, and the efforts for China mobilized protrade groups and the Clinton war room more effectively. Creative ways of co-opting groups of legislators were found.

120. One hypothesis is that in the early years Democrats were unwilling to vote against the president. But in fact, almost as many Democrats supported giving George Bush fast track to negotiate NAFTA (91) as eventually voted for the agreement itself (102). It is more likely, however, that in the first two years Republicans were more willing to support NAFTA and the Uruguay Round, which had been initiated by Republican presidents, than they were later on.

These conflicts were apparent internationally. In the Uruguay Round, the issue of culture (protecting the domestic movie industry) became a major point of contention between the United States, Canada, and France. In the Uruguay Round, as well as in many bilateral negotiations, the use of trade to enforce intellectual property protection was a source of friction between developed and developing countries. It was China's poor record on human rights that threatened the ability to provide it with permanent normal trade relations. The differences between the United States and Europe on beef were a harbinger of problems relating more generally to fundamentally different views of the dangers of advances in biotechnology, such as genetically modified organisms (GMOs).

But conflicts were also in evidence in the U.S. domestic debates about trade. There were important economic issues debated during the passage of NAFTA, but it was the questions about environment and labor rights that really ignited passions. Disagreements over the appropriate role for labor and environment in trade agreements served as the stumbling block to obtaining fast-track authority in the United States and were partly responsible for the failure to launch a new trade round at Seattle. The concern that rules on expropriation could unduly hinder environmental policies was important in the failure of the MAI.

As all these issues were raised, the controversy over trade agreements changed from a debate over economics to a debate over policies that had once been considered matters of purely domestic concern or matters for nontrade international organizations. This shift dramatically changed the nature of the politics. To achieve traditional liberalization, it used to suffice to create coalitions of export interests whose gains outweighed import-competing interests. For the most part, the major players were firms and workers with relatively narrow economic interests on both sides. And generally, while there were always opponents of liberalization in the Congress, they tended to reflect relatively narrow, often regionally based, economic interests. It was, therefore, possible to craft bipartisan support for agreements. But as trade policy moved to deal with these other questions, it became the battleground in which controversial questions were fought. Groups that had not previously engaged in trade policy found they had interests at stake. Trade policy tended to divide more strongly along partisan lines, with the Democratic Party strongly opposed to liberalization.

5.4.3 The Negotiating Record

On the one hand, trade agreements are often crafted to reflect the demands of particular political actors rather than the requirements of good policy. On the other hand, congressional critics have often complained that the United States does not advance its commercial interests with sufficient fervor, suppressing them in favor of geopolitical and foreign policy goals. Indeed, the Omnibus Trade Act of 1988 with its Super and Special 301 provisions reflected efforts on the part of Congress to pressure the president to be tougher.

But there can be little doubt that the Clinton administration was an extremely tough negotiator, fully prepared to walk away from agreements that failed to achieve its objectives. Examples include the refusal to paper over disagreements in the first Clinton-Hosakawa meeting in 1993, the insistence on reopening NAFTA to include surge protection and provisions on minimum wages, the refusal initially to sign the multilateral agreement on financial services because of inadequate commitments to liberalize, the refusal to conclude the agreement with China despite Zhu Rongji's visit in 1999, and the refusal to bring antidumping into the new WTO round even when it meant Seattle would fail.

The administration was also quite prepared to impose sanctions to back up its demands, even on other major developed countries—for example, on Japanese automobile imports in 1994, on European beef, and on bananas in response to the European Union's failure to comply with WTO rulings on China in the negotiations over intellectual property. One reason is that the Clinton administration in particular viewed toughness as desirable. The president appointed two USTRs, Kantor and Barshefsky, who were both professional negotiators par excellence.

A more basic reason that the United States is such a tough bargainer internationally is the structure of the U.S. political system. Unlike parliamentary systems, each agreement must muster sufficiently large support in Congress to ensure passage. The combination of a weak president—a Democrat who needed Republicans—and the breakdown of the congressional consensus in support of free trade made striking bargains particularly difficult. This situation afforded individual members and other special interests the ability to exert influence that is far greater than they would achieve in a system with party discipline or broader free trade support. Thus the U.S. system serves to bring to the fore issues that may matter intensely to just a few decision-makers. This fact can have a detrimental impact on coherence.

The passage of the NAFTA and China-PNTR in particular stand as testimony to the success of U.S. negotiating tactics. But from the viewpoint of its long-term interests, ironically, the United States can be "too tough," too responsive to short-term political considerations and insufficiently attentive to the long-run system in which it has an interest. A prime example here is the position taken by the administration on the issue of the antidumping rules. Not being willing even to place these on the table severely impaired the ability of the administration to lead.

5.5 Final Reflections: The Only Game in Town

Trade policy is currently in a precarious position because trade policy has in many respects become the only game in town. It has become the forum in which debates reflecting many domestic and international concerns take place. In part, this development is testimony to trade policy's success. A rule of law has been established to govern trade, and now many are seeking to have their concerns enforced by it. But there is a great danger when success leads to mission creep. Indeed, it seems that trade policy will be overloaded with issues until it will eventually fail. This problem, at an institutional level, resembles Peter's explanation for why things always go wrong. His Peter Principle states, "In a hierarchy, people are always promoted to their level of incompetence."[121] Do something well, and you'll be promoted until they find something you can't do well.

Part of the solution lies outside the arena of trade policy. It requires strengthening other international institutions so that they can be more effective in achieving goals such as enforcing labor and human rights, environmental standards, and competition policies. But part of the solution also requires dealing better with these issues at home. It is striking that among developed countries, the United States is probably the most vocal advocate of bringing core labor and international environmental standards into trade agreements. Yet, at the same time, it is among the weakest in supporting these standards at home. It is astonishing, given its international posture, that the United States has actually ratified only two of the conventions that enforce the four core ILO labor standards in its domestic legislation, having failed to act on the conventions covering nondiscrimination and rights to bargain collectively.[122] By contrast, several other developed countries with much more extensive social rights at home seem less insistent on labor standards internationally.

Apparently, trade policy has served as a focal point for domestic political conflicts and frustrations. Indeed, the U.S. labor movement has been diverted to focus more on trade issues and standards, in part because domestic labor-rule reform has made so little progress. Likewise, the United States, which has failed at home to ratify the Convention on Biodiversity and which passed a resolution critical of the Kyoto Protocol by a vote of 95–0, is scarcely in a position to insist on international environmental standards as a precondition for trade.

More fundamentally, Americans fear open trade because of job insecurity and the impact on their incomes of job loss. Again, the solution lies in enhanced

---

121. See Peter and Hull (1969).
122. See Shaffer (2000).

programs to facilitate trade adjustment in particular and to deal with dislocation more generally. Likewise, concerns over inequality are better met through redistribution through the tax system and measures such as the earned income tax credit.

It is also striking that U.S. efforts to enhance labor and environmental standards have raised the specter of enforcement through government-imposed trade sanctions. This position detracts from approaches that provide countries with positive inducements to improve their records in these areas. Providing open markets is important for developing countries, but technical assistance and adequate financial assistance should be part of the package.

When it comes to trade policies specifically, it will take compromise from both trade purists and those seeking more extensive rules on labor and the environment so that we will be able to enjoy the benefits of globalization in a system that commands widespread support. Above all, it will take imagination. The side agreements to the NAFTA have their critics, but the approach should be improved upon rather than discarded.

None of these ideas is particularly novel. And indeed, the Clinton administration sought to implement many of them. But its success was limited, in part because measures such as labor-market and labor-law reform and foreign aid are not exactly popular in Congress. In the American system for conducting trade policy, no single actor, even one with presidential power, is ever in control. The result is outcomes that are not always rational or coherent.[123] At the end of the day, however, the Clinton administration should be credited with promoting more major trade liberalization agreements than any of its postwar predecessors. It was also particularly successful in avoiding "extralegal" quota protection at home and unilateral sanctions that violated WTO rules abroad. These policies helped create an economy whose performance was remarkable. Free trade critics may carp that the president has deviated from their blueprints, but as good economists, they should understand what it is to maximize "subject to constraints." While the third way for trade policy remained a work in progress, the achievements of the Clinton administration were especially impressive because the president came from a party in which two-thirds of the members were often against his policies. The fact that many of his trade policy actions weakened his domestic political base is compelling evidence of his personal courage and commitment to free trade. These achievements were also impressive because in the 1990s the politics of trade has become increasingly entangled with other issues.

---

123. As Roger Porter has observed, "What [the U.S. system] has not produced are consistently coherent policies" (Porter, 1988).

References

Baldwin, Richard. 1996. "A Domino Theory of Regionalism." In R. Baldwin, P. Haaparanta, and J. Kiander, *Expanding Membership in the European Union*. New York: Cambridge University Press for the Center for Economic Policy Research.

Baldwin, Robert, and Christopher S. Magee. 2000. *Congressional Votes: From NAFTA Approval to Fast-Track Defeat*. Washington, DC: Institute for International Economics.

Barshefsky, Charlene. 2001. "Trade Policy for a Networked World." *Foreign Affairs*, 80(2): 134–147.

Bergsten, C. Fred. 2001. "America's Two-Front Economic Conflict." *Foreign Affairs*, 80(2): 16–27.

Bhagwati, Jagdish. 1999. "Did Clinton Take a Dive in Seattle?" *The Washington Post*, Dec. 7, 1999. Reprinted in *The Wind of the Hundred Days*, Chapter 34. Cambridge, MA: MIT Press.

———. 2000. *The Wind of the Hundred Days: How Washington Mismanaged Globalization*. Cambridge, MA: MIT Press.

Bhagwati, Jagdish, and Arvind Panagariya, eds. 1996. *The Economics of Preferential Trade Agreements*. Washington, DC: American Enterprise Institute.

Bhagwati, Jagdish, and Hugh Patrick. 1990. *Aggressive Unilateralism*. Ann Arbor: University of Michigan Press.

Birdsall, Nancy, and Robert Z. Lawrence. 1999. "Deep Integration and Trade Agreements: Good For Developing Countries?" In I. Kaul, I. Grunberg, and M. A. Stern, *Global Public Goods*, 128–151. New York: Oxford University Press for the United Nations Development Program.

Burtless, Gary, Robert Lawrence, et al. 1998. *Globaphobia: Confronting Fears about Open Trade*. Washington, DC: Brookings Institution.

Destler, I. M. 1995. *American Trade Politics*. Washington, DC: Institute for International Economics and the Twentieth Century Fund.

Destler, I. M., and Peter J. Balint. 2000. "The New Politics of American Trade: Trade, Labor, and the Environment." Washington, DC: Institute for International Economics.

Deveraux, Charan. 2001a. "The Eagle and the Dragon: Charlene Barshefsky, the November 1999 U.S.-China Bilateral Agreement, and the Battle over PNTR." Cambridge, MA: John F. Kennedy School of Government.

———. 2001b. "Food Fight (Or, Where's the Beef?)." Cambridge, MA: John F. Kennedy School of Government.

Dryden, Steve. 1995. *Trade Warriors*. New York: Oxford University Press.

Elliott, Kimberly Ann. 2001. (Mis)Managing Diversity: Worker Rights and US Trade Policy. *International Negotiation* 5:97–127.

Flamm, Kenneth. 1996. *Mismanaged Trade: Strategic Policy and the Semiconductor Industry*. Washington, DC: Brookings Institution.

Frankel, Jeffrey A. 1997. *Regional Trading Blocs in the World Economic System*. Washington, DC: Institute for International Economics.

Freeman, Richard. 2000. "The US Economic Model at Y2K: Lodestar for Advanced Capitalism?" Cambridge, MA: National Bureau of Economic Research.

Graham, Edward M. 2000. *Fighting the Wrong Enemy: Antiglobal Activists and Multinational Enterprise*. Washington, DC: Institute for International Economics

Kennedy, Paul. 1987. *The Rise and Fall of the Great Powers: Economic Change and Military Conflict from 1500 to 2000*. New York: Random House.

Krueger, Anne O. 1995. *American Trade Policy: A Tragedy in the Making*. Washington, DC: American Enterprise Institute.

Lawrence, Robert. 1993. "Japan's Different Trade Regime: An Analysis with Particular Reference to Keiretsu." *Journal of Economic Perspectives*, 7 (Summer): 3–19.

Lawrence, Robert Z. 1995. *Regionalism, Multilateralism and Deeper Integration*. Washington, DC: Brookings Institution.

————. 1996a. "Regionalism and the WTO: Should the Rules be Changed?" In J. J. Schott, *The World Trade System: Challenges Ahead*, 41–56. Washington, DC: Institute for International Economics.

————. 1996b. *Single World, Divided Nations? International Trade and OECD Labor Markets*. Washington, DC: Brookings Institution and OECD Development Center.

————, ed. 1999. *Brookings Trade Forum*. Washington, DC: Brookings Institution.

Lawrence, Robert Z., and Charles L. Schultze, eds. 1990. *An American Trade Strategy: Options for the 1990s*. Washington, DC: Brookings Institution.

Lincoln, Edward J. 1999. *Troubled Times: US-Japan Trade Relations in the 1990s*. Washington, DC: Brookings Institution Press.

Lindsey, Brink, Daniel T. Grisworld, et al. 1999. "The Steel 'Crisis' and the Costs of Protectionism." Washington, DC: Cato Institute.

Mayer, Fredrick W. 1998. *Interpreting NAFTA: The Science and Art of Political Analysis*. New York: Columbia University Press.

Mishel, Lawrence, Jared Bernstein, and John Schmitt. 2000. *The State of Working America, 2000–01*. Washington, DC: Economic Policy Institute.

Peter, Laurence J., and Raymond Hull. 1969. *The Peter Principle: Why Things Always Go Wrong*. New York: Morrow.

Porter, Roger. 1988. "The President, Congress and Trade Policy." *Congress and the Presidency*, 15(2): 165–184.

Prestowitz, Clyde V., Jr. 1988. *Trading Places: How We Allowed Japan to Take the Lead*. New York: Basic Books.

Richardson, J. David. 1994. "Trade Policy." In Martin Feldstein, ed., *American Economic Policy in the 1980s*, 627–690. Chicago: University of Chicago Press for the National Bureau of Economic Research.

Rosegrant, Susan. 1999. "Banana Wars." Cambridge, MA: John F. Kennedy School of Government.

Sanger, David E. 2001. "A Grand Trade Bargain." *Foreign Affairs*, 30 (January/February): 65–75.

Saxonhouse, Gary. 1993. "What Does Japanese Trade Structure Tell Us about Japanese Trade Policy?" *Journal of Economic Perspectives*, 7(3): 21–44.

Scheve, Kenneth F., and Matthew J. Slaughter. 2001. *Globalization and the Perceptions of American Workers*. Washington, DC: Institute for International Economics.

Shaffer, Gregory. 2000. "WTO Blue-Green Blues: The Impact of U.S. Domestic Politics on Trade-Labor, Trade-Environment Linkages for the WTO's Future." *Fordham International Law Journal*, 24(1&2): 608–651.

Tyson, Laura. 1992. *Who's Bashing Whom: Trade Conflict in High-Technology Industries*. Washington, DC: Institute for International Economics.

U.S. Council of Economic Advisers. 2000. *Economic Report of the President*. Washington, DC.

U.S. Council of Economic Advisers. 2001. *Economic Report of the President*. Washington, DC.

U.S. International Trade Commision. 1997. *The Year in Trade: 1996*. Washington, DC.

U.S. Trade Representative. 1996. *1996 Trade Policy Agenda and 1995 Annual Report*. Washington, DC.

U.S. Trade Representative. 1998. *1998 Trade Policy Agenda and 1997 Annual Report*. Washington, DC.

U.S. Trade Representative. 1999. *1999 Trade Policy Agenda and 1998 Annual Report*. Washington, DC.

Waldman, Michael. 2000. *POTUS Speahs*. New York: Simon and Schuster.

Wilson, John Douglas. 1996. "Capital Mobility and Environmental Standards: Is There a Theoretical Basis for a Race to the Bottom?" In J. Bhagwati and R. E. Hudec, *Fair Trade and Harmonization: Prerequisites for Free Trade?*, 393–428. Cambridge, MA: MIT Press.

Comments

Charlene Barshefsky

The trade agenda has faced both substantive and political challenges. Let me start with the general observation that we used to think of trade as simply a practical choice, one that had effects, for example, on living standards; but in the 1990s we saw that trade policy illuminated very different perceptions about our present economic circumstances, about our role in the world, and about issues of social justice. This is a very different role for trade than what we have been accustomed to.

A word on background. The genesis of the modern trading system and the WTO, of course, was one of the postwar institutions, the General Agreement on Tariffs and Trade—the GATT, which I used to call the "gentleman's agreement to talk and talk." That system was born of war and economic depression. You had seen in the world before 1914 a trading system that was actually rather globalized. In the interregnum between the two wars you saw political isolationism, economic protectionism, and the other isms—fascism, communism, and so on. The net effect, between our Smoot-Hawley tariff in the 1930s and Europe's colonial preference schemes, was to choke off trade, exacerbating the depression and helping to foment the political strife that led to war. That was how the postwar leaders saw it.

The basis for Smoot-Hawley was, in Herbert Hoover's famous injunction, that we can't compete with low-wage countries, and if we trade with them, they will pull down our wages and pull down our standard of living. This has familiar echoes today. Along came Franklin D. Roosevelt and Harry S. Truman who said that this is all wrong. If countries trade with each other, two things will happen: one, prosperity increases overall and, two, you have a firmer foundation for peace because countries that become economically interdependent will tend not to go to war with each other. The result was the postwar creation of a number of institutions we depend on to this day—the UN, NATO, the IMF, World Bank, and the GATT, now the WTO.

The GATT had 23 founding members, one of which, interestingly, was China, a fact which most people have forgotten. The system over the ensuing 50-plus years served to help reintegrate countries into the international system. This process began with Japan and Germany after the war in the 1950s, followed by the countries that emerged from the colonial preference schemes of Europe, and beginning in the 1980s, the integration of countries breaking with central planning, including China.

We have had a 55-year period of relative economic prosperity around the globe. Global production has increased sixfold, global trade 15-fold. Global per capita income is up threefold. World life expectancy has increased by 20 years, though now threatened by HIV-AIDS. Infant mortality is down by two-thirds, as countries have become wealthier over time. All of this proceeded in the context of periodic rounds of trade negotiations: eight global rounds reducing the barriers that had risen between World Wars I and II. Indeed, the tariffs that we are still working to reduce today, the tariff peaks, stem from the original Smoot-Hawley tariffs.

We had this rather stable system of liberalization; and then something happened in the late 1980s and 1990s. Trade returned to the center of American economic and foreign policy and to the center of public debate as at no time since the war. In retrospect this was a natural development. Profound changes were roiling the waters. First, as we all remember, came the view that "America can't compete," that we are losing out around the world, that American leadership globally was on the wane. Second, the domestic debate was heating up as our own barriers were coming down. Working people felt more and more vulnerable as trade became ever more important to our economy, with attendant job dislocation. Third, we saw changes in technology that recast or dispensed with former jobs. Fourth, we saw a major change in the political landscape. The end of the cold war eroded the assumptions that underlied many of our global relationships, and economics began to take their place. That process further exacerbated the tensions and anxieties that people already felt.

These were the converging trends that Bill Clinton saw during the 1992 campaign and during the early years of his presidency. The administration's response was to look to the vision of Roosevelt and Truman, to say that the right path is market opening and integrative. We negotiated more than 300 trade agreements. We brought 31 countries into the global system in the span of eight years. We created or nurtured new forums, such as the Asia-Pacific Economic Cooperation Group (APEC) forum, the Free Trade Area of the Americas forum, the African Trade Ministers series, and the Transatlantic Economic Partnership (with Europe). Among all the negotiations were perhaps a half dozen agreements that I would identify as signal achievements: the NAFTA, the Uruguay Round, the Japan Framework, the high-tech agreements of the mid-1990s (global telecom, global financial services, global information technology products, and duty-free cyberspace), and historic agreements with Vietnam and especially China, including PNTR—permanent normal trading relations. We also saw the passage of five major pieces of trade legislation and over 30 smaller ones.

This body of work, over the course of the Clinton presidency, contributed to five trends in the world economy of particular note. One, world markets are far more open today than they were eight or ten years ago. We see this openness in the sharp reduction of global tariffs overall. We see it in the diminution of government subsidies to favored industries. We see it in an absence, in large part, of industrial quotas. The U.S. market is more open, though I know Jagdish will say not nearly as open as it should be, and he's right.

Second, the trading system is stronger and broader. The membership of the old GATT system, now the WTO system, increased by 50 percent between 1991 and the end of Bill Clinton's term. The range of issues covered by global rules increased dramatically, intellectual property rights being one good example.

Third, we built a foundation of rules for the 21st-century global economy, from intellectual property rights all the way through to cyberspace.

Fourth, we see a stronger peace. Look at the countries that came into this global system as they were breaking from communist central planning and wanted to reform economically: Albania, Armenia, Bulgaria, Croatia, Cambodia, Georgia, Kurdistan, Latvia, Lithuania, Estonia, Mongolia, Slovenia. It is unbelievable. We've not seen this kind of shift internationally in decades. The negotiating forums and agreements, and the trading system more broadly, have helped create an additional framework for American foreign policy. Where we have seen an acceleration of reform in past cold-war rivals like China, Vietnam, Laos, and Cambodia, it is trade that is used as the basis for normalizing relations, not traditional forms of diplomacy alone.

I was overwhelmed by the analysis that Robert Lawrence applied to this mass of issues in his paper, for its thoroughness and its incisiveness. As you can tell from these comments, we are largely in agreement.

This is a remarkable record. So, what's the problem? Why are we in this big public debate? There is a substantive problem, and there is a political problem. They intersect. Let me spend one minute on each side of the coin.

On the substance, I put to one side the extremes: the far, far right, and the far, far left. I also put to one side what I call recreational revolutionaries who seem to think social injustice increases in April, May, and June and decreases in

December, January, and February. I put all of that aside. I think that there are four principal concerns of the central critics of trade.

Number one: the fear of the pace of economic change as trade transforms old jobs. Included in that is the problem of income inequality, which I thought Robert Lawrence addressed well. A good example is the following:

I happened to be at the American Federation of Labor (AFL) headquarters the day the AOL/Time Warner merger was announced. People were saying that hundreds of 25-year-olds had become multimillionaires overnight. One of the folks at the AFL asked, What do I tell the guy who has been on the assembly line for 35 years?

Number two: concern about the role and authority of international institutions, which tend to operate in a rather opaque way.

Number three: concern for the global environment. Increased trade does tighten the strain on our national and global heritage. The presence of persistent pollutants and global warming are huge issues. The critics of trade tend to pin the blame on increased trade flows, increased competitive pressures, a dumbing down of environmental standards, and so forth.

Fourth: humanitarian sympathy. Exploitative child labor. Slave labor. Inhumane working conditions. These are not more prevalent as many argue, but they are certainly more visible.

These separate concerns, though they come from different directions, converge. The critics of trade say that only the renegade companies will benefit. It is sort of a Hobson's choice that is presented. Substantively, most of the arguments of the trade critics can be responded to with data or information. If you look at the United States in the 1990s, an increasingly open economy didn't dumb down our standards: our drinking water got cleaner, our air got cleaner, our wetlands became more protected than they were previously. We had a rising standard of living during the period of greater market opening. You see something similar as well globally. No part of the world has developed without trade. Contrast East Asia and Latin America with the Asian subcontinent, sub-Saharan Africa, and the Middle East.

Last, what is really interesting is that it tends to be the countries with the highest labor and environmental standards that attract the most investment—certainly from U.S. companies—not the countries with the low standards. Two facts. In the 1990s, Singapore attracted more U.S. investment than the rest of Southeast Asia combined, even though Singapore is a high-standard country in many of these areas and the rest of Southeast Asia tends to be lower-standard.

Second fact: Britain and the Netherlands, two very high-standard countries, received as much U.S. direct investment as the entire developing world put together. The notion that renegade companies will move jobs to the poorest nations simply is not borne out.

That's on the substantive side. Two points on the politics. Trade education is going to be ever more critical. The politics of trade are difficult and complicated, and not particularly positive.

First, the gains from trade are widely disbursed. Trade-related job loss tends to be highly concentrated. Members of Congress hate to vote for trade agreements because they don't know if their constituents are going to be on the winning or the losing side.

Second, the shift to the political center that has characterized domestic economic policy has not happened on the trade front. It's the opposite. It has become more polarized. Third, the business community is less united for various reasons, including the fact that more time-sensitive economic issues tend to grab the bulk of their attention, rather than long-running trade negotiations or general trade policy. Fourth, there is less confidence in the ability of our trade remedy laws to protect U.S. workers. Fifth, trade adjustment assistance, the traditional sop to labor, is viewed as funeral insurance. Sixth, the debate on labor and the environment polarizes even the center core of both political parties.

Thus we are polarized on the substance and polarized on the politics. These are topics that deserve substantial analysis and thought if the center-core coalition on trade is to be rebuilt on a genuinely bipartisan basis.

Comments

Jagdish Bhagwati

I face three distinguished members of the Clinton administration—U.S. Trade Representative Charlene Barshefsky; the White House adviser on trade to the president, Lael Brainard; and the author, Robert Lawrence, who also served as a member of the Council of Economic Advisers. They will proclaim the administration's success with trade policy, whereas I hold the diametrically opposed and published view that the administration's trade policy left much to be desired, and in key respects was a disaster.[1] I feel, therefore, very much like Gary Cooper in *High Noon*. But let me assure the chair that, unlike Gary Cooper, I shall not turn in my badge and ride my buggy away from the scene even if I win. I have every intention of staying on, fighting the good fight for a better trade policy, for one's task is never done if one is a free trader, and a multilateral one to boot, as I happen to be.

I must compliment Lawrence on a characteristically splendid paper. It is a bird's-eye view of virtually the entire trade policy scene, and every reader will profit from reading it. The bird is, however, the American eagle, and, despite the author's cosmopolitan temperament and record, I shall argue that the evaluation of Washington's trade policy under the Clinton administration is a trifle, even excessively, indulgent.

But, ignoring the inevitable disagreements on details that a paper of such scope entails, let me raise at the outset three general issues about the Clinton hagiography. First, Lawrence talks at times, and so do most former officials of the administration, of Clinton "believing" this or that. I am not privy to the former president's beliefs; and I doubt if these officials are either. Indeed, at the beginning of his first term, many of us were doubtful about President Clinton's commitment to free trade; and I said mischievously at a Washington meeting that, while the problem with President Bush, his predecessor, was that one could

---

1. I have argued this thesis in my latest collection of public policy essays, *The Wind of the Hundred Days: How Washington Mismanaged Globalization* (Cambridge, MA: MIT Press, 2001).

not read his lips, the problem with President Clinton was deeper: one did not know whether to read his upper lip or his lower lip. But, whatever the truth of the matter, we cannot go even by his speeches. After all, with American politicians, we know that others write their speeches, a practice that we deplore even in the weaker version such as the notorious Milli Vanilli episode, and which we academics cannot emulate: I have never succeeded in getting an assistant professor to write my article for me, leave aside hogging the credit for his work instead.

Second, since Lawrence addresses the 1990s and the Clinton administration record, more or less as if the two were the same, let me say that the Clinton administration did not start until 1993. More important, we have a problem that afflicts every assessment of an administration's record: initiatives and work that began under earlier ones will cross over into the one we are assessing, and initiatives begun under the latter will likely bear fruit in the succeeding administrations. In the case of the Clinton administration, it can be fairly said that the Uruguay Round was begun earlier and was close to completion when the Clinton folks came in: they simply completed it, standing on the shoulders of their predecessors and grasping the prize. I do not deny that they had to work very hard to do so, balancing themselves precariously and reaching out at the definite risk of falling off these shoulders. The Clinton administration deserves some credit for sure, but the toast must be drunk to its predecessors on this one.

But both good and bad things were inherited. Thus the discredit (in my view) for having gone after NAFTA—which, as I will argue, has had important adverse effects on multilateralism—belongs also to the previous administration, and especially to Messrs. James Baker and Robert Zoellick, who were and are energetic proponents not just of NAFTA but also of the bilateral preferential trade agreements (PTAs) that now disfigure the world trading scene and to which Mr. Zoellick now plans to devote his new duties. (Of course, despite all this, there are some defining and huge events [such as the Seattle debacle at the WTO ministerial meeting] and almost completed but minor initiatives [such as the PTA with Jordan] that are virtually entirely to be attributed to the Clinton administration; but more on this later.)

Third, Lawrence should not suggest, however fleetingly, that the critics of the Clinton trade policies and performance are either far out on the right (like Pat Buchanan) or on the extreme left (like Ralph Nader) and that the "pure free traders,"[2] whatever that means, such as myself are also somehow on the "right"

---

2. I am not sure that Nader could be described as being on the extreme left. He is totally misguided on trade policy, but his views on the need for countervailing corporate power are shared widely and were reflected even in the Gore campaign's central themes.

and that they belong to either the American Enterprise Institute or the Cato Institute. As it happens, I am a Democrat myself, and my affiliations are multiple and have extended also in varying ways to Brookings, the Council on Foreign Relations, the United Nations, the GATT, the WTO, Human Rights Watch, and on and on. I have the certain knowledge that this statement is true also of many trade economists who have misgivings about the Clinton administration record. Also, whenever I have organized petitions on trade issues faced by the Clinton administration (and its predecessor as well since I am an equal opportunity critic of bad policies), the signatories have included numerous Democrats who have been unhappy with Washington.

Indeed, this is important to remember also since many defenders of the Clinton administration's failings in trade policy come back by saying that Reagan or Bush did worse. Maybe. But perhaps things were worse in the Garden of Eden too: if, *in lieu of* autarky, the wretched apple had only been traded for something more innocuous, Adam and Eve would have continued in bliss. It is better to measure each administration against itself, its challenges and whether it met them, its potential and whether it rose to it. In short, at least in the reflective atmosphere of academe, we ought to be able to avoid making our analysis captive to a partisan spirit, difficult as it is to do so.

But let me now get down to real business. The administration's success could be judged by reference to two broad, and generally distinct, criteria:

• *Criterion 1.* How much did trade expand; how many trade agreements were signed; etc.: an approach that dominates certainly Ambassador Barshefsky's comments and is present also in Lawrence's paper at various points.

• *Criterion 2.* Did the administration affect the atmospherics of trade, and the architecture of the world trading system, in the right way?

Criterion 1

Yes, indeed, Lawrence is right to argue that, by the criterion of trade expansion, the Clinton record is pretty good. But, since Lawrence implies (and Ms. Barshefsky has also suggested in her comments) that this was courtesy of Washington's policies, and particularly because of the numerous trade agreements signed under Ms. Barshefsy's watch, let me make a few important qualifiers.

We must recognize that trade has grown rapidly, even as a proportion of GNP, worldwide and for some time going back way before the 1990s. We therefore need to take the partial derivative here. How much did these agreements add to what would have happened anyway?

Thus, for example, service trade has been growing phenomenally even prior to the Uruguay Round's General Agreement on Trade in Services (GATS), whose aim is not just to open markets further but to introduce some discipline and rules in this trade, these latter objectives translating more into better quality than into increased quantity of trade flows.

Again, much of the expansion reflects not only agreements to liberalize trade, but also a great amount of unilateral trade liberalization worldwide that has had little to do with agreements or even aid conditionality.[3] It is hard to say whether this accelerated in the 1990s, but in such areas as South America, Central Europe, and India there is indeed evidence that it did.

Moreover, Lawrence tends to attribute more to the preferential trade agreements than is legitimate. Our PTAs with Chile and Singapore are, of course, still not negotiated, whereas Jordan is not yet approved. But the former two represent agreements with countries that have unilaterally liberalized their trade. They seek PTAs with us because they face trade diversion against them from our preferential policies, leaving aside political reasons. So, the bottom line is that they have already opened their markets and are happy to finish their job unilaterally, whereas it is we who are indulging in preferential agreements to bring them into the PTA fold with us! It makes no sense for us to take credit for such a situation by suggesting that we are "opening the markets of the world" through these PTA agreements.

In this vein, I should also remind Lawrence, who surely knows this well, that all agreements should not be lumped together with equal weights. I can understand Ms. Barshefsky, who is a lawyer, claiming that she has signed nearly 300 trade agreements. So did USTR Mickey Kantor, of course. To a trade negotiator, perhaps every agreement is another feather in her cap. But these agreements surely include several sectoral trade-restricting agreements, such as those under the MFA, I guess. Are trade-restricting agreements to be equated with trade-liberalizing ones? And, even among the trade-liberalizing ones, is a piffling U.S.-Jordan FTA of the same value as the Uruguay Round? And, is a failure such as Seattle, to be balanced off against the success of a sectoral agreement, however large in scope?

Criterion 2

But, even if all these qualifiers and nuances were reflected in the assessment, the verdict on the Clinton years would be woefully incomplete and misleading.

---

3. I recently directed a project on the subject of unilateral trade liberalization. The volume resulting from it is being published shortly. Cf. Jagdish Bhagwati, ed., *Going Alone: The Case for Relaxed Reciprocity in Freeing Trade* (Cambridge, MA: MIT Press, 2002).

The real problem with the Clinton administration was that it contributed adversely to the atmospherics of trade policy, and hence undermined unwittingly but surely the architecture of the multilateral world trading system. Consider just a few important points.

1. It can fairly be said that the Clinton administration elevated allegations of "unfairness" into a major problem in dealing with trade openness and liberalization. President Clinton came into office with Japan baiting and Japan obsession at center stage. Charges of Japan's unfair trade practices were the hallmark of the administration. Revival of Super 301 was right inside the party document, *Putting People First*. The infamous U.S.-Japan auto dispute, which (contrary to Lawrence's approbation)[4] turned into a fiasco for the administration, both reflected the obsession with unfair trade and contributed to its exacerbation.

2. Taking NAFTA through Congress for a successful outcome was, from the viewpoint of the increasing encroachment of "fair trade" notions, another turning point. Protectionists who feared free trade with Mexico, and these included labor unions that feared a decline in their worker's real wages and loss of jobs across the Rio Grande, could zero in on the warts on Mexico's face and turn them into "fair trade" issues. This was true of Mexico's labor and environmental state and standards, for sure: the protectionists claimed that free trade with Mexico was unfair trade by Mexico unless labor and environmental restrictions were put into the NAFTA treaty. This was not the case with the Uruguay Round, where the multiplicity of nations precluded zeroing in on one country's nontrade situation. Thus, in debates that I had with antitrade activists over NAFTA, I was often told, "You can have the Uruguay Round but NAFTA we will give you only over your dead body." NAFTA helped make credible the notion that nontrade issues, with persistent lobbying, could be made into "fair trade" preconditions for trade liberalization.

The United States has had to live with the consequences ever since: the failure to secure fast track, the Seattle debacle, and the present impasse over the Trade Promotion Authority have their origins, to a large extent, in the NAFTA debate and outcome. Was NAFTA worth it all? I doubt it, leaving aside also the fact that it has pushed the United States still further and decisively into the embrace of a trade policy of proliferation of bilateral and plurilateral PTAs, which I believe to be a mistake.

In fact, the cancer of "fair trade" has spread so deeply into the American body politic by now, and the Clinton administration must take its share of blame for

---

4. Cf. my detailed analysis of the dispute and how the USTR had declared victory but was only masking defeat, which is in an essay published in *International Affairs*, and reprinted in my public policy essays, *A Stream of Windows: Unsettled Reflections on Trade, Immigration and Democracy* (Cambridge, MA: MIT Press, 1998).

it,[5] that even the present President Bush, who had studiously avoided the invocation of fair trade when endorsing free trade, succumbed to it in announcing his 201 action against foreign steel. This is a safeguard action (which has nothing to do with whether the market disruption is due to unfair or fair trade), but the administration announced it while claiming that foreign nations were "unfairly" exporting steel to us.[6] The action was bad enough from the viewpoint of free trade in steel; but the language of unfair trade made it far worse in stroking the monster that the previous administration had fed and raised.

3. The Clinton administration also fed the virus of unfair trade by a frequent resort to Section 301, which, of course, relies for the most part heavily on the notion of unfair trade by others. President Bush had reluctantly signed on to the 1988 Omnibus Trade and Competitiveness Act, which had made this a more deadly instrument; but remember that President Clinton's administration was more enthusiastic, in light of the Japan obsession with which it came into office.

The panelists today suggest that the Clinton administration sheathed this nasty sword. But surely, only after the high-profile U.S.-Japan auto dispute debacle and the massive criticisms abroad,[7] and in the end only when the WTO dispute-settlement panel in 1999 virtually made use of 301 de facto WTO-illegal, while giving us a face-saving victory and the European Union the real victory, can we claim that this sword was finally sheathed.

4. That brings me to the Seattle debacle. It outweighs any success that the Clinton administration may claim. It was a direct blow to the multilateral system and has also served to accelerate the shift to bilaterals in Asia, a region that had been generally free from this affliction.

Was it something that could be blamed on Mike Moore (as many in Washington would like to believe) or on the disorder in the streets that came (presum-

---

5. My position is only that the Clinton administration gave this cancer an immense boost. I had actually talked about this cancer, and its spread, and raised an alarm over it in my 1990 Harry Johnson Lecture in London, published later as *The World Trading System at Risk* (Princeton, NJ: Princeton University Press, 1991).

6. This misled even our "newspaper of record," the *New York Times*, into editorializing as if this was an antidumping action! Our trade policy coverage in the best newspapers can border on the abysmal, unlike that in the "foreign legion" represented by *The Financial Times* and *The Economist*.

7. I remember Arthur Dunkel, then director general of GATT, whom I was Economic Policy Adviser to in 1991–93, telling me that nothing had unified the GATT members as much as their opposition to the 301 legislation and actions of the United States. For a proper assessment of 301 legislation, we must remember, however, that one part of it dealt with enforcement of existing obligations and another with creating new ones; it was the latter that created the resentments, not the former (when it followed favorable GATT dispute-settlement panel findings that were blocked from being adopted by the GATT council). See, in this regard, the chapters by me and Robert Hudec in Jagdish Bhagwati and Hugh Patrick, *Aggressive Unilateralism* (Ann Arbor: University of Michigan, 1990).

ably exogenously to our actions and inactions) from the foes of free trade and of the WTO? Some have even argued that the problem was that the conference hall was not available over the weekend to complete negotiations that were "close to completion" because the optometrists had booked it for their convention: apparently if we had only consulted them and restored our 20/20 vision, we could have kept the hall away from them and for our glorious purpose.

I will only briefly assert, as I and others have argued at length elsewhere, that Washington gets the lion's share of the blame. There was little effective preparation for Seattle, to secure the kind of negotiating text with which we could operate at the speed necessary. Washington had also disregarded the obvious signs of impending disorder, making no preparation for the chaos that followed. Reliance on Seattle authorities to manage the meeting without significant federal input was surely a mistake as well. I have returned to Seattle several times after the debacle, to debate antitrade activists; and I must say that Seattle is an ultraliberal city that makes even Massachusetts seem conservative! And then President Clinton's gaffe over trade sanctions for labor issues was critical; whatever his reasons for this—I myself do not think it was unwitting and believe that it was calculated—it did finally kill the Seattle Round.

5. This brings me to other ways in which the Clinton administration appears to have failed us. With Seattle goofed up, the effect was to create the notion that the NGOs and the unions had "won the battle of Seattle." President Clinton did not confront the street violence and demonstrators in the clear tone of condemnation that Prime Minister Tony Blair has firmly deployed, calling them "louts." He was instead accommodating and indulgent. As for the unions' fears of free trade and their inappropriate demands to amend the WTO to apply trade sanctions to countries and their products apropos of lapses from a social clause, he did not forcefully refute these fears and demands.

Recall that the turning point in the NAFTA debate came with Al Gore's success in the debate with Ross Perot. We needed a debate where Clinton would slay John Sweeney, but we never got it. Nor did we get a direct attack on Mr. Sweeney's fears and demands from the White House. Nor were there any new creative initiatives at ILO and other agencies where social and environmental issues could be pursued without the use of trade sanctions nor any systematic argumentation about the relative demerits of a WTO-based, trade-sanctions-using approach. In short, President Clinton at Seattle got what he deserved, but not what we deserved.

6. Finally, let me say that while, under the Clinton administration's watch, there have been important sectoral liberalization agreements, this achievement must be set against the fact that these agreements take the affected business groups out of the multilateral arena in the future. If you have already gotten

your liberalization through sectoral agreements, why waste time and lobbying resources for the new round? Hence, the politics of getting multilateralism going becomes more difficult. This situation is in contrast to the sectoral trade-restricting agreements such as the MFA in the past: they took the difficult sectors out of the negotiations and enabled multilateralism to flourish instead!

This observation is equally true of the bilateral and plurilateral PTAs. If you invest in getting NAFTA, you (in an exporting business) get the benefits of your lobbying efforts all to yourself, since NAFTA is a PTA. But if you invest in the Uruguay Round or a new Qatar Round, the liberalization that follows would be on an MFN basis: other "free riders" benefit too.

Then again, if you have negotiated a special preferential benefit for yourself, you have no real interest in pursuing it for all at Geneva. This is seen in the fact that, in the latest antidumping dispute (over the Byrd legislation awarding revenues from antidumping duties to the "injured" complainants) where several countries have joined as plaintiffs against the United States, Canada and Mexico did not join but are now likely to because they have discovered that they too can be charged with dumping.

So, getting support for multilateral efforts on trade liberalization gets more difficult. Interest in the WTO then wanes. Though Lester Thurow was wrong in declaring the GATT was dead, we must then begin to worry about the WTO beginning to suffer from neglect, even atrophy, though not a certain death. Meanwhile, the world trading system would see a continuing proliferation of bilaterals, which Ambassadors Kantor and Barshefsky may celebrate as feathers in their cap, but which are rapidly creating a maze of preferences that I have called a "spaghetti bowl" and which are a blight on the world trading system. Let my last vignette for Lawrence be that the European Union, the chief sinner in this regard, now has only five countries enjoying MFN tariff access to it, with all others enjoying some special preference or the other. So, the MFN tariff has now become the LFN tariff: it applies to the least favored countries! And so our cynicism, and not just our distress, multiplies.

Comments

Lael Brainard

Trade was important in the 1990s. Both opponents and proponents agree that trade was much in our national consciousness, in our domestic politics, in our economic performance, and in our diplomatic relations. Many of the major trade achievements of the 1990s will leave their mark for years to come.

Trade takes place at the interface of domestic politics, economic policy, and foreign policy, and it has an intimate relationship with international finance. In this comment, I organize my reflections on trade in the 1990s around these poles, hopefully without losing the complexity of the interrelationship among them. I also provide a brief discussion of the process of trade policy-making in the 1990s, which reflected the multifaceted nature of the enterprise to a degree not achieved earlier.

The 1990s opened with the United States in a defensive crouch on competitiveness and a broad political consensus that the United States needed to be more aggressive in promoting its commercial interests. This posture changed dramatically over the decade, as the United States regained international preeminence in the industries emerging as growth drivers and in macroeconomic performance. By the end of the 1990s, America had compiled one of the most impressive records seen in decades on forging trade agreements with key regional and bilateral partners and providing leadership on the multilateral trading system, with profound implications for economic and foreign policy.

In security policy, the big event of the last decade was the collapse of the Soviet Union and the end of the cold war. In international economics, the big event of the 1990s was the decline of Japan and the associated "Asian model" of capitalism. By the middle of the decade, the United States found itself in an unexpectedly dominant—some would say hegemonic—position in the international economy, due to a combination of unexpected, rapid decline in Japan and resurgence at home. At the same time, the "Washington consensus" recipe for growth was increasingly adopted around the world. This trend presented the United States with opportunities that scarcely could have been imagined in the previous decade, but equally with responsibilities on the global stage. In parallel, the domestic debate on trade grew increasingly polarized, in great part because of the very success of the trade agenda and America's newfound dominance. So the United States concluded the decade in a position of unchallenged economic dominance on the global scene, but simultaneously beset by popular opposition to trade.

The result was unevenness. Sometimes the United States seized the opportunities and took ambitious leadership positions, finalizing the Uruguay Round, NAFTA, and global agreements in telecommunications, financial services, and information technology, launching the Free Trade Area of the Americas (FTAA), elevating the Asia-Pacific Economic Cooperation Group (APEC) forum, driving the international financial rescue of Mexico and later of East Asia, negotiating the U.S.-Jordan Free Trade Agreement (FTA) and the U.S.-Vietnam bilateral trade agreement, and brokering China's entry into the World Trade Organization (WTO). But sometimes the polarization at home led to paralysis abroad, most notably with the collapse of WTO negotiations in Seattle and the symbolically important defeat of fast track in 1997. And in those instances where U.S. domestic politics got in the way of exerting leadership, rivals were only too happy to step in, most notably the European Union (EU) on the WTO and Japan in Asia.

Economic Policy

The course of trade policy over the 1990s was integrally shaped by the interaction with the overall state of the economy—as it had been, in mirror image, during the 1980s. When the Clinton administration entered office in 1993, the overriding imperative was the "economy, stupid." America's economic posture abroad was overwhelmingly colored by the realities of the 1980s: severe macroeconomic imbalance associated with loose fiscal policy and tight monetary policy and severe erosion of international market share and "competitiveness" in key manufacturing sectors. Japan was seen as the major competitive threat to be challenged where possible and imitated where not. In fact, one of the main points of agreement among the Clinton administration's new economic team coming into office was that with the cold war over, American policy-makers could take off their gloves vis-à-vis Japan.

But just as in the 1980s, when America's twin deficits and dollar overshooting contributed centrally to a loss of competitiveness vis-à-vis Asian rivals, so too in the 1990s, trade developments were heavily conditioned by the Clinton administration's commitment to fiscal discipline and the stunning performance of the information technology sector in the United States, as well as the deepening economic slump in Japan. By the mid-1990s, U.S. economic performance was strong—with trade making a significant contribution. On a sectoral level, it was becoming clear that the industries where the United States was on the cutting edge were increasingly dominating economic performance all over the globe.

The resulting confidence left room for trade advances across a variety of fronts. And it put the United States in a position to act as a stable anchor in the international financial system, first in the Mexican peso crisis of 1995 and later in the Asian financial crisis of 1997–98, helping to support accelerated recoveries and to maintain the commitment to open trade regimes.

And expanding trade in turn contributed centrally to America's stellar performance. In the early to mid-1990s, trade was an important stimulant to growth. But as the decade progressed, trade's contribution was increasingly to be a brake on inflation, probably providing the Federal Reserve a little more leeway in navigating its way through the financial crisis in 1998.

Trade Policy

It is also important to assess progress on the goal of advancing open trade as an economic policy in its own right. The record of the Clinton administration on trade is very strong—perhaps not compared with the economist's ideal of free trade but certainly when compared with previous administrations facing similar political constraints. Although the administration's early rhetoric could have been construed as favoring results-oriented managed trade, in fact the record is strongest on forging market-opening agreements and quite respectable on managing trade disputes and trade remedies. By any measure, the trade record in the 1990s stacks up very well against the 1980s—despite polarization in the domestic debate. A combination of factors contributed to this record of achievement, including America's economic resurgence and the sea change in attitudes toward trade in Latin America and other developing countries, but some credit must be given to President Clinton and the extraordinary group of people he selected to make trade policy.

Market Opening

When it comes to market-opening agreements, it is hard not to recognize the momentous achievements of the 1990s. The Reagan administration initiated the Uruguay Round and negotiated the U.S.-Canada FTA and the U.S.-Israel FTA, and the Bush administration initiated NAFTA. In comparison, the Clinton administration concluded negotiation and achieved legislative passage of both

NAFTA and the Uruguay Round, concluded WTO agreements on telecommunications, financial services, and information technology, launched negotiations toward the FTAA and a free trade agreement with Chile, negotiated a free trade agreement with Jordan, secured legislative approval of significantly expanded Caribbean trade preferences and a generous new trade preference program with Africa, and negotiated and won legislative approval for China's entry into the WTO.

Free trade purists tend to critique the Clinton administration's market-opening record as too ambitious rather than too modest, citing the eager pursuit of a "spaghetti bowl" of free trade agreements. In fact, there were two big developments on this front: NAFTA and the commitment to pursue an FTAA starting with Chile. In both cases, the agreements would seem to meet all of the criteria that economists believe make trade agreements more likely to be building blocks than stumbling blocks to multilateral free trade. Although the U.S.-Jordan agreement does not fit this mold, surely it should be seen primarily as an instrument of foreign policy rather than of trade policy, like the U.S.-Israel FTA that went before it.

Trade Remedies and Protection

Many economists judge any implementation of trade remedies as effectively protectionist and antitrade. Those who live in the world of policy and politics make finer distinctions. First, there is a vast difference between implementing protectionist measures on an ad hoc basis and doing so in accordance with U.S. trade laws and WTO rules. Second, there is a strong political rationale for our trade remedy statutes as a safety valve, helping support a remarkably open trade regime overall. Indeed, it is likely that the only politically feasible alternative would be a regime that builds in comparable insurance by maintaining higher levels of bound protection across the board.

With these provisos, the Clinton administration's performance was strong—especially in contrast to the 1980s. The 1980s witnessed a series of ad hoc mechanisms restricting imports in a number of politically important industries: steel quotas covering 27 countries, quotas on Japanese car imports, a worldwide price cartel on semiconductors, restraints on machine tool imports, and quotas on Canadian softwood lumber imports (although the Reagan administration also ended the Orderly Marketing Agreement in the footwear industry). In nearly all cases, the protection was instituted outside the framework of U.S. trade laws, and in many cases, findings under the statutory processes were ignored or rejected.

In contrast, the Clinton administration early on made clear that it saw strong implementation of U.S. trade laws—in accordance with international obligations—as an integral component of sustaining domestic support for the international trading system. In practice, this meant that the president took action in all cases where the ITC recommended it, from the minute broomcorn broom industry to the powerful steel industry. But the administration refrained from imposing protectionist measures outside the context of the legal process (with the sole exception of two agricultural cases with Canada, where it extended negotiated solutions established under previous administrations).

Perhaps the most prominent example differentiating the Clinton administration's approach is the case of steel. The Asian financial crisis was in full swing when the U.S. steel industry was thrown into crisis, with layoffs affecting fully 10 percent of the workforce, capacity utilization plummeting, and firms filing bankruptcy. The industry pursued a strategy centered on antidumping cases, in parallel with an all-out effort to secure legislation imposing worldwide quotas on steel imports. The Clinton administration responded with aggressive implementation of the antidumping laws and intense engagement on industry adjustment measures, but early on made clear they would veto any quota legislation inconsistent with WTO rules. Because of concern over the fragility of international financial markets, the Clinton administration steadfastly resisted taking any extralegal measures or even self-initiating a safeguards case—even when the steel quota legislation passed in the House by a bipartisan vote of 289 to 141. President Clinton's position—which would later have consequences for America's negotiating position in Seattle and for the China permanent normalized trade relations (PNTR) vote—stands in sharp contrast to actions by previous administrations.

Trade Disputes and Unilateralism

During the 1980s there was increasing sentiment in Congress and among policy experts that the multilateral trading rules were inadequate to address key foreign barriers faced by U.S. firms because the dispute settlement system was weak, "hidden" barriers were not subject to trade disciplines, and key trade partners such as China remained outside the rules. Indeed, the single biggest piece of trade legislation produced during the 1980s, the 1988 Omnibus Trade Act, mandated action to address systematic unfair trade barriers under the so-called Super 301 provision. This legislation and U.S. attempts to deal with barriers in Japan and South Korea led to growing international concern about U.S. unilateralism in the late 1980s and early 1990s.

When the Clinton administration assumed office in 1993, it placed significant emphasis on taking aggressive action to deal with trade barriers abroad. And indeed, 1993 to 1995 witnessed several high-profile bilateral negotiations, first with Japan in the context of the U.S.-Japan framework, and then with China.

Concerns about U.S. unilateralism spread to Europe and Canada with the passage of the Helms-Burton Cuba sanctions legislation in 1996, whose provisions were alleged to impose a burden of extraterritoriality.

But beginning with the passage of the Uruguay Round legislation in 1994 and the associated strengthening of the WTO dispute-settlement system, there was an important change in America's approach. The Clinton administration determined to pursue trade disputes through the WTO system; although the administration continued to invoke Section 301, in fact all Section 301 actions were pursued in parallel with—and subject to—WTO rulings. Perhaps the most striking example is the Kodak-Fuji case, where the administration terminated the action under Section 301 following a WTO loss. Exceptions to this rule were limited to cases against China, because it remained outside the WTO, as well as intellectual property cases mandated under the statutory "Special 301" standards, where eligibility requirements for U.S. trade preference programs exceed WTO standards.

Some free trade purists have criticized the aggressive use of the WTO dispute-settlement system. However, the Clinton administration consciously adopted a policy of availing itself of the mechanisms available under international law in order to affirm the primacy of the multilateral system and to demonstrate to domestic critics that the United States could use the new system to advance its interests. This strategy came under attack from Congress and domestic interests when the United States won cases at the WTO only to find its trade partners, and particularly the European Union, opting to accept retaliation rather than implement changes to the disputed provisions. For its part, the United States established a record of coming into compliance with adverse WTO rulings, but this may prove more difficult in the months ahead.

Foreign Policy and International Financial Policy

The Clinton administration entered office with a stated determination to end the perceived subordination of trade policy to security, reflecting the end of the cold war and the need to address America's relative economic decline. In the early years, this policy was given concrete expression in a series of high-profile trade disputes with Japan. But over the course of eight years in office, several new developments pushed in the direction of mutual reinforcement between international economic policy and security policy (with notable exceptions in the areas of sanctions and export controls). Perhaps most important, the turnaround in the U.S. economic position permitted a reorientation of the trade agenda more in the direction of pursuing opportunities rather than redressing inequities. Second, President Clinton, who entered office with a much stronger vision and mandate on domestic and economic policy than on foreign policy, gradually developed a strong interest in foreign policy and a keen instinct for using economic tools to advance U.S. interests abroad. And third, the international financial system presented critical challenges that dominated trade policy-making at several key junctures.

Ultimately, the Clinton administration was able to advance U.S. core economic and security interests in tandem on several fronts: in the western hemisphere, in East Asia, and to some degree with Africa. The relationship with Japan improved over time, because of the sharp change in the relative economic positions of the United States and Japan and because of a course correction by the administration. The Clinton administration can also be credited with providing important international leadership on systemic issues, helping to strengthen the multilateral trading system, and helping to galvanize international financial stabilization. But the administration ended with some notable failures as well, bequeathing to its successor a dispute-riddled relationship with the European Union and doubt abroad about whether America could muster the political will to continue providing international leadership on trade.

Mexico

The early years of the Clinton administration were a defining time for the U.S. relationship with Mexico—America's most important economic relationship with a middle-income country because of the 2000-mile shared land border. The first challenge confronting the new administration was determining how to handle the endgame on NAFTA given a hostile Congress and strong opposition within the Democratic Party. The Clinton administration followed a strategy of elaborating the agreement to address areas of particular concern to Democrats and then waging an all-out effort to secure passage, on the strength of claims about NAFTA's job creation potential in the United States. Scarcely a year later, Mexico plummeted into the most severe financial crisis in its history. With the support of the congressional leadership, President Clinton used executive authority to assemble the biggest ever financial rescue package, in the face of broad opposition from the American people and Congress. Mexican President Ernesto Zedillo's tenacity and strong economic policies made the investment one of the best of its kind. Moreover, the framework of rules mandated by NAFTA held strong throughout the financial crisis, helping Mexico to recover in record time.

From a foreign policy vantage point, these policies were a clear win. They fundamentally transformed the relationship with Mexico, putting in place an economic framework that will govern relations for years to come and will form the basis for a hemisphere-wide system of trade and investment rules. But the fight over NAFTA and the sharp deterioration in trade balances following the peso crisis galvanized a powerful coalition of trade opponents and generated a fierce backlash on trade that, perhaps more than any other single factor, helped defeat fast track in 1997 and undermine the Seattle trade talks in 2000.

Western Hemisphere

Spurred in part by the competitive dynamic set off by NAFTA and in part by a profound change in Latin American attitudes toward market liberalization, the United States was able to put in place an ambitious negotiating agenda toward the goal of achieving FTAA by 2005. Although hard issues such as agriculture subsidies and antidumping will not be addressed until the endgame of the negotiations, the ambitious trade goals and the initiation of a regularized hemisphere-wide summit process are major achievements in U.S. relations with the Caribbean, Central America, and Latin America, in a clear case where trade and security interests proceed in tandem.

Japan

In the early days of the administration, the policy that most united the international economic team was broad determination to achieve concrete sectoral results with Japan. Major emphasis was placed on the U.S.-Japan framework negotiations aimed at addressing impediments in important Japanese sectors where U.S. market share was low. There is little doubt that this put strains on the overall relationship with this key ally. But even as the Clinton administration approached the moment of peak tension with Japan, threatening punitive sanctions in order to exact concessions on opening Japan's auto and auto parts market, Japan's economy was slipping into a severe and protracted slump.

The turnaround in the relationship to Japan and the trade agenda bears analogy to the breathtaking demise of the Soviet Union and end of the cold war. Starting with the rapid turnaround in the relative economic positions of Japan and the United States, and reinforced by the challenge to the Japanese model of capitalism posed by the Asian financial crisis, America's trade agenda was turned on its head. By early 1998, trade disputes had taken a back seat to the imperative of prodding Japan's supine economy back to life. Although trade negotiations continued on key areas of U.S. priority (telecommunications, pharmaceuticals, insurance, and autos) the tenor became more muted, and greater weight was placed on the overall relationship and the common security agenda. The contrast can be seen in President Clinton's bookend visits to Japan in 1993 and 2000. When President Clinton traveled to Japan in 1993 for his first G-7 meeting, Japan's trade barriers and U.S. imbalances topped the agenda. When President Clinton traveled to Japan in 2000 for his final G-7/8 meeting, the United States and Japan collaborated closely on a major new effort to address development challenges including HIV/AIDS, the digital divide, primary education, and debt relief, as well as a showcase agreement on information technology.

China

The Clinton administration also made a major breakthrough on relations with China through trade policy, after several years of rocky relations on the security and trade fronts. The early years were characterized by a series of high-profile trade disputes that culminated in a landmark intellectual property agreement signed under the threat of sanctions. Although the administration early on identified WTO accession as one of the few levers available to the United States for influencing China's development and advancing the rule of law, negotiations did not intensify in earnest until the Chinese leadership, in particular Premier Zhu Rongji, embraced WTO membership as a critical complement to the domestic reform agenda and determined that the United States would be the key broker of a deal.

The terms of China's entry into the WTO will have a profound impact on U.S.-China relations, on the terms of China's integration into the international economy, and on the WTO itself for years to come. Nevertheless, several interactions between trade and foreign policy are worth noting. First, President Clinton's decision to actively pursue congressional approval for PNTR before the WTO accession process was completed and during his final year in office, which was critical to the breakthrough with China, incurred heavy political costs and displaced other trade legislation priorities such as fast track. Second, as is common in trade negotiations, the twists and turns in the negotiations with China—reflecting domestic politics on both sides—severely strained the relationship. Third, it is clear that the endgame on the China WTO negotiations, coming as they did in November 2000, distracted high-level attention from the Seattle WTO preparations at a critical time.

South Korea and ASEAN

With respect to relations with South Korea and the ASEAN nations, President Clinton early on signaled the importance he attached to these relationships by elevating APEC to an annual summit process and by pursuing an ambitious trade liberalization agenda within APEC. But, ultimately, it was the Asian financial crisis that defined the tenor of U.S. relationships in East Asia and to some degree even APEC.

Three things are notable here as they relate to the interaction of international economic and foreign policy. First, although it is widely recognized that the United States played a key leadership role on financial stabilization in Asia, foreign perceptions of America's role suffered from the highly partisan debate over the U.S. financial contribution to the IMF and America's inability to pledge financing for Thailand, a treaty ally, because of restrictions on the Exchange Stabilization Fund imposed during the peso crisis. Second, analogous to the course of many trade negotiations, although our security agenda is well served by coming to the aid of friends and allies at times of financial crisis, the "take your medicine" tenor of America's involvement implicates America in the onus associated with strict IMF conditionality, which can place strains on our relationships. Third, trade policy was an integral part of the rapid recovery from crisis. Although there was some experimentation with financial conditions, no crisis country deviated significantly from its open trade commitments. And the strength of the U.S. economy, coupled with President Clinton's commitment to maintain open markets, made a central contribution to recovery—despite recession in Japan and low growth in Europe.

The Poorest Nations

Over the course of the 1990s, trade preference programs for developing countries were significantly expanded, starting with expansion of the Generalized System of Preferences for the poorest countries, extending to the proposal for Southeast Europe Trade Preferences, and culminating in the expansion of Caribbean Basin preferences to approximate parity with NAFTA and the creation of a new preference program for Africa. Africa deserves particular attention; the Clinton administration elevated trade and investment relations with the nations of Africa to a degree not seen before as part of a broader effort to develop a new framework of partnership with Africa. Moreover, these efforts were complemented by initiatives on debt forgiveness for the poorest, massive increases in spending on the infectious disease crisis in developing countries, and modest increases in spending on basic education. But it is worth noting that it took years to bring the trade initiatives to fruition because of opposition from key domestic interests. And the Clinton administration was unable to obtain congressional approval for sufficient funding to help the poorest countries realize the full potential of expanded trade access or to make sufficient offers of expanded market access to turn the tide in Seattle.

Europe

With respect to the European Union, the best that might be said is that the Clinton administration succeeded in deepening and broadening the overall relationship with the European Union and key European allies at a time of deepening integration, *despite* a series of high-stakes trade disputes. The United States and the European Union have a pattern of testing the limits of the world trade dispute settlement system and then trying to fix the system in a subsequent negotiating round. The past decade was no exception. But the escalation to the point where America now faces a WTO ruling reaching into the minutiae of domestic tax law that could result in billions of dollars of retaliation, despite an apparent lack of any clear European Union constituency that is harmed by the alleged violations, puts some strain on the relationship and on domestic support for the trading system more generally.

Separately, substantial progress was made on identifying policies that could significantly facilitate trade and investment ties across the Atlantic. The launch of the Transatlantic Economic Partnership, the efforts of the Transatlantic Business Dialogue, and the substantial progress on achieving mutual recognition of product standards have yielded commercially important outcomes.

Domestic Politics

Many see the 1990s as a watershed in the politics of trade. But any such analysis should make a distinction between politicization of the public debate and congressional activity. My assessment is that there was much greater intensity around trade issues in the public debate and greater activism on globalization generally, but the congressional politics of trade were not greatly changed.

Certainly, public awareness of trade rose in the 1990s, as did activism among NGOs and students. In the United States this trend reflected two converging forces. First, a powerful alliance of interests was formed in the crucible of the fight against NAFTA, bringing together disparate groups from the left and right. NAFTA provoked intense opposition and backlash because it was the first attempt at deep integration with a low-wage country, Mexico's geographical proximity made the consequences more concrete, and the public conflated NAFTA's impact with the surge in imports and immigration associated with the peso crisis. Subsequently, the same coalition succeeded in defeating fast track in 1997 (although they did not prevail in the votes on fast track in 1994, the Uruguay Round, or China PNTR). What is most interesting about the NAFTA and fast track debates is that trade opponents—and particularly the labor union

Trade Votes in the 1990s

	Yes				No		Total[1]	
	Dem	%Dem	Rep	%Rep	Dem	Rep	Yes	No
House of Representatives								
Disapprove fast track 1991	170	65	21	13	91	140	191	231
NAFTA	102	40	132	75	156	43	234	199
Fast track 1994	145	59	150	87	102	23	295	125
Uruguay Round	167	65	121	68	89	56	289	145
Fast track 1998	29	15	151	68	171	71	180	243
Steel quota	197	94	91	42	13	128	289	141
WTO withdrawal Sec. 125	21	10	33	15	181	182	56	363
China PNTR	73	35	164	74	138	57	237	197
Senate								
Disapprove fast track 1991	31	57	5	12	23	36	36	59
NAFTA	26	48	35	78	28	10	61	38
Fast track 1994	39	76	37	90	12	4	76	16
Uruguay Round	41	75	35	78	14	10	76	24
Fast track 1997	26	58	42	78	19	12	68	31
Steel quota	27	60	15	28	18	39	42	57
IMF quota	43	96	41	75	2	14	84	16
China PNTR	37	84	46	85	7	8	83	15

1. Includes independents.

movement—struck a chord that resonated with the American people by raising questions about the distributional consequences of trade agreements.

Second, there was a striking increase in activism among groups opposing globalization. Initially, the activism was organized around particular goals, such as the antisweatshop movement on college campuses, debt forgiveness for the poorest countries, and addressing the HIV/AIDS crisis in Africa. But starting with the Seattle WTO protests in 2000 and continuing with every international meeting since then, antiglobalization has become a rallying cry for a much more diffuse set of interests. Ironically, this loose movement is itself a product of the globalization of ideas.

It is more difficult to see evidence that the congressional politics of trade were much changed in the 1990s or that partisanship increased. If anything, the partisan lineup may have softened modestly, with greater numbers of moderate Democrats voting in favor of trade and greater numbers of Republicans voting against trade for ideological or constituency reasons. For instance, 42 percent of House Republicans voted in favor of steel quotas in 1998, and 26 percent opposed China PNTR in 2000.

Although critics allege that the congressional trade consensus eroded during the 1990s, it is worth noting that the singular accomplishment of this so-called consensus during the 1980s was the 1988 Omnibus Trade Act, whose provisions were more notable in the area of fair trade than that of trade opening. Moreover, the partisan lineup on fast track does not look enormously different between the Bush and Clinton administrations. Contrasting the Bush fast-track vote of 1991 with the Clinton fast-track vote of 1994, it is worth noting that only 13 percent of Democrats in the House and 43 percent in the Senate supported fast track in 1991, compared with 59 percent in the House and 76 percent in the Senate in 1994. Republican support in the House held steady at 87 percent and rose slightly in the Senate from 88 to 90 percent. (Fast track never came to a vote in the House in 1997, so there are no official tallies, and the 1998 fast-track vote in the House is not a useful benchmark, since it was widely recognized to be a political vote and there was no concerted effort to build support.)

Indeed, when one compares the tallies for trade votes in the 1990s, the most important factor distinguishing successes from failures appears to be whether there were calculable concrete benefits in the offing sufficient to galvanize supporters. A simple comparison makes the case. In 1997, with no trade agreement pending, fast track failed in the House, but in 1994, when the hard-won gains of the Uruguay Round hung in the balance, the vote was 295 to 125 in the House, with 59 percent of Democrats in support. Similarly, in 2000 the China PNTR vote succeeded, despite the unpopularity of trade votes in election years, because of the strength of the underlying trade agreement with China.

Policy-Making Process

Finally, it is worth noting briefly the distinctive way in which trade policy was coordinated during the Clinton administration. President Clinton entered office determined to strengthen international economic policy-making by establishing a new White House coordinating body. Despite numerous turf battles, variations in leadership styles and structure, and limited resources, the National Economic Council evolved a viable, effective model for integrating the competing considerations that go into international economic policy-making and coordinating the diverse institutional actors. The quality of the process and the participants helped ensure an overall logic and consistency between policies, strengthened the voice of policy officials within the overall decision-making process, and elevated the profile of trade issues. Over the course of the administration, the International Economic Deputies evolved as a policy-development body that helped tee up policy recommendations and oversee consistent implementation. And at the principals level, coordination evolved over time as a shared responsibility between the national economic and national security advisers in close consultation with the chief of staff.

Lessons of the 1990s

The last decade presents a rich period for the study of trade policy. I will briefly suggest several lessons that can be drawn from the experience of the 1990s, although more systematic study in the future will no doubt yield a more definitive list:

• Negotiating a trade agreement is like planning a wedding. Although economic and security interests may be closely aligned at the outset, the process of negotiating the agreement tends to be dominated on each side by domestic commercial and political considerations (the in-laws) that can at least temporarily strain diplomatic relations. And the ultimate agreement may have some negative foreign policy consequences or generate domestic political backlash that makes future trade liberalization more difficult. For that reason, it is important for a new administration to prioritize and sequence carefully.

• Don't go for fast track unless there is a locomotive. Fast track in the abstract is a hard sell. Asking Congress for an open-ended grant of authority to pursue trade agreements whose benefits are as yet undefined and far into the future is a recipe for trouble. A powerful coalition of trade opponents has demonstrated that they can mobilize effectively to oppose trade legislation. But supporters are only galvanized to mount a full-fledged offensive when there are concrete benefits in the offing.

• The president is well served by instituting a White House process for coordinating international economic policy. Because of its growing complexity, trade policy affects a diverse set of interests and has a relatively large number of institutional players, making the payoff to coordination very high.

• It is very risky for the United States to host major international ministerial meetings or summits while at the same time pursuing an ambitious agenda. Far better for the United States to work closely with a more neutral host.

• Don't create separate trade adjustment assistance programs associated with particular trade agreements. Trade adjustment assistance is a critical complement to any trade liberalization initiative, particularly in light of the inadequacy of America's general social insurance for dealing with the distributional consequences of trade. However, there are both political and efficiency reasons to maintain a single overarching trade adjustment assistance program.

Summary of Discussion

Henry Aaron opened the discussion by expressing skepticism regarding the claim that economic inequality had narrowed in the 1990s, and regarding the statistical accuracy of the Gini coefficient referred to in Lawrence's paper. Citing a CBO report on the trends in income and tax burden over the period of 1979 to 1997, he stated that the leveling off of the Gini coefficient in census statistics is an artifact of "top coding," and that in reality, income inequality may have deteriorated further in the late 1990s. He pointed to the fact that the before-tax income of the top 1 percent of the income distribution rose by 30 percent between 1995 and 1997, about four to five times larger than that of all the other groups. *Aaron* also asked, as trade negotiations started by one administration are often completed only in subsequent administrations, what specific trade policy process initiated during the Clinton administration can we expect to see coming to fruition in the next four to six years.

Alan Blinder commented on three points. First, while he concurred with the view that the time frame for trade policy progress often spans across administrations, he objected to *Jagdish Bhagwati's* characterization of the effort by the Clinton administration in completing the Uruguay Round as a mere "closer" role. He emphasized that the administration was confronted with an enormous number of unresolved issues, and successful completion of the round was far from easy. He then declared his position as a "free trader against fast track." Concurring with *Lael Brainard's* point, he believes that "fast track in the abstract," with no concrete agenda to push for, is bound to fail in the current political environment where the broad public and congressional sentiment is against free trade in the abstract. (*Charlene Barshefsky* signaled that she agrees.) Finally, *Blinder* lamented that despite a decade of achievements on free trade by the Clinton-Gore administration, the national belief in mercantilism seems stronger today than a decade ago. As economists since Adam Smith have not been effective in dispelling this belief, *Blinder* suggested that perhaps the presidential bully pulpit is the only megaphone loud enough to make it end.

Jeffrey Frankel recalled that the White House decision to invite the WTO ministerial conference to the United States in an election year—which in retrospect was a mistake in light of the resulting debacle in Seattle—began precisely as an effort to use the presidential bully pulpit to explain the virtues of free trade to the American people. Presidential speeches on free trade, part of the campaign to persuade Congress to grant fast track, had not previously been reported in the press.

Gregory Mankiw asked why ideas such as unilateral trade liberalization and the repeal of the antidumping laws are so seldom mentioned in the policy arena in Washington, even by economists there, despite wide agreement on their benefits among professional economists outside the District of Columbia. *Frankel* thinks that the name "antidumping" gives the public the impression that these laws have something to do with fighting predatory practices or promoting competition, and that economists need to keep explaining that this is not the case.

Martin Feldstein believes that the past decade has witnessed an "innovation" in antitrade politics, in that the opponents of trade liberalization have discovered issues such as environmental and labor standards as a new device to support protectionism. Asserting that the organized push behind these movements is ultimately antitrade, Feldstein felt that strengthening the ILO or global environmental standards would not help make trade liberalization easier. He then referred back to *Blinder's* point concerning the presidential bully pulpit, and felt that the Clinton administration might not have taken the opportunity to educate the public about the appropriateness of keeping these issues separate from trade.

Larry Mishel commented that among those who are 100 percent for expanding trade, one doesn't observe a corresponding intensity in support for domestic reforms to help protect the families and workers that are the losers from trade. In fights over trade agreements, economists often mention domestic assistance, but they are mostly absent when it comes to the fight to implement these measures. He wondered where the economists are when it comes to helping the losers.

Richard Cooper, chair of the session, began his comment with the disclaimer that as both the Uruguay Round and NAFTA represent continuations of efforts started by earlier administrations, his question is meant to be nonpartisan. He asked the panelists to address whether, on reflection, it was a mistake to have brought intellectual property rights (IPR) into the WTO regime in the Uruguay Round, as it is not exclusively a trade issue. As trade sanctions are now legitimately used to enforce IPR despite the inherent ambiguity of its benefits, how would the panelists respond to arguments that trade sanctions should also be used to enforce other nationally agreed objectives, such as the quality of the workplace or environmental standards?

The panelists responded to these questions in turn:

Barshefsky agreed that trade policy progress spans across administrations; as such, it should be viewed as a continuum rather than broken down along partisan lines. She mentioned Free Trade Area of Americas, China's entry into the WTO, the Jordan and Vietnam agreements, and the Chile and Singapore negotiations as examples of efforts initiated during the Clinton administration that will likely be concluded during the new Bush administration.

With respect to fast track, she believed that it is a mistake to push for it now, as it is polarizing and, while desirable, is unnecessary, and would only become a net constraint, not an asset, to the administration. She posed the question whether Congress would have granted fast-track authority to President Clinton to conclude the China negotiations. While the answer is a clear no, she argued, the deal itself passed the House by 40 votes. In the case of China, as with all trade agreements that go before Congress, a concrete agreement was needed to energize the constituencies in the districts that would benefit.

Barshefsky concurred that the belief in mercantilism and trade as a zero-sum game is indeed a serious problem, and admitted that members of the Clinton administration might not have defended open markets as rigorously as they should have. She attributed this failure to politics, as the base of the president's party was extremely antitrade. She further illustrated the crucial role that politics plays in the trade policy arena. The political protection afforded to dumping laws in Congress and the role that campaign finance played in the debate over environmental and labor standards serve as examples. IPR differs from labor/environmental issues also in its political potency, despite substantive similarity. "It's just different."

Finally, on helping the losers from trade, *Barshefsky* felt there are fundamental problems: trade adjustment assistance programs are widely discredited (viewed by the unions as "burial insurance"). The necessary social safety net has eroded. And it is extremely difficult to convince workers to give up their jobs in exchange for transitory economic compensation.

Bhagwati contended that rather than giving credit to various administrations for signing more agreements, we should recognize the overproliferation of these rules and agreements as a systemic problem facing today's world economy. Although seldom mentioned in the United States, the number of agreements on rules of origin, trade barriers, and tariff rates, depending on which FTA a country belongs to, has multiplied out of control and become extremely difficult for developing countries to handle. *Bhagwati* urged us to reflect on why we have taken such an utterly chaotic approach to trade liberalization, and to avoid giving in to the politics of signing more agreements without looking at their economics first.

In addition, *Bhagwati* conjectured that mercantilism is not the real issue behind protectionism; instead, the public is increasingly doubting the merits of free trade. While free traders used to have the moral high ground over protectionists, labor unions and environmentalists have since gained this position by calling the free traders a "special interest group." Thus it has become more difficult to argue for free trade, and *Bhagwati* believed a proper WTO design is essential for addressing this problem. The organization of the WTO needs to be based on consistent guiding principles, such as mutuality in gains. As such, it is not appropriate to bring in issues such as IPR protection, which involves mainly the transfer of benefits from one country to another.

Last, *Bhagwati* raised the distinction between labor versus environmental standards, and argued that lumping the two together adds confusion to the debate. Many environmental issues have already been dealt with in the WTO, while labor standards are yet to be introduced.

Brainard emphasized the relevance of political climate in trade policy making. As an example, the Europeans are fervent about bringing environmental and food safety issues into the trade arena because they do not have the corresponding domestic regulatory safety systems to address public concerns, whereas they do have a very well developed social safety net to address the labor issues. In addition to the political imperatives, she felt that there are indeed real policy issues to be addressed internationally regarding environmental and labor concerns, as domestic environmental production standards would not work unilaterally if imports violating such standards can enter the country freely. The case for IPR is similar in that we face extremely powerful domestic lobbying groups on this issue, and there are substantive policy issues to be worked out.

In response to *Mankiw's* question on unilaterally opening our borders, *Brainard* stated that while the United States would not want it, as we have market power in many markets and thus are able to influence relative prices in our favor, many countries are too small to affect their "terms of trade" and so should see unilateral liberalization as beneficial. She suggested domestic politics as the main reason why we do not see more Singapores and Hong Kongs. In terms of unilateral actions to address the overproliferation of regional agreements, she maintained that an ideal situation for the United States would be to set out a template offering the same terms to all countries willing to follow certain rules. Unfortunately, while this may be an effective way to exercise our market power, it is not feasible politically.

Robert Lawrence felt that despite the political impossibility of removing the dumping laws, the administration should have been at least willing to talk about them in Seattle. According to *Lawrence*, the refusal of any discussion on dumping was a strategic mistake and might have contributed to the impasse. *Lawrence* felt that for the United States to play the role of the world leader, it needs to take the middle stance, with a willingness to discuss and improve these laws, despite a letter from 300 members of Congress stating their objection to such initiatives.

On the issue of mercantilism, *Lawrence* emphasized that from the standpoint of a policy-maker, enacting trade agreements is painful and difficult, in that the losers are created as the result of one's own explicit actions. *Lawrence* further gave credit to Clinton for his courage in standing behind free trade when every action taken in this direction cost him within his own party. *Lawrence* concluded by pointing out that while the antitrade groups might be advancing their goals using labor and environmental issues as a tool, the fact that they are gaining resonance with the larger public suggests that these concerns have not been adequately addressed. Here, *Lawrence* emphasized the need for creative solutions, such as the side agreements within NAFTA and the human rights discussion associated with China's PNTR status, to help effectively isolate the antitrade extremists.

6   Information Technology

The "New Economy" and Information Technology Policy

Pamela Samuelson and Hal R. Varian

PANELISTS: *Martin N. Baily, Esther Dyson, and Paul Romer*

6.1   Introduction

The growth of the information technology (IT) sector in the 1980s was an important development for the economy, but it spurred relatively little policy or media interest. True, IT was recognized as a driver of comparative advantage for the United States, and there were a few initiatives involving industrial policy and military preparedness, but IT was of interest primarily to specialists. In the 1990s, however, things changed dramatically when the Internet became a topic of intense public discussion. Suddenly computers were not only a way to manipulate information, but also a way to *communicate* information. This ability led to a dramatic rise in the public and political awareness of the importance of information policy issues such as intellectual property, privacy, and security.

The rapid adoption of the Internet stimulated Wall Street's interest as well. Previously arcane topics like venture capital and IPOs became part of the common vernacular. The stock market boom that followed had a dramatic effect on individual wealth, leading to robust consumption demand.[1] Meanwhile, the triple stimulus from telecommunications deregulation in 1996, the "year 2K"

We gratefully acknowledge support from National Science Foundation grant SEC-9979852, and comments by Martin Bailey, Esther Dyson, Jeffrey Frankel, Brian Kahin, Tom Kalil, Michael Katz, Peter Orszag, and Paul Romer. We are, of course, responsible for any remaining errors. E-mail comments to hal@sims.berkeley.edu or pam@sims.berkeley.edu.
1. See Chapter 1 (Mankiw) of this volume.

problem in 1998–99, and the Internet stock market bubble in 1999–2000 led firms to dramatically increase their investment in information technology.[2] The significant increase in both consumption and investment demand led to the robust economic growth documented elsewhere in this volume.[3] It also appears that at least some of the productivity growth in the 1990s can be attributed to the deployment of information technology, though this point is still somewhat controversial, as we explain later in this chapter.

Some have asserted that the 1990s witnessed the emergence of a "new economy." That term dates back to the 1980s when it referred to an economy driven by services rather than manufacturing. The fear then was that the service economy would result in slow growth, rising prices, and low-wage jobs. In 1996, Michael Mandel published an article in *Business Week*, called "The Triumph of the New Economy," that emphasized the development of a technology-driven, fast-growing, low-inflation economy, which he referred to as "the New Economy."[4] This connotation came to dominate popular discussion, although economists as a whole remain somewhat skeptical of the concept.

A unique confluence of forces certainly came together in the 1990s: rapid technological advances in the information technology sector; widespread recognition that computers could be used to communicate information as well as process it; the rapid spread of a simple, inexpensive, and powerful wide-area computer network based on nonproprietary standards; and financial institutions ready to fund investment in advanced technology. These forces led to very rapid growth of the Internet. As firms and consumers flocked to the Internet in large numbers, it became evident that information policy issues—including, importantly, intellectual property, security, and privacy—required serious attention.

In this chapter we will describe the technological and economic developments that faced the Clinton administration in the mid-1990s and examine how the administration responded to the challenges raised by these developments.

6.2   The National Information Infrastructure Initiative

The Clinton administration "got the Net" very early. In 1993 it issued an "Agenda for Action" to articulate and implement a vision for a National Information Infrastructure (NII).[5] This initiative was widely praised at the time as a forward-looking technology policy initiative that would simultaneously pro-

---

2. See the editors' introduction to this volume.
3. Ibid.
4. See Mandel (2000), p. 153.
5. See Information Infrastructure Task Force (1993).

mote economic growth, improve the lives of citizens, and allow governments to provide better services and information to the public—all without significant new expenditures by the government. The agenda embraced information technologies as an enabling, and indeed as transformative, means for achieving a broad range of economic, social, and political goals. The agenda characterized the United States as having become primarily an information-based economy and asserted a bright future for communications and information industries. The agenda sought to marshal attention to the emerging NII so that "business, labor, academia, the public, and government" could work together to build the NII for the benefit of all.

A notable feature of the agenda was its endorsement of private-sector leadership for development of the NII. The agenda sought to ensure there would be adequate incentives for private-sector investment to build, extend, and develop applications for the NII, for example, by adoption of appropriate tax and regulatory policies. Government action should "complement" private sector leadership, not compete with it. The role of the government, in its view, was mainly to forge partnerships, coordinate activities, and promote technological innovation and new applications for the NII. The government could also improve allocation of radio frequencies, protection of intellectual property rights, and access to government information as well as government procurement of goods and services from the private sector—all of which, in turn, would promote private investment in the NII or applications for it.[6]

It is noteworthy that the initial documents describing the NII[7] make little mention of the Internet. The term "information superhighway" was used, but it was meant in a broader sense than the Internet, including cable TV, dial-up computer bulletin boards, and many other components of infrastructure to store and communicate information. The Internet was referred to only in its traditional role, as a communications network for educational and scientific purposes.[8]

Tom Kalil describes the administration's vision of the NII as "a seamless web of communications networks, computers, databases, and consumer electronics

---

6. On the reinvention of government using information technology, see the National Partnership for Reinventing Government (1997).

7. The historical documents are available at http://www.iitf.nist.gov/index-old.html.

8. Note in particular the discussion in the chapter of the Agenda for Action titled "Benefits and Applications of the National Information Infrastructure," available at http://www.ibiblio.org/nii/NII-Benefits-and-Applications.html. There were, however, voices within the administration that recognized the value of an "open platform" for the NII. See, for example, Al Gore's address to the National Press Club in 1993 where he says, "We need to ensure the NII, just like the PC, is open and accessible to everyone with a good idea who has a product they want to sell" (http://iitf.doc.gov/documents/speeches/gore_speech122193.html).

that will put vast amounts of information at users' fingertips."[9] This vision was realized, albeit through a rather different route than had been envisioned in the Agenda for Action. It was the Internet (a "bit player," in the agenda's view) and the World Wide Web (not even mentioned in the agenda), more than any other technologies, that defined the NII of the 1990s.[10]

6.3 The Internet as Enabling Technology

The Internet was the enabling technology for the 1990s. Most of the policy issues discussed later in the chapter revolve around the Internet, so it is worthwhile describing briefly where it came from and why it surfaced in the 1990s to become a mass-market medium.

6.3.1 Origins and Evolution of the Internet

The term "Internet" made its first appearance in a research paper written by Vinton Cerf and Robert Kahn in 1974. It described a "network of networks" that would link together computers across the country, and eventually the world.[11] Recognizing the strategic importance of this concept, the Department of Defense, via its Advanced Research Projects Agency (ARPA), funded networking research for many years. The evolution of the Internet was overseen by the Internet Engineering Task Force (IETF), an organization of volunteers that codified various standards for technological interoperability. By 1986, when the National Science Foundation (NSF) wanted to provide access to five new supercomputer centers, the Internet technology was sufficiently mature to deploy for this purpose. The NSF called its new network program the NSFNET, and it quickly became the principal infrastructure of the Internet.[12]

As the Internet grew, it became clear that the NSF could no longer play a central role in its management, and it searched for a way to spin off responsibility for backbone maintenance. These discussions were particularly intense during 1990–92. NSF finally concluded that privatization of the Internet was the right path to follow. On April 30, 1995, the NSF stopped funding the NSFNET backbone. Though dire predictions had been made about the Internet grinding to a halt, this privatization went off without a hitch—a tribute to the careful planning and coordination by all involved.

---

9. See Kalil (1995).
10. For more on this period, see Kahin (1996).
11. The next goal for the Internet is the solar system; planning is now in progress for an Internet host on Mars.
12. See, for example, Barry M. Leiner et al., "A Brief History of the Internet," http://www.isoc.org/internet/history/brief.html.

The Internet grew from 313,000 hosts in 1990 to 43,230,000 in 2000, and currently stands at over 110 million hosts. The remarkable growth testifies to the huge success of the technology. All in all, the development and subsequent privatization of the Internet is a textbook case of technology transfer. The Internet, with its open protocols and highly extensible nature, would have likely never been developed, much less deployed, by the private sector. Open standards of the sort that made the Internet possible may well require some sort of industry-wide, or publicly sponsored, research and development. But once the Internet reached critical mass, the government wisely decided to facilitate privatization of the infrastructure. Though, in retrospect, there were a few things that could have been done differently, overall the process was hugely successful.

6.3.2 The World Wide Web

The Internet was a creation of computer engineers. As such, it had an elegant design but a terrible user interface. File transmission, remote login, e-mail, and other applications all were based on command-line interactions, which involved a steep learning curve.

In the summer of 1991, Tim Berners-Lee, a computer systems analyst at CERN, released the first World Wide Web software to the high-energy physics community. Shortly thereafter an NSF-funded team at the National Center for Supercomputing Applications (NCSA) at the University of Illinois incorporated the WWW architecture into Mosaic, a user-friendly Internet browser. Marc Andreessen, a 23-year-old research assistant at the NCSA who worked on the Mosaic development team, subsequently became one of the founders of Netscape Communications Corporation.

The Web put a friendly face on the Internet, providing an interface that a 10-year-old, or even a 50-year-old, could easily understand. Perhaps more importantly, the back-end protocols for authoring and distributing Web pages (HTML and HTTP) were easy to understand and use as well, facilitating the rapid deployment of Web servers. The first Web sites were in universities and research centers, but other organizations soon followed.

The next step in the development of the Web was to bring in the for-profit sector. In March 1994, Jim Clark, founder of Silicon Graphics, initiated talks with Marc Andreessen about forming a company. The company, initially named Electric Media, was formed in April 1994 with the goal of developing browserlike technology for interactive TV.

Within a few weeks, the founders realized that interactive TV was less attractive a market than the Internet itself, and they decided to try to develop a commercial version of the NCSA browser. Accordingly they changed the company's name to Mosaic Communications and started programming. After a dispute with the University of Illinois, the name was changed once more in November 1994 to Netscape Communications.[13]

By 1995 everything was in place to create fertile ground for widespread Internet deployment. The critical components were the following:

• *Personal computers.* Universities, major corporations, many small businesses, and a significant number of home users had access to personal computers.

• *Local area networks.* Most businesses had networked personal computers together to make them easier to manage. Standardized technologies like ethernet had become commoditized and were widely available at low prices.

• *Wide area networks.* The basic standards underlying the Internet protocols developed by network researchers for connecting together disparate networks were mature. These standards described basic services for address assignment, e-mail, file transfers, and the like that were nonproprietary, robust, and well documented. Universities and research organizations had embraced the Internet as the primary network for wide area communications; the technology for home access through dial-up modems was widely available; and there was a thriving culture of dial-up access to computer bulletin boards.

• *The Web.* Mosaic had provided a standardized interface for both users and information providers that allowed for easy deployment of, and access to, on-line information.

6.4   Growth of Private Investment in Internet Companies

Recall that the Clinton administration's vision for the National Information Infrastructure was that the private sector would play a major role in investing in its development. This hope was to succeed beyond the administration's wildest dreams, through the vehicle of the Silicon Valley venture capital industry.

Soon after partnering with Andreessen, Clark turned to venture capitalist John Doerr of the venture capital firm Kleiner, Perkins, Caufield, and Byers. This VC firm had financed some of Clark's other undertakings, such as the Silicon Graphics workstation, and was well positioned to fund the development of Netscape.[14]

Venture capital has been used for financing technology development in the United States for decades, but Netscape decided to adopt an unusual model.

---

13. http://www.wired.com/news/business/0,1367,16440,00.html.
14. For an entertaining history of Clark, see Lewis (1999).

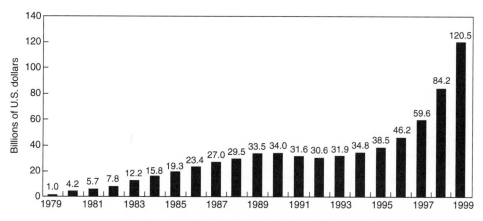

Figure 6.1
Amount of Money Invested in Venture Capital. (*Source:* Jerome Engle and Venture Economics.)

Normally, VCs finance companies for three to five years, allowing them to establish a track record and achieve profitability before they went public. But in Netscape's case, public interest in the Web was so high that the founders decided to proceed with an initial public offering when the company was barely a year old.

The August 1995 offering was originally intended to be 3.5 million shares at $12 a share, but this was raised to 5 million shares at $28 each shortly before the IPO. The stock closed at $52 on opening day, after reaching levels as high as $71. Jim Clark, the founder, had a net worth of $565 million after the first day of trading.

The Netscape IPO set off a wave of interest in venture capital funding of Internet companies. As Figure 6.1 shows, the amount of investment funded by venture capital grew extremely rapidly during the Clinton years. The bulk of the VC capital was invested in information technology, particularly in the latter part of the decade, as shown in Figure 6.2. Of this IT investment, most went to Internet-related businesses: in the fourth quarter of 1999 and the first quarter of 2000, roughly 75 percent of all VC funding went to "dot coms."

During the second Clinton term the rates of return on venture capital investments were very high, as shown in Figure 6.3. These high rates of return were due, in large part, to the run-up in the stock market as a whole, but in part to "Internet mania." The media hoopla surrounding the 1995 Netscape IPO led other "dot coms" to adopt the Netscape model of taking the company public as quickly as possible. The resulting dramatic increase in the number of VC-backed IPOs is shown in Figure 6.4.

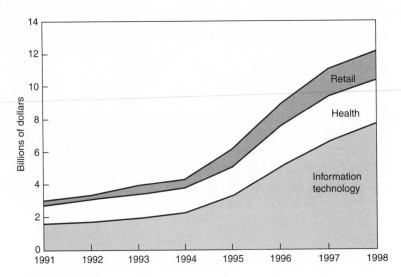

Figure 6.2
Venture Capital Investment by Types. (*Source:* Jerome Engle and Venture Economics.)

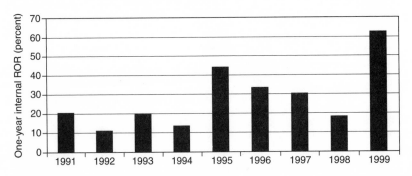

Figure 6.3
Rate of Return to VC Firms. (*Source:* Jerome Engle and Venture Economics.)

6.4.1 The Internet Bubble

The market developed an insatiable appetite for all things Internet during 1998–99. In March 2000, the NASDAQ hit a high of 5,132 just before reality set in. By December 2000, the NASDAQ had fallen more than 50 percent to 2,288, with many Internet companies losing 90 percent of their value.

Figure 6.5 depicts the total return on the NASDAQ and S&P 500 from January 1993 to January 2001. Note how closely the two indexes tracked each other

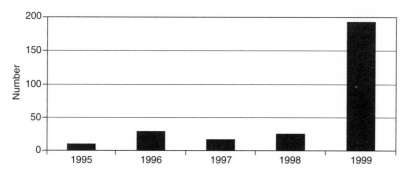

Figure 6.4
VC-Backed Internet Firm IPOs. (*Source:* Jerome Engle and Venture Economics.)

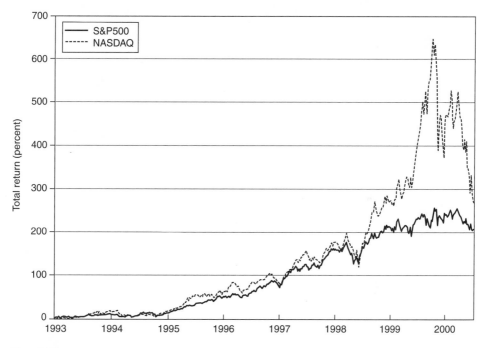

Figure 6.5
The NASDAQ Bubble

up until January 1999, at which time the NASDAQ began its roller-coaster ride. In December 1990 the technology component of the value-weighted S&P 500 was 6.5 percent. By March 2000 it was over 34 percent. The number of technology companies in the S&P 500 doubled in essentially the same period.[15] The stock market boom of the late 1990s was primarily a technology boom, which was fueled by the public interest in the Internet and IT in general.

We think that the behavior depicted in Figure 6.3 has to be classified as a speculative bubble. Although the exact definition of a financial bubble is a matter of dispute, there is ample evidence that the rates of growth necessary to warrant the valuations at the peak of the bubble were simply not credible.

In 1996, Federal Reserve Board Chairman Alan Greenspan warned that the stock market was perhaps exhibiting "irrational exuberance." But this pronouncement was significantly before the Internet boom; most of the irrationality was yet to come. Even during the height of Internet mania, many sober observers pointed out that the valuations for "dot coms" were simply not sustainable. Here is but one example, published in July 1999.

Yahoo's revenue per page view consistently has been $\frac{4}{10}$ of one cent.... If it takes Yahoo 250 page views to get $1 in revenues, then to reach $35 billion in revenues [a level which would justify its stock price] will require 8.75 trillion page views per year, or about 24 billion page views per day. If the world population is 6 billion, then on average everyone in the world, regardless of age, language, or access to the Internet, will have to view 4 pages on Yahoo per day.[16]

Even proponents of Internet technology recognized the problem. Anthony Perkins and Michael Perkins, founding editors of *The Red Herring*, a magazine devoted to the new economy, published a book in November 1999 called *The Internet Bubble: Inside the Overvalued World of High-Tech Stocks*. Traditional value investors like Warren Buffet warned that a crash was coming, but few investors listened.

Should the Federal Reserve Board have done something to dampen the swings of the stock market? Was this, in fact, the motivation behind the interest rate increases of 2000? The Fed was worried about the stock market bubble, but ultimately decided not to respond in any dramatic way. In part, this decision was due to Greenspan's belief that the real economy was fundamentally sound and to the recognition that the bubble was located primarily in one category: "new economy" stocks (see Figure 6.5 again). There was little the Fed could do to deflate one group of stocks without having adverse effects on others. The Fed continued to maintain a low-interest-rate policy during the late 1990s, ap-

---

15. See Henry (2001).
16. Arnold Kling, http://arnoldkling.com/~arnoldsk/aimst2/aimst209.html.

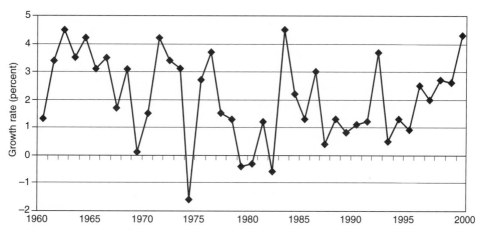

Figure 6.6
Labor Productivity Growth Rates. (*Source:* Department of Commerce.)

parently believing that there was little danger of inflation. Chairman Greenspan argued in several speeches that the widespread adoption of information technology had shifted the aggregate supply function outward, so that the economy could produce more output without experiencing upward pressure on prices. It was widely believed that IT had made the economy more competitive, more responsive, and more productive.

6.5 Impact of Information Technology on Productivity

Since the Federal Reserve Board's interest-rate policy was premised on the belief that the economy had become more productive, it is important to examine the evidence for this view.

The historical facts are not in dispute. From 1959 to 1973 labor productivity growth averaged a healthy 3 percent per year. Then in 1973 it abruptly slowed down: from 1973 to 1992 it was about 1.4 percent. During the Clinton years labor productivity growth seems to have picked up to about 2.7 percent, almost returning to its previous rate of growth (see Figure 6.6).

This acceleration was greeted with great acclaim, but there is considerable debate about what fraction of this increased productivity growth was cyclical and what fraction was sustainable.

Consider first the hypothesis that the productivity increase of the late 1990s was simply cyclical. During economic slowdowns, firms tend to hoard labor; and during booms, they encourage employees to exert extra effort. Consequently, measured labor hours tend to underestimate the hours worked during booms and overestimate them during busts. Hence measured labor productivity appears to rise when economic activity is high and fall when it is low.

The United States emerged from a small recession during 1990–91, so it is not surprising that productivity grew in the early 1990s. According to Alan Blinder, "Similar surges in productivity can also be found in 1990–1992, 1983–1986, and 1977–1978. But they all followed recessions. And they were all subsequently reversed."[17] Indeed, recent evidence of declining productivity in 2001 suggests that there was a strong cyclical component in the productivity growth in the mid- and late 1990s.

However, many observers think that a significant part of the productivity growth in the 1990s was due to increased investment in computerization and networking, and thus reflects a sustainable increase in productive capabilities. One difficulty with this hypothesis is that the growth in labor productivity from 1959 to 1973 apparently had nothing to do with computers. Since we don't have a good explanation of why productivity fell in 1973, we aren't in a very good position to explain why it has resumed rapid growth in the last few years.

If the productivity growth in the 1990s was due to computerization, why did it take so long to show up? After all, mainframe computers became widespread in the 1960s and 1970s, and personal computers were widely deployed in the mid-1980s. Paul David has offered one explanation for this lag.[18] David points out that it took nearly 20 years for the U.S. productivity figures to reflect the benefits due to electrification, so presumably the benefits from computerization would similarly take several years to emerge. Perhaps the acceleration in productivity in the 1990s is simply the delayed impact of earlier computerization in the 1980s. If so, this explanation would be very good news, since it means that we have yet to experience the productivity increases from the even larger investment during the late 1990s.

Brynjolfsson and Hitt extend David's argument by asserting that investment in computers only achieves its full impact on productivity when work processes and practices change as well.[19] Changing organization structures is quite time-consuming and prone to failure. Hence, the delayed response of measured productivity to computerization is due to the slow pace of organizational change.

A second explanation for the slow response of productivity to computerization is measurement error. Many of the benefits from computers show up on

---

17. http://www.cisp.org/imp/april_2001/04_01blinder.htm.
18. See David (1990).
19. See Brynjolfsson and Hitt (2000).

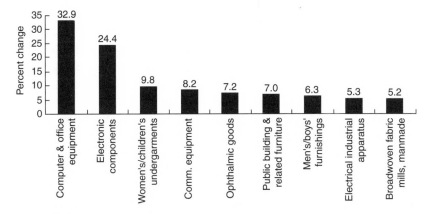

Figure 6.7
Change in Output per Hour in Selected Manufacturing Industries, 1990–98. (*Source:* http://www.bls.gov/opub/ted/2000/dec/wk1/art02.txt.)

the services side of the economy, and it is notoriously difficult to measure improvement in the quality of services. As Brynjolfsson and Hitt put it:

According to official government statistics, a bank today is only about 80 percent as productive as a bank in 1977; a health care facility is only 70 percent as productive, and a lawyer only 65 percent as productive as they were in 1977. These statistics seem out of touch with reality. (page 42)

Services currently comprise over 75 percent of GDP, so the measurement problem is clearly significant.

However, there are skeptics. Robert Gordon analyzed macroeconomic data and found that most of the productivity increase in the 1990s due to computerization was in durable goods manufacture, and the bulk of that was in industries that produce computers.[20] See Figure 6.7, which shows that more than half of the productivity growth in the 1990s occurred in computers and electronic components.[21]

In part, these findings reflect another sort of measurement problem. The official statistics on the output of the computer industry attempt to adjust for quality improvement using hedonic regression techniques. Since the performance of chips has grown extremely rapidly (as described by Moore's law), the quality-adjusted output of the computer industry has also grown extremely rapidly.

---

20. See Gordon (2000).
21. For other contributions to "the productivity debate," see Steindel and Stiroh (2001), Stiroh (2001), the Council of Economic Advisers (2000, 2001), Oliner and Sichel (2000), and Jorgenson (2001).

Since the computer manufacturing industry also uses computers intensively, the result is a large increase in productivity in that industry.

Some might argue that Moore's law is essentially exogenous technological progress and that the dramatic output of the computer industry is not really due to computerization per se. However, experts in the industry are quite clear that computer-aided design and computer-aided manufacture (CAD/CAM) have made very significant contributions to the productivity of the chip industry. Today's chips simply couldn't be built without today's computers. So perhaps the chip industry is just far ahead of other manufacturing industries, and other manufacturers will eventually catch up to the computer industry in terms of productivity growth.

Kevin Stiroh[22] recently examined aggregate data for 61 industries. Consistent with the Gordon results, he found that high-tech producing industries and electronics industries exhibited dramatic growth in labor productivity. However, he also found more modest, but still significant, acceleration in productivity for 38 out of the 61 industries examined. In general, he found that IT-producing and IT-using industries accounted for almost all of the productivity growth effects in the 1990s. It is difficult to determine whether this difference occurred because IT is not useful in the industries that didn't adopt it, or whether these industries just haven't yet caught on to the benefits of IT.

Dedrick, Gurbaxani, and Kraemer[23] recently summarized some of their ongoing research on the IT investment patterns of 400 Fortune 1,000 manufacturing firms during 1986–93. During this period the IT capital per worker of an average firm increased from $4,000 per worker to $27,000 per worker. This capital deepening would be expected to increase output by about 0.4 percent a year. However, the estimated return was about 1.3 percent per year for consumer durables manufacture. Curiously, the researchers find that there is almost no productivity impact of IT in nondurables. Even if one omits computer manufacturing itself from the sample, the productivity effect on durables is very strong.

The differential impact of computers on durables and nondurables remains a puzzle. The durable goods sector is both more labor intensive and more computer intensive than the nondurable goods sector. Gilchrist et al. (2001) note that investment in PCs, especially networked PCs, is highly correlated with productivity growth in this sector. Perhaps the role of computers as communication and coordination devices is particularly important for durable goods.

---

22. See Stiroh (2001).
23. See Dedrick, Gurbaxani, and Kraemer (2000).

The Fall 2000 *Journal of Economic Perspectives* symposium describes several different ways to tackle the productivity impact of computers.[24] Suffice it to say that there are many unanswered questions.

6.6 Government Policy Initiatives

As pleased as the administration must have been about the high level of investment and growth in IT and the NII, it knew it could not rely solely on the private sector. The rest of this paper describes four areas of policy initiatives that were, in various ways, responses to the success of the Internet.

First, we describe how the administration responded with respect to federal funding for research and development. Given the bountiful yield from previous research, it made sense to plant some seed corn for future development.

Second, the boom in financial markets and IPOs stimulated a number of reforms by the Securities and Exchange Commission (SEC) and the Financial Accounting Standards Board (FASB). In retrospect, it is clear that there were some abuses of financial accounting during this period, and, to its credit, the SEC attempted to stem the most egregious of these abuses.

Third, there was a need for new institutions to govern the global information infrastructure. The most immediate need was for a new institutions to administer the Domain Name System (DNS). Although the Internet was remarkably scalable in most respects, the DNS, which matched site names to numeric addresses, was not. As we describe in more detail later, dissatisfactions with DNS administration led to the Clinton administration's decision to contract with a nonprofit corporation, known as the Internet Corporation for Assigned Names and Numbers (ICANN), to administer the DNS. This story highlights two of the difficult issues that Internet governance faced and will continue to face in the future: its international nature, and its impact on intellectual property concerns.

Finally, we turn to the fundamental information policy issues mentioned in the introduction: security, privacy, content regulation, and intellectual property. These issues form the core of what we have called information policy. The Internet's emergence as a medium for mass communication had undeniable benefits. But it also made it easier to infringe copyrights, transmit child pornography, and commit various types of consumer fraud. Thus "information policy," which has always been with us, gained a new and broader significance in both the public eye and the halls of Congress.

---

24. See vol. 14, no. 4 (Fall 2000), http://www.e-jep.org/archive/Fall2000.html.

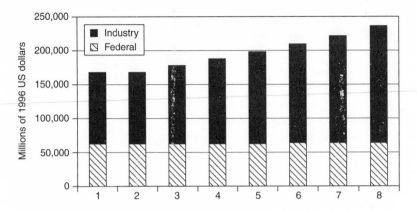

Figure 6.8
U.S. R&D Funding. (*Source:* National Patterns of R&D Resources, 2000 Data Update, National Science Foundation. http://www.nsf.gov/sbe/srs/nsf01309/start.htm.)

Because of space limitations, we will not discuss numerous other initiatives of the Clinton-Gore administration in this area. Among the omitted topics are the allocation of spectrum for new licensed and unlicensed services, liberalization of export controls on computers and telecommunications, efforts to bridge the "digital divide" both domestically and internationally, and policies to promote applications of the Internet and other information technologies in areas such as electronic government, K-12 education, lifelong learning, e-health, digital libraries, and improving the quality of life for people with disabilities.

6.7 R&D Funding

The boom surrounding the Internet can be traced back to university research sponsored by ARPA in the 1970s and 1980s. To its credit, the Clinton administration recognized the source of its good fortune and attempted to rebuild and expand federal research funding.

Between 1994 and 2000, total R&D grew from $176 billion in 1994 to $249 billion (1996 dollars), an annual real growth rate of 6.0 percent.[25] This is the largest six-year growth rate period in the history of the R&D data series. However, most of this increase was for industry-funded R&D, which grew at a rate of 8.5 percent during this period. See Figure 6.8 for the growth and composition of R&D expenditures during this decade.

Federal funding of R&D was stagnant between 1993 and 1998, but growth picked up in the latter part of the 1990s, leading to an overall 1 percent real in-

---

25. See Payson and Jankowski (2000).

crease per year since 1994, much of this increase going to the National Institutes of Health. Since privately funded R&D grew much more rapidly, the federal share of R&D funding in 2000 was 26.9 percent, the lowest it has been since the start of the time series in 1953.

In summary, the federal R&D budget expanded modestly during the Clinton years, especially during the second term, but the private R&D budget grew by substantially more. Since industry funding tends to focus on more applied research, overall research drifted more toward applied, rather than basic, research. The NSF and ARPA recognized this trend and, at least in their rhetoric, attempted to return to their original mission of high-risk/high-reward initiatives.

There were several notable but relatively small IT-related initiatives during this period, including the Digital Library initiatives, the continuance of the High Performance Computing and Communications Program, and the Information Technology Research Program. The National Science Foundation became more sensitive to issues surrounding the economic and social impact of information technology and encouraged technology proposals to addresses some of these issues, as well as funding some programs focused on these issues.[26]

There were also a number of initiatives in biotechnology, such as the Human Genome Project. The same debates between role of the private sector and public sector emerged in this area. Computers, of course, played a key role in gene sequences. Bioinformatics gained new prominence in the 1990s, along with the related fields of medical and health informatics. These topics are outside the scope of this chapter, but it is noteworthy that information technology played such a key role in understanding these fundamental biological processes. Indeed, computers have become integral tools for every type of scientific research, and will no doubt continue to play this role in the future.

6.8 Financial Market Regulation

Given the importance of stock market boom of the 1990s, it is important to examine some of the financial accounting issues that came before the regulatory authorities during this period. We examine four issues: options compensation, merger accounting, safe harbor provisions, and fair disclosure rules. All four of these issues have to do with financial reporting requirements: the accounting treatment of compensation and acquisition strategies, the liability associated with forecasts by corporate officials, and the requirements for equitable disclosure of material information. Though these topics are of interest to all publicly held companies, they were particularly important to Silicon Valley firms.

---

26. See National Research Council (1998).

These four issues were addressed by the Securities and Exchange Commission and the Federal Accounting Standards Board. The SEC is an independent regulatory agency that tends to be resolutely nonpolitical, but it is, of course, subjected to political pressures of various sorts. The FASB is a private standards-setting body. So far as we can tell, the White House did not intervene explicitly in these issues, preferring to leave the policy choices up to the agencies themselves.

6.8.1 Options Compensation

During these period there were at least three different accounting rules governing options-based compensation. The most favorable, APB 25, indicated that a company that granted an option to purchase its stock with a strike price set at the value of the stock when the option was issued did not have to declare this as a labor compensation expense. This rule has been in place, essentially unchanged, for at least 63 years.[27]

As options-based compensation became more and more prevalent, especially in high-growth technology firms, questions were raised about whether the rule made sense. One side argued that options-based compensation simply hid a real expense from the investing public; the other side argued that options were a powerful incentive mechanism.

In 1995 the FASB decided that publicly owned companies should estimate the impact of options on income and earnings per share using an options-pricing model such as the Black-Scholes model, and report this estimate as a footnote in its financial statements.[28] The options-pricing rule had a significant impact on reported profit: according to some studies, profits had been mismeasured by as much as 50 percent.[29] This was something of a compromise as there were people who wanted to require that options be expensed at some appropriate valuation, while others didn't want to see options compensation reported at all. There was even a demonstration of hundreds of Silicon Valley workers who supported not counting options as an expense when the FASB met there in 1999. Of course, the demonstrators expected their options to end up in the money, so it's not clear how they would view this issue now that the Internet bubble has burst.[30]

---

27. http://www.manitouinvestment.com/content/longviewoct.html. There two types of options, qualified and nonqualified, which have different tax consequences for individuals when exercised. Though this treatment is also economically questionable, our primary concern in this section is with firm accounting, not individual tax liabilities.

28. http://www.fed.org/onlinemag/july00/trends1.htm.

29. http://www.manitouinvestment.com/content/longviewoct.html.

30. http://www.americanbusinessconf.com/pooling.html.

Despite the accounting treatment of options for earnings statements, options are deducted from corporate earnings for purposes of tax collection. This double standard of what counts as an expense made options an extremely attractive method of compensation, and they were widely adopted in the 1990s.

But options weren't just used for compensation purposes. During the Internet boom of 1998–2000, many technology companies such as Dell Computer, Microsoft, and Intel aggressively issued put options on their stock. They were essentially betting against the market that their stocks would continue to rise. This practice tended to amplify earnings: if the stock did go up, the put options would finish in the money, making earnings even larger. This practice was fine while the stock was going up, but when the market turned down, it led to serious problems. To cite just one example:

Dell pocketed $59 million in proceeds from option sales. But if the company's stock remains at its current depressed price of $25.63 until its put options expire by September of this year, the company will have to pay $1.06 billion if the options are exercised at the average price of the range noted in the company's filings. That figure is 64 percent of Dell's net income last year.[31]

There is nothing wrong with options-based compensation and sales of puts per se. Each can be an appropriate financial tool in the right circumstances. However, it can be argued that investors should be fully aware of the use of these tools by firms. The SEC actions were helpful in this respect.

6.8.2 Merger Accounting

When one business acquires another, the acquisition is normally accounted for by the "purchase" method. This treats the purchase price of the acquired firm as similar to the purchase of an asset. The difference between the purchase price and the "fair value" of the acquired company is known as an intangible asset known as "goodwill" and is assumed to be subject to depreciation. This difference is then charged against earnings over the life of the goodwill.

Companies whose stock market value far exceeds the value of their physical assets, such as technology firms, prefer to use an alternative accounting method known as "pooling." This can only be used in stock-for-stock mergers and acquisitions. Furthermore, such acquisitions must also satisfy several other financial criteria, making it a relatively rare form of M&A accounting; only 5 percent of such transactions use pooling. Under pooling, firms simply combine their balance sheets, with no change in financial value for either firm.[32]

---

31. See Morgenson (2001).
32. http://www.americanbusinessconf.com/pooling.html.

Here is an example of the difference in the two methods:

If a company founded by an initial investment of $100,000 has increased revenues to $1 million per year, and is acquired by a public company for $10 million in stock, pooling accounting allows the purchaser to continue to state $100,000 as the target's assets. Consequently, the purchaser appears to earn $1 million per year on an investment of only $100,000 instead of earning $1 million on the actual $10 million paid for the target.[33]

The report from which this quote was taken goes on to say, "The United States is unique in allowing its public companies to apply pooling accounting to report acquisitions through using the target's asset values, ignoring the price actually paid for the target's assets." Pooling was widely used by Silicon Valley companies such as Cisco, which acquired 72 companies between 1993 and 2000.[34] In January 2001, the FASB voted to eliminate the pooling method of accounting, but agreed to allow special treatment of intangible assets in purchases.

6.8.3 Safe Harbor for Forward-Looking Statements

In December 1995, Congress enacted the Private Securities Litigation Reform Act of 1995, overriding President Clinton's veto. One of the more controversial elements of that act consisted of provisions designed to encourage "forward-looking" statements about a firm's prospects by executive officers of the firm.

In particular, the safe-harbor provisions protect certain employees of the firm from liability for a forward-looking statement if the statement is identified as forward looking and accompanied by a "meaningful cautionary statement identifying important factors that could cause actual results to differ materially" from those in the statement. It eliminates liability for such statements unless the plaintiff can show that it was made with actual knowledge that the statement was false or misleading.

Many firms have availed themselves of the opportunity to make such forward-looking statements under the safe-harbor provision.[35] It is an interesting topic for future research to see if forward-looking safe-harbor disclosures have a different impact on stock prices from traditional backward-looking accounting announcements.

6.8.4 Fair Disclosure of Corporate Information

Corporate announcements of financial information have traditionally been leaked to industry analysts prior to their official announcement. Sometimes this

---

33. http://www.mmmlaw.com/articles/pooling.html.
34. http://www.cisco.com/warp/public/750/acquisition/summarylist.html.
35. Type "safe harbor" into any Web search engine to see some examples.

leaking was explicit, as in conference calls. Sometimes it took place behind the scenes by way of "whisper numbers" or cocktail party conversations. Such information release was generally tolerated as long as it was not abused. During the 1990s intense public interest in the stock market raised issues of fair treatment of small investors vis-à-vis information disclosure.

In August 2000 the SEC adopted Regulation FD, which governed "selective disclosure and insider trading."[36] This rule prohibited public companies from selectively disclosing important information to analysts and institutional investors before individual investors. In particular, the SEC warned that private discussions by a corporate official with an analyst giving direct or implicit guidance on the analyst's earnings estimates will generally violate Regulation FD. The SEC's rule was motivated by two considerations: first, that analysts appeared to have favored access to information, and second, that advances in technology meant that the general public could be included in any disclosures at negligible cost.

There have been many critics of FD. Some have argued that information released directly to the general public will tend to make stock prices more volatile; in this view the filtering of news by financial analysts presumably has a calming influence on stock prices. Other observers have argued that Regulation FD will discourage companies from releasing information. However, Arthur Levitt, the Chair of the SEC from 1993 to 2001, felt that FD was one of his most important achievements.

The FD rule could well have a significant influence on financial markets through a circuitous route. On the one hand, the Grossman-Stiglitz model of information dissemination in financial markets recognizes that analysts must be compensated for their efforts by higher returns. Presumably, reducing selective access to information will reduce their incentive to collect it. But, on the other hand, better access to information by the public is worth something too. The impact of regulation FD is a promising topic for both theoretical and empirical research in financial economics.

6.9   Governance of the Internet

The Internet is, in one sense, simply a set of computer protocols and standards that govern the interchange of data among networks. These standards are overseen by various standards bodies, such as the Internet Engineering Task Force and the World Wide Web consortium.[37] Individuals and groups in these organizations propose, debate, and recommend standards, but have no partic-

---

36. http://www.sec.gov/rules/final/33-7881.htm.
37. See http://www.ietf.org and http://www.w3.org.

ular enforcement power. Their membership is made up of technologists, whose goal has generally been the smooth operation of the Internet and the Web. Although the privatization of the Internet has interjected considerable commercial tension into the IETF and the W3 Consortium, they continue to function reasonably well as technical standards bodies.

However, there is a fine line between "standards" and "policies." Many of the technical decisions involving the Internet also involve other issues of information policy such as intellectual property, content, speech, and the like. The Domain Name System, for better or worse, has been at the center of a number of these issues.

The Domain Name System is basically the telephone book of the Internet: it consists of a large database that relates domain names such as Amazon.com to the actual numeric Internet address (208.216.182.15). In the early days of the Internet, the Defense Advanced Projects Research Agency (DARPA) funded network researchers at the University of Southern California's Information Sciences Institute to manage this database.[38]

As the burden of registering domain names grew, it became attractive to outsource this service to a commercial party, and in 1993 the NSF awarded a five-year contract for this task to a small, minority-owned business in Virginia named Network Solutions International (NSI). The contract was worth about $6 million a year at that time. It is safe to say that no one anticipated how valuable it would later become: in March 2000 VeriSign paid more than $21 billion to acquire NSI.

When the Internet was privatized in 1995, the NSF terminated its funding contract with NSI, extracting agreements about what prices it would subsequently charge for domain name registration. Scientific Applications International Corporation (SAIC), a large government contractor, acquired NSI as a wholly owned subsidiary in May of 1995, and in September 1995, NSI instituted a charge of $50 to register names and maintain the supporting databases for the .com, .net, and .org domains.

There was considerable dissatisfaction in the Internet community with this arrangement: some people felt that such a critical task should not be under the control of a private firm, others objected to the price and service quality provided by NSI, and yet others wanted to compete with NSI, hoping to profit from the seemingly insatiable demand for domain names. Intellectual property owners were beginning to wake up to the potential conflicts involving their trademarks and domain names. Jon Postel, the USC researcher who had managed the DNS for many years, attempted to design an administrative system

---

38. The following historical account is drawn from Mueller (1999) and from Froomkin (2000).

that would provide some competition for NSI, which eventually grew into an organization known as Internet Corporation for Assigned Names and Numbers (ICANN). Unfortunately, Postel died soon after ICANN was created, removing a highly respected and knowledgeable player from the scene.

In December 1996, Ira Magaziner initiated an interagency group to study the domain name problem as part of his working group on electronic commerce. In July 1997, President Clinton issued an executive order asking the Department of Commerce to "support efforts to make the governance of the domain name system private and competitive and [to deal] with the potential conflicts between domain name usage and trademark laws on a global basis." This relieved the NSF from responsibility for these matters. After two rounds of public comment, the Department of Commerce issued a "White Paper" on domain name registration in June 1998.[39]

The Department of Commerce entered into an agreement with ICANN in November 1998 to "coordinate the technical management of the Internet's domain name system, the allocation of IP address space, the assignment of protocol parameters, and the management of the root server system."

ICANN is a unique institution: it is international in scope and yet it is not directly affiliated with any government or government agency. Essentially it is a standards-setting body, similar to, yet different from, internationally chartered organizations like the International Telecommunications Union (ITU).

ICANN faced, and continues to face, numerous challenges:

1. From where does it get its authority? The Internet is obviously a global institution, while ICANN has been associated closely with the U.S. Department of Commerce.

2. From where does it get its funding? The Department of Commerce made no provision for this.

3. How does it govern? Who are its constituents, and how should members be chosen? Who votes on ICANN issues, and to whom is it accountable?

4. What, exactly, should it do?

ICANN has thus far focused on two significant issues: first, setting up a dispute-resolution procedure for resolving conflicts between trademark holders and domain name registrants, and second, finding ways to make domain name registration more competitive.[40] We describe ICANN's Uniform Dispute

---

39. http://www.icann.org/general/white-paper-05jun98.htm.
40. ICANN has also wrestled with the issue of expanding the number of top-level domains. Recently it has created seven new domain names such as .biz, .info, and .museum to complement the existing TLDs such as .com and .edu.

Resolution Policy in our discussion of trademark policy in section 6.12.3. Here we focus on the management of the DNS itself.

The White Paper recognized that the management of the DNS database is probably a natural monopoly.[41] However, the *registration* process itself is not necessarily a monopoly, and there can, potentially, be many *registrars* even if there is only one *registry*.

Magaziner thought that that NSI should continue to manage the registry, at least for a while, in the interests of Internet stability. However, as the White Paper argued, there was ño reason not to allow competition in the registration process, and the Department of Commerce encouraged this policy change. Significantly, NSI would continue to function as both a registry administrator and a registrar, and would be paid a wholesale price for maintaining the database of $9 per name per year (which was subsequently reduced to $6 per name per year).

NSI's five-year contract with the NSF required it to give the government a copy of the database when the contract expired, but was, unfortunately, unclear on whether it could continue to register names on its own after the contract expired. The ownership of the domain name database was also unclear. These ambiguities led to tortured behind-the-scene negotiations, lobbying, and negotiation between a variety of public and private parties. Finally, in September 1999 an acceptable agreement was reached that partially clarified the rights and responsibilities of ICANN and NSI.

In March 2000, NSI was acquired by VeriSign, a Web infrastructure service provider. In March 2001, under intensive pressure from the federal government, VeriSign/NSI agreed to give up management of the .org database in December 2002, but will maintain the .com database until 2007. It will continue to collect $6 per name per year for the maintenance of these databases, and it will continue to function as a registrar as well as the registry administrator.

As of June 2001, it is still unclear how ICANN will deal with its mission of managing the domain space. Part of the problem is that ICANN itself has a rather narrowly defined mission, but tangential issues relating to Internet governance continue to arise. Since there is no governing body for the Internet as a whole, ICANN has been called upon to deal with a variety of matters. So far, it has generally resisted this temptation. But the problem of Internet governance will continue to be with us for many years.

---

41. There are those who say that the technology can be decentralized, and many technologists believe that one can layer directory services on top of the DNS that would provide a better framework for users to locate relevant Web sites.

6.10   A Framework for Global Electronic Commerce

As commercial interest in the Internet started to accelerate in 1996, it became clear that that the administration should provide some guidance to the private sector concerning its thoughts about an appropriate information policy. The president appointed Ira Magaziner to develop policy guidelines for electronic commerce on the Internet. Magaziner was chiefly responsible for the policy report entitled "A Framework for Global Electronic Commerce" (but widely known as the Magaziner Report) issued on July 1, 1997.[42]

This report was notable for its hands-off approach to regulation, as reflected in the report's five principles for e-commerce policy:

1. The private sector should lead.

2. Governments should avoid undue restrictions on electronic commerce.

3. Where governmental involvement is needed, its aim should be to support and enforce a predictable, minimalist, consistent, and simple legal environment for commerce.

4. Governments should recognize the unique qualities of the Internet.

5. Electronic commerce over the Internet should be facilitated on a global basis.[43]

The report examined nine policy issues in light of these principles:

1. Customs and taxation

2. Electronic payment systems

3. "Uniform Commercial Code" for electronic commerce

4. Intellectual property protection

5. Privacy

6. Security

7. Telecommunications infrastructure and information technology

8. Content

9. Technical standards[44]

Almost nothing happened during the 1990s at a policy level with respect to electronic payments, so we will have nothing further to say about that issue. Each of the other eight policy areas is discussed in its own subsection below.

---

42. See Clinton and Gore (1997).
43. See Clinton and Gore (1997), pp. 2–3.
44. See Clinton and Gore (1997), pp. 3–4.

Telecommunications policy issues were particularly prominent during the
1990s, but are somewhat outside the scope of this chapter. Chapter 7 describes
some of the antitrust issues relating to telecommunications, and we will provide a very brief overview of developments in this area.

6.11   Taxation

The Magaziner Report recommended that governments refrain from imposing
special taxes or customs duties on Internet transactions that would inhibit the
growth of e-commerce.[45] The Clinton administration supported a congressional
moratorium on *new* e-commerce taxes and lobbied with some success in international forums for similar moratoriums by other governments.[46]

The moratorium on new Internet taxes was effective. However, the growth of
e-commerce in 1998 and 1999 resurrected an old problem: what to do about
sales tax treatment of remote purchases.

There is no question that residents of a state are supposed to pay a sales
tax (or, more properly, a "use tax") on the items they purchase from out-of-
state vendors. Individual consumers, however, are rarely audited by state tax
authorities and therefore generally escape payment of these taxes.

States have long wanted to require out of state vendors to collect use taxes
when sales are made. But in 1992 the U.S. Supreme Court ruled that one state
could not demand that vendors in other states be required to collect taxes for it,
as this requirement would be inconsistent with the Commerce Clause of the
U.S. Constitution.[47] However, this same clause gives Congress the power to
regulate interstate commerce, and the Supreme Court suggested that Congress
could grant states the power to compel vendors in other states to collect taxes
on mail order purchases if it chose to do so by passing enabling legislation.

Some bills were introduced in Congress to establish conditions under which
out-of-state commerce could be taxed, but they were never enacted. Taxation of
out-of-state purchases was subsequently relegated to the back burner until the
rapid growth of Internet commerce again brought this issue to the fore.

In 1998, Congress passed the Internet Tax Freedom Act, which created the
moratorium already alluded to.[48] In addition, this act created the Advisory
Commission on Electronic Commerce, which was supposed to revisit the issues
surrounding sales tax. The commission held several public meetings around the

---

45. See Clinton and Gore (1997), pp. 4–5.
46. See U.S. Government's Working Group on Electronic Commerce, First Annual Report (1998),
available at http://www.doc.gov/ecommerce/E-comm.pdf, p. 7 (discussing Internet Tax Freedom
Act), p. 12 (discussing negotiations about foreign tax initiatives).
47. *Quill Corp. v. North Dakota*, 504 U.S. 298 (1992).
48. Public Law 105-277, 112 Stat. 2681 (1998). See generally Forst (1999).

country and issued a report in April 2000, but the commission was unable to reach any consensus on what to do about the sales tax collection problem.

The subsequent demise of the "dot coms" reassured Main Street merchants and state governments that they were not about to be "Amazoned" out of existence, and the sales tax issue has again been relegated to the back burner. Political forces are likely to keep it there. Congress is understandably reluctant to be blamed for enabling a "new" tax, especially if they don't get to spend any of the revenues from it. States are reluctant to simplify and unify their sales tax codes unless there is a clear and present danger to revenues. For these reasons, we expect progress in extending sales and use taxes to remote purchases will be slow.

6.12 Intellectual Property

Several factors contributed to a heightened significance of intellectual property issues in the 1990s, both at the policy level and in broader popular discourse. One was the growing importance of information and information technology products to the gross national product and to U.S. export markets. By 2000, for example, exports of information technology products constituted 29 percent of all U.S. exports.[49] Billions of additional exports were attributable to motion pictures, sound recordings, and other products of traditional copyright industries.[50] A second factor was the seemingly greater vulnerability of intellectual property works to infringement because of the increasing distribution of such works in digital form. Third, many copyright, software, and Internet industry groups were supporters of President Clinton, as well as significant contributors to the Clinton-Gore campaigns, and the administration was understandably receptive to the industry's concerns. Fourth, the expansion of intellectual property rights in the 1990s meant that these rights affected the wider public and captured public attention as never before.[51]

Hence it is not surprising that intellectual property was an especially active policy area during the 1990s. There were major pieces of legislation in the copyright, patent, and trademark fields. Even trade secrecy, long protected only by state law, was federalized with the enactment of the Economic Espionage Act of 1996.[52] Also significant were several appellate court decisions that changed the intellectual property landscape, such as *Feist Publications, Inc. v.*

---

49. See, for example, Mark (2001).

50. See, for example, NII IP White Paper, supra note 39, p. 131 (reporting $45.8 billion in annual exports of copyright products in 1993).

51. See, for example, Computer Science and Telecommunications Board, National Research Council (2000) (cited hereinafter as "Digital Dilemma"), pp. 45–47.

52. 18 U.S.C. secs. 1831–39.

Rural Telephone Service Co. (no copyright in uncreative compilations such white pages listings of telephone directories),[53] *State Street Bank & Trust v. Signature Financial Services* (business methods are patentable),[54] and *Computer Associates, Inc. v. Altai* (no copyright for computer program interface specifications).[55] Even more significant were two international treaties, one setting minimum standards for intellectual property protection for all member states of the World Trade Organization (WTO) and another establishing an international consensus on the application of copyright in the digital environment. These treaties provided new assurances to technology firms and other content providers that they could count on intellectual property law to protect their investments in information products and services.[56]

6.12.1   Copyright Law: The Digital Millennium Copyright Act

In 1993 the Clinton administration's Task Force on the National Information Infrastructure (NIITF) formed the Working Group on Intellectual Property (IPWG) to study how intellectual property should be applied in the emerging NII. Unless such property could be adequately protected, there was concern that rights holders would not make their works available via the NII, and the great promise of the NII would not be fulfilled. Bruce Lehman, a former copyright industry lawyer-lobbyist who became head of the Patent and Trademark Office and assistant secretary of commerce, chaired this working group. The IPWG finalized its conclusions and recommendations and issued a White Paper on "Intellectual Property and the National Information Infrastructure," published in September 1995.[57]

The White Paper's main substantive conclusions and recommendations were as follows: (1) Copyright owners have the legal right to control temporary as well as permanent copies of their works in digital form (which arguably renders every access to or use of a work via the NII as a copyright-significant activity). (2) Fair use and other copyright exceptions (e.g., archival copying by libraries) will no longer be necessary because it will be possible to license uses needed via the NII. (3) Internet service providers and other intermediaries were and should be strictly liable for any infringing copies made by users because ISPs were in the best position to monitor user behavior. (4) New legislation should be enacted to make it illegal to make or distribute technologies, the primary

---

53. 499 U.S. 340 (1991).
54. 149 F.3d 1368 (Fed. Cir. 1998).
55. 982 F.2d 693 (2d Cir. 1992).
56. See section 6.12.5 for discussion of these developments.
57. See NII IP White Paper, supra note 39.

purpose or effect of which was to circumvent a technical protection measure used by copyright owners to protect their works. (5) New legislation should also prohibit the alteration or removal of copyright management information (CMI) that copyright owners might attach or associate with copies of their works to identify the rights holder and the set of rights licensed to a particular user.

The White Paper was received with considerable praise among traditional copyright industry groups, such as the Motion Picture Association of America and the Association of American Publishers. However, it was heavily criticized by other groups, including telephone companies, Internet Service Providers (ISPs), computer companies, universities, libraries, and scientific organizations, as to its interpretation of existing law and as to its legislative proposals.[58]

Not until October 1998 did Congress enact the legislation to deal with the challenges of digital technology.[59] The most contentious and heavily lobbied issue in this legislative struggle concerned ISP liability that pitted the lobbying strengths of the major copyright industries against those of telephone companies and Internet service providers. Congress was eventually able to broker a compromise by establishing "safe harbors" for ISPs (e.g., no liability for user infringement if service takes down infringing material after having been notified about it).[60] This cleared the way for enactment of the Digital Millennium Copyright Act (DMCA). This law included provisions to regulate anticircumvention technologies and to protect the integrity of CMI similar to the White Paper proposals.[61] The anticircumvention regulations have been criticized as ambiguous, overbroad, confusingly complex, and harmful to innovation.[62]

Looking back with the benefit of 20–20 hindsight at the "Agenda for Action" and the IPWG's White Paper, several things are noteworthy. First, the model of the NII in these documents more closely resembles a 500-channel cable TV system than the Internet and World Wide Web that became the predominant new economy phenomenon of the waning years of the 20th century. Second, even before Congress granted the copyright industries stronger intellectual property rules, millions of individual creators and even many established copyright firms put substantial amounts of content on the Internet and Web despite the absence of technical protection systems to stop the copying of this content. Third, although many content providers have tried to fund electronic publishing activities through advertising, few have successfully transitioned to paying

---

58. See, for example, Samuelson (1997) (discussing controversies over NII IP White Paper proposals and their equivalents in the proposed WIPO Copyright Treaty).
59. Digital Millennium Copyright Act, Public Law 105-304, 112 Stat. 2860 (1998).
60. Now codified at 17 U.S.C. sec. 512.
61. Now codified at 17 U.S.C. secs. 1201–04.
62. See, for example, Samuelson (1999).

sites, either by subscription or pay-per-use systems. Fourth, the ease with which digital copies can be made and shared has made it easier than ever to infringe copyrights; while personal use copying and noncommercial sharing of music and other copyrighted works has long been regarded as acceptable behavior, the Internet has so changed the scope and scale of such activities (e.g., Napster, Gnutella, and Freenet) that copyright industries have good reason to be afraid that they will lose control of their works. Fifth, it remains uncertain whether the technically protected content will meet with commercial success in the market-place. Sixth, intellectual property policy is hampered by the lack of serious analysis of the economic impact of changes in both the law and operating prac-tices. It would be worth considering ways to create an organizational frame-work under which economic considerations could be brought to bear on IP issues, given their increasing importance for the economy at large.

6.12.2   Patent Law: Software and Business Method Patents

Before computer software and the Internet, inventive ways to organize, pro-cess, or present information were considered unpatentable, as were business methods.[63] Since the mid-1960s, inventors of software and business method concepts sought to chip away at these old patent rules, arguing that emerging information industries needed and deserved patents as much as any other in-dustry. Yet, until the early 1990s, software was generally patented, if at all, as part of an automated industrial process (for example, as a step in an improved method for curing rubber) or as a virtual device for performing some function. By the early 1990s, however, patents were issuing for algorithms, data struc-tures, and user interface devices (e.g., icons) as well. Although there continues to be controversy within the computing field about whether software patents promote innovation, an increasing number of software firms have sought pat-ents for their innovations. Toward the end of the 1990s, business methods were finally ruled to be patentable subject matter in the United States, even without some computer-related implementation.[64] This ruling has considerable signifi-cance for Internet commerce.

Opponents of software, business method, and other information innovation patents typically make three kinds of arguments against them.[65] First, they as-sert that these innovations are not really technological in character and hence

---

63. See, for example, Samuelson (1990) (discussing these limiting doctrines and pre-1990s patent case law on software, information, and business method innovations).
64. *State Street Bank & Trust v. Signature Financial Services*, 149 F.3d 1368 (Fed. Cir. 1998). Interest-ingly, the European Union has not embraced a similar expansion of patentable subject matters.
65. See, for example, Samuelson, Davis, Kapor, and Reichman (1994); Thomas (1999).

are not patentable. This theory draws upon the Supreme Court's 1972 *Gottschalk v. Benson* decision in which the Court ruled that a method for converting binary decimals to pure binary form was a mathematical idea, not a technological process.[66] Second, they argue that the patent system cannot do a good job with such applications because of the lack of sufficiently knowledgeable examiners, the lack of a sufficiently well-developed classification system for such innovations, and most importantly, the lack of access to databases of prior art from which to judge whether a claimed invention is novel and nonobvious. Third, opponents sometimes argue that the affected industries are unsuitable for patenting. In the software industry context, critics note that the industry rose to prominence without patents because copyright, trade secret, and licensing protected their creations, that innovation in this industry is overwhelmingly incremental in nature, and that there is such a rapid pace of innovation in the industry that a patent is likely to be irrelevant by the time it issues. In the context of business methods, opponents argue that major investments are rarely necessary to bring about innovation in business methods, making patents unnecessary. Fourth, software, no matter how complex its design, is typically constructed from scratch, there being no market for software components by which inventors can be compensated in an efficient way as there is for other manufactured items, the purchase of which allows them to be assembled into larger devices (e.g., airplanes). The dangers of inadvertent infringement of software inventions, by means of independent development of the same or a similar idea, are omnipresent, and costs of searching the tens of thousands of software patents to determine what has been patented is prohibitively high.

The principal response of the Patent and Trademark Office (PTO) to complaints about software and business method patents has been to announce steps to improve the administration of patents in these areas. These steps have included hiring new examiners, providing additional training for examiners, issuing new guidelines or stricter processes for judging the patentability of these innovations, and licensing access to new sources of prior art information. In the case of obvious mistakes (for example, Compton New Media's claim to have a patent covering all multimedia products), the commissioner announced his willingness to reexamine such patents (and in the case of the Compton's patent, the PTO upon reexamination invalidated it). Notwithstanding the PTO's efforts to improve its processes, many continue to believe that the quality of decisions about software and business method patents is unacceptably low.[67] The perception that patenting is easy in these fields may contribute to the flood

---

66. *Gottschalk v. Benson*, 409 U.S. 63 (1972). For critical commentary on this decision, see, for example, Chisum (1986). For commentary supportive of the decision, see, for example, Samuelson (1990).
67. See, for example, Digital Dilemma, pp. 192–198.

of applications that only exacerbates the problem. For all the complaints about software and business method patents, there has been very little litigation to enforce such patents, so it is unclear whether they are as much of a drag on innovation and competition as some critics have asserted.

Notwithstanding the paucity of litigation on software and business method patents, these patents do have significance in the marketplace. The principal strategy of many software developers is to engage in "defensive patenting" and acquire a portfolio of patents so that the firm will have something to trade if another firm threatens to sue it for patent infringement. IBM is one of the few firms with a substantial patent portfolio from which it derives significant revenues. Business method patents, particularly for electronic commerce concepts, seem to be particularly important to start-up firms seeking venture capital.

More general developments with implications for new economy firms included progress in the 1990s toward harmonization of U.S. patent law with world norms. For example, U.S. law finally requires publication of most patent applications 18 months after filing.[68] Congress also made some improvements to the patent reexamination process.[69] Overall, patent rights got stronger in the 1990s, as is evident from the higher rate of appellate court affirmances of patent infringement decisions and reversals of rulings of noninfringement after establishment of the Court of Appeals for the Federal Circuit.[70]

6.12.3   Trademark: Cybersquatting

One new economy business model that was consigned to the dustbin of history in 1999 was speculation in domain names, now widely known as "cybersquatting." A journalist may have gotten this speculative frenzy started when he wrote a story in the mid-1990s about his registration of various famous trademarks as domain names (mcdonalds.com, coke.com, and the like) and the cluelessness of these major business enterprises about the desirability of registering their marks as domain names.[71] Although the journalist registered these famous names in pursuit of his story, others began speculating in trademark domain names, offering to sell the names to the owners of trademarks in a registered word or phrase for hefty sums. Many trademark owners were outraged by this behavior, bringing lawsuits charging domain name registrants with trademark infringement or dilution. Some of these lawsuits were successful because the

---

68. 35 U.S.C. sec. 122. See Boss (1999) (discussing the U.S. 18-month publication rule).
69. 35 U.S.C. sec. 304–306. For a discussion of the new procedures, see Janis (2000).
70. See, for example, Merges (1988) (reporting higher rate of affirmances of infringement decisions after establishment of the Federal Circuit).
71. See Quittner (1994).

domain name registrant was using the domain name in a manner likely to cause consumer confusion or dilute the distinctiveness of the name.[72] However, courts sometimes stretched trademark law beyond traditional bounds to reach "cybersquatters."[73]

This was an important problem because old economy firms began to realize in the late 1990s the potential revenues they might derive from electronic commerce, and they wanted to be sure that their trademark rights would not be nullified by domain name registrations by cybersquatters. The U.S. Congress passed the Anticybersquatting Consumer Protection Act of 1999 to make it illegal to register a trademark as a domain name in bad faith.[74]

The Clinton administration sought to address the global problem of cybersquatting by encouraging ICANN to formulate a uniform dispute resolution process (UDRP) for trademark-domain name disputes. ICANN has now put a UDRP in place, requiring all registers and registrars of domain names to require applicants to agree to use of UDRP for resolving these kinds of disputes.[75] Hundreds of disputes have been resolved, most of which have resulted in the transfer of domain names to the trademark owner. The UDRP addresses the most pressing of the international trademark–domain name problems in a remarkably cost-efficient way.

6.12.4 Database Legislation

Commercial databases are an important new economy industry. The call for legal protection for the data in databases arises from the obvious fact that data, especially when in digital form, are cheap and easy to copy, seemingly making them vulnerable to market-destructive appropriations. Given this fact, it is unsurprising that legal protection for databases became an important policy issue in the 1990s. Up until 1991, U.S. courts had generally protected data compilations, such as white pages of telephone directories, on a "sweat of the brow" rationale, that is, on the theory that the expenditure of substantial time, money, and energy in compiling and updating information allowed the compiler to assert copyright protection to prevent appropriation of all or a substantial part of the contents of the compilation.[76]

---

72. See, for example, *Panavision International v. Toeppen*, 141 F.3d 1316 (9th Cir. 1998).

73. See, for example, *Intermatic, Inc. v. Toeppen*, 40 U.S.P.Q. 2d 1412 (N.D. Ill. 1996).

74. 15 U.S.C. sec. 1125(d).

75. See Rules for Uniform Domain Name Dispute Resolution Policy, http://www.icann.org/udrp/udrp-rules-24oct99.htm. For a helpful essay discussing the UDRP and the circumstances leading up to its adoption as well as controversies concerning ICANN and the UDRP, see, for example, Litman (2000).

76. This history is well recounted in Ginsburg (1990).

All this changed in 1991 when the Supreme Court ruled in *Feist Publications Co. v. Rural Telephone Service, Inc.* that copyright law could not protect the white pages' listings of telephone directories or other uncreative compilations.[77] Copyright protection required some creativity in the selection or arrangement of the data such that the compilation as a whole satisfied the statutory requirement that a compilation be "an original work of authorship."[78] In *Feist*, the Supreme Court repudiated the utilitarian rationale for protecting unoriginal compilations by copyright law, saying that Congress lacked constitutional power to do so under the copyright clause, even if it wanted to.

Although some commentators worried that *Feist* was a threat to the stability of the U.S. database industry,[79] no legislation to protect the contents of databases from *Feist*-like appropriations was introduced in the U.S. Congress until 1996. Even then, the bill was mainly an accommodation to certain Clinton administration officials who wanted to assert that such a law was being considered in the United States in order to strengthen the U.S. negotiating position on a draft international treaty on the legal protection of databases scheduled to be considered at a diplomatic conference in December 1996. In each session of Congress since then, database protection bills have been proposed, but so far none has been enacted.[80]

The principal impetus for U.S. database legislation since 1996 has been a set of rules that the European Union created to protect the contents of databases.[81] The expenditure of substantial resources in developing a database gives the maker 15 years of protection against the extraction and reuse of all or a substantial part of the contents of that database. To induce other countries to adopt equivalent laws and to ensure that European databases would not suffer from inadequate protection on foreign shores, the Europeans decided that databases of non-EU nationals would not be eligible for the benefits of the new legal regime unless their nations had adopted an equivalent law.[82] Because U.S. firms were the leading providers in the European database market, they had some reason to fear losses unless the U.S. Congress adopted an equivalent law.

Even though the 1997 Framework for Global Electronic Commerce identified database protection as a priority,[83] the administration later opposed EU-like

---

77. 499 U.S. 340 (1991).
78. 17 U.S.C. sec. 102(a).
79. See, for example, Tyson and Sherry (1997).
80. See, for example, Reichman and Uhlir (1999) (discussing U.S. legislative activity on database protection).
81. Council Directive 96/9/EC of March 11, 1996 on the Legal Protection of Databases, 1996 O.J. (L77) 20. For a critique of the directive, see, for example, Reichman and Samuelson (1997).
82. Council Directive, supra note 81, art. 11.
83. Clinton and Gore (1997), p. 10.

database legislation as overbroad.[84] It drew upon concerns expressed by the science community and new economy companies such as Yahoo! Yahoo! recognized that an overbroad database law would make it illegal for them to extract information on the World Wide Web to make directories for their search engine.

Even without a new form of intellectual property protection for the contents of databases, the U.S. database industry has continued to grow.[85] Copyright still provides significant protection to data compilers. In addition, database firms rely on their reputations for high-quality, up-to-date information, as well as on licensing contracts and technical controls.

6.12.5 International Developments: TRIPs and the WIPO Copyright Treaty

Among the most significant information policy achievements of the Clinton administration was its leadership in the successful conclusion of the Agreement on Trade-Related Aspects of Intellectual Property Rights (TRIPs) as an annex to the agreements establishing the World Trade Organization in 1994.[86] The TRIPs initiative had begun during the Reagan-Bush years as U.S. officials came to believe that the U.S. global comparative advantage in innovative technology was being eroded because many nations turned a blind eye to local infringements of intellectual property rights of foreign nationals.[87] Use of unilateral sanctions against nations with inadequate IPRs produced only limited success in changing the policies of other governments, so the United States and its allies in the developed world sought international recognition that inadequate IPRs distorted international trade. It was no small feat to convince developing and least developed countries to agree to abide by TRIPs norms.

TRIPs not only requires member states of the WTO to conform their national laws to certain minimum standards of protection as to seven categories of intellectual property rights, but it also requires them to enforce those rights. Nations aggrieved by the deficiencies of another nation's intellectual property laws or enforcement of rights can now submit their grievances to the WTO. If the dispute cannot be resolved through mediation, a dispute-resolution panel will be appointed to consider the merits of the complaint and to issue a ruling.

---

84. See Reichman and Uhlir (1999), pp. 822–823 (discussing the Clinton administration's opposition to an EU-style database law).

85. See, for example, Maurer (2001).

86. Among the many fine commentaries on the TRIP Agreement and its implications are the following: Dreyfuss and Lowenfeld (1997), Geller (1995), and Reichman (1995).

87. See, for example, Ryan (1998).

In the last few years, WTO dispute panels have resolved several significant IP disputes.[88]

The overwhelming majority of the TRIPs norms derive from longstanding international intellectual property treaty provisions. However, TRIPs also addresses some new economy technology policy concerns as well. Because of some uncertainty about whether computer programs and databases were protectable under the leading international copyright treaty known as the Berne Convention for the Protection of Artistic and Literary Works, Clinton administration officials insisted that the TRIPs Agreement should require WTO member states to provide copyright protection for programs and databases.[89] They also used TRIPs to strengthen international norms on the legal protection for the topography of integrated circuits.[90] By insisting that patents must issue to protect inventions "in all fields of technology,"[91] U.S. officials set the stage for possible challenges to the patent laws of some nations that do not as yet protect computer software or genetically engineered inventions.

Also ongoing during the early 1990s were negotiations hosted by the World Intellectual Property Organization (WIPO) to consider a possible treaty to update application of copyright law to the Internet and the World Wide Web. In 1996, largely at the instigation of U.S. officials, WIPO convened a diplomatic conference of representatives of 170 nations that resulted in the adoption of the WIPO Copyright Treaty.[92]

The WIPO Copyright Treaty establishes several norms with important implications for the new economy.[93] Like TRIPs, the WIPO treaty requires signatory nations to protect computer programs and databases as literary works under the Berne Convention. It affirms that copyright owners have the right to control reproductions of their works in digital form. Owners also have the right

---

88. For instance, the United States challenged a Canadian law that allowed manufacturers to stockpile generic versions of drugs whose patent rights were about to expire so that the generic firms could begin selling products as soon as the patent expired. The WTO panel ruled that this violated the TRIPs norm that patent laws of WTO member states must grant patentees exclusive rights to make, use, and sell the invention during the life of the patent. See WTO Dispute Panel decision in *United States v. Canada Concerning Pharmaceutical Patents*, http://www.wto.org/english/ tratop_e/dispu_e/7428d.pdf.

89. TRIPs, art. 10.

90. Ibid, arts. 35–38.

91. Ibid., art. 27(1).

92. The history of this and a similar treaty to protect sound recordings is recounted in Samuelson (1997).

93. WIPO Copyright Treaty, adopted Dec. 20, 1996, WIPO Doc. CRNR/DC/94. Its sister treaty for sound recordings is WIPO Performances and Phonograms Treaty, adopted Dec. 20, 1996, WIPO Doc. CRNR/DC/96. The implications of the treaty for the new economy are discussed at length in Samuelson (1997).

to control communications of their works to the public via the Internet or other communications medium, although clarifying that merely providing a communications facility should not give rise to liability, thereby allowing nations to limit the responsibility of Internet service providers for user infringement. Exceptions and limitations to copyright continue to apply, as appropriate, in the digital networked environment, and new exceptions and limitations may also be adopted as appropriate for the digital networked environment.

The WIPO treaty established two new wholly international norms. One deals with the removal or alteration of copyright management information that may be attached to or associated with digital copies of protected works to identify the copyright owner and licensed rights in the copy.[94] The other requires nations to provide "adequate protection" and "effective remedies" against circumvention of technical protection measures copyright owners use to protect their works against infringing uses.[95] As indicated previously, the United States implemented these new international norms in 1998.[96] The WIPO Copyright Treaty was a significant achievement of the Clinton era's technology policy, for it paved the way for the emergence of the global market in digital information envisioned in the Information Infrastructure Task Force's Agenda for Action and in the 1997 Framework for E-Commerce.

6.13   Commercial Law

The 1995 NII IP White Paper and the 1997 Framework for Global Electronic Commerce report emphasized the need for harmonization of contract law to promote global electronic commerce.[97] These documents imagined a global market for digital information in which anyone anywhere on the globe could search electronically for information of interest and make a contract via the GII for delivery of the information directly to them. To bring this vision to fruition, there needed to be some international consensus about contract formation rules in cyberspace and default terms of such contracts (e.g., which jurisdiction's law will apply to the transaction and in which forum[s] disputes should be resolved).

Although the Clinton administration initiated legislation on other NII and e-commerce policy matters, it did not initially propose new cyberspace contract rules in part because contract and commercial law rules have traditionally

---

94. WIPO Copyright Treaty, Art. 12.
95. Ibid., art. 11.
96. See section 6.12.1.
97. NII IP White Paper, supra note 39, pp. 49–59 (discussing licensing and the need for contract rules for on line transactions); Clinton and Gore (1997), pp. 6–8.

been matters for state rather than federal law. The Clinton administration was also aware that the National Conference of Commissioners of Uniform State Laws (NCCUSL) had been at work for some years to develop two model laws for electronic commerce: the Uniform Electronic Transactions Act (UETA) and that now known as the Uniform Computer Information Transactions Act (UCITA).[98]

UETA was needed because the laws of many states require that contracts be memorialized in "writings" and bear the "signatures" of persons authorized to enter into the contract. Prior to UETA, it was unclear whether electronic signatures and electronic records would satisfy such state law requirements. UETA updates contract law so that signature requirements can be satisfied by electronic signatures and writing requirements by electronic records. NCCUSL promulgated UETA in the summer of 1999, and about half of the country's state legislatures have now enacted it. To spur additional uniform adoptions, the U.S. Congress enacted the "E-Sign" legislation that essentially makes UETA a national standard.[99] Proponents of UETA hope that it will eventually be an international standard as well.

UCITA is NCCUSL's model law for commercial transactions in computer information.[100] Among other things, UCITA would validate shrink-wrap, click-through, and other mass-market licenses for software, databases, Web sites, and the like, as long as the user of the information has had an opportunity to review the terms of the license.[101] UCITA has been highly controversial because it is complex, poorly drafted, overbroad, hostile to consumer interests, and imbalanced in other ways.[102] Some key provisions of the law are likely to be preempted by federal intellectual property law and policy (e.g., UCITA would seem to validate anti–reverse engineering clauses of software licenses even though reverse engineering is permissible under federal law).[103] Despite a strong push by leading new economy firms, such as Microsoft and AOL, only two states have adopted UCITA so far, one of which made significant changes to enhance consumer protection and the other of which deferred its enforce-

---

98. See Framework, p. 7.
99. Public Law 106-229, 114 Stat. 464, codified at 15 U.S.C. secs. 7001–06. See Stern (2001).
100. For an overview of the principal features of UCITA and the main arguments supporting it, see, for example, Nimmer (1998), Gomulkiewicz (1998). Nimmer was the chief drafter of UCITA; Gomulkiewicz is a senior attorney for Microsoft Corporation and head of the Business Software Alliance's Working Group on UCITA.
101. Uniform Computer Information Transactions Act, sec. 211.
102. See, for example, Samuelson and Opsahl (1999) (reviewing criticisms).
103. See, for example, Nimmer, Brown, and Frischling (1999) (arguing that many UCITA terms would be preempted), and Lemley (1999) (discussing preemption and other doctrines likely to be employed to limit UCITA licenses).

ment for two years out of concern about imbalance in the law. Although a number of state legislatures are still considering UCITA, there is reason to doubt that this law will provide the clarity and uniformity in rules that proponents had hoped for. Thus an important part of the legal infrastructure for the new economy remains uncertain.

6.14 Security Policy

The proliferation of computers and networks as critical infrastructure for government and private-sector activities meant that computer security and encryption policy took on a new importance in the 1990s.[104] Computer security was in part a national security issue, and encryption was one of the key technologies for strengthening computer security. The market for encryption technologies grew rapidly during these years for a wide range of uses, for instance, to enable businesses to transfer sensitive data, to enable individuals to engage in secure communications, and to enable the transfer of credit card numbers to complete commercial transactions over the Internet.

A significant barrier to growth of the market for software using encryption was the U.S. export control regulations that forbade the export of encryption technologies beyond a certain strength (typically measured by the length of keys).[105] American firms faced the dilemma of making two products—one with strong encryption for the American market and another with weaker encryption for foreign markets—or making one product with weak encryption for both markets. Their concern was not only the higher costs of developing two products, but also that foreign developers of encryption technologies often operated under looser or no export control constraints. U.S. firms complained they were losing market share both domestically (because foreign competitors could import strong encryption products into the United States) and abroad because of the export control regulations. They lobbied vigorously for changes to these controls. Over the course of the 1990s, encryption rules were loosened considerably to the evident relief of the American software and related high-technology industries.[106]

The principal reason that the FBI and other intelligence agencies opposed loosening encryption controls was that advances in information technologies made it more difficult for them to get access to information affecting national and international security. These agencies sought to encourage the adoption of

---

104. See generally Dam and Lin (1996).
105. See 15 C.F.R. sec. 734 et seq.
106. See, for example, Levy (2001), pp. 282–312 (discussing the loosening of export controls affecting cryptography during the 1990s).

technologies that would facilitate the access they regarded as essential to their mission, such as fostering "voluntary" industry adoption of the "Clipper Chip" in information technology devices.[107] Clipper was a superior security technology in some respects as compared with previously endorsed government encryption standards, but it provided the government with a "back door" through which to access encrypted communications if doing so became necessary. Civil libertarians and the high technology industry strongly objected to installation of the Clipper Chip on both practical and philosophical grounds. The discovery of technical flaws in the Clipper Chip reinforced industry objections to this technology. Subsequently, the administration proposed a "key escrow" system as an alternative way to ensure their access to encrypted communications.[108] Proposals varied somewhat, but the core idea was that users of strong encryption would deposit keys to their encrypted information with the government or a third party so that the government could get access to the information in appropriate cases. The technology industry and civil liberties groups received these proposals with little enthusiasm. The decade ended without resolution of this important encryption and computer security issue.

In the late 1990s it became increasingly evident that use of strong encryption was essential to the growth of e-commerce. This need may have been a crucial factor in the Clinton administration's decisions to relax export controls considerably and to cease promotion of the Clipper Chip and key escrow initiatives.[109]

6.15 Telecommunications

Describing the details of telecommunications policy during the 1990s could easily require a whole book, so we can provide only the most cursory overview of major developments in this section.[110]

The biggest single topic is, of course, the Telecommunications Act of 1996, and we will use it to organize our discussion. This act, coming 12 years after the historic breakup of AT&T in 1984, was a valiant attempt to clean up the detritus left from half a century of regulation.[111]

---

107. For a discussion of the Clipper Chip initiative and its aftermath, see, for example, Froomkin (1996).
108. For a discussion of key escrow systems, see, for example, Levy (2001), pp. 294–296, and Dam and Lin (1996).
109. See, for example, Levy (2001), pp. 311–312 (crediting e-commerce with bringing about change in the crypto policy environment).
110. For an insider's account, see Hundt (2000).
111. For a brief summary of the act, see the Benton Foundation's review at http://www.benton.org/Policy/96act/.

The main provisions of the act were as follows:

1. To encourage competition for incumbent local exchange carriers (ILECs) by allowing entrants (competitive local exchange carriers, or CLECs) to interconnect with the ILECs and to lease lines and other "unbundled network elements" from the ILECs at wholesale prices, allowing for physical collocation of equipment, as well as several related measures such as mandating number portability. Some of these changes were already under way in various states, but the act made these provisions a nationwide policy.

2. To allow regional Bell operating companies to enter the long-distance market, once their local markets were sufficiently competitive, as determined by the FCC. This provision superseded the provisions of the Modified Final Judgment in the AT&T breakup.

3. To set forth explicit principles of universal service as a matter of federal communications policy, and to require the FCC to advance this goal. In particular, the act created the so-called E-rate, which provided subsidized access to the Internet by schools and libraries.

4. To encourage the FCC to relax various restrictions on over-the-air radio and TV broadcast, and to grant additional spectrum rights to TV in order to allow for a transition to high-definition digital TV.

5. To deregulate cable TV by repealing many provisions of the 1992 Cable Act.

6. To deal with content-related issues, such as pornography and violence, using measures such as the V-chip. The Communications Decency Act, described in section 6.17, was attached to the 1996 Telecommunications Act.

7. To deal with a large number of other miscellaneous measures to further the deployment of advanced services.

The Telecommunications Act of 1996 was widely hailed by officials in the Clinton administration, Congress, and the communications industry as a whole. Congress passed the act by 414 to 16 in the House and 91 to 5 in the Senate.

Significantly, the act mentions the Internet only in two places, one of which had to do with school and library access to the Internet, the other being the various provisions of the Communications Decency Act.

How successful has the act been? We think that it is safe to say that progress has been made, but not as much as had been hoped for. In particular, it is widely believed that requiring ILECs to provide access to their "unbundled network elements" has not worked particularly well. There is considerable debate as to whether this lack of success was due to foot-dragging by the ILECs or a poor business model by the CLECs, but the fact of the matter is that the local market continues, for all practical purposes, to be monopolized. The major beneficiaries of competition at the local exchange level have been businesses that have purchased discounted telephone services from CLECs.

The act appears to have stimulated a number of telecommunications mergers, which are described in by Robert Litan and Carl Shapiro in Chapter 7. These include SBC–Pacific Bell–Ameritech, Bell Atlantic–Nynex–GTE, Quest–US West, and Worldcom–MCI. There were also a few divestitures, most notably AT&T's spinoff of Lucent in 1997.

With respect to item 2, progress has also been slow. In 2000, Bell Atlantic became the first "Baby Bell" to be approved to offer long-distance services between local areas to customers in New York.

The most notable aspect of the universal service provision was the E-rate, which subsidized access by schools and libraries via a tax on telecommunications carriers. The act has definitely been successful in connecting up schools: in 1994 only 30 percent of public elementary schools had Internet access, but by 1998 over 80 percent had Internet access, and by now virtually all public schools have at least some degree of Internet access.[112]

However, the E-rate has cost between $1 billion and $2 billion a year, a cost covered by a "hidden" tax on telecommunications service providers. Though the E-rate program enjoys wide popular support, there are still many critics of the telecommunications tax used to fund it.

Item 5, the deregulation of cable TV, has not had as much of an impact at the consumer level as its critics had feared. It may have contributed to consolidation of the industry, as represented by the AT&T acquisition of TCI in 1998 and the AOL–Time Warner merger in 2001. However, such consolidation was well under way prior to the act.

Finally, item 6, having to do with content regulation, is discussed in section 6.17.

Consistent with the vision of the NII, there was considerable deployment of Internet access in the United States during the 1990s. In August 2000, roughly 40 percent of U.S. households had access to the Internet, with 4.4 percent of U.S. households having broadband access, through either cable modems (50 percent) or DSL (34 percent).[113] Nearly half of Internet users reported that they had access to broadband, but only 12 percent had actually adopted it by the end of 2000.[114]

---

112. See http://www.speakout.com/Issues/Briefs/1164/.
113. See the October 2000 NTIA report, "Falling Through the Net," available at http://www.ntia.doc.gov/ntiahome/fttn00/Falling.htm.
114. See "Telecommunications: Characteristics and Choices of Internet Users," General Accounting Office AO-01-345, Feb. 16, 2001.

In summary, significant progress was made during the 1990s in terms of attempting to deregulate telecommunications and deploy new services. Many states were already moving in this direction; the act's primary contribution was to set a nationwide policy. Deployment of new services did not occur as rapidly as their proponents had hoped, but the fact that they occurred at all stands as a stark contrast to previous decades.

6.16 Information Privacy

Advances in information technology, especially those adapted for use on the Internet and World Wide Web, made it easier than ever before to collect data about individuals (what they looked at, how long they looked at it, what they did next, etc.), often in ways of which the individuals were unaware. The economic value of personal data motivated firms to collect and process these data, for example, by generating profiles of user behavior for internal marketing purposes or for sale to other firms wanting customers of that type. Polls consistently show that an overwhelming majority of people in the United States are concerned about their lack of control over personal data, especially on the Internet and Web. Among other things, this concern makes them less willing than they might otherwise be to purchase goods and services over the Internet and World Wide Web. Privacy thus became a key issue for e-commerce policy in the 1990s.[115]

One pressure point for U.S. information privacy initiatives was the decision of the European Union in the mid-1990s to require member states to adopt a comprehensive legal regime to protect personal data.[116] The regime protected individuals against unauthorized collection or processing of personal data. It also granted individuals rights to access data about themselves in the hands of private-sector firms, to demand correction or deletion of the data, and to sue for violations of data privacy rules. EU member states are also obliged to establish data privacy bureaucracies to ensure compliance with the data protection rules. The European data protection rules authorize blockage of transnational data flows if the nations through which the data would pass do not have satisfactory privacy rules. During much of the 1990s, European officials expressed serious doubts that U.S. rules met this standard,[117] resulting in considerable tension

---

115. For a discussion of this and other economic reasons why legal protection for personal data is warranted, see, for example, Swire and Litan (1998).

116. See Council Directive 95/46/EC of the European Parliament and of the Council of 24 October 1995, on the Protection of Individuals with Regard to Processing of Personal Data and the Free Movement of Such Data, 1995 O.J. (L281) 31.

117. For a discussion of the extent to which U.S. law conforms to European privacy standards (and why it mostly does not), see Schwartz and Reidenberg (1996).

between the United States and the European Union about data privacy issues. To overcome this potential barrier to trade, U.S. and EU officials engaged in lengthy negotiations aimed at establishing "safe harbor" rules so that American firms willing to abide by such rules could transfer and process data in or through the European Union without fear of blockages.[118] Although safe harbor rules were eventually adopted, the European Parliament and EU data privacy officials have expressed some reservations about them. For now, the safe harbor rules, if followed, provide some assurance for businesses operating in the global market that information flows will not be interrupted.

Another pressure point for U.S. information privacy initiatives came from domestic concerns about information privacy. For the most part, the Clinton administration relied on the private sector to develop self-regulatory measures to protect information privacy.[119] The Federal Trade Commission (FTC) took action against some firms that failed to abide by posted information privacy policies, thereby committing an unfair or deceptive trade practice under section 5 of the FTC Act.[120] The FTC also began issuing annual reports to Congress on privacy on the Internet, reporting, for example, on the proportion of Web sites that informed consumers about uses they intended to make of data collected about them.[121] The FTC articulated a set of principles for judging the meaningfulness of self-regulatory measures. During the mid- to late 1990s, Clinton administration officials frequently stated that if the private sector did not engage in meaningful self-regulation, the administration would support information privacy legislation. Yet it bristled when the FTC announced in 2000 that self-regulation had been a failure and endorsed enactment of legislation in addition to that adopted in the late 1990s to protect against online gathering of information from children.

Notwithstanding the lack of comprehensive privacy legislation in the United States, electronic commerce did grow during the 1990s. However, e-commerce may grow more rapidly if the American public has more confidence that their personal data will not be abused. If state legislatures become more active in adopting Internet privacy rules, industry groups may press for national legislation as a way of achieving uniformity in rules. In addition, many other nations are adopting EU-style privacy rules. American firms engaged in international business transactions already have to comply with EU rules and increasingly with other similar national privacy rules. To promote business certainty, one harmonized set of privacy rules may be desirable.

---

118. See U.S. Department of Commerce (2000).
119. See, for example, U.S. Department of Commerce (1997).
120. See, for example, *In re Geocities* (consent decree excerpts in Mark A. Lemley et al. [2000], pp. 991–1001).
121. See, for example, Federal Trade Commission (2000).

6.17   Content Regulation as E-commerce Policy

Just as advances in IT have made it easier to infringe copyrights and invade privacy, they have also made it easier than ever before to disseminate harmful content, such as hate speech, child pornography, and defamation. The global nature of the Internet makes it difficult to know what content regulations will apply to Internet communications. The Framework for Global Electronic Commerce announced the Clinton administration's general opposition to content regulations.[122] Commerce in content obviously flows more freely when there are few or no content regulations with which to deal. In addition, free speech values of American law disfavor content regulations. One source of tension between the United States and other nations during the 1990s arose because some nations sought to regulate Internet availability of hate speech and the sale of Nazi memorabilia, which are legal in the United States.[123] Another source of tension concerned national rules limiting the amount of "foreign" content. Although other nations defend such rules as necessary to preserve cultural heritage, American firms tend to regard them as discriminatory protectionism against foreign competition and market access. Clinton administration officials argued that such rules should not apply to the emerging GII.[124]

Yet content regulation was viewed differently by the administration when the question was whether the law should protect children against "indecent" or "harmful" materials on the Internet. The administration joined a majority in Congress in support of legislation to outlaw such material and to require schools and libraries to use filtering software to block access to such material. One such law was the Communications Decency Act (CDA), enacted as part of the 1996 telecommunications deregulation package. It outlawed, among other things, the use of an interactive computer service to display patently offensive materials on a site accessible by persons under the age of 18.[125] Although Internet service providers persuaded Congress to exempt them from indirect liability for harmful speech on their sites, anyone who uttered patently offensive words using an interactive computer service could have gone to jail for up to two years—at least until the U.S. Supreme Court ruled that the CDA's strictures violated the First Amendment.[126] The term "patently offensive" gave inadequate notice about what would and would not violate the law and was therefore likely to chill expression of protected speech. As important as it was to protect children from harmful materials on the Internet, the Supreme Court

---

122. Clinton and Gore (1997), pp. 18–20.
123. Ibid., pp. 18–19.
124. Ibid., p. 19.
125. 47 U.S.C. sec. 223.
126. *Reno v. ACLU*, 117 S.Ct. 2329 (1997).

concluded that Congress could not reduce the level of discourse on the Internet to be that suitable for five-year-olds. An important aspect of this ruling was its designation of the Internet as a robust forum for democratic discourse that is entitled to the highest level of protection under the First Amendment. Thus, content regulations aimed at the Internet will likely be carefully scrutinized in the future.

The economic significance of content regulations aimed at protecting children is considerable, partly because of the breadth of their application, the strictures they impose on sites, and the burdens they impose on online services. The Child Online Protection Act (COPA), for example, encourages sites to adopt identification systems, such as credit card systems.[127] Operators of pornographic sites will find it easy to comply with COPA because they do not object to imposing credit card obligations on those wanting to have access to their content. Other firms or individuals with open Web sites are at risk, if their content includes questionable words (such as references to breast cancer or beavers). Schools and libraries that receive federal funding are now required to purchase, install, and maintain filtering technologies, even though most reports on filtering technologies suggest that they both under- and overblock content.[128] This regulation too is being challenged as unconstitutional under the First Amendment.[129] In the meantime, this law will be a boon to new economy firms in the filtering software industry.

6.18 Standards

The Clinton administration recognized that standards were critical to the development of an open information infrastructure. However, they also realized that standards development was something typically best left to the private sector. For example, the National Institute of Standards and Technology funded the Advanced Technology Program, which awarded grants to private companies that developed standards for information interchange, among other things.

The Internet Engineering Task Force (IETF), which had evolved as a volunteer effort to standardize various aspects of the Internet, suddenly found itself at the center of numerous political and commercial interests. It is still the center of much debate, and there are some that question how well it will be able to deal with the stresses and strains associated with its much-enlarged role. However,

---

127. 47 U.S.C. sec. 231.
128. Children's Internet Protection Act, codified at 20 U.S.C. sec. 9134 and 47 U.S.C. sec. 254(h).
129. The ACLU has sued to enjoin the mandatory filtering by schools and libraries receiving federal funding. The complaint is available at http://www.aclu.org/court/multnomah.pdf.

since there is no alternative organization that can command the loyalty of the engineers that make the Internet run, it will likely continue to play its critical role in developing Internet standards.

The World Wide Web Consortium (W3C) was created in 1994 by Tim Berners-Lee "to lead the World Wide Web to its full potential by developing common protocols that promote its evolution and ensure its interoperability."[130] It has also played a very significant role in making the Web work more effectively. Currently more than 500 member organizations contribute to its standards development.

The 1990s saw a plethora of ad hoc standards bodies arise, often focused on a single technology or even a single standard. Given the deliberative and slow-moving nature of the more established standards bodies, it was natural that the fast-moving IT industry would want decisions made more quickly. However, sometimes the rapid development of standards led to poor decisions, and some of the traditional standards bodies have attempted to respond to industry needs more expeditiously. Competition is effective, even in the domain of standards setting.

6.19 Conclusion

The Clinton administration presciently conceived of a National Information Infrastructure that, if properly nurtured, would promote economic growth, better government services, broad public access to information, and cultural enrichment. From the beginning, the administration was committed to the idea that the private sector should lead in developing and deploying NII technologies. And invest the private sector did in a wide variety of innovative Internet infrastructure and applications technologies. This investment, in turn, produced an unparalleled stock market boom, especially notable in the late 1990s. The market was, as Alan Greenspan observed, irrationally exuberant, and the stock market correction of 2000 was to be expected.

Among the many hopes for the NII was that it and concomitant investments in IT would enhance productivity more generally. There are some signs that productivity did improve during the 1990s as a result of investments in IT, although economists continue to debate important questions about the impacts of IT on productivity.

Consistent with the administration's policy of promoting private-sector initiatives was its encouragement of private-sector self-regulatory measures, such as nudging firms to post information privacy policies on Web sites so that

---

130. Mission statement at http://www.w3.org/Consortium/.

privacy legislation would be unnecessary. Also encouraged were industry consortium initiatives to address policy issues, such as the Platform for Privacy Preferences initiative of the W3C, so that users could program their browser software so that they would not visit Web sites whose privacy policies did not conform to their preferences. In addition, the administration supported turning over a significant Internet policy-making function, namely, administration of the domain name system, to the newly created nonprofit corporation ICANN.

While relying principally on the private sector for NII development, the Clinton administration introduced new policies when necessary either to correct abuses or to create incentives for certain desired activities. The FASB, for example, formulated new accounting rules for valuing stock market options that are widely used in the IT sector, and the SEC issued a rule requiring disclosure of nonpublic information to the market at one time so that industry analysts and institutional investors did not enjoy undue advantages from, for example, pre-IPO IT road shows.

More proactively, the administration sought to promote NII development by supporting deregulation of the telecommunications industry, opposing new Internet taxes or customs that might inhibit the growth of electronic commerce, proposing new intellectual property rules, and articulating the need for new commercial law rules for the Internet. Noneconomic considerations (e.g., protecting children and national security) were significant driving forces behind some controversial information policy proposals the administration supported such as the Communications Decency Act rules forbidding indecent communications over the Internet and export control regulations that limited the use of strong encryption in software or Internet applications. Critics of both policies relied on economic arguments (e.g., the rules unduly inhibited commerce) and noneconomic arguments (e.g., the rules also violated civil liberties).

The administration's record on intellectual property policy would be more praiseworthy had it been more consistently guided by economic analysis. The administration deserves praise, for example, for expressing doubts on economic grounds about a European-style database law that would have outlawed many uses of information on the Internet. However, the administration can fairly be criticized on economic grounds for its support of an extension of copyright terms for an additional 20 years and of overbroad anticircumvention rules that the content industry has been using to challenge innovative IT applications.

In the international arena, the Clinton administration achieved notable successes on key electronic commerce policies, such as the successful conclusion of the TRIPs Agreement and of the WIPO Copyright Treaty, safe harbor information privacy rules, and moratoria on electronic taxation.

Undoubtedly it will take years, and perhaps decades, to reach satisfactory resolutions of all the policy issues examined in this chapter. We can only hope that future administrations will be as appropriately supportive of private-sector initiatives and as successful in their proactive policies to promote beneficial development of the information infrastructure as the Clinton administration was.

References

Boss, Aimee. 1999. "Comment: The 21st Century Patent System Improvement Act: Is It Really an Improvement?" *John Marshall Law Review*, 32:725.

Brynjolfsson, Erik, and Lorin M. Hitt. 2000. "The Resurgence of Growth in the Late 1990s: Is Information Technology the Story?" *Journal of Economic Perspectives*, 24, no. 4 (Fall): 23–28.

Chisum, Donald S. 1986. "The Patentability of Algorithms." *University of Pittsburgh Law Review*, 47:959.

Clinton, William J., and Albert Gore, Jr. 1997. "*A Framework for Global Electronic Commerce.*" Available at http://www.iitf.nist.gov/eleccom/ecomm.htm.

Computer Science and Telecommunications Board, National Research Council. 2000. *The Digital Dilemma: Intellectual Property in the Information Age*. Washington, DC: National Academy of Sciences Press.

The Council of Economic Advisors. 2000 and 2001. *Economic Report of the President*.

Dam, Kenneth, and Herbert Lin, eds. 1996. *Cryptography's Role in Securing the Information Society*. Washington, DC: National Academy of Sciences Press.

David, Paul. 1990. "The Dynamo and the Computer: An Historical Perspective on the Modern Productivity Paradox." *American Economic Review*, 80, no. 2 (May): pp. 355–361.

Dedrick, Jason, Vijay Gurbaxani, and Kenneth L. Kraemer. 2001. "Information Technology and Economic Performance: Firm and Country Evidence." Working Paper, Center for Research on Information Technology and Organizations, University of California, Irvine.

Dreyfuss, Rochelle Cooper, and Andreas F. Lowenfeld. 1997. "Two Achievements of the Uruguay Round: Putting TRIPS and Dispute Settlement Together." *Virginia Journal of International Law*, 37:275.

Federal Trade Commission. 2000. "Privacy Online: Fair Information Practices in the Electronic Marketplace, A Report to Congress," http://www.ftc.gov/reports/privacy2000/privacy2000text.pdf.

Forst, David L. 1999. "Old and New Issues in the Taxation of electronic Commerce." *Berkeley Technology Law Journal*, 14:711.

Froomkin, A. Michael. 1996. "It Came from Planet Clipper." *University of Chicago Law Forum*, 15.

Froomkin, A. Michael. 2000. "Wrong Turn in Cyberspace: Using ICANN to Route Around the APA and the Constitution." *Duke Law Journal*, 50:17. Available at http://www.icannwatch.org/icann4beginners.php.

Geller, Paul Edward. 1995. "Intellectual Property in the Global Marketplace: Impact of TRIPS Dispute Settlement?" *International Lawyer*, 29:99.

Gilchrist, Simon, Vjay Gurbaxani, and Robert Town, "Productivity and the PC Revolution," CRITO Working Paper ITR-169, UC Irvine, 2001.

Ginsburg, Jane C. 1990. "Creation and Commercial Value: Copyright Protection for Works of Information." *Columbia Law Review*, 90:1865.

Gomulkiewicz, Robert W. 1998. "The License Is the Product: Comments on the Promise of Article 2B for Software and Information Licensing." *Berkeley Technology Law Journal*, 13:891.

Gordon, Robert. 2000. "Has the 'New Economy' Rendered the Productivity Slowdown Obsolete?" *Journal of Economic Perspectives*, 14, no. 4 (Fall).

Henry, David. 2001. "Behind the S&P 500." *Business Week Online* (March 23). Available at http://www.businessweek.com/bw50/content/mar2001/bf20010323_409.htm.

Hundt, Reed. 2000. *You Say You Want a Revolution*. New Haven, CT: Yale University Press.

Information Infrastructure Task Force. 1993. "The National Information Infrastructure Initiative: Agenda for Action." Washington, DC (September 15).

Janis, Mark A. 2000. "Inter Partes Patent Reexamination." *Fordham Intellectual Property, Media, and Entertainment Law Journal*, 10:481.

Jorgenson, Dale W. 2001. "Information Technology and the U.S. Economy." *American Economic Review*, 91, no. 1 (March): 1–32.

Kahin, Brian. 1996. "The Market, the Web, and the Virutal Project." In *National Information Infrastructure Initiatives: Vision and Policy Design*, ed. Brian Kahin and Ernest Wilson. Cambridge, MA: MIT Press.

Kalil, Thomas. 1995. "Public Policy and the National Information Infrastructure." *Business Economics*, 30, no. 4 (October): 15–20.

Lemley, Mark A. 1999. "Beyond Preemption: The Law and Policy of Intellectual Property Licensing." *California Law Review*, 87:111.

Lemley, Mark A. et al. 2000. *Software and Internet Law*. New York: Aspen Law and Business.

Levy, Stephen. 2001. *Crypto: How the Code Rebels Beat the Government Saving Privacy in the Digital Age*. New York: Viking Press.

Lewis, Michael. 1999. *The New New Thing*. New York: W. W. Norton.

Litman, Jessica. 2000. "The DNS Wars: Trade Marks and the Internet Domain Name System." *Small and Emerging Business Law*, 4:149.

Mandel, Michael. 2000. *The Coming Internet Depression*. New York: Basic Books.

Mark, Roy. 2001. "U.S. High Tech Exports Surge." *The New York Times*.

Maurer, Steven M. 2001. "Across Two Worlds: Database Protection in the U.S. and Europe," for Industry Canada Conference on Intellectual Property and Innovation in the Knowledge-Based Economy, May 23–24 (on file with the authors).

Merges, Robert P. 1988. "Commercial Success and Patent Standards: Economic Perspectives on Innovation." *California Law Review*, 76:803, 820–821.

Morgenson, Gretchen. 2001. "If Earnings Depend on Investing, Watch Out." *New York Times*, Jan. 21.

Mueller, Milton. 1999. "ICANN and Internet Governance." *info*, 1: 6, 497–520. Available at http://www.icannwatch.org/archive/from_the_archives.htm.

National Partnership for Reinventing Government. 1997. "Access America: Reengineering Through Information Technology" (February), available at http://govinfo.library.unt.edu/npr/library/announc/access/acessrpt.html.

National Research Council. 1998. *Fostering Research in the Economic and Social Impact of Information Technology*. Washington, DC: National Academy of Sciences Press, http://www.nap.edu/readingroom/books/esi/.

Nimmer, David, Elliot Brown, and Gary Frischling. 1999. "The Metamophosis of Contract into Expand." *California Law Review*, 87:17.

Nimmer, Raymond T. 1998. "Breaking Barriers: The Relation Between Contract and Intellectual Property Law." *Berkeley Technology Law Journal*, 13:827.

Oliner, Stephen, and Daniel Sichel. 2000. "The Resurgence of Growth in the Late 1990s: Is Information Technology the Story?" Federal Reserve Board of Governors, Finance and Economics Discussion Series 2000–20 (March).

Payson, Steve, and John Jankowski. 2000. "Sixth Year of Unprecedented R&D Growth Expected in 2000." *NSF Data Brief* (November 29), http://www.nsf.gov/sbe/srs/databrf/nsf01310/sdb01310.htm.

Quittner, Joshua. 1994. "Billions Registered." *Wired*, 2: 10, 50.

Reichman, J. H. 1995. "Universal Minimum Standards of Intellectual Property Under the TRIPS Component of the WTO Agreement." *International Lawyer*, 29:345.

Reichman, J. H., and Pamela Samuelson. 1997. "Intellectual Property Rights in Data?" *Vanderbilt Law Review*, 50:51.

Reichman, J. H., and Paul Uhlir. 1999. "Database Protection at the Crossroads." *Berkeley Technology Law Journal*, 14:793.

Ryan, Michael P. 1998. *Knowledge Diplomacy: Global Competition and the Politics of Intellectual Property*. Washington, DC: Brookings Institution Press.

Samuelson, Pamela. 1990. "*Benson* Revisited: The Case Against Patent Protection for Algorithms and Other Computer Program-Related Inventions." *Emory Law Journal*, 39:1025.

———. 1997. "The U.S. Digital Agenda at WIPO." *Virginia Journal of International Law*, 37:369.

———. 1999. "Intellectual Property and the Digital Economy: Why the Anti-Circumvention Regulations Need to Be Revised." *Berkeley Technology Law Journal*, 14:519.

Samuelson, Pamela, Randall Davis, Mitchell D. Kapor, and J. H. Reichman. 1994. "A Manifesto on the Legal Protection of Computer Programs." *Columbia Law Review*, 94:2308, 2361–64.

Samuelson, Pamela, and Kurt Opsahl. 1999. "Licensing Information in the Global Information Market: Freedom of Contract Meets Public Policy." *European Intellectual Property Review*, 21:386.

Schwartz, Paul M., and Joel R. Reidenberg. 1996. *Data Privacy Law*. Charlottesville, VA: Michie Press.

Steindel, Charles, and Kevin J. Stiroh. 2001. "Productivity: What Is It and Why Do We Care?" (April 12). Available at http://www.ny.frb.org/rmaghome/staff_rp/2001/sr122.pdf.

Stern, Jonathan E. 2001. "The Electronic Signatures in Global and National Commerce Act." *Berkeley Technology Law Journal*, 16:391.

Stiroh, Kevin. 2001. "Information Technology and the U.S. Productivity Revival: What Do the Industry Data Say?" *Federal Reserve Bank of New York Staff Report Number 115*. Available at: http://www.ny.frb.org/rmaghome/economist/stiroh/papers.html.

Swire, Peter P., and Robert E. Litan. 1998. *None of Your Business: World Data Flows, Electronic Commerce, and the European Privacy Directive*. Washington, DC: Brookings Institution Press.

Thomas, John R. 1999. The Patenting of the Liberal Profession. *Boston College Law Review*, 40: 1139.

Tyson, Laura D'Andrea, and Edward Sherry. 1997. "Statutory Protection for Databases," in Hearings on H.R. 2652 Before the Subcommittee on Courts and Intellectual Property of the House Committee on the Judiciary, 105th Congress.

U.S. Department of Commerce. 1997. "Privacy and Self-Regulation in the Information Age." Available at http://www.ntia.doc.gov/reports/privacy_rpt.htm.

———. 2000. "International Safe Harbor Privacy Principles." Available at http://www.ita.doc.gov/ecom/shprin.html.

Comments

Martin N. Baily

This is a very good chapter. There were places where the authors were a little hard on the Clinton administration and places where they may have been a little too easy on the administration. The main issue that I disagreed with, and that I will talk most about, is productivity. The title of the chapter, "Information Policy," is a little different from the title of the session, which invokes the new economy. And the relatively brief treatment that the authors give to the acceleration of productivity implies that this was not a big deal. I will argue that productivity is a key element in the emergence of what people are calling the new economy.

Before turning to that topic, however, I will start with three specific topics developed in the paper itself. First, the paper would benefit from a more developed discussion of the life sciences sector, a sector that has become an information technology sector. The human genome project, the growth of biotech, and the incorporation of information technology into biotech were major developments in the 1990s. This sector was helped by Clinton administration policies, including greater certainty on the regulatory side, faster FDA approval for biotech and drug products, and better patent protection in that area.

The second specific issue from the paper is the discussion of R&D and related policies. One thing the administration tried to do—and sometimes it was not able to enact the policies that it wanted—was to develop a comprehensive approach to R&D policy. This comprehensive approach included tax credits for private R&D; direct spending by agencies, the Department of Defense, and others; and grants to universities and to the Advanced Technology Program (ATP) or the National Institutes of Health (NIH).

This approach tried to avoid using the technology budget only to increase spending at NIH or on health research. It is vital to make sure there are sufficient funds for other areas, including developments in basic science. In the end, developments in basic science are essential to enhance R&D in health care and other applied areas. In other words, the comprehensive approach attempted

to make sure there were multiple options that encouraged R&D in the private
sector, encouraged the demand for technology by agencies, and provided direct
grants for basic and precommercial R&D. This triple push was seen as the best
way to push technology forward.

The third point from the paper is on the issue of pooling. The authors argue
that there is a clear-cut case for using the purchase method of accounting rather
than the pooling method. I think the case is far from clear-cut. Many companies
today, especially technology companies, have market values that are much
higher than, indeed bear little relation to, the value of their tangible assets. They
are valued for their intangible assets, including patents, technological knowledge, brands, and so on. These intangible assets have been acquired through
investments in R&D, business system development, and advertising, which
were all expensed at the time they were incurred. In other words, the investment to create the intangible assets has already been depreciated once.

Consider the case of a software company valued for its intangible assets.
Under the purchase method, supported by Samuelson and Varian, a company
that acquires this software company must depreciate the value of the company,
including the value of its intangible technology assets. Given that the software
company is presumably continuing to invest in upgrading its software business
and is expensing the costs of doing this, the result could well be that the acquisition adds little or nothing to the reported profit of the combined company.
A thriving software company that was quite profitable operating on its own is
now reported as a zero-profit activity within a large company after acquisition.
That hardly seems like a good way to inform investors of what is going on.

I recognize that there are two sides to this story, and the authors present the
other side. Moreover, I recognize that there are concerns about inconsistency, if
some companies use the purchase method and others the pooling method. But
from an economic point of view, there is a case for the pooling approach. Fortunately, the evidence is that investors are able to pierce the accounting veil
and in practice value companies about the same regardless of the accounting
approach used.

I am now going to talk about the issue of the increase in productivity growth
and the new economy. I will draw on the material that was in the *Economic
Report of the President* (ERP) this January or in the NBER paper that Robert Lawrence and I put out. First, did a new economy develop? We argued that it did,
and this argument was based, first, on the fact that in the 1990s expansion there
was unusually rapid growth of real GDP, including very fast growth in the four
years 1997 to 2000. Second, there was an unusual combination of low unemployment and low inflation. Third, there were rapid increases in family incomes
and reductions of poverty. Fourth, there was a sustained and large increase in

the market value of U.S. corporations. And perhaps most important, there was a sharp acceleration of productivity that took place after 1995 that was linked to information technology.

The use of the term "new economy" has its pitfalls. To some people it implies a complete transformation of the economy or a complete change in the rules of economics, neither of which is correct. Moreover, it suggests that the acceleration of productivity is permanent, whereas in fact there is great uncertainty about the likely duration of the productivity surge. Some of the indicators of a new economy have been around for a while, but the increase in productivity growth has only lasted five years.

Despite these misgivings, I continue to use the term "new economy," along with many other economists. It appears that during the last long expansion, the forces of globalization, information technology development, and heightened competition have resulted in a much more efficient and productive economy. Improved performance in computer hardware, software, and telecommunications are changing the way old economy companies are doing business.

One obvious approach to understanding the changes that took place is to carry out a growth-accounting exercise to figure out what caused the productivity acceleration. I have been comparing the estimates made by Steve Oliner and Dan Sichel, by Robert Gordon, by Dale Jorgenson and Kevin Stiroh, and in the ERP. There are important differences in approach and results, but also similarities. Everyone agrees that the high-tech sector was a key contributor, both because its own productivity accelerated and because the resulting decline in computer prices fueled a wave of capital deepening. There is little agreement as to the extent to which the productivity surge was cyclical. As the ERP reported, we found that there was only a very small cyclical effect, based on the typical pattern of productivity over a business cycle. Gordon disagrees. But my current view is that some of the productivity surge was probably temporary, the result of unusually favorable circumstances, especially in 2000. So despite the disagreements on this issue, Gordon and I get to similar points. The other authors do not make specific cyclical adjustments. The bottom line that remains is the residual estimate that a portion of the productivity acceleration was attributable to an increase in the rate of multifactor productivity (MFP) growth in the broad or noncomputer part of the economy.

In interpreting the results of this growth decomposition, the aspect where I disagree most with other writers is in describing the drivers of change. There is sometimes an implication that there is a mechanical link running from faster MFP growth in the computer sector (exogenously occurring), to capital deepening, to faster labor productivity growth in the rest of the economy. That mechanical connection does not exist. The ability of traditional industries to make productive use of new technology was something new. It required a revamping of business systems in order to take advantage of the technology. The current authors discussed this point, and the work of Eric Brynjolffson points in this direction. It says that if companies just acquire the hardware, that doesn't do much.

I would even go further. There is a sense in which the growth and innovativeness of the high-tech sector and the extent of capital deepening in the economy were driven by the effect of powerful competitive forces, as well as the forces of globalization that were occurring in the rest of the economy. If there is a conventional wisdom that the productivity surge started in high tech and that drove the rest of the economy, I might try and turn that around: The demand for best practices. The demand for innovation. The demand to improve productivity. The competitive pressure to expand the range of services being offered. These were driven by a highly competitive, globalizing economy, the bulk of which is in the service sector, and which then encouraged innovation in the high-tech economy.

I recognize that the technological opportunities in the high-tech sector had to be there, and obviously you had to have the brilliant people that had the innovative ideas. And the decline in the prices of high-tech goods was an essential part of the story. But the growth of the new economy was a two-way street involving the traditional and the high-tech parts of the economy.

To what extent was the emergence of the new economy linked to the policies of the Clinton administration, or more broadly to economic policies during the 1990s? The first important policy drivers of the strong overall economic performance are fiscal and monetary policy, both of which helped substantially. Fiscal discipline shifted the federal budget from large deficits to surpluses. And then monetary policy was made in a way that accommodated the more rapid growth of the U.S. economy that took place after 1995. There was a favorable fiscal policy, monetary policy mix that kept interest rates down and encouraged rapid growth. Those policies did not create the new economy, but bad fiscal and monetary policy could easily have aborted some of the benefits of the strong investment. And this in turn could have hampered the development and availability of new technologies.

On the technology side, the funding for research was helpful in supporting investment in basic research to the extent possible under the budget conditions that prevailed. Doing more would have helped more, but that was not possible. And in the event, the private sector provided its own rapid increases in R&D funding.

The policies to increase educational opportunities were important. To a degree they contributed to the availability of the skilled workers needed in the new economy. But I want to put the education and training initiatives into a broader context. These comments may get too much into political economy for the taste of those of you around the room. But I think the broader context is important. President Clinton and Vice President Gore both embraced the new economy, and they embraced the idea that economic change was going to take place. This meant that workers were not necessarily able to stay forever in the same jobs they currently had. Workers could no longer expect to maintain lifetime employment in a particular place. Companies were going to rise and fall.

There were some missteps in the embrace of change. The political pressures can be very extreme from communities where a plant is closing or shedding workers. In particular, the pressure for trade restraint becomes very great if trade is the source of the economic change, or is perceived to be the source. But despite these missteps, the overall thrust of the policy dialogue that took place in the administration was supportive of technology and the new economy.

One might argue that another administration would have been just as good at embracing change. But the difference is that the Clinton administration also supported policies like the EITC and increased education and training opportunities. It supported concern for the environment. Doing these things made economic change and adjustment more acceptable to the population at large. The president could say to people, yes you may lose your job here, but we're going to create educational opportunities for you to get a new job and potentially a better job.

The administration in the 1990s had to baby-sit the economy into the 21st century, and I would draw a contrast here between the United States and the other developed economies of Europe and Japan. The policy dialogue there is very different. It is much more about preserving the existing structure of industries and jobs. Yes the new economy is fine, but only as long as it does not disrupt the old economy. The end result has been much less benefit from the new economy, and slower growth. GDP per capita in the European Union is 69 percent of the U.S. level. It's 74 percent in Japan. A key reason for this difference is the unwillingness to embrace change in the way that this past U.S. administration has done.

Finally, I will comment on the future prospects for the new economy. It is perhaps foolish to prognosticate, given that much more will be known at the time these comments are published. But it may be useful to look back and see how the future appeared from this vantage point. I am optimistic that the U.S. economy will recover from its current slowdown in pretty short order, maybe by the end of 2001, and if not, by mid-2002. The forces that drove the strong performance of the economy in the 1990s are largely still in place. The technology still has a way to run, and the forces of globalization and competition are still very much in play. I would expect to see a trend of labor productivity around 2 to 2.5 percent emerging in the future. This estimate is made with great uncertainty, and most of the risks are on the downside. Productivity growth could return to its old level of 1.4 percent a year (I guess that covers me from future ridicule).

Given this uncertainty, I am concerned that fiscal policy has shifted. Even if there is good news on long-term growth, the long-run fiscal position of the U.S. economy is not good, given the retirement of the baby boom generation. Moreover it is a mistake to lower national saving at a time when the current-account deficit is so large. If the news on long-run productivity and growth is not so good, then on-budget deficits are very likely to occur. Fiscal discipline was one of the great policy achievements of U.S. economic policy in the 1990s. It will be sad if it is a casualty of the first decade of the new century.

Comments

Esther Dyson

I'd like to start by taking just a minute to explain who I am. On such a panel of distinguished economists and academics and policy makers, I'm more a specimen than an articulate academic observer.

I got into this subject thinking that the most benign policy the administration, any administration, could have for the Internet would simply be neglect. And I'd argue that to a large extent that was true for the commercialization of the Internet. But I have since learned a lot from two things. One was going to Russia and seeing what a market is like when there really is no policy and no regulation, no controls, no rules for disclosure. Any leanings I had toward complete libertarianism were completely smashed by my experience in Russia.

The second was that, without really meaning to be, I was quite involved with the administration's efforts in this area. It started (for me) with the National Information Infrastructure Advisory Council, which was indeed the body that told Al Gore, who was the person designated to listen to us, that by and large the best policies were to leave this thing alone, and just let it grow and commercialize. But there were some issues that were going to come up: content control and trying to avoid it, privacy issues, copyright, and so on.

Then later on I joined a little informal group that Ira Magaziner assembled to help him as he thought about what the Clinton administration should do about the Internet. Eventually, he produced the "Framework for Global Electronic Commerce" paper that is described in this chapter. Some of it had to do with privacy, and some of it had to do with the government's administration of the domain name system, the Internet's infrastructure.

This Internet infrastructure thing struck me as being very complicated and full of opposing parties who all hated each other. Ira's idea—and there's an interesting question, Would a Republican administration have done the same thing?—Ira's idea was that the U.S. government should not be running the infrastructure of the Internet. Because after all, it wasn't something that America owned. It was now at this point worldwide. Most of its constituent parts, at least in the United States, were owned by the private sector. Thus, he thought, this thing should be governed by the Internet community itself. That was a combination of some notion of let the market do it with an incredible idealism which unfortunately was probably overoptimistic. When Ira put out this paper and said, "Let's let the DNS be run by the Internet community," all hell broke loose.

The academics thought it was some kind of commercialization plot. The engineers thought it was an attempt to wrest the Holy Grail from their hands and hand it over to unwashed idiots. A lot of the U.S. Congress people thought it was a plot to give away an American birthright to a bunch of dirty foreigners. And the dirty foreigners thought the U.S. government was absolutely nuts— but if it didn't want to run the Internet, they would be happy to take over the task.

(There are some fundamental principles at the bottom of all this. This whole thing is poorly understood, and it's unfortunate that it is. What Ira tried to do was in fact very clever—probably so clever that nobody could understand it.)

The first thing is, ICANN is nothing like the ITU or the WTO or any of these other organizations you've heard of. Because those are all treaty organizations. They are set up by treaties between governments. One way or the other they inherit the statutory authority of the governments that created them. Ira's idea was quite different. He said, we want the Internet community to do it themselves. You guys create something that's legitimate. And then the U.S. government will hand it over.

One big problem with ICANN is that people keep asking, Where's the legitimacy? Who appointed you? Ironically you could argue—I'm sure this has been done in many academic circles—that no power is legitimate. You could certainly ask, Well, where did the U.S. government get the power or the authority to run this thing? As you read in the paper correctly, it was being administered under a contract with the U.S. government. There was the National Science Foundation (NSF); there was the Defense Research Projects Agency (DARPA). There was a guy called John Postel, who unfortunately died in September or October of 1998, just as ICANN was formed. He had moral legitimacy to make the policies. Everybody on the Internet trusted him. He was clearly a disinterested party concerned only for the public welfare. He was wise. He had hair down to the bottom of his back. (Ira loved taking him to the White House mess for lunch because it caused a stir each time.) Unfortunately, the idea of legitimacy due to being created by the Internet community turned out to be something of a fiction because the Internet community itself never came to much of a consensus. But it was very specifically not created by the U.S. Department of Commerce. It was instigated by it.

That's a fine distinction, but in the annals of ICANN history it's a very important one. In theory at least, ICANN should have as much legitimacy as the government of the United States did when it was created, because it was indeed created bottom-up by the people who decided to create it.

The other distinction is that ICANN is not in fact a government. It doesn't control people. It controls resources. It's something like a waterworks. But of course it runs into a lot of political and economic and commercial implications, because it controls the domain name system. It does in fact administer resources worldwide. And that fact led to the second problem it ran into: Ira's notions of liberty and freedom, accountability, openness, and so forth were not shared by a lot of people in other countries—and specifically not by their governments, most of whom couldn't really understand this notion of bottom-up governance.

So in theory at least, ICANN should be more legitimate than almost any government around. In practice it had an appointed board of which I was one of the members. I became chairman of it because no one else was crazy enough to take on that job. ICANN exerts its authority by contract, not by statute. Its initial challenge was to redo the U.S. government's contract with Network Solutions, which, as you read in the chapter, was a monopoly contract.

It's an interesting question whether a monopoly that you earn in whatever fashion, as Microsoft did, is better or worse than a monopoly you get through a contract that you don't necessarily earn. In either case, Network Solutions was widely considered to be close to abusing its monopoly. It was making huge profits and providing rather poor service. ICANN's initial goal was simply to try to eliminate Network Solutions' monopoly. In the United States, in contrast to many other countries, if you have a contract with the government, you can hang onto it. You don't have to give it up if the government comes to you quietly in a smoke-filled room and tells you, sorry, things have changed. Accordingly, Network Solutions fought bitterly and hard over the renegotiation of this contract, which finally concluded about a year after ICANN was created.

Meanwhile, ICANN created competition, as the chapter said, in the retail service business of registration of names, but not in the wholesale business of maintaining the registry of those names. Now, in the second phase, ICANN is creating competition for the NSI registry, with a new set of domain names coming up.

I don't want to go into too much more detail, but all we've got so far is halfway competition—a very unstable transition. Because there's now competition for dot com, but it's not very effective. What they've done is essentially to duplicate the domain space, rather than carve it up into new space by creating a new space for dot air or dot banks or something like that. So you still have the problem of a word like United. United dot biz, United dot com could refer to anything, whereas if you had United dot air, it would be more useful.

So if you look at this not as a U.S. policy decision but as the result of U.S. policy decisions, I'd say the result so far has been imperfect. Still, it's going in the right direction. It's one of the most interesting and innovative things to happen in governance around the turn of the century. It foreshadows some of the fundamental questions we're going to face as a world, not just a government.

How do you manage and allocate worldwide resources? Here we need to consider not just the impact of the government of the Net, but the impact of the Net on governments. What you're seeing is the creation of new jurisdictions that extend across political boundaries. They don't extend vertically; they don't cover everybody's behavior. But they extend horizontally across countries, and they cover specific kinds of behavior or specific resources worldwide. In this case particularly, they're dealing with intellectual property laws that apply to domain names, which of course intersect with and frequently conflict with trademark laws.

Five, ten, fifteen years ago, it was common for rich people to change their domiciles for tax reasons. Now it's getting easier and easier to do so because of the Internet. If you're a business, you may want to change your business domicile, so to speak, for reasons of the kind of content you produce: whether you offer gambling services, the delivery of spam to people, all kinds of things. We need to figure out ways to deal with some of these questions. Most of the answers, I would argue, are some form of private-sector governance, rules that apply to a specific domain and jurisdiction. People enter those voluntarily, because they want the benefits of the regulation there.

Much as right now, foreign companies will come to the United States to raise money—not so much because they want to be regulated by the SEC, but because they want to reach the investors who are regulated by the SEC. They want the level of prices that companies can get in securities markets where fair disclosure is the norm.

Now, very briefly on privacy, I foolishly believed that it should be left up to consumers and disclosure. I still think so in principle. But in practice, I think what's necessary to make privacy and disclosure work is much greater involvement by the financial sector. That means, first, disclosure requirements for public companies, so they include in their financial statements representations about their privacy practices and their security policies, and second, getting insurance companies to start paying a lot more attention to security and data protection. Probably the most important thing to make that happen is the establishment of visible precedents of liability where there have been security or privacy breaches. You are probably going to see that happen soon.

Comments

Paul Romer

This chapter is a survey of key policy issues in the area of information technology and a history of the events from the 1990s that brought us to where we are today. A quick look back at recent history is helpful when you are trying to keep track of a rapidly changing field such as information technology. Remember the Clipper Chip, proposed back in 1994 as the government's solution to the conflict between privacy and law enforcement? If you blinked you might have missed it.

The chapter also reminds us of how different the world seemed as recently as the mid-1990s. Both the Clinton administration, in preparing its National Information Infrastructure Initiative, and Jim Clark and Marc Andreessen of Netscape, in their initial business plans, assumed that the killer application of the networked economy would be interactive television. So just six years ago, no one had any sense of how people would actually be using digital communications networks at the beginning of the 21st century.

Events of the past sometimes look as if they were inevitable. For example, we sometimes write and speak as if it had been preordained that cheaper transistors, hard disks, and bandwidth would bring us to where we are today. The clarity of hindsight tempts us to overestimate our ability to see into the future. Thinking back to 1995 should help us resist this temptation. When we look back in 2007 we will probably remark that in 2001, no one had any clear understanding of what will then seem like an inevitable set of developments.

Overview

The chapter begins with a quick history of the Internet and a discussion of the National Information Infrastructure Initiative. Then it sets up the issue of the "new economy" and adopts a sensible "wait and see" stance. The most widely cited new-economy claim is that the trend rate of growth has permanently

increased. The basic statistical reality is that we will not know what, if anything, has happened to long-run trends until more time has passed. From a
theoretical point of view, the more interesting and important claim is that the
information technology revolution caused the conjectured increase in the trend
rate of growth. If our experience with the productivity slowdown of the 1970s
and 1980s is any guide, even if it becomes clear that the trend rate of growth
has increased, we may never be able to say with confidence what caused this
change.

The chapter then moves through a series of subtopics: research and development, financial markets, governance of the Internet, taxation, intellectual property, commercial law, security, privacy, and content regulation. To cover all of
them, the chapter has to move quickly. I won't even try to comment on all of
them. I want to focus on just one, R&D.

Government Support for Technology

When we look back at the 1990s, we should be troubled by the weak government support for R&D.

During this decade, the public became increasingly aware of the importance
of technological developments, as news outlets brought into common parlance
such topics as the progress of Moore's law for transistors and the dramatic
improvements in data storage and digital communications. The media also
covered new software applications and the business opportunities the hardware and software made possible. The public seems to have grasped more fully
than ever the basic lesson about long-run economic performance: New technologies create profit opportunities and raise standards of living. Economists
agree that such innovations as cheaper bandwidth, transistors, and hard disks
offer returns to society that are substantially larger than the returns captured
by private investors. They recognize that government support for science and
technology can therefore lead to important increases in the public welfare.
In 1993 the Clinton administration came into office convinced that the government could play a constructive role in fostering the development of new technologies. Then, through a combination of good luck and good policy (pick your
own weights), Clinton presided over a remarkably long and stable economic
expansion.

Given all these favorable circumstances, one might have thought that we
would make substantial progress toward increased government support for
research and development. If science and technology could generate such dramatic benefits in information technology, why not try to get more benefits where
these came from?

In fact, as the chapter reports, government spending on R&D increased very little in the 1990s. If you look carefully, the numbers are even worse than the chapter suggests. If you eliminate spending on medical research by the NIH, the rest of R&D grew in real terms by only a couple of percent between 1994 and 2001. Furthermore, a glance at the proposed 2002 numbers from the Bush administration shows that R&D spending outside of medical research will drop back to where it was in 1994.

Stop for a moment and examine the special treatment that medical research received during the 1990s and continues to receive under the new administration. This is important for my argument. If you believe that the returns from medical research are higher than returns in other areas of science and technology, it may have been a reasonable strategy to increase spending more rapidly there. Increased support for R&D targeted on biomedicine could be interpreted as a sign of continued overall support for government spending on R&D.

In contrast, if you believe, as I do, that growth in spending on biomedical research is the result of a unique political dynamic, one that is driven by the evident suffering of people with the "disease of the month," then spending there is not a sign of a broad base of support for R&D spending that is matched with a careful judgment about where highest scientific returns lie. You are then left with the challenge of explaining why an administration determined to encourage technological progress was unable to marshal additional resources in support of R&D at a time when the economy was booming and the public was unusually appreciative of the role that technology plays in sustaining economic growth. And why the new Bush administration should feel compelled, as one of its first acts in office, to cut real spending in the nonmedical part of the R&D portfolio.

The Morrill Era

To understand these puzzling developments, we need to look at the 1990s from a much longer historical perspective.

Begin in 1862 with the passage of the Morrill Act, named for Senator Justin Morrill of Vermont. This law gave federal land to the states for the establishment of colleges that came to be known as the land grant schools. The language of the act stipulated that at these colleges "the leading object shall be ... to teach such branches of learning as are related to agriculture and the mechanic arts." Because of the act's clear utilitarian focus, these schools did not push the United States to the forefront of basic science. But they did dramatically increase the supply of skilled workers and engineers who could put the new technologies of the era to use.

Farmers who used new seed varieties and new cultivation methods; manufacturers that assembled goods from interchangeable parts; railroads that deployed new types of rails, engines, and rolling stock; electrical utilities that built the first generating plants and transmission networks; petrochemical refiners that supplied the fuel for lighting and the automotive industry—none of these groups relied on scientists who were working at the cutting edge of basic research. Good thing too, because until World War II, the United States had hardly any of these researchers. What America wanted then was engineers trained in the practical application of the new technologies of the day, people who were ready to put their knowledge to work exploiting emerging commercial opportunities. In what I have labeled the Morrill era of science and technology policy, the states and the federal government supported technology-driven economic growth in the private sector by subsidizing the production of human capital.

The Bush Era

Jump forward to the years after World War II, to the Bush era in science and technology policy. Not the George H. W. Bush era. Nor the George W. Bush era. The Vannevar Bush era. In his report for President Franklin D. Roosevelt, "The Endless Frontier," Vannevar Bush, the head of the Office of Scientific Research and Development during World War II, articulated an entirely different vision from the one that guided Senator Morrill. Morrill wanted the government to subsidize the production of human capital. Bush wanted to subsidize basic research.

Bush outlined what has come to be called the linear model of research, wherein the path from science to the economy is like an assembly line. Things start with basic scientists who follow their curiosity with no regard for practical application. They put new insights on the beginning of the conveyor belt. Down the line, applied scientists take these general insights and look for ways to put them to use. In the last stage, people working for private firms convert applied science into new goods and better production processes. In this vision, the discovery of new basic scientific insights is the rate-limiting step in the innovation process. The government, Bush suggested, could best encourage economic growth and other practical benefits by subsidizing basic scientific research on university campuses and in government laboratories.

U.S. practice did not conform immediately to the Bush prescription, nor did it ever conform fully. For example, the Department of Defense developed a notion of "mission-oriented basic research" that could not exist in Bush's model. For Bush, basic research was defined by the absence of any concern for possible application. But in the decades after World War II, the balance of funding did shift toward the kind of curiosity-driven basic science that Bush advocated, and the Bush vision became the guiding ideology for government support of science and technology.

The Battle During the 1990s

By the 1980s, scholarly criticism of the linear model of science and technology became too loud to ignore. Vannevar Bush's vision misses many important pathways in the innovation process. In particular, there were too many cases where new technologies emerged first in the private sector and academic science came along later to figure out what was going on. The transistor, the key to the entire digital information revolution, emerged from inside the Bell telephone system. Technologists in the phone company realized that it would take lots of amplifiers to run a network that stretched across the continent. They searched for a way to build them without using the unreliable vacuum tube. University-based physics professors did not think improving the reliability of amplifiers was an important basic research challenge. The people working on this problem did, nevertheless, win a Nobel Prize. The subsequent growth of university-based solid-state physics was caused by the discovery of the transistor, not the other way around.

As it became clear that important new technologies could emerge from innovation in the private sector, people began to suggest that the government should do more to subsidize innovative activity in that realm. This suggestion received extra impetus from the difficulties that the U.S. manufacturing sector experienced in the 1980s and from the perception that Germany and Japan were benefiting from a much more interventionist technology policy. In retrospect, the advantage enjoyed by the manufacturers from these other countries probably had more to do with an overvalued dollar than wise government leadership of their industries. But in the early years of the 1990s, many people still believed that manufacturing in the United States would be doomed if we stuck with a policy of laissez-faire, and that government-led technology policy would guide Japan and Germany to positions of world economic and technological leadership.

This was the backdrop when the Clinton administration took office. The new administration seems to have understood that there is a logical justification for government support of innovation in the private sector as well as in the university and the government lab. They also seem to have been swayed by the example of mission-oriented research carried out by Defense Advanced Research Projects Agency (DARPA) in the Department of Defense. DARPA had produced important practical benefits for the economy, the most obvious of which was the Internet. Also, the Clintonites were almost certainly influenced by angst about the survival of manufacturing in the United States and the arguments coming out of the 1980s in favor of a more active government role in technology policy.

The new administration set aggressive goals for creating new government technology programs and expanding existing programs. These programs were explicitly designed to support innovation at private-sector firms. The highest-profile approach was the Advanced Technology Program (ATP) in the Department of Commerce. This program directly funded research proposals from private firms. In addition, the Clinton administration expanded the Small Business Innovative Research Grant program, which also gave government funds directly to private firms. It created the Partnership for the Next Generation of Vehicles (PNGV), which provided support to the automotive industry through the Department of Energy, the Department of Commerce, and a variety of other government agencies.

The amount of money involved in this little-noticed program was not small. ATP received funding of $142 million in fiscal year 2000. That same year, the Department of Energy spent $128 million on PNGV.

These kinds of programs were controversial when they were first discussed in the late 1980s. They become even more contentious when the Clinton administration decided to press ahead and implement them despite the misgivings that many people felt about programs that were targeted so explicitly at helping specific firms.

When the Republicans took control of the House under Newt Gingrich in 1994, one of their key policy initiatives was to cut these programs back. The ATP program became a key symbolic target. Throughout the 1990s, Republicans pushed repeatedly to abolish it. Although they did not succeed immediately, they did manage to cut funding back from the ambitious expansion path that the Clinton administration had outlined.

The Republicans won the larger political and public relations battle about the direction of science policy. Groups such as Ralph Nader's Public Citizen now attack the ATP program as a form of corporate welfare. In 1998 the House Science Committee, with the backing of such mainstream groups as the Committee on Economic Development, issued its report "Unlocking Our Future: Toward a New National Science Policy." It articulated the new consensus. It explicitly stated that "there is a risk that using federal funds to bridge the mid-level research gap could lead to unwarranted market interventions and less funding for basic research." It also said that priority for federal funding should be placed on "fundamental" or "understanding-driven" research.

The Clinton effort to create a new vision of technology policy failed. Policy-makers retreated to the Vannevar Bush prescription for science policy.

Why Did Support for R&D Stagnate?

In the debate during the 1990s over the direction of government science policy, the traditional bipartisan coalition in favor of government support for research and development fractured. Many of the research initiatives sponsored by the Clinton administration were tainted by suspicions that they supported a hidden industrial policy agenda or suffered from bad blood from fights over programs that did. Research funding outside of medical research stagnated. Meanwhile, in medicine, Congress routinely added more funding than the administration asked for.

The pressure created by spending caps surely contributed to slow growth in all areas of discretionary spending, but as the example of support for medical research suggests, growth in the overall R&D budget would still have been possible had it been backed by a strong bipartisan coalition.

The aftershocks from the battle over science policy continue to be felt today. When the George W. Bush administration took office in 2001, it zeroed out funding for new research projects by ATP, pending a review of the program, and it proposed cuts in many research programs (notably in the Department of Energy) or increases that were smaller than inflation. Only funding for medical research continued to grow.

Missed Opportunity

In addition to the stagnant funding for R&D, another telling statistic from the 1990s is worth a mention. In the mid-1980s, more than 40,000 computer science majors graduated each year from undergraduate institutions. After the Clinton administration took office in 1992, this number fell below 25,000 majors per year.

Unfortunately, many policy-makers seem to have ignored the fact that it would take people, actual human beings, to carry forward the information technology revolution. When business firms began clamoring for more skilled workers in the late 1990s, the Clinton administration and Congress did work together to raise the number of temporary visas that the United States could issue to foreign workers. The 1998 report by the House Science Committee also pointed to the widening gap between the demand for skilled workers in the marketplace and the supply produced by our educational system. But neither the Republicans, speaking through this report, nor the Democrats, as represented by the Clinton administration, offer any concrete steps that the federal government could take to resolve the shortage of skilled talent.

Things might have turned out differently if the Clinton administration had pushed science policy in United States back toward its 19th-century roots. It could have pushed toward Justin Morrill's emphasis on government support for the training of highly skilled human capital and away from Vannevar Bush's exclusive focus on support for research projects carried out by university professors. It did not have to turn toward the problematic new vision of powerful civilian technology agencies modeled on DARPA.

Instead of giving grants to firms, the government could have supported more students. As the Morrill era suggests, subsidies for human capital can be an effective way to encourage technological development in the private sector, precisely the goal that the Clinton administration wanted to achieve. Subsidies for students do not raise the many troubling questions that sprang from the administration's chosen programs: Can the government pick the right firms to fund? Will lobbying and campaign contributions begin to influence which firm is supported? How can the government draw distinctions between U.S. firms (which are supposed to get help) and excluded foreign firms (which are not). In the Partnership for the Next Generation Vehicle, Mercedes Benz eventually bought its way in alongside GM and Ford. None of these companies is selling the type of hybrid electric car that PNGV was supposed to foster. Honda and Toyota continue to be excluded but have already managed to introduce their own hybrids anyway.

The land grant university system was a powerful driver of economic growth in the first part of the 20th century. A renewed commitment to its goal of training more people might have slowed the splintering of the bipartisan coalition that supported science through the end of the cold war. It would have left us in a stronger scientific, economic, and technological position as we move into the 21st century.

William Niskanen asked why the White House had assigned Ira Magaziner to write the framework report on information technologies. He also asked about Magaziner's "dramatic conversion" from the interventionist perspective that was reflected in the 1993 health care proposal.

Esther Dyson, who noted that she had known Magaziner for 15 to 20 years, explained that he may have learned something from his 1993 experience in health care policy, particularly about the importance of openness and transparency. She also noted that, according to Magaziner, health care involved significantly different issues (in particular, regarding social welfare) than did the Internet.

Hal Varian added that another lesson that Magaziner learned is that less is more. Varian added that the Clinton administration's handling of the Internet was, in general, relatively good.

Bill Hogan asked about self-regulation. He expressed skepticism based on two cases, the gas industry standards board in the United States and the experience in New Zealand. He attributed the success of the former to its avoidance of dealing with hard problems, which it left to official regulators. In New Zealand, he argued, the numerous self-regulatory bodies are actually reinforced by significant, albeit not entirely transparent, government intervention. He was therefore skeptical about the prospects for success with self-regulation, especially in a large group with no carefully identified and common interests.

Dyson responded to the question by noting that ICANN was de facto a monopoly. She also suggested two flaws in the ICANN structure. First, the contracts ICANN is currently signing with domain name registries are too intrusive: They control too much of the firms' business plans. Second, ICANN's contracts do not effectively address consumer protection issues, an area that she believes ICANN will have to address in the future.

Joseph P. Newhouse then asked Hal Varian why productivity growth in durables could be so different than in nondurables. Newhouse observed that price indexes for the services sector are often inaccurate and suggested that productivity may be growing even faster than we think it is. *Varian* clarified that he was only looking at manufacturing. He also agreed that in the area of services, measurement problems are severe.

Martin Baily noted that if you look at the Bureau of Economic Analysis's data on gross output originating by industry, you find quite a substantial acceleration of labor productivity in service industries. In fact, Baily said, labor productivity growth rose by more in the service sector than in the goods sector, although the goods-producing sector includes both durables and nondurables. He then noted that data from the Bureau of Labor Statistics tell a slightly different story, but concluded that there were some signs of improvement in productivity in services industry. In the case of medical care, he explained that productivity growth went from a substantial negative number to a smaller negative number. In many other service industries, particularly wholesale and retail trade and financial services, very substantial increments to productivity growth occurred.

Baily also stated that while he understood the difficulties inherent in the term "new economy," we must not lose sight of the spectacular economic performance in the 1990s, particularly during the period after 1995. Baily urged that although we may not like the term "new economy," a lot depends on whether strong productivity growth continues or not.

Alice Rivlin raised the issue of the digital divide. She asked the panelists about the potential for closing the digital divide and for the use of the Internet in education. *Pamela Samuelson* explained that the chapter for the session framed the information-policy issues based on the Magaziner reports, which did not mention the digital divide until the second or third annual report. She observed that there was more rhetoric than actual policy in this area, with the exception of the e-rate program and the efforts to connect schools to the Internet.

Dyson expressed her view that the productivity gains in the United States are not necessarily due to computers, but rather to how people use computers, the openness of the American economy, and the education of American workers. She contended that the digital divide led people astray and that the real issue was education, on the one hand, and marketplace culture, on the other. She noted that Europe did not experience the same kind of productivity gains as the United States, even though Europeans had access to the same technology. The reason for the difference, according to Dyson, is the U.S. market culture.

Robert Samuelson then asked Paul Romer to elaborate on his proposal for the government to subsidize the development of human capital. Samuelson expressed puzzlement because, to his knowledge, the government already subsidized college education. He asked why more students don't become scientists and engineers, and, if we think it is desirable in a social sense that they do, how far should we go in either subsidizing them or coercing them to do so.

Paul Romer responded by highlighting a peculiar feature of universities in the United States: the institution does not collect more revenue if it sends a student through a more expensive as opposed to a less expensive training program. He contrasted the United States with other countries, in which governments allocate more money to universities that train people on an engineering track than on a humanities track.

Romer then argued that because of the incentives created by our system of funding, U.S. institutions are structured to deter students who enroll with a desire to study science from continuing along those tracks. He asserted that cost considerations are reinforced by an elitist view that only a select few should continue along the science path. Romer concluded by arguing that the ultimate rationale for encouraging more science and engineering training is to increase the supply of inputs into innovative activity. Because the social return to innovation is higher than the private return, the market will encourage too few people to acquire the scientific and engineering training needed to be on the cutting edge of discovery. If society wants more innovation, it will have to have train more innovators.

7 Industrial Organization

Antitrust Policy in the Clinton Administration

Robert E. Litan and Carl Shapiro

PANELISTS: *Robert Pitofsky, Richard Schmalensee, and Robert Willig*

7.1 Introduction

For at least 20 years a broad, bipartisan consensus has prevailed regarding the goal of U.S. antitrust policy: to foster competitive markets and to control monopoly power, not to protect smaller firms from tough competition by larger corporations. The interests of consumers in lower prices and improved products are paramount. When these interests are served by large, efficient firms, even firms with substantial shares of well-defined markets, the consensus view is that antitrust policy should applaud, not stand in the way. However, when those large and powerful firms wield their power to exclude rivals in unreasonable ways, antitrust policy should act to preserve competition, both on prices and regarding product improvements stemming from innovation. Since the 1970s these principles have been widely accepted, and antitrust law and policy have fundamentally been about economics—promoting competition and consumer benefits—not about broader social objectives such as favoring domestic firms, preserving employment, or protecting small businesses.

Within these confines, antitrust policy turned more activist during the Clinton years than in the prior Bush administration, and sharply more active than during the Reagan administration. To the general public, the most visible symbol of this activism was surely the Microsoft antitrust trial, which led in May

The authors are grateful for the very helpful comments and suggestions provided by the editors and by Robert Pitofsky.

2000 to a dramatic court order (largely upheld on appeal in June 2001) that Microsoft be broken up. To practicing antitrust lawyers and academicians who specialize in the field, the upturn in antitrust activity was evident in many more ways: in challenges to several large corporate mergers, in the uncovering and prosecution of some large national and international price-fixing conspiracies, and in the many active investigations of monopolization practices by dominant firms other than Microsoft.

To a significant extent, the enhanced activity reflected a more activist philosophy of the officials in charge of the two major federal antitrust enforcement agencies—the Antitrust Division of the Department of Justice (DOJ) and the Federal Trade Commission (FTC)—than was on display during the preceding 12 years. This statement was most clearly true of enforcement activity directed at various business practices of dominant firms, although an observable shift was also evident regarding certain proposed corporate marriages, especially in comparison with the second term of the Reagan administration.

The Microsoft case illustrates a key shift during the Clinton administration that explains in part the more aggressive approach taken at the DOJ and the FTC: greater attention was paid to long-term competition in the form of innovation, in comparison with the traditional focus of antitrust on shorter-term competition, namely pricing. We believe the increased emphasis on innovation can be attributed to the confluence of two fundamental factors.

First, the 1990s covered a period during which new technologies had a marked impact on a range of markets, with the Internet and information technology leading the way. Increasingly, the fruits of competition are seen in the form of new technologies that lead to new and improved products. At the same time, intellectual property rights, in the form of patents, copyrights, and trade secrets, increasingly have become a key source of competitive advantage for firms controlling such rights. How natural, then, that antitrust authorities have paid more attention to "innovation competition" and intellectual property rights.

Second, antitrust officials in the Clinton administration combined a willingness to predict the medium- to long-term effects of mergers and various commercial practices, a necessary element of enforcing the antitrust laws in the area of innovation, with a confidence that they could correct market failures in the realm of innovation. Unlike traditional pricing competition, the effects of which can be seen on a day-to-day basis and occur in the short term, innovation competition by its nature requires time to unfold and is far less amenable to quantification. Hence, the underlying philosophy of antitrust officials can greatly affect their actions (or inactions) in the area of innovation: the Clinton team's activism can be traced to its greater confidence regarding the ability of government officials to predict future outcomes in markets subject to technological change, along with greater skepticism that markets will correct problems over time and greater suspicion regarding the strategies employed by large or dominant firms.

Ultimately, the more active antitrust policy we have seen over the past eight years, in contrast to the policy we saw in the previous 12 years, can be traced to a greater confidence of Clinton appointees in their ability to correct market failures by banning business practices and blocking mergers thought to harm competition. We fully expect to see a shift back to a more cautious antitrust enforcement effort over the next several years, all within the boundaries of the broad consensus described previously.

We do not mean to suggest that a focus on innovation during the Clinton years in any way distracted from the most traditional, and least controversial, aspect of antitrust enforcement, namely, the breaking up of cartels and conspiracies in restraint of trade. To the contrary, the Antitrust Division had unprecedented success during the Clinton years, and especially during the second Clinton administration, in prosecuting price fixers. We see this as an area where an apparently small change in policy had a major impact. The change in prosecutorial policy—little noticed at the time—was the introduction by DOJ in August 1993 of a corporate amnesty program. Under the corporate leniency or amnesty program, immunity was granted for criminal prosecution to the first participant in a price-fixing or other collusive conspiracy to turn itself in. This seemingly innocuous policy change helped identify some of the largest price-fixing conspiracies ever uncovered, and eventually led to far and away the largest fines for antitrust violations ever imposed.

Antitrust policy during the Clinton years also became much more international in scope, both by necessity and design. The necessity arose from the greater frequency of cross-border mergers and price-fixing conspiracies brought to the attention of the American officials and their foreign counterparts (in part because of the corporate amnesty program). Cross-border antitrust cooperation—especially between American, Canadian, and European antitrust enforcement officials—also intensified, especially after the enactment by Congress (at the urging of the Justice Department and the FTC) of the International Antitrust Enforcement Cooperation Act of 1994. With few exceptions (such as temporary disagreements over how to analyze certain mergers), the Clinton years marked a major advance toward enhanced international antitrust cooperation. We forecast even more cross-border cooperation and interaction—and quite possibly conflict—among antitrust enforcement agencies in the years ahead.

The Clinton years also saw significant increases in the antitrust enforcement budgets of both federal agencies. The increased resources allowed sizable staffing increases among attorneys, economists, and staff support. In addition, DOJ in particular abandoned the prior practice of having staff attorneys handle all antitrust trials, and for its major cases—notably Microsoft, but also for certain other high-profile investigations—turned to highly experienced private attorneys to supervise these assignments. This change in tactics brought greater expertise to the prosecution of these cases and helped impart cutting-edge trial skills to the government's permanent staff attorneys (who played major supporting roles in these trials and investigations).

The antitrust agencies during the Clinton years were also aided by state attorneys general and private litigants who brought information to the enforcement officials, and in some cases assisted with the prosecution of the cases. The increased involvement of the state attorneys general, however, has been a mixed blessing, in our view, since more prosecutors can complicate efforts to obtain prompt resolution of investigations, especially settlements that promise similar results to litigation but can achieve them much more quickly.

Looking ahead, a key challenge confronting antitrust enforcement is how to adapt to the increasingly rapid pace of technological change, with the concomitant expansion in the role played by intellectual property. On the one hand, technological change can reduce the need for prompt antitrust action, by eroding more quickly any market power held by dominant firms. On the other hand, patents and copyrights can serve as significant barriers to entry. We fully expect the enforcement agencies and the courts to continue to explore the antitrust limits on the use or abuse of intellectual property. The challenge of fashioning antitrust policy in a world of rapid technological change is heightened by the presence of "network effects," primarily demand-side economies derived from compatibility, in some high-tech markets. Network effects, in conjunction with intellectual property rights, can result in durable market power even in the presence of rapid technological change. A firm that achieves dominance by taking advantage of network externalities—a perfectly lawful vehicle—may be able to thwart challenges from new competitors and technologies by having large numbers of existing customers "locked in" to the use of existing products and services. As a result, barriers to entry to new competitors can be significant in high-tech markets. In such situations, heightened antitrust scrutiny is needed to ensure that dominant positions are not being abused. Complicating the antitrust response, however, is the fact that the judicial process—even with quick disposition of pretrial motions and expedited discovery and trial—is often slower than ongoing market developments. How to deal with this disjunction between "technology time" and "judicial time," so evident in the Microsoft case, is likely to be one of the central challenges to antitrust enforcement in the future.

We assume that readers of this chapter will come to the material with varying levels of background in antitrust. For those with relatively little experience
in the subject, we begin by outlining the basic antitrust laws in section 7.2, and
the agencies that enforce them in section 7.3; these sections can be skipped by
those already familiar with the basics of antitrust law and enforcement procedures. We then proceed in section 7.4 to provide a brief history of antitrust
enforcement, concentrating especially on the two decades preceding the 1990s.
This discussion provides the predicate for the heart of the chapter, the discussion of the Clinton antitrust enforcement record. After an introduction to the
Clinton record in section 7.5, we explore the three key areas of antitrust enforcement: criminal prosecutions (section 7.6), civil nonmerger enforcement activity
(section 7.7), and review of mergers (section 7.8). We then provide a discussion
of the increased level of international cooperation and extraterritorial enforcement of U.S. antitrust laws in section 7.9. We conclude in section 7.10 by presenting our assessment of the Clinton antitrust record and by offering some
thoughts about the future of antitrust, intellectual property, and high tech.

We caution readers at the outset that each of us brings to the subject our
own experiences at the Antitrust Division at DOJ during two separate periods
of the Clinton era, along with our private-sector experience on specific cases.
We acknowledge that this personal history has the potential for introducing
bias, and because we are aware of this possibility, we make great efforts to
avoid it by discussing the issues in what we believe is a neutral manner. How
successful we are in this effort is for readers to judge.

7.2   Some Basics of Antitrust Law

Antitrust law in the United States dates from the passage in 1890 of the Sherman Act, which prohibited contracts, combinations, conspiracies in restraint of
trade (Section 1), and actions taken to monopolize or attempt to monopolize
markets (Section 2). Almost a generation later, Congress added the Clayton
Act of 1914, which, among other things, prohibited (1) firms with dominant
power in one market from forcing consumers to buy entirely different products
(tying); (2) competing firms from having overlapping boards of directors; and
(3) mergers between firms that threatened to substantially reduce competition
in any line of commerce.[1] In the 1930s, Congress supplemented these two
basic statutes with the Robinson-Patman Act, aimed at preventing firms from
charging different prices to different customers that were not based on costs

---

1. The Clayton Act was amended in 1950, mostly to broaden its coverage of mergers. The Hart-
Scott-Rodino Act further strengthened merger enforcement procedures in the 1970s.

(i.e., from engaging in price discrimination) when such pricing harmed competition. The Robinson-Patman Act, roundly criticized, has rarely been enforced by the government in the past 20 years. Indeed, selective price discounting has for the most part come to be welcomed by antitrust authorities.[2] Most states have their own versions of one or all of these federal statutes, and so do most other industrialized countries, including Australia, Canada, European nations, and even Japan.

Broadly speaking, the antitrust laws punish conduct designed to impair the *competitive process*—that is, conduct likely to lead to higher prices and restricted output relative to a state of unfettered competition—not the economic fortunes of *individual firms*. Of course, as a practical matter, information about potential violations often is brought to the attention of the enforcement authorities (discussed section 7.3) by competitors of possible antitrust violators. The antitrust proscriptions can be and often are categorized in different ways.

One categorization, for example, distinguishes among the proscription of *collective conduct* aimed at restraining competition (price fixing, bid rigging, dividing markets among competitors, boycotts, and the like); *unilateral conduct* (acts designed to entrench or establish a monopoly that have little or no legitimate business purpose and that are only profitable because of their tendency to exclude competitors); and *mergers*, which very often pose no threat to the competitive process (and often enhance it by producing more efficient combinations) but in some cases so reduce the number of players in a market that the most likely result is higher prices or reduced innovation after the merger is consummated (in which case the merger almost certainly will be challenged by one, or several, antitrust agencies).

Another common distinction is based on the different penalties that apply to antitrust violations, at least in the United States. Where juries are able to conclude *beyond a reasonable doubt* that two or more companies have conspired to restrain commerce, the law provides for criminal penalties: fines and potential incarceration of the individuals involved. As a practical matter, criminal prosecutions tend to be brought primarily by the Justice Department, and then only for forming cartels to fix prices (perhaps the most naked form of anticompetitive conduct) or divide markets. Where the agencies, or private parties, cannot meet the high criminal standard of proof, antitrust violations are punishable by judicial decrees ordering the end of the offending conduct and actions that may resemble it (in cases brought by the government), by disgorgement

---

2. In contrast, discounting by foreign suppliers selling into the U.S. market has often been attacked as illegal "dumping." Conflicts between trade policy and antitrust policy are not uncommon, with antitrust officials welcoming import competition as a check on the market power of domestic firms.

of the unlawful gains from the violations (if the FTC has brought the action), or by treble damages to victims of the offensive conduct (in cases brought by private litigants). Unlawful mergers, meanwhile, can be prevented or undone by the courts; more often, they are restructured (often with divestitures of certain assets or activities) as part of a negotiation with the antitrust agencies. Other countries have different antitrust penalties. Notably, European Union law provides for no criminal sanctions; enforcers typically resort to fines or injunctions against the offending conduct. Furthermore, while private antitrust lawsuits are available in Europe, they are not nearly as common as they are in the United States.

A final distinction that antitrust specialists often draw is between conduct that is deemed to be a per se violation and conduct that is judged under a "rule of reason." The notion of per se offenses has been developed by the courts over time to eliminate the need for extensive proof of the anticompetitive effect of certain conduct that, on its face, has been determined to lack any legitimate justification, regardless of how much market power the actors may possess. Examples include such collective conduct as fixing prices, dividing markets, and a narrow range of group boycotts and tie-in sales. In virtually all other cases, courts take a case-by-case approach when examining the alleged unlawful behavior, requiring the plaintiff(s) to prove that the conduct, on balance, does more harm than good to the competitive process.

The standards for assessing the competitive impact of mergers have also become clearer over time with the development and refinement of Horizontal Merger Guidelines by the DOJ and the FTC, which set forth the methodology that enforcement officials use to decide whether to challenge particular business combinations involving direct competitors. Although these decisions must still be made case by case, antitrust practitioners and the courts have come to value the use of a common framework for understanding and assessing these decisions—in particular, standards for defining the "relevant" markets in which the effects of the merger will be assessed and measures of market concentration—that are likely to affect whether the merger will be judged to lead to higher prices or reduced innovation, thus justifying a challenge.

7.3 Antitrust Enforcement Procedures and Institutions

In the antitrust chapter of the last exercise of this kind—the volume edited by Martin Feldstein for the National Bureau of Economic Research that assessed economic policy in the 1980s—one of the leading academic authorities in this field identified the courts as the key institution for developing, articulating, and enforcing at least the federal antitrust laws.[3] Because the words of the antitrust laws are inherently vague—and seemingly so all encompassing—there is a sense in which this claim must be right. All contracts, for example, "restrain" trade; it has been left to the courts to identify which types of contracts do so unlawfully. The same applies to other "magic" words in the antitrust laws, such as "monopolization."

In practice, however, as in so many other areas of the law, the day-to-day decisions about enforcement are made by government antitrust law enforcement officials—primarily at the federal level, but also in the states.[4] Moreover, beyond appointing the key antitrust officials—the head of the Antitrust Division at Justice and the members of the Federal Trade Commission—the president and other members of the executive branch play essentially no role in day-to-day antitrust enforcement. On broad policy issues, it is possible that the president and his advisers may voice their views, but even these occasions are rare.

The key enforcement decisions are whether to launch an investigation, and then whether to file a formal legal complaint. Typically, right before formal action is taken, however, officials give targets of their investigations their "last rites": a final chance to settle, analogous to a plea bargain in the criminal context. In fact, it is our experience from serving in the DOJ during the Clinton years that most serious antitrust investigations are settled without a formal trial; this is one reason that we believe so much enforcement power is actually lodged in the prosecutors.

At the same time, however, there was a discernible shift in the willingness of the DOJ, in particular, to settle or litigate—at least between the two Clinton terms. Settlements were more the rule than the exception during the tenure of Anne Bingaman, the first Clinton assistant attorney general for antitrust at DOJ, for all types of antitrust matters. Both the department and the FTC became more willing to litigate, at least with respect to some high-profile matters, during the second term, under the direction of Joel Klein, the second Clinton appointee as assistant attorney general for antitrust, and at the FTC, under the chairmanship of Robert Pitofsky. In part, we attribute this willingness to the de-

---

3. Areeda (1994), p. 575.

4. The competition policy laws in most foreign countries, while distinct, are no less vague. Officials in other jurisdictions, most notably the European Union, are actively exploring the limits of their enforcement authority and interpreting their own statutes as they fashion competition policy. Since more and more firms, American and foreign, are doing business both in the United States and abroad, and since the very same business practices (ranging from Intel's pricing and licensing strategies to the merger of Boeing and McDonnell Douglas) affect commerce around the world, companies increasingly must be mindful of competition policy rules in multiple countries as they conduct their business affairs.

sire of Joel Klein and Robert Pitofsky to establish legal precedents, not "merely" to fix particular competition problems in specific matters that they happened to come across. As we shall see, both the DOJ and FTC met with mixed success when their cases were actually subjected to rigorous review by a trial court (and in several cases, appellate review as well).

This brief commentary highlights the fact that antitrust enforcement jurisdiction at the federal level is split between Justice and the FTC. This dual responsibility is unusual, but not completely atypical. In the tax field, for example, both the IRS and DOJ share jurisdiction. The same is true for civil rights enforcement, which is shared by the Equal Employment Opportunity Commission and the DOJ. In the antitrust field, the FTC was created in 1914 because of a perception then that DOJ was insufficiently aggressive in pursuing antitrust violations. Over the years, the two agencies have informally divided enforcement responsibility by industry—DOJ has handled airlines and telecommunications matters, for example, while the FTC has specialized in the oil industry and pharmaceuticals—but in many cases there are overlaps. Where these occur, responsibility is divided on a case-by-case basis, although sometimes with tension between staff or political appointees. We witnessed such tension during our tenure at DOJ, but found it to be the exception rather than the rule, and it is usually most pronounced in high-profile cases such as the AOL–Time Warner merger where each agency could claim real industry or company expertise.

As we have noted, most states have antitrust statutes that parallel one or more of the federal statutes. These give enforcement authority to state attorneys general. In the past, the states for the most part confined their antitrust enforcement activities to prosecuting local price-fixing conspiracies, often against competitors in bid-rigging schemes. During the 1990s, however, the states began to play a much higher profile role, not only bringing matters to the attention of the federal agencies, but also seeking a share of litigation responsibilities, as occurred during the Microsoft trial during the second Clinton term. One of the interesting developments to look for during the next administration not only is whether the federal antitrust agencies will become less activist in any sense (a subject we address at the end of the chapter), but also, if they do, whether and to what extent the states will take up any of the slack by becoming more aggressive.

The 1990s also saw more cooperation between U.S. and foreign antitrust agencies, especially the European Union. This was due in large part to two factors: the European Union significantly strengthened its merger enforcement procedures in the early 1990s, and the 1990s witnessed an increased number of mergers involving parties on both sides of the Atlantic, thus giving EU enforcement officials jurisdiction over the transaction along with U.S. officials. Except in rare cases (notably the Boeing–McDonnell Douglas and the General Electric–Honeywell mergers), the U.S. and EU agencies viewed transactions very similarly, with the EU agencies taking the lead in some, the U.S. agencies in others.[5]

Since the Clayton Act of 1914, the U.S. antitrust laws have allowed—many would say encouraged—private parties injured by antitrust violations to sue for damages. Under Section 4 of the Clayton Act, winning plaintiffs are entitled to three times the amounts by which they can prove they were injured,[6] a provision that provides very strong incentives for private litigants and their attorneys to investigate potential violations, and thus equally strong incentives for firms and individuals subject to treble damages to avoid violations of the antitrust laws.

We would like to emphasize the uniquely strong character of the U.S. system as regards financial penalties imposed on companies violating the antitrust laws. The United States has put into place a powerful combination of forces operating to benefit private antitrust plaintiffs: private antitrust cases are permitted and involve treble damages; private plaintiffs have extensive discovery rights; plaintiffs can demand a jury trial; and lawyers representing a class of plaintiffs often face a low hurdle to have their proposed class action certified. Antitrust hawks see these proplaintiff rules as a great virtue of the U.S. system. Others believe that the U.S. system allows plaintiffs' lawyers to extract substantial sums of money from corporations that have done nothing to violate the antitrust laws.

The unflattering view of private antitrust enforcement in the United States runs roughly as follows: lawyers for antitrust plaintiffs face a very low hurdle to obtain class certification. Once a class is certified, defendants face the possibility of a very large damages award (after trebling), such as claims based on overcharges from an alleged conspiracy. Plaintiffs then benefit from extensive rights to discovery of defendants' files and data, which often turns up at least a few unflattering statements or e-mails, perhaps written by low-level employees. These documents, in conjunction with the less-than-favorable views held by some jurors about large corporations, and the willingness of jurors to infer that a conspiracy may exist even absent direct supporting evidence, imply that a perceived risk to the defendant of an adverse jury decision exists in virtually any case. Given this risk, many executives will be inclined to pay substantial sums of money rather than face a jury trial, even if they are confident that their company's conduct has not harmed competition. The net result is many

5. See Evenett, Lerhmann, and Steil (2000). We discuss the substantive nature of this international antitrust enforcement activity later in the chapter.

6. As developed by the courts, only those plaintiffs who have suffered "antitrust injury"—such as having had to pay higher prices—can sue for damages. Under some circumstances, this limitation means that competitors of a defendant may not have standing to sue.

private antitrust lawsuits of dubious merit, imposing a type of tax on corporate America. Of course, there is an obvious counterargument: U.S. laws empower an army of private antitrust enforcers who collectively have a pronounced effect on improving compliance with the antitrust laws, thus stifling cartels and preserving competitive markets.

In any event, the dual nature of antitrust enforcement—government actions against companies that violated the antitrust laws along with private actions to collect damages—leads to various complex interactions between public and private enforcement, for a number of reasons.

First, because antitrust litigation can be so expensive—especially when launched against defendants with deep pockets—private litigants often bring their complaints to the government and wait for official prosecutions in court, either civil or criminal, to provide proof of a violation. With such judgments in hand, as a practical matter private plaintiffs rarely need to prove more than damages. In part for this reason, defendants that are targets of government antitrust investigations often settle by signing consent decrees, which involve no admission of unlawful conduct but simply agreement to change conduct in some manner to meet the government's objections. In such instances, private plaintiffs must therefore prove that a violation has occurred as well as any damages they might have suffered.

Second, because of the importance of private antitrust actions in the United States, confining attention to government enforcement actions, much less federal government enforcement actions, does not give a complete picture of the antitrust landscape. Enforcement of the antitrust laws is more stable over time than is reflected in federal antitrust policy, in part because of lags between federal activity, subsequent court decisions, and the resulting payoffs to private plaintiffs in antitrust actions.

Third, federal antitrust policy tends to have a multiplier effect: targets of antitrust investigations understand well that a lawsuit with federal officials (or even a settlement, which then becomes public) will almost invariably trigger one or more private antitrust lawsuits. Since private actions can involve hundreds of millions of dollars (such as the price-fixing cases involving the NASDAQ and the auction houses, which we will discuss later), increased enforcement activity by the FTC and the DOJ very quickly sends a message to companies throughout the economy that they are at real risk if they do not stay on the safe side of the line currently being drawn by federal antitrust officials.

7.4 Historical Cycles in Antitrust Enforcement

Before considering the antitrust enforcement record of the Clinton administration in some detail, it is useful first to place it in some historical perspective.

Accordingly, we will review here very briefly some of the developments and waves in federal antitrust enforcement in particular over the last century.[7] These cycles in enforcement reflect shifting views over time in public attitudes toward business as well as scholarly thinking about the appropriate role of government intervention in the market with the aim of ensuring competition. Although in the last several decades there has been convergence among antitrust legal scholars and economists on the basic structure that prosecutors and courts should use for analyzing markets, differences in views remain. It is these differences that account for the continued fluctuations in antitrust enforcement philosophy and activity that persist to this day.

Given the vagueness of the first antitrust law, the Sherman Act, the courts spent considerable time in the first few decades after the act was passed giving content to the meaning of terms like "contract in restraint of trade" or "monopolization." Broadly speaking, the courts condemned only those contracts under Section 1 of the act where direct rivals agreed to restrict output and raise price, or in other words, agreed to act like a monopolist.[8] The Supreme Court also condemned "vertical" agreements by manufacturers and their retailers on minimum prices above which retailers would sell.[9]

After some early cases in which the Supreme Court tolerated mergers that produced large or even dominant firms—examples being the Sugar Trust, General Electric, International Harvester, du Pont, Eastman Kodak, U.S. Steel, and Standard Oil—the Court in 1904 finally blocked the merger between the Northern Pacific and Great Northern railroads on monopolization grounds. Seven years later, the Court found that Standard Oil had achieved monopoly status with 90 percent of the market for refined oil products and abused its dominance by various forms of exclusionary conduct (all thoroughly documented in Ron Chernow's *Titan*, published in 2000). The following year, the Court handed down another antimonopolization decision in *Terminal Railroad Association of St. Louis*, holding that various railroads could not use their control over terminal facilities at a main crossing of the Mississippi River to discriminate against rivals. Both *Standard Oil* and *Terminal Railroad* would be widely

---

7. This section draws heavily on Kovacic and Shapiro (2000).

8. A notable example is *United States v. Addyston Pipe & Steel Co.* (85 Fed. 271 [6th Cir. 1898]).

9. *Dr. Miles Medical Co. v. John D. Park & Sons Co.* (220 U.S. 373 [1911]). This case has since been much criticized. A general problem with the development of the law regarding vertical restraints of trade is that the courts have attempted to take a distinction that makes sense in the horizontal realm—that between unilateral conduct and "agreements"—and apply it in the vertical area, where buyers and sellers necessarily "agree" to do business. In the area of "vertical price fixing" the courts have struggled long and hard to draw a line between conduct that constitutes an "agreement" between a manufacturer and a retailer versus conduct that is "unilaterally" imposed by the manufacturer.

cited as important precedents in the Justice Department's antimonopolization case brought against Microsoft in the 1990s (discussed later).

The monopolization cases of the early 1900s proved to be a temporary high-water mark for antitrust enforcement, however, as the next decades saw a movement by prosecutors and courts to adopt case-by-case "rule-of-reason" standards for assessing wrongdoing. The shift in attitude was due to several sources: a widespread consensus after World War I that cooperation between business and government was a good way to organize the economy; a strong sentiment after the Depression began in 1929 that prices were *too low* rather than too high; and a narrow interpretation by courts of the antitrust enforcement mandate of the Federal Trade Commission (created in 1914 in response to fears of excessive concentration of enforcement power in the executive branch).

The enforcement cycle turned in a different, more aggressive direction by the mid-1930s and continued on this path until the early 1970s. Interestingly, the shift in direction was prompted by Chicago-school economists—Henry Simons, Jacob Viner, and Frank Knight—who argued that economic planning was not getting the United States out of the Depression and that antitrust enforcement was needed to deconcentrate American industry.[10] Antitrust enforcement against various forms of collusive behavior—price fixing, tying, nonprice vertical restraints, group boycotts, and exclusive sales territories—was revitalized and eventually condemned by the Supreme Court using per se rules. In contrast to a rule of reason standard, per se rules required proof only that the conduct took place, not of its anticompetitive effects. The courts also became more willing to find fault with excessively aggressive behavior by dominant firms, most notably in the famous Alcoa case in 1945, when Judge Learned Hand found that the preemptive addition of capacity by a firm with most of the aluminum market was wrongful. In subsequent cases, the Supreme Court condemned a locally dominant newspaper's effort to destroy a small radio station by refusing to sell it advertising (*Lorrain Journal Co. v. United States*, 342 U.S. 143 [1951]); prevented the "lease only" policy of the United Shoe Company, which dominated the market in shoe-making equipment (eventually authorizing the breakup of the company); and found a nationally dominant bakery's localized price cuts to be wrongful (*Utah Pie Co. v. Continental Baking Co.*, 386 U.S. 685 [1967]). With the exception of *Lorrain Journal* and the price-fixing and tying cases, it is not clear that many of the others would be brought by enforcement officials (or supported by the courts) today.

Antitrust enforcement also became much more aggressive against corporate mergers, inspired by the "structure, conduct, performance" paradigm associated

---

10. See Kovacic (1989), p. 1134.

with Harvard economist Joe Bain, which posited a strong correlation between even relatively low levels of market concentration and industry profitability, and thus potentially anticonsumer outcomes. In a series of decisions in the 1960s, in particular, the Supreme Court approved government challenges to horizontal mergers (those among competitors in the same geographic and product markets) whose combined market shares would fall well below those that would be challenged now. Indeed, in a famous dissent in *Von's Grocery* (384 U.S. 270, 301 [1966]), in which the majority condemned a merger that would have generated a market share of only 7 percent in a generally unconcentrated market, Justice Potter Stewart summed up the prevailing judicial environment then with the declaration "The Government always wins."

Beginning in the 1970s, the three-decade-long pattern of antitrust activism began to attract strong criticism from various law professors and economists associated with the University of Chicago (where a previous generation of scholars, as just indicated, ironically helped launched the very trend that this newer generation of scholars attacked). Among other things, the Chicago School critique was leveled at the Supreme Court's per se rule against nonprice vertical restraints (which were argued to be procompetitive) and at the Court's various merger decisions for failing to define markets accurately or for stopping transactions without proof of competitive harm. Over time, more judges were appointed to the federal bench who were sympathetic to this line of argument, including Richard Posner and Frank Easterbrook, who were prominent contributors to the Chicago School critique of the earlier antitrust policy.

As a result, by the 1980s, the federal courts began to grow more skeptical of antitrust cases. Moreover, with the notable exception of the breakup of AT&T— where the evidence was clear that a dominant company had abused its market power—and various prosecutions against bid rigging, government antitrust authorities became much more reticent to mount antitrust challenges of all types. The shift in attitude was also reflected in personnel and resources, especially at the Department of Justice, where the number of attorneys was significantly reduced through much of the 1980s. This trend began to be reversed under James Rill, the assistant attorney general during the Bush administration of 1989–93. As noted earlier, antitrust enforcement resources were augmented throughout the two Clinton terms.

Although the Clinton antitrust appointees became more aggressive in pursuit of antitrust violations of various types, it is fair to say that a "post-Chicago" synthesis has emerged, reflecting a significant degree of consensus among antitrust scholars and practitioners on two key items. One important area of agreement is on the framework used to analyze mergers, especially to define markets, which were totally revamped during the first Reagan term (under the guidance of Assistant Attorney General William Baxter). As we will discuss later, the so-called Horizontal Merger Guidelines have since been revised under both the Bush and Clinton administrations, but the revisions have been more in the nature of tweaking—and certainly not rejecting—the initial framework. The second area of agreement is that collusive activities are to be punished. As we will discuss, one of the important features of the Clinton antitrust years is how many large price-fixing conspiracies were uncovered or investigated, often international in scope. To us, this development was a surprise. Prior to coming to the Justice Department, neither of us would have suspected how extensive collusive practices turned out to be.

7.5 The Clinton Antitrust Record: Introduction

7.5.1 Measures of Enforcement Activity

Antitrust enforcement activity can be measured and described. Here we do both, first by presenting some summary statistics from the Antitrust Division of the Justice Department that confirm the overall impression of increased activity during the Clinton years. The data only begin, however, in 1991, and thus provide an incomplete picture of enforcement in the pre-Clinton era. Nonetheless, we will accept the conventional wisdom that the number of investigations and cases initiated in the 1980s was below that of the 1990s and thus use the data primarily to concentrate on the latter decade when the Clinton antitrust team was in place. In addition, the data reported here are only for Justice Department cases, not those launched by the FTC. We do not believe this limitation is significant, however, since both DOJ and the FTC during the Clinton years shared similar antitrust enforcement philosophies.[11]

---

11. We do have some FTC data, but we lack a time series of FTC enforcement actions. The FTC data are from "Summary of Bureau of Competition Activity: Fiscal Year 1996 Through March 31, 2000," pp. 52–58. During this $3\frac{1}{2}$-year period, the FTC reports the following merger enforcement activity: 9 preliminary injunctions authorized, 2 Part III administrative complaints, 89 Part II consent agreements, 14 civil penalty actions, and 34 transactions abandoned after a second request was issued, for a total of 148 merger actions. On the nonmerger side, there were 5 Part III administrative complaints, 31 Part II consent agreements, 1 civil penalty action, and 1 injunction, for a total of 38 nonmerger actions. This same document lists all of these cases and describes a number of them. See http://www.ftc.gov/bc/abafy96thru00.pdf. During the subsequent year ending March 31, 2001, the FTC reports the following activity in the merger area: 4 preliminary injunctions, 20 consent agreements, and 7 mergers abandoned during the FTC investigation. On the nonmerger side, the FTC obtained a $100 million consent judgment in one case (Mylan) and entered into eight consent agreements. See http://www.ftc.gov/speeches/other/boastmollys.htm.

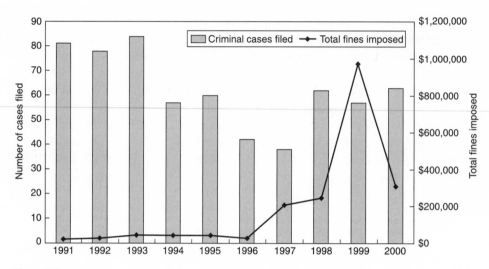

Figure 7.1
Criminal investigations. (*Source:* U.S. Department of Justice, Antitrust Division, *Workload Statistics FY 1991–2000*.)

The pictures are shown in Figures 7.1–7.4 and pretty much speak for themselves. Figure 7.1 illustrates that although the simple number of criminal prosecutions filed in court actually declined somewhat from a peak in the early years of the 1990s, the magnitude of fines collected jumped sharply, especially toward the end of the decade. As we will discuss shortly, this pattern reflects increased priority given by the DOJ to large national and international price-fixing conspiracies, leaving local bid-rigging cases to be investigated and prosecuted by the states.

Figures 7.2 and 7.3 illustrate the significant increase through much of the decade in both categories of civil nonmerger cases—restraint of trade under Section 1 of the Sherman Act and monopolization cases under Section 2—that the DOJ has brought and won. These graphs clearly evidence heightened activism on both these fronts during the Clinton era.

Figure 7.4 shows a more uneven pattern for merger enforcement activity. While the numbers of mergers requiring notification under the Hart-Scott-Rodino Act (any combination involving an entity with more than $15 million in assets) increased throughout the decade, the percentage of those mergers that were actually investigated seriously rose briefly and then fell back by the end of the decade. Even more strikingly, the percentage of mergers actually challenged was small—less than 1 percent of the total—and relatively stable throughout the period. The falling share of mergers investigated most likely

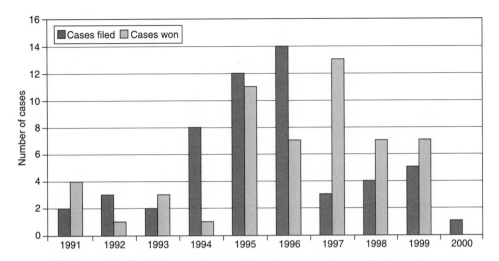

Figure 7.2
Restraint of trade cases (Sherman Act Section 1). (*Source:* U.S. Department of Justice, Antitrust Division, *Workload Statistics FY 1991–2000.*)

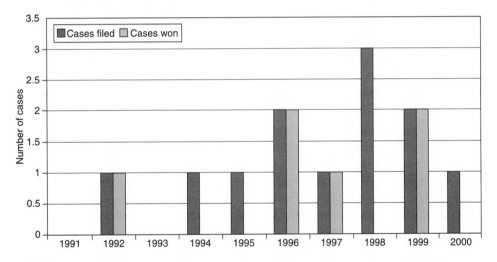

Figure 7.3
Monopoly cases (Sherman Act Section 2). (*Source:* U.S. Department of Justice, Antitrust Division, *Workload Statistics FY 1991–2000.*)

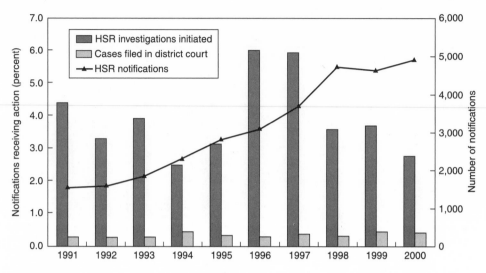

Figure 7.4
Hart-Scott-Rodino merger notifications and actions. (*Source:* U.S. Department of Justice, Antitrust Division, *Workload Statistics FY 1991–2000.*)

reflects the fact that, even with more staff, the antitrust agencies had to ration their time in light of the substantial increase in the numbers of mergers that needed at least to be preliminarily reviewed.

The low and stable share of mergers actually challenged reflects several aspects of merger enforcement. First, the DOJ was cautious in merger enforcement, insisting upon a solid factual and theoretical basis before bringing a challenge. Second, the Antitrust Division was inclined through much of the period to reach agreements with the parties to solve anticompetitive problems through divestitures of assets in markets where postmerger concentration was deemed to be excessive, or through consent decrees restricting the activities of the combined entity to prevent any future anticompetitive effects. Third, and perhaps most important, is the fact that companies contemplating a horizontal merger or acquisition can predict with reasonable accuracy how their proposed merger will be received at the DOJ and the FTC, based on the Horizontal Merger Guidelines. In other words, with enforcement policy well articulated, surprises at DOJ's enforcement stance, as well as the need for Court review to draw the line, are both relatively rare.

Numbers and trends provide only a glimpse of the true nature of antitrust enforcement activity. For a more in-depth look, we need to delve into some of the more important cases and developments surrounding them. We do that in the four subsequent sections of this chapter.

7.5.2   Guidelines and Hearings

Since so few antitrust cases actually involve litigation, much less an actual trial, a great deal of antitrust policy is set through either consent decrees (settlements) or through the enforcement guidelines that the agencies publish to inform the business community of their policies.[12]

Probably the most influential antitrust guidelines are the Horizontal Merger Guidelines, which are issued and followed by both the Justice Department and the FTC. These "Merger Guidelines" were totally reworked in 1982 under the first Reagan administration, then revised in 1992 under the Bush administration. The only change in the Horizontal Merger Guidelines during the Clinton years was the release in 1997 of an expanded explanation of how the agencies will treat efficiencies—namely, the ability of the merged company to achieve lower costs or improved product performance—as a result of the merger. While in principle the new treatment of efficiencies is more generous to merging companies than were the prior guidelines, practitioners generally believe that both agencies continue to apply a rather tough "screen" before they credit a merger with real efficiencies. In particular, both agencies are wary of efficiency *claims* that will not in fact be achieved, or that would be achieved even without the proposed merger. Only efficiencies that are "merger-specific" are given any weight.

Three major new sets of guidelines were issued during the Clinton administration.[13] First came the Statements of Antitrust Enforcement Policy in Health Care, issued in 1994 (later revised in 1996), which explain, among other things, how physician networks will be treated. Second were the Antitrust Guidelines for the Licensing of Intellectual Property, issued in 1995, which have been highly influential in mapping the role of antitrust policy in high-technology industries. Third came the Antitrust Guidelines for Collaborations among Competitors, issued in 2000, which address the very complex issues that arise when direct rivals seek to cooperate in various ways such as to set standards or participate in joint ventures.

In addition to these guidelines, Chairman Pitofsky revived an old tradition at the FTC of holding hearings on important current antitrust topics. Two sets of hearings stand out as offering rich and valuable information on topical issues: (1) Hearings in 1995 that led to a staff report, "Anticipating the 21st Century:

---

12. All the FTC and DOJ guidelines and reports are available at their web sites, www.ftc.gov and www.usdoj.gov/atr. These sites also offer a wealth of information about specific antitrust cases brought by these two agencies.

13. In addition, the Antitrust Enforcement Guidelines for International Operations were updated in 1995.

Competition Policy in the New High-Tech Global Marketplace," issued May 1996; and (2) hearings held June 29–30, 2000, that led to a staff report, "Competition Policy in the World of B2B Electronic Marketplaces," issued in October 2000.

7.5.3 Competition Advocacy

The DOJ and the FTC have long played advisory roles, essentially acting as advocates within the federal government on behalf of market competition. As part of the executive branch, the DOJ (often along with the Council of Economic Advisers) takes the lead as the competition advocate in the context of interagency discussions, from trade issues to privatization to a range of regulatory issues. Both agencies also serve as sources of expert advice to Congress regarding legislation that has implications for competition and monopoly.

The DOJ played an especially large role in the developments and negotiations that led to the Telecommunications Act of 1996. DOJ's role was natural because the act was intended, in part, to replace the Court oversight of the Bell system, itself arising from the 1984 consent decree between AT&T and the DOJ, with regulatory oversight and deregulation. In particular, DOJ officials met regularly with other administration officials, led by Vice President Al Gore, on legislative strategy while the act was being considered by Congress. In addition, just prior to the act's enactment, the department negotiated a waiver of the consent decree to allow Ameritech to enter the long-distance market in Chicago, as a trial. The district court never issued a ruling on the waiver, however, because the act preempted that experiment. Nonetheless, many of the conditions set forth in that waiver for entry by the regional Bell operating companies (RBOCs) into long-distance telecommunications—largely relating to the openness of the local markets to effective competition—found their way into Section 251 of the act.

In addition, the act gave DOJ a special advisory role to the Federal Communications Commission on RBOC applications for entry (although the department and the administration had initially sought more—actual joint decision-making authority). Throughout the second Clinton term, DOJ took a relatively hard line on RBOC applications for permission to enter long-distance markets, recommending to the FCC denials in several cases because, in the view of the department, the RBOC applicants had not sufficiently opened up their own local markets to competition, as required by the 1996 act. Nonetheless, by the end of the administration, even DOJ's opposition started to soften. DOJ recommended, and in December 1999 the FCC agreed, to allow Bell Atlantic (now Verizon) entry into long distance in New York. The following year, the FCC permitted SBC to enter long distance in Texas. Shortly after the Bush administration came to office, in early 2001, the FCC granted Verizon's long-distance application in Massachusetts, and as this is written, it is widely expected that the FCC quickly will open up many more states to RBOC entry into long-distance service.[14]

DOJ also cooperated closely in the mid-1990s with the Securities and Exchange Commission during the investigation by both agencies into price fixing by securities dealers on the "bid-ask spreads" on certain highly traded stocks listed on the NASDAQ (a case we will discuss later). While the DOJ included in its consent decree with the dealers an injunction against certain practices that had the effect of facilitating collusion, the SEC also took important regulatory actions that compelled disclosure of "limit orders" (orders to buy or sell at, above, or below specific prices) that also helped ensure that collusion among market makers would not take place.

7.6   Cartel Enforcement in the Clinton Years

DOJ was extremely active during the Clinton years in investigating and prosecuting cases against companies and individuals involved in price fixing and bid rigging. While there is broad agreement across the political spectrum that such activities should be vigorously pursued, the Department in the two previous administrations had concentrated its enforcement activities in significant part on price fixing and bid rigging in limited geographic areas. The Clinton years saw a major pickup in enforcement uncovering not only national, but also international, conspiracies, resulting in incarcerations of key company executives, record fines, and in the civil area, some major changes in the way key industries did business.

7.6.1   Criminal Price Fixing

The Antitrust Division got off to a very poor start in its battle against price fixing with an embarrassing loss in the case against General Electric for price fixing in industrial diamonds. The government believed that a major reason for its failure was its inability to compel testimony of key foreign witnesses and to obtain documents abroad. The latter problem helped motivate the department to seek broader authority to cooperate with antitrust prosecutors in other countries, which we will discuss later. In any event, the DOJ's setback in the GE case was not a portent of things to come.

---

14. If the FCC does not approve a number of these applications in the near future, several influential members of Congress have vowed to seek legislation that would speed up such entry.

To the contrary, as shown in the figures already referenced, the DOJ imposed far greater fines for price fixing during the Clinton administration that had ever been assessed before. Gary Spratling, the deputy assistant attorney general in charge of criminal enforcement, was widely recognized for his expertise in guiding the department's enforcement effort, aided by the amnesty program discussed earlier.[15] Table 7.1 lists the price-fixing violations that led to fines of $10 million or more.

The citric acid and lysine cartels, which included Archer-Daniels Midland (ADM), led the way in FY97. ADM paid a fine of $100 million, at that time by far the largest such fine ever assessed. Total fines collected in FY1997 were $205 million, some five times the previous record. This number was exceeded in FY1998 with total fines of $265 million. Then, in FY1999, a breathtaking $1.1 billion in fines were obtained. During that year, the single largest fine ever assessed, $500 million, was imposed on Hoffmann–La Roche in the vitamins price-fixing case. This case involved an international cartel that operated from 1990 through 1999 covering certain vitamins used in human food, animal feed, and pharmaceuticals. The graphite electrodes case led to fines of over $400 million.

These are merely the most visible of the many price-fixing and bid-rigging cases brought by the DOJ, ranging from school milk and highway bid rigging to electrodes. As noted earlier, more and more cases had an international scope. Cases against Canadian producers of plastic dinnerware and Japanese manu-facturers of thermal fax paper provide additional examples in this regard. Later we will discuss the international component of cartel enforcement more specif-ically. The United States has been quite successful in exporting its version of cartel enforcement to other countries, with the exception that other countries remain unwilling to make price fixing a *criminal* violation.

To put these fines in perspective, the annual fines during the previous Bush administration (1990–92) ranged from $20 million to $24 million. During the first Clinton administration (FY1993–FY1996), the annual fines collected ranged from $27 million to $42 million. From FY1997 through FY1999, the division collected more than $1.5 billion in fines, of which over 90 percent was based on international cartel activity.[16]

Clearly, there has been a sea shift, with cartel enforcement more effective and more active than in recent memory. Though it is unlikely that these dramatic numbers could be sustained under any administration, there is no doubt that

---

15. Indeed, the U.S. Department of Justice noted in its 1999 annual report (p. 8) that the amnesty program at that point was generating applications for amnesty at the rate of two per month.
16. Starting in FY1990, here are the total annual price-fixing fines collected by the Antitrust Divi-sion, rounded to the nearest million dollars: $24, $20, $24, $40, $42, $40, $27, $205, $267, $1,107.

Table 7.1
Sherman Act Violations Yielding a Fine of $10 Million or More

Defendant (FY)	Product	Fine ($ Millions)	Geographic Scope	Country
F. Hoffmann-La Roche, Ltd. (1999)	Vitamins	$500	International	Switzerland
BASF AG (1999)	Vitamins	$225	International	Germany
SGL Carbon AG (1999)	Graphite electrodes	$135	International	Germany
Mitsubishi Corp. (2001)	Graphite electrodes	$134	International	Japan
UCAR International, Inc. (1998)	Graphite electrodes	$110	International	United States
Archer Daniels Midland Co. (1997)	Lysine and citric acid	$100	International	United States
Takeda Chemical Industries, Ltd. (1999)	Vitamins	$72	International	Japan
Daicel Chemical Industries, Ltd. (2000)	Sorbates	$53	International	Japan
ABB Middle East & Africa Participations AG (2001)	Construction	$53	International	Switzerland
Haarmann & Reimer Corp. (1997)	Citric acid	$50	International	German Parent
HeereMac v.o.f. (1998)	Marine construction	$49	International	Netherlands
Sotheby's Holdings Inc. (2001)	Fine arts auctions	$45	International	United States
Eisai Co., Ltd. (1999)	Vitamins	$40	International	Japan
Hoechst AG (1999)	Sorbates	$36	International	Germany
Showa Denko Carbon, Inc. (1998)	Graphite electrodes	$32.5	International	Japan
Philipp Holzmann AG (2000)	Construction	$30	International	Germany
Daiichi Pharmaceutical Co., Ltd. (1999)	Vitamins	$25	International	Japan
Nippon Gohsei (1999)	Sorbates	$21	International	Japan
Pfizer Inc. (1999)	Maltol/sodium erythorbate	$20	International	United States
Fujisawa Pharmaceuticals Co. (1998)	Sodium gluconate	$20	International	Japan
Dockwise N.V. (1998)	Marine transportation	$15	International	Belgium
Dyno Nobel (1996)	Explosives	$15	Domestic	Norwegian Parent
F. Hoffmann-La Roche, Ltd. (1997)	Citric acid	$14	International	Switzerland
Merck KgaA (2000)	Vitamins	$14	International	Germany
Degussa-Huls AG (2000)	Vitamins	$13	International	Germany

Table 7.1 (continued)

Defendant (FY)	Product	Fine ($ Millions)	Geographic Scope	Country
Ueno Fine Chemicals Industry, Ltd. (2001)	Sorbates	$11	International	Japan
Eastman Chemical Co. (1998)	Sorbates	$11	International	United States
Jungbunzlauer International AG (1997)	Citric acid	$11	International	Switzerland
Lonza AG (1998)	Vitamins	$10.5	International	Switzerland
Akzo Nobel Chemicals, BV & Glucona, BV (1997)	Sodium gluconate	$10	International	Netherlands
ICI Explosives (1995)	Explosives	$10	Domestic	British Parent
Mrs. Baird's Bakeries (1996)	Bread	$10	Domestic	United States
Ajinomoto Co., Inc. (1996)	Lysine	$10	International	Japan
Kyowa Hakko Kogyo, Co., Ltd. (1996)	Lysine	$10	International	Japan

cartel enforcement activity remains high. The most visible recent price-fixing case is against the auction houses of Christies and Sotheby's. This case received a great deal of media attention, both because it occurred in the rarified world of art auctions in New York and because it led to a shake-up at both auction houses. Sotheby's has already agreed to pay a $45 million fine, and in December 2001 a federal district court convicted its former chairman of participating in the price-fixing conspiracy.

7.6.2   Civil Price-Fixing Cases

There were also some very prominent *civil* price-fixing cases brought by the DOJ during the Clinton years. While the penalty and deterrent—imprisonment—is plain for criminal price-fixing cases, readers might wonder what penalty is associated with *civil* price-fixing cases, where the companies involved typically agree to cease the alleged price fixing, a "sin no more" remedy, and perhaps some additional "fencing in" provisions designed to prevent related antitrust abuses in the future. An important part of the answer comes in the form of follow-on *private* antitrust actions. Virtually every DOJ case triggers a private case, in which customers asserting overcharges seek treble damages. These cases can be enormously costly to the companies involved. For example, in the NASDAQ case immediately following, the brokerage houses ultimately agreed to pay nearly $1 billion to settle the private cases that followed on DOJ and SEC enforcement actions.

The NASDAQ dealer case stands out as a signature case during Anne Binga-man's tenure. In this case, the DOJ alleged that the major brokerage houses had agreed to limit competition by only quoting NASDAQ stocks in even eighths, thus ensuring that spreads would not be any smaller than one-fourth. This investigation involved close cooperation between the DOJ and the SEC, which was simultaneously bringing its own enforcement action against NASDAQ dealers. The NASDAQ case raised some very interesting issues of evidence (tape recordings of dealer conversations), focal point theories (odd eighths versus even eighths), the role of academic research (an academic paper by Professors William G. Christie and Paul H. Schultz of Vanderbilt University initially brought this matter to the attention of the DOJ and SEC), and appropriate remedy (regulation versus antitrust). The final remedy agreed to by NASDAQ, which led to an SEC rule opening up the "limit order" books, has significantly increased on the exchanges.

In a similar if less visible case, four exchanges that trade options allegedly had an agreement not to engage in multiple listing at different exchanges of "grandfathered" options,[17] that is, options that had been exclusively assigned to individual exchanges by the SEC during an era when the SEC actively discouraged competition among exchanges, preferring instead that all trading take place at a given location. This case provides an interesting example of prior regulation being lifted and competition taking a long time to take root.

7.7 Civil Nonmerger Cases in the Clinton Years

The civil nonmerger antitrust enforcement effort covers several types of possible violations: unlawful conduct by dominant firms, or monopolies; unlawful cooperation among competitors (so-called horizontal conduct); and unlawful activities between firms in different levels of commerce, such as prices imposed by manufacturers on retailers (vertical conduct). The Clinton antitrust team was active on all these fronts, and we review the major efforts here.

7.7.1 Monopolization Cases: Microsoft, Intel, and American Airlines

Antitrust cases challenging the unilateral conduct of dominant firms are among the most controversial, although they also resonate well with a large body of the public, which sometimes distrusts the activities of monopolies. Nonetheless, a major reason for the controversy is that antitrust attacks on dominant firms inevitably involve challenges to the business practices of some of our

---

17. *U.S. v. American Stock Exchange, Chicago Board Options Exchange, Pacific Exchange, and Philadelphia Stock Exchange*, September 2000. See http://www.usdoj.gov/atr/cases/indx262.htm.

most successful firms. These criticisms are not new: they were heard when the government challenged Standard Oil, Kodak, Alcoa, IBM, and AT&T over the decades.

During the Clinton era, the most visible targets of antitrust activity in general were investigations or cases brought against the largest, most powerful firms. We explore three such cases in this subsection: Microsoft, Intel, and American Airlines. But readers should recognize that several less visible monopolization cases were also brought against smaller companies who nonetheless were viewed as dominant in their own spheres by the DOJ or the FTC. These include DOJ's 1996 case against General Electric regarding GE's licenses for medical-imaging-equipment software; DOJ's 1999 exclusive dealing case against Dentsply, the leading supplier of artificial teeth; and the FTC's 1998 case against Mylan Laboratories regarding two antianxiety drugs.

7.7.1.1 United States v. Microsoft

As we hinted at the outset, the Clinton antitrust years probably will be most remembered for the DOJ's continued investigation and ultimately its court action taken against Microsoft for conduct the department asserted constituted unlawful abuse of monopoly power.[18] Although the litigated case during the second Clinton term brought by Joel Klein was the most visible effort in this regard, the DOJ in the first term settled a less sweeping investigation with the company under the direction of Anne Bingaman. Because of its importance, we summarize here some of the key issues from the perspective of each side and then provide our own assessments of each of them. These issues are not unique to Microsoft, but also pose a challenge to competition policy generally with respect to high-technology industries.[19] We include arguments and relevant decisions up through the court of appeals decision in July 2001, which upheld much of the district court's original ruling, but reversed it in part.[20] At this writing, Microsoft had reached a settlement agreement with the DOJ and nine of the 18 plaintiff states, which was pending before the district court.

From the government's perspective, the following propositions seemed evident and well supported by the evidence in the trial (a judgment the court of

---

18. Both authors were involved in investigations of Microsoft when at the Antitrust Division, and Shapiro has offered testimony as an expert witness for the government in the remedy phase of the trial.

19. For excellent overviews of the economics of the Microsoft case from different perspectives, see Gilbert and Katz; B. Klein; and Whinston, all in the Spring 2001 issues of the *Journal of Economic Perspectives*.

20. The decision of the Court of Appeals for the District of Columbia in the Microsoft case is one of the most significant antitrust decisions in recent years and will have lasting implications for the application of the antitrust laws in the software industry and beyond. See http://msft.cadc. uscourts.gov/cadc/00-5212a.pdf.

appeals essentially confirmed). First, Microsoft has a clear monopoly over desktop operating systems, and that monopoly is protected by the "applications barrier to entry," which makes other operating systems (such as the Apple OS or Linux) far less attractive because many fewer applications are written to run on those operating systems: this is network effects in action. Second, Microsoft saw a threat to its operating system in the form of the Netscape browser combined with Sun's Java, which together offered the promise of "cross-platform" middleware that would provide a neutral platform to which applications could be written, thus paving the way (in a two-step entry process) for other operating systems to overcome the applications barrier to entry. Third, Microsoft acted during 1995–98 at least to eliminate the threat to its monopoly by engaging in a series of practices with the intent and effect of limiting the distribution and use of Netscape's browser and of Sun's Java. These practices, such as exclusive dealing arrangements and tying, involved the use of Microsoft's monopoly power over operating systems to stifle the adoption of Netscape and Sun software. Microsoft realized that it would be sufficient to prevent these middleware products from becoming ubiquitous and thus serving as an alternative platform that could "commoditize the operating system." Finally, as a result of Microsoft's conduct, consumers were deprived of a chance to pry open the Microsoft monopoly, which instead persists. While we do not know just how competition would have played out in the absence of Microsoft's conduct, we do know that one major threat to the monopoly (and these do not come along all that often) was eliminated through conduct that did not lead to benefit consumers, and thus cannot be construed as competition on the merits.

Microsoft challenged each of the government's propositions and counters with those of its own. First, the company argued that the software industry is extremely dynamic and fluid, making any monopoly power fleeting and insignificant. Microsoft asserted that it was forced to price competitively because of a multitude of threats that are ever present, since there can be no monopoly over software programming skills, which is all that is needed to design and sell an operating system. The "applications barriers to entry" allegedly are a fiction: applications companies often write software for multiple platforms and would readily do so if those platforms offered superior value to the Microsoft operating system. For example, the Apple system runs a great deal of software, and in fact Microsoft itself ports Office to the Mac OS. Second, Microsoft argued that Netscape and Java were not any unique threat to the company, and in fact did not even constitute a rival operating system as such. Netscape was a competitor in providing browser functionality, but did not offer a substitute to Windows. Third, Microsoft maintained it had done nothing more than innovate, improving the functionality of the operating system by incorporating browser functionality into Windows. This is a natural extension of the operating system, one that all other operating systems have also made as the Internet and computer networking have become important. Microsoft saw the government's attack on its design decisions for Windows as a direct attack on Microsoft's ability to innovate in ways that clearly benefit consumers. Finally, Microsoft claimed there was no consumer harm from any of its conduct, pointing to the fact that Netscape in fact achieved widespread distribution, and Internet Explorer has been able to gain share (against Netscape's initially dominant position) only by offering superior functionality and by leading the way in making its browser available for free. All of this has led to significant consumer benefits, in the company's view.

So, how did these respective arguments play out in the district court and ultimately at the court of appeals? We consider each argument in turn, beginning with the first point, whether or not Microsoft has monopoly power. No doubt Microsoft software has improved over time; no doubt, either, that the mere cost of writing an operating system is modest in comparison with Microsoft's market capitalization (in the hundreds of billions of dollars) and perhaps even in comparison with the annual revenues from Windows. And Microsoft's pricing for Windows—which Microsoft said indicated that entry was an ever-present threat—presented something of a puzzle for the government. But many antitrust economists would agree that Microsoft's durable and very high share of sales of personal computer operating systems, in conjunction with the compatibility issues that hinder Apple and Linux (for example), give Microsoft meaningful monopoly power. The trial record also left little doubt that Microsoft wielded significant power over personal computer makers such as Gateway and Compaq, who have no practical alternative to Microsoft if they want to actually ship personal computers to their customers. In short, software markets, like some other high-technology markets, involve a different set of entry barriers: here, compatibility and copyright, not traditional entry barriers such as specialized manufacturing facilities or trade restrictions. In June 2001, the Court of Appeals for the District of Columbia (CADC) upheld the district court's conclusion that Microsoft did indeed have a monopoly over desktop operating systems.

What about the second point—whether or not Netscape and Java posed a real threat to Windows? Here we get into some of the thorniest issues in "high-tech antitrust." We may imagine as a general principle that a high-tech company—monopoly or not—will be better placed than antitrust officials to identify at an early stage the threats to its position. Especially in software, which is inherently so malleable, the greatest threat may not come from a frontal assault, but rather from a complementary product that can be transformed into at least a partial substitute over time. Let us suppose that the high-tech monopolist, seeing a possible threat, acts to block it before it matures into a full-fledged and "obvious" direct threat. Surely sound competition policy cannot conclude that such behavior is immune from antitrust challenge merely because the threat was immature at the time it was eliminated. And surely it makes sense, as a matter of enforcement policy, to give considerable weight to the company's own documents and views about the likely market evolution. But it is equally clear that predictions of market effects will be very difficult to make if the threat is in its early stages and the market is inherently dynamic. Thus we have an unavoidable policy dilemma: if antitrust officials act early to prevent the incumbent from eliminating the threat, they will necessarily have a difficult time showing definite harm to competition; but if they wait until the harm is shown, it will be too late to correct the problem and far less likely to deter such conduct in the future. On this issue, the court of appeals came down squarely on the government's side, ruling that it would be inconsistent with the purpose of the Sherman Act to allow monopolists free reign to "squash nascent, albeit unproven, competitors at will"—especially in industries marked by rapid technological advance.

The third point—evaluating the actual economic effects of Microsoft's conduct—suffers the same problem just described with respect to the identification of anticompetitive effects. This problem has always been present in monopolization cases, although it is arguably exacerbated in the high-tech setting. The most heated debate revolves around the government's claim that Microsoft "tied" Internet Explorer to Windows. Many commentators harbor considerable unease about having the courts "second-guess" product design decisions, even those by dominant firms. And the antitrust law revolving around tying has always had problems stemming from the necessity of defining just when two "functions" constitute two separate "products," which can be tied, rather than a single product. All the long-standing thorny issues surrounding the law of tying are brought into sharp relief when software is involved, since the boundaries of one piece of software, or one piece of code, and another are inherently hard to define. In fact, the court of appeals remanded the district court's tying decision against Microsoft, indicating that while the application of a per se rule was inappropriate, the government could try again to make its tying case again using the rule of reason, which would require a balancing of the exclusionary effects and the beneficial effects of Microsoft's tying of Internet Explorer to Windows. The DOJ, however, under new leadership, declined the court's offer.

There is less debate surrounding Microsoft's contractual practices, such as exclusivity provisions in various contracts, although even there the effectiveness of these contracts to actually impede Netscape was hotly disputed. The court of appeals fully supported the district court's ruling that Microsoft violated the Sherman Act by defending its monopoly using exclusive contracts with a range of parties.

Finally, we face here the tricky question of whether Microsoft was defending its operating system monopoly or attacking Netscape's browser monopoly (or both). If we take network effects and compatibility seriously, as Microsoft clearly does, Netscape's browser posed a threat to Microsoft precisely because it was the *dominant* browser, and thus an attractive "platform" to which other software could be written. Thus, by attacking Netscape's "monopoly"—something normally encouraged under the antitrust laws—Microsoft was eliminating a threat to its own monopoly—actions which can amount to illegal "monopoly maintenance." Indeed, Microsoft documents indicate that Microsoft's primary goal was simply to match Netscape in browser share, not necessarily to "win" the browser war. Viewed this way, and looking for general principles beyond this particular case, limits on the conduct of one incumbent monopolist can potentially strengthen the position of *another* incumbent monopolist. The court of appeals fully accepted the findings of the district court that Microsoft engaged in "monopoly maintenance" by preventing Netscape's browser and Sun's Java from gaining sufficient acceptance to become an alternative software "platform." Furthermore, the appeals court held that it was an act of monopolization for Microsoft to meld the computer code for the browser and the operating system, given the potential of the browser (plus Java) to become a competing platform for a wide range of applications programs. As a practical matter, this part of the appellate ruling means at the very least that Microsoft must enable consumers and computer manufacturers to remove Internet Explorer from Windows. The proposed settlement before the district court at this time would require this to be done.

In sum, the June 2001 court of appeals decision sends a clear message, especially since is was written by a 7–0 Court: high-technology companies are not immune from antitrust scrutiny. Even if Microsoft ultimately survives with a settlement or court-imposed remedy that is no more than a slap on the wrist, we believe few dominant companies in the future will want to take on the legal risks, and face the public relations problems, that Microsoft has endured by acting so aggressively in wielding its economic power. Whatever happens next, we believe that the legacy of the Microsoft case is clear: powerful companies, even in industries experiencing rapid technological change, must compete on the merits, not by using their power to exclude competition, even competition offered by nascent technologies.

7.7.1.2   Federal Trade Commission v. Intel

The case brought against Intel by the Federal Trade Commission in 1998 is a useful contrast to the Microsoft case.[21] When Intel was faced by patent infringement suits by some of its customers (Intergraph and Digital being the leading examples), Intel withdrew certain valuable Intel intellectual property (including trade secrets valuable to customers building systems incorporating Intel microprocessors) from those customers. The FTC viewed this conduct as a monopolistic abuse by Intel, since these customers would suffer significant economic harm if deprived of the Intel intellectual property. The FTC took the view that Intel should not be able to engage in "self-help" to resolve patent claims brought against it, but rather should resolve such claims in court. Intel viewed its conduct as a natural defensive response, refusing to share its intellectual property with companies that were bringing their own intellectual property cases against Intel.

The parallels between the Microsoft and Intel cases are clear enough: Intel, like Microsoft, is a powerful company in the personal computer business; Intel, like Microsoft, sells a critical component (microprocessors) of personal computers and has a very large share of the sales of this component; Intel, like Microsoft, has enjoyed this large share for years.

But the similarities end there. The Intel conduct challenged by the FTC was very narrow, confined to Intel's response in situations in which an Intel customer sued Intel for patent infringement. Intel's conduct was directed at certain customers, not at Intel's competitors (such as AMD, Intel's primary competitor in making x86 compatible microprocessors, or IBM and Sun, two of Intel's leading competitors in making microprocessors for servers). Unlike the Microsoft case, the FTC never identified any evidence that Intel was attempting to do anything more than defend itself, and reduce its exposure, in the face of patent infringement cases brought against it. Nor was the FTC able to point to any adverse effect of Intel's conduct on competition in microprocessors. The final difference is the disposition of the two cases: shortly before (and not after) trial, Intel settled its case with the FTC, agreeing to partially alter its business practices to meet the FTC's concerns. The Intel case is now seen as a leading example of the boundary between intellectual property and antitrust, as well as a good example of how a leading company can minimize its antitrust exposure by compromising with antitrust enforcers.

Both the Intel and Microsoft cases illustrate the willingness of Clinton antitrust officials to make predictions about how specific business practices will affect competition well into the future. In the Microsoft case, the DOJ necessarily

---

21. Shapiro served as an expert witness on behalf of Intel in this proceeding.

was predicting that Netscape's browser and Sun's Java could, in time, have posed a genuine threat to Microsoft's monopoly position. One reason the government case was so strong in court is that Microsoft itself took precisely this view. Some would say that Microsoft overreacted to the Netscape/Java threat, but who was better placed to judge the severity of the threat than Microsoft itself? Clearly, the efforts of Microsoft executives to distance themselves from their own earlier documents and e-mails undermined their credibility with Judge Thomas Jackson. In the Intel case, the FTC predicted that Intel's conduct inevitably would have a chilling effect on companies that might otherwise engage in innovation to challenge Intel's position in microprocessors. But again we see the importance of the documents and internal assessments of the company itself: the FTC had an underlying theory but virtually no evidence, either from Intel or from third parties, in support of its position. Intel's own documents showed that it was fighting back in the context of patent litigation in an effort to limit its exposure to patent infringement suits. Intel's stated objective was to reduce the royalties it might have to pay and thus lower its costs. And Intel's actions were primarily directed at its customers, not its competitors.

What lessons can we learn from these two signature cases at the intersection of antitrust, intellectual property, and high technology? The lesson for powerful companies subjected to antitrust scrutiny is clear: they must be prepared to defend themselves based on their contemporaneous assessment of their own actions combined with economic analysis of the likely effects of those actions, not based on a reconstruction of why they pursued the strategies they did. The lesson for antitrust officials: court challenges to the conduct of dominant firms based on predictions about future effects on competition and innovation are unlikely to have much force without a solid evidentiary basis for those predictions combined with a sound economic theory of harm to competition.

7.7.1.3   United States v. American Airlines

A third monopolization case stands out from the Clinton years: the predatory-pricing case brought against American Airlines in 1999 by the DOJ. The government challenged American's strategy of cutting prices on flights into and out of its Dallas–Fort Worth (DFW) hub in response to competition from new entrant airlines seeking to serve certain spokes out of that hub.[22]

What was remarkable about the American Airlines case is that the DOJ sued even though there was no evidence that the airline was pricing below average

---

22. Earlier, the Department of Transportation had proposed promulgating rules regarding the pricing and frequency decisions of airlines at their hubs. Meeting resistance by the larger carriers, these rules were never put into place. The DOJ case against American Airlines was an attempt to control aggressive behavior by hub airlines using antitrust rather than regulation.

variable cost or marginal cost, the conventional test for assessing whether predatory pricing was present that is applied by courts, as recommended by antitrust scholars Philip Areeda and Donald Turner. The government none-theless asserted in its complaint that American Airlines intended to drive new entrants out of business with extraordinarily low fares and expected success precisely because marginal costs in the industry—the cost of filling an additional seat on an airplane—were so low.[23] In late April 2001, however, the federal district court in Wichita, Kansas, that was hearing the case threw it out on summary judgment, in effect affirming the Areeda-Turner test. As a result, predatory-pricing law remains where it was before the American Airlines case was brought.[24] In our view, it is unlikely we will see many such cases in the future.[25]

7.7.2   Horizontal Activity

Whatever one may believe about the wisdom of government challenges of conduct by dominant firms, there is much more consensus among antitrust scholars and practitioners that the government should be vigilant in prosecuting various types of horizontal, or collusive, arrangements to fix prices and divide markets. Nonetheless, even this consensus can break down when confronted with the facts of particular cases. The Clinton antitrust years were marked by some rather novel investigations and prosecutions of horizontal conduct, not merely plain vanilla price fixing. A review of the most notable efforts follows.

7.7.2.1   DOJ's Credit Card Case

DOJ sued Visa and MasterCard in October 1998 for their rules regarding dual governance and exclusivity. Dual governance refers to the fact that many of the banks in control of Visa also play a lead role in running the MasterCard system. Exclusivity refers to the rules that prohibit banks that are members of Visa or MasterCard from issuing rival cards such as American Express or Discover.

---

23. As usual in predatory pricing cases, the measurement of "marginal cost" or "average variable cost" is both contentious and tricky. In this case, the treatment of the cost of aircraft was a central issue. DOJ sought to have the opportunity cost of an aircraft, namely, the profits that could be earned by flying that aircraft on an alternative route, included in the measurement of variable cost (at least when evaluating decisions to add more flights to the routes in question). Courts historically have been reluctant to include opportunity costs in their measurement of incremental costs.

24. In June 2001 the DOJ announced that it would appeal the district court's ruling in the American Airlines case.

25. Prior to the American Airlines case, the government had not brought a predatory-pricing case for years. Generally, the courts have become less and less receptive to predatory-pricing cases over the past 25 years.

DOJ asserted that dual governance and exclusivity had impeded competition among and innovation by credit card systems (such as Visa, MasterCard, American Express, Discover). A trial was held in the summer of 2000 in this case. After a trial in the summer of 2001, the district court judge who heard the case struck down the exclusivity rules, but rejected the government's claim that dual governance stifled innovation in the credit card market.

7.7.2.2 FTC Cases Challenging Patent Settlements by Drug Companies

Starting in 1999, the FTC moved aggressively to challenge agreements reached between incumbent companies holding pharmaceutical patents and would-be challengers offering generic drugs. Several of these cases display variations on the same fact pattern. First, the challenger files with the FDA for permission to introduce a generic version of a popular branded drug. Next, the incumbent supplier, who holds a patent, asserts that the challenger would infringe the patent, which (under the Hatch-Waxman Act) freezes the generic challenger for 30 months while the patent infringement issues are sorted out in court. Then the incumbent and the challenger reach a settlement, which specifies a date at which the challenger is licensed to enter the market.

The FTC has objected strongly when these patent settlements involve a cash payment from the patent holder to the challenger. The FTC asserts that incumbents are effectively paying to delay the entry by the generic challenger, thereby depriving consumers of the benefits of generic competition, which typically involves much lower prices than are charged by the branded incumbent supplier. In some cases, due to the operation of the Hatch-Waxman Act, a settlement between the patent holder and the first company to file with the FDA to offer a generic can also freeze *other* generic suppliers out of the market. The FTC has filed several of these cases and has opened a broader industry investigation into this type of settlement agreement.[26]

7.7.2.3 Patent Pools

As intellectual property becomes a more and more important element of competition, the antitrust limits on agreements involving intellectual property loom larger in the antitrust enforcement world. The FTC generic drug cases just described fit into this category. So does the Intel case, which was in many respects about cross-licensing: Intel would not license its patents and trade secrets unless the licensee also shared its intellectual property with Intel. As explained in Shapiro (2000), the surge in patenting activity has created a "patent

---

26. For a more complete discussion of these cases, see Gilbert and Tom (2001). On the broader question of the antitrust limits on settlements of patent disputes between direct rivals, see Shapiro (2001).

thicket" that companies must cut through to commercialize products in a number of high-tech industries, inevitably leading to more licensing and cross-licensing activity.

Patent pools are yet another type of intellectual property agreement. Under this form, two or more companies contribute their patents to the pool, which then licenses out a package of patents to companies seeking to manufacturer products using those patents. Patent pools have long raised red flags in antitrust circles, as they can easily involve an agreement on pricing (at least to set the price charged by the pool) between actual or potential competitors.[27]

The Clinton Justice Department was quite supportive of patent pools, with suitable protections. The DOJ recognized that pooling the *complementary* patents necessary for a product or technology can be highly procompetitive. In theory, forming a patent pool can lower licensing costs for two reasons: by offering convenient, one-stop shopping for licensees whose products make use of several patents, and by internalizing the "Cournot complements" problems that leads to inefficiently high prices when two complementary monopolists price their products (or patents) independently. Using this sound economic reasoning, DOJ issued favorable business review letters for a patent pool involving the MPEG video compression technology and for two patent pools involving DVD technology.

In contrast, the FTC took a distinctly more hostile approach to patent pools, challenging the patent pool formed by Summit and VisX, the two key suppliers of technology for laser eye surgery. Despite the fact that Summit and VisX appeared to have held complementary blocking patents (this being the standard used by the DOJ for allowing the formation of a pool), the FTC challenged their pool, Pillar Point Partners. In the Summit/VisX case, the parties agreed to abolish their pool and give each other royalty-free cross-licenses. Although this agreement served the short-run interests of consumers, the FTC approach may discourage the formation of efficient and procompetitive patent pools in the future, and may discourage innovation by failing to give sufficient returns to innovators who must deal with others holding complementary blocking patents.

7.7.2.4 Standard Setting

The FTC's case against Dell Computer articulated an important principle regarding the use of intellectual property in the standard-setting process: after Dell had agreed not to assert any patents against other companies for the purpose of

---

27. See J. Klein (1997) for a discussion of cross-licensing and patent pools, including a nice description of an airplane patent pool dating back to World War I, which was approved by the Justice Department.

complying with a certain hardware standard, Dell indeed tried to assert such patents. The FTC challenged this practice, and Dell agreed not to assert its patents on this standard. The key principle here is that companies must meet the promises they make in a standard-setting context with respect to the licensing of their patents necessary to comply with the standard. For a further discussion of the antitrust treatment of standard-setting activities, see Shapiro (2000).

7.8 Merger Control Policy During the Clinton Years

For reasons having nothing to do with antitrust policy, there was a massive merger wave during the mid- to late 1990s. The merger wave washed over large sections of the economy, ranging from banking to telephones, from defense to health care, from railroads to radio. Inevitably, many of these mergers involved dominant firms or direct competitors, and thus triggered antitrust review. As shown in Figure 7.4, the number of Hart-Scott-Rodino merger notifications received by the FTC and the DOJ more than tripled from the early 1990s to the late 1990s.[28] Even more dramatic was the increase in the *value* of U.S. merger activity. During the 1990–92 time period, the average annual value of U.S. merger activity was $151 billion. During the 1998–99 time period, this average had jumped more than tenfold to $1.7 trillion. While some of this increase reflects the overheated stock market valuations of 1998–99, the real economic value of merger activity clearly rose dramatically during the 1990s. Naturally, this increase put more pressure on the resources of the DOJ and the FTC and increased their crucial role ensuring that mergers and acquisitions do not substantially reduce competition.[29]

We find it notable, however, that the rate of *challenges* of mergers as a percentage of HSR filings (again, see Figure 7.4) did not rise significantly from the early 1990s to the late 1990s. In fact, despite the huge number of mergers proposed and consummated, virtually none of these mergers were challenged and litigated on antitrust grounds. In large part, the dearth of litigation reflects a clear articulation of merger control policy—less uncertainty means less litigation. In no year were more than 6 percent of proposed mergers subjected to a full investigation (second request for information); in no year were more than 0.5 percent of proposed mergers challenged in court. And, in the vast majority of deals that were modified as a result of the HSR review, these modifications (usually divestitures) were achieved through a settlement with the DOJ or the FTC.

---

28. During 1990–92, an average of 1,366 HSR filings were made per year. During 1998–2000, an average of 4,584 HSR filings were made.
29. Data are taken from the Antitrust Division's *Annual Report* for FY1999.

We also should note a reality of today's capital markets: few companies are prepared to fight in court a DOJ or FTC challenge to their merger. The ensuing litigation inevitably takes several months, if not more, during which time the target company is likely to suffer, both in terms of its stock price and in terms of its ability to operate effectively. As a result, merging parties often abandon their mergers once DOJ or the FTC makes it clear that a challenge will ensue and if the agency's requirements to "fix" the deal are unacceptable to the merging parties.

7.8.1 The Predictable Nature of Merger Enforcement Policy

We attribute the low level of merger litigation in no small part to the relatively predictable nature of merger enforcement, at least as regards horizontal mergers, following the 1992 Horizontal Merger Guidelines. Recall that the guidelines have been largely in place for nearly 20 years. In other words, the small amount of litigation should not be taken as indicating that antitrust policy was somehow lax or irrelevant. To the contrary, companies are continually counseled on which proposed mergers will pass, or fail, antitrust scrutiny. In this very real sense, merger control policy has an ongoing, profound, if largely hidden effect on the very structure of American industry.

As noted earlier, the economic principles behind merger control policy have not shifted since the Reagan administration. Rather, the differences across administrations have been one of judgment and emphasis. For example, in the Reagan years, antitrust officials were quite receptive to "entry arguments," namely, arguments put forward by merging parties that they could not exercise market power postmerger because any attempt to do so would be met with easy and rapid entry into the market. Clinton administration officials also acknowledged that entry *can* eliminate concerns, but tended to require much more solid evidence of ease of entry before giving significant weight to these arguments.

There has been one clear shift in merging thinking throughout the 1990s. Early on, the primary theory used by lawyers at the DOJ and FTC was a collusion theory: after the merger, with one fewer player in the market, the remaining suppliers would find it easier either to form a cartel (explicit collusion) or simply to adopt "live and let live" strategies (tacit collusion) rather than to compete actively and aggressively. By the mid-1990s, an alternative theory, known in antitrust circles as "unilateral effects," became much more common in merger analysis. This is effectively the theory that the post-merger competitive equilibrium (formally, some type of Nash equilibrium) would involve reduced output and higher prices than before the merger. Based as it is on noncooperative oligopoly theory, unilateral effects analysis is highly amenable to economic modeling and estimation. As a result, the emphasis on unilateral effects has led to a great expansion in the role of oligopoly theory and econometric analysis in merger review. This has been evident especially in cases where considerable data are available, such as mergers involving consumer goods where super-market (or comparable) scanner data are available. Some of the most detailed empirical work on differentiated products, pricing, and oligopoly now takes place in the context of merger analysis, in part because economists conducting such analysis have exceptional access to detailed company records as well as high-frequency, disaggregated price and quantity data.

7.8.2   General Approach to Remedies

We did see some general shifts in the approach taken at the FTC and the DOJ regarding three broad classes of merger "remedies": (1) blockage of the merger; (2) requiring the merged firms to divest certain assets to preserve competition (a so-called structural remedy); or (3) requiring the merged entity to operate its business subject to certain limitations (a so-called behavioral remedy).

As a general rule, both agencies have long been unwilling to enter into be-havioral remedies in horizontal mergers. For example, an agreement to lower prices 5 percent per year after the merger would typically not be accepted as a substitute for premerger competition between the merging parties. Underlying this view is the judgment that the benefits of competition cannot be replicated through consent agreements: perhaps competition would lead to much better products, or to prices falling at a rate greater than 5 percent per year. Concerns about enforceability also argue against behavioral remedies, especially in hori-zontal mergers.

In contrast, behavioral remedies are often accepted in vertical mergers. For example, in the Time Warner/Turner merger, the FTC accepted a commitment by Time Warner to provide access on the Time Warner cable systems to either MSNBC or Fox News, the two leading competitors to CNN, which was part of Turner Broadcasting and was being acquired by Time Warner. This behav-ioral remedy was intended to address the concern that Time Warner might use its cable properties to exclude rivals to CNN from obtaining needed cable distribution.

Returning to horizontal merger cases, where divestitures are the typical rem-edy, there still remains the question of how big a package of assets must be divested. The operative rule at both agencies is that the divestiture should create a viable competitor so that there is no significant loss of competition in comparison with the premerger state of affairs. In most cases, the competitive vitality of the divested assets depends both on the package of assets that is divested *and* the identity of the company acquiring those assets. For example, in the proposed acquisition of Intuit by Microsoft, which the DOJ asserted would have reduced competition in the market for financial software (Intuit's Quicken competed against Microsoft's Money), the divestiture offered by Microsoft was rejected by the DOJ. Simply spinning off Money (even if a full package of assets had been offered) was inadequate, since it was unlikely that any firm picking up the Money assets would be as strong a competitor in the financial software market as Microsoft was viewed to be prior to the proposed merger.

The implication: before accepting a divestiture remedy in a merger case, antitrust officials are interested in knowing not just what assets will be divested but also the likely identity of the firm acquiring the divested assets. On this score, we observe the DOJ, and especially the FTC, taking a tougher stance in the second Clinton term than during the first. The FTC went so far as to issue a report in 1999 on the divestiture process, reaching the conclusion that certain "partial" remedies had not been as effective as hoped. The unavoidable policy conclusion: divestitures should be more complete, and the FTC should make sure that the buyer of any divested assets will be a highly capable competitor in the relevant markets at issue. In short, the prevailing approach during the first term was to accept surgical fixes, while a "clean sweep" of assets was more likely to be required during the second term. Leading examples in which the agencies required the divested operations to be full-fledged, viable businesses on their own were Exxon/Mobil, BP/Amoco, BP/ARCO, Time Warner/Turner, and Worldcom/MCI.

7.8.3   Major Merger Challenges

We cannot do justice here to the many mergers investigated and challenged during the Clinton years. Rather, we will simply mention a handful of the more visible cases at each agency, with very brief commentary on the substance of these cases, what they tell us about merger enforcement policy during the Clinton years, and their implications for future merger enforcement.

7.8.3.1   Department of Justice
The Antitrust Division challenged Microsoft's acquisition of Intuit in 1995. Intuit's Quicken financial planning software was a direct competitor to Microsoft's Money software. Microsoft and Intuit abandoned the deal prior to litigation. This case shows the DOJ rejecting arguments that entry barriers into software markets are inevitably low, and viewing Microsoft as a strong force capable of adding significant competition in an area where Intuit was the leader. The case also shows that DOJ was unwilling to accept a partial divestiture of Money assets by Microsoft.

In 1996 the division urged the Surface Transportation Board (STB) not to approve the proposed merger between the Union Pacific and Southern Pacific railroads, two of the three major railroads in the western United States. Analysis of this merger at DOJ involved extensive econometric work to define relevant railroad markets and the impact of competition from trucking and waterborne freight transportation. The DOJ also expressed skepticism over the large efficiency claims put forward by the merging parties. The STB approved the merger over DOJ objections. After the merger, Union Pacific experienced very substantial disruptions to its operations—effectively an antiefficiency. Later, following a complex deal by which CSX and Norfolk Southern split up Conrail, the STB imposed a ban on railroad mergers, which was only lifted by the Bush administration in the summer of 2001. This case shows how resting final authority over mergers in the STB, rather than DOJ, is likely to lead to a more lenient policy, just as it did during the 1980s when the Department of Transportation approved several airline mergers over DOJ objections.

DOJ challenged several hospital mergers during the first Clinton term, but was less active in controlling hospital mergers after facing several defeats in court, including a 1994 setback in the merger of the only two hospitals in Dubuque, Iowa, Mercy Health Center and Finley Hospital, and a 1997 defeat in the merger of Long Island Jewish Medical Center and North Shore Health System.

Throughout the Clinton administration, and especially after the passage of the Telecommunications Act of 1996, the Antitrust Division was faced with a series of proposed mergers in the telecommunications sector. The radio industry experienced a wave of consolidations, with the DOJ (not the FCC) serving as the gatekeeper limiting concentration of radio assets in various cities. Likewise, DOJ faced several huge telephone mergers, including SBC/Pacific Bell, SBC/Ameritech, Bell Atlantic/Nynex, Bell Atlantic/GTE, and Qwest/U.S. West. Generally, DOJ approved these mergers with relatively minor divestitures or other conditions. DOJ effectively took the view that adjacent regional Bell operating companies (RBOCs), such as Bell Atlantic and Nynex, either were not significant potential competitors in each other's regions or that the merging parties were only one of several potential competitors. One telecom merger in which the DOJ required a significant divestiture was the merger between Worldcom and MCI in 1998: the DOJ required the sale of a major MCI unit to preserve competition in Internet backbone services. Various antitrust observers have noted that preserving competition among the various underlying pipes that constitute the Internet—itself often viewed as a technology that breaks down entry barriers and enables wide-open competition—requires vigilant antitrust enforcement.

During the second Clinton term, several very large mergers or acquisitions were abandoned in the face of DOJ challenges: Alcoa and Reynolds in aluminum (1997); Lockheed Martin and Northrop Grumman in defense contracting, at $11.6 billion the largest merger ever blocked on antitrust grounds at that time (1998); the acquisition of Primestar, a direct broadcast satellite service, by several cable companies (1998); and the merger of Worldcom MCI and Sprint in telephone and Internet services (2000). In some respects, these are the most visible merger enforcement actions of all: major deals that are not merely restructured, but flat-out abandoned because of antitrust problems.

7.8.3.2   Federal Trade Commission

One of the most important merger cases brought by the FTC was against Staples and Office Depot, two office supply "superstores" that sought to merge in 1997. The case was a significant test of the "unilateral effects" theory described earlier. The FTC, relying on extensive econometric evidence showing that prices were lower in cities served by multiple office superstores, claimed that this was a three-to-two merger in a market for office supply superstores. The parties asserted that the market included all suppliers of office supplies, and that their combined share was too small to pose a serious antitrust problem. By winning this case, the FTC strengthened merger enforcement by convincing a court that direct evidence of pricing effects could overcome more qualitative arguments about "reasonable substitutes" that have often been used by courts to define antitrust markets.

One of the most sensitive mergers reviewed by the FTC was Boeing's acquisition of McDonnell Douglas. In 1997 the FTC cleared this merger, despite the fact that Boeing's share of the market for large commercial aircraft was roughly 60 percent and the fact that McDonnell Douglas was one of only two rivals, the other being Airbus Industrie. In a statement explaining their decision, three commissioners explained that they had not acted to further a "national champion," but rather had simply concluded that "McDonnell Douglas, looking to the future, no longer constitutes a meaningful competitive force in the commercial aircraft market."[30] The case caused some tension across the Atlantic when the European Commission required that Boeing modify some of its exclusive contracts with airlines as a condition for approving the merger.

Like the DOJ, the FTC experienced an acceleration of its merger enforcement duties in the second Clinton term. Generally speaking, the FTC displayed a far greater appetite to look for behavior remedies in vertical cases than the DOJ,

---

30. See the statement by Chairman Pitofsky and Commissioners Steiger, Starek, and Varney at http://www.ftc.gov/opa/1997/9707/boeingsta.htm. Shapiro served as an outside economic consultant to the commission on the Boeing/McDonnell Douglas merger.

which was more inclined to simply let vertical deals proceed. Two of the most significant vertical mergers reviewed by the FTC were the acquisition of Turner Broadcasting by Time Warner (1997) and the merger of AOL and Time Warner in 2000. In both cases, the FTC insisted on behavioral provisions before approving these deals.

The FTC also found itself in the middle of a major consolidation in the oil industry during the second Clinton term. After extensive reviews, the FTC insisted on major divestitures in the BP/Amoco merger (1998), the Exxon/Mobil merger (1999), and the BP/ARCO merger (2000). The entire vertical chain in the oil industry was implicated in these various mergers, from exploration and drilling (BP/ARCO in Alaska) to retail gasoline stations. As usual, oil industry mergers are highly visible and politically sensitive. The FTC did not block any of these mergers outright, but was aggressive in the divestitures sought. For example, in the BP/ARCO deal, the FTC insisted that BP divest ARCO's entire Alaskan operations, on the theory that BP had monopoly power in the sale of Alaskan North Slope crude oil on the U.S. West Coast, even though the State of Alaska was satisfied that a much smaller divestiture would preserve competition in bidding for exploration rights on the Alaska North Slope, and despite a consensus among experts that the market for crude oil is a worldwide market, with no separate market for Alaskan crude oil used on the U.S. West Coast. After entering into litigation with the FTC, BP agreed to the divestiture sought by the FTC, averting a trial.[31]

A final FTC case worthy of note is the FTC's challenge to the proposed acquisition of Beechnut's baby food business by Heinz. The FTC challenged this merger in 2000, expressing concern that Heinz and Beechnut were the only two rivals to Gerber, the dominant supplier of baby food in the United States. The merging parties argued that they would achieve significant efficiencies by joining forces and thus be better able to take on Gerber. The district court agreed with the parties on this point and refused to grant a preliminary injunction blocking the merger. However, the FTC appealed this decision. Such appeals are very rare, since most merging parties lack the patience to appeal unfavorable merger decisions by the lower courts, and the agencies at times choose not to appeal if the merger in question is consummated after a request for preliminary injunction is denied. Because they are so rare, decisions by the appeals court on merger matters are highly influential. In this case, Heinz and Beechnut were able to hold their merger together through the appeals process. In a blow to the "efficiencies defense" in mergers, the appeals court ruled that the merging parties had *not* established sufficient efficiencies to offset the presumed re-

---

31. Shapiro served as an expert witness for BP and ARCO in this case.

duction in competition based on the increase in concentration in the market for baby food. This case is significant because it raises the hurdle even further for companies seeking to justify their mergers based on achieving efficiencies.

Several major mergers were also abandoned in the face of a potential FTC challenge, including Barnes & Noble's proposed marriage with Ingram and the Air Liquide–Air Products merger. As with threatened actions by the DOJ, the potential for challenge by the FTC also discourages some anticompetitive mergers from ever seeing the light of day.

7.9 The Rise in International Antitrust Enforcement in the Clinton Years

There is no doubt that antitrust enforcement became more international in scope during the Clinton years. For more detail on how U.S. companies and U.S. antitrust officials must be mindful of international issues, see the final report of the International Competition Policy Advisory Committee (ICPAC), which was issued in February 2000. The ICPAC was established by the attorney general in November 1997 to address global antitrust problems.[32]

The increasingly global nature of antitrust enforcement should be expected to some degree, since the U.S. economy itself was become more integrated during these years—as measured by rising shares of imports and exports and capital flows as a share of total output (for more details, see Chapter 5 in this volume). Nonetheless, the international nature of the enforcement agenda was surprising in one respect. Normally, one would assume that the greater the competition from foreign imports, in particular, the more competitive pressure would be applied to domestic firms; and thus the need for antitrust scrutiny would be reduced. But while this effect almost certainly did materialize, increasing cross-border economic activity led to a more active international agenda for at least four important reasons.

First, there were mounting numbers of highly visible mergers involving companies that had international operations, and thus which triggered antitrust review in multiple jurisdictions—especially Europe, where antitrust enforcement had been centralized since the early 1990s in the European Commission. Some of the best-known examples included several major telecommunications alliances—British Telecom and MCI, and then with AT&T; Deutsche Telecom and France Telecom with Sprint; MCI's marriage with Worldcom; Boeing's purchase of McDonnell Douglas; and most recently, General Electric's plan to acquire Honeywell (which was blocked by the European Commission in July 2001).

---

32. The report is available on-line at http://www.usdoj.gov/atr/icpac/icpac.htm.

Second, as we indicated earlier, the U.S. corporate amnesty program eventually uncovered a number of price-fixing conspiracies that were international in scope. Indeed, the vitamins case—which resulted in the largest criminal antitrust fine in U.S. history—had a number foreign defendants. However, there were other price-fixing cases—notably, fax paper involving Japanese defendants and dinner flatware involving Canadian defendants—where U.S. authorities successfully mounted a court challenge (or agreed to a settlement) even though most, if not all, of the evidence and illegal activity were located abroad. Nonetheless, U.S. law is sweeping in scope: well-established cases allow U.S. antitrust prosecution as long as the offending activity adversely affects U.S. consumers. The problem of international cartels is not simply a problem for the United States, but has been recognized as an important global issue (WTO, 1997).

Third, both European and U.S. antitrust authorities have become involved in investigating and prosecuting dominant-firm abuses where the target of the investigation conducts business and engages in similar activities in both jurisdictions. A prominent example is the first Microsoft investigation during 1993–94. In that case, Microsoft actually consented to a joint investigation—and ultimately to a joint settlement—because the company did not want potentially inconsistent rulings from both authorities (see Litan, 2000). A more recent example is the initiation of an investigation of Intel by the EC in 2001 after the FTC had conducted and then closed its own investigation. In this instance, the EC investigation apparently is proceeding without much U.S. involvement or cooperation—a possible harbinger of things to come, as we will note shortly.

Finally, the Clinton Justice Department carved out new ground in the international arena when it acted on a potentially important policy change that was announced in 1992 under Assistant Attorney General James Rill: the prosecution of foreign defendants for taking steps outside the United States that violated our antitrust laws in a way that harmed U.S. *exporters*, not just importers. The initial target of this change in policy was a British company, Pilkington, which the DOJ asserted had a dominant position worldwide in the provision of technology for the manufacturing of glass. The Justice Department charged Pilkington with using exclusive territories and other restrictive licensing practices to entrench its monopoly position. Eventually, the company agreed to a consent decree to abandon these practices.

Where antitrust investigations or matters involve multiple jurisdictions, it is appropriate—indeed necessary—for U.S. authorities to cooperate with their counterparts in other countries. As early as 1967, the OECD went on record urging such cooperation, a recommendation that has been modified a number of times since (OECD, 1995). U.S. antitrust authorities have followed up this recommendation by entering into a number of bilateral cooperation agreements with similar authorities in other countries, including Australia, Canada, the European Commission, and Germany. During the Clinton years, Brazil, Israel, Japan, and Mexico were added to this list. Each of these agreements obligates the parties to notify the other of a pending investigation, contemplates the sharing of information about planned actions that may affect the interests of the other party, and outlines efforts to cooperate in actual investigations, to the extent permitted by applicable law. None of these agreements, however, overrides domestic laws that prohibit the sharing of confidential information without the consent of the target of the investigation. The United States does have one other agreement, however, with Canada—a "mutual legal assistance treaty" (MLAT)—that allows the sharing of information obtained in criminal investigations that otherwise might be confidential.

While these bilateral agreements have been important, they do not require the sharing of all information, nor can they compel foreign witnesses to testify or produce any documents they may have in their possession, unless home country authorities compel such production. The latter shortcoming was arguably the main reason why the Justice Department failed to survive a motion for directed verdict in the criminal price-fixing case it brought against General Electric during 1993–94 involving industrial diamonds. Shortly after that case, however, the department was more successful in persuading Congress to authorize U.S. antitrust agencies to enter into bilateral MLATs to share otherwise confidential information in *civil* cases. That authority was granted in the International Antitrust Assistance Act, and the government has since entered into such an agreement with Australia.

Given the relatively heavy volume of mergers and other investigations involving joint jurisdiction with the European Commission (EC), much of the cooperative activity of the U.S. authorities during the Clinton years was with the European Commission's competition directorate, DG IV (now known as DG-Comp). By and large, the U.S. and EC authorities saw eye-to-eye, with perhaps the notable exception of the Boeing–McDonnell Douglas merger, where the European Commission was more insistent on conditions (which it eventually got, in the form of a ban on exclusive contracts between Boeing and certain airlines). In the first Microsoft investigation, Justice and EC officials sat side-by-side in the negotiations with Microsoft that led to the first consent decree. In other cases, notably the MCI–Worldcom merger, the U.S. authorities let the EC take the lead in imposing conditions (a divestiture of Internet backbone operations).

While the trend toward increasing cooperation with foreign authorities exists, some rough spots remain. In our view, the Justice Department during our tenure was somewhat frustrated with what it saw as a less-than-aggressive posture by the Japanese Fair Trade Commission. The department also ruffled feathers abroad with its insistence on extraterritorial application of our antitrust laws, not just in the Japanese fax paper case, but also in the Pilkington matter, where the primary harm was to U.S. exporters in third-country markets rather than to U.S. consumers. Meanwhile, European officials appear to be frustrated with the resistance of our antitrust authorities to add antitrust harmonization to the list of issues to be negotiated under the auspices of the World Trade Organization (WTO). The main reason for recalcitrance on our part has been a fear of U.S. officials that any international agreement could water down our own antitrust standards. Nonetheless, shortly before he left office, Assistant Attorney General Joel Klein endorsed a recommendation by an advisory board report that the United States seek to harmonize merger reporting requirements so as to facilitate the review, approval, or where necessary, opposition of authorities to mergers invoking the jurisdiction of multiple countries.[33]

Both antitrust and trade officials in the U.S. government have also been extremely hesitant about putting antidumping reform on the trade agenda. Intellectually speaking, this reluctance is difficult to justify. The antidumping law punishes behavior by foreign companies—selling below average cost and engaging in price discrimination—that is lawful for domestic firms selling in the U.S. market and certainly not in violation of U.S. antitrust law. Less developed countries, in particular, have been fond of pointing this out and have insisted that antidumping policy reform be added to the agenda of any future trade negotiating round. Until USTR Robert Zoellick boldly agreed at the November 2001 WTO ministerial to add antidumping to the next trade work plan, U.S. trade officials, in both Democratic and Republican administrations, had strongly resisted such a course, as a large majority of Congress continues to do. In our view, the strong congressional support of the antidumping laws is the major reason why U.S. antitrust officials have not so far pressed for antidumping reform.[34]

Finally, it is possible that any material changes in antitrust policy during the current Bush administration will lead to more friction with antitrust officials abroad, especially in Europe, where the Competition Directorate in recent years appears to have become even more aggressive in antitrust enforcement. If this

---

33. Ibid.

34. One of us (Litan) has suggested a reform of the antidumping laws that would not require their repeal (and replacement with just antitrust law): eliminating the cost of production test or changing it to penalize only sales below average *variable* cost for goods bought from countries that have reasonably adequate antitrust enforcement and that do not maintain significant barriers to imports of the same goods. This modification is designed to satisfy those who claim that an antidumping law is necessary to prevent firms in countries with closed markets from "dumping" their goods abroad, and especially in our market. But if foreign markets are not really closed, then arguably a different (more reasonable) antidumping test should apply. See Burtless et al. (1998).

friction emerges, then major multinational companies that might have anticipated benefits from a more relaxed antitrust enforcement policy in this country
could end up being sorely disappointed. At the same time, disagreements over
antitrust policy between the United States and Europe could make an already
difficult trade relationship even more contentious. Most recently, the July 2001
opposition of the European Union to the proposed General Electric and Honeywell merger—a deal that was cleared by the DOJ with selected divestitures—
has occasioned significant comment, most of it adverse, from the U.S. press and
political leaders. Since the EC's concerns are difficult to justify on traditional
antitrust grounds,[35] the events surrounding the GE/Honeywell merger could
be the harbinger of further tensions between the United States and European
antitrust authorities in the future.

7.10   Challenges Ahead: Antitrust in an Era of High Tech[36]

Looking ahead, questions have been raised about whether antitrust enforcement
is up to the challenges posed by certain aspects of what has come to be called
the new economy. One challenge grows out of the sheer speed of technological
change, especially in the information technology sector, where new generations
of microprocessors have been doubling the speed of computers every 12 to 18
months. Ever faster computer chips lead to the creation and production of very
powerful personal computers and other chip-based devices, which in turn require new and more powerful software. Technological change in the biotech
sector also seems extraordinarily rapid, with potentially even more far-reaching
benefits for society.

It is tempting to conclude that the quickened pace of technological change
makes antitrust irrelevant. If technology, firms, and markets can change so
rapidly, how long can any single firm retain monopoly power? More to the
point, given the relatively slow pace of the judicial process—even after the
relatively rapid trial in the Microsoft case, more than three years elapsed between the filing of the government complaint and a decision by the appeals
court, and we still have no definitive outcome—how can antitrust enforcers
expect to contribute more good than harm when litigating?

---

35. The European Commission opposed the merger in part on the grounds that GE would be able
to offer Boeing, Airbus, and others discounts on packages of GE engines and Honeywell avionics
and other products. The commission feared that this discounting would put pressure on rivals and
ultimately create or strengthen a dominant position by GE. Needless to say, blocking a merger
based on concerns that it will lead to discounting is not in the mainstream of economic thinking
about merger control policies, nor in keeping with U.S. antitrust law. Shapiro has provided economic assistance to GE and Honeywell during their merger review process.
36. This section draws on Litan (2001) and Shapiro (2000).

There are several answers to this techno-pessimism about antitrust. One is that even in the face of rapid technological change, incumbent monopolies enjoy tremendous advantages that make it difficult for new entrants to dislodge them even when technology advances. Microsoft, for example, has maintained a monopoly in operating systems for personal computers over a decade. Likewise, Intel has enjoyed a high share of desktop microprocessor sales for over a similar period. Incumbents not only have the advantage of deep pockets, but they also can take advantage of lead time in designing upgrades or new products that are "backward compatible" with their preexisting versions. Accordingly, there is time for litigation—and often early settlement—to make a real difference where monopolies are believed to be abusing their market power. The appeals court in the Microsoft case certainly did not back away from the application of the antitrust laws in the rapidly changing software industry.

A second answer is that rapid technological change underscores the *importance* of antitrust in the review of mergers among firms in high-technology markets. An ounce of prevention is worth more than a pound of cure when market conditions are subject to change. Accordingly, mergers in high-tech markets should face an extra degree of scrutiny precisely because the relative sluggishness of the judicial process makes it more difficult after the fact to unscramble in a timely and meaningful fashion concentrations of markets made possible by mergers.

A third answer concedes the problem that rapid change poses for antitrust enforcement but then seeks to speed up the judicial process so that resolution of antitrust litigation can occur much more quickly. One approach, which is difficult to legislate but nonetheless should be copied, is to conduct trials in the streamlined way in which the Microsoft trial was conducted. That is, discovery can be limited, the parties can be confronted with a real, early trial date, and the trial itself can be streamlined by limiting the number of witnesses each side is able to present. Requiring all judges to conduct their litigations this way is difficult, if not impossible, to mandate, as the experience with the Civil Justice Reform Act of 1990 has demonstrated.[37] But Judge Jackson demonstrated in the Microsoft case that a major antitrust liability trial could be conducted relatively quickly (even if he then got himself into trouble by attempting to impose a structural remedy without sufficient evidentiary hearings and by discussing the case with the press after his decision). Nonetheless, it is not clear that a lag of

---

37. There was uneven adoption of expedited procedures in the ten "model" district courts that were funded to experiment with ways to streamline their cases. The CJRA experience highlights the fact that procedural reform depends almost exclusively on the willingness of particular judges to adopt such approaches as early trial dates and limits on discovery and witnesses.

more than three years from complaint to final judgment is truly workable and effective in high-tech industries.

Continued advances in technology undoubtedly will raise many more fascinating antitrust issues in the years ahead. One of them is how the emerging business-to-business (B2B) exchanges on the Internet—many of which are joint ventures among competing firms—will be treated by the antitrust authorities. In theory, of course, joint ventures of this type pose the dangers of collusion, not just among the competing buyers but also among the suppliers from whom bids are sought, and so need to be scrutinized carefully. To give another current example, American, Continental, Delta, Northwest, and United Airlines recently launched their Orbitz venture to sell tickets on-line, over the strong objections of travel agents (but approved by the Transportation Department). Will this venture streamline ticket sales and cut out middlemen, or will it serve as a mechanism for collusion?

The Federal Trade Commission staff indicated in its October 2000 staff report that antitrust concerns over B2B exchanges can usually be eliminated by adopting well-crafted operating rules. B2B exchanges are likely to pass muster as long as they meet a number of conditions designed to ensure that pricing is transparent, that the price quotes are "firm" (and not signals of what suppliers intend to charge), that confidential information is protected, and that exchanges avoid being "overinclusive" while also making sure that they are not used to exclude buyers or suppliers from the market. At this writing, we are aware of no exchange that has failed to meet these conditions.

We close simply by flagging two potentially broader and deeper issues that we believe the antitrust authorities will inevitably be forced to deal with more and more frequently in the years ahead: tying and intellectual property rights.

Tying is a storied topic in antitrust law and policy. Traditionally, the courts and the enforcement agencies have been very wary of commercial tying, whereby a company with a dominant product (the tying product) sells that product only on the condition that buyers take another of its products (the tied product). The Microsoft case involved allegations of tying the browser to the operating system. At this writing, Microsoft has recently launched its new operating system, XP, that integrates additional features, including Microsoft's own audio and video player, a "single passport" identification system for doing commerce on the Net, and other features. The problem posed for antitrust authorities by such efforts at integration is to find justifiable and easily administrable ways of distinguishing between a single, integrated product (in which case there can be no tying) and two distinct products (in which case tying is possible). The courts have struggled to fashion a broadly applicable rule to determine whether two distinct "functions" are one product or two. Is the browser part of the operating system? Is the car radio part of the car? What about the tires or the engine? The decision by the appeals court in the Microsoft case offers some guidance regarding tying cases by calling for a rule of reason inquiry rather than a per se treatment. This decision nonetheless means that what will constitute one product or two will require a more complex, exhaustive, and time-consuming inquiry conducted in each case.

As this conclusion implies, the Microsoft appellate decision suggests that longstanding difficulties with tying doctrine are likely to become more pronounced in various high-tech industries in the future, given the trends toward *integrated* products.[38] For example, Intel's microprocessors and chip sets now handle the functions that were handled by many more parts 10 or 20 years ago. Indeed, the name "Intel" stands for "integrated electronics." The Microsoft court explicitly noted the example of integration of the microprocessor with the math coprocessor as an example of apparently beneficial integration of two products into one. If customers value integration and technology makes integration efficient, surely the antitrust laws should not stand in the way. Worse yet, the boundary between one "functionality" and another is especially messy in the software industry. We predict that a number of sharp antitrust issues in the years ahead will revolve around integrated products, interfaces, and the meaning of "tying" under antitrust law.

Finally, we see a continuation of the clear trend toward a greater role for intellectual property within antitrust.[39] As we noted previously, patents, copyright, and trade secrets—not production facilities or access to raw materials—increasingly are the key sources of competitive advantage in the "knowledge economy." This being the case, it is inevitable that owners of intellectual property rights will push to the limit the advantages such rights confer upon them. These limits are defined not only by the scope of the intellectual property rights themselves, but also by antitrust principles. While former FTC Chairman Robert Pitofsky and former Assistant Attorney General Joel Klein were both keen to point out that the laws governing intellectual property serve the same underlying goal as the antitrust laws—to promote innovation and thus benefit our economy—there is no getting around the fact that tensions arise between these two bodies of law. We expect those tensions to be actively explored in the years ahead by the private litigants, the antitrust enforcement agencies, or both.

---

38. For one recent survey of the antitrust issues surrounding bundling in high-tech markets, see Sidak (2001).
39. Gilbert and Tom (2001) document this trend nicely in the enforcement actions taken by the DOJ and the FTC during the Clinton years.

References

Areeda, Phillip. 1994. "Antitrust Policy." In Martin Feldstein, ed., *American Economic Policy in the 1980s*. Chicago and London: University of Chicago Press/NBER.

Burtless, Gary, et al. 1998. *Globaphobia: Confronting Fears of Open Trade*. Washington, DC: Brookings Institution Press, Progressive Policy Institute, and Twentieth Century Fund.

Chernow, Ronald. 2000. *Titan*. New York: Random House.

Evenett, Simon J., Alexander Lehmann, and Benn Steil, eds. 2000. *Antitrust Goes Global: What Future for Transatlantic Cooperation*? Washington, DC: Brookings Institution Press.

Federal Trade Commission (FTC). 1996. "Competition Policy in the New High-Tech Global Marketplace." Staff Report, May.

Gilbert, Richard J. and Michael L. Katz. 2001. "An Economist's Guide to *U.S. v. Microsoft*." *Journal of Economic Perspectives*, 15, no. 2 (Spring).

Gilbert, Richard, and Willard Tom. 2001. "Is Innovation King at the Antitrust Agencies?: The Intellectual Property Guidelines Five Years Later."

Klein, Benjamin. 2001. "What Can a Dominant Firm Do to Defend Its Market Position?" *Journal of Economic Perspectives*, 15, no. 2 (Spring).

Klein, Joel I. 1997. "Cross-Licensing and Antitrust Law." Available at http://www.usdoj.gov/atr/public/speeches/1123.htm.

Kovacic, William E. 1989. "Failed Expectations: The Troubled Past and Uncertain Future of the Sherman Act as a Tool for Deconcentration." *Iowa Law Review*, 74:1105–50.

Kovacic, William E., and Carl Shapiro. 2000. "Antitrust Policy: A Century of Economic and Legal Thinking." *Journal of Economic Perspectives*, 14(1): 43–60.

Litan, Robert E. 2000. "The First Microsoft Case." In Evenett, Lerhmann, and Steil (2000), pp. 174–177.

———. 2001. "Antitrust and the New Economy." *University of Pittsburgh Law Review*, 62:429.

Organization for Economic Cooperation and Development (OECD). 1995. "The 1995 Recommendation of the OECD Council Concerning Cooperation Between Member Countries on Anticompetitive Practices Affecting International Trade." OECD Doc. C(95)130, at http://www.oecd.fr/daf/clp/rec8com.htm.

Shapiro, Carl. 2000. "Navigating the Patent Thicket: Cross Licenses, Patent Pools, and Standard-Setting." In *Innovation Policy and the Economy*, ed. Adam Jaffe, Joshua Lerner, and Scott Stern. National Bureau of Economics. http://haas.berkeley.edu/~shapiro/thicket.pdf.

———. 2001. "Antitrust Limits to Patent Settlements." Available at http://haas.berkeley.edu/~shapiro/settle.pdf.

Sidak, J. Gregory. 2001. "An Antitrust Rule for Software Integration." *Yale Journal on Regulation*, 18, issue 1 (Winter).

U.S. Department of Justice (DOJ), Antitrust Division. 1999. *Annual Report FY/1999*.

Whinston, Michael D. 2001. "Exclusivity and Tying in *U.S. v. Microsoft*: What We Know, and Don't Know." *Journal of Economic Perspectives*, 15, no. 2 (Spring).

World Trade Organization (WTO). 1997. *Annual Report 1997*. Geneva, Switzerland: World Trade Organization.

Comments

Robert Pitofsky

The central theme of the Litan-Shapiro chapter is that antitrust enforcement at the federal level was "noticeably more activist" during the eight years of the Clinton administration than in the previous two administrations. That is true as far as it goes, but the substance of antitrust enforcement in the 1990s might be more fully appreciated if examined in a larger historical perspective.

In the 1960s, U.S. antitrust enforcement was extremely aggressive. Practices and transactions were added to the zone of illegal behavior (e.g., conglomerate mergers, agreements based on expectations of reciprocity); abbreviated treatment to find illegality—the so-called per se approach—was expanded to cover additional categories of behavior (e.g., tie-in sales, boycotts, nonprice vertical limits on marketing); antitrust considerations regularly trumped exclusivity rights granted to innovators of intellectual property; price discrimination was frequently challenged under the Robinson-Patman Act; and many transactions among small players in unconcentrated markets were blocked on what would now be regarded as tenuous theories. The most extreme examples of questionable enforcement occurred in the merger area. In one notable case (*Brown Shoe*),[1] a vertical merger in the shoe business was declared illegal when a manufacturer with 4 percent of the production market acquired a distributor with less than 2 percent of the nation's retail sales despite the fact that there was low concentration and moderate or low barriers to entry at both the manufacturing and retailing level; in another example of extreme activism (*Von's Grocery*),[2] a horizontal merger between retail supermarkets in Los Angeles, producing a combined market share of between 8 and 9 percent, was blocked, though there were low barriers to entry and a trend among the leading firms in the market toward deconcentration. The Warren Court, convinced that Congress was committed to an extreme effort to prevent concentration and preserve competitive markets, supported federal enforcement almost without exception.

---

1. *Brown Shoe Co. v. U.S.*, 370 U.S. 294 (1962).
2. *U.S. v. Von's Grocery Co.*, 384 U.S. 270 (1966).

The heightened level of 1960s antitrust enforcement, and particularly enforcement that was insensitive to legitimate claims of efficiency, was subjected to strong and cogent criticism by many academics and most of the bar. Economists and economically trained lawyers at the University of Chicago are usually credited with the major role in changing the nature of thinking about antitrust, and they did represent the cutting edge. In fact, however, challenges to overenforcement were heard from most points of the academic and legal spectrum.

The result was a substantial diminishing of antitrust enforcement in the 1970s and a reconsideration of some previous draconic rules, especially in the area of scope of per se application to vertical agreements and in merger review. Perhaps demonstrating a rule of life that almost all "revolutions," especially revolutions in ways of thinking, go too far, the 1980s saw a sharp decline in both the number and scope of enforcement activities. Toward the end of the decade, all that remained of antitrust enforcement was an admirably aggressive effort against hard-core cartels (horizontal price fixing and market division) and challenges to a few relatively large mergers and joint ventures among direct competitors. There was a complete or close to complete disappearance of enforcement against exclusionary practices by monopolists or attempts to monopolize, vertical or conglomerate mergers, all vertical distribution arrangements including minimum price fixing (despite the fact that the Supreme Court and Congress had indicated that such practices were anticompetitive), exclusive dealing arrangements and tie-in sales, all boycotts, and all forms of discriminatory pricing. To the extent that enforcement did occur, it was against practices so clearly illegal (like hard-core price fixing) that defendants rarely appealed to the courts, or the cases were settled with agreements on fairly easy remedies. As far as federal enforcement was concerned, the courts were dealt out of the game.

The minimalist enforcement efforts of the 1980s began to change during the four years of the Bush administration. Except for price discrimination enforcement under the Robinson-Patman Act, many of the types of behavior and transactions stricken from the antitrust agenda in the early 1980s were restored.[3]

Now to antitrust enforcement in the Clinton years. In my view, the goal of Clinton antitrust was to focus on basic competitive values and to find a

---

3. It bears noting that these vast changes in domestic antitrust—bouncing from maximum enforcement to minimalist enforcement and then to something of a middle ground—occurred without participation, other than some commentary from the sidelines, from Congress. It is characteristic of American antitrust in recent decades that virtually all changes in direction occur as a result of prosecutorial discretion (i.e., who to sue and on what grounds) and a few judicial pronouncements. The Supreme Court has rarely reviewed substantive competition rules since the end of the decade of the 1960s.

sustainable middle ground between the overenforcement of the 1960s and the underenforcement of the 1980s—that is, an active but careful program that hopefully would survive the results of future elections. The program was designed with considerable input from economists and from the academic community and characterized by an effort to be sensitive to claims of efficiency, especially when those claims were based on incentives to innovate. Aside from continuation of enforcement against practices restored to the agenda by the Bush administration, the eight years saw a more activist stance with respect to mergers (including challenges for the first time in many years to vertical mergers), challenges to a wide variety of distribution practices including restoration of tough enforcement against minimum resale price maintenance, and challenges to allegedly unreasonable behavior by monopolists—the two leading examples, as the Litan-Shapiro chapter points out, involving challenges to Microsoft and Intel, two giants of the new technology.

Thus, the theme of the Litan-Shapiro chapter—that federal antitrust enforcement was "noticeably more activist"—is valid. However, the differences in antitrust enforcement were probably greater between the Reagan and Bush years than between the Bush and Clinton enforcement efforts. Also, despite an unprecedented merger wave during the 1990s, the percentage of mergers challenged during the Clinton years was about the same as during the first Bush administration, and challenges continued to be organized around the excellent merger guidelines introduced by Assistant Attorney General William Baxter in the early 1980s.

Two aspects of federal antitrust enforcement in the 1990s, noted in the Litan-Shapiro chapter, deserve comment: first, a much greater willingness on the part of the Antitrust Division and the Federal Trade Commission to litigate their cases and, second, imposition across the board—both in criminal and civil enforcement—of more severe penalties.

Far more cases were litigated rather than settled in the 1990s than any decade since the 1960s. This trend had several useful consequences. Once private parties realized that litigation was an option, and the agencies each would throw maximum resources into any litigation effort, they were likely to be more accommodating in settlement negotiations. More important, I believe the bipartisan consensus in the United States that supports reasonable antitrust enforcement depends on a sense that any government initiative eventually must be passed on by the courts. If enforcement initiatives are untested, and yet the parties decline to litigate because of the enormous cost, burden, and delay caused by litigation, concerns arise about the influence of an unreviewed bureaucracy.

Incidentally, it is interesting that the judiciary, clearly more conservative as a result of appointments in the 1980s, nevertheless backed government initiatives in the 1990s to a very high degree. For example, the Federal Trade Commission won nine of eleven cases that resulted in opinions after the parties appealed to the courts.

Finally, more active judicial participation had the desirable consequence of clarifying the law. Much antitrust doctrine in the previous decades had been elaborated in the form of joint Department of Justice–FTC guidelines, including the immensely important and influential horizontal merger guidelines published in 1982 and revised in 1992 and 1997. By litigating, the courts were given an opportunity to embrace and close the gap between the guidelines and pre-1980 law. Thus in the merger area, courts adopted the guidelines approach to measurement of market power (*Staples*),[4] took a more demanding stance when claims were advanced that entry would defeat any price increase occasioned by a merger or other business behavior (*Microsoft*),[5] appeared comfortable with the guideline adoption of various levels where alarms were set off about undue concentration, and elaborated upon and qualified what private parties must do to take advantage of the more generous treatment of efficiencies as a mitigating factor introduced into the merger guidelines in 1997 (*Heinz–Beech Nut*).[6]

In my view, it is not correct to suggest that the Clinton administration litigated for the sake of establishing precedent. But where the parties are unwilling to consent to an order that will fully restore competitive conditions as they existed before the anticompetitive effects of the transaction, the government in my view can only act responsibly by litigating.

The Litan-Shapiro chapter is correct to conclude that remedies, both criminal and civil, became much more severe in the decade of the 1990s. On the criminal side, Antitrust Division enforcement, particularly against international cartels, was extraordinarily successful, and unprecedented fines frequently amounting to hundreds of millions of dollars were imposed and prominent business people were sent to jail. The Criminal Fine Improvement Act of 1987, which had not been used in the antitrust area prior to the Clinton administration, and which provided for an alternative minimum fine of twice the gross pecuniary gain or loss resulting from a violation, had much to do with permitting fines at unprecedented levels. On the civil side, until quite recently the principal non-merger remedy consisted of conduct orders in effect telling the parties that

---

4. *FTC v. Staples, Inc.*, 970 F. Supp. 1066 (D.D.C. 1977).

5. *U.S. v. Microsoft*, Civil Action No. 00–5212 (D.C. Cir. 2001).

6. *FTC v. Heinz*, 246 F.3d 708 (D.C. Cir. 2001).

if they engage in the same or similar conduct again, they would be subject to civil penalties. Unfortunately, the parties often were allowed to keep the illegal gains of the first transaction—subject only to the possibility of private treble-damage actions, which themselves face formidable procedural barriers. In *FTC v. Mylan*,[7] a generic drug company allegedly cornered the market on an essential ingredient for its product and promptly raised the price to consumers by about 3000 percent. By the time the government had put together a challenge a little over a year later, the company allegedly had taken in over $100 million in illegal profits. Relying on the court's equitable powers, the FTC persuaded a district court that the proper remedy in these circumstances would be disgorgement, and in fact an elaborate system was introduced that required repayment to exploited consumers of over $100 million. It is far too early to tell, but it may be that the disgorgement approach to civil remedies may in the future have a significant impact on the nature of antitrust law enforcement.

Finally, I would like to offer some thoughts on a set of questions raised in the Litan-Shapiro chapter and in some important cases: did Clinton administration antitrust enforcement depart in serious ways from past practice in discharging its burden of proving anticompetitive effects on competition? The chapter introduces the discussion by noting that Clinton-era enforcers were more comfortable with long-term predictions about market effects.

I would put the point differently. Virtually all antitrust enforcement involves predictions of competitive effect. When the government initiates litigation, it is offering its prediction that the transaction will have an adverse effect on the competitive process and then on consumers. But when the government fails to challenge a transaction, it is similarly making a prediction of long-term effects. In the 1980s, government enforcers regularly declined to challenge mergers on grounds that if the merger led to coordinated behavior and higher prices, the higher prices (in the absence of barriers to entry erected by government action) would attract new entry and defeat the price increase. That is also a long-term prediction. My conclusion is that there is little difference between Clinton-era and earlier enforcement efforts in terms of willingness to make predictions, but rather the difference is in indulging some premises in those predictions. Specifically, Clinton-era enforcement was much less comfortable with the theory that the overwhelming majority of anticompetitive effects would be better addressed through assumed market responses than the enforcement efforts of a band of bureaucrats.

The Litan-Shapiro chapter concludes its discussion of the market-effects point with some expressions of mild skepticism about the validity of the Federal

---

7. *FTC v. Mylan Labs, Inc.*, 99 F. Supp. 221 (D.D.C. 1999).

Trade Commission's 1998 complaint against Intel. The facts of the FTC-Intel controversy frame the issue of proof of effects so nicely that the case is worth some elaboration. The government had alleged that Intel had achieved and maintained a monopoly position with respect to microprocessors, an essential component of all personal computers. It licensed its technology widely and generally without attempts at coercion, with one striking exception. When it found itself in a controversy involving intellectual property (IP) with one of its licensees, and controversies did arise with respect to at least three licensees, it tried to settle the matter with cross-licenses. But if the negotiations proved unsuccessful and the IP rival refused to agree to terms, Intel withdrew previously provided IP and refused to supply additional IP or advance samples to its challenger. The government alleged that Intel was a monopolist, and, without access to the IP and samples, it would be difficult for the rival company to remain competitively effective in the marketplace.

All agree that the plaintiff's burden is to show "likely" competitive effects. If there are no anticompetitive effects, there can be no antitrust violation. The narrow but critically important issue is, What is the government's burden to establish anticompetitive effects when a monopolist cuts off access to essential technical information as a result of being sued by a rival? Should a monopolist be allowed to engage in self-help in those circumstances? One possible resolution is to infer "likely" competitive effects from the cutoff. If self-help is permitted to a monopolist, the strong will prevail over the weak every time, regardless of the merits of their cases. Existing or potential rivals would then be aware of the consequences if they had the temerity not to reach agreement with the monopolist with respect to intellectual property controversies, and would cave in during future negotiations. Preventing this kind of self-help would not lead to the monopolist giving up its legitimate rights to intellectual property; rather the issue would be settled, as intellectual property disputes are commonly settled, by judges in court.

An alternative approach to the question of the rights of monopolists to terminate relations with IP challengers is to require proof of marketplace effects— as a practical matter, proof that as a result of the monopolist's behavior, prices went up, output declined, or there was a chilling effect on innovation. In the past, antitrust decisions have not required direct proof of price or output effects (see *Lorain Journal, Aspen Ski*)[8] because the burden of demonstrating whether prices went up, went down, or stayed the same as a result of a particular line of behavior is a difficult if not impossible burden to discharge.

---

8. *Lorain Journal Co. v. U.S.*, 342 U.S. 143 (1951); *Aspen Skiing Co. v. Aspen Highlands Skiing Corp.*, 472 U.S. 585 (1985).

The Litan-Shapiro chapter concludes with the prediction that resolution of problems at the intersection between intellectual property and antitrust will be among the most severe challenges to sensible economic regulation in the future. I agree and particularly admire the analysis in that portion of the paper. I do not believe, however, that limits on self-help by a monopolist when sued by a rival are an example of a difficult area to reconcile. We build courthouses and pay judges to solve that sort of problem.

Comments

Richard Schmalensee

The core of U.S. antitrust enforcement involves cartel behavior and horizontal mergers. In these areas, what's remarkable about the Clinton years is the extent of policy continuity. By any mainstream standard, DOJ's cartel enforcement results during this period are absolutely outstanding. In the merger area, the survival of Bill Baxter's 1982 merger guidelines to 2001 with only "tweaking" is a tribute to Bill and those who worked with him.

Outside these core areas, the Clinton years saw marked increases in antitrust activism, most obviously at the federal level. Before discussing federal enforcement policy in more detail, though, I want to say a few words about what happened outside of the Beltway—at the states and the European Union.

The state attorneys general have become more active on a number of fronts in recent years, particularly and visibly in antitrust. Most recently, they participated in the *Microsoft* litigation and were reliably reported to have blocked its settlement in early 2000. The European Union's antitrust authority, DG Comp, has recently killed the proposed GE/Honeywell merger, even though U.S. authorities had approved it. A few years ago, DG Comp belabored the Boeing/McDonnell Douglas merger after DOJ had approved it.

The causes of these changes at the states and the European Union are complex, and there is no obvious reason to expect them to be reversed in the near term. Thus substantive and procedural concerns raised by greater antitrust activism outside the Beltway are likely to be with us for some time.

Substantively, neither the European Union's statute or case law nor the state unfair competition laws, under which state attorneys general may sue, have the kind of tight focus on consumer welfare that has served to discipline U.S. antitrust policy at the federal level for at least the last two decades. In addition, neither the states nor the European Union can match the economic expertise on which the federal agencies have long relied. DG Comp in Europe pays much more attention to competitors' complaints than the U.S. agencies and, notably in GE/Honeywell, has embraced economic models that have been out of the U.S. mainstream for decades. Indeed, merger-specific efficiencies that U.S. agencies treat as virtues are apparently treated as vices in the European Union if they would be hard for competitors to match. In light of all this, it should be no surprise that Brussels is full of U.S. companies complaining to DG Comp about U.S. competitors.

In terms of procedure, lawsuits by state attorneys general in state courts against out-of-state corporate defendants are not always models of due process. In Europe, DG Comp is prosecutor, judge, and jury. Defendants have very limited opportunity to cross-examine adverse witnesses or even to see adverse evidence, and the appeals process is time-consuming and not defendant-friendly. Add private plaintiffs to the states and the European Union, and we obtain what Judge Richard Posner has called "the cluster bomb" of antitrust: a single complaint about anybody by anybody else may result in a host of lawsuits involving a variety of plaintiffs in different forums under different substantive and procedural rules. The outcome may bear little or no relation to the original injury to consumers, if any. There is every reason to expect this problem to intensify and to be on the agenda at the next one of these conferences a decade hence.

Let me now return to the increase in antitrust activism at the federal level. I find it interesting that Litan and Shapiro, who ought to know, attribute this in part to the rise in the importance of "innovation competition." In industries in which competition focuses on the generation and use of intellectual property, network effects are often important, and, as a consequence of both attributes, competition often centers on winner-take-most struggles *for* the market, rather than price/output competition at the margin *in* the market.

Now it is not obvious, without some argument, why an increase in the relative importance of this sort of dynamic or Schumpeterian competition *for* the market calls for a more activist antitrust policy. Indeed, as Litan and Shapiro discuss, the speed of change in innovation-driven industries poses serious problems for antitrust. (They suggest that expedited process, as in the *Microsoft* case, can mitigate some of these problems. But, particularly in complex cases with high stakes, putting a high weight on procedural efficiency risks denial of due process. And, despite an expedited process, it is very unlikely that any final settlement or court-imposed remedy in the Microsoft case will take effect before 2002—five or six years after the acts that were the focus of the case. This is an eternity in the computer business.)

The rise in innovation competition seems to have been linked to the increase in antitrust activism in the Clinton administration by a particular view of the competitive process in innovation-driven industries. At the core of this view are the notions, present as assumptions in much of the theoretical literature, that competition *for* the market generally happens only once and that network effects are very strong. Relying on these assumptions, it is argued that once any firm somehow acquires even a small market share lead over its competitors, the market tends to tip in its favor, and it is very hard thereafter to dislodge it from market dominance.

To say the least, this is a very static view of what have historically been very dynamic industries; it was surely not Schumpeter's view. The basic notion that competition *for* the market happens only once is blatantly inconsistent with history in many sectors—word processing is an obvious example.

Even if the static, one-shot view of dynamic competition were generally correct, however, it would not imply that increased antitrust activism—which in this context must mean tightening conduct restrictions on market leaders—would in practice make consumers better off. In the first place, this view implies that monopoly is inevitable in high-tech industries; the only issue is which firm gets it. But, despite various urban legends, there is no real evidence that unregulated markets ever get this sort of choice wrong in any important sense. That is, there is little or no evidence of suboptimal performance in innovation-driven markets. Moreover, the substantial probability of judicial error in the face of conflicting testimony about cutting-edge technologies makes it likely that courts would not on average choose monopolists as well as the market.

One other aspect of the treatment of new-economy industries by the DOJ and FTC deserves comment. During the Clinton administration, these agencies sometimes seemed to treat the advantages given to incumbents by network effects as less worthy than, say, the tremendous advantages that Henry Ford once enjoyed because of economies of scale in the production of Model T's. The agencies sometimes seemed to feel that if an incumbent's advantages stemmed in part from network effects, antitrust should be tilted against it to level the playing field for its competitors. Of course, there is no theoretical or empirical support for such a position: network effects provide both advantages to incumbents and real economic benefits to consumers.

Though Litan and Shapiro do not make this point, an important underlying source for the rise in antitrust activism in the Clinton years was surely the erosion of the Chicago consensus in antitrust economics. Through the early 1980s, the Chicago School used basic price theory to argue that some practices, like tying, to which antitrust has been hostile can never harm consumers, even when engaged in by monopolies. These arguments had a strong influence on federal antitrust policy during the Reagan years. By the 1990s, however, game-theoretic tools had been used to show that many of the practices at issue, including tying, can in fact produce anticompetitive results under some, specific conditions.

Unfortunately, this recent work rarely provides simple, practical rules that can reliably sort procompetitive from anticompetitive conduct.

There are several kinds of policy responses one could make to this state of intellectual affairs. The Clinton administration's response is reflected in the paper's observation that increased activism stemmed in part from the greater confidence of Clinton officials "in their ability to correct market failures." That is, in the Clinton years the DOJ and FTC adopted what might be called a *regulatory* approach to antitrust: rather than concentrating on the hard task of establishing economically sound general rules to define lawful conduct and guide business behavior, they concentrated on developing market-specific remedies to correct what they perceived to be market failures. With a market failure identified and a remedy in hand, liability was to be established by any available means.

Full disclosure requires me to admit that I was involved in the 1970s as an expert witness in an earlier instance of this regulatory approach: the FTC's *Ready-to-Eat Cereals* case. I still believe that the remedy the commission proposed in that case would likely have improved market performance. But I have no doubt that basing decisions to prosecute on market performance more than on business conduct—in the *Cereals* case and in the Clinton years—gives rise to significant uncertainty in the business community about the boundaries of acceptable conduct. And though the economic costs of increased uncertainty are rarely visible, they are nonetheless real.

What about the Clinton administration's antitrust legacy? I agree with Litan and Shapiro that the increased activism of the Clinton years will likely be reversed in substantial measure in the George W. Bush administration. Will the civil, nonmerger cases brought in the Clinton years benefit consumers substantially or establish economically sound precedents? At least as regards four of the important cases highlighted by Litan and Shapiro, I think the answer is no on both counts.

The American Airlines case, in which I have not been involved, seems to have been based on the post-Chicago theoretical result that prices can be above cost and yet, by discouraging entry, can injure consumers. As I understand it, the DOJ attempted to persuade the district court to replace the below-cost component of the *Brooke Group* test for predation with a test involving the profitability of increments to capacity and to apply that test to established firms that merely matched prices set by entrants. The district court, which threw out the DOJ's case on summary judgment, was obviously troubled by the departure from previous law. I am more troubled by the difficulty of reliably implementing the standard that the DOJ proposed. If this standard is ultimately adopted by the courts, which seems possible but unlikely, I believe the main result will be to chill price competition. Today, prices above variable cost are almost surely legal; the DOJ's proposed standard would remove this relatively clear safe harbor and, I believe, cause established firms to hesitate to match entrants' price reductions—thus raising prices paid by consumers, at least in the short run.

At least two other panelists know a lot more about the FTC's case against Intel than I do. But I do want to note that it is not obviously sound economic policy to compel market leaders to share intellectual property with customers who are suing them. It is my understanding that the FTC's economic expert admitted there was no way to show that Intel's refusal to share under these conditions harmed consumers. It thus seems unlikely that the settlement ultimately agreed upon by the FTC and Intel will benefit consumers noticeably, and, of course, the case established no precedent.

The DOJ's case against Visa and MasterCard, which is mentioned only briefly by Litan and Shapiro, is a high-water mark of regulatory antitrust. This case would take too much space to describe in any detail, but it is fair to say that the government proposed a thorough reorganization of the credit-card industry based on an organizational design that to my knowledge, and to that of the government's economic expert, has never been tried here or abroad. And, in essence, the antitrust violation alleged was the failure to adopt the government's remedy. (One novel wrinkle was that the remedy proposal ultimately adopted by the DOJ differed in nontrivial ways from the proposal about which its economic expert testified.) As this is written, the trial has been over for almost a year, but the district court has not yet announced a decision. Whatever the final outcome, this case represents an attempt to impose complex regulation of organizational form on an industry that by almost any standard is performing well. Thus, whatever happens, industry performance will not be improved much, and it may well be degraded, and no general rule will be established.

Finally, let me turn to the *Microsoft* case, on which the Circuit Court of the District of Columbia spoke about an hour before this session began. I agree with much, though not all, of what Litan and Shapiro say about the issues in this case, but I do want to add one important issue that, presumably for tactical reasons, neither side stressed. It seems clear from the documents that Microsoft was concerned with the determination of standards for the Internet. In the Microsoft e-mail quoted most prominently by the District Court (Finding of Fact No. 377), for instance, a Microsoft employee says, "we set out on this mission 2 years ago to not let netscape dictate standards and control the browser api's [sic]." Microsoft clearly accomplished this mission, and I would argue that the public interest has been better served by open Internet standards than it would have been if Netscape (or anyone else) had been able to impose proprietary standards.

I believe that *Microsoft* can also be fairly characterized as a regulatory case. The DOJ began with the belief that it had encountered a market failure it should correct. Initially, the core of the liability case was the contention that under the *Jefferson Parish* test, the addition of a browser to a market-leading operating system should be considered a per se illegal tie—illegal regardless of its effects on competition or consumers. I doubt that any economist in the Antitrust Division believes that this standard should be applied broadly to block product integration by leading firms—particularly in high-technology industries. But, until the *Jefferson Parish* standard was apparently rejected by the DC circuit court in a related case, it seemed a convenient club with which to beat Microsoft. After that DC circuit decision, the government elected to try the Microsoft case essentially as a RICO matter, with a wide range of "bad acts" waved before the judge. This approach worked: Judge Jackson has made it clear to the press and in his Findings of Fact that he came to regard Microsoft and its witnesses as corrupt. Very few of these "bad acts" survived examination by the appeals court, although, of course, some did. At the end of the day, I do not believe this case will have a substantial impact on the software industry (unless private plaintiffs obtain ruinous judgments against Microsoft) or that it will contribute to the establishment of clear and economically sound standards for the conduct of dominant firms.

Tying arose in two ways in the Microsoft case. I don't think the attempt to have the addition of Internet Explorer to Windows declared illegal per se, regardless of its costs and benefits, can be characterized as an attempt to clarify the rules. There is, as I said earlier, no economic support for a rule declaring tying illegal per se. I think the only way to describe the per se tying claim in the Microsoft case is as an attempt to find some doctrine under which Microsoft's conduct could be found illegal, thus leading to a remedy that, DOJ believed, would improve market performance.

Tying also arose in the Microsoft case as part of a long list of practices that the DOJ described as illegal monopoly maintenance and as part of a substantially shorter list that the DC circuit court described the same way. In this context, tying by a monopolist is illegal only if it has substantial anticompetitive effects that are not outweighed by efficiency benefits. I have no objection in principle to this sort of analysis of tying, though I would note that the discussion of this issue by both the district and circuit courts (particularly on the issue of "commingling of code") gives one no confidence in the courts' ability to distill understanding of complex technical matters from conflicting testimony.

I think it may be difficult to keep politics out of antitrust policy, depending on what DG Comp does over the next few years and on whether or not its actions are viewed as outrageous. If they are viewed as outrageous by an appreciable fraction of the American people, there will be a political response. I don't think the result will be to politicize prosecutorial decisions by the federal agencies, however. Rather, antitrust would be put on the agenda for high-level international negotiations, and the federal agencies might operate under politically driven instructions when dealing with their counterparts abroad.

Comments

Robert Willig

Robert Litan and Carl Shapiro have produced an excellent chapter. It is a real contribution to the literature and will be extremely helpful in teaching students about antitrust policy in the 1990s. On my next class syllabus, I will put a "star" next to it, signifying that it is a must-read. The paper is both accessible and lively, a rare combination for a paper on antitrust policy. The paper also provides a significant amount of background information and depth about both the policy process and relevant economic theory.

The paper asserts that it tries to be neutral in its reporting. And maybe it did try. But like most lively reporting, it did not succeed in being truly neutral in many important respects. While this failure does not really bother me, I will have to put an extra "star" next to the paper on my reading list so that the students understand that it includes a lot of personal judgments about certain cases. It is important to note that the authors are not always biased toward the Clinton administration. In some instances, an author worked on a case against the administration. The paper often reflects such involvements, and these personal expressions should be noted by the reader.

Let me point to one bias that I take very personally. The paper shows excellent team spirit by taking credit for the good things that happened during the Clinton administration. But a number of these "good things" were really continuations of policies developed during the first Bush administration—or even earlier during the Reagan administration. The Clinton administration did implement a number of sound policies, but we should not forget the broad and strong shoulders that preceded it.

Since it is still June, I'm still in academic mode. Therefore, I have decided to develop a report card for the Clinton administration's antitrust policies. (The grading is on the typical Princeton University curve, which means that a comfortable amount of grade inflation is included.) Emulating every good elementary school report card, I have not produced an overall grade. Rather, I have produced a grade for each subject.

Subject one: breaking up international cartels. The administration deserves an A++. The administration's efforts were off the scale; as the chapter notes, there was a real sea change on breaking up international cartels. Looking to the future, it is important to discuss how the administration achieved such remarkable success. The paper suggests that we should thank the corporate amnesty program. Evidently, the program was responsible for helping kick-start the dramatic string of prosecutions, which broke all previous records by a factor of 10 (in terms of impact on commerce and on penalties collected). If the causal relationship between the corporate amnesty program and the busting of international cartels is right, it should lead us to think seriously about using that kind of tool more pervasively in other government-business relationships. I should note for the record that the amnesty program was engineered by a Bush administration appointee, whom the Clinton administration had the good sense to keep on and to listen to.

Subject two: policy guidelines. Here, the administration deserves an A−, on a senior thesis scale. The administration had some creativity. But the administration largely maintained the Bush administration's guidelines and acted upon them, and where the Reagan administration had good sense, the Clinton administration borrowed from their efforts too. In summary, the policy guidelines were just fine: a little creativity, but not that much, combined with a lot of good judgment.

Subject three: policy overlaps with other agencies. Here again I give the Administration an A−. The paper discusses this issue, and I've had some personal experience in these areas. Thus, I want to grade subcategories.

The first subcategory is overlaps with the Federal Communications Commission (FCC). The Department of Justice (DOJ) provided excellent guidance to the FCC on telecommunications policy. The administration did a good job all around. In this subcategory, it deserves an A+.

The second subcategory is the Department of Transportation (DOT). Here the Clinton administration deserves an A−. The Justice Department did a great job controlling DOT's excesses and stopping DOT's efforts to interfere with airline competition. DOJ was there both explicitly and behind the scenes to keep DOT on track, and with the help of Congress, actually succeeded in holding DOT at bay. Finally, the DOJ made the wise decision to bring a predatory-pricing case against American Airlines with a novel but sound logical structure—although I don't know if the asserted facts are interpreted accurately. Why the A− rather than a better grade? DOJ did not do a very good job interacting with the railroad regulators. DOJ seemed to be influenced by the attitude that it, not the railroad regulators, should analyze rail mergers. Given the DOJ's attitude, I am glad that DOT wound up making the call.

The third, and final, subcategory is the Department of Energy (DOE) and the Federal Energy Regulatory Commission (FERC). The Justice Department failed to muster sufficient energy to show DOE and FERC how to promote competition in the energy sector. While no one else has succeeded in this effort either in the energy area, an opportunity was lost.

Subject four: process. Many people do not understand that process is extremely important in antitrust policy. It is very important in providing U.S. businesses with a road map on mergers, acquisitions, and conduct. Here, I give the administration a B+. The administration made little progress on the age-old problems of process. The Federal Trade Commission (FTC) deserves congratulations on their efforts toward greater transparency. The FTC held terrific hearings, produced great reports, and advanced policy on the foundations of the lessons adduced. Thus, good job to the FTC, but a not-so-great job at the DOJ.

Subject five: the cases. In the end, it is perhaps the cases brought that constitute the most important legacy. Here I cannot assign a single grade. There's very high variance from A+ all the way to C− (and, at Princeton, C− is a failing grade).

Case 1: The American Airlines predatory pricing case. The administration deserves an A+. DOJ showed a lot of courage in bringing this case. It articulated just the right economic theories and linked the evidence to them with strength. While I am not a partisan on the case, I appreciate it as an outside observer.

Case 2: The Microsoft and Intuit merger. Many people are not aware of this other Microsoft case. Microsoft tried to buy Intuit, the maker of Quicken—a marvelous financial software package. The antitrust agencies said no, which was probably the right decision. I give the administration an A for the theory. DOJ carefully articulated a brilliant, far-reaching theory of how to analyze competitive effects in the Microsoft-Intuit case. The view was that it is not concentration per se that ought to be the indicator of competition or the lack thereof. The department did not argue about concentration as measured by market shares, which is the traditional way to undertake such analyses. Rather, DOJ made it perfectly clear that the issue involved platforms for competitive advantage and success. The DOJ decided that it was important to count competitive platforms, and that a merger between the two leading platforms would be anticompetitive.

In this case, the two platforms consisted of Microsoft's operating system and Quicken's financial software installed base. As with Microsoft's operating system, people who use Quicken tend to stay with Quicken. Thus the Department argued that combining these two platforms would illegally diminish competition, and I think they probably got that decision right.

Case 3: The Microsoft case. Microsoft was the signature case of the Clinton administration, in the view of the press as well as the Litan-Shapiro chapter. And

I have to give them a C or C− on it. All of my remarks are based on knowledge prior to the appellate decision. Every curve needs a bottom, and for the Clinton administration, the Microsoft case was the bottom of the curve. How did it happen? I think the DOJ got carried away in formulating its complaint and in making its litigation decisions during the course of the case, for reasons that were understandably human. Microsoft, and almost everybody involved in the case on behalf of Microsoft, acted with various degrees of arrogance. But meeting extreme with extreme and arrogance with arrogance is not necessarily conducive to good competition policy.

In my personal view, some of the exclusivity contracts that Microsoft imposed on those dealing with the company were basically measures for self-protection from competition in the economic sense (and dirty tricks in a business sense) that were made possible only because of Microsoft's market power over operating systems. I should note that some prominent economists do not think that Microsoft had the market power from which those dirty tricks were levered. My read on the issue is that Microsoft did have sufficient market power. And those dirty tricks were imposed in an anticompetitive way, which probably was actionable in a properly tailored case.

As the case unfolded, the main issue had to do with the characterization of the bundling of the Explorer browser with the Windows operating system, and the characterization that that bundling was a "tie." Under the law, tying is per se illegal. Unfortunately, this characterization in the case was substantially flawed. The claim that the bundling of Explorer with Windows significantly maintained Microsoft's monopoly is a dramatic reach for a per se theory, since the bundling may have provided important consumer benefits that should be weighed against the asserted foreclosure.

Even Judge Jackson could not find successful monopolization of the browser space. All computer users certainly had Netscape available to them. The bundling that actually occurred in no way displaced rival browsers. You could have downloaded Netscape, even though you had Explorer given to you with your computer. Thus, if there were an adverse impact on competition, it should not be viewed as a per se consequence of bundling that might very well be an important source of consumer benefits, both in the Microsoft context and in other dynamic and progressive industries too.

In closing, let me note that I agree with the chapter that high tech is not immune from antitrust, and I think the world has received that message. In fact, the behavior of Microsoft, Intel, and others has improved in the last few years because of the attention paid by antitrust regulators to the high-tech sector. Nonetheless, as an economist, I am worried about the deterrence of good, aggressive conduct that benefits consumers that may result from treatment like that received by Microsoft by the antitrust regulators and the district court.

Victor Fuchs opened the discussion by referring to the correlation between merger activities and the stock market noted in the paper, and asking whether one can predict a falloff in such activity from the recent decline in the stock market relative to its early-2000 height.

Joseph P. Newhouse opined that the FTC had been right in its cases against hospitals and thought some of the negative outcomes strange. He further questioned the reason for the silence of the FTC in this domain. He had in mind both sides of the market—the health plan side as well as the buyer side.

Robert Pitofsky, in response, pointed out that the FTC has only lost two cases in the last eight years, achieving the best batting average ever. Furthermore, the two hospital merger cases that were lost were both local markets in relatively small cities. Hence, it is not discouragement from losing cases that is keeping the FTC quiet about the issue. The message from the local judges was that they did not think Washington ought to be telling them how many hospitals should be present in their community. In this light, he said that although he is troubled by the trend in hospital mergers in smaller cities, resulting in monopolies in some cases, he thinks it is more sensible to put the FTC's resources to use elsewhere. Concerning the health plan side, Pitofsky noted that the practice has been that the Department of Justice handles this area, not the FTC.

Gregory Mankiw argued that "pushing the envelope" of antitrust laws, as Antitrust Division chief Joel Klein did, is always dangerous, because it creates uncertainty as to what the rules are in any business. He questioned what the guideline is that the government is trying to establish in the Microsoft case, particularly concerning the complaints surrounding the internet browser. There are many firms with dominant positions in their markets; is the government telling all of them, "Once you get a dominant position, you can't use it to introduce new products"?

Carl Shapiro agreed that pushing the envelope creates uncertainty. However, he presumed that Joel Klein and others would say, "We were just trying to keep you on the right side of the line we think was always there, in the context of a new industry." In the American Airlines case, the Supreme Court, among others, was trying to draw a bright line—if you are above cost measured in a certain way, you are clean, and otherwise not. With respect to the Microsoft case, there were already tying cases and tying law, and the question is how those can be applied to software. Working this problem out may inevitably entail some un- certainty, but the lines need to be drawn and clarified in new and emerging industries.

Richard Schmalensee followed up by stating that tying played two roles in the Microsoft case. First, the government charged that integrating the browser in Windows was illegal per se—that is, regardless of its effects. There is no economic justification for this approach, except as an attempt to establish liabil- ity and justify imposing a legal remedy. Second, the government charged that tying was illegal monopoly maintenance. To establish this sort of charge, one has to look at the effects of the tie. The Microsoft case began as an attempt to use the per se rule as a club to force Microsoft to change; the case ended up being tried as a RICO proceeding instead, and the judge was clearly convinced by the government that the company, its employees, and its experts were all corrupt.

Peter Orszag asked the panel's views on the progress of the Telecom Act. *Litan* responded that the issue is divisive, and there will be no agreement among the panel. After the Telecom Act had passed, long-distance and local phone companies did not agree with each other, and cable companies were thrown in. It is a combustible mix. He thinks that the act was an improvement, but it was a mistake to pretend that the act was somehow going to lead to nirvana and introduce a lot of competition.

Robert Willig complimented the administration on its telecom policy as far as supporting the FCC statutory law. The Modified Final Judgment (MFJ) set- tlement against AT&T was a marvel in its time in the 1980s, but it became an albatross around the neck of the industry and policy-makers by the time of the 1990s. Hence, the Telecom Act of 1996 was a remarkable success in replacing the MFJ. The Telecom Act has been litigated up to the Supreme Court a couple of times already, and there is high hope that the Supreme Court will get it right. Arguments are there for the Court to find correctly regarding the economics of the future of the industry.

Robert Lawrence raised a question about the roles played by the Congress and the president in the decision-making process of antitrust policy, as opposed to leaving it up to the competition agencies. He stressed the importance of this point, for it tells us something about how difficult it would be to bring antitrust policy into international trade negotiations, where executives and parliamentary bodies must be involved.

Pitofsky addressed the question posed by Lawrence. For more than 110 years, U.S. antitrust has been judge-made law, more so than in any other country. In the Clinton administration especially, the White House took a more hands-off position in antitrust than at any time in recent history. With high stakes and powerful companies, the entry of the White House into antitrust policy would be a sure road to political scandal. As for Congress, in recent years members have been active in commenting, but not in legislating, in this area.

Litan pointed out that the White House tried to stay as far away as it could for two reasons. First, there were other investigations going on, and second, it is convenient for the White House to have distance, since it did not want to be accused in the press of getting involved. Congress has very intensive interest in cooperation with both the FTC and Justice, and on selective cases it did play a role in heightening the visibility of certain mergers. Congress certainly also took an interest in the Microsoft case. Litan suggested that the role of Congress is to put heat on the DOJ and FTC at various points to avoid a particular outcome.

Willig emphasized the enormous amount of discretionary power in the hands of the assistant attorney general and FTC chairman. The power of appointment takes on remarkable influence in antitrust policy. The individual personas of various past leaders of the antitrust division of the DOJ and of the FTC have been very influential in the conduct of policy, though their influence to some extent reflected deliberate choices by the administration.

Alan S. Blinder asked for panelists' comments on the issue of separation of politics from international antitrust enforcement.

Schmalensee answered that he does not think decisions regarding international enforcement will be politicized in response to recent EU actions, but that there will be a political response if EU actions are viewed as outrageous by an appreciable fraction of the American public.

Shapiro, continuing on the theme of international antitrust enforcement, referred to the recent GE–Honeywell case, in which the European Union's competition authority blocked the merger. He viewed it as extraordinary that President Bush made remarks that the EU decision troubles him. He raised the possibility of retaliation in other areas, which gets into the trade policy issue. He responded to Lawrence's question, agreeing that it is White House tradition not to get involved in mucking around with individual antitrust cases. The Antitrust Division of the DOJ and the Bureau of Competition of the FTC want to describe what they are doing as "law enforcement" rather than "regulation," since law enforcement is straightforward but regulation opens up another whole set of boxes.

Paul Joskow gave the enforcement agents a B– for not playing a more active role in the electricity restructuring and competition initiatives at the Federal Energy Regulatory Commission (FERC). There were staff at the Justice Department and at the FTC who tried to interact with FERC, but limited resources were devoted to these initiatives. He said that one of the problems at FERC has been that there was very little interest in serious economic analysis, although there was much interest in competition. It is crucial that FERC develop a group of economists, like those in the antitrust division of the DOJ or FTC, who can play a more active role on market design issues, market monitoring, and mitigation of market flaws. Currently they do not have enough people with skills necessary to play that role, and the commission is poorly organized to use the skills of those economists it does have effectively. At the DOJ and FTC, economists are fully integrated into antitrust enforcement. At FERC the economists seem to be peripheral to important decisions about market design, market imperfections, and market power mitigation.

Willig added that the staff of the DOJ and FTC had some sound ideas about what was going right and wrong in electricity deregulation, long before anyone thought of it as a crisis. But the problem from the Justice's point of view was that, at FERC or the Energy Department, there was no leadership from the top, no attempt to use the executive branch to try to get such ideas in play.

8 Energy Policy

Energy Policy During the 1990s

Paul L. Joskow

PANELISTS: *Charles B. Curtis, Philip R. Sharp, and Daniel Yergin*

8.1 Introduction[1]

This chapter discusses U.S. energy policy and the associated evolution of energy supply, energy demand, energy prices, and the industrial organization of the domestic energy industries during the period 1991 through 2000. This period covers the last two years of the George H. W. Bush administration and the entire Clinton administration. It begins with an "energy crisis" stimulated by the invasion of Kuwait and the subsequent Gulf War and ends with an "energy crisis" caused by significant increases in oil and, especially, natural gas prices, the collapse of California's new competitive electricity markets, and the threat of electricity shortages throughout the western United States. Both "energy crises" led the sitting presidents' administrations to develop national energy

I gratefully acknowledge financial support from the MIT Center for Energy and Environmental Policy Research (CEEPR). I have benefited from discussions with Denny Ellerman, John Deutch, Luis Tellez, and Ernie Moniz, and comments from Charles Curtis, Daniel Yergin, Bill Hogan, Philip Sharp, and participants in recent CEEPR workshops. Erich Muehlegger provided excellent research assistance.

1. *Data note*: I have relied extensively on data reported in the Energy Information Administration's (EIA) publications *Annual Energy Review 1999* (July 2000) and *Monthly Energy Review* (April 2001). I have included revisions to some data originally included in the *Annual Review* which appeared either in the *Monthly Energy Review* or in more recent data distributed by EIA and available on its Web site. Unless otherwise indicated, the data utilized and referred to in this essay come from these sources.

strategies and to try to convince Congress to enact comprehensive energy legislation to implement them. Neither "energy crisis" had the kind of severe economic impact or led to the kinds of dramatic, and often ill-conceived, policy responses observed following the two oil shocks of the 1970s. The 1990–91 "energy crisis" was short-lived, and interest in energy policy soon faded. It would not be surprising if the latest "energy crisis" follows a similar course.

Most of the decade between these two "energy crises" was characterized by abundant supplies of energy, stable or falling real energy prices, and relatively little public or political interest in national energy policy issues. Energy demand continued to grow modestly, energy intensity continued to decline modestly, and the mix of fuels satisfying demand changed remarkably little. Energy supplies were able to expand to meet growing demand without major increases in prices until the end of the decade.

Because energy prices were stable or falling during most of the decade and there were no serious supply disruptions, there was little interest among the voters in energy policy issues. Major new energy policy initiatives never rose very high on the Clinton administration's policy agenda. After an early failed effort to convince Congress to pass legislation to impose a large "Btu" tax on energy, the Clinton administration's energy policy initiatives became more modest and less urgent, largely working within the existing statutory framework and budget constraints. No sweeping new energy policy legislation was passed by Congress after President George H. W. Bush signed the Energy Policy Act of 1992. The Clinton administration's belated and cautious effort to get national electricity deregulation and regulatory reform legislation passed was not successful.

The Clinton administration's energy policies were heavily influenced by concerns about the environmental impacts of energy consumption and production, including their impacts on greenhouse gas emissions and climate change. The administration trumpeted programs to encourage renewable energy, energy efficiency, alternative-fuel vehicles, and increased use of natural gas in electricity generation and vehicles. However, some of these efforts were hampered first by federal budgetary constraints that limited increased R&D expenditures and tax subsidies, then by a Republican Congress that restricted the administration's efforts to tighten vehicle and appliance efficiency standards and provide larger tax incentives for renewable energy, alternative fuel vehicles (natural gas, electric, and hybrid vehicles), and finally by an unexpected acceleration in the pace of electricity-sector restructuring and competition programs that undermined the administration's efforts to use regulated monopoly utility "integrated resource planning" programs to subsidize energy efficiency, renewable energy, and electric vehicle infrastructure.

While the Clinton administration pursued federal land-use policies that further restricted oil and gas drilling activity on some federal lands in the West, it also quietly supported or acceded to Republican policy initiatives that encouraged oil and gas drilling in deep water in the Gulf of Mexico, along with tax and royalty relief for small oil and gas wells. The administration also opened up additional federal lands in Alaska to oil drilling, proceeded with the privatization of federal uranium enrichment facilities and the Elk Hills Naval Petroleum Reserve, supported federal funding for development of new technologies to increase oil extraction productivity, continued the slow process of licensing a federal nuclear waste storage facility, supported the relicensing of operating nuclear power plants and continued research on advanced reactor technology, and initiated a cooperative program with the U.S. automobile industry to develop more fuel-efficient vehicle technology. Foreign policy initiatives endeavored to strengthen relationships with the governments of oil-producing states, to diversify the nation's oil imports, and to foster the independence from both Iran and Russia of oil-producing states that were created after the breakup of the Soviet Union.

An important component of energy policy during the 1990s involved the completion of the restructuring and deregulation of natural gas production and transportation begun during the 1980s, as well as major new initiatives to restructure the electric power sector so that it would rely on competitive wholesale and retail markets for power supplies. The wholesale electricity market competition initiatives were undertaken initially by the Federal Energy Regulatory Commission (FERC). The retail competition programs were driven primarily by state rather than federal policy initiatives. Harmonizing diffuse state retail competition programs with federal wholesale market and transmission access and pricing reforms became a major policy challenge. The Clinton administration supported these initiatives by appointing sympathetic individuals to serve as commissioners at FERC and, belatedly, by proposing comprehensive federal electricity industry reform legislation in competition with numerous Republican electricity reform bills; none of which made it through Congress during the administration's tenure.

Though the 1990s was a decade of limited major new federal energy policy initiatives, it was also a decade in which the country finally reaped the benefits of the end of many inefficient energy policies first implemented during the 1970s and the early 1980s and subsequently abandoned: oil and gas price controls, fuel-use restrictions, protectionist policies for oil refiners, and publicly funded megaprojects to promote specific supply sources all came to an end. Traditional market forces were given the opportunity to operate with less government intervention in oil, gas, and coal markets; the restructuring of the

natural gas pipeline industry was largely completed; and major electricity restructuring and competition initiatives began and progressed more rapidly than
had been expected. Even the Clinton administration's controversial privatization of the United States Uranium Enrichment Corporation (USEC) reflected
broad acceptance of relying primarily on market forces to govern the energy
industries.[2] Moreover, the transition to competition in electricity, the spread of
performance-based regulation, and the like provided powerful incentives to
improve the performance of nuclear and coal-fired generating facilities.

Because much of the regulatory apparatus of the 1970s and early 1980s had
been dismantled by 1990, some of the tools for doing mischief in response to
energy supply and price shocks were not readily available. As a result, there
was little of a regulatory nature that could be easily done in the short run to
respond to oil price shocks during 1990–91 and oil and gas price shocks in 2000
and 2001. This inability was a good thing and made it easier for these sectors
to adapt smoothly to changes in supply and demand conditions. The 1990s
benefited from the legacy of failed regulatory policies of the 1970s and 1980s in
another important, though indirect way. The decade began with substantial
excess production and distribution capacity and a variety of inefficiencies on
the supply side. They provided significant opportunities for cost reduction and
innovation in energy production and distribution. These factors made it easier
for supply to expand to meet growing demand without significant price shocks
or supply disruptions during most of the decade, and allowed energy issues to
fade into the background on the national policy agenda. The legacy of regulatory and energy policies of the 1970s and 1980s also was a major stimulus for
electricity-restructuring initiatives in California and the Northeast that had inherited high-cost assets and contracts from the 1970s and 1980s and whose costs
for regulatory purposes were often far above their 1990s competitive market
values.

The Clinton administration largely embraced and supported increased reliance on market forces to allocate energy resources and continued efforts begun
by the previous administration to remove barriers to good market performance.
It viewed the proper role of energy policy to be to respond to market imperfections, especially as they related to the environmental impacts of energy
production and consumption and federal regulations limiting competition. However, the favorable performance of the energy sectors during most of the 1990s
also led to some complacency on the energy policy front, especially regarding
investments in energy supply infrastructure. While the decade began with sub-

---

2. For a discussion of the nature of this controversy, see Orszag (undated, 2000, 2001b) and
Falkenrath (2000).

stantial excess capacity in electricity generation and transmission, natural gas production and transportation, and oil-refining capacity, the capacity of these infrastructure facilities was being stressed by the end of the decade. Tight supplies and growing demand led to rising prices for oil, natural gas, and wholesale electricity by the end of the decade. Regulatory and environmental constraints, as well as continued problems with and uncertainty about the future of electricity-sector restructuring, contributed to tight supplies, price volatility, and some spot shortages of electricity and natural gas during 2000 and early 2001.

The rest of this essay proceeds in the following way. Section 8.2 discusses the public policy rationales for national energy policies. In section 8.3 I provide an overview of energy policies and energy sector developments during the George H. W. Bush and Clinton administrations, focusing primarily on the Clinton administration.[3] Four segments of the energy sector and policy initiatives affecting them are discussed in more detail in sections 8.3–8.7: petroleum, natural gas, electricity, and energy efficiency and renewable energy. I conclude with a discussion of energy policy challenges that are a legacy of the 1990s.

8.2   Why Do We Need National Energy Policies?

It is useful to begin with a brief discussion of the reasons why we might need national policies targeted specifically at energy supply, demand, and pricing that go beyond broader public policies (tax, antitrust, environmental, R&D, etc.) affecting American industry generally. Energy policies are derivative policies reflecting a number of higher level policy objectives and considerations.[4]

8.2.1   Important Infrastructure Sectors Essential for Economic Growth and Development

Economical and reliable supplies of energy play an important role in fostering economic growth and development. Energy, like transportation and telecommunications services, is a key intermediate input into most sectors of a developed economy. Distortions in prices, consumption, supply, or reliability of energy infrastructure services can lead to large economic and social costs. Moreover, because the short-run demand for energy tends to be quite inelastic

---

3. A more detailed discussion of all energy sectors can be found in Joskow (2001b).
4. The list is not meant to be exhaustive. Clearly, income distribution concerns have played a role in energy policy formation and implementation. So too have market imperfections that may make it difficult for consumers to make rational investments in energy-using structures, equipment, and appliances.

and dependent on long-lived capital investments, it takes time for consumers to respond fully to long-term shifts in price levels by changing consumption patterns. Key segments of the energy system (electricity and natural gas networks) have (or had) natural monopoly characteristics and have been subject to economic regulation for most of the 20th century. The performance of these regulatory institutions has profound implications for broader indices of economic performance.

8.2.2   National Security Concerns

A growing fraction of U.S. energy consumption is supplied by imports of energy, primarily petroleum, from other countries. World petroleum reserves in countries exporting oil are concentrated in North Africa, the Persian Gulf, Russia, and countries that were formerly part of the Soviet Union.[5] These regions are politically unstable and have governments that are not always friendly to the United States. Because energy, and in particular petroleum, is an important input supporting economic growth and development, energy market instability is potentially very costly to the U.S. economy and those of our oil-importing allies. Accordingly, enemies of the United States or its allies may use energy supply strategically in an effort to influence other U.S. policies.[6]

8.2.3   Environmental Impacts

The combustion of fossil fuels is the primary source of air pollution targeted by environmental policies aimed at cleaning the air (NO_x, SO_2, CO, etc.) and accounts for most of the production of CO_2, a greenhouse gas generally thought to be a major contributor to global climate change. Energy production and delivery also have significant potential impacts on water quality, water temperature, and land use. Since air and water pollution are generally acknowledged to be "externalities" that require policy intervention, environmental policies will have significant effects on energy supply, demand, and prices and vice versa. Environmental policies necessarily affect energy markets, and energy policies necessarily have environmental effects. Sensible environmental policy should be matched with compatible energy policies. Moreover, because the United States has been reluctant to use the best available instruments to internalize environ-

---

5. Countries in the Middle East and North Africa account for over 70 percent of world crude oil reserves.

6. This is not my area of expertise, but it seems to me that the oil import situation for both the United States and other G-7 countries in the aggregate is an important consideration in evaluating energy security issues.

mental externalities (e.g., environmental taxes and/or property rights–based cap and trade systems), second (third, fourth, or more) best policies may involve interventions that work directly on the supply of and demand for the resources that have adverse environmental impacts.

8.2.4   Competition Policy

General U.S. economic policy is oriented toward promoting the development of competitive markets and relying on price and entry regulation only when unregulated markets have "natural monopoly" characteristics and are expected to perform poorly absent regulation. Important segments of the U.S. energy sector, in particular electric power and natural gas, have been subject to price and entry regulation for almost a century. As already noted, these regulatory institutions have important implications for the performance of these important infrastructure sectors and, therefore, for the performance of the economy. U.S. competition policies continually reexamine the rationale for and performance of price and entry regulation. Poor sector performance, as well as technological and economic changes that undermine the case for price and entry regulation, can make it desirable to design and implement competition policies that restructure regulated industries to expand opportunities for competition and shrink the expanse of price and entry regulation.

8.2.5   Use of Publicly Owned Resources

A significant fraction of domestic energy resources lie on or under land that is controlled by the federal government (and to a lesser extent state governments), and this fraction has been increasing.[7] Hydroelectric resources lie on rivers and in locations subject to state or federal jurisdiction. The federal government has no choice but to develop and implement policies that define how these lands can be used for energy exploration and production. Whether and how these public lands are made available for exploration, development, and production of energy can have important implications for energy supply and prices. These policies also have impacts on the environment that further complicate the interactions between energy and environmental policies. Sound federal land-use policies cannot be developed independent of complementary energy and environmental policies.

---

7. Largely because of increased production from federal offshore tracts, the share of domestic oil production from federal lands increased from 16.3 percent in 1989 to 26.9 percent in 1997; similarly, the federal share of natural gas production increased from 30.2 percent in 1980 to 39.3 percent in 1997.

8.2.6   Federalism Issues

Responsibility for energy policy involves both the states and the federal government. However, state energy policy decisions can have impacts on other states and on suppliers of energy and energy-using equipment that affect consumers in many states. Conflicts between state policies have emerged in electricity and natural gas industry reform initiatives. Moreover, individual uncoordinated state programs defining appliance efficiency standards, air and water emissions standards, the composition of gasoline, certification of energy facilities, and the like can increase the overall national costs of achieving energy policy and environmental goals. Federal policies may be necessary to harmonize state programs to reduce their costs and to alleviate barriers to interstate commerce created by individual state policies.

8.3   Energy Policy Overview: 1990 Through 2000

8.3.1   Energy Supply, Demand, and Prices During the 1990s

Total U.S. energy consumption grew steadily after 1991, increasing by about 17 percent between 1990 and 2000. Consumption grew in all sectors (residential, commercial, industrial, transportation) during the decade, and the distribution of energy consumption between residential, commercial, industrial, and transportation sectors changed little between 1990 and 2000 (Figure 8.1). The econ-

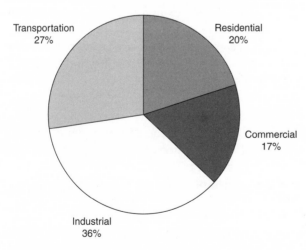

Figure 8.1
U.S. Energy Consumption by Sector, 2000

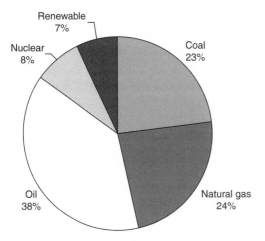

Figure 8.2
Energy Consumption by Fuel, 2000

omy continued to become more electricity intensive as electricity consumption grew by over 25 percent during the decade. Energy consumption per real dollar of GDP continued its long historical decline, though the rate of decline was slower than during the 1980–90 period when energy prices were higher. However energy consumption per capita increased steadily after 1991.

The overall fuel supply mix in 2000 was little different from that in 1990, with a small increase in the share of natural gas and a small decrease in petroleum's share (Figure 8.2).

Aggregate domestic energy production was roughly constant during the decade, while imports of oil and natural gas increased to balance supply and demand. Domestic oil production continued to decline. Domestic natural gas production increased slightly, as offshore production and production from nonconventional sources increased more than conventional onshore production declined. Imports of natural gas from Canada increased significantly as the demand for natural gas increased much more quickly than did domestic supplies. Net imports of energy increased overall by more than 50 percent during the decade, with all of the increase coming after 1992 (Figure 8.3).

Coal production continued to increase slowly but steadily along with the continuing shift of production from the eastern producing areas to those in the West. Electricity produced from nuclear power plants increased significantly, despite the fact that few new plants were completed and nearly a dozen plants closed, as nuclear plant availability increased dramatically during the decade. Definitive resolution of a site for permanent storage of nuclear waste continued

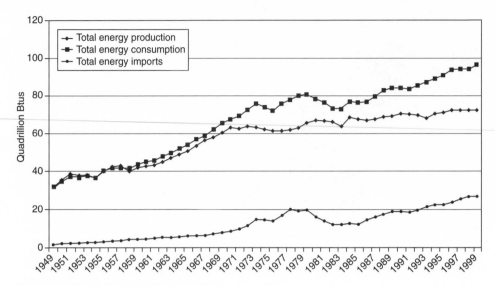

Figure 8.3
Energy Production, Consumption and Imports, 1949–2000

to elude policy-makers, though some military waste began to move to a site in New Mexico. Renewable energy supplies increased modestly and accounted for about the same fraction of domestic energy production in 2000 as in 1990.[8]

Real fossil fuel prices declined 20 percent (average for decade) from their 1990 peak through 1999, though there was considerable volatility in oil and natural gas prices. By 1998–99 the real price of fossil fuels reached a level about equal to prices prevailing just before the 1973–74 oil embargo. A further dramatic drop in world oil prices in 1998 quickly reversed itself in 1999 as OPEC implemented a supply reduction program, facilitated by Mexico, and oil prices continued to increase during 2000. Wellhead prices of natural gas, which had remained in the range of $2 to $3 per million Btu through most of the 1990s, increased dramatically beginning in the summer of 2000, with delivered prices rising to as high as $10 per million cubic feet (Mcf) in most regions by the end of 2000 and (briefly) to as high as $60/Mcf in southern California in mid-December 2000, before falling back to $3/Mcf by July 1, 2001. Real electricity prices fell during the decade, with the first nominal price increases in many years starting to be observed in late 2000 in response to increases in natural gas

---

8. Almost all of the increase in renewable energy is associated with the use of wood, waste, and alcohol fuels. The data for these uses are not very reliable. Solar and wind energy supplies increased by about 50 percent during the decade, but represented only about 0.1 percent of total domestic energy production in 2000. More on renewable energy later.

and wholesale electricity market prices. There was excess electric generating and transmission capacity in all regions of the country at the beginning of the decade. Little new generating or transmission capacity was added after 1992. With growing demand and little new supply, the excess capacity margin gradually disappeared. Rising natural gas prices, tight supplies, and delays in the completion of new generating plants led to dramatic increases in wholesale market prices in 1999 and especially in 2000. Spot shortages of electricity occurred in California in late 2000 and early 2001.

8.3.2 Energy Policy, 1990–92

The decade began with the invasion of Kuwait by Iraq, the curtailment of oil exports from the area, and a rapid and significant run-up in oil prices in mid-1990. This in turn led to the now familiar, though episodic, process of hand-wringing by politicians and the media about rising oil prices, dependence on Middle East oil, and the absence of any sustained coherent U.S. energy policy. The Department of Energy developed a "national energy strategy" that presented policy options to President George H. W. Bush.[9] In February 1991 the Bush administration proposed federal energy policy legislation to Congress. It focused on increasing oil, natural gas, and nuclear power production, including oil and gas exploration in the Arctic National Wildlife Refuge (ANWR). The proposals were very controversial and aggressively opposed by Democrats, environmentalists, and some Republican congressmen as well. Congress spent the rest of the year debating the administration's proposed energy policy measures. The core features of the Bush administration's bill were finally rejected by Congress in June 1991.

The debate about energy policy continued in 1992, though the public concern about high oil prices, potential shortages, and dependence on imported oil faded quickly away with the end (so to speak) of the Gulf War. Indeed, in retrospect, the oil shock of 1990–91 was much more modest and short-lived, and had much less impact on other fuels than did the previous two oil shocks. It is surprising that it generated so much media attention and legislative activity. Apparently, eager energy "supply-sider" friends of George saw this as an opportunity to promote their favorite policy initiatives. They may have regretted doing so.

The debate subsequently shifted away from the Bush administration's supply-side initiatives to a very different energy policy program advocated by

---

9. There was a big increase in media coverage of energy policy issues during this period. A Herb Block cartoon (August 12, 1990) depicted the White House staff searching for an energy policy, which was last heard of during the Jimmy Carter administration. Numerous editorials in major newspapers during the rest of 1990 called for a national energy policy.

House Democrats. The Energy Policy Act of 1992 (EPAct92) was passed in October 1992. It was the only piece of major energy policy legislation passed during the 1990s. It grew out of legislation proposed by Congressman Phil Sharp entitled the "National Energy Efficiency Act of 1991." It was a very different piece of energy legislation than the Bush administration had proposed in 1991. Rather than being a supply-side program oriented toward conventional fuels, it focused on creating tax and direct subsidies for energy efficiency and renewable energy technologies and on encouraging all states to develop and implement "integrated resource planning" programs for their utilities that were to include utility-sponsored energy-efficiency programs in their resources-planning processes. The associated costs were to be included in regulated retail electricity and gas prices.

EPAct92 also made changes in the Federal Power Act (FPA) and the Public Utility Holding Company Act (PUHCA) that helped to make electricity industry restructuring and competition initiatives feasible. Ironically, these restructuring and competition programs in turn eventually undermined the state integrated resource planning and energy-efficiency programs that EPAct92 promoted, since the structure and financing of these programs relied heavily on the institution of regulated monopoly to support what were effectively a set of "taxation by regulation" policies.[10]

In 1992, FERC also issued Order 636, the culmination of nearly a decade of policy initiatives to open up access to natural gas pipelines by unbundling the sale of transportation service, the sale of gas storage services, and the sale of natural gas itself, allowing buyers and sellers of "commodity" natural gas to negotiate supply contracts directly and then to buy pipeline transportation service to deliver the gas from field to destination.

8.3.3 Energy Policy, 1993–2000

EPAct92 embodied what was largely a Democratic congressional energy policy framework inherited by the Clinton administration soon after it was signed by President George H. W. Bush. It became the foundation for most of the Clinton administration's subsequent energy policy initiatives. The focus of EPAct92 on energy efficiency, renewable energy, and environmental impact mitigation was well matched to the positions that the Clinton-Gore team had advanced during their election campaign. Vice President Al Gore was a champion of environmental improvement and had expressed deep concerns about CO_2 emissions

---

10. See Joskow (1992). Expenditures on electric utility energy efficiency and demand-side management programs peaked in 1994 and have declined significantly since then. See Energy Information Administration (2000), p. 228.

and their impacts on global climate change. The administration's appointments to the Department of Energy were consistent with these views. Promoting improvements in energy efficiency, renewable energy, alternative-fuel vehicles, and new technologies for extracting and using conventional energy sources were their highest priorities.

Soon after his inauguration, President Clinton proposed the implementation of a large broad-based tax on energy (an energy "Btu tax"). The proposal's motivation was to raise revenue to reduce the federal budget deficit, to promote energy conservation, and indirectly to reduce pollution associated with the combustion of fossil fuels. The proposal was widely criticized in Congress, was unpopular with industry and individual consumers, and eventually went down in flames. The only remnant of the initial proposal that eventually was passed by Congress was a small increase in the federal gasoline tax to bolster the Highway Trust Fund. No new major energy policy legislation was passed by Congress during the rest of the decade.

Energy policy during the rest of the decade relied heavily on the framework and policies embodied in the Energy Policy Act of 1992, associated state initiatives to restructure the electricity industry to promote wholesale and retail competition, the continued implementation of FERC regulations supporting the evolution of the restructured natural gas industry, new state initiatives to expand "customer choice" of natural gas supplier to residential and commercial customers served by local distribution companies (LDCs), and the effects of the Clean Air Act of 1990 on coal use in the electric power industry. The major energy policy venues for gas and electricity policies were the FERC (natural gas, electricity) and state regulatory commissions. In April 1999 the Clinton administration finally did propose comprehensive electricity industry restructuring and competition legislation, but neither it nor Republican alternatives got very far in Congress.

The Department of Energy's (DOE) policies were heavily influenced by the administration's environmental policy agenda, including concerns about global climate change. The DOE gradually reallocated R&D funding and policy initiatives away from coal and nuclear R&D programs toward programs focused on promoting energy efficiency and renewable energy supplies, as well as the development of more efficient vehicles that use fuels other than petroleum. Federal expenditures supporting energy efficiency, renewable energy technology, and alternative-fuel vehicles increased significantly, while funding for coal and nuclear technology declined.[11] The administration's efforts in these areas

---

11. There was a significant increase in appropriations for fossil energy and nuclear science and technology programs in FY2001.

were first hampered by federal budgetary constraints that placed pressure on the DOE's budget. After 1994 these initiatives were impeded by a Republican Congress that was hostile to the DOE in general and the Clinton administration's favorite energy programs in particular. In response to budget constraints and a hostile Congress, the Clinton administration began to work with industrial groups on voluntary programs to develop policies to respond to global warming concerns (Climate Change Action Plan) and new motor vehicle technologies that would improve fuel economy and reduce air emissions (Partnership for a New Generation of Vehicles).

Early in the administration, the DOE was an active cheerleader for spreading the gospel of state "integrated resources planning" (IRP) programs for regulated gas and electricity utilities. However, most of the states that had been leaders in applying IRP were veering quickly toward initiatives to restructure their gas and electric utilities in order to promote wholesale and retail competition or "customers' choice." The Clinton DOE team had to play "catch-up" on the electricity competition front as the states (e.g., California, New York, Maine, Massachusetts) that had been the primary test beds for integrated resource planning and utility demand-side-management (DSM) programs began to focus primarily on the problem of high electric rates and the potential for industry restructuring and competition to bring them down. The electricity restructuring bandwagon also undermined the Climate Change Action Plan initiative as many of the utilities that had been active on climate change issues became occupied with industry restructuring, stranded cost recovery, and competition issues. The administration did not propose its own federal electricity restructuring legislation until early 1999, and it too had a number of provisions designed to preserve utility energy-efficiency and renewable energy programs and to tilt deregulated markets toward renewable energy through electricity generation "portfolio" standards requiring suppliers to have minimum fractions of their power supplies from renewable energy sources. Neither the administration's bill nor several Republican alternatives ever gathered enough political support to come close to being passed.

The administration also quietly supported or acceded to Republican policy initiatives that encouraged oil and gas drilling in deep water, as well as tax and royalty relief for small, relatively inefficient oil and gas wells; opened up additional federal lands in Alaska to drilling; proceeded with the privatization of federal uranium enrichment facilities and the Elk Hills Naval Petroleum Reserve; supported federal funding for development of new technologies to increase oil extraction productivity; continued the slow process of licensing a federal nuclear waste storage facility; supported the relicensing of operating nuclear power plants and continued research on advanced reactor technology;

and initiated a cooperative program with the U.S. automobile industry to de-velop more fuel-efficient vehicle technology. Foreign policy initiatives endea-vored to diversify the nation's oil supplies and to foster the independence of oil-producing states that were created after the breakup of the Soviet Union. The administration also supported increases in the oil stored in the Strategic Petroleum Reserves (SPR) and the development of policies to use the SPR to respond to oil supply crises.

It is important to recognize that the Clinton administration demonstrated a commitment to relying primarily on market forces to allocate energy resources. It did not try to return to the failed price control, rationing, and energy-allocation policies of the 1970s and early 1980s. The Clinton administration viewed the proper role of energy policy to be to respond to market imperfec-tions, especially as they related to the environmental impacts of energy pro-duction and consumption. It believed in using limited financial incentives to encourage consumers and suppliers to change their behavior. It had faith that new technologies could reduce the costs of energy efficiency, renewable energy, alternative-fuel vehicles, and production of conventional fuels. It also viewed increased supply diversity from renewable and alternative fuels as playing an important role in promoting national security interests as well. Thus the Clin-ton administration's policies reinforced what has become a bipartisan rejection of the aggressive energy market intervention policies of the 1970s and early 1980s, and bipartisan support for policies focused on allowing energy markets to work, breaking down regulatory barriers restricting markets from working efficiently, and reflecting environmental and national security externalities in energy policies through financial incentives and market-based mechanisms.

8.4 Petroleum

8.4.1 Petroleum Industry Behavior and Performance

Petroleum accounted for about 38 percent of domestic energy consumption in 2000, down from 40 percent in 1990. Petroleum consumption grew by 15 per-cent between 1990 and 2000,[12] and in 1998 surpassed the previous peak con-sumption level reached 20 years earlier (Figure 8.4). The transportation sector, primarily passenger cars and trucks, accounted for about 68 percent of U.S. oil consumption in 2000, up from about 64 percent in 1990. Most of the rest is accounted for by the industrial sector, with little oil being used in the residen-tial and commercial sectors or to generate electricity.

---

12. This is about the same growth rate experienced by the OECD countries as a whole and for OECD Europe.

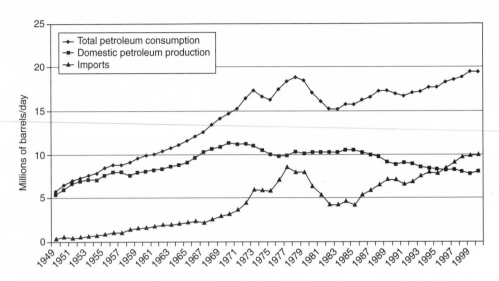

Figure 8.4
U.S. Petroleum Consumption, Production, and Imports

Domestic oil production continued to decline steadily during the 1990s as imports increased. Petroleum imports increased by 40 percent during the decade, and by the end of 2000, the United States was importing 56 percent of its petroleum. Overall, imported energy increased from 17 percent of total energy consumption in 1990 to 25 percent in 2000. In the mid-1990s aggregate energy imports surpassed the previous peak level reached in 1977 and by 2000 had exceeded that import level by 36 percent. By the end of the decade, the United States was far more dependent on imported energy in general and imported petroleum in particular than it had been since the mid-1970s, just before the second oil shock.[13] However, it is also important to recognize that the energy intensity of the U.S. economy declined significantly during this period; energy consumption by dollar of real GDP in 2000 was about 60 percent of what it had been in 1977.

Crude oil prices declined from their 1990 peaks during most of the decade, though there is significant year-to-year price volatility (Figure 8.5). Crude oil prices plummeted during 1998, apparently as a result of declining imports by Asian countries experiencing an economic contraction and subsequent economic problems in Russia. Gasoline prices followed a similar pattern (Figure 8.6). Domestic oil and gas drilling activity followed these price trends fairly closely.

---

13. Petroleum supplied by OPEC countries increased to 43 percent of world production in 2000 from 38 percent in 1990. However, OPEC accounted for a much smaller proportion of world production in 2000 (43 percent) than it did in 1973 (56 percent).

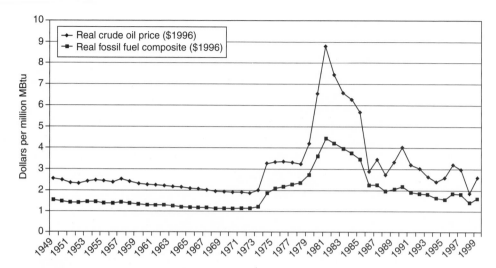

Figure 8.5
Real Fossil Fuel Production Prices

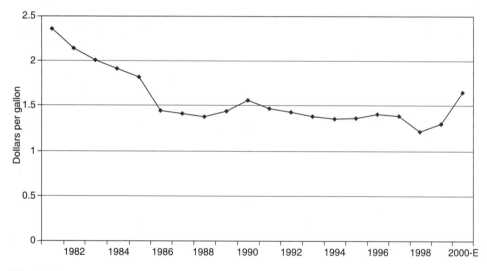

Figure 8.6
Real Price of Regular Unleaded Gasoline

Falling crude prices had a significant adverse impact on oil-exporting countries. In 1999 the Mexican minister of energy worked closely with Venezuela, Saudi Arabia, and other OPEC countries to curtail supplies in an effort to drive up prices. Although these efforts initially met with little success, they eventually led to coordinated supply curtailments. World petroleum demand subsequently increased as well, as the economies of countries in Europe and Asia recovered and oil prices began to rise rapidly. Oil prices rose significantly in 1999 and increased further in 2000 as world demand continued to increase as supplies tightened. Oil prices peaked at an average price of about $31 a barrel for crude oil during the fall of 2000 and then fell back to the $25–$27 range during the first four months of 2001. The increase in crude oil (and natural gas) prices stimulated a very significant increase in domestic drilling activity, with the number of oil and gas wells drilled each month doubling from mid-1999 levels by the end of 2000. And despite the significant price increases that occurred after mid-1999, real oil and product prices remained at levels far below their peaks during 1980–81, though higher than the local price peaks reached in 1990.

As U.S. petroleum consumption has increased, the availability of domestic capacity to refine crude oil into petroleum products has become a growing problem. The United States experienced a steep decline in refining capacity since its peak in 1981, though most of this decline occurred before 1987 (Figure 8.7). About 3 million barrels per day of refining capacity were closed during the 1980s, after price controls and allocations ended. These regulations had propped up small, inefficient refineries, which exited the market as these regulations were repealed. Though the number of refineries has continued to decline and no new refineries have been built in many years, total refining capacity was roughly constant during the decade, with a significant expansion in capacity after 1994, resulting from capacity expansions at existing refineries.[14] Growing demand for refined products and roughly constant refining capacity led to increasing refinery capacity utilization rates during the 1990s, with capacity utilization reportedly increasing to 98.5 percent by the end of 2000. It is unlikely that major new refinery sites will be developed in the United States unless regulatory restrictions on siting new refineries change significantly. Future expansions in refining capacity are expected at some existing refineries and outside the United States, including in Mexico and South America.

The unprecedented high levels of refinery capacity utilization mean that refined product supplies and prices are very sensitive to unplanned refinery

---

14. See Energy Information Administration (2000). Contrary to some conventional wisdom, refining capacity did not decline during the 1990s. It increased slightly overall, with more than 100 percent of the increase between 1990 and 2000 coming after 1994.

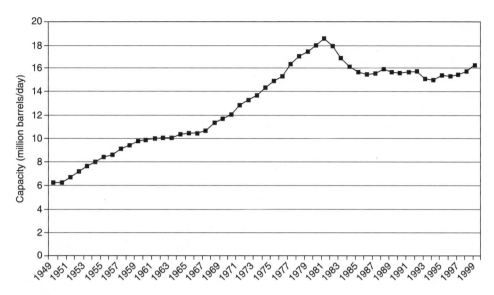

Figure 8.7
U.S. Crude Oil Refining Capacity

outages resulting from equipment breakdowns, fires, and so on, since there is essentially no reserve capacity in the system. Accordingly, product demand and supply availability fluctuations must be fully absorbed by product inventories, which had also declined in the last few years. This sensitivity of product prices to refinery (and oil pipeline) outages has increased as a consequence of the growing regional differentiation in the composition of gasoline required to meet environmental regulations on a seasonal basis. There are now as many as 40 "microbrews" of gasoline (including octane differences) sold in the United States.

8.4.2 Policy Initiatives

The 1990s was a decade in which U.S. policies relied primarily on unregulated market forces to operate to allocate resources to and within the petroleum sector. While there were no major domestic petroleum policy developments during the decade, the administration supported Republican-sponsored legislation to stimulate offshore drilling for oil and natural gas in deep water of the Gulf of Mexico by reducing federal royalty payments,[15] urged Congress to reauthorize the Strategic Petroleum Reserves, proposed the establishment of regional

---

15. See Deep Water Royalty Relief Act, Public Law 104–58, November 28, 1995.

heating oil reserves, sold the Elk Hills Naval Petroleum Reserve,[16] initiated a set of modest technology transfer and support programs to increase productivity from small high-cost oil wells, and opened up federal lands for oil and natural gas drilling, including the National Petroleum Reserve in Alaska and additional areas adjacent to existing production areas on the North Slope of Alaska. The administration also pursued foreign policies to strengthen relationships with governments of oil-producing countries and to encourage Caspian Sea countries and U.S. oil companies developing resources in these countries to build a pipeline under the Caspian Sea to Turkey in order to avoid routes through Iran and Russia, reducing dependence on these two countries. Environmental regulations also affected petroleum supply and demand during the decade. In particular, the implementation of environmental regulations affecting the composition of gasoline burned in automobiles in several cities resulting from the Clean Air Act Amendments of 1990 and growing constraints on domestic refining capacity began to have a visible affect on gasoline supply and prices in some regions by the end of the decade. Gasoline price spikes in 1999 and 2000 in California and the Midwest led to calls for price controls, which the administration resisted.

In the last ten years, the refinery industry has had to respond to five sets of new environmental regulations affecting motor gasoline product composition.[17] These regulations have required significant changes in refinery operations and investments in plant and equipment. In total, the regulations have been estimated to have increased gasoline prices by amounts in the range of 7 to 10 cents a gallon.[18] Perhaps more importantly, because different states have different requirements for gasoline composition, some states and regions have become more dependent on a small number of refineries that can produce gasoline meeting local requirements.[19] As a result, regional demand or supply-side shocks can have larger impacts on prices in particular areas of the country than would be the case if there was more refinery capacity producing approved fuels available to meet supply and demand shocks. The benefits of giving states

---

16. The federal government began studying the sale of Naval Petroleum Reserve No. 1 (Elk Hills in California) and No. 3 (Teapot Dome in Wyoming) in 1986. The DOE initiated the process of evaluating and selling Elk Hills in 1995. The sale was completed in 1998 for $3.65 billion. Since the Teapot Dome reserve contained relatively little remaining oil, it was decided to produce it out rather than to sell it. The administration also initiated policies to lease or transfer to the private sector the federal Shale Oil Reserves. The primary motivations for these efforts were to raise funds for the federal government and to increase productivity from these properties.

17. See Lidderdale (2001).

18. Lidderdale (2001) and references cited there.

19. Some states have voluntarily adopted restrictions on gasoline composition during different seasons, and states retain some flexibility regarding the precise "microbrew" they rely on to meet environmental regulations.

flexibility in choosing whether and how to restrict gasoline compositions to meet ambient air quality standards may not be worth the growing costs of this flexibility.

The introduction of the EPA's Phase II regulations for summer-blend reformulated gasoline in high-ozone urban areas likely contributed to the localized gasoline price spikes experienced in the Midwest during the first half of 2000. As discussed previously, crude, gasoline, and product prices rose dramatically during the second half of 1999 and during 2000 throughout the United States. However, the increase in gasoline prices was much more extreme in a few midwestern cities than it was in most of the rest of the country during this period of time.

Midwestern governors and congressmen put pressure on the administration to take actions to constrain rising gasoline prices and to curb alleged anticompetitive abuses by gasoline suppliers. The administration resisted calls for price controls and allowed responsible agencies to respond to complaints about anticompetitive behavior. A subsequent FTC study found that the new, more-stringent environmental regulations governing the compositions of gasoline required in several midwestern cities, may have contributed to abnormally low inventories and made gasoline prices in these cities very sensitive to supply and demand shocks.[20] The FTC concluded that supplier behavior that caused the midwestern gasoline price spikes during summer 2000 did not violate the antitrust laws.[21]

The Strategic Petroleum Reserve (SPR) was created in late 1975 pursuant to the Energy Policy and Conservation Act (EPCA). EPCA provided for the establishment of a petroleum reserve of up to 1 billion barrels. Salt caverns were subsequently acquired along the Gulf coast to store the oil, and crude oil began to be stored there in 1977. Oil stored in the SPR peaked in 1994 at 592 million barrels and, after some test sales, settled at 570 million barrels by the late 1990s. Under EPCA, the president must determine if a drawdown is required by "a severe energy supply disruption or by obligations of the United States" under the International Energy Treaty. EPCA goes on to discuss the characteristics of such a severe supply disruption, and these include that the supply disruption be of significant scope and duration, and cause major adverse impact on national safety or the national economy. Prior to September 2000, the SPR had been drawn down for a couple of test sales and during Operation Desert Storm in early 1991.

---

20. Final Report of the Federal Trade Commission (2000). See also the FTC's Interim Report, available at http://www.ftc.gov/os/2000/07/gasprice.htm.
21. In May 2001 the FTC closed an investigation of gasoline price spikes in the western United States, which it began in 1998, concluding that the prices at issue were not the result of behavior that violated the antitrust laws. http://www.ftc.gov/opa/2001/05/westerngas.htm.

On September 22, 2000, President Clinton authorized the release of 30 million barrels of oil from the SPR over a 30-day period. The objective was to increase domestic supplies during the prevailing tight supply situation and, in particular, to increase supplies of heating oil, which were projected to be short during the coming winter. Heating oil inventories were at unusually low levels during 2000, and oil prices continued to increase as the year progressed. Very low heating oil stocks going into the fall of 2000 were of particular concern given the lags between crude oil deliveries, refining, and delivery to local oil terminals.

The proposed release from the SPR was very controversial both inside and outside the administration. The release was opposed by Treasury and State. Those opposed were concerned that the federal government was marching down the path of speculating on future oil price movements, that these interventions would be ineffective because private oil inventory and production decisions would simply work in the opposite direction, and that they would anger major oil-exporting countries. In the end, with the presidential election rapidly approaching, the White House decided to release oil from the SPR to demonstrate that it was doing something to respond to rising prices and potential heating oil shortages. The release was structured as a "swap" rather than a sale of oil, apparently partly to avoid dealing with EPCA's criteria for selling SPR oil. Under a swap arrangement, oil was released from the SPR and would be replaced later by a larger amount of oil, with the terms of the swap determined by competitive bidding. It is hard to know what, if any, effects this modest release had on heating oil stocks or prices. There is no obvious change in the trajectory of heating oil stocks after the release, though crude oil and product prices did fall significantly after November 2000.

The Clinton administration's "let the market work" approach to petroleum markets did have some potentially adverse consequences. Imports of petroleum increased to their highest levels in history. U.S. imports of petroleum now exceed 10 million barrels per day. The Energy Information Administration projects a continuing decline in domestic production and increasing imports of petroleum over the next two decades. By 2020, imports are projected to account for roughly 75 percent of U.S. petroleum consumption. There is little chance that much can be done to significantly change this trend through domestic "supply-side" initiatives, despite the fact that real oil prices are projected to increase significantly over the next 20 years in all EIA cases. As I will discuss presently, the Clinton administration did little to curtail oil demand growth by tightening vehicle fuel efficiency standards, largely because Congress made it virtually impossible for the administration even to study changes in vehicle fuel economy standards.

For those concerned about U.S. dependence on imported oil, the 1990s did not end well. While the United States and other oil importing countries are much less dependent on Middle Eastern oil producers than was the case in the 1970s, the share of world production accounted for by Middle Eastern and North African countries has begun to grow once again. Moreover, these countries account for 70 percent of world petroleum reserves, and dependence on them is likely to continue to grow. The administration's primary direct response to the national security implications of rising oil imports focused on strengthening relationships with governments of oil-producing countries, on encouraging Caspian Sea countries and producers to choose an export pipeline route that did not cross Iran or Russia, and on maintaining a significant military presence in the Middle East.

8.5 Natural Gas

8.5.1 Natural Gas Industry Behavior and Performance

Natural gas accounted for 24 percent of U.S. energy use in 2000, up from 23 percent in 1990. U.S. natural gas consumption increased by 22 percent between 1990 and 2000. Electricity produced with natural gas increased by 57 percent between 1990 and 2000, and almost all new electric generating plants under construction at the end of the decade were fueled by natural gas.[22] Natural gas consumption is projected to continue to grow rapidly in the next two decades, increasing by roughly 50 percent by 2020.[23] Natural gas's share of total energy consumption is projected to grow to 33.1 percent in 2020. This increase in projected natural gas consumption is dominated by rapidly growing utilization of natural gas to produce electricity, using combined-cycle gas turbine (CCGT) generating technology.

Domestic natural gas production increased by only about 8 percent between 1990 and 2000; domestic production was roughly constant from 1994 to 1999 before increasing again in 2000 in response to significantly higher prices. Production from offshore wells, unconventional sources, and gas associated with the production of oil all increased during the decade.[24] From 1994 to 1997 natural gas reserve additions exceeded actual production; however, in 1998 and

---

22. Based on second quarter 2001 data on generating plants actually under construction provided to me by Argus. Natural gas used to generate electricity likely increased at a slower rate during the decade as more efficient combined-cycle gas turbine (CCGT) capacity was completed. However, the EIA data presently available do not make it possible to derive accurate estimates of natural gas utilization to generate electricity after 1998.
23. See Energy Information Administration (2000), pp. 82–86.
24. See Mariner-Volpe (2000).

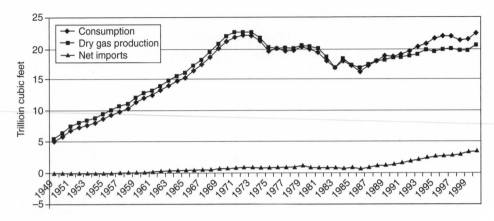

Figure 8.8
Natural Gas Consumption, Production, and Net Imports

1999 reserve additions fell short of actual production, and this statement is likely to have been true as well during 2000.[25] After declining significantly during the 1980s, gas-finding costs appear to have stabilized, partly because of increased drilling in the Gulf of Mexico facilitated by royalty relief legislation signed by President Clinton.

With rapidly growing consumption and stagnant domestic production, a large increase in imports of gas was required to balance supply and demand (Figure 8.8). Imports from Canada increased by about 50 percent during the 1990s, new reserves were developed offshore of eastern Canada, and new pipelines were built, providing a new supply of natural gas for New England and the Northeast. The deteriorating reserve additions situation, the leveling out of declining gas-finding costs, stagnant domestic production, the "separation" of gas from oil prices owing to what was characterized as a "gas bubble," and the growing demand for gas in the electricity sector probably should have been a warning that natural gas prices would soon rise. However, this was not widely predicted by experts at the time.[26]

Real natural gas prices were roughly constant through most of the decade, though there was considerable year-to-year price variation (Figure 8.9). However, beginning in mid-2000, natural gas prices began to rise rapidly to levels far above prevailing predictions or historical experience. By late summer 2000, natural gas prices had risen to about $5/million Btu at Henry Hub and climbed to near $10 by the end of the year, before declining back to about $5/million Btu by late March 2001, about $4 by June 1, 2001, and $3 by July 1, 2001. Prices

---

25. Mariner-Volpe (2000). Year 2000 data on reserve additions were not yet available in June 2001.
26. Most pre-2000 forecasts were for natural gas prices in the $2 to $3 range in 2010.

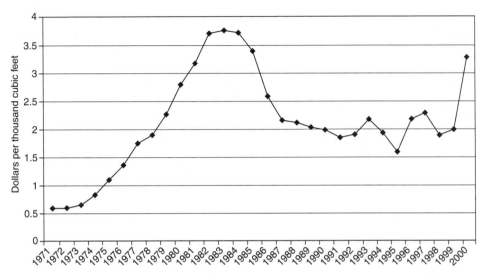

Figure 8.9
Real Wellhead Natural Gas Prices ($1996)

in California reached much higher levels as pipeline constraints caused delivered natural gas prices in California to rise to levels far above those prevailing in the rest of the country during the winter of 2000–01.[27] However, by July 2001 the gap between prices in California and the rest of the country returned to historical levels.

8.5.2   Policy Initiatives

During the 1990s natural gas was widely viewed as "the fossil fuel of choice." It is relatively clean (its combustion produces less CO_2, SO_2, and NO_x than do coal and oil yielding equivalent useful energy), it was relatively cheap, and it could fuel new, efficient CCGT electric generating facilities. The CCGT facilities in turn were ideally suited for supporting the evolving competitive electricity markets because they could be built quickly, at relatively small minimum efficient scale, they were less capital intensive, and they could be more easily sited than conventional generating plants. The primary policy initiatives related directly to natural gas focused on completing the program begun in the 1980s to open up access to interstate natural gas pipelines to competing marketers and brokers who could then buy gas in the field at unregulated

---

27. Whether the high prices in California were caused by real pipeline and local storage constraints or reflected (at least in part) the market power of those controlling pipeline capacity into southern California is an issue in dispute and litigation.

markets. The Clinton administration's support for the Republican-sponsored Deep Water Royalty Relief Act of 1995 encouraged exploration, development, and continued production of natural gas from marginal reserves in the Gulf of Mexico.

Putting aside the excitement in gas markets during 2000, natural gas policy during the post-1992 period focused on the continued implementation of the open access and unbundling provisions of Order 636 issued by FERC in 1992. Order 636 supported continued development of competitive natural gas markets, natural gas marketing, natural gas financial derivatives markets, natural gas storage, and secondary markets for natural gas pipeline capacity. It represented the culmination of eight years of efforts by FERC to respond to the consequences of the failed natural gas regulatory policies of the 1970s and early 1980s and the subsequent collapse of the existing regulatory and contractual framework governing the natural gas industry. As FERC continued to restructure the pipeline industry, states began to extend the "unbundling" concept to local gas distribution companies (LDCs), allowing industrial and larger commercial consumers to purchase unbundled transportation service from their LDC as well. The Clinton administration supported, but did not lead, these state gas policy initiatives. These state policies further expanded the base of retail customers purchasing in competitive gas commodity markets and working with gas marketers and brokers. These developments also had important implications for related changes in the electric power industry that came later in the decade. In addition, federal and state policies supporting restructuring and competition in the electricity sector were viewed as an indirect way to encourage increased use of natural gas to generate electricity.

8.6 Electricity

8.6.1 Background

The electric power sector experienced the most profound structural and regulatory changes of any of the energy sectors during the 1990s and received the most attention by the Clinton administration. These changes were facilitated by a combination of wholesale market reforms initiated by FERC as it implemented portions of the EPAct92 and individual state initiatives to restructure the electric utilities under their jurisdiction to take advantage of competitive wholesale markets and to create competitive retail markets as well. The Clinton administration's role in these important developments was modest. The rapid evolution of federal and state restructuring activity surprised the DOE, and the administration played catch-up during the last half of the decade.

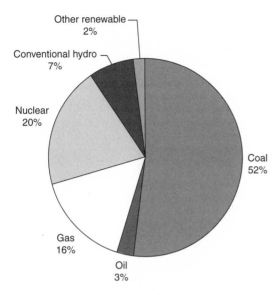

Figure 8.10
Fuels Used to Generate Electricity, 2000

Electricity accounts for about 36 percent of U.S. energy consumption, after taking account of the thermal losses associated with the transformation of fossil fuel into electricity.[28] In 2000, coal accounted for 52 percent, nuclear for 20 percent, and natural gas for 16 percent of the electricity supplied. Conventional hydro (7 percent), oil (3 percent), and renewable energy (2 percent) accounted for the rest of the electricity supplied in 2000 (Figure 8.10). The proportions of fuels used to generate electricity changed relatively little between 1990 and 2000, with natural gas accounting for a larger fraction (16 percent versus 12 percent) and conventional hydro (10 percent versus 7 percent) a smaller fraction. Electricity consumption grew by about 28 percent, and peak demand grew by about 25 percent between 1989 and 1999.

The United States began the decade with substantially more generating and transmission capacity than "needed" to meet current demand according to standard reserve-margin criteria. Relatively little investment in new electric generating facilities was made during the decade, however. Generating capacity available to meet peak demand grew by only about 7 percent during the 1989–99 period, while (noncoincident) peak demand increased by nearly 30 percent

---

28. The actual number is somewhat higher when electricity produced by industrial generators and cogenerators is fully taken into account. The measurement of the fuel used by these facilities is buried in commercial and industrial fossil fuel consumption data.

during this time period. Investments in new high-voltage transmission lines also increased by only about 7 percent during this period as well. Accordingly, electricity consumption grew much more rapidly than did generating and transmission capacity during the decade.

By the end of the decade, the excess capacity had largely disappeared, and spot shortages of power began to appear in some regions of the country, especially in the West. The real price of retail electricity continued to fall during the 1990s, reaching real price levels prevailing in 1974 by the end of the decade. However, retail electricity prices began to rise again in a number of areas in late 2000, following the increases in natural gas and wholesale power prices.

For most of the 20th century, the U.S. electric power industry was organized primarily around investor-owned electric utilities that had de facto exclusive franchises to serve all consumers in designated geographic areas.[29] The prices that the utilities could charge to retail consumers were regulated by state public utility commissions, based on their "cost of service," including a "fair rate of return" on investment. In return for their exclusive franchises, utilities had an obligation to serve all consumers requesting service at the prices approved by their state regulatory commissions. Utilities met their obligation to serve by investing in distribution, generation, and transmission facilities. That is, utilities were vertically integrated into the three primary electricity supply segments and provided "bundled" retail service to their franchise customers.

Unlike most other countries, the United States had a large number of vertically integrated utilities serving relatively small geographic areas rather than a single dominant electricity-supply enterprise serving most of the country. Over time, however, transmission and generating technology evolved in ways that made the economic supply areas regional rather than local. Rather than encouraging horizontal mergers to create much larger utilities to span economical supply areas, U.S. policies since the 1930s encouraged utilities to interconnect their transmission systems with one another, to build facilities jointly, to coordinate and share operating reserves, and to trade power among themselves in wholesale markets when a utility with surplus energy could produce more cheaply than could a proximate utility from its own generating facilities. The prices of third-party transmission service ("wheeling") and wholesale trades of power between utilities have been regulated by the Federal Energy Regulatory Commission (FERC), formerly the Federal Power Commission, since 1935. However, prior to EPAct92, FERC had no authority to order utilities to provide transmission service or to require utilities to build power plants or transmission facili-

---

29. A more detailed discussion of the structure and regulation of the electric utility industry prior to the late 1990s can be found in Joskow (1989, 2000).

ties to provide wholesale power or transmission service. As a result, regulatory authority for utility investments, operating costs, and prices lay primarily with individual state regulatory agencies.[30] In addition, the Public Utility Holding Company Act (PUHCA) of 1935 gave the SEC regulatory jurisdiction over the structure of public utility holding companies, their geographic expanse, internal transfer prices, and the kinds of businesses that they could engage in.[31]

The Public Utility Regulatory Policies Act of 1978 (PURPA) played an important role in stimulating interest in expanding opportunities for nonutility suppliers to compete to build and operate power plants to supply electric generation service to utilities for resale and created a powerful interest group to promote it. Title II of PURPA required utilities to purchase power produced by certain "qualified facilities" (QFs) using cogeneration and renewable energy technology at a price reflecting the utility's "avoided costs" of supplying the power from its own facilities. These provisions of PURPA were motivated by a desire to encourage more efficient electricity production technologies (cogeneration) and nonfossil technologies (renewables), and they reflect the 1970s goals of reducing dependence on foreign oil (though little oil is used to generate electricity) and reducing emissions of air pollution from fossil-fueled power plants.

Some states embraced PURPA with gusto, pressed utilities to rely as much as possible on PURPA facilities, and required them to enter into high-priced long-term contracts to encourage third-party investment in PURPA generating facilities. These states were primarily those with politically powerful environmental groups and high retail electricity prices such as California, New York, the New England states, and a few others along the east and west coasts. Other states were indifferent and placed little pressure on their utilities to turn to third-party suppliers for power. By 1991 nearly 10 percent of electricity supplies was coming from nonutility generating facilities, primarily PURPA facilities heavily concentrated in California, the Northeast, Texas, and a few other states. Few utility-owned power plants were built in these states after the mid-1980s.

The enthusiastic implementation of PURPA by California, New York, the New England states, and a few others was heavily influenced by environmental interests and concerns. In conjunction with the implementation of PURPA, these

---

30. IOUs historically accounted for about 80 percent of industry supplies. The rest is accounted for by municipal, cooperative, and federal power supply and distribution entities. I will not discuss these entities here.

31. A public utility holding company is a company that owns more than one utility operating company. PUHCA placed draconian restrictions on public utility holding companies with utility subsidiaries in more than one state. These restrictions severely limited the geographic areas in which a public utility holding company could operate, the lines of business that it could engage in (only those closely related to its utility operations), foreign investments in utilities in other countries, and investments by foreign utilities in U.S. utility businesses.

states adopted complex public planning processes to review utility investments and power purchase arrangements with PURPA suppliers, and to encourage utilities to "invest in customer energy efficiency" as an alternative to acquiring additional power supplies through ownership or contract. They also required utilities to give preference to cogeneration and renewable energy sources by placing "environmental adders" on the direct costs of power supplies. These planning processes were referred to as integrated resource planning (IRP) or least-cost planning (LCP). They were a way to use the institution of regulated monopoly to pay for environmentally friendly supply sources and energy-efficiency programs that traditional utility planning protocols would not have viewed as being "least cost."

Most of these states also experienced significant increases in the regulated retail prices of electricity during the 1970s and 1980s. By the mid-1990s retail prices in many of these states were far above the national average. The high prices reflected the high capital costs and poor operating performance of nuclear power plants commissioned during the 1970s and 1980s, the high prices reflected in PURPA/QF contracts, and the costs of excess capacity that got rolled into regulated prices.

8.6.2   FERC Takes the Lead

Probably the most important contribution to the development of competitive wholesale and retail electricity markets made by the Clinton administration was the appointment of a new set of FERC commissioners who were committed to creating well-functioning competitive wholesale electricity markets and providing open nondiscriminatory access to interstate transmission facilities to support the development of these markets. It turned out as well that these commissioners were willing and able to work closely with California and a few other states as they went further than Congress required, or the administration expected, to restructure their utilities and to create competitive retail markets as well.

Soon after the new FERC commissioners were appointed in 1993, they proceeded aggressively to implement the wholesale transmission access provisions included in EPAct92. The focus was on providing transmission access to utilities seeking to buy power in the loosely regulated wholesale market from independent producers, as well as from other utilities with excess generating capacity, to meet a portion of the demand of their regulated retail customers franchises rather than building their own generating capacity that would be subject to cost-based regulation. However, these early initiatives only required utilities to respond to transmission service requests on a case-by-case basis.

Utilities were not required to file generic transmission tariffs that specified generally available transmission service offerings and associated maximum prices. Moreover, the nature of the transmission services that transmission owners were obligated to supply, and the associated prices, remained fairly vague, and utilities defined the kinds of transmission services and the pricing principles applicable to them in a variety of different ways. Transmission service requests sometimes became lengthy and contentious negotiations.

Both FERC and transmission service customers became frustrated by the slow pace at which transmission service was being made available to support wholesale market transactions, and FERC continued to receive complaints about discriminatory terms and conditions (real or imagined) being offered by transmission owners. Moreover, California's electricity restructuring initiatives that began in April 1994 (more on this topic later) and similar initiatives in a few other states began to make it clear to FERC that its transmission access and pricing rules might have to support far more radical changes in the structure of the utility industry—the functional separation of the generation of electricity from distribution service and the opening of retail electric service to competition—and deal with a variety of new issues regarding state versus federal jurisdiction over transmission, distribution, wholesale power sales, and the treatment of "above market" costs of generating capacity and QF contracts (what came to be called the "stranded cost" problem).

In 1995 these considerations led FERC to initiate rule-makings on transmission service that ultimately served as the basis for two major sets of new rules issued by FERC in 1996. These rules are Order 888—"Promoting Wholesale Competition Through Open Access Non-Discriminatory Transmission Service by Public Utilities; Recovery of Stranded Costs By Public Utilities and Transmitting Utilities,"[32] and Order 889—"Open Access Same-Time Information Systems."[33] These rules now serve as the primary federal foundation for providing transmission service, ancillary network support services, and information about the availability of these services to support both wholesale and retail competition in the supply of generating services.[34]

Order 888 requires all transmission owners to file with FERC pro forma open-access transmission tariffs that transmission-service customers can rely upon to define the terms and conditions of transmission services that will be made available to them. Order 888 specifies the types of transmission services that

---

32. Final Rule issued April 24, 1999, 75 FERC, para. 61, 080.
33. Final Rule issued April 24, 1999, 75 FERC, para. 61, 078.
34. FERC Order 2000 regarding Regional Transmission Organizations issued in December 1999 is likely to become equally important. *Regional Transmission Organizations*, 89 FERC, para. 61, 285 (1999).

must be made available, the maximum cost-based prices that can be charged for these services, the definition of available transmission capacity and how it should be allocated when there is excess demand for it, the specification of ancillary services that transmission owners must provide and the associated prices, and requirements for reforms of power-pooling arrangements to comply with Order 888. All transmission owners and power pools have now filed open access transmission tariffs with FERC.[35]

Order 888 also recognizes the sanctity of preexisting commercial, contractual, and regulatory arrangements associated with the historical use of transmission systems and is generally sensitive to providing a smooth transition from the old regime to the new regime. Importantly, Order 888 establishes federal principles governing the recovery of stranded costs.[36] FERC established the public-policy case for allowing for stranded cost recovery in light of the long-established regulatory rules in effect when the investments and contractual commitments were made and in light of the public-policy interest in facilitating restructuring and the creation of competitive wholesale power markets. Most states subsequently adopted the same principles in conjunction with their retail competition initiatives.

8.6.3   California Takes Over the Lead

FERC's initial efforts to implement the transmission provisions of EPAct92 were based on the traditional model in which utilities had exclusive franchises and an obligation to provide power supplies as well as transmission and distribution capacity to serve the retail consumers in these areas at state-regulated

---

35. Order 889, issued at the same time as Order 888, requires each public utility or its agent (e.g., a power pool) that owns, controls, or operates facilities used for the transmission of electric energy in interstate commerce to create or participate in an Open Access Same-Time Information System (OASIS). This system must provide information, by electronic means, regarding available transmission capacity, prices, and other information that will enable transmission service customers to obtain open access nondiscriminatory transmission service in a time frame necessary to make effective use of the transmission system to support power transactions. Order 889 also required public utilities to implement standards of conduct to functionally separate transmission and unregulated wholesale power merchant functions to ensure that a vertically integrated transmission owner's wholesale market transactions are not advantaged by virtue of preferential access to information about the transmission network. Utilities must also make the same terms (e.g., service price discounts) available to third parties as they do to their wholesale power marketing affiliates.

36. For utility-owned generating plants, stranded or "strandable" costs are defined conceptually as the difference between the net book value of a generating plant used for setting cost-based regulated prices and the market value of that plant if it were required to sell its output in a competitive market. For a QF contract, stranded costs are generally defined as the difference between the present value of the contractual payment obligations and the present value of the competitive market value of the electricity delivered under the contracts.

"bundled" prices. EPAct92 and FERC's subsequent initiatives assumed that this basic model would continue to prevail, anticipating that state regulators would encourage their utilities to buy power to meet their franchise obligations in competitive wholesale power markets rather than building their own new power plants subject to cost-based regulation. Then something rather unexpected happened. In the midst of the recession of the early 1990s, which hit California and the Northeast especially hard as defense contractors and aerospace firms suffered from federal budget cuts, large industrial consumers revolted against the high electricity prices in these states. They wanted "retail competition" or "retail wheeling" rules requiring their local utilities to provide them with unbundled distribution and transmission service so that they could buy power supplies in the wholesale market where prices were lower than the bundled regulated retail prices that they were then obligated to pay their local utility. The latter prices in turn reflected the historical costs of investments in nuclear power plants and expensive power supply contracts with QFs. They were supported by independent power producers and energy marketers who emerged and matured with the earlier PURPA QF projects and the transformation of the natural gas industry. The utilities in these states generally opposed "retail competition" because it would "strand" the costs of investments and contracts entered into years ago.[37]

In early 1993 the California Public Utilities Commission (CPUC) launched a comprehensive review of the structure and performance of California's electricity industry. It was motivated primarily by pressure from industrial consumers to reduce electricity prices that were among the highest in the United States. High prices in turn were blamed on failures of the existing system of regulated vertically integrated monopolies: the high costs of nuclear power plant investments, expensive long-term contracts with independent power suppliers, excess generating capacity, and costly and ineffective regulatory institutions. There was broad agreement that the existing industry structure and regulatory system were seriously broken and needed to be fundamentally reformed.

In April 1994 the CPUC articulated a reform program for the electricity sector. It was built around a new industry structure in which the production of electricity from existing generating plants and the entry of new plants would be deregulated and their power sold in a new competitive wholesale market. Retail consumers would have the choice of using the transmission and distribution wires of their local utility to obtain "direct access" to these new competitive wholesale markets or continuing to receive power from their local

37. There are many states where the regulated cost of generation service is below market levels. There has been little interest in unbundling and retail competition in those states.

utility at prices reflecting the costs the utilities incurred to buy or produce it. This vision for reform was heavily influenced by reforms implemented in Britain in 1990, where several CPUC commissioners and staff visited in early 1994.

California's well-funded interest groups then spent the next four years arguing about exactly how this reform vision would be implemented. The new industry structure that eventually emerged from this contentious regulatory, legislative, and market design process was the most complicated electricity market ever created with many features that had never been tried before.[38] The operation of the utilities' transmission networks was turned over to the newly created nonprofit Independent System Operator (ISO), which was responsible for managing the operation of the transmission network efficiently and reliably by relying on hourly spot markets for ancillary services and energy to balance supply and demand in real time. The nonprofit public Power Exchange (PX) was also created to operate a day-ahead hourly energy market and (ultimately) markets for a number of longer term forward contracts. Utilities were required to divest most of their fossil-fueled generating plants and to buy and sell energy in the PX and ISO hourly spot markets. Other power suppliers were free to enter into bilateral contracts and simply submit schedules to the ISO. The most complicated set of auction markets for energy and operating reserves ever created on earth was developed to govern spot market trading managed by the PX and the ISO.[39]

It is inaccurate to characterize California's electricity reforms as "deregulation." The reforms are more properly viewed as "regulated competition." Wholesale market prices were deregulated, but retail prices were fixed for up to four years. The utilities were forced to sell their generating plants, in order to facilitate the creation of a truly competitive wholesale market and to value any prudent costs "stranded" by competition. But they also retained the obligation to buy power in the new wholesale market to provide service to retail consumers who did not choose a competitive retail supplier and to resell it to them at a fixed price regardless of its cost. The CPUC rejected utility requests to meet their default retail-supply obligations, accounting for about 85 percent of demand, by negotiating fixed-price long-term contracts with power suppliers to hedge wholesale market price risks. As a result, a large fraction of California's electricity demand was being served through the utilities' purchases in a volatile wholesale spot market; the utilities in turn were selling at a regulated fixed retail price and buying at an unregulated wholesale spot market price. Several

---

38. See Joskow (2000) for a more detailed discussion of California's wholesale and retail market institutions.
39. See Joskow (2000) for a more detailed discussion of these markets.

knowledgeable people argued that there were numerous design flaws that would lead to problems once the wholesale markets began to operate. Importantly, the excess capacity situation that contributed to the pressures for reform in 1993 gradually disappeared as electricity demand grew and no new generating capacity was completed during the four-year period of uncertainty over the new rules of the game.[40]

Following California's lead, nearly two dozen states decided to implement wholesale and retail competition reforms, though only about a dozen states had proceeded very far with the restructuring of their electricity industries by 2000. These states include five of the six New England states, New York, Pennsylvania, New Jersey, and Illinois. Most of these "pioneer states" shared many attributes with California: high retail rates, excess generating capacity, expensive nuclear plants and QF contracts, and angry industrial customers (Table 8.1). Nearly 100,000 megawatts of utility generating capacity were divested to independent power suppliers, primarily affiliates of electric and gas utilities with franchises in other parts of the country, by utilities in these and other states from 1997 though 2000. Power supplied from "nonutility" generating plants increased by 400 percent during the 1990s.[41] Note that, so far, the state reform initiatives have proceeded with no new federal mandates or obligations beyond those included in EPAct92 and FERC wholesale-power-market and transmission regulations made under its existing legislative authority.

8.6.4 The Clinton Administration Plays Catch-up

The Clinton administration largely played catch-up with these developments during much of the decade, and its initial support for retail competition was muted, reflecting opposition from environmental groups and (small) consumer protection advocates and disagreements about stranded cost recovery principles. Early in the administration's tenure the DOE's policies focused on exploiting the institution of regulated monopoly to promote utility funding of renewable energy and energy conservation options, whose costs were paid for

---

40. Once these rules were defined, developers quickly applied for permits to build many new power plants, only to confront a time-consuming environmental review process and community opposition to power plants located near where citizens lived or worked. These things slowed the pace of investment in and completion of new power plants. The first new plants came on line in June and July 2001.

41. Until 1996 the increase in nonutility generation reflected primarily the completion of PURPA facilities and a few non-PURPA-independent power projects. Since 1996 the increase has reflected primarily the divestiture of generating plants by regulated utilities subject to electricity restructuring programs in California, the Northeast, Illinois, and Montana to independent power suppliers and the entry of new capacity developed by independent power producers in these and other states.

Table 8.1
Comprehensive State Retail Competition Programs (Start date/All consumers eligible date)

1996	1997	1998	1999
California (1998/1998)	Massachusetts (3-98/3-98)	Arizona (10-99/1-2001)	New Jersey (11-99/11-99)
New Hampshire (1998/1998-Delayed)	Illinois (10-1999/5-2002)	Connecticut (1-2000/7-2000)	Arkansas (1-2002/6-2003)
New York (1998/2001)	Maine (3-2000/3-2000)		Delaware (10-99/10-2000)
Pennsylvania (1-99/1-00)	Montana (7-98/7-2000)		Maryland (7-2000/7-2002)
Rhode Island (1-98/1-98)			New Mexico (1-01/1-2002)
			Ohio (1-2001/12-2005)
			Oregon (10/01 except residential)
			Texas (1-02/1-02)
			Virginia (1-02/1-04)

Average IOU Electricity Prices (1997):

| | 8.3 cents/kWh | 9.5 cents/kWh | 6.8 cents/kWh |

10.4 cents/kWh

Other States: 5.6 cents/kWh

in regulated retail prices. The states that had pioneered these "integrated resource planning" programs also happened to be the pioneers on the restructuring and retail competition front. As the debates about restructuring and retail competition spread across the country, interest in IRP and related programs evaporated. The DOE tried to get back into the action by sponsoring a set of electricity policy forums, but DOE simply was never a major player on the electricity reform front. The administration's support for these reforms grew as several traditionally Democratic states became electricity restructuring pioneers.[42]

However, it was not until April 15, 1999, that the administration proposed comprehensive electricity restructuring and deregulation legislation. Because it tried to accommodate states rights interests, pressures from environmental groups to incorporate energy-efficiency and renewable-energy programs into federal "deregulation" legislation, and pressures from utilities and independent power producers to repeal the Public Utility Holding Company Act (PUHCA) and PURPA, the administration was slow in proposing comprehensive electricity reform legislation. The legislation that it did propose in April 1999 had something for almost every interest group in it, but broad support for the entire package was lacking, and it did not get very far in Congress.

The primary features of the administration's proposed legislation were as follows:

1. Provided that all retail electricity consumers would be permitted to choose their power supplier (retail wheeling) and that local distribution companies would provide unbundled distribution and transmission service to allow them to do so by January 1, 2003, *except* if a state decided to opt out of this retail competition system.

2. Clarified FERC's authority to order utilities to provide wholesale and retail transmission service, enshrined the provisions of Order 888 in federal law, and gave FERC authority to require the creation of independent regional system operators.

3. Established a Public Benefits Fund that would disburse federal matching funds to participating states to provide subsidies to low-income consumers, energy efficiency programs, education, and other programs. The fund would be financed by generators with a fee of up to 0.1 cent per kilowatt-hour.

4. Established a Federal Renewable Energy Portfolio Standard (RPS) that would have required electricity retailers to include specified minimum percen-

---

42. Most of the states that pioneered radical restructuring and retail competition were carried by Vice President Gore in the 2000 presidential election: California, Massachusetts, Maine, Rhode Island, New York, New Jersey, Pennsylvania, and Illinois.

tages of designated renewable energy sources (e.g., wind, solar) in their supply portfolios.

5. Repealed the "must buy from QF" provisions of PURPA, while preserving existing QF contracts.

6. Repealed the Public Utility Holding Company Act while expanding access to books and records of holding companies and affiliates by FERC and state regulatory authorities.

7. Expanded FERC's authority to remedy market power problems in wholesale power markets.

8. Expanded FERC's authority to approve and oversee a national Electric Reliability Organization and affiliated regional entities to prescribe and enforce mandatory reliability standards.

9. Clarified the authority of EPA to require an interstate trading system for NO_x reductions by electric generating plants.

10. Included provisions for stranded cost recovery.

Numerous other pieces of proposed restructuring legislation were filed in the House and Senate during 1999 and 2000 by both Democrats and Republicans.[43] Several bills included many of the key provisions of the administration's bill, while others focused on a narrower set of issues—for example, repealing PURPA, repealing PUHCA, transmission access, creating regional system operators, and reliability issues. However, neither the administration's proposed legislation nor competing legislation proposed by Republican senators and representatives garnered sufficient support to come close to being passed by Congress. Nor does it appear to me that the administration pushed its electricity reform legislation very aggressively.

8.6.5   California Runs into Major Problems[44]

California's new competitive wholesale and retail electricity markets began operating in April 1998. Within a few months significant problems already began to emerge as a result of wholesale market design flaws and suppliers' ability to exploit them. Flaws were identified in the congestion management system, with the local reliability contracts, with the protocols for planning and

---

43. See U.S. Department of Energy (2001).
44. For a detailed discussion of California's electricity market problems see Joskow (2001a). For an overview of the evolution of electricity restructuring and competition programs in the United States see Joskow (2000).

investment in transmission, with the real-time balancing markets, in the ancillary services markets, and in other areas. Within the first two years of operation, the ISO had filed 30 major revisions to its protocols with the FERC. The PX had filed for numerous changes in its operating protocols as well. Responding to a never-ending series of problems and proposed fixes for them, FERC ordered the ISO to seek to identify and implement fundamental reforms rather than just piecemeal fixes to individual problems as they arose. The complex "Noah's Ark" governance arrangements, with all major interest groups represented on the board of the PX and ISO, made agreement on any sensible reforms very difficult. Moreover, because of California's very difficult and time-consuming regulatory process for getting siting and environmental approvals for new power plants, the anticipated flood of new generating capacity was being delayed, while demand continued to grow along with the economy.

Despite these problems, competitive wholesale market prices for power were reasonably close to prereform projections, averaging 3 cents per kilowatt-hour ($30 per megawatt-hour) between April 1998 and April 2000, only a little higher than what had been projected in 1996. All things considered, prices were perhaps 10 percent higher than they would be in a system without these design flaws. As late as March 2000, the California Energy Commission published projections for wholesale market prices for 2000 and beyond that were in the $30 to $35 per megawatt-hour range.[45] Nevertheless, California's new market arrangements were an accident waiting to happen. And in mid-2000 the flawed wholesale market institutions and the partial deregulation program suddenly confronted a run of very bad luck.

Wholesale prices began to rise above historical levels in May 2000 and stayed at extraordinarily high levels for the rest of the Clinton administration's tenure (Table 8.2).[46] As wholesale prices rose above the fixed retail prices that California's two largest investor-owned utilities could charge their retail customers, they began to lose a lot of money. The CPUC refused to raise retail prices to cover rising wholesale power costs until early January 2001, and the 1 cent per kilowatt-hour surcharge approved in early January 2001 was far too little to allow the utilities to cover their ongoing wholesale power costs, let alone their past-due bills. By December 2000 some suppliers had run up against their credit limits and stopped selling electricity to California utilities. In mid-January the utilities had run out of cash and stopped paying their bills for

---

45. See California Energy Commission (2000).
46. The prices reported in Table 8.2 are average hourly day-ahead prices in the PX. The PX went out of business at the end of January 2001. The prices listed for February, March, April, and May 2001 are the average prices paid by the ISO for real-time energy during those months.

Table 8.2
California PX Day-Ahead Prices ($/Mwh: Weighted Averages 7 × 24)

	1998	1999	2000	2001
January	—	21.6	31.8	260.2
February	—	19.6	18.8	363.0 (ISO)
March	—	24.0	29.3	313.5 (ISO)
April	23.3	24.7	27.4	370.0 (ISO)
May	12.5	24.7	50.4	274.7 (ISO)
June	13.3	25.8	132.4	
July	35.6	31.5	115.3	
August	43.4	34.7	175.2	
September	37.0	35.2	119.6	
October	27.3	49.0	103.2	
November	26.5	38.3	179.4	
December	30.0	30.2	385.6	
Average	30.0	30.0	115.0	

wholesale power. As the Clinton administration left office, the California electricity reform was in shambles as buyers had no credit and suppliers threatened to stop supplying.

During the administration's final month in office the secretary of energy issued emergency orders requiring generators in California and Federal Power Marketing agencies to continue to supply to keep the lights from going out in California as credit problems led suppliers to withdraw supplies from the market. An angry battle developed between DOE and FERC, with the DOE arguing that FERC could and should have done more to fix market failures and mitigate market power. A divided FERC did little until 2001. The secretary of the Treasury tried to facilitate a negotiated settlement with the governor of California, California utilities, and the major independent generators and marketers. His efforts were not successful. The California electricity mess would be left for the new Bush administration to deal with.

The serious problems that emerged with the new market and regulatory arrangements in California during summer 2000 cast a dark cloud over the electric utility restructuring and competition programs implemented during the Clinton years. Several states that had planned to initiate retail competition and other industry reforms delayed doing so as a result of the events in California. Many other states that had not yet adopted any reform policies became even more committed to resisting reforms.

California's electricity market meltdown was at least partially a consequence of the failure of the federal government to articulate and promote a clear model for electricity-sector restructuring and competition initiatives. Instead, it accommodated a wide range of state approaches to restructuring and interest group concerns. This "let a thousand flowers bloom" approach may have been politically convenient, but it led to an uncoordinated and sometimes incompatible and poorly designed patchwork of state efforts to respond to interest-group views on the appropriate directions for electricity restructuring and competition. It is possible that the passage of the comprehensive federal restructuring legislation proposed by the administration would have (eventually) improved the situation, largely by expanding and clarifying FERC's authority in a number of important areas. However, I don't think that the passage of the legislation in 1999 would have forestalled the problems in California. The legislation does not specify a particular restructuring framework and does not deal with many important "details" that have led to problems in California and other states. It would have taken FERC some time to develop a more comprehensive framework and to use its new authority to implement it. Moreover, the state opt-out provision would have inevitably given the states a lot of discretion to proceed along their individual paths.

8.7 Energy-Efficiency, Renewable-Energy, and Alternative-Energy Policies

8.7.1 Energy-Efficiency and Renewable-Energy Trends

The energy efficiency of the U.S. economy, as measured by energy consumption per dollar of real GDP, continued to improve during the decade. Energy consumption per dollar of real GDP declined by nearly 15 percent between 1990 and 2000. However, it declined by 22 percent from 1980 to 1990, a period with significantly higher average energy prices. In 2000, renewable energy, *including conventional hydroelectric energy*, accounted for 7 percent of U.S. energy consumption, about the same fraction as in 1990. Excluding conventional hydro, renewable energy accounted for 3.7 percent of total U.S. energy consumption in 2000, only slightly higher than in 1990. Most of the nonhydro renewable energy is accounted for by wood, waste, and alcohol fuels. Wind and solar energy accounted for only 0.1 percent of total U.S. energy consumption in 2000, though wind energy supplies did grow quickly during the decade from (and to) a very low base. There were about 400,000 alternative fuel vehicles, mostly light trucks and buses, in operation in 1999. Most of these vehicles use liquid petroleum gas or compressed natural gas. There were only about 6,500 electric vehicles in operation in 1999. While alternative fuel vehicles represent a tiny fraction of the vehicles on the road, the number of such vehicles nearly doubled during the decade.

8.7.2 Policy Initiatives

The case for government programs to promote energy efficiency, renewable energy, and alternative fuels is often based on the argument that energy markets are plagued by a variety of market imperfections: poor consumer information, imperfect capital and rental markets, regulated energy prices that are too low, the failure to internalize fully or properly environmental and national security externalities, and other market barriers. That is, there is a proper role for government policies to promote energy efficiency, renewable energy, and alternative fuels because market imperfections lead to underinvestment in them. Needless to say, the existence and importance of such market imperfections are controversial.

A variety of policy instruments have been used to promote energy efficiency, renewable energy, and alternative fuels. These include vehicle, appliance, and equipment energy efficiency standards, tax subsidies, government R&D expenditures, fuel-use mandates, and subsidies funneled through regulated gas and electric utilities and paid for in the prices they charge to consumers. Federal policies supporting improvements in energy efficiency and expanded supplies of renewable energy are reflected in federal energy legislation that began in the late 1970s and was enhanced during the 1980s. As noted earlier, the Energy Policy Act of 1992 has numerous provisions aimed at providing tax subsidies, R&D funding, and other forms of encouragement for energy efficiency and renewable energy. Several states in the Northeast and West began to use their regulated monopoly electric utilities to stimulate investments in cogeneration, renewable energy, and energy efficiency during the 1980s.

The Clinton administration's appointments to the DOE in 1993 reflected the Clinton/Gore team's strong interest in promoting renewable energy, energy efficiency, and integrated resource planning, and in recognizing the close linkages between energy production and use and environmental impacts in energy policy, including the impacts of CO_2 emissions on global climate change. Secretary Hazel O'Leary drew together an energy policy team whose members were very "green" and had been closely involved with the development of integrated resource planning, renewable energy, and demand-side management programs in their respective states.[47] Team members saw the opportunity to bring the lessons they had learned in New England, New York, and California about the wonders of using electric and gas utilities as instruments for promoting energy efficiency, renewable energy, and related programs to the rest of the country. Promoting improvements in energy efficiency, renewable en-

---

47. A large fraction of the DOE budget is devoted to nuclear-weapons-related programs and the cleanup of radioactive waste on sites associated with these programs. I will not discuss these important aspects of DOE activities in this chapter.

ergy, alternative-fuel vehicles, and new technologies for extracting and using conventional energy sources were their highest priorities.

The instruments that the Clinton-era DOE had at its disposal from existing laws were limited, however. It could seek authorizations to fund R&D, demonstration, and grant programs for energy-efficiency, renewable-energy, and alternative-energy projects. It had opportunities to review and update appliance efficiency standards. It could use moral suasion and federal grants to convince more states to adopt integrated resource planning programs to promote the use of regulated monopoly utilities to support energy efficiency and renewable-energy programs.[48] And within the restrictions imposed by existing laws, the Clinton DOE team tried to use these instruments to their fullest potential. However, no major new laws to promote energy efficiency, renewable energy, or alternative fuels were passed after 1992.

The Clinton team's efforts to move forward aggressively to promote energy efficiency, renewable energy, and alternative-fuel vehicles were heavily constrained. During the first several years, a significant constraint was the federal budget deficit and congressional spending limits. The DOE's budget had been reduced significantly during the previous decade and continued to be under pressure at the beginning of the Clinton administration as well. Republican senators continued to propose the DOE's abolition. After 1994 the administration's efforts to pursue its agenda were further hampered by the Republican Congress.

Beginning in 1995 (FY1996), Congress included language in the Department of Transportation's annual appropriations bills forbidding it to even spend any money to study tightening the Corporate Average Fuel Economy Standards (CAFE). Congress also placed roadblocks in the way of the administration's efforts to review and tighten appliance efficiency standards as provided for under existing laws.[49] Although President Clinton vetoed a 1995 DOE appropriations bill that would have prohibited further DOE efforts to change appliance efficiency standards, the DOE proceeded cautiously afterward, delaying the promulgation of new standards for several appliances until the very end of the second term. State programs to promote energy conservation and renewable energy that are funded through electric and gas utility rates increased significantly from 1990 to 1996 and then declined as state regulators turned their attention toward industry restructuring and competition.[50] Finally, the Republican Congress rejected most Clinton administration proposals to create or

---

48. However, they had to play catch-up as the policy focus at the states quickly shifted from using the institution of regulated monopoly to subsidize energy-efficiency and renewable-energy projects to breaking up the monopolies and promoting competition.

49. See "House Conservatives Step Up Assault on Regulations" (1995).

50. See Energy Information Administration (1999), p. 228.

increase tax subsidies for renewable-energy technologies and alternative-fuel vehicles.

Despite these problems, the DOE gradually shifted funds toward renewable-energy, energy-efficiency, and alternative-fuel-vehicle programs, and, as federal budget surpluses appeared, total funding expanded. During FY2001, the DOE received appropriations of about $2.2 billion for expenditures on "energy resources," of which about $1.2 billion was allocated to energy-efficiency, renewable-energy, and alternative-fuel-vehicle programs.[51] Of this amount, about one-third went to renewable-energy and two-thirds to energy-efficiency programs. The FY2001 budget included $540 million for fossil-energy research and development.[52] This sum includes $70 million of funding for fuel cells and carbon sequestration and about $200 million for research focused on improving thermal efficiency and reducing emissions from fossil-fueled power plants. Finally, about $240 million was budgeted in FY2001 for nuclear energy science and technology.[53]

Between FY1996 and FY2000, energy-efficiency and renewable-energy resource expenditures increased by about 50 percent, while expenditures on fossil and nuclear resource development declined by about 20 percent. There was a significant increase in fossil energy expenditures in FY2001. DOE eventually was able to move forward to review and promulgate appliance efficiency standards pursuant to the National Appliance Energy Conservation Act of 1977 and the National Appliance Energy Conservation Amendments of 1988.

DOE claims that its appliance efficiency standards have reduced consumer energy expenditures by $2 billion per year.[54] Appliances are clearly more energy efficient today than they were prior to 1987. For example, a full-size refrigerator uses about half the energy today that it did 20 years ago.[55] The new efficiency standards proposed at the end of the Clinton administration would require washing machines to be 22 percent more energy efficient by 2004 and 35 per-

51. The Bush administration's budget proposes to cut expenditures in these areas by about 15 percent in FY2002.

52. I have excluded funds reported in the same line of business for the SPR and the federal power marketing agencies.

53. An additional $34 million was appropriated for advanced particle accelerators in FY2001. Unpacking the DOE's R&D budget is not easy. In FY2001 the DOE budget included about $7.7 billion of R&D expenditures. However, this figure includes weapons-related research at the national labs, basic and applied science research funded through the DOE budget (e.g., nuclear physics, human genome research, computer science), and other items. The nuclear science and technology research figure includes some funds that are pure research (e.g., university research reactors, medical research, etc.). Other departments also provide some support for related energy resource and conservation programs, but I have not tried to identify them.

54. http://www.eren.doe.gov/building/consumer_information/, March 11, 2001.

55. However, appliance choices also changed. The fraction of households with central air conditioning increased by 21 percent and with personal computers 120 percent between 1990 and 1997.

cent more energy efficient by 2007. Hot water heater efficiency is to increase by 8 percent for gas units and 4 percent for electric units by 2004. The proposed rules would have required central air conditioners to be 30 percent more energy efficient by 2006.[56] However, the cost-effectiveness and energy-savings estimates attributed to federal appliance-efficiency standards and state-sponsored utility-energy-efficiency programs have been the subject of considerable controversy. The costs and benefits associated with these initiatives have relied heavily on engineering estimates of costs and energy savings rather than actual field experience, fail to take into account all relevant costs, and ignore behavioral responses by consumers (e.g., purchasing larger refrigerators and air conditioners).[57]

One contributor to the deterioration in the rate of decline in the energy intensity of the economy since the late 1980s is likely to be the relative trends in vehicle fuel economy. Between 1980 and 1990, aggregate (passenger cars, light trucks, and trucks) average vehicle fuel efficiency for the then existing stock of vehicles increased by about 20 percent. Between 1990 and 1999 it increased by less than 4 percent.[58] The average fuel economy of *new* passenger cars and *new* light trucks (as measured by the EPA) has been essentially flat for the last 15 years. Due to the shift toward SUVs, which are classified as light trucks and have lower average fuel economy than passenger cars, the average fuel economy of new light vehicles in the aggregate (passenger cars plus light trucks) deteriorated by about 7 percent between 1988 and 2000.[59] Sales of light trucks (including SUVs) now make up almost half of new vehicle sales, more than double their share 20 years ago.

---

56. The Bush administration subsequently approved the first two new standards and reduced the central air conditioner standard to a 20 percent improvement in energy efficiency by 2006.

57. See Greening and Greene (1997), Greene et al. (1999), Eto et al. (2000), and Wirl (2000).

58. A variety of different data on vehicle fuel economy are available. The Energy Information Agency produces estimates of actual average mileage achieved by vehicles in operation each year. These are the numbers used for the calculations in this sentence. The Department of Transportation (DOT) and EPA publish estimates of the mileage for new "model year" vehicles in various categories. These data are based on laboratory tests, not actual driving experience. The DOT and EPA numbers also differ slightly from one another because the DOT incorporates other factors (e.g., ethanol credits) into the mileage calculations that are related to the agency's enforcement responsibilities. These mileage numbers are higher than the actual mileage achieved by new vehicles in each model year, the mileage reported on the stickers on the windows of new vehicles, and the actual mileage of the current *stock* of vehicles, which includes vehicles from a large number of model years. For example, DOT reported that the average fuel economy for 1999 model year passenger cars was 28.3 miles per gallon. EIA reports actual vehicle mileage of 21.4 miles per gallon in 1999 for the entire fleet of operating passenger cars.

59. The data in the last two sentences are based on the EPA's "new model" mileage data discussed in the previous footnote. See Automotive Fuel Economy Program, National Highway Traffic Safety Administration, http://www.nhtsa.dot.gov/cars/problems/studies/fuelecon/index.html and U.S. Environmental Protection Agency (2000).

The Energy Policy and Conservation Act of 1975 established Corporate Average Fuel Economy (CAFE) standards for each automaker, with domestically produced and imported vehicles counted as separate fleets. For passenger cars, the CAFE standards started at 18 miles per gallon with the 1978 model year and gradually increased to 27.5 miles per gallon for the 1985 model year. For light trucks, including SUVs, the CAFE standard began at 17.2 miles per gallon in 1979 and rose to 20.5 miles per gallon by 1987. These standards are based on laboratory tests and have not changed since 1985 and 1987, respectively. Actual vehicle mileage has continued to improve, at a declining rate, since then as new cars replaced older vehicles from model years with lower CAFE standards.

The effects of the CAFE standards on vehicle efficiency and utilization, and their merits compared to alternative instruments (e.g., gasoline taxes), have been the subject of much study and remain a subject of considerable controversy.[60] Efforts to tighten the CAFE standards have been opposed by domestic automobile manufacturers for the last two decades. Since the standards were phased in during a time of rising gasoline prices, some studies suggest that vehicle mileage would have improved significantly without the standards. Other studies suggest that the shift to light trucks (SUVs) is partially explained by the more lenient mileage standards applicable to these vehicles, though changes in consumer preferences and incomes are a more likely explanation. Still other studies find that the improvements in fuel efficiency have led to an increase in miles driven (the so-called "rebound effect"), reducing the impact of the standards on gasoline consumption. Finally, studies have suggested that when manufacturers reduced vehicle weights to increase mileage, this weight reduction led to an increase in the severity of accidents.[61]

There are several things that are fairly clear about the CAFE standards. First, they have almost certainly been binding constraints on domestic automobile manufacturers since the mid-1980s as gasoline prices fell from their previous peak levels. Second, the efficiency of the CAFE standards could be substantially improved if manufacturers could trade mileage "credits" among one another and the "two-fleet" averaging rules were eliminated. Third, special credits for alternative fuel capabilities (i.e., ethanol) are ineffective in promoting use of alternative fuels. Fourth, EPA automobile emissions regulations are constraining the diffusion of diesel-fueled vehicles with higher mileage. Finally, cost-effective

---

60. See Goldberg (1998), Crandall and Graham (1989), Mayo and Mathis (1988), Crandall (1990), Bresnahan and Yao (1985), and Greene et al. (1999).
61. Vehicle performance (e.g., acceleration) probably suffered as well during the first decade of experience with the CAFE standards, as manufacturers responded by reducing engine horsepower.

improvements in automobile mileage appear to be available with new technology, but stimulating consumer interest in fuel economy continues to be a major challenge.

As a result of roadblocks created by budgetary constraints and a hostile Congress, the administration also embarked on cooperative programs with industry to develop new technologies. The most important program involved cooperation between the federal government and the automobile industry to develop commercial technologies to increase automobile fuel efficiency, with a goal of commercializing vehicles that could get 80 miles to the gallon of gasoline by 2010 (Partnership for a New Generation of Vehicles). Another program to encourage energy companies voluntarily to begin to reduce greenhouse gas emissions themselves or to finance reductions in emissions or increases in carbon sinks was initially successful, but faded as the attention of the major participants, electric utilities, turned to industry restructuring and competition initiatives (Climate Change Action Plan).

Despite all the Clinton administration's hopes and plans for aggressive energy efficiency and renewable energy, and the efforts of the DOE to shift funds to develop and promote more energy efficiency and renewable energy, these initiatives had little if any effect on trends in energy supply and demand during the 1990s. To the extent that these efforts have any significant effects, they will only be realized over a significant future period of time.

8.8   Conclusions

Overall, the decade of the 1990s was a period in which energy markets performed reasonably well, federal energy policy-makers focused primarily on implementing and completing policy initiatives that began before or at the very beginning of the decade, and the energy supply sectors evolved slowly and relatively smoothly. The overall fuel supply mix that satisfied growing energy demand changed very little between 1990 and 2000. Aside from the "energy crises" at the very beginning and very end of the period examined here, which were not nearly of the magnitude of those of the 1970s, energy supply was able to expand easily to meet growing demand and to support a rapidly growing economy without triggering significant sustained price increases or supply disruptions. Real energy prices were stable or falling for most of the period, and there were significant productivity improvements in several energy sectors. The performance of the nuclear energy and coal sectors was especially impressive in terms of continuous performance improvement. It was simply not a decade where there was much public interest in energy policy issues.

The good performance of energy markets during the seven or eight years following the Gulf War is likely to have masked a number of continuing and emerging energy policy challenges that derive from higher order domestic and foreign policy goals discussed at the beginning of this essay. The changes in world oil, domestic natural gas, and electricity markets in 1999 and especially 2000 likely reflect the impacts of ignoring some of these challenges. I conclude this essay by briefly discussing a few energy policy challenges that are legacies of the 1990s.

8.8.1   Energy Supply Infrastructure, "Reserve" Capacity, and Market Volatility

By the end of the decade the energy supply infrastructure was being stressed in most of the energy sectors, reflecting the end of a decade in which demand grew faster than did infrastructure capacity. This is certainly the case with regard to the generation and transmission of electricity, the production and transportation of coal, the refining of oil, and in some areas the transportation and storage of natural gas. The tightening infrastructure situation reflects, in part, the fact that the decade began with excess capacity in several of these sectors and, as demand grew, existing capacity was naturally utilized more fully before major new investments were economical. Moreover, as prices have risen in the last couple of years, there has been a significant supply response, though there are necessarily lags between project identification, construction, and operation.

However, the current tight supply situation reflects more than simply a traditional adjustment of supply to demand. Major changes took place in important infrastructure segments during the 1990s that are likely to make supplies tighter on average in the future than we have experienced in the past; these changes are leading to more reliance on the equivalent of "just in time" manufacturing than was the case in the past. These changes are likely to lead energy industries to carry less "reserve capacity" and to be more vulnerable to supply and demand shocks with attendant increases in price volatility. Moreover, because the 1990s was a decade in which significant increases in demand could be accommodated without major expansions of energy infrastructure facilities in several sectors, we have been able to avoid resolving conflicts between the need to get approvals to site and develop major new infrastructure facilities and federal, state, and local siting and environmental policies which, at the very least, make it costly and time-consuming to obtain necessary government approvals. These siting and infrastructure investment issues can no longer be avoided.

8.8.2 Electricity-Sector Restructuring Is Incomplete and Balkanized and Suffers from Serious Market-Design and Regulatory Imperfections

The restructuring of the electricity sector has been driven by individual state initiatives affecting an industry that physically and economically is increasingly organized (or should be organized) around wholesale energy and transmission markets covering large geographic areas encompassing many states. Federal policies have taken a "let a thousand flowers bloom" approach, and federal policy-makers have cheerfully pointed to electricity-sector reform as an example of "cooperative federalism" where policy reforms are benefiting from the "50 laboratories of democracy" that characterize our federal system. This rhetoric sounds very nice, and there is certainly something to it. However, in my view the electricity-sector reform program is in trouble and needs more attention and direction at a national level. The "thousand flowers bloom" approach reflects more the absence of political backbone and weak political support for comprehensive restructuring than it does sensible electricity policy.

The United States needs a comprehensive set of federal electricity policies governing industry structure, wholesale market design, regional transmission ownership and network operating institutions, and options for arranging power supplies for retail consumers. Continuing to rely on the current mix of federal and state jurisdictions, the absence of a clear model that these reforms should follow, and a federal regulatory agency (FERC) whose skills, legal authority, and procedures are poorly matched to presiding over the creation of competitive electricity markets with good performance attributes is not going to lead to a good result. Succeeding in making the electricity restructuring and competition program work well is not going to be easy. It requires dealing with difficult issues of states' rights, powerful utility and energy marketing companies with private interests that may diverge from the public interest, and consumers and their representatives in many states who think that the old system worked just fine.

8.8.3 Dependence on Imported Petroleum Is Growing[62]

If one believes that U.S./G-7 dependence on imported petroleum creates national economic and defense security problems whose costs are not fully internalized, then the 1990s may not look like it was a good decade at all.[63] U.S.

---

62. I offer these observations as an observer rather than as an expert on national security issues.

63. It is important to note, however, that the U.S. economy is less dependent on petroleum than it was during the 1970s, that the United States and other oil-importing countries are less dependent on Middle Eastern oil, and that we seem to better understand how to use monetary policy to manage the macroeconomic effects of oil shocks.

oil imports increased substantially, and imports grew in other G-7 countries as well. While world oil production remains less concentrated in the Persian Gulf than was the case in 1973, world crude oil reserves available to support exports are concentrated in the Middle East and North Africa. Current forecasts indicate that U.S. petroleum imports will continue to grow as a fraction of domestic consumption in the future. It is not credible to believe that realistic domestic supply-side initiatives will significantly alter these trends. Moreover, while plausible demand-side policies aimed at improving vehicle efficiency, as well as new cost-effective technologies that will make their way into the market without new regulations, may slow the rate of growth in gasoline consumption and imports, it will be a long time before gasoline consumption actually starts to decline,[64] even under the most optimistic credible assumptions about cost-effective improvements in vehicle fuel efficiency. Accordingly, growing dependence on imported oil looks like it is something that we are going to have to live with for a long time. Accordingly, our foreign and domestic policies will need to adapt to this reality.

8.8.4 Energy and Environmental Policies Can Be Better Coordinated

It is quite clear to me that many of the Clinton administration's energy policies were driven, by design or default, by its environmental goals. It would make sense to recognize more formally the fundamental interdependence between energy and environmental policies and coordinate them more effectively. If and when the United States implements a serious program to control carbon emissions, close coordination between energy and environmental policies will be even more important. One issue that deserves immediate attention involves older coal-fired power plants that were built before the New Source Performance Standards (NSPS) were adopted. The NSPS standards do not apply to these plants unless investments in generating unit upgrades lead the units to cross an uncertain line that triggers their applicability. The rationale for exempting these plants from NSPS was the expectation that the plants would be retired in due course. It is now clear that many of these plants can continue to operate economically for many years into the future as long as additional investments in maintenance, replacement equipment, and modern boiler and turbine monitoring and control equipment are made.

On the one hand, from an energy policy perspective it doesn't make much sense to discourage owners of coal-fired power plants from investing in effi-

---

64. The reasons are that (a) projections are that miles driven will continue to grow, (b) it takes a long time for the vehicle stock to turn over, and (c) new, more fuel-efficient technologies will be introduced into new vehicles gradually over the next decade.

ciency and reliability improvements or life extensions that are economical. On the other hand, from an environmental policy perspective it doesn't make much sense to permanently apply different environmental standards to old plants than to new plants. This policy could make plant enhancements economical only because they allow the owner to avoid current environmental standards applicable to new plants. A solution to this policy conflict is to adopt more flexible environmental policies that integrate old and new sources, but that do not apply specific uniform emissions requirements to all plants. The SO_2 cap and trade program created by the Clean Air Act Amendments of 1990 provides a successful example of how economic mechanisms can be used to harmonize emissions restrictions applicable to all sources producing the same product (electricity in this case) while giving individual sources the flexibility to adapt to emissions constraints in the most cost-effective ways.

8.8.5 We Need to Reevaluate Policies Toward Nuclear Power

The 1990s were an especially good decade for nuclear energy. The U.S. nuclear industry has finally learned how to *operate* the existing fleet of nuclear plants economically and safely. Moreover, their improved performance during the 1990s helped to reduce air emissions, since if they had not improved their capacity factors, older fossil plants would have been the substitute sources of electricity. Existing nuclear power plants increasingly have to sing for their supper, in the sense that they must cover their going-forward costs based on the market value of the electricity they produce. Plants that can't make it economically will continue to close. Those that can should continue to be given the opportunity to extend their operating licenses.

While nuclear plants do not produce SO_2, NO_x, CO_2, and so on, they do produce long-lived nuclear waste (as well as safety and nuclear weapons proliferation challenges). It is now accumulating primarily in storage ponds on nuclear plant sites around the country. This is not a long-term solution to the nuclear waste problem. The federal government has defaulted on its commitment to take back the waste and store it safely. It's time for the federal government to make a more concerted effort to license, construct, and begin operating a waste fuel depository.

Whether or not it will prove to be profitable for a developer to build a new merchant nuclear plant that will sell its output in competitive wholesale electricity markets is very uncertain, perhaps even doubtful. However, for the first time in nearly two decades, a few generating companies are talking seriously about the possibility of making investments in new nuclear plants, and without the security of cost-based regulation. At the very least, policies should be adopted to ensure that unnecessarily burdensome federal licensing and state siting regulations, as well as unresolved waste disposal policies, do not represent a barrier to making these investments if investors are willing to take on the ordinary electricity market risks associated with construction and operating costs and plant performance.

8.8.6 We Need to Reevaluate and Perhaps Refocus Energy-Efficiency and Demand-Side Management Programs

When the Energy Policy Act of 1992 was passed, energy efficiency advocates expected that electric and gas utility "DSM" programs would provide an important platform for introducing and diffusing more energy-efficient lighting, appliances, equipment, and building standards, using revenues collected out of regulated retail gas and electricity rates to finance the costs of the programs, including subsidies given to consumers to induce them to adopt approved equipment. These initiatives were to be and have been supported by DOE's energy-efficiency and renewable R&D and deployment initiatives. While these programs have not disappeared with the changes affecting the electric power and natural gas industries, the funding available through utilities has been reduced and the effectiveness of the programs has become more uncertain, especially in states where industry restructuring initiatives have taken distribution utilities out of the "retail" business.

I have felt for many years that the energy and economic savings attributed to these programs have been overstated, that many of them were poorly designed, and that program performance was poorly monitored and evaluated. Moreover, they have not been as successful as many had hoped in "jump-starting" more rapid market diffusion of the energy-efficient appliances and equipment they have promoted. Nevertheless, it is clear even to me that there are a number of energy-efficiency opportunities that clearly both are economical for consumers and can save significant amounts of energy (though less than is often claimed). There continue to be market barriers to their diffusion, but the nature of these barriers and how they can be reduced are not well understood.

I would like to see more attention paid to identifying the nature of the market barriers that significantly slow diffusion of more efficient appliances, buildings, and equipment and more research on the strengths and weaknesses of alternative mechanisms to reduce them. (More marketing experts and fewer economists and engineers are needed.) I would also like to see more rigorous and complete evaluations done of the costs and benefits of energy-efficient technologies based on actual experience with real people in real homes and businesses, not engineering calculations of energy savings and costs. Finally, deployment and third-party funding programs need to adapt to the changes taking place in the electricity and natural gas industries, especially the gradual spread of retail competition.

References

Bresnahan, T., and D. Yao. 1985. "The Nonpecuniary Costs of Automobile Emissions Standards." *Rand Journal of Economics*, 16:437–455.

California Energy Commission. 2000. "Market Clearing Prices under Alterative Resource Scenarios: 2000–2010," March.

Crandall, R. W. 1990. "The Changing Rationale for Motor Vehicle Fuel-Economy Regulation." *Regulation*, 13, no. 3 (Fall): 10–13.

Crandall, R. W., and J. Graham. 1989. "The Effects of Fuel Economy Standards on Automobile Safety." *Journal of Law and Economics*, 32(1): 97–118.

Energy Information Administration. 1999. *Annual Energy Review*.

Energy Information Administration. 2000. *Winter Fuels Outlook*.

Energy Information Administration. 2000. *Annual Energy Outlook, 2001*.

Eto, J., et al. 2000. "Where Did All the Money Go? The Cost and Performance of the Largest Commercial Sector DSM Programs." *Energy Journal*, 21(2): 23–49.

Falkenrath, Richard. 2000. "Uranium Blues: Economic Interest vs. National Security." *Milken Institute Review*, 4th Quarter.

Federal Trade Commission. 2000. *Midwest Gasoline Price Investigation*, March 29. Available at http://www.ftc.gov/os/2001/03/mwgasrpt.htm.

Goldberg, P. K. 1998. "The Effects of the Corporate Average Fuel Efficiency Standard in the U.S." *Journal of Industrial Economics*, 46, no. 1 (March): 1–33.

Greene, D. L., et al. 1999. "Fuel Economy Rebound Effect for U.S. Household Vehicles." *Energy Journal*, 20(3): 1–31.

Greening, L. A., and D. L. Greene. 1997. "Energy Use, Technical Efficiency and the Rebound Effects: A Review of the Literature." Report to the Office of Policy Analysis and International Affairs, U.S. Department of Energy, Washington, DC, December.

"House Conservatives Step Up Assault on Regulations." 1995. *Washington Post*, July 19, Section A, p. 4.

Joskow, Paul L. 1989. "Regulatory Failure, Regulatory Reform and Structural Change in the Electric Power Industry." *Brookings Papers on Economic Activity: Microeconomics* (Special Issue), pp. 125–208.

———. 1992. "Emerging Conflicts Between Competition, Conservation, and Environmental Policies in the Electric Power Industry." Prepared for the California Foundation on the Environment and the Economy conference on the regulatory compact, April 2–3.

———. 2000. "Deregulation and Regulatory Reform in the U.S. Electric Power Sector." In *Deregulation of Network Industries: The Next Steps*, ed. S. Peltzman and Clifford Winston. Washington, DC: Brookings Institution Press.

———. 2001a. "California's Electricity Crisis," July. Available at http://web.mit.edu/pjoskow/www/.

———. 2001b. "Energy Policy During the 1990s," July 10. Available at http://web.mit.edu/pjoskow/www/.

Lidderdale, Tancred C. M. 2001. "Environmental Regulations and Changes in Petroleum Refining Operations." Energy Information Administration. Available at http://www.eia.giv/emeu/steo/pub/special/enviro.html.

Mariner-Volpe, Barbara. 2000. "The Evolution of Gas Markets in the United States." A presentation made available by the Energy Information Service, May.

Mayo, J., and J. Mathis. 1988. "The Effectiveness of Mandatory Fuel Efficiency Standards in Reducing the Demand for Gasoline." *Applied Economics*, 20(2): 211–219.

Orszag, Peter R. (undated, but written prior to the privatization of USEC). "Privatization of the U.S. Enrichment Corporation: An Economic Analysis."

———. 2000. "Nuclear Proliferation: Implications of the U.S. Purchase of Russian Highly Enriched Uranium." U.S. General Accounting Office, December.

———. 2001. "Commercial Nuclear Fuel from U.S. and Russian Surplus Defense Inventories: Materials, Policies, and Market Effects." Energy Information Administration. Available at http://www.eia.doe.gov/cneaf/nuclear/com_fuel, March 11.

U.S. Department of Energy. 2000. *Federal Restructuring Legislation 106th Congress*, June 29. Available at http://www.eia.doe.gov/cnea/page/restruct_bills/bill_sums_106.html.

U.S. Environmental Protection Agency. 2000. *Light-Duty Automotive Technology and Fuel Economy Trends 1975 through 2000*. December. Washington, DC: U.S. Environmental Protection Agency.

Wirl, F. 2000. "Lessons from Utility Conservation Programs." *Energy Journal*, 21(1): 87–108.

Comments

Charles B. Curtis

I would like to begin by acknowledging Paul Joskow's fine work. His chapter on U.S. energy policy during the 1990s is a true tour de force, capturing the intricacies of the policies that helped shape the energy markets of the last decade as well as the shaping influences of earlier policy successes and failures. It is a remarkable piece of scholarship, and I agree with most, but not all, of its characterizations of the events of the past.

I will try to correct the historical record where I see the need during the course of this discussion. But the important part of this exercise is not to construct a definitive history of the last decade. Rather, it is to learn from that history so that we may better understand the present and predicate the future fate of energy policy and our economy. Toward that end, Paul Joskow's paper is an especially well thought out guide. I commend it to you and I want to commend to your consideration, in particular, what Paul has identified in his conclusion as "a few energy policy challenges that are legacies of the 1990s." These are the hard questions. Only some of them have entered the contemporary policy debate in Washington.

This conference is convened on the threshold of yet another attempt to define a national energy policy. One is reminded of Samuel Johnson's observation about second marriages, a state of affairs he considered to be the evidence of "the triumph of hope over experience."

I have been witness to the struggles of six administrations and more than ten Congresses in an on-again, off-again attempt to define a coherent and comprehensive energy policy. The experience has not exactly been confidence building.

It might be useful to reflect a moment on just why it has been so difficult in the past.

There are two principal reasons. First, energy policy should be seen as a derivative policy—it derives from the broader and more fundamental national goals of economic health, environmental quality, and national security. Any attempt to define energy policy goals must first attempt to understand the full scope of these more comprehensive goals and then attempt to fit energy policy objectives to them. This process is not exactly linear. It is more iterative in character, because often energy policies that serve one of these broader goals are in conflict with the others. This type of balancing is often simply beyond the grasp of congressional committees and subcommittees acting within narrowly defined jurisdictional boundaries. Administrations have a broader reach. But the constitutional construct is that the president proposes and Congress disposes. The jurisdictional diffusion of congressional committees works against rational energy policy.

The second reason has to do with a point Dan Yergin made almost a decade ago in a *Newsweek* essay. "America's energy economy is huge and complex, and the interests involved—of regions, producers, and consumers—are often conflicting." Energy policy choices often involve high dollar stakes and correspondingly high passion.

Most of the really important decisions were made on the strength of one- or two-vote margins in committee or on the Senate and House floors. As President Gerald Ford's chief policy adviser on energy, Frank Zarb, observed some years back "[in energy policy] our political system produced what the public would support—no more, no less." Compromise born of necessity and pragmatism shaped the legislative product. Energy policy, as a consequence, lacked a discernible theme or even a recognizable form. Can we do better this time around? Let's hope so.

I am entirely doubtful, however, of the success of an attempt to define a *comprehensive national energy policy*. Rather, I would recommend we attempt to articulate *comprehensible* national energy policies, a series of individual initiatives with a coherent theme. As Paul Joskow has put it, we need sustained national *policies that are specific to the energy sector*. A fine point perhaps, but I believe an important one.

At the beginning of this last decade, energy policy took the form of Norman Schwartzkopf and the military intervention in Kuwait. The events in the desert were a clear reminder of how intertwined are our strategic interests in the Middle East and our energy economy. The Bush administration set out to articulate a new comprehensive energy policy. At the threshold of that undertaking, in 1991, Dan Yergin recommended that the administration propose "an ecumenical policy"—one that appealed to, and comprehended, the diversity of stakeholder interest and the regional differences of our society. In 1991—in testimony before my colleague on this panel, Phil Sharp—I counseled the administration to include a policy component addressed to energy efficiency, which I labeled the starting point of analysis for the Democratic Congress of that day. Supply-side incentive, I believed, would garner political support only if, and after, Congress had first evaluated what could be done to expand the resource base by improving on energy efficiency.

The Bush administration of 1991 heeded neither Dan Yergin's nor my admonition and, ignoring also the advice of its own Department of Energy, submitted a one-sided, supply-side initiative. Congress largely ignored it and evolved an energy policy that focused on expanding renewables and energy-efficiency options and on the restructuring of the electric power sector. That was the essence of the Energy Policy Act of 1992, and, not surprisingly, the implementation of this policy became the focus of the first Clinton term—the period of my service.

The Clinton administration saw the Energy Policy Act of 1992 as a call for diversification. In the sphere of international policy, the Clinton administration worked hard to diversify from Middle Eastern supply dependency. Here, I think Paul's paper is deficient in failing to recognize the administration's high-level efforts to develop the Caspian resources, to help Russia recover its oil and gas productive capacity, and to develop western hemisphere resources.

At home, the administration worked equally hard to diversify our energy options. All was not as quiet on the domestic oil policy front as the paper suggests.

For example, the Clinton administration proposed and Congress enacted royalty relief for production in the deep waters of the central and western Gulf of Mexico. Both the *Wall Street Journal* and *Texas Monthly* credited this initiative with increased exploration and development activity in the Gulf. The same legislation gave permission to allow exports of Alaskan oil, making it possible to increase Alaskan oil production as well as Californian oil production. Also, we were able to change onshore royalty requirements to reduce royalties due to high-cost oil supplies, such as California heavy oil. And we privatized the Elk Hills Naval Petroleum Reserve, lowered industry costs by working to reform the Oil Pollution Act of 1990, and reduced royalties on declining production.

I also think Paul's paper is somewhat off the mark in criticizing the Clinton administration's devotion to renewables and energy efficiency. That's exactly what the Congress of 1992 directed the administration to do. That was our job. Indeed, the role of the Congress is too little acknowledged in the energy policy history of the 1990s. It both defined the administration's obligation for action and constrained its capacity for initiative.

For example, there was no change in CAFE—that is, fuel efficiency standards—because the Republican House that was elected in 1994 banned any change in the standards—a ban that was kept in place for the remaining six years of the administration. Appliance efficiency standards were locked up in the appropriations process and delayed by three years. There were no tax in-centives for many of the things the George W. Bush administration now wants to provide incentives for—such as combined heat and power systems and hy-brid fuel vehicles—because in the budget crunch of the first four Clinton years, there were no credits to give out, and in the last four Clinton years, Congress refused to provide them when the president asked. Indeed, the Clinton admin-istration asked and was refused such incentives for the last three years of its term.

And, throughout its tenure, the administration waged an eight-year fight to restore R&D funding to diversify our energy options. Consider this historical footnote: the investment in renewable and energy-efficiency R&D in President Jimmy Carter's last budget year, 1981, was $3 billion in constant 1998 dollars. President Ronald Reagan cut it by 60 percent in his first year, and by 1990 the budget had fallen by more than 80 percent to $500 million. After the 1991 energy policy called the Gulf War, the R&D budget began to recover, and it stands today at around $1.3 billion in 1998 dollars. In President George W. Bush's April budget, however, the administration proposed a 50 percent cut in renew-able R&D and a 25 percent cut in energy efficiency. So much for "sustainable" national policies to diversify the domestic suite of energy options. However, I believe in redemption, and I note with appreciation that the House recently voted to restore these funds. The Senate will do likewise.

The Clinton administration's stewardship of energy policy was shaped fun-damentally by the hard-earned lessons from past experience—namely, that government policies that are intended to work against market forces, at best, can only be justified as short-term transitional devices. Over time they will fail and prove costly. That was the dominant lesson of the oil-sector and natural-gas producer price controls of the 1970s. The policy-makers of 1992 had learned that government action is most effective and most justified when directed at removing or compensating for market imperfections. So they set out on a course of reliance on markets and competitive forces to shape our energy future. The Clinton administration took these lessons to heart and vigorously introduced competition to the electricity and natural gas markets. Given the experience in California and the price volatility in natural gas markets, it is perhaps a fair criticism that the Clinton administration's embrace of markets was a little too enthusiastic and too unqualified. Given the complexity of the task, more thought and planning might have been invested in developing monitoring tools and mitigation measures in the event things went wrong. But that comment is easy to make with the benefit of hindsight.

I believe the Clinton administration's record is—directionally—pretty good. One can always quibble with the details. Throughout the 1990s it was directionally correct to foster the development of competitive markets in the gas and electric sectors. It was directionally right to push for comprehensive—and still needed—federal legislation to better rationalize the restructuring and operation of the electric power market. Throughout its eight years the Clinton administration "stayed the competitive market course" at home and abroad. Over the span of the Clinton years, the 1980s vocabulary of demand-side management and integrated resource planning largely gave way to the decade's dominant fashion of energy infrastructure privatization and market liberalization. I still believe that directionally this is a good thing and the right path. Could more have been done? Yes. Was there much political opportunity to do more? With better or more attentive leadership? I doubt it.

The reasons lie in the first few lines of Paul Joskow's conclusion. I quote:

Overall, the decade of the 1990s was a period in which energy markets performed reasonably well, federal energy policy-makers focused primarily on implementing and completing policy initiatives that began before or at the very beginning of the decade, and the energy supply sectors evolved slowly and relatively smoothly.... Real energy prices were stable or falling for most of the period, and there were significant productivity improvements in several energy sectors.

Hardly a clarion call for new policy initiatives or new legislation. Hardly a political justification for stirring up the stakeholders. The events of this last year—a full five years after I left office I might observe—have now given birth to a new attempt to articulate a comprehensive national energy policy. There are clearly things that should be done—as Paul has so well documented. But I think Paul and I would join in trying to discourage thinking of this as an "energy crisis." That term has been a justification for too much legislative mischief in the past.

As I observed at the outset of these remarks, energy policy is a derivative of the broader and more fundamental national goals of economic health, environmental quality, and energy security. Clearly the first and second Clinton terms were overwhelmingly focused on restoring the economic health of the nation. And on balance the Clinton administration emphasized environmental quality. Energy security issues were also attended to but in, perhaps, a not too visible way—and with not nearly the emphasis they are expected to receive in the new Bush administration. The nuclear option was preserved; advanced light water reactor designs were completed with government R&D funds and certified. Fossil R&D programs were revamped with the advice of outside experts, such as Dan Yergin, to make them of greater relevance and value to industry. And, as noted earlier, within the fiscal constraints we faced, the administration acted to reduce domestic exploration and production costs for oil and natural gas.

We also worked to get environmental and energy policy better coordinated—albeit with only minor success. The Bush administration intends to do better. I wish them success.

It is also my hope—not my experience, but my hope—that our political process will be up to the challenge of defining a new, comprehensive energy policy that will best serve the needs of the 21st century. Yet the early political posturing—like past experiences—has not been confidence building. The new Bush administration allowed its policies to be portrayed as a one-sided, supply-side initiative—although they ended up more "ecumenical" than critics acknowledge. The Democrats, sensing a presidential "note" out of tune with the body politic, have hammered away. It's hard to find anyone in search of common ground, and many of the most important elements of the administration's proposal remain under study. Yet, as I noted earlier, I believe in redemption and the future may be better than the past.

Comments

Philip R. Sharp

My remarks will focus on three energy policy themes from the 1990s: internationalizing energy markets, greening markets, and liberalizing markets. These themes reinforce, consolidate, and accelerate where we were headed in energy policy even before the 1990s.

On internationalizing energy markets, Charlie Curtis has already alluded to specific foreign policy efforts. It was of fundamental importance to the country's energy future that the opening of international energy markets continued during the 1990s. An example was NAFTA. (Although NAFTA itself did not have a direct liberalizing effect on Mexico's energy markets in the 1990s, many of us expected it would eventually have an indirect effect.) The end result of this continued internationalization of energy markets is that we can purchase energy from more places around the world. And this is quite a contrast from the energy policy in the 1970s, when Democrats and Republicans competed over who could outdo whom on energy independence. We now recognize that we are critically dependent on the rest of the world and must keep the markets open.

The second theme is the greening of the markets. The administration had a desire to be green. But was the administration wearing dark green glasses or light green? If you are from the environmental community, they were light green. If you are from the business community, they were dark green. It is hard to get a perspective on what was real. Remember that the Btu tax was the administration's first proposal out of the box, although that was primarily put forward for budgetary reasons, not environmental reasons. The interesting thing on the Btu tax was that one national association did support it: The National Coal Association, believe it or not, initially supported the Btu proposal. It thought a Democratic Congress would follow the lead of a Democratic president. They were relieved that at least it was a Btu tax, and not a carbon tax, so they supported the proposal. Little did they know that Democrats don't follow.

In certain R&D areas, the administration succeeded in securing more funding—for example, in renewables development. But again there is the question of perspective. The interesting thing that is missed by critiques of the administration is that it put a lot of money in R&D for drilling efficiencies, 3-D seismic activities, and other efforts that would also enhance production, not just improve end-use efficiency. And given the Democratic constituency on coal, the administration proposed a research program on carbon sequestration as a part of the broader global warming issue.

Regarding public lands, the administration succeeded in locking up more lands, especially with the national monuments designations. Interestingly enough, what is often missed is the lands that the administration opened up—against environmental complaints. For example, consider the National Petroleum Reserve in Alaska to the west of Prudhoe Bay, where the exploratory wells are proving as lucrative as expected.

The administration clearly exhibited a significant policy preference for natural gas. It articulated that preference frequently, and a number of decisions enhanced the economic viability of natural gas in the system. One of the most important was a significant increase in sitings for the natural gas pipeline system in the country, which could be critical in the future.

Finally, let me turn to the issue of market liberalization. Here the administration was true to its "new Democratic" rhetoric on electricity: there was a dramatic movement toward deregulation. The Federal Energy Regulatory Commission made a very significant move in 1996 with Order 888, to bring open access to the transmission grid. This order was a follow-on to the 1992 Energy Policy Act, but it actually went much farther than many observers ever dreamed it would. Ironically, on the American scene, federal regulators have been the strongest advocates of open markets. You may find some wavering on that, but in general they have been an important driver.

Coupled to this advocacy by regulators, the administration itself took on an advocacy role. The administration offered a major piece of legislation on electricity restructuring. It didn't *require* liberalization, but it did pressure states to adopt what we call retail access. The administration added to this legislation a mandatory requirement for renewables through the so-called renewable portfolio standard. That reflected a political bind, and it was the subject, as I understand it, of a huge argument within the administration. Many at the Department of Energy did not want to adopt this policy—and the Treasury, CEA, and a variety of places were also opposed to an aggressive renewable portfolio standard. But it was difficult to argue that the administration's proposal should not include such a requirement when the conservative chair of the Energy and Power Subcommittee had legislation that included a renewable portfolio standard (and also was more aggressive in mandating that states give up their authority over the electric utilities). That fact made it hard for the Clinton administration to tell its environmental friends that "we can't do it" when the environmental advocates could point to Congress and say, "What do you mean? The strongest proponents of competition on Capitol Hill are doing it."

Let me turn quickly to the issue of price controls. The debate over price controls on oil and natural gas has ended. Even the farthest left in the Democratic Party no longer supports such price controls—they just don't come onto the radar screen. A strong political test of the lack of support for price controls has occurred in the last two years, we had persistent high prices in natural gas, oil, and heating oil. Yet neither the Clinton administration nor (less surprisingly) the Bush administration advocated price controls. Nor were they being pressured by anybody to advocate such controls. That is a remarkable thing. (Admittedly the situation is somewhat different in California. We are in such a scrambled mess betwixt and between a competitive marketplace that the advocacy for controls on electricity prices has some resonance there.)

Finally, let me mention the auto industry. The Partnership for a New Generation of Vehicles (PNGV) was a significant investment in R&D in conjunction with the American domestic automobile industry (if one could define "domestic" in this context). PNGV was clearly a way to finesse the CAFE issue politically. But it was also a philosophy intended to achieve a dramatic gain, rather than the incremental gains that regulation could bring.

Comments

Daniel Yergin

I'm very grateful and very pleased to be part of this panel and this conference. I want to congratulate Paul on his comprehensive and excellent chapter. One of the very interesting parts is the beginning, in which he sets out six reasons why energy policy takes place. I recommend that people look at how he brings it together. As you read and think about his chapter, you may—as I did—find yourself having the sense that energy policy is happening all the time, directly and indirectly. A lot of the time it is not explicit.

Energy policy loomed large, explicitly, at the beginning of the 1990s and then again at the end—and not much in between. At the beginning of the decade, as Charlie observed, big things were happening—the Gulf crisis. The first post–cold war crisis was about oil and geopolitics, although a lot of effort went into saying it was not about oil. Terms were used like "jobs, jobs, jobs," which were actually a code for "oil, oil, oil." But this comment underlines how extremely important were the security dimensions, for the risks were about economic and political power—and about military power and weapons of mass destruction. The Gulf crisis had a big impact on the outcome of the 1992 election, although not, as one would have thought, as a result of the military victory, but rather because of the impact on economic growth. And it certainly stands as a very high mark. There was the 1992 energy policy act in which Phil was so involved. And then there was the fight over the Btu tax. At the end of the decade the conjunction of high prices and disruption and opinion polls pushed energy policy forward again.

In between we had the annual spring cycle of the driving season, which traditionally is said to begin with the Memorial Day weekend. The cycle seems to be the same: higher gasoline prices and charges of price manipulation, and then many months later the FTC study comes out saying that actually it was just the market working. But that gets much less attention. So there is lots of energy policy but not a high focus. During the time that Charlie was serving in the

Department of Energy, I was a member of the secretary of energy's advisory board. Thinking back on it, I remember that many of those meetings were not about energy: they were about nuclear waste, they were about labs, and they were about research. During that period when Charlie had responsibility for science and technology, I headed a task force on energy R&D. It was just after the Contract with America, and much of what we were doing was about how to make decisions about R&D. After all, the Department of Energy is also the department of science. We examined the relationship to what's happening in the market and how to prioritize.

Most noteworthy, when you look at what happened in the 1990s, is what both Charlie and Phil referred to: this continuing process of transforming the traditional vertically integrated utility—a natural monopoly and biggest contributor and booster to the local United Way campaign—into a deintegrated competitive brand-driven business. This reflects what both of them have talked about, which was a shift in confidence, in the balance of confidence, toward markets—our subject in *The Commanding Heights.* You can detect from both of their remarks that the battle over natural gas price control and then deregulation had a very big impact on Democrats, in particular, in terms of setting the stage for the kind of market liberalization that we are talking about. This impact was so large because when prices were deregulated, they went down, not up. The general premise became that competitive markets, as Phil has observed, can serve consumers better and protect them.

Before the Clinton administration finished, of course, there was the vexing issue of thinking through "market power." Paul would say that issue has become much more vexing in the last year. Accordingly, we have to pause for a moment on the electrical power crisis in California. It straddles the decades. After all, we are talking here both about the Clinton administration and the decade—and California's partial deregulation. Paul questions in this chapter whether the term "deregulation" should have even been used for describing what happened in California. And I think that's a very good point.

It is striking to think back that the issues today are a product of the mid-1990s. California was coming out of recession, and the view was that the surplus would last forever. No one had yet heard of the "new economy." There was no real World Wide Web. Three big errors stand out. First, there was no provision for encouraging sufficient capacity. Second, as Paul points out, retail was not deregulated. As a result, price signals did not reach consumers. And, third, you certainly can't say that the siting and permitting process was deregulated. There was no new construction. So what you had has been an old-fashioned shortage. In five years the economy of California grew 29 percent; electricity demand grew 24 percent. But over ten years, no new plants.

There are two further things that one might observe about the California imbroglio. California really does loom large globally as something that is being
assessed. Innumerable countries seem to be sending task forces to California
to understand the imbroglio. In many countries, it has become the "reason" to
slow or stop electric power reform. The consequences of that trend are still to
be played out. The other thing—and Paul mentioned this last night—is the
governance issue. Yes, there are energy issues. But there is also a real question
of governance and the leadership—or the lack of leadership—that brought
California to this pass.

Paul observes in the chapter that—surprisingly or not surprisingly—over
the decade there was no big change in the supply picture. And conservation
continued to work. The country is 43 percent more energy efficient than it was
in 1973. Some may say conservation stopped, yet the nation became 15 percent
more efficient over the 1990s. And I think Charlie made a very interesting
comment, if I heard it correctly. He said that there is a gap between how the
new Bush energy policy is being presented and portrayed in the press coverage
and its actual content.

The big issue of course that wasn't dealt with in the 1990s is SUVs—sport
utility vehicles. When the original fuel efficiency standards were passed, farmers drove pickup trucks. And that was about it. Now one out of every two new
vehicles more or less is an SUV, and six years of not dealing with this change
can be measured in our consumption. The obvious way that most people in this
room would look to promote conservation is through price, but that is because
most of you are economists. That approach, as Paul points out, is—for politicians—political suicide. Many advocates say we need more conservation. But,
if some of you in this room say, "Okay, raise the price," the conversation changes
from conservation.

Much of what we are seeing in markets now began in Asia in 1997 when the
Asian economy collapsed, Asian oil demand collapsed, and the price collapsed.
This price decrease led to an enormous contraction in the oil industry, a severe
reduction in activity and much less production capacity in the world today
than would otherwise have been expected.

And something else happened. This has been the real impact of growing
shareholder value on the oil and gas industry. Shareholders—institutional
investors—seem unwilling to let there be a drilling boom. They will punish
companies that spend too much money. And that tendency has reinforced the
contraction that already took place. And so we are seeing the consequences
today.

Growth came back more quickly than many anticipated after the Asian collapse. Korea, instead of having no growth in 1999, had about 12 percent. So

demand rebounded. The producers were already very scared about the sharp decline in their revenues, and they were cutting back. And the result? We went from an oversupplied market to a very tight market. We have seen that reflected in prices. Natural gas has had parallel developments. Phil pointed out the shift in natural gas. Some in this room will remember that one of the ten commandments of energy policy in the 1970s was that "thou shalt not burn natural gas in electric power generation." That turned around. And over the last few years it has been anticipated that 95 percent of new electric capacity will in fact be fired by natural gas. This expectation is premised on inexpensive gas.

However, because of the collapse in prices and warm weather, gas development decreased. And we have had tight gas markets. But we are now, with a delay, seeing the supply response at a time of recession and weaker demand. But here the preceding environmental panel and this energy panel converge. Natural gas development is really part of achieving our environmental objectives. What has happened with oil and gas has brought back energy as a policy issue. There was a view that energy was not very important in terms of the overall economy anymore, because we have a new economy. Alas, the new economy has come and gone—at least in its first incarnation—and as of around October or November 2000, people started to see that, in fact, what was happening in energy prices would have considerable impact.

These markets will change again. They will be affected by what happens with overall economic growth. Indeed, they will not be immune by any means to a global economic downturn. But—and this is one of the themes in Paul's chapter—we are in more of a "just-in-time" economy. There is less surplus in the system; competitive pressures are squeezing out surplus. Shareholder pressures are driving it out. As a result, there is a need for greater flexibility in the energy supply system. The drive for renewables will increase. There will be a lot of innovation. But to go back to that recognition of our huge and complex energy supply system in Paul's chapter, 93 percent of our $10 trillion economy is supported by oil, natural gas, coal, and nuclear. After all the efforts on renewables, wind and solar are 0.1 percent of our energy supplies. We are seeing increasing focus on an aging, inadequate infrastructure. It needs to be modernized. How do you get things done? I remember attending in the 1990s the dedication of a natural gas pipeline that took seven years just to get the permits before any dirt could be turned. The scale of projects is growing. We are seeing a return of LNG.

What is not in the chapter, as Charlie observed, is the international aspect—the encouragement of international development that Charlie was much involved in, the diversification, the Caspian region. This led to a very interesting contrast. Domestically, sometimes there was definite confrontation between the

U.S. government and companies. Yet overseas, the U.S. government was acting almost as though these companies were national champions in the way it was promoting development—and seeking a speed of development that was unlikely in the regulatory system of the United States itself. This impetus by the U.S. government was driven both by energy considerations and by a desire to see the independence of the newly independent countries consolidated.

One thing I am perplexed about in Paul's chapter is that he refers to what he says is better coordination of energy and environmental policies. I might have misread that. I'm puzzled. I find that hard to see. We just looked at the micro-brew gasolines. The so-called boutique fuels. One pipeline system that used to carry seven grades of gasoline, now has to carry 90 different grades of gasoline. You lose the flexibility in the system to respond to changes in supply and demand. In a way it is like the allocations and controls of the 1970s, because you cannot move supplies around. And I think that's just one example. In the last panel it was remarked that people think the environment is getting worse. You see these charts showing how air quality is dramatically improved in San Francisco. But people's conviction that air quality is getting worse is also dramatically increasing. Access for exploration and production will be a big battle coming out of the 1990s, as Phil has noted. Despite the very considerable environmental advances and the love affair with the SUVs, there is clearly a well of animosity toward the energy industries—an antipathy to developing supply. That is evident in the debate on the new energy policy document. And, of course, the arguments about new infrastructure. "NIMBY," "Not in My Back-yard," has given way to—and I may not have it quite right—to "BANANA," "Build Almost Nothing Anywhere Near Anybody." But when you need new infrastructure, it's hard to accept that limitation.

And finally I think Richard Zeckhouser in the session on environmental policy (Chapter 11) left a very intriguing question: "Will climate change concerns provide a rationale for a serious reconsideration for the first time in 22 years of nuclear power?" That discussion will continue. Thank you.

Very briefly, I think that part of the answer is that it is there, and there will be future crisis for sure. To add to what Phil said, the other aspect is of course just diversification. The more countries, the more parts of the world. And we have seen that. And that's what the Caspian was about.

Very quickly, I think of four reasons in response. One is that the industry is digesting the regulatory burdens in terms of these microbrews—all these different gasolines. And it is uncertain about the investment levels. So I think that's a very dominating thing. Second, what I've observed in the business is that it's much more sensitive to the pressure from shareholders and pleasing shareholders. And that sensitivity is just taking over the psychology. Third is that, although, as you say, it's a good business now, I think for most people who have been kind of decision-makers for most of their careers, refining has been a crummy business, and they expect it to return to being a crummy business. And they spent many years shedding capacity as you very well know. I think, fourth, with all these things, I'm sure some entrepreneurs and some people will come forward with the thought that the regulatory hurdles to site and build a new refinery, as opposed to expanding capacity in existing refineries, would make it a pretty distasteful activity to undertake. Because you may never get there anyway.

Can I just say one other thing? The futures markets are one guide. The other guide is the physical supply and demand and how tight the balance is. And that has turned out in both oil and gas to be a better guide than the futures markets themselves.

Summary of Discussion

Richard Cooper noted that the discussion focused on liberalization in domestic energy markets and failed to recognize that oil is a global, not solely domestic, industry. Furthermore, world supply decisions often reflect political, not economic, considerations. Cooper asked if the panelists could address the disconnect between the noncompetitive world oil market structure and the desire for and usual assumption of competition within the U.S. market.

Paul Joskow responded that the question is one probably best addressed by experts on international security. However, he noted that the nation should not expect to produce its way out of its oil problem, if it is a problem. Sound policy would combine international security initiatives, efforts to continue to diversify oil supplies, and perhaps activities on the demand side to reduce consumption.

Philip Sharp responded by noting that it is a delusion to think the nation can do anything about foreign dependence on oil. This delusion influenced policy in the 1970s, but the nation discovered it was unwilling to pay the requisite price in terms of regulations or cost. He described the outcome as a victory of economists over politicians. He then argued that the United States can have only a modest impact on prices through efforts on either the production or the conservation side, and that at times of crisis the critical issue is surge capacity (which is largely, if not entirely, outside the United States). He concluded by noting that "we are stuck living with everybody else in this world."

Daniel Yergin added that the key to dealing with future crises is to work toward diversification of supply today. U.S. energy interests are increasingly protected when more countries from more regions of the world produce oil.

Robert Pitofsky commented that FTC reports on high gasoline prices have all found no evidence of collusion among suppliers. These investigations, however, highlighted a very unusual fact: by the end of the 1990s, the refining industry was operating at 95 percent of capacity year-round, with some parts of the country at nearly 100 percent of capacity. These figures compare to the average for other industries of about 82 percent of capacity. The high capacity-utilization rates in refining, according to Pitofsky, reflect the fact that no new refineries have been built in the United States in 25 years. He asked why firms are not building refineries now, despite the relatively high prices.

Charlie Curtis argued that price volatility discouraged investment in both capacity and inventories. To address price volatility, he supported continued diversification of supply to reduce the influence of OPEC. Curtis also suggested that domestic policy could be formulated to create incentives for holding inventories. He also urged efforts to facilitate the siting and construction of critical infrastructure, through financial incentives and expedited regulatory processes.

Joskow argued that the problem is very difficult. First, the extensive differentiation of gasoline products now means that fewer and fewer refineries are capable of producing any particular variant of fuel, making each specific niche market more vulnerable to supply disruptions. In addition to the supply-side issues, Joskow pointed to unresolved questions about how consumers and intermediaries will respond to "just-in-time" supply in electricity, natural gas, and oil. For example, gas and electric utilities are no longer entering into long-term contracts for natural gas supplies and for storage. In today's environment, consumers are supposed to engage in such contracting, but their time horizons tend to be very short, for whatever reason. Either the nation will have to live with the volatility that results, or consumers will have to take advantage of risk-management options to hedge their supplies. Long-term contracts between consumers and suppliers would in turn provide more capability to finance energy infrastructure, presuming the siting issues can be addressed.

Yergin provided several reasons for the dearth of new refineries. First, the industry is digesting regulatory burdens in terms of the microbrew fuels. Second, sensitivity to shareholders' concerns has limited capital investments. Third, for most decision-makers in this industry, for most of their careers, refining has been an unattractive business, and they expect it to return to being an unattractive business. Fourth, the regulatory burden to site and build a new refinery as opposed to expanding capacity at existing refineries discourages new investment.

Sharp noted that the discussion hinted at the need for government to interfere in the marketplace in order to encourage investment, contrary to the overall trend toward liberalization. He also commented that when firms upgraded their refineries to comply with new environmental regulations under the 1990 Clean Air Act Amendments, the investments also increased efficiency, which helped increase refinery output.

Martin Baily commented on the difficulty of forecasting energy prices. He suggested that the Council of Economic Advisers did not provide timely information to the president regarding the spike in gasoline prices and the events in California. One reason for this failure was a triumph of economics—administration economists looked at futures markets to understand future oil and gasoline prices. The futures markets suggested lower expected future spot prices, so the economists claimed that prices would decline. However, some people warned that the administration should not pay any attention to the futures markets because of OPEC's limited excess capacity and the shortage of refining capacity. In hindsight, Baily asked if it would have been better to give less weight to the futures markets, and if so, asked what that approach implies for the standard view about how financial markets work.

Curtis noted that it was well known in regulatory circles that a significant problem was developing in California. Perhaps the administration could have done more to get the state regulators to respond earlier to what was emerging. In addition, Curtis noted that in retrospect the administration could be criticized for being overly enthusiastic in its embrace of markets in the electricity sector. For example, he argued that at the federal level anticipatory market monitoring mechanisms and market mitigation measures could have been created so that the problem in California would have been foreshadowed and acted on earlier.

Joskow responded that no one could have predicted the spike in natural gas prices: there was simply no information available in March 2000 to allow one to predict a more than tripling in the price of Henry Hub natural gas by the end of the year. In fact, with natural gas at $5.50 per thousand cubic feet in August, most market players believed that the natural gas price could only fall, and so no one stored gas, only to find natural gas prices at $9.00 in December.

Regarding electricity, Joskow noted that in 1996 FERC created the Market Surveillance Committee in California, which began issuing warnings about the state's electricity market in 1998. Moreover, the committee offered suggestions to address the state's problems, but these were basically ignored by federal officials. He argued that FERC and state officials erred in not responding to the growing evidence of the serious flaws in these markets.

Yergin commented that the futures markets are only one guide to expected future prices. The other guide is physical supply and demand conditions, and how tight the balance between the two is. This latter guide has served to explain oil and gas prices better than the futures markets themselves.

Baily responded that any economist who believes in efficient markets would note that information regarding the balance of supply and demand was available to traders in the futures market. He then noted that the silver lining of being optimistic about future energy prices is that the optimism may have prevented the implementation of ill-advised policies.

Robert Stavins asked what credit the Clinton administration deserved for keeping the nuclear option alive. He also asked about the path forward for related public policy, including the economic merits or demerits of the Price-Anderson Act.

Sharp noted that the administration's first effort in support of nuclear power was the relicensing of the Calvert Cliffs Plant. Many observers had thought that relicensing was too difficult politically and that it would therefore never happen. But now such relicensing is almost a certainty for most plants, unless they develop severe, plant-specific operating problems. Second, the administration continued the technical work necessary for the Yucca Mountain site, allowing a presidential decision to be made later in 2001 on whether to go forward with nuclear waste storage at that site. Third, the Clinton administration maintained the R&D program for advanced nuclear plant designs. Building on this work, the Nuclear Regulatory Commission has already prelicensed and preapproved several new designs, easing the regulatory approval process for a firm to pursue the development of a new nuclear facility.

Carl Shapiro asked whether policies impeded the construction of new capacity, specifically oil refinery capacity and electricity capacity in California. Further, he raised the issue of whether the hurdles to developing new refineries have been identified and eliminated.

Joskow pointed to the electricity siting regulations in California, noting that although the state restructured part of its electricity system, it did not address siting rules. With the rules designed for the old 10-year utility planning system, the process for siting new facilities took too long. On oil, Joskow noted that oil refineries are not considered to be very profitable by those in the industry. The industry therefore prefers to expand existing refineries, a process which does not involve the additional cost of siting and permitting.

Alice Rivlin asked about the performance of the Partnership for a New Generation of Vehicles and whether it was worthwhile given the experience with the program.

Curtis described the program as an attempt to increase by a factor of three the fuel economy of a passenger vehicle while maintaining performance characteristics. He argued that significant progress has been made and that the automobile industry would agree with that assessment. While subsidizing R&D along these lines may not be the most efficient way to increase fuel economy, more efficient policy instruments, such as the Btu tax, were not politically viable during the 1990s.

William Niskanen asked why the government should promote energy conservation measures when energy prices are no longer controlled.

Sharp responded that energy efficiency is one approach for addressing the environmental externalities associated with energy use.

Joskow seconded the point by Sharp. He noted that the price of energy does not fully reflect the social cost of consuming energy, because environmental externalities and national security concerns have not been internalized. Such internalizing would best be achieved with economic instruments, but without such tools at one's disposal for political reasons, policy-makers are left with the second-best, third-best, and even fourth-best types of approaches. Further, although it may be difficult for economists to accept the argument, some people believe that energy efficiency programs are a form of consumer protection. The argument is that consumers don't know that somehow they can save lots of money by buying a highly efficient refrigerator that has a higher purchase price, but quickly pays for the difference through lower electric bills. Publications for the past 20 years have suggested a significant "free lunch" in these programs. Although Joskow noted the imperfections in markets for energy-efficient equipment, he was not sure whether the imperfections justified the kinds of efficiency regulations that have been implemented.

9   Environmental Policy

National Environmental Policy During the Clinton Years

Robert W. Hahn and
Robert N. Stavins

PANELISTS: *George T. Frampton, Paul R. Portney, and Murray Weidenbaum*

9.1   Introduction

We examine, from an economic perspective, major developments in national environmental policy during the two terms of the Clinton administration, 1992 through 2000. We define environmental policy broadly to include not only the statutes, regulations, and policies associated with reducing environmental pollution, but also major issues in natural resource management. Issues that might fall within a comprehensive assessment of environmental and natural resource policy, but which are covered by other chapters in this book, such as energy policy and trade policy, are not included in our investigation.

Our analysis is primarily descriptive, although in some of the cases in which environmental policies have been analyzed from an economic perspective, we

Sheila Cavanagh, a Ph.D. student in Public Policy at Harvard, provided exceptionally valuable research assistance, contributing to all aspects of the work. This chapter benefited from the discussion at the conference American Economic Policy in the 1990s, sponsored by the Center for Business and Government at Harvard's Kennedy School. We thank conference panelists George Frampton, Paul Portney, and Murray Weidenbaum and panel chair Richard Schmalensee. Helpful comments on previous versions were provided by Arthur Fraas, Myrick Freeman, Alan Krupnick, Randall Lutter, Albert McGartland, Richard Morgenstern, Paul Portney, and Jason Shogren. Financial support was provided by the Savitz Family Fund for Environment and Natural Resource Policy and the Ford Fund at Harvard University. The authors alone are responsible for any remaining errors. A related paper by Cavanagh, Hahn, and Stavins (2001) includes comprehensive tables describing specific environmental and resource statutes and regulations. For surveys of environmental and resource policy in the 1980s, see Portney (1984) and Viscusi (1994).

discuss those analytical results. Moreover, the analysis is not exhaustive. While our choice of policies and programs to discuss in depth has inevitably been somewhat arbitrary, we include the most important and the most prominent issues in economics and environment over the decade. Finally, while we do mention a number of policies and programs administered by agencies other than the U.S. Environmental Protection Agency (EPA), rules promulgated by EPA comprise a substantial majority of total costs and benefits of federal environmental regulation. We therefore give considerable attention to the use and acceptance of economics at EPA.

A fundamental issue that confronts our assessment is the choice of an appropriate basis of comparison for evaluating policy initiatives. It might appear reasonable to contrast first-term Clinton administration initiatives with what might have been anticipated from a hypothetical second-term Bush administration, but what would be the appropriate counterfactual for the second term of the Clinton years? The impossibility of providing a definitive answer to that question leads us to take a different approach, adopting economic criteria for policy assessment—principally efficiency, cost effectiveness, and distributional equity.[1]

Five themes emerge from our review of national environmental policy during the years of the Clinton administration. First, *over the course of the decade, environmental targets were made more stringent, and environmental quality improved*. Most important among the new targets were the National Ambient Air Quality Standards (NAAQS) for ambient ozone and particulate matter, issued by EPA in July 1997, which could turn out to be one of the Clinton administration's most enduring environmental legacies, both in terms of potential benefits and potential costs. Environmental quality improved overall during the decade, continuing a trend that started in the 1970s, although trends in water quality were less clear than trends in air quality. Environmental quality improvements were much less than during the previous two decades—not surprising given that the low-hanging fruit had already been picked.

Natural resource policy during the Clinton years was heavily weighted toward environmental protection. The administration proposed initiatives to reduce subsidies for private resource extraction on public lands. In addition, the U.S. Forest Service shifted priorities away from a focus on timber production to

---

1. We follow the standard definition of an *efficient* environmental policy as being one that involves a target—such as a 50 percent reduction in sulfur dioxide (SO_2) emissions—that maximizes the difference between social benefits and social costs, that is, a target level at which marginal benefits and marginal costs are equated. By *cost-effective* policies, we refer to those which take (possibly inefficient) targets as given by the political process, but achieve those targets with policy instruments—such as a tradable permit system in the SO_2 case—that minimize aggregate costs. Assessments of the distributional implications of environmental policies include analyses of the distribution of costs and benefits.

resource protection, placing 60 million acres of federal forests off limits to road building. Clinton also designated more than 20 new national monuments, thus restricting permissible activities on 6 million additional acres of federal lands.

Second, *the use of benefit-cost analysis for assessing environmental regulation was controversial in the Clinton administration, while economic efficiency emerged as a central goal of the regulatory reform movement in the Congress during the 1990s.* When attention was given to increased efficiency, the locus of that attention during the Clinton years was Congress in the case of environmental policies but the administration in the case of natural resource policies.

Despite a series of supportive executive orders, economic efficiency appears not to have been accepted as a legitimate criterion for environmental policy during the Clinton years. In contrast, economic efficiency was a central goal of regulatory reform efforts in Congress. Major amendments to the Safe Drinking Water Act were passed, containing the most stringent requirement for benefit-cost analysis of any environmental statute. Legislators were less successful at reforming other environmental statutes that had been criticized on efficiency grounds, but Congress did pass a variety of cross-cutting regulatory reform initiatives, aimed at increasing the efficiency of environmental, health, and safety regulations. Ironically, the increased attention given to benefit-cost analysis may not have had a marked effect on the economic efficiency of environmental regulations. The evidence indicates that the overall benefits of air pollution regulation have exceeded its costs, but the picture is mixed when one examines specific air pollution regulations. In general, there appears to be a downward trend in aggregate net benefits of such regulations over time, although there are important exceptions among individual regulations, such as the new NAAQS for particulate matter.

Third, *cost-effectiveness achieved a much more prominent position in public discourse regarding environmental policy during the 1990s.* From the Bush administration through the Clinton administration, interest and activity regarding market-based instruments for environmental protection—particularly tradable permit systems—continued to increase. The administration promoted cost effectiveness by supporting the implementation of existing market-based initiatives, including the sulfur dioxide allowance trading program, and by proposing new initiatives, exemplified by the strong U.S. support for tradable permit programs for reducing greenhouse gas emissions. The performance of market-based instruments that have been implemented in the past two decades has been encouraging, including the leaded gasoline phasedown in the 1980s and the SO_2 allowance trading program in the 1990s.

Fourth, *the Clinton administration put much greater emphasis than previous administrations on expanding the role of environmental information disclosure and voluntary programs.* EPA expanded the list of chemicals to be reported under the

Toxics Release Inventory (TRI), lowered reporting thresholds, and launched a number of other information programs. EPA also initiated dozens of programs designed to encourage sources to reduce emissions on a voluntary basis, many under the "Common Sense Initiative." While such programs may potentially be cost-effective ways of reaching environmental policy goals, we know very little about their actual costs or their actual effectiveness.

Fifth and finally, *the Environmental Protection Agency reduced the role of economic analysis in its decision-making during the 1990s*. During the Clinton years, EPA was more hostile toward economic analysis than it had been during the prior Bush administration, and EPA leadership made organizational changes to reflect this shift. When economics did play a role, economic analysis was more likely to be focused on increasing the cost effectiveness of regulations than on weighing benefits against costs.

This chapter is divided into five parts. In section 9.2 we analyze cross-cutting issues that stand out from the hundreds of statutes, regulations, and administrative decisions of the Clinton years, focusing separately on congressional initiatives and those that had their primary origin within the administration. In section 9.3 we review the most important national environmental policy developments from an economic perspective, and in section 9.4 we summarize performance, employing three metrics: environmental quality, cost effectiveness, and efficiency. In section 9.5 we offer some conclusions.

9.2   Cross-Cutting Environmental Policy Developments

A number of broad-based initiatives of the Clinton years—not linked with specific environmental problems—potentially had significant impacts on the conduct of environmental policy, including initiatives that were intended to affect (or could have affected) the efficiency, cost effectiveness, or distributional equity of environmental policies and programs. Our examination of such cross-cutting initiatives considers them as either executive or congressional, although this division is not always clear-cut. In some cases, it can be difficult to discern whether an initiative began in the executive branch or Congress, and any initiative that becomes law must have received the approval of both branches.[2]

---

2. For example, in 1994, the Clinton administration proposed Superfund reform that would give more weight to cleanup costs and greater consideration of future uses in site remedy selection (U.S. Council of Economic Advisers, 1996). Legislation was proposed and considered by the 103rd, 104th, and 105th Congresses, but no Superfund reform bills were enacted. In 1995 the administration proposed expediting pesticide registration and other reforms to the Federal Insecticide, Fungicide, and Rodenticide Act (FIFRA), which were achieved in large part by legislation passed by the 104th Congress in 1996.

9.2.1   Executive Initiatives

We consider cross-cutting executive branch initiatives under three categories: efficiency-enhancing initiatives; those targeted at distributional equity; and those that addressed cost-effectiveness.

9.2.1.1   Efficiency and Environmental Regulation

Since 1981, federal regulatory agencies have been required to conduct economic analyses for regulations with expected annual costs greater than $100 million.[3] Throughout the Reagan and Bush administrations, these Regulatory Impact Analyses (RIAs) were required under Reagan Executive Orders 12291 and 12498.[4] President George H. W. Bush also created a Council on Competitiveness, chaired by Vice President Dan Quayle, which reviewed the impact on industry of selected regulations. Shortly after taking office in 1993, President Clinton abolished the Council on Competitiveness and revoked both the Reagan orders, replacing them with Executive Order 12866, Regulatory Planning and Review, which itself required benefit-cost analysis.[5]

The Clinton Executive Order (EO) on benefit-cost analysis was substantively and administratively similar to the Reagan orders, requiring benefit-cost analysis and cost-effectiveness analysis of major rules. It was qualitatively different in tone, however, signaling a less strict efficiency test, as well as a new emphasis on distributional concerns. While the Reagan orders required that benefits *outweigh* costs, the Clinton order required only that benefits *justify* costs. The Clinton EO allowed that (1) not all regulatory benefits and costs can be monetized; and (2) nonmonetary consequences should be influential in regulatory analysis (Viscusi, 1996). The Clinton order also imposed a 90-day limit on the

---

3. The threshold is not indexed for inflation and has not been modified over time. Elsewhere in this chapter, we refer to year 2000 dollars, unless we indicate otherwise.

4. Executive Order (EO) 12291 required agencies to conduct a benefit-cost regulatory impact analysis for all proposed and final rules that were anticipated to have an effect on the national economy in excess of $100 million. Executive Order 12498 required, in addition, a risk assessment for all proposed and final environmental health and safety regulations. EO 12291 has been called the "foremost development in administrative law of the 1980s" (Morgenstern, 1997b). The Reagan EOs were not the first presidential effort at regulatory efficiency, however. President Richard Nixon required a "Quality of Life" review of selected regulations in 1971, and President Gerald Ford formalized this process in EO 11281 in 1974. President Jimmy Carter's EO 12044 required analysis of proposed rules and centralized review by the Regulatory Analysis Review Group. It appears that President George W. Bush will continue the RIA requirements of Clinton's EO 12866 in some form (Card, 2001).

5. In discussing Clinton's EO 12866, many investigators also mention EO 12875, Enhancing the Intergovernmental Partnership, which limited "unfunded mandates." While EO 12875 was part of the administration's regulatory reform agenda, it did not make reference to the efficiency or cost effectiveness of environmental regulations.

review process by the Office of Management and Budget (OMB), a process that had frequently extended for years under previous executive orders (Morgenstern, 2000).

While attention to regulatory efficiency may have grown during the 1990s, it would be impossible to attribute this growth to the Reagan or Clinton EOs, or any other executive actions. Regulatory reform was a major focus of Congress in the 1990s, as we will discuss later. In addition, regulatory impact analysis has continued to be required only for major rules, a small fraction of all rules issued by EPA and other agencies.

9.2.1.2 Incorporation of Distributional Concerns

During the 1990s, the regulatory review process acquired a new focus on distributional concerns. In addition to requiring RIAs, Clinton's EO 12866 instructs agencies to select regulatory approaches that maximize net benefits, *including distributive impacts and equity*, unless a statute requires another regulatory approach. The language of the EO implicitly includes equity in the objective function to be maximized, although it is not clear how equity can be "maximized." In practice, agencies have responded to the order by including a separate distributional impact analysis within RIAs.

In 1994, Executive Order 12898 formalized the president's stance on what was by then called "environmental justice," instructing each federal agency to identify and address "disproportionately high and adverse human health or environmental effects of its programs, policies, and activities on minority populations and low-income populations." The administration also supported the filing of environmentally related claims under Title VI of the Civil Rights Act of 1964, which allows citizens to file complaints against EPA alleging discriminatory intent or effect based on race, color, or national origin, resulting from the issuance of pollution control permits by state and local government agencies receiving EPA funds.[6]

9.2.1.3 Cost-Effectiveness and Environmental Regulation

Executive Order 12866 also mandated selection—when appropriate—of cost-effective regulatory alternatives, specifically user fees, marketable permits, and information programs. The use of market-based environmental policy instruments grew in the 1990s (Stavins, 1998; Hahn, 2000; U.S. Environmental Protection Agency, 2001a; Stavins, forthcoming). The proliferation of cap-and-trade

---

6. EPA's approach to Title VI complaints, issued in February 1998, complicated urban brownfields cleanup and was received poorly by the U.S. Conference of Mayors, suggesting that the means of the focus on distributional issues may have been at odds with its goals. See Carol M. Browner, "Letter to the U.S. Conference of Mayors Forum on Title VI in Detroit, Michigan" (July 1998), available at http://www.epa.gov/swerosps/bf/html-doc/confmayo.htm.

programs through the implementation of the 1990 Clean Air Act Amendments is one example; the Clinton administration's aggressive promotion of international market-based policy instruments for greenhouse gas emissions control (specifically, emissions trading) is another. Information programs, another type of potentially cost-effective market-based environmental policy instrument, received special emphasis at EPA during the Clinton years through expanded use of existing policies and creation of new ones. We cannot attribute federal agencies' increased use of market-based instruments to the Clinton EO, because we have no appropriate counterfactual against which to measure this kind of change.[7]

9.2.1.4 Political and Administrative Changes in the Use of Economic Analysis at EPA

We noted earlier the ambivalence of the major environmental statutes with respect to the role of economic analysis.[8] Such statutory ambivalence was accompanied during the Clinton years by a mixed record of political and administrative integration of economic analysis within EPA. Although EPA is constrained from using the economic efficiency criterion within particular dimensions of environmental policy, there is a good deal of flexibility in the extent to which economic analysis influences EPA processes and decisions. As a result, the use of economic analysis has varied substantially from one administration to another. This variance can be directly observed as changes in the channels through which economic advice reaches the administrator and other decision-makers, and indirectly as shifts in agency "culture"—broadly, the level of acceptance of economic advice as a valid contributor to agency decision making.

Historic Role of Economics at EPA   The channels through which economic advice historically has reached the EPA administrator have been threefold: (1) passive applied economic analysis; (2) economic guidance, benefit studies, and computable general equilibrium modeling; and (3) economic policy advising (Stavins, 2000). The RIAs and Regulatory Flexibility Analyses mandated by

---

7. Although not discussed in this chapter, state, regional, and international use of market-based environmental policy instruments also increased in the 1990s (Stavins, forthcoming).

8. The term "major environmental statutes" in this chapter refers to the following federal laws (and all amendments thereto): the Clean Air Act (CAA); Federal Water Pollution Control Act (Clean Water Act, CWA); Toxic Substances Control Act (TSCA); Federal Insecticide, Fungicide, and Rodenticide Act (FIFRA); Comprehensive Environmental Response, Compensation, and Liability Act (CERCLA); Resource Conservation and Recovery Act (RCRA); and Safe Drinking Water Act (SDWA). The major statutes alternately "forbid, inhibit, tolerate, allow, invite, or require the use of economic analysis in environmental decision making" (Morgenstern, 1997b). For a thorough and early assessment of EO 12291, see V. Smith (1984). For a broader treatment of the role of economic analysis in environmental regulation, see Fraas (1991).

Table 9.1
Evolution of Organization of Economic Analysis at EPA

Applicable Years	Organizational Location of Core Economics Staff at EPA
1980–83	Benefits Staff, Office of Policy Evaluation, Office of Policy and Resource Management
1983–87	Benefits Branch, Office of Policy Analysis, Office of Policy, Planning, and Evaluation
1987–90	Economic Analysis Branch, Office of Policy Analysis, Office of Policy, Planning, and Evaluation
1990–96	Economic Analysis and Research Branch, Office of Policy Analysis, Office of Policy, Planning, and Evaluation
1996–99	Economy and Environment Division, Office of Economy and Environment, Office of Policy, Planning, and Evaluation
1999–2000	Economic and Policy Analysis Division and Economy and Environment Division, Office of Economy and Environment, Office of Policy and Reinvention
2000–01	National Center for Environmental Economics, Office of Policy, Economics, and Innovation

Source: U.S. Environmental Protection Agency, National Center for Environmental Economics World Wide Web site, available at http://www.epa.gov/economics/.

executive orders and legislation throughout the 1980s and 1990s fall within the first category, passive applied analysis. EPA routinely performs benefit-cost analyses of major rules, and limits most of its economic analyses to cost-effectiveness and distributional analyses, as required by statute. The second category includes studies and advice generated by the core economics staff at EPA, which has been housed in an assortment of administrative entities since 1980, as summarized in Table 9.1. The third category includes advising by economists internal and external to the agency.

The background against which economic advice generated through these channels is evaluated is the culture of EPA, which historically has found the goal of economic efficiency tolerable, at best (Morgenstern, 1997b). Aversion to economic analysis within EPA is not surprising, given the agency mandate to protect human health and the environment through the administration of the major statutes; the constraints on economic analysis inherent to many of those statutes; and the relatively thin representation of economists within most EPA offices, particularly at the level of the Senior Executive Service.[9] Despite their

---

9. See Morgenstern (1997b). Of the 196 EPA Senior Executive Service members with graduate degrees in 1996, only four (2 percent) held graduate economics degrees; in contrast, almost one-third held law degrees, and one-fifth held graduate science degrees. Between 1996 and 2000, the share of EPA employees with graduate degrees who held either masters or doctoral degrees in economics increased by 15 percent, compared to a 7.7 percent overall increase in EPA employees with graduate degrees (Morgenstern, 2000).

minority status, relative to lawyers, scientists, and engineers, EPA employs more economists working on environmental issues than any other single institution (Morgenstern, 1997b). The extent to which economic analysis influences regulatory policy, however, depends critically on agency culture and on the extent to which the administrator and others are receptive to such analysis. Without support within the agency, economic analysis moving through the channels described will have little effect.

Changes in the Role of Economics at EPA During the 1990s   Significant changes in the role of economics at EPA, both in terms of channels of influence and the culture of acceptance, occurred during the 1990s: (1) during the Clinton years, economics had to "fight harder for its place at the table" than it had at EPA during the prior Bush administration; and (2) when it did have a place at the table, economic analysis was more likely to be focused on increasing the cost effectiveness of regulations than on weighing benefits against costs (Morgenstern, 1997b; Nichols, 1997).

Given the increase in requirements for and attention to benefit-cost analysis by Congress during the 1990s, EPA probably was required to perform more (passive) applied economic analysis during the 1990s than at any other time in its 30-year history. While these analyses satisfied internal and external requirements, they were not done to provide economic information to key agency decision-makers.

The organizational influence (and location) of the "economics policy shop" at EPA changed significantly during the Clinton years. When the Clinton administration took office in 1992, the core economics staff at EPA was located within the Office of Policy, Planning, and Evaluation (OPPE), as it had been since at least 1980. OPPE reviewed all draft regulations and provided the administrator with an independent economic perspective, which could differ significantly from program office analyses.[10] Within weeks of the Clinton inauguration, however, this role was eliminated, and economic analyses were rarely forwarded to Administrator Carol Browner during her eight-year tenure. The substantive role of economic analysis in the development and review of EPA regulations was abandoned by the agency in 1995, when the program offices, rather than the administrator, became the "clients" of these analyses (Morgenstern, 2000). In 1999, OPPE was eliminated, shifting the core economics staff to the new Office of Policy and Reinvention.

Policy advising by economists external to the agency was active during the 1990s. Deputy Administrator Fred Hansen worked closely with the Envi-

---

10. This practice was especially active under Administrator William Reilly, 1988–92, who regularly sought the opinion of the economics staff.

ronmental Economics Advisory Committee (EEAC) within EPA's Science Advisory Board to develop an aggressive mission statement for EEAC that focused on giving expert advice on broad issues of importance to the agency, rather than simply carrying out end-of-pipe reviews of agency RIAs.[11] Projects executed by the EEAC during the 1990s included (1) the first comprehensive review and revision in 15 years of EPA's Economic Analysis Guidelines; (2) a thorough review of EPA's methodology for valuing reductions in cancer-induced mortality; and (3) the reinstatement of the Pollution Abatement Cost and Expenditure survey. External economists also served on the Advisory Council on Clean Air Act Compliance, required under the 1990 Clean Air Act (CAA) amendments to provide technical and economic input on EPA's benefit-cost analyses of CAA impacts. The council had a major impact on the identification of key research issues and the treatment of uncertainty in these analyses (Morgenstern, 2000).

While most of the channels for economic policy analysis at EPA remained fairly active during the 1990s, the "cultural acceptance" of economic analysis of environmental regulations was almost certainly lowered (Morgenstern, 1997b). Administrator Browner was skeptical, indeed dismissive of economics as an appropriate framework for environmental decisions, a view which is by no means unique to environmental policy-makers and advocates. In her remarks in honor of the 30th anniversary of the first Earth Day, she commented on the establishment of the EPA and recalled that "the nation committed itself to the task of eliminating pollution, to restoring our lands and waters to their uses, and to protecting public health without regard to cost. Let me repeat those last four words—*without regard to cost*" (Browner, 2000). The administrator went on to refer to the introduction of benefit-cost analysis into EPA regulations intended to protect public health as "poisoning the well".[12] The reduction in acceptance of economic analysis at EPA was likely influenced by Vice President Albert Gore, who was known to be deeply skeptical about the application of benefit-cost analysis to environmental policy (Gore, 1992).[13]

---

11. The Environmental Economics Advisory Committee was established by the Science Advisory Board in 1990.

12. Although she referred to benefit-cost analysis, what Administrator Browner described was a strict benefit-cost test that would disallow rules unless quantified benefits outweighed costs. The influence of Administrator Browner's views was particularly great, given her eight-year tenure in the position. The next-longest-serving EPA administrators, William Reilly and Lee Thomas, each served four years.

13. While the vice president was understood to have a strong influence over environmental policy in the Clinton White House, his influence was frequently exercised behind the scenes, with his views represented by Katie McGinty, director of the Council on Environmental Quality (CEQ) from 1993 to 1998.

Thus, while requirements for regulatory benefit-cost analysis expanded in the 1990s, policy-makers' receptiveness to benefit-cost analysis at EPA declined significantly.

Although efficiency analysis was more controversial under Clinton's EPA than under the earlier Bush administration, EPA's interest in cost effectiveness (in particular, the use of market-based instruments) and distributional analysis continued to grow. In the same Earth Day speech that was critical of benefit-cost analysis, Administrator Browner took pride in highlighting EPA's cost-effective regulatory measures and flexible approaches to pollution reduction (Browner, 2000).

EPA and Reinventing Government   EPA's Office of Reinvention was created in 1997, although efforts to reform processes at EPA had been under way since the 1980s, when Administrator Lee Thomas asked the agency to manage its resources and activities to (1) account for relative risks, (2) recognize the cross-media nature of environmental problems, and (3) achieve measurable environmental results. Vice President Gore's National Performance Review Report and the Government Performance and Results Act of 1993 brought increased attention to these issues at EPA, and the agency launched the centerpiece of its "reinvention" program, the Common Sense Initiative (CSI) in 1994.[14]

Each of the CSI goals can be considered within the umbrella of cost effectiveness, but it is unclear whether the CSI improved the cost effectiveness of environmental regulation in the 1990s. The CSI engaged six major industries in dialogue with EPA with the purpose of reducing compliance costs, introducing flexibility into regulatory instruments (in particular, moving toward regulation by industry, rather than by pollutant), and reducing costly litigation through stakeholder participation.[15] But in 1997, two GAO reports found that too many CSI resources had been spent on process issues, and too few on substance and tangible results. In addition, progress had been limited by the inability of the individual industry work groups to reach consensus, especially on the most

14. Other organizations and institutions may also have played a role in EPA's focus on reinvention. A 1995 National Academy of Public Administration report suggested reforms at EPA, including better use of risk and cost information to rank priorities. In 1996, the Center for Strategic and International Studies launched "Enterprise for the Environment," an effort to build consensus for systematic environmental management reform. And the regulatory reform focus of the 104th Congress may also have prompted EPA to emphasize reform efforts, in part to forestall congressionally mandated changes (Copeland, 1996).

15. The participating industries were auto manufacturing, computers and electronics, iron and steel, metal finishing, petroleum refining, and printing.

important issues, and the effort lacked results-oriented measures to assess progress (U.S. General Accounting Office, 1997a, 1997b).

In 1995, Vice President Gore and Administrator Browner announced a set of 25 specific reinvention reforms at EPA, in addition to CSI. One of these new programs was Project XL ("Excellence and Leadership"), which set a goal of 50 pilot projects allowing regulated firms to propose alternatives to existing command-and-control regulations that would attain higher levels of pollution control at lower cost. The National Environmental Performance Partnership System sought to give states greater flexibility in achieving environmental goals by allowing them to convert some types of categorical federal grants into more flexible block grants. Criticisms of these and many other parts of EPA's reinvention program were similar to criticisms of CSI, but they included another important factor. The GAO report noted that EPA's effort could have only limited success in introducing cost-effective changes into processes like permitting and grant awards to the states, given that the major statutes regulate by environmental medium or by pollutant. Substantial progress would, therefore, depend on reform of the legislative framework for environmental protection, rather than process reforms within EPA. In addition, the GAO noted a lack of "buy in" among agency staff accustomed to traditional medium-by-medium regulations.[16] The GAO report also noted some confusion among stakeholders due to the large number of initiatives launched under the banner of reinvention (U.S. General Accounting Office, 1997a).[17]

Death and Resurrection of the PACE Survey While the 103rd and 104th Congresses were increasing the efficiency and cost-effectiveness analysis responsibilities of federal agencies, one vital source of information on the costs of environmental regulation was being disassembled. The U.S. Bureau of the Census conducted the annual Pollution Abatement Costs and Expenditures

---

16. Agency staff may not have been the only ones reluctant to "buy into" this shift in regulatory focus—the public and environmental organizations were nervous, as well. A report in the *Boston Globe* criticized the New England regional EPA office for embracing the national movement to "combine enforcement with 'compliance assistance,' a program whereby [EPA] tells companies what they should be doing and allows them to voluntarily fix pollution problems to avoid penalties." The journalist interviewed a number of EPA regional enforcement officials, who felt that the agency's new collaborative approach meant that it had "become subservient to business, sending a dangerous message to polluters that penalties can be avoided." See David Armstrong, "U.S. Lagging on Prosecutions," *Boston Globe*, November 16, 1999, p. A01.

17. Appendix I of the GAO's broad report on EPA reinvention efforts lists all reinvention programs—the list is almost three pages long (U.S. General Accounting Office, 1997a). Larger programs include the CSI, Project XL, permitting reform, and the National Environmental Performance Partnership System focused on EPA's relationship with the states.

(PACE) survey from 1979 to 1994 but suspended it in 1995 for budgetary reasons.

The PACE database comprised operating and capital expenditures on pollution abatement from all manufacturing plants with more than 20 employees, selected electric and gas utilities, and some petroleum companies. Despite questions about the survey's comprehensiveness and reliability, it had been the primary data source of its kind for industry, government, and the research community. EPA itself used PACE data in many RIAs and in broad efficiency and cost-effectiveness analyses, including the *Cost of Clean*, the Section 812 retrospective benefit-cost analysis of the Clean Air Act, and sector-specific studies.

In 1998, the EPA Science Advisory Board's Environmental Economics Advisory Committee (EEAC) urged that the PACE survey be reinstated. Two months later, Assistant Administrator for Policy, Planning, and Evaluation David Gardiner announced EPA's support for reinstating the PACE program and pledged significant funding to make it happen, citing EEAC's arguments and support as critical to the decision (Gardiner, 1999). With financial and technical support from EPA, the Bureau of the Census requested that OMB reinstate funds for PACE in February 2000, noting that the survey was "essential for monitoring impact of environmental programs on the U.S. economy and responsiveness to these programs" (U.S. Department of Commerce, 2000). The survey was reinstated, with revisions, after a five-year hiatus.

9.2.1.5 Role of Economists at Agencies Other Than EPA

Having described the rather diminished role of economics at EPA during the Clinton years, it is important to note that economists external to EPA, in particular within the Council of Economic Advisers (CEA) and the OMB, had considerable influence over environmental policy in the 1990s. Economists within the Treasury Department also had more influence on environmental issues than in the previous Bush administration. The extent to which economic thinking outside of EPA influenced environmental decision-making varied depending on the nature of the issue. For example, the White House economic agencies' fingerprints can be found on the administration's negotiating position on climate change, especially its strong advocacy for international emissions trading and other cost-effective elements, and on the natural resource management elements within the president's 1993 deficit-reduction plan. Economists outside EPA, similar to economists within the agency, had less influence over more traditional regulatory matters, however, such as the NAAQS for ozone and particulate matter. All of these are discussed in greater detail later in the chapter.

9.2.2   *Congressional Initiatives*

Environmental regulation emerged as a major target of the congressional regulatory reform effort of the 1990s. This development is not surprising, given that EPA is the source of most of the major rules subject to Regulatory Impact Analysis under the various benefit-cost executive orders, as measured by their estimated benefits and costs.[18] We discuss both comprehensive and specific regulatory reform proposals considered by the 103rd through 106th Congresses.

9.2.2.1   General Themes of Regulatory Reform Proposals

The 103rd Congress (1993–95), the Clinton administration's first legislative "partner," actively debated benefit-cost analysis and risk analysis as methods for informing environmental protection decisions (Blodgett, 1995; Lee, 1995). Three of the lightning rods for regulatory relief interests were "takings" issues or private property rights, unfunded mandates, and risk analysis, all of which are prominent aspects of environmental regulation (Lee, 1995). With Democratic majorities in both houses, none of the 103rd Congress's initiatives were enacted into law, or even offered for presidential signature.

The regulatory reform movement gained momentum when the members of the 104th Congress (1995–97) took their seats after the 1994 midterm election, in which the Republican Party gained control of both the Senate and the House of Representatives. Reform-oriented bills during 1995–96 included mandates for benefit-cost analysis, maximum likelihood risk assessments (rather than upper bounds), and regulatory process reforms (Viscusi, 1996). Under this last category, process reforms, Congress considered requiring regulatory agencies to (1) prepare special plans and analyses, (2) report to Congress on priority-setting and benefit-cost analysis, (3) submit rules for peer review by panels of scientific experts, and (4) submit rules for judicial review.

9.2.2.2   Comprehensive Regulatory Reform: The Contract with America

Most of the 104th Congress's comprehensive regulatory reform proposals either failed to pass both houses or were vetoed by President Clinton. The 1994 Contract with America's item 8, the "Job Creation and Wage Enhancement Act," did not pass as legislation. It would have made Reagan's Executive Order 12291 statutory, superseding the Clinton executive order—as well as the language in several other important statutes—and would have required that the

---

18. Fifty-four percent of the total annual regulatory benefits and 50 percent of the total annual regulatory costs identified by OMB in 1997 were attributed to environmental regulations (Dudley and Antonelli, 1997; U.S. Office of Management and Budget, 1997).

benefits of regulations outweigh their costs.[19] Although these components of the Contract with America did not become law, the contract itself was a major political event, symbolic of the shift in power in Congress and a consequential public debate over regulatory reform, in which benefit-cost analysis was a central issue.

9.2.2.3 Specific Regulatory Reform Proposals

The Small Business Regulatory Enforcement Fairness Act (SBREFA, Public Law 104–121) amended the 1980 Regulatory Flexibility Act. As one of the affected agencies, EPA must prepare a regulatory flexibility analysis of all rules with "significant economic impact" on a "substantial number" of small entities (businesses, nonprofits, and small government organizations). These analyses, which must be reviewed by Congress, examine the type and number of small entities potentially subject to the rule, record-keeping and compliance requirements, and significant regulatory alternatives. The statute does not require formal benefit-cost analysis beyond that already required by environmental regulations and executive order; rather, it requires that EPA submit to Congress "a complete copy of the benefit-cost analysis of the rule, if any," along with the regulatory flexibility analysis. From an economic efficiency perspective, the focus on small entities makes little, if any sense, and the SBREFA requirements were viewed by EPA staff as little more than a time-consuming diversion from more important analyses and other activities.

Embedded within SBREFA, but for the most part unrelated to its other provisions, was the Congressional Review Act, which established a process of congressional review and possible rejection of agency rules. Agencies must submit all new rules to the House and Senate leadership, in addition to the GAO. Within 15 days, GAO must provide a report on each major rule to the agency's authorizing committee, after which any member of Congress may introduce a "resolution of disapproval," which is treated as a bill in the House and somewhat differently in the Senate. Congress then has 60 session days in which to act on the measure; if the resolution of disapproval passes both

---

19. Item 8 also focused on the reduction of so-called "unfunded mandates," and on strengthening the Regulatory Flexibility Act of 1980, which resulted in the Small Business Regulatory Enforcement Fairness Act of 1996 and the Unfunded Mandates Reform Act of 1995. There were many other unsuccessful attempts at regulatory reform legislation during the 104th Congress, including H.R. 1022, Risk Assessment and Cost-Benefit Act of 1995; H.J.Res. 27 and 54, which proposed a constitutional amendment to ban unfunded mandates; H.R. 47, Regulatory Relief and Reform Act; and H.R. 122 to establish a Regulatory Sunset Commission. Detailed discussion of these is beyond the scope of this study. We mention them only to emphasize the scope and depth of the 104th Congress's focus on regulatory reform.

houses, it must be signed by the president in order to lead to rejection of the given rule.[20]

In 1995, the 104th Congress enacted the Unfunded Mandates Reform Act (Public Law 1044), which requires quantitative assessment of benefits and comparison of benefits to costs for all proposed and final rules, including environmental regulations, with an expected cost to state, local, and tribal governments, or to the private sector, greater than or equal to $100 million. In addition, the act mandates that agencies choose the least-cost regulatory alternative, or explain why the least-cost alternative was not chosen, and that they submit rules to the GAO, which reports to appropriate congressional committees on agency compliance with statutory and executive order requirements.

In late 1996, the 104th Congress attached a benefit-cost requirement to Section 645(a) of the Treasury, Postal Services, and General Government Appropriations Act of 1997 (Public Law 104–208).[21] The Office of Management and Budget would be required to submit to Congress a report estimating the "total annual costs and benefits of federal regulatory programs, including quantitative and non-quantitative measures." The legislation also required OMB to estimate individually the benefits and costs of rules with annual costs to the economy of $100 million or more. Importantly, OMB also was required to recommend the reform or elimination of any regulation that appeared to be inefficient. This reporting requirement has remained in place, and reports were submitted in each year, 1997 through 2000.[22] The requirement has further centralized regulatory oversight in the hands of OMB, which already had been charged with reviewing the RIAs required by executive orders since 1981.

Although the benefit-cost and cost-effectiveness legislation promulgated by the 104th Congress had a limited effect on agency rule-making, congressional regulatory reform efforts continued through the end of the Clinton administration. The 105th and 106th Congresses considered establishing further checks on agency regulation. The Regulatory Improvement Act of 1999 (also known as the Thompson-Levin bill) would have allowed courts to remand or invalidate rules formulated by an agency that fails to perform sufficient benefit-cost

---

20. The Congressional Review Act was the basis for the George W. Bush administration's overturning of the Occupational Safety and Health Administration's ergonomics rule in 2001. The CRA has not been used to reject any environmental regulations.

21. This provision was typically referred to as regulatory accounting.

22. The continuation of this provision was proposed by the Regulatory Right-to-Know Act of 1999 (S. 59). Introduced as H.R. 1074 in the House, the bill would have required much more stringent analysis by OMB: an annual accounting statement of total costs and benefits of federal regulations, including direct and indirect impacts on federal, state, local, and tribal government, the private sector, small business, wages, and economic growth.

analysis.[23] While this bill never became law, the 106th Congress did pass a major piece of regulatory reform legislation, the Truth in Regulating Act (TIRA), which was signed into law (Public Law 106–312) by President Clinton in October 2000. The TIRA established a three-year pilot project beginning in early 2001 in which GAO will review RIAs to evaluate agencies' benefit estimates, cost estimates, and analysis of alternative approaches, upon request by Congress.[24]

9.3 Economics and Specific Environmental Policies of the 1990s

One major challenge of summarizing the most important environmental policy developments of the 1990s from an economic perspective is that the number of environmental policies for which efficiency and cost-effectiveness analyses exist is relatively small. In addition, many important environmental policy developments may not be important economic developments, and vice versa. The specific policies we analyze are a mixture of the most important environmental developments and the most important applications of economic analysis and market-based instruments to environmental policy.

We consider Clinton era statutes and regulations that focused on specific environmental problems under five principal categories: congressional changes to individual environmental statutes (including the Safe Drinking Water Act amendments of 1996 and the Food Quality Protection Act of 1996); implementation of the Clean Air Act amendments of 1990 (including new national ambient air quality standards for ozone and particulates, SO_2 allowance trading, new air toxics regulation, and the regional NO_x trading program); expansion of information-based regulatory programs; natural resource policy initiatives; and global climate change initiatives.

9.3.1 Congressional Changes to Individual Environmental Statutes

In addition to their attempts at cross-cutting regulatory reform, the congresses of the Clinton years pursued efficiency and cost effectiveness within environmental statutes themselves.[25] In general, Congress was more successful during

---

23. The Regulatory Improvement Act was proposed as S. 981 in 1997 and carried on with the same title into 1998. It was introduced in various versions in both houses of Congress throughout 1997–99, and took on the Thompson-Levin moniker in May 1999. A similar bill was introduced in the House in late 1999, but without the judicial review mandate.

24. The initiation of GAO review under TIRA is contingent on appropriations. As of May 2001, funding had not been authorized.

25. During the 1990s, Congress also pursued reforms of nonenvironmental statutes that affect environmental regulation. For example, the Accountable Pipeline Safety and Partnership Act of 1996 (104th Congress) requires the secretary of transportation to issue pipeline safety regulations only

the 1990s at passing cross-cutting regulatory reform bills than it was at reforming individual environmental statutes, although important exceptions were the
1996 Safe Drinking Water Act (SDWA) amendments, and the partial reform of
pesticide permitting under the Federal Insecticide, Fungicide, and Rodenticide
Act (FIFRA) and the Federal Food, Drug, and Cosmetic Act (FFDCA). The
104th Congress also pursued efficiency-oriented reform of the Clean Water Act
through the reauthorization process, but the effort failed in the Senate. All
efforts to reform the Comprehensive Environmental Response, Compensation,
and Liability Act (CERCLA) failed, as did attempts to reform the Resource Conservation and Recovery Act (RCRA) and other statutes.

9.3.1.1 Safe Drinking Water Act Amendments of 1996

The 1996 SDWA Amendments (Public Law 104–182) include the most far-
reaching requirement for economic analysis in any environmental statute. The
amendments focus EPA regulatory efforts on contaminants that pose the greatest health risks by (1) requiring benefit-cost analysis of new rules, (2) removing
the mandate that EPA regulate 25 new contaminants every three years, (3)
allowing EPA to use cost information to adjust its "feasibility standards" for
water system reduction of contaminants, and (4) requiring the administrator
to balance risks among contaminants to minimize the overall risk of adverse
health effects (Tiemann, 1999). While the amendments require EPA to determine whether the benefits of each new drinking water maximum contaminant
level (MCL) regulation justify the costs, they also allow the agency to adopt more
stringent standards than those that maximize net benefits, explaining the reasons for not selecting the efficient standard.[26]

The decisions made on MCLs since the SDWA amendments have not placed
great weight on the results of required benefit-cost analyses. Two major rules
proposed since the 1996 amendments are those regulating allowable levels of
arsenic and radon in drinking water. The arsenic rule was finalized on January
22, 2001, but is under review by the George W. Bush administration, while
no final action was taken on radon.[27] EPA's benefit-cost analyses for the radon
and arsenic MCLs can be interpreted as indicating that monetized costs exceed

---

upon justification that benefits exceed costs (Blodgett, 1998). Discussion of these reforms is beyond
the scope of this study.

26. See Safe Drinking Water Act sec. 300g–1 (4) (C). The amendments do not allow old standards to
be subjected to an ex post benefit-cost analysis.

27. On March 20, 2001, EPA Administrator Christine Todd Whitman announced the agency's intention to withdraw the pending arsenic standard in order to seek independent reviews of both the
science behind the standard and the estimates of the benefits and costs of implementing the rule. In
May 2001 the administrator announced that the National Academy of Sciences will review a range
of possible arsenic standards, and that the effective date of the standard will be postponed until
February 2002.

monetized benefits for both rules (by more than $50 million annually for radon and $30 million annually for arsenic). The agency maintained, however, that benefits of both rules justify their costs when unquantified benefits are included (Burnett and Hahn, 2001).[28] Although this claim may be true, the fact that both the radon and arsenic rules result in net monetized costs has caused some to be skeptical of EPA's commitment to applying the SDWA amendments' benefit-cost requirement. Moreover, these analyses did not consider cost-effective alternatives, such as limiting compliance to large public drinking water systems.

There will be more rule-makings under the SDWA over the next decade—in 1998 EPA published a list of 50 chemical and ten microbiological contaminants that will be investigated for possible regulation. The impact of the SDWA amendments' requirement for benefit-cost analysis in deciding both which drinking water contaminants to regulate and how to regulate them will be an important area for further research.

9.3.1.2 Food Quality Protection Act of 1996

The Food Quality Protection Act of 1996 (Public Law 104–170) amends both FIFRA and the FFDCA, removing pesticide residues on processed food from the group of Delaney "zero-risk standard" substances. The Delaney standard has long been a target of economic criticism. While the standard continues to apply to nonpesticide food additives, the Food Quality Protection Act of 1996 eliminated the distinction between pesticide residues on raw foods (which had been regulated under FFDCA section 408) and processed foods (which had been regulated under FFDCA section 409—the Delaney Clause). The act also mandates that EPA coordinate pesticide regulation under FIFRA and FFDCA.[29]

9.3.1.3 Debates over Changes to Superfund and the Clean Water Act

Two of the environmental statutes most frequently criticized on efficiency and cost-effectiveness grounds—Superfund and the Clean Water Act (CWA)—remained relatively untouched by Congress in the 1990s, despite its focus on regulatory reform. Superfund's critics have focused on the low benefits per dollar spent (Viscusi, 1992; Breyer, 1993; Hamilton and Viscusi, 1999). Reauthoriza-

---

28. EPA's cost and benefit figures for these rules were presented as annualized 1999 dollar values using a 7 percent discount rate. The AEI-Brookings Joint Center for Regulatory Analysis performed its own benefit-cost analysis of the arsenic rule, which concluded that the cost per life saved by the rule would not be less than $6.6 million, and that in the most likely scenario, cost per life saved would be approximately $67 million. See Burnett and Hahn (2001).

29. For example, once a pesticide registration is canceled under FIFRA, the food-use tolerance under FFDCA must be revoked within 180 days, rather than the average six-year time frame noted in a 1994 GAO report (Schierow, 1996; U.S. General Accounting Office, 1994).

tion and reform were considered during the 105th Congress, but no legislation was passed. Rather than efficiency or cost effectiveness, liability issues and the financing of Superfund were at the center of legislative discussion of this statute in the late 1990s. The taxes that support the Superfund trust fund (primarily excise taxes on petroleum and specified chemical feedstocks and a corporate environmental income tax) expired in 1995 and have not been reinstated.[30]

During the 104th Congress, the House passed a comprehensive Clean Water Act reauthorization (H.R. 961) that would have been more flexible and less prescriptive than the current statute, but the Senate did not take up the bill.[31] No reauthorization legislation was considered in the 105th or 106th Congress, but the legislature did oppose nonpoint-source water pollution control initiatives under Section 303(d).

Section 303(d) of the Clean Water Act requires states to establish a total maximum daily load (TMDL), something like a "pollution budget," for each water body that does not meet ambient water quality standards for its designated use, despite point-source pollution control.[32] Until recently, EPA did little to enforce this part of the CWA, but state courts ordered the development of TMDLs in the 1990s in response to lawsuits by environmental groups.[33]

EPA convened a federal advisory committee to develop a consistent national TMDL program in 1996, proposed regulations to clarify and strengthen the TMDL program in August 1999, and issued a final rule in July 2000. The proposed and final rule generated controversy over the costs of state implementation of TMDLs and about their impact on agriculture and forestry. As a result, the 104th Congress attached a rider to an appropriations bill that prevents EPA from spending funds to implement the rule in FY2000 and FY2001. Should states be required to fully enforce TMDLs, the economic implications are likely to be very large—the most current list of impaired waters under Section 303(d), which would be subject to TMDL enforcement, includes almost 22,000 water bodies.

---

30. The revenues now flowing into the trust fund come from so-called potentially responsible parties, interest on the fund's investments, fines, and penalties. House Ways and Means Chairman Bill Archer (R-TX) has made it known that no reinstatement of the Superfund taxes will be considered without major reforms of the statute's liability provisions and other features. See Reisch (2000).

31. The 103rd Congress had considered similar legislation (H.R. 3948, S. 2093), but no floor action on CWA reauthorization was taken in either house.

32. The TMDL should be set at a level necessary to attain the applicable water quality standard for the water body's designated use. Designated uses include recreational use, public water supply, and industrial water supply, for example, and each designated use has an applicable water quality standard.

33. Through October 2000, environmental groups had filed 40 legal actions in 38 states. EPA is under court order or consent decree in many states to ensure that TMDLs are established either by the state or by EPA itself (U.S. Environmental Protection Agency, Office of Water, 2000).

Table 9.2
EPA Ranking of Sources Contributing to Water Quality Impairment, 1996

Rank	Rivers	Lakes	Estuaries
1	Agriculture	Agriculture	Industrial discharges
2	Municipal point sources	Unspecified nonpoint sources	Urban runoff/storm sewers
3	Hydrologic modification	Atmospheric deposition	Municipal point sources
4	Habitat modification	Urban runoff/storm sewers	Upstream sources
5	Resource extraction	Municipal point sources	Agriculture

Source: U.S. Environmental Protection Agency (1996), quoted in Boyd (2000).

The TMDL program takes an ambient approach to water quality regulation and emphasizes watershed-level water quality trading over the traditional technology standards promulgated under the CWA's National Pollutant Discharge Elimination System permits. Both of these would be welcome changes to traditional water quality regulation from an economic perspective, but it is very difficult to link particular sources to ambient water quality. In addition, attaining the TMDL generally involves regulating nonpoint-source pollution, given that point-source permitting has been insufficient to achieve compliance with water quality standards. Identification of the sources and pathways of pollution in compiling a TMDL requires a "kind of holistic accounting exercise" in which all permitted sources and land uses within a waterbody's drainage area are inventoried and allocated portions of the pollution budget (Boyd, 2000).[34] In addition, while the theoretical economic gains from point-nonpoint-source water quality trading could be substantial, the number of actual trades under the 15 current and past federal and state water quality trading programs has been negligible (Boyd, 2000; Stavins, forthcoming).

From a cost-effectiveness standpoint, the focus on nonpoint sources is theoretically sound; there is no reason, ex ante, to impose further restrictions on point sources merely because the legal, technical, and institutional bases for regulating nonpoint sources are murky. Recognition is widespread that nonpoint sources of pollution are of greater concern for most of the nation's impaired water bodies than permitted point sources from which reductions have been achieved over 25 years (see Table 9.2). The potentially high costs of establishing, monitoring, and enforcing pollution budgets for nonpoint sources, however, may offset any gains that would be achieved from bringing the marginal abatement costs of point and nonpoint sources into closer alignment.

---

34. In addition, data sources and modeling techniques can be standardized only to a very small degree, since each listed water body (lakes, river segments, ponds, estuaries) has unique hydrology, transport pathways, pollutant sources, weather patterns, etc. See Boyd (2000).

9.3.2 Implementation of the 1990 Clean Air Act Amendments

A substantial portion of air quality regulation during the 1990s had to do with implementation of the Clean Air Act Amendments of 1990. The 1990 amendments addressed efficiency and cost effectiveness of air quality regulations in a variety of ways.[35] First, the amendments required a retrospective benefit-cost analysis of the 1970 CAA and its 1977 amendments, and biennial prospective analyses of the 1990 amendments themselves. The results of these benefit-cost analyses are discussed in section 9.4.3.1, where we consider the efficiency of the major environmental statutes.

In addition, although they did not allow for the consideration of costs in setting ambient standards, the amendments occasionally provided the basis for implementation of cost-effective regulation. For example, under Title IV of the amendments, Congress directed EPA not to mandate specific pollution control technologies for sulfur dioxide (SO_2) emissions from power plants, while it required the agency to oversee SO_2 emissions reduction from these sources by nearly 50 percent over 10 years. The result was the SO_2 permit trading system. Not all regulations promulgated under the 1990 CAA amendments were equally as cost effective, however. The amendments explicitly required EPA to issue technology standards for 188 toxic air pollutants, perhaps one of the most expensive and least cost-effective components of the CAA (Portney, 1990). Highlights of the implementation of the 1990 CAA amendments, from an economic perspective, are discussed in the following subsections.

9.3.2.1 Use of Market-Based Instruments in Clean Air Act Amendment Implementation

EPA provided averaging, banking, and trading opportunities for most of the new standards promulgated under the direction of the 1990 CAA amendments, including those aimed at mobile sources. EPA's implementation of the reformulated gasoline provisions of Title II of the amendments allowed refinery-level trading of oxygen, aromatics, and benzene content.[36] Title II also authorized EPA to regulate particulate matter, nitrogen oxide (NO_x), and other emissions from heavy-duty trucks. The resulting regulations were promulgated at the ve-

---

35. However, the judiciary in the 1990s (and subsequently) upheld CAA statutory provisions preventing EPA from taking costs into account when setting the National Ambient Air Quality Standards; see U.S. Supreme Court (2001). The 2001 decision regarding the National Ambient Air Quality Standards is discussed further in section 9.3.2.4.

36. The initial guidance for the reformulated gasoline trading programs was issued in October 1992, during the Bush administration. Trading at the refinery level has been very active (U.S. Environmental Protection Agency, 2001a).

hicle engine–manufacturing level and allow averaging, banking, and trading.[37] The Tier 2 emissions standards for cars and light-duty trucks, issued in February 2000, allow vehicle manufacturers to average NO_x emissions throughout their fleets to meet the new national tailpipe standards. They also allow refiners and gasoline importers to average, bank, and trade gasoline sulfur content to meet new Tier 2 standards.[38]

With respect to stationary sources, the regional NO_x cap-and-trade program in the Northeast is another significant market-based policy instrument developed and implemented under the aegis of the 1990 Clean Air Act Amendments. Although the SO_2 trading program was created under the Bush administration, implementation of Phase I and Phase II occurred during the 1990s and is one of the world's most frequently studied market-based instruments for environmental policy. These two programs are described in the following subsections, as are two significant rule-makings that have been more heavily criticized from an economic perspective: the revised ambient air quality standards for ozone and particulate matter, and new regulations on toxic air pollutants.

9.3.2.2 Sulfur Dioxide Trading Phase I and Phase II

The tradable permit system that regulates SO_2 emissions, the primary precursor of acid rain, was established under Title IV of the Clean Air Act Amendments of 1990. The system is intended to reduce SO_2 and NO_x emissions from 1980 levels by 10 million tons and 2 million tons, respectively.[39] The first phase of SO_2 emissions reductions was started in 1995, with a second phase of reduction initiated in the year 2000.[40]

A robust market of bilateral SO_2 permit trading emerged in the 1990s, resulting in cost savings on the order of $1 billion annually, compared with the costs under some command-and-control regulatory alternatives (Carlson et al., 2000). Although the program had low levels of trading in its early years (Burtraw, 1996), trading levels increased significantly over time (Schmalensee et al., 1998; Stavins, 1998; Burtraw and Mansur, 1999).

---

37. While a great deal of averaging and banking has taken place, only one trade was completed through 2000 (U.S. Environmental Protection Agency, 2001a).

38. The banking and trading allowances under the Tier 2 standard are limited. The average sulfur content cap drops annually between 2004 and 2006, and credits produced within that time frame have a limited life, while credits produced after the introduction of the strictest standard (2006) have unlimited life.

39. For a description of the legislation, see Ferrall (1991).

40. In Phase I individual emissions limits were assigned to the 263 most SO_2-emissions-intensive generating units at 110 plants operated by 61 electric utilities, and located largely at coal-fired power plants east of the Mississippi River. Under Phase II of the program, beginning January 1, 2000, almost all electric-power-generating units were brought within the system.

Table 9.3
Benefits and Costs, Revised NAAQS for Ozone and Particulate Matter

	Annual Monetized Benefits	Annual Monetized Costs
Ozone	$2.0 billion to $11.2 billion	$12.7 billion
Particulate matter	$26.4 billion to $145 billion	$48.8 billion

Source: U.S. Office of Management and Budget (1998), reporting EPA estimates from Regulatory Impact Analyses. EPA estimates were in constant 1990 dollars; those reported here are 2000 dollars. Cost and benefit estimates assume full attainment.

9.3.2.3   Regional NO_x Budget Program in the Northeast

Under EPA guidance, 12 northeastern states and the District of Columbia implemented a regional NO_x cap-and-trade system in 1999 to reduce compliance costs associated with the Ozone Transport Commission (OTC) regulations of the 1990 CAA Amendments.[41] Required reductions are based on targets established by the OTC and include emissions reductions by large stationary sources. The program is known as the Northeast Ozone Transport Region (Farrell, Carter, and Raufer, 1999).

EPA distributes NO_x allowances to each state, and states then allocate allowances to sources in their jurisdictions. Each source receives allowances equal to its restricted percentage of 1990 emissions, and sources must turn in one allowance for each ton of NO_x emitted over the ozone season. Sources may buy, sell, and bank allowances. Potential compliance cost savings of 40 to 47 percent have been estimated for the period 1999–2003, compared to a base case of continued command-and-control regulation without trading or banking (Farrell, Carter, and Raufer, 1999).

9.3.2.4   National Ambient Air Quality Standards
for Ozone and Particulate Matter

EPA issued new, stricter National Ambient Air Quality Standards (NAAQS) for ozone and particulate matter in July 1997. The revised standards were immediately controversial; both the decision to tighten the standards and the quality of the research used to support the new standards came under fire. Table 9.3 lists EPA's estimated monetized benefits and costs for the revised ozone and particulate matter NAAQS. EPA's cost estimates for the ozone standard were singled out for criticism; some analysts found them to be too low by a considerable margin (Shogren, 1998; Lutter, 1999).

The regulated community challenged the new NAAQS in the courts, and the case reached the U.S. Supreme Court in October 2000. Under the Clean Air Act,

---

41. Seven OTC states have also implemented state-level NO_x trading programs: New Jersey, Connecticut, Delaware, New York, Massachusetts, New Hampshire, and Maine (Solomon, 1999).

EPA is required to set standards for these pollutants at levels that will "protect public health with an adequate margin of safety," a provision that had been interpreted over the years by the judiciary as requiring that cost considerations be ignored when setting the standards. A group of academic economists and the AEI-Brookings Joint Center for Regulatory Studies filed a brief *amici curiae* in the Supreme Court, suggesting that benefit-cost analysis should be considered in the setting of ambient air quality standards, to the extent permitted by law (AEI-Brookings Joint Center et al., 2000). But the Supreme Court ruled unanimously in February 2001 that the CAA does *not* allow EPA to consider costs in setting NAAQS for the criteria pollutants, and that the statute's mandate that the NAAQS protect the public health with "an adequate margin of safety" allows an acceptable scope of discretion to EPA. The Court acknowledged that EPA and the states could continue to take costs into account in implementing the standards, which may serve as an impetus for cost-effective policy instruments.[42]

Given that monetized costs appear to outweigh monetized benefits in the case of the new ozone standard, EPA has been under pressure to revise the standard despite the Court's decision on cost consideration.[43] The situation is different for particulate matter, where monetized benefits appear to outweigh monetized costs. In any case, the NAAQS represent a majority of all economic effects of environmental policy changes during the 1990s. Should the courts continue to uphold the standards and should the statutes preventing cost considerations remain unchanged, the stricter NAAQS for ozone and particulate matter may be one of the Clinton administration's most enduring environmental legacies, in terms of both potential benefits and potential costs.[44]

9.3.2.5 Maximum Available Control Technology for Air Toxics

The air toxics regulations necessitated under the 1990 CAA amendments could be the least cost-effective component of the Clean Air Act. The amendments mandated that EPA issue standards for 188 toxic air pollutants, substances that

---

42. The Supreme Court decision was supported by EPA Administrator Christine Todd Whitman: "Congress delegated to EPA the standard-setting function, and EPA carried it out appropriately" (U.S. Environmental Protection Agency, 2001b).

43. EPA has agreed to reconsider its analysis of ozone NAAQS benefits in at least one respect; the agency's initial analysis did not consider the possible damages associated with *decreases* in ground-level ozone, which lead to increases in some ultraviolet radiation (UV-B) exposure. These damages, which include increases in skin cancer and cataracts, may be comparable to the benefits associated with reductions in ground-level ozone (Lutter and Wolz, 1997).

44. It remains to be seen whether some urban areas will be able to comply with the new ozone standards. One analyst estimates that the costs to Los Angeles of meeting the ozone standard in 2010 will be about $15 billion in constant 2000 dollars, assuming a 5 percent decrease in current abatement costs due to technological change (Lutter, 1999).

are less common than the criteria pollutants for which NAAQS are promulgated, but nonetheless might pose threats to human health. Like the NAAQS, the statute's treatment of toxic air pollutants requires EPA to set standards so that resulting concentrations provide an "ample margin of safety" against human health effects. Unlike in the case of the NAAQS, however, the EPA administrator is directed to require the maximum degree of emissions reduction achievable, taking costs into consideration.

Although EPA is allowed to take costs into account when determining standards for hazardous air pollutants, the type of regulation required is a technology standard—Maximum Achievable Control Technology (MACT)—not a market-based approach. From 1992 through August 2000, EPA issued technology standards for 45 of these substances, covering 82 categories of industrial sources. While there are no estimates of the total monetized costs and benefits of this new set of technology standards for hazardous air pollutants, one analyst in 1990 estimated that when fully implemented, compliance costs would range from $7.9 billion to $13.2 billion per year, and benefits would range from $0 to $5.3 billion per year (Portney, 1990).[45] The lower bound of zero on potential benefits is indicative of the considerable uncertainty over risks posed by these pollutants to human health. Some analysts have been particularly critical of EPA's very conservative estimates of risks to human health from air toxics in its promulgation of standards (Stroup, 2000; Gray and Graham, 1991).

9.3.3 Expansion of Information Programs

EPA increased its use of information disclosure regulations, one form of market-based instrument for environmental policy, during the 1990s. The Toxics Release Inventory (TRI) was initiated in 1988 under the Emergency Planning and Community Right-to-Know Act, Section 313, and requires firms to report on use, storage, and release of hazardous chemicals. A 1993 Clinton executive order required TRI reporting by federal facilities. In 1994, EPA added 286 new chemicals to the list requiring TRI reporting, nearly an 80 percent increase in the number of listed chemicals. In 1999, EPA lowered reporting thresholds for many persistent bioaccumulative toxic chemicals and added more of these chemicals to the TRI list.[46] The 104th Congress considered but

---

45. These figures were Portney's "educated guess" in 1990, based on George H. W. Bush administration estimates and those of a 1990 consulting firm study. We have converted them to 2000 dollars, assuming that they were originally stated in 1990 dollars. See Portney (1990).

46. The EPA under Clinton also continued the 33/50 program, started under the Bush administration, which engaged TRI-reporting industries in achieving voluntary accelerated emissions reduction targets in exchange for public "certification" and its associated goodwill.

did not enact legislation that would have restricted EPA's ability to require TRI reporting.[47]

Releases reported under TRI declined by 45 percent from 1988 to 1998, but it is unclear how much, if any, of that reduction represents true emissions reductions and whether such reductions can be attributed to the policy itself. There is some evidence that publicly available information about firms' TRI emissions, either in absolute terms or relative to some benchmarks, negatively affects stock prices (Hamilton, 1995; Konar and Cohen, 1997; Khanna et al., 1998). Other possible avenues through which the TRI may influence emissions are green consumerism, redirection of firms' attention toward measures that increase environmental performance while saving costs, and community pressure, but there is currently little solid evidence that any of these forces are at work with respect to the TRI (Snyder, 2001).

In addition to the Toxics Release Inventory, EPA also focused on establishing new and expanding other existing information programs during the 1990s. In 1997, EPA expanded the existing Energy Star Buildings program, consolidating it with the newer Green Lights program. In 1998 the agency began requiring public water systems to issue annual Drinking Water Consumer Confidence Reports. In 2000 it posted automobile "pollution rankings" on the EPA web site, ranking vehicles based on hydrocarbon and NO_x tailpipe emissions. While these programs could, in theory, be cost-effective ways to reach environmental objectives, we cannot conclude from existing empirical evidence whether they are responsible for any portion of the trends in air and water quality in the 1990s. Not surprisingly, given the lack of evidence regarding the benefits of these programs, no formal benefit-cost analyses of TRI or any of the other information disclosure programs have been conducted.

9.3.4 Natural Resource Policy

From an economic perspective, five aspects of natural resource policy during the Clinton years stand out: the natural resource subsidy reductions included within the administration's 1993 economic stimulus and deficit-reduction proposal; the shift in priorities of the U.S. Forest Service; President Clinton's designation of monument status for almost 6 million acres of federal public lands under the 1906 Antiquities Act; changes to federal wetlands policy and the

---

47. The Clinton administration announced another expansion of TRI on January 17, 2001, considerably lowering the threshold for reporting lead emissions. The previous standard required reporting by facilities that manufacture or process more than 25,000 pounds of lead annually, or that use more than 10,000 pounds annually. The new standard requires reporting by any facility that manufactures, processes, or uses more than 100 pounds annually. The Bush administration announced its intention to uphold the new threshold on April 17, 2001.

Endangered Species Act; and attempts to introduce natural resource capital and
environmental quality into the national income and product accounts.[48]

9.3.4.1   Natural Resources and the 1993 Clinton Budget Proposal

The administration proposed a variety of policies related to natural resource
subsidy reduction within its 1993 economic stimulus and deficit reduction proposal. First, it proposed increasing the baseline federal grazing fee on public
lands by almost 200 percent, resulting in a Senate filibuster on FY1994 Interior
appropriations during the 103rd Congress. The baseline federal grazing fee had
been calculated at only 56 to 83 percent of federal costs per animal unit month
in 1990 and was a much smaller percentage (perhaps 18 to 40 percent) of private market rates (Cody, 1996). In theory, below-market fees for grazing livestock on public lands cause economic overgrazing. In practice, low fees have
also been criticized from a budgetary perspective, since current fees do not cover
the costs of federal public range management.[49]

Similarly, below-cost timber sales from federal lands theoretically lead to
logging at greater-than-efficient rates. The administration's 1993 proposal sought
to phase out below-cost timber sales from federal forests. By U.S. Forest Service
(USFS) estimates, 77 of the 120 national forests showed net losses from timber
sales over the period FY1989–FY1993, and 60 reported losses in every year over
this period. The plan to reduce below-cost sales was eliminated from Clinton's
final budget proposal, however, and a USFS draft plan to phase out below-cost
sales on one-half of forest service lands over four years was not adopted by the
administration.

The 1993 deficit-reduction plan also included a British thermal unit (Btu) tax,
one of the first and most visible environmental initiatives of the Clinton presidency.[50] The proposal, which would have taxed essentially all fuels, faced stiff

---

48. Land use change emerged as an important issue during the 1990s and received substantial rhetorical attention from President Clinton and, in particular, Vice President Gore. While initiatives
under this umbrella term could be considered as natural resource policy, most of the policies
designed to address land use change, including those promoting "smart growth," "livable communities," and limiting "urban sprawl" were related to transportation policy and other areas beyond the scope of this chapter. Land use change is, therefore, omitted from our discussion.

49. The baseline grazing fee for federal lands in 1990 was $1.81 per animal unit month (AUM),
while the various livestock grazing programs' cost to government ranged from $2.18 to $3.24 per
AUM. The fair market value of grazing on federal land was last updated in 1986, and ranged from
$4.68 to $10.26 per AUM for cattle and horses, varying by region (Cody, 1996). (These figures have
not been converted to constant dollars.) The administration continued to lobby for fee increases,
and the 104th Congress established a new fee formula that resulted in a small increase in the baseline fee, still many times lower than the average private market rate.

50. The tax would have been imposed on coal, natural gas, liquid petroleum gases, nuclear electricity, hydroelectricity, and all imported electricity (almost 3 cents per million Btu); a higher tax
(about 6 cents per million Btu) would have been imposed on refined petroleum products.

opposition in the first session of the 103rd Congress, but it narrowly passed the House. Recognizing that the proposal did not have enough votes in the Senate, the administration removed the Btu tax from its budget proposal.[51] The administration proposed another energy tax in 1997 as part of its climate-change strategy, but faced similar opposition.

The administration's experience with the Btu tax merits additional discussion. Numerous CEA economists and staff note that this experience constrained their future input to subsequent discussions regarding alternative environmental policy instruments in the contexts of climate change and other issues. While the receptivity of the president, EPA officials, and others to tradable permit systems remained strong, the word "tax" was, after the Btu tax experience, forbidden to appear within administration memos and other public documents; taxes were never again seriously considered as potential environmental policy instruments during the Clinton years.

The administration's focus on natural resource policy in the 1993 budget proposal also included introduction of royalties for hardrock mining on public lands governed under the 1872 General Mining Law, and increased fees for recreational use of federal public lands (U.S. Council of Economic Advisers, 1997).[52] Congress opposed all the natural resource initiatives in the 1993 Clinton proposal, with one exception—the 104th Congress established a framework for user fee demonstration projects within the National Park Service (Public Law 104–134).[53]

9.3.4.2　U.S. Forest Service Changes

While the administration's proposed phasedown of below-cost timber sales failed, the Forest Service under Clinton underwent a substantial shift in priorities, emphasizing resource protection over timber production and extraction. In two speeches delivered in 1998 and 1999, USFS Chief Mike Dombeck summed up these changes in the agency's "Natural Resource Agenda for the 21st Century," emphasizing (1) watershed protection, (2) sustainable ecosystem manage-

---

51. The Senate later passed a much watered-down Transportation Fuels Tax in 1993, with revenues flowing to the general fund. This was a retail tax on gasoline of less than 5 cents per gallon, paid by consumers.

52. The administration also supported electricity deregulation and agricultural subsidy reduction, but those initiatives are beyond the scope of this chapter.

53. During the 1990s, Congress also opposed the application of market incentives to fisheries management. The Sustainable Fisheries Act of 1996 (Public Law 104–297) amended the Magnuson-Stevens Fishery Conservation and Management Act, imposing a four-year moratorium on new individual tradable quota programs among the nation's eight regional fishery management councils and repealing one such program that had been created in 1995 (Buck, 1996). The act did not, however, repeal the five other existing ITQ programs.

ment, (3) forest roads, and (4) recreation.[54] Prior to these statements, however, substantial changes had already been implemented.

The volume of timber sold from U.S. National Forests fell from about 11.5 billion board feet per year in 1987 to less than 4 billion board feet per year in 1997, a decrease of almost 70 percent (U.S. General Accounting Office, 1999).[55] This decrease was due, in part, to the increased costs to producers associated with the USFS shift to offering timber sales to improve forest health, rather than to provide wood fiber—most of the trees removed to reduce the risk of fire have little commercial value. In addition, the USFS 1992 policy reducing clear-cutting in national forests dramatically increased the costs of logging, especially in the Pacific Northwest, which experienced per-unit cost increases of 150 percent between 1980 and 1997 (U.S. General Accounting Office, 1999). No efficiency estimate exists for this aggregate policy shift, and no analysis of the potentially substantial environmental and recreational benefits and economic costs has been undertaken.

The Forest Service also was the focus of the Clinton administration's Roadless Initiative, hailed by environmentalists as one of the decade's most important environmental policy initiatives, but perhaps less important economically than the shift discussed previously. President Clinton announced the initiative in October 1999, instructing the USFS to develop regulations for long-term protection of inventoried roadless areas within the National Forest system. The USFS Roadless Rule, submitted to the *Federal Register* in January 2001, placed 58.5 million acres of unroaded federal forest lands in 39 states off limits to new road building.[56]

The efficiency implications of this rule are unclear. Inventoried roadless areas comprise 2 percent of the U.S. landmass and 31 percent of the forest system. They are characterized by rugged terrain and low-value timber or are considered ecologically sensitive, all of which may suggest relatively low costs to leaving

54. This change was not driven exclusively by the executive branch. Congress has increasingly designated portions of National Forest lands for conservation, so that about 25 percent of national forests were being managed for conservation by 1994. The Endangered Species Act (ESA) has also played a role. The number of threatened and endangered species on National Forest system lands rose from about 50 to almost 350 between 1973 and 1997, and the USFS is required by Section 7 of the ESA to give greater priority to species protection than other missions on such lands. See U.S. General Accounting Office (1999).

55. Over this same period, the number of visitor-days in National Forests increased from about 225,000 to almost 350,000, indicating an increase in recreational benefits (U.S. General Accounting Office, 1999).

56. President George W. Bush placed a 60-day "stay" on this and all federal rules published in the *Federal Register* and not yet in effect as of January 20, 2001. The Bush administration announced on May 4, 2001, that it will allow the rule to take effect but will propose changes to the rule in June. Through May 2001, six lawsuits had been filed challenging the roadless rule. Plaintiffs include timber companies and industry associations, Boise County, various off-road vehicle groups, livestock companies, the Kootenai Tribe, and the states of Alaska, Idaho, and Utah.

them in their current state and relatively high environmental benefits from preservation.[57] In addition, by Forest Service calculations, less than 0.2 percent of the U.S. timber harvest and less than 0.4 percent of U.S. oil and natural gas reserves will be affected by the roadless rule (Dombeck, 2001). Any benefit-cost calculation would have to take into account the cost of maintaining forest system roads. USFS currently maintains a road system of more than 386,000 miles and has a maintenance backlog in excess of $8 billion.

Also in January 2001, Forest Service Chief Michael Dombeck announced a new USFS policy directive on old-growth cutting. This was a substantial reversal of previous policy, which had promoted the cutting of the largest, oldest trees first. The Forest Service estimates that the change could affect 20 percent of the U.S. timber harvest from national forests scheduled in the coming year, and as much as 50 percent in the forests of the Pacific Northwest.[58] The combined effect of these three policies—the change in priorities of the USFS, the Roadless Initiative, and the directive on old-growth cutting—is that significant portions of the system of National Forests are being managed more as national parks. This may well reflect a change in social preferences, but if commercial uses are prohibited, it will conflict with the system's statutory framework, which supports management for multiple uses (Sedjo, 2000). In addition, the distributional implications of the Forest System changes have made them very controversial in western states, which bear much of the cost of the shift away from extractive use.

9.3.4.3 Designation of New National Monuments

One of the most visible natural resource policy developments of the 1990s was the Clinton administration's designation of more than 20 new national monuments and expansion of three existing national monuments, under the 1906 Antiquities Act. The designations and expansions gave monument status to almost 6 million acres of federal public lands, restricting uses relative to prior designations.[59] Clinton also created the largest protected area in U.S. history,

57. Clinton Forest Service Chief Michael Dombeck makes the point that these areas were the 58.5 million acres of Forest Reserves created between 1891 and 2000 that had remained roadless through 20 presidencies.

58. This policy directive does not have the force of law and can be overturned at will by the USFS chief.

59. A notable exception was the Arctic National Wildlife Refuge (ANWR). Clinton was lobbied heavily to declare the 1.5-million-acre coastal plain of ANWR a national monument, but he did not make the designation. Environmental groups thought the designation would better protect the refuge from future oil and gas exploration, a possibility raised by several congressional bills during the 1990s. The 1995 shutdown of the federal government was due in part to a budget legislation rider that would have allowed drilling in ANWR, which contributed to Clinton's veto. In contrast, the Clinton administration opened 4.6 million acres of the National Petroleum Reserve–Alaska, 23 million acres situated between the Brooks Range and the Arctic Ocean, to oil and gas leasing during the 1990s. Clinton directed Interior Secretary Bruce Babbitt to initiate a planning process for the

the 84-million-acre Northwest Hawaiian Islands Coral Reef Ecosystem Reserve. During the 1990s, Congress created one new national monument of 272,000 acres, and one national preserve (the Mojave Desert) of 1.6 million acres.

Taken together, Clinton's national monument designations constitute the largest withdrawal of U.S. federal lands from commercial activity since President Jimmy Carter withdrew 56 million acres of Alaskan lands in 1978 (Vincent, 1998). All but one of Clinton's designations were declared in the final year of his presidency, from January 2000 to January 2001. The final-hour nature of some of the declarations raised objections from western legislators, property-rights activists, and others.[60] The efficiency and cost-effectiveness aspects of these declarations have not been assessed; unlike rules issued by regulatory agencies, presidential actions under the 1906 Antiquities Act are not subject to benefit-cost-analysis requirements. The economic costs and benefits of many of these monument declarations are likely to be quite large and merit further study.[61]

9.3.4.4 Changes to Federal Wetlands Policy and the Endangered Species Act

Wetlands policy and the Endangered Species Act were major targets of property-rights activists and others in the regulatory reform movement during the 1990s. Congress did not succeed in passing any major changes to federal wetlands regulation, although the executive branch did attempt some important administrative changes.

The Clinton administration expanded wetlands permitting requirements to include excavation in 1993, a move that was overturned by the U.S. District Court for the District of Columbia in 1997. A U.S. Supreme Court decision in 2001 overturned the U.S. Army Corps of Engineers' 1986 "Migratory Bird Rule," which had allowed regulation of intrastate waters that provide habitat for migratory birds. These court decisions halted administration attempts to augment the scope of federal wetlands regulation. In 1998, the Army Corps greatly reduced the scope of nationwide permit 26, which authorizes discharges into nontidal headwaters and isolated waters, a change that resulted in lawsuits by

reserve in 1997, and the Bureau of Land Management held an oil and gas lease sale for portions of the northeast corner of the reserve in May 1999, despite the filing of a lawsuit by environmental groups in 1998.

60. The George W. Bush administration, however, has announced that it does not plan to overturn Clinton's monument designations, but will seek to adjust the rules governing commercial activities within the monuments and also their boundaries.

61. For example, the 1.7-million-acre Grand Staircase–Escalante National Monument, declared in 1996, may hold low-sulfur coal reserves worth more than $200 billion (Vincent, 1998). The Giant Sequoia National Monument, declared in 2000, receives more than 10 million recreational visits per year (White House, 2000).

the development and commercial communities.[62] In addition, the Clinton administration endorsed the concept of wetlands mitigation banking in 1993, a market-based policy instrument, resulting in EPA framework guidance issued in 1995.

Attempts to reauthorize the Endangered Species Act in the 1990s failed, but the Clinton administration made some important administrative changes. It implemented three provisions that had been included within many of the unsuccessful congressional reauthorization attempts and had broad bipartisan support. All of these sought to reverse one of the major economic criticisms of the ESA: that it discourages landowner efforts to improve species populations, since larger populations require expanded protections. First, voluntary "safe harbor" agreements guarantee that increases in species populations on private lands will not restrict future land use decisions. Second, the controversial "no surprises" rule guarantees that a landowner properly carrying out a habitat conservation plan will not experience further restrictions or costs without mutual consent. Third, "candidate conservation agreements" allow landowners to protect declining species that are not yet listed, in exchange for assurance that no additional measures will be required if the species is listed. The administration also emphasized habitat conservation plans (HCPs) as a tool to manage endangered and threatened species on nonfederal lands.[63] HCPs are considerably more flexible than direct enforcement of the act.

As with wetlands issues, timber subsidies, and other natural resource policy issues, the distributional implications of the ESA were the focus of much debate during the 1990s. Private landowners objected to use restrictions they believed amounted to de facto seizure of private property under the "takings clause" of the Fifth Amendment to the U.S. Constitution. From an economic perspective, the fact that private property owners may be expected to bear the costs of public goods provision is a significant distributional concern.

9.3.4.5 Green Accounting
Critics of the conventional National Income and Product Accounts (NIPA) have long recognized that the omission of a variety of nonmarket activities, such as

---

62. The so-called nationwide permits authorize landowners to proceed with specified categories of activities without obtaining individual permits, reducing regulatory burdens. The waters governed by permit 26 are often difficult to identify as wetlands because they may appear dry for much of the year and do not exhibit the vegetation characteristic of wetlands, but scientific evidence is mounting for their important function within aquatic ecosystems (Copeland, 1999).

63. Under Section 10 of the ESA, private landowners applying for an "incidental take" permit must submit a HCP, in which they agree to restrict some uses in the interest of species and habitat protection in exchange for the permit. More than 250 habitat conservation plans were completed between 1992 and 2000, compared to 14 between 1982 and 1992.

household production, unpaid work, and the depletion of natural resource and environmental capital, distorts gross domestic product (GDP) as a measure of economic activity (Darmstadter, 2000). The rationale for including natural resource depletion and environmental quality changes within the national accounts, "green accounting," is grounded in economic theory (Weitzman, 1976; Solow, 1992; Nordhaus and Kokkelenberg, 1999), and the idea has received additional impetus in the United States from environmentalists.

Interest in green accounting in the United States was academic in nature until 1992, when the Department of Commerce's Bureau of Economic Analysis (BEA) began work on the issue. Following hearings by the Joint Economic Committee, the 103rd Congress appropriated funds to BEA specifically for this purpose. The bureau produced the first official U.S. environmental accounts, the Integrated Environmental and Economic Satellite Accounts (IEESA), in 1994. BEA's initial effort accounted only for selected mineral commodities, including oil, gas, and coal (U.S. Department of Commerce, Bureau of Economic Analysis, 1994). Shortly after the BEA released the IEESA, however, Congress suspended BEA's work on environmental accounting, pending external review by a blue-ribbon panel convened by the National Research Council's (NRC) Committee on National Statistics.

The NRC panel's review, released in 1999, strongly supported BEA's efforts and endorsed further efforts to extend the NIPA system to include assets and production activities related to natural resources and the environment (Nordhaus and Kokkelenberg, 1999).[64] It encouraged the BEA to include natural resource and environmental flows in satellite or supplemental accounts, rather than redefining the core NIPA. The panel also expressed concern that the United States may have fallen behind the ongoing efforts of other countries, as a result of the congressional stop-work order in 1994, and recommended that Congress authorize and fund recommencement of work on natural resource and environmental accounts by the BEA. Through May 2001, Congress had not funded further work on the IEESA.[65]

9.3.5 Global Climate Change

No environmental issue gained in national visibility and political attention more during the Clinton years than the threat of global climate change. We

---

64. The panel also supported incorporating other nonmarket activities that are not related to the environment. See Nordhaus and Kokkelenberg (1999).

65. There is no sign in the *Congressional Record* or in the text of bills proposed during the 105th or 106th Congress that additional funding for BEA's work on the IEESA has been considered. The issue may be tied up in "environmental politics" (Nordhaus, 2001).

explore the implications of this political attention by reviewing the history of executive and legislative activities during the 1990s, highlighting the Clinton administration's emphasis on cost-effectiveness considerations, in particular, the use of market-based instruments, both domestically and internationally.

9.3.5.1 Climate Change Policy Developments During the 1990s

In June 1992, the United Nations Framework Convention on Climate Change (FCCC) was negotiated at the Conference on Environment and Development, the so-called Earth Summit, held in Rio de Janeiro, Brazil. The convention required signatories to "achieve stabilization of greenhouse gas concentrations in the atmosphere at a level that would prevent dangerous anthropogenic interference with the climate system" (United Nations, 1992). Further, it established the idea that, because of the global-commons character of the problem, all nations must be engaged in the pursuit of a solution, although different countries could participate in different ways. This was the notion of "common but differentiated responsibilities." For industrialized countries, the specific challenge was to return greenhouse gas emissions "individually or jointly to their 1990 levels by the year 2000."

President George Bush signed the FCCC, and the U.S. Senate ratified the convention in October 1992,[66] but the Bush administration did not commit the United States to specific reductions. This position changed with the new administration. On Earth Day, April 21, 1993, President Bill Clinton announced that the United States would reduce its emissions of greenhouse gases to 1990 levels by the year 2000, and ordered federal agencies to establish a plan to achieve this goal. Congressional legislation would have been required to actually commit the country to this goal, but the announcement was significant, nonetheless.

In October, the administration released its Climate Change Action Plan, which recommended 52 voluntary measures to meet the emissions goal. The initiatives in the plan are not different in nature from those that might have been expected from a second-term Bush administration, with their emphasis on voluntary programs, government-industry cooperation, cost effectiveness, use of market incentives, and minimal mandatory government intervention.[67] But, even if not different in substance, the Clinton administration's Climate Action Plan differed greatly in tone from what had been Bush administration policy.

---

66. By March 2001, 84 nations had signed and 33 countries had ratified or acceded to this agreement.

67. In 1993, the administration established the U.S. Initiative on Joint Implementation under the Climate Change Action Plan. Joint implementation arrangements allow firms or other entities in one country to meet part of their greenhouse gas reduction commitments by financing mitigation in another country. The U.S. Initiative through 2000 had approved 26 arrangements whereby U.S. firms agreed to finance projects in 11 other countries.

This complex set of voluntary initiatives had relatively little effect, however, and by 1995 the United States acknowledged that it would fall short of its goal by at least 50 percent.

In an important departure from previous policy, in July 1996, at the second Conference of the Parties (COP-2) to the U.N. Framework Convention on Climate Change, meeting in Geneva, the chief of the U.S. delegation, Undersecretary of State for Global Affairs Timothy Wirth, issued a statement supporting legally binding targets and timetables for greenhouse gas emissions reductions for 34 industrialized countries (and no targets for the 154 other nations).[68]

This new approach of binding commitments only for industrialized countries caused substantial concern in the business community and in the U.S. Senate, leading to passage in July 1997, by a vote of 95 to 0, of Senate Resolution 98, subsequently known as the Byrd-Hagel Resolution. The resolution stated that the United States should not approve any agreement at the upcoming third Conference of the Parties (COP-3), to be held in Kyoto, Japan, that did not impose binding emission reduction targets on all nations.

Just five months after passage of the Byrd-Hagel Resolution, the nations of the world met at COP-3 in Kyoto, and what came to be known as the Kyoto Protocol on Climate Change was negotiated, following the approach laid out by the Berlin mandate and inconsistent with the (nonbinding) Byrd-Hagel Resolution. The industrialized nations agreed to legally binding emission reductions, with the United States directed to reduce its emissions 7 percent below 1990 levels by the compliance period, 2008–12.[69] The Clinton administration, in particular Vice President Gore, enthusiastically supported the Kyoto Protocol, and the United States became the 60th signatory of the protocol in November 1998. At the same time, however, because the protocol clearly did not meet the Senate's stipulations as outlined in the Byrd-Hagel Resolution, the administration made clear that it did not intend to submit the protocol to the Senate for ratification unless or until key developing countries had agreed on "meaningful participation."

In 1998, the U.S. Energy Information Administration (EIA) released its analysis of the potential costs of U.S. compliance with the Kyoto Protocol emissions targets, at the request of the House of Representatives Committee on Science (U.S. Department of Energy, Energy Information Administration, 1998). The

---

68. The position statement released at COP-2 also noted U.S. acceptance of the scientific findings on climate change summarized by the Intergovernmental Panel on Climate Change (IPCC) in its Second Assessment Report, released in 1995, and rejected uniform harmonized policies in favor of flexible policy instruments, including market-based instruments. See Morrissey (2000).

69. Note that because of economic growth, it is anticipated that this 7 percent reduction would translate into approximately a 30 percent reduction below baseline emissions, that is, what they would be in the absence of policy action.

report estimated a 4 percent reduction in annual GDP through 2010, compared to business as usual, a 53 percent increase in gasoline prices, and an 87 percent increase in average electricity prices. Note that these cost estimates assumed that the U.S. target would be met entirely by reducing U.S. carbon dioxide emissions, that is, with no offsets from carbon sequestration ("sinks") resulting from land-use changes, no reductions in other greenhouse gases, and no international emissions trading.

At about the same time, the U.S. government released another analysis, one which yielded considerably lower cost estimates, mainly because of more generous assumptions on some of the factors just mentioned. In particular, the 1998 analysis by the CEA estimated costs on the order of 0.5 percent of annual GDP if flexible (market-based) policy instruments were employed. The CEA study also predicted no negative effects on the U.S. trade deficit, relatively small increases in gasoline prices ($0.05 per gallon), and no significant effects on aggregate employment.[70]

It is important to note that a key component of the Clinton administration's climate change policy was its strong support for cost-effective approaches, in particular, tradable-permit mechanisms.[71] The administration's formal proposal released in preparation for Kyoto called for domestic and international emissions trading, and international joint implementation. It was largely because of the efforts of the U.S. negotiating team that the Kyoto Protocol included significant provisions for international emissions trading and joint implementation projects among the industrialized nations, as well as what came to be known as the Clean Development Mechanism for offsets in developing countries.

Subsequently the United States proposed rules for international emissions trading in 1998, at preparatory talks for the Fourth Conference of the Parties in Buenos Aires. The U.S. proposal faced substantial opposition, most significantly from the European Union. No agreement was reached on emissions trading at the Fourth (1998), Fifth (1999), or Sixth (2000) Conference of the Parties. Indeed, at the Sixth Conference of the Parties, which met in The Hague in November

---

70. Note that both analyses were exclusively of the costs of addressing global climate change. Because of the considerable uncertainty regarding the nature and degree of damages resulting from anticipated climate change, there have been fewer analyses of the benefits of policy action. Nevertheless, there is now a growing literature of what have come to be known as integrated assessment models, which examine both sides of the ledger. The range of results from some of the best analyses indicate that relatively small taxes on the carbon content of fossil fuels would be warranted in the short run, to keep from rendering large parts of the capital stock prematurely obsolete while providing an "insurance policy," with gradually increasing carbon taxes over time. The earliest work was by Nordhaus (1977, 1982), and the literature is summarized by Kolstad and Toman (forthcoming).

71. The prior Bush administration had taken a similar position. See, for example, Stewart and Wiener (1992).

2000, disagreements between the United States and the European Union on the role of carbon sequestration and emissions trading led to the breakdown of the talks. Thus, at the end of the Clinton administration in January 2001, there was less than full agreement among the countries of the world on the ultimate shape of the international agreement, no action toward ratification in the United States, and no significant domestic initiatives, other than the voluntary programs of the administration's 1993 Climate Action Plan.[72]

9.3.5.2   Role of Economic Considerations in Climate Change Policy Development

Economic considerations appear to have played a much more substantial role in the development of the administration's international negotiating position on climate change than they did in the development of domestic regulatory policies with substantial economic costs, such as the NAAQS for ozone and particulate matter. Within the White House, weekly (and even more frequent) meetings on climate change leading up to the Kyoto conference were chaired by the National Economic Council (NEC), the coordinating body for economic policy during the Clinton years. In contrast, EPA was relatively disengaged on this issue.

The major role of the economic agencies in developing U.S. climate change policy began at least as early as July 1997, when then-CEA Chair Janet Yellen testified before the House Commerce Committee, Subcommittee on Energy and Power. The administration's two representatives at this hearing on "the economic and environmental impact of the proposed international global climate change agreement" were Yellen and Wirth.

CEA testimony on this occasion and many other occasions emphasized the enormous cost savings to be achieved through emissions trading and through participation by developing countries, virtually locking in the administration's position and possibly contributing to the Senate's passage of Byrd-Hagel. In addition, the CEA resisted pressure to adopt in its own 1998 report on the costs of complying with the Kyoto Protocol's targets overly optimistic assumptions about technological change and energy efficiency floated by the so-called "DOE

---

72. During the presidential campaign, candidate George W. Bush stated that he recognized global climate change to be a serious problem but believed the Kyoto Protocol to be an inappropriate approach, largely because key developing countries are exempt from targets. In March 2001, President Bush indicated unequivocally that the administration did not intend to submit the protocol to the Senate for ratification and believed that another approach to the problem was needed. See Eric Pianin, "U.S. Aims to Pull Out of Warming Treaty; 'No Interest' in Implementing Kyoto Pact, Whitman Says," *Washington Post*, March 28, 2001, p. A01; and Eric Pianin and William Drozdiak, "U.S. Angers Allies over Climate Pact; Europeans Will Ask Bush to Reconsider," *Washington Post*, March 29, 2001, p. A01.

Five Lab study," and again by the Interagency Analytical Team study on the economic effects of global climate change policies (Interlaboratory Working Group, 1997; Interagency Analytical Team, 1998).

Shortly before the Kyoto conference, Wirth resigned and was replaced as undersecretary of state for global affairs and head of the U.S. delegation to climate change negotiations by Stuart Eizenstadt, previously undersecretary of commerce for international trade and a career senior political appointee to business- and economics-related posts. Eizenstadt worked closely with the CEA and with the NEC, then directed by Gene Sperling. In March 1998, Eizenstadt testified before the House Subcommittee on Energy and Power that the U.S. negotiating team would not accept restrictions on international trading, locking in a U.S. negotiating position with cost-effective implementation as a cornerstone. It should also be noted, however, that Clinton administration economists had virtually no influence in formulating emissions targets agreed upon at Kyoto, one more example of cost-effectiveness as an easier and more successful "sell" than efficiency.

9.4   What Do We Know about Efficiency, Cost Effectiveness, and Environmental Quality?

Having reviewed both cross-cutting and specific environmental initiatives of the Clinton years, we summarize in this part of the chapter what is known about the performance of environmental regulation, employing three metrics: environmental quality, cost effectiveness, and efficiency.

9.4.1   Environmental Quality

The improvements in aggregate U.S. air quality since the 1970s have been summarized often in the literature. Most notably, between 1979 and 1998, concentrations of carbon monoxide fell by 58 percent, sulfur dioxide by 53 percent, nitrogen dioxide by 25 percent, and ambient ground-level ozone by 17 percent (Portney, 2000). Changes in aggregate emissions of the criteria air pollutants over the period 1970–98 are listed in Table 9.4.

Improvements in ambient water quality have been less visible, but substantial nonetheless. Between 1974 and 1981, industrial and municipal biological oxygen demand loads in the United States decreased by 71 percent and 46 percent, respectively (R. Smith, Alexander, and Wolman, 1987).[73] From 1975 to 1994, the

---

73. These improvements, as well as many local improvements in dissolved oxygen, might be attributed in part to increased wastewater treatment. Between 1970 and 1985 the fraction of U.S. residents served by wastewater treatment facilities increased from 42 to 74 percent (Boyd, 2000).

Table 9.4
U.S. Emissions of Seven Major Air Pollutants, 1970–98

	SO_2	NO_x	VOCs	CO	Lead	PM_{10}	$PM_{2.5}$
1970	100	100	100	100	100	N/A	N/A
1980	83	117	85	91	34	N/A	N/A
1989	75	114	73	82	3	100	N/A
1990	76	115	68	76	2	54	100
1991	74	116	68	78	2	53	97
1992	73	118	67	75	2	53	96
1993	72	119	67	76	2	50	92
1994	70	121	70	79	2	56	100
1995	62	119	67	72	2	48	90
1996	61	118	60	74	2	61	103
1997	63	119	61	73	2	63	107
1998	63	117	58	69	2	64	105

Sources: U.S. Environmental Protection Agency, Office of Air Quality Planning and Standards (2000a, 2000b).

Notes: Figures are indexed from EPA data, with 1970 aggregate U.S. emissions equal to 100 for all pollutants except PM_{10} (1989 = 100) and $PM_{2.5}$ (1990 = 100). Data for 1970 and 1980 are drawn from U.S. Environmental Protection Agency, Office of Air Quality Planning and Standards (2000a); data for 1989, 1991–95, and 1997 are drawn from U.S. Environmental Protection Agency, Office of Air Quality Planning and Standards (2000b). Data for 1990, 1996, and 1998 appear in both reports. (Data for PM_{10} differ between the two reports—for this pollutant, the 2000b data were used exclusively.) Data for particulate matter include only directly emitted PM. No figures are shown for PM_{10} and $PM_{2.5}$ in 1970 or 1980; while estimates exist, they do not include natural sources, agriculture, forestry, fugitive dust, and other sources which together comprised almost 90 percent of directly emitted PM_{10} and almost 70 percent of directly emitted $PM_{2.5}$ in 1990.

share of measured water quality readings in violation of federal standards for dissolved oxygen declined by more than 80 percent, total phosphorous by 20 percent, and fecal coliform bacteria by 19 percent (Freeman, 2000).

But downward trends in emissions and upward trends in environmental quality or compliance are not sufficient evidence of the impact of environmental regulations. In order to assess individual regulations or aggregate statutes, we must compare actual emissions to what they would have been in the absence of the regulation. Although it is difficult to attribute marginal environmental quality improvements to federal environmental regulations, it has been easier for some media than for others. Trends in air quality have been attributed to federal regulations both by EPA itself (U.S. Environmental Protection Agency, 1997, 1999) and by independent analyses (Freeman, 1982; Portney, 2000). The impacts of federal legislation on water quality are much less clear. One study of the period 1972 to the mid-1990s estimates that increases in the

Table 9.5
Changes in Average Ambient Concentrations, Five Major Air Pollutants, 1989–98

	Ambient Concentration, 1989	Ambient Concentration, 1998	Percent Change, 1989–98
CO	6.2 ppm	3.8 ppm	−39
Lead	0.09 ppm	0.04 ppm	−56
NO_x	0.021 ppm	0.018 ppm	−14
PM_{10}	31.7 μg/m^3	23.7 μg/m^3	−25
SO_2	0.0087 ppm	0.0053 ppm	−39

Source: U.S. Environmental Protection Agency, Office of Air Quality Planning and Standards (2000b).
Notes: CO measured as arithmetic mean, 2nd maximum 8-hour concentration. Lead measured as arithmetic mean, maximum qtr. arithmetic mean. NO_x measured as daily average arithmetic mean. PM_{10} and SO_2 measured as annual average arithmetic mean.

number of U.S. river miles meeting water quality standards for swimming, fishing, and boating attributable to federal water quality legislation were only 6.3 percent, 4.2 percent, and 2.8 percent, respectively, over the 18-year period (Bingham et al., 1998; Freeman, 2001).[74]

These small changes in national compliance with standards are indicators of a substantial difference between air and water quality in the United States. On average, water quality in the preregulation period (in this case, before the Federal Water Pollution Control Act of 1972) was fairly good. Improvements, then, would be more appropriately analyzed regionally or locally, since the small national changes mask the fact that some local pollution problems have improved dramatically, while other areas already supported their designated water uses (Freeman, 2001). In addition, improvements in water quality have been achieved largely through point-source regulation. The nonpoint sources that are of principal concern have not been part of the regulatory strategy (see Table 9.2).

What about trends in air and water quality in the 1990s? Changes in average ambient concentrations of five major air pollutants between 1989 and 1998, the last year for which such aggregate data are available, are described in Table 9.5. Concentrations appear to have decreased significantly over the decade, although emissions of most of the criteria pollutants declined much more dramatically over the 20 years prior to 1990, when the "low-hanging fruit" of air quality

---

74. Improvements were assessed only for conventional water pollutants; almost no data are available with which to assess trends in toxic water pollutants over the past three decades (Freeman, 2000). Boyd (2000) notes that Toxics Release Inventory data, available only since the late 1980s, show a decrease in toxic discharges to surface water of more than 50 percent between 1987 and 1990.

Table 9.6
Summary of National Annual Emissions Projections (Thousands of Tons)

	1990 Base Year	2000 Pre-CAA	2000 Post-CAA	1990–2000 Percent Change
VOC	22,715	24,410	17,874	−27
NO$_x$	22,747	25,021	18,414	−26
SO$_2$	22,361	24,008	18,013	−25
CO	94,385	95,572	80,919	−15
Primary PM$_{10}$	28,289	28,768	28,082	−2
Primary PM$_{2.5}$	7,091	7,353	7,216	−2

Source: Table adapted from Freeman (2001), data obtained from U.S. Environmental Protection Agency (1999).

regulation was being harvested. Based on EPA modeling of trends in emissions with and without the Clean Air Act, the observed decreases in concentrations of these major air pollutants between 1990 and 2000 can "reasonably be attributed to" the Clean Air Act and its amendments (Freeman, 2001). During the 1990s emissions of VOC, NO$_x$, and SO$_2$ are estimated to have fallen by about one-quarter, CO emissions by 15 percent, and particulate matter by about 2 percent (Table 9.6). Following the pattern of 30-year trends, trends in water quality over the past decade have been much more modest than trends in air quality, and in some cases (particularly nonpoint-source pollution in the form of runoff from cities and agricultural areas) may have been negative (Freeman, 2001).

9.4.2 The Cost of a Clean Environment

At the beginning of the decade of the 1990s, two general equilibrium analyses were carried out of the effects of environmental regulations on the U.S. economy (Hazilla and Kopp, 1990; Jorgenson and Wilcoxen, 1990), and an EPA assessment was developed on the costs of the major environmental regulations (U.S. Environmental Protection Agency, 1991). Neither of the general equilibrium analyses attempted to quantify the benefits of environmental regulation, but both illustrated the fact that costs, correctly calculated, include more than the capital and operating costs of compliance (Table 9.7). The magnitude of the cost estimates ($977 billion from 1981 to 1990, according to Hazilla and Kopp) indicated that the long-run aggregate social costs of regulation are considerable.[75]

---

75. While only 13 business sectors in the United States made direct pollution control investments, all 36 sectors experienced increased costs and decreased output and labor productivity as a result of environmental regulation (Hazilla and Kopp, 1990). Jorgenson and Wilcoxen (1990) estimated that environmental regulation reduced U.S. Gross National Product by about 2.6 percent per year. For additional analysis of the aggregate costs of regulation, see Hahn and Hird (1991).

Table 9.7
Component Parts of the Costs of Environmental Regulation

Government administration of environmental statutes and regulations
Monitoring
Enforcement
Private-sector compliance expenditures
Capital
Operating
Other direct costs
Legal and other transaction
Shifted management focus
Disrupted production
General equilibrium effects
Product substitution
Discouraged investment
Retarded innovation
Transition costs
Unemployment
Obsolete capital
"Negative costs"
Natural resource inputs
Worker health
Innovation stimulation

Source: Jaffe et al. (1995).

The 1991 EPA report, *Environmental Investments: The Cost of a Clean Environment*, was drafted in response to Section 312(a) of the Clean Air Act and Section 516(b) of the Clean Water Act. The report provided estimates of the direct costs of pollution control regulations in the United States from 1972 to 2000, including public-sector implementation and private-sector compliance.[76] No attempt was made to monetize the benefits of regulation, or even to establish a link between the environmental quality statistics generated and the regulations for which costs were calculated.[77] The report estimated annualized regulatory implementation and compliance costs of more than 2 percent of U.S. gross national product (GNP) in 1990.

No conclusions about economic efficiency can be drawn from these analyses because benefits were not monetized, but these studies focused attention on the

---

76. The cost estimates included expenditures related to CAA; the Radon Gas and Indoor Air Quality Research Act of 1986; Radon Pollution Control Act of 1988; CWA; Marine Protection, Sanctuaries, and Research Act; SDWA; RCRA; CERCLA; TSCA; FIFRA; Energy Security Act; and Title III of the Superfund Amendments and Reauthorization Act.

77. It did attempt to estimate counterfactual (without regulation) emissions of air pollutants and precursors from 1970 to 1988, and provided comparisons of these counterfactual statistics with actual emissions.

rising costs of environmental regulation in absolute terms and as a fraction of GNP. In addition, a relatively recent literature in environmental economics has noted that the ultimate costs of any given environmental policy initiative depend on interactions between the new policy and existing regulations or tax policies. Additional costs can arise from interactions between environmental policies and preexisting distortions in the economy, such as those due to taxes on labor (Goulder, 1995). Some policy instruments, such as taxes and auctioned permits, generate revenues, which can be used by governments to reduce preexisting taxes, thereby reducing what the overall costs of the policy would otherwise be.

9.4.3   What Do We Know about the Efficiency of Environmental Policies?

In writing environmental statutes, Congress has sent mixed messages regarding the use of benefit-cost analysis to decide when and what to regulate and to choose among regulatory alternatives.[78] We would therefore expect the relative efficiency of the major environmental statutes to vary widely. Available analyses range from aggregate assessments of the costs and benefits of environmental regulation as a whole to assessments of individual rules.

9.4.3.1   Efficiency of the Major Environmental Statutes

Aggregate benefit-cost analysis of statutes is problematic for both technical and practical reasons. The establishment of an appropriate counterfactual is technically difficult—we need to establish what emissions would have been in the absence of the Clean Air Act, for example, to attribute emissions reductions over time to the act. Practically, typical policy problems do not lead to creation or elimination of entire statutes, but rather marginal changes to individual regulations (which will be discussed later). Nonetheless, the few existing efficiency analyses of the major statutes can be illuminating.

Two of the most important federal environmental statutes, the Clean Air Act and the Clean Water Act, have been the subjects of benefit-cost analysis. Under

---

78. The Flood Control Act of 1936 may include the first U.S. legislative mandate to use benefit-cost analysis: "The Federal government should improve or participate in the improvement of navigable waters or their tributaries, including watersheds thereof, if the benefits to whomsoever they may accrue are in excess of estimated costs." See National Center for Environmental Decision-Making Research, "Cost-Benefit Analysis," 2000, available at http://www.ncedr.org/tools/othertools/costbenefit/module1.htm.

Several statutes have been interpreted to restrict the ability of regulators to consider benefits and costs, such as the RCRA and the Delaney Clause of the FFDCA. Others, including TSCA and FIFRA, explicitly order regulators to consider benefits and costs (Arrow et al., 1996). For a comprehensive review of the inclusion or exclusion of benefit-cost criteria from regulatory action under most major federal environmental legislation, see Schierow (1994).

Section 812 of the 1990 CAA Amendments, Congress required EPA to undertake (1) a retrospective benefit-cost analysis of the 1970 CAA and its 1977 amendments, and (2) biennial prospective analyses of the 1990 amendments. By EPA's calculations, the 1970 CAA and 1977 and 1990 amendments pass benefit-cost tests by very wide margins. The retrospective study, presented to Congress in 1997, estimated direct costs of CAA regulatory implementation and compliance from 1970 to 1990 to be $689 billion and direct benefits to be $29.3 trillion. In 1999, EPA presented its first prospective study (1990–2010) to Congress, with positive net benefits estimated for the period to be $672 billion.[79]

These estimates are highly controversial. According to the retrospective analysis, benefits of the CAA from 1970 to 1990 exceeded costs by a factor of 42, a difference much greater than estimated by other studies (Freeman, 1982, 2000). The estimates appear improbable. EPA's "best estimates" of net benefits of the CAA through 1990, $22 trillion, were estimated to be approximately equal to aggregate U.S. household net worth in that year (Lutter and Belzer, 2000). Further, the number of annual avoided deaths attributed to the CAA was 10 percent of all annual deaths in the United States (Portney, 2000). Others have criticized the retrospective and prospective studies on the grounds that they exclude the indirect costs of increased prices for goods and services due to the act, exclude the costs of meeting some of the act's costly provisions, and potentially exaggerate the risk-reduction benefits associated with particulate matter reduction, which account for more than 90 percent of the benefits estimated for the 1990 CAA Amendments (Lutter and Belzer, 2000).[80]

However, what is perhaps most important is that the general finding that the benefits of air pollution regulation have exceeded its costs is well supported by other studies (Freeman, 1982; Portney, 2000). We understand less about how marginal benefits and costs of *specific* air pollution regulations have varied over time, though it appears many such individual regulations would not pass a benefit-cost test. In addition, there appears to be a downward trend over time in net benefits of air pollution regulation, indicated by the results of the retrospective and prospective studies and the individual efficiency analyses for recent rules (Morgenstern, 2000; Freeman, 2001).[81]

---

79. The 90 percent confidence interval of net benefits ranged from −$26.4 billion (net cost) to +$1.8 trillion. The first prospective study estimated the benefits of selected ecological effects; the retrospective study did not. EPA's figures were calculated in constant 1990 dollars; these have been converted to 2000 dollars.

80. Freeman (2001) emphasizes another aspect of EPA's analysis; while the stationary source regulations under the CAA appear to have benefits greatly exceeding costs, in aggregate the mobile source regulations taken together appear to have substantial net costs.

81. An important caveat is that the cited studies did not review recent regulations on particulate matter nor potential regulations affecting CO_2 emissions associated with global climate change, which may not conform to the observed downward trend in measured net benefits.

The Clean Water Act also has been analyzed in a benefit-cost framework, with considerably less favorable results. Estimates of annual benefits of the CWA range from $24.8 billion in 1985 (Freeman, 1982) to $38.4 billion in 1990 (Carson and Mitchell, 1993).[82] Cost estimates range from $46.6 billion in 1985 to $59.7 billion in 1990 (U.S. Environmental Protection Agency, 1991).[83] While subject to much uncertainty, a rough comparison of these estimates supports the conjecture that the CWA's overall costs outweigh its benefits (Freeman, 2000). Estimates by others have shown that the incremental costs of specific CWA rules also exceed their benefits (Lyon and Farrow, 1995).

It should not be surprising, perhaps, that the CWA measures up less favorably than the CAA in terms of economic efficiency. The stated goals of the Federal Water Pollution Control Act of 1972 were (1) the attainment of fishable and swimmable waters by July 1, 1983, and (2) the elimination of *all* discharges of pollutants into navigable waters by 1985. Although those deadlines were postponed, and a distinction made between organic pollutants and toxics by the 1977 Amendments, the CWA continues to emphasize a target of zero emissions and fails to distinguish among bodies of water with different uses. In addition, applications of market-based instruments have come more slowly to water-pollution than to air-pollution policy.

The other major federal environmental statutes are more difficult to assess, because few, and in some cases, no aggregate benefit-cost studies have been carried out. FIFRA and TSCA are the two major statutes that explicitly allow benefit-cost considerations in rule-making.[84] One of EPA's responsibilities under FIFRA is pesticide registration, which triggers a benefit-cost test that results in either cancellation, suspension, continuation of registration with restrictions, or unrestricted continuation. EPA *does* appear to take benefits and costs into account in these decisions, but its decisions from 1975 to 1989 imply a value per statistical cancer case among pesticide applicators of more than 580 times the implied value for consumers of pesticide residues on food (Cropper et al., 1992). While benefit-cost tests are applied under FIFRA, they do not appear to be applied consistently.

---

82. The 90 percent confidence interval for the Carson and Mitchell (1993) estimate is $29 billion to $54 billion, and for the Freeman (1982) estimate it is $9.1 billion to $44.3 billion. No CWA benefit estimates have included potential benefits to commercial fisheries and diversionary uses, indicating that true benefits may be somewhat higher than those cited above. Freeman (1982) does not include the benefits from control of toxic pollutants and heavy metals, which are both included in EPA's cost calculations. However, the counterfactual for many benefit calculations, including Carson and Mitchell (1993), is taken to be "no control," which may substantially overstate CWA benefits.

83. All CWA cost and benefit figures are expressed in constant 2000 dollars.

84. One reason that benefit-cost procedures were written into FIFRA and TSCA, while explicitly written out of other regulatory statutes, may be that these two statutes regulate commodities, rather than wastes (Morgenstern, 1997c).

CERCLA, or Superfund, is a frequent target of critics on efficiency grounds. One particularly comprehensive assessment of the efficiency of Superfund considered a representative sample of 150 cleanup sites, and found mean remediation cost per cancer case avoided to be $3.6 million (Hamilton and Viscusi, 1999). This mean cost estimate masks considerable variance, however, since both risks and costs are highly concentrated at a small number of sites. About 70 percent of sites with nonzero cancer cases averted had costs per case averted greater than $100 million.[85]

The analysis of Superfund is illustrative because it shows how aggregate analyses of statutes or programs can obscure great differences in the net benefits of individual rules or activities. Within the CAA, for example, a handful of individual rules, like those governing lead in gasoline and reductions in fine particulate matter, are responsible for a substantial portion of the health benefits attributed to the statute. Counterbalancing the regulations that confer large net benefits are other regulations, such as the NAAQS governing ozone precursors, that do not pass a benefit-cost test. Economists generally agree on the need to look at the incremental impacts of such regulations for policy-making, but only recently have they begun to devote substantial resources to this task.

9.4.3.2 Efficiency of Individual Rules

Since 1981 federal agencies have been required to submit Regulatory Impact Analyses to OMB for all new rules expected to have aggregate costs of $100 million or greater. The increased visibility of benefits and costs that has resulted from the RIA process has led to greater scrutiny of the analyses and the rules that trigger them.

There are many examples of environmental rules for which RIAs have estimated positive net benefits, including the lead-in-gasoline rule (Nichols, 1997) and the NAAQS for particulate matter (U.S. Office of Management and Budget, 1998). Likewise, the estimated benefits of the SO_2 emissions trading program under Title IV of the 1990 CAA Amendments are greater than its estimated costs by an order of magnitude (Burtraw et al., 1998).

The requirements for Regulatory Impact Analysis, however, have not necessarily improved the efficiency of individual federal environmental rules. One study compared the cost per life saved of 33 individual risk-reducing rules (a mix of proposed and final rules) from federal regulatory agencies, 15 of them from EPA (Viscusi, 1992).[86] Of the EPA rules, only one had a cost per life saved

---

85. These figures have been converted from constant 1993 dollars to 2000 dollars. They are substantially greater than reasonable estimates of willingness-to-pay numbers, which typically range from $4 to $9 million, in constant 2000 dollars (Viscusi, 1992).

86. Viscusi's statistics were drawn, in large part, from Morrall (1986) and updates to Morrall (1986) through unpublished communication.

Table 9.8
Cost of Selected EPA Regulations per Statistical Life Saved

	Year	Net Cost/ Discounted Statistical Life (Millions of 2000$)
Toxicity characteristics to determine hazardous wastes	1990	−9,400
Underground storage tanks: technical requirements	1988	−400
Asbestos prohibitions: manufacture, importation, processing and distribution in commerce (total)	1989	21
National primary and secondary water regulations—Phase II: MCLs for 38 contaminants	1991	28
Hazardous waste management system—wood preservatives	1990	57
Sewage sludge use and disposal regulations, 40 CFR Part 503	1993	215
Land disposal restrictions for third scheduled waste	1990	215
Hazardous waste management system: final solvents and dioxins land disposal restrictions rule	1986	226
Prohibition on land disposal of first third of scheduled wastes ("second sixth" proposal)	1988	452
Land disposal restrictions, Phase II: universal treatment standards and treatment standards for organic toxicity, characteristic wastes, and newly listed wastes	1994	1,030
Drinking water regulations, synthetic organic chemicals, Phase V	1992	10,800
Solid waste disposal facility criteria, 40 CFR Parts 257 and 258	1991	40,700

Source: Adapted from Hahn, Lutter, and Viscusi (2000).

Notes: All values are millions of 2000 dollars annually; rules are ranked in order of decreasing cost effectiveness.

of less than $6.7 million. In a more recent study that included 12 EPA rules, only two reduce risk, while the other 10 could increase risk by reducing private expenditures on risk-reducing investments (Hahn, Lutter, and Viscusi, 2000). Table 9.8 summarizes the cost of selected EPA regulations per statistical life saved.[87]

In the first 11 years of the RIA review process, the lowest cost per life saved of any rule rejected by OMB was $142 million, indicating that OMB may have succeeded in eliminating only some of the most inefficient regulations (Viscusi,

87. To the extent that there are important nonmortality benefits, these studies may be misleading, although Hahn, Lutter, and Viscusi (2000) tried to control for these by examining rules that focus on mortality benefits.

1996). In the first 15 years of the review process, about two-thirds of the federal government's approved environmental quality regulations failed these statutory benefit-cost tests, using the government's own numbers (Hahn, 2000). One example is the NAAQS for ozone, for which EPA submitted an RIA that listed $2.0 to $11.2 billion in monetized benefits and $12.7 billion in costs through 2010, assuming full attainment (U.S. Office of Management and Budget, 1998).

In another study of a dozen proposed rules at EPA that required economic analysis, only four clearly passed a benefit-cost test performed by the agency itself (Morgenstern, 1997a). However, the estimated benefits of just three of the rules studied exceeded the estimated cost of all 12 rules combined, reinforcing the fact that aggregate analysis of a group of rules can be misleading (Morgenstern, 1997b). In all cases, economic analysis contributed to changes in rules that decreased costs, and in five cases to changes that increased benefits, demonstrating that RIAs can be used to improve cost effectiveness, even if the standard to be set is not economically efficient.[88]

After agencies submit RIAs to OMB for review, interest groups can submit comments for the public record. In addition, in the last few years, independent groups have begun to submit formal comments that enter into the public dialogue as working papers and published articles. These efforts often target rules that appear to be inefficient or ineffective, particularly in cases where interest groups wish to reduce the cost of the rule imposed on them. These analyses have helped identify important patterns in the economics of regulatory decision-making.

First, economic analyses prepared by regulatory agencies frequently fail to provide sufficient information to make valid benefit-cost comparisons. Less than 30 percent of new environmental, health, and safety regulations from mid-1996 to mid-1999 quantified net benefits, and few provided quantitative comparisons of regulatory alternatives (Hahn, Lutter, and Viscusi, 2000). Second, in many cases, the environmental statutes themselves limit the extent to which RIAs could affect policy outcomes by, for example, forbidding the consideration of costs in decision-making.

Third, the existence of a large public database of ex ante estimates of the costs and benefits of environmental regulations has made it possible to begin comparing ex ante and ex post estimates, which may be the best way to gauge the quality of agencies' efficiency calculations. The first major study to attempt

---

88. In some cases environmental statutes necessitate that RIAs not be the primary decision factor in rule-making (Caulkins and Sessions, 1997; Rasmussen, 1997; Anderson and Rykowski, 1997). Barring legislative changes in these cases, use of RIAs to improve the cost effectiveness of regulations may be the most that can be expected. In addition, many RIAs do not contain enough information to compare the cost effectiveness of multiple regulatory alternatives, which, in general, prevents them from being useful cost-effectiveness tools. See Hahn, Lutter, and Viscusi (2000).

this comparison reviewed more than two dozen major environmental and occupational safety regulations, and found that ex ante estimates of costs systematically exceeded actual costs, although when EPA regulations were considered in isolation, no evidence of systematic bias in either direction was found (Harrington, Morgenstern, and Nelson, 2000).[89]

9.4.4 What Do We Know about the Cost Effectiveness of Environmental Policies?

It has frequently been pointed out that environmental laws are not cost effective, often requiring specific technologies or uniform emissions limits, despite tremendous variation in firm abatement costs (Newell and Stavins, 2001; Tietenberg, 1990). While uniform standards may effectively limit emissions of pollutants, they typically exact relatively high costs in the process, by forcing some firms to resort to unduly expensive means of controlling pollution. For example, under current regulations the marginal cost of abating lead emissions ranges from $13 per ton in the nonmetal-products sector to $56,000 per ton in the food sector (Hartman, Wheeler, and Singh, 1994; Morgenstern, 2000).

Market-based approaches to environmental protection can be used to achieve the least-cost allocation of pollution reduction, even when the aggregate target is not efficient; thus cost effectiveness can be seen as a criterion quite separate from efficiency (Baumol and Oates, 1971). Since the 1970s, the advantages of economic-incentive approaches to environmental regulation have received serious political attention, and there have been increasing numbers of applications in the United States and other countries (Stavins, forthcoming).

Analysts have compared the costs of some of the larger U.S. market-based environmental policies with those of alternative (hypothetical) command-and-control policies.[90] One survey of eight empirical studies of U.S. air pollution control found that the ratio of actual aggregate costs of the conventional command-and-control approach to the aggregate costs of least-cost benchmarks ranged from 1.07 for sulfate emissions in the Los Angeles area to 22.0 for hydrocarbon emissions at all domestic DuPont plants (Tietenberg, 1985). One should not make too much of these numbers, however, since actual command-and-control instruments are being compared with theoretical benchmarks of cost effectiveness (that is, what a perfectly functioning market-based instrument

---

89. Another analysis of the chlorofluorocarbon (CFC) phaseout in the United States also indicates that EPA may overestimate costs ex ante (Hammitt, 2000).

90. Like benefit-cost analysis, cost-effectiveness analysis is required by the 1993 Clinton EO 12866, which directs agencies to identify and assess alternative policies (with an emphasis on incentive-based mechanisms).

would achieve in theory). A fair comparison among policy instruments would involve either idealized versions of both market-based systems and likely alternatives, or realistic versions of both.

EPA's Emissions Trading Program, which started in 1974 as the "offset" policy and was codified in 1986, is one individual program for which cost savings have been estimated. The only comprehensive study of cost savings based on actual trades estimates that the program achieved savings of $1.6 to $21.5 billion over its first 14 years (Hahn and Hester, 1989).

Another program that has been analyzed for cost effectiveness is EPA's lead-in-gasoline rule, which allowed interrefinery trading of lead credits beginning in 1982 and banking of credits in 1985. EPA estimates that trading and banking generated cost savings of 20 percent per year over alternative regulation through 1987, when the phasedown was complete (U.S. Environmental Protection Agency, 1985). Although no other actual cost savings estimate exists, an independent analysis of the level of trading activity and the rate of the lead phasedown suggests that the program was indeed cost effective (Kerr and Maré, 1997).

The market-based policy instruments resulting from the 1990 CAA Amendments were discussed earlier. The market for tradable SO_2 emission permits among U.S. electric utilities established under Title IV has the potential to save more than $280 million annually through Phase I (1995–2000), and more than $880 million annually during Phase II (after 2000), compared with a uniform emissions rate standard (Carlson et al., 2000).[91] The regional NO_x cap-and-trade system in the Northeast may generate compliance cost savings of 40 to 47 percent compared with continued command-and-control regulation of ozone precursors (Farrell, Carter, and Raufer, 1999).

One state-level market-based environmental program has also been analyzed in a cost-effectiveness framework. The South Coast Air Quality Management District, which is responsible for controlling emissions in a four-county area of southern California, launched a tradable permit program in January 1994 to reduce NO_x and SO_2 emissions in the Los Angeles area. While no analysis of actual cost savings has been performed, one prospective analysis predicted 42 percent cost savings annually over traditional regulation (Anderson, 1997).

While these results are heartening for economists who advocate applying market-based instruments to environmental policy, they barely scratch the surface of environmental regulation as a whole. Although agencies are required to

---

91. These figures have been converted to constant 2000 dollars. Highlighting the difficulty of estimating cost savings compared with a hypothetical policy alternative, Carlson et al. (2000) also estimate actual cost savings during two program years, 1995 and 1996, and suggest that the allowance market has not realized these potential "gains from trade" to date.

perform cost-effectiveness analysis within RIAs, more than one-quarter of RIAs discuss no policy alternatives, and barely one-third of RIAs quantify the costs and benefits of alternative policies (Hahn, Burnett, et al., 2000).

9.5 Conclusions

Looking back over the past decade of environmental policy, it is striking how much of it is independent of the identity of the particular administration. Much policy is determined by existing laws and regulations and by the political equilibrium among the courts, Congress, the president, and the key departments and agencies in the administration. Nevertheless, Congress and the administration can and do make a significant difference. Here we identify five themes that emerge from our review of national environmental policy during the eight years of the Clinton administration, and we comment briefly on the political context that may affect the future use of economics in environmental and resource policy.

First, *environmental targets were made more stringent, and environmental quality improved significantly during the decade.* Most important among the new targets were the National Ambient Air Quality Standards for ambient ozone and particulate matter, issued by EPA in July 1997. These could turn out to be one of the Clinton administration's most enduring environmental legacies, both in terms of potential benefits and potential costs.

Environmental quality improved overall during the decade, continuing a trend that started in the 1970s. Emissions of major air pollutants fell significantly, and these changes can be attributed, in part, to the Clean Air Act and its amendments. The decreases were much less than during the previous two decades, however, which is not surprising given that the low-hanging fruit had already been picked. Trends in water quality over the decade of the 1990s were less clear, and in some cases reflected increased pollution levels.

Natural resource policy during the Clinton years was heavily weighted toward environmental protection. A number of initiatives were proposed to reduce subsidies for private resource extraction on public lands, targeting below-market timber sales, grazing fees, and subsidized mining of nonrenewable resources. More importantly, there was a significant shift in priorities at the U.S. Forest Service away from a focus on timber production to resource protection. One aspect of this was the administration's proposal, in its last month, to place some 60 million acres of federal forest land off limits to new road building. In addition, the administration designated more than 20 new national monuments and expanded three others, thus restricting permissible activities on about 6 million acres of federal lands.

Second, *the use of benefit-cost analysis for assessing environmental regulation was controversial in the Clinton administration, while economic efficiency emerged as a central goal of the regulatory reform movement in Congress during the 1990s.* When attention was given during the 1990s to increased efficiency, the locus of that attention during the Clinton years was Congress in the case of environmental policies and the administration in the case of natural resource policies.

Despite a series of supportive executive orders, there is little evidence that economic efficiency was accepted as a legitimate criterion for environmental policy during the Clinton years. The administration's support for benefit-cost analysis in environmental, health, and safety decision-making was—with some exceptions—no more than modest. At the Environmental Protection Agency, there was significantly more opposition to the use of this analytical tool for decision-making.

In contrast, economic efficiency was a central goal of regulatory reform efforts in Congress, especially after the Republican takeover in the 1994 mid-term elections. Major amendments to the Safe Drinking Water Act were passed, containing the most stringent requirement for benefit-cost analysis of any environmental statute. Legislators were less successful at reforming other environmental statutes that had been criticized on efficiency grounds, but Congress did pass a variety of cross-cutting regulatory reform initiatives, aimed at increasing the efficiency of environmental, health, and safety regulations.

Ironically, the increased attention given to benefit-cost analysis may not have had a marked effect on the economic efficiency of environmental regulations. The evidence indicates that the overall benefits of air pollution regulation have exceeded its costs, but the picture is mixed when one examines specific air pollution regulations. In general, there appears to be a downward trend in net benefits of such regulations over time. Furthermore, the Clean Water Act measures up much less favorably than the Clean Air Act in terms of economic efficiency.

Third, *cost effectiveness achieved a much more prominent position in public discourse regarding environmental policy during the 1990s.* From the Bush administration through the Clinton administration, interest and activity regarding market-based instruments for environmental protection—particularly tradable permit systems—continued to increase, while support for taxes was lukewarm. The administration promoted cost effectiveness by supporting the implementation of existing market-based initiatives, including the sulfur dioxide allowance trading program, and by proposing new initiatives, exemplified by the strong U.S. support for tradable permit programs for reducing greenhouse gas emissions. The performance of market-based instruments that were implemented—from the 1980s through the 1990s—was encouraging, including the leaded gasoline phasedown in the 1980s and the SO_2 allowance trading program in the 1990s.

Fourth, *the Clinton administration put much greater emphasis than previous administrations on expanding the role of environmental information disclosure and voluntary programs.* In 1994, EPA expanded the list of chemicals to be reported under the Toxics Release Inventory (TRI) by 80 percent; it lowered reporting thresholds, and later expanded the list again. In addition, EPA launched a number of other information programs, focusing on energy efficiency and contaminants in drinking water. While such programs can provide cost-effective ways of reaching environmental policy goals, we know very little about their actual costs or their actual effectiveness. EPA also initiated dozens of programs designed to encourage sources to reduce emissions on a voluntary basis, many under the "Common Sense Initiative." These too have the potential to be cost effective, but it is unclear whether the programs were actually successful.

Fifth and finally, *the Environmental Protection Agency reduced the role of economic analysis in its decision-making during the 1990s.* During the Clinton years, the EPA was more hostile toward economic analysis than it had been during the prior Bush administration, and EPA leadership made organizational changes to reflect this shift. When economics did play a role, economic analysis was more likely to be focused on increasing the cost effectiveness of regulations than on weighing benefits against costs.

These five themes emerge within the broader political context of environmental policy. On the one hand, in simple terms, Democrats, supported by environmental advocacy groups, have typically opposed benefit-cost analysis as a criterion for identifying environmental targets, because it has been seen by many as a mechanism to reduce environmental protection efforts. Republicans, supported by business interests, have usually supported greater use of benefit-cost analysis of environmental regulations for precisely the same reason. On the other hand, in the context of public lands and natural resource management, the application of benefit-cost analysis typically implies limited extractive resource use. Hence, in this case, we observe significant support from Democrats to implement policies that could enhance efficiency, but consistent opposition from most Republicans. Each side supports the use of economic criteria in the environmental/resource realm only when and where related economic analysis is likely to affirm its predisposed ideological position.

In contrast to efficient policies, cost-effective policies and thus market-based instruments are far easier for both Democrats and Republicans to endorse. If a goal is set, why not find the least costly way of achieving it? There are exceptions, of course, most notably when there are identifiable losers from particular policies. But, by and large, cost-effectiveness analysis and market-based instruments have evolved from political anathema for many to political correctness for virtually all.

Much can be explained as business as usual in Washington, but politics is only part of the explanation. Ideas also matter. The very notions of applying economic analysis in environmental and resource policy design and using economic instruments in policy implementation are becoming more widely accepted. We expect the future to bring more benefit-cost analysis, more risk analysis, more cost-effectiveness analysis, and more use of market-based policy instruments. Whether or not such analysis will improve policy is less clear, but we believe that environmental policies are likely to become more cost effective over time, if only because policy-makers and interest groups will have better information at their disposal. More broadly, the efficiency of environmental and resource policy in the future will depend, to some extent, on the ability of economists to convince the broader policy community of the value of this way of thinking about the world.

References

AEI-Brookings Joint Center for Regulatory Studies et al. 2000. Brief Amici Curiae in the Supreme Court of the United States No. 99–1426, *American Trucking Associations, Inc., et al. v. Carol M. Browner, Administrator of the Environmental Protection Agency et al.* (21 July).

Anderson, Robert C. 1997. *The U.S. Experience with Economic Incentives in Environmental Pollution Control Policy.* Washington, DC: Environmental Law Institute.

Anderson, Robert C., and Richard A. Rykowski. 1997. "Reformulated Gasoline." In Richard D. Morgenstern, ed., *Economic Analyses at EPA: Assessing Regulatory Impact*, 391–418. Washington, DC: Resources for the Future.

Arrow, Kenneth J., Maureen L. Cropper, George C. Eads, Robert W. Hahn, Lester B. Lave, Roger G. Noll, Paul R. Portney, Milton Russell, Richard Schmalensee, V. Kerry Smith, and Robert N. Stavins. 1996. "Is There a Role for Benefit-Cost Analysis in Environmental, Health, and Safety Regulation?" *Science* 272 (April): 221–222.

Baumol, W. J., and Wallace E. Oates. 1971. "The Use of Standards and Prices for Protection of the Environment." *Swedish Journal of Economics*, 73:42–54.

Bingham, Tayler H., Timothy R. Bondelid, Brooks M. Depro, Ruth C. Figueroa, A. Brett Hauber, Susan J. Unger, and George L. Van Houtven. 1998. *A Benefits Assessment of Water Pollution Control Programs Since 1972.* Revised draft report to the U.S. Environmental Protection Agency. Research Triangle Institute, Research Triangle Park, NC.

Blodgett, John E. 1995. "Environmental Policy and the Economy: Conflicts and Concordances." Congressional Research Service Report for Congress 95–147 ENR. Congressional Research Service, Washington, DC.

———. 1998. "Environmental Reauthorizations and Regulatory Reform: From the 104th Congress to the 105th." Congressional Research Service Report for Congress 96–949 ENR, updated February 10, 1998. Congressional Research Service, Washington, DC.

Boyd, James. 2000. "The New Face of the Clean Water Act: A Critical Review of the EPA's Proposed TMDL Rules." Discussion Paper 00–12. Resources for the Future, Washington, DC.

Breyer, Stephen. 1993. *Breaking the Vicious Circle: Toward Effective Risk Regulation*. Cambridge, MA: Harvard University Press.

Browner, Carol M. 2000. Speech marking the 30th anniversary of Earth Day. John F. Kennedy School of Government, Harvard University (17 April).

Buck, Eugene H. 1996. "Magnuson Fishery Conservation and Management Act Reauthorization." Congressional Research Service Issue Brief for Congress 95036. Congressional Research Service, Washington, DC.

Burnett, Jason K., and Robert W. Hahn. 2001. "EPA's Arsenic Rule: The Benefits of the Standard Do Not Justify the Costs." Regulatory Analysis 01–02 (January). AEI-Brookings Joint Center for Regulatory Studies, Washington, DC.

Burtraw, Dallas. 1996. "The SO_2 Emissions Trading Program: Cost Savings Without Allowance Trades." *Contemporary Economic Policy*, 14:79–94.

Burtraw, Dallas, Alan Krupnick, Erin Mansur, David Austin, and Deirdre Farrell. 1998. "Costs and Benefits of Reducing Air Pollutants Related to Acid Rain." *Contemporary Economic Policy*, 16 (October): 379–400.

Burtraw, D., and E. Mansur. 1999. "The Environmental Effects of SO_2 Trading and Banking." *Environmental Science and Technology*, 33(20): 3489–94.

Card, Andrew H., Jr. 2001. Memorandum for the Heads and Acting Heads of Executive Departments and Agencies, Regarding Regulatory Review Plan (January 20). White House, Washington, DC.

Carlson, Curtis, Dallas Burtraw, Maureen Cropper, and Karen L. Palmer. 2000. "Sulfur Dioxide Control by Electric Utilities: What Are the Gains from Trade?" *Journal of Political Economy*, 108(6): 1292–1326.

Carson, Richard T., and Robert Cameron Mitchell. 1993. "The Value of Clean Water: The Public's Willingness to Pay for Boatable, Fishable, and Swimmable Quality Water." *Water Resources Research*, 29(7): 2445–54.

Caulkins, Peter, and Stuart Sessions. 1997. "Water Pollution and the Organic Chemicals Industry." In Richard D. Morgenstern, ed., *Economic Analyses at EPA: Assessing Regulatory Impact*, 87–130. Washington, DC: Resources for the Future.

Cavanagh, Sheila M., Robert W. Hahn, and Robert N. Stavins. 2001. "National Environmental Policy During the Clinton Years." Working Paper Number RWP01–027. John F. Kennedy School of Government, Harvard University, Cambridge, MA.

Cody, Betsy A. 1996. "Grazing Fees: An Overview." Congressional Research Service Report for Congress 96–450 ENR (May). Congressional Research Service, Washington, DC.

Copeland, Claudia. 1996. "Reinventing the Environmental Protection Agency and EPA's Water Programs." Congressional Research Service Report to Congress 96–283 ENR. Congressional Research Service, Washington, DC.

———. 1999. "Nationwide Permits for Wetlands Projects: Permit 26 and Other Issues and Controversies." Congressional Research Service Report for Congress 97–223 ENR (January). Congressional Research Service, Washington, DC.

Cropper, Maureen L., William N. Evans, Stephen J. Berard, Maria M. Ducla-Soares, and Paul R. Portney. 1992. "The Determinants of Pesticide Regulation: A Statistical Analysis of EPA Decision-Making." *Journal of Political Economy*, 100:175–197.

Darmstadter, Joel. 2000. "Greening the GDP: Is It Desirable? Is It Feasible?" *Resources*, 139 (Spring): 11–15.

Dombeck, Mike. 2001. "Roadless Area Conservation: An Investment for Future Generations." Statement on Final Rule on Roadless Area Conservation, Washington, DC (5 January).

Dudley, Susan, and Angela Antonelli. 1997. "Shining a Bright Light on Regulators: Tracking the Costs and Benefits of Federal Regulation." Heritage Foundation *Backgrounder* (September 30).

Farrell, Alex, Robert Carter, and Roger Raufer. 1999. "The NO_x Budget: Market-Based Control of Tropospheric Ozone in the Northeastern United States." *Resource and Energy Economics*, 21:103–124.

Ferrall, B. L. 1991. "The Clean Air Act Amendments of 1990 and the use of Market Forces to Control Sulfur Dioxide Emissions." *Harvard Journal on Legislation*, 28:235–252.

Fraas, Arthur. 1991. "The Role of Economic Analysis in Shaping Environmental Policy." *Law and Contemporary Problems*, 54:113–125.

Freeman, A. Myrick. 1982. *Air and Water Pollution Control: A Benefit-Cost Assessment.* New York: Wiley.

———. 2000. "Water Pollution Policy." In Paul R. Portney and Robert N. Stavins, *Public Policies for Environmental Protection*, 169–214. Washington, DC: Resources for the Future.

———. 2001. "Environmental Policy in the U.S. Since Earth Day I—What Have We Gained?" Working Paper, Department of Economics, Bowdoin College, Brunswick, ME.

Gardiner, David. 1999. Letter to Robert Stavins, Chair, Environmental Economics Advisory Committee, Science Advisory Board, U.S. Environmental Protection Agency, April 6.

Gore, Albert, Jr. 1992. *Earth in the Balance: Ecology and the Human Spirit.* New York: Houghton Mifflin Company.

Goulder, Lawrence H. 1995. "Effects of Carbon Taxes in an Economy with Prior Tax Distortions: An Intertemporal General Equilibrium Analysis." *Journal of Environmental Economics and Management*, 29:271–297.

Gray, George M., and John D. Graham. 1991. "Risk Assessment and Clean Air Policy." *Journal of Policy Analysis and Management*, 10(2): 286–295.

Hahn, Robert W. 2000. "The Impact of Economics on Environmental Policy." *Journal of Environmental Economics and Management*, 39:375–399.

Hahn, Robert W., Jason K. Burnett, Yee-Ho I. Chan, Elizabeth A. Mader, and Petrea R. Moyle. 2000. "Assessing Regulatory Impact Analyses: The Failure of Agencies to Comply with Executive Order 12866." *Harvard Journal of Law and Public Policy*, 23:859–885.

Hahn, Robert W., and Gordon L. Hester. 1989. "Where Did All the Markets Go? An Analysis of EPA's Emissions Trading Program." *Yale Journal of Regulation*, 6:109–153.

Hahn, Robert W., and John A. Hird. 1991. "The Costs and Benefits of Regulation: Review and Synthesis." *Yale Journal on Regulation*, 8(1): 233–278.

Hahn, Robert W., Randall W. Lutter, and W. Kip Viscusi. 2000. *Do Federal Regulations Reduce Mortality?* Washington, DC: AEI-Brookings Joint Center for Regulatory Studies.

Hamilton, James T. 1995. "Pollution as News: Media and Stock Market Reactions to the Toxics Release Inventory Data." *Journal of Environmental Economics and Management*, 28:98–113.

Hamilton, James T., and W. Kip Viscusi. 1999. "How Costly Is Clean? An Analysis of the Benefits
and Costs of Superfund." *Journal of Policy Analysis and Management*, 18(1): 2–27.

Hammitt, James K. 2000. "Are the Costs of Proposed Environmental Regulations Overestimated?
Evidence from the CFC Phaseout." *Environmental and Resource Economics*, 16(3): 281–301.

Harrington, Winston, Richard D. Morgenstern, and Peter Nelson. 2000. "On the Accuracy of Regulatory Cost Estimates." *Journal of Policy Analysis and Management*, 19:297–322.

Hartman, Raymond S., David Wheeler, and Manjula Singh. 1994. "The Cost of Air Pollution
Abatement." World Bank Policy Research Working Paper No. 1398. Washington, DC (December).

Hazilla, Michael, and Raymond J. Kopp. 1990. "Social Cost of Environmental Quality Regulations:
A General Equilibrium Analysis." *Journal of Political Economy*, 98(4): 853–873.

Interagency Analytical Team. 1998. *The Kyoto Protocol and the President's Policies to Address Climate
Change: Assessing the Costs and Benefits of Reducing Greenhouse Emissions, Administration Economic
Analysis*. Washington, DC, July.

Interlaboratory Working Group. 1997. *Scenarios of U.S. Carbon Reductions: Potential Impacts of Energy-
Efficient and Low-Carbon Technologies by 2010 and Beyond*. Oak Ridge, TN, and Berkeley, CA: Oak
Ridge National Laboratory and Lawrence Berkeley National Laboratory. ORNL-444 and LBNL-
40533. September.

Jaffe, Adam B., Steven R. Peterson, Paul R. Portney, and Robert N. Stavins. 1995. "Environmental
Regulation and the Competitiveness of U.S. Manufacturing: What Does the Evidence Tell Us?"
Journal of Economic Literature, 33:132–163.

Jorgenson, Dale W., and Peter J. Wilcoxen. 1990. "Environmental Regulation and U.S. Economic
Growth." *RAND Journal of Economics*, 21(2): 314–340.

Kerr, Suzi, and D. Maré. 1997. "Efficient Regulation Through Tradable Permit Markets: The United
States Lead Phasedown." Department of Agricultural and Resource Economics, University of
Maryland, College Park, Working Paper 96–06 (January).

Khanna, Madhu, Wilma Rose H. Quimio, and Dora Bojilova. 1998. "Toxics Release Information: A
Policy Tool for Environmental Protection." *Journal of Environmental Economics and Management*,
62:243–266.

Kolstad, Charles D., and Michael A. Toman. Forthcoming. "The Economics of Climate Policy." *The
Handbook of Environmental Economics*, ed. Karl-Göran Mäler and Jeffrey Vincent. Amsterdam: North-
Holland/Elsevier Science.

Konar, Shameek, and Mark A. Cohen. 1997. "Information as Regulation: The Effect of Community
Right to Know Laws on Toxic Emissions." *Journal of Environmental Economics and Management*,
32:109–124.

Lee, Martin R. 1995. "Environmental Protection: From the 103rd to the 104th Congress." Congressional Research Service Report for Congress 95–58 ENR, Congressional Research Service, Washington, DC.

Lutter, Randall. 1999. "Is EPA's Ozone Standard Feasible?" Regulatory Analysis 99–6, AEI-Brookings
Joint Center for Regulatory Studies, Washington, DC (December).

Lutter, Randall, and Richard B. Belzer. 2000. "EPA Pats Itself on the Back." *Regulation*, 23(3): 23–28.

Lutter, Randall, and Christopher Wolz. 1997. "UV-B Screening by Tropospheric Ozone: Implications for the National Ambient Air Quality Standard." *Environmental Science and Technology*, 31:142A–146A.

Lyon, Randolph, and Scott Farrow. 1995. "An Economic Analysis of Clean Water Act Issues." *Water Resources Research*, 31:213–223.

Morgenstern, Richard D. 1997a. "Introduction to Economic Analysis at EPA." In Richard D. Morgenstern, ed., *Economic Analyses at EPA: Assessing Regulatory Impact*, 1–4. Washington, DC: Resources for the Future.

———. 1997b. "The Legal and Institutional Setting for Economic Analysis at EPA." In Richard D. Morgenstern, ed., *Economic Analyses at EPA: Assessing Regulatory Impact*, 5–23. Washington, DC: Resources for the Future.

———, ed. 1997c. *Economic Analyses at EPA: Assessing Regulatory Impact*. Washington, DC: Resources for the Future.

———. 2000. "Decision making at EPA: Economics, Incentives and Efficiency." Draft conference paper, EPA at Thirty: Evaluating and Improving the Environmental Protection Agency, Duke University (7–8 December).

Morrall, John F., III. 1986. "A Review of the Record." *Regulation*, 10(2): 13–24, 30–34.

Morrissey, Wayne A. 2000. "RL30522: Global Climate Change: A Survey of Scientific Research and Policy Reports." Congressional Research Service Report for Congress (April), Congressional Research Service, Washington, DC.

Newell, Richard G., and Robert N. Stavins. 2001. "Abatement Cost Heterogeneity and Anticipated Savings from Market-Based Environmental Policies." Working Paper, John F. Kennedy School of Government, Harvard University, March 2001.

Nichols, Albert. 1997. "Lead in Gasoline." In Richard D. Morgenstern, ed., *Economic Analyses at EPA: Assessing Regulatory Impact*, 49–86. Washington, DC: Resources for the Future.

Nordhaus, William. 1977. "Economic Growth and Climate: The Case of Carbon Dioxide." *American Economic Review*, May.

———. 1982. "How Fast Should We Graze the Global Commons?" *American Economic Review*, 72:242–246.

———. 2001. Personal communication, 19 March.

Nordhaus, William D., and Edward C. Kokkelenberg, eds. 1999. *Nature's Numbers: Expanding the National Economic Accounts to Include the Environment*. Washington, DC: National Academy Press.

Portney, Paul R. 1984. *Natural Resources and the Environment: The Reagan Approach*. Washington, DC: Urban Institute Press.

———. 1990. "Policy Watch: Economics and the Clean Air Act." *Journal of Economic Perspectives*, 4(4): 173–181.

———. 2000. "Air Pollution Policy." In Paul R. Portney and Robert N. Stavins, *Public Policies for Environmental Protection*, 77–124. Washington, DC: Resources for the Future.

Portney, Paul R., and Robert N. Stavins. 2000. *Public Policies for Environmental Protection*. Washington, DC: Resources for the Future.

Rasmussen, Sara. 1997. "Municipal Landfill Management." In Richard D. Morgenstern, ed., *Eco-

nomic Analyses at EPA: Assessing Regulatory Impact, 233–266. Washington, DC: Resources for the Future.

Reisch, Mark. 2000. "IB10011: Superfund Reauthorization Issues in the 106th Congress." Congressional Research Service Issue Brief for Congress (October), Congressional Research Service, Washington, DC.

Schierow, Linda Jo. 1994. "Risk Analysis and Cost-Benefit Analysis of Environmental Regulations." Congressional Research Service Report for Congress 94–961 ENR, Congressional Research Service, Washington, DC.

———. 1996. "Pesticide Legislation: Food Quality Protection Act of 1996." Congressional Research Service Report for Congress 96–759 ENR, Congressional Research Service, Washington, DC.

Schmalensee, R., P. L. Joskow, A. D. Ellerman, J. P. Montero, and E. M. Bailey. 1998. "An Interim Evaluation of Sulfur Dioxide Emissions Trading." *Journal of Economic Perspectives*, 12(3): 53–68.

Sedjo, Roger A. 2000. "Does the Forest Service Have a Future? A Thought-Provoking View." In *A Vision for the U.S. Forest Service: Goals for Its Next Century*, ed. Roger A. Sedjo. Washington, DC: Resources for the Future.

Shogren, Jason F. 1998. "A Political Economy in an Ecological Web." *Environmental and Resource Economics*, 11(3–4): 557–570.

Smith, Richard, Richard Alexander, and M. Gordon Wolman. 1987. "Water Quality Trends in the Nation's Rivers." *Science*, 235:1607.

Smith, V. Kerry. 1984. *Environmental Policy under Reagan's Executive Order*. Chapel Hill: University of North Carolina Press.

Snyder, Lori D. 2001. "Regulating Pollution Through Information Disclosure: Modeling Firm Response to the Toxics Release Inventory." Draft Working Paper, Kennedy School of Government, Harvard University, Cambridge, MA.

Solomon, B. D. 1999. "New Directions in Emissions Trading: The Potential Contribution of New Institutional Economics." *Ecological Economics*, 30:371–387.

Solow, Robert. 1992. "An Almost Practical Step Toward Sustainability." Invited Lecture on the Occasion of the Fortieth Anniversary of Resources for the Future (October), Resources for the Future, Washington, DC.

Stavins, Robert N. 1998. "What Have We Learned from the Grand Policy Experiment: Lessons from SO_2 Allowance Trading." *Journal of Economic Perspectives*, 12(3): 69–88.

———. 2000. "A Somewhat Personal Perspective on the Role of Economics at the U.S. Environmental Protection Agency." Comments delivered in panel session, North Carolina State University, Raleigh (14 November).

———. Forthcoming. "Experience with Market-Based Environmental Policy Instruments." In Karl-Göran Mäler and Jeffrey Vincent, *The Handbook of Environmental Economics*. Amsterdam: North-Holland/Elsevier Science.

Stewart, Richard B., and Jonathan B. Wiener. 1992. "The Comprehensive Approach to Global Climate Policy." *Arizona Journal of International and Comparative Law*, 9:83.

Stroup, Richard L. 2000. "Air Toxics Policy: Liabilities from Thin Air." In *Cutting Green Tape: Toxic Pollutants, Environmental Regulation and the Law*, ed. Richard L. Stroup and Roger E. Meiners. Oakland, CA: Independent Institute.

Tiemann, Mary. 1999. "Safe Drinking Water Act Amendments of 1996: Overview of P.L. 104–182." Congressional Research Service Report for Congress 96–722, updated February 8, 1999. Congressional Research Service, Washington, DC.

Tietenberg, Tom H. 1985. *Emissions Trading: An Exercise in Reforming Pollution Policy*. Washington, DC: Resources for the Future.

———. 1990. "Economic Instruments for Environmental Regulation." *Oxford Review of Economic Policy*, 6(1): 17–33.

United Nations. 1992. "United Nations Framework Convention on Climate Change." Climate Change Secretariat, Geneva, Switzerland (June).

U.S. Council of Economic Advisers. 1996. *Economic Report of the President*. Transmitted to the Congress February 1996. Washington, DC: U.S. Government Printing Office.

———. 1997. *Economic Report of the President*. Transmitted to the Congress February 1997. Washington, DC: U.S. Government Printing Office.

———. 1998. *The Kyoto Protocol and the President's Policies to Address Climate Change: Administration Economic Analysis*. Washington, DC: Council of Economic Advisers.

U.S. Department of Commerce. 2000. "Submission for OMB Review: Comment Request." *Federal Register*, 65(27), February 29.

U.S. Department of Commerce, Bureau of Economic Analysis. 1994. "Accounting for Mineral Resources: Issues and BEA's Initial Estimates." *Survey of Current Business* (April).

U.S. Department of Energy, Energy Information Administration. 1998. *Impacts of the Kyoto Protocol on U.S. Energy Markets and Economic Activity*, SR/OIAF/98–03. Washington, DC: U.S. Department of Energy.

U.S. Environmental Protection Agency. 1985. *Costs and Benefits of Reducing Lead in Gasoline, Final Regulatory Impact Analysis*. Washington, DC: U.S. Environmental Protection Agency.

———. 1991. *Environmental Investments: The Cost of a Clean Environment*, EPA–230–90–083. Washington, DC: U.S. Environmental Protection Agency.

——— 1996. *The Quality of Our Nation's Water: Overview of States' Sec. 303(b) Water Quality Reporting for the Year 1996*. Washington, DC: U.S. Environmental Protection Agency.

———. 1997. *The Benefits and Costs of the Clean Air Act, 1970 to 1990*. Prepared for the U.S. Congress. Washington, DC: U.S. Environmental Protection Agency.

———. 1999. *The Benefits and Costs of the Clean Air Act, 1990 to 2010*. Prepared for the U.S. Congress. Washington, DC: U.S. Environmental Protection Agency.

———. 2001a. *The United States Experience with Economic Incentives for Protecting the Environment*, EPA–240–R–01–001. Washington, DC: National Center for Environmental Economics.

———. 2001b. "Supreme Court Upholds EPA Position on Smog, Particulate Rules." EPA Headquarters Press Release (27 February), Washington, DC.

U.S. Environmental Protection Agency, National Center for Environmental Economics. 2001. *The United States Experience with Economic Incentives for Protecting the Environment*, EPA 240–R–01–001, January. Washington, DC: U.S. Environmental Protection Agency.

U.S. Environmental Protection Agency, Office of Air Quality Planning and Standards. 2000a. *National Air Pollutant Emission Trends, 1900–1998*, EPA–454/R–00–002. Research Triangle Park, NC.

————. 2000b. *National Air Quality and Emissions Trends Report, 1998*, EPA–454/R–00–003. Research Triangle Park, NC.

U.S. Environmental Protection Agency, Office of Water. 2000. "Total Maximum Daily Load (TMDL) Program," EPA841–F–00–009. Washington, DC.

U.S. General Accounting Office. 1994. *Pesticides: Reducing Exposure to Residues of Canceled Pesticides*, GAO/RCED–95–23. Gaithersburg, MD.

————. 1997a. "Environmental Protection: Challenges Facing EPA's Efforts to Reinvent Environmental Regulation," GAO/RCED–97–155 (July). Washington, DC.

————. 1997b. "Regulatory Reinvention: EPA's Common Sense Initiative Needs an Improved Operating Framework and Progress Measures," GAO/RCED–97–164 (July). Washington, DC.

————. 1999. "Forest Service Priorities: Evolving Mission Favors Resource Protection Over Production," GAO/RCED–99–166 (June). Washington, DC.

U.S. Office of Management and Budget. 1997. *Report to Congress on the Costs and Benefits of Federal Regulations*. Washington, DC: Office of Management and Budget.

————. 1998. *Report to Congress on the Costs and Benefits of Federal Regulations*. Washington, DC: Office of Management and Budget.

U.S. Supreme Court. 2001. Syllabus, *Whitman, Administrator of Environmental Protection Agency, et al., v. American Trucking Association, Inc., et al.*, Certiorari to the United States Court of Appeals for the District of Columbia Circuit, No. 99–1257, Argued November 7, 2000–Decided February 27, 2001.

Vincent, Carol Hardy. 1998. "Grand Staircase–Escalante National Monument." Congressional Research Service Report for Congress ENR 98–993 (December). Congressional Research Service, Washington, DC.

Viscusi, W. Kip. 1992. *Fatal Tradeoffs: Public and Private Responsibilities for Risk*. New York: Oxford University Press.

————. 1994. "Health and Safety Regulation." In *American Economic Policy in the 1980s*, ed. Martin Feldstein. Chicago: University of Chicago Press.

————. 1996. "Regulating the Regulators." *University of Chicago Law Review*, 63:1423–61.

Weitzman, Martin L. 1976. "On the Welfare Significance of National Product in a Dynamic Economy." *Quarterly Journal of Economics*, 90(1): 156–162.

White House, Office of the Press Secretary. 2000. "Giant Sequoia National Monument." Press Release (15 April).

Comments

George T. Frampton

I thought that the chapter prepared for this session was terrific, very thorough and a very good summary of most of the major environmental initiatives and programs that the Clinton administration mounted over the last eight years.

I want to focus on four areas where I think the Clinton administration changed and redefined the direction of environmental policy for the next 15 or 20 years, all in the domestic arena, then discuss a fifth area—that of global issues—where the intersection of economics and environmental policy is going to be most difficult and most problematic. It is the global issues which I think, by and large, the Clinton administration barely touched in the past eight years.

The first area has to do with the future of our air quality. The second with ecosystem management, public land management, and water management. The third is the exploding area of environmental information. The fourth area I would call the operational reform of some of the original 1970s environmental statutes that by the early 1990s appeared to be broken and in need of fixing. With one exception, the Food Quality Protection Act (pesticides), Congress didn't fix these laws; therefore, the executive branch had to try to reform them administratively. I think the first two areas, air quality and ecosystem management, are the areas which, when we look back 10 years from now, will stand out as the major environmental achievements of the Clinton administration.

Bob and Robert's paper talks a lot about the so-called soot and smog rules and the battle over setting new levels for these criteria air pollutants as required by the Clean Air Act. But I think, as well, the new so-called Tier II regulations governing tailpipe emissions for cars and trucks, requiring cleaner fuels—reducing sulfur in both regular gasoline and diesel fuel—were equally important. The Tier II regulations came in the second four years and were somewhat less controversial than the soot and smog rules, in part because Carol Browner and her colleagues at EPA did a fantastic job of negotiating out in advance, with various interests—including health and environmental groups, the automobile manufacturers, the oil companies—what was an acceptable outcome.

If you look at these two sets of air quality rules that were promulgated in the last five years of the Clinton administration, we pretty much defined the rules for most stationary sources and mobile sources for air pollution for the next 15 years. I would add to these a third rule, on regional haze, which the Bush administration has just decided to implement. These regulations were driven, as the paper notes, by statute. They follow from the original Clean Air Act and the 1990 amendments. These statutes in 1990 forced EPA to come up with a whole new generation of standards, and those standards have now been promulgated, and I think probably, for the most part, a few court challenges notwithstanding, will stick.

The second area I want to highlight is ecosystem management. The need to come up with new approaches to federal land management was originally triggered by the fact that there was gridlock in the Pacific Northwest over forest policy and the spotted owl. It's a little hard to remember now, but our whole public lands regulatory system was in a crisis when Clinton was elected. What the administration developed there, in its broad regional plan for the Pacific Northwest forests, balanced sustainable timber cutting with environmental protection. It became a model for addressing contentious land and resource management issues on a regional basis, bringing different interests to the table to work out some kind of compromise that would allow on-the-ground management to go forward without court interference but would also try to provide some kind of predictability and sustainable production.

The same basic approach then got applied in other places where, without some sort of a state/federal stakeholder process, you would have had litigation gridlock. To deal with the California water wars, the California Bay Delta Accord was reached in 1994, and then finally a long-term strategy ("CalFed") was put in place in 2000 for dividing up California water in the northern part of the state between agriculture, urban water interests, and environmental needs. In south Florida, the Everglades were threatened with a total litigation breakdown; instead, the administration designed what now has become an $8 billion restoration plan, approved by Congress and the state, which I think is supported by both parties. It's also supported by a diverse set of interest groups. Finally, flowing out of the Northwest forest plan, the evolutionary but very important changes in forest policy that were made by the Forest Service in the last couple of years, including new forest planning rules, I think will define the way we manage our public forests over the next 10 or 15 years. Here, I think these new approaches are now the accepted model for land use management.

Now, going back and looking at the intersection of economics and the environment, the paper for this session suggests that cost-benefit analysis of environmental initiatives played less of a role in the Clinton administration than it did, let's say, in the Bush administration or the Reagan administration. My impression, from participating in internal White House debates, is that, in fact, in the case of environmental rule-making, the ultimate choices between policy alternatives were very intensively debated on the basis of relative costs versus environmental benefits. Now, the ecosystem management issues were a little different. There, long-term plans tended to be developed through a stakeholder process, and the economic issues were equity issues: for example, between competing uses of forestland or water resources. In the major restoration initiatives like the Everglades and CalFed, a key economic issue was who would end up paying the bills between state and federal government taxpayers, resource users, those who derived benefits from government projects, and so on.

But in the case of air quality and other pollution issues, cost-benefit analysis was an important template for policy-making—perhaps not so much at EPA, but certainly when proposed rules moved to the White House for interagency review at OMB, you had the full panoply of players within the administration, the Council of Economic Advisers, the Energy Department, all weighing in, and you had a robust debate with interest groups from outside that were trying to bring their own set of pressures to bear on that process. Cost-benefit analysis became, really, the structure for the internal dialogue.

Now, that's not to say that cost-benefit analysis necessarily dictated the outcome or was determinative, as some economists would like to see. Let me give you an analogy. In the environmental community, over the last few years, there's been a great hue and cry about how we have to have environmental policy built on sound science. To the extent this position suggests that science can tell you the right answer, that's not true. Science can help you evaluate risks and make predictions about outcomes, but there's a point at which science isn't going to take you any further. Science helps you define the choices and make educated guesses about results, but ultimately the choices are policy choices and, perhaps, one would say political choices. In the same way, I think that's the way cost-benefit analysis, from my point of view, functioned in the Clinton administration. It helped define the range of choices, the terms of the debate, the risk and probability of certain outcomes likely to result from competing choices—but it didn't ultimately dictate or totally control the policy and political choices that had to be made.

With respect to the third category of issues I want to address, environmental information, the Clinton administration started to do something that's very important. I'm personally convinced that as more and different kinds of information are made available in different ways to the public and to consumers, the availability of environmental information is going to displace a great deal of environmental regulation in the future. In the past few years, through expan-

sion of substances covered by the Toxic Release Inventory reporting requirements and lowering reporting thresholds, and through agreements such as
the one reached by EPA with the Chemical Manufacturers' Association to test
thousands of chemicals and post the results on the Internet, we've begun the
process of making relevant and eventually real-time information available to
the public.

In these areas, it's a little harder to figure out how to apply cost-benefit
analysis. You can predict with reasonable accuracy what the costs will be to an
industry of reporting much lower levels of certain toxic releases, but it's very
difficult to try to evaluate what the benefit of more information is to the public.

The fourth area that I wanted to mention is reforming and updating major
statutes that by the early 1990s were simply not working very well. The Superfund program and Endangered Species Act are the two that, in my judgment,
stick out. In both cases there were consensus reform legislative proposals that
should have passed Congress and didn't. So it was left to the administration to
try to fix these statutes by executive action. I think we did a fairly good job on
both. The Endangered Species Act wasn't necessarily a statute that was broken
as applied to public lands. But as applied to private lands, it was headed for a
total breakdown in a sense that the way the statute was written, the landowner
was faced with enormous threats, but the species weren't going to get very
much benefit, so you had a lose-lose proposition there. What the administration
tried to do was work out a whole new program of voluntary agreements to
substitute for regulation. In the case of the Superfund program, cleanups were
vastly accelerated.

In this area of reforming statutes administratively, significant positive economic *and* environmental benefits will flow from our actions, because we reduced the costs to those being regulated at the same time as the environmental
payoff is increased.

Having had some months now to look back, I think it's fair to say that the
area where the Clinton administration made the least impact was on global
issues. The Kyoto Protocol is an exception. Of course, we are now having a debate, which we should be having, about whether Kyoto is the right vehicle for
addressing global climate change. Whether we're going to go sideways, backward, or forward remains to be seen. But Kyoto was an international milestone.
With the exception of Kyoto, however, look at the major global issues that were
identified by 1990: climate change, and the intersection of energy and the environment; biodiversity loss; ocean pollution; the challenge of biotechnology; the
intersection between our international financial architecture and the environment; and trade policy. The administration really didn't grapple with these

issues very effectively. I'm not making a judgment about it. I think it's just a fact. And those are the big issues we will confront in the next 15 to 20 years.

Are these issues amenable to cost-benefit analysis? I would go further and say that these issues—energy, climate, carbon release, biotechnology, international lending—are issues that are entwined with the global economy. So we must bring effective economic analysis and economic information to bear on how we—the United States—and the entire world community approach them. In fact, these "environmental" issues will be largely determined by economic policy-making. I don't think we can derive very many lessons from what the Clinton administration did on those issues, and I am sure it's not going to be easy to structure a way to bring effective economic analysis and information to those issues in the future. Doing so, it seems to me, is the major environmental challenge that we face in the next 10 or 15 years.

Comments

Paul R. Portney

It's particularly distinguished company at this conference, and it's nice to be a part of it. I'm going to make a few direct remarks on the really nice chapter that Rob Stavins and Bob Hahn have written. Then I'm going to use their chapter as a point of departure to make a few broader observations about environmental policy and the role that economics did play in the 1990s and might play in the years ahead.

With specific reference to the chapter, the authors have really done a terrific job. I once had the responsibility to write a similar paper on the role of economics in environmental and natural resource policy in the Reagan administration. These are very difficult papers to write because a lot of laws and regulations get passed during an administration, and it's easy to get very focused on not just the trees, but even the branches and the twigs. The authors have looked at the forest, trees, branches, and twigs. I have no doubt that for me or for anybody else who is interested in going back and trying to figure out what happened during the 1990s in environmental policy, particularly from an economic standpoint, this will become the definitive reference.

I particularly like the fact that the authors talk not just about EPA-type pollution policy under the environment rubric, but that they also talk about what happened with respect to the Forest Service, endangered species, water policy, and other public land management issues. The latter tend to get much shorter shrift in discussions of environmental policy. I especially found helpful, and I think you will too, or have already, their racking up of individual regulations, major regulatory decisions, and major statutory changes that bear on the use of economics in environmental regulation during that eight-year period.

Let me step back just a bit and emphasize several things that Hahn and Stavins talked about, though somewhat obliquely, in their chapter, and then conclude by mentioning one thing that they didn't say very much about, but that I think might have been a constructive focus for a discussion about environmental policy in the 1990s. With any luck, it might be one of the things that we'll talk about in this area in the years ahead.

Rob and Bob allude to the downplaying of economics at EPA during the two Clinton terms. They are fairly direct, but I would have used even stronger language myself if I had written this chapter. In some respects, the period 1992 to 2000 was the low-water mark for the application of economics to environmental regulatory decision-making over the 25 years that I have followed environmental policy. The policy office at EPA—which was arguably the best, or certainly one of the best, policy offices in any of the federal agencies—was really eviscerated, and I don't think that that's too strong a word. I think it was done fairly purposefully. At various times, economics, and even economists, were vilified in speeches by the EPA administrator.

Lest this sound like a partisan screed, I want to be quick to say that I think the Republicans bear some, perhaps an equal share, of the blame for all this. When they regained control of Congress in 1994, we began to see the Contract with America and a number of regulatory reform bills introduced that used the words "benefit-cost analysis" and "quantitative risk assessment" and "sound science" a lot. But for most of the people who were proponents of this legislation, very few of them knew a benefit from a cost, or knew anything about benefit-cost analysis, other than having the unshakable view that if this got applied to regulation, there would be less of it in the future. Those proponents of benefit-cost analysis who didn't know very much about it, I would argue, set it back at least as much as the EPA administrator did, though for very different reasons. So when I say it was a low-water mark for the use of economics in environmental policy, I mean sincerely that there's plenty of blame to go around on this issue.

Why should we care about the application of economics to environmental policy anyway? First of all, because it is expensive. As best we can tell, the nation spends somewhere between $150 billion and $200 billion annually to comply with federal environmental regulations on the books now. Now, think about that for a minute—$150 billion to $200 billion annually to comply with environmental regulation. That does not include consumer product safety. That does not include occupational safety and health. And it does not include transportation regulation or any other form of "social regulation." For that reason, it is essential that we put in place only those regulations that, at the margin, balance incremental benefits and costs. Incidentally, meeting the goals the United States committed itself to in the Kyoto Protocol would probably add $50–75 billion per year more to environmental compliance cost.

This $150 billion to $200 billion per year that we spend on environmental compliance is somewhere in the vicinity of 2 percent of GDP. The next time you hear people in Europe complaining that they do more on the environment than we do, keep in mind that, as best we can determine, the Netherlands and Germany probably spend 1.6 to 1.8 percent of their GDP to comply with their respective environmental regulations. So the United States, in my opinion, is not lagging behind anybody in terms of share of GDP devoted to environmental compliance costs.

I've talked a bit about the cost of regulation here. Don't conclude that I think that environmental regulation is necessarily out of control. As Bob Hahn and Rob Stavins point out in their paper, there are at least some regulatory programs, including some big expensive programs, that generate benefits that are in excess, and on occasion well in excess, of their costs. My view of a sophisticated society, at least in the regulatory realm, is one that's developed the ability to somehow filter out the clear regulatory home runs from the clear turkeys. I would argue that we still don't do a very good job even of that. So that's why we need careful economic analysis of environmental regulations, both inside and outside of the Environmental Protection Agency.

Let me say a word about Congress here. Those of us who have had the opportunity to testify before Congress on regulatory reform regularly hear members of Congress say that regulation is "out of control." Congress speaks as if our regulatory statutes were the 11th commandment, that they came down from God, and that there's nothing that Congress can do about them. But our legislators are the ones that pass the laws that give the regulatory agencies all their powers. So instead of wringing their hands and gnashing their teeth about how regulation is out of control, Congress should make the changes they want to see in our regulatory laws. Congress is the body that creates the regulatory agencies, can abolish them, and passes the laws that give them all their powers.

Furthermore, in addition to changing the statutes, if we want information about the compliance costs of other regulatory agencies—CPSC, NHTSA, OSHA, and so on—Congress could pass a law saying that every so often the agency must make an estimate of annual compliance costs and benefits, as it has done in the case of the EPA. That's why we have some idea what the nation spends to comply with environmental regulation; in 1972, Congress amended the Clean Water Act to require a regular cost estimate.

Let me conclude by talking about the one issue that wasn't raised in Rob and Bob's chapter that I think merits some discussion. That is the role of environmental federalism. Going back to the early 1970s, Congress quite appropriately federalized clean air and clean water, because of the obvious interstate spillovers. I think a mind-set developed then in Washington that environmental problems were automatically federal responsibilities. When we began to pass other environmental statutes having to do with solid or hazardous waste, drinking water, and other environmental problems, the mind-set in Congress was that this has to be a federal statute.

In fact, if one looks carefully at such things as the standards that landfills ought to meet, there's no reason why the standards have to be the same everywhere. If California wants to have 45-foot-thick clay liners with leachate collection systems, and make these landfills gold plated, that's fine. But I don't see why if the adjacent state of Nevada wants thinner and less protective landfill liners, preferring to spend money on other things, that's a problem. I don't see interstate spillovers from differences in solid waste regulation that come anywhere close to the kind of spillovers that exist in air and water pollution control.

I think it's time to have a debate in the United States about what level of government is the appropriate level to set standards for various environmental programs. The one warning I would make is this: if you think that applying benefit-cost analysis to environmental regulation is controversial in the advocacy community, try talking about defederalizing some environmental programs that may lend themselves better to regulation at the state and local level!

Comments

Murray Weidenbaum

Let us see if we have this right. The air is getting cleaner; the water is getting purer. The environment generally is getting better. Americans are living longer. The policy regime seems to be working.

So how do policy-makers respond to this good news? They go for tougher standards and do so while brushing aside those green-eyeshades economists who seem determined to make life complicated for the good guys in the white hats. Hahn and Stavins pretty much say this, but as good researchers, they are a bit more circumspect.

Here is an example of my concern. In early 1993, the outgoing members of the Clean Air Act Advisory Committee were asked for advice. As the lone economist, I recommended that the Clinton administration reconsider the number of economists on the committee. They followed my advice to the letter. They went from one economist to none.

Hahn and Stavins have provided a most comprehensive review of the Clinton environmental policies and a very good place to start a discussion of the topic. Despite the great attention that the economics profession has lavished on emissions trading, I believe that Hahn and Stavins are correct in concluding that, on balance, economic analysis has had little effect on the substance of environmental programs in the Clinton administration.

Unfortunately, there is some precedent for that. This situation reminds me of a press conference in early 1981 when I was trying to explain the Reagan administration's approach to regulatory reform. A *Washington Post* reporter got a good laugh when he said, "Professor Weidenbaum, when I took your course in public finance at Washington University, you said that the Corps of Engineers used benefit-cost analysis to sanctify the pork barrel. Have you changed your mind?"

In that same spirit, in the 1990s by and large the environmental regulators went through the motions of performing the required economic analysis, but they primarily used and abused it to justify decisions made on noneconomic grounds. When the EPA said that its best estimate was that, through 1990, the Clean Air Act generated net benefits of $22 trillion, they were telling us that they did not take economic analysis seriously and were playing games.

In this regard, economists are more forgiving than other groups involved in public policy. If any university or think tank researcher had estimated the cost of the Clean Air Act at $22 trillion, they would have been pilloried and subject to intense public ridicule. I still remember the vehement attack by Al Gore and Ralph Nader when I dared to estimate that the cost of complying with all federal regulations at a modest $100 billion a year (in the late 1970s).

There is no need to be too partisan. Environmental policy during the 1990s began with the landmark Clean Air Act Amendments of 1990, enacted during the first Bush administration. That legislation set the tone for the decade that followed. I recall that Paul Portney prepared a rough-cut analysis of an early version of the bill. He demonstrated—with the usual caveats of a good scholar—that the bottom end of the range of costs was greater that the top end of the range of benefits. The analysis did not dampen the enthusiasm of the proponents of the legislation. The 1990 law provided the statutory basis for some of the most burdensome EPA rule-making in the Clinton administration.

In contrast, it is good to be reminded that the benefits of the SO_2 emissions trading program are far greater than the costs. That is an impressive tribute to the economists who designed this innovative concept.

Nevertheless, I have an uneasy feeling that these very useful efforts, which provide a fine precedent, are being devoted to an end that may be of questionable value. I say this because Congress enacted the SO_2 requirements while ignoring the huge amount of research—almost $1 billion—it had sponsored which tended to conclude that the basic acid rain problem was not nearly as serious as the regulatory proponents had described.

A note on information. At times the EPA reporting system is somewhat rigged. For example, the toxics release inventory data are used to develop annual lists of the major polluters. That is useful information. However, when I asked EPA why no government agencies or nonprofit institutions are on the lists, they replied that the law is limited to business firms. The narrow coverage yields misleading conclusions, which in turn influence the public policy environment (e.g., XYZ corporation is listed as the biggest polluter in the state when a DOD or DOE facility is generating far more emissions).

Let us turn to more macro aspects that policy-makers rarely consider: the opportunity costs of the massive outlays for compliance required by the various environmental statutes and the implementing regulations. Aggregate estimates are in the neighborhood of $150 billion a year. From time to time intrepid researchers have estimated how many more lives would be saved if a small fraction of these huge outlays were diverted to such other uses as the provision of emergency medical treatment. The imagination can supply other examples.

Unfortunately, many of the alternatives lack the special attractiveness of environmental compliance costs. They are truly off the federal budget, mainly buried in the accounts of the private sector. This is precisely why regulatory programs, of which the environmental activities are the largest part, need to be subject to probing examination such as benefit-cost analysis, cost-effectiveness analysis, and risk-benefit analysis.

Hahn and Stavins have demonstrated both the difficulties and the potentialities of using economic analysis in the conduct of environmental policy. When the patient is so unwilling, the physician trying to administer the medicine must be both persistent and resourceful. The impacts of environmental regulations are too great for economists to become discouraged and abandon the task—even though the Clinton administration EPA effectively sandbagged most of the efforts to apply economic analysis to environmental decision-making.

It is far more than a matter of numerical estimation, important though that may be. There is an environmental mind-set that is difficult to deal with. Consider the highly touted project XL—one of the EPA's "reinvention" reforms. EPA is so proud that companies are encouraged to propose alternatives that would attain higher levels of pollution control at lower cost. Why not encourage alternatives that attain the same level of pollution control at lower cost? We do not have to guess why that approach is absent. When some of us raised it at an EPA advisory committee in the early 1990s, we encountered implacable resistance from the environmental members. We also learned how to guarantee creating a donnybrook at committee meetings. You do not have to shout "fire." You merely whisper "trade-off."

To those who continue the battle, good luck!

Summary of Discussion

Paul Joskow started off the discussion by asking the panelists and authors to comment on the lawsuits brought by the EPA toward the end of the Clinton administration against several coal-burning utilities which it claimed had over the years modified their plants sufficiently to be subject to the New Source Performance Standards.

Robert Stavins emphasized that new source review is a favorite target of economists because it entails very high costs and strong disincentives for capital stock turnover, possibly resulting in lower environmental quality. The recent EPA lawsuits arose because utilities were going to great lengths to disguise new construction as regular maintenance in order to maintain their grand-fathered status under clean air regulations.

George Frampton argued that the real problem is that 50 percent of electric power in the United States is generated by coal-fired power plants built in the 1970s. These plants emit a large percentage of greenhouse gases in the United States and pose both an efficiency problem and a health problem. *Paul Portney* noted that when the George W. Bush administration issued its energy proposal, the Democratic response noted expansions in electric generating capacity during the Clinton administration. But the response did not mention that EPA then proceeded to sue all of the plants that expanded.

Brad DeLong noted that the Clinton administration's environmental policy was a very odd combination of bold and aggressive environmental rhetoric, a fair measure of command and control, and aversion—except in a very narrow range—to the use of incentives. In his experience, when people within the administration would suggest incentive-based policies, they would meet an immediate objection along the following lines: "We tried that by including the Btu tax in the 1993 budget. It did not work. There is substantial political support for command-and-control environmental policies. There is no support in the United States today for incentive-based environmental policies."

DeLong therefore asked whether industry shot itself in the head by opposing the Btu tax so strongly and successfully. Wasn't this a powerful demonstration that "efficient" incentive-based policies were politically unwise? *Robert Hahn* maintained that it is very hard to convince industry that linking issues is a good idea. Hahn recalls counseling the George H. W. Bush administration that if they really wanted to take a risk, they should support the "polluter pays" principle and shift the tax system around to incorporate revenue-neutral environmental taxes. This was a hard sell. *Stavins* reviewed a few of the many reasons why taxes have much less support in the United States than other market-based instruments. First, while in theory a tax and a tradable permit system have equal total social costs, the cost of a tax to the regulated sector is much higher than the cost of a permit system (unless the permits are auctioned, but typically they are not). In addition, taxes are very transparent. Politicians and environmental activists like benefits to be visible and costs to be invisible. Taxes are incompatible with these priorities.

William Niskanen brought up the Supreme Court decision in *American Trucking Association v. Whitman*, suggesting that the decision was correct, given the current requirements of the Clean Air Act. "Not every dumb law is unconstitutional." He asked the panelists what the likely outcomes of this decision would be. *Portney* maintained that even if Congress changed the Clean Air Act and included a directive to balance benefits and costs, we still would not see a big change in regulations. Administrations will still advocate either stricter or less strict regulations, depending on their political viewpoint, rather than any kind of commitment to efficiency.

Josh Gotbaum questioned why the session chapter and discussion did not distinguish between the use of analysis for decision-making versus its later use for advocacy in support of decisions, two very different uses. He argued, contrary to Hahn's view, that some analyses should not necessarily be required to be publicized, to permit an honest presentation of views to the president. Because EPA's analyses are publicly available, they are not capable of showing all of the nuances and uncertainties that, as part of the Executive Office of the President, the Office of Management and Budget (OMB) can. *Hahn* agreed that this observation may be true—agency analyses play a different role than objective analyses. Hahn asked how economists could encourage the OMB analyses to be made more public and thereby act as a counterweight to analyses by EPA and other agencies. *Gotbaum, Jeffrey Frankel*, and others argued that this would not be the best role for OMB analyses. If analysis is written with publication in mind, they maintained, it cannot discuss the subtler trade-offs and compromises inherent in regulatory policy-making.

Robert Litan asked the panel to explain a paradox: there has been a steady improvement in environmental quality, but still public support for more aggressive regulations is stronger than ever. Does this contradiction persist because we have a high income elasticity for public goods? Or does it continue because interest groups cannot declare victory, since doing so would put them out of business? *Portney* mentioned again that the costs of environmental regulation are approaching $200 billion per year in the United States, but added that no household understands that it is paying about $2,000 per year as its share of these costs. If households did understand, they would probably apply more scrutiny to the regulatory process and the scope of regulation. *Frampton* asked whether the same thing was true of health care, and the panelists responded that it probably was true of health care, as well. *Murray Weidenbaum* suggested that people think of firms as the bearers of the costs of environmental regulation, and consumers as recipients of the benefits. While this assumption is clearly not true, it is a simple picture that makes more regulation an attractive option.

Richard Zeckhauser noted that in pharmaceutical regulation, the time to marketing of drugs became much shorter during the Clinton administration. This change was due at least in part to the pressure applied by AIDS activists. Are there some areas in environmental regulation in which we saw this kind of progress during the 1990s? Going forward, will the California energy crisis shift U.S. preferences toward less regulation, and perhaps toward more nuclear power? Were there any wake-up calls in the 1990s for the costs of environmental regulation?

Portney suggested that the influence of economic analysis has improved over the past 25 years, in terms of its application to environmental regulation. For example, environmental advocates are now sometimes advocates for cost-effective regulations, realizing that they can get more regulation for the same amount of money. Also, the business community realizes that environmental protection is an important public value, and it is in some cases precluding regulation by doing things on its own.

Frampton suggested that economists have complained in the past two decades that they are not listened to enough in regulatory decision-making. The big issues of the next 50 years, like climate change and the intersection of trade and the environment, will be resolved through economic policy, because they will be determined by the direction of economic growth, including carbon intensity of industry and the shape and scope of international trade regimes. So economists will be making many of these decisions and will see their role expand.

Stavins noted that interest in efficiency and cost-effectiveness analysis was very encouraging in the 1990s, compared to preceding decades, especially with respect to potential global climate change policies. For example, think about the position of the United States vis-à-vis other countries in the negotiation of international climate change agreements, as well as our aggressive promotion of market-based instruments in that context.

Frankel seconded Stavins's point, noting that the economic team was included far more integrally in the White House decision-making process on climate change, and had a greater impact on the outcome, than was true of the economics agencies in the governments of other countries participating in the international negotiations. However, he noted, good economic analysis is being threatened in the executive branch by a number of issues surrounding the concern for transparency. Congressional committee document requests and subpoenas, Freedom of Information Act requests, leaks to the press and to NGOs and other interest groups, and risks to the international U.S. negotiating position and domestic White House strategy have resulted in caution about putting things in writing. And good economic arguments, unlike political arguments, must be made in writing in most cases, often with charts or tables. The written record is becoming less useful from an analytical standpoint because of the self-imposed censoring that has followed the introduction of these various kinds of "transparency." So we should not be pushing for OMB analyses or other in-house deliberations to be made more public as a counterweight to agency analyses. To do so would threaten the usefulness of the analyses.

Hahn noted that many of the benefit-cost analyses put out by the administration were biased. Is there a way to organize an administration so that we do not end up with this phenomenon? *Gotbaum* suggested that making all economic analysis public constrains a full discussion of alternatives and their consequences. *Hahn* said that he was not suggesting making the analysis of every small rule public, but rather, he was referring to the big rules, like NAAQS and ergonomics, for example. According to Hahn, we should, at minimum, be able to expect agencies to follow OMB guidelines in the conduct of these analyses.

III

Economics and Social Policy

10

Labor and Education

Putting Students and Workers First? Education and Labor Policy in the 1990s

Alan B. Krueger and Cecilia E. Rouse

PANELISTS: *Lawrence Mishel, Roger B. Porter, and Robert B. Reich*

10.1 Introduction

"Putting people first," "It's the economy, stupid," and "Making work pay" are three familiar slogans from Bill Clinton's presidential campaign in 1992. All three of these slogans place labor and education policy at the top of the agenda. This paper discusses and evaluates the major thrusts in federal education and labor policy in the 1990s. The budget deficit-reduction efforts sidetracked and delayed the education and labor agenda, as did the shift in Congress in 1994. Nevertheless, several small steps and new programs were introduced that helped forge a more rational and efficient federal role in the education and training system, and addressed the diverse concerns of many groups. In addition, labor policy made modest steps to address concerns generated by the changing composition of the workforce and shifts in labor demand.

Table 10.1 presents basic labor market and education indicators corresponding to the peak and trough years (in terms of unemployment) since 1979. The

We thank Lisa Lynch, Susan Dynarski, Jane Hannaway, and Peter Orszag for useful conversations and comments. We also thank Thomas Kalil (White House National Economic Council [NEC] from 1993 to 2001 and most recently deputy assistant to the president for technology and economic policy and deputy of the NEC [2000–01]), Robert Shireman (legislative assistant and then chief education adviser to U.S. Senator Paul Simon [D-Ill.] [1989–94], legislative director for Senator Simon [1995–96], and senior policy adviser at the NEC [1997–98]), and Marshall Smith (undersecretary of education [1993–2000]) for extremely helpful and insightful background. Heather Morr and Nisreen Salti provided expert research assistance. All errors in fact or interpretation are ours.

central motivation for education and labor policy in the 1990s is easy to discern from the developments in the 1980s. Most prominently, in the 1980s and early 1990s wage dispersion increased dramatically. Real earnings for workers at the bottom of the wage distribution, in particular, fell considerably. Between 1979 and 1989, for example, the average real hourly wage of the worker at the 10th percentile of the wage distribution fell by 16 percent. The average real wage fell by 17 percent for male high school dropouts in this period, and by 12 percent for male high school graduates. A decline in fringe benefits, such as health insurance, further eroded the position of lower-wage workers. Additionally, earnings in the middle of the distribution were stagnant, at best. Although it is possible that biases in price deflators exaggerate the fall in real wages, the rise

Table 10.1
Economic and Educational Outcomes over Recent Business Cycles

	Peak 1979	Trough 1982	Peak 1989	Trough 1992	Peak 2000
Unemployment Rate[a]					
Overall	5.9%	9.7%	5.3%	7.5%	4.0%
White	5.1%	8.6%	4.5%	6.6%	3.5%
Black	12.3%	18.9%	11.4%	14.2%	7.6%
Hispanic	8.3%	13.8%	8.0%	11.6%	5.7%
Poverty Rate[*b]					
Overall poverty rate	11.7%	15.0%	12.8%	14.8%	11.8%
Extreme poverty (<.5 poverty line)	3.8%	5.6%	4.9%	6.1%	4.6%
Average Household Income[*c]					
Bottom 20 percent	$9,262	$8,719	$9,433	$8,654	$9,940
Middle 20 percent	$37,136	$35,193	$38,862	$36,373	$40,879
Top 20 percent	$96,786	$95,850	$114,912	$108,189	$135,401
Real Wage Levels[*d]					
10th percentile	$6.67	$6.14	$5.60	$5.70	$6.05
50th percentile	$11.89	$11.60	$11.60	$11.59	$11.87
90th percentile	$23.31	$23.25	$24.35	$23.95	$26.05
Wage Ratios[*d]					
50/10 ratio	1.78	1.89	2.07	2.03	1.94
90/50 ratio	1.95	2.00	2.10	2.07	2.24
90/10 ratio	3.48	3.78	4.35	4.20	4.36
Educational Wage Differentials[*d]					
Exactly college/high school ratio	1.40	1.47	1.58	1.63	1.74
High school/high school dropout ratio	1.12	1.16	1.22	1.25	1.34

Table 10.1 (continued)

	Peak 1979	Trough 1982	Peak 1989	Trough 1992	Peak 2000
Educational Indicators					
HS dropout rate[e]	14.6%	13.9%	12.6%	11.0%	11.8%
College enrollment rate[f]	25.0%	26.6%	30.9%	34.4%	35.6%
NAEP Scores for 17-Year-Olds[†g]					
Whites, mathematics	306	304	309	312	315
African Americans, mathematics	268	272	289	286	283
Whites, reading	293	295	297	297	295
African Americans, reading	243	264	267	261	264

*Data for 2000 are not yet available, so 1999 data are used. Income and wages are in 1999 dollars, deflated by CPI-U.

[†] Data for 1979, 1989, and 2000 are not available for mathematics; data from 1978, 1990, and 1999 (respectively) are used. For reading, data from 1979, 1980, and 1989 are not available; data from 1980, 1984, and 1999 are used instead.

[a] *Source:* U.S. Bureau of Labor Statistics, http://www.bls.gov.

[b] *Source:* U.S. Bureau of the Census, http://www.census.gov.hhes/poverty/histpov/hstpov22.html.

[c] *Source:* U.S. Bureau of the Census, March Current Population Survey; http://www.census.gov/hhes/income/histinc/h03.html.

[d] *Source:* Based on Mishel, Bernstein, and Schmitt (2001), Table 2.6; http://epinet.org/.

[e] *Source:* U.S. Department of Commerce, Bureau of the Census, Current Population Survey, October (various years); http://nces.ed.gov/pubs99/1999082.pdf.

[f] *Source:* U.S. Department of Commerce, Bureau of the Census, Current Population Survey, unpublished data. (This table was prepared August 2000.)

[g] *Source:* National Center for Education Statistics.

in inequality is indisputable. *Putting People First* (Clinton, 1992, p. 2) put it this way: "While the rich cashed in, the forgotten middle class—the people who work hard and play by the rules—took it on the chin. . . . The working poor had the door of opportunity slammed in their face."

Much of the rise in wage dispersion is associated with formal education, cognitive ability, and work experience. For example, the college–high school wage ratio increased from 1.40 in 1979 to 1.63 in 1992. This trend led to increased emphasis on improving job prospects through human capital development. The rise in college tuition costs and popularity of education programs among the public also made enhancing college access a major policy thrust.

With unemployment high in 1992—and the recession of the early 1990s affecting white-collar workers to a greater extent than past recessions—policy also focused on improving employment services, especially for middle-class workers. President Clinton set a goal of creating 8 million jobs in his first term of office, which influenced much economic policy-making.[1]

In our view, four core principles underlay most of the Clinton administration's initiatives in the labor and education arena; these principles connect the programmatic summary that follows. The first was an effort to make work pay and to narrow wage gaps, broadly (and often ambiguously) defined. Examples of specific policies motivated by this principle include the minimum wage increase and expansion of the Earned Income Tax Credit. The second was a desire to increase the skills and productive capacity of the workforce, through improved preschool and K–12 education, greater college access, and lifelong learning. The third was the reinvention of programs to make the federal role more cohesive, coordinated, and efficient. Goals 2000, the reauthorization of the Elementary and Secondary Education Act in 1994, student loan reform, and the Workforce Investment Act of 1998 are examples of policies motivated in large part by this principle. The final principle was a desire to make it easier for workers and students to cope with change in a volatile economy. Examples include the School-to-Work Opportunities Act, One-Stop Centers, and the Lifetime Learning Tax Credit.

In the next section we consider education policy during the 1990s. Following that we discuss major developments in labor policy. Both sections describe the policies and motivation for the policy developments, and provide an assessment of the likely effects of the programs based on available research. The conclusion provides an assessment of labor and education policy in the 1990s.

10.2   Education Policy

10.2.1   Background

10.2.1.1   Rationale for Government Involvement in Education

Three common economic justifications for government involvement in education are inequities in readiness for school, positive externalities to education, and imperfect credit markets. At the preschool level, one could make a case for government involvement out of concerns for equity. Rather than attempt to equalize outcomes, the government can attempt to compensate for unequal endowments through publicly funded early education (Currie, 2001). In addition, positive externalities arise when the social benefits to an individual be-

---

1. The 8 million jobs target was based in part on the advice of Lawrence Katz of Harvard. Katz derived his estimate assuming that the labor force would grow at the rate predicted by the Bureau of Labor Statistics and that unemployment would return to what was then considered a "full employment level" of 5.5 to 6.0 percent. Actual job growth between January 1993 and January 1997 was 9.4 million based on the household survey and 11.3 million based on the establishment survey.

coming educated are greater than the individual benefits (Friedman, 1962). If the government did not subsidize education in the presence of such externalities, then individuals would not obtain as much education as is socially desirable. The case for positive externalities has usually been made to justify government subsidies at the preschool and elementary and secondary school levels, because such externalities include the ability to be an informed voter and to support oneself.[2] At higher levels of education, however, economists have traditionally believed there are likely fewer positive externalities to education. (An exception is growth externalities, which we interpret to be small or uncertain; see Krueger and Lindahl, in press.) As a result, most of the justification for government subsidy of higher education has rested on imperfect capital markets, although evidence on the importance of such credit constraints is the subject of some debate, as discussed in section 10.2.4. Most economists probably agree that some level of government support of education at all levels is justified. The debate is over the level and form of that support.

10.2.1.2   Backdrop for Education Policy in the 1990s

In addition to the economic trends discussed in the introduction, education policy in the 1990s was also motivated by a fear that the educational system was in "crisis." The evidence came from three sources. First, wages of those without a high school degree had been in decline since the early 1980s, as discussed in the introduction. Second, in 1983 the influential *A Nation At Risk* (Gardner, 1983) cited the decline in SAT scores—despite years of increasing school expenditures—in declaring that our educational system had become a "rising tide of mediocrity." The test scores of American students allegedly floundered, despite years of increasing expenditures. This sentiment continued throughout the 1980s. However, the composition of students taking the SAT changes over time.

The only nationally representative and continuing evidence on student test scores comes from the National Assessment of Educational Progress (NAEP). Since the early 1970s the NAEP has periodically tested a sample of students at ages 9, 13, and 17 in mathematics, reading, and science. These series comprise what are referred to as the NAEP long-term assessments. The long-term average raw scores in mathematics and reading for 17-year-olds by race are shown in Table 10.1. Among white students, math scores in the early 1990s were slightly higher than those from the early 1970s. The gains among African American students were larger. The overall trend in reading scores suggests only a minor increase since the early 1970s. Thus, the trends in NAEP scores do

---

2. Note that the existence of positive externalities is used to justify government subsidization of education but not necessarily government provision of education.

not suggest a "crisis" in education in the early 1990s. Many were concerned, however, that the overall levels of achievement were low and that the racial gap remained large.

The perception of low national test scores was reinforced by comparisons of American students with those in other countries. For example, Bishop (1990) reports on results from international studies conducted during the 1980s by the International Association for the Evaluation of Education Achievement. U.S. students scored lower than their counterparts in almost all other countries tested in subjects such as algebra, biology, chemistry, and physics.[3]

It was in response to this statistical picture of the American elementary and secondary school system that education policy was shaped during the 1990s. Tables 10.2 and 10.3 summarize the main education legislation and administration initiatives during President Clinton's time in office. The programs reflect the administration's attempts to refocus the federal government's role in K–12 education to support the reforms already occurring in the states, and in postsecondary education to restructure financial aid. The programs also reflect the administration's belief that a diversified strategy was required. To improve education one must improve schooling inputs (such as class size and technology) while also increasing flexibility and competition from within the public school system.

10.2.2   Early Education

While there is debate over the value of education and training for some groups of adults, few dispute the value of early education. Those children who arrive at kindergarten not ready to start learning to read and write, as well as to learn mathematics, are at great risk of never catching up. In addition, the public is sympathetic to young children. Therefore, many believe that the most effective educational programs target the youngest children (although recent findings from the National Job Corps study that we will describe later may lead to a reassessment of that view). The primary federal program in this area is Head Start. The program was started in 1965 as part of President Johnson's War on Poverty (Zigler and Muenchow, 1992). Although it began as a summer program serving 500,000 children aged 4–5, it was soon expanded to a full-year program that served children aged 3–5. The program has always enjoyed bipartisan support, since it is hard to argue with the basic premise: give children from disadvantaged families the skills they need to succeed in elementary school.

---

3. The achievement of U.S. students has continued to lag behind those in other countries as reported by the Third International Mathematics and Science Study (TIMSS) from 1995 and the Third International Mathematics and Science Study–Repeat (TIMSS-R) from 1999.

Table 10.2
Major Federal Early and Elementary and Secondary Education Legislation
Enacted and Programs Created Since 1992

Legislation/Program	Year	Brief Description
Goals 2000: Educate America Act	1994	Provides funding to schools, communities, and states to raise their educational standards. It was amended in 1996.
Head Start reauthorization	1994	Instituted performance standards and attempts to improve quality; created Early Head Start to serve low-income families with pregnant women, infants, or toddlers.
Improving America's Schools Act	1994	Reauthorized the ESEA of 1965 and was designed to encourage local approaches to improving schools.
Public Charter School Program (Title X, Part C of ESEA)	1994	Provides grants to states to assist in the planning, program design, and initial implementation of charter schools.
School-to-Work Act	1994	Provides funding to states and districts to develop "School-to-Work" systems that are designed to attain high academic standards through contextual, applied, and focused learning.
Technology Innovation Challenge Grants Program	1994	Provides competitive grants to support demonstration projects designed to generate models of effective uses of educational technology in schools.
Technology Literacy Challenge Fund	1994	Provides states and school districts with funding to invest in educational technology and to integrate such technology into the curriculum.
Telecommunications Act of 1996 (created the "E-rate" program)	1996	FCC-adopted Universal Service Order that provides discounts ("e-rates") for low-income and rural schools for telecommunications services.
21st Century Learning Centers	1997	Authorized under Title X, Part I of the ESEA; provides competitive grants to districts for community education centers for after-school programs.
Charter School Expansion Act	1998	Extends the authorization of the Public Charter School program through FY2004. Amends the program to target funds to states with strongest statutes and increases accountability.
Head Start Amendments	1998	Reauthorized Head Start; expanded Early Head Start.
Preparing Tomorrow's Teachers to Use Technology (PT3)	1998	Authorized under Title III of the ESEA; provides competitive grants to schools of education to train new teachers to use information technology in their future classroom practice as part of the teacher education curriculum.
Class Size Reduction Program	1999	Authorized under Title VI of the ESEA; provides grants to states to help schools recruit, hire, and train teachers in order to reduce class sizes in grades 1–3.
Education Flexibility Partnership Act of 1999	1999	Authorizes the secretary of education to allow all states to participate in the Education Flexibility Partnership program.
Reading Excellence Act	1999	Provides competitive grants to states, which in turn distribute them to needy districts to promote the ability of children to read independently by the third grade.

Table 10.3
Major Federal Postsecondary Education Legislation Enacted and Programs Created since 1992

Legislation/Programs	Year	Brief Description
Student Loan Reform Act	1993	Created the Federal Direct Student Loan program.
Student Loan Interest Deduction (Taxpayer Relief Act of 1997)	1997	Allows up to $2,000 (in 2000/$2,500 in 2001) of interest on student loans to be tax deductible for the first 60 months of loan repayment.
Emergency Student Loan Consolidation Act of 1997	1997	Amends the Higher Education Act to provide for improved student loan consolidation services.
Reauthorization of the Higher Education Act	1998	Substantially amended, and reauthorized, through fiscal year 2003, the Higher Education Act of 1965.
HOPE Scholarship	1998	Nonrefundable tax credit of 100% of first $1,000 of college tuition and 50% of second $1,000 for first two years of college; phased out for higher income filers. Available on a per-student basis.
GEAR UP	1998	Provides grants to partnerships between high-poverty middle schools, colleges and universities, community organizations, and business to provide tutoring, mentoring, information on college preparation and financial aid to entire grades of low-income students.
Lifetime Learning Credit	1999	Nonrefundable 20% tax credit for first $5,000 tuition through 2002 and for the first $10,000 thereafter for those beyond the first two years of college or those taking classes part-time; phased out for higher income filers. Available on a per-taxpayer (family) basis.

A unique aspect of the Head Start program is its "whole-child" approach. Children receive medical care and meals, in addition to developing the educational and social skills that they will need in order to succeed in school and later life. Head Start has also emphasized educating the "whole family" and was designed to provide "spill-overs" to the families of participating children. In 1992 there were just over 620,000 children enrolled in Head Start at a (federal) cost of $4,100 (in 2000 dollars) per child. By 2000 enrollment had increased by 38 percent, or by about 250,000 children. In addition, the federal funding per child had increased to about $6,100, for a total of $5.3 billion (U.S. Administration for Children, Youth, and Families, 2001b). Despite this size, the program only serves about 35 percent of eligible children, mostly because the program has never been fully funded by Congress (Currie, 2001).

The Clinton administration sought to "expand and improve" Head Start through the 1994 reauthorization of the Head Start Act as well as amendments passed in 1998. The primary goal of these pieces of legislation was to improve the quality of Head Start programs through better staff training and career development, higher salaries for Head Start workers, improved federal oversight, and better facilities. Further, under the new performance standards, grantees would lose federal funding if their performance fell below a minimum quality level and they failed to correct problems quickly.[4]

The 1994 reauthorization of the Head Start Act also created Early Head Start, a program designed to serve low-income families with children under the age of three and pregnant women. The Early Head Start programs provide child development services to improve cognitive and language development, social-emotional behavior, and health as well as develop family and community partnerships. Services may be provided exclusively at centers, exclusively through home visits, or a combination of the two. In 2001 the program was expected to serve 55,000 children with a budget of $560 million. An early (randomized) evaluation of Early Head Start by Mathematica Policy Research suggests positive effects on child development (U.S. Administration for Children, Youth, and Families, 2001a).

One of the primary criticisms of Head Start is that it does not generate long-run effects. Rather, the early evidence suggests that children who had participated in Head Start had short-run improvements in IQ test scores, but that these gains "faded out" by the third grade. The cause of the "fade-out" is not clear. However, a leading hypothesis is that the school quality of the subsequent elementary schools attended by Head Start participants does not sustain the intellectual advantages incurred by the preschool program. In addition, the single-minded focus on IQ rests on the undocumented belief that IQ test scores are all that matters for labor market success. As it turns out, studies on the effects of compensatory preschool programs on longer-run tangible outcomes (such as college attendance, welfare receipt, employment, and criminal activity) have tended to find that attendance at preschool makes a significant long-term difference.[5]

Although they report large benefits, the most famous long-term randomized evaluations of compensatory preschool, the Perry Preschool and Carolina Abcedarian projects, are distinguished by the fact that they were more expensive and intensive than current Head Start programs.[6] Therefore, the question remains whether the benefits of Head Start outweigh the costs. Based on a back-

---

4. Since 1993 approximately 200 grantees have been identified as "seriously deficient," and about 150 have lost their federal funding (U.S. Administration for Children, Youth, and Families, 2001b).
5. See Barnett (1992, 1995) for an excellent review of several studies on compensatory education programs, as well as Garces, Thomas, and Currie (2000) for more recent nonexperimental evidence. The oldest of the studies using randomized evaluation to examine the long-run effects is based on the well-known Perry Preschool Project (Schweinhart, Barnes, and Weikart, 1993). A second, more recent, randomized study is the Carolina Abcedarian Project, which began in 1972 (Campbell, Pungello, et al., 2001 and Campbell, Ramey, et al., in press).
6. A recent estimate by researchers at the RAND corporation suggests that the cost of Head Start is 71 percent that of the Perry Preschool project (Karoly et al., 1998).

of-the-envelope cost-benefit analysis, Janet Currie of UCLA concludes, "Given the short- and medium-term benefits ... Head Start would pay for itself if it yielded long-term benefits that were even a quarter as large as those of Perry Preschool" (Currie, 2001). Further, because many of the studies report greater impacts for the most disadvantaged children, the net benefits may be even greater for those most in need. Thus it appears that publicly funded compensatory preschool programs have the potential to significantly improve the adult lives of their participants.

10.2.3 Elementary and Secondary (K–12) Education

Elementary and secondary school policy in the United States is largely determined at the state and local levels. In 1999 approximately 45 percent of revenues came from local governments, 48 percent from state governments, and the remaining 7 percent from the federal government (U.S. Department of Education, 2000b). In the early 1990s the federal role in education was dominated by Chapter 1 (now called Title I) of the Elementary and Secondary Education Act (ESEA), which attempts to address perceived inequities in education by redistributing funds to low-income and disadvantaged schools and districts. Thus one of the challenges President Clinton faced in establishing a legacy in education (and seeking to be known as the "education president") was to have significant influence in an area over which the federal government has little budget authority and little direct control.

During the 1980s many states and districts began to reform their educational systems by instituting policies such as teacher accountability programs, high school graduation requirements, smaller class sizes, longer school years, and site-based management. The aim was to increase school accountability and to provide the resources to help schools succeed. While few disputed the need for educational reform, how to achieve greater accountability and whether or not greater resources were needed were controversial issues.

A simplistic characterization of the debate was (and still is) of two camps. In one camp are those who believe that the fundamental problem with our educational system is a lack of school choice. Because children are assigned to attend their neighborhood schools, schools have a kind of "monopoly" power and very little incentive to provide a quality education. Therefore, as we will discuss, the educational system should be reformed by introducing more competition into the marketplace, either through vouchers to help children attend private schools or through greater choice within the public school system. Through the forces of market competition, schools would be held accountable and forced to improve to attract students. Many who subscribe to the market model believe the educational system is not in need of more resources (such as smaller class sizes) as the United States already has one of the highest expenditures per capita among industrialized countries (Hanushek, 1986, 1997; U.S. Department of Education, 2000b).

In the second camp are those who believe that introducing private school vouchers to hold schools accountable is counterproductive.[7] Rather, many of them believe that there is already ample competition within the public school system arising from "residential (Tiebout) choice," or the fact that many families choose the neighborhood in which to live based on the quality of the local schools (Tiebout, 1956). Furthermore, many argue that one can construct an accountability system in which schools that do not attain certain predetermined goals are sanctioned by, for example, withholding funding. Underlying this view is a belief that the system can be reformed within the existing structure, provided it is given ample resources to lower class sizes, lengthen the school day or year, provide professional development, and improve other inputs. However, providing such additional resources is difficult for state and local governments facing many competing demands on their revenues. In addition, the challenge of this approach is to devise a sensible and fair accountability system. Because there are so many inputs to education, it is difficult to isolate the contribution of the school from the contributions of the family, peers, and other external forces.

The route most states and school districts took during the 1980s was to attempt reform from within the public school system. The federal government, however, remained relatively uninvolved with these reforms. In fact, some would argue that many of the federal government's requirements conflicted with the reform efforts of states. In an attempt to modernize and expand the federal government's role in K–12 education, President George H. W. Bush along with state governors (members of the National Governor's Association) held an Education Summit in 1989. Then-Governor Bill Clinton of Arkansas was cochair of a task force on national goals that formed the basis for the agenda of the summit (Schwartz and Robinson, 2000). During the summit, six National Education Goals were endorsed. Although President Bush attempted to translate these six education goals into legislation (called America 2000), he did not succeed, largely because of his support of school vouchers and the inclusion of voluntary national tests.[8]

Thus was the scene when President Clinton took office.

---

7. In fact, some of these writers would argue that any large-scale voucher program would also need a structure by which to hold schools accountable, eventually leading to a new bureaucracy and entailing substantial cost (Levin, 1998).

8. Chester Finn, president of the Fordham Foundation, is reported to have quipped when the Clinton administration's own proposal for voluntary national tests failed, "Republicans don't like 'national,' Democrats don't like 'test'" (cited in Schwartz and Robinson, 2000).

10.2.3.1   Standards-Based Reform

In view of his involvement in their development, it is not surprising that one of President Clinton's first legislative actions was to propose legislation that would resuscitate the National Education Goals. His proposal, which did not include school vouchers, resulted in Goals 2000: Educate America Act of 1994, the foundation upon which much of the administration's subsequent education policy was built.

Through Goals 2000, the federal government has authorizing authority to provide grants to states (which in turn provide grants to districts and schools) to encourage comprehensive educational reform. The idea was to move the federal government's role in education away from supporting categorical programs toward supporting the reform efforts that states and districts were already undertaking, or encouraging them to do so. To qualify for federal funding, states must submit "State Plans" that describe the standards to which schools and districts will be held and the policies in place to help the educators achieve them. The aim was to have states articulate "content standards" (what students should know) as well as "opportunity-to-learn standards" (what resources districts will devote to helping students achieve the content standards).[9] A key element of the legislation is for states to set clear, high academic goals and for the federal government to relax regulations and requirements that interfere with state reform efforts. Thus, Goals 2000 was an attempt to promote "standards-based" reform and accountability throughout the American educational system. Secretary of Education Richard Riley describes it as "nothing less than landmark legislation, as important in its own way as the Morrill Act and the Elementary and Secondary Education Act" (Riley, 1995). In his remarks at the signing ceremony for Goals 2000, President Clinton said, "Goals 2000 is a new way of doing business in America. It represents the direction our government must take in many problems in the 21st century" (cited in Riley, 1995).

The reauthorization of the ESEA in 1994, known as the Improving America's Schools Act (IASA), attempts to reinforce Goals 2000. It strives to move away from programs ascribed by the federal government that often bear no relation to the reform efforts of states, and toward more federal-government-assisted state- and district-initiated reform. Further, it pushes states and districts to include *all* students in their reform efforts (including low-income students and those receiving special services) and to help *all* students achieve the same high

---

9. One controversial aspect of the Goals 2000 legislation was the creation of the 19-member National Education Standards and Improvement Council (NESIC) to help states develop their standards (and help provide some quality control over the program). Republicans viewed the proposed NESIC as too much federal involvement in state reform efforts, and it "died" in 1995 when Representative William Goodling (R-PA) introduced legislation to eliminate it (Schwartz and Robinson, 2000).

standards. As an example of its attempt to increase flexibility, the Department of Education moved to administratively drop every regulation not required by law. The attempt to allow more flexibility made it difficult for the administration to simultaneously impose tough performance standards, for it is difficult to introduce new regulations on accountability while also decreasing the overall level of regulation. As a result, the performance accountability provisions that were ultimately included in the legislation were relatively lax (some with time lines that extended past the five years of the reauthorization of the ESEA, for example) and enforcement of some of the standards in the IASA was not as tough as lawmakers envisioned (Smith, Scoll, and Plisko, 1995; phone interview with Marshall Smith, 2001).

Critics of Goals 2000 and the IASA, such as Bruno Manno, formerly of the Hudson Institute in Washington, DC, believe that the Clinton administration's approach to accountability and standards-based reform is just government "business as usual." In particular, Manno contends that Goals 2000 puts more emphasis on schooling inputs (class size, spending per pupil, how teachers teach) than outputs (student achievement) because of the "opportunity-to-learn" standards that measure school resources. Further, he argues that the State Plans reflect a "top-down" centralized view of education with the secretary of education as central planner (Manno, 1995).

Has the standards-based reform worked? If one defines the central goal of Goals 2000 as encouraging states to implement content standards and other elements of the standards-based reform, then the policy has been a success. While only a few states had defined standards in the early 1990s, today 47 states plus the District of Columbia have content standards, and 25 have performance standards (Goals 2000 Fact Sheet, 2001). Further, although only funded at $92 million in 1994, in the year 2000 Goals 2000 was appropriated $458 million, which suggests continuing (and growing) congressional support. But ultimately the goal of Goals 2000, and of the IASA, is to raise student achievement. And, unfortunately, it is difficult (if not impossible) to separately identify the impact of the federal contribution from the state reform efforts and from other secular trends.[10]

Although Goals 2000 was the foundation for the administration's education policy, over time it faded from the forefront and was overtaken by other initiatives, such as class size reduction and school construction.

---

10. There is a small economics literature on the impact of grading standards on student achievement. See, for example, Costrell (1994) and Betts (1998) for theoretical models, and Bishop (1990), Betts and Grogger (2000), and Figlio and Lucas (2000) for empirical papers. Both the theoretical models and empirical evidence seem to suggest that higher standards primarily improve the achievement of already high-achieving students, although Figlio and Lucas report as well that this result depends on the average achievement of the students' peers.

10.2.3.2   The School-to-Work Opportunities Act

Soon after Goals 2000 was passed, a complementary piece of legislation, the School-to-Work Opportunities Act of 1994, was signed into law. School-to-Work was motivated by concern that a majority of students enter the workforce without a bachelor's degree and that many are not adequately prepared to face the changing workplace of the "new economy." As such, it attempts to create systems (not just programs) that promote the education and career preparation of young people beginning in middle school (School-to-Work Opportunities Act of 1994, Public Law 103–239, Hughes, Bailey, and Mechur, 2001). Jointly administered by the Departments of Education and Labor, the program provides funds to states and local communities to form partnerships among local educational institutions, employers, community-based organizations, parents, and students. These partnerships are meant to expand promising activities, such as career academies and apprenticeship programs, as well as to use workplaces as learning environments (such as through "job shadowing").[11] A key part of the legislation from the standpoint of Congress is that these school-to-work activities are meant to further the national education goals in Goals 2000 by providing states with an alternative way of reforming their high schools (Jennings, 1995).

Critics, most notably Phyllis Schlafly of the Eagle Forum, view School-to-Work as a vocational track that discourages the learning of basic academic subjects. Advocates respond that the goal of such activities is to help students attend college or receive additional training if they so choose, as well as provide students with the knowledge and skills needed to obtain a well-paying job directly out of high school. The idea is to motivate students by providing them with knowledge of career opportunities in the labor market.

While more than 90 percent of secondary school students in states that had received federal School-to-Work grants attended schools in districts with partnerships between their school and local partners, only 3 percent had received all three components that advocates of School-to-Work believe are necessary: career-related academics, comprehensive career development activities, and paid or unpaid work experience linked to school (Hughes, Bailey, and Mechur, 2001). Rather, most programs have focused on the less intensive (but easiest to implement and least controversial) activities such as "job shadowing" and brief work-site visits.

---

11. Career academies are "schools within schools" in which each year groups of students take several classes together with the same group of teachers. Each academy focuses on a particular career theme around which the teachers organize the academic and occupation-related classes. Academies also develop partnerships with local employers for help in planning the program and as a source of mentors and internships (Kemple and Snipes, 2000).

Recently, researchers at Teachers College at Columbia University released a report reviewing the research on School-to-Work, including a careful study by the Manpower Demonstration Research Corporation (MDRC) that used random assignment to evaluate career academies (Hughes, Bailey, and Mechur, 2001; see also Kemple and Snipes, 2000). Results from the MDRC study suggest that at the end of their scheduled 12th grade year, students in career academies at risk of dropping out of high school had improved attendance and increased academic course taking; among all students there was only a slight reduction in dropout rates, however. Further, the students in career academies did not have improved standardized reading and mathematics test scores. The researchers at Teachers College conclude that other evidence is generally supportive of School-to-Work (Hughes, Bailey, and Mechur, 2001). However, all such results must be taken as preliminary. For example, the MDRC study is only based on results as of the 12th grade; a second phase of the study will follow the students for up to four years after high school.

School-to-Work is another initiative that received much focus in the first part of the Clinton administration, but faded as attentions turned to other priorities. And although authorization is due to expire in 2001 (with little or no momentum to attempt reauthorization), school-to-work type activities are allowed under the new job-training legislation, the Workforce Investment Act (see section 10.3.2).

10.2.3.3 School Vouchers

The Clinton administration chose not to support school vouchers, programs that would provide vouchers for children to attend private schools. Advocates of vouchers argue that teachers' unions and bloated bureaucracies impede improved resources from reaching the classroom and increasing student achievement (e.g., Chubb and Moe, 1990). Further, because children are required to attend their neighborhood school, the system has no incentive to change (e.g., Chubb and Moe, 1990; Friedman, 1962). While wealthier parents can voice dissatisfaction with their residential school by moving to another neighborhood or enrolling their child in a private school, advocates argue that poorer parents cannot. Vouchers would, at a minimum, provide disadvantaged children more educational options. If, in addition, they were to receive a better education in the private schools, the program might offer a cost-effective way to improve student achievement, at least for those students who use the vouchers.

Some argue that a large voucher program would also improve the schooling of all children, including those who remain in public schools. In the most unrestricted program, all (or a substantial fraction) of the students in the public schools would be eligible to attend a private school. Since state funding would be tied to student enrollments, the public schools would have to "compete" for students, as in the marketplace, which would give the public schools an incentive to improve. One of the theoretical advantages of a voucher program is that it shifts the burden of standards and accountability to the marketplace. If a school is not performing to the standards demanded by parents (the consumers), then the schools will not attract students. Thus, the government does not need to assess, through an elaborate bureaucracy, whether or not a school or district has reached its academic goals, and the government does not have to find itself in the awkward position of having to sanction (such as by withholding funds) "failing" schools.

While vouchers have many supporters, others question the validity of applying the simple, competitive economic model to the education market (e.g., Bagley, Woods, and Glatter, 1996; Frey, 1992; and Garner and Hannaway, 1982). Because public schools are not "profit-maximizing" enterprises, the nature and extent of their responses to competitive pressures is not obvious. Opponents also worry that vouchers would lead to a widening of the achievement gap between various groups of students because family resources, including information about school quality, are unequal (e.g., Schneider, 1999).[12] Similarly, vouchers could lead to reduced public support for public schools, in terms of both desire to fund the public sector and volunteer efforts in the public sector (particularly if the most motivated parents leave for the private sector). All these factors could lead to increased inequality in student outcomes and reduced student outcomes for those "left behind" in the public schools.

The best evidence on school vouchers to date comes from experiments in which one group of students is randomly offered a voucher and a second group of students is (randomly) denied a voucher. This type of experiment is currently being conducted in several cities around the country, mostly by Paul Peterson of Harvard University. The longest running experiment is being conducted in New York City, with vouchers funded by the School Choice Scholarships Foundation. This program, which began in the spring of 1997, provides scholarships worth up to $1,400 annually that can be used at both religious and secular private schools for at least three years. A report issued by Mathematic Policy Research, Inc., based on two years of data suggests that the parents of children offered a voucher are more satisfied with their child's school (Myers

---

12. In addition, Fernandez and Rogerson (1996) and Glomm and Ravikumar (1992) suggest that more decentralized school systems generate more income inequality. And Epple and Romano (1998) and Nechyba (1996) predict increased ability sorting within schools with the introduction of private school vouchers. At the same time, by decoupling the residential and schooling decisions of families, racial and income stratification within schools could also decrease with the introduction of school vouchers.

et al., 2000). However, it also reports that, overall, the test scores of students offered a voucher are about the same as the test scores of students who were denied a voucher. One exception to this overall finding is that the test scores of African American students who were offered a voucher did improve relative to those who were not offered one. This result, though suggestive, only holds for students who were in the 6th grade; there were much smaller (statistically insignificant) gains among African American students in grades 3–5. In fact, the finding of positive impacts on test scores for African Americans, but not for Hispanics or whites, holds across two other, more recent, experiments in Dayton, Ohio, and Washington, DC, as well (Howell et al., 2000).

Researchers have also used nonexperimental evidence to assess whether attending a private school improves the achievement of the students who use vouchers. Evidence from the Milwaukee Parental Choice Program, the oldest publicly funded voucher program in the nation, suggests mixed effects on student achievement. Specifically, students selected to attend a voucher school experienced significantly faster gains in math scores, but showed no differential gains in reading (Rouse, 1998a, 1998b). This pattern of results also held for African Americans, although Hispanic students who attended a voucher school showed significantly faster gains in their math as well as reading test scores (Rouse, in press).

These early results from the voucher experiments are encouraging in that voucher parents are more satisfied with their children's schools. And, there is some evidence that the achievement of African American students offered vouchers improves as well. There are, however, several unanswered questions. For example, these results are only from relatively early years of the programs; over time the effects may become even stronger or may diminish—it is too early to tell. In addition, all of these programs are too small (or were too small at the time of analysis) to reveal the effects of a larger-scale program. That is, they cannot determine whether the achievement of students that remain in the public schools would also improve and whether the public schools would become more efficient.

Thus the academic research to date (and even more so back in the early 1990s) cannot help to evaluate whether or not overall student achievement would have shown more improvement had the Clinton administration chosen to support vouchers. And, given the paucity of evidence, it is not surprising that the decision of whether or not to do so rested primarily on politics and other concerns. Back in 1992, the administration's decision was heavily influenced by four factors. The first was that the teacher's unions, major supporters of Clinton, were strongly opposed to vouchers. The second was that in the early 1990s the default rates for student loans were at record high levels as a result of financial aid improprieties at many vocational proprietary schools.[13] The experience from this market at the postsecondary level led many administration officials to be concerned that similarly disreputable schools could open in a market at the elementary and secondary level. They feared that students, particularly children of low-income parents, would suffer unless there was substantial regulation that would, in turn, diminish the theoretical value of the vouchers. Third, there were concerns about the constitutionality of providing vouchers for students to attend religious private schools. Given that only 21 percent of private schools are nonsectarian (accounting for 15 percent of private school enrollment), the administration believed that unless the vouchers could be redeemed at religious schools, they would not provide the majority of students with significantly more educational choice (U.S. Department of Education, 2000b). (Of course, if a large number of vouchers had been provided, new private schools at which students were eligible to use the vouchers might have opened.) Finally, President Clinton strongly supported a public education system and believed that private school vouchers would drain money from public schools.

And so the decision was made not to support a policy of providing vouchers for students to attend private schools.

10.2.3.4 Charter Schools

Charter schools are public schools that have a contract with the state or the school district. The contract, or charter, specifies the terms of their operation and obligations in order to receive state funds. And, as long as the school meets preestablished accountability goals, charter schools have more autonomy than do regular public schools in decisions regarding staffing, curriculum, and school organization (Nelson et al., 2000). In 1999, 70 percent of charter schools were newly created schools; the rest were preexisting public or private schools that chose to convert to charters. Further, charter schools were relatively small in size. The median charter school had about 140 students, whereas the median for all public schools in charter states was about 475 (Nelson et al., 2000). In 1992, only two states had charter legislation, Minnesota and California, and the only two charter schools in existence were in Minneapolis. By 1999, 36 states and the District of Columbia had charter legislation covering more than 1,400 charter schools. In the same year, more than 250,000 children were enrolled in charter schools (Nelson et al., 2000).

---

13. The schools would help students to apply for student loans without properly explaining the repayment obligations to them. Default rates on student loans soared. At the peak in 1990, nearly one-quarter of borrowers defaulted within one year of beginning repayment, allowing schools to profit at the taxpayers' expense (U.S. Department of Education, 2001).

The arguments advanced by charter school advocates are quite similar to those advanced by voucher advocates. Namely, charter schools are more innovative and responsive to the needs of students than are public schools. Because they only exist if parents choose to enroll their children, the schools must provide relatively high-quality education. Because they provide an alternative to the local public school, charter schools inject additional competition into the local education market and should therefore stimulate the local public schools to improve as well. At the same time, charter schools are often supported by those who oppose vouchers for private schools because they operate within the public school system (with fewer regulations).

Although he was opposed to private school vouchers, President Clinton supported the notion that public schools needed additional competitive pressure to become more efficient. He was also sympathetic to the argument advanced by voucher proponents that parents should have more choice about the kind and style of education their children would receive. (As candidate Clinton wrote, "Every parent should have the right to choose the public school his or her child attends" [Clinton, 1992].) Such choice would stimulate more "market" accountability as well as increase parental satisfaction with schools. As a result, one of the administration's early and major policy initiatives was to support the creation of more charter schools (and other forms of public school choice).

The first piece of legislation was the Public Charter School Program under Title X, Part C of the reauthorization of the ESEA in 1994. Because the start-up cost is one of the most commonly cited problems for new charter schools, the program aimed to assist in the planning, program design, and initial implementation of charter schools through grants to states. The Charter School Expansion Act of 1998 extended the authorization of the Public Charter School Program through fiscal year 2004 and amended it to target funds to states with the strongest charter statutes (thereby allocating funds to the most autonomous charter schools). Federal support for charter schools grew along with their expansion across the states. In 1995 this program was funded at $6 million; by the 2001 fiscal year budget it received $1.9 billion.

As with vouchers, there is not much evidence on charter schools mostly because they are relatively new, are heterogeneous, and tend to be relatively small. In one of the few statistical evaluations, Case Western Reserve University's Eric Bettinger (1999) examined the effect of charter schools in Michigan on student achievement. He reports that the test scores of students in charter schools did not improve relative to those in similar public schools; he also finds that charter schools had little effect on the test scores of students in the neighboring public schools. Thus his results suggest that charter schools may not be more effective than local public schools and that competitive pressure from nearby charter schools does not cause public schools to improve. These results are far from definitive, however, as the study only looked at test scores over a two-year period, which may not be enough time for any impacts to emerge.

10.2.3.5 Class Size Reduction

While Goals 2000 emphasizes content and performance standards, it also includes standards based on school inputs, so-called "opportunity-to-learn" standards. One such input is class size. The administration argued that its initiative to reduce class sizes in the early grades to a national average of 18 students per class was motivated by the research on class size (discussed in this subsection), but it is also clear that reducing class sizes was a favored policy by the teacher's unions and the public. A Gallup Poll conducted in June 1998 asked respondents whether they would favor or oppose "providing funds to be used to reduce class size in grades 1, 2, and 3"; 80 percent of respondents favored such a policy (Phi Delta Kappa, 1998). A March 1997 NBC News/*Wall Street Journal* poll found that 70 percent of adults believed that reducing class size would lead to big improvements in public schools.[14] In 1999 the administration created the Class Size Reduction Program. The program provides grants to states to help schools recruit, hire, and train teachers to reduce class sizes in grades 1–3. The ultimate goal of the program is to hire "100,000 New Teachers" to reduce class sizes. In structuring its initiative, the administration attempted to learn from the experience in California which reduced its class sizes to a maximum of 20 students in grades K–3 in 1996 in a program championed by then-Governor Pete Wilson (CSR Research Consortium, 2000). In the first years of the California program, schools struggled with a lack of classroom space and a "shortage" of qualified teachers. As a result, the Clinton administration attempted to phase in the Class Size Reduction Program over several years and to package it with other programs to improve the quality of teachers and increase classroom space (programs such as State Grants for Improving Teacher Quality and Transition to Teaching as well as the school construction and modernization bonds), although these supporting efforts were less successful in Congress.

Researchers' views of the evidence on the effect of class size on student achievement from observational studies is mixed. On the one hand, Eric Hanushek of the Hoover Institution has argued that studies of the effect of class size (and other school resources) tend to find unsystematic and often statistically insignificant results (see, for example, Hanushek, 1986, 1997). Larry Hedges of the University of Chicago and his coauthors, on the other hand, perform a

---

14. Hart and Teeter Research Companies, NBC News/*Wall Street Journal* poll, question 108, March 1997.

meta-analysis that aggregates the literature and find sizable class-size effects (Hedges, Laine, and Greenwald, 1994). Moreover, Alan Krueger (2000a) re-analyzes Hanushek's overview of the literature and finds that Hanushek's pessimistic conclusion about the efficacy of class size depends critically on how studies are assigned (implicit) weights. Hanushek places more weight on studies from which he extracted more estimates. If every study is assigned an equal weight, however, the literature does indicate that smaller classes are associated with higher achievement. He also argues that many studies estimate specifications that are fundamentally flawed. This debate highlights that a direct assessment of whether class size reduction works is difficult, at best, with observational data.

Probably the best available evidence on class size comes from Project STAR. In the 1985–86 school year, approximately 6,000 kindergarten students in Tennessee were randomly assigned to one of three groups: small classes, regular-sized classes, and regular-sized classes with a teacher's aid. The students were followed for four years and after the third grade were returned to regular-sized classes. The data have been analyzed by a variety of researchers, and the results have been remarkably consistent.[15] The results suggest that students initially placed in a small class had higher test scores that persisted through high school, were more likely to take the ACT or SAT college entrance exam and scored higher on the exam, and were less likely to be arrested or convicted of a crime. Further, the gains were highest for African American students and those eligible for a free or reduced-price lunch.

Although the results from Project STAR suggest there are benefits to reducing class sizes, there are also costs—which can be considerable, as additional teachers must be hired and classrooms built. Krueger (2000a) estimates that the internal real rate of return from reducing classes by 7 students in grades K–3 is about 6 percent, assuming that productivity grows by 1 percent per year. Although this calculation suggests that the benefits of class size reduction may exceed the costs, the question remains whether this relatively expensive intervention is the most efficient use of public funds to improve education. Unfortunately, other initiatives have not been evaluated as thoroughly as class size reduction.

10.2.3.6 Technology

Information technology (IT) is becoming increasingly important in the American job market. In 1997 more than half of all workers directly used a computer keyboard on the job. Further, workers who use a computer in their daily routine

---

15. See Word et al. (1990), Finn and Achilles (1990), Folger and Breda (1989), Krueger (1999), and Krueger and Whitmore (2001a, 2001b).

are paid more than those who do not (Krueger, 1993; Holzer, 1996; Autor, Katz, and Krueger, 1998). At the beginning of the decade, 52 percent of students reported using a computer in school, although the percentages differed by race, with 54 percent of whites reporting using a computer compared to only 39 percent of blacks and 41 percent of Hispanics (Krueger, in press). And, a recent report by the Department of Education documents that in 1994 only 35 percent of all public schools, and only 3 percent of classrooms, had Internet access (Cattagni and Farris, 2001). There was also unequal access to IT in education, as rural schools and those that served a high proportion of minority or low-income students had less computer equipment than did schools in suburban and more affluent areas. In the early part of the decade there was clearly a digital divide in elementary and secondary schools.

Concern that IT literacy had become one of the "new basics"—as important as reading, writing, and arithmetic—was one of the motivations for the Clinton administration's focus on technology in education. The administration also feared that without a national effort to encourage investment in IT, the existing inequities in access to IT in schools would continue to grow and that these would become yet another force driving inequality in the labor market. The assumption underlying this strategy is that technology can help to improve student achievement, an assumption to which we will return.

The administration had four main policies to promote the use of technology at the K–12 level. The first, and by far the biggest, was known as the "E-rate." For more than 60 years prior to 1996, person-to-person voice communication through telephones was provided to high-cost (such as rural) areas and low-income users through a set of subsidies known as "Universal Service." For example, urban areas (with lower costs of provision) subsidized rural areas; wealthier users subsidized low-income users; and commercial users subsidized residential users. In the 1996 Telecommunications Act, Universal Service was expanded to also include new advanced telecommunications, such as enhanced phone and computer networks that would allow users access to the Internet. The new Universal Service Order implementing this expanded definition allows up to $2.25 billion annually to provide schools and libraries with discounts, referred to as the "E-rate" for services beginning in January of 1998. The discounts are allotted on a sliding scale from 20 to 90 percent (with the poorest schools [and libraries] receiving the maximum discount). This program has been fairly controversial. Because the major long-distance telephone companies started to itemize the Universal Service on phone bills, it became known as the "Gore tax." Further, there have been legal challenges over specific design elements of the program, such as whether it would cover internal wiring of the schools in addition to Internet access.

At face value, it would appear that the E-rate program has succeeded in expanding Internet access (Puma, Chaplin, and Pape, 2000). By the third year of the program (December 2000), approximately $1.8 billion was allocated to schools and districts, funding more than 20,000 applicants. Thirty percent of the subsidies went to the poorest 16 percent of schools and districts—those in which 75 percent or more of the students are eligible for the national school lunch program (Universal Service Administrative Company, 2001). Further, by the year 2000, 98 percent of schools had access to the Internet; 77 percent of classrooms had Internet access. The gap between suburban and rural and between low-income and high-income schools had closed substantially (Cattagni and Farris, 2001). Despite these gains, it is difficult to isolate the specific impact of the E-rate on this growth in IT in elementary and secondary schools from the growth that would have occurred in its absence.

Other administration programs to increase and improve IT in schools include the Technology Literacy Challenge Fund, which distributes funds on a formula basis to help states invest in education technology; Preparing Tomorrow's Teachers to Use Technology (known as PT3), which attempts to train new teachers in the use of technology; and the Technology Innovation Challenge Grants, which are competitive grants to states also designed to promote innovation in the use of technology. These programs are in addition to "bully pulpit" initiatives, such as promoting private and volunteer efforts (e.g., "Net Day," a day during which communities wire the local schools for Internet access).

The most important question for these policies is whether technology actually makes a difference for student achievement. Surprisingly, there is little compelling evidence that it does. In part, the problem arises because technology changes so quickly. Different studies evaluate different hardware and software products, and by the time the study is completed the technology is often obsolete. In addition, virtually all studies of computers and student learning are based on observational data. After reviewing several meta-analyses, single studies, and critical reviews on the effect of computer use on student achievement, Stanford University's Larry Cuban and Heather Kirkpatrick (1998) conclude, "We are unable to ascertain whether computers in classrooms have in fact been or will be the boon they have promised to be."[16]

We believe that a fair reading of the evidence is that computer-aided instruction (CAI), when done correctly, can probably help reinforce traditional classroom learning. But the curriculum has to be tailored to the student with clear goals in mind, and CAI may be ineffective, or perhaps harmful, if done

---

16. In the late 1970s a study described in Ragosta, Holland, and Jamison (1982) used randomized assignment. See Angrist and Lavy (1999), Kulik and Kulik (1991), and Wenglinsky (1998) for recent studies.

incorrectly. A set of randomized studies would go a long way to answering whether CAI works, what modes work, and for whom it works.

10.2.4 Postsecondary Education

The Clinton administration's policies in higher education were motived by three economic trends and a desire to cut taxes. The first trend was the increasing income inequality in the United States, which was driven in large part by the declining wages of those with only a high school degree, as discussed earlier. The second was increasing college tuition. College tuition has been increasing steadily since the early 1980s, jumping by more than 50 percent between 1980 and 1990.

Finally, the administration was concerned that intergenerational income mobility would slow because postsecondary enrollment varies by family income. Analysis by David Ellwood and Thomas Kane (2000) of Harvard University suggests that the percentage of students enrolling in higher education increases with parental income, even accounting for student test scores. Such a pattern of enrollment may be explained by several factors, such as differences in college preparedness not captured by test scores, information about college and financial aid, and the existence of credit constraints. The explanation is important because it should affect the direction of policy.

The first explanation suggests a policy of focusing more on K–12 education. The second is an information deficiency that could potentially be addressed through informational campaigns or mentoring programs for youth.[17] The third potential explanation, credit constraints, arises because more affluent students can finance postsecondary education by drawing on family wealth while lower-income students may need to borrow. Since students are unable to offer their future earnings as collateral to secure a loan on the private market, the cost of borrowing may exceed the expected return to attending college. If credit constraints are important, then policies to either lower the cost of higher education or to decrease the cost of borrowing are appropriate.

Heckman and Lochner (2000) argue that college preparedness is the dominant force driving the differences in college attendance by family income, and that it swamps any potential borrowing constraints faced by families during the college-going years. In contrast, Ellwood and Kane (2000) offer evidence consistent with the existence of borrowing constraints. More generally, a wide array of evidence from outside of education suggests that many people, particularly those close to college age, are credit constrained. For example, Warner

---

17. GEAR-UP, which funds partnerships between high-poverty middle schools, colleges and universities, community organizations, and businesses, is one such program.

and Pleeter (2001) find that, when offered the choice between an annuity and a lump-sum bonus as a separation payment, the vast majority of members of the armed forces selected the lump sum; the discount rate that would justify their decision typically exceeded 20 percent. Additional evidence comes from credit card usage. Gross and Souleles (2000), for example, find that well over one-half of households with at least one credit card regularly roll over debt, with the median revolving account equal to about $7,000. Interest rates on such debt run around 15 percent. They also find that when credit limits are increased, there is an immediate and significant rise in credit card debt, especially for those who were already close to their previous credit limit. In addition, many families pay college tuition bills with credit cards and roll over the resulting debt.

In fact, one could characterize the administration's policy toward higher education as attempting to address all three potential explanations of the relationship between family income and college attendance.

10.2.4.1 Expansion of Pell Grants

Created in 1973, the Pell Grant program provides grants to low-income students who have yet to complete a bachelor's degree so they can attend a post-secondary institution. It is the federal government's primary means-tested grant program in higher education. A student's grant is calculated as the maximum Pell Grant minus the expected family contribution (largely determined by income and assets). The maximum Pell Grant in 1993 (in 2000 dollars) was $2,616; by 2000 it had increased to $3,300.[18] The total federal appropriation for Pell Grants in 2000 was $7.6 billion (Budget of the United States Government, 2001). In *The Price of Admission: Rethinking How Americans Pay for College*, Thomas Kane (1999) explains that while Pell Grants lower the cost of attending college, they have little effect on the marginal cost of attending a more or less expensive college among those who would attend college in the absence of the program. There is little effect because tuition is usually not a factor in calculating the grant amount. In theory, Pell Grants should, however, have an effect on students who are on the margin of attending college. The empirical evidence on the effect of Pell Grants on college attendance is relatively sparse. For example, when looking for changes in enrollment among low-income youth before and after the introduction of the Pell Grant, Kane (1999) finds no effect on attendance. In contrast, researchers who have attempted to study the effect of college cost on enrollment tend to find that a $1,000 decrease in net price is associated with a 3–5 percentage-point increase in attendance (see, for example, Leslie and

---

18. The administration also expanded the Supplemental Educational Opportunity Grants (SEOG), which provide grants up to $4,000 to low-income students.

Brinkman, 1988, and Kane, 1994) with most of that accounted for by the enroll-ment response of students attending two-year colleges (Rouse, 1994).

Because this could not be claimed as a "new Clinton initiative," increases in Pell Grants were never a front-line initiative of the administration, and they paled in comparison to the new education tax credits (discussed in section 10.2.4.3), which primarily benefit middle-income students.

10.2.4.2 Student Loan Reform

Federal student loans comprise the largest share of federal aid to postsecondary students—about $21 billion in new loans were made to 3.5 million students in 1999 (Smith, 1999). Under the Guaranteed Student Loan (GSL) program (for-mally renamed the Federal Family Education Loan Program in the 1992 amend-ments to the Higher Education Act, or HEA),[19] loans are made through private companies, although the government ensures the lenders a return that covers the cost of providing the loans as well as a profit. As Representative Bill Good-ling summarizes, "Federal student loans were made and serviced by the private sector but were guaranteed and subsidized by the federal government" (Good-ling, 1994). And yet throughout the 1980s and early 1990s there were signs that the program was in trouble. As noted earlier, default rates were unacceptably high in some sectors of higher education; and a General Accounting Office re-port concluded that the GSL program was "vulnerable to waste, fraud, abuse, and mismanagement" (Kunin, 1994). Although proposals to reform the fed-eral student loan system had been floating around Washington for years— including consideration of direct lending by the Bush administration for the 1992 reauthorization of the HEA—little had been accomplished.

During the 1992 presidential campaign, Bill Clinton pledged that

[to] give every American the right to borrow money for college, we will scrap the exist-ing student loan program and establish a National Service Trust Fund. Those who bor-row from the fund will be able to choose how to repay the balance: either as a small percentage of their earnings over time, or by serving their communities for one or two years. (Clinton, 1992)

The idea was that the need to repay their student loans should not discourage students from taking low-paying community service–oriented jobs and that individuals who complete national service should receive some reward. This pledge resonated with Americans who felt that more should be done to en-courage national service and who were seeking ways to pay for rising college tuition. And, this pledge was among those that Clinton kept. The National Service Trust Act of 1993 created AmeriCorps, which provides volunteers with

---

19. Despite the name change, we will refer to federally subsidized student loans as the more familiar "GSL" both before and after the 1992 reauthorization.

an educational award to help pay for postsecondary education or to pay off student loans; that same year, the Student Loan Reform Act was passed.

The centerpiece of the Student Loan Reform Act is the creation of the Direct Loan program.[20] The idea was to reform the GSL program to "work better and cost less" and to use the cost savings to subsidize the national service corps as well as alternative forms of loan repayment (such as income-contingent loans). Through the Direct Loan program, funds are provided directly to schools that, in turn, make loans to students. As a result, the financial intermediaries in the existing GSL program (the lenders, secondary markets, and guaranty agencies) play no role. The Department of Education estimates that the program has thus far saved the federal government $6 billion (U.S. Department of Education, 2000a).

The Direct Loan program benefits students because it can provide them with more flexible repayment options and loans at lower cost. Under the program, students have the option of the standard 10-year repayment period, graduated repayment (smaller payments at the beginning of the repayment period and increasing over time), extended repayment (smaller payments extended over more than 10 years), income-contingent repayment, or a combination of these alternatives (Ford, 1994). The cost savings derive from the fact that the federal government's cost of funds is less than that of the private sector, from the fact that the federal government does not need to receive a profit in order to have an incentive to provide student loans, and from increased competition in the market for student loans (Ford, 1994). In fact, although the program has never been fully implemented, many observers agree that the increased competition (resulting from the lower-cost loans offered by the federal government) is one of its most important effects. An evaluation of the program in 1999 concluded, "Virtually no one disputes that the operation of an alternative loan program has produced a competition that inspired innovation and service—to the benefit of all borrowers and schools"[21] (cited in Smith, 1999). The Department of Education estimates that the students have saved $9 billion in interest and fees to date (U.S. Department of Education, 2000a).

---

20. It is widely accepted that direct lending could not have been enacted had it not been for the Credit Reform Act of 1990, which changed the way in which loans were scored. Direct lending is substantially less costly under the new rules than under the old. The fact that the cost savings are a result of a change in scoring method is one of the controversial aspects of the Direct Lending program.

21. In addition, a senior executive from a bank providing GSLs reported, "[Direct Loans] have introduced some ways of doing business and some delivery mechanisms that made the private enterprise wake up a little bit. To be perfectly honest, as a private enterprise we thought we were doing almost an A-plus job. When we stepped back a little bit, we saw some of the things that the Department of Education was doing and we realized we weren't. . . . It's been relatively good for the industry, particularly for the recipients in terms of students and schools" (cited in Smith, 1999).

Although initially opposed by members of the banking and guaranty agency community, student loan reform may be one of the more significant unsung accomplishments of the Clinton administration. It injected competition into a market that by many accounts had become uncompetitive while also giving students greater options and attempting to reform a large government program. Whether these changes actually encouraged the marginal student to attend college is, however, unclear.

10.2.4.3 Education Tax Credits

The newest, and perhaps most controversial, of the administration's policies in higher education was the creation of additional education tax credits. Available since 1998, the Hope Scholarship is a nonrefundable $1,500 tax credit for the first two years of college for tuition and fees (minus certain tax-free funds, such as scholarships and Pell Grants). It is phased out for joint filers between $80,000 and $100,000 of income and for single filers between $40,000 and $50,000 of income. The credit can be claimed in two taxable years on an individual basis (for students enrolled on at least a half-time basis) and cannot be claimed after the student completes the first two years of college. As President Clinton often declared when proposing the Hope Scholarship in 1996, "Our goal must be nothing less than to make the 13th and 14th years of education as universal to all Americans as the first 12 are today" (U.S. Department of Education, 2000a). The Hope Scholarship roughly achieves this goal for students attending community colleges, where in the spring of 1997, tuition averaged about $1,500 per year (U.S. Department of Education, 2000b). In 2000, the government budgeted $5 billion for the Hope Scholarship tax credit.

The Lifetime Learning Tax Credit (available since 1999) allows college juniors and seniors, graduate students, and workers enrolled in a postsecondary institution to upgrade their skills with a 20 percent tax credit for the first $5,000 of tuition and fees (minus certain tax-free funds) through 2002 and for the first $10,000 thereafter. It is available on a per-family basis and phased out at the same levels as the Hope Scholarship; a taxpayer cannot claim both the Hope Scholarship and the Lifetime Learning Tax Credit in the same year. Although not currently as large as the Hope Scholarship, in 2000 it was budgeted at almost $3 billion. The credit was motivated by the concern that in the "new economy" in which the skill demands of the labor force change rapidly, workers need to engage in a "lifetime" of learning.[22]

---

22. These credits were enacted under the Taxpayer Relief Act of 1997. Other tax benefits for higher education in that act include (among others) a deduction for interest paid on student loans, penalty-free withdrawal from Individual Retirement Accounts (IRAs) for education purposes, and an expansion of education IRAs.

These credits are opposed by many in the higher education establishment because they institute a new system of financial aid that is disconnected from the existing system, and add complexity to the financial aid system with the introduction of a new regulator (the Internal Revenue Service). Further, observers argue that public institutions with tuition levels below the financial aid limits have an incentive to raise tuition with little effect on college cost for low-income students, but with a shift in the subsidy from the state to the federal government (see, e.g., Kane, 1999, and Wolanin, 2001). Finally, public finance economists decry the complexity that the tax credits add to an already complicated tax code.

Another important policy question is the extent to which these scholarships encourage students to attend college who otherwise would not have done so. Susan Dynarski (2000) of Harvard University analyzes the enrollment effects of Georgia's HOPE (Helping Outstanding Pupils Educationally) scholarship program, the model and namesake for the federal Hope Scholarship tax credit. Through this program state residents with at least a B average in high school can attend Georgia's public colleges for free. Dynarski estimates that Georgia's HOPE scholarship has had a sizable impact on the college attendance of 18- and 19-year-olds. About 20 percent of the college attendance after the introduction of the HOPE scholarship appears to have been induced by the scholarship. Thus, 80 percent of the scholarships go to students who would have gone to college even in the absence of the program.[23]

Finally, it is important to note that while Pell Grants are targeted to low-income students, the Hope Scholarship and Lifetime Learning Tax Credits are not. Four features of the credits limit their usefulness for low-income families: (1) they are not refundable (such that those with no tax liability receive no benefit from the program); (2) the amount of the tuition and fees that can be counted toward the tax credits is reduced by the amount of tax-free educational assistance received by the student (including Pell Grants); (3) only tuition and fees can be included rather than the full cost of college attendance (which also includes room and board, books, and transportation); and (4) the credits are available several months after the tuition payments have been made (Wolanin, 2001). Figure 10.1 shows the distribution of tax credits by taxpayer income for 1998. Only about 12 percent of the tax credits go to taxpayers with an adjusted gross income of less than $20,000; almost 50 percent go to those with incomes greater than $50,000. This pattern has led some analysts to be concerned that such tax credits may actually serve to widen the gap in postsecondary en-

---

23. Based on a simulation, Cameron and Heckman (1999) forecast that more than 90 percent of the expenditure of the Hope Scholarship would go to students who would have enrolled in college in the absence of the program.

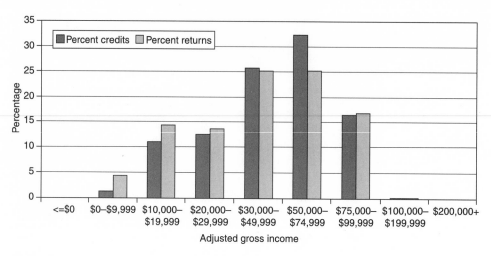

Figure 10.1
Distribution of Education Tax Credits by Income, 1998 Tax Year. (*Source:* Unpublished data from
the U.S. Department of the Treasury.)

rollment between low- and upper-income families. For example, Dynarski finds
that Georgia's HOPE scholarship program had widened the gap in college
attendance between low- and high-income families, as well as between African
Americans and whites.

Why did the administration elect to focus on tax credits rather than increases
in Pell Grants? Because they were largely motivated by providing tax relief to
middle-income families, and the goal was immensely popular among the public.[24] They did not expect the credits to help low-income students to attend college. As David Longanecker, assistant secretary for postsecondary education,
said in 1997 regarding the Hope Scholarship, "Most lower-income families will
not benefit from the tax credit" (Wolanin, 2001). Rather, it was designed to
counter the across-the-board rate and capital gains tax cuts proposed by Senator Robert Dole in 1996 (Wolanin, 2001). And although most observers do not
believe that the credits make much economic sense (at least if motivated by
concerns about college access), it appears that the Bush administration is continuing and expanding them.[25]

---

24. Former Clinton adviser Dick Morris writes, "[The] idea for tax deductions for college tuition
had resonated deeply with the public at a visceral level, with 55 percent saying they strongly support it and another 25 percent somewhat support it, far better numbers than any other tax-cut proposal we'd tested" (Morris, 1997).
25. For example, the new tax cut legislation signed by President Bush expands the Lifetime Learning Tax Credit, Education IRAs, and student loan interest reduction.

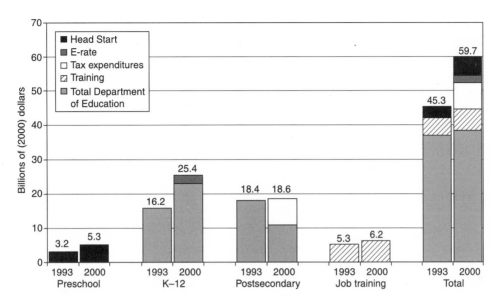

Figure 10.2
Federal Budget for Education and Training, 1993 and 2000. (*Sources:* Departments of Education, Health and Human Services, and Labor.)

Notes: The total for the Department of Education includes other departmental programs. The job training budget for 2000 is the actual appropriation for 1999, assuming 3 percent growth.

10.2.5 Discussion

Figure 10.2 shows the federal budget for education and training (human capital development) in 1993 and 2000. In addition to the budget from the Department of Education, we have also included the appropriations for Head Start, the E-rate, the Student Loan Interest Deduction, the Hope Scholarship and Lifetime Learning Tax Credits, and job training. Overall, federal education spending increased by about 30 percent; with the addition of job training spending increased by about 32 percent.[26] There was an increase in the Department of Education's spending at the K–12 level due to increases in special education, Title I of the ESEA, and the Class Size Reduction program. Simultaneously, there was a decrease in the department's budget at the postsecondary level arising from the savings from student loan reform. Note, however, that overall appropriations to the Department of Education were relatively constant. Thus the Clinton administration increased the federal investment in education

---

26. We note that there are other education programs throughout the federal government that are not included in these figures.

through nontraditional educational programs such as the E-rate and the tax code.[27]

Part of the administration's strategy resulted from the fact that it was hemmed in because of congressional budget rules. Health, education, and labor—three priorities—all fell in the same budget committee. As a consequence, to a large extent the allocation of the budget for these functions was zero-sum: if Title I funding increased, then funds for another priority would have to be decreased. The budget restrictions in part motivated the administration to look for ways of achieving education and labor goals outside the usual channels, often through targeted tax cuts. Overall, throughout his eight years in office President Clinton helped to solidify the federal role in education. His policies made the federal government's contribution to elementary and secondary education more complementary to efforts by state and local governments, and student loan reform at the postsecondary level brought savings and flexibility to students and taxpayers. Further, they promoted education in nontraditional ways, such as through the tax code. Although larger, the federal role nevertheless remains small compared to those of state and local governments.[28]

10.3 Labor Department Policy

To provide an overview of the size of the Department of Labor, Figure 10.3 reports the department's budget outlays in constant 2000 dollars from 1962 through 2000. The figure indicates that DOL's budget fluctuated between $14 billion and $20 billion in the 1960s, increased by approximately threefold to a peak of $67 billion in 1976, fell by almost half in the 1980s, spiked up during the recession of the early 1990s, and returned to its late 1980s level by the end of the 1990s. The department's outlays clearly reflect a countercyclical pattern, typically peaking a year after the trough of a recession. The correlation between year-over-year changes in the department's real outlays and changes in the unemployment rate is 0.62. The countercyclical pattern is largely driven by spending on unemployment insurance benefits, which naturally rise during a recession, and comprise a large share of the department's budget.

Figure 10.4 displays DOL's budget as a percent of overall federal budget outlays. The department's budget fell gradually relative to the overall federal

---

27. We discuss the small overall increase in funding for job training in section 10.3.2.

28. One missed opportunity for the federal government that the administration did not emphasize is the promotion and dissemination of high-quality research in education. As one of us has argued, the Department of Education could play a role in education much as the Food and Drug Administration does in medicine.

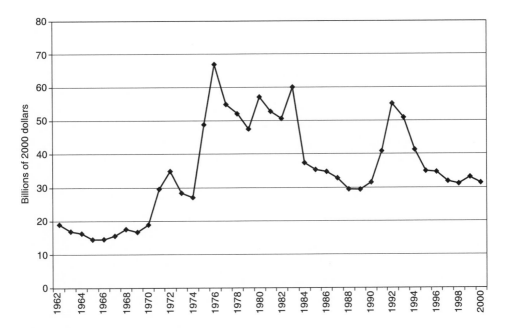

Figure 10.3
Department of Labor Outlays, 1962–2000

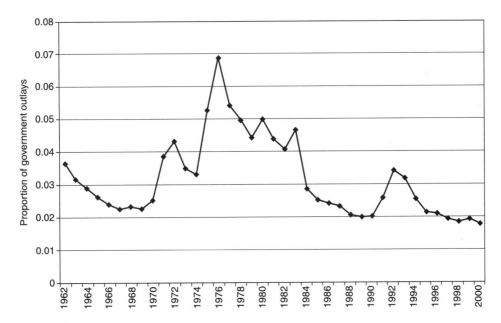

Figure 10.4
Department of Labor Outlays Relative to Federal Budget, 1962–2000

government in the 1960s, grew sharply in the 1970s, and declined in the 1980s and 1990s. By 2000, DOL's share of the federal budget fell below 1.8 percent, its lowest level in over four decades. The Bush administration's initial budget proposal cuts the DOL budget further, reducing discretionary spending (mainly job training) by $600 million in 2002.

The budget gives a crude picture of the scale and scope of government activity, especially if regulatory functions—which tend to require low government expenditures but can have a profound effect on the economy—are involved. An alternative measure is the number of employees involved in carrying out particular functions. Table 10.4, taken from Krueger (2000b), summarizes the allocation of DOL employees across various agencies over the last 40 years. The bottom of the table shows employment grouped into four broad functions, based on the mission of the agencies. Employment from currently defunct agencies was categorized into the succeeding agencies, although in some cases this task was difficult.[29] Nonetheless, several shifts in the general direction of policy are evident from the table. Total employment doubled in the 1960s, and then again in the 1970s, and then fell by 20 percent during the 1980s and by another 7 percent in the 1990s. The increase in employment in the 1960s and 1970s coincided with an increase in the regulatory functions performed by the department.

Much of the decline in DOL employment since the 1970s was associated with a decline in training activities. In 1969, 37 percent of DOL employees were engaged in job training and administering the unemployment insurance system; by 1999, such employment fell to just 8 percent of the department's total employment. The training budget declined substantially since the 1970s as well. In constant 1999 dollars, spending on training and employment services exceeded $12 billion in 1979 but was only $4.8 billion in 1989. Although job training was a stated priority of the Clinton administration, expenditures on training and employment services increased by just 2 percent between 1992 and 1999.[30] The decline in federal funding for job training in the early 1980s was not made up by an increase in state funding. In 1999 state spending on employer-centered job training (both incumbent workers and new hires) was $593 million, just 11 percent of the total federal expenditures. At this level of expenditures, it is impossible that any state increase would have offset the nearly $8 billion de-

---

29. For example, in 1969 it was probably the case that many of the functions of the Office for Administration and Management were handled by the secretary's office.

30. The 1979 data are from DOL's annual reports. The post-1980 data are from "Historical Summary of Actual Budget Authority" provided by DOL. The figures pertain to "Training and Employment Services." The GDP deflator was used to convert to 1998 dollars.

Table 10.4
Number of DOL Full-Time-Equivalent Employees by Agency, 1959–99

Agency	1959		1969		1979		1989		1999	
	Number	Percent	Number	Percent	Number	Percent	Number	Percent	Number	Percent
Employment and Training Administration	1,356	24.8	3,887	37.2	3,507	16.1	1,696	9.6	1,350	8.3
Labor-Management Services/Standards	254	4.6	617	5.9	1,272	5.9	959	5.4	0	0.0
Employment Standards Administration	1,824	33.3	2,805	26.8	4,991	23.0	4,047	23.0	3,830	23.5
Occupational Safety and Health Administration	0	0.0	0	0.0	2,855	13.1	2,270	12.9	2,154	13.2
Mine Safety and Health Administration	0	0.0	0	0.0	3,703	17.0	2,671	15.2	2,202	13.5
Bureau of Labor Statistics	958	17.5	1,537	14.7	2,087	9.6	2,097	11.9	2,406	14.7
Solicitor of Labor	329	6.0	462	4.4	818	3.8	722	4.1	689	4.2
International Labor Affairs	0	0.0	178	1.7	376	1.7	83	0.5	69	0.4
Office of the Secretary	187	3.4	961	9.2	860	4.0	247	1.4	211	1.3
Administration and Management	124	2.3	0	0.0	1,250	5.8	926	5.3	890	5.5
Inspector General	0	0.0	0	0.0	0	0.0	524	3.0	412	2.5
Veterans' Employment Services	64	1.2	0	0.0	0	0.0	267	1.5	254	1.6
Pension Benefit Guarantee Corporation & PWBA	0	0.0	0	0.0	0	0.0	520	3.0	1,432	8.8
Other	380	6.9	0	0.0	0	0.0	575	3.3	420	2.6
Total DOL FTE employment	5,476		10,447		21,719		17,604		16,319	

Table continued on following page

Table 10.4 (continued)

	1959		1969		1979		1989		1999	
	Number	Percent	Number	Percent	Number	Percent	Number	Percent	Number	Percent
Summary of DOL FTEs by Function										
Regulation	2,078	37.9	3,422	32.8	12,821	59.0	10,467	59.5	9,618	58.9
Training	1,420	25.9	3,887	37.2	3,507	16.1	1,963	11.2	1,604	9.8
BLS	958	17.5	1,537	14.7	2,087	9.6	2,097	11.9	2,406	14.7
Management, executive direction, and program development	640	11.7	1,423	13.6	2,928	13.5	2,419	13.7	2,202	13.5
Total	5,096	93.1	10,269	98.3	21,343	98.3	16,946	96.3	15,830	97.0

Sources: Author's analysis of *DOL Annual Reports* 1959–89 and DOL Budget Office unpublished tables 1999.

Notes: International Labor Office is not classified into a function, and neither is "other." The DOL employment data for 1959 are number of positions; all other years are FTEs.

cline in federal expenditures in the early 1980s.[31] Section 10.3.2 provides a more detailed analysis of developments in federal job training in the 1990s.

The trend toward enacting legislation that regulated more aspects of the labor market continued in the 1990s. Examples of such legislation include the Americans with Disabilities Act (ADA), which added individuals with disabilities to the groups protected by Title VII of the Civil Rights Act in 1990; the WARN Act, which required employers to give two months of advance notification prior to a mass layoff or plant closing; and the Family and Medical Leave Act—the first bill signed by President Clinton—which mandates unpaid leave in the event of certain medical emergencies. In addition, increasing numbers of employers became covered by existing regulations as a consequence of reductions in the minimum size of covered establishments under many standards and the elimination of many employer exemptions.

Table 10.5 summarizes the main labor legislation and executive branch initiatives begun in the 1990s. By and large, the initiatives continue the past trend of increased labor market regulation. In addition, a new model, based on greater worker choice, was initiated for federal job training. In the remainder of this section we describe the political, intellectual, and economic forces that led to the major labor policy thrusts of the 1990s, along with relevant research bearing on the impacts of the policy initiatives.

10.3.1 Family and Medical Leave Act

When he signed the Family and Medical Leave Act (FMLA) in February 1993, President Clinton said, "I believe that this legislation is a response to a compelling need—the need of the American family for flexibility in the workplace. American workers will no longer have to choose between the job they need and the family they love."

Support for FMLA had existed in Congress for some time. The FMLA permits covered workers to take up to 12 weeks of unpaid, job-protected leave in a 12-month period for specified medical and family reasons, such as the birth of a child or a seriously ill relative. The changing characteristics of the workforce—in particular, the steady rise in employment of women, who tend to be care givers, and the increase in the number of workers with elderly parents—are

---

31. State expenditures on job training are available from Duscha and Graves (1999). States operate many different types of programs. For Texas, for example, the figures include expenditures on the Smart Jobs Fund for direct grants to companies and the Skills Development Fund for customized training through community colleges or vocational schools. From 1989 to 1999, state job training expenditures increased by 21 percent, after adjusting for changes in the CPI. Data for earlier years are unavailable.

Table 10.5
Major Executive Branch and Congressional Initiatives in Labor Market Policy in the 1990s

Legislation/Initiative	Year	Brief Description
Americans with Disabilities Act	1990	Prohibits discrimination and requires equal opportunity for persons with disabilities in employment, state and local government services, public accommodations, commercial facilities, and transportation.
Family and Medical Leave Act	1993	Grants family and temporary medical unpaid leave under certain circumstances for up to 12 weeks.
North American Agreement on Labor Cooperation (NAFTA side agreement)	1993	Establishes Commission for Labor Cooperation run by representatives of the United States, Mexico, and Canada to provide a public forum for issues of mutual concern, monitoring enforcement of existing national laws, investigating complaints, and recommending fines or sanctions.
Worker Profiling and Reemployment Services (WPRS) program	1993	Required each state to implement a system in which unemployed workers were statistically profiled for reemployment services; greatly expanded the use of Job Search Assistance.
OSHA Regulations on Indoor Air Quality	1994	OSHA-adopted standards regulating air quality in indoor work environments, such as ventilation and smoking.
President's Affirmative Action Review	1995	Review committee chaired by George Stephanopolous and Christopher Edley that made recommendations leading to the president's "Mend it, don't end it" speech.
Striker Replacement Executive Order	1995	Executive order prohibiting federal agencies from making contracts to buy goods and services sold by companies that permanently replace workers striking for economic reasons; ruled unconstitutional by U.S. Court of Appeals in 1996.
Minimum Wage Increase	1996	Increased the hourly minimum wage from $4.25 to $4.75 on October 1, 1996, and to $5.15 on September 1, 1997.
Workforce Investment Act	1998	Replaced the Job Training Partnership Act of 1983. Established one-stop system for job training and introduced greater flexibility in training venues.
H-1B Visa Program	1998, 2000	H-1B visas permit foreign nationals with advanced training to work in the United States for a renewable three-year term. In 1998 the maximum number of visas was increased from 65,000 to 115,000 a year, and in 2000 it was increased to 200,000+ for three years.

probably the main driving forces behind public support for the FMLA. About two-thirds of the U.S. labor force works in a firm that is covered by FMLA, and about one-half of the workers also meet the FMLA's requirement in terms of length of service and hours.

Relatively little research has been done on the effects or use of FMLA. The most comprehensive analysis of FMLA is contained in the Commission on Leave's congressionally mandated report, *A Workable Balance*, released in 1996. This study commissioned two surveys in 1995, one of employers and one of employees to assess views toward FMLA. Although it is difficult to assess the impact of the FMLA, the commission found that 16.8 percent of all employees took leave for a reason covered by the FMLA, and about 1.2 percent of all workers *said* they took an FMLA leave in the preceding 18 months. This is a low utilization rate, and it is possible that leave would have been taken in many of these cases without the FMLA. Almost 90 percent of covered employers knew they were covered by the act, while only 58 percent of employees at covered work sites had heard of the act. The vast majority of employers also said that compliance with FMLA entails no costs or only small costs. The survey was done shortly after FMLA was enacted, and it is possible that utilization and costs have increased since then. Nevertheless, the commission found widespread support among workers for the view that "every employee should be able to have up to 12 weeks of unpaid leave in a year from work for family and medical problems." In addition, the commission found that 40 percent of employees think they will have need to take a leave for an FMLA reason some time in the next five years.

In a competitive labor market, employees should pay for the option of taking unpaid leave through a lower salary. If employees value leave at the cost it takes employers to provide it, then wages would fall by that cost. If constraints or frictions prevent wages from adjusting, then one would expect mandated leave to cause employment to decline. If employees do not value mandated leave rights, then FMLA would be equivalent to a tax on employers, which would result in lower pay and employment. Because the likelihood of employees taking leave is small, however, the wage and employment responses would probably be small as well. Moreover, from society's perspective, protected leave for medical emergencies and family reasons could be desirable, as caring for a sick child or parent or for a newborn or nursing oneself back to health can have benefits to society at large that are not taken into account in individual decisions over leave.

Ruhm and Teague (1997) provide a longitudinal analysis of the effect of leave entitlements on GDP, the employment-to-population rate, and the unemployment rate using data for 17 countries during the 1960–89 period. They conclude,

"The econometric estimates provide little support for the view that moderate periods of parental leave reduce economic efficiency but rather hint at a modest beneficial impact, particularly when considering paid time off work." In the United States it is likely that the effect of leave policies are so small as not to noticeably influence macroeconomic outcomes; there still may be effects, however, on microeconomic outcomes such as pay for certain subsets of affected workers.

10.3.2 Job Training

Federal job training undergoes a major reform about once a decade. In 1962 the John F. Kennedy administration introduced the Manpower Development and Training Act (MDTA), which provided training for unemployed and underemployed workers and created public service employment jobs. The Comprehensive Employment and Training Act (CETA), passed in 1973, continued this mission. In 1983, CETA was replaced by the Job Training and Partnership Act (JTPA), which delegated discretion over the choice and oversight of training providers to local Private Industry Councils (PICs) and did away with public service employment. In 1998, JTPA was replaced by the Workforce Investment Act (WIA). Even before WIA took effect, however, major changes in the allocation of the job training budget took place in the 1990s.

As preparation for seeking reforms in job training, in 1994 and early 1995 DOL's Office of the Chief Economist prepared a 71-page report entitled *What's Working (and What's Not): A Summary of Research on the Economic Impacts of Employment and Training Programs*. The effects of job training on participants' employment and earnings have been thoroughly studied by economists, often with the benefit of randomized assignment of subjects into participant and control groups. Although possible general equilibrium effects of training and long-term effects on participants (especially youth) are not well understood, a great deal of progress has been made in this field.[32] The *What's Working* report summarized and synthesized much of the available literature on employment and training, relying heavily on Bloom et al.'s (1994) analysis of the National JTPA Study and earlier studies of the Job Corps, CETA, and summer youth employment programs. The main conclusions of the report can be summarized as follows:

• For disadvantaged out-of-school youth, relatively short-term training programs such as JTPA IIC have been found to be unsuccessful in raising participants' employment and earnings.

---

32. Heckman, LaLonde, and Smith (1999) provide a comprehensive overview of the literature. LaLonde (1995) provides a less technical summary.

· The residential, high-intensity Job Corps program has had a positive effect on participants' future earnings and propensity to commit crime; Mallar's (1982) benefit-cost analysis suggests that the benefits outweigh the costs by 45 percent.

· The traditional school program produces returns for disadvantaged students. Effective strategies to prevent students from dropping out of school would have a high payoff.

· The Summer Youth Employment and Training Program increases the likelihood that participants are employed during the summer months and does not appear to displace other potential workers.

· Contextual training, where skills are taught in the context of a particular job, appears to be more successful.

· For disadvantaged male adults, those who participated in JTPA earned about 10 percent more than those in the control group who did not participate. For disadvantaged female adults, JTPA participants earned about 15 percent more than control group members. "The total additional earnings of participants were about 50 percent greater than the total additional costs expended on that group compared to the control group," within 2.5 years, and probably larger over a longer time horizon.

· Job search assistance produces benefits for all groups that have participated in the program.

· "Both successes and failures among training programs have been common. This argues against a 'one-size fits all' approach and for an attempt to make a wide variety of choices available to those who need to upgrade their skills."

Jodie Allen described the *What's Working* report as "an honest report and many of the findings are honestly disappointing though not surprising."[33] The conclusions of the *What's Working* report were consistent with other, independent, studies. For example, LaLonde (1995) argued: "JTPA dollars are misallocated to the extent that sites must deny services to eligible adult women to reserve some of their funds for adult men and especially for youths," and, "Because Job Corps appears to be the only program that benefits disadvantaged youths, it would make sense to allocate more JTPA funds to this program."

To some extent, training funds moved in the direction suggested by the research findings. Table 10.6 summarizes DOL's training budget authority from 1989 to 1999, in constant 1999 dollars. It is difficult to compare the figures by recipient group over the full 1990s because separate JTPA figures for youth and adult training are only available beginning in 1993.

---

33. Jodie Allen, "Why Retooling Workers Is No Quick Fix for Anxious America," *Washington Post*, January 22, 1995, p. C3.

Table 10.6
Actual Budget Authority for DOL Job Training Programs in Millions of 1999 Dollars

	1989	1990	1991	1992	1993	1994	1995	1996	1997	1998	1999
Job Corps	951	985	1,025	1,077	1,082	1,138	1,165	1,148	1,189	1,271	1,308
Summer Youth	909	859	807	1,144	1,148	972	198	656	897	888	871
JTPA Youth Training Grants					758	721	82	133	131	133	130
JTPA Adult Training Grants					1,137	1,081	1,066	892	922	974	955
JTPA Block Grant	2,291	2,142	2,101	2,039							
JTPA Dislocated Workers	364	569	623	663	729	1,223	1,314	1,146	1,325	1,372	1,406
School-to-Work							131	178	206	204	125
Youth Opportunity Grants							0	0	0	0	240
National Programs	334	268	264	263	313	390	222	192	189	245	485
Total	4,848	4,824	4,819	5,186	5,168	5,524	4,177	4,346	4,859	5,088	5,280

Source: Authors' calculations based on unpublished data provided by Mark Wichlin of DOL. Data are on a fiscal year basis. National programs include several miscellaneous programs, such as demonstrations and administration.

Notes: Data are adjusted to 1999 dollars based on the GDP deflator. An inflation rate of 2 percent is assumed for 1999. Numbers may not add to the total due to rounding.

The various youth training programs and the Summer Youth Employment Program (which is not really a training program) are highlighted in boldface type. Notice first that JTPA Youth Training Grants were eviscerated in FY1995, falling from $721 million to $82 million. The program rebounded somewhat in the subsequent years, but still remains a skeleton of its former self. The Summer Youth Employment Program was gutted in 1995, although much of the funding was subsequently added back. In arguing for a cut in Summer Youth Employment, Congressman John Kasich cited the *What's Working* report as evidence that the program has not been found to have long-term effects, which seems like a lot to ask of a six-week program that is primarily intended to increase employment while youth are out of school. By contrast, expenditures on the Job Corps program increased in nine of the last ten years, although the program is still not nearly large enough to accommodate every eligible youth. These shifts in the relative allocation of the youth training budget are consistent with LaLonde's recommendations, although the deep cuts in youth programs are more a result of the Republican takeover of Congress than administration intent.

In 1995, Senator Nancy Kassenbaum (R-KS), chairwoman of the Senate Labor and Human Resources Committee, sought to reduce or eliminate the Job Corps program. The administration relied primarily on Mallar's (1982) dated matched-comparisons study and a letter from two-time heavyweight champ George Foreman, a Job Corps alumnus, to defend the program. Recent results of Mathematica's ongoing "National Job Corps Study" suggest that the program was worth fighting for.[34] Mathematica is studying the experiences of 9,409 applicants to the Job Corps between November 1994 and December 1995 who were randomly assigned to the program, and another 6,000 applicants who were randomly assigned to a control group. Applicants were surveyed 12, 30, and 48 months after applying to the program; analyses of the first two waves are available. Participants received about 1,000 more hours of education and job training than the control group. Participation in the program raised participants' weekly earnings by an estimated 12 percent four years after they applied to the program. Participants were also less likely to have been arrested, charged, or convicted of a crime, and if convicted, they served less jail time. They were also less likely to utilize welfare. The residential feature of Job Corps appears to be critical, as those slated for a nonresidential center were less successful. Overall, the results of the National Job Corps Study are qualitatively similar to—and even stronger than—Mallar's (1982) earlier study. Mathematica estimates that every dollar spent on Job Corps returns more than $2 to society, a return that is as large as is found for the most successful preschool programs.

---

34. See Burghardt et al. (2001).

New youth training initiatives have also begun. As discussed previously, one goal of School-to-Work is to improve the transition to the job market for non-college-bound students. In 1999 youth training was partially restored in the form of a new Youth Opportunity Grants program. This program provides funding for training for long-term employment in empowerment zones and other high-poverty areas.

The training budget for disadvantaged adults declined over the last six years, while the budget for dislocated workers increased by a greater amount. As a consequence, total spending on adult training increased. Budget figures are not available on adult training by gender. However, data on JTPA-II adult training participants (economically disadvantaged) indicate that between 1990 and 1997 the fraction of program terminees who were women steadily increased from 58 to 68 percent, also consistent with the higher percentage earnings payoffs for women from participation.[35] In general, training dollars shifted toward dis-located middle-class workers and away from economically disadvantaged male workers. Because there is a paucity of research on the effects of training for dislocated workers, this shift should not be viewed as a response to research findings. Instead, it is probably best viewed as a reflection of the fact that middle-class workers vote in higher numbers, experienced stagnant real wage growth in the 1980s and early 1990s, and felt anxious in the aftermath of the 1990–91 recession.

Because job training is also provided by some federal agencies outside DOL and by many other public and private sources, one should be cautious about interpreting the trends shown in Table 10.6 as reflecting shifts in the national training budget. Individuals who are denied access to DOL's job training pro-grams may gain access to other programs, and the prevalence of such training may have changed over time. Substitution of other programs may be particularly important for youth: Heckman, LaLonde, and Smith (1999, Table 5.1), for example, find that 34 percent of male youth and 42 percent of female youth who were randomly denied admission to JTPA nonetheless received some training services. Nonetheless, in looking over the training budget, one is struck by how small the budget is compared to the magnitude of the problems caused by low skills. Even with the Clinton administration's new tax breaks to promote education and training, the federal effort devoted to upgrading the skills of the workforce is still small.

During the 1992 campaign Clinton proposed that every employer be re-quired to spend 1.5 percent of payroll for continuing education and training. The training would be provided to the entire workforce, not just executives.

---

35. See Committee on Ways and Means (2000; Table 15–38a).

This grandiose objective was a nonstarter with Congress and was quickly jettisoned.

Fundamental changes to the structure of the job training system occurred when the Workforce Investment Act (WIA) of 1998 was passed. Support for WIA stemmed primarily from (1) a feeling that there were "too many" job training programs and lines of funding, (2) a desire to have a coordinated employment services delivery system, (3) a desire to give participants more flexibility over their type of training and training provider, and (4) a desire to require more accountability of service providers. The intention to reinvent job training dates back to the 1992 campaign; in *Putting People First* (p. 17), for example, Bill Clinton promised to "streamline the confusing array of publicly-funded training programs."

The WIA grew out of training bills that were initially proposed by DOL under Secretary Robert B. Reich. Major changes introduced by the bill are as follows: (1) participants will have Individual Training Accounts (ITAs) to use to select training services, rather than have JTPA contract with a training provider to which participants are referred; (2) states will have the option of developing a unified plan to implement a number of federal programs; (3) each state, or a group of states, will be authorized to establish regional performance measures and coordinate services among local areas; (4) the four funding streams under JTPA will be aggregated into three funding streams; (5) training providers will be required to meet performance-based eligibility criteria; (6) states will be subject to a penalty equal to 5 percent of their federal funding if they fail to meet statewide performance goals; (7) states are required to establish one-stop centers that partner with other programs (such as TANF or Trade Adjustment Assistance) to provide training and other services to adults; and (8) Workforce Investment Boards take the place of PICs.

The use of ITAs, which are not different from training vouchers (although the White House frowned on the use of that word), is a particularly radical departure for federal job training. It is unclear whether participants will chose as wisely as the PICs did, however. Moreover, publicizing information on providers' job placement rates may not be very helpful to potential participants if social scientists have difficulty inferring causality from such nonexperimental data (unless a great deal of effort is devoted to collecting data on comparison samples). One could question whether the participants and Workforce Investment Boards will have the expertise to evaluate such data. Nonetheless, on general principles, it is hard for economists to argue with providing more choice and information.

The states are responsible for phasing in many aspects of the WIA program. Although WIA is no longer a "new" program, having been in effect for three years, many of the kinks (e.g., forming partnerships) are still being worked out. We suspect that results of earlier research on JTPA are still relevant for evaluating training effects in the new WIA regime, however, because many of the JTPA providers and training services carry over from those that worked under JTPA, and because the *group* undergoing training seems at least as important for the success of the treatment as the services they receive. This reasoning suggests that one should expect normal rates of return to the training dollars, on the order of 5 to 12 percent. But, like most legislation, the devil will lie in the details. An important detail is the level of funding for the ITAs. Secretary Reich's goal of universal access to training accounts is unlikely to be realized any time soon. Also, if the past pattern holds, we would not be surprised to see another wave of job training reform in a decade or so.

10.3.3   Minimum Wage

One of the more contentious areas of labor policy in the 1990s involved the minimum wage. During the 1992 campaign, Bill Clinton endorsed increasing the minimum wage to make work pay, and make up for past erosion in the value of the minimum due to inflation. Raising the minimum wage took a backseat when universal health insurance funded by an employer mandate was under active consideration, but was resurrected primarily by Secretary Reich and Senator Edward Kennedy shortly after it became clear that health care reform was off the table. Secretary Reich sought a higher minimum wage to raise the earnings and living standards of lower-wage workers. President Clinton proposed raising the minimum wage (by an unspecified amount) in his 1995 State of the Union Address, in the following passage:

The goal of building the middle class and shrinking the underclass is also why I believe that you should raise the minimum wage. It rewards work....

Now, I've studied the arguments and the evidence for and against a minimum wage increase. I believe the weight of the evidence is that a modest increase does not cost jobs and may even lure people back into the job market. But the most important thing is, you can't make a living on $4.25 an hour, especially if you have children, even with the working families tax cut we passed last year. In the past, the minimum wage has been a bipartisan issue, and I think it should be again. So I want to challenge you to have honest hearings on this, to get together, to find a way to make the minimum wage a living wage.

Of course, conventional economic models predict that a minimum wage that is set above the market-clearing level will cause employment to decline. If the elasticity of demand for labor is less than one, total payroll of low-wage workers would nonetheless rise, as the loss in employment would be more than offset by higher wages, so the minimum wage will still transfer resources to low-wage workers, but at an efficiency cost.[36] This is an example of Okun's leaky bucket.

The size of the leak in the bucket is a matter of some dispute in the economics profession. (Disclosure: one of the authors of this paper has been a participant in this debate.) First, some theoretical models yield the prediction that minimum wage increases initially lead employment to increase, and then to decrease (e.g., search models). In these models, an appropriately set minimum wage would generate an efficiency gain and redistribute income from employers to employees. Second—and more important for policy—the strength of empirical evidence linking the minimum wage and employment came into question in the early 1990s. The traditional time-series approach to estimating the impact of the minimum wage found that a 10 percent increase in the minimum reduced employment by about 1 percent (see Brown, Gilroy, and Kohen, 1983). This relationship fell apart when the experience of the 1980s was included in the sample, however. As Brown (1999, p. 2154) notes, "Time series estimates that centered on an elasticity of −0.10 moved closer to zero in samples that included the 1980s."

Alternative methods of estimating the impact of the minimum wage have yielded ambiguous results as well. Card and Krueger (1994), for example, found that an increase in New Jersey's minimum wage in 1992 did not appear to cause job loss in fast-food restaurants, either when New Jersey as a whole was compared to Pennsylvania, or when low-wage restaurants were compared to high-wage (unaffected) restaurants within New Jersey. Card's (1992a) analysis of California also found that an increase in the minimum wage there in 1988 did not meaningfully affect employment. And probably most convincingly, Card's (1992b) cross-state analysis of the 1990–91 minimum wage increase, which exploited the fact that a national minimum wage increase affects different parts of the country differently, also found that employment growth was not slower for teenagers in states that were more likely to have wages boosted by the minimum wage increase than in other states. This research is summarized and extended in Card and Krueger (1995).

These new research findings and politics figured into the administration's decision to support a minimum wage increase. For example, Secretary Reich (1997, p. 227) describes a conversation that he had with the president on the issue in which, after several attempts to persuade the president, Reich contended, "New research shows a modest hike won't cost jobs. New Jersey recently raised its state minimum to $5.05, with no effect on employment. Another study looked

---

36. A full distributional analysis would take into account any effect of changes in prices (see Card and Krueger, 1995). This effect is likely to be spread throughout the income distribution.

at California ..." At this point, Reich reports the president cut him short to say, "You can stop lobbying, Bob. I'll propose it in the State of the Union."

But the role of research in this area should not be exaggerated. Deeper political forces (e.g., strong public support, support by unions) were also very much at work. There were minimum wage increases prior to the new research findings, so too much credit (or blame, depending on your point of view) should not be attributed to the research. Moreover, in many areas public policy has not changed despite the support of compelling economic research, so the research alone is not sufficient.

In a speech presented at the National Restaurant Association, Speaker of the House Newt Gingrich greeted the president's endorsement for a higher minimum wage with characteristic combativeness:

The President came up and graciously offered to raise the minimum wage. It was part of a continuing commitment to having no understanding of the free enterprise system.... When you raise the minimum wage, you lay-off black male teenagers more than any other group. This is an objective fact. I mean, the White House has some spurious new evidence that a couple of their friends concocted. But the fact is, every study for a long period of time says the higher the cost of entry, the more the marginally unemployable will be dispossessed and not have a job.

Others were less generous. For example, Dick Armey called the new research "unscientific and counterintuitive," and he vowed to fight the minimum wage with "every fiber of my being." Representative James Saxton (R-NJ) held a hearing to publicize alleged "revelations" concerning the Card-Krueger study based on a small, nonrandom sample of data collected by a lobbyist for restaurants, and then wrote an op-ed criticizing the *Washington Post* for not reporting on his hearing.

The national hourly minimum wage increased from $4.25 to $4.75 on October 1, 1996, and then to $5.15 on September 1, 1997. Many business tax breaks were attached to the minimum wage bill, which was formally called the Small Business Job Protection Act of 1996.

Before turning to systematic evidence on the effect of the 1996–97 minimum wage increase, we feel compelled to examine Speaker Gingrich's prediction concerning black teenage unemployment. Figure 10.5 reports the unemployment rate for teenagers by race and sex in August 1996 and 1998, before and after the minimum wage increases. The figure shows a sharp decline in the unemployment rate for black male teenagers and black female teenagers. Of course, cyclical factors have contributed to the improved employment situation for black teenagers, but so much for objective facts. (We also note that conventional economic theory makes an unambiguous prediction about employment, not unemployment, when it comes to the minimum wage.)

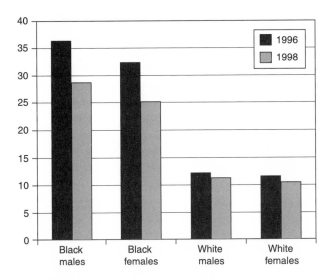

Figure 10.5
Teenage Unemployment Rates, August 1996 and August 1998

Bernstein and Schmitt (1997) have carefully reestimated four models that had been previously used to examine the effect of the minimum wage on employment. These included the approach in Card (1992b) and Deere, Murphy, and Welch (1995), which argued that the 1991–92 minimum wage increases had a severe adverse effect on employment. In all cases, applying the same methods (even using Deere, Murphy, and Welch's computer code) to the later data they find that the 1996–97 increase in the minimum wage did not have an adverse effect on employment.

Additional cross-state evidence on the impact of the 1996–97 minimum wage increases, based on Card's (1992b) approach, is summarized in Figures 10.6 and 10.7.[37] In the year preceding the October 1996 minimum wage increase, the percent of teenage workers who earned between the old minimum ($4.25) and the new one ($5.15)—the percent affected—ranged from 11 percent in Hawaii to 73 percent in Mississippi. Using the state-level data derived from the *Current Population Survey*, Figure 10.6 shows a scatter diagram of the percentage change in the mean wage of teenagers between the 12 months before the 1996 minimum wage increase and the 12 months after the 1997 increase versus the percentage of teenagers in the range affected by the minimum wage increases prior to the increase. The upward-sloping relationship indicates that wages grew most in states that had a higher proportion of teenagers in the affected range, as

---

37. These data were provided by John Schmitt and are analyzed in Schmitt (1999).

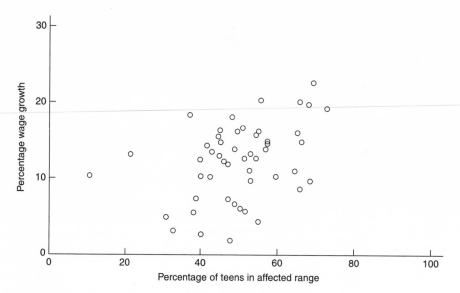

Figure 10.6
Teenage Wage Growth Versus Percentage Affected by the 1996–97 Minimum Wage Hike

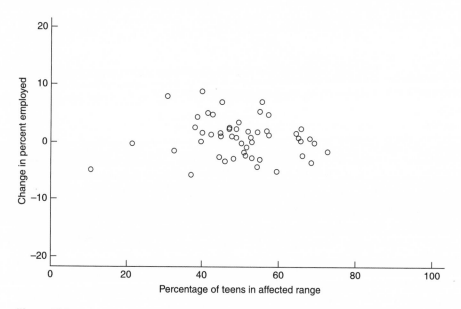

Figure 10.7
Change in Percentage of Teenagers Employed Versus Percentage Affected by 1996–97 Minimum Wage Hike

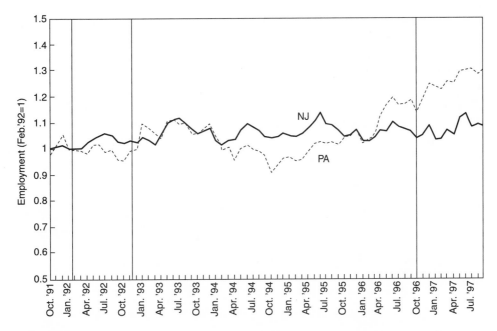

Figure 10.8
Employment in New Jersey and Eastern Pennsylvania Fast-Food Restaurants, October 1991 to September 1997. BLB Payroll Data. (*Source:* Card and Krueger [2000], Figure 2.)

one would expect if the minimum wage increase were binding. Figure 10.7 displays a scatter diagram of the change in the employment-to-population rate over the years surrounding the minimum wage increases. Although the standard model predicts a downward-sloping relationship, no systematic relationship is evident.[38] Schmitt (1999) finds that this conclusion is not altered if controls for past employment growth are held constant in a regression.

In addition, Card and Krueger (2000) reexamined and extended their earlier work with employer-reported payroll data. Figure 10.8 summarizes their main results. The 1992 New Jersey minimum wage has no apparent impact on employment in New Jersey fast-food restaurants relative to that in eastern Pennsylvania. Moreover, the 1996 increase in the federal minimum wage enables the researchers to look at the experiment in reverse, as New Jersey's state law already superseded the federal law. Yet there is no apparent evidence that Pennsylvania's employment grew more slowly than New Jersey's after the federal minimum wage increase.

The evidence suggests that the minimum wage increases in 1996 and 1997 did just what supporters had hoped for: raise wages for low-wage workers

---

38. The *p*-value for the weighted correlation between the two series is 0.75.

without adversely impacting employment growth. Even Alan Greenspan felt obliged to answer, "At this particular stage, none," when he was asked what negative effects he had detected from the 1996–97 minimum wage increases at a hearing held in July 1998.[39] *The New York Times* aptly described the jobs debate in an article titled, "After the Shouting; A Minimal-Impact Minimum Wage."[40] The impact was not minimal on the low end of the wage distribution, however, where real wages grew after years of decay as soon as the minimum wage increased.

10.3.4 Union Policy

Relatively few fundamental changes took place in policy toward unions in the 1990s. In March 1993, Labor Secretary Reich and Commerce Secretary Ronald H. Brown established the Commission on the Future of Worker-Management Relations, widely known as the Dunlop Commission, after its chair, former Labor Secretary John T. Dunlop. The commission's charge was to make recommendations to modernize labor policy for the 21st century. The commission's report in January 1995 contained several recommendations, such as quicker representation elections and employee participation programs. The commission also released a trenchant and sobering fact-finding analysis of developments in the labor markets in May 1994. We think it is fair to say that the commission will be remembered more for its analysis of labor market developments than for its specific policy recommendations, which did not become law. More than anything else, the Dunlop Commission suffered from poor timing. Reaching consensus on labor policy is difficult enough, but doing so in the midst of a change in Congress makes it even more complicated.

In March 1995, President Clinton signed Executive Order 12954, which prohibited federal agencies from making contracts to buy goods and services sold by companies that permanently replace workers striking for economic reasons. Striker replacement legislation had been a priority of labor unions. Such legislation was passed by the House of Representatives in 1993, but filibustered in the Senate. The executive order was ruled unconstitutional by the U.S. Court of Appeals in 1996 and not appealed to the Supreme Court. Even had striker replacement been in effect, it is unlikely that it would have had a major effect on labor relations or the labor market. Strikes are increasingly rare in the United States. The number of strikes involving 1,000 or more employees declined from 51 in 1989 to 17 in 1999, according to the BLS. Although the threat of being

---

39. Federal News Service Transcript, Hearing of the Domestic and International Monetary Policy Subcommittee of the House Banking and Financial Services Committee, July 22, 1998.
40. Peter Kilborn, "After the Shouting; A Minimal-Impact Minimum Wage," *New York Times*, Week in Review section, April 6, 1997, p. 5.

permanently replaced may dissuade some bargaining units from going on strike, it is unlikely that striker replacement protection would have much impact on labor relations, or on the labor market more generally, in the near future.

Although there were changes in the administration of union policy as a result of appointments to the NLRB, and probably proactive federal involvement in labor strikes (such as the baseball strike and UPS strike), a fair summary is that there were no significant changes in policy toward unions in the 1990s. Moreover, union membership as a share of the workforce continued to asymptotically approach zero in the 1990s. In view of the role that unions play in expanding the middle class (see, e.g., Card, 1998) and providing voice to workers, the 1990s were a lost opportunity to revitalize policy toward unions to further the Clinton administration's goal of narrowing wage gaps.

10.3.5 Occupational Safety and Health Administration

The Occupational Safety and Health Administration planned to initiate two major sets of regulations during the 1990s, one dealing with ergonomic standards and the other with indoor air quality. OSHA, which considered the ergonomics standards a higher priority, made a strategic error in issuing the indoor air quality standards first. When the 104th Congress came to power in 1994, it quickly moved to prohibit OSHA from issuing ergonomics standards.[41] After threatening deep cuts in OSHA's budget, Congress was able to wring an agreement from the administration that OSHA would not issue ergonomics standards. The moratorium was written into the budget. In the words of House Whip Tom Delay (R-TX), this moratorium "would force OSHA to cease its activities on the promulgation of an ergonomics standard that is paternalistic in concept and a menace in its implementation."[42]

Ergonomic injuries cost industry an estimated $50 billion per year in terms of missed work, compensation costs, and medical costs.[43] OSHA estimated that its ergonomics regulations would cost business $4.5 billion for compliance and generate $9 billion in benefits. The Small Business Administration, by contrast, estimated that the compliance costs were between $11 and $63 billion. Because most of the costs and benefits are borne privately by the parties directly involved, it would be surprising that the benefits of a standard would exceed the

41. This timing was not entirely OSHA's responsibility, however, because the DOL Chief Economist's Office raised frequent objections to OSHA's benefit-cost analysis of the ergonomic standards, which held up the development of the standards.

42. Quoted in Cindy Skrzycki, "OSHA Abandons Rules Effort on Repetitive Injury: Opposition by GOP, Business Cited," *Washington Post*, June 13, 1995, p. D1.

43. This figure is from the National Academy of Sciences and is quoted in Yochi J. Dreazen, "White House's Ergonomics Rules Aided by Study," *Wall Street Journal*, January 18, 2001, p. A4.

costs by as much as OSHA predicted—unless there was profound ignorance about the efficacy of injury prevention methods.

To bring the story to full circle, shortly before the presidential election in November 2000, OSHA did issue ergonomics regulations, causing great consternation in Congress. On March 20, 2001, however, President Bush signed a measure repealing the proposed ergonomics rule.

Another change in OSHA policy was greater emphasis on compliance assistance instead of safety inspections. Indeed, in 1995, OSHA was awarded the Kennedy School's "Innovations in American Government" award for the Maine Top 200 program, which targeted inspections toward employers who had the greatest risk of injury based on workers' compensation insurance records. Under this program, which started in 1993, OSHA encouraged employers to identify workplace hazards themselves and to take corrective actions before injuries and illnesses occurred. This approach is a contrast to OSHA's past practice of fining employers if violations are discovered during inspections. Given the relatively small force of OSHA inspectors, encouragement of voluntary compliance makes a fair amount of sense.

Work-related injury and illness rates declined considerably during the 1990s. From 1992 to 1998, for example, the work injury and illness rate fell by 25 percent.[44] This decline is all the more remarkable because work injuries usually rise during the upswing of a business cycle. The decline in work-related injuries and illnesses represents a major improvement in the working conditions of American workers. Some analysts have attributed the decline in injuries and illnesses to OSHA's shift in enforcement from safety inspections toward compliance assistance. While this interpretation is possible, the decline in the injury rate began before OSHA's shift took place, and was slightly steeper in the states that administer their own state OSHA program than in those that are administered by federal OSHA. Moreover, injury rates declined in Canada and the United Kingdom as well, so the trend appears to be a universal one.

10.3.6 Unemployment Insurance

On November 24, 1993, Congress passed legislation requiring states to implement a Worker Profile and Reemployment Services (WPRS) program for unemployed workers through their unemployment insurance (UI) systems. Worker profiling involves using a statistical model (which varies across states) to identify those UI recipients who are likely to eventually exhaust their benefits and have difficulty finding a job, and then channel them to reemployment services, including job search workshops, counseling, job clubs, and referrals to employ-

---

44. See Krueger (2000b).

ers. The program focuses on serving individuals who are predicted to suffer long-term unemployment, based on characteristics such as their recall status, first payment, industry or occupation, employment history, job tenure, education, and the local unemployment rate. Claimants referred to employment services are required to participate in those services as a condition of eligibility for UI.

The WPRS initiative represents a break from the traditional approach of the UI program in the United States, which primarily has been concerned with providing temporary cash compensation to eligible unemployed workers while they search for a job. By implementing WPRS and related One-Stop Career Centers, the UI service has embarked on a course of playing a more active role in reducing unemployment.

A major part of the motivation for the administration's proposal of WPRS was that several studies have found that job search assistance (JSA) programs are effective at reducing the duration of unemployment spells. Meyer (1995), for example, provides a summary of the effects of JSA in five states (South Carolina, New Jersey, Washington, Nevada, and Wisconsin) that have randomly selected eligible claimants to receive various forms of JSA and compared their performance to a randomly selected control group. He finds that (1) JSA participants found a new job more quickly—their average duration of UI benefits was reduced by about 0.5 to 4 weeks compared to the control group, with most estimates falling near the bottom of this range; (2) the reduction in UI benefits and increased tax revenue from faster reemployment made the JSA programs cost effective for the government; and (3) on average, JSA participants found jobs that paid about as much as the jobs found by the control group.[45] Indeed, based on this evidence, the job search assistance component of WPRS was scored by the Congressional Budget Office as not raising costs, on net.

WPRS was phased in rather quickly: all states phased in WPRS systems between 1994 and 1996. This new system has had the effect of channeling many additional UI recipients through inexpensive reemployment services, including job search workshops, counseling, and job clubs. In 1994, only 10,773 workers reported for at least one type of reemployment service under WPRS, and 9,990 completed at least one service. In 1998, fully 999,208 reported for at least one type of service, and 747,904 completed a service.[46] Evidence in Wandner, Messenger, and Schwartz (1999) suggests that most of the JSA services provided under WPRS are a net addition to the total amount of JSA that UI claimants receive.

---

45. More recently, work by Ashenfelter, Ashmore, and Deschenes (1998) suggested that the instructional component of JSA is essential for it to be effective; stricter enforcement and verification of worker search behavior alone do not appear to reduce unemployment spells.
46. These figures are from Katz and Krueger (1999).

The unemployment rate fell rapidly after WPRS was passed. This fortuitous development was just coincidental, however. Katz and Krueger (1999) find that it is unlikely that WPRS has had a noticeable effect on aggregate unemployment because the effect of job search assistance on unemployment duration tends to be modest and because UI claimants only account for a minority of the unemployed. Unemployment did not fall more rapidly in the states that implemented WPRS earlier than in those that implemented it later.

Of course, the failure of WPRS to explain the record low unemployment in the late 1990s is not a mark of failure for the program. WPRS has probably modestly reduced unemployment durations for participants, and reduced UI expenditures, on net. It is an example of a policy that nudged the reemployment system toward a more rational and coordinated approach.

One feature of the UI system that received inadequate attention from the Clinton administration during the booming economy in the late 1990s is the reserve funds. State UI reserve funds usually accumulate funds when unemployment is falling so they can be drawn down when unemployment rises. A number of states, however, failed to adequately replenish their UI funds during the late 1990s. As a consequence, about a quarter of the states are in danger of having their fund become insolvent if they are hit by a moderate recession, according to Levine (2000). New York and Texas, in particular, have the lowest reserve ratios (accumulated reserves as a percent of payroll) in the country.

10.3.7 NAFTA Supplemental Agreements

Public opinion polls find that Americans are of two minds about international trade in general and NAFTA in particular.[47] On the one hand, they think that reducing trade barriers will be good for consumers, businesses, and investors. On the other hand, they think that reducing trade barriers will be bad for workers. Indeed, polls find that Americans think that NAFTA has made more jobs available in Mexico and Canada, but fewer jobs available in the United States. (Given the U.S. employment growth after NAFTA passed compared to our partner countries, this belief is quite a puzzle.) There is also a strong educational divide: low-educated workers are much more skeptical about the benefits of expanding trade, and are more likely to believe companies will send jobs overseas, than are highly educated workers.

With this background, it is not surprising that the public also favors—and the Clinton administration sought—side agreements to protect labor and the environment. The NAFTA supplemental labor agreement, formally known as

---

47. See Krueger (1997).

the North American Agreement for Labor Cooperation (NAALC), established the Commission for Labor Cooperation (CLC), which is run by representatives of the United States, Mexico, and Canada. The CLC provides a public forum for addressing issues of mutual concern, monitors enforcement of existing national labor laws, investigates complaints, and recommends fines or sanctions.

The administration also sought and received congressional funding for the NAFTA Worker Security Act in 1993. That program, which went into effect on January 1, 1994, provides workers who have been certified by DOL as having been adversely affected by NAFTA with NAFTA Trade Adjustment Assistance (TAA). NAFTA TAA entitles laid-off workers to 52 weeks of additional unemployment compensation beyond their ordinary 26 weeks of benefts. In addition, workers can receive job training and the related costs of tuition, books, and materials, a job search allowance, and relocation expenses. Although NAFTA was strongly opposed by labor unions, the NAFTA TAA has become the gold standard for adjustment assistance because workers can receive up to 1.5 years of unemployment benefits while undergoing training. In FY2000, $66 million was appropriated for NAFTA TAA.[48] The NAFTA side agreements and the Trade Adjustment Assistance probably generated some support for NAFTA among the public.

10.4 Conclusion

In a statement that in retrospect is both prescient and exaggerated, candidate Clinton argued, "I know economic growth will be the best jobs program we'll ever have. But economic growth does not come without a national economic strategy to invest in people and meet the competition." The first claim is undoubtedly true. The rapid economic growth of the Roaring '90s certainly did much to improve the economic standing of working Americans (see Table 10.1). But were the investments in people in the 1990s—that national economic strategy to invest in people—necessary for this growth? We would argue that reforms to the education and training system helped make small steps toward creating a more rational and efficient system, but they were not an essential contributor to the record economic growth of the 1990s given the modest increase in the investment in people, as well as "normal" rates of return on such investments.

Some would have preferred a different strategy to improve human capital and reduce inequality. A different vision would have been to (1) divert funds from existing youth training, K–12, and tuition assistance programs, in order to pay

48. *Green Book* (Committee on Ways and Means, 2000), p. 346.

for preschool programs and vouchers for private schools, and (2) address rising inequality by a system of wage subsidies for low-wage jobs or a negative income tax credit.[49]

Still others would have preferred to have pursued many of the reforms to the education and training system that took place, but fund the system at a much more generous level. As Robert Reich and George Stephanopoulos chronicle in their books, the desire to reduce the deficit prevented a major effort in investing in people.[50] Consequently, the administration followed a diverse strategy of initiating many small programs, under a broad, more coordinated umbrella, and shifted funds to programs that were believed to have higher returns.

Would it have made more sense to use the monies allocated for training and education for a negative income tax type program? Preliminarily, we note that politically such a strategy was likely to have been—and still be—infeasible. Redistributing income to low-wage workers through education and training, and raising the minimum wage, were among the few options available to make progressive changes. Moreover, these policies were very popular. As Voltaire might say, the best—and we are not convinced a negative income tax is the best policy—should not be the enemy of the good.

And the best might not have been the enemy of the good anyway. On intellectual grounds, we think a strong argument could be made for pursuing a diverse set of policies to achieve the goals of making work pay, reducing wage gaps, raising skills, and reducing anxiety about economic change. First, it makes sense to pursue policies to achieve a given aim to the point that the marginal payoff from each policy is equal. Under most circumstances, this approach would suggest that diverse policies should be pursued. Second, if there are many goals and target groups, then one policy may not dominate in achieving all of the goals. For example, expanding Head Start may have the highest return on the margin, but it does nothing to help 16-year-old youths who are at risk of becoming involved in crime and social dependence. Third, economic change, such as globalization, creates winners and losers. It is only reasonable to expect those who will lose to go along with change—even if the change greatly increases national income—if they feel they will receive some of the benefits of the change. So, for example, NAFTA Trade Adjustment Assistance and the side agreements probably engendered some additional support for expanding trade.

Fourth, according to economic theory, if one starts from a first-best situation, any attempt to redistribute income (short of unattainable lump sum taxes and transfers) will create distortions. In this situation, it is quite plausible that pur-

49. Heckman (1999), for example, argues, "Public-sector training programs are an inefficient transfer mechanism and an inefficient investment policy for adult workers with few skills."
50. See Reich (1997) and Stephanopoulos (1999).

suing a multiplicity of approaches can help minimize the aggregate distortions. For example, the EITC is expected to cause labor supply to increase for workers with very low wages because a dollar of additional earnings brings home more than a dollar after tax when the EITC is on the upswing. This shift in labor supply would be expected to depress the market wage, possibly offsetting much of the benefit of the EITC. The minimum wage limits the fall in the market wage. Moreover, many low-income people do not file taxes or request the EITC even if they are eligible. For these reasons, the EITC and minimum wage are best viewed as complimentary policies. The fact that, at moderate levels, increases in the minimum wage appear to have no adverse impact on employment only strengthens the case for pursuing both policies (and suggests that the economy is not starting from a "first-best" solution). Likewise, summer employment would raise demand for low-wage workers, and training would lift their marginal products above the wage floor. A good analogy is a doctor who prescribes chemotherapy to try to cure cancer, and then prescribes additional medications to offset the undesired side effects of chemotherapy, and so on.

The best evidence suggests that education and job training programs have rates of return of about 10 percent—about the same as is expected from a year of formal schooling. Some programs may have higher returns, and some lower, but 10 percent is a good figure to have in mind. The spectacular economic growth of the late 1990s had a much more profound effect on narrowing income gaps and raising employment than reasonably could be hoped for by education policy, at least in the short run. For that reason, *if* deficit reduction was responsible for the spectacular growth of the late 1990s, then it might have been sensible to defer massive human capital investments for the future. But if deficit reduction was not the key to the recent economic growth, then a unique opportunity might have been lost to strengthen the skills and knowledge of the workforce by not investing more in education and training in the 1990s.

References

Angrist, Joshua, and Victor Lavy. 1999. "New Evidence on Classroom Computers and Pupil Learning." Mimeo, MIT, Cambridge, MA, May.

Ashenfelter, Orley, David Ashmore, and Olivier Deschenes. 1998. "Do Unemployment Insurance Recipients Actively Seek Work? Randomized Trials in Four U.S. States." Princeton University Industrial Relations Section Working Paper No. 412.

Autor, David, Lawrence Katz, and Alan Krueger. 1998. "Computing Inequality: Have Computers Changed the Labor Market?" *Quarterly Journal of Economics*, 113, no. 4 (November): 1169–1213.

Bagley, Carl, Philip Woods, and Ron Glatter. 1996. "Barriers to School Responsiveness in the Education Quasi-Market." *School Organization*. 16(1): 45–58.

Barnett, W. Steven. 1992. "Benefits of Compensatory Preschool Education." *Journal of Human Resources*, 27, no. 2 (Spring): 279–312.

Barnett, W. Steven. 1995. "Long-term Effects of Early Childhood Programs on Cognitive and School Outcomes." *The Future of Children*, 5(3): 25–50.

Bernstein, Jared, and John Schmitt. 1997. "The Sky Hasn't Fallen." Mimeo, Economic Policy Institute, Washington, DC.

Bettinger, Eric. 1999. "The Effect of Charter Schools on Charter Students and Public Schools." National Center for the Study of Privatization in Education (Teachers College, Columbia University), Occasional Paper No. 4 (November).

Betts, Julian R. 1998. "The Impact of Educational Standards on the Level and Distribution of Earnings." *American Economic Review*, 88, no. 1 (March): 266–273.

Betts, Julian R., and Jeff Grogger. 2000. "The Impact of Grading Standards on Student Achievement, Educational Attainment, and Entry-Level Earnings." National Bureau of Economic Research Working Paper No. 7875 (September).

Bishop, John. 1990. "Incentives for Learning: Why American High School Students Compare So Poorly to Their Counterparts Overseas." *Research in Labor Economics*, 11:17–51.

Bloom, Howard, et al. 1994. "The National JTPA Study: Overview of Impacts, Benefits and Costs of Title IIA." Bethesda, MD: Abt Associates.

Brown, Charles. 1999. "Minimum Wages, Employment, and the Distribution of Income." In D. Card and O. Ashenfelter, eds., *Handbook of Labor Economics*, 2101–64. Amsterdam: North Holland.

Brown, Charles, Curtis Gilroy, and Andrew Kohen. 1983. "Time-Series Evidence of the Effect of the Minimum Wage on Youth Employment and Unemployment." *Journal of Human Resources*, 18 (Winter): 3–31.

Budget of the United States Government. 2001. Washington, DC: Office of Management and Budget.

Burghardt, John, Peter Sochet, Sheena McConnell, Terry Johnson, R. Mark Gritz, Steven Glazerman, John Homrighausen, and Russell Jackson. 2001. "Does Job Corps Work? Summary of the National Job Corps Study." Princeton, NJ: Mathematica.

Cameron, Stephen, and James J. Heckman. 1999. "Should College Attendance Be Further Subsidized to Reduce Rising Wage Inequality? Does Family Income Foster Ability or Is It an Important Cash Constraint Limiting College Attendance?" In *Financing College Tuition: Government Policies Social Priorities*, ed. Marvin Kosters. Washington, DC: AEI Press.

Campbell, Frances A., Elizabeth P. Pungello, Shari Miller-Johnson, Margaret Burchinal, and Craig T. Ramey. 2001. "The Development of Cognitive and Academic Abilities: Growth Curves from an Early Childhood Educational Experiment." *Developmental Psychology*, 37:231–242.

Campbell, Frances A., Craig T. Ramey, Elizabeth P. Pungello, Joseph Sparling, and Shari Miller-Johnson. In press. "Early Childhood Education: Young Adult Outcomes from the Abecedarian Project." *Applied Developmental Science*.

Card, David. 1992a. "Do Minimum Wages Reduce Employment? A Case Study of California, 1987–89." *Industrial and Labor Relations Review*, 46 (October): 38–54.

———. 1992b. Using regional variation in wages to measure the effects of the federal minimum wage. *Industrial and Labor Relations Review*, 46 (October): 22–37.

————. 1998. "Falling Union Membership and Rising Wage Inequality: What's the Connection?" NBER Working Paper No. 6520, April.

Card, David, and Alan B. Krueger. 1994. "Minimum Wages and Employment: A Case Study of the Fast Food Industry." *American Economic Review*, 84 (September): 772–793.

————. 1995. *Myth and Measurement: The New Economics of the Minimum Wage*. Princeton, NJ: Princeton University Press.

————. 2000. "Minimum Wages and Employment: A Case Study of the Fast Food Industry: Reply." *American Economic Review*, 90(5): 1397–1420.

Cattagni, Anne, and Elizabeth Farris. 2001. "Internet Access in U.S. Public Schools and Classrooms, 1994–2000." National Center for Education Statistics, Statistics in Brief (NCES 2001–071), U.S. Department of Education (May).

Chubb, John E., and Terry M. Moe. 1990. *Politics, Markets, and America's Schools*. Washington, DC: Brookings Institution.

Clinton, Bill. 1992. *Putting People First: A National Economic Strategy for America*. Little Rock, AR: Clinton for President Committee.

Committee on Ways and Means, U.S. House of Representatives. 2000. *Green Book*. Washington, DC.

Costrell, Robert M. 1994. "A Simple Model of Educational Standards." *American Economic Review*, 84, no. 4 (September): 956–971.

CSR Research Consortium. 2000. "CSR Fact Sheet No. 1: Class Size Reduction in California" (June).

Cuban, Larry, and Heather Kirkpatrick. 1998. "Computers Make Kids Smarter—Right?" *Technos*, 7, no. 2 (Summer): 26–31.

Currie, Janet. 2001. "Early Childhood Education Programs." *Journal of Economic Perspectives*, 15, no. 2 (Spring): 213–238.

Deere, Donald, Kevin M. Murphy, and Finis Welch. 1995. "Employment and the 1990–1991 Minimum-Wage Hike." *American Economic Review: Papers and Proceedings*, 85, no. 2 (May): 232–237.

Duscha, Steve, and Wanda Lee Graves. 1999. "State Financed and Customized Training Programs." Submitted to U.S. Department of Labor, Office of Policy and Research, F-6827-30-00-80-30, May.

Dynarski, Susan. 2000. "Hope for Whom? Financial Aid for the Middle Class and Its Impact on College Attendance." National Bureau of Economic Research Working Paper No. 7756 (June).

Ellwood, David T., and Thomas J. Kane. 2000. "Who Is Getting a College Education? Family Background and the Growing Gaps in Enrollment." In *Securing the Future: Investing in Children from Birth to College*, ed. Sheldon Danziger and Jane Waldfogel. New York: Russell Sage Foundation.

Epple, Dennis, and Richard E. Romano. 1998. "Competition Between Private and Public Schools, Vouchers and Peer Group Effects." *American Economic Review*, 88, no. 1 (March): 33–62.

Fernandez, Raquel, and Richard Rogerson. 1996. "Income Distribution, Communities, and the Quality of Public Education." *Quarterly Journal of Economics*, 111, no. 1 (February): 135–164.

Figlio, David N., and Maurice E. Lucas. 2000. "Do High Grading Standards Affect Student Performance?" National Bureau of Economic Research Working Paper No. 7985 (October).

Finn, Jeremy D., and Charles M. Achilles. 1990. "Answers and Questions About Class Size: A Statewide Experiment," *American Educational Research Journal*, 27, no. 3 (Fall): 557–577.

Folger, John, and Carolyn Breda. 1989. "Evidence from Project START about Class Size and Student Achievement." *Peabody Journal of Education*, 67:17–33.

Ford, William D. 1994. "The Direct Student Loan Program: Acknowledging the Future." In *National Issues in Education: Community Service and Student Loans*, ed. John F. Jennings. Bloomington, IN, and Washington, DC: Phi Delta Kappa International and the Institute for Educational Leadership.

Frey, Donald E. 1992. "Can Privatizing Education Really Improve Achievement? An Essay Review." *Economics of Education Review*, 11(4): 427–438.

Friedman, Milton. 1962. *Capitalism and Freedom*. Chicago: University of Chicago Press.

Garces, Eliana, Duncan Thomas, and Janet Currie. 2000. "Longer Term Effects of Head Start." National Bureau of Economic Research Working Paper No. 8054 (December).

Gardner, David P., et al. 1983. *A Nation at Risk* (Washington, DC: U.S. Department of Education).

Garner, W. T., and Jane Hannaway. 1992. "Private Schools: The Client Connection." In *Family Choice in Schooling*, ed. M. Manley-Casimir. Lexington, MA: D. C. Heath.

Glomm, Gerhard, and B. Ravikumar. 1992. "Public Versus Private Investment in Human Capital: Endogenous Growth and Income Inequality." *Journal of Political Economy*, 100, no. 4 (August): 818–834.

Goodling, Bill. 1994. "Direct Student Loans: A Questionable Public Policy Decision." In *National Issues in Education: Community Service and Student Loans*, ed. John F. Jennings. Bloomington, IN, and Washington, DC: Phi Delta Kappa International and the Institute for Educational Leadership.

Gross, David B., and Nicholas Souleles. 2000. "Consumer Response to Changes in Credit Supply: Evidence from Credit Card Data." Mimeo, University of Pennsylvania (February).

Hanushek, Eric A. 1986. "The Economics of Schooling: Production and Efficiency in Public Schools." *Journal of Economic Literature*, 24 (September): 1141–77.

———. 1997. "Assessing the Effects of School Resources on Student Performance: An Update." *Educational Evaluation and Policy Analysis*, 19(2): 141–164.

Heckman, James. 1999. "Doing It Right: Job Training and Education." *The Public Interest*, 135 (Spring): 86–107.

Heckman, James, Robert LaLonde, and Jeffrey Smith. 1999. "The Economics and Econometrics of Active Labor Market Programs." In *Handbook of Labor Economics*, ed. Orley Ashenfelter and David Card. Amsterdam: North Holland, pp. 1865–2097.

Heckman, James, and Lance Lochner. 2000. "Rethinking Education and Training Policy: Understanding the Sources of Skill Formation in a Modern Economy." In *Securing the Future: Investing in Children from Birth to College*, ed. Sheldon Danziger and Jane Waldfogel. New York: Russell Sage Foundation.

Hedges, Larry V., Richard Laine, and Rob Greenwald. 1994. "Does Money Matter? A Meta-analysis of Studies of the Effects of Differential School Inputs on Student Outcomes." *Educational Researcher*, 33:5–14.

Holzer, Harry. 1996. *What Employers Want*. New York: Russell Sage Foundation.

Howell, William G., Patrick J. Wolf, Paul E. Peterson, and David E. Campbell. 2000. "Test-Score Effects of School Vouchers in Dayton, Ohio, New York City, and Washington, DC: Evidence from Randomized Field Trials." Program on Education Policy and Governance Working Paper (August).

Hughes, Katherine, Thomas R. Bailey, and Melinda J. Mechur. 2001. "School-to-Work: Making a Difference in Education: A Research Report to America." Institute on Education and the Economy, Teachers College, Columbia University report (February).

————. 1995. "Commentary on the Nature of an Omnibus Bill." In *National Issues in Education: Elementary and Secondary Education Act*, ed. John F. Jennings. Bloomington, IN, and Washington, DC: Phi Delta Kappa International and the Institute for Educational Leadership.

Kane, Thomas J. 1994. "College Entry by Blacks since 1970: The Role of College Costs, Family Background, and the Returns to Education." *Journal of Political Economy*, 102(5): 878–911.

————. 1999. *The Price of Admission: Rethinking How Americans Pay for College*. Washington, DC: Brookings Institution Press.

Karoly, Lynn A., Peter W. Greenwood, Susan S. Everingham, Jill Houbé, M. Rebecca Kilburn, C. Peter Rydell, Matthew Sanders, and James Chiesa. 1998. *Investing in Our Children: What We Know and Don't Know about the Costs and Benefits of Early Childhood Interventions*. Santa Monica, CA: Rand Corporation.

Katz, Lawrence, and Alan Krueger. 1999. "The High-Pressure U.S. Labor Market of the 1990s." *Brookings Papers on Economic Activity*, no. 1: 1–87.

Kemple, James J., and Jason C. Snipes. 2000. "Career Academies: Impacts on Students' Engagement and Performance in High School: Executive Summary." Manpower Demonstration Research Corporation report (February).

Krueger, Alan. 1993. "How Computers Have Changed the Wage Structure: Evidence from Microdata, 1984–1989." *Quarterly Journal of Economics*, 108, no. 1 (February): 33–61.

————. 1997. "Labor Market Developments, Trade and Trade Agreements." *Income and Productivity in North America*. Dallas: Commission for Labor Cooperation and Bernan Press.

————. 1999. "Experimental Estimates of Education Production Functions." *Quarterly Journal of Economics*, 114, no. 2 (May): 497–531.

————. 2000a. "Economic Considerations and Class Size." Princeton University, Industrial Relations Section Working Paper No. 447 (September).

————. 2000b. "Labor Policy and Labor Research since the 1960s: Two Ships Sailing in Orthogonal Directions?" *Economic Events, Ideas and Policies: The 1960s and After*, ed. George L. Perry and James Tobin, 299–331. Washington, DC: Brookings Institution Press.

————. In press. "The Digital Divide in Educating African American Students and Workers." In *Education and Training for the Black Worker in the 21st Century*, ed. Cecilia Conrad and Margaret Simms.

Krueger, Alan B., and Mikael Lindahl. In press. "Education for Growth: Why and for Whom?" *Journal of Economic Literature*.

Krueger, Alan B., and Diane M. Whitmore. 2001a. "The Effect of Attending a Small Class in the Early Grades on College-Test Taking and Middle School Test Results: Evidence from Project STAR." *Economic Journal*, 111:1–28.

————. 2001b. "Would Smaller Classes Help Close the Black-White Achievement Gap?" Industrial Relations Section Working Paper No. 451 (March).

Kulik, Chen-Lin, and James Kulik. 1991. "Effectiveness of Computer-Based Instruction: An Updated Analysis." *Computers in Human Behavior*, 7:75–94.

Kunin, Madeleine M. 1994. "Student Loan Reform Act of 1993." In *National Issues in Education: Community Service and Student Loans*, ed. John F. Jennings. Bloomington, IN, and Washington, DC: Phi Delta Kappa International and the Institute for Educational Leadership.

LaLonde, Robert J. 1995. "The Promise of Public Sector–Sponsored Training Programs." *Journal of Economic Perspectives*, 9, no. 2 (Spring): 149–168.

Leslie, Larry, and Paul Brinkman. 1988. *The Economic Value of Higher Education*. New York: Macmillan.

Levin, Henry M. 1998. "Educational Vouchers: Effectiveness, Choice, and Costs." *Journal of Policy Analysis and Management*, 17(3): 373–418.

Levine, Phillip B. 2000. "Cyclical Welfare Costs in the Post-Reform Era: Will There Be Enough Money?" Mimeo, Wellesley College.

Mallar, Charles, et al. 1982. *Third Follow-up Report of the Evaluation of the Economic Impact of the Job Corps Program*, Mathematica Policy Research.

Manno, Bruno V. 1995. "Reinventing Education in the Image of the Great Society." In *National Issues in Education: Elementary and Secondary Education Act*, ed. John F. Jennings. Bloomington, IN, and Washington, DC: Phi Delta Kappa International and the Institute for Educational Leadership.

Meyer, Bruce. 1995. "Lessons from the U.S. Unemployment Insurance Experiments." *Journal of Economic Literature*, 33:91–131.

Mishel, Lawrence, Jaren Bernstein, and John Schmitt. 2001. *The State of Working America 2000–01*. Washington, DC: Employment Policy Institute.

Morris, Dick. 1997. *Behind the Oval Office: Winning the Presidency in the Nineties*. New York: Random House.

Myers, David, Paul Peterson, Daniel Mayer, Julia Chou, and William G. Howell. 2000. "School Choice in New York City after Two Years: An Evaluation of the School Choice Scholarships Program." Mathematica Policy Research, Inc., interim report (August).

Nechyba, Thomas J. 1996. "Public School Finance in a General Equilibrium Tiebout World: Equalization Programs, Peer Effects, and Private School Vouchers." NBER Working Paper 5642 (June).

Nelson, Beryl, Paul Berman, John Ericson, Nancy Kamprath, Rebecca Perry, Debi Silverman, and Debra Solomon. 2000. *The State of Charter Schools 2000: Fourth-Year Report*. Washington, DC: U.S. Department of Education, Office of Educational Research and Improvement.

Phi Delta Kappa. 1998. "Attitudes Toward the Public Schools 1998 Survey." Roper Center at University of Connecticut, Public Opinion Online (August).

Puma, Michael J., Duncan D. Chaplin, and Andreas D. Pape. 2000. "E-Rate and the Digital Divide: A Preliminary Analysis From the Integrated Studies of Educational Technology." Urban Institute Report (September 21).

Ragosta, Marjorie, Paul Holland, and Dean Jamison. 1982. "Computer-Assisted Instruction and Compensatory Education: The ETS/LAUSD Study." Final Report, Princeton, NJ, Educational Testing Service, April.

Reich, Robert. 1997. *Locked in the Cabinet*. New York: Knopf.

Riley, Richard W. 1995. "The Goals 2000: Educate America Act: Providing a World-Class Education for Every Child." In *National Issues in Education: Goals 2000 and School-to-Work*, ed. John F. Jennings.

Bloomington, IN, and Washington, DC: Phi Delta Kappa International and the Institute for Educational Leadership.

Rouse, Cecilia Elena. 1994. "What to Do after High School? The Two-Year vs. Four-Year College Enrollment Decision." In *Contemporary Policy Issues in Education*, ed. Ronald Ehrenberg. Ithaca, NY: ILR Press.

————. 1998a. "Private School Vouchers and Student Achievement: An Evaluation of the Milwaukee Parental Choice Program." *Quarterly Journal of Economics*, 113, no. 2 (May): 553–602.

————. 1998b. "Schools and Student Achievement: More on the Milwaukee Parental Choice Program," *Economic Policy Review*, 4, no. 1 (March): 61–78.

————. In press. "School Reform in the 21st Century: The Effect of Class Size and School Vouchers on African American and Hispanic Students." In *Education and Training for the Black Worker in the 21st Century*, ed. Cecilia Conrad and Margaret Simms.

Ruhm, Christopher J., and Jackqueline L. Teague. 1997. "Parental Leave Policies in Europe and North America." *Gender and the Family Issues in the Workplace*, ed. Francine D. Blau and Ronald Ehrenberg, 133–156. New York: Russell Sage Foundation Press.

Schmitt, John. 1999. "Testing the Employment Impact of the 1996–97 Increases in the Federal Minimum Wage: Another Look at Card (1992) and Deere, Murphy and Welch (1995)." Mimeo, Economic Policy Institute, Washington, DC.

Schneider, Mark. 1999. "The Role of Information in School Choice." State University of New York at Stony Brook mimeo.

Schwartz, Robert B., and Marian A. Robinson. 2000. "Goals 2000 and the Standards Movement." In *Brookings Papers on Education Policy, 2000*, ed. Diane Ravitch. Washington, DC: Brookings Institution Press.

Schweinhart, Lawrence J., Helen Barnes, and David Weikart. 1993. *Significant Benefits: The High/Scope Perry Preschool Study Through Age 27*. Monograph of the High/Scope Educational Research Foundation, Number 10. Ypsilanti, MI: High-Scope Educational Research Foundation.

Smith, Marshall S. 1999. Testimony on the Federal Direct Student Loan Program for the Subcommittee on Criminal Justice, Drug Policy, and Human Resources of the Committee on Government Reform (June).

Smith, Marshall S., Brett W. Scoll, and Valena White Plisko. 1995. "The Improving America's Schools Act: A New Partnership." In *National Issues in Education: Elementary and Secondary Education Act*, ed. John F. Jennings. Bloomington, IN, and Washington, DC: Phi Delta Kappa International and the Institute for Educational Leadership.

Stephanopoulos, George. 1999. *All Too Human: A Political Education of George Stephanopoulos*, New York: Little, Brown.

Tiebout, Charles M. 1956. "A Pure Theory of Local Expenditure." *Journal of Political Economy*, 64, no. 5 (October): 416–424.

U.S. Administration for Children, Youth, and Families. 2001a. "Building Their Futures: How Early Head Start Programs Are Enhancing the Lives of Infants and Toddlers in Low-Income Families—Summary Report." U.S. Department of Health and Human Services (January).

————. 2001b. "Head Start Fact Sheet, 2001." U.S. Department of Health and Human Services (February).

U.S. Department of Education. 1995. *Third International Mathematics and Science Study (TIMSS).* Washington, DC.

———. 1999. *Third International Mathematics and Science Study-Repeat (TIMSS-R).* Washington, DC.

———. 2000a. "Expanding College Opportunity: More Access, Greater Achievement, and Higher Expectations" (June). Washington, DC.

———. National Center for Education Statistics. 2000b. *Digest of Education Statistics, 2000.* Washington, DC.

———. 2001. "National Student Loan Default Rates." http://www.ed.gov/offices/OSFAP/defaultmanagement/defaultrates.html.

U.S. Department of Labor, Office of the Chief Economist. 1995. *What's Working (and What's Not): A Summary of Research on the Economic Impacts of Employment and Training Programs.* Washington, DC: U.S. Department of Labor.

Universal Service Administrative Company. 2001. www.sl.universalservice.org/funding.

Wandner, Stephen, Jon Messenger, and Suzanne Schwartz. 1999. "Worker Profiling and Reemployment Services Policy Workgroup: Final Report and Recommendations." U.S. Department of Labor, Washington, DC, February.

Warner, John T., and Saul Pleeter. 2001. "The Personal Discount Rate: Evidence from Military Downsizing Programs." *American Economic Review*, 91, no. 1 (March): 33–53.

Wenglinsky, Harold. 1998. "Does it Compute? The Relationship Between Educational Technology and Student Achievement in Mathematics." Policy Information Center, Research Division, Educational Testing Service, Princeton, NJ, September.

Wolanin, Thomas R. 2001. "Rhetoric and Reality: Effects and Consequences of the HOPE Scholarship." Institute for Higher Education Policy Working Paper (April).

Word, Elizabeth, J. Johnston, Helen Bain, et al. 1990. "The State of Tennessee's Student/Teacher Achievement Ratio (STAR) Project: Technical Report 1985–1990." Nashville: Tennessee State Department of Education.

Zigler, Edward, and Susan Muenchow. 1992. *Head Start: The Inside Story of America's Most Successful Educational Experiment.* New York: Basic Books.

Comments

Lawrence Mishel

I'm going to start by picking up a theme that was in the chapter and relates this panel to the earlier fiscal policy discussion. There was unadulterated praise for a maximal prosaving, fiscally conservative budget policy yesterday that was bipartisan (stretching all the way from the moderate Democratic to the conservative Republican participants, which comprises the political spectrum of this conference) and rather shocking to me. I want to draw out the issue that Krueger and Rouse raise about whether the Clinton plan to invest in people was sacrificed to deficit and debt reduction.

To set the context, before the administration came into office, domestic discretionary spending was 4.7 percent of GDP in 1980, and it had fallen to 3.4 percent by 1992. That's about a one-third reduction in domestic spending relative to GDP, a sizable disinvestment in my view. By 1999 the share had fallen to 3.1 percent. So under the Clinton administration, domestic spending fell relative to GDP. If you look at the 10-year budget projections in the last Clinton budget, you can see that the share was expected to fall another half a percent of GDP. Thus the domestic spending squeeze that began in the GOP administrations, 1980 to 1992, continued under Clinton and was expected to continue (as a matter of policy) thereafter for another 10 years, providing a 30-year period of domestic spending austerity.

It shouldn't be surprising that, within this context, spending on education and training—investing in people—was pretty paltry, as the paper documents. Where does this come from? In *Putting People First* (the Clinton campaign book), a stated goal was reducing the fiscal deficit in half, when the deficit was 5 percent of GDP. I could understand on both political and economic grounds that it was necessary to pursue steady deficit reduction—this was the Perot era and voters wanted to see that spending, taxes, and the fiscal situation were under control. However, deficit and debt reduction later became a political maneuver to defeat GOP tax cuts, and, as Robert Kuttner has written, debt and deficit reduction gradually was elevated from a tactic to a principle among Democrats.

The policy target kept shifting, originally targeting a deficit of only 2.5 percent of GDP, then targeting a balanced budget. The target later moved to achieving balance excluding the Social Security surplus and then moved further to a target of balance exclusive of the Social Security and the Medicare surpluses. By the end of the Clinton administration the issue was "In how many years can we pay down the public debt?" We shouldn't be surprised that these goals precluded much investment in people.

Education provides a very good illustration of how fiscal policy strangled a popular human investment. It is remarkable how the issue of spending money in education was transformed in the 1990s. The first Bush administration, for instance, clearly claimed that spending more money on education was not worthwhile and not even a part of the solution to improve schools. This was made very clear, for instance, in the Education Summit with governors. By the end of the 1990s, however, there was a broad bipartisan political consensus that spending more on education was at least popular, if not good policy. For instance, last year we saw Senate Republicans outbidding Democrats on education. President Bush's campaign and first budget give further testament to this popularity.

But did bipartisan and broad public support translate into spending? In fact, budget data show that spending on higher education and elementary and secondary (K–12) education as a share of GDP was totally flat in the 1990s and rather substantially down from what it was in the 1980s and the 1970s. (This analysis ignores the tax expenditures for college tuition because, as the chapter shows, this policy was really about a middle-class tax cut and not about raising college enrollment.) One can only conclude that fiscal restraint offset the bipartisan and broad public support for more spending on education. This fiscal restraint set by increasingly austere policy targets also prevented the expansion of well-regarded programs such as the Job Corp and Head Start, as the chapter shows.

I think it is worth questioning whether we've gone too far by shifting our goals from deficit reduction to paying down the public debt. Productivity growth is a wonderful thing. Capital formation is a wonderful thing. But capital formation is responsible for only 15–25 percent of productivity growth. So fiscally conservative budget policies are targeting a narrow piece of the growth puzzle—attempting to influence investment by increasing saving and lowering interest rates. The main factor in productivity growth is multifactor productivity growth, and there's also labor skills and labor quality, so it is curious that more attention isn't paid to these other growth factors. At this point, it's hard for me to see what problem we're trying to fix with debt reduction. We've had a productivity acceleration in the late 1990s, so the problem is certainly not a productivity crisis. Even if we're seeking more investment, the source of investment funds is from firm cash flow and profitability, which did not constrain investment in the 1990s. In fact, firm profitability in the late 1990s was higher than it had been in 30–40 years. So there was and is ample cash for investment.

My fear, and my appraisal, is that the problem to be solved is "more savings" and that this goal cannot and will never be met. Whether purposeful or not, this savings quest serves as an all-purpose justification for constraining domestic spending regardless of the country's fiscal position—deficit, balance, or surplus. The reality is that debt reduction has a modest, long-term impact on incomes, so the benefits are rather modest in my view.

Unfortunately, there's not much attention paid to the opportunity costs of debt reduction, such as the reduced social spending and the failure to meet unmet social needs in early education, child care, health coverage, housing, and other areas. Domestic spending programs have productivity, equity, and quality-of-life goals that need to be balanced against fiscal policy–induced capital formation. Those praising and/or proud of the Clinton era fiscal policy at the conference do not even bother to argue that the consequences of fiscal restraint are superior to the outcomes from greater public investment in people and technology or the benefits of greater social spending. Debt reduction reflects a growth model solely focused on capital formation—a very narrow growth perspective, especially for Democrats. I suspect Krueger and Rouse agree, which is why they raised this issue, though softly, in the chapter.

Next, I want to comment on the Krueger and Rouse framing of education and training policy. Krueger and Rouse correctly note that the whole issue of growing wage inequality and the poor performance of wages for the "less educated" has framed labor and education policy: the solutions for these problems are said to be more and better education and training. This view is based on a notion that non-college-educated workers have fared poorly because of a "skills deficit," or in more technical circles, because of skill-based technical change. Although, I favor policies to increase and improve skills and education, I do not believe that education and training policy can be the major solution to the wage gap that developed over the 1980s and early 1990s.

I think that the chapter pulls together some facts that shed light on all this. In particular, the chapter shows that there was not much of a skills explosion in the 1990s: test scores turned up, but there was not much investment on education and training. Yet the wages of low-wage workers grew rapidly from 1996, and the wage gap at the "bottom"—the ratio of the median to the 10th percentile wage, the 50/10 wage gap—has been narrowing since the late 1980s among both men and women. In fact, the 50/10 wage gap for men has now returned to the level where it was in 1979. Among women, however, the 50/10 wage gap has been narrowing for more than 10 years but remains well above its late 1970s level. This narrowing of the 50/10 wage gap is especially surprising given that there was fast immigration and welfare reform, factors that added a whole wave of "less skilled" workers. Consequently, you would expect the 50/10 wage gap to have widened just because of a composition effect.

So we have seen a diminution of wage inequality in the bottom half (wage inequality in the upper half continued to grow in the 1990s just as it did in the 1980s) despite no clear improvement in skills and education. Clearly then, we were able to make progress on the wage inequality front without closing any "skill deficits." Rather, we made progress because of persistent low unemployment and increases in the minimum wage. I think one lesson to be learned is that persistent low unemployment is a critical component in improvements in living standards and equity. Let me be clear that I am not arguing that improved schools and a better trained workforce would not have led to desirable growth and equity outcomes. Rather, I am only pointing out that the policy discussion around addressing wage inequality is too often narrowly constrained to be solely about improved education and training policies.

Let me shift to talking about training policy for a bit. The Clinton campaign articulated a vision of a very broad-based, expanded training system that involved not just youth but a broad swath of the work force, including incumbent workers. This vision was drawn from the *America's Choice* report, the product of a commission cochaired by former Secretaries of Labor Ray Marshall and Bill Brock. There were two policies that were most prominent in that vision. The first was a "pay or play" training scheme that would increase workplace skills and increase training. In this scheme, employers had to either pay the tax, 1.5 percent of payroll, to a government training fund or use it for training "front-line workers." The second policy component was an improved school-to-work transition program. What ended up happening is that not much progress was made in either area. The "pay or play" scheme was abandoned before the Inauguration. I don't think the "pay or play" scheme failed because of insufficient congressional support, as the chapter suggests. Rather, I think the scheme was abandoned because the Clinton administration was thinking that a new health care scheme was going to be financed by a payroll tax and that adding another payroll tax to the mix was too much. The school-to-work transition program ended up as a small experimental program that helped "10s if not 100s of kids across the country."

There was also not much progress on the dislocated-worker policy area. I'm not talking about a better trade adjustment assistance program or a better adjustment assistance program for NAFTA-related dislocations. Everyone knows that any serious dislocated worker program has to be a universal system for all dislocated workers. It's got to be generous; it's got to have income support, ample training, job search, all those sorts of things. The reason why we get these small programs related to particular types of layoffs is that, because of budget restraints, we can have a somewhat more generous system only if we can restrict the eligibility to a limited group. What's needed is something that has broad eligibility and is comprehensive in terms of services. For an administration whose top goals include expanding trade, it's a shame that a comprehensive adjustment program was not established. True, there was an effort made during the NAFTA fight. But the time to move on a new dislocated worker policy is not when trade agreements are before Congress. When done in this way, the adjustment policy is really being used to obtain votes for a trade treaty, to provide "cover" for a trade vote.

It is also worth commenting on the minimum wage policy of the Clinton administration. Legislation was passed that raised the minimum wage in 1996 and 1997. It should be noted, however, that the impetus for this effort arose from congressional Democrats and the labor movement. The White House viewed the minimum wage as an "Old Democrat" policy and was initially hesitant to get behind the increase. The momentum shifted dramatically after the AFL-CIO ran issue ads in the districts of moderate Republicans, resulting in a group of House Republicans proposing a higher minimum wage than that proposed by the administration.

From that moment on it was clear that there would be a minimum wage increase. Strong polling results helped as well. One unfortunate by-product of this effort was that congressional Republicans were able to tie a package of tax cuts to the minimum wage legislation. Although the argument was that these tax cuts were meant to soften the blow on business, an examination of the specifics clearly shows these tax cuts were not in any way targeted on the particular sectors affected by a minimum wage increase. Rather, the minimum wage bill became a vehicle for totally unrelated tax cuts.

The consequence is that tax cuts are also now being considered as part of the minimum wage package now before Congress. Other than political and legislative opportunism, the logic eludes me. The last bill's tax cuts were permanent and provided more tax relief than the wage increase generated by the minimum wage increase. Moreover, the minimum wage increase is temporary, as inflation and wage growth reduce its "bite" over time. It's unfortunate that the legacy of the last round of legislation is that we now face another round of permanent, unrelated tax cuts attached to the minimum wage bill.

Let me shift to my last topic, the Dunlop Commission. We have both John Dunlop and Bob Reich here, so I think it will be interesting to discuss the mistakes made by many people. The Dunlop Commission was about the reform of employment law generally, not just the National Labor Relations Act (NLRA) which governs collective bargaining. I think that the whole enterprise was based on a mistaken political assumption: that there was some common ground between labor and business on these issues, especially the tough issues around the NLRA.

In the context where business can veto any labor law reform with 40 senators on its side, there was no basis to believe that business would make any compromise regarding NLRA reform. This is especially the case since the status quo was and is very favorable to management, a system that does not protect workers' rights to organize and bargain and helps propel the continued erosion of unionism. Rather than operate in some realm looking for common ground with a business partner, which wasn't there, I think the goal should have been to speak loud truths about what's needed and the problems workers and unions face. I think the labor movement was at fault for thinking that the commission could be a vehicle for labor law reform, when in fact what was needed was a broad public campaign to raise the issue and an elaborated union policy agenda.

It is interesting that unions enter the conference discussion only in so far as people are worried about unions being an obstacle to bad trade policy. It seems to me the people in this room ought to consider the value of unions to industrial democracy, to our political democracy, and see workers' rights to organize as a human right and a civil right. Until folks here as well as elsewhere take workers rights and industrial democracy seriously, we won't be able to obtain the legal changes needed that allow people to obtain their rights.

Comments

Roger B. Porter

Presidential Interest in Education Policy

The range of responsibilities, interest, and involvement varies enormously across the large number of foreign, economic, and domestic issues to which presidents devote their attention. Certain responsibilities are difficult to delegate, others relatively easy. Some issues are substantively intractable, others less so. Presidents also weigh, implicitly and explicitly, the amount of time and political capital they must invest relative to the expected rate of return.

Education is a policy area that has consistently engaged recent presidents—certainly Ronald Reagan, both Bush presidents (father and son, or "41" and "43" as they refer to themselves), and Bill Clinton. Indeed, the 1990s and the preceding decade represent the high-water mark in presidential involvement in education policy.

Perhaps this more intense engagement by recent presidents flows from their background as governors. From Harry Truman through Gerald Ford—a period of nearly three decades—no president had previously served as a state governor. A quarter of a century ago the pendulum swung, and since the 1976 election, we have had former governors in the Oval Office for all but four years.

Perhaps presidents (and presidential candidates) are drawn to education because of its salience with voters. In the 2000 election the focus groups and opinion surveys consulted by both major party candidates encouraged them to raise education to the top of their domestic agendas. Public interest in education has remained remarkably high over a sustained period.

It is also more than possible, even probable, that recent presidents have devoted considerable attention to education because of a genuine interest in the subject area and a conviction that education is important to long-term economic prosperity as well as to addressing a wide number of problems facing those less fortunate. Whatever the reason or combination of reasons, the phenomenon of presidential interest in education seems genuine.

The Nature of Education Policy

Yet, as the excellent review of education and labor policy by Alan Krueger and Cecelia Rouse reveals, education is an area where the leverage of the president and his administration is limited. Federal officials face a deep attachment to local control of education, an attachment that has persisted for more than a century and a half and that is sustained by more than 100,000 elected school board officials.

One common lever, financing, places the federal government in a distinctly inferior position given that the overwhelming bulk of funds for elementary and secondary education (and for higher education) come from state and local governments. A separate cabinet-level U.S. Department of Education was not created until the first of this recent phalanx of former governors, Jimmy Carter, became president. Moreover, the federal government has little control over the delivery system. It runs no elementary and secondary schools domestically, does not establish graduation requirements or dictate a national curriculum as in some countries. Not least, there is widespread skepticism among most citizens about the federal government's role in education.

At first blush, education is not a likely candidate for a policy area where the president will devote a good deal of energy and political capital. At the same time, given the deep national attachment to local control, presidents and their administrations recognize that voters are not likely to hold them accountable for education outcomes in the way they do on national security, trade policy, or federal tax issues.

Prelude to the 1990s

In assessing education policy in the 1990s, it is important to start at the beginning of the decade. It was in January 1990 that President Bush on behalf of himself and the nation's governors announced six national education goals in his State of the Union Address. What preceded that announcement is instructive in understanding the decade that followed.

In the 1980s, while the number of students in elementary and secondary school in the United States changed little, per-pupil spending adjusted for inflation rose by 30 percent, demonstrating a remarkable commitment—mostly by state and local governments—to investing funds in education. Early in the decade, in 1983, the Reagan administration's Commission on Excellence in Education issued a widely publicized report entitled *A Nation at Risk*, sounding a warning regarding elementary and secondary schools and proposing much more rigorous curricula and greatly strengthened graduation requirements.

By the end of the decade a majority of states had changed their graduation requirements and altered their curricula, yet scores on standardized tests such as NAEP showed little improvement. The best that one could wring from the data after making the appropriate adjustments for an increased number of students taking a wide range of standardized tests (SATs and ACTs largely because college and universities were requiring such scores) was that student performance was not deteriorating. At the same time, the increased financial investment in elementary and secondary education had little to show in the way of positive results.

The Early 1990s

George Bush campaigned on the pledge to be "the education president." Once in office he pursued a three-pronged approach. First, he sought to raise the visibility of the issue by participating in a large number of education events as well as proposing the Excellence in Education Act. Second, he advanced a series of ideas—school choice, alternative certification of teachers, merit schools, site-based management, New American Schools—to help stimulate a national debate on education. Third, he established a partnership with the nation's governors, holding a summit conference in Charlottesville in late September 1989.

The President's Summit Conference on Education provided an opportunity, although neither of them had any idea they would face each other in the 1992 election, for a current and a future president, George Bush and Bill Clinton, to work together. As his White House economic and domestic policy adviser, I received the assignment to organize the summit and immediately reached out to the National Governors Association (NGA). The NGA operates through a series of task forces, each cochaired by a Democrat and a Republican governor. The cochairs for the NGA Education Task Force were two southerners, Carroll Campbell (R-South Carolina) and Bill Clinton (D-Arkansas). Together we negotiated an agenda for the two-day conference, as well as the joint statement that was issued at its conclusion. In this exercise, I got a glimpse of how the issues played out among Democrat and Republican elected officials. The joint statement issued by the president and all 50 governors said that they would work together to establish national education goals and pursue greater flexibility in the use of federal education funds, and that the governors would commit to a state-by-state restructuring of their education systems.

In the aftermath of the education summit, intense negotiations over the next three and a half months yielded six national education goals. This exercise produced agreement that the goals should cover a 10-year period, until the year

2000; that reaching the goals would require a bipartisan effort; that the goals should focus on outcomes rather than inputs; and that a systematic process to measure progress toward achieving the goals was essential.

The Bush approach toward education was organized around the six goals and drove his education spending proposals. George Bush sought to cement his relationship with the governors by appointing a new secretary of education, Lamar Alexander, the first former governor to serve in that cabinet post.

Four key ideas animated education policy during the early years of the decade: first, greater accountability as evidenced in the establishment of standards for what students should know and be able to do and assessments as to whether students had met those standards; second, greater competition as evidenced in school choice, vouchers, and charter schools; third, greater flexibility as evidenced in fewer restrictions on states in the use of federal funds; and fourth, greater innovation as evidenced in break-the-mold schools and the use of technology.

Interestingly, none of these themes envisioned large increases in federal spending, a constraint necessitated by virtue of the federal budget situation during most of the decade.

The Clinton Approach

Given the legacy of budgetary constraints he inherited, Alan Krueger and Cecelia Rouse identify several interesting patterns in Bill Clinton's approach to education policy. First, to his credit, as president, Bill Clinton embraced the national education goals that he had helped to negotiate and made them a central part of his policy. Second, he continued seeking to engage the governors in part by appointing a former governor, Richard Riley, as his secretary of education and appointing another former governor, Madeleine Kunin, as deputy secretary of education. Indeed, throughout the entire decade of the 1990s, the position of secretary of education was held by a former governor. Third, Bill Clinton embraced accountability, competition, flexibility, and innovation as guiding principles, but in his own way.

Accountability is almost always a challenging and, with regard to education, an extremely contentious principle. In this respect, Bill Clinton needed to reassure members of his political party who were concerned not only about outcomes but also traditionally were inclined to emphasize inputs. Thus the idea of content standards (what students should know and be able to do) was supplemented by "opportunity to learn standards" (the resources that districts would devote to helping students achieve the content standards).

Second, Clinton's approach to increased competition was both substantively and politically skillful. As president, he embraced a limited form of increased competition through encouraging charter schools and expressing support for public school choice. At the same time, he reassured his base, the teachers unions, that he would steadfastly oppose school choice that would include private schools or any form of a voucher program.

Third, to get the states to embrace a partnership whereby they would undertake desired reforms, Bill Clinton proposed additional incentives, and ultimately funding, through Goals 2000: Educate America Act of 1994. This legislation reflected more carrot than stick in the effort to generate reform.

It is instructive to note two developments in Bill Clinton's approach to education during his eight years as president. The first is that the continuing emphasis on accountability, as Krueger and Rouse put it, "faded from the forefront" and was overtaken by more standard input-oriented initiatives such as reducing class size and federal financing of school construction. The second is that President Clinton's enthusiasm for giving states greater flexibility gave way in the last years of his administration to calling for federal guidelines for teacher training, student discipline, school performance, and promotion policy with the threat of a loss of federal education funding for those states that did not comply. By his second term he was clearly a president and no longer a governor.

Conclusions

What are we to make of this? The comprehensive survey of education and labor programs during the Clinton administration by Krueger and Rouse reveals, among other things, much continuity in policy across administrations. There is a powerful impulse with each new administration to define and describe the policies it articulates and pursues as new, different, and innovative. This impulse is particularly strong when the new administration involves a change of party. The reality is that while political imperatives encourage rhetoric to emphasize sharp policy departures, much change is incremental. There is often considerable continuity in policy direction over time. Head Start, the Earned Income Tax Credit (initiated by President Gerald Ford and increased by each succeeding president), and the national education goals are simply well-known examples.

This survey also reveals that enormous resistance to change persists despite a decade of reform efforts. In the case of elementary and secondary education much of this resistance comes from large unions that dominate the ranks of teachers and administrators. As president, Bill Clinton was willing to take on his labor base by supporting the North America Free Trade Agreement (NAFTA), but he was reluctant to also challenge a core labor constituency on the issue of education beyond his support for charter schools.

Third, the old adage that where you stand depends on where you sit proved durable once more with respect to the Clinton approach on education and labor policy. Genuinely embracing flexibility in the use of federal funds is worth pursuing when you are a governor. It is somewhat less attractive when you are the president.

Comments

Robert B. Reich

Undoubtedly, the best thing I did as labor secretary was to create the Office of Chief Economist within the Department of Labor. The first incumbent of that office was Larry Katz; the second was Alan Krueger; and the third was Lisa Lynch, who unfortunately is not here with us today.

Another person who deserves mention, my secret weapon, is former labor secretary John Dunlop. It's a pleasant sensation to have Larry Mishel on my left and Roger Porter on my right, and therefore be in the center as I am on most issues.

In the third week of November 1992, I was sitting minding my business in my office here at the Kennedy School, having just finished teaching a class, when President-elect Bill Clinton called and asked if I would head up his economic transition team. I said I would have to check with my wife and students, but first wanted to know what he had in mind. He said, "Oh, it's not a big deal; we just need to prepare the groundwork for the administration." He asked me to gather together all the people who had given him economic advice during the campaign—some 20 or so people—and "figure out some way of integrating macro with micro." This theme motivated the founding of the National Economic Council.

The president-elect also said at the time that he wanted to advance his "investment agenda" in his first budget proposal to Congress. None of us who worked on the campaign was terribly clear on what exactly the "investment agenda" entailed, but we generally understood it to refer to public spending involving substantial positive externalities—in such areas as education, job training, public infrastructure, and basic research and development.

Let me confess our political naïveté, in many respects. For example, the federal government was supplying only seven cents of every dollar spent on primary and secondary education, but candidate and then President Clinton believed the federal government had more leverage than this figure suggested. And he also believed the power of the bully pulpit could be used to leverage even more power over education. Even though he had been a governor and had been deeply involved in educational policy, he may not have fully appreciated the degree to which educational policy at the federal level is a highly contested political terrain involving sharp ideological disputes. Interested groups run the gamut from the religious right to the teachers' unions. The question "What is to be taught in our schools?" raises some of the most fundamental moral and political issues this nation faces in terms of how its young people are to understand the world. The question "Who is to decide education policy?" raises some of the most basic issues of federalism, and of the proper roles of our communities.

Labor policy proved to be another highly contested terrain. We had no illusions about that at the start; labor and management had been battling it out in America for more than a century. But we didn't fully appreciate just how contentious the battle had become since the 1980s. When we began raising possible reforms of labor law, job training programs, or efforts to help working people adjust to structural changes in the economy, the reactions were sharp and swift from both camps. There seemed precious little room for compromise.

We soon discovered that job training had no political constituency other than the rather small number of people and institutions in the business of doing the training. Organized labor doesn't particularly like job training because the unions, understandably, don't relish the prospect of their members being trained for jobs that are not unionized or that are outside of the union in which they currently exist. Nor are union leaders confident that job training will help their members maintain their standard of living, certainly not as definitively as a strong union. On the other side, the business community gives a great deal of lip service to the importance of job training, but, in fact, dedicates relatively little money to training blue-collar or pink-collar workers.

This lack of constituency for job training became evident in the effort to gain congressional approval for the North American Free Trade Act. When we explored including in the NAFTA legislation a comprehensive approach to job training, which would pool all the government's separate training programs into one overarching and well-funded workforce investment system, Democrats who opposed NAFTA hollered. They were not willing to support anything that might provide "a fig leaf" for NAFTA or make it more palatable. The business community, for its part, was unwilling to support a substantial increase in job training funds. To simplify, the two opposing positions were either (1) preserve the jobs as they are and don't push international trade or (2) embrace international trade but don't spend very much money on helping people adapt to the new economy and new jobs.

NAFTA, of course, involved an unfortunate sparring match with labor, in which the major question at issue was a false one—how many jobs NAFTA would create or destroy. NAFTA would do neither. Like any trade-opening agreement, it would affect the composition of jobs, not the total number. Yet, we found ourselves pulled into that debate, including several of us around this very table.

Health care also loomed high on the early agenda of the administration. Bill Clinton did not want to confuse the issue by suggesting an additional payroll tax that might support job training, or an increase in the minimum wage, until health care reform had been considered. The defeat of his health care proposal in 1994 and the subsequent Republican takeover of Congress proved to be the pivotal events in the Clinton administration's domestic policy. Microeconomic policy-making changed substantially after January 1995, as, of course, did the role of the National Economic Council. Those of us who played a role in economic policy-making may not want to admit it, but I think it is fair to say that from early 1995 through November 1996, Dick Morris was the president's major economic adviser.

The widening inequality of income and wealth during the 1980s and first half of the 1990s was never a central focus of Bill Clinton's policy agenda. Many of us who worked for him were concerned about these trends, but the president rarely talked explicitly about them. Nor did he seek to justify his policies as means of countering them. The nation made some headway nonetheless, for two reasons. First and foremost, Alan Greenspan and his Federal Reserve Board decided that the natural rate of unemployment was not 6 percent, as had been assumed at the start of the Clinton administration, but significantly lower. They sensed that technology permitted the economy to grow faster than before, with a lower level of unemployment. The Fed's interest-rate policies helped to keep the labor market reasonably tight and thereby, at least by the late 1990s, to boost wages at the bottom.

Second, the Earned Income Tax Credit proved to be a much larger and more significant antipoverty program than anyone had envisioned when we prepared the initial budget in 1993 and sought to expand the program. It is now the largest antipoverty program in the federal government. In combination with the 1996 increase in the minimum wage, it also clearly helped boost wages of low-income workers.

On the so-called investment agenda, I think it is fair to conclude that we did accomplish some important things, incrementally. We didn't spend much money, but we did rationalize many of these programs and thereby laid the foundation for a future administration to fund them to greater effect. One example is the Workforce Investment Act, by which many of the government's myriad training programs are now combined, and people seeking job training have much easier access to training, job counseling, and job-search assistance.

Our great failing was to allow the public debate over macroeconomic policy to shift ground substantially. At the start of the administration it was generally understood that public deficits and public debt are not bad in and of themselves. It is always a question of what the borrowing is to be used for and whether the social benefits of the public spending outweigh the borrowing costs. On these grounds the president felt he had no choice but to aim to reduce the deficit, which by 1993 had ballooned to some $300 billion a year. During the 1992 campaign he had promised to reduce the deficit by half, and his initial budgets made progress toward that end. But after the Republican takeover of Congress in November 1994, the administration's goal shifted. Balancing the federal budget now became paramount. The president first agreed to balance the budget in 10 years, then in seven.

All the while, economic growth was itself reducing the deficit, then causing the budget to be balanced well in advance of the seven-year goal, and finally generating a substantial budget surplus. But the administration's initial premise—that public spending must be judged in its own terms, by whether its benefits exceed its costs—had meanwhile been lost in the political shuffle. Fiscal restraint is not an end in itself, but, at best, a means. Large public needs must still be addressed. There is nothing magical about a balanced budget, nothing prima facie wrong with public debt, and no good reason why eliminating the debt should be an object of public policy.

As the surplus ballooned, the pursuit of "fiscal responsibility" became a political tactic for the administration in countering Republican proposals for an across-the-board tax cut. Rather than offer bold plans for education, job training, infrastructure, basic research and development, or health care, the president opted for what was considered a politically safer route. "Save Social Security first," he cautioned, thereby implying that as long as the surplus was adequate to accomplish this objective, it would be perfectly fine to apply the remainder to a tax cut. By the election of 2000, candidate Al Gore was urging that part of the surplus be used to eliminate the debt.

My final point concerns the ways in which policy analysis was utilized politically by our opponents in ways we did not fully anticipate. One example is the fine report to Congress prepared by then Labor Department chief economists Alan Krueger and Larry Katz, pointing out which job training policies worked well and which did not. At the time, we assumed that such a frank admission would only add to our credibility and encourage Congress to allocate more funds to programs that proved to be most effective. To some extent, that was the case. But in significant measure our strategy boomeranged. Members of Congress used the evidence we amassed against us and defunded not only programs that were less successful, such as short-term training for disadvantaged young people, but even programs that served beneficial purposes other than achieving long-term wage gains, such as the summer jobs program.

Policy analysis also played a major role in the debate over raising the minimum wage. Alan Kruger and David Card's work, strongly suggesting that any negative employment effects from a moderate increase in the minimum wage would be insignificant, figured prominently and was enormously helpful. But it should be noted that almost immediately congressional opponents of increasing the minimum wage used academic studies purporting to show far more significant negative employment effects. Rather than debate the larger ethical and normative questions embedded in the question of whether to raise—or even have—the minimum wage, or look at the historic record of how low the minimum wage had dropped in real terms, the public was treated to an almost incomprehensible and inconclusive debate about whose studies were better.

In all these respects, economic policy-making cannot be divorced from politics. Good economic policy-making depends on educating the public about the issues and the stakes at hand.

Rebecca Blank suggested that welfare-to-work activities of the 1990s represented a significant labor market issue. During the decade, more people were directly involved in job placement and job search activities than at any previous time, and with a greater level of cooperation between the private sector and those programs.

Murray Weidenbaum then asked *Robert Reich* if he really meant to say that business is lukewarm in its support of government training programs. Reich responded by pointing to the lack of support from major business groups during 1993, when the administration was trying to pass a comprehensive training program. Businesses do provide a considerable amount of training for their own workers, according to Reich, but most of that is targeted to white-collar workers. The data suggest that very few training dollars are devoted to blue-collar and pink-collar workers.

Ron Haskins commented that education vouchers appear to be promising. He asked *Lawrence Mishel* if he agreed with the Clinton administration policy of opposition to vouchers. He also asked whether Democrats should at least agree to additional research to see if vouchers produce beneficial effects. Mishel responded that he does not support vouchers and is not sure he would support large-scale experimentation. *Reich* commented that the evidence is still out on vouchers. Current programs are too small, resulting in large sampling error in the research and questions about whether the results hold more broadly. He does not believe vouchers will become policy for a long time, but argued that expansion of charter schools is more likely.

Alan Krueger suggested that limited experimentation with vouchers for research purposes would make sense. Krueger noted that Paul Peterson of Harvard has done an impressive job raising funds to conduct private school choice experiments, and that the results were mixed. These experiments provided a voucher to children from overwhelmingly below-average public schools to attend a private school of their choice. The effects for whites and Hispanics were basically nil, while the average effect for blacks as a whole was positive and statistically significant (but that average effect arose solely from the 104 sixth graders who participated; there was no significant benefit from the third, fourth, or fifth graders). But he noted potential problems in the experiments also. For example, he would like to see the experiment done in reverse—that is, to take students from below-average private schools and offer them a payment to attend average public schools. Voucher advocates would predict that test scores would decline in this experiment, which Krueger thought was unlikely to be the case.

Roger Porter commented that he is surprised by the reluctance to try vouchers, given the high level of dissatisfaction many Americans have with the public system's performance, as well as our country's tendency to experiment with new approaches when something is not working well.

John Dunlop then offered what he believes to be the most important contribution of the Dunlop Commission: a protocol for facilitating mediation and arbitration in employment disputes. Instead of taking disputes to the agencies and then to court, increasingly these issues are being taken to mediation within and outside the agencies, and in some cases to private arbitration. The Equal Employment Opportunity Commission has reduced its backlog inventory from 110,000 cases to approximately 40,000 to 50,000 over the course of several years by using the protocols advanced by the commission.

Reich then asked Dunlop to what he attributes the labor-management animosity of the 1990s, and if he had a sense that such animosity was greater in the 1990s than in the 1950s, 1960s, and 1970s. *Dunlop* responded that he believes the events of the late 1970s and early 1980s, in particular the labor law and reform fight of 1978 and 1979, was a major contributor to the current animosity. He added that labor-management relations in Washington are poisoned very badly, but that there are many other places in the country where it is possible to work out issues on a practical basis.

Martin Feldstein argued that one of the significant events during the 1990s was the collapse of household saving, from about 10 percent of disposable personal income at the beginning of the decade to essentially zero by the end of the decade. National saving survived the decline of household saving because the federal budget balance went from a deficit of 2 percent of GDP to a surplus of 2 percent of GDP. This improvement allowed us to finance, although not fully, the significant increases in investment that have been associated with technological change. Even so, we have relied on an increasing capital inflow from the rest of the world. Until we find ways of increasing private savings, large budget surpluses are very helpful, Feldstein argued.

Feldstein also noted the benefits of persistent low unemployment. He argued that a number of factors, including temporary agencies and unemployment insurance reform, contributed to a reduction in the permanent level of unemployment during the 1990s. Nonetheless, once the unemployment rate began dropping below 5.5 percent in 1995, total compensation began to increase rapidly. That compensation growth did not translate into price inflation because unusually rapid productivity growth temporarily restrained inflationary pressures. We were thus lucky that rising wages did not translate into higher prices. However, Feldstein concluded, it is not a long-term, viable policy to have an unemployment rate that begins with the number 4.

Larry Katz argued that there is some coherence to having "little programs here and there." A large program that redistributes income or distorts behavior excessively may involve substantial efficiency costs. A lot of more modest programs, he suggested, could be more attractive. Katz then noted two attempts to strengthen labor market institutions during the 1990s—the Dunlop Commission and the minimum wage increase—and suggested that there was modest progress in these areas. Especially given the significant expansion in labor supply from welfare to work and unskilled immigration in the United States, the higher growth in wages for the bottom end in the 1990s than in the 1980s says something about the interaction of the strong economy with these policies. Finally, Katz noted that social science research occasionally played an important role in getting the Congressional Budget Office to agree that new labor programs would actually save the government money.

Reich concluded the session by observing that the Clinton administration had a coherent approach to improving the labor market. The problem, he said, was that the administration continually ran into the problem of scale. The Democrats tended to be more interested in preserving and protecting existing programs, while the Republicans tended to be more interested in not having any programs at all. All the attempts to adjust and improve labor markets were jeopardized by that political divide.

11 Poverty and Welfare

The Clinton Legacy for America's Poor

Rebecca M. Blank and
David T. Ellwood

PANELISTS: *Robert Greenstein, Ron Haskins, and Bruce Reed*

I believe people on welfare ought to go to work and I've been doing something about it in our state where we've moved 17,000 people from welfare to work, and I have a plan to do even better, to end welfare as we know it and make it a second chance, not a way of life.

Governor Bill Clinton, Economic Club of Detroit, August 21, 1992

"End welfare as we know it" must be one of the two or three most memorable policy promises offered by candidate Bill Clinton. And no one disputes that at the close of his administration, welfare as we "knew" it was gone. Whether the reforms actually offered a "second chance" is subject to more debate. But caseloads had fallen from their peak of more than 14 million persons in 1993 to fewer than 6 million toward the end of 2000. Fewer people were collecting welfare than in any year since 1968—in spite of population growth and a significant increase in single-mother families, the group most likely to receive welfare. Work by single mothers was up. And poverty was down.

Much of the debate over Clinton's social policy legacy is centered on the wisdom of the welfare reform bill he signed and how much credit or blame he should get for it. Yet the real Clinton social policy legacy is far more complex and provocative than a focus on this bill alone might suggest. In fact a combina-

The authors thank Elisabeth Scott and Lucie Schmidt for excellent research assistance. We also thank Seth Kirshenbaum for his editorial support. We benefited from excellent comments from Robert Greenstein, Ron Haskins, Wendell Primus, Bruce Reed, Sandra Clark, Peter Orszag, and participants at the conference.

tion of policy changes radically transformed several critical elements of social policy, modestly changed others, and altered the economic incentives facing low-income parents. And these changes raised new questions about the vulnerability of low-income families to economic cycles and high unemployment.

11.1   The Original Clinton Vision of Social Policy Reform

During the campaign, Clinton offered a fairly specific vision of how he wanted to shift social policy. There were three critical elements, all presented here in Clinton's own words:

• *Make work pay.* "... people who work shouldn't be poor. In a Clinton Administration, we'll do everything we can to break the cycle of dependency and help the poor climb out of poverty. First, we need to make work pay by expanding the Earned Income Tax Credit for the working poor.... At the same time, we need to assure all Americans that they'll have access to health care when they go to work."[1]

• *Strengthen child support enforcement.* "If this new covenant is pro-work, it must also be pro-family. That means we must demand the toughest possible child support enforcement."[2] "I want a national system of national child support enforcement because governments don't raise children; people do."[3]

• *Work-oriented welfare reform.* "We'll still help people who can't help themselves, and those who need education and training and child care. But if people can work, they'll have to do so. We'll give them all the help they need for up to two years. But after that, if they're able to work, they'll have to take a job in the private sector, or start earning their way through community service."[4]

Clinton clearly wanted to enforce work and responsibility, as evidenced by work requirements and time limits on welfare as well as strict child support enforcement. But he also envisioned a sizable role for government in rewarding work, ensuring health coverage, and providing training, child care, and even community service jobs. Clinton's agenda focused primarily on families with children, presumably because of a special concern with the next generation and because federal policies have rarely done much to aid childless individuals and couples, outside of programs for the aged and disabled.

Clinton did not call for an end to government, but a redirection of its efforts. Implicitly he sought to move away from long-term cash welfare and toward

1. Clinton (1991).
2. Clinton (1991).
3. Clinton (1992).
4. Clinton (1991).

greater support for work and workers, including greater investment in human capital, though this emphasis was muted when he talked about welfare reform.

Note that candidate Clinton also made a number of remarks that seemed to be in tension with each other. In the opening quote, he says he does not believe in big government, but he calls for government to do much more to support workers. He says he believes in a national child support enforcement system *because* parents (not governments) raise children. He would often indicate that the best ideas did not come from Washington and call for state flexibility, even as he described in detail the ideas that his administration would adopt nationally.

We next turn to an examination of what actually transpired during the administration, how the enacted policies altered incentives, and whether the president deserves the credit or blame for these changes.

11.1.1 Make Work Pay

The administration moved almost immediately to make good on its pledge to ensure that families with a full-time worker wouldn't be poor. In his first budget Clinton proposed a dramatic expansion in the Earned Income Tax Credit (EITC) and explicitly chose levels to ensure that the combination of wages, EITC, and food stamps available to a family of four with a full-year full-time minimum wage worker would be sufficient to move that family out of poverty.[5] The expansion was passed as part of the first budget for the new administration. The EITC is an earnings credit with benefits tied to level of earnings and the number of children. For each dollar earned up to a maximum, the parent gets a refundable tax credit from the government. For a parent with two or more children, the credit is currently 40 percent of earnings up to a maximum credit of roughly $3,800—roughly triple the maximum for such families in 1992. For a minimum wage worker, this is the equivalent of a 40 percent pay raise. But as a family's income rises above $13,000, the credit is gradually reduced (at a rate of 21 cents per additional dollar earned) and the credit is fully phased out for families with incomes over $30,000.

Clinton had not talked much about raising the minimum wage during the 1992 campaign, and it was not emphasized in his first two years, but as the issue gained momentum in 1996, he embraced the idea, and the minimum wage was raised from $4.25 per hour, where it had stood since 1992, to $5.15 in 1997.

Clinton had also promised universal health coverage, but when his reform proposal collapsed (Cutler and Gruber, Chapter 12 of this volume), a series

---

5. Ellwood (1996).

of more modest expansions in Medicaid, particularly for children, continued. Starting in 1986, Congress had adopted a series of expansions in Medicaid coverage for children and pregnant women.[6] As of June 1991, states were required to cover all poor children born after September 1983 until they reached age 19. Thus, by 1999, all poor children under 17 were covered. States were given considerable flexibility to cover older and near-poor children, and many chose to cover many additional children.

As we will discuss, the Personal Responsibility and Work Opportunity Reconciliation Act of 1996 (PRWORA—the welfare reform legislation) gave states dramatically more flexibility in determining eligibility for public aid. To protect children from losing medical coverage as a result of welfare reform, states were required to maintain an entitlement to Medicaid and to use eligibility criteria at least as generous as they had in place in 1996.

The most important low-income health insurance expansion passed during the Clinton administration was the State Children's Health Insurance Program (CHIP or S-CHIP), established under the Balanced Budget Act of 1997. The program provides federal matching funds for state-designed programs to provide health insurance to low-income children. States have much more flexibility with respect to benefit structures and eligibility than under Medicaid. All states except one (Arkansas!) have made children eligible if their family's income is below 133 percent of poverty, with the majority adopting even higher eligibility limits.[7] Some $24 billion in federal dollars was appropriated over five years for CHIP.

Child care funding was expanded considerably over the Clinton years. Prior to 1996 there were four major federal funding streams with varying requirements. Under PRWORA, these were consolidated into the Child Care and Development Block Grant (CCDBG), and child care funding was expanded. Moreover, states were given flexibility to transfer up to 30 percent of their cash assistance block grant into child care programs, and nearly all states have transferred some monies.

Finally the Taxpayer Relief Act of 1997 included a $500 per child *nonrefundable* tax credit that also offered support for working families. In 1999, two-parent families with two children and incomes below $18,000 ($15,000 for a one-parent two-child family) owed no federal income taxes and could not receive the credit. Since the poverty line for a family of four was $17,029 ($13,290 for a family of three) in 1999, the child tax credit primarily benefited near-poor families. Two-parent, two-child families earning $25,000 and two-child, one-parent families earning $22,000 would have qualified for the full credit.

---

6. Committee on Ways and Means (2000), p. 894.
7. Committee on Ways and Means (2000), Table 15–27, pp. 932–933.

Figure 11.1 indicates the dramatic increases in expenditures on four of these five major programs. The child tax credit is not included, since it was not refundable.

• Between 1992 and 1999, annual real federal spending on these programs increased by more than $30 billion. To put this figure in perspective, in 1995, the year before the passage of PRWORA (and a peak year in welfare spending), the federal government spent a total of $17.3 billion (1999 dollars) on the old Aid to Families with Dependent Children (AFDC) program. The EITC *increase* alone was nearly as large as the *total* amount the federal government was spending on AFDC when Clinton took office.[8]

11.1.1.1   Impacts on Incentives and Sources of Concern

These policy changes had dramatic effects on the incentives to work, particularly among single parents. For 1988, 1992, and 1999, Table 11.1 indicates how much a single mother of three could expect to receive if she did not work and collected welfare versus if she worked full time at the minimum wage. Welfare benefits vary state to state, and child care expenses vary across people, but the table gives a sense of how a typical person might fare.[9]

• The payoff to working has increased dramatically since 1988, and particularly during the Clinton years. A full-year full-time minimum wage single parent who would otherwise be on welfare in 1988 would have a net gain of only $2,325, and she would likely lose her Medicaid benefits, which might easily be worth more than that gain. By 1992 when Bush departed, the same woman would gain $4,142 by working and her younger children would not lose Medicaid. In 1999 the gain to work had grown to over $7,000, the children would keep Medicaid and even the woman would be eligible to keep it for a time.

A higher minimum wage and slightly lower welfare benefits contributed to this gain, but it is mainly the result of a sizable rise in the EITC and greater child care support.

---

8. The chart excludes spending for AFDC/TANF, food stamps, and housing aid for working families because these figures are not available. There was a sizable recent increase in the number and share of AFDC/TANF who were working, so adding these values would magnify the changes shown. The EITC increases reflect changes enacted under both the Clinton and the Bush administrations. Large as the numbers are, Figure 11.1 may understate the long-term increase in spending. The chart is based on actual expenditures. The State Children's Health Insurance Program has grown far more slowly than expected. Rather than spending the more than $4 billion appropriated, only $600 million was actually spent. Since that time, S-CHIP has been expanding rapidly.

9. Welfare benefits are based on the weighted average of state benefits, weighted by the share of all single parents who reside in the state.

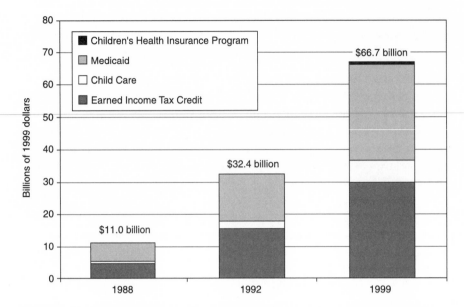

Figure 11.1
Spending for Programs Other Than AFDC/TANF, Food Stamps, and Housing That Are Targeted on Low-Income Working Families.

Sources: Earned Income Tax Credit: Committee on Ways and Means (2000, Table 13–14). Child Care: Committee on Ways and Means (2000, Tables 9–26, 9–30, 10–1, 10–4), Committee on Ways and Means (1996, Tables 10–13, 10–15), Committee on Ways and Means (1992, p. 974, for estimated share of Title XX funding spent on child care). Medicaid numbers based on adjustments to form 2082 data done at the Urban Institute and provided by Leighton Ku. 1999 Medicaid data are not yet available by group, thus 1999 represents aggregate 1999 spending (Committee on Ways and Means, 2000, Table 15–13) times 0.156, which is the share we project will be spent on these groups based on trends through 1998.

Notes: Medicaid is money spent on children and nonelderly, nondisabled adults not receiving cash assistance. Child care includes money spent under the Child Care Development Block Grant (CCDBG), AFDC transitional and at risk, TANF child care, TANF transfers to CCDBG, and estimated share of Social Services block grant spent on child care. The chart excludes spending for AFDC/TANF, food stamps, and housing for working families because these figures are not available. There was a sizable recent increase in the number and share of AFDC/TANF who were working, so adding these values would magnify the changes shown.

Table 11.1
Income and Benefits for a Single Mother with Two Children When Working and Not Working in 1988, 1992, and 1999

	1988		1992		1999	
	Not Working	Working Full-Time, Minimum Wage	Not Working	Working Full-Time, Minimum Wage	Not Working	Working Full-Time, Minimum Wage
Total earnings	0	$9,813	0	$10,497	0	$10,712
Payroll taxes	0	−737	0	−803	0	−819
TANF (AFDC) and Food Stamps	8,612	2,630	8,393	2,697	7,967	2,310
Earned Income Tax Credit	0	1,231	0	1,643	0	3,816
Child care expense	0	−2,000	0	−2,000	0	−2,000
Child care support	0	0	0	500	0	1,000
Disposable income	$8,612	$10,937	$8,393	$12,535	$7,967	$15,018
Government paid health insurance? (Medicaid)	Yes	No	Yes	Children under 9	Yes	Children under 16
Net financial gain from working		$2,325		$4,142		$7,051

Source: Authors' tabulations.

On the one hand, Table 11.1 may understate the real change in incentives for work among single parents. By 1999 revised welfare programs were putting increasing pressure on welfare applicants and recipients to eschew welfare and enter the workforce. Thus the option to not work and collect welfare was increasingly unavailable. Over the past 12 years and particularly during the Clinton era, the incentives and pressures for lone parents to work expanded dramatically. On the other hand, Table 11.1 might overstate the changes, since it assumes that women were receiving food stamps, child care supplements, and Medicaid if eligible. As we will discuss later, many eligible families appear not to have received support from these programs in the late 1990s.

Note also that the table assumes relatively modest child care expenses. Many families, particularly those with older children or who have relatives who could care for the children, report less, but many families also report spending far more. If child care expenses are much greater, the returns to working would be less in both years, though the changes would look the same.

But these expansions in support for the working poor did not create unambiguously positive work incentives for all workers. In particular, they sometimes diminished work incentives for second workers married to low earners.

Above $13,000 in income, the EITC is reduced by roughly 21 cents per dollar earned. This phaseout adds to the high marginal tax rate that low-income workers may already face. This includes payroll taxes, whose employer and employee share totals 15 percent. If a family is collecting food stamps, they face a benefit reduction rate of 24 percent. Other assistance such as housing, child care, and medical benefits may also be phased out slowly. As of the year 2000, at approximately $25,000 in income, a family would begin paying federal income taxes of 15 percent.

Few persons will face all of these reductions simultaneously, but

• A significant number of working families would face an EITC phaseout, payroll taxes, and either benefit reductions or federal taxes, resulting in a marginal tax rate of 50 percent or more. Candidate George W. Bush emphasized this problem when he described the "tollgate to the middle class." A mother married to a man earning $15,000–$25,000 who considers entering work would face a high tax rate on her earnings, above and beyond any child care or other costs.[10]

• The expanded worker supports targeted at the working poor also altered marriage incentives—generating both rewards and penalties. If a nonworking mother contemplates marrying a working childless man, her children and his earnings would allow them to qualify for the EITC and effectively create a marriage bonus. But if a working mother earning $10,000 considers marrying a working man, she will lose much or all of the EITC. His earnings will reduce her EITC. Thus they will face a marriage penalty.[11]

Phasing in benefits as family earnings rise creates a strong work and marriage incentive for nonworking parents. Phasing them out once people get above some income threshold creates adverse work and marriage incentives in cases where someone is near or above that threshold.

11.1.1.2 Does Clinton Deserve the Credit (or Blame) for These Expansions?

Figure 11.1 indicates that support programs for low-wage workers clearly did not originate with Clinton. The first EITC was adopted in the mid-1970s and was significantly expanded under President Ronald Reagan, who labeled it "the best antipoverty, the best profamily, the best job creation measure to come out of Congress." It rose again during the George H. W. Bush administration.

---

10. The recently passed Economic Growth and Tax Relief Act of 2001 raised the tax threshold considerably by doubling the child tax credit. The child tax credit was also made partially refundable, further benefiting lower-income working families. This significantly lowered the marginal tax rates facing people in the $15,000 to $30,000 category.

11. The recent tax cut improved this situation for low-income families by making the child tax credit partially refundable and by changes in the EITC plateau for married persons. A sizable marriage penalty remains.

Medicaid for children in working families was also sharply expanded during this period. Altogether work supports rose by nearly $21 billion between 1988 and 1992.

But neither Reagan nor Bush ever focused much attention on the working poor. Clinton, by contrast, spent considerable time and political energy on the issue. The Clinton role was particularly clear during the years after 1994 when the Republicans gained control of Congress. Key Republicans, particularly Don Nickles, chairman of the Finance Subcommittee on Taxation and IRS Oversight, emphasized problems with the EITC, focusing on its high error rates and large cost. Some GOP lawmakers sought to limit expenditures, but Clinton was very clear that he would not accept cuts in the EITC.

Similarly Clinton's emphasis on work support influenced the final legislation that was passed. Clinton vetoed the first two Republican versions of welfare reform, noting that Congress should "provide sufficient child care to enable recipients to leave welfare for work" and "restore the guarantee of health coverage for poor families."[12] The bill he finally signed left Medicaid intact and included significantly more child care money than the ones he had vetoed. However, the bill Clinton signed had major cutbacks for immigrants and childless food stamp recipients, both low-income groups that are employed at high rates, though these were not provisions Clinton favored.[13]

Clinton probably should not get much credit for the $500 per child tax credit. After all, the 1994 GOP Contract with America called for a $1,000 per child tax credit. But here too Clinton played a role in supporting low-income workers. When the child tax credit was initially voted on, it included an EITC offset, effectively denying the new child credit to low-income workers between roughly $18,000 and $25,000 who were getting an EITC benefit. Clinton threatened a veto and the provision was eliminated.

• Thus, while plenty of momentum had built up for supporting working families prior to his administration, Clinton should get substantial credit for giving priority to specific policies. Without his political attention to this issue, work supports for low-income families would almost surely have been much less.

11.1.2 Strengthen Child Support Enforcement

Child support enforcement involves several basic steps. One must establish paternity, get an award in place and determine the amount of the award, locate the noncustodial parent, and collect the award. Until recent years, paternity

---

12. Clinton (1996).
13. For a detailed discussion of the legislative maneuvering that preceded passage of the 1996 legislation, see Weaver (2000).

establishment was rare and cumbersome. Awards were set once in nominal dollar values and rarely adjusted for changing circumstances. Locating absent fathers was hampered by limited information, lack of automated systems, and a high proportion of interstate cases. Data and tracking systems were often in terrible shape. It should not be surprising that by some estimates the system was collecting perhaps a third of what an ideal system would.[14]

During the past eight years, the administration and the Congress moved aggressively to adopt new measures:[15]

• *Streamlined and more immediate paternity establishment, including in-hospital paternity establishment and civil procedures for voluntary acknowledgement of paternity.* Nearly 80 percent of fathers are present at the birth of the child or visit the hospital, and both parents at the child's birth typically indicate a strong desire that the child's father be known. Yet paternity establishment often does not begin until several years after the birth and then only for purposes of collecting aid. After two years, roughly half of the original relationships had ended. In-hospital establishment has proven far more effective.

• *More automatic use of genetic testing.* Court procedures dating back to a time when blood tests were vastly less reliable often placed limits on testing and on their admissibility. New legislation required states to create a "rebuttable presumption" of paternity if the probability of paternity in the genetic tests exceeds a threshold established by the state.

• *New rules for updating awards.* States were required to update awards more often and to adopt one of several alternatives for moving toward more automatic updating.

• *Federal registry of child support orders and automated systems.* States were required to create automated registries of orders, collections, and arrearages and to provide this information in a new federal registry. Prior to this time many states did not even have a registry. And even though interstate cases constitute roughly 30 percent of all cases,[16] there was no national database of cases or arrearages.

• *National new-hire reporting system.* Employers were required to collect and immediately report to the state the names and Social Security numbers of all new hires. State and federal officials were required to compare these to state and national registries of child support orders. If an arrearage was found, states were required to have the employer begin wage withholding immediately.

---

14. Sorenson (1995).
15. The following discussion draws heavily on Committee on Ways and Means (2000) and Department of Health and Human Services (2000).
16. Weaver and Williams (1989).

• *New penalties.* New laws expanded wage withholding, provided for the re-vocation of drivers' licenses and the suspension of professional licenses, denial of passports, and many other measures for those with unpaid child support.

• *Expanded data matching.* Data matching of the child support registries with information from various sources, particularly financial institutions, was man-dated, allowing easier access to information on the assets of delinquent parents.

• *"Pay parents first"—priority for families when both states and families have child support claims.* States have a right to claim most child support payments owed to mothers on welfare during the time they collect aid. Often large arrearages build up. When a mother leaves welfare, many states were insisting that any child support money paid after that time go first to the state to pay off this arrearage, leaving the mother with nothing even though she was no longer on welfare. The new policies required that payments owed to families had priority.

• *Access and visitation grants and experiments.* Money was also provided for grants to help states increase and improve visitation by fathers. In addition, money was provided for various state-initiated demonstrations.

• *Altered state reimbursement formula.* Reimbursement formulas and incentive payments were adjusted to take account of more than just the dollars collected per dollar spent. Previous formulas discouraged pursuit of all but the cases that promised the most immediate and largest potential for collections.

Collectively these were radical changes in the child support enforcement system, changes that proponents hoped would significantly increase collections and enhance the economic position of children in lone-parent families. But one change in welfare reform may have had negative consequences for child sup-port collections and support of children:

• *Elimination of mandatory $50 pass-through.* The welfare reform legislation elim-inated a requirement that states automatically pass through the first $50 per month of child support collected for a child on welfare without any reduction in welfare benefit. The new legislation allowed states to simply use all child support money collected for TANF recipients to reduce benefits, thus providing no net gain to the child.

11.1.2.1 Impacts on Incentives and Sources of Concern
Child support collections also have mixed incentives.

• Increased child support collections coupled with a "pay families first" policy creates unambiguous work incentives for custodial parents. If they remain on welfare, the state will keep any child support they collect as an offset for wel-fare (less any pass-through if the state so chooses). But if a custodial mother goes to work and no longer receives welfare benefits, she would get all that child support that was owed and collected. This would be added to her wages, EITC, and other supports.

Thus on Table 11.1, if child support collections added another $500 per month, a mother's incentive to work would rise accordingly.

• Child support may also serve as a tax on noncustodial parents. Whether or not such payments are perceived as taxes will depend on the use of the money. On the one hand, if the money goes to the support of the child, the noncustodial parent need not see this as a tax in the same way that custodial parents do not consider the support of their children a tax on earnings. On the other hand, if the money is just going to offset state expenditures when the custodial parent is on welfare, child support payments are close to a pure tax.

And in cases where the noncustodial parent resents providing support or believes the money is wasted by the custodial parent, it may be even more psychologically upsetting than an income tax of an equivalent size. Relatively little work has been done about the incentive effects of child support payments.

Child support enforcement also raises questions about the appropriate role for males in separated families. Some scholars and father's rights advocates complain that men are increasingly seen only as a source of financial support, not as people who could offer nurturing and direction. Some also worry that young black men are being further stigmatized and unfairly burdened by excessive child support obligations that they cannot pay.

11.1.2.2 Does Clinton Deserve the Credit (or Blame) for These Changes?

Child support enforcement has always enjoyed bipartisan support in Congress. Still, the complexity of the issues and the need to understand the variation across states makes it difficult for Congress to take the lead in such legislation. In our view, Clinton probably deserves almost full credit for these initiatives. Most of the child support reforms were included either in Clinton's original budget proposal for 1993 or in the Work and Responsibility Act of 1995—Clinton's original welfare reform bill. Indeed more pages of that bill were devoted to child support enforcement changes than to classic welfare reform provisions. In 1996, when Republicans gained control of Congress, they crafted their own welfare reform bill that included no child support enforcement provisions. Pressed for such measures by both Democratic and Republican members (notably Republican women), the drafters largely adopted the Clinton proposals wholesale with only minor changes. The major omission was money for a demonstration of child support assurance, a plan by which custodial parents with an award in place would be guaranteed some amount for child support even if the state failed to collect the money.

• Here too, then, Clinton deserves considerable credit. Though support for these measures was bipartisan, they had been crafted by the administration.

11.1.3   Welfare Reform

After taking office the Clinton administration continued and expanded the practice of issuing "waivers" to states that wanted to experiment with substantial revisions in the delivery of public assistance programs. As more and more states became interested in welfare reform, waiver applications increased, and waiver proposals became more extensive. By 1996, 26 states had major statewide waivers in operation, mostly allowing them to run more extensive and more strictly enforced welfare-to-work programs than the AFDC program would normally allow. The state waivers were an important precursor to federal welfare reform legislation and created a constituency in the states for greater state flexibility and control over public assistance.

In 1994 the Clinton administration proposed a welfare reform bill. The original Clinton plan called for all recipients to begin training or job search activities immediately upon beginning welfare. It set a two-year time limit on cash aid, but certain activities stopped the clock, such as part-time work if one had a preschooler or full-time work if children were over 6. After two years, recipients would be required to work. If they could not find an unsubsidized job, a subsidized one would be created. States were given greater flexibility, but welfare remained an entitlement, meaning that all who qualified were guaranteed aid.

The Clinton bill died when Republicans took control of Congress in 1996. The Personal Responsibility and Work Opportunity Reconciliation Act (PRWORA), passed and signed in the summer of 1996, was very different from Clinton's original conception. Among other things it abolished the Aid to Families with Dependent Children (AFDC) program and replaced it with the Temporary Assistance for Needy Families (TANF) block grant. Its major provisions were the following:

• *Block grants replaced matched funding.* States were given fixed block grants equal to or greater than what their average spending had been in the 1992–94 period.[17] This provision shifted the financial risk of changes in demand for

---

17. States were given the maximum of the annual average during 1992–94, the spending in 1995, or a rather complicated third formula.

public assistance onto the states, whereas this risk was shared under the older matching grant system.

• *Seventy-five percent maintenance of effort (MOE) requirement.* States were required to spend 75 percent of what they used to spend on AFDC on their TANF programs. What could be counted toward this MOE was relatively broad (including "any other expenditures which further the goals of" the act).

• *Entitlement eliminated.* States were no longer required to cover everyone who met their income and eligibility requirements.

• *Fully flexible eligibility.* States could determine whatever eligibility criterion they chose. Thus benefits need not be limited to single parents as they largely were under AFDC. States could determine benefits, maximum asset levels, earnings disregards to reward work, and the like. They could require work or participation or any other activity as a condition of eligibility.

• *Five-year maximum time limit.* PRWORA set a lifetime limit of five years on TANF-funded aid. States can exempt up to 20 percent of the caseload under a "hardship exemption." States are free to set shorter time limits if they choose, or to continue funding after five years entirely out of state funds.

• *Work requirements or caseload reductions.* By 2002 at least 50 percent of all recipient families and 90 percent of two-parent families were required to be working. However, the law stated that any caseload reductions below the 1995 level were treated as equivalent to work. Thus a state that reduced its caseload by 50 percent would meet its work requirement regardless of how many current or former recipients were working. States were also mandated to require "work" by recipients after two years, but states could define work in almost any manner they chose, and there were no penalties associated with failure to meet this provision.

• *Significant expansions in child care.* Several child care programs were consolidated into a single block grant. Significantly more child care money was included for women leaving welfare. And states could transfer some of the regular TANF funds into child care.

• *Bonus funds for reducing nonmarital birth rates.* States that reduced out-of-wedlock child bearing without raising abortion rates qualified for special bonuses.

• *Reductions in food stamp eligibility.* States were given more discretion about how they enforced the food stamp rules (and more ability to sanction noncompliant recipients). Work rules were added for 18–50-year-olds without dependents.

· *Reductions in eligibility for aid among* legal *immigrants.* Illegal immigrants were already denied nearly all federal aid. The bill added new restrictions on receipt of TANF, food stamps, and Supplemental Security Income (SSI, the program for the aged and disabled) for many legal immigrants who were not (yet) citizens, particularly those who were admitted because they were relatives of citizens.[18]

11.1.3.1 Impacts on Incentives and Sources of Concern

Supporters of this approach emphasized several features. States would finally be given the flexibility they had been seeking to implement real welfare reforms. Governors emphasized that they cared as much about the welfare of their citizens as federal bureaucrats did. This bill would allow them to implement genuine work-focused reform without using the cumbersome waiver process. Conservatives also proclaimed the end of the entitlement as an important signal. No one was guaranteed welfare anymore. Recipients could and would be expected to take responsibility for themselves.

The immigrant and food stamp cuts were themselves quite controversial, and though benefits were partially restored in 1997, tough rules remain in place for recent legal immigrants and for many nonelderly, nondisabled adults.

· The potential negative impact on green card holders and their families will grow over time. Given the recent rise in immigration, notably among very poorly educated persons, an increasing number of families who have come to the United States legally will be at risk of extreme poverty if they are unable to find work.

Critics also identified three major sources of concern regarding the TANF provisions: its greater emphasis on time limits and caseload reductions than on work, the dangers of a block grant system of financing, and the question of whether recipients could get decent jobs or any jobs at all.

Work Versus Caseload Reductions   Opponents argued that, for all the talk about work, the bill was crafted to produce caseload reductions. The lifetime five-year cutoff seemed particularly draconian, since a sizable majority of those on welfare at a point in time would eventually reach the limit under the current AFDC program.[19] Unlike Clinton's original proposal, states were not even

---

18. Sponsoring relatives must sign an affidavit indicating that the entering relatives will not become a "public charge." Virtually all of the cost savings from this legislation occurred because of the food stamp and immigrant cuts.

19. Bane and Ellwood (1994).

allowed to use federal funds to help create subsidized jobs for people who hit the five-year federal time limit without finding work. Even more striking was the provision that called for high levels of work *or* equivalent levels of caseload reductions. In fact, states could meet the requirement of this bill without putting one more person to work, simply by moving them off welfare.

Note, however, that a closer examination of the bill suggests that pressures to push people off welfare were easily avoided if states chose to do so. The five-year cutoff applied only to federal aid. State money, including money counted toward maintenance of effort, could be used to support people beyond the five-year limit.

Moreover, states could completely redefine who was eligible for aid and under what conditions. Thus states could add working poor persons to aid and count their work. With some creative design and bookkeeping, states were given essentially complete authority to arrange public assistance as they saw fit. If they chose to largely maintain the present system, they could. If they wanted to implement the original Clinton vision, they could. If states wanted to essentially end welfare entirely, they could.

What is harder to gauge, but potentially just as important, is the extent to which the rhetoric of PRWORA led states to adopt more radical reforms. The whole tone of the reform sent a strong message to state administrators that the mission of welfare offices was no longer to determine eligibility and compute the proper amount of the check, but rather to move people quickly off welfare, and, hopefully, into employment.

Matching Versus Block Grants   The switch from matching to block grants was another source of controversy. Under a matching grant system, the marginal cost of spending another dollar on public aid was reduced by the amount of the match. States such as Connecticut or California got a dollar-for-dollar match, so the price of support was cut in half. In Mississippi, the state had to cover only 20 percent of the costs. For each dollar they spent in state money, the federal government would provide another four.

Simple economic theory suggests that if one lowers the cost of providing a service, more will be provided. The federal match could be justified in part to deal with the externalities of operating a solely state-based system. States might worry that high benefits would attract recipients from other states, and thus would set benefit levels lower than they otherwise might.

• Several prominent scholars, most notably Peterson (1995), expressed concern that by removing the incentives inherent in a match, a block grant system would lead to a race to the bottom as states compete to discourage poor families from living in their borders.

Table 11.2
Median Family Income and TANF Grants per Poor Child, Selected States

	Median Family Income (1996–97)	Approximate TANF Dollars per Poor Child per Year (1996–97)
Arkansas	$31,300	$297
California	$44,200	$1,585
Connecticut	$55,700	$1,854
Florida	$37,000	$798
Mississippi	$32,750	$412
Wisconsin	$49,800	$1,765

Sources: TANF grant: Committee on Ways and Means (1998, Table 7–40, p. 504). Median family income and number of poor children: Authors' tabulations of March 1997 and March 1998 Current Population Survey data.

In addition, differences in wealth across states might leave some states less able to provide for their poorer citizens. A subsidy that varied by the income and wealth of the states helped overcome this problem.

• Another fear was the loss of the automatic stabilizer effect. When economic conditions worsen in a state, the caseload rises. With matching grants, the federal government covered at least half of the new costs, thus stimulating the troubled economy. Under a block grant, states get no new aid during recessions.

• Overlooked in the worries about block grants was their upside potential in strong economic times. When caseloads and expenditures fall, so do federal matching funds. But the TANF block grant amount was based on a expenditures when caseloads were at historic highs. As the economy improved in the late 1990s and caseloads began to fall, states suddenly had substantial excess resources. They could devote far more to services and supports for people leaving welfare, and many chose to do so. Thus there was no immediate pressure to race to the bottom, since government budgets were not stressed.

One other feature of the block grants got almost no attention. The block grants locked in place a remarkably uneven distribution of federal funds. Table 11.2 shows the median family income and TANF grants per poor child in a representative group of states. The dates 1996–97 were selected to illustrate that the variability was built in from the start.

• By locking in place existing allocations, TANF grants per poor child are much higher for richer states than for poorer ones. Indeed Arkansas and Mississippi with median family incomes of close to $32,000 received grants of $297 and $412 per poor child. Connecticut and Wisconsin with family incomes of $50,000 or more, nonetheless received roughly $1,800 per poor child.

Even though Arkansas and Mississippi had a much higher match rate, Connecticut and Wisconsin spent so much more on welfare that they got much more federal aid per poor child under the AFDC program. PRWORA simply locked in place those differences. It seems inconceivable that a block grant program designed from scratch would give four or five times more per poor child to rich than to poor states.

Availability of Jobs for Welfare Recipients   Welfare recipients are often poorly educated. In 1995 nearly 40 percent were dropouts, and only 16 percent had any schooling beyond high school. Some 45 percent had children under the age of 6. Almost 60 percent were never-married mothers. Some 37 percent were black and another 20 percent Hispanic.[20] At least 40 percent had not worked in the past two years.[21] Danziger et al. (2000) report that a quarter have major depressive disorders and 22 percent have children with significant health problems.

• Opponents feared that even in good times many of these mothers may not be particularly employable. There were also fears that a major influx of welfare mothers could not be absorbed into the economy. And even if the women were employed, several studies cast doubt on whether they would be able to support themselves and whether their wages would actually grow over time.[22]

In response to these and related concerns, the administration and Congress enacted several measures designed to increase the demand for welfare leavers. They extended the Work Opportunity Tax Credit, which provides employers with a credit of 40 percent of wages up to a maximum of $2,400 for the first-year pay of persons in target groups, including TANF leavers. The Welfare-to-Work Tax Credit was adopted, which provides employers with a credit of 35 percent of the first $10,000 in pay in the first year and 50 percent of the first $10,000 in pay for the second year of employment of a TANF leaver. The Welfare-to-Work Grant Program created a two-year, $3 billion fund to be used for programs aimed at hard-to-serve welfare clients. Clinton sponsored transportation and housing initiatives designed to help mothers leaving welfare. And the president helped set up the Welfare-to-Work Partnership, a nonprofit organization chaired by key business leaders with a mission "to provide innovative workforce solutions for companies through hiring, retaining and promoting welfare recipients and other unemployed and low-income

20. Committee on Ways and Means (1998), Table 7–19, p. 441.
21. Bane and Ellwood (1994).
22. Burtless (1997).

workers."[23] This group worked to inform employers of the opportunities to hire recipients and the tax and other benefits of doing so.

11.1.3.2 Does Clinton Deserve the Credit (or Blame) for These Changes?
Unlike in the make-work-pay and child support enforcement arenas,

• The welfare bill that emerged was dramatically different from Clinton's original vision. It enacted a devolution of program and financial responsibility from the federal government to the states, coupled with incentives and strong rhetorical signals about the need for states to reduce caseloads and move people into work.

Clinton did influence the final bill. He vetoed two earlier versions, primarily on the grounds that they also block-granted Medicaid, but also because of insufficient child care dollars. These elements were changed in the final bill. Even when he signed the bill, he complained about harsh treatment of legal immigrants and food stamp cuts, and promised to work to change those provisions—and he was partially successful at doing so. But he never took a stand opposing the basic structure of the Republican welfare plan, and its basic structure changed little from the first to the last Republican bill.[24] This was a bill largely shaped by Republican governors, notably Tommy Thompson of Wisconsin and John Engler of Michigan. As a former governor himself, Clinton always seemed very comfortable with such dramatic devolution.

• But, if a major effect of the bill was to alter the political and social climate (rather than changing the locus of control over welfare), then Clinton's role may loom larger. Many observers argue that Clinton's rhetoric about "ending welfare as we know it" and "two years and you're off"[25] sharply altered the political landscape and legitimized a far more energetic attack on the present welfare system.

Clinton often talked about the present system being broken. Clinton again and again signaled his enthusiasm for state experimentation, even if he did not like the particulars. And his was the rhetoric of work and responsibility that came to dominate the discussion.

There is real irony for Clinton here. Those who are deeply troubled by the bill place considerable blame on Clinton, decrying his incendiary rhetoric and his

---

23. www.welfaretowork.org.
24. Weaver (2000).
25. To our knowledge, Clinton never actually used this phrase. But it was widely used to describe the basic Clinton principle, and the administration never sought to rephrase it as the more accurate "two years and you work."

unwillingness to veto the final bill even though most of his cabinet urged him
to do so.[26] Those who like the bill give the Republican Congress and governors
the credit, since the bill was so far from the original Clinton vision.

11.1.4 Housing and Urban Economic Development

Candidate Clinton said much less about housing and urban policy during the
1992 campaign than about work and welfare proposals. But the need to establish enterprise zones—special zones within urban (or rural) areas targeted for
community development where businesses could qualify for special tax treatment and residents might get special services—was a frequent theme. He did
not offer a new vision of housing policy, but he talked publicly and regularly
about the problems of urban areas, and he decried past failures and the concentration of poverty that public housing sometimes yields.

11.1.4.1 Urban Economic Development

Throughout his administration, Clinton emphasized the need to develop and
"empower" poor urban communities. Clinton tended to emphasize devolution
and a public-private partnership. Major initiatives included the following:

• *Empowerment zones and enterprise communities (EZ/EC).* The Omnibus Budget
Reconciliation Act of 1993 authorized the establishment of empowerment zones
(heavily funded areas) and enterprise communities (less richly supported areas)
as part of Clinton's Community Empowerment Agenda. Communities competed for designation as one of the zones and had to demonstrate that business,
government, residents, and community organizations were involved in developing a community revitalization plan. The first round designated 11 zones and
94 enterprise communities in 1993 and 1994. EZ/EC provided approximately
$2.5 billion in tax incentives and $1.3 billion in flexible grants to these areas. An
additional 15 urban and 5 rural communities were designated as empowerment
zones in a second round in January 1999.

• *Community Development Financial Institutions (CDFI).* The CDFI Fund, created
in 1994, was designed to bring more capital to areas inadequately served by
traditional financial institutions. CDFIs include community development banks,
credit unions, loan funds, venture capital funds, and microenterprise loan funds.
The fund invests in these institutions using a variety of vehicles including equity
investments, loans, and grants. The CDFI can provide funding for a range of
services including mortgages, commercial loans, housing rehabilitation, and the

---

26. See especially Edelman (1997).

like. By 1999 there were 270 designated CDFIs, and more than $190 million had been distributed.[27]

• *Economic Development Initiative (EDI) and other changes in the Community Development Block Grant (CDBG).* A number of changes were made to the existing CDBG program (originally created in 1974), which provides federal resources for local development activities. Overall funding increased from roughly $3.5 billion to $5 billion (in 2000 dollars). Under EDI (begun in 1994), current and future CDBG grants are held as security for loans that enable communities to pursue initiatives in public/private housing rehabilitation, economic development, and physical development.

• *New Markets Initiative.* On December 14, 2000, as Clinton was preparing to leave office, he signed an initiative jointly created with House Speaker Dennis Hastert designed to "encourage private sector equity investments in underserved communities."[28] It included a series of tax credits, low-interest loans, and equity matching plans to reward both those who invest in low-income communities and persons who provide capital to institutions that finance business loans in those areas. It also increased the Low-Income Housing Tax Credit (LIHTC) cap on money available for low-income housing from $1.25 to $1.75 per capita.[29]

In addition, the administration had a variety of microenterprise programs totaling roughly $60 billion to help low-income individuals begin small businesses.[30]

11.1.4.2 Housing Policy

There are a variety of ways in which housing is supported by the federal government. The deductibility of home interest, FHA and VA loan guarantees, and various grant and loan programs through which local jurisdictions can subsidize the purchase of homes by moderate-income families all support homeownership. And the administration expanded a number of these, including some programs to help those getting rental assistance become homeowners.

Rental assistance serves more low-income families than homeownership programs. Such aid typically comes in one of four ways: public housing, federal subsidies paid to private firms to construct housing to be occupied by low-income families or individuals, negotiated agreements with existing landlords providing subsidized rents for particular units, and tenant-based assistance whereby the rent of particular *households* is subsidized. In some, but not all

---

27. Office of the Press Secretary (1999).
28. Office of the Press Secretary (2000).
29. U.S. Department of Housing and Urban Development (2000).
30. Else and Gallagher (2000).

cases, tenant-based assistance is portable, meaning it can be used to rent any apartment meeting certain standards.

Housing aid is not an entitlement, and availability varies widely across cities. Kingsley (1997) reports that only about one-quarter of those eligible actually get aid. Among those on AFDC the number is closer to one-fifth. Long waiting lists for housing assistance are common, with priority often given to the homeless.

Originally, the design, construction, and control of public housing was almost entirely left to local public housing authorities. Federal public housing support came in the form of fully subsidized construction costs, while maintenance had to be covered by local authorities out of rents. Predictably, many public housing projects were massive high-rise cement buildings that maximized capital and minimized operating costs.[31] The combination of capital subsidies and an allocation scheme that sometimes targeted aid on the poorest of the poor meant that housing, particularly public housing, often concentrated and isolated poor families.

Starting with the Reagan years and continuing into the Bush years, net new construction in both public and subsidized private housing largely stalled. Most growth came in the form of increased numbers of household/tenant-based renter assistance. Eligibility rules further targeted the poor.

• Perhaps surprisingly, the Clinton years were a time of even less growth in new commitments for rental assistance than under the previous Republican administrations.

During some years of the Carter administration, there were more than 350,000 new commitments for subsidized housing. These averaged more than 100,000 a year during Reagan. The Bush administration provided roughly 75,000 new commitments per year. But during the 1994–99 period, just over 30,000 net new commitments were made each year. Finally in 2000 and 2001, the number jumped above 100,000, in part as a result of 50,000 new vouchers committed for special "welfare-to-work" housing vouchers.

• The Clinton era did coincide with important changes in the nature and shape of housing assistance. The general goal was to reduce the high concentration of poverty families that scholars such as Bill Wilson had pointed to as being so pernicious.

With the passage of the HOPE VI program in 1993, HUD embarked on a new strategy designed to replace the old high-density public housing projects inhabited by concentrated poor populations with lower density projects for a mix of income classes. HUD also sought to provide improved support ser-

---

31. Muth (1973).

vices to residents. Displaced residents who could not be accommodated in the new buildings were given vouchers to purchase rental housing in the larger marketplace.[32]

For the first time since 1950, the number of public housing units actually declined noticeably.[33] There were more than 1.4 million public housing rental units when Clinton took office in 1993. By the time he left, the number had fallen by 10 percent,[34] offset by increases in tenant-based supports. HUD also sought to tighten rules that forced out drug dealers and others who had been convicted of criminal activity.

The 1998 Quality Housing and Work Responsibility Act included a wide range of reforms designed to further reduce poverty concentrations in public housing, target new voucher aid on the lowest income families, make vouchers more "portable" so that people could move to other regions for better employment, and hold rents fixed for a time for people leaving welfare for work. And in 1994, HUD began a series of Moving to Opportunity experiments designed to test, using randomized controls, whether or not helping low-income families move to higher income neighborhoods would improve their economic prospects and school performance.

11.1.4.3 Impacts on Incentives and Sources of Concern

This was not a period of revolutionary change. The number of families getting housing aid was essentially the same at the end of the period as before it. There were modest alterations in rent and eligibility rules, but benefits did not change much. Still there was a serious push to encourage investment in low-income communities. And there was a clear attempt to reduce the impact of assisted housing on concentrating poor families.

• Evaluations of earlier enterprise zone policies have shown mixed results.[35] Clinton's EZ/EC policy clearly sought to deal with some of the criticisms of previous enterprise zone policies—particularly their failure to address issues of social isolation and job readiness—by requiring a comprehensive plan and by making cities compete for funds. Still the obvious questions remain whether targeted investment strategies merely rearrange jobs in the metropolitan area and whether they actually reduce poverty and improve the lives of poor residents.

There is near unanimous support for the principle of poverty deconcentration and economic integration. Recent changes in housing programs seem to reduce

---

32. The program received an Innovations in Government Award from Harvard's Kennedy School of Government.
33. Quigley (2000), Figure 1.
34. Table supplied by Chad Chirico, Congressional Budget Office.
35. See, for example, Vidal (1995), Wolf (1990), Papke (1993).

somewhat strong opposite incentives imbedded in past housing policies. Moving toward greater use of housing vouchers, particularly for the very poor, and redesigning public housing should help. But the number of housing projects replaced is still modest. And over the eight Clinton years, the shift from public housing to tenant/voucher-based support amounted to a shift of roughly 5 percent of the assisted population—which in turn implies that only about 2–3 percent of all poor households were switched, since only a portion of poor families get housing.

The administration also moved to reduce at least for a time the high cumulative marginal tax rate faced by housing-assisted families moving from welfare to work. Families in assisted housing typically must pay 30 percent of their income toward rent. This adds to the high marginal tax rates already mentioned. By delaying rent increases that would normally be required of families getting more income as they moved from welfare to work, these incentive problems were presumably reduced somewhat, though only temporarily.

The administration did not tackle the larger questions in housing policy, like whether cash support would be more effective than earmarked housing aid; why housing assistance is provided to only a subset of those eligible; and whether the mix of aid for families versus incentives for new construction is appropriate. But it does appear that over the Clinton years, the benefits of housing support were maintained while some of the negative consequences were lessened.

11.1.4.4 Does Clinton Deserve the Credit (or Blame) for These Changes?

Clinton inherited a Department of Housing and Urban Development beset by severe management problems. Clinton, himself, cut the HUD budget. Particularly when Republicans took control, there was enormous congressional skepticism about the department and its policies. Budget cuts led to the possibility of HUD being unable to even continue existing commitments to subsidized families. By most accounts this situation is significantly improved today, and there has even been some resumption in the issuance of new housing vouchers.

• In general the Clinton administration continued and improved upon policy directions that were already in place for significantly improving the administration of HUD.

Republicans such as Jack Kemp had long been advocates of enterprise zones, and Bush had proposed them. He had vetoed a bill that created them only because it included tax increases. Clinton gets credit for the size and shape of his EZ/EC proposal and for keeping it a program of sizable aid for a few cities rather than a small amount of aid for a plethora of cities, the way Model Cities became in an earlier era.

Similarly the growing preference for housing vouchers over public housing reflects a long-term trend dating back at least 20 years. But Clinton did more to change the nature of public housing than previous administrations had, and he accelerated the move toward encouraging greater geographic mobility among poor families.

11.2 Outcomes That Changed During the Clinton Administration

In this section we focus on a key set of outcomes that are closely related to the policy changes discussed in section 11.1. In particular, we look at caseload declines, at changes in labor force behavior among less-skilled persons, at changes in poverty and income among low-income families, at changes in child support collection and paternity establishment, and at changes in housing and poor neighborhoods.

In most cases, we are able to document the coincidental timing of policy changes and changes in behaviors and outcomes with some reliability. It is much harder to prove causality or to nail down exactly what share of the behavioral change was due to policy, although we cite a variety of research studies that try to do just this.

11.2.1 Caseload Declines

The number of families receiving AFDC rose sharply during the economic slowdown of 1990–91 and continued to rise through the early years of the 1990s. Concern about these rising caseloads was one reason governors were so actively involved in supporting major welfare reform in the mid-1990s. Figure 11.2 plots AFDC/TANF caseloads between 1970 and 2000; the 1996 welfare reform is marked with a vertical line (we discuss the food stamp trends shown in Figure 11.2 in section 11.2.1.2).

· Caseload numbers peaked in 1994 and started to turn down, two years before PRWORA was passed. They plummeted for the remainder of the decade. By 2000 the number of households receiving support from the TANF block grant was less than half of what it had been in 1994.

While the magnitude of decline differed slightly across states and geographic regions, all areas of the United States experienced unprecedented caseload declines in the last half of the 1990s.

These declines are all the more striking because they surprised the supporters of welfare reform as much as the opponents. In debating the 1996 legislation, no one predicted more than mild reductions in caseloads in the near future. The speed of this decline took observers by surprise. Proponents of the legislation

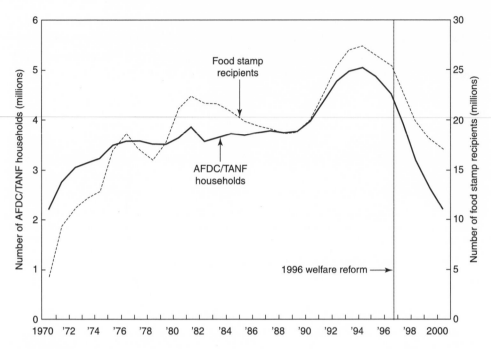

Figure 11.2
Total AFDC/TANF and Food Stamp Caseloads. (*Sources:* http://www.fns.usda.gov and http://www.acf.dhhs.gov.)

(and governors who were implementing new TANF-funded programs) claimed this result as evidence of the success of their initiatives, while opponents worried about how families who had left welfare were faring. Indeed, one of the best determinants of a person's welfare politics in the late 1990s was whether or not the individual saw declining caseloads as a good outcome or a serious problem.

11.2.1.1 Was Policy Change Responsible for the Caseload Declines?

A rapidly growing literature relating to these caseload changes has sprung up in the past five years. Most of the caseload studies utilize state panel data over the 1980s and 1990s to investigate caseload changes over time within states.[36] These papers attempt to separate the effects of the economy (typically mea-

---

36. For instance, see Council of Economic Advisers (1997, 1999), Wallace and Blank (1999), Figlio and Ziliak (1999), Ziliak et al. (2000), or Blank (2001b). Grogger (2000) uses microdata from the CPS rather than aggregating to state panel data, in order to control for individual family characteristics. Moffitt (1999) and Schoeni and Blank (2000) use state panel data, but differentiate between age and education groups within states. Blank (2001a) provides a more detailed and technical review of this literature, while Bell (2001) provides a more policy-oriented review.

sured by state unemployment rates) from the effects of policy (typically measured by a variety of variables, including AFDC/TANF benefit levels and dummy variables to indicate the timing when welfare waivers or TANF-funded programs were implemented within a state). Some studies also control for a range of political and demographic variables within states, although these controls appear to have little effect on estimated economic and policy effects.

These studies also include state fixed effects, to control for any state-specific variables that might affect overall caseload levels within a state. The resulting estimates, therefore, can be interpreted as showing how economic and policy variables influence caseloads over time within a state, without explaining differences in cross-state variation. Most studies also include year fixed effects (to remove any common national "shocks"); this approach has the effect of removing variation due to increases in the EITC or national minimum wage, since these policies are enacted everywhere at the same time.

The earliest studies focused on measuring the effects of state waivers on caseloads, utilizing data from *before* the enactment of the 1996 PRWORA legislation. The fact that different states enacted waivers at different times (and some states never enacted waivers) provides variation from which to measure the impact of these policy changes. Later studies have tried to measure the additional effects of states adopting new TANF-funded programs. Such measurements, however, are difficult to make, since most states switched from AFDC to TANF at about the same time, providing no variation in implementation by which to identify the separate effect of enacting a TANF program within a state. For instance, Schoeni and Blank (2000) try several different ways to estimate a separate TANF effect on caseloads (and other variables) and discuss the problems of interpretation in these estimates.

• Not surprisingly, most studies find a significant effect for both policy and the economy. The stellar economic growth of the late 1990s produced low unemployment rates and growing wages even among low-skilled workers. Simultaneously the combination of expanded work supports (such as the enhanced EITC) and PRWORA ushered in the biggest change in U.S. social policy toward the poor since the 1930s.

One commonly cited study is that done by the Council of Economic Advisers in 1999. This study finds that a one-point decline in the unemployment rate causes state caseloads to fall by about 6 to 7 percent over the long term. The implementation of a state waiver reduced caseloads by 8 to 9 percent, on average, while the implementation of TANF reduced caseloads by another 18 to 19 percent—though a portion of this growth is probably attributable to changes in the EITC as well. These results are consistent with those found in Schoeni and Blank (2000), as well as with earlier studies that focused on waivers only, such as Council of Economic Advisers (1997), Blank (2001b), and Wallace and Blank (1999).

A few studies have argued that policy effects were unimportant to the caseload decline, notably Ziliak et al. (2000) and Figlio and Ziliak (1999). Frankly we are quite skeptical. These studies tend to use complex specifications, which involve multiple lags of economic and policy effects as well as lagged independent variables.[37] The very strong economy of the late 1980s pushed down unemployment sharply yet did not produce very noticeable effects on caseloads. The idea that a somewhat stronger economy alone can explain a 50 percent reduction in caseloads when previous economic changes produced barely noticeable effects strikes us as highly implausible. The correlation between state caseload declines and state economic improvement is modest. Meanwhile, those who actually run welfare offices report that the nature of their work has changed dramatically and testify that this fact has changed recipient behavior.

At some level, it may be impossible to truly separate out policy effects from economic effects over the 1990s. The two obviously interact with each other. The strong economy allowed states to move faster in redesigning their welfare programs to emphasize work. The EITC rewarded work. And recipients pushed off welfare entered a market relatively rich with jobs. We believe that these factors reinforced each other in a simultaneous process that produced unprecedented behavioral changes.[38]

· Overall, we believe that the evidence suggests quite strongly that the welfare policies of the 1990s—state waivers as well as the enactment of PRWORA—were an important factor in reducing caseloads. But by themselves, these policies would not have produced the really dramatic caseload declines of the past five years. The strong economy and increases in the returns to work (such as the increase in the EITC) were also important and reinforced the incentives for women to leave welfare more quickly or to avoid receiving it in the first place.

11.2.1.2 Food Stamps and Medicaid

So far, we have focused on the utilization of AFDC/TANF. But AFDC was the "gateway" program through which many women and children also became

---

37. In our opinion, these estimates are "overspecified." Klerman and Haider (2000) argue that all these caseload studies are misspecified and utilize separate data on welfare entrants and welfare exits from the state of California to test their preferred specification. They find that both policy and economy variables matter.

38. The issue of identifying separate policy effects also arises in attempts to measure the impacts of the EITC versus welfare reform on increasing labor force participation, discussed in section 11.2.2.1. Several authors, including Ellwood (2000) and Meyer and Rosenbaum (1999), suggest that the effects of welfare change, expanded work supports, and the economy are interactive and cannot be meaningfully disentangled.

eligible for food stamps and for Medicaid. Reductions in the use of cash public assistance have had a major impact on the utilization of other public assistance programs as well. Declines in caseloads are more troubling if they are correlated with declines in food stamp and Medicaid usage as well.

The dotted line in Figure 11.2 shows how food stamp caseloads have changed over time. Food stamps expanded in the late 1970s (due to a variety of program changes that made them more accessible). With the advent of welfare-to-work programs, however, many expected food stamp utilization to remain high even as welfare caseloads fell.

· While some welfare falls were anticipated, large food stamp declines were a particular surprise. As women moved into low-wage jobs, it was expected that they would still need the additional income supplementation provided by food stamps; most women working in near-minimum-wage jobs remained eligible for some food stamp assistance. As Figure 11.2 indicates, however, food stamp usage has plummeted almost as quickly as AFDC/TANF usage, although this decline has slowed down in the past year.

The historical determinants of food stamp usage are quite similar to those of AFDC,[39] even though food stamp eligibility rules are quite different from AFDC. Food stamps have historically covered *all* low-income persons, not just families with children, and also provided assistance at higher income levels than most state AFDC programs. But in reality, most families who received food stamps also received AFDC.

Food stamp offices did little to bring eligible working families onto their rolls. Indeed, most offices were set up to discourage food stamp use among working families. They were open only during work hours and required regular visits by recipients. Furthermore, working adults were more difficult cases to process, since their earnings had to be regularly verified and their food stamp benefits would vary as their earnings varied. Quality control rules imposed by the federal government made it difficult to serve working families without increasing the caseload error rate.[40] While implementing welfare reform, few states focused on trying to maintain food stamp eligibility for ex–welfare recipients. Many women who have left welfare appear to believe that they are no longer eligible for food stamps.

A variety of legislative and regulatory changes have been implemented and proposed, trying to increase the access of working low-income families to the food stamp program. At present, however, a significant number of those who

---

39. Wallace and Blank (1999).
40. Greenstein and Guyer (2001) discuss these provisions in the food stamp program in detail.

have left cash public assistance appear to be forgoing food stamp assistance, although their family incomes are very low.

The Medicaid program is more complicated. As described previously, eligibility for children in poor families was established in the mid-1980s regardless of their AFDC utilization. Furthermore, women who leave welfare through work have ongoing Medicaid eligibility for a year (and longer at state discretion). This provision suggests that Medicaid utilization should have been less tied to welfare usage than were food stamps.

• Yet, there was a significant and completely unexpected decline in Medicaid usage among both children and nondisabled adults immediately following the implementation of TANF programs in the mid-1990s. Concerns about getting poor children to access health care was a primary reason for Clinton's CHIP proposal, discussed earlier.

The evidence suggests that Medicaid usage among children has begun to increase again in the late 1990s, perhaps because of the special efforts made by states using the CHIP funding, but coverage of low-income children in 1999 remained below where it was in 1995. Medicaid usage among adults who have left welfare remains quite low, and many of these adults (mostly women) go without insurance even though they may be eligible for transitional Medicaid.[41] These changes increase the probability that some women (and their children) might be worse off after leaving welfare, a topic we will return to later.

11.2.2 Work Behavior

Caseload declines will leave families more impoverished unless welfare leavers are able to replace welfare dollars with earnings. Hence, many researchers have looked closely at increases in work among low-skilled ex–welfare recipients.

Table 11.3 shows labor force participation rates among less-skilled persons by gender and race in 1989 (the peak of the last economic expansion), 1993 (the beginning of the Clinton administration), and 2000 (the end of the Clinton administration). The table demonstrates the strong increases in labor force involvement among less-skilled women over the past decade, particularly during the Clinton years. Between 1993 and 2000, among all female high school dropouts, labor force participation rates rose by 7 percentage points (from 43 to 50 percent), while they rose 11 percentage points among black female dropouts. Increases among female high school graduates also occurred, but were smaller in magnitude.

---

41. Greenstein and Guyer (2001).

Table 11.3
Selected Labor Force Participation Rates (Ages 20–65)

	1989	1993	2000
High School Dropouts			
Female			
Total	44.5	43.1	50.0
Black	43.6	40.0	51.1
White/other	45.2	43.9	49.0
Hispanic	43.8	43.3	50.6
Male			
Total	75.5	74.3	74.7
Black	65.3	64.0	58.7
White/other	74.4	72.5	70.2
Hispanic	86.7	85.0	87.4
High School Graduates			
Female			
Total	68.0	68.1	70.8
Black	72.3	67.6	73.0
White/other	67.6	68.5	71.0
Hispanic	64.1	64.9	66.6
Male			
Total	88.2	86.8	85.3
Black	83.3	79.2	78.2
White/other	88.8	88.0	86.0
Hispanic	90.4	88.1	89.4

Source: Authors' tabulations of Current Population Survey March supplement data.
Note: Black and white/other categories do not include Hispanics.

It is, of course, the women who are more likely to have access to welfare and to be most affected by the policy changes of the 1990s. In contrast, the less skilled men actually show flat or declining labor force participation over the Clinton years, a particularly striking result given the strong labor market boom of this time period. These strong increases among women versus men in labor market involvement are at least consistent with the idea that the welfare policy changes had a strong effect on labor force involvement among women. The ongoing declines in male labor force participation, even in the strong economy of the 1990s, is often attributed to increases in disability benefits and workers compensation claims.[42]

---

42. See Ellwood (2001) for a summary.

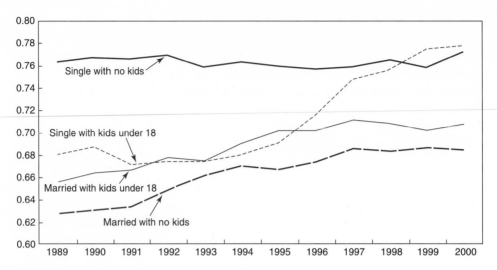

Figure 11.3
Labor Force Participation Rates for Women by Marital Status and Children (Ages 20–65). (*Source:* Tabulations of March Current Population Survey data.)

Further evidence that these labor force changes are closely correlated with policy changes is visible in Figure 11.3, which plots labor force participation among women by marital status and children over the 1990s. While married women show moderate increases in labor force participation (continuing a decades-long trend), the largest increases are among single mothers with children under age 18. This group experienced a 10-point increase in labor force participation between 1993 and 2000. Furthermore, this effect really takes off in 1995, just as the debate about welfare reform heats up and a majority of states are implementing waivers to move more welfare recipients into work. The changes are even larger among single mothers with children under age 6.[43]

Focusing on actual welfare recipients, the data also show dramatic changes in behavior. For instance, one can look at the share of women who are actively working while also receiving welfare payments. This number rose from 7 percent to 33 percent between 1992 and 1999.[44] A variety of studies follow welfare leavers over time in specific states, and these studies indicate that a clear majority of these women are working at some future date.[45] For instance, using the National Survey of America's Families, Loprest (2001) finds that 71 percent of former TANF recipients were employed in 1999.

---

43. For more discussion of these changes, see Blank and Schmidt (2001).
44. U.S. Department of Health and Human Services (2000).
45. Brauner and Loprest (1999).

11.2.2.1 Was Policy Change Responsible for the Increases in Employment?

The research that we have cited provides circumstantial evidence that policy changes were important to increases in employment among single women. As noted earlier, however, there were at least three things going on in the mid-1990s. The welfare reforms occurred at about the same time the economy started to expand strongly. And in these same years there were expansions in the minimum wage and in the EITC. All these changes pushed in the same direction, increasing the returns to work at the same time that programmatic changes encouraged women to leave public assistance and enter the labor market.

• Unlike the literature on caseload effects, there is near unanimity in the current literature that the combination of the expanded EITC and other work supports and various welfare reforms dramatically increased work by single parents, though debate remains about the relative contribution of each component.

A wide range of researchers, including Eissa and Liebman (1996), Meyer and Rosenbaum (1999), Moffitt (1999), Blank et al. (2000), Ellwood (2000), Schoeni and Blank (2000), and O'Neill and Hill (2001) all find that a sizable component of the growth in labor force participation can be linked to welfare reform, the EITC, or both.

A key methodological question is whose labor force participation should be examined. Most, including Meyer and Rosenbaum (1999), Ellwood (2000), and Moffitt (1999), have focused on single mothers with children. But, if policy also influences fertility and marriage choices, this group might be endogenously selected. Others such as Schoeni and Blank (2000) compare the impacts among high school dropouts (both mothers and nonmothers) with those who have education beyond high school, arguing that more educated women were less affected by the policy reforms, although they were affected by the strong economy, and hence might provide a reasonable comparison group to study the impact of policy. Regardless of the comparison group, the research on work involvement finds that both policy and economy seem to have mattered.

There is much more uncertainty about the relative contributions of the EITC changes versus the welfare reform changes. Meyer and Rosenbaum (1999) indicate that about half of the labor force increases among single mothers between 1984 and 1996 are due to the EITC expansions. Schoeni and Blank (2000), while showing that the implementation of waivers increased employment prior to the passage of welfare reform, find that the implementation of TANF-funded programs had much less impact on labor market participation. They indicate that the EITC and the strong economy played a critical role. And Ellwood (2000) suggests that the combination of the EITC and welfare reform had a very sizable impact, but argues that the independent effects cannot be accurately separated because many of the welfare reform changes were administrative in nature and interacted with the strong economy and the existence of EITC supports.

The impact of the minimum wage increases in the 1990s has been less studied, perhaps surprisingly given the controversy over minimum wage effects that erupted in the early 1990s. While minimum wage increases should raise the returns to work among low-skilled workers, if they also result in a loss of jobs then the net effect is uncertain. Of course, in the very strong and expanding labor market of the mid-1990s, this effect is more likely to show up as slower growth in jobs rather than a net loss. Bernstein and Schmitt (1998) investigate the minimum wage increases of 1996 and 1997 and conclude that there is little evidence of job loss and some real evidence of wage gains due to these policy changes. This conclusion is relatively consistent with the work of Neumark (1999), which suggests that the minimum wage changes in the mid-1990s affected only unskilled teen workers.

One additional strand of research investigates employer behavior rather than worker behavior, and focuses on the willingness of employers to hire less-skilled workers (and particularly ex–welfare recipients.) Holzer and Stoll (2001) analyze survey data from employers in four major cities in 1998 and 1999 and find that 3 percent of all job openings went to ex–welfare recipients. Of course, the tight labor market almost surely made employers more willing to hire and train lower-skilled workers in the late 1990s, an effect which would have added to the employment opportunities of women leaving welfare.

• The striking declines in caseloads were clearly matched with striking increases in labor force participation among exactly the population likely to be most affected by welfare changes. The evidence suggests that policy changes, both in welfare and in wage support programs, played an important role in increasing the labor force involvement of less-skilled women and particularly single mothers.

There is far less literature on whether the higher marginal tax rates on second earners or the changing rewards and penalties for marriage influenced behavior. Dickert, Houser, and Scholz (1995), Eissa and Hoynes (1999), and Ellwood (2000) all suggest that the labor supply of low-skill married women may have been depressed slightly by the higher marginal tax rates created by EITC phaseouts. The findings on marriage are far more mixed, perhaps reflecting the fact that the social policy changes created marriage rewards for some and marriage penalties for others. Eissa and Hoynes (2000) report that marriage penalties created a small increase in female headship. Dickert-Conlin and Houser (1999) find that a rise in the EITC increases female headship for whites and reduces it

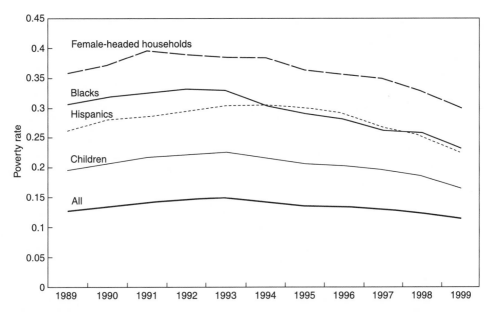

Figure 11.4
Selected Poverty Rates. (*Source:* Bureau of the Census [http://www.census.gov/].)

for blacks. Ellwood (2000) finds limited impacts, but argues that there may be longer term impacts.

• Overall, it appears that the social policy changes increased work by single mothers fairly dramatically. They may also have reduced work somewhat by wives married to low-earning males. Impacts on marriage are uncertain.

11.2.3 Poverty and Income

Declining caseloads and increased earnings need not result in increased income if the earnings are no greater than the welfare income they replace. One of the key debates over the late 1990s was whether welfare reform's primary goal should be to get women into the workforce, or whether it should reduce poverty. Ideally, one would like to do both. But policies that increase work and reduce poverty might be more costly than policies that only move women off welfare.[46]

By most measures, low-income families became better off during the 1990s. Figure 11.4 presents poverty rates for selected groups.

---

46. The 1996 legislation had four stated goals which notably did *not* include poverty reduction.

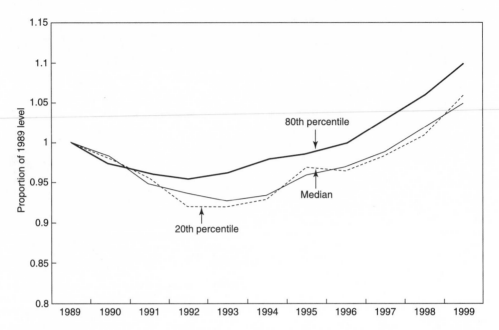

Figure 11.5
Growth in Real Family Income, 1989–99. (*Source:* Department of Commerce, Bureau of the Census.)

• While overall poverty declined slightly between 1993 and 1999, poverty rates among blacks and Hispanics, as well as among female-headed households (those most affected by welfare reform) declined more rapidly, and all three groups experienced their lowest recorded poverty levels in 1999. This trend suggests that, at least in the short run, the altered social policies did not cause deterioration in the economic situation of households as some had predicted.

Schoeni and Blank (2000) suggest that the welfare policy reforms of the mid-1990s (both waivers and TANF) reduced poverty rates by 2 percent among less-educated women.

Figure 11.5 shows the growth in real family income at the 20th percentile, the median, and the 80th percentile over the 1990s.

• While income at the median and below fell more rapidly between 1989 and 1992, all groups grew at about the same rate from 1993 to 1999. These increases in income at the bottom of the distribution are the most substantial since the economy-wide income growth of the 1960s.

Several analyses have focused on income changes among female-headed families with children at the bottom end of the income distribution, the group

Table 11.4
Impact of the Safety Net on Poverty Gaps per Person
(All Persons in Families with Children, 1999 Dollars)

	1993	1995	1997	1999
Poverty Gap				
Cash income	$2,737	$2,562	$2,562	$2,370
Plus social insurance[a]	$2,559	$2,394	$2,338	$2,185
Plus means-tested benefits[b]	$1,488	$1,419	$1,529	$1,547
Plus federal taxes (including EITC)	$1,447	$1,386	$1,514	$1,524
Percent Reduction in Poverty Gap due to:				
Social insurance	16.1	15.8	18.4	17.7
Means-tested benefits	43.8	44.7	37.2	34.0
Federal taxes	1.1	4.4	5.7	6.8

Source: Center on Budget and Policy Priorities (2001).

[a] Includes Social Security, disability, and worker's compensation.

[b] Includes cash benefits, food stamps, housing subsidies, and school lunch.

most likely to be affected by welfare reform. All these studies agree that the median single-parent family gained income over the 1990s, as a result of sharp increases in earnings that more than offset the decline in public assistance income (Primus et al., 1999; Haskins, 2001; Center on Budget and Policy Priorities, 2001). For instance, the Center on Budget and Policy Priorities (2001) reports that female-headed families in the middle of the income distribution saw their real income rise by 23 percent between 1993 and 1999, from $16,200 to almost $20,000.

There is also agreement that some groups of disadvantaged women lost income in the mid-1990s. The Center on Budget and Policy Priorities (2001) indicates that the bottom quintile (the bottom 20 percent) of income recipients among all female-headed families with children lost income from 1995 to 1999, although they gained sharply from 1993 to 1995. Somewhat contrasting evidence comes from data on consumer expenditures (versus income), which show increases in consumption spending throughout the 1990s among even very-low-income single mothers with children (Haskins, 2001).

Supporting evidence that some among the most disadvantaged may have become worse off in the 1999s is apparent by looking at poverty gaps, a better measure of economic well-being than a simple poverty count. Table 11.4 shows the poverty gap per person among all families with children below the poverty line in four years in the 1990s. The poverty gap based on cash income only falls by almost $400 between 1993 and 1999, reflecting the earnings gains in this population. But after social insurance and means-tested benefits are taken into account, the per person poverty gap goes up slightly, from $1,447 to $1,524. The bottom of Table 11.4 makes clear that the poverty-reducing effects of means-tested benefits declined as these benefits declined, and this decline more than offset the rise in earnings and the rise in benefits from the growth of the EITC.

· Our reading of the evidence suggests that there are clearly a group of the poorest single-mother families that have probably made only minimal gains over the 1990s and some at the very bottom who have lost ground, although the size of this group is unclear. This evidence is consistent with the belief that some more-disadvantaged women who are not work-ready have been sanctioned or time-limited off welfare and not been able to replace their welfare income with other income sources.

There are at least three other reasons to view all these income calculations with a bit of skepticism. First, studies of welfare leavers indicate that a substantial minority of leavers appear to be unemployed at some point after leaving welfare.[47] The best guess about what these women are doing is that they are surviving by relying more upon their boyfriends or upon other family members for income. Though such arrangements may work as a short-term strategy, they may fall apart over time and are unlikely to produce long-term economic stability for either the women or their children.

Second, the income reported in these calculations may overstate disposable income. For instance, these calculations do not take account of increased expenses associated with work. While we know that child care subsidies have expanded enormously with welfare reform, many women still receive no or low subsidies. If out-of-pocket work expenses—child care and transportation costs—were netted out of earnings, these families might have much less disposable income. Further, some of these calculations assume that women receive food stamps, EITC, or child support as well. To the extent that women do not receive these other types of support after they leave welfare, their incomes will be lower.[48]

Third, most available evidence focuses on income-related measures. Measures of hunger have changed little over the 1990s, despite the strong economic boom.[49] Changes in health outcomes, educational outcomes, criminal victim-

---

47. Brauner and Loprest (1999).
48. Not surprisingly, immigrants appear to be particularly affected by the loss of noncash benefits. This problem is likely to worsen as a rising share of immigrants will have arrived since August 1996 and be ineligible for any public assistance support, except at state discretion.
49. Survey data on food security are available since 1994. See www.usda.gov.

ization, or other measures of well-being among female-headed families have received little attention. Thus we are left without a full picture of how the welfare reforms have affected the overall well-being of those most affected by them.

The evidence seems to indicate clearly that the average woman who might have been affected by welfare reform has increased her cash income, largely by working more than in the past. Both increased earnings and expansions in the supports for working families have been important. Whether these changes have left her better off remains a debatable point, once increased expenses are taken into account. Certainly, the modest income gains over the late 1990s for mother-headed families at the bottom of the income distribution suggest that anything that disrupts their earnings (such as a future recession) could sharply increase poverty rates if public assistance is no longer readily available.

11.2.4 Child Support Enforcement

The bulk of the major child support changes were passed in 1996, and many of these required that states set up new systems and coordinate with larger national ones. Thus it is still relatively early to determine how much difference the child support changes adopted during the Clinton administration will ultimately make. And tragically, in our view, only a limited amount of scholarly work is being done to examine how the new child support measures are changing collections, and far more importantly, behavior and well-being.

On at least one dimension, it is possible to measure progress. Major changes in paternity establishment, notably the move toward in-hospital paternity establishment, were adopted in 1993.

• Largely because of the use of voluntary, in-hospital paternity establishments, between 1992 and 1999 paternity establishment tripled, rising from 512,000 to 1,546,000.[50] Given that there were roughly 1,300,000 out-of-wedlock births,[51] it follows that paternity was being established in a large share of new births and that states were beginning to "catch up" on establishing paternities for previous births.

Since paternity establishment is the vital first step in child support, these developments are very important. One other measure is widely cited:

---

50. Data for 1992 from Committee on Ways and Means (2000), Table 8–1, p. 467; for 1991, Office of Child Support Enforcement (2001), Table 2.
51. Ventura et al. (2000) report that there were 1.293 million out-of-wedlock births in 1998. Data for 1999 are not yet available.

• Since 1993 the amount of child support collected through the child support enforcement program rose in real dollars from roughly $9 billion to nearly $16 billion. This increase has occurred before most of the new system changes are fully implemented.

Still this is not the whole story. There is a sizable share of child support collections that do not go through the child support enforcement program at all. Some of these are handled directly through parents. Others go through the court system. Some of the apparent increase in collections may simply be a change in accounting, as payments that were formerly collected privately are now part of the public system.

Unfortunately there is no reliable measurement of all the child support payments made in the United States. What data we have are based on survey reports and are likely to be seriously underreported. One important reason is that child support collected for women while on welfare goes mostly to the state, with only a small pass-through going to the recipient in the form of a slightly higher welfare check. But the evidence suggests child support collections are rising.

Current Population Survey data show that reported child support grew by roughly 30 percent between 1992 and 1999, rising from $10.7 billion to $13.5 billion. The fraction of never-married mothers who are not on welfare and who reported getting any child support grew from 0.13 to 0.23.[52]

Sorenson and Halpern (1999) point out that one of the particular challenges for the child support system is that it is faced with an ever-growing share of cases among never-married mothers, for whom collections are much harder to achieve. As a result, the fraction of all mothers getting child support has been relatively flat, growing from 0.28 to 0.30 over this period. It is too soon to tell whether the fairly radical changes in child support will really change the rate and level of collections. There are some promising signs, but the current fractions getting child support remain low.

11.2.5   Urban Poor Neighborhoods

As discussed earlier, the Clinton administration explicitly focused on poor urban neighborhoods in a variety of their initiatives. The 1990s were generally good years for the cities. The 2000 census indicates that population rose strongly in 8

---

52. These are authors' tabulations of March CPS data. Note that in looking at the fraction of never-married mothers getting child support we looked only at those not on welfare who are more likely to know if child support was being collected. If we look at all never-married mothers, the share reporting child support grew from 0.14 to 0.20.

of the 10 largest cities in the country between 1990 and 2000.[53] Of course, much of this growth was due to the economic expansion of that decade.

Changes in the well-being of low-income populations within these cities over the 1990s are largely still unknown. The 2000 census will ultimately allow us to look at whether population in neighborhoods of concentrated poverty—the so-called underclass neighborhoods—increased or decreased over the 1990s, but these data are not yet available. Indeed, census data on overall poverty rates and income levels within cities are not yet available.

Until we have the 2000 census data, the best we can do is look to see how well cities fared relative to the country as a whole. Table 11.5 shows our own tabulation of poverty rates and median income during 1988–89, 1992–93, and 1998–99 for the 10 largest cities using the March CPS data and averaging across two years for a larger sample. Poverty declined in all of these cities between 1992–93 and 1998–99, but it is up in four of the cities between 1988–89 and 1998–99, and it changes very little in three others. The last column of Table 11.5 shows poverty rates excluding immigrants who arrived since 1993. In several of the southwestern cities the improvement in poverty is slightly greater if the effect of immigration is removed.

• There was a great deal of heterogeneity in poverty changes across cities. Between 1992–93 and 1998–99 poverty fell in all but one city among the 10 largest cities. But in some cities the falls were sizable; in others they were minor. And to our surprise, poverty rose in four of the cities between 1988–89 and 1998–99, and changed very little in three others, in spite of the fact that national poverty rates fell significantly over the last decade, particularly for blacks.

Median income changes mirror poverty changes. While median incomes rose in almost all cities during the economic boom of the 1990s, they fell in half of these cities when compared with 1988–89.

• Like poverty, median income changes are quite diverse across cities. Some cities experience income declines, even in the midst of the national economic boom; other cities show strong income gains.

An alternative way to evaluate well-being among low-income populations is to look at how their housing conditions changed. As discussed previously, an ongoing thrust of reform during the Clinton administration was to provide funds for low-income housing construction and rehabilitation, or to improve the delivery of housing assistance. Because housing is often the largest budget item for low-income families, changes in housing prices can have major effects

---

53. The exceptions are Philadelphia and Detroit.

Table 11.5
Poverty Rate and Median Income for the Ten Largest Central Cities

	1988–89	1992–93	1998–99	1998–99 (Excluding Post-1993 Immigrants)
Poverty Rate (Percent)				
New York	20.8	25.6	21.7	21.5
Los Angeles	18.9	25.0	22.7	21.6
Chicago	25.9	27.5	16.2	15.9
Houston	20.6	21.5	19.6	18.5
Philadelphia	18.3	26.1	27.2	26.5
San Diego	12.2	20.1	12.0	11.3
Dallas	17.5	25.6	15.8	14.9
Phoenix	12.3	14.7	14.2	13.4
Detroit	29.0	38.3	28.2	28.0
San Antonio	29.4	32.2	18.0	17.8
Median Income (Dollars)				
New York	34,756	27,551	32,093	32,867
Los Angeles	33,236	29,134	29,797	31,530
Chicago	30,287	26,604	37,300	37,606
Houston	29,699	30,481	33,291	34,291
Philadelphia	32,563	27,315	26,930	27,513
San Diego	42,531	35,614	40,039	40,008
Dallas	29,933	24,324	36,441	38,362
Phoenix	42,004	34,684	37,247	38,575
Detroit	26,517	20,338	24,699	25,582
San Antonio	20,568	21,030	34,765	35,274

Source: Authors' tabulations of Current Population Survey March supplement data. All estimates are calculated from two-year averages.

on housing choices. Table 11.6 presents a few key indicators of housing quality, from the 1991 and 1999 American Housing Survey, which is conducted in major urban areas in selected years.

• Measures of physical housing conditions all improve over the 1990s, continuing a long-term trend. There is less crowding and fewer people living in houses with structural problems by 1999 versus 1991.

• Housing rent burdens present a more ambiguous picture. While the share of families paying 30–49 percent of their income on housing declined somewhat, the share of families paying over 50 percent of their current income on housing

Table 11.6
Housing Indicators

Percent of All Occupied Units with	1991	1999
High Rent Burden		
Housing costs 30–49% of current income	16.8	15.5
Housing costs over 50% of current income	12.3	14.2
Crowding		
1.01 to 1.50 persons per room	2.2	2.1
1.51 or more persons per room	0.6	0.4
Physical Structure Problems		
Moderate physical problems	4.9	4.7
Severe physical problems	3.1	2.0

Source: U.S. Bureau of the Census, American Housing Survey.

Table 11.7
Homeownership Rates by Race and Ethnicity

	1989	1993	1999
Total	64.0	64.1	66.7
White Non-Hispanic	69.3	70.2	73.0
Black Non-Hispanic	42.1	42.0	46.1
Hispanic	41.6	39.4	45.2

Source: U.S. Bureau of the Census tabulations from March Current Population Survey.

went up by two percentage points. While low-income families typically benefit from earnings and employment gains during an expansion, these benefits may be offset by increases in housing costs that also occur in an expansion. The incomes of the very poorest families many not be keeping up with the rise in housing prices.

Several initiatives, including the CDFI Fund, were focused on encouraging homeownership through affordable mortgages. Many community-based groups used this program to develop low-income housing and encourage homeownership, and homeownership did rise in these years. Table 11.7 shows homeownership rates by race and ethnicity in 1989 (the previous economic peak), 1993, and 1999.

• Homeownership rises dramatically between 1993 and 1999, particularly among Hispanic and black households (and is at an all-time high for these groups by the end of the 1990s).

We know of no research that tries to untangle whether these changes in housing quality or homeownership in the 1990s are due to policy changes or to overall economic expansion. To the extent that the Clinton administration wanted to improve housing quality and homeownership, there certainly appeared to be ongoing gains on these fronts over the 1990s.

The 1990s brought a wide variety of changes in public housing and housing assistance, as well, most of which have not been seriously evaluated. Efforts to "clean up" public housing by reducing crime and drug dealing were ineffective in many cases.[54] As discussed earlier, partly out of frustration with the ineffectiveness of these efforts, a number of communities explicitly started to remove high-rise public housing units, replacing them with either low-rise scattered-site units or with Section 8 vouchers. The impact of these changes deserves evaluation.

Overall, we know much less about the changes in American cities as a result of the policies implemented in the 1990s than we do about the effects of welfare reform, in part because much of our detailed city-specific knowledge must come from census data that are not yet available. Researchers have focused less on the housing and neighborhood issues than they have on the welfare and employment issues. The currently available evidence suggests that life in most big cities improved in the 1990s—crime rates came down, poverty came down, and income went up. But there are worrisome signs that poverty often did not come down much and that rent burdens were rising for some families. A more nuanced evaluation that looks at how specific urban populations were faring and that measures the effects of specific policies is still to be done.

11.3 What Was the Clinton Legacy?

The Clinton years were a period of remarkable social change. Revolutionary changes in social policy dramatically increased support for low-income working families, while families where no adults were employed generally could get cash aid only on a short-term basis (and they were often required to perform some work-related activities to continue to receive it). The strong economy created the strongest employment opportunities since the 1960s.

· The result was a transformation of behavior among low-income single mothers. They left welfare (or avoided entering welfare) in much larger numbers than anyone expected, and they entered the labor market in greater numbers

---

54. Popkin et al. (2000) describe these efforts in Chicago, as well as their ultimate failure.

than expected. The result was a substantial increase in their earnings, which was reinforced through expanded work-related supports such as the EITC. Their overall disposable income grew less than their earnings, in part because they lost public assistance income and in part because work expenses such as child care ate into their dollars.

But this major transformation off welfare and into work did not produce increases in poverty, and in fact, most of these families appear to be doing at least as well as or a little better than before (based on cash income measures). As we will discuss, it remains to be seen whether this trend will continue in a slower-growth economy.

• These changes transformed the political discussion about welfare and the programmatic organization of public assistance. Devolution to the states has given state governors much greater involvement in program design and oversight. The perceived success of work-oriented programs has led to political support for welfare-to-work programs and for welfare reform among a broad spectrum of political leaders.

Five years after welfare reform was passed, many people are invested in making it succeed; criticisms come primarily from grassroots and community advocacy organizations that often have difficulty making their voices heard in the policy process. Sharp criticism of welfare mothers—so-called welfare bashing—has receded as well, as more recipients combine work and income. Public support for the current work-oriented welfare programs appears to be relatively strong. Of course, the extent to which this translates into a long-term legacy for the Clinton administration depends not just upon recent history, but upon the long-term effects of these changes.

• The Clinton-era policies are extremely well suited to a strong economy. Public assistance changed its focus from supporting nonworkers to supporting workers. Block grant funding for TANF does not fall even as the economy improves. And recent immigrants are readily employed in good times.

But there remain a variety of key questions and concerns about these social changes that will only be answered over time.

• The first question involves what to do with people who are not very successful in their efforts to find and retain work, even in a strong economy.

Most state welfare-to-work programs are still designed to serve women who are relatively work-ready. Programs are not designed for the hard-to-serve families, in which the adults face multiple barriers to work.[55] Serving populations with learning disabilities, substance abuse problems, or family legal or health problems, or families in situations of domestic violence is not only difficult but almost surely more expensive. It may be more expensive to help women in these circumstances become work-ready than it is to simply continue to pay them a monthly welfare check. States are increasingly facing the question of how to serve these more difficult (and needy) populations in their welfare-to-work efforts.

• A second issue involves ensuring that supports for working families actually reach them. Unexplained declines in food stamp and Medicaid usage are troublesome, though there is evidence that things may be improving.

Ultimately we believe the nation may need to dramatically simplify these programs. They still are cloaked in the administrative and rhetorical framework of welfare-based supports, with their intensive and intrusive application process and their complex regulations.

• Most important is the question of how many of the behavioral changes observed in the 1990s are strongly tied to the unusually strong labor market of that decade. Any serious future recession could cause major disruptions for the newly designed system of public assistance.

The changes have converted public support from a countercyclical program—helping people the most when they are unemployed—to a procyclical one. In the next recession, as people lose their jobs, they will also be faced with losing their worker supports. The problems will be particularly acute for recent legal immigrants who are not citizens, since they are no longer eligible for most TANF and food stamp benefits regardless of their income and employment situation.

If private-sector jobs for less-skilled workers become much less available in a future recession, it is simply unclear how the newly unemployed families will cope with this situation or what sort of public assistance will be available to them. Indeed, in the presence of time limits, sanctions, and immigrant prohibitions, it is not even clear how many families would be eligible for cash public assistance. The human cost of a serious downturn could therefore be much larger than in the past.

• Of course, much will depend on how states react. The TANF fixed block grant funding pushes most of the residual responsibility for changes in the demand

---

55. For instance, see the research by Danziger et al. (2000) that describes these barriers.

for public assistance onto the states. Federal dollars will not increase in the next recession, so any increase in the need for public assistance will fall on state coffers. Since most states operate under balanced budget requirements, an economic slowdown could bring substantial cuts in welfare support, even as more individuals lose their jobs and apply for public assistance.

It is not at all clear how the currently designed system operates in a slower-growth economy with fewer jobs. States have so far had the luxury of operating their programs only in a time of strong economic expansion. In different economic circumstances, state programs could face substantial economic and political strains that might lead to major programmatic changes at both the state and the federal level.

In short, while the public assistance system has been significantly transformed, the new system is still being tested and strained. The social policy changes of the 1990s were enacted in a charmed world of growing employment and earnings opportunities. If we return to more normal economic times—and particularly if wage and employment opportunities for less-skilled workers shrink in the years ahead—it remains unclear what the final outcome of the revolutions of the Clinton years is likely to be. Since much of the legacy is one of devolution, one must look to how the states will react when things get tough.

The Clinton years could be a springboard for further policy change. If economic pressures make it difficult for states to continue their work-support efforts, they may pursue changes that allow them to build a more recession-proof but still work-oriented system. For instance, states may run more extensive public-sector job programs for workers unable to find private-sector jobs; they may demand health care reforms that make it easier to provide low-wage workers with health insurance; they may work on expanding unemployment insurance coverage, so that workers who lose their jobs have an alternative to public assistance. Should some of these things occur, then the changes of the 1990s will appear to be the beginning of a series of social policy changes that may be much more substantial than currently enacted. Of course, some states may use tight budgets and hard economic times to enforce time limits and sanctions even more strongly and to limit public assistance to fewer families.

• In the short run, Clinton's legacy is one of radical change in social policy. Programs have devolved to a different level of government, their funding structure has been dramatically changed, and there has been a massive increase in the incentives to work and a concomitant decrease in the availability of cash support. This legacy has been strongly intertwined with and dependent upon the strength of the economy.

It is currently impossible to fully understand how many of the behavioral and program changes of the 1990s are fundamentally reliant upon the expanding economy, and how much will change when the economic environment changes. What will happen when the next serious recession comes is still unknown.

• The long-term legacy of the Clinton-era reforms will depend upon how these newly configured programs evolve over time, including how well they operate in a weak economy as well as a strong. It will also depend on what happens to the nature of the poor and poverty. If poverty becomes even more identified with single parents and inner city residents, there may be less sympathy for addressing future poverty-related issues. But if the policy changes transform the nature of poverty, the Clinton legacy may be a more hopeful, if somewhat more insecure, future.

Clinton and the Republican Congress really did end "welfare as we know it." In the near term, more people are working, and fewer people are poor. A judgment as to whether the policy reforms of the 1990s fundamentally moved the nation closer to ending poverty as we know it awaits the more measured perspective of history.

References

Bane, Mary Jo, and David T. Ellwood. 1994. *Welfare Realities: From Rhetoric to Reform*. Cambridge, MA: Harvard University Press.

Bell, Stephen H. 2001. "Why Are Welfare Caseloads Falling?" Assessing the New Federalism, Discussion Paper No. 01–02, March. Washington, DC: Urban Institute.

Bernstein, Jared, and John Schmitt. 1998. "Making Work Pay: The Impact of the 1996–97 Minimum Wage Increase." Washington, DC: Economic Policy Institute.

Blank, Rebecca M. 2001a. "Evaluating U.S. Welfare Reform." Unpublished manuscript, University of Michigan.

———. 2001b. "What Causes Public Assistance Caseloads to Grow?" *Journal of Human Resources*, 36, no. 1 (Winter): 85–118.

Blank, Rebecca, David Card, and Philip Robbins. 2000. "Financial Incentives for Increasing Work and Income Among Low-Income Families." In *Finding Jobs: Work and Welfare Reform*, ed. Rebecca Blank and David Card. New York: Russell Sage.

Blank, Rebecca M., and Lucie Schmidt. 2001. "Work, Wages and Welfare." In *The New World of Welfare*, ed. Rebecca M. Blank and Ron Haskins. Washington, DC: Brookings Institution.

Brauner, Sarah, and Pamela Loprest. 1999. "Where Are They Now? What States' Studies of People Who Left Welfare Tell Us." Assessing the New Federalism Project, Series A, No. A–32. Washington, DC: Urban Institute.

Burtless, Gary T. 1997. "Welfare Recipients' Job Skills and Employment Prospects." *The Future of Children*, 7, no. 1 (Spring): 39–51.

Center on Budget and Policy Priorities. 2001. *Poverty and Income Trends, 1999.* Washington, DC: CBPP.

Clinton, Bill. 1991. "The New Covenant: Responsibility and Rebuilding the American Community." Remarks at Georgetown University, October 23.

————. 1992. "Economic Policy Address." Economic Club of Detroit, August 21.

————. 1996. "Veto Message on H.R. 4 (Welfare Reform)." White House, January 9.

Committee on Ways and Means. 1992. *1992 Green Book: Background Material and Data on Programs under the Jurisdiction of the Committee on Ways and Means.* Washington, DC: U.S. Government Printing Office.

————. 1996. *1996 Green Book: Background Material and Data on Programs under the Jurisdiction of the Committee on Ways and Means.* Washington, DC: U.S. Government Printing Office.

————. 1998. *1998 Green Book: Background Material and Data on Programs under the Jurisdiction of the Committee on Ways and Means.* Washington, DC: U.S. Government Printing Office.

————. 2000. *2000 Green Book: Background Material and Data on Programs under the Jurisdiction of the Committee on Ways and Means.* Washington, DC: U.S. Government Printing Office.

Congressional Budget Office. 1998. "Policy Changes Affecting Mandatory Spending for Low-Income Families Not Receiving Cash Welfare." Washington, DC: U.S. Congress, September.

Council of Economic Advisers. 1997. "Technical Report: Explaining the Decline in Welfare Receipt, 1993–1996." Washington, DC: Executive Office of the President, April.

————. 1999. "Economic Expansion, Welfare Reform, and the Decline in Welfare Caseloads: An Update." Technical Report. Washington, DC: Executive Office of the President, September.

Danziger, Sandra, Mary Corcoran, Sheldon Danziger, Colleen Heflin, Ariel Kalil, Judith Levine, Daniel Rosen, Kristin Seefeldt, Kristine Siefert, and Richard Tolman. 2000. "Barriers to Employment of Welfare Recipients." In *Prosperity for All? Economic Boom and African Americans,* ed. Robert Cherry and William M. Rodgers III. New York: Russell Sage.

Department of Health and Human Services. 2000. "Fact Sheet: Child Support Enforcement: A Clinton/Gore Priority." ACF Press Office. http://www.acf.dhhs.gov/news/fschsupt.htm. Accessed May 7, 2001.

Dickert, Stacy, Scott Houser, and John Karl Scholz. 1995. "The Earned Income Tax Credit and Transfer Programs: A Study of Labor Market and Program Participation." In *Tax Policy and the Economy,* ed. James M. Poterba, 9, 1–50. Cambridge, MA: MIT Press and National Bureau of Economic Research.

Dickert-Conlin, Stacy, and Scott Houser. 1999. "EITC, AFDC and the Female Headship Decision." Mimeo, Syracuse University.

Edelman, Peter. 1997. "The Worst Thing Bill Clinton Has Done." *The Atlantic,* March. 43–58.

Eissa, Nada, and Hilary Hoynes. 1999. "The Earned Income Tax Credit and the Labor Supply of Married Couples." Mimeo, University of California at Berkeley.

————. 2000. "Good News for Low-Income Families? Tax-Transfer Schemes and Marriage." Mimeo, University of California at Berkeley.

Eissa, Nada, and Jeffrey B. Liebman. 1996. "Labor Supply Response to the Earned Income Tax Credit." *Quarterly Journal of Economics,* 112, no. 2 (May): 605–637.

Ellwood, David T. 1996. "Welfare Reform as I Knew It." *The American Prospect*, 26 (May–June).

———. 2000. "The Impact of the Earned Income Tax Credit and Social Policy Reforms On Work, Marriage, and Living Arrangements." *National Tax Journal*, 53, no. 4 (part 2) (December): 1063–1106.

———. 2001. "The Sputtering Labor Force of the 21st Century: Can Social Policy Help?" NBER Working Paper No. W8321. Cambridge, MA: National Bureau of Economic Research.

Else, John F., and Janice Gallagher. 2000. "An Overview of the Microenterprise Field in the U.S." International Labor Organization. http://www.ilo.org/public/english/employment/finance/reports/us1.htm. Accessed May 10, 2001.

Figlio, David N., and James P. Ziliak. 1999. "Welfare Reform, the Business Cycle, and the Decline in AFDC Caseloads." In *Economic Conditions and Welfare Reform*, ed. Sheldon H. Danziger. Kalamazoo, MI: W. E. Upjohn Institute for Employment Research.

Greenstein, Robert, and Jocelyn Guyer. 2001. "Supporting Work Through Medicaid and Food Stamps." In *The New World of Welfare*, ed. Rebecca M. Blank and Ron Haskins. Washington, DC: Brookings Institution.

Grogger, Jeff. 2000. "Time Limits and Welfare Use." National Bureau of Economic Research Working Paper No. 7709. Cambridge, MA: National Bureau of Economic Research.

Haskins, Ron. 2001. "The Second Most Important Issue: Effects of Welfare Reform on Family Income and Poverty." In *The New World of Welfare*, ed. Rebecca M. Blank and Ron Haskins. Washington, DC: Brookings Institution.

Holzer, Harry J., and Michael A. Stoll. 2001. "Employers and Welfare Recipients: The Effects of Welfare Reform in the Workplace." San Francisco: Public Policy Institute of California, January.

Kingsley, G. Thomas. 1997. "Federal Housing Assistance and Welfare Reform: Uncharted Territory." New Federalism: Issues and Options for States Series No. A–19. Washington, DC: Urban Institute.

Klerman, Jacob, and Steven Haider. 2000. "A Stock-Flow Analysis of the Welfare Caseload: Insights from California Economic Conditions." Mimeo, Rand.

Loprest, Pamela. 2001. "How Are Families That Left Welfare Doing? A Comparison of Early and Recent Welfare Leavers." New Federalism, Series B No. B–36. Washington, DC: Urban Institute.

Meyer, Bruce D., and Dan T. Rosenbaum. 1999. "Welfare, the Earned Income Tax Credit, and the Labor Supply of Single Mothers." NBER Working Paper No. W7363. Cambridge, MA: National Bureau of Economic Research.

Moffitt, Robert A. 1999. "The Effects of Pre-PRWORA Waivers on Welfare Caseloads and Female Earnings, Income, and Labor Force Behavior." In *Economic Conditions and Welfare Reform*, ed. Sheldon H. Danziger. Kalamazoo, MI: W. E. Upjohn Institute for Employment Research.

Muth, Richard E. 1973. "Capital and Current Expenditures in the Production of Housing." In *Government Expenditures and Land Values*, ed. C. L. Harriss, 65–78. Madison: University of Wisconsin Press.

Neumark, David. 1999. "The Employment Effects of Recent Minimum Wage Increases: Evidence from a Pre-Specified Research Design." NBER Working Paper No. W7171. Cambridge, MA: National Bureau of Economic Research.

Office of Child Support Enforcement. 2001. "Child Support Enforcement FY99 Preliminary Data Report." Administration for Children and Families, Department of Health and Human Services. http://www.acf.dhhs.gov/programs/cse/rpt/99report/index.html. Accessed May 31, 2001.

Office of the Press Secretary. 1999. "The Clinton-Gore Administration's Record of Strengthening Families and Communities." White House. http://clinton6.nara.gov/1999/11/1999-11-04-fact-sheet-on-strengthening-families-and-communities.html. Accessed May 7, 2001.

————. 2000. "Fact Sheet: President Clinton's New Market Initiative: Revitalizing America's Underserved Communities." White House. Accessed May 10, 2000.

O'Neill, June, and Anne M. Hill. 2001. "Gaining Ground? Measuring the Impact of Welfare Reform on Welfare and Work." Civic Report No. 17, Center for Civic Innovation. New York: Manhattan Institute, July.

Papke, Leslie. 1993. "What Do We Know about Enterprise Zones?" *Tax Policy and the Economy*, 7:37–72.

Peterson, Paul. 1995. "State Response to Welfare Reform: A Race to the Bottom?" In *Welfare Reform: An Analysis of the Issues*, ed. Isabel Sawhill. Washington, DC: Urban Institute Press.

Popkin, Susan J., Victoria E. Gwiasda, Lynn M. Olson, Dennis P. Rosenbaum, and Larry Buron. 2000. *The Hidden War: Crime and the Tragedy of Public Housing in Chicago*. New Brunswick, NJ: Rutgers University Press.

Primus, Wendell, Lynette Rawlings, Kathy Larin, and Kathryn Porter. 1999. "The Initial Impacts of Welfare Reform on the Incomes of Single-Mother Families." Washington, DC: Center on Budget and Policy Priorities.

Quigley, John M. 2000. "A Decent Home: Housing Policy in Perspective." *Brookings-Wharton Papers on Urban Affairs*, pp. 53–88.

Schoeni, Robert F., and Rebecca M. Blank. 2000. "What Has Welfare Reform Accomplished? Impacts on Welfare Participation, Employment, Income, Poverty, and Family Structure." NBER Working Paper No. W7627. Cambridge, MA: National Bureau of Economic Research.

Sorenson, Elaine. 1995. "Noncustodial Fathers: Can They Afford to Pay More Child Support?" Washington, DC: Urban Institute.

Sorenson, Elaine, and Ariel Halpern. 1999. "Child Support Enforcement: How Well Is it Doing?" Assessing the New Federalism, Discussion Paper No. 99–11. Washington, DC: Urban Institute.

U.S. Department of Health and Human Services. 2000. "Temporary Assistance to Needy Families: Third Annual Report to Congress." Washington, DC: Department of Health and Human Services, August.

U.S. Department of Housing and Urban Development. 2000. "State of the Cities 2000: Megaforces Shaping the Future of the Nation's Cities." June.

Ventura, Stephanie J., Joyce A. Martin, Sally C. Curtin, T. J. Mathews, and Melissa M. Park. 2000. "Births: Final Data for 1998." National Vital Statistics Report, No. 28. Hyattsville, MD: National Center for Health Statistics, March.

Vidal, Avis C. 1995. "Reintegrating Disadvantaged Communities into the Fabric of Urban Life: The Role of Community Development." *Housing Policy Debate*, 6, no. 1: 169–224.

Wallace, Geoffrey, and Rebecca M. Blank. 1999. "What Goes Up Must Come Down? Explaining Recent Changes in Public Assistance Caseloads." In *Economic Conditions and Welfare Reform*, ed. Sheldon H. Danziger. Kalamazoo, MI: W. E. Upjohn Institute for Employment Research.

Weaver, R. Kent. 2000. *Ending Welfare as We Know It*. Washington, DC: Brookings Institution.

Weaver, R. L., and R. G. Williams. 1989. "Problems with URESA: Interstate Child Support Enforcement Isn't Working but Could." Mimeo, American Bar Association Third National Child Support Conference.

Wolf, Michael Allan. 1990. "Enterprise Zones: A Decade of Diversity." *Economic Development Quarterly*, 4(1): 3–14.

Ziliak, James P., David N. Figlio, Elizabeth E. Davis, and Laura, S. Connolly. 2000. "Accounting for the Decline in AFDC Caseloads: Welfare Reform or the Economy?" *Journal of Human Resources*, 35, no. 3 (Summer): 570–586.

Comments

Robert Greenstein

If one is talking about the Clinton administration's legacy with regard to poverty, one should start by noting, as other chapters in this volume do, that administration policies contributed to economic growth that produced a 4 percent unemployment rate and real wage growth for low-income workers in the latter part of the 1990s. These economic improvements had a significant effect in reducing poverty.

The Blank/Ellwood chapter, however, is not about that aspect of the administration's record; it focuses on the administration's social program legacy. As the chapter notes, this is a complex legacy with numerous elements. Legislatively, two areas stand out as the most significant, although many other pieces of legislation also are important. The two most significant pieces of legislation were the EITC expansion contained in the 1993 deficit-reduction law and the 1996 welfare law.

The EITC expansion enacted in 1993 was substantial. It represented one of the largest expansions in a low-income program of the last quarter century. The administration established a goal that the combination of full-time earnings at the minimum wage plus the EITC and food stamps should lift a family of four to the poverty line. After the minimum wage was raised in 1996, this goal was achieved, although we are now somewhat short of it as a result of the erosion of the minimum wage to inflation in the past few years. Of particular note, the EITC now lifts more children out of poverty than any other program or category of programs.

Furthermore, there is more to the administration's strong EITC record than the 1993 expansion. The administration made intensive efforts in the mid-1990s to combat large reductions in the EITC that both the Senate and the House passed in 1995. In substantial part as a result of the administration's resistance, those reductions did not become law.

I am going to focus in these comments, however, not on the EITC, but on issues related to the welfare law. I do so not because that law should be the sole focus in evaluating the administration's legacy—it should not be—but because important issues related to the welfare law often get insufficient attention. As a result of the focus here on some of the less attractive aspects of the welfare law, those comments may give an impression that I hold a less sanguine view of the administration's overall legacy in this area than I do.

The Welfare Law and Poverty

The record-low poverty rates of the late 1990s are often cited as evidence that the welfare law has been highly successfully in reducing poverty. However, given the growth in the economy and the achievement of a 4 percent unemployment rate—the lowest unemployment rate in more than 30 years—as well as the fact that we had much smaller social programs when the unemployment rate was last that low, one would expect there would have been record-low poverty rates at the end of the 1990s. It is difficult to ascertain what effect the welfare law had on these record-low rates. The welfare law clearly increased employment among single-mother families and increased earnings among those families. EITC expansions and the economic boom, however, also contributed to employment gains, and it is difficult to disentangle the effects.

Furthermore, the welfare law resulted in larger-than-expected reductions in means-tested benefits. While the increases in earnings reduced poverty, the reductions in benefits increased poverty. Here, also, sorting out the effects is difficult.

To add to the complexity of this issue, when you look at poverty rates, you see dramatic declines in the rates for key groups in the late 1990s, but those doesn't tell you anything about the depth of poverty. To understand more about the depth of poverty, you have to look at the "poverty gap," which measures the aggregate amount by which the incomes of the poor fall below the poverty line. One would expect that if poverty rates declined dramatically, poverty gaps also would drop sharply. Yet that is not what happened in the later half of the 1990s.

As Table 11.8 shows, between 1993 and 1995 the poverty gap for families with children—as measured *before* taxes and government benefits are taken into account—declined by $12 billion. (These figures are in 1999 dollars.) After taxes and government benefits (including the EITC and in-kind benefits) are counted, the poverty gap fell by $7 billion between 1993 and 1995. Thus, while the increase in earnings among low-income households in this period resulted in some reduction in mean-tested benefits, the net reduction in the poverty gap still was large. But in the 1995–99 period a different pattern emerged. The poverty gap, as measured *before* taxes and government benefits, went down an im-

Table 11.8
Poverty Gap for Families with Children (in Billions of 1999 Dollars)

	1993	1995	1999	Dollar Change		Percent Change	
				1993–95	1995–99	1993–95	1995–99
Before taxes and government benefits	85.0	73.0	55.9	−12.0	−17.1	−14.1	−23.4
After taxes and government benefits	32.0	24.8	22.5	−7.2	−2.3	−22.5	−9.3

Table 11.9
Poverty Gap per Poor Child (After Taxes and Government Benefits, in 1999 Dollars)

1979	1984	1993	1995	1999
$1,479	$1,454	$1,501	$1,503	$1,640

pressive $17 billion, but it went down only $2 billion *after* taxes and government benefits are taken into account, a surprisingly small reduction given the robust economic growth in this period. In these years, most of the gain in earnings was offset by large reductions in government benefits. It is possible that in the absence of the welfare law, the poverty gap would have gone down more.

Indeed, it is possible that the welfare law caused the poverty *rate* to decline more than it otherwise would have, while simultaneously resulting in a smaller reduction in the poverty gap than otherwise would have occurred. This could be the case if more people went to work than otherwise would have, causing more people to rise above the poverty line, but those who stayed poor became poorer, on average, primarily as a result of the large reductions in means-tested benefits.

There is some evidence that this result may have been what occurred. If you look at the poverty gap per poor child, you find that the poverty gap per poor child remained fairly flat at about $1,500 per child (in 1999 dollars) over the 16-year period from 1979 to 1995. But the poverty gap per poor child increased 10 percent between 1995 and 1999 and reached its highest level on record in 1999, at $1,640 per child (see Table 11.9).

In addition, if you look at changes in the average disposable income of the poorest fifth of female-headed families with children, you find that the average income of this group increased between 1993 and 1995, but declined between 1995 and 1999 (see Table 11.10). In the 1995–99 period, as in the 1993–95 period, there were large increases in earnings among the bottom fifth of single-mother families. In the 1993–95 period, this increase in earnings, along with the increase

Table 11.10
Changes in Average Disposable Income of Poorest Fifth of Female-Headed Families with Children (in 1999 Dollars)

				Percent Change		Dollar Change	
	1993	1995	1999	1993–95	1995–99	1993–95	1995–99
Female-headed families with no other adults	7,714	8,532	7,835	10.6	−8.2	818	−697
Female-headed families with other adults (includes the other adults' income)	8,519	9,551	9,281	12.1	−2.8	1,032	−270

in EITC benefits, substantially outweighed the reductions in other benefits. By contrast, between 1995 and 1999 there were further increases in both earnings and the EITC (in part because the EITC expansions enacted in 1993 were still phasing in), but these gains were outweighed by large reductions in other government benefits.

Declines in Means-Tested Benefits

What factors contributed to the unusually large decline in means-tested benefits in the 1995–99 period? The role of the economy and the declines in welfare caseloads are well known. But several factors that often receive insufficient attention were important as well. For one thing, there was a dramatic reduction in food stamp receipt. As Figure 11.6 shows, between 1994 and 1999 the number of people receiving food stamps declined nearly twice as fast as the number of people who were poor. Some of this decline resulted from provisions of the welfare law that made certain categories of low-income individuals, such as most legal immigrants, ineligible for food stamps, but those provisions leave the bulk of the food stamp decline unexplained. The key factor appears to be a decline in food stamp participation rates. As Table 11.11 shows, some 74 percent of those eligible for food stamps received them in 1994. In 1999, the latest year for which we have these data, 57 percent did.

In recent congressional testimony, Ron Haskins notes that at the time the welfare law was enacted, the Congressional Budget Office forecast that food stamp expenditures would total $190 billion over the six years from fiscal year 1997 through fiscal year 2002, but that CBO now projects these expenditures will total $120 billion. Some of this $70 billion difference is the result of lower-than-expected unemployment and a stronger-than-expected economy, but a substantial portion of it cannot be explained by economic factors.

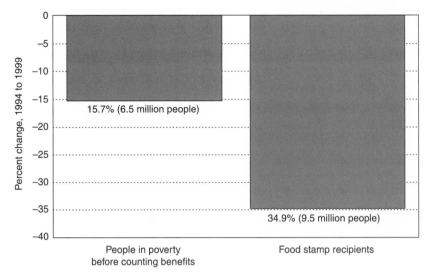

Figure 11.6
Poverty and Food Stamp Participation, Calendar Years 1994 to 1999. (*Sources:* Poverty statistics calculated using U.S. Census Bureau's Current Population Survey Food stamp participation decline calculated from food stamp administrative data.)

Table 11.11
Proportion of Eligible Individuals That Receive Food Stamps (Percent)

	All Individuals	Children under 18
1994	74.3	89.5
1999	57.4	67.7

Source: Trends in FSP Participation Rates: 1994 to 1999. Mathematica Policy Research, Inc. for USDA/FNS, October 2001.

Figure 11.7 illustrates this point. The top line shows CBO's estimate, made prior to enactment of the welfare law, of food stamp expenditures in fiscal years 1997 to 2000. The middle line shows the estimate CBO made at the time the welfare law was enacted of what expenditures would be in these years (taking into account the provisions of the welfare law), adjusted downward to reflect the differences between actual economic conditions in these years and those that CBO forecast at that time. The bottom line shows actual food stamp expenditures in the 1997–2000 period.

The bottom line in Figure 11.7 reflects the large reduction in food stamp participation rates. Many people who went off welfare ceased to receive food stamps despite remaining eligible for them. Of particular note, the participation rate declined significantly among working poor families with children.

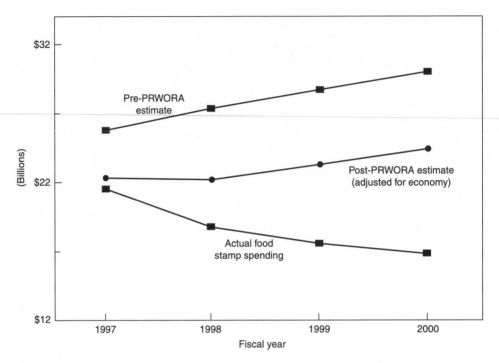

Figure 11.7
Estimated Versus Actual Food Stamp Expenditures. (*Source:* Congressional Budget Office, program information data.)

Here, unfortunately, the Clinton administration made a miscalculation with the best intentions. Following enactment of the welfare law, which included large food stamp benefit cuts—and almost included a food stamp block grant provision that the administration strenuously opposed—the administration concluded that one way to strengthen the food stamp program politically for the future was to become more aggressive in seeking reductions in food stamp error rates and to do so by intensifying threats that states would face fiscal penalties if they did not succeed in lowering their error rates significantly.

This intensified emphasis on precise payment accuracy in the food stamp program came at the same time that the food stamp caseload was shifting toward working families, with many families moving from welfare to work and the economy bringing more people into the workforce. Unfortunately, food stamp error rates are higher among working families than among welfare families, because the earnings of working-poor families tend to fluctuate while welfare payments generally remain flat from month to month. The increase in the proportion of the food stamp caseload consisting of working families thus

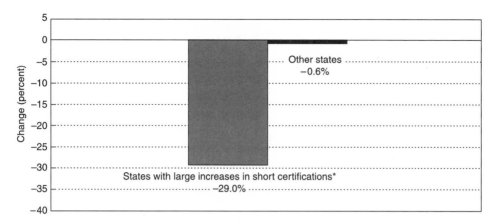

Figure 11.8

Change in Number of Families with Earnings and Children from 1994 to 1999 for States with Large Increases in Short Certifications*

*These states increased their use of certification periods between 1 and 3 months by 50 percentage points for families with children and earnings. Twelve states met this standard: Arizona, Maine, Missouri, North Carolina, Ohio, Oklahoma, Texas, Utah, Virginia, West Virginia, Wisconsin, and Wyoming.

exerted upward pressure on state error rates at the same time that the federal government was ratcheting up pressure on states to lower error rates. This induced many states to institute changes in the late 1990s that were designed to drive down errors among working families but had the effect of impeding access to the program by these families.

For example, a substantial number of states moved during the second Clinton term to require working families receiving food stamps to come back to the food stamp office every three months to be recertified. The states that did so experienced substantially larger reductions in food stamp participation among working families with children (and much larger reductions in food stamp participation rates) than states that did not institute such policies (see Figure 11.8). In the final 18 months of the Clinton term, the administration began to change course and to move to ease barriers to participation among low-income working families.

The administration moved much more quickly in the health insurance area to try to prevent the large reductions in the welfare rolls from causing reductions in Medicaid enrollment and increases in the ranks of the uninsured. In addition, the 1997 budget agreement established the Children's Health Insurance Program. A common view is that the result of these efforts was substantial progress in reducing the numbers of uninsured low-income children.

Table 11.12
Health Insurance Status of Children by Income Level

	Medicaid	Other Coverage	Uninsured
Poor Children (Family Income below 100% of Poverty)			
1995	62.1%	15.0%	22.9%
1998	54.9%	18.1%	26.9%
1999	55.6%	18.6%	25.8%
Near-Poor Children (Family Income Between 100% and 200% of Poverty)			
1995	25.5%	52.5%	22.0%
1998	24.6%	51.7%	23.7%
1999	27.4%	51.9%	20.6%

Source: Analysis of 1995–2000 Current Population Survey data.

Here, also, the data show the actual story to be more complicated. Table 11.12 disaggregates low-income children into poor children—those who are below the poverty line—and near-poor children, those between 100 percent and 200 percent of the poverty line. It shows that progress was made between 1995 and 1999 in reducing the proportion of *near-poor* children who are uninsured but that the proportion of *poor* children who are uninsured increased during this period (1999 is the latest year for which these data are available). Specifically, between 1995 and 1999, the percentage of poor children who were uninsured rose from 22.9 percent to 25.8 percent. Moreover, among *parents*, the percentage who are uninsured rose among poor and near-poor parents alike. The percentage of poor parents who are uninsured increased from 36.5 percent in 1995 to 41.4 percent in 1999 (see Table 11.13). Among both poor children and poor parents, the percentage with employer-based insurance increased, but by less than the percentage with Medicaid declined.

Last but not least, one must take note of the large changes in the safety net for legal immigrants. Some may mistakenly think that the welfare law initially made dramatic changes in the safety net for immigrants, but these changes were reversed in 1997. To be sure, the immigrant benefit restrictions were reversed to a substantial degree in 1997 for immigrants who entered the country before the welfare law was signed. These reductions were not reversed at all, however, for immigrants who entered the country after the date the welfare law was signed. (Also, many of the food stamp benefit restrictions for legal immigrants who entered the country before the welfare law was signed were not reversed and remain in effect.) This point is of major significance from a

Table 11.13
Health Insurance Status of Parents by Income Level

	Medicaid	Other Coverage	Uninsured
Poor Parents (Family Income below 100% of Poverty)			
1995	43.4%	20.2%	36.5%
1998	35.4%	24.9%	39.8%
1999	34.2%	24.7%	41.4%
Near-Poor Parents (Family Income Between 100% and 200% of Poverty)			
1995	12.8%	59.7%	27.5%
1998	10.6%	60.2%	29.2%
1999	10.6%	60.6%	28.8%

Source: Analysis of 1995–2000 Current Population Survey data.

legacy standpoint; with each passing year, a larger percentage of the immigrant population consists of people who entered the country after the welfare law was signed. (With each passing year, more of the immigrants who entered *before* the law was signed naturalize or die.) Over time, the welfare law's restrictions on legal immigrants will affect the vast majority of such immigrants.

As a result, the immigrant benefit restrictions will have increasingly large effects over time. The effects on children are likely to be quite substantial. One of every four poor children in the United States today is a child who lives in an immigrant family. These include both citizen children with immigrant parents (i.e., children born in the United States to immigrant parents) and children who themselves are immigrants.

Some who hear this statistic may respond that 80 percent of the children in immigrant families are citizen children and that these children did not lose eligibility for anything in the welfare law. That statement is true, but the welfare law, along with the 1996 immigration law, appears nevertheless to have had far-reaching effects in depressing participation in some means-tested benefit programs by these citizen children. These laws engendered confusion in immigrant communities and appear to have had chilling effects on participation in some means-tested programs by eligible members of immigrant families, including citizen children.

For example, USDA data show that in 1994 some 1.35 million citizen children with legal immigrant parents received food stamps. In 1998 only 350,000 such children did. The number of these children receiving food stamps fell by 1 million, or 74 percent, in these years (the 1998 data are the latest available).

Similarly, a Mathematica study found that the food stamp participation rate among citizen children living in households with a noncitizen member fell from 76 percent in 1994 to 38 percent in 1998.

A recent Urban Institute study contains other disturbing findings about immigrant children and families. The percentage of children in immigrant families who were uninsured was, by 1999, double the percentage of children in native families who were uninsured. The percentage of children without a regular source of health care was three times higher in immigrant families, while the percentage of children in poor or fair health was more than twice as high. The percentage of children living in overcrowded housing was four times as high among children in immigrant families. There were, of course, substantial disparities in these areas before the welfare law was enacted, but these gaps between children in immigrant families and children in native families appear to have widened following enactment of the welfare law.

Conclusion

As noted at the outset of these comments, in the EITC and some other areas, the administration's accomplishments in reducing poverty are strong. As the Blank/Ellwood chapter ably shows, substantial expansions occurred in the 1990s in various benefits for low-income working families. Overall, the "work-support" system was considerably stronger at the end of the decade than at its start.

It also bears noting that the administration secured some food stamp budget improvements in 1993, although a number of these were repealed in the welfare law, and sought to alleviate many of the welfare law's restrictions on legal immigrants and some of its food stamp cuts after the law was enacted. (The administration achieved major success in rolling back the benefit restrictions on immigrants who entered the country before the welfare law was signed, no success in easing the restrictions on immigrants who entered after the law was signed, and limited success in easing the severity of the food stamp eligibility and benefit reductions.) In other words, in most areas where adverse developments occurred, the administration sought to moderate them at some point.

The welfare law was, however, a momentous piece of legislation whose full effects—while not yet fully known—seem mixed so far. As a result, the administration's overall legacy in the social program area appears to be mixed, with the principal achievements being the EITC expansion, other increases in supports for low-income working families with children, and the substantial increase in employment and earnings among poor families, and the principal negative development being the near elimination over time of the federal safety net for poor individuals and families who are legal immigrants.

Comments

Ron Haskins

President Clinton was at the center, some would say was a major cause, of two perfect storms. The first was the political alignment that produced the remarkable welfare reform law of 1996. The second was the combination of conditions that shaped the law's implementation and helped it become one of the most successful social policies for the poor in the nation's history. More specifically, the law was implemented in the midst of one of the strongest economic expansions ever and was accompanied by the maturing of a diverse system of federal and state benefits that supported poor and low-income working families (food stamps, Medicaid, child care, the child tax credit, and above all the Earned Income Tax Credit).

The superb chapter by Rebecca Blank and David Ellwood is a balanced assessment of these forces that assigns a great deal of credit to Clinton for welfare reform and its largely positive effects. In general, I concur with both conclusions: welfare reform has been successful, and Clinton deserves credit. But a historical perspective suggests a more complex story about the relative contributions of Clinton and his Republican adversaries.

Since the Great Depression, Democrats have eagerly accepted the mantle of the party of the poor and minorities. In 1935, when President Franklin D. Roosevelt signed the Social Security Act, he also authored the first major federal program for the poor, the forerunner of the Aid to Families with Dependent Children program (AFDC). But President Roosevelt was uncomfortable with welfare programs. In his 1935 message to Congress, he talked of welfare as a "narcotic" and as a "subtle destroyer of the human spirit." He even promised that the nation "must and shall quit this business of relief."[1] Conservatives couldn't have put it better.

But the nation did not quit the business of relief, although for 30 years the federal government did not much expand its policy for the poor beyond AFDC.

---

1. See Roosevelt (1935).

Then in 1965, President Lyndon B. Johnson launched his War on Poverty by creating the Office of Economic Opportunity and fitting it out with a bevy of new programs including Head Start, the Jobs Corps, and various community development programs. In that same year, Johnson played a key role in getting Congress to enact Medicaid, now the biggest of the means-tested programs ($200 billion in 2000), which pays for health care for the poor. Johnson did not see himself as simply the chief dispenser of "relief." His speeches are full of rhetoric about a "hand up, not a hand out"; he viewed his programs as designed primarily to help the poor get a better education, more work, better work, more political influence. Thus, like Roosevelt, he was uncomfortable with the welfare side of helping the poor and tried to balance welfare provisions with programs intended to strengthen self-reliance and work.

Despite the best intentions of Roosevelt and Johnson, in the years after 1965 the nation embarked on a 30-year expansion of welfare programs that did not emphasize self-reliance and work. Rather, under the guidance of Democrats, but with plenty of help from Republicans, the federal government took the path of welfare entitlement. This concept held that government owed a guaranteed package of benefits to the poor that gave them a legal claim against government to have "their" benefits paid. These welfare entitlements included, in addition to AFDC and Medicaid, the food stamp and Supplemental Security Income programs; all four programs were firmly in place by the mid-1970s. On the eve of the welfare reform debate of 1995–96, poor mothers who had children outside marriage and who didn't work could claim an entitlement package of cash, food stamps, and Medicaid benefits worth about $12,000 in the typical state. Moreover, by 1995 federal and state governments were spending around $350 billion on over 300 means-tested programs, up from a mere $40 billion or so (in 1995 dollars) in 1965. Roosevelt would not have been pleased.

As programs and spending multiplied rapidly, many liberals and Democrats continued to be concerned with the negative effects of welfare on people's behavior. President Jimmy Carter continued the Roosevelt tradition of trying to mix benefit increases with self-help and work. The Program for Better Jobs and Income (PBJI), unveiled by Carter in 1977, was an attempt to create what amounted to a guaranteed income to replace the AFDC, food stamp, and Supplemental Security Income programs as well as a public jobs program. Note which goal got top billing.

After Carter's PBJI failed in Congress, yet another major attempt to reform welfare occurred during 1987–88 at the end of Ronald Reagan's second term. This round of reform was initiated by congressional Democrats and was again an attempt to combine benefit increases with work requirements. The final bill signed by Reagan contained a rough balance of both benefit increases, including a mandate that every state offer AFDC-like benefits to two-parent families, and work inducements, including the $1 billion per year Job Opportunities and Better Skills (JOBS) program. JOBS required work of families in the two-parent caseload and either training or work of some single parents. In addition, the law contained standards that required states to place a given percentage of their caseload in education, training, or work programs. However, there were many exemptions, the percentage standards were very low, and there were only weak sanctions against individuals and states that refused to comply. At best, JOBS was a modest step toward building a welfare system that emphasized work and personal responsibility.

It goes almost without saying that throughout this period, conservatives deeply questioned the growth of programs and spending, especially the growth of entitlements.[2] But as these repeated attempts to reform welfare by requiring more work and individual responsibility failed or produced ambiguous changes, many prominent liberals seemed almost to join conservatives in criticizing the growing welfare system, especially AFDC. By the 1970s research had clearly established that welfare reduced work among single males and females and among spouses.[3] Although there was less agreement on whether welfare reduced marriage and led to illegitimacy,[4] most people believed that it did.[5] Based in part on research, and even more on judgments about the values held by most Americans, by the mid-1980s a large number of notable liberals were writing serious critiques of AFDC and entitlement welfare.[6]

I provide some detail about this history to make two points. First, while it is true that liberals were far more committed to entitlement welfare than conservatives, there nonetheless is a consistent strand in the thought and actions of many liberals and Democrats that emphasized the importance of self-reliance and work. But the second point is that liberals were not willing to actually require work of mothers on welfare. They always tried to accompany modest work tests that were not truly mandatory with guaranteed benefits. The reason appears to be that liberals feared that many poor mothers would not be able to find jobs, would not be able to keep them even if they found them, and would receive low wages even if they managed to keep the jobs. In a word, mandatory work subjected the poor to too much risk.

Enter Bill Clinton. During the 1992 presidential campaign, Clinton was consistently to the right of George H. W. Bush on welfare. He amazed Republicans

---

2. See Anderson (1978), Mead (1986), and Murray (1984).
3. See Danziger et al. (1981) and Lynn and Whitman (1981).
4. See Moffitt (1992) and Haskins (1996).
5. See Jencks (1992).
6. See Ellwood (1988), Jencks (1992), Kaus (1992), and Lemann (1988, 1989).

by repeatedly calling for "two years and out" (meaning that welfare recipients would be required to work after a maximum of two years on the rolls) and stating his intention to "end welfare as we know it" (his slogan for converting welfare into a program that required work).

The legislation signed by President Clinton on August 22, 1996, fulfilled his promises to the American public. Thus any assessment of President Clinton's role in the sweeping 1996 reforms must begin with the straightforward acknowledgment that Bill Clinton initiated the debate, that his slogans nicely and provocatively captured the general substance of the needed reforms, and that he signed the final legislation. By actually signing the bill, Clinton went beyond his Democratic predecessors and showed that he had the determination and resolve to take an action that was certain to be opposed, even ridiculed, by members of his own party. There is a lot to praise here.

However, examining the actual provisions of the 1996 law shows that they were authored by Republicans and went far beyond the provisions favored by the Clinton administration. Clinton lost control of welfare reform. Early in his first year, he made the decision to table welfare reform in favor of health care reform. This decision gave conservatives an opening to claim that Clinton was typical of other Democrats in saying he favored work but failing to deliver. By the time the administration had produced a bill, it was too late in the 103rd Congress (1993–94) to take action. It seems reasonable to fault Clinton for choosing to pursue health care reform before welfare reform, thereby allowing himself to be portrayed as a liberal and presenting Republicans with an opening to create their own legislation.

However, Clinton and his advisers were undoubtedly assuming that he would have plenty of time in the 104th Congress to focus his efforts on welfare reform. But one of the most surprising events in the history of American politics intervened. For the first time in more than 40 years, in the off-year elections of 1994, Republicans captured both Houses of Congress. Only slightly less amazing, a determined group of House Republicans—including Bill Archer of Texas, Clay Shaw of Florida, Nancy Johnson of Connecticut, and Jim Talent of Missouri—had been working on welfare reform legislation for several years and were ready with a bill that enjoyed nearly universal support among House Republicans, including the 73 newly elected Republicans. Between election day and the opening of Congress in early January 1995, Republicans worked with governors to modify their bill enough so that every Republican governor and most Democratic governors also supported the bill.

The legislation as introduced by Republicans and as signed by Clinton 20 months later replaced AFDC with the Temporary Assistance for Needy Families (TANF) program. The TANF program had five major characteristics, all radical changes from AFDC: the entitlement to cash welfare was ended; open-ended entitlement funding was replaced with a block grant; states were required to place an increasing percentage of their caseload in work programs or suffer financial penalties; individuals who did not cooperate with state efforts to help them find or prepare for work were sanctioned by having their cash benefit reduced or even eliminated; and recipients, with some exceptions, were subjected to a federal five-year time limit. As Blank and Ellwood show in convincing detail, the result of the reforms has been historic declines in the welfare caseload, huge increases in work by single mothers (especially never-married mothers), and substantial reductions in child poverty. These are remarkable outcomes, more spectacular than anything associated with any previous reforms.

If welfare reform produced these exceptionally positive outcomes, what particular features of the reforms were most responsible? Although Blank and Ellwood do not examine the five features of the new TANF program outlined earlier, some combination of these features is probably responsible for the increases in work and decreases in welfare rolls and poverty. Examination of the legislative history of the 1996 reforms reveals that all five were introduced by Republicans and that Republicans, sometimes with strong opposition from Democrats, defended them and refused to allow any to be dropped from the final bill or even substantially modified. All five were in the two bills vetoed by Clinton (in December 1995 and January 1996); all five were in the bill he signed in August 1996. However, the president was very circumspect in his criticism of these five defining features throughout the welfare debate. Even as House and Senate Democrats often used invective to attack these features of the Republican bill, Clinton did not. Thus, even if Clinton included at most two of these features (work requirements and sanctions) in his own bill, he must be given substantial credit because he did not directly attack these features and signed the final bill that contained all five. My own guess, based on observations of Clinton and discussions with his staff both at the time and since, leads me to believe that if he had had a choice, Clinton would have retained the entitlement, retained the open-ended funding, and substantially modified the time limit by guaranteeing a government job for persons who couldn't find their own. But he didn't have many choices. In the end, because of Republican dominance of Congress and their insistence on the bill they had developed, Clinton had only the choice of whether to accept or veto the bill.

The political perfect storm that produced the 1996 reforms occurred at the time of the second perfect storm made up of a hot economy and an expanded federal work support system. Republicans believe that the 1980s tax cuts were a major factor in the booming economy of the 1990s; Democrats and Clinton administration officials claim it was the 1993 tax increase and the balanced budget legislation of 1997 that Clinton negotiated with Republicans that produced the boom. These claims and counterclaims will probably never be resolved, but there is no getting around the fact that Clinton presided over a spectacular economy and that Clinton deserves as much credit as Republicans for the balanced budget measures. So, on the economy and its role in making welfare-to-work reforms so successful, even stingy Republicans like me must again give Clinton high marks.

Another element in the perfect storm that greeted the 1996 welfare reforms was the work support system. Starting in approximately the mid-1970s, Congress created a series of programs that provide benefits to working families. The motivation for the origination and expansion of most of these programs probably owed more to the desire to simply provide benefits to low-income families rather than provide incentives for work.

The exception is the EITC, which provides cash benefits only to working families. Both Republicans and Democrats have understood the advantages of the EITC in rewarding work, and both parties played a central role in expanding the EITC in 1986 and 1990. However, by far the biggest increase in the history of the program was the increase Clinton engineered as part of the 1993 tax legislation. This reform increased the maximum credit from 25 percent to 40 percent for a parent with two children. Thus, by 1996 when the welfare reform legislation was signed, the EITC would provide a maximum of nearly $3,600 to a family in the maximum income range. To gain some idea of the magnitude of the Clinton increase and the level of help provided to working families, total expenditure on the EITC increased from about $15 billion in 1993 to $30 billion in 2000.[7] A mother with two children earning $10,000 in 2000 would qualify for an EITC of $4,000. Combined with a food stamp benefit worth around $2,000, her total income increased from $10,000 to $16,000. Plus she and her children retained Medicaid coverage.

There is a lot of credit to go around for the EITC and the other benefits in the work support system, but it must again be recognized that Clinton played the most important role in the biggest increase in the history of the EITC. To use his own slogan, Clinton deserves major credit for "making work pay."

My interpretation of events that preceded and surrounded passage of the seminal 1996 welfare reform law does not differ markedly from that presented by Blank and Ellwood. However, it does show that Clinton broke with a long line of liberals and Democrats who, despite their concerns with the unintended effects of AFDC, did not support tough reforms such as ending the entitlement and imposing time limits. Some liberals are still resentful of Clinton's support

---

7. See U.S. House of Representatives (2000).

for the welfare reform law. But even they must balance their criticism against Clinton's expansion of the EITC and the dramatic declines in welfare rolls, increases in work, and reductions in child poverty (especially among black children) that followed enactment of the reforms. My interpretation also creates a more prominent place for Republican policies and aggressive actions in fashioning the actual provisions of the new law. The exact meaning of "ending welfare as we know it" was closer to the Republican than the Clinton definition.

References

Anderson, Martin. 1978. *Welfare: The Political Economy of Welfare Reform in the United States*. Stanford, CA: Hoover Institution.

Danziger, Sheldon, Robert Haveman, and Robert Plotnick. 1981. "How Income Transfers Affect Work, Savings, and the Income Distribution: A Critical Review." *Journal of Economic Literature*, 19 (no. 3): 975–1028.

Ellwood, David. 1988. *Poor Support: Poverty in the American Family*. New York: Basic Books.

Haskins, Ron. 1996. "Does Welfare Encourage Illegitimacy?" *American Enterprise*, 7, no. 4: 48–49.

Jencks, Christopher. 1992. *Rethinking Social Policy: Race, Poverty, and the Underclass*. Cambridge, MA: Harvard University Press.

Kaus, Mickey. 1992. *The End of Equality*. New York: Basic Books.

Lemann, Nicholas. 1988. "The Unfinished War." *Atlantic*, 262:37–56.

———. 1989. "The Unfinished War." *Atlantic*, 263:53–68.

Lynn, Laurence E., and David F. Whitman. 1981. *The President as Policymaker: Jimmy Carter and Welfare Reform*. Philadelphia: Temple University Press.

Mead, Lawrence M. 1986. *Beyond Entitlement: The Social Obligations of Citizenship*. New York: Free Press.

Moffitt, Robert. 1992. "Incentive Effects of the U.S. Welfare System: A Review." *Journal of Economic Literature*, 30:1–61.

Murray, Charles. 1984. *Losing Ground: American Social Policy, 1950–1980*. New York: Basic Books.

Roosevelt, Franklin D. 1935. *The Public Addresses of Franklin D. Roosevelt*. New York: Random House.

U.S. House of Representatives, Committee on Ways and Means. 2000. *2000 Green Book: Background Material and Data on Programs within the Jurisdiction of the Committee on Ways and Means*, WMCP: 102–9. Washington, DC: U.S. Government Printing Office.

Comments

Bruce Reed

I want to thank the organizers of this event for being the first to recognize that for many of us, the rest of our life is just one long conference on the 1990s.

The Bush administration has given me hope. There will be seven more presidential elections before I'm Donald Rumsfeld's age. So we're not has-beens. We're retreads in waiting.

I want to commend my two former colleagues, David Ellwood and Becky Blank, for their fine, evenhanded summary of the Clinton legacy on welfare reform and poverty policy. I'm only sorry they both chose to apply the two-year time limit to their own service in the Clinton administration.

Ron Haskins and Robert Greenstein have done a good job of laying out the facts of the case, pro and con. I would like to put those facts in philosophical and historical perspective. I'd like to touch briefly on two questions: First, why did we do what we did on welfare reform and poverty? Second, on balance was it the right thing to do?

First, why'd we do what we did? Critics of the Clinton administration have offered two schools of thought on that question: incompetence and spinelessness. As we used to say in the Clinton White House, this is a false choice.

To be sure, the first two years of the Clinton administration proved the old adage that one should never ascribe to conspiracy what one can ascribe to incompetence. You have to give the George W. Bush administration credit: they promised a more efficient White House, and they've delivered. It took us two whole years to lose the Congress. They did it in just four months.

Likewise, there is some circumstantial evidence on the spinelessness front, primarily in the form of that other famous victim of our two-years-and-out policy, Dick Morris. I am perhaps the only person ever to be called "a sensitive, sober soul" by Dick Morris and a man of "principle and conviction" by George Stephanopoulos. I figure the only character reference I'm missing is to be called "loyal" by Linda Tripp.

As they used to say of Joe DiMaggio's brother Vince, we made it all look difficult. But no one should sell short what we set out to do. When it came to welfare reform, our ideas were not small ideas. From the beginning, our goal was a radical transformation of America's policies toward the poor. Bill Clinton never promised to tinker around the edges, or phase change in over time. In October 1991, in the first major policy address of his campaign, he said, "We're going to put an end to welfare as we know it," "People who work shouldn't be poor," and "No one who can work can stay on welfare forever."

We set out to create a new social contract based on work, not dependence—a contract that expanded opportunity, but demanded responsibility in return, by both rewarding and requiring work. Expansion of the EITC, the end of permanent welfare, the expansion of child care and health care were all part of the same vision that social policies would neither succeed nor be sustained unless they were inextricably linked to work.

We believed that three decades of reforms had fallen short either because they relied on cutting benefits instead of helping people go to work, or because they provided benefits without insisting that people go to work in return. We wanted to get the incentives and the values right: making every job pay better than welfare, but at the same time requiring all who can work to do so.

Obviously, not every aspect of our grand vision went according to plan. Universal health care, a key element of a social contract in which good things happen to those who work, died on the operating table. The Gingrich Congress insisted on mean-spirited and politically suicidal cuts in immigrant benefits. As David and Becky note, we had to accept a greater level of uncertainty than we originally proposed in order to achieve our goal of a system based on work, not welfare.

But in the end, the reason we ended welfare had little to do with Newt Gingrich or Dick Morris. We did it because we had promised to do it, and we promised to do it because we believed that we would never succeed in helping the poor unless we put work, more than certainty, back at the heart of every policy we proposed.

That said, the second question has to be, Was it the right thing to do? As to whether the president should have signed the welfare bill, I haven't changed my mind on that question, and I suspect neither has anyone else here. David and Becky have ably summarized the real-world outcomes of welfare reform, good, bad, and indifferent.

I'd like to address a different question, which is whether we had the right vision in the first place—whether we were right that the national government should make work the new basis of America's safety net. At the outset of the 1990s, that was a highly controversial notion. Some objected on practical grounds, that we didn't know whether people would actually go to work if we rewarded work and required them to do so, or whether state welfare bureaucracies would be willing or able to help clients find jobs, or whether employers would hire them.

Others objected on principle. In a way, the old welfare system was an unfortunate compromise between conservatives who didn't want the federal government to spend too much on poor people and liberals who didn't want it to ask too much of them. With the EITC and welfare reform, we were doing both.

A decade later, I believe the right's fears about the EITC and the left's fears about work requirements should be put to rest. Whatever one thinks of lifetime time limits, whatever concerns one may still have about how best to help the long-term recipients who remain on the rolls, whatever challenges lie ahead in conquering poverty, I believe that the 1990s have settled this question once and for all: work is the most effective, most sustainable basis for social and anti-poverty policy.

The evidence is overwhelming. Single mothers have entered the work force in record numbers. Labor market participation by single mothers with children under 18 went up 10 points between 1992 and 2000. For those who doubt the value of unprecedented caseload reduction, consider the equally remarkable fact that people still on the welfare rolls are nearly five times more likely to be working than in 1992.

Why is this so important? Because it destroys the debilitating premise that the old system had come to represent, that the poor are irreparably broken people, and that the underclass was stuck forever outside the mainstream of American life. We said it time and again, even though the pollsters told us no one else in America believed it, that people on welfare wanted to work, we just had to give them the chance to go to work. And sure enough, legions of them did so, and employers welcomed them with open arms.

In the process, we have fundamentally changed the political debate by ushering in a day when all the poor can be the deserving poor. We have taken much of the hate out of the debate. I am not a big fan of compassionate conservatism. I believe a compassionate conservative is someone who wants to keep the Confederate flag, but fly it at half-mast. A compassionate conservative is someone who calls for a new War on Poverty, as President Bush did last month, and starts it with a $2 trillion tax cut for the wealthy.

But I will say this: the success of our antipoverty policy in the 1990s put the nail in the coffin of compassionless conservatism. I think we've seen the last of Republican crusades to cut immigrant benefits. I doubt we'll see another serious Republican assault on the EITC. Indeed, in the last tax bill, Republicans joined us in providing a refundable child tax credit to low-income families.

Meanwhile, the combined impact of a good economy, the EITC, welfare reform, and a higher minimum wage helped 7 million people lift themselves out of poverty. I was pleased to see David and Becky conclude that most (though not all) people who've gone to work have gained more in income than they've lost in benefits. But I would argue that they've gained something even more important than that, because in ways we can't begin to measure, their children are better off to be growing up in households and communities where people go to work. That gives them a shot at the promise of American life, and it gives policy-makers a foundation for the work we have left to do.

The road ahead is long and hard, for people struggling to work their way out of poverty and for policy-makers struggling to help them, now that the Bush administration has ended the surplus as we knew it. We have a heap of unfinished business—health care, child care, expecting as much of low-income fathers as we have of low-income mothers. But the 1990s give us the right road map.

That new synthesis—helping people help themselves—provides a philosophical basis for activist government that could prove as enduring in this century as the New Deal was in the last. The real Clinton legacy on the poor comes down to one word: work.

In response to a question from the audience about whether the "on the ground" reality of welfare reform was more negative than the broad statistics revealed, *Rebecca Blank* replied that the question was a crucial one. She noted that there was far less information available about actual living conditions than about trends in, say, caseloads or labor force participation rates. Blank added that the use of food banks and temporary feeding programs had risen, although the link between those trends and declines in food stamp use was uncertain. It would be valuable, she suggested, to look across states that have run different types of welfare reform programs over the late 1990s and examine indicators such as health, homelessness, food consumption, and children's performance in school—measures not typically examined by economists.

Robert Greenstein added that it was important to look at trends in the poverty gap, not just the poverty rate. He also argued that restrictions in the mid-1990s on SSI and Medicaid receipt by substance abusers—even those in treatment— probably led to increased hardship, although no studies have examined that issue. In response to this point, *Ron Haskins* noted that the debate in Congress revealed that there was no support from either Republicans or Democrats for providing a guaranteed income or Medicaid to those addicted to illegal drugs.

Larry Katz said it was important to consider how individuals assess their own happiness, well-being, and health status when they shift from welfare to work. Survey data from the United States and Europe, he said, found large differences between the self-reported happiness and well-being of individuals who work compared to those who do not—independent of differences in incomes between these two groups. He also noted that evidence from several random assignment demonstrations had shown, on the one hand, that children appeared to benefit little when their parents moved from welfare to work in the absence of extra income supplements. On the other hand, he said, there were positive effects for children whose parents began work *and* received a generous EITC or wage subsidy. Katz also commented that any discussion of social policy in the 1990s should reflect the fact that the largest increase in social policy spending during the decade was for incarceration. He noted that 2 million people, mostly minority men from poor neighborhoods, were now incarcerated.

Haskins argued that results from Minnesota's Family Investment Program showed that mandatory work combined with income supplements, medical care, and child care programs produced several positive effects: improved school performance and behavior among children, reductions in domestic violence, and expansions in marriage.

Discussing the effect of welfare reform on children, *Blank* said that there was some evidence that in states with significant work support policies, younger children had better outcomes when their mothers entered welfare-to-work programs compared to similar children whose mothers did not enter such programs. She said the results appear to stem from the higher-quality child care available to those in the welfare-to-work programs (both preschool and after-school programs). However, Blank said that some studies had found negative effects on teenaged children when their parents transitioned to work. She noted that while direct evidence was limited, those negative effects might be due to decreased supervision of older children by their working parents.

Commenting on the use of monthly wage supplements, *Greenstein* pointed out that in all but a handful of states, these supplements count against the five-year lifetime time limit for welfare. This requirement puts poor families in a bind, he said, because if they receive wage supplements (bringing them closer to the time limit), they risk not qualifying for assistance later on during a recession, for example. Another concern, Greenstein noted, was that the majority of states implemented child support laws after PRWORA that funnel to the state every dollar paid by noncustodial fathers for the support of children receiving public assistance—with none going to the mother. This was a particular problem for women who leave welfare for work; in some cases, such women have all their child support payments diverted to the state in order to "repay" prior welfare assistance. Greenstein also pointed out that results from Minnesota as well as several other studies during the 1990s found that gains in employment and earnings were disproportionately concentrated among families receiving housing assistance. He suggested that it would be useful to learn more about the interactions between the program that provides Section 8 housing vouchers to low-income families and welfare reform efforts.

Martin Feldstein provided a final comment, noting the remarkable difference between the United States and Europe in terms of social policy. He pointed to two specific differences: the work-based approach to income maintenance in the United States, and the degree to which individual states in the United States act as laboratories for innovations in policy-making.

Health Care and Tobacco Policy

Health Policy in the Clinton Era: Once Bitten, Twice Shy

David Cutler and Jonathan Gruber

PANELISTS: *Victor R. Fuchs, Joseph P. Newhouse, and W. Kip Viscusi*

At the dawn of the Clinton era, health care was poised to be one of the major issues of the coming decades. Health care costs were rising at a rapid rate and had been doing so for well over a decade. The number of uninsured was steadily rising, and the recession of 1990–91 had brought fears of uninsurance to the ranks of the middle class. Employers were increasingly shifting the costs of insurance to their employees, and employees were afraid to switch jobs for fear of losing their health insurance. Despite leading the world by a large margin in health care spending, health outcomes in the United States were no better than other developed countries in dimensions such as life expectancy and infant outcomes. This combination of rising costs, high uninsurance, and poor outcomes led to a crisis mentality in the U.S. health care system

Moreover, a defining political event of the early 1990s brought health care to the national stage. The election of Senator Harris Wofford of Pennsylvania on a platform of major health care reform showed that this was an issue the public cared about. Candidate Bill Clinton embraced health care reform. The public responded favorably. Public opinion polls showed that health care ranked third on the list of voter concerns in the 1992 election, behind the economy and the federal budget deficit. With Clinton's ascension to the White House, there was every expectation that major health care reform would follow.

We are grateful to Gary Claxton, Nancy Ann DeParle, Jeff Frankel, Victor Fuchs, Larry Levitt, Joe Newhouse, Len Nichols, Peter Orszag, Kip Viscusi, and Richard Zeckhauser for helpful comments and to the National Institute on Aging for research support.

Clinton took on the issue full force. The Health Security Act (HSA) was one of the first major initiatives of the new administration. Demonstrating his commitment to the issue, the president appointed his wife, Hillary Clinton, to draft the plan. It was the first time that a first lady had ever had direct involvement in the policy process. The HSA was an impressive and ambitious proposal that provided a detailed blueprint for a national health plan.

But it went spectacularly awry. The HSA failed dismally in the legislative process, resulting not only in the defeat of the plan but ultimately in loss of Democratic control of the Congress. Republicans at one time hoped to use the issue to unseat President Clinton in 1996 as well. The defeat of the HSA was felt not only in future health care debates, but in everything the administration accomplished, or attempted to accomplish, over the remainder of its tenure. It taught the administration a central lesson: no longer would the administration attempt to get out in front of the legislative branch or lead the public on major health initiatives (or, in general, in areas outside of health care either). Rather, it would pursue bite-sized, less controversial policies with limited scope for legislative failure and reliance on executive order as much as possible. The administration never approached another problem like the HSA. Once bitten, twice shy; the administration learned the lesson of the HSA extremely well.

The irony is that bite-size policy was quite successful. The Clinton administration accomplished an enormous amount in health care. The record looks small only in comparison to what might have been, not in comparison to past administrations. Out of the ashes of failure came significant success, although significant problems remain.

In this chapter we review the health care accomplishments and failures of the Clinton era. We begin, in section 12.1, by discussing the health care market in the early 1990s. This is key to understanding the Health Security Act, the central health care initiative of the administration. We review the politics and policy of the HSA in section 12.2. We then turn to other areas in which health policy was made, or attempted to be made, throughout the Clinton years. With universal coverage out, the administration pursued incremental insurance expansions. We discuss these policies in section 12.3. In section 12.4 we turn to insurance market reform, another residue from the HSA. Section 12.5 focuses on initiatives in the area of long-term care.

Sections 12.6 and 12.7 then turn from health insurance and health care to public health issues. We first discuss tobacco policy, a particularly interesting area because it represents the one other arena in which the administration tried another ambitious initiative. It too failed—legislatively, if not substantively. In truth, the tobacco wars were ultimately favorable for the administration's goals. We then turn to other public health initiatives, which were much more modest but also much more successful. Section 12.8 concludes.

At the outset, we note for the reader our own biases. We each took part in the administration as insiders—Cutler in the HSA and Gruber in the CHIP and tobacco debates. We do not attempt to hide our personal views. A retrospective cannot be written in a vacuum, and ours has perhaps a sympathetic tilt. Readers can apply a different filter if they choose. We also leave aside issues of Medicare. Medicare proposals were constant throughout the administration, from the HSA to calls for prescription drug coverage later on. These topics are reviewed in Chapter 13.

12.1 The Economic Setting

To understand the essential parts of the Clinton health care agenda, it is important to revisit the state of health care in 1992. Health care financing had been a perennial topic on the public agenda at least since the presidency of Franklin Roosevelt. The United States was (and is) the only major country without universal health insurance coverage. Universal insurance coverage became the defining health care issue. Enacting universal health insurance coverage would make whichever president did so the successor to Franklin Roosevelt, who enacted Social Security, and Lyndon Johnson, who initiated Medicare. The moral case for universal health insurance coverage was strong as well. Harris Wofford was elected to the Senate in 1990 arguing that if prisoners had the right to basic medical care, middle-class people should as well.

But there was an economic rationale as well. One argument made in the 1980s against increased government support for health insurance was that a period of economic growth would substantially alleviate social problems of this form. It would give employers incentives to provide health insurance and workers access to the type of jobs that came with health insurance.

As Figure 12.1 shows, however, such was not the case. The share of the population that was uninsured actually increased over the 1980s, a pattern to be repeated in the even more spectacular growth of the 1990s. True, the recession of 1990–91 particularly exacerbated this trend, with the number of people who were uninsured rising by 4 million from 1989 through 1992 (Employee Benefits Research Institute, 2000). But, looking at these trends, an increasing share of analysts came to the view that the lack of health insurance was a structural problem requiring substantial government involvement, not a temporary problem to be solved by increased economic growth.

Uninsurance was not just a problem of the very poor. Figure 12.2 shows insurance coverage in 1990 by family income. Among those with income below the poverty line (roughly $15,000 for a family of four in 1990), about one-third were uninsured. A similar share of the "lower middle class" (between poverty and twice poverty) were uninsured as well. This group was to be a key

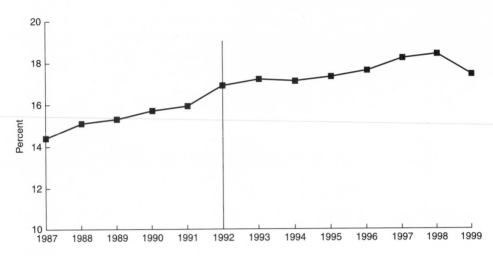

Figure 12.1
Share of Nonelderly Population Without Health Insurance. (Data are from the Current Population Survey.)

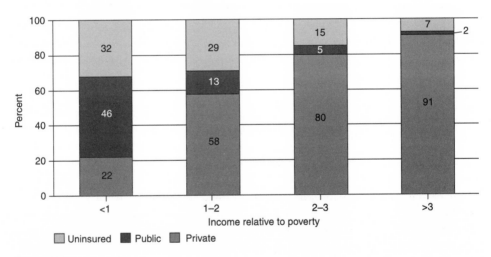

Figure 12.2
Insurance Coverage by Income, 1990. (Data are from the March 1991 Current Population Survey.)

constituency in the rise and fall of the Clinton health plan, as we will discuss. It wasn't until higher up in the income scale (roughly $50,000 in annual income) that the share of people who are uninsured became very low.

Middle-class anxiety about health care was relatively new. Where middle-class jobs had previously been a key to lifetime health security, that was no longer perceived to be the case. The fact that many people in this group knew people who were uninsured, particularly in the recession, contributed to this perception.

But structural changes of the 1980s also explain the increased anxiety of the middle class about health care. After the recession of the early 1980s, cost cutting became a key issue for employers. Health insurance costs were high and growing rapidly. Thus they became a natural target. Employers cut back on health coverage or increased its costs to employees. This trend concerned workers greatly.

Some intrusion of economic theory is appropriate here. Economic theory does not view employers (or shareholders, their manifestation) as paying the cost of health insurance. Rather, if workers value health insurance at its cost, they will pay for it in the form of lower wages (Summers, 1989). Indeed, empirical evidence generally finds a negative correlation between benefit costs and wages in settings that are designed to test for this issue (Gruber, 1994; Sheiner, 1999). Thus employers should not have cared about the increasing cost of health insurance in the 1980s.

But employers clearly did not have that view, nor did workers. Employers saw themselves as paying for health insurance costs through higher prices for their products or lower profits. Individuals saw a clear distinction between their employer paying for health insurance and paying themselves. Politicians, hearing from workers and businessmen, mirrored this view. Thus, "political incidence" or "public incidence" was very different from economic incidence.

There are several possible reasons for this discrepancy, some substantive and some reflecting misperception. First, the offset reasoning is based on general equilibrium points that are not always obvious. No employer perceives himself as paying lower wages when health insurance costs rise. Rather, overall demand for labor falls, and the result would be downward pressure on wages in general. But any individual employer could reap the benefits if he could lower health insurance costs on his own. And conversely, if his competitor lowered costs and he did not, his competitor would drive him out of business. Thus, businessmen thinking in a partial equilibrium framework might not perceive that they did not bear the burden of health insurance costs.

Second, the ability to pass costs back to workers may also be limited for low-wage workers or workers with a higher-earning spouse. Where high-wage workers might be willing to pay for health insurance in lower wages, low-wage workers were less willing to: minimum wage constraints bind for some of these workers, low incomes in general reduce the demand for medical care, and the ability of these workers to receive free or publicly subsidized care reduces their willingness to pay for costly employer benefits. Further, workers obtaining coverage from a spouse would be unwilling to give up cash income to pay for insurance through their own employer as well. Firms with a predominance of married women, for example, might not be able to pass costs back to employees as easily as firms with married men.

Third, the economics model of incidence is distinctly a long-run model. Adjustment to labor market equilibrium may occur quite slowly. This observation can be particularly true if incidence occurs not through cutting (sticky) nominal wages but rather by eroding the growth of real wages. At the time (as now), inflation was low, so real wage cuts were difficult. But workers and employers may be much more focused on the very short run, so that the long-run adjustment of wages is less relevant to their deliberations than it is to economists' models.

Finally, the discrepancy may reflect a difference in time perspective. In the short run, one would expect less offset than in the long run, since wages become more flexible over time. Employers and workers may have been focusing on this short-run situation rather than the long-run analysis that most economists typically use.

For some combination of these reasons, health insurance costs became a target for employers in the newly competitive economy. Employers responded with a sustained effort to reduce their health insurance coverage, particularly for the poor (Cutler and Madrian, 1998). Jobs that could be outsourced were, to firms that generally did not pay for health insurance for their workers. Workers were made part-time or temporary in part to save on benefits costs. Employee costs for health insurance were increased to induce some people to drop coverage: the share of employers paying the full cost of insurance for family policies fell from 46 percent in 1983 to 24 percent in 1993, and for single policies it fell from 67 percent in 1983 to 39 percent in 1993 (Gruber and McKnight, 2001). And employers increasingly moved workers into managed care, which had lower premiums but less provider choice. Where managed care accounted for 8 percent of the privately insured population in 1980, it had risen to 45 percent by 1992.

Many of these measures reduced insurance coverage among the working poor. It is interesting to note that this decline was *not* due to reduced employer offering of insurance, but rather reduced take-up by employees, perhaps as a result of higher employee premium shares and outsourcing (Cooper and Schone, 1997; Farber and Levy, 2000).

Changes in the insurance industry added to this problem. Historically, health insurance was community rated: all groups paid close to the same cost, regardless of the expected cost of the group. Community rating arose because insurance was perceived to be a community activity (the first health insurers were not-for-profit) and because determining the expected cost for any particular group was too difficult. The spread of computer power and increased competitiveness among insurers led to a change in this policy.

Increasingly, health insurance became experience rated: groups were charged on the basis of their expected cost (Cutler, 1994b). This practice was followed even among small firms, where average costs can be quite variable (if one person develops AIDS, for example). Thus people became concerned that their insurance coverage would be dropped if they became sick or that their premiums would increase so much that they could not afford insurance.

The economics of risk segmentation are worthy of some discussion. If insurers can differentiate sick from healthy and charge appropriate premiums, why should we care? The market is superficially efficient: everyone can get full insurance, and they do so at actuarially fair rates. Understanding the problem requires an ex ante assessment, before people know if they are sick or healthy. Risk-averse people without knowledge of their future health status would choose to insure against the risk that they will become sick and then face high premiums, by guaranteeing to pay more when they are healthy. Such insurance is not carried out ex post, however, when the sick are charged more than the healthy. The loss from risk segmentation is this inability to buy insurance at average rates when sick. The risk of moving into the outer tail of the risk distribution was what people were concerned about.

An outgrowth of risk segmentation was the increasing fear that workers had about changing jobs. People were worried that if they changed jobs, they would lose their insurance coverage, either because they would move to a job without insurance, or because their preexisting conditions would not be covered under their new insurance policy. Such "job lock" was commonly listed as a concern in public opinion polls, and a number of economic studies over the past decade have shown that job lock may reduce mobility among those with insurance by as much as one-quarter.[1] It was these fears that led to the title of the Clinton health reform plan: the Health Security Act.

The final concern was about the cost of medical care. Public and private health insurance costs had been increasing for decades at rates well above the growth of national income. As the cost of medical care increased, however, the dollar increases associated with these high growth rates became larger. Figure 12.3

---

1. The classic reference on "job lock" is Madrian (1994). See Gruber (2001a) for a review of the literature on this topic.

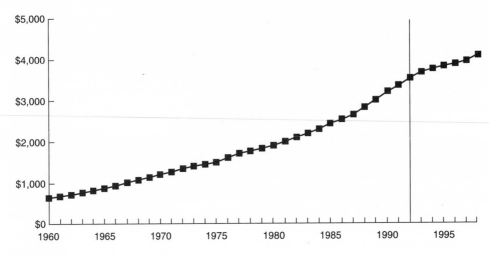

Figure 12.3
Real Medical Spending. (Data are from the Center for Medicare and Medicaid Services.)

shows average spending per person on medical care in real (1990) dollars. Where medical care costs averaged $650 in 1960 and $1,900 in 1980, they averaged $3,500 in 1992.

At least in the political arena, the increase in medical care costs over time was largely seen as a problem of price inflation, not increased service utilization. This assumption applied particularly to pharmaceutical costs, the most noticeable out-of-pocket cost, but was perceived to be true about other items of medical spending as well. The judgment that price inflation was the source of medical care cost increases contributed to the view that costs could be reduced without substantial adverse impact on health—just stop providers from raising prices so much. Economic research that was begun early in the decade but particularly research done afterward suggests that this conclusion is wrong (Newhouse, 1992; Cutler, 1995; Peden and Freeland, 1995). Medical care cost increase is now seen as predominantly, if not exclusively, a result of increased service utilization. The price-increase view justified public involvement in controlling medical care. The new service-increase view makes the welfare analysis of limiting spending more difficult. With the exception of pharmaceuticals, where concern is still expressed about price inflation, this view has made substantial inroads in the policy arena as well.

These cost increases were a burden for the public and private sectors. In the private sector, employers were (irrationally, according to economic theory) concerned about their health insurance costs. They responded to rising costs by changing their benefits substantially. The problem was particularly acute in the public sector. Medicare and Medicaid together spent $200 billion in 1992, about 14 percent of the federal budget. Rising costs were also a significant factor contributing to future budget deficits. According to projections in 1992, federal health care spending would increase by 10 percent per year between 1992 and 2000. Tax revenues, in contrast, were projected to increase by only half that amount.

For an activist president who wanted to spend money on social policies, the only way to do so was to reduce the growth of federal medical care costs. President Clinton put it directly in introducing his health reform plan in September 1993:

The budget we just adopted had steep cuts in defense, a five-year freeze on the discretionary spending, so critical to reeducating America and investing in jobs and helping us to convert from a defense to a domestic economy. But we passed a budget which has Medicaid increases of between 16 and 11 percent a year over the next five years, and Medicare increases of between 11 and 9 percent in an environment where we assume inflation will be at 4 percent or less. We cannot continue to do this. Our competitiveness, our whole economy, the integrity of the way the government works, and ultimately, our living standards depend on our ability to achieve savings without harming the quality of health care.

This was the situation facing the Clinton administration in 1992: persistent and increasing rates of uninsurance; a middle class that was concerned about being dropped or forced out of insurance coverage; and rising medical care costs that made employers, and particularly the government, nervous. The proposed solution to this problem was the Health Security Act.

12.2   The Health Security Act

The Health Security Act (or HSA) was a defining issue for the Clinton administration in many ways. It was extremely high profile. The president's wife led the reform effort, an unprecedented step historically. It was also the most spectacular failure of the administration, and it led to the strategy that subsequently infused the administration throughout: take small, popular steps to achieve commonly sought goals, but don't overreach.

12.2.1   Structure of the HSA

The HSA was designed to address each of the problems discussed in the previous section; see Cutler (1994a) for a longer discussion. It is useful to review the HSA in some detail even though it did not pass; the HSA demonstrates more than anything else the health care goals of the Clinton administration. We focus on the provisions of the HSA for the nonelderly population. Changes for the elderly were fewer and involved mostly new benefits for prescription drugs and long-term care. The provisions for the nonelderly were the heart of the proposal.

Universal coverage was the most notable feature of the plan. Everyone would be insured, in all situations. Universal coverage requires a mandate that some-one pay for health insurance; it also requires subsidies, since the poor cannot afford all of the costs for insurance on their own. There are three types of pay-ment systems that can be enacted to guarantee universal coverage. The first is an employer/individual mandate: require employers to pay for most of health insurance costs and individuals to pay for the rest. Nonworkers are covered through their own payments, along with subsidies. The second strategy is an individual mandate alone: require individuals to pay for insurance, regardless of whether their employer contributes part of the cost. Single payer, funded by general taxation—for example, through a consumption tax—is a third option.

The Health Security Act chose the first option: a combination employer/individual mandate was proposed, with subsidies for low-income families to afford their payment and for small firms. The choice of an employer mandate reflected the "political incidence" noted earlier; people thought it was better if their employer paid for health insurance than if they did. This was also the situation that was familiar to most Americans, who worried that without a mandate for employers to pay for health insurance, employers would drop or eliminate their current payments (without increasing their wages).

One also had to specify how people would get insurance and the price they would pay. It does no good to require a family to pay for insurance if one mem-ber is very sick and the price is high. The risk segmentation problems noted earlier were particularly important here; because of changes in the insurance market, the plan had to group people together to get community rates. The so-lution was to set up regional "health alliances." All firms except the very largest ones (who in effect operated their own alliance) had to purchase insurance from a common pool, set up on a regional basis. Insurers would be required to offer standard plans—an HMO, PPO, or indemnity plans—and enroll all who wanted. Rates would be the same for everyone in the pool.

In addition to guaranteeing insurance coverage, the regional alliances were a key element of cost containment. "Managed competition" was the buzzword; the idea is that by standardizing benefits and prohibiting selection, competition among insurers would focus on price and quality, not selection of risk. Anec-dotal evidence from the effect of competition in lowering premiums in Califor-nia (Zwanziger and Melnick, 1988) and Minnesota (Feldman and Dowd, 1993) supported the concepts behind the plan.

Regional health alliances became a bureaucratic nightmare that partly explained the defeat of the Clinton plan. But it is interesting to note as a historical matter the resurgence of regional alliances (under different names) in the subsequent years. Periodic Republican proposals have also supported regional purchasing pools to achieve cost savings in insurance. And a sizable share of recent proposals for incremental health insurance reform as part of a project sponsored by the Commonwealth Fund (Glied, 2000) also centered around some type of pooling mechanism; the Federal Employees Health Benefit Plan repeatedly is used as a popular example of such a type of mechanism. One way or another, the concept of regional pools has survived the Health Security Act.

Low-income families cannot pay for all of the cost of health insurance, and it was perceived that low-wage firms could not either. Thus subsidies were designed to reduce the cost of health insurance for these groups. The employer subsidies in particular were somewhat awkward. Small firms were believed to need subsidies, but only small firms with low average wages. Redistribution is difficult at the firm level, and the targeting could have led to substantial gaming by employers. Because health insurance is expensive and the subsidies would apply to everyone in an income group, not just those who were currently uninsured, the subsidy system was expensive. The subsidies were estimated to cost about $70 billion per year when fully phased in.

The money for these subsidies had to be found somewhere. Broad-based new taxes were not a politically realistic option. The only tax increase in the proposal was an increase in the federal excise tax on cigarettes, from 24 cents per pack to 99 cents per pack. This was not a significant share of the revenue needed, however.

Most of the money for the subsidies came from slowing the growth rate of health care costs, particularly Medicare and Medicaid, but also private insurance premiums. The rationale for public savings was explicitly to free up money for expanded insurance coverage. The limit on private insurance premiums was intended partly to serve the same purpose. Since the federal government would be paying for a large part of private health insurance costs (through subsidies and the tax exclusion of employer-provided health insurance payments), the government had an interest in managing those costs. Further, the perception that cost increases reflected inflationary price increases on the part of providers and insurers justified premium controls to limit spending. And the premium limits were also implemented to provide some certainty to businesses now facing the cost of a health insurance mandate. But the cap on private insurance premiums was thought of as a backstop by many advocates of managed competition, who believed competition among plans in regional alliances would reduce costs more than sufficiently.

12.2.2   The Demise of the Health Security Act

When the administration began designing its health reform plan in the spring of 1993, 71 percent of people approved of what they heard or read about the plan. By the middle of 1994, only 33 percent of people believed the Health Security Act would be good for the country. Ultimately, nothing emerged directly from the Health Security Act.

What happened? That is a complicated question, well beyond the scope of this (economic) chapter. But some factors bear mentioning.[2] The first explanation for the failure of the HSA was a poor policy-design process. Appointing the president's wife to lead the health reform effort limited internal debate. This was coupled with the seeming intransigence of Ira Magaziner, the reform's chief architect, to listen to alternative points of view. As a result, debates were stifled internally, and an acceptable plan was never put forth. Chapter 14 of this volume, by Orszag, Orszag, and Tyson, concludes that the policy process used in the health reform effort was a very poor one compared to the process used in other economic matters. In a complex matter such as health care, producing a high-quality reform plan may be particularly important.

Process was also important in the interaction with Congress. The administration decided early on to draft the HSA without any pretense of bipartisan cooperation. Rather than working quickly to use the constellation of a Democratic Congress and White House to introduce the outlines of a health plan in the initial days of a new administration, the process was laboriously dragged out, going past the middle of 1994. This approach was partly designed to give the president's other priorities time to work their way through the legislative process (NAFTA, the economic plan), but also gave opponents time to galvanize around key issues as they (inevitably, despite attempts at secrecy) leaked out.

A second explanation stresses not process but political fighting. In 1993 and 1994 far right Republican leaders were beginning to assert their power over the Republican Party, and they saw defeating the Health Security Act as a key to doing so. Newt Gingrich led the opposition to the HSA and was followed by other, like-minded Republicans. This was combined with intense lobbying from groups opposed to aspects of the HSA. Most prominent among these were the National Federation of Independent Businesses (NFIB), the trade group for small businesses, and the Health Insurance Association of America (HIAA), the lobbying organization for health insurers.

---

2. Victor Fuchs' comments on this chapter, as well as his previous writings, discuss this question in more detail.

In each case, the opposition was economic. The NFIB opposed the employer mandate, fearing that they would bear the burden of the mandate—again, not agreeing that they would be able to fully pass through the costs. The HIAA was dominated by small insurers, who made profits by finding healthy groups to insure and charging them below-market rates. The inability to do so under the HSA was a chief concern for this group. The HIAA sponsored the famous Harry and Louise ads, featuring the middle-aged couple discussing the Health Security Act and concluding, "There must be a better way."

In the immediate aftermath of the failed health reform effort, the Clinton administration blamed these political considerations for the failure of the health reform plan. To our eyes, though, these explanations look less credible over time than they did at the time. Not only did the Clinton plan fail, but other reform efforts in this cycle and past political cycles failed as well. Perhaps there is a structural reason why health care reform is difficult to enact in the United States.

One such explanation is distributional: the Health Security Act, as would any universal coverage effort, involved significant redistribution, and this has historically been difficult to achieve.[3] The redistribution was at several levels: by income, by geography, by family type, and between firms providing and not providing insurance. Income redistribution was probably the most important. The primary beneficiaries of the coverage increases were lower-income groups—not the very poor, who were already covered by Medicaid, but the lower-income working population, which did not have access to either Medicaid or employer-sponsored insurance. With the exception of an increase in the cigarette excise tax, the money for the subsidies was to come from reduced growth rates of health insurance premiums.

But this source of revenues was ultimately not convincing. There were two, ironically contradictory reasons for this. First, people did not believe the savings would materialize. The lack of any explicit revenues led many people to believe that the plan would lead to increased deficits. This belief was supported by Congressional Budget Office projections that the plan would cost more than the administration estimated. In an era of mounting concern about the deficit, people feared alternately that the Health Security Act would increase the deficit, or that a future tax increase would be necessary to pay for it.

Second, people thought that if the savings were realized, they would come at too high a price. Fears that the Health Security Act would lead to rationing of

---

3. An earlier example of this difficulty could be found in the 1988 Medicare Catastrophic Care Act, which raised the Medicare premiums on higher-income elderly to improve the benefits package for lower-income elderly. This plan proved vastly unpopular with seniors and was repealed after two years.

health care were widespread. And asking the middle class to pay for health care for the poor by rationing their own use of services was not popular. Support for the Clinton plan fell most prominently among those who would be asked to sacrifice.

Indeed, the entire focus on universal insurance coverage and transfers to the poor drove attention away from what the middle class was supposed to get out of the plan. Research by political scientists has suggested (Blendon, Brodie, and Benson, 1995) that middle-class people turned from the Clinton plan because they wanted the focus to be on their *personal* health care problems, not the problems of the health care *system*. The middle class perceived itself as having three goals: (1) making sure they don't lose insurance coverage when they change or lose their job; (2) making sure they are not charged more if someone in their family gets sick; and (3) reducing the insurance premiums and out-of-pocket costs they and their employers had to pay. Universal coverage is not on this list; regional health alliances are only dimly related to these goals and sound like big government. Government-enforced caps on insurance premiums might lead to rationing.

The decline in support by the middle class was the most notable change in public opinion over the course of the Clinton plan. Where three-fifths of those earning $20,000 to $30,000 supported the Clinton Plan in September 1993, only two in five did so in April 1994.

In summary, the middle class wanted to have more but pay less. But this goal is of course impossible, and until this fact is widely accepted, there is bound to be disappointment among those endeavoring to achieve national health insurance. The failure of health reform may be a result of the fact that no administration can meet the unreasonable expectations of the vast majority of people.

A fourth explanation for the decline of the Health Security Act is that the problems driving the health care concern abated. Health concerns were most prominent in the recession of 1990–91, when people feared losing their job and thus health insurance. As the economy expanded in 1993 and 1994, fear of job loss receded. It is an ironic feature that the administration's successful effort to promote macroeconomic growth helped to kill one of its signature social insurance programs.

Whatever the reason, the Health Security Act failed badly in the political arena. After a lengthy congressional debate, the HSA was pulled in 1994. It was a bitter time for the administration.

12.2.3 Lessons from the HSA

The administration drew several lessons from the failure of the Health Security Act, which drove health policy for the remaining years. We summarize these lessons and in the remainder of the chapter discuss how and when they were applied.

12.2.3.1 Lesson 1: Broad-Based Coverage Expansions Are Out

The administration never again proposed a large-scale expansion of insurance coverage. Rather, coverage expansions were targeted to specific groups in the population where a strong case could be made that insurance coverage was a clear need. We term this the "Titanic strategy," because in practice it meant saving the women and children first.

Thus the administration's most notable coverage expansion—quite a large policy, albeit small relative to the Health Security Act—was the Children's Health Insurance Program (CHIP), which provided public health insurance coverage to low-income children. It was always easy to sell coverage expansions for children. Even in the 1980s the Democrats forced the Reagan Administration to expand Medicaid coverage for children. The administration's focus on children was a clear case where the public could be convinced to spend additional money.

The other initiatives were even more targeted: a buy-in to Medicare for the near elderly; coverage for the unemployed; coverage for the parents of CHIP children (it's unfair for the children to have coverage but not the parents); and substantial new benefits for the elderly.

It is ironic that the administration was never again able to approach the issue of broad-based coverage expansions, since the "structural" view of the problem seems even more correct in retrospect. Figure 12.1 shows the rate of uninsurance over the 1990s. Even in the boom economic times of the 1990s, rates of uninsurance rose. There is no longer any credible case that if the economy just grew faster, the health insurance problem would get better. Indeed, it is quite possible that the next recession will reawaken the fears about health insurance coverage that propelled the Health Security Act.

12.2.3.2 Lesson 2: Focus on Middle-Class Concerns

The fear of being dropped from coverage, losing coverage when changing jobs, or having insurance premiums increase when someone becomes sick did not go away with the demise of the Health Security Act. At first, states took up the issue. State governments passed legislation limiting the extent to which insurers could discriminate against the sick. The federal government followed the states in 1996, with the Health Insurance Portability and Accountability Act (HIPAA, also called the Kassebaum/Kennedy legislation). This legislation reduced some of the most complained-about features of private insurance and attempted to reduce costs by standardizing medical record keeping, but it was not entirely successful, as we will review subsequently.

12.2.3.3 Lesson 3: Don't Get Too Far Out in Front

The final lesson is that it is dangerous to get too far out in front of the public. After the Health Security Act, the Clinton administration generally waited for issues to bubble up from the public, judging the public mood and proposing policies appropriate to it. Thus the administration was a latecomer to tobacco litigation, pushed HMO regulation only when the problem garnered substantial public attention (and even then not with the full vigor of many Democrats), and seized on smaller issues such as privacy protection, medical errors, record keeping, and the like. As with the CHIP program, many of these were successful interventions, but they frequently rode the wave of public opinion, rather than leading the public to a new position.

12.2.4 *The Health Care Market, Post-HSA*

The failure of the HSA was a defining event in private markets as well. Since the mid-1980s it had been widely expected that some health care legislation would be enacted, probably with universal insurance coverage. Thus employers were shy about making long-term changes in their benefits plans that would be changed again soon. With the failure of the HSA, employers realized this change would not happen. Given their view of incidence, employers became increasingly concerned about how they would afford health care benefits.

The result was a headlong rush into managed care. Employers that had offered managed care plans before the HSA tilted their pricing to encourage employees to enroll in them. Those that offered only conventional plans often gave those up for managed care options. By 1996 less than 5 percent of the privately insured population was enrolled in traditional fee-for-service insurance. The rest were in some form of managed care—managed indemnity insurance sometimes, PPOs, HMOs, and other combinations as well.

The result of all this, when combined with very rapid economic growth, was a substantial reduction in the share of GDP that was going to health care, at least relative to baseline projections. Where forecasts in 1992 predicted that health care would rise from 14 percent of GDP to nearly 20 percent by 2000, actual health spending in 2000 was still but 14 percent of GDP. The implied reduction in spending was about $100 billion.

The reductions carried over to public programs as well. With managed care cutting fees for physicians in the private sector, Medicare and Medicaid did the same. Where managed care lowered utilization volume for privately insured people, providers carried these reductions over to the elderly as well. As a result, Medicare and Medicaid experienced very low rates of cost growth over the 1990s, particularly from 1997 onward. Indeed, this factor contributed significantly to the improved budgetary position of the federal government. This result is exactly what the administration had hoped the HSA would bring about, but it happened even in the HSA's defeat.

But all was not rosy. The share of people without insurance continued to climb in the 1990s, even with moderate health care cost increases and a stunning period of economic growth. Policies such as the CHIP expansion (discussed in section 12.3.3) mattered, but not enough to offset the tide of other factors. And providers and patients alike are growing increasingly dissatisfied with managed care as a "solution" to our health care problems. So, we enter the 21st century with an even more structural problem than when President Clinton took office—there is no conceivable hope that insurance coverage will increase without substantial public policy action. With HSA-like options off the table, however, it is not clear where the answers lie.

12.3   Incremental Approaches to Expanding Health Insurance Coverage

In the wake of the HSA's failure, the Clinton administration, as well as many legislators who wanted to expand insurance coverage, clearly recognized that incremental approaches to coverage expansions were the only feasible route. For some, incremental approaches to coverage were desirable on policy grounds, as the most cost-effective means of addressing particularly important parts of the uninsured population. For others, incremental approaches were a means to an end, national health insurance coverage. But both groups recognized that, whatever their goal, politics dictated that this was the route to take.

In this section, we review the incremental approaches to expanding health insurance coverage pursued during the Clinton years. We first set the stage by discussing the economics of incremental insurance expansions and by briefly reviewing the evidence on the incremental insurance expansions that preceded the Clinton years. We then turn to a discussion of the major initiatives of the Clinton era, within the context of this theory and evidence. We conclude with an overview of what was and wasn't accomplished.

12.3.1   The Theory and History of Incremental Insurance Expansions

There are many potential goals for incremental expansions, and they are often in conflict. The most straightforward goal would be to maximize the number of newly insured for a given budgetary cost, or to maximize the "bang for the buck" of insurance policy. This is often called target efficiency.

Target efficiency, in turn, is related to "crowdout." The uninsured population is not very distinct from the insured population. As the saying goes, dolphins and tuna swim closely together. Almost 60 percent of the uninsured have family incomes over $20,000 per year; indeed, 21 percent of the uninsured have family incomes over $50,000 per year. Yet among those with family incomes of more than $20,000 per year, only 14 percent of persons are uninsured, and 82 percent are privately insured. So any policy that is targeted purely to income, as most incremental approaches are, will by its nature be operating in a range where there are many insured persons for every uninsured person that the program is trying to attract.

The potential problem is that those enrolling in the program will not just be the uninsured, but also those insured who find public insurance attractive. As Cutler and Gruber (1996) note, typical insured persons pay about one-third of the total costs of their medical care, while public insurance has traditionally been completely free. Thus, if many of those with private insurance are made eligible for public insurance, they may be "crowded out" of their private plans onto the public rolls. This effect will reduce the bang for the buck of public insurance expansions, as dollars of spending rise but net insurance coverage does not.

It is fundamentally impossible to target a policy purely to those who are currently uninsured, since there is no way to tell exactly who would or would not be insured in the absence of the new program. Rather, minimizing crowdout means finding mechanisms that best cull out those who would otherwise be uninsured from the total population. One way to do so is to change the benefits that are offered. Less generous benefits, either less attractive coverage or charging people more, attract fewer of those with private insurance than do more generous benefits. But they also confer fewer benefits on recipients. Other barriers to enrollment, "ordeal mechanisms" such as waiting lists, that make public insurance less attractive to those who would otherwise be insured while still making it useful for those who are uninsured may help (A. Nichols and Zeckhauser, 1982).

The trade-off is, of course, the desire to help the needy. Many analysts express concern that these mechanisms will have significant adverse effects on accomplishing the goals of the program. Moreover, if low-income persons move from a poor private insurance policy to a good public insurance policy, health may improve, even though people are officially crowded out. It may be better to live with target inefficiency than to try to remove it through costly ordeal mechanisms. And even when there is crowdout, it is not without benefits: effectively, crowdout transfers income to those who would otherwise have had to finance their own private insurance coverage.

How one chooses the target group reflects these and other factors. Some groups have low crowdout but not much benefit from insurance. Other groups may have high benefits but severe crowdout. For policy and political reasons, there has always been special concern about ensuring high levels of insurance coverage among children. But doing so means raising income limits for public insurance eligibility into ranges where there is likely to be significant crowdout. For example, among those children in households with incomes between 200 percent and 250 percent of the federal poverty line, only 14 percent are uninsured, and almost 80 percent already have private health insurance.

Prior to the Clinton era, concerns about efficiency were not paramount.[4] Until 1997 the predominant tool of public insurance policy was the Medicaid program, which provided coverage for low-income families; Medicaid also provides coverage for the disabled and elderly that will be discussed in section 12.5. Before the mid-1980s, Medicaid eligibility was tied to cash welfare policy, which meant that eligibility was largely restricted to very-low-income families headed by a single mother. Starting in the mid-1980s and continuing into the Clinton era, the federal government and individual states expanded insurance coverage for two distinct populations: children and pregnant women (for the expenses of pregnancy only). Children were a natural group for obvious political reasons: they could not provide for themselves. Pregnant women were also particularly important because some evidence suggested that the savings in costs for low-birth-weight infants from covering pregnant women could more than offset the direct costs of the insurance expansion (Institute of Medicine, 1985).

By 1992 states were required to cover all pregnant women and children under the age of 6 up to 133 percent of poverty (independent of family composition) and were allowed to expand coverage up to 185 percent of poverty. In addition, children born after September 30, 1983, were mandatorily covered at incomes up to 100 percent of the poverty line (once again independent of family composition). And a number of states had gone beyond these limits, using their own state funds.

These Medicaid expansions tremendously increased the eligibility of low-income women and children for public health insurance coverage. By 1992 almost one-half of all women were eligible for Medicaid in the event they became pregnant, and almost one-third of children age 0–14 were eligible for all of their medical spending (Gruber, 1997).

However, many of those made eligible for public insurance already had their own private coverage; roughly two-thirds of eligibles were privately insured before becoming eligible (Gruber, 1997). The fact that such a large share of the newly eligible population under the Medicaid expansions had access to private

---

4. For detailed discussions of the history of public insurance policy, see Gruber (1997, 2000).

insurance raises the prospect that many of the new enrollees on the program may have been "crowded out" of private insurance purchases. There is a large literature devoted to the study of crowdout, and it generally concludes that crowdout is significant, although there are debates over the magnitude of this phenomenon; see Gruber (1997, 2001a) and Cutler (in press) for reviews.

At the same time, several studies argue that the expansions of the Medicaid program were beneficial to public health. Currie and Gruber (1996a, 1996b) find that Medicaid eligibility expansions were associated with increased use of preventive care and reduced infant and child mortality. But these improvements were costly; Currie and Gruber estimate a cost per infant life saved of roughly $4 million from the Medicaid expansions of the late 1980s and early 1990s.[5] This high cost may reflect the relative lack of targeting of these expansions.

12.3.2   First the Defense: The 1995 Government Shutdown

After the defeat of HSA, the next battle over insurance coverage in the 1990s was really a battle over the basic structure of Medicaid. Riding the wave of their "revolutionary" 1994 retaking of Congress, the Republicans in 1995 proposed in their budget to block-grant the Medicaid program, giving states almost total control of what has been traditionally a very centralized federal program.

The Clinton administration strongly opposed this block-grant plan, as well as the associated dramatic cuts in the Medicare program. There was enormous concern that a block grant would lead to significant reductions in insurance coverage, particularly in a downturn. The opposition to the health care provisions of the 1995 Republican budget plan (including very significant cuts in the Medicare program that are discussed elsewhere in Chapter 13) was the nexus of the battle that led to government shutdown in the winter of 1995. Ultimately, the administration won. The Republicans compromised and the basic structure of Medicaid was preserved.

The administration's principled, and ultimately successful, stand against block-granting the Medicaid program stands in interesting contrast to its support of a welfare reform bill less than one year later that block-granted cash welfare programs. These contradictory positions likely reflect several factors. The debate in 1995 was over a set of Medicare and Medicaid policies that were very unsavory as a package, whereas the welfare reform debate was focused on a single program. In addition, the variation in the Medicaid entitlement across states was much smaller than the existing variation in cash welfare benefits; in a sense, cash welfare had already been much more decentralized, so there was

---

5. This conclusion is not supported by some other studies in this area; see Gruber (2000) for a review.

less to "lose" (from the perspective of Democrats who prefer federal standards) from turning the program over more fully to the states. And the president had campaigned on welfare reform, so, in the face of a reelection battle, it was very hard to veto a bill that did fundamentally reform the program.

12.3.3 Further Expansions for Children: The CHIP Program

As the Clinton administration entered its second term, at a time when the wounds from HSA and the 1995 budget battle had started to heal, the focus returned to health insurance coverage expansion. The fact that a steadily growing economy had not reduced the number of uninsured was a clear precipitating factor. Of particular concern was rising uninsurance of children, which was occurring not only in the face of a growing economy, but also despite dramatic growth in the Medicaid program. Thus children became the natural target.

The administration, in its 1997 budget, proposed $8 billion for children's health insurance. In May 1997 the administration and the Republican congressional leadership reached agreement on the broad parameters of a deal to balance the budget within five years, and in the context of this agreement the Senate Finance Committee raised the amount earmarked for children's health insurance to $16 billion over 5 years. But the agreement contained essentially no detail on the nature of this new spending. Republicans, led by Phil Gramm, wanted block grants to the states to use as they saw fit for childrens' health care. They saw the existing public programs as failing and wanted to focus more directly on delivering medical services. Democrats viewed the failures of the existing system as ones of scope, and wanted an expansion of existing public programs. In addition to this fight, concerns over crowdout had now entered the policy vocabulary. Finally, there were complaints from states about the rigidity of the Medicaid program and its expensive mandates.

A compromise was hammered out that resulted in the adoption of the Children's Health Insurance Program (CHIP). The compromise was much closer to the Democrats' original position, in part because Republicans gained so much else through what became the Balanced Budget Act (BBA) of 1997 (including significant reductions in capital gains taxation and the introduction of Roth IRAs). But Republicans were successful in denying a simple expansion of Medicaid. Rather, states were given the choice of either expanding their Medicaid programs or introducing an entirely new insurance program for CHIP. This new program could offer an insurance package that was less generous than the Medicaid package, although it had to be at least as generous as one of (a) Medicaid, (b) the typical HMO offered in the state, or (c) plans offered to state employees. Moreover, states were allowed to introduce premiums and cost sharing for children enrolled in families with incomes above 150 percent of the poverty line, a significant departure from the free entitlement to Medicaid that had traditionally existed.

As with traditional Medicaid, this program was not a mandate, but states were motivated to introduce CHIP programs by the promise of vast federal subsidies. In particular, the federal government offered to pay an even larger share of CHIP costs than of Medicaid costs—30 percent of the base match rate—so that on average the federal government would pick up about three-quarters of the program costs. But, unlike Medicaid, CHIP is not an individual entitlement, raising concerns that it will not be sufficient in difficult economic times. Finally, at the end of the debate, a 15-cent increase in the tobacco excise tax was added to the BBA, funding an additional $8 billion for the program over five years.

The enactment of CHIP was clearly the high-water mark of the Clinton years in terms of insurance coverage expansion. The resultant $24 billion program (over five years) was hailed by the administration as the largest expansion in public insurance since the introduction of Medicaid, and the administration asserted that the program would insure 5 million of the 10 million uninsured children at its time of passage.

Both claims are, in fact, somewhat questionable. Some of the Medicaid-mandated expansions of the 1980s and 1990s, particularly the Omnibus Budget Reconciliation Act of 1989 (OBRA 1989), which mandated coverage of pregnant women and all children under age 6 to 133 percent of the poverty line, resulted in an increase in spending on new health insurance coverage that may have been equally large. And the OBRA expansions probably resulted in more new insurance coverage. Whether the CHIP program will ultimately enroll 5 million children is unknown. To date, CHIP programs have only enrolled roughly 3.3 million children (Domestic Policy Council, 2001). Part of this low enrollment, relative to the initial goals, was slow state action in taking up their CHIP entitlements. Despite the increased flexibility CHIP afforded, states did have to submit a very detailed plan on how they would spend their CHIP entitlement before they could receive their share of funds. This process took time. Recently enrollment has been increasing rapidly, and it rose by 70 percent in 2000 (Domestic Policy Council, 2001).

The key question is whether the CHIP program creates more in benefits than it costs, including crowdout. By allowing states some flexibility, CHIP did establish the kind of "ordeal" mechanisms that should minimize crowdout. In addition, states were explicitly mandated to have a strategy for minimizing crowdout, and a number of states have considered or enacted approaches such as waiting periods. At the same time, CHIP was expanding insurance coverage into the income range where there were many more insured per uninsured child. Because real expansions are so recent, there is little evidence to date on the net insurance increase from CHIP. One promising sign is that the number of uninsured children declined in 1999 for the first time in a decade.

12.3.4 Medicaid and CHIP Refinement

Throughout the HSA debate and continuing afterward, a major tool of incremental coverage expansion has been innovation within the Medicaid program. States are allowed to apply for "waivers" that permit them to deviate from standard program guidelines. The administration approved a wide variety of Medicaid waivers throughout its tenure. And, almost immediately after the passage of CHIP, states began applying for waivers from the structure of this program as well.

Most of the waivers from Medicaid applied for by states and approved by the administration were relatively minor deviations from the standard benefit package. But some were more major initiatives, in essence transforming Medicaid funds for women and children into coverage for entire families. The motivation for these waivers was partly the split in family coverage induced by Medicaid that lowered overall rates of coverage. Families may not enroll children in Medicaid if only some children in the family are eligible for care, or if only the children are eligible and the parents are not. Thus making entire families eligible may be a way of increasing take-up among children. Indeed, recent estimates suggest that almost 7 million low-income uninsured children in the United States are actually eligible for some form of public insurance (Broaddus and Ku, 2000). Evidence from states with plans to cover all family members suggests that this policy raised coverage of children as well.

Other reforms were proposed by the administration. Over time, there arose an increasing sense that there were much higher returns to covering low-income adults than continuing to cover somewhat higher income children. Over two-fifths of all adults below the poverty line are uninsured, compared to "only" one-quarter of children (Employee Benefits Research Institute, 2000). Thus the Clinton administration's last major proposal on the uninsured (largely a symbolic gesture included in the 2001 budget in support of similar proposals made by candidate Al Gore) was to extend Medicaid and CHIP coverage to parents of the children on these programs. This proposal did not make much headway in legislative discussions.

Finally, the administration turned its efforts to increasing enrollment among groups eligible for Medicaid but not taking it up, particularly children. To a significant extent, public policy has already created the mechanism for near-universal coverage of children, so that now 95 percent of low-income children are eligible for public insurance (Broaddus and Ku, 2000). The major problems at this point are extending eligibility to other groups, as in the proposal just discussed, and enrolling those children who are eligible but uninsured.

One group of particular emphasis is children losing insurance when they leave welfare, an important but unintended byproduct of the 1996 welfare reform act. The decline in the uninsured from 1998 to 1999, the first decline in more than a decade, partly reflects the success of efforts to enroll these eligible but not insured populations, along with the CHIP expansions.

12.3.5   Other Initiatives

While the incremental approach to insurance expansion was more successful than the HSA, not all incremental expansions were politically successful. Foremost among these was a proposal to provide public insurance to those between jobs, through state unemployment insurance (UI) programs. This proposal, included in various forms in the administration's 1994 through 1997 budgets, would have provided free or subsidized coverage to those unemployed collecting UI.

Given concerns over job lock and insurance portability, this group would seem to be an attractive one for coverage expansions. But the proposal never really gained political traction. One significant drag may have been the insistence of tying the program to UI programs, which raised both administrative and expenditure concerns among the states, as well as concerns among conservatives about the dangers of expanding UI.

Another unsuccessful proposal was to expand coverage to those early retirees who are not eligible for Medicare. As Gruber and Madrian (1996) document, early retirees face significant medical risk. Compared to those age 35–44, for example, those age 55–64 are twice as likely to report themselves in fair health and four times as likely to report themselves in poor health. They are four times as likely to have had a stroke or have cancer, seven times as likely to have had a heart attack, and five times as likely to have heart disease. They are twice as likely to be admitted to a hospital (spending twice as many nights in the hospital if admitted) and 40 percent more likely to have a prescribed medicine (having twice as many medicines if they have a prescription). As a result, the medical spending of 55- to 64-year-olds is twice as high, and twice as variable, as that of 35- to 44-year-olds. Yet this is a group with no access to public insurance options, other than if disabled.

The administration proposed in its 1999 budget a package of options designed to increase insurance coverage for the near-Medicare population. Foremost among these was the ability for 62- to 64-year-olds to buy into Medicare at its average price (about $300 per month), with an additional premium paid once they turn 65 to cover adverse selection costs.[6] There was also a similar buy-in option for 55- to 62-year-old workers who involuntarily lost their jobs (and health insurance), as well as extensions of COBRA coverage to those early retirees whose retiree health insurance coverage was terminated (a group internally labeled the "promisebreaker" population).

Once again, however, this proposal did not get very far in congressional deliberation. In terms of the buy-in, there was enormous concern among fiscal conservatives about expanding the Medicare entitlement at a time when Medicare did not seem on stable financial footing. And there remains significant resistance to any expansion of the COBRA entitlement among the business community, which also resulted in the quick rejection of the administration's 2000 budget proposal of a 25 percent tax credit for COBRA costs.

It is unclear why these proposals did not go further in the political process. They were tightly targeted to a relatively narrow interest group, meeting the seeming preconditions for political success in the Clinton era. But the affected interest groups, for example, unions, never really rallied to the cause. Perhaps this reluctance reflected their concern that partial reform would undercut the demand for more aggressive interventions later on. The result was the quick death of all these proposed initiatives.

12.3.6 Tax Policy

A final incremental approach deserves mention, as much for the future as for the past—tax-based incentives for insurance coverage. A constant debate throughout the academic community has been over the possibility of using the tax code as a means of stimulating insurance coverage. The tax code is already a major determinant of health insurance decisions, through the existing tax subsidy to employer-provided insurance, whereby employer payments through wages are taxed and employer payments through health insurance are not. This subsidy was partially extended to the self-employed in 1986, as they were allowed to deduct 25 percent of the cost of their insurance from their taxes, and fully extended to the self-employed in the Balanced Budget Act of 1997.

Toward the end of the Clinton years and throughout the 2000 campaign for president, focus shifted more heavily onto tax policy as a vehicle for addressing the problem of the uninsured. For example, George W. Bush's campaign platform included a credit for the purchase of nongroup insurance of $1,000 for

---

6. This was a somewhat odd means of financing the adverse selection cost, since it would mean the highest lifetime premiums for those healthy enrollees who lived the longest.

individuals and \$2,000 for families; this mirrored a multitude of congressional proposals for similar tax credits. Former Senator Bill Bradley had also proposed a tax credit approach in the Democratic primary.

As discussed in Gruber and Levitt (2000), however, there are important limitations to tax policy that make it much less efficient than public insurance program expansions: the fact that about half of uninsured families don't pay taxes; that even a refundable credit would face the daunting administrative problem of advancing the credit in time to finance insurance purchases; and that any politically realistic credit amount still leaves the uninsured with very large insurance costs (for example, the Bush credit would pay only about one-third of the cost of a nongroup family policy). As a result, take-up would not be substantial. Gruber and Levitt estimate that roughly three-quarters of the spending on such a tax credit actually accrues to those already covered by insurance. This is even lower target efficiency than is seen with public programs. Thus, despite their limitations, public insurance expansions remain the natural means of pursuing further reductions in the uninsured.

12.4   Insurance Market Reforms: Feeding the Middle Class

The failure of the Health Security Act did not diminish the view that some reform of insurance markets was needed. After all, the middle class was upset about their fragile ability to obtain health insurance. And there were growing concerns, particularly toward the end of the administration's tenure, about the quality of the health care being delivered by managed care plans. These concerns led to a series of reforms and proposed reforms that were politically exciting, but ultimately economically insignificant. Insurance market reforms were more hype than true change.

12.4.1   *The Health Insurance Portability and Accountability Act*

After suitable time for reflection after the defeat of the HSA, the idea of more limited health care legislation gained currency. In particular, middle-class concerns about "job lock"—losing or being denied insurance simply because a person was sick or changed jobs—had never really been addressed. Federal legislation along these lines was enacted in the Health Insurance Portability and Accountability Act (HIPAA) of 1996, also commonly known as the Kassebaum-Kennedy legislation, after its two chief sponsors.

To understand what the HIPAA did, some knowledge of the health insurance system and arcane aspects of health insurance regulation is needed. People get private health insurance in one of three ways. Some people have insurance through a large firm, a firm with sufficiently many employees that the variance of average health costs is fairly small. Firms with more than 5,000 employees are generally considered large for insurance purchases, but some insurance companies consider firms with as few as 50 employees large. Large firms frequently self-insure their medical risks. An insurer runs the insurance policy, but the firm takes all risk for the cost of its employees.

Other people obtain insurance as part of a small firm (a market often termed the small-group insurance market). These firms have average costs that are quite variable. Thus, when insurers moved to experience rating at small group sizes in the 1980s, these firms faced increasingly variable premiums. Premiums were low for healthy firms or firms with good claims experience in the immediate past, but rates could jump dramatically when one employee got sick. Finally, a residual share of people purchase insurance as individuals or families in the nongroup market.

The different markets are also characterized by differing degrees of adverse selection. Essentially all large firms provide insurance, while a minority of small firms do, and an even smaller share of individuals. Thus insurers pay particular attention to small firms wanting to purchase insurance, to guarantee that these firms are not the sickest ones. This is especially true of the individual insurance market. Insurers have long feared that individuals purchasing insurance in the nongroup market were the sickest of those without group coverage. Thus insurers either avoided that market entirely or employed substantial underwriting criteria before selling insurance to those people.

Most of the regulation of health insurance up until, and in the early years of, the Clinton administration took place at the state level. While it has been clear since the Supreme Court's 1944 decision in *United States v. Southeast Underwriters* that the federal government had the right to regulate insurance as interstate commerce, the McCarran-Ferguson Act passed the next year legislated that the federal government would devolve regulatory responsibility to the states, so long as state regulation was consistent with "federal purpose," which at that point was primarily focused on price fixing (Nichols and Blumberg, 1998).

The largest federal involvement in insurance regulation was to prohibit state involvement in regulating large, self-funded insurance plans. Most self-funded plans were operated by large, multistate employers, the large firms discussed earlier. These firms were worried about dealing with 50 state governments, each with different insurance rules. Thus, the Employee Retirement and Income Security Act (ERISA) of 1974 removed state insurance authority for self-funded plans.[7] States that wanted to restrict preexisting condition restrictions for all employees, therefore, were unable to do so.

To address the issue of job lock and ability to buy insurance, HIPAA had to deal with these three markets: the large-firm market, the small-firm market, and the individual market. HIPAA addressed each of these situations, with varying degrees of bite.

While the HIPAA legislation was complex, its essential elements were two-fold. Most importantly, HIPAA mandated changes in group insurance markets to guarantee access to insurance in situations where people might otherwise have lost it. HIPAA imposed maximum preexisting condition exclusions on group insurance. No firm—including ERISA-exempt firms—can exclude from coverage for more than one year any condition known about in the six months prior to starting on the insurance policy. Further, these preexisting condition exclusions were waived for people moving from one job with insurance to another job with insurance, provided the person had 18 months of coverage prior to the job change. Both these provisions were designed to deal with the insurance portability problem.

An important point about these changes, though, is that they did not specify the price at which insurance must be offered. Thus insurers could charge substantial amounts for people with preexisting conditions, and these charges would be allowed under HIPAA. The omission of premium restrictions was by design; there was no bipartisan support for premium restrictions at the federal level, although states were allowed to enact them on their own.

HIPAA had further provisions for insurance sold to small firms—defined as firms with 2 to 50 employees. HIPAA required insurers in the small-group market to sell insurance to all small groups wishing to buy it; groups could not be excluded simply because a member of the group was sick. The rules under which firms could obtain this insurance—in particular the plans they had access to and the price they had to pay—were complex, depending on other regulations the state enacted (as we will discuss further later on).

---

7. Contributing to the desire for federal regulation was the growing belief that insurance companies were using ERISA as a loophole. For example, a state might mandate that all insurers (except self-funded companies) provide a minimum level of mental health benefits. Insurers and companies that did not want to provide these benefits might convert the insurance product being sold into a self-funded plan. If the firm buying insurance were small, this conversion would seem to open it up to substantial risk of claims expense. But nothing prohibited the company from buying stop-loss coverage—often from the same insurer—to limit its maximum expense for any individual. This stop-loss insurance was not health insurance and thus was not subject to the mental health mandate. As a result, companies of all sizes could effectively skirt the regulatory mandates by becoming self-funded with little increase in risk.

Finally, HIPAA made smaller changes in the nongroup market. Requiring firms to offer insurance to anyone in this market was not an option; insurers were too worried about adverse selection to go along with that. Rather, the act made it easier for certain people to get insurance without being denied care. Insurers could not exclude from coverage or impose preexisting condition restrictions on people with at least 18 months of continuous private coverage, who most recently had group coverage, who had exhausted their benefits under federal continuation of coverage (COBRA) legislation, and who were not eligible for public coverage or employer-sponsored insurance through a spouse. This is a small set of people, to be sure. Again, the price at which these people could get such insurance was not specified in federal legislation; it was left to the states to regulate this (and most do not).

HIPAA left so much to the states because the states were substantially ahead of the federal government in this area. Indeed, the right way to view HIPAA is as the federal government codifying what the majority of states had already done, not imposing a wealth of new requirements on them.

Over the course of the 1980s, states had become increasingly worried about small-group health insurance issues. Unlike the federal government, which concentrated on covering more of the uninsured, states focused much more on the problems of those with insurance. Many small businesses wanted restrictions on insurance practices. And insurers were often out-of-state companies, so their lobbying counted less in state capitals. Thus state government acted long before the federal government.

As early as 1989 states began passing legislation designed to help small firms obtain insurance. By the time of the HIPAA, nearly all states had some small-group market reforms in place. The state legislation was generally similar to the HIPAA as it applied to small firms: it required insurers to offer at least some insurance products (HIPAA mandated *all* insurance products) to all groups of people, and it prohibited preexisting condition restrictions in some cases. Most importantly, many states limited the variability of premiums that insurers could charge to less healthy groups. Typically, states set rating bands that insurers could not exceed. For example, some states required insurers to price all policies within 15 percent (plus or minus) of the average premium. Others required insurers to contribute to a high-risk pool for very expensive nongroup cases, which would be run by the state. The HIPAA legislation allowed states to continue these rating reforms if they wished, effectively putting some teeth in the HIPAA regulations.

What HIPAA effectively accomplished, then, was relatively minor. It codified these state regulations, making them more uniform and expanding them in minor ways.[8] It extended prohibitions on preexisting-condition exclusions to ERISA-exempt firms. It brought reform to the few states that had not passed legislation already. And it made minor changes increasing access to nongroup insurance for some people.

Not surprisingly, essentially all analyses of the effect of HIPAA on health insurance markets suggest that the HIPAA legislation by itself had virtually no effect on rates of insurance coverage, premiums paid, or job mobility (Pollitz et al., 2000; Nichols and Blumberg, 1998).

And yet, as with the HSA before it, passing the HIPAA legislation was quite a struggle. Congress had protracted negotiations over the issue, far disproportionate to what the legislation actually accomplished. Indeed, to get passage of the legislation, the White House and congressional Democrats had to agree to a demonstration program for Medical Savings Accounts.[9] Given its incremental progress, why all the fighting? Why even pass HIPAA in the first place?

The desire for reform was largely political. In 1996 congressional Republicans had lost the budget fights of the previous year and were on the verge of losing the presidential election and possibly control of Congress. They wanted some positive health care accomplishment to run on (and their leadership was very focused on making at least a symbolic gesture in favor of MSAs, for ideological and constituent service reasons). Democrats wanted to establish the principle that the federal government could act on health care, and they wanted a bipartisan statement that some insurance market regulation was needed. They knew this legislation was not major, but hoped that it would set the stage for later action. That is also the reason why insurers opposed it. They did not fear the provisions of the HIPAA per se, but worried that it would lead to other federal legislation that would be more onerous.

Even if HIPAA itself had no major effect, one might wonder whether the state legislation it built upon was successful. Those laws were more consequential, as they preceded federal action. In answering this question, one needs first to decide what the goals of the legislation were. Premiums were supposed to be compressed by the legislation. There is little data on health insurance premiums paid by employers, however, so testing this issue is not easy. The legislation was also supposed to reduce job lock and increase labor market mobility. In principle, this assumption can be tested. The few studies that have been done suggest no large changes in mobility as a result of the HIPAA. Fi-

---

8. For example, not all states imposed small-group restrictions for firms with as few as 2 employees or as many as 50 employees.

9. Medical Savings Accounts (MSAs) are a catastrophic insurance product that provides low-cost insurance with very high deductibles and/or copayments. Very few people took up these accounts, however, so we do not spend much time on them.

nally, one hope was that more people would become insured, since the ability of insurers to deny coverage would be reduced. The literature to date suggests this outcome did not happen.

Indeed, some studies find that insurance coverage *declined* slightly as a consequence of the legislation, although the estimates of insurance decline are small and a number of studies find no significant effect. A decline in coverage could be explained by the fact that insurance reform lowers premiums for high-risk firms but raises premiums for low-risk firms. As a result, some low-risk firms choose to drop coverage, or their employees choose not to take it up. Of course, this result may not be bad; public policy may well want to insure high-risk people at the expense of low-risk people. But it does not promote overall insurance coverage.

However, the small overall effects suggest a more basic problem with the insurance reform legislation. Fundamentally, the legislation did not materially impact the insurance market. To a great extent, this failure is a result of the complexity of insurance markets. Insurers offer more than one insurance policy and do so in many different settings. Some of the legislation required only that insurers offer a "basic" and "comprehensive" package to everyone. Insurers complied with these restrictions but priced the required policies very high. Purchasing firms that were good risks were offered access to different policies that had lower prices.

Other times, state mandates regarding purchased insurance were met by increases in the share of firms becoming self-insured. Insurers and firms worked out such arrangements to avoid the new legislation. HIPAA might have extended the full range of state insurance regulations to these ERISA-exempt firms, but it chose not to do so. As a result, self-insurance remains a mechanism to avoid most of the reforms that states required.

In retrospect, these actions should not be a surprise. People who are healthy do not want to pool with those who are sick. Insurers would like to cater to these desires. Thus legislation regulating health insurance needs to constrain what both firms and insurers naturally want to do. Without very onerous regulations, it is impossible to do so. The lesson from the HIPAA, and the state regulations that preceded it, is that partial legislation cannot constrain markets from acting in profit-maximizing ways. HIPAA was perhaps a political success, but was close to an economic nonevent.

12.4.2 Benefits Mandates

A similar conclusion can be drawn from studying the other major insurance market reforms of the Clinton era. These other reforms were focused on addressing perceived limitations in the benefits being offered by private insurance plans in the managed care era. Principal among these was mental health parity. The administration, led in this instance by the vice president's wife, Tipper Gore, was disenchanted with the discrimination in the common limitations on mental health coverage in private insurance plans relative to the coverage afforded somatic illnesses. Insurers were long reluctant to cover mental health on parity with other illnesses, because of a higher elasticity of demand for mental health services. This was often termed the Woody Allen effect, after the famous actor's many years in therapy. In fact, research supported the insurers' position; for example, the RAND Health Insurance Experiment found that mental health services were more responsive to patient cost sharing than physical health (Newhouse et al., 1993). Economic theory dictates that optimal insurance policies feature less generous coverage for more elastically demanded services, such as mental health.

Two countervailing arguments were made by advocates of more generous mental health coverage. First, they stressed there would be significant "offset" effects: increased generosity of outpatient mental health coverage would reduce spending on inpatient mental health. While there is little evidence to support this claim, this was a strongly held belief in the administration. Second, the development of managed health care limited the impact of cost sharing alone on mental health utilization. A health insurer with tight utilization management on mental health care could afford to reduce cost sharing on use of psychiatric services without worrying about significant cost increases.

After considerable debate, the administration was able to secure passage of Public Law 104–204 in 1996, which prohibited health plans from establishing separate lifetime and annual limits for mental health coverage. The evidence since this legal change took place suggests that, consistent with the preceding arguments, plans did not spend much more on health care, as costs were managed in other ways.

A stronger step was an executive order, in 1999, mandating that all Federal Employees Health Benefit Program (FEHBP) plans have full mental health parity. This guaranteed benefit parity for all federal employees. The executive order was one example of a way that the administration could avoid the pitfalls of dealing with a hostile Republican Congress on health issues: bypass Congress.

Other benefits mandates were passed as well, such as regulations stipulating that all women receive at least a two-night stay in the hospital for childbirth. Once again, there is little evidence on the costs and benefits of these regulations.

A more important insurance debate was over the "Patients' Bill of Rights." Managed care grew rapidly in the 1980s and early 1990s, particularly after the demise of the HSA, as employers abandoned traditional fee-for-service insurance plans in favor of managed care. The rise of managed care drew increasing concern in public discussion. People worried that managed care would restrict access to necessary care. This concern was fueled by horror stories of patients being denied "necessary" care and being gravely injured as a result.

In fact, research suggests that such horror stories were not widespread. Quality of care in managed care plans, as best it can be measured, is virtually identical to quality of care in traditional indemnity plans (Miller and Luft, 1997). But the vast majority of people clearly felt otherwise. By the start of the second term of the Clinton administration, the "managed care backlash" was in full swing.

To its credit (given the evidence), the administration never really joined the managed care bashing full throttle. The administration worried about managed care abuses but never went as far as many opponents of managed care hoped. Given the tenet of managed competition, with its emphasis on a diversity of health plans, bashing managed care at length would have been a large about-face.

The administration's response to the managed care backlash was the establishment in 1997 of a "quality commission" that was charged with developing a patient's bill of rights. This bipartisan commission recommended that there should be guaranteed access to needed health care specialists; access to emergency room services when and where the need arose; continuity of care protections; and access to a fair, unbiased, and timely internal and independent external appeals process (Domestic Policy Council, 2001). These recommendations were immediately adopted by the administration, setting off a fierce congressional debate over patient protections that continues today. The major issue around which the current debate revolves is the right of patients to sue their HMOs for denial of care or other perceived abuses.

The administration was unable to reach agreement in Congress. Instead, Congress slowly wound its way around this topic, with no agreement by the term's end. Perhaps as a result, Clinton left office with little progress on insurance restrictions, other than the HIPAA and using his executive powers to put some patient protections in place for FEHBP enrollees.

12.5   Health Policy for the Elderly and Disabled

Medicaid policy was essential to the children's health insurance expansion in 1997. But Medicaid is more than insurance for poor children and their moms. Two-thirds of Medicaid spending is for the elderly and disabled, paying for cost sharing Medicare does not cover and coverage Medicare omits, primarily prescription drugs and institutional long-term care. In this section, we discuss the evolution of Medicaid policy toward those groups during the Clinton years.

12.5.1   Long-Term Care Reforms

After the failure of the HSA, which had a significant long-term care expansion, the administration took an incremental approach to long-term care. And, as with coverage initiatives for the nonelderly population, the record was mixed.

The Clinton administration, like the Reagan and Bush administrations before it, was interested in developing and promoting the private market for long-term care insurance. Public-sector cost was the driving force; private long-term care insurance would be cheaper than public expansions. One of the few remnants of HSA that actually made its way into law was legislation in 1996 that gave employer-sponsored long-term care insurance the same tax-preferred status that is conferred on employer-provided health insurance, while at the same time implementing basic quality standards that any tax-preferred product had to meet.

That this provision made it into law is not surprising, given the bipartisan support for tax-induced private coverage. Further, at the very end of its tenure, the administration was also able to pass a proposal to introduce long-term care products as a benefit for federal employees, with the hope that this would jump-start the private employer market. Even with this legislation, though, the private long-term care insurance market remains tiny, numbering no more than a few million policies. Employers burned by rising acute-care costs for several decades do not appear eager to embark on the same path with long-term care.

Another potentially important change of the Clinton years was the repeal of the Boren Amendment, which governed long-term care reimbursement rates. This amendment, passed in 1980, allowed states to move to their own methodologies for reimbursing these providers, so long as rates were "reasonable and adequate." In the wake of a long history of lawsuits brought under the Boren Amendment ruling that reimbursement rates were not reasonable and thus mandating higher payments, the amendment was repealed as part of the Balanced Budget Act of 1997. After BBA, states had only to provide public notice of their proposed rates for reimbursing hospitals, nursing facilities, and intermediate-care facilities and the methods used to establish those rates. While this change was viewed as a major victory for states, so far it has had little impact. Medicaid rates for nursing homes have risen at roughly the same rate since the repeal as before, and there has not been any concerted movement among the states to more restrictive nursing-home payment methodologies.[10]

---

10. Based on data kindly provided to us by David Grabowski of the University of Alabama at Birmingham.

By far the most expansive post-HSA effort on long-term care came late in the administration, with the proposal of a tax break for those with long-term care needs and their caregivers. The initiative was developed after the 1997 BBA enacted many new benefits for children, including tax breaks for the cost of college education and the CHIP expansion. But these policies did the elderly and near elderly little good. Long-term care (and prescription drug coverage) would rectify this potential political oversight.

Long-term care costs are very high for a relatively small number of persons. Insurance principles argue for covering this population first. But past experiences with incremental approaches had convinced administration officials that they needed a broad base of support for a new policy. This required benefits at a lower level of spending. The compromise was to provide a credit of modest size, $3,000, that would apply to any person, or his or her caregiver, who was somewhat but not totally disabled (defined as having three or more activities of daily living, or ADLs). In addition, a proposal was made for tax deductibility for private expenditures on long-term care insurance, to complement the deductibility of employer spending passed in 1996. Even this somewhat broad proposal, however, found very little public support, and it did not become law.

Finally, the administration actively pursued regulatory changes to improve long-term care. One such change was growing endorsement of state Medicaid waivers for the provision of home and community-based care for the elderly and disabled. Spending on these waivers rose from $2.2 billion in FY1992 to $10.6 billion in FY1999. In theory, states must show that these waivers pass cost-effectiveness tests before they can be approved by HCFA, in terms of offsetting increased community care costs with lower institutionally based care costs. In practice, it seems unlikely that they can meet these cost-effectiveness standards, given the existing (albeit dated) evidence on the subject. The channeling experiment of the 1970s randomly assigned to some families more exhaustive community-based care; but, while this improved quality of living, it had no impact in terms of reducing institutionally based care use (Kemper, 1988). A second initiative, pursued at the very end of the administration's tenure, was an aggressive campaign to improve nursing home quality through the Medicare and Medicaid programs.

12.5.2   Policy for the Disabled

Incremental, but meaningful, accomplishments were made in policy for the disabled. Fewer than 1 percent of recipients return to work after starting on disability insurance (DI) (U.S. General Accounting Office, 1998). One barrier to returning to work is the high cost of health insurance, leading to a reluctance to drop the public Medicare entitlement that comes with enrollment in disability insurance (after two years). The Jeffords-Kennedy Work Incentives Improvement Act, passed in 1999, addressed this problem by extending Medicare coverage for another $4\frac{1}{2}$ years after someone leaves the DI program; the law also allowed some disabled not on the program to buy into their state's Medicaid insurance pool.

This law is an example of where the incremental approach to health reform was both a policy and political success. It is eminently sensible to extend incentives to work for a population receiving many other benefits: in the worst case, the policy has no effect and no cost; in the best case, it saves money overall by inducing the disabled to work. In political terms, by addressing such a clearly needy population, and at such a low cost, the law was hard to resist.

12.6 Tobacco Policy

As is reflected in the discussion thus far, the primary focus of the administration's health policies was on health insurance coverage and market reforms. This reflects a basic view among administration officials, shared by many health care analysts, that health insurance coverage was the primary policy tool available for improving the health of the U.S. population. But this view is not universal. Many prominent observers suggest that medical care is a secondary influence on health relative to individual decisions to engage in healthy, or unhealthy, behaviors (e.g., McGinness and Foege, 1993).[11]

Perhaps the most widespread unhealthy behavior in the U.S. population is smoking. An aggressive public information campaign has led to a massive, three-decade-long decline in smoking in the United States. Still, more than a fifth of the adult population continues to smoke. Smoking is the largest cause of preventable illness in the United States, accounting for more than 400,000 deaths per year, more than AIDS, alcohol, cocaine, heroin, homicide, suicide, motor vehicle crashes, and fires combined (U.S. Department of the Treasury, 1998). The typical smoker's life expectancy is about six years less than if the person did not smoke (Cutler et al., in press).

There were two new elements in the Clinton administration. The first was the rise in youth smoking. Beginning in 1993, youth smoking ended a long period of decline and began a sustained increase. As shown in Figure 12.4, by 1997

---

11. The economist Victor Fuchs (1994) noted that the tobacco tax used to fund part of the Health Security Act was the part of the plan most likely to improve health—this is a plan guaranteeing universal coverage with a generous set of benefits!

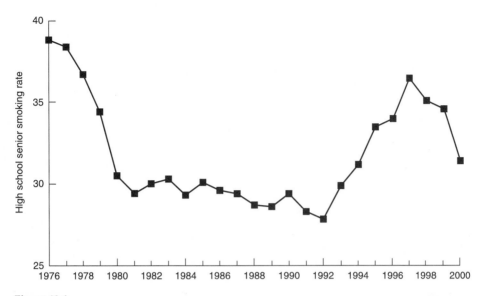

Figure 12.4
Youth Smoking over Time. (*Source:* Based on data kindly provided to us by David Grabowski of the
University of Alabama at Birmingham. Data are from the Monitoring the Future Survey.)

youth smoking had risen by roughly one-third from its 1992 trough, before
declining again after 1997 (due to price increases that will be discussed later).

Three-quarters of smokers start as youths (Gruber and Zinman, 2000), so increasing youth smoking initiation could reverse the recent trend toward lower
overall cigarette usage. Moreover, youths have demonstrated a clear lack of appreciation for the addictive nature of their smoking habit. Among high school
seniors who smoke, 56 percent say that they will not be smoking five years later,
but only 31 percent of them in fact quit within five years. Moreover, among those
who smoke more than one pack a day, the smoking rate five years later among
those who stated that they *would not* be smoking (74 percent) is actually higher
than the smoking rate among those who stated that they *would* be smoking (72
percent) (U.S. Department of Health and Human Services, 1994).

The second factor was the shift of tobacco companies from a business like any
other, and thus not deserving of special government punishment, to a pariah
among business because of deceptive advertising and attempts to hook youths.
The emergence of the "Joe Camel" campaign, along with the negative public
reaction to it as an obvious attempt to woo young smokers, was a symbol of
this transition in public perceptions.

Of course, from an economics perspective, the fact that smoking is inherently
harmful is not justification for regulating or taxing it. In the standard economics

paradigm, the only justification for regulating or taxing an activity is the externalities it causes to others; damage to self is presumed to be incorporated into the rational decision to smoke (Becker and Murphy, 1988). And the externalities from smoking may be quite low, since much of the health care cost increases of smoking appear to be offset by savings to the Social Security program and other defined-benefits pensions from early mortality. Gravelle and Zimmerman (1994) estimated the net externalities of smoking at only 33 cents per pack, although this estimate ignores potentially important factors such as secondhand smoke and long-term health consequences of low-birth-weight babies (Gruber, 2001b). This level of externalities was actually lower than the actual tax per pack of cigarettes when the Clinton administration took office.

Of course, this "rational addiction" model is not readily accepted outside of economics. Even within formal economics, recent analyses have suggested alternatives for moving beyond this formulation in thinking about optimal taxation of addictive bads such as cigarettes (Gruber and Koszegi, 2000; Laux, 2000). Considerations such as the underprediction of addiction for teens, the fact that adults express strong desires to quit smoking but seem unable to, and the popularity of "self-control" devices such as self-imposed punishments for continuing to smoke, all point to alternative models with "time-inconsistent" consumers who do not fully appreciate the future consequences of their actions. In such a situation, the fact that smoking harms one's own health can be a rationalization for government action, as government regulation acts as the type of "self-control device" craved by smokers who cannot quit even though they would like to do so over the long run. This becomes an important consideration because, while the externalities of smoking may be low, the "internalities" (or damage to self) are enormous; the cost per pack of cigarettes through increased mortality alone is $30 per pack using standard estimates of the value of a life (Gruber and Koszegi, 2000). Estimates such as those in Gruber and Koszegi (2000), who compute an internality correction tax of $1.00 for even very modest time inconsistency, suggest that taxes were indeed too low in the early 1990s.

Public policy toward smoking had been stymied for years by the profitable and well-connected tobacco companies. As a result, beyond informational campaigns, there had been little effective increase in government regulation of this industry since the 1960s. Indeed, by 1995, real federal and state excise taxes on cigarettes were one-third below their peak level of the mid-1960s.

The administration ultimately took on the tobacco industry, haltingly at first and with vigor later on. Antitobacco policy became a significant accomplishment of the administration, despite the lack of legislative actions. The social actions in isolating tobacco companies and focusing attention on youth smoking could have significant long-term benefits for public health.

12.6.1   Early Initiatives

The administration made tobacco taxes part of its agenda early on, with a proposed 75-cent rise in the federal excise tax on cigarettes as part of the HSA. By comparison, the federal tax at that point was 24 cents. The tobacco tax was the only explicit tax in the proposal. But the rhetoric was not explicitly punitive. Rather, smoking was an obvious target because it cost money and lives, and some revenues were needed for the HSA. The administration actually rejected a higher tobacco tax in formulating its plan, for fear of antagonizing tobacco-state Democrats. Of course, when the HSA was defeated, this tax was not passed. Tobacco taxation reemerged as a source of insurance expansion funding in 1997, and a 15-cent increase in tobacco taxation in the Balanced Budget Act of 1997 was a source of funding for CHIP.

The real driving force for substantial tobacco regulation in the first Clinton term was not the White House or Democratic political operatives, but rather FDA Commissioner David Kessler (Kessler, 2001). Early in his and the administration's tenure, Kessler decided to push the envelope of what the FDA might do in terms of regulating tobacco, a topic of interest but little action for previous FDA regimes. Kessler's charge led to the announcement in August 1996 of the nation's first comprehensive program to prevent children and adolescents from using cigarettes or smokeless tobacco. This program would mandate proof of age 18 for tobacco purchase; cigarette vending machines would be banned from locations frequented by children such as supermarkets; tobacco advertising on billboards near schools and playgrounds would be forbidden; all billboards advertising tobacco would be printed in black and white and contain no pictures; and tobacco companies would be forbidden from aiming their marketing campaigns at young people and within two years would be banned from sponsoring sporting events.

In March 1997 the FDA regulation requiring retailers to have all tobacco customers up to age 27 prove that they are at least 18 years old went into effect. The FDA then planned to implement the regulations pertaining to tobacco advertisements over the next six months, but in April 1997 a federal judge in North Carolina ruled that the FDA could not control tobacco advertising aimed at young people. However, the judge also ruled that the FDA could regulate cigarettes as drugs, giving the FDA the potential to control nicotine levels in cigarettes. The FDA was collecting data on the effects of varying nicotine levels when a federal appeals court ruled that the FDA lacked the authority to regulate cigarettes or smokeless tobacco in 1998. In March 2000 the Supreme Court also ruled that the FDA did not have the authority to regulate tobacco as an addictive drug in a 5-to-4 decision.

12.6.2 Litigation[12]

The next round in the battle over tobacco was fought early in the second term, and once again the genesis was not the administration, but rather state attorneys general and the industry itself. There was a long history of private individuals suing the tobacco industry for premature morbidity and mortality, dating back to 1954. Historically, the tobacco industry had won every legal case it faced, with the single exception of a $400,000 judgment against the Liggett group that was overturned on appeal. The failure of individuals' suits was often attributed to the fact that it was difficult to tell for any given death whether the case was smoking-related or due to some other factor (the fact that cigarette smokers often don't exercise, for example).

Clever lawyers decided to counter this defense by suing as a group. Thus no individual death need be attributed to tobacco, only deaths on average. In 1994 the first class action lawsuit was filed against the industry in *Castano et al. v. American Tobacco Company*. Sixty-five law firms pooled their resources to file this case, which alleged that the tobacco industry had failed to warn adequately about the addictive properties of cigarettes. This suit was ruled too unwieldy by the Fifth Circuit Court of Appeals in 1996, perhaps reflecting the difficulty of pursuing these types of class actions across state lines given very different state regulatory guidelines (Bulow and Klemperer, 1998). But it set the stage for the state lawsuits to follow.

On March 23, 1994, the state of Mississippi filed a lawsuit against the tobacco industry to recover the costs to the state of treating smoking-related illness under its Medicaid program. No state had ever attempted such litigation before. This lawsuit posed two particular problems for the industry (Bulow and Klemperer, 1998). First, it relied on the argument that the industry was liable to the state for medical costs, even if smokers knowingly contributed to their illness. Thus individual decisions to smoke were less relevant. Second, it was filed shortly after the passage of Florida's Medicaid Third-Party Liability Act of 1994 (and the consideration of similar legislation in other states), which allowed the state to sue a manufacturer of an allegedly harmful product for the medical expenses of a group, relying on statistical evidence instead of proving causation and damages in each case. Tobacco litigation was the first application of this principle.

In the wake of the Mississippi suit, most other states filed similar suits for Medicaid cost recovery. Under pressure, the largest "fringe" manufacturer, Liggett, broke ranks with the major industry participants in early 1996 to settle with

---

12. The discussion in this section draws heavily on Gruber (2001b).

five states, in the process providing a host of secret documents that detailed industry knowledge of the damages of smoking and marketing to youth. These "smoking gun" documents provided further ammunition for additional cases and account for a significant change in the public's perception of the tobacco industry. The legal risks from state and private class action suits were an enormous drag on the market value of the industry; indeed, Bulow and Klemperer (1998) reported that the implicit market value of the domestic tobacco side of RJR Nabisco had become roughly *zero* in the mid-1990s.

In the face of this enormous legal risk, the tobacco industry sat down early in 1997 with the attorneys general of the states filing lawsuits and the lawyers behind the *Castano* class action suit to attempt to hammer out a comprehensive agreement. In April 1997 a proposed settlement was announced. The key components were that the industry would agree to pay $368 billion over 25 years to the states, in return for (1) dismissing the state suits; (2) immunity from future punitive damages as part of individual suits; and (3) immunity from future class action suits. In effect, this industry was buying legal peace. The financing of the payments was largely through taxation, although this fact was not directly stated. A key component of the payments was a "volume adjustment" that would tie each company's payment to its volume of cigarette sales. This in effect converted the settlement into a tax (with the exception of a $10 billion up-front payment), as both linked payments to sales, and all evidence suggests that past taxes on tobacco had been fully passed on to prices, so that this "settlement" would be as well.[13] Bulow and Klemperer (1998) calculate that, given the inelasticity of demand for cigarettes, the industry could pass this tax on to prices and suffer only a $1 billion per year reduction in profits while transferring $13 billion per year to the states.[14]

While the attorneys general had the right to settle their state lawsuits, the approval of Congress was needed to grant other legal immunities. It was at this point that the White House became involved.

12.6.3   *The Administration Acts*

In September 1997 the Clinton administration announced that it was not satisfied with the parameters of this tobacco deal and would not endorse legislation to implement it. The key concern was that the payments were not large

---

13. Indeed, this settlement actually explicitly *mandated* that the payments be passed forward to prices!

14. The impact on industry profitability computed by Bulow and Klemperer ignores the collusive aspects of price setting in this industry. As we will argue, the settlement of state lawsuits by the industry may have actually *increased* profitability.

enough. It had not escaped the administration's notice that tobacco stock prices jumped significantly on the day the deal was announced, and Wall Street analysts suggested that the enormous discount at which tobacco stocks had historically traded relative to comparable investments would disappear under this deal. In addition, there were concerns about restrictions in FDA jurisdiction over tobacco and other perceived weaknesses.

In spring 1998 the Clinton administration worked with Senator John McCain and others to develop a legislative alternative to the settlement of the attorneys general. This alternative differed in a number of key ways from the original settlement. First, there was a much larger payment—$516 billion over 25 years compared to $368 billion. Second, the Food and Drug Administration (FDA) was given full regulatory authority over tobacco products, as it has over other pharmaceuticals and medical drugs. Third, regulations on youth smoking were increased, including greater enforcement of youth access restrictions and a very sizable "youth lookback penalty" that imposed both industry-wide and company-specific payments if youth smoking did not decline in the future. Finally, the legal protections provided against private lawsuits were more limited, although the state suits were settled in full. Partly because of limitations on legal protections designed to woo key Democrats, the proposed legislation was voted almost unanimously out of the Commerce Committee in the Senate. But, after several weeks of debate, it died on the floor of the Senate in June 1998.

The demise of tobacco legislation is interesting in comparison to the experience of the HSA. The administration clearly learned from its HSA experience. There was constant caution about getting ahead of Congress on the issue, as well as a genuine effort to work in a bipartisan fashion with Senator McCain. But still a consensus could not be formed. The bill could not pass Congress with anything approximating the legal protections on future lawsuits of the settlement originally reached by the attorneys general. Indeed, during floor debate the remaining protections were actually stripped out. This action, in turn, turned the tobacco industry from ally to opponent, leading to the bill's demise.

Tobacco regulation did not fail because it was too Democratic, because it was drafted in secret, or for any of the other arguments made about the HSA. It failed rather because it was too big and did not offer enough benefits to the tobacco industry. It is simply too hard to undertake such ambitious legislation in today's political climate. Perhaps this is what happened to the HSA as well.

After the demise of the tobacco legislation, the industry and states went back to the negotiating table. A more limited settlement was hammered out in November 1998. Under this Master Settlement Agreement (MSA), the industry would pay $206 billion to the states over 25 years, the equivalent of roughly 45 cents per pack; Cutler et al. (in press) calculate that the present discounted value of these payments through the year 2025 was $105 billion. The MSA also included some voluntary advertising restrictions, such as the removal of billboard advertisements for cigarettes, and a ban on using cartoon characters in advertisements. There was no restriction on private litigation.

The individual state settlements, the Master Settlement Agreement, and the proposed McCain bill all shared some important limitations, which are highlighted by Bulow and Klemperer (1998). First, these approaches provide contracts only with the major tobacco producers and leave other brands without an obligation to make payments, resulting in a substantial cost advantage for these other brands (which make up only a few percentage points of the market, at least at the time of this deal), conferring a windfall profit on them. These windfall profits are capped by a feature of the MSA—the "nonparticipating manufacturers adjustment"—that essentially mandates that states levy taxes on any sales of nonparticipating manufacturers that exceed 125 percent of their 1997 market share; if states do not pass such taxes, they risk losing most or all of their state payments (Cutler et al., in press).

A second area of concern is the enormous payments going to lawyers from this settlement. Under the Master Settlement Agreement, lawyers representing the 46 settling states received $1.25 billion initially and $500 million per year thereafter. These payments appear disproportionate to the actual work done by lawyers in many states, some of whom had not even filed cases before the MSA was signed. Jeremy Bulow estimated that the lawyers fees based on the actual damage payments would have been about one-fortieth of the actual payments they are scheduled to receive (Nasar, 1998).

The way to solve both of these problems would be with a straight-out tax increase rather than a complicated settlement. Such a tax increase would certainly be better social policy. But the outlook for a tax increase was poor. The indirect taxation of the settlement was really the only option. In this sense, the payments to lawyers and excess profits to small producers, while inequitable, can be viewed as the political economy costs that must be paid to impose cigarette taxes.

The tobacco industry responded to the MSA by raising prices. In fact, price increases in 1997 and 1998 *exceeded* the amount required to pay the costs of state settlements by roughly 20–25 cents per pack (Black, 1998). A price increase this large, given the highly inelastic demand for cigarettes, would imply that tobacco industry profits would actually rise as a result of the settlement, as the profit lost from the relatively small declines in sales is more than offset by the additional profit earned on the remaining packs sold. This excessive rise in prices was also a feature of the industry's reaction to previous federal tax increases; Harris (1997) suggests that the tobacco companies may use these events as focal points to achieve higher industry-wide prices, a story of implicit collusion. Another (perhaps complementary) explanation may be that the industry was convinced in the wake of its failed attempt at a comprehensive settlement that the domestic tobacco industry was in rapid decline, so that its past strategy of keeping prices low to induce new smokers to take up the habit is no longer worthwhile.

The fact that prices rose above settlement costs raises a central tension in tobacco control policy (and one that was never really fully resolved inside the administration): Is the goal to punish the managers or shareholders in tobacco companies, or to raise cigarette prices and thereby discourage smoking? If the former, then the MSA or the equivalent excise tax would not have the desired effect. If the latter, the additional price increase is a positive outcome of the settlement.

Despite this settlement, however, the industry's legal woes are far from over. In 1997, Lorillard paid more than $1.5 million to the family of Morton Horowitz, the first time a U.S. cigarette maker had ever paid a smoking-related personal injury claim. The industry paid out $350 million in the *Broin* case to airline attendants who had illness claims related to secondhand smoke exposure. The tobacco industry has also lost several other high-profile cases in recent years, culminating in the *Engle* case in Florida in July 2000, in which a jury awarded a class of 500,000 smokers in Florida $145 billion in damages. These payments are lump sum and not subject to future sales of cigarettes, so incorporation into prices may not be so immediate. While all of these recent decisions remain subject to appeal, the past invulnerability of the industry to private lawsuits is clearly being penetrated. New information about the tobacco industry has clearly affected its public image.

Finally, in September 1999, the U.S. Department of Justice filed suit against the industry to recover the costs to the federal government of smoking-related illness. According to the complaint, the costs of smoking to Medicare, the Veterans Administration, and the Federal Employees Health Benefit Program amount to more than $20 billion per year. The complaint also seeks additional damages under a racketeering charge against the industry, resulting from its (alleged) conspiracy since the early 1950s to defraud the American public concerning the dangers of smoking. But the courts have so far rejected the medical-costs part of this claim, and the outlook for this case under the watch of the Bush administration is unclear.

12.6.4 Summary

Despite the failure of comprehensive legislation, the efforts of the Clinton administration had enormous impacts on tobacco policy. The 15-cent rise in the tobacco excise tax in the Balanced Budget Act of 1997 was the first major increase in federal tobacco taxation in 15 years. And, although the administration was not able to craft an alternative to the original settlement of the attorneys general, it did reject a deal that was likely too soft on the industry. The result was a major settlement of just the state suits and ongoing legal woes for the industry.

And perhaps more important, the tide has turned against the tobacco industry. The public is outraged about past behavior, and private lawsuits are increasingly leading to price increases, deterring future smokers. The industry is no longer invincible.

Looking forward, the federal government faces two possible paths in terms of regulating the tobacco industry. The first is to sit back and let the lawsuits proceed—both private lawsuits and those of the U.S. Department of Justice. The disadvantage of this approach is that the tort system is a haphazard and inefficient mechanism for reducing tobacco use, with large deadweight losses and uncertain outcomes.[15] Moreover, if the existing industry participants are pushed into bankruptcy, the market may pass to new companies who do not face such enormous legal liabilities from past poor conduct.

At the other extreme, the government can act legislatively, providing the industry with the kind of legislative shield against legal risk that it sought through the proposed 1997 attorneys general settlement, perhaps in return for some level of payment and tighter regulation of tobacco products. But providing a legal shield for the industry is a risky strategy as well. There is enormous uncertainty about the "optimal" cigarette price that would accurately capture at least the externalities—and perhaps also some of the internalities—of smoking. In addition, the federal government does not have an enviable track record for regulating this industry, and once the lobbying begins, there is some risk that the tobacco companies would get off very easy. A trade-off that involves settlement of current lawsuits but no new lawsuits would also be inequitable for smokers who have not yet brought smoking-related claims. This could set a disturbing precedent if future corporations see a possibility of avoiding tort liability by signing government agreements.

---

15. For example, the state settlement alone featured up-front payments to lawyers of $1.25 billion and ongoing payments of $500 million per year.

12.7   Other Public Health Issues

Tobacco was not the only area of activity for the administration in the public health arena. We group as our last set of policies a series of public health actions enacted throughout the administration, but particularly in the latter half. Several policies fall under this rubric. They include substantially increased funding for childhood vaccinations (beginning in 1993) and encouraging outreach efforts to find children needing immunization; increased funding for HIV prevention and treatment, including the Ryan White Care Act, which funds HIV and AIDS care for poor and uninsured people; agreement with Congress in 1998 to double the NIH budget (at the time, about $15 billion per year) over the course of five years; requiring more reporting of medical errors and mandating error-reduction programs in hospitals; and increased funding for and coordination of community care clinics serving the uninsured.

In addition, the president used his bully pulpit to call attention to health issues that had not had a high profile. These include women's health, including family planning and reproductive health; mental health, including a White House conference and the first surgeon general's report on the topic; and racial and ethnic disparities in health, including setting as a goal for Healthy People 2010 the elimination of racial and ethnic disparities in health.

It is too soon to evaluate most, if not all, of these policies. Public health changes improve health over a span of decades, not years. For example, the surgeon general first warned of the dangers of smoking in 1964. Over the next quarter century, smoking rates declined by half. If repeated reports from the surgeon general about mental health lead to a change in mental health care and behavior of anywhere near that magnitude in the next quarter century, this will rank as one of the greatest actions of the Clinton administration.

These initiatives had several features in common. First, they each responded to a particular public health need or concern and kept the focus on that one issue. For example, the requirement that hospitals report medical errors was a direct response to a National Academy of Sciences report on the high rate of errors in hospital practice. But rather than using the occasion to begin a major program of hospital auditing or error detection, the administration settled for the smaller, easier policy of requiring reporting of medical errors. As a result of this small focus, these policies were easy to justify. To a public seeing on the evening news stories about medical errors and hearing a report estimating thousands of deaths from such errors, it was straightforward to accept targeted actions to reduce errors.

Second, the policies are generally cheap. Even the most expensive of these programs, the doubling of the NIH budget, cost about $10 billion dollars per year, not the $60 to $70 billion of a major coverage expansion. The universal vaccine program for children cost only $1 billion. Third, the policies often help with an overall goal of increasing insurance coverage and reducing medical care costs, but they do not form any natural bridge from here to there. Consider again the policies about reducing medical errors. Medical errors are costly; reducing errors would reduce overall medical care costs. But this factor is small in relation to the overall increase in medical care costs over time. It is difficult to imagine any big changes in overall medical care spending (and thus overall rates of insurance coverage) from such legislation.

12.8 Conclusions

In health care, the Clinton administration will be remembered most readily for a spectacular failure—the Health Security Act. Less well known will be a series of other, oftentimes successful policies: coverage expansions for children, changes in long-term care and care for the disabled, and a dramatic change in the public's view of cigarettes. Our recall of the Clinton administration in years hence should include these successes as well.

Still, a lot of health care work remains. The Clinton administration wanted to expand access to insurance, make the middle class feel safe, and control the costs of medical care. The private market took care of the last of these goals, at least for a few years. There are indications that health care costs are beginning to increase again. While policy-makers might once have viewed these changes as adverse, the new view that cost increases in medical care represent the expansion of valuable technology to more people (Cutler and McClellan, 2001) reduces a lot of concern about rising health costs.

Policy did a little, but not much, to make the middle class feel safe. The federal government, along with state governments, tried to regulate what insurance companies could do. But success was limited. Fundamentally, people felt safer in their health insurance at the end of the Clinton administration because they felt safer in their jobs. When job safety declines, so will confidence in having health insurance.

The private sector did very little to help advance toward the last goal, increasing insurance coverage. Despite the best economy in generations, the share of people without insurance coverage rose. Our personal forecast is that this trend will have a major impact on public policy over the next decade and beyond. We have learned that the private sector will not guarantee insurance coverage to the vast majority of the uninsured. Unfortunately, we have also learned that the political process is not particularly willing to deal with the issue either. Where these lessons leave policy in coming years is not entirely clear.

References

Becker, Gary S., and Kevin Murphy. 1988. "A Theory of Rational Addiction." *Journal of Political Economy*, 96:675–700.

Black, Gary. 1998. "Big Price Increase: Early Trade Liquidation Should Lower 1998, Raise 1999 Estimates," report available at www.tobacco.org/news/Blackf/981124black.html.

Blendon, Robert J., Mollyann Brodie, and John Benson. 1995. "What Happened to Americans' Support for the Clinton Health Plan?" *Health Affairs*, 14, no. 2 (Summer): 7–23.

Broaddus, Matthew, and Leighton Ku. 2000. "Nearly 95 Percent of Low Income Children are Now Eligible for Medicaid or SCHIP." Washington, DC: Center on Budget and Policy Priorities.

Bulow, Jeremy, and Peter Klemperer. 1998. "The Tobacco Deal." *Brookings Papers on Economic Activity: Microeconomics*, 323–394.

Cooper, Philip, and Barbara Schone. 1997. "More Offers, Fewer Takers for Employment-Based Health Insurance: 1987 and 1996." *Health Affairs*, 16, no. 6 (November/December): 142–149.

Currie, Janet, and Jonathan Gruber. 1996a. "Saving Babies: The Efficacy and Cost of Recent Expansions of Medicaid Eligibility for Pregnant Women." *Journal of Political Economy*, 104:1263–1296.

———. 1996b. "Health Insurance Eligibility, Utilization of Medical Care, and Child Health." *Quarterly Journal of Economics*, 111:431–466.

Cutler, David M. 1994a. "A Guide to Health Care Reform." *Journal of Economic Perspectives*, Summer, 3–17.

———. 1994b. "Market Failure in Small Group Health Insurance." Mimeo.

———. 1995. "Technology, Health Costs, and the NIH." *National Institutes of Health Roundtable on the Economics of Biomedical Research*.

———. In press. "Health Care and the Public Sector." In Alan Auerbach and Martin Feldstein, eds., *Handbook of Public Economics*, vol. 3. Amsterdam: Elsevier.

Cutler, David, and Jonathan Gruber. 1996. "Does Public Insurance Crowd Out Private Insurance?" *Quarterly Journal of Economics*, 111:391–430.

Cutler, David, Jonathan Gruber, Raymond Hartman, Mary Beth Landrum, Joseph P. Newhouse, and Meredith Rosenthal. In press. "The Economic Impacts of the Tobacco Settlement." *Journal of Policy Analysis and Management*.

Cutler, David, and Brigitte Madrian. 1998. "Labor Market Responses to Rising Health Care Costs." *RAND Journal of Economics*, 29, no. 3 (Autumn): 509–530.

Cutler, David, and Mark McClellan. 2001. "Is Technological Change in Health Care Worth It?" Mimeo.

Domestic Policy Council. 2001. "Health Care Accomplishments of the Clinton Administration." Washington, DC: The White House.

Employee Benefits Research Institute. 2000. "Sources of Health Insurance and Characteristics of the Uninsured." Washington, DC: EBRI.

Farber, Henry, and Helen Levy. 2000. "Recent Trends in Employer-Sponsored Health Insurance Coverage: Are Bad Jobs Getting Worse?" *Journal of Health Economics*, 19(1): 93–119.

Feldman, Roger, and Bryan Dowd. 1993. "The Effectiveness of Managed Competition in Reducing the Costs of Health Insurance." In Robert Helms, *Health Policy Reform: Competition and Controls*, 176–217. Washington, DC: American Enterprise Institute.

Fuchs, Victor. 1994. "The Clinton Plan: A Researcher Examines Reform," *Health Affairs*, 13(1): 102–114.

Glied, Sherry. 2000. "Challenges and Options for Increasing the Number of Americans with Health Insurance." Commonwealth Fund Publication Number 415, December.

Gravelle, Jane, and D. Zimmerman. 1994. "Cigarette Taxes to Fund Health Care Reform: An Economic Analysis." Congressional Research Service Publication 94–214E. Washington, DC: Library of Congress.

Gruber, Jonathan. 1994. "The Incidence of Mandated Maternity Benefits." *American Economic Review*, 84:622–641.

———. 1997. "Health Insurance for Poor Women and Children in the U.S.: Lessons from the Past Decade." In *Tax Policy and the Economy 11*, ed. James Poterba, 169–211. Cambridge, MA: MIT Press.

———. 2000. "Medicaid." Forthcoming in Robert Moffitt, ed., *Means-Tested Transfer Programs in the U.S.* Chicago: University of Chicago Press.

———. 2001a. "Health Insurance and the Labor Market." In Joseph Newhouse and Anthony Culyer, eds., *The Handbook of Health Economics*, 645–706. Amsterdam: North Holland.

———. 2001b. "Tobacco at the Crossroads: The Past and Future of Smoking Regulation in the U.S.." *Journal of Economic Perspectives*, 15, no. 2 (Spring): 193–212.

Gruber, Jonathan, and Botond Koszegi. 2000. "Is Addiction 'Rational'? Theory and Evidence." NBER Working Paper No. 7507, January.

Gruber, Jonathan, and Larry Levitt. 2000. "Tax Subsidies for Health Insurance: Costs and Benefits." *Health Affairs*, 19:72–85.

Gruber, Jonathan, and Brigitte Madrian. 1996. "Health Insurance and Early Retirement: Evidence from the Availability of Continuation Coverage." In David Wise, ed., *Advances in the Economics of Aging*, 115–143. Chicago: University of Chicago Press.

Gruber, Jonathan, and Robin McKnight. 2001. "Why Are Employee Health Insurance Contributions Rising?" Mimeo, MIT.

Gruber, Jonathan, and Jonathan Zinman. 2000. "Youth Smoking in the U.S.: Evidence and Implications." In Jonathan Gruber, ed., *Risky Behavior among Youth: An Economic Analysis*, 69–120. Chicago: University of Chicago Press.

Harris, Jeffrey. 1987. "The 1983 Increase in the Federal Cigarette Excise Tax." In Lawrence Summers, ed., *Tax Policy and the Economy*, 87–112. Cambridge, MA: MIT Press.

Institute of Medicine. 1985. "Preventing Low Birth Weight." Washington, DC: National Academy Press.

Kemper, Peter. 1988. "The Evaluation of the National Long Term Care Demonstration. 10. Overview of the Findings." *Health Services Research*, 23(1): 161–174.

Kessler, David. 2001. *A Question of Intent: A Great American Battle with a Deadly Industry*. New York: Public Affairs.

Laux, Fritz. 2000. "Addiction as a Market Failure: Using Rational Addiction Results to Justify Tobacco Regulation." *Journal of Health Economics*, 19:421–438.

Madrian, Brigitte C. 1994. "Employment-Based Health Insurance and Job Mobility: Is There Evidence of Job-Lock?," *Quarterly Journal of Economics*, 109:27–51.

McGinnis, J. Michael, and William H. Foege. 1993. "Actual Causes of Death in the United States." *Journal of the American Medical Association*, 270, no. 18 (November 10): 2207–2212.

Miller, Robert H., and Harold Luft. 1997. "Does Managed Care Lead to Better or Worse Quality of Care?" *Health Affairs*, 16:7–25.

Nasar, Sylvia. 1998. "The Ifs and Buts of the Tobacco Settlement." *New York Times*, November 29, 1998, Section 4, p. 1.

Newhouse, Joseph. 1992. "Medical Care Costs: How Much Welfare Loss." *Journal of Economic Perspectives*, 6, no. 3 (Summer): 3–21.

Newhouse, Joseph, et al. 1993. *Free for All? Lessons from the RAND Health Insurance Experiment.* Santa Monica, CA: RAND Corp.

Nichols, A., and Richard Zeckhauser. 1982. "Targeting Transfers Through Restrictions on Recipients." *American Economic Review*, 72:372–377.

Nichols, Len, and Linda J. Blumberg. 1998. "A Different Kind of New Federalism? The Health Insurance Portability and Accountability Act of 1996." *Health Affairs*, 17, no. 3 (May/June): 25–42.

Peden, Edgar A., and Mark S. Freeland. 1995. "A Historical Analysis of Medical Spending Growth, 1960–1993." *Health Affairs*, 14, no. 2 (Summer): 235–247.

Pollitz, Karen, Nicole Tapay, Elizabeth Hadley, and Jalena Specht. 2000. "Early Experience with 'New Federalism' in Health Insurance Regulation." *Health Affairs*, 19, no. 4 (July/August): 7–22.

Sheiner, Louise. 1999. "Health Costs, Aging, and Wages." Mimeo, Federal Reserve Board.

Summers, Lawrence H. 1989. "Some Simple Economics of Mandated Benefits." *American Economic Review, Papers and Proceedings*, 79, no. 2 (May): 177–183.

U.S. Department of Health and Human Services. 1994. *Preventing Tobacco Use Among Young People: A Report of the Surgeon General.* National Center for Chronic Disease Prevention and Health Promotion, Office of Smoking and Health.

U.S. Department of the Treasury. 1998. "The Economic Case for Comprehensive Tobacco Legislation."

U.S. General Accounting Office. 1998. *Social Security Disability Policy: Factors Affecting Beneficiaries' Return to Work.* Testimony before the Subcommittee on Social Security and Family Policy, Committee on Finance, U.S. Senate, July 29, 1998.

Zwanziger, Jack, and Glenn A. Melnick. 1988. "The Effects of Hospital Competition and the Medicare PPS Program on Hospital Cost Behavior in California." *Journal of Health Economics*, 7:301–320.

Comments

Victor R. Fuchs

The failure of the Clinton health care initiative was the most important health policy event of the 1990s. Indeed, it was arguably the *only* important health policy event of the 1990s. In my view, however, the widespread misunderstanding of *why* it failed is also very important because future progress in health policy requires a candid, clearheaded view of that experience.

The finger of blame has been pointed in many directions: "The plan was unworkable"; "It was poorly explained"; "The political strategy was misconceived"; "Special interests were too powerful"; and still others. Each explanation has some merit, but they do not go to the heart of the matter. The fundamental problem was the unwillingness of policy-makers and the public to make the difficult choices implicit in any comprehensive health care reform.

A bit of historical background helps to put the 1990s in perspective. The Clinton Health Security Act was far from the first attempt at national health insurance in the United States. Beginning in 1912, there have been numerous proposals in a wide variety of formats, and there have always been opponents. At first, organized labor, led by Samuel Gompers, was opposed because the legislation was viewed as interfering with labor-management relations. Physicians, at that time, were mostly in favor. After World War II, unions supported national health insurance, but organized medicine, led by the American Medical Association, was opposed. The detailed fate of each proposal is of secondary importance; the key point is that not one of them came close to success, despite the popularity of national health insurance around the world.

It is also important to note that Clinton's Health Security Act was not the only attempt at health care reform during 1993–94. There were proposals from the left of Clinton, and there were proposals from the right of Clinton. There was the so-called "mainstream proposal," and there was a "bipartisan coalition." Again, the key point is that not one of the proposals even made it out of committee. To imagine, as so many commentators have, that if only the Clinton proposal had been less complex, or the Clintons more politically adept, or special interests not so effective, the proposal would have sailed through Congress is to misunderstand not only the 1990s but almost a century of failed efforts at comprehensive medical care reform in the United States.

What is the problem? Simply put, the Clinton proposal, like other attempts at comprehensive reform, tried to accomplish three incompatible objectives: (1) Provide universal insurance coverage; (2) constrain the rate of growth of health care spending; and (3) preserve freedom of choice and behavior for patients and providers. With skillful plan design, and even more skillful administration, it might be possible to achieve any two of the objectives, but not all three—not in the United States; not in any country in the world.

Consider the goal of universal insurance. To achieve it there must be cross-subsidization for those who are too poor or too sick to pay their own way, and there must be compulsion for the free riders, the gamblers, and those who are unwilling to pay *more* than their own way, that is, provide the subsidies. No nation achieves universal coverage without cross-subsidization and compulsion; the United States could have it next year if the public and the policy-makers were prepared to bite those two bullets.

Why is the United States virtually alone among industrialized nations in not having national health insurance? Twenty-five years ago I wrestled with this question and proposed four explanations (Fuchs, 1976). First, except in times of great national stress, Americans have always been distrustful of government. It was Thomas Jefferson, not some right-wing Republican, who articulated an enduring tenet of American political philosophy: "That government is best which governs least." Second, the heterogeneity of the population has contributed to a reluctance to embrace national health insurance. Unlike Swedes, Germans, Japanese, and many other peoples, Americans do not share centuries of common language, culture, and traditions; thus there is less instinctive, nationwide empathy for the poor and the sick. Third, relatively few Americans have a strong sense of "noblesse oblige," a feeling that motivates many well-born conservatives in other countries to vote for social programs to aid the less fortunate. Finally, the United States traditionally has had strong private not-for-profit institutions that carried out quasi-governmental functions. The Blue Cross and Blue Shield plans used to charge equal premiums throughout a community; not-for-profit hospitals provided for cross-subsidization through cost shifting.

When I revisited my analysis of why the United States did not have national health insurance in 1991, the first three reasons seemed as strong as or stronger than ever, but the fourth was not (Fuchs, 1991). The unraveling of community-wide insurance premiums and the growth of managed care had substantially eroded the redistributive role of not-for-profit health organizations. I concluded, however, that most Americans were still unwilling to forgo their own health care arrangements for a more egalitarian government program—their replies to pollsters notwithstanding.

Consider the goal of slowing the growth of health care expenditures. To achieve that over the long run, it is necessary to slow the growth of services to patients. This requires slowing advances in medical technology, the primary cause of rising expenditures. In the short run, it is possible to dampen expenditures by cutting drug prices or by squeezing the incomes of physicians, nurses, and other health care personnel, or by eliminating gross inefficiencies. But these are typically one-time gains; they cannot be repeated year after year without seriously eroding the quantity and quality of care. In short, universal coverage combined with cost containment requires abandoning the objective of freedom of choice for patients and providers.

Will the United States ever embrace some form of national health insurance? I believe it will, but the timing will depend largely on factors external to health care. Major changes in health policy, like major changes in most areas, are political acts undertaken for political purposes. That was true when Bismarck introduced national health insurance to the new German state more than a hundred years ago. It was true when England adopted national health insurance after World War II, and it will be true in the United States as well. National health insurance will probably come to the United States in the wake of a major change in the political climate, the kind of change that often accompanies a war, a depression, or large-scale civil unrest.

When it comes, what will be its effects? Improved access to care for some; probably less ready access for others. Barring constraints on technology and personnel, expenditures will accelerate, but sooner or later such constraints will be imposed. As for health levels and inequalities in health outcomes, decades of experience with national health insurance in other countries tell us the effects will be minimal. Most improvements in health will come from advances in medicine, public health measures such as those that lead to less air pollution and more road safety, and changes in cigarette smoking, diet, exercise, and other personal behaviors.

Postscript on the Cutler-Gruber Chapter

The invitation to the panelists emphasized the desire for an independent statement rather than a critique of the chapter. This postscript, however, may contribute to an understanding not only of health policy in the 1990s, but also to this volume's goal of writing the history of policy-making in the Clinton administration.

The Cutler-Gruber chapter seems to me to be perceptive and balanced in most respects. Two statements, however, while not inaccurate, require additional comment. First, Cutler and Gruber write, "At least in the political arena, the increase in medical care costs over time was largely *seen* [italics added] as a problem of price inflation, not increased service utilization" (p. 832). One must ask, "Seen by whom?" Health care expenditures deflated by the GDP deflator were $2\frac{1}{2}$ times larger in 1990 than in 1970. Such rapid growth in real expenditures could not possibly have been primarily the result of health care price inflation—where was the extra money going? The Clintons made much of high drug industry profits, but excess profits accounted for less than 1 percent of health care expenditures. High incomes of physicians were another popular target, but if American physicians' incomes had been cut to the level of Canadian physicians, the savings would have been less than 3 percent of health care expenditures. Much more relevant was the fact that health services employment in 1990 was more than $2\frac{1}{2}$ times larger than in 1970. What were the millions of additional physicians, nurses, technicians, and others doing if not producing more inpatient and outpatient services? Also relevant were Medicare records that showed very rapid rates of growth of age-specific, per capita utilization of angioplasties, coronary artery bypass grafts, hip and knee replacements, and many other major surgical and diagnostic procedures. These were real surgeons providing services to real patients, not price inflation.

That the administration espoused the price inflation line there can be no doubt. In so doing, they were echoing (and reinforcing) the public's misperception that drug company profits and physicians' incomes were mainly responsible for rising expenditures. That the administration could find some "analysts" to support these views is also true. But there was no shortage of leading health economists who could have told them they were wrong—if they had chosen to seek such advice. Once policy-makers decide what they want to do, they usually get the advice they want to hear.

The second problematic statement comes toward the end of the Cutler-Gruber chapter when they write,

As is reflected in the discussion thus far, the primary focus of the administration's health policies was on health insurance coverage and market reforms. This reflects a basic view among administration officials, *shared by many health care analysts* [italics added], that health insurance coverage was the primary policy tool available for improving the health of the U.S. population. (p. 860)

Again one must ask, "Which analysts?" Was the administration making use of the best evidence and expert advice available at the time, or were they choosing their policies for other reasons and finding advisers who would support their decisions?

The most widely cited book in health economics, *Who Shall Live? Health, Economics, and Social Choice* (Fuchs, 1974), had as its main point the importance of *nonmedical* factors in health outcomes. The RAND health insurance experiment (1980s), the most credible, prospective social experiment ever carried out in the United States, had clearly shown that variation in the amount of insurance coverage had minimal effects on health (Newhouse, 1993). Did the administration pay any attention to such views? If not, why not? The answers to *these* types of questions could help to illuminate policy-making in health and possibly in some of the other areas discussed in this volume.

References

Fuchs, V. R. 1974. *Who Shall Live? Health, Economics, and Social Choice.* New York: Basic Books.

———. 1976. "From Bismarck to Woodcock: The 'Irrational' Pursuit of National Health Insurance," *Journal of Law and Economics*, 19(2) (August): 347–359.

———. 1991. "National Health Insurance Revisited," *Health Affairs*, 10(4) (Winter): 7–17.

Newhouse JP and the Insurance Experiment Group. *Free for All: Lessons from the RAND Health Insurance Experiment.* Cambridge, MA: Harvard University Press, 1993.

Comments

Joseph P. Newhouse

I focus most of my remarks on the Health Security Act (HSA), but also comment briefly on the growth of managed care and the growth of the NIH budget.

Arguably the most important event in the entire eight years of the Clinton presidency—other than perhaps the failure to convict the president in the impeachment proceedings—was the defeat of the HSA. Not only did the president lose one of his most important objectives, but the defeat was also a key factor in the Republican takeover of Congress in 1994, which foreclosed much of the agenda with which the administration came to office.

The defeat of the HSA links to at least three other chapters in this book. One is the discussion in Chapter 14, by Orszag, Orszag, and Tyson, of the contrast between the decision-making process for the HSA and that for other major economic and social policy initiatives. Their chapter points out that the economics team was not brought into the deliberations over the health care plan until it had been shaped. But my sense was that more than the economics team felt excluded. For all the publicity about the 500-person health care reform task force, those I knew in the administration thought the key decisions were made by the president and the first lady, with much of the input to the Clintons filtered through Ira Magaziner. In short, not only was the economics team excluded in the early going, but other key executive branch officials as well thought they had limited ability to convey their views directly to the president, as did members of Congress and outsiders. I infer that this highly controlled but ultimately dysfunctional process is what the president wanted; in retrospect, it was a fateful decision.

The HSA also links to the chapters on trade and welfare reform. The administration had to make an important decision in 1993 about the timing of submitting NAFTA, the HSA, and welfare reform legislation, since the House Committee on Ways and Means and the Senate Finance Committee could only consider these measures seriatim. Proponents of each measure argued for their favored legislation to take precedence, with the decision going to NAFTA. One can only speculate about whether history would have differed if health reform had gone first. Some think a version of universal coverage would have passed had health care taken priority over NAFTA in September 1993—and that the chances of passage would have been even higher had something been sent to Capitol Hill in May, a time when the task force had largely completed its work. My own view is that passage of the HSA would have been difficult irrespective of when it was submitted, although submitting a less detailed and comprehensive plan earlier would surely have increased the chances of passage. Of course, had health care reform gone first, NAFTA might well not have passed.

One can also speculate about what might have happened with welfare reform had it had gone before both NAFTA and health care reform. The then Democratic Congress would likely have enacted a more generous bill than was ultimately passed; for example, there might have been a public service job guarantee.

Books have been written about the reasons for the demise of the HSA (Johnson and Broder, 1995; Skocpol, 1997; Hacker, 1999). I only wish to make two points about its fate. First, passing any form of universal coverage, the president's key goal, was and remains exceedingly difficult because of the redistribution it necessarily entails. Second, I agree with Cutler and Gruber that the HSA had features that would not have worked well and would likely have required change.

The American political system has only limited tolerance for substantial redistribution, at least in times other than major depressions and wars, but substantial redistribution is an inevitable corollary of universal coverage. Indeed, a key decision on the architecture of the plan, the choice of an employer mandate, probably stemmed from the president's desire to minimize redistribution. Cutler and Gruber note the three broad approaches to universal coverage: an employer mandate, an individual mandate, and an entirely tax-financed plan. Redistribution is least with the employer mandate, but keeping employment-based insurance in place undoubtedly leads to a more complex architecture than the other two options, since one must in effect create arrangements for those with no access to employment-based insurance while preserving much of current employment-based insurance. Most likely one would also want to keep states from shifting their Medicaid obligations to the federal government. The administration decided it needed to work out the necessarily complex architecture of the employer mandate in great detail, a decision that both contributed to the delay in submitting the legislation and allowed the opponents of the plan to attack its complexity when it was submitted.

Although the employer mandate minimized redistribution relative to the other two approaches, the HSA nonetheless entailed substantial redistribution. Most obvious was the redistribution to finance benefits for the uninsured, largely the traditional redistribution from higher to lower income groups. This amount of redistribution would have been nontrivial but not overwhelming; the additional care the uninsured would have received would have added around 5 to 10 percent to personal health care spending.

But there would also have been substantial redistribution within income groups. This redistribution largely stemmed from two sources, the alliances and the treatment of one- and two-worker families. The HSA called for health care alliances, geographic areas within which health care spending would have been pooled. Health care spending varies substantially across not only large areas such as states but also across small areas such as towns in Vermont and counties (Basu, 1996; Chassin et al., 1986; Wennberg and Gittelsohn, 1973; Newhouse, Chapter 13 of this volume). As a result, averaging spending within the alliance necessarily entails redistribution and controversy about which areas should be grouped together. An analogous situation occurs in the case of automobile insurance, where central cities generally want to be pooled with suburbs for rating purposes, but the suburbs do not share the same affinity for the central city. In health care, however, the stakes are considerably higher (at the time of the HSA, spending on personal health care services among the under 65 was around $2,000 per person in today's dollars). In addition to the redistribution the alliances would have caused, uncertainty about how their governance would work in practice was an additional barrier to passage.

The HSA would also have led to redistribution between one- and two-worker families and across employment groups. It called for employers to pay 80 percent of the alliance-wide premium for each worker, with workers paying the remaining 20 percent. One-worker families typically insure their spouses and children through their place of work; two-worker families may insure through one or both of their respective employers. In the case of two-worker families insuring through one employer, the HSA would have split the cost between the two employers, presumably leading in equilibrium to an increase in cash wages at the employer who had previously insured the family and a decrease at the other. Moreover, to the degree any employer paid more or less than 80 percent of the alliance average premium—and that would have been just about all employers—there would have been redistribution within each work group as cash wages adjusted to account for the changes in employer health care payments.

Yet another source of redistribution was the proposed Medicare drug benefit, which, given the subsequent growth in drug spending, would have been nontrivial. As described in my chapter on Medicare in this volume (Chapter 13), 31 percent of retired workers have coverage for drugs through their former employer. The Medicare drug benefit would thus have been a tax-financed windfall to the shareholders of the firms providing this coverage. In sum, the redistribution that the HSA would have caused, though doubtless less than with a tax-financed plan or individual mandate, was nonetheless large enough so that enactment would have been difficult.

Cutler and Gruber point to two features of the HSA that would likely have had to change had the bill passed: subsidies to low-wage firms and the expenditure limits. I agree that these features would have had to change. Subsidies to low-wage firms, which were in addition to subsidies to low-wage workers, would have encouraged firms to subcontract out work done by low-wage workers or possibly form a new firm for low-wage workers. This type of gaming would have been costly for little overall gain.

The HSA would have limited premium increases to the increase in GDP (in the first few years the limit was somewhat more generous). The limits were in the plan so the administration could claim that new taxes would not be required. It is exceedingly unlikely, however, that the limits would have held over the long run in light of the historical rate of increase in health care spending. Reflecting the increase in medical capabilities, the average annual real rate of increase in health care spending by decade for the past six decades is 4.4 percent per person (this value updates the figures in Newhouse, 1992), whereas the average rate of growth of real GDP is 2.5 percent.

Interestingly, however, in the 1996–99 period the proposed spending limits would not have been binding because of the below-average increases in health care costs and the above-average increases in GDP. Most observers attribute the slowdown in health care spending in the mid- and late 1990s to the spread of managed care (e.g., Newhouse, 2001), but the resulting public backlash against managed care would probably have also applied to the HSA's expenditure limits.

Managed care in principle is an effort to reduce moral hazard, the use of services for which the marginal social benefit falls short of the marginal social cost. The insured patient, however, wants all health care services with a private benefit greater than the copayment, which under managed care is typically minimal. Rather than demand-side cost sharing, managed care addresses moral hazard through command-and-control methods such as prior authorization and financial incentives to providers such as capitation. These methods, however, have generated a political demand for patient protection legislation, since there is no guarantee that they eliminate only low or negatively valued services. (The consumer has no ready mechanism to express willingness to pay at the point of service.) And there is every reason to think the same forces would have been at play had the HSA's premium limits forced greater rationing of health care services.

A striking development in the administration's second term was large increases in the budget for the National Institutes of Health (NIH). Starting in 1998, NIH received 14 and 15 percent annual increases in nominal appropriations, part of a bipartisan effort to double its budget over a five-year period. Forecasting the consequences of these increased appropriations is an exercise in crystal ball gazing, but they could be substantial both for human health and for health care spending. One plausible scenario is that the revolution in molecular biology that the investment in medical research has spawned will lead to individually tailored pharmaceuticals and biotech compounds. These advances potentially open the door to greater price discrimination, but how these products will be priced is an open issue that could well be part of the chapter on health care in a conference a decade hence.

References

Basu, Joy. 1996. "Border-Crossing Adjustment and Personal Health Care Spending by State." *Health Care Financing Review*, 16(1): 215–236.

Chassin, Mark, Robert H. Brook, Rolla Edward Park, et al. 1986. "Variations in the Use of Medical and Surgical Services by the Medicare Population." *New England Journal of Medicine*, 314(5): 285–290.

Hacker, Jacob S. 1999. *The Road to Nowhere: The Genesis of President Clinton's Plan for Health Security*. Princeton, NJ: Princeton University Press.

Johnson, Haynes, and David S. Broder. 1995. *The System: The American Way of Politics at the Breaking Point*. New York: Little Brown.

Newhouse, Joseph P. 1992. "Medical Care Costs: How Much Welfare Loss?" *Journal of Economic Perspectives*, 6(3): 3–21.

———. 2001. "Lessons from the Medical Marketplace." *Governance Amid Bigger, Better Markets*, ed. Joseph S. Nye, Jr., and John D. Donahue. Washington, DC: Brookings Institution Press.

Skocpol, Theda. 1997. *Boomerang: Health Reform and the Turn Against Government*. New York: W. W. Norton.

Wennberg, John, and Alan Gittelsohn. 1973. "Small Area Variations in Health Care Delivery." *Science*, 182:1102.

Comments

W. Kip Viscusi

Evaluating the Clinton Performance

My comments will focus primarily on tobacco policy during the Clinton era. However, before beginning this assessment, it is useful to specify the appropriate criteria for assessing whether the Clinton administration health and tobacco policies were successful. Several different approaches can be distinguished.

The first approach, which is often taken in the chapter by Cutler and Gruber, is that legislation enacted that is consistent with the administration's objectives is viewed as a success. Although this may be the case within the narrow confines of political success, whether everything that was desired by the Clinton administration was in fact in the national interest is not at all clear.

A second criterion one might apply is that the world is better on some dimension. Have we exhibited improvements in individual health, decreased rates of smoking, or some other dimension that the authors view as a measure of a successful outcome? This approach is a useful beginning, but it does not resolve the question of whether policies are in fact successful because in many cases the improvements discussed in the chapter simply follow a long-term trend.

As a result, one might wish to turn to a third measure of success, which is that the trend on some dimension has shifted in a beneficial manner. Has there in fact been an increase in the extent of the improvements that would have occurred because of the influence of Clinton administration policy?

A final criterion is that one might assess whether society is better off in terms of the benefits of the policies exceeding their costs. Ideally, such an assessment would be based on actual policy effects, but given the short period of time since the Clinton administration, perhaps the best that can be done is to provide an assessment of the prospective expected effects. These criteria provide at least a useful checklist of the kinds of concerns one could highlight in assessing the Clinton administration performance.

Was HSA a Failure?

Although the Clinton administration's efforts to mount a massive overhaul of the health insurance system in the United States was not passed by Congress, there did seem to be two noteworthy dividends of this effort that were not discussed by Cutler and Gruber. First, as part of the Clinton administration health care proposal, there were suggestions that cigarette taxes be used to finance this health care initiative to a substantial extent. Indeed, Hillary Clinton and Senator George Mitchell made reference to the social cost of cigarettes and the fact that a substantial tax was needed to defray these costs, where this tax could be used to finance such a health insurance scheme. Although no major increase in cigarette taxes was ever enacted, perhaps in large part because of concerns about the severe regressive character of cigarette taxes, this discussion did at least put on the national agenda the social costs of cigarettes and the link of these costs to cigarette taxes. Making this linkage perhaps served to inspire some of the state litigation efforts against the cigarette industry.

As part of the HSA debate there was also discussion of rising medical prices, particularly with respect to prescription drugs. The jawboning efforts that ensued and perhaps other changes in the health care system other than those attributable to actions of the Clinton administration, such as the increased influence of managed care, led to a substantial abatement of medical price inflation. Medical prices increased by 54.8 percent from 1987 to 1993 and by only 17.18 percent from 1993 to 1998. Although the causes of this dampening of inflation are not clear, this shift certainly represents a major improvement in one of the long-term inflationary trends in the economy.

Tobacco Policy

Cutler and Gruber claim that "antitobacco policy became a significant accomplishment of the administration, despite the lack of legislative actions." My view on this assessment is twofold. First, the dominant governmental player with respect to tobacco during the 1990s was the states, not the federal government. Second, the changes that did occur were on balance harmful to society rather than beneficial.

A useful starting point for assessing the Clinton administration's performance with respect to tobacco is to examine the social costs of cigarettes. All studies in the literature of the financial externalities associated with cigarettes indicate that on balance there is a net savings, even excluding the role of excise taxes, provided that one uses a reasonable discount rate. My estimates of the cost to the federal government and to the average state government reported in

Viscusi (1999) extend my national estimates in Viscusi (1995) to specific governmental entities. To the best of my knowledge my study provides the only estimates that break out the effects in terms of these different governmental entities. There are in fact increased costs of medical care due to cigarettes, on the order of $0.24 per pack for the federal government and $0.03 per pack for the average state. Sick leave and life insurance are also minor cost components. However, there are also cost savings, including nursing home care and retirement pensions, which dwarf the medical care costs. Because smokers die sooner, they pay fewer payroll taxes and make fewer contributions to pension plans than they otherwise would. Overall, there is a net cost savings to the federal government of $0.53 per pack and to state governments of $0.09 per pack, using a 3 percent discount rate. Excise taxes paid on cigarettes are in addition to this amount.

The existence of medical care costs gave rise to suits by state governments in an effort to recoup these costs. These suits had nothing whatsoever to do with welfare losses to individual smokers but focused solely on the financial costs to the states. The basis for these lawsuits was unprecedented. To the extent that there was no basis for an individual claim against the cigarette industry because of smokers' assumption of the risk, these defenses would travel with claims filed by the states. The Iowa Supreme Court threw out the state suit against the industry, concluding that there was no legal basis for the state to recoup Medicaid costs attributable to smoking. In some cases, such as Maryland and Florida, the states passed legislation to change the legal rules ex post in order to provide a legal basis for recouping these costs.

The flurry of these state suits against the industry, which eventually numbered more than 40, led to the Proposed Resolution in 1997 that the industry pay $368.5 billion over 25 years to settle the state suits. This proposal had two distinctive features. First, it was not a damages settlement in any conventional sense. Rather, it was effectively a $0.62 per pack excise tax on cigarettes that would continue indefinitely. Second, this proposal included sweeping new regulations that would have affected the cigarette industry. The FDA would have been given the authority to regulate cigarettes as a drug. There also would have been nine new rotating warnings for cigarettes, bans on cigarette outdoor advertising and cartoon characters, and a series of other regulatory reforms.

This proposal was drafted principally by the Mississippi attorney general and cigarette industry attorneys and was forwarded to Congress as a basis for legislation. However, all legislative proposals based on it languished. Particularly noteworthy is that no proposal was ever endorsed by the Clinton administration, which in effect sat on the sidelines as the Proposed Resolution unraveled. Based on the public debate, it seemed that the extreme positions staked out by former FDA Commissioner David Kessler, former U.S. Surgeon General C. Everett Koop, and Senator Edward Kennedy prevented the Clinton administration from taking any action that might have alienated the strong antitobacco contingency.

When this legislation failed, the cigarette industry pursued separate agreements with individual states and eventually reached separate deals with four states and a Master Settlement Agreement with the remaining 46 states for $206 billion, shortly after the 1998 elections. As with the Proposed Resolution, this settlement did not involve a conventional damages payment but in effect imposed a cigarette excise tax that would be borne by smokers, not by the industry. Moreover, it included extensive regulatory provisions, including prohibition of cartoon characters in advertising and limitations on cigarette advertising. These limitations have the potential for strong anticompetitive effects, with respect both to locking in the market shares in a highly concentrated industry and to preventing the advertising of new safer cigarettes.

The cigarette settlement not only was record setting in terms of the scale of the funds being transferred, but also led to huge payoffs to attorneys in the billions of dollars. These funds in turn have spawned litigation against a variety of other products, including HMOs, firearms, and lead paint. Other products, such as alcoholic beverages, may follow the same pattern in the future.

What is unfortunate about this outcome is that regulation through litigation usurps the traditional authority for levying excise taxes and imposing regulatory policies. If cigarette taxes are too low, then the legislature should increase these taxes. Similarly, if there is a need for regulatory change, there should be regulatory change, but this should go through the rule-making process in which the agency examines the regulatory alternatives, disseminates the details of the regulation for public debate, and engages in an open process subject to the agency's legislative mandate and congressional review. There was no such engaging of the public with respect to the secret deals negotiated as part of the cigarette settlement, as this agreement was brokered without any public input whatsoever.

The settlement also prevented the courts from resolving the legal issues involved in the case. As a result, we have no guidance as to whether other similar suits have any standing and, if there are damages to be considered, how these damages should be calculated. In this instance, given the novelty of this line of litigation, there would have been a positive informational externality to other industries from knowing more about the legal status of this untested legal approach.

Noteworthy in its absence from the discussion of the policy developments in this area was any role for the federal government. There were, however, two efforts to be involved. First, with respect to the state settlements, the U.S. Office of Management and Budget and the Clinton administration suggested that the federal government should share in the settlement amount. This request was in fact consistent with the way in which the states calculated costs, as they sought to recoup both the state and federal share of Medicaid costs when assessing the damages. However, this attempt by the federal government to reap some of the winnings was rebuffed by the states, which simply saw this as a money grab by a party not involved in the litigation.

After the states settled with the industry, the federal government decided to launch a suit of its own near the end of the Clinton administration. However, much of the basis for the suit was rejected by the courts, leaving the federal suit to rest largely on a dubious racketeering claim against the industry, which is highly speculative and in all likelihood difficult to prove. Now that the case has been inherited by the Bush administration, the Justice Department has indicated a desire to settle the litigation. However, if the litigation has no merit, it should be dropped altogether. If it does have merit, the Bush administration should pursue it to obtain legal resolution of the novel legal issues at stake so that other industries will have reliable guidelines with respect to the legal status of such claims.

Environmental Tobacco Smoke

A major policy concern over the past decade has been environmental tobacco smoke (ETS). However, with respect to actual policy initiatives, the major players once again have been state and local entities rather than the federal government. Indeed, the two principal federal initiatives with respect to ETS were in large part failures.

Consider first the study by EPA assessing the scientific literature pertaining to risk of environmental tobacco smoke.[1] No study in the literature identified by EPA found that there was statistically significant risk associated with ETS using a 95 percent confidence interval. However, EPA's meta-analysis of these studies using a procedure that is not discussed by the agency indicates that there is a significant risk at the looser 90 percent confidence level. Rather than providing scientific guidance with respect to the risk of environmental tobacco smoke, this agency assessment in fact has stirred considerable concern with respect to the risks of secondhand smoke. The scientific merits of the EPA review are, however, questionable, as a federal court has thrown out the EPA analysis as being without scientific merit.[2] In particular, the court concluded that the

---

1. See U.S. Environmental Protection Agency (1992).
2. See *Flue-Cured Tobacco Cooperative Stabilization Corp. v. U.S. Environmental Protection Agency et al.*, 4 F. Supp. 2d 435 (M.D.N.C. 1998).

EPA "cherry-picked" the studies that it chose to report, choosing not to include studies that showed a weaker relationship between risks and ETS exposures. In addition, the court concluded that, based on the usual scientific criteria for statistical significance, there was no statistically significant relationship.

The Occupational Safety and Health Administration also ventured forth with a proposal to ban workplace smoking except in specifically designated smoking lounges. However, the OSHA analysis did not include any recognition of the benefits of smoking to the smokers themselves. These benefits loomed particularly large among workers affected by the proposal, as opposition to the proposed regulation from labor unions served to kill this regulatory proposal.

These failures do not indicate that environmental tobacco smoke does not merit regulatory concern. There are many clear-cut costs associated with ETS, not the least of which is the smell and annoyance to nonsmokers. However, by not taking a more balanced assessment of ETS risks, the Clinton administration failed to be a significant policy player in any constructive way.

Youth Smoking

Youth smoking is a policy concern shared by all, including the cigarette industry. However, it is difficult to identify any major initiatives by the Clinton administration against youth smoking, apart from frequent references to youth smoking as an effort to justify higher cigarette taxes. In terms of policy performance, the youth smoking rates had been in long-term decline until 1992 and then increased throughout the Clinton administration until 1998. The only concrete policy initiative against youth smoking undertaken by the Clinton administration seems to have been pointless.[3] The symbol of the youth smoking problem was Joe Camel, the cartoon character used in recent Camel cigarette advertising. While Joe was the visible symbol of the youth smoking problem, there is no statistical evidence suggesting that there is any causal link between youth smoking and Joe Camel. Indeed, roughly two out of every three cigarettes smoked by underage smokers are Marlboros, not Camels. Nevertheless, after the states had begun their litigation efforts against the cigarette industry, the FTC launched its own independent case against Joe Camel, perhaps not wishing to be left out of the litigation frenzy. What was curious about this case is that Joe Camel had already been voluntarily retired by R. J. Reynolds in 1997. Perhaps because the case was not going well, the FTC eventually dropped it, taking advantage of the face-saving opportunity provided by the state settlements, which formally banned the use of cartoon characters in advertising.

---

3. I discuss other youth smoking issues, such as young smokers' risk beliefs, in Viscusi (1992).

Overall Assessment

By any standard the Clinton administration was not a leader in the development of tobacco policy in the 1990s. Rather, it was states and local governments that had the greatest policy influence on almost all dimensions of tobacco policy. A particularly disturbing trend has been the emergence of the phenomenon of regulation and taxation through litigation, in which high-stakes court cases are used as leverage against industries to extract tax and regulatory changes that circumvent the usual governmental processes. The Clinton administration certainly deserves some of the blame for this development, as it failed to develop a legislative solution to the litigation and instead left matters to the secret deals negotiated by the litigants.

References

U.S. Environmental Protection Agency, Office of Health and Environmental Assessment, Office of Research and Development. 1992. *Respiratory Health Effects of Passive Smoking: Lung Cancer and Other Disorders*. EPA/600/6–90/006F. Washington, DC: U.S. Environmental Protection Agency.

Viscusi, W. Kip. 1992. *Smoking: Making the Risky Decision*. New York: Oxford University Press.

———. 1995. "Cigarette Taxation and the Social Consequences of Smoking." In James M. Poterba, ed., *Tax Policy and the Economy*, 51–101. Cambridge, MA: MIT Press.

———. 1999. "The Governmental Composition of the Insurance Costs of Smoking." *Journal of Law and Economics*, 42(2): 575–609.

Bradford DeLong began the discussion by responding to Victor Fuchs and David Cutler's assertion that the Health Security Act (HSA) legislation failed because of fundamental issues rather than political mismanagement. At the start of the Clinton administration, DeLong argued, large businesses were terrified of accelerating health care costs, small businesses were angry at the fact that they paid high prices, and insured consumers were nervous that their health care coverage would vanish if they lost their jobs. A well-designed program that provided universal coverage seemed attractive to all three groups. The administrative inefficiency of health care suggested that the long-run costs of reform would not be unreasonably high. So it seemed likely in 1993 that health care reform would pass. The Clinton administration would develop a policy by hammering out an internal compromise within the executive branch. The compromises and concessions made within the policy-planning group would perform a very important external purpose: just as they brought people within the process on board, so they would bring other people outside the process who thought in a similar fashion on board as well.

But the process failed, DeLong noted. He argued that its head—Ira Magaziner—seemed uninterested in assembling a coalition to support reform. So internal objections were never addressed, and those objections were subsequently repeated in stronger form by the Congressional Budget Office, by key senators like Daniel P. Moynihan, John Breaux, and John Chafee, and by others. Precisely because these objections were not answered in the internal executive branch policy process, there was no one to persuade the center of the Senate to support Magaziner's reform. The structure of American politics made reform difficult, but in DeLong's view it was errors on the part of the White House that made reform impossible.

Victor Fuchs suggested that the failure to pass the HSA had to be viewed in the context of a series of political failures in this area throughout the 20th century. That history, in turn, could be partly explained by another underlying reality of the U.S. political system: As H. G. Wells observed to Lenin, the United States lacks not only a socialist party, but also a conservative party in the European sense. Instead, we have the left and right wings of a traditional European liberal party. In part, this means that both parties share a commitment to individual choice and to private enterprise, which makes any national health care plan suspect on both sides of the aisle. Fuchs also responded to Cutler's argument that, despite the failure of the HSA, the Clinton administration did achieve a number of legislative successes. In Fuchs' view, the correct measure is not legislation but health outcomes, where he thinks little progress resulted from policy changes. For example, the number of uninsured Americans was higher at the end of the decade than at the beginning, despite record prosperity and the Clinton administration's policy efforts. Furthermore, relative to the trend, improvements in mortality in the 1990s were less than might have been predicted.

Joseph Newhouse commented that the degree of redistribution in policies is important to their political success or failure. Most of the policies that were actually passed during the 1990s hardly affected middle- or upper-income Americans. He added that another reason for the political failure of the HSA was that, despite the evident inefficiencies of the status quo system at the beginning of the Clinton administration, people had little faith that the government would solve the administrative inefficiencies. Most physicians and hospital administrators complain not only about HMOs but also about Medicaid and Medicare. The administrative side of Medicare would not have been affected by the proposed changes, and whatever replaced Medicaid, he suggested, would also generate quite a bit of paperwork.

David Cutler agreed with Fuchs' focus on health outcomes, but pointed out that such outcomes are hard to evaluate. We seldom know what would have happened in the absence of the policy that was enacted and therefore don't know what benchmark we should use to judge whether a policy was successful.

Jonathan Gruber added that when considering the benchmark for evaluating the Clinton administration's success or failure, it was important to realize that after the fiasco of HSA, no further progress on health care policy seemed likely. Compared to that baseline, the S-CHIP (State Child Health Insurance Plan) program, for example, would have to count as a significant success, since it was partly responsible for last year's decline in uninsurance rates among children, the first decline in 20 years.

Allan Meltzer asserted that HSA did not encourage people to consider the marginal cost of health care, which it should have done. Meltzer also picked up on Newhouse's point regarding inefficiencies, noting that the HSA accounting assumed that the government would pay for 37 million uninsured people by reducing paperwork, which Meltzer suggested was thoroughly implausible. In his view, the program was doomed when Representative Dan Rostenkowski recognized that the alleged savings would not materialize and raised this issue publicly.

Robert Reischauer responded to Cutler's claim that S-CHIP was a major Clinton administration success by pointing out that the program's main goal is to counter the negative and unanticipated effect of welfare reform in pushing people out of Medicaid into uninsurance. A policy that partially repairs the collateral damage done by another administration policy, he suggested, is not the same as a success that improves the situation relative to a pre-administration benchmark. The reason uninsurance rates increased since the middle of the decade is that Medicaid enrollment fell rapidly, and S-CHIP represents an attempt to counter that trend.

Reischauer agreed with DeLong's analysis of conditions in 1993 and argued that the possibility of passing HSA or any fundamental health care reform rested on middle-class insecurity regarding health insurance. Such insecurity was high in the early 1990s as a result of macroeconomic conditions, the S&L crisis, military downsizing, and related events. Since the economy subsequently expanded and people became more secure, and since the proposed reforms appeared to have more to do with redistribution than security, support for the administration's plan disappeared. Inefficiencies remained, but in the absence of personal insecurity, most people were relatively unconcerned about overall spending levels. He suggested that Americans have no idea how their health insurance is being paid for now, as they do not experience the marginal cost of their own care.

Gruber wondered why the Clinton administration had been willing to shut down the government to prevent block-granting Medicaid to the states, whereas they allowed an equally if not more radical restructuring of welfare without nearly so much opposition.

Martin Feldstein voiced his opinion that crowding out was the central problem that led to the failure of HSA. Too much money was spent on covering or subsidizing those who were already covered in the private market, so the final cost of the plans was too high per additional person covered. It was very hard, he felt, to make a case for such a large subsidy to raise the insurance rate from 85 percent to 90 or 95 percent of the population.

Cutler observed that if the targeted population is viewed as deserving, such as the beneficiaries of S-CHIP, political support is strong even if the cost is high. Policy-makers knew S-CHIP would cause crowdout, and instructed the states to take measures against it, but were willing to put up with some inefficiency to benefit a deserving population.

Jeffrey Frankel noted that health care reform may affect welfare reform. Frankel related that, according to Ira Magaziner, urban hospitals that expanded as a result of S-CHIP were in the neighborhoods where jobs were most needed to move people off welfare.

Peter Orszag asked the panelists about the reasonability of employers' opposition to employer mandates, based on the view that they would bear the cost of increased premiums. How much of the employer opposition was due to rational factors (including limits, such as implied by the minimum wage, on the degree to which health care costs are passed through to wages) versus misunderstanding or misperception?

Cutler answered that workers do pay, but they don't know it; firms don't pay, but they think they do. As Reischauer suggested earlier, said Cutler, nobody really knows who's paying. When you ask firms why they oppose mandates, they argue that such mandates would raise costs and are skeptical that the costs would be passed back to employees in the form of lower wages. Only unions seem to recognize the wage offset: Their political lobbying reflects an understanding that their members would bear any increase in health care costs, in part because management makes this argument to them in collective bargaining sessions; that is, "We can't give you a wage increase because health care costs are going up." In Cutler's view, the overwhelming business opposition to employer mandates is quite surprising. Opposition was also due to concerns about regulatory burden and so on, but views regarding the incidence of health benefit costs differ starkly between economists and practitioners.

Newhouse added that small businesses may also oppose employer mandates because their workers prefer higher wages to health insurance, perhaps because they are gamblers or because they have coverage from other sources. If small firms have optimized their compensation structure between cash wages and fringes, imposing a mandate on them makes them worse off by making it more difficult for them to compete in the labor market.

Ira Jackson asked *Cutler* and *Gruber* how the administration decided which incremental reforms to push for after the failure of large-scale reform. Why HIPAA and S-CHIP, for example, as opposed to something else? Were the political consultants, like Dick Morris, driving the decisions? What process led to this particular alphabet soup of incremental legislative successes?

Gruber answered that in the wake of HSA's failure, the administration chose the most politically viable approaches, even if they were not the most sensible from a policy standpoint. Gruber suggested that S-CHIP, for example, which covered children between 150 percent and 200 percent of the poverty line, may have been less socially valuable than covering adults below 50 percent of poverty, who are much less likely to be insured. But there was no political constituency for low-income adults, whereas there was for mothers and children. A similar logic led to the support for HIPAA, since even after the recession ended people were afraid of losing coverage if they changed jobs (because of the failure of insurance markets to provide long-term contracts). HIPAA appealed to this insecurity, and that appeal made it more politically viable.

Cutler added that even on the incremental policies, the administration did not get everything passed that it wanted. Administration proposals on the disabled, long-term care, the near elderly, and other issues were never implemented. So rather than a strategic decision to tackle a few issues, the administration actually pursued lots of incremental reforms—and some of them made it through Congress.

Richard Zeckhauser, the moderator, then directed the discussion toward the tobacco issues.

Robert Stavins asked *Gruber* and *Kip Viscusi* to clarify the sources of their disagreement over the costs of smoking. Stavins suggested that, according to Gruber, the sum of the internal damages to smokers plus the out-of-pocket cost of cigarettes is greater than the utility smokers receive. He asked both Gruber and Viscusi whether they believe, based on this method of analysis, that the costs are larger than the benefits. Second, he asked them whether this is really the appropriate welfare analysis, given the addictive nature of the product.

Gruber said he would attempt to answer the question from a somewhat different perspective. The traditional public finance course teaches that cigarettes are different from apples because of externalities, like health care costs, which are offset by saving money on Social Security. Adding these things up, you get a figure between positive and negative 50 cents. However, according to Gruber, the model for cigarettes should not be the hyperrational model we use for apples. People's decisions to use cigarettes too often reflect misinformation, the age at which smokers begin to smoke, failures in long-run discounting, and other factors. Gruber did not think that he and Viscusi disagreed significantly about the external costs to smoking, which are fairly small and less than the current tax (which, including the cost of the litigated settlement, is about $1.50 per pack). The appropriate place for debate now, he claimed, is on whether or how internal costs (of perhaps $30 per pack) should count in the analysis. Gruber concluded that such costs had to be included, at least partially, in the analysis unless people make decisions about cigarettes the same way they make decisions about apples, an assumption which he asserted is implausible.

Viscusi replied that his calculations focused only on the financial cost, not the losses to smokers. The lawsuits, however, were also not concerned with individuals but with finances. He then expressed his willingness to consider the broader question Gruber raised of whether cigarettes are costly from a social perspective, which he agreed depended on whether the private costs were internalized in the smoker's decision or whether smokers were making mistakes. His research suggests that people substantially *overestimate* the risk associated with smoking, a finding which would suggest that they do internalize the costs (indeed, perhaps internalize too high a cost). Gruber gave credence to surveys in which younger people do not expect to continue smoking, but Viscusi was more inclined to place evaluative weight on other surveys in which almost everybody says that smoking is a habit, an addiction, or both. So he agreed with Gruber about how to think about this issue, but they disagree about the extent to which smokers are making mistakes.

Benjamin Friedman asked two questions. First, are there data on the ages at which Americans begin to smoke broken down by age of the smoker? The answer could determine whether smoking was a children's protection issue, or whether only the addictive nature of cigarettes complicated the analysis. Second, Friedman commented that somewhere in the spectrum between health and tobacco policy is the issue of drugs. He was interested in the panel's views regarding U.S. policy on drugs.

Gruber responded that about 75 percent of smokers start smoking before 19, but noted two caveats. First, the starting age has been dropping over time, but slowly. Second, starting young does not necessarily imply addiction: There are currently more ex-smokers than smokers. However, Gruber's current research suggests that starting as a teenager leads to a 50 percent chance of smoking as an adult, so he believes there is a strong link. What that implies for policy, he said, depends on how we feel about the decision-making process of 16-year-olds.

Gruber argued that drugs really highlight the external-internal cost debate. The external costs to drugs, he said, are primarily the costs of battling drugs. If drugs were legal, they would impose little external cost to society. The vast majority of the cost is internal to the users themselves. So, Gruber argued, those who believe that we should not tax tobacco because only the external costs matter should also support legalization of drugs because the external costs are low.

Fuchs closed the session by noting that he was not going to answer the very good questions posed by Friedman, but rather by bringing up a new issue: the distributive aspects of cigarette smoking. Heavy cigarette smoking is concentrated among the people with the least education. Though this element did not enter into the present discussion, Fuchs believes it should in the future.

13

Medicare

Joseph P. Newhouse

PANELISTS: *Nancy-Ann DeParle, Mark McClellan, and Robert D. Reischauer*

Medicare, which accounts for about an eighth of the federal budget, covers health care costs for three groups of beneficiaries.[1] The great bulk of the spending, approximately 85 percent, provides benefits for those over 65.[2] About 10 percent covers those eligible for Disability Insurance, and the remaining 5 percent covers those of any age with end-stage renal disease (kidney failure).[3] Enacted in 1965 as part of the Great Society, the program was implemented in

I wish to thank David Cutler, Victor Fuchs, Michael O'Grady, Jon Gruber, Peter Orszag, and Bruce Vladeck for comments. Any errors are my responsibility.

Note: Newhouse's vantage point on Medicare comes from serving on the various commissions that Congress created to advise it with respect to Medicare. He was a commissioner of the Physician Payment Review Commission from 1993 to 1996 and the chair of the Prospective Payment Assessment Commission in 1996 and 1997. The Balanced Budget Act (BBA) of 1997 combined these two commissions into the Medicare Payment Advisory Commission (MedPAC), and he has served on that commission from 1997 to the present. As a result of this experience, his viewpoint likely gives a larger role to Congress and a lesser role to the executive branch than might a chapter written by someone who served in the executive branch.

1. The one-eighth figure includes the Part B payments financed by beneficiary premiums. If they are not considered, Medicare accounts for about 11 percent of outlays.

2. Medicare is a secondary payer for those over 65 actively employed with group insurance through their employer. Those few elderly not eligible for Social Security must pay a premium for Medicare Part A.

3. Medicare eligibility for the disabled begins two years after eligibility for disability insurance. Those with renal disease are to be covered through any employer-based coverage for the first 30 months of eligibility.

July 1966 and extended to the disabled and those with renal disease in 1972. It now enrolls approximately 40 million individuals.

Given that Medicare pays an average of more than $5,000 per beneficiary, it should not be surprising that it is a voting issue for the elderly and near elderly and hence an issue that no president or member of Congress can ignore. Of those voters 60 years of age and over who responded in exit polls following the 1996 presidential election, Medicare/Social Security ranked as the top issue (Blendon et al., 1997). And the elderly vote disproportionately; 61 percent of those 65 and over voted in the 1994 congressional elections versus 20 percent of those 18 to 24 and 32 percent of those 25 to 34 (Blendon et al., 1995).

In this chapter I first describe Medicare as the 1990s began and then discuss some of the important changes made to the program in the 1990s. I next analyze current issues, dividing them into relatively short-term issues of reimbursement methods, longer-run issues of financing, and potential future benefit expansions. I conclude by commenting on certain administrative issues. A more extensive economic analysis of many of the issues discussed here can be found in (Newhouse, 2002). Because Medicare is complicated, describing it and the changes to it during the 1990s does not always make for easy reading. Nonetheless, I have tried to minimize the detail.

Much of the public debate of the last several years has been about financing Medicare a decade or more hence when the baby boomers start to swell the ranks of the beneficiaries. Although I touch on this issue, my focus is more on Medicare in the here and now. Medicare relies on administered price systems that are not likely to see us through the next decade. But improving those systems raises difficult substantive and political issues.

13.1   Medicare at the Beginning of the 1990s

13.1.1   Benefits

The Medicare insurance contract remains patterned after the indemnity policies that prevailed in the 1960s. Part A, an entitlement financed from payroll taxes, covers services of institutional providers, most notably hospitals and skilled nursing facilities.[4] It accounts for roughly 60 percent of Medicare spending. Part B is a voluntary insurance program covering physician and other out-

---

4. The payroll tax rate is currently 2.9 percent on all earnings, with half nominally paid by the employer. Prior to 1991, the upper limit on taxable earnings was the same as Social Security. The Omnibus Budget Reconciliation Act of 1990 (OBRA90) raised the limit to $125,000 from $51,300; the limit was removed entirely in OBRA93, effective in 1994.

patient services. It is financed 75 percent from general revenues and 25 percent from premiums paid by the elderly; given this degree of subsidy, more than 95 percent of the elderly purchase Part B.[5] Importantly, Medicare was designed to cover the cost of acute medical services and not chronic long-term care. As we shall see, however, in practice this distinction has become somewhat blurred.

Reflecting the insurance policies of the 1960s, Medicare does not cover outpatient prescription drugs, nor does it have a stop-loss feature that limits a beneficiary's out-of-pocket spending in a year. Hospital coverage, in fact, gives out entirely after a 90-day stay.[6] Hospital services have a deductible equal to the average cost of a day in the hospital ($792 in 2001), well above the deductible in almost all employer-provided policies for the under 65; Part B services have a $100 annual deductible and a 20 percent coinsurance rate. Home health services are an exception and have no cost sharing.

Probably because Medicare lacks a stop-loss feature, a supplementary insurance industry has grown up. More than 90 percent of beneficiaries have some form of supplementary insurance that covers much of the cost sharing, thereby converting cost sharing at the point of service to premium payments. This supplementary insurance comes from four sources: employer-provided retiree health insurance (36 percent of beneficiaries in 1999); individually purchased coverage ("Medigap," 27 percent); additional benefits provided to those who join a Health Maintenance Organization (HMO, 17 percent); and Medicaid (11 percent) (Rice and Bernstein, 1999).

Overall Medicare covers about two-thirds of expenses among those elderly living in the community. Supplementary insurance, both employer provided and individually purchased, covers 11.5 percent, Medicaid covers 2.5 percent, and 15.2 percent is paid for out of pocket (Medicare Payment Advisory Commission, 1999b).[7]

13.1.2   Reimbursement

Medicare also emulated the insurance policies of the 1960s in giving its beneficiaries freedom to choose among almost all providers with little or no difference in price to the beneficiary. Moreover, Medicare's designers did not want

---

5. The elderly with incomes below the federal poverty line have their Part B premiums as well as their cost sharing paid for by Medicaid, and there is also premium assistance but no cost-sharing assistance for those between 100 and 120 percent of the poverty line.

6. Medicare covers 90 days of a hospital stay within an episode of illness. A new episode of illness begins after a beneficiary has been out of the hospital or the skilled nursing facility for 60 days. Beneficiaries have an additional 60 days of coverage from a one-time "lifetime" reserve.

7. The remainder comes from other sources such as the Veterans Administration.

providers to bill beneficiaries additional amounts, or at least wanted to limit such "balance billing."[8] Not only could balance billing undermine freedom of choice, but it would defeat the entire purpose if providers charged patients what they would have charged without Medicare and collected Medicare reimbursement in addition. If Medicare was to shoulder the bulk of the reimbursement load and there was to be freedom of choice, Medicare had to pay physicians and other providers at rates that virtually all of them would accept. Of course, Medicare could not agree to reimburse any price a provider named, and it therefore developed administered pricing systems that have grown steadily more elaborate. Initially the program followed the methods of Blue Cross and Blue Shield insurance plans by reimbursing institutional providers such as hospitals its share of costs and physicians their usual fees, subject to an area-wide ceiling.[9]

In FY1984 a major change occurred in hospital reimbursement, which increased the incentive for efficient production (Shleifer, 1985). A Prospective Payment System (PPS) was introduced over a five-year transition. The PPS reimbursed a fixed amount per admission rather than Medicare's share of hospital costs. The amount paid varied with the patient's diagnosis and whether certain procedures were performed; this information was used to classify the patient into one of about 500 diagnosis-related groups (DRGs), to which a relative weight was attached. Congress legislated a "conversion factor" that translated the weight into a dollar figure, which was "updated" each year. The payment also varied with the hospital's area wage index, the number of interns and residents per bed at the hospital, and the size of the city in which the hospital was located (McClellan, 1997).

Other institutional providers, including hospital outpatient departments, continued to be reimbursed on the basis of cost, a policy which not only offered no incentive for efficient production, but gave hospitals an incentive to adopt accounting conventions that shifted as much joint cost as possible from prospectively reimbursed inpatient services to other parts of the hospital, such as the outpatient department, the skilled nursing facility (SNF), and the rehabilitation unit.[10]

---

8. From the outset hospitals and other institutional providers could not balance bill. OBRA86 prohibited physicians charging more than 10 percent above the fee schedule.

9. Medicare's share of costs was defined as its share of patient days; costs were determined from audited cost reports filed by providers.

10. In the case of the institutional providers not covered by the PPS, I am greatly oversimplifying a set of complex reimbursement rules; Medicare sometimes reimbursed a function of a prior year's cost per case updated for inflation (e.g., rehabilitation units), sometimes simply cost (e.g., ancillary services in SNFs), and sometimes costs subject to maximums (e.g., routine costs in SNFs and home health agencies).

13.1.3   HMO Reimbursement

When it began in 1966, Medicare had no mechanism for paying HMOs a set amount per member per month, the method by which they were paid for their under-65 members. Rather, HMOs billed Medicare like any other provider, that is, on a fee-for-service basis.[11] Medicare enrollment in HMOs was modest; indeed, in 1966 when Medicare began even the enrollment of the under 65 in HMOs was modest.[12]

By the early 1980s the notion grew that HMOs might be an efficient means to deliver care and that Medicare should be more accommodating toward them. The 1982 Tax Equity and Fiscal Responsibility Act authorized risk contracts under which HMOs would be reimbursed a fixed amount per member per month. This amount, called the adjusted average per capita cost (AAPCC), was, for an average enrollee, 95 percent of traditional Medicare's average payment in the enrollee's county of residence. The 5 percent off-the-top reduction was taken so that Medicare could share in the assumed efficiencies of HMOs.

The AAPCC payment was adjusted for the enrollee's age, sex, institutional status (e.g., whether the person's residence was a nursing home), and whether the person was eligible for Medicaid. For example, if 65–69-year-old females, living at home and not on Medicaid, spent 93 percent as much as the average Medicare beneficiary, the HMO received 93 percent of the AAPCC amount for enrolling a person with those characteristics. In addition to the AAPCC, HMOs could charge their members a premium up to the actuarial value of the cost-sharing provisions in traditional Medicare. If HMOs could provide services for less than the AAPCC payment plus the allowable premium, they were to reduce the premium or provide additional services to beneficiaries or both.[13]

---

11. In 1972 an option was added for Part B services to be reimbursed on the basis of cost, and in 1982 this was extended to all services. These contracts are now being phased out.

12. I have not found data on the number of HMO beneficiaries in the early years, but in the 1980s the HMO Medicare market share was only 3 percent. It almost certainly was less than that at the outset of the program. Indeed, the term HMO was not even coined until 1971, although entities such as the Kaiser Health Plan had existed for several decades.

13. The applicable regulations used the adjusted community rate (ACR), which was the rate charged by the HMO in its private business, adjusted for benefit and demographic differences with the Medicare population. If the cost of services to the Medicare population plus a private business profit rate was less than the ACR, the HMO was to provide additional benefits, lower the premium, or refund the excess to the government. The adjustments in the ACR calculation have considerable arbitrariness and are probably not binding; even so, competition in metropolitan areas among HMOs forced any rents in HMO reimbursement to be passed through to beneficiaries in the form of additional benefits or lower premiums, as I will come to later.

13.2   Changes to Medicare in the 1990s

13.2.1   *The First Six Years*

Compared to the second half of the 1990s, the first part of the decade was relatively quiet for Medicare. The major change was to physician payment.

13.2.1.1   Changes in Physician Payment

The Omnibus Budget Reconciliation Act of 1989 (OBRA89) enacted a major reform of physician payment, which began to be implemented in 1990. Despite attempts in the 1980s to restrain fees, physician spending had grown very rapidly. An increased quantity of services had more than offset the fee cuts, and by 1989 Part B spending, 75 percent of which was for physician services, was the largest domestic program funded from general revenues. At a time of large deficits, Congress sought additional constraints on Medicare physician spending. In addition, many felt that Medicare fees for procedures were too high relative to those for evaluation and management services such as taking a history. As a result, Congress legislated a series of ad hoc reductions in certain "overpriced" procedures in the late 1980s.[14]

The essence of the 1989 reform addressed both the issues of spending growth and the structure of relative prices across physician services. Effective in 1990 it put in place a formula, the Volume Performance System (VPS), that set a target for the total amount of money Medicare would pay to physicians in a year. Under the VPS a target increase ("performance standard") in physician spending was set. The target was a function of a five-year moving average of the annual increase in the quantity of physician services, on the grounds that this value would reflect scientific and technical advances for which Medicare should pay. If the quantity of services ("volume") increased above its five-year trend, unit prices two years later (the "conversion factor") would be proportionately decreased to constrain total spending on physician services. Conversely, a fall in volume below the five-year trend caused unit prices to rise in the short run. As volume stayed low, however, the five-year moving average would start to fall, and the target would fall, thereby lowering future updates. Although not realized at the time, this method was to cause substantial instability in physician fees and would be changed in 1997.

The VPS, however, was effective in constraining spending growth on physician services (Figure 13.1). The real growth rate in spending declined from the 9.7 percent rate of the prior 15 years to 2.8 percent between 1990 and 1997.

---

14. That Medicare was overpaying for some procedures was plausible. In the case of several newer, high-tech procedures, productivity had improved considerably, but Medicare's administered prices were rigid downward and had no ready way of adjusting for these improvements.

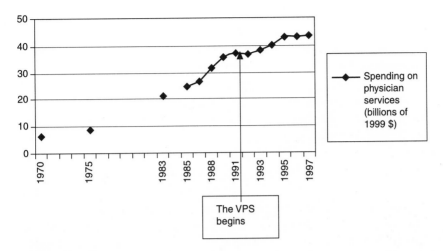

Figure 13.1
Growth in Real Physician Expenditure, Calendar Years 1970–97. (*Source:* Health Care Financing Administration, "Medicare and Medicaid Statistical Supplement, 1999," Table 55, adjusted by the GDP chain-type price index.)

In addition to the VPS, Medicare adopted a new schedule of relative prices for physician services that reflected the amount of "work" for each service (Hsiao et al., 1988). The new relative fees implied a substantial redistribution across specialties. In particular, procedure-oriented specialties, such as surgeons and certain medical subspecialists such as invasive cardiologists, were to have fees for many services reduced, whereas primary care physicians were to receive higher fees.

Not surprisingly the losers resisted the reform. As a result, the potential redistribution was initially mitigated in two ways. First, the implementation of the new fee schedule (but not the VPS) was put off three years, until 1992, after which time there was a four-year (linear) transition to the new fee schedule, so that the new relative prices were not fully in place until 1996. Second, "practice costs" were excluded from the reform, and continued to be passed through under the earlier reimbursement rules. Practice costs refer to the approximately half of physician revenue that is not net physician income; that is, they encompass "overhead" costs such as office rent, salaries of assistants, supplies, and so forth. Excluding practice costs from the reform, therefore, approximately halved the redistributional effect.

Although some practice costs can be directly associated with individual services, many are joint costs, the allocation of which to any specific service is arbitrary (e.g., the rent, the telephone bill). Nonetheless, there was continuing political pressure from the potential winning specialties to include practice costs, and in the Balanced Budget Act (BBA) of 1997 the Congress mandated the inclusion of "resource-based" practice costs. After an initial unsuccessful try at allocating such costs empirically, the Health Care Financing Administration (HCFA) resorted to physician judgment to allocate practice costs among procedures. (On June 14, 2001, Secretary Thompson announced that HCFA would be renamed as Centers for Medicare and Medicaid Services; for convenience I will refer to the agency as HCFA.)

A curious development arose from the rhetoric that accompanied the 1989 reform—that by setting a target spending level, physicians would have an incentive to reduce volume in order to increase their fees. Such rhetoric was economic nonsense, since it ignored each physician's incentive to free-ride and increase income by providing more services. Around the time of the reform, however, the rate of increase in the volume of surgical procedures fell substantially for reasons that even today are not entirely clear. Seizing upon the rhetoric, surgeons took credit for this fall and successfully argued that their services should not be pooled with those of other, more profligate physicians. As a result, Congress in 1990 created a separate performance standard for surgical services effective in 1991, which implied a separate conversion factor (price per relative value unit) for surgical services. Primary care physicians then asked to have a separate target and conversion factor for evaluation and management and other primary care services, so that the increasing volume of nonsurgical procedures such as endoscopy and coronary angiography would not drag down their fee increases. In OBRA93 Congress also granted this request, effective in 1994, so there were then three conversion factors.

By law the increases in the three conversion factors were inversely related to volume increases for each of the three groupings of services, and the increases differed across the three targets each year. After a few years the conversion factors differed by 21 percent, with surgical services having the highest conversion factor.[15] But this spread undid whatever logic there was to the effort in the relative price scale to achieve equal pay across specialties for equivalent work. Congress addressed this issue in the BBA, as described subsequently.

13.2.1.2 Two Nonevents in the 1990–96 Period

Two proposals from the 1990–96 period were not enacted into law but set the stage for future events. From the beneficiaries' perspective the Health Security Act left Medicare mostly alone, reflecting its political sensitivity, but it did contain an outpatient drug benefit for Medicare, a topic I will take up later.

---

15. As a result of low volume increases, surgeons in 1994 and 1995 received 10.0 and 12.2 percent (nominal) increases in their conversion factor, whereas other nonsurgical, nonprimary care services only received increases slightly over 5 percent in each year.

From the providers' perspective, however, the act proposed numerous payment reductions to finance coverage for the uninsured.

Second, Medicare was a prime target for budget savings for the Republican Congress that came to office in the November 1994 elections. Among other issues was the elderly's share of Part B premiums. In 1966, when Medicare was enacted, the elderly paid 50 percent of Part B premiums and the other 50 percent came from general revenues. Part B spending, and hence the elderly's premium payments, increased more rapidly than the elderly's income, however, so in 1972, Congress limited the increase in the elderly's premiums to the cost-of-living increase in Social Security payments. With this limit in place, over the next decade the elderly's share of Part B spending fell to 25 percent. At that time Congress began to regularly pass legislation setting the premium at 25 percent of the cost. In 1990, however, Congress mandated specific dollar increases in premiums rather than a percentage for the 1991–95 period; the dollar amounts were intended to keep the elderly's share at about 25 percent. Part B costs, however, grew less rapidly than Congress had projected, so that the elderly's share of the premium rose from 25 to 31.5 percent.

In 1995, Republicans proposed keeping the share at 31.5 percent to achieve budgetary savings, but Democrats wished to return to 25 percent. Given the projected increases in Part B spending, even a constant share of 25 percent implied an increase in beneficiary premiums that would be greater than the increase in income among the elderly. This particular Republican proposal was among the most salient issues in the three-week shutdown of the federal government in late 1995, and both it and the shutdown were used to great political advantage by President Clinton in his 1996 reelection campaign.

Republicans made numerous other proposals for reductions in provider payment at this time, many of which echoed the administration's proposals from the Health Security Act. Despite the administration's rejection of the overall Republican package in 1995, it was clear that Medicare could not keep on doing business as it had in the past. The groundwork for the Balanced Budget Act of 1997 had been laid.

13.2.2   The Balanced Budget Act

By far the most important piece of legislation affecting Medicare in the 1990s was the Balanced Budget Act (BBA), enacted in 1997. Federal budget deficits were still projected as far as the eye could see in the 1997 era, and the administration and the Republican Congress agreed on the desirability of reducing the deficits. Part B of Medicare, with its large budget share, could not be left unscathed. Moreover, in 1996 the Trustees of the Medicare Hospital Insurance

Fund ("Part A") had estimated that the Part A Trust Fund would have a zero balance in 2001. Outlays had slightly exceeded income in 1995 and were expected to exceed income by ever greater amounts in all subsequent years. And the budgetary picture would become much grimmer when the leading edge of the baby boomers started to turn 65 in 2010 and especially when they started to turn 75 in 2020.

The projection of a zero balance in the Part A Trust Fund in 2001 was translated in the press as Medicare's "going broke," the political equivalent of shouting "fire" in a crowded theater. Thus the pressure was on both Congress and the administration to reduce the rate of growth in Medicare spending, and especially Part A spending, since there was no appetite on either side of the aisle for an increase in payroll taxes to finance Part A.

This pressure resulted in the BBA, which made sweeping changes in how Medicare paid health care providers. Fundamentally it all but eliminated the considerable portion of cost reimbursement that remained in the program. In doing so, however, it created a new set of problems. I first describe several of the changes made by the BBA and then turn to some problems those changes created. I focus especially on post-acute care services, HMO reimbursement, and physician payment.

13.2.2.1 Post-Acute Services

After 1988 the use of post-acute services—home health services, skilled nursing facility (SNF) services, rehabilitation services, and long-term hospital services— began to rise at very high rates (Table 13.1). From 1988 to 1997 home health visits per beneficiary increased by nearly a factor of 7 and SNF days per beneficiary by nearly a factor of 5. Spending on post-acute services rose from about 3 percent of Part A spending in the mid-1980s to 26 percent of Part A spending in 1996, a time when Part A spending itself was rising at rates well in excess of the growth in tax revenues.[16] Spending on post-acute services appeared out of control.

The fundamental causes for the increased spending were several: reimbursement that was primarily cost based (though this was a readier explanation for high rather than increased spending); generous reimbursement of new entrants; the incentive the PPS offered to unbundle inpatient hospital services to post-acute sites; and, in the case of home health services, an ill-defined criterion for eligibility for benefits. In addition, court decisions in 1986 and 1988 held that prior HCFA regulations and interpretations of law, which had been used to

---

16. Nominal spending in Part A grew by a factor of 3 between 1984 and 1996, whereas federal tax revenue grew only by a factor of 2.2.

Table 13.1
Substitution of Post-Acute Care for Medicare, Inpatient Hospital Days

Year[a]	Inpatient Days per 1,000 Beneficiaries	Skilled Nursing Facility Days per 1,000 Beneficiaries	Home Health Visits per 1,000 Beneficiaries	Rehabilitation Admissions per 1,000 Beneficiaries
1981	3,827			
1982	3,889			
1983	3,786			
1984	3,217			
1985	2,823			
1986	2,784	268	1,106	2.8
1987	2,815	229	1,104	3.3
1988	2,804	334	1,104	3.7
1989	2,721	889	1,350	4.0
1990	2,749	749	2,052	5.1
1991	2,728	669	2,880	6.0
1992	2,642	812	3,763	6.6
1993	2,474	948	4,661	7.2
1994	2,436	1,006	6,020	7.8
1995	2,317	1,053	7,125	8.8
1996	2,056	1,053	7,546	
1997	1,979	1,519	7,519	
1998	1,895	1,527	4,590	
AAGR[b]	−4.1%	15.6%	12.6%[c]	12.1%

Sources: Inpatient days through 1993, *Health Care Financing Review,* "Statistical Supplement, 1996," Table 23. Inpatient days, 1994 and 1995, *Statistical Abstract of the United States, 1997,* pages 115–116. 1996–98 inpatient days from http://www.hcfa.gov/stats/stats.htm. Other values calculated from Prospective Payment Assessment Commission, "Medicare and the American Health Care System," June 1997, Chapter 4. SNF values for 1997 and 1998 and home health value for 1997 are unpublished data from the Health Care Financing Administration. 1996–98 data for rehabilitation admissions are not available.

[a] Calendar year for hospital days through 1993; fiscal year for other values. 1994 value from *Statistical Abstract* because 1994 value in Statistical Supplement excludes managed care enrollees and so is biased upward.

[b] AAGR is average annual growth rate. Value is calculated from initial year shown in the table to final year.

[c] Value through 1997 is 20.5 percent. The sharp decline in visits in 1998 reflects some undetermined mix of greater antifraud enforcement efforts and changes in payment that were effective in October 1997.

hold down home health and SNF spending, were illegal.[17] Furthermore, states became more aggressive about shifting some chronic long-term care spending from the Medicaid budget to Medicare, adding to the increase in SNF spending. Because it remains a problem, I now analyze Medicare payment policy for post-acute services in more detail.

Reimbursement for Post-Acute Services Prior to the BBA   I focus on the three largest components of post-acute spending, home health services, SNF services, and rehabilitation hospitals and units. In 1996, Medicare spent $16.8 billion on home health services, $9.6 billion on SNFs, and $4.6 billion on rehabilitation facilities (Health Care Financing Administration, 1999; Medicare Payment Advisory Commission, 1999a).

Prior to the BBA, home health agencies were paid their cost per visit up to a limit of 112 percent of the national mean cost per visit.[18] SNFs were paid their cost per day for routine expenses up to a limit of 112 percent of the national mean.[19] Ancillary services delivered to SNF patients—for example, physical and speech therapy—were reimbursed on a reasonable cost basis, as were capital costs.[20] At rehabilitation hospitals and units, reimbursement per admission was related to a target figure, a base-year cost per admission trended forward by the Consumer Price Index. Hospitals and units shared half of any deviation from this target within a band of 90 to 110 percent. Outside that band the government bore all costs and kept all savings.

New Entrants   New home health agencies and SNFs received cost reimbursement, just as older entities did. New rehabilitation hospitals and units (units were units within acute care hospitals) were reimbursed their costs for the first three years; the costs in the second full cost-reporting period were used to set their target value for future reimbursement. Not only did cost reimbursement give little incentive to economize on initial costs, to the degree that the new rehabilitation units could subsequently economize or reduce per-case costs as

17. The case on home health was *Duggan v. Bowen*, 691 F. Sup. 1487 (D.D.C. 1988) and on SNF services was *Fox v. Bowen*, 656 F. Sup. 1236 (D. Conn. 1986).

18. The text oversimplifies in that there was a cost limit of 112 percent for each type of covered service (e.g., physical therapy, home health aide), although the limit was applied to aggregate agency payments. Also, the labor portion of the limit was adjusted by the hospital wage index for the area.

19. Routine services are room, board, and nursing services. This was the rule for freestanding SNFs. Reimbursement for hospital-based SNFs was somewhat greater.

20. Ancillary services at SNFs grew particularly rapidly. In 1990 charges for physical, occupational, speech, and respiratory therapy were 15 percent of total Medicare SNF charges; by 1994 they were 30 percent (U.S. House of Representatives, 1996).

volume increased, they could keep half of the cost reductions from their target values to a maximum of 10 percent.

The generous reimbursement rules for new entrants caused the number of post-acute care facilities to rise rapidly. The number of SNFs grew 6.8 percent per year between 1990 and 1996, the number of rehabilitation hospitals and units rose 4.3 percent annually, and the number of home health agencies grew 9.3 percent annually (Prospective Payment Assessment Commission, 1997). Hospitals had an additional incentive to open or acquire these entities, because they could allocate some joint costs to these units (e.g., the CEO's salary), where they would be reimbursed, and away from inpatient services, where reimbursement was fixed by the PPS. Relative to freestanding entities, therefore, the number of hospital-based SNFs and rehabilitation units grew particularly rapidly in the 1990–96 period, at annual rates of 10.5 percent and 5.8 percent, respectively.

Unbundling The fixed PPS payment per inpatient admission together with the additional reimbursement for post-acute services offered hospitals an incentive to unbundle inpatient services, that is, to substitute post-acute care services for the last days of stay in the hospital. As a result, length of stay and beneficiary days per thousand fell, and post-acute services rose (Tables 13.1 and 13.2). That much of this fall could be attributed to the payment system can be seen by comparing the fall in length of stay between 1988 and 1996 for Medicare beneficiaries and all others, whose inpatient stays were usually paid on a per-day rather than a per-admission basis. Medicare length of stay fell 27 percent; length of stay for all patients (including Medicare) fell 15 percent.[21] Moreover, among the ten DRGs with the largest number of post-acute care users, average length of stay dropped 1.3 to 2.0 days between 1994 and 1996 among post-acute care users, but only 0.6 to 1.8 days among nonusers (Medicare Payment Advisory Commission, 1998a).[22] Finally, hospitals that operated post-acute services had greater drops in length of stay (Prospective Payment Assessment Commission, 1996).

At the time of the BBA, hospitals were enjoying the highest margins the industry had experienced since the first two years of the PPS in 1984 and 1985 (Table 13.2).[23] The Medicare Payment Advisory Commission (MedPAC) estimates that unbundling was responsible for a substantial portion of this fiscal

---

21. Although this comparison does not control for any age-specific factors affecting length of stay (it is not clear which direction they would go), it understates the contribution of the payment system because several private payers changed from paying hospitals a daily rate to a DRG basis of payment in this period.
22. And the drop for users was greater than for nonusers in each of the ten DRGs.
23. Although it was to have been introduced on a budget-neutral basis, the PPS was misnormed so that initial payments were too great.

Table 13.2
Length of Stay, Medicare Inpatient and Total Hospital Margins

Year	Length of Stay (days)		Medicare Inpatient Margin (%)[a]	Total Margin (%)	Update Factor (%)
	All Patients	Medicare Patients			
1981	7.2	10.4	[b]	Not available	[b]
1982	7.2	10.2	[b]	Not available	[b]
1983	7.0	9.8	[b]	Not available	[b]
1984	6.7	8.9	13.4	7.3	[b]
1985	6.5	8.6	13.0	6.6	Not available
1986	6.6	8.7	8.7	4.3	Not available
1987	6.6	8.9	5.9	3.6	Not available
1988	6.6	8.9	2.7	3.5	Not available
1989	6.6	8.9	0.3	3.6	3.3
1990	6.6	8.8	−1.5	3.6	4.7
1991	6.5	8.6	−2.4	4.4	3.4
1992	6.4	8.4	−0.9	4.3	3.0
1993	6.2	8.0	1.3	4.4	2.7
1994	6.0	7.5	5.6	5.0	2.0
1995	5.7	7.0	11.1	5.8	2.0
1996	5.6	6.5	15.9	6.1	1.5
1997	5.4	6.2	16.9	5.9	2.0
1998	5.3	6.1	13.7	4.3	0.0
1999	5.2	6.0	12.0	2.8	1.1

Sources: All patients length of stay through 1996: Prospective Payment Assessment Commission, "Medicare and the American Health Care System: Report to the Congress," June 1997, page 89; 1997–99 calculated from Medicare Payment Advisory Commission, "Report to the Congress," March 2001, Table B-1. Medicare length of stay through 1996: *Health Care Financing Review: Medicare and Medicaid Statistical Supplement, 1998,* page 206; 1997–99 calculated from Medicare Payment Advisory Commission, "Report to the Congress," March 2001, Table B-1. Margins to 1993: Medicare Payment Advisory Commission, "Report to the Congress: Medicare Payment Policy," March 1999, pages 53 and 55. 1993 and later: Medicare Payment Advisory Commission, "Report to the Congress," March 2001, Tables B-4 and B-18. The Medicare inpatient margin is the ratio of Medicare revenue to the allocated cost of Medicare cases; the total margin is the ratio of hospital revenue from all payers to total hospital cost. Operating updates from Medicare Payment Advisory Commission, "Report to the Congress," March 2001, Table B-1.

[a] Excludes graduate medical education payments. Including these payments would raise the margins.

[b] Not applicable because of cost reimbursement.

improvement by lowering hospital costs per Medicare (inpatient) case by about 10 percent with no corresponding adjustment in payment (Medicare Payment Advisory Commission, 2001a).

The BBA Provisions for Post-Acute Care   The BBA addressed the unintended overpayment to hospitals in five ways. First, in an effort to better match payment for inpatient services with the cost reductions from unbundling, which had not been accounted for in setting prior hospital updates, the hospital update factor for 1998 was zero. Further, the BBA mandated that future updates to the PPS be below the rate of increase in hospital input prices. MedPAC estimates that these reductions to date have offset about two-thirds of the overpayment from unbundling; in other words, the payment rate for inpatient services is still about 3 percentage points above where it would have been if the rate had been adjusted for the unbundling—and of course hospitals have profited from the unbundling in the interim.

Second, the BBA attempted to end cost reimbursement for post-acute services by mandating that HCFA develop prospective payment systems for those services. In particular, HCFA was to put in place prospective payment systems for SNFs in 1998, for home health in 1999, and for rehabilitation services in 2000, and was to develop (but not implement) a system for long-term hospitals in 1999. Despite the short time frames and the lack of experience with prospective payment systems for post-acute facilities, the agency largely met its targets. It introduced the Resource Utilization Group (RUG) system for SNFs in July 1998. This system had been developed for chronic long-term care services, and when transplanted to the post-acute environment it proved to have problems. Nonetheless, this was probably the only option open to HCFA if the schedule mandated in the BBA was to be met. In October 2000 the agency introduced a prospective case-based system for home health agencies, the Home Health Resource Groups (HHRGs), and in January 2002 it will introduce a prospective system for rehabilitation hospitals and units. Despite the problems with reimbursement for post-acute care that I will describe later, HCFA's performance in introducing these systems in the space of a few years, largely on the timetable mandated in the BBA, was commendable.

Third, just as with inpatient hospital services, the BBA substantially reduced the growth rate of reimbursement for post-acute services. In the case of SNFs, these reductions came through the RUG system, which ended cost reimbursement and gave Congress control over rate increases. In the case of home health care, HCFA was given two years to develop a prospective payment system. In the interim the BBA mandated a payment system that substantially tightened the limits on cost reimbursement. Previously the limit on cost reimbursement was 112 percent of the mean cost of freestanding agencies; this was reduced to the lesser of 105 percent of the median cost or a 75–25 blend of the agency's *1994* cost and the average cost in the census region. Because of the increase in cost after 1994, the blend was usually the binding constraint. Moreover, the BBA provided that when the prospective payment system was ultimately introduced, there was to be a 15 percent reduction from a budget-neutral amount. Congress clearly considered home health spending excessive and was intent on rolling back spending to earlier levels.

Fourth, the BBA substantially tightened the rules for new entrants. As of 1998 target amounts for new rehabilitation facilities were limited to 110 percent of the national mean target amount even if their initial costs were greater. New SNFs were subject to the prospective payment system for SNFs that was implemented in 1998, and new home health agencies were subject to the revised payment limits in the interim system.

Fifth, the BBA modified the DRG payment for patients in certain DRGs who were discharged after a relatively short stay and who used post-acute services. In particular, for patients in ten DRGs who were discharged before the geometric mean length of stay for that DRG, the hospital would be paid per day rather than per admission. In implementing this regulation HCFA chose ten DRGs with high use of post-acute services. For those ten DRGs this change made the payment system more neutral (lower powered in contract theory jargon) with respect to whether the marginal day would be spent as an inpatient or in a post-acute setting.

In addition to these changes, the BBA attempted to clarify eligibility rules for home health services. Patients are eligible for Medicare home health benefits even without a hospital stay if they are homebound and need part-time or intermittent skilled nursing services or physical or speech therapy.[24] These terms had, however, not been defined in statute. After the 1988 court decision substantial ambiguity about the meaning of the terms remained; the BBA defined these terms.[25]

---

24. Prior to 1981 eligibility required a hospital stay, but that requirement was dropped on the argument that making home health services more available would pay for itself by reducing nursing home costs, an argument that later data have not supported (Kemper, 1988). The lack of a hospital stay has led to a heterogeneous population of users. Some receive post-acute services (e.g., a few visits to verify normal recuperation), while others receive almost daily visits because they can barely manage to live independently. The 1988 court decision was directed at earlier regulations that required patients to need part-time *and* intermittent services rather than part-time *or* intermittent services.

25. For the purpose of initial eligibility, intermittent care is care that is needed (strictly) less than 7 days a week or less than 8 hours a day for 21 days or less. Once eligible, an individual can receive services for any number of days per week, as long as the total is less than 8 hours per day and 28 hours per week.

Because no prior hospital stay was required for eligibility, under the old definition a number of home health services that were essentially chronic long-term care rather than post-acute services had de facto become covered Medicare services. For example, in 1994 more than half of all home health visits went to the 12 percent of users who had more than 150 visits per year. This group averaged 275 visits per user per year, or nearly daily visits, and they received a disproportionately high percentage of nurse aide as opposed to nurse visits (Prospective Payment Assessment Commission, 1997). Aide visits are more likely to be for a chronic problem; the aide, for example, might give an elderly person assistance with bathing. I doubt that the BBA's definitions of eligibility will much reduce this kind of service, although the new prospective payment system may well do so.

One change the BBA made was mainly an accounting change. It shifted the cost of all home health visits in excess of 100 in a year plus all visits that did not follow a hospital stay from Part A to Part B. Although this change did not affect payment rates by beneficiaries (the BBA waived the Part B coinsurance on such services) or payment rates to home health agencies, both the administration and the congressional Republicans could take credit for prolonging the life of the Part A trust fund. The only real effect, however, was to shift the cost of these services from payroll tax to general revenue financing.

Shifting State Monies to Medicare   Another cause of increased post-acute care spending was left untouched by the BBA. Patients are eligible for the SNF benefit if they stay in the hospital at least three days.[26] The SNF benefit then covers up to 20 days of a stay in the facility with no copayment and another 80 days with a copayment of one-eighth the hospital deductible (in 2001 this is just under $100). Although intended to apply to patients who need a period to recuperate from their illness but do not need the intensity of service that a hospital provides, states have aggressively pursued Medicare reimbursement for Medicaid-eligible nursing home residents who are hospitalized and then return to the nursing home, which will typically have a SNF. If Medicare rather than Medicaid pays for any of the nursing home stay, of course, the state saves its share of Medicaid reimbursement of the nursing home. Medicare's responsibility in principle ends when the episode of illness that caused the hospitalization ends (up to a maximum of 100 days of SNF care), but defining the end of the episode is often ambiguous, especially in the nursing home population.

---

26. The three-day stay requirement for SNF services has been contentious for many years. The Catastrophic Coverage Act of 1988 abolished the three-day requirement, and SNF usage shot up in 1989 (Table 13.1). When the act was repealed in 1989, the three-day stay requirement was reinstituted.

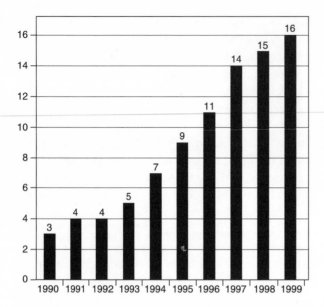

Figure 13.2
Percentage of Medicare Beneficiaries Enrolled in HMOs. (*Source:* Medicare Payment Advisory Commission, Report to the Congress, March 1998, page 5, and unpublished data.)

As a result of state efforts to shift the financing of nursing home residents from Medicaid to Medicare, the proportion of nursing home revenues that come from Medicare has risen substantially. Only 2 percent of nursing home revenues came from Medicare in 1980, and even as late as 1991 only 3 percent came from Medicare. By 1998, however, this proportion had risen to 12 percent, another example of chronic long-term care services being covered by Medicare (Cowan et al., 1999). Whether this trend has run its course is unclear.

13.2.2.2   The BBA Provisions for Medicare + Choice

During the 1990s the share of beneficiaries enrolled in HMOs grew from 3 to about 15 percent (Figure 13.2). This growth was prompted in large part by inefficiencies in traditional Medicare that were then transmitted to HMO reimbursement through the AAPCC and that HMOs could exploit. (Recall that the AAPCC was 95 percent of traditional Medicare payment in a county.) HMOs were concentrated in larger metropolitan areas, where there were often several HMOs, and competition among them forced the efficiency gains through to beneficiaries in the form of additional benefits and reductions in premiums. The estimated value of these benefits was directly related to the level of plan pay-

Table 13.3
Standardized Extra Benefits as a Function of Plan Payment, 1996

Decile	Plan Payment Index	Standardized Extra Benefits
U.S. Average	1.00	$77
10	1.29	121
9	1.15	86
8	1.09	80
7	1.06	86
6	1.03	92
5	0.99	78
4	0.94	68
3	0.88	57
2	0.82	53
1	0.75	48

Source: Prospective Payment Assessment Commission, "Medicare and the American Health Care System," June 1997, Table 2-8. Plans are grouped in deciles of equal numbers of plans according to the level of the AAPCC. The value of extra benefits is the actuarial value of any waived premium for noncovered services and reduced cost sharing, divided by the hospital wage index for the area.

ment, averaging $121 for the highest decile, 29 percent above the national average, but only $48 in the lowest decile (Table 13.3).[27]

The growth in HMO enrollment posed two issues. First, the geographic dispersion in reimbursement became more visible. As long as Medicare simply sent checks to individual physicians and hospitals on a service-by-service basis, the geographic dispersion in payments, which was well known to researchers, seemed to remain below the political radar screen. When it was summarized by the AAPCC, however, it did not. And the dispersion, which mirrors large variation in rates of procedures in the Medicare population, was large (Chassin et al., 1986) (Table 13.4).[28]

Politically this dispersion created a demand for more equality, especially from rural areas, which are well represented on the Senate Finance Committee. But the demand also came from metropolitan areas such as the Twin Cities and Portland, Oregon, which had AAPCCs that were only around 50 to 60 percent

27. The dollar values in Table 13.3 almost certainly understate the spread in the value of the benefits, because they have been standardized by the area wage index. The major supplementary benefit, however, is some drug coverage, and drug prices undoubtedly vary less from area to area than the wage index does.
28. The dispersion cannot be explained by variation in factor prices. The spread in the wage rate index is a factor of two, and several inputs are purchased in national markets with the same factor price. The fraction of inputs purchased in national markets varies by provider type, but is around 30 percent for hospitals.

Table 13.4
The AAPCC in the Six Highest and Six Lowest Counties, 1997

County	State	Annual Rate
The Six Highest Counties		
Richmond	NY	$9,208
Dade	FL	8,979
Bronx	NY	8,739
Plaquemines	LA	8,733
St. Bernard	LA	8,638
New York	NY	8,557
The Six Lowest Counties		
Arthur	NB	$2,651
Banner	NB	2,656
Holmes	OH	2,700
Chippewa	MN	2,728
Presidio	TX	2,756
Saline	NB	2,773

as large as those of Miami and New York City. The congressional representatives from these low-rate areas argued that their constituents were not being treated fairly by a program that was to provide uniform benefits across the nation.

Second, because of favorable selection into the program, the growth of HMO enrollment cost the government money; that is, the government was paying more for the beneficiaries that joined an HMO than it would have paid for them had they remained in traditional Medicare. Estimating just how much more the government was paying was controversial, but the most widely cited estimates were in the 6 to 8 percent range, even net of the 5 percent that the government took off the top (Brown et al., 1993; Riley et al., 1996; Congressional Budget Office, 1997).

An influential study by the Physician Payment Review Commission found that those who enrolled in HMOs in the 1989–94 period spent 38 percent less in the six months before they joined than the control group who did not join, after adjusting for age, sex, institutional status, welfare status, and county of residence. By contrast, those disenrolling spent 42 percent more than the control group (Physician Payment Review Commission, 1996). In other words, the healthy appeared to be joining HMOs, and the sick appeared to be leaving them. The same study compared mortality rates of those who joined HMOs in the year following enrollment with a control group who never joined HMOs, controlling for age, sex, and county of residence. The mortality rate among those who joined was 25 percent less than in traditional Medicare.[29] Although an HMO lobbyist might claim some health benefits from the more integrated care that HMOs could in principle provide, no one could seriously maintain that an HMO could cause anything like a 25 percent reduction in mortality.

The HMO industry's response to these findings was to assert that they were based on data from a period when HMO enrollment was only a tiny share of Medicare, but by 1997 the share was much higher and therefore it was likely that HMOs had a more representative risk mix. Moreover, HMOs asserted that it gave a misleading picture to use data from the period around the time of enrollment because as HMO beneficiaries remained in the HMO they would age and therefore their spending and mortality experience would regress toward the mean. This latter argument, of course, did not deny that some overpayment existed around the time of enrollment.

In response to these arguments, the BBA mandated a study by MedPAC similar in method to the Physician Payment Review Commission study of selection just discussed, but one that used more recent data. Although this subsequent study had some methodological differences with the earlier study, it essentially confirmed its findings. In particular, it showed that those enrolling in 1997 spent 28 percent less in the 12 months before enrollment than those in traditional Medicare (Medicare Payment Advisory Commission, 2000a). (But it found no difference in spending between those disenrolling and the control group.) Moreover, in the first year after enrollment (1998) there was a 21 percent mortality difference. Although this mortality difference fell as beneficiaries were in the HMO longer, it never returned to the mean, and for all HMO enrollees the difference was 15 percent (Figure 13.3).

Furthermore, the selection was threatening to create ever worse overpayment through a death spiral. If those joining HMOs in any time period are drawn from the population of the best risks remaining in traditional Medicare, as seems likely, mean costs for the groups in traditional Medicare and in HMOs will both rise but will steadily diverge (Cutler and Reber, 1998). That is, the traditional Medicare mean will increase by a greater amount than the HMO mean, so that payment in traditional Medicare, the basis for the AAPCC, will become ever more overstated as a measure of the cost of treating HMO enrollees. In 1997, HMO enrollment in some counties was approaching 50 percent of beneficiaries; thus the bias could be appreciable.

In addition to addressing geographic differentials in payment and overpayment from selection, many congressional Republicans wished to increase enrollment in HMOs.[30] But HMOs had several complaints about how Medicare

---

29. With low mortality rates, HMOs profit by avoiding high end-of-life spending.
30. And many in both parties saw HMOs as a way to provide drug benefits to constituents.

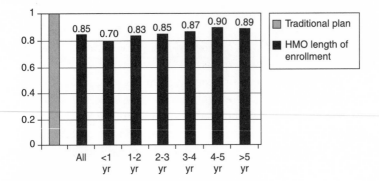

Figure 13.3
Selection: Mortality in 1998, HMO Enrollees as a Proportion of Traditional Medicare Enrollees, by Length of HMO Enrollment. (*Source:* Medicare Payment Advisory Commission, 2000a.)

paid them, which they argued reduced their willingness to participate. First, payment could change substantially from year to year, especially in rural areas, for reasons that had little to do with HMO costs (Table 13.5). Second, within metropolitan areas payment rates could differ substantially by county (Table 13.6). Just because a person moved her residence across the line from the District of Columbia to Montgomery County, Maryland, for example, did not justify a thousand dollars less annual payment for that person's care. Finally, physicians lobbied for the rights to form their own HMOs, since they wished to appropriate monies that were otherwise going to health plans.

The BBA and HMOs   The BBA responded to these various complaints and ills in several ways. To address the differences in payment rates by area, it created a floor of $367 per month ($4,404 per year) for the AAPCC in 1998. This floor was binding in counties with about 12 percent of beneficiaries, or about half of all nonmetropolitan beneficiaries. The BBA also moved the AAPCC partway toward a national payment rate by making it a blend of the county rate and the national mean rate. For each of the next five years, the weight on the national rate was to increase by 10 percentage points, so that by 2003 there would be a 50–50 blended rate. In order to protect the high-payment areas, however, all HMOs would get at least a 2 percent annual update. Thus payment to an HMO was to be the maximum of the floor payment, the blended rate, or the 1997 rate updated by 2 percent per year.

In the Benefits Improvement and Protection Act (BIPA) of 2000, Congress went further along this road, increasing the floor payment in nonmetropolitan areas by 18 percent, from $402 per month in 2000 to $475 in 2001, and intro-

Table 13.5
Instability in AAPCC Rates, Change in 1997 Rates Relative to 1996 Rates (Percent)

County	State	Percent Change, 1996–97
Rural Counties with Large Changes		
Culberson	TX	+37
Refugio	TX	+33
Logan	WV	+29
Gilliam	OR	−17
Delta	CO	−24
Loving	TX	−40
Rate Changes among Large Metropolitan Areas		
Los Angeles	CA	6.0
Maricopa	AZ	3.8
Dade	FL	8.9
Wayne	MI	1.8
New York	NY	−0.2
Middlesex	MA	7.0

Source: Medicare Payment Advisory Commission, unpublished materials.

Table 13.6
Payment Rates Within the Washington, DC, Metropolitan Area, 1997

County	Annual Rate
Prince Georges, MD	$7,224
Washington, DC	7,008
Montgomery, MD	5,904
Arlington, VA	5,412
Fairfax, VA	4,812

Source: Medicare Payment Advisory Commission, unpublished materials.

ducing a floor of $525 ($6,300 per year) for metropolitan areas with more than 250,000 population. These increases make the floor rates binding for 40 percent of the beneficiaries.

In response to selection, the BBA took two actions. First, it lengthened the lock-in period for enrollees who opted for HMOs, although implementation of this provision was deferred for five years. Previously, enrollees had been allowed to opt into or out of health plans on the first of every month, unlike the private sector where enrollees are typically locked into their plan for a year. Although enacted as a beneficiary protection measure, the ability to change plans monthly clearly increased the opportunity for selection. The BBA changed the monthly lock-in to an annual lock-in period starting in 2002.[31]

Second, the BBA mandated that by 2000 HCFA introduce a risk adjustment method based on health status. In other words, in addition to the age and sex of the beneficiary, HCFA was to account for the health status of the beneficiary in determining how much to pay the HMO. On the correct assumption that HCFA would want to use a method that accounted for a beneficiary's diagnosis, the BBA mandated that health plans report information on diagnosis to HCFA. Many health plans only had accurate diagnostic information on those who had been hospitalized, so the BBA required that only inpatient diagnostic information be reported initially, but it also set a requirement that outpatient information ultimately be reported. Because it would partially correct for selection, risk adjustment based on health status would reduce payment for the average health plan; as a result, the BBA provided for a transition to fully risk-adjusted payment, a transition that BIPA lengthened.

In response to the volatility of rates, the BBA fixed in statute annual updates to the AAPCC as a percentage increment from the prior year's rate, so that updates were no longer a function of the past year's spending in traditional Medicare. This provision also eliminated the possibility of ever increasing overpayment at the national level, or a death spiral, since annual updates in payment to HMOs and to traditional Medicare could now differ. In response to physicians' wishes to form HMOs, the BBA permitted them to do so, but there has been minimal response to this provision.

Two New Options   The BBA also created two new options for beneficiaries, medical savings accounts (MSAs) and a private fee-for-service option; the ensemble of these options, plus the HMO option, was termed Medicare + Choice to distinguish it from traditional Medicare. MSAs are plans with a large deductible (the legislation set this between $3,000 and $6,000 per person annually). If a beneficiary elected an MSA, he or she would receive the AAPCC, adjusted by the relevant risk adjusters, less a premium for the large deductible plan. This amount would not be taxable if it was spent for medical care. Unspent balances could accrue and could ultimately be used to finance long-term care or used as a bequest.[32]

There was intense political activity around MSAs. Many Republicans saw MSAs as a way to reduce moral hazard; most congressional Democrats and the

31. In 2002 beneficiaries can disenroll for the first six months of the period, and in 2003 and later they can disenroll monthly for the first three months of the period.
32. If used as a bequest, it would be taxable.

administration saw them as a further opportunity for selection, because only good risks would profit from choosing a plan with a large deductible. Because of inadequate risk adjustment, such selection would benefit well-off and healthy seniors at the Treasury's expense. The compromise was an agreement on a demonstration project that would be capped at 300,000 participants. Subsequently, however, no insurance company entered the market offering MSAs, so the issue was moot.

The private fee-for-service option stemmed from complaints by physicians that Medicare's limitations on balance billing abridged their freedom and the freedom of the beneficiary to contract for a fee. This had been a longstanding issue with physicians, who, at the time of Medicare's enactment, had often price discriminated among patients according to ability to pay (Kessel, 1958). When it began, therefore, Medicare offered weak incentives to not balance bill, but in OBRA86 these limitations were greatly strengthened, and physicians were not permitted to bill more than 10 percent above the fee schedule. Particularly in the light of the changes in relative fees that were being introduced, physicians lobbied for "freedom to contract."

The religious right also supported the private fee-for-service option. They were concerned that increasing fiscal constraints in the Medicare program would lead to restrictions on care near the end of life. They therefore supported structuring the private fee-for-service option so that physicians must be paid on a fee-for-service basis (i.e., no element of capitation) and their fees could not be reduced as a function of utilization (i.e., no bonus to the physician for keeping utilization low).

Thus beneficiaries electing the private fee-for-service option buy an insurance policy that insures Medicare-covered services. The insurer is allowed to contract with physicians at any rate mutually agreed upon and can charge beneficiaries a premium to cover any increment in fees above the Medicare fee schedule. To help pay the premium for this policy, the beneficiary receives the AAPCC. Unlike the MSA option, the private fee-for-service option appears as if it will have considerable consequences, as I will come to subsequently.

13.2.2.3 The BBA and Physician Payment

At the time of the BBA, payment to physicians suffered from two problems, one related to the effort to cap physician spending and one related to relative prices. First, as described previously, under the VPS increases in target spending for physician services were in part a function of a five-year average of the rate of increase in the number of units of services. The five-year average was to measure the cost of technological change. But the volume of surgical procedures had stopped increasing very much. Because their initial spending target was based on much higher historical volume, the fall in volume led to very large short-run increases in surgeons' fees, 10 percent in 1994 and 12.2 percent in 1995. In the longer run, however, the low annual rates of increase in volume started to reduce markedly the five-year average rate of increase, and by the time of the BBA, it had affected the average enough so that, together with other actions that Congress had instituted to reduce spending on physician services, nominal physician fees were projected to fall for at least the next ten years.[33] This result was not tolerable politically, in part because fees in the commercial market were not expected to fall in nominal terms, and a substantial divergence between Medicare and commercial fees might lead some physicians to refuse to see Medicare patients.

Congress therefore abandoned the VPS and substituted the Sustainable Growth Rate (SGR) system. Under this method, increases in target spending are a function of real GDP growth rather than past increases in units of service. The rationale was to tie physician payment to the government's ability to pay. Because GDP growth was very robust in the immediate post-BBA years, physicians did well. I will discuss later whether any spending cap for physician services is good policy.

There was also a problem with relative prices. As described earlier, Congress had established three conversion factors, which were diverging, thereby undermining whatever rationale the relative value scale had. In the BBA, Congress therefore returned to a single conversion factor. Because this was done in a budget-neutral fashion, the conversion factor for surgical procedures was reduced a little more than 10 percent. Hence, surgeons took a double hit; the conversion factor for surgical services was reduced, and so-called resource-based practice costs were phased in, as described previously. Both these changes have now been accomplished, and, as far as is known, most surgeons continue to accept Medicare patients, suggesting that there were rents in surgical fees.

13.2.2.4   Other Changes Made by the BBA

The BBA made a host of other changes in Medicare, four of which I briefly describe here. These relate to hospital outpatient departments, teaching hospitals, disproportionate share payments, and additional preventive care benefits.

Hospital Outpatient Departments   If a physician treats a patient in the outpatient department or in an ambulatory surgery center rather than in an office, Medicare reimbursement is complicated. The physician receives payment under the physician fee schedule, but for 650 services there is a "site-of-service" ad-

---

33. The most important of the other actions were arbitrary continuing reductions in the target, which had reached 4 percentage points per year by the time of the BBA.

justment, a 50 percent reduction in payment for practice cost on the grounds that Medicare is also paying the outpatient department or ambulatory surgery center a "facility fee" to cover the costs of personnel and supplies. Between 1984, the beginning of the PPS, and 1996 these facility fees grew by more than 12 percent per year, amounting to $10.5 billion in 1996.[34] Both the growth and the cost-based nature of these fees led Congress to mandate that HCFA develop a prospective payment system for hospital outpatient departments and ambulatory surgery centers. Later I will turn to the resulting problems.

A second provision applying to outpatient departments concerned beneficiary cost sharing. Because of a defect in the way the law had been written in the late 1980s, hospital outpatient departments were able to increase revenues from patients by raising charges, but this had the effect of raising the cost-sharing percentage for beneficiaries to an average around 50 percent, far above the standard 20 percent figure for Part B (Medicare Payment Advisory Commission, 1998b).[35]

The BBA sought a remedy, but to bring all services back to a 20 percent coinsurance rate was estimated to cost $4 billion in an act that was trying to reduce Medicare spending.[36] The BBA therefore put in a very lengthy transition to reduce beneficiary coinsurance. It held that nominal coinsurance amounts for each service would be fixed at 1999 levels until they reached 20 percent, something that was estimated could take up to 40 years for some services!

Teaching Hospitals   Because they had higher costs per admission, even controlling for DRG, teaching hospitals had been paid more per admission than nonteaching hospitals since the inception of the PPS in FY1984. The amount of the increment was a function of the house-staff-to-bed ratio, which created an incentive to increase the number of house staff. Moreover, the initial reimbursement was at twice the rate that house staff added to cost, generating a subsidy that reinforced the incentive to increase house staff. This subsidy for teaching hospitals was financed by lower reimbursement for nonteaching hospitals..

---

34. This figure is understated because it does not include HMO enrollees, the fraction of which grew substantially over this period.

35. Medicare continued to base its reimbursement to outpatient departments on 20 percent of their costs, but hospitals were permitted to charge beneficiaries 20 percent of their charges. When this law was enacted, charges and costs were not much different, but over time they differed sharply as hospitals raised charges. Moreover, the cost-sharing percentage varied substantially by service. For some outpatient department services the cost sharing was at or near the statutory 20 percent for other Part B services; for others, it was in the 60 to 80 percent range.

36. Because more than a third of beneficiaries had employer-provided retiree health insurance that paid much or all of the cost sharing, the incidence of reducing the coinsurance rate would partly redound to shareholders.

Consistent with the incentives, the number of residents increased by about a third from 1985 to 1993, after which it stabilized, suggesting teaching hospitals had adjusted to the new financial regime (Newhouse and Wilensky, 2001). Because the output of U.S. medical schools has been approximately constant since the mid-1970s, this increase came from hiring residents trained at non-U.S. medical schools and from lengthening training periods. The increase in residents occurred at a time when many felt the United States had at least an adequate supply of physicians. And the additional payment to teaching hospitals, of course, increased approximately proportionately to the increase in residents, reaching $7 billion by the mid-1990s, whereas in 1985 it was only $1.4 billion (Newhouse and Wilensky, 2001).[37]

Preserving the additional payments to teaching hospitals was especially important to Senator Daniel P. Moynihan (D-NY), the chairman of the Senate Finance Committee from 1992 to 1994 and the ranking minority member after 1994 until his retirement in 2000, but the teaching hospital subsidy attracted bipartisan support.[38] As a result, Congress did not eliminate the subsidy, but after 1984 it steadily chipped away at it in several budget bills. By the time of the BBA the payment had been reduced from an 11.59 percent increment for every 0.1 change in the house-staff-to-bed ratio to a 7.5 percent increment. The BBA further reduced this by 0.5 percentage points per year for four years, down to a 5.5 percent increment. The Balanced Budget Refinement Act of 1999 (BBRA) and the BIPA legislation of 2000 have stopped the transition at 6.5 percent, a figure now scheduled to drop to 5.5 percent for 2003 and beyond. Even the 5.5 percent figure, however, represents a subsidy to teaching hospitals.[39]

The BBA also capped the number of residents that a hospital could count toward reimbursement at 1996 levels. Thus the hospital could no longer gain by expanding its number of residents, but it could still lose monies by contracting.[40] Because of the stability in the number of residents since 1993, however, the cap at 1996 levels is not very binding. The problem remains of how to pay teaching hospitals without distorting the market for house staff.

Disproportionate Share Payments   In the mid-1980s, Congress enacted the Disproportionate Share Hospital (DSH) program. This program paid higher DRG

37. The amounts include both Direct and Indirect Medical Education payments.
38. Although New York received a disproportionate share of these monies, Senator Moynihan's concern for teaching hospitals went well beyond such parochial interests. He viewed these monies as critical for the advances in knowledge being generated at teaching hospitals. During the debate over the Health Security Act he said on the Senate floor that to reduce these payments would be "a sin against the Holy Ghost."
39. No subsidies would imply about a 3 percent increment for each 0.1 change in the ratio.
40. The BBA gave some transition funds to hospitals that reduced the number of residents.

rates to hospitals that treated many Medicaid patients. Initially this program had the rationale that such patients were more expensive to treat, a finding based on an analysis of data from the state of Massachusetts (Epstein, Stern, and Weissman, 1990). A later study using national data replicated the finding for Massachusetts, but showed that the Massachusetts finding did not generalize; there was no difference in the cost of Medicaid and non-Medicaid patients using national data (Kominski and Long, 1997).

Not surprisingly, recipients of DSH monies had an interest in continuing to receive them, and so the program acquired other rationales. Many legislators, especially Democrats, wanted to use Medicare monies to aid safety-net hospitals with their burden of uncompensated care for the under 65 population. Such safety-net hospitals were usually large urban public hospitals. Aid for safety net hospitals would have been more logically financed from general revenues, but it did not appear likely that general revenues would be appropriated for this purpose. Another rationale, more specific to Medicare, was that the safety-net hospitals were important sources of care for those Medicare beneficiaries that lived near them.

At the time of the BBA the Medicare DSH monies amounted to $4.5 billion, up from $1.1 billion in 1989. Given the various articulated and unarticulated goals for the DSH program, the formula for allocating the monies among hospitals had several important defects. The formula set a threshold before a hospital was eligible for any funds based on the proportion of its total admissions (including the nonelderly) that were eligible for Medicaid and its share of Medicare admissions that were Medicaid eligible. Importantly, the formula did not include a measure of uncompensated care or the hospital's share of patients who lacked insurance coverage. This was a critical omission to the degree that the program was intended to support safety-net hospitals, because the correlation between Medicaid and uncompensated care admissions was weak. Fundamentally the low correlation arose because Medicaid patients were insured; hence, other things equal, the more generous the eligibility for the state's Medicaid program, the fewer uninsured in the state. The situation was exacerbated in the mid-1990s when certain states began to expand Medicaid eligibility dramatically, most notably Tennessee and Oregon, thereby expanding their share of DSH monies.

DSH payments to hospitals were structured as a percentage increment to their DRG rate, but the increment was sharply progressive in the percentage of Medicaid patients, reflecting the desire to target the urban safety-net hospitals. These hospitals not only had the largest uncompensated care burdens; they had a relatively small share of *Medicare* patients, and DSH monies were simply additional reimbursement for each Medicare patient. Making the formula progressive, therefore, was a way to give the safety-net hospitals more money in spite of their relatively small number of Medicare admissions. Rural hospitals, however, had many Medicare patients (often they were the only local hospital in a community with a high proportion of elderly persons), and Congress did not intend the progressive formula to apply to rural hospitals. Congress therefore put in place a much higher eligibility threshold for rural than for urban hospitals. The threshold was so much higher, however, that 96 percent of the DSH monies went to urban hospitals.[41] Not surprisingly, rural hospitals lobbied against this unequal treatment.

Finally, there was a notch at the threshold where DSH payments began; urban hospitals at the threshold received 2.5 percent more for each Medicare admission, whereas hospitals just below the threshold received no increment.

Simply to save money the BBA reduced the funds available for the DSH program by 1 percent a year for five years and asked for studies to lay the groundwork for later reform of the DSH program. Importantly, it mandated that hospitals start to report the share of admissions from uninsured patients, so a measure of uncompensated care could be included in the formula for allocating DSH monies. Subsequently the BBRA and BIPA have mostly restored the BBA cuts in the DSH program; under current law there is only a 2 percent cut in 2001, 3 percent in 2002, and no reductions at all after 2003.

Preventive Care Benefits   The BBA added several preventive benefits to Medicare. For example, coverage for mammograms went from biennial to annual and for Pap smears from every three years to annual. Coverage for prostate cancer screening was instituted for the first time, and a number of other preventive benefits were added. These cost relatively little, but they generated beneficiary support to offset the resistance from providers for the reductions in reimbursement and kept the BBA from being portrayed as simply a takeaway.

13.2.3   The Effects of the BBA and Some Givebacks

The BBA succeeded in its main goal of reducing the rate of growth in Medicare outlays. Nominal spending in 1998 and 1999 was below spending in 1997, an event which had never happened before, and in real terms spending in 2000 was still below the 1997 level (Table 13.7). The reductions were concentrated in post-acute care. Between 1997 and 1999 home health spending fell 45 percent, from $17.5 billion to $9.7 billion, and SNF payments fell 17 percent, from $11.0

---

41. Although rural hospitals do not receive a proportionate share of DSH funds, many provisions in the PPS subsidize rural hospitals, including the Critical Access Hospital program, the Sole Community Hospital program, the Medicare Dependent Hospital program, and the Rural Referral Center Hospital program.

Table 13.7
Real Medicare Spending, CY1970–2000

Year	Spending[a]	Percent Increase	Part A[a]	Part B[a]
1970	27.6	—	19.4	8.1
1975	43.6	9.6[b]	30.9	12.6
1980	69.0	9.6[b]	47.9	21.1
1985	104.9	8.7[b]	70.2	34.6
1990	137.1	5.5[b]	82.8	54.4
1991	144.8	5.6	86.5	58.3
1992	158.1	9.2	99.0	59.2
1993	173.0	9.4	107.3	65.7
1994	183.6	6.1	116.4	67.2
1995	200.8	9.4	128.2	72.6
1996	214.2	6.7	138.9	75.3
1997	224.0	4.6	146.3	77.7
1998	221.0	−1.3	140.6	80.4
1999	217.3	−1.7	133.3	84.0
2000	221.8	2.1	131.1	90.7

Sources: Board of Trustees (2001a, 2001b). Deflated by the chain-weighted GDP deflator for the corresponding calendar year.

[a] Spending in billions of 2000 dollars. Total may not add because of rounding error.

[b] Annualized rate over the prior five years.

billion to $9.4 billion (nominal dollars). The number of home health users per beneficiary fell more than 20 percent, and SNF discharges declined over 8 percent (Medicare Payment Advisory Commission, 2001a, 2001b).

Not all the reductions, however, can be attributed to the changes in the BBA. Approximately concurrently with the BBA the federal government greatly increased the resources it devoted to antifraud and antiabuse efforts in the Medicare program. These resources were especially targeted on home health services, but they were applied throughout the program. As a result, in 1998 hospitals coded similar cases in lower-weighted DRGs than in 1997, the first time they had done so.

Because of the confounding of the BBA's reimbursement changes and the antifraud efforts, a good estimate of the savings attributable purely to the BBA cannot be made. But the low Medicare outlays in 1998 and 1999 were well below the outlays projected at the time of the BBA, leading providers to lobby for higher payments on the grounds that the BBA was unexpectedly harsh.[42]

---

42. In August 1997 the CBO estimated the BBA would save $112 billion between 1998 and 2002. By July 1999 this value grew to $217 billion (http://www.cbo.gov/).

Partly because the long-run fiscal outlook for the Part A Trust Fund had greatly improved (as I will discuss when I come to issues of long-term financing), the Congress in the 1999 BBRA and again in the 2000 BIPA increased payment rates for almost all providers above the BBA provisions. In particular, it increased payments to SNFs in 1999 and again in 2000, and it increased monies for home health in 2000. It also stayed the 15 percent reduction in home health rates that the BBA called for when the home health prospective payment system was implemented.

Nonetheless, the givebacks in 1999 and 2000 were modest on the scale of the entire program. The Congressional Budget Office (CBO) estimated that the BBRA givebacks would cost $17.2 billion over 10 years; the BIPA givebacks were estimated to cost substantially more, $81.5 billion over 10 years.[43] But the January 2000 CBO projection for total Medicare spending over the next 10 years was $3,226 billion; using that as a denominator, the givebacks raised Medicare spending above what it otherwise would have been by about 3 percent. The givebacks were also small in comparison with the BBA cuts; in August 1997 the CBO expected the BBA to save $385 billion over the following 10 years. Two years later it had doubled its estimate of savings in the 1998–2002 period.[44]

In sum, the BBA almost certainly reduced Medicare outlays, thereby helping to restore the long-run fiscal health of the program. It increased the incentives for efficient production by mandating the development of prospective reimbursement systems for post-acute care and for hospital outpatient departments, thereby ending cost-based reimbursement virtually throughout the Medicare program. It addressed the geographic differences in payment in the Medicare + Choice program, though not in traditional Medicare, and it changed physician payment from a course that appeared unsustainable. In my judgment, however, the changes the BBA made have left a new set of serious problems. Before discussing the program's long-range financing, I take up the problems the BBA created in post-acute care and hospital outpatient reimbursement, the Medicare + Choice program, and physician payment.

13.3 Some Current Issues

13.3.1 Post-Acute Care and Hospital Outpatient Departments

As noted earlier, HCFA has implemented new prospective schemes for home health agencies, SNFs, rehabilitation facilities, and outpatient departments, and did so on or near the very tight deadlines specified in the BBA. Nonetheless,

---

43. See http://www.cbo.gov/.
44. See http://www.cbo.gov/.

I doubt that the new schemes will function tolerably well. The problems are fourfold.

First, and fundamentally, for all the post-acute services the new payment methods largely do not pay more for additional services; in contract theory jargon they are high powered. Our ability to specify a priori and monitor a desired bundle of services for these services, however, is markedly less than for inpatient services. Hence, economic theory suggests that payment should be lower powered, so the BBA's changes seem to have gone in the wrong direction. Put another way, providers now have a financial incentive to underserve or stint on these services. The home health reimbursement system is particularly high powered, with zero marginal revenue for all visits past five within a 60-day period.[45] And monitoring is particularly difficult in home health, where auditing what actually happened during a visit is a daunting task.

Second, the new payment systems set different prices for the same service in different settings, yet many patients can obtain the service in multiple settings. Physical therapy, for example, can be given in a hospital outpatient department, in a SNF, in a rehabilitation hospital or unit, or, if the patient is well enough to go home, through home health. Both the level and basis of reimbursement vary considerably across these sites. Because the most intense treatment is given in rehabilitation hospitals and units and the least intense at home and because the new systems were implemented in a budget-neutral fashion for each site, reimbursement is highest in rehabilitation facilities and lowest at home. Furthermore, patients in rehabilitation facilities are reimbursed per stay, SNF patients reimbursed per day, and home health patients per 60-day episode. As a result, the payment system is far from neutral as to where a given patient should be treated. We have few data, however, about whether the nonneutral incentives have affected patient care.[46]

Third, 18 percent of patients discharged from a hospital use multiple post-acute providers (Medicare Payment Advisory Commission, 1999b). In effect, many, if not most, of these patients receive part of their treatment at one site (e.g., a SNF) and then transfer to another site to complete their treatment (e.g., home). Accounting for partial episodes of treatment in various sites introduces substantial additional complexity, as well as possibilities for gaming.

Fourth, the difficulty of securing reliable data on what services were delivered at the patient level has hampered the development of case-level adjustments.

---

45. There is a modest outlier provision.
46. Regulations limit the ability to shift patients to rehabilitation hospitals and units, where the payment is highest. Such patients must receive an average of three hours of therapy per day, and 75 percent must be in one of 10 DRGs. Many patients, especially the frail elderly, cannot tolerate three hours of daily therapy.

Partly for this reason MedPAC's judgment in March 2001 was that the RUG system, which was initially developed for chronic long-term care, could not be adapted for the post-acute care of SNF patients. It therefore recommended that HCFA stop work on refining the RUG system and focus on developing a new system (Medicare Payment Advisory Commission, 2001a). Although this view is controversial, it indicates the depth of the problems with the new post-acute payment methods. Furthermore, the large reduction in the number of home health visits after the BBA suggests that the HHRG weights based on historical data are inappropriate.

In my view the ultimate solution for post-acute services will be to bundle payment for them with the DRG payment to the hospital, with a reasonably high fraction of cases receiving some kind of payment at the margin (i.e., lowering the power of the system). Freestanding post-acute providers, however, are fiercely opposed to such a solution because they would then become contractors to the hospital. Although they have carried the day for now, I doubt that any other system will work well.[47]

The problem of payment rates for the same service that vary by site also appears in reimbursement for ambulatory services. Virtually all of these services can be delivered in at least two of three settings: the hospital outpatient department, the ambulatory surgery center, or the physician's office. But the rates Medicare reimburses differ substantially among these sites (Table 13.8). Additionally, some patients can be treated on either an inpatient or outpatient basis, for which payment also differs. Thus the payment system is far from neutral in this domain as well. Moreover, the rules for determining whether the building adjacent to the hospital will be reimbursed as the outpatient department or the medical office building, or for that matter the ambulatory surgery center, are ambiguous. As with post-acute care, the importance of the nonneutrality of payment across sites is unclear.

13.3.2 *Medicare + Choice*

There were three salient effects of the BBA on the Medicare + Choice program: reductions in reimbursement in response to selection, an effort to narrow geographic differences in spending within the Medicare + Choice program, and the introduction of diagnostic-based risk adjustment.

---

47. If hospitals were given responsibility for post-acute care and contracted with certain providers, there could be a court challenge that such contracting abridged patients' freedom of choice. At issue would be whether, when using a hospital, the patient agrees to use certain providers, as for example the patient does with respect to the laboratory with which the hospital contracts for services.

Table 13.8
Base Payment Rates for Selected High-Volume Ambulatory Services

Type of Service	Description	OPD	Practice Expense	ASC
Surgical	Upper GI endoscopy	$347	$139	$425
	Diagnostic colonoscopy	387	192	425
	Colonoscopy with lesion removal	387	260	425
	Extract cataract, inset lens	1,287	—	934
Radiology	Chest X-ray, one view	38	21	—
	Mammography, both breasts	34	56	—
Diagnostic	Cardiovascular stress test	79	63	—
	Echo exam of heart	213	171	—
Clinic visit	Office or outpatient visit, new patient	48	23	—
	Office or outpatient visit, established patient	48	22	—

Source: Medicare Payment Advisory Commission (2000b), p. 39.

OPD is the hospital outpatient department, and ASC is ambulatory surgery center. The practice expense column shows the amount paid for services in the office that is intended to cover practice expenses, as opposed to the physician take-home or work component, which is the amount that corresponds to the other two columns for office services.

13.3.2.1 Taking Back the Profits of Selection

In response to the reductions in payment to HMOs mandated by the BBA, HMOs pulled out of several counties on January 1 of each subsequent year. These pullouts attracted a great deal of publicity for at least two reasons. Some saw competition among health plans as the future of the program, but the withdrawals cast doubt on whether this expectation was realistic. Second, growth in HMO enrollment before the BBA had been rapid, and no plans had previously pulled out. As a result, most thought growth would continue. The CBO, for example, had projected in 1997 that HMO penetration would reach 30 percent by 2005, a projection that four years later looks distinctly optimistic (Congressional Budget Office, 1997).

The pullouts had serious consequences for some beneficiaries. On the one hand, those enrolled in HMOs that no longer contracted with Medicare potentially had to change physicians and probably lost some supplementary benefits. On the other hand, it would be poor policy for the program to pay a rate sufficiently high to keep every health plan in business, no matter how poorly run. And enrollments in HMOs tended to climb back in the months after the January

1 pullouts, so that although the share of beneficiaries enrolled in Medicare + Choice has fallen from its high of 16 percent, it remains at around 15 percent (Figure 13.2). Nonetheless, enrollment is now stagnant after growing rapidly in the 1990s.

13.3.2.2 Payment Floors

Congress established floors on payment to health plans in response to perceived geographic inequity; in particular, beneficiaries in the high-rate areas were getting drug benefits and those in low-rate areas were not or were getting fewer benefits. Perhaps some conservatives may have also had an eye toward reducing pressure for enacting an outpatient prescription drug benefit by giving beneficiaries an option to join HMOs to obtain drug coverage. But the effort to address geographic equity has the potential to change the nature of the Medicare + Choice program radically, because it has unbalanced local health care markets. That is, because Congress did nothing about variation in spending in traditional Medicare, traditional Medicare is now more attractive in the high-rate areas and less attractive in the floor areas.

In the high-rate areas, rate increases for Medicare + Choice plans are now limited to 3 percent per year (up from 2 percent in the BBA). To the degree costs rise faster than this and the plan market is competitive, which for the most part it is in the high-rate areas, supplementary benefits will be taken off the table, and beneficiaries will tend to drift back toward traditional Medicare.

Congress put the floors in place in an effort to attract HMOs—preferably bearing drug benefits—to small-population counties that lacked them. This policy assumed that the reason HMOs were not in these areas was the low rate of payment, but this assumption is likely misplaced. The structure of small markets is not attractive to HMOs. In many small areas there is one local hospital, and there may be only one type of a given specialist. Thus in many instances HMOs are unable to obtain rates below the Medicare fee schedule, because their threat to shift business to another provider is not credible. In short, the market structure means HMOs have difficulty making a profit. Similarly, a threat to terminate a provider from the HMO's network for not following quality guidelines is not credible. Consistent with this argument, HMOs have not entered in response to the higher floors.

But in the floor counties there is a good deal more money now in Medicare + Choice plans than in traditional Medicare, more than $2,000 per beneficiary per year in some counties. These additional funds make the private fee-for-service option attractive in the floor counties. There were very few utilization controls within traditional Medicare, so equivalent medical care can be delivered under the private fee-for-service option at considerably less than the payment. In short, there are rents to be appropriated. Economics would predict that providers with market power will ultimately capture most of these rents. But until there is competition among private fee-for-service insurers, many of the rents will accrue to the early insurer entrants in this market. Some of the rents may go to beneficiaries to induce them to leave traditional Medicare, but physicians in the floor counties may simply stop participating in traditional Medicare and tell their patients to choose the private fee-for-service plan. In nonfloor counties, private fee for service is unlikely to succeed. Because almost all physicians accept Medicare beneficiaries in those counties, there is no incentive for beneficiaries to pay more for a private fee-for-service plan. In the floor counties, however, beneficiaries will not have to pay more.

Thus far only one private fee-for-service plan has entered the market, although it has entered in 35 states. It disproportionately serves floor counties. HCFA is currently reviewing the application of a second private fee-for-service plan.

13.3.2.3 Risk Adjustment
HCFA did carry out the risk-adjustment mandate of the BBA by proposing a method based on Diagnostic Cost Groups (DCGs). Like the DRGs for hospital patients, DCGs group patients by their diagnosis (if any), and pay health plans more for their enrollees with costly diagnoses. Confirming favorable selection, HCFA estimated that the average health plan would lose 7 percent of its revenues when this method was fully implemented. Health plans, arguing that reimbursement was already inadequate, lobbied for budget-neutral risk adjustment. This they did not obtain. But the health plans also argued that the risk-adjustment method HCFA proposed gave an incentive to distort their treatment choices. This problem arose because HCFA had to employ diagnostic information from the inpatient setting only.

Reliable diagnostic information is available on inpatients because the DRG and hence hospital reimbursement is a function of diagnosis. If hospitals do not report diagnosis accurately, they are liable for criminal penalties. Although physicians are to report diagnosis on their Part B claims, their reimbursement does not depend on diagnosis; as a result, there is substantial undercoding of diagnosis for office visits. One study examined those who had a claim in 1994 with a diagnosis of a serious chronic condition, such as stroke, coronary artery disease, and diabetes. Among those who survived, only a little over half had a Part B claim with the given diagnosis in 1995 (Medicare Payment Advisory Commission, 1998a).

As a result, HCFA faced two problems. First, the weights for a given DCG were likely in error because patients were misclassified. Second, there was an enormous potential for upcoding if HCFA were to pay on the basis of outpatient diagnoses. That is, given the new financial incentive to code accurately, many more patients would appear in higher weighted DCGs than was the case in the historical data being used to set rates on a budget-neutral basis. Given that likelihood, HCFA opted to introduce risk adjustment using inpatient data only. But this option gave health plans an incentive to hospitalize patients merely to record the diagnosis and hence obtain the higher payment. HCFA recognized the problem; it therefore proposed not only a four-year transition to a fully risk-adjusted payment but also basing only 10 percent of the reimbursement on the risk-adjusted payment in the first year. This percentage would rise to 35 in the second year and 80 in the third year, and in the fourth year outpatient data would be incorporated. The transition also mitigated the payment reduction from risk adjustment.

The plans subsequently lobbied to defer diagnosis-based risk adjustment indefinitely. Although Congress did not agree to this request, it did slow the transition. Payment is still only 10 percent risk adjusted, so most of the incentives for plans to select healthy beneficiaries within age-sex classes are still in place. Moreover, if and when outpatient data are used, there will almost certainly have to be another transition to estimate and allow for effects of upcoding.

More fundamentally, although the DCGs are a substantial improvement over the prior methods, or at least will be once outpatient data are incorporated, no one knows whether they will suffice to render selection behavior negligible. They will, however, lessen the profitability of certain selection strategies. If a plan enrolled a random sample from the 20 percent of traditional Medicare enrollees who spent the least in 1991, it would earn $2,134 per enrollee in 1992 if the risk-adjustment method used only the demographic adjusters of the AAPCC (and if the patient received the same care as in traditional Medicare). With the DCG method (and using outpatient diagnoses) the profit would be $424 per enrollee, still a healthy profit rate on mean spending of $3,800, but much less than $2,134. At the other extreme, if the plan enrolled a random sample of the 20 percent who spent the most in 1991, it would lose an average of $4,425 in 1992 with demographic adjustment but only $1,311 with the DCG method (Ellis et al., 1996). Thus a plan that can devise inexpensive methods to select still stands to profit handsomely at the expense of the government.

For that reason I and others have proposed what is variously termed partial capitation or supply-side cost sharing (Ellis and McGuire, 1986, 1993; Newhouse, 1986, 1996, 1998; Newhouse et al., 1989; Newhouse, Beeuwkes, Buntin, and Chapman, 1997). In its simplest formulation, reimbursement to the plan would be a weighted average of what would otherwise be paid under a risk-adjusted capitation and what would be paid under traditional Medicare, but nonlinear formulations are also possible. Such a formulation sacrifices incentives for efficiency in production in order to reduce both incentives for selection and incentives to stint or underserve (Laffont and Tirole, 1993). MedPAC and its two predecessor commissions have all recommended this, but health plan opposition has blocked the proposal legislatively. Health plans' reasoning is clear; just as with risk adjustment, partial capitation reduces the profit from the favorable selection that they now enjoy.

13.3.3 Physician Payment

The BBA, as mentioned earlier, made increases in spending on physician services a function of, among other things, real GDP growth. This method of setting total spending differs from the method used for other providers, where Congress sets rates or prices with no explicit or formulaic account taken of past changes in the quantity of services or of GDP growth. The method stemmed from the rapid increase in physician spending in the 1970s and 1980s and the belief that if fees were reduced, physicians would simply order more services to offset the loss in income.

There was empirical support for the view that physicians increased services when fees fell, strong enough support in fact so that when the new fee schedule was introduced in 1992, HCFA actuaries allowed for a "behavioral offset." Specifically, the actuaries assumed physicians would offset a third to half of the fee cut by increasing the quantity of those services whose fees were being reduced. Hence, they applied an additional reduction to the conversion factor to reach the desired spending cut (Physician Payment Review Commission, 1993). In fact, the actuaries overestimated. Although physicians did on balance increase those services whose fees had been reduced, they also decreased services whose price had increased. These effects approximately netted out (Zuckerman, Norton, and Verrilli, 1998).

Nonetheless, the view has persisted that a physician can simply order services to reach his or her desired income, so that policy must cap total spending. I think the evidence against this view is compelling. But even if this view is correct, a cap is problematic as policy because of the possibility of substitution of care among sites. As shown in Table 13.8, hospitals are paid substantial amounts to cover costs for outpatient department services (e.g., nurse salaries, supplies). Because physicians do not bear these costs in the outpatient department but do bear them in their offices, the practice cost component of physician reimbursement is reduced 50 percent for services performed in the outpatient department and in ambulatory surgery centers (relative to the physician's office), as described previously. But outpatient physician services move across various outpatient sites in response to technological change, as well as from the inpatient

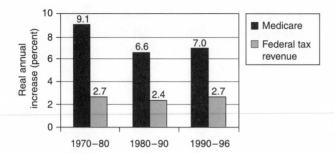

Figure 13.4
Medicare Outlays Increased at a Rate Much Faster Than Federal Tax Revenues. (*Sources:* Statistical Abstract, Economic Report of the President, Congressional Budget Office. Deflators: GDP deflator to 1990, CPI XI 90–96.)

to the outpatient setting, in ways that a fixed target cannot accommodate. As a result, MedPAC has recently recommended that Congress abandon its approach to controlling spending on physician services and set physician fees in a fashion similar to rates for hospitals and other institutional providers (Medicare Payment Advisory Commission, 2001a).

13.4   Financing Medicare in the Long Term

13.4.1   The Bipartisan Commission

The BBA set up a Bipartisan Commission on the Future of Medicare, whose chair was Senator John Breaux (D-LA) and whose administrative chair was Congressman William Thomas (R-CA). The commission's main agenda was to consider how to finance Medicare over the longer term. Medicare had for many years grown at rates far in excess of the growth rate of federal tax revenues, and in 1997 this trend seemed likely to continue indefinitely (Figure 13.4). The 1996 Report of the Trustees of the Medicare Trust Fund, the backdrop for the BBA, projected that the Part A Trust Fund would have a zero balance in 2001; the 1997 Report pushed that date back to 2005. And, if Medicare was going to be gasping for funds in 2005, matters were going to become much worse after 2010. In short, at the time of the BBA the long-run financing of Medicare appeared to be a very serious substantive and political problem.

Senator Breaux and Congressman Thomas favored shifting Medicare toward a defined-contribution approach that would include traditional Medicare. That is, the government would pay a lump sum, as those employers that offer multiple plans often do, and the beneficiary would be responsible for paying the marginal dollar. Such an approach has been endorsed by a wide variety of economists of varying political persuasions, including myself (e.g., Cutler, 1995; Aaron and Reischauer, 1995; Butler and Moffit, 1995; Wilensky and Newhouse, 1999).

Those advocating this approach saw several advantages. First, it would make the government neutral among choices of health plan. At present, a lower-cost plan has a limited ability to pass on lower costs in the form of lower premiums. Specifically, the plan may not offer rebates, so that the most money a beneficiary can save by joining a health plan is any Medigap premium plus the expected value of any remaining cost sharing.[48] Any additional savings must be taken in the form of more covered services, which the beneficiary may or may not value at their cost to the plan. Second, a defined-contribution approach may lead to more efficient production by freeing up pricing underneath the plan rather than relying on the current administered pricing systems and the distortions they induce. It may also avoid some of the problems in introducing new products that I will describe later.

Those opposing a defined-contribution approach worried that traditional Medicare will become more expensive because better risks would tend to leave it. In the extreme, traditional Medicare could go into a death spiral. In other words, true neutrality among competing health plans assumes adequate risk adjustment, something that at present requires a leap of faith, although use of partial capitation can reduce the load that risk adjustment needs to bear. Additionally, there were concerns about geographic adjustment; if enrollees from low-cost areas were pooled with those from high-cost areas with no geographic adjustment, for example, they would be worse off. Finally, there were concerns among some that low-income Medicare beneficiaries not eligible for Medicaid could be coerced into plans with skimpy benefits or high cost sharing.

The commission of 17 members operated under rules that required a supermajority of 11 to make formal recommendations. Initially it was hoped there might be a deal that involved changing Medicare to a defined-contribution approach and adding an outpatient prescription drug benefit. But only 10 votes could be mustered for the chairs' proposal that embodied defined contribution principles and addressed the drug issue. Specifically, the chairs proposed a new fee-for-service option involving private-sector insurers partnering with HCFA to offer policies with a stop-loss provision and drug benefits, although there would be no commingling of money or management between HCFA and the

---

48. The 36 percent of beneficiaries with retiree health insurance are unlikely to find anything other than traditional Medicare attractive unless employers offer them something to give up their retiree health insurance. Defined-contribution arrangements might stimulate employers to do so. BIPA allows premium rebates starting in 2003.

private companies. Medicare HMOs would simply have the actuarial value of the stop-loss and drug benefits added to the AAPCC, so that they could offer additional benefits (e.g., a higher drug maximum). When 11 votes for this proposal could not be found, the commission did not file a formal final report, but the Chairmen's Report, transcripts, and other commission documents can be found on the commission's website.[49]

At the time the commission disbanded in 1998, the administration attacked the suggestion that Medicare move to a defined-contribution framework. This response may have resulted from pressure from congressional Democrats who wished to run on this issue, hewing to the successful 1996 strategy of not changing traditional Medicare for the 85 percent of the beneficiaries who had elected it. In 1999, however, the administration did an about-face and introduced a proposal that could probably have been compromised with the proposal that attracted 10 votes from the commission.

The administration's 1999 proposal made one important change from the proposals that the 10-person majority on the bipartisan commission favored. Whereas the commission had proposed that the government's contribution be increased in the future at the rate of the weighted average premium across plans, the administration proposed that it increase it at the rate of increase in the premium for traditional Medicare. Thus the administration protected beneficiaries who chose to remain in traditional Medicare against an increase in their Part B premium. Initially, however, both proposals kept the Part B premium at the level of current law. This position left open a possible compromise of making the government-beneficiary split less favorable to beneficiaries over time, as seems likely to happen if health care costs increase at historical rates (Fuchs, 2001). Second, if enrollees chose a lower-cost plan, they would only receive 75 percent of the savings, rather than the 100 percent under the commission's proposal, though under both plans if they chose a more expensive plan they would pay 100 percent of the excess.

The administration's proposal, while an important departure for a Democratic administration, came a little over a year before the 2000 elections, a time when congressional Democrats—and probably a number of Republicans—did not want to take up major reform of the Medicare program. As a result, nothing came of it.

Moreover, the increase in payroll taxes from the economic boom along with the unexpectedly large reductions in spending from the BBA and the antifraud efforts meant the long-term finances of the program looked dramatically better. By 1999 the Trustees Report projected that the Part A trust fund would not

---

49. See http://medicare.commission.gov/.

have a zero balance until 2015, the 2000 report pushed that date out to 2025, and the 2001 Report set a date of 2029 (Board of Trustees, 2001a). As the date receded, the political impetus for large-scale reform decreased. Changing Medicare to a defined-contribution approach involved sufficient political pain that many members of Congress were happy to leave this job to their successors. Although President George W. Bush campaigned on the issue of converting Medicare to a defined-contribution plan, I believe its chances of enactment in this Congress are slim unless a deal is struck to add a prescription drug benefit in exchange for moving Medicare to a defined-contribution arrangement.

In my view, however, the trustees are overly optimistic about the long-run rate of Medicare cost increase, and therefore the long-run financing problem is more serious than their estimates imply. The projections using the intermediate assumptions, which are those commonly cited and the basis for the dates cited previously, assume that between now and 2025 real hospital payments per beneficiary will increase annually at approximately the rate of per capita GDP plus 1 percentage point, whereas the rate of increase between 1975 and 1996 was GDP plus 2.25 percentage points (Board of Trustees, 2001a).[50] Even the trustees' "high" estimate assumes that costs only grow about 2 percentage points more than GDP.

In the case of Part B spending, the trustees seem even more optimistic, assuming that annual spending per beneficiary increases only 0.7 percentage points faster than the rate of GDP between now and 2025 (Board of Trustees, 2001b). Between 1975 and 1996, however, spending per beneficiary on Part B grew a full 4.15 percentage points more than GDP. Although Part B spending per beneficiary is unlikely to grow as rapidly in the future as in the past, I find the trustees' projection improbable.

Finally, none of the trustees' projections includes a prescription drug benefit, which, depending on its structure, could add perhaps 10 to 20 percent to Medicare spending on a once-and-for-all basis. And most analysts expect the rate of increase in drug spending to exceed that of other health care services, so the steady-state rate of growth in Medicare would also probably increase if a drug benefit were enacted.

13.4.2 Paying for Technological Change

Two quite different issues are created by welfare-increasing but costly technological change, something that seems to happen almost daily in medical care.

---

50. I use 1996 as an endpoint to avoid correcting for the BBA shift of home health spending from Part A to Part B, and 1975 as a beginning point to be past the inclusion of the disabled and those with end-stage renal disease.

The first is how to share the burden of paying for such change between the elderly and the nonelderly. Under the current, mainly tax-financed program most of the cost of technological change inevitably falls on the nonelderly. In a defined-contribution approach, the division between the elderly and nonelderly turns on how the government's contribution will be updated to account for cost-increasing change.

Two formulaic proposals for updating a defined contribution both appear unsatisfactory. One would index the government's contribution by a medical care price index. Setting aside the important upward biases in the current official indices (Berndt et al., 2000; Newhouse, 2001), conceptually such a proposal would put the entire burden of costly new products on the elderly. A second approach would index the contribution by a measure of change in private insurance premiums, which would put almost all the burden on the nonelderly, since they pay a disproportionate share of the taxes. In practice a defined-contribution approach is likely to steer between these two approaches, although a proper price index might be a reasonable lower bound for an update.

The second issue around new products is how Medicare's administered price methods reimburse for them, a traditional problem for administered price systems. The problem is most acute for the physician and outpatient department systems. In those systems if there is no billing code for a new product, there is no reimbursement. The situation is only marginally better in the hospital system, where there is no immediate change in the DRG payment if a cost-increasing but welfare-raising product comes to the market. In the hospital case, however, if the product is sufficiently better that it is introduced despite no incremental reimbursement, its costs will begin to be reflected in the updates to the DRG weights (relative prices).[51]

In the case of the outpatient reimbursement systems, obtaining a billing code may require a coverage decision, but even if it does not, there is generally a substantial lag. The BBRA attempted to rectify the resulting bias against new products by mandating pass-through payments for certain drugs and devices in the new hospital outpatient payment system, to be implemented in August 2000. But allowing the hospital to simply pass through its costs for specific products invites manufacturers of drugs and devices with high Medicare outpatient shares to set high prices. It also undercuts price competition among substitute products. To limit potential federal spending under this provision, Congress capped these payments beginning in 2003, but political pressure precluded imposing any cap before that time. Thus spending in this area could rise substantially; indeed, whether the caps now in law will in fact be imposed seems problematic (Medicare Payment Advisory Commission, 2001a).

---

51. Kane and Manoukian (1989) describe a product whose diffusion the PPS deterred.

13.5   A Prescription Drug Benefit

The two principal services Medicare does not cover are outpatient prescription drugs and chronic long-term care. Proposals to cover long-term care within Medicare have occasionally been made, but the cost and the availability of Medicaid as coverage of last resort have deterred serious policy consideration. Cutler and Gruber in this volume (Chapter 12) discuss the Clinton administration's initiatives in long-term care.

By contrast, adding a prescription drug benefit to Medicare has not only been considered for many years but was in fact enacted as part of the Medicare Catastrophic Coverage Act of 1988. Starting in 1991, the act would have provided a benefit of 50 percent coinsurance above a $600 deductible. By 1993 the coinsurance was to drop to 20 percent, and the deductible was to rise so that about a sixth of the beneficiaries would exceed it in any one year. The act was to be financed entirely by the elderly, through an increase in the Part B premium and a surcharge on beneficiaries with incomes above $40,000. The surcharge was as much as $800 in 1989 and was projected to rise to over $1,000 in 1993. Many higher-income beneficiaries already had drug coverage through employer-provided retiree health insurance and were unenthusiastic about paying the surcharge for no additional benefit to themselves. Their political opposition was strong enough so that Congress repealed most of the provisions of the act a year later, including the drug coverage. Thus the drug benefit never went into effect.

The 1993 Health Security Act proposed a more generous Medicare drug benefit than the Catastrophic Act, namely a $250 deductible, 20 percent coinsurance, and a $1,000 stop-loss provision. The deductible and stop-loss amounts were to be indexed so that slightly over half the beneficiaries would receive some benefits. The benefit was to be added to Part B, with about 75 percent of the financing from general revenues and about 25 percent from additional Part B premiums. The act also proposed mechanisms to control drug prices. Manufacturers were to give Medicare rebates equal to the greater of the difference between average wholesale and retail prices or 17 percent of retail prices, with an additional rebate for drugs whose price increased faster than inflation. To address the resulting incentive to price new drugs higher than otherwise, the secretary could exclude new drugs from coverage if an agreement on price could not be reached.

Not surprisingly, the pharmaceutical industry intensely opposed these provisions to control its prices, arguing that they would deter new drug development. Although the principal cause for the defeat of the Health Security Act was its employer mandate to provide insurance, the pharmaceutical provisions were a contributing factor.

The impetus for a drug benefit has remained, however, spurred by the increased spending on drugs in recent years and by price discrimination, whereby those without drug insurance pay higher prices. Largely because of the growth in the number of efficacious drugs, Medicare beneficiaries spent 4.1 percent of their income on prescription drugs in 1998, up from 2.4 percent in 1988 (Medicare Payment Advisory Commission, 2000b; Berndt, 2001). The elderly disproportionately use drugs; although only 13 percent of the population, those over 65 account for more than a third of the (domestic) spending on drugs.

Responding to the financial burden of drug spending for the elderly, as well as potential distortions in care from failing to cover drugs, the administration in 1999 introduced a proposal to cover drugs through a Medicare Part D. Coverage was to be offered by private health insurers or pharmacy benefit managers (PBMs), who would compete for a single contract for the business of a local area. Benefits were much less generous than in the Health Security Act; beneficiaries would pay 50 percent coinsurance, up to a maximum of $2,000 initially, after which there was no coverage (i.e., a maximum of $1,000 in government payments). The $2,000 maximum was to increase to $5,000 by 2008. There was no deductible. Coverage would be voluntary, but general revenues would subsidize 50 percent of the premium to reduce the burden on the elderly and to combat selection. To reduce selection further, beneficiaries would only be allowed to purchase drug insurance when they first became eligible for Medicare or if their employer dropped drug coverage from retiree health insurance.

The concern over selection certainly seemed warranted given the experience in the individual Medigap market. The additional premium for those Medigap policies that cover drugs, plans H, I, and J, exceeds the value of the benefit even for those who spend the maximum amount on drugs (the maximum covered amount is $1,250 or $3,000, depending on the policy). Table 13.9 compares premiums for Plans C and I in five cities; the differences are much greater than the $500 benefit someone spending the maximum on drugs would obtain, so that Policy C is close to strictly dominating Policy I because of selection.

To assist the low-income elderly, the administration proposed that both the premiums and the coinsurance would be fully subsidized for those elderly with incomes below 135 percent of the federal poverty level, with partial premium subsidies for those with incomes between 135 and 150 percent of poverty. To prevent crowdout of existing retiree health insurance, employers who offered drug coverage to retirees that was at least as generous as the Medicare benefit would receive a subsidy equal to two-thirds of the Medicare benefit. HMOs would also be given the value of the benefit as an addition to their reimbursement, so whatever drug coverage they had in place could be improved. The administration estimated the cost of its proposal at $118 billion over ten years;

Table 13.9
Premiums for Individual Medigap Plans with and Without Drug Coverage, 1999

	65-Year-Old		75-Year-Old	
	Policy C[a]	Policy I[a]	Policy C[a]	Policy I[a]
Dallas, TX	$1,046	$2,294	$1,295	$2,974
Denver, CO	974	2,589	1,199	3,221
Los Angeles, CA	1,502	3,362	1,820	4,437
Miami, FL	1,510	3,428	1,890	4,158
Manchester, NH	917	1,945	1,247	2,581

Source: Gluck (1999).

[a] Policy C does not cover drugs. Policy I covers 50 percent of drug spending above a $250 deductible to a $1,250 maximum expenditure, so the maximum value of the drug benefit is $500. Policy I also covers any physician fees in excess of Medicare's reasonable charges, but these are limited to an additional 10 percent of physician fees, and few physicians charge additional fees. Policy I also covers up to 40 home health visits during recovery from an acute illness. Medicare beneficiaries who are homebound and need part-time or intermittent care already have this benefit; for others benefits are limited to $40 per visit. In addition, Policy C, but *not* Policy I, covers the Part B deductible of $100, which anyone using physician services is likely to satisfy. The actuarial value of the Part B deductible coverage in Plan C likely exceeds the actuarial value of the excess physician fee and home health visit features in Plan I, but in any event the premium differences of $1,000 to 2,000 would seem to vastly outweigh the additional benefits in Plan I, even for those spending the maximum amount on drugs.

CBO estimated costs of $168 billion. Steady-state costs would be substantially more than either estimate, because of the phase-in of the benefit through 2008.

In addition to the demands on the budget, this and other proposals for Medicare drug coverage raise five issues that deserve further discussion: (1) The lack of stop-loss coverage, (2) the universality of the benefit, (3) possible selection among competing insurers, (4) the provisions to reduce crowdout of retiree health insurance, and (5) how much authority insurers or PBMs would be given to exclude certain drugs in order to achieve lower prices.

13.5.1 Stop-Loss Provisions and Cost Sharing

The front-end nature of the benefit in the administration's proposal violated elementary insurance principles, but would have paid something to the 86 percent of beneficiaries who have at least one prescription in a year rather than the sixth of beneficiaries who would have received some payment given the deductible of the Health Security Act. However, the 6 percent of beneficiaries who spent more than $3,000 on prescription drugs in 1999 would have been left with open-ended liability.

Senator Edward Kennedy (D-MA) and Congressman Pete Stark (D-CA) introduced a bill that was considerably more generous than the administration's proposal, as well as more in accord with traditional insurance principles. It had a deductible of $200, coinsurance of 20 percent rather than 50 percent, and a stop-loss feature, set initially at $3,000 per year. I have not found a cost estimate for this proposal, but in 1999 the CBO estimated a cost of around $30 billion per year for a similar but somewhat less generous proposal. Subsequently the administration proposed earmarking $35 billion from 2006 to 2010 for catastrophic drug spending, but details were unclear.

More generally, the cost-sharing provisions in the administration bill were much greater than most drug coverage for the under 65. Under-65 persons with drug benefits typically pay a modest copayment if they use a generic drug or a drug that is on a formulary, for example, $10 for a month's supply. (A formulary is a list of favored drugs within a therapeutic class, such as antihypertensives, for which the plan has negotiated a low price.) Off-formulary drugs may carry a copayment of $25 or even $50 for a month's supply. The cost sharing in virtually all Medicare proposals is much greater than this example to keep costs down, but the disparity with the benefits among the under 65 means that there will be continuing political pressure to reduce the cost sharing, should any Medicare drug benefit be enacted. Reductions in cost sharing, however, if not compensated for by premium increases, raise the issue of the division of the Medicare spending burden between the elderly and taxpayers.

13.5.2 Provisions for the Low-Income Population and the Universality of the Benefit

The administration would have required Medicaid to pay both the premiums and the 50 percent coinsurance for those with incomes under 135 percent of poverty, about 30 percent of the Medicare beneficiaries.[52] The average state share of the Medicaid program is 43 percent; thus the proposal would have created a substantial new burden for states to cover the drug spending of those between 100 and 135 percent of poverty.[53] Whether Congress would have imposed this additional financing requirement on states is problematic.

Senator Breaux and Congressman Thomas, however, proposed limiting the drug benefit to those with incomes below 135 percent of poverty. This proposal would, of course, have substantially reduced the cost of the plan and would

---

52. For those between 135 and 150 percent of poverty, premium subsidies would have phased out. In addition to the notch from dropping coinsurance subsidies at an income of 135 percent of poverty, the phaseout of premium subsidies implies an addition of 40 to 50 percentage points to the marginal tax rate between 135 and 150 percent of poverty.

53. Medicaid already covers drug costs for those below 100 percent of poverty.

also have largely avoided the crowdout issue with respect to retiree health insurance, because few low-income beneficiaries have such insurance. It would, however, have violated the social insurance principle of universality upon which Medicare is based. Furthermore, there is little correlation between income level and drug coverage currently, so substantial numbers of Medicare beneficiaries would have remained without drug coverage (McClellan, Spatz, and Carney, 2000).

13.5.3 Selection Among Competing Insurers

In structuring competition among insurers, the administration favored competition for a local contract. The winner would receive a temporary local monopoly, for example, for three years. I agree with this approach (Huskamp et al., 2000). Under this arrangement the government would specify classes of drugs, and at least one drug from each class would have to be covered. Such an arrangement should achieve competitive pricing while preventing selection.

An alternative is that insurers or PBMs compete for individual beneficiaries. Under this arrangement it is unclear whether the government would require that any competing plan cover at least one of a certain type of drug (e.g., antidepressant, antiarthritis drug). If there were such a requirement, prices drug manufacturers receive should be similar to competition for a contract, but there would be additional marketing costs for little gain. If there were not such a requirement, selection would divide the risk pool; certain beneficiaries would opt for the plan that, for example, includes Viagra and excludes antidiabetic drugs, while diabetics would need to ensure that their plan covered the drugs they needed.

The structure of competition at the retail level is also important, because distribution costs account for about 20 percent of drug spending. Most current plans among the under 65 use pharmacy networks chosen in part on the basis of price; thus a drug will cost substantially more at a nonnetwork pharmacy. In determining the number of network pharmacies, there is usually a constraint to ensure access, such as a certain percentage of beneficiaries living within a certain distance of a network pharmacy. Use of a network of pharmacies could help Medicare minimize retail costs, but this implies excluding some pharmacies, a politically problematic outcome.

13.5.4 Provisions to Reduce Crowdout

Thirty-one percent of beneficiaries have drug coverage through their former employer. The administration sought to keep this coverage in force by offering a subsidy of two-thirds of the value of the Medicare benefit to employers. It assumed that the remaining third of the cost would be covered through the tax deductibility of the drug benefit. Although the subsidy would have arguably kept existing insurance in force, it would not have prevented crowdout in a fiscal sense. By assumption, the full cost of the plan for those with retiree health insurance would be covered entirely by the government, two-thirds by the on-budget subsidy costs and one-third by the tax expenditure. Without such a provision, however, one would expect employers to drop or restructure their retiree health insurance if a Medicare drug benefit were enacted. In other words, it appears that crowdout is simply part of the price of a universal Medicare drug benefit.

13.5.5   Price Determination for Pharmaceuticals

Among those under 65, 70 percent of drug coverage is contracted to PBMs. As already described, PBMs employ differential copayments to direct consumers to those drugs on their formulary. Formularies lower drug prices by increasing the elasticity of demand that manufacturers face; they are the drug analogue of a network of physicians and hospitals. Because the PBM market is reasonably competitive, most discounts are passed on to consumers. I have advocated the analogous procedure of reference pricing for Medicare; under this method drug manufacturers would submit bids within classes of drugs, and consumers would pay the entire marginal dollar for drugs that are not the cheapest (Huskamp et al., 2000). Pharmaceutical manufacturers would be paid at their bid prices. In effect, the resulting insurance is a lump-sum transfer for specific drugs, with the amount of the lump sum set through a bidding process.

But traditional Medicare has avoided the use of bidding arrangements and differential pricing to consumers that favor low-bidding suppliers, perhaps because of the tradition of freedom of choice of provider with which it began and the resistance to change from the affected providers. Rather, it has used administered price systems, such as the PPS, with minimal or no difference among alternative suppliers in prices to the beneficiary. For example, the amount beneficiaries pay for hospital care is completely independent of the hospital they use, and for practical purposes this statement is true for physician services as well. There is no reason in principle why prescription drugs could not be an exception, but this approach runs counter to the political pressure to cover services from all or almost all potential suppliers.

Although price competition among pharmaceutical manufacturers can be effective when there are competing drugs, some branded drugs have no close substitutes. If Medicare covers such drugs, there must be some kind of price control, because Medicare cannot agree to reimburse any price a manufacturer names. In private insurance the PBM can negotiate with the pharmaceutical firm and potentially not cover the drug if its price is too high. It is not clear that Medicare in practice could exclude the drug. Not surprisingly, the pharmaceutical industry remains strongly opposed to any element of price control, arguing correctly that the monopoly rents on a few blockbuster drugs support the industry's research and development effort (Scherer, 2000). Indeed, the industry's fear of price controls has been an important obstacle to prior efforts at Medicare prescription drug coverage.

Medicare does now in fact spend about $2 billion per year to cover certain outpatient drugs, and its procurement of those drugs does not inspire confidence in its ability to operate an efficient administered price scheme for drugs. For those suffering from end-stage renal disease (ESRD) Medicare covers erythropoetin, a product to stimulate red blood cell production. It appears that the rate HCFA pays dialysis centers for the erythropoetin they dispense has been well above the price that the centers pay for the drug. Indeed, the margin appears large enough that the centers can offset losses they incur on other services. (The composite rate that centers receive for a dialysis session has been approximately constant in nominal terms since 1983, a fall of one-third in real terms; Medicare Payment Advisory Commission, 2001a.)

Medicare also covers certain cancer chemotherapy drugs. It reimburses for those drugs at 95 percent of the average wholesale price, a price that, as in the erythropoetin case, appears to be well above the transaction prices at which oncologists actually purchase the drugs.[54]

No legislation resulted from the administration's 1999 proposal to cover drugs, in part because of industry opposition and in part because congressional Democrats were happy to run on this issue in 2000 if they could not obtain their preferred outcome of a universal drug benefit. Both candidates for president in 2000 made enacting a Medicare prescription drug benefit a high priority, as did many candidates for Congress. Nonetheless, the prior experiences at adding such a benefit are sobering for those like me who think such a benefit would be good policy, and much disagreement remains on the issues just discussed.

13.6 The Administration and Governance of Medicare

One view of HCFA, typically found among Republicans, is that it is a hidebound agency, committed to preserve traditional Medicare. Adherents of this view frequently want to take the Medicare + Choice program out of HCFA and create a new agency to administer it (Institute of Medicine, 1996). Some would go further and create an independent board to administer all of Medicare, with

---

54. See HCFA Program Memorandum AB-00-86.

HCFA perhaps continuing to administer the traditional program under the supervision of the board. Supporters of this view prefer to have Congress less involved in the management of the program (they would say micromanagement of the program) than it now is.[55]

A radically different view is that HCFA has been performing admirably under almost impossible conditions. On this view Congress has steadily increased the workload on HCFA, especially in what it asked in the BBA, without commensurate increases in administrative resources. Moreover, until the BBA's changes in HMO reimbursement, the Medicare + Choice program was expanding smartly, suggesting no bias on the part of HCFA. My own opinion is that HCFA is starved for resources (Butler et al., 1999), but that some organizational changes hold promise.

13.6.1 Administrative Resources

Supporters of traditional Medicare often point to its low administrative costs, but in my view they are too low. They were probably too low even in the 1980s, but the changes that have been made in the program over the 1990s have substantially added to HCFA's administrative load.

There are many areas in which the lack of resources manifests itself. One is the accuracy of the data used as the basis for the administered price systems. Those data in several instances are very old; in other instances they are unaudited. For example, the current payment system for dialysis relies on cost reports from 1977–79, and cost reports from ESRD providers were unaudited between 1991 and 2000, when HCFA undertook an audit of 1996 cost reports.[56] As another example, the hospital wage index is used to adjust payment for skilled nursing facilities and home health agencies, although they use a different mix of labor than hospitals. Further, the wage index areas do not correspond to labor market areas (e.g., nonmetropolitan areas of a state are considered one labor market), necessitating a cumbersome appeals process, whereby hospitals can ask to be reclassified to other geographic areas for the purposes of the wage index.[57]

---

55. A recent example of the level of congressional management is that when HCFA proposed to use transaction prices as the basis of reimbursement for the cancer chemotherapy drugs described in the previous section, oncologists protested, and Congress legislated a moratorium pending a study by the General Accounting Office. The oncologists did not deny the markups but claimed they compensated for inadequate reimbursement for providing chemotherapy. See *AMNews*, October 2, 2000.
56. As one indicator of a problem, the costs reported by hospital-based dialysis centers far exceed those reported by freestanding facilities, although there is no evidence that the outpatients they treat are sicker or more costly (Medicare Payment Advisory Commission, 1998b).
57. See Medicare Payment Advisory Commission (2001a) for a critique of the wage index. Indeed, it is not a proper index, since it does not hold occupational mix constant.

Furthermore, the wage data used to determine relative wages across areas are four years old.

13.6.2 Organizational Issues

A key issue with respect to an independent board is the degree of independence the Congress is willing to afford such a board. In as large and politically sensitive a program as Medicare, Congress may not be willing to be substantially less involved than it is now. If not, the creation of a board probably gains little.

But short of establishing a board, the Medicare program would be well served by shifting some functions out of HCFA to other parts of the department (Etheredge, 2000; Wilensky, 2001). These functions include Medicaid and the State Child Health Insurance Program (S-CHIP); although HCFA was originally created in the Carter administration to bring together the administration of Medicare and Medicaid, there is not much synergy between them. Other functions, such as the survey and certification of nursing homes, the conditions of participation for hospitals, and the certification of clinical laboratories, could also usefully be moved out of HCFA, possibly to the CDC or the FDA. This change would allow HCFA to concentrate its scarce management resources on the Medicare program.

Congress has its own set of management issues. First, the division of jurisdiction over Medicare between two House committees is not helpful. Second, although there are some outstanding individual staffers, in my view the overall expertise of congressional staff on the key committees of jurisdiction has declined over time, whereas the complexity of the program has grown. Third, partisanship has steadily increased, perhaps reflecting the more nearly equal division of power between the parties in the 1990s, making legislation more difficult.

13.7 Conclusion

The main substantive changes in Medicare during the Clinton years were those enacted in the Balanced Budget Act of 1997. By reducing the rates Medicare paid providers and by ending cost reimbursement, the act generated an unprecedented slowdown in the rate of growth of Medicare spending. It thus importantly contributed to the administration's great economic achievement of the first budget surpluses in decades. It also greatly prolonged the expected life of the Part A trust fund, which surely helped the administration maintain political support among the elderly.

Much of the recent public discussion of Medicare has focused on how it should be financed after 2010 and especially after 2020. Although this issue is certainly important, the administered price methods that Medicare is now using have serious problems and are likely to need large-scale revision over the next several years. Within traditional Medicare the separate "silo" method of paying by provider or site of service does not appear likely to work well for two reasons. First, the same service is reimbursed at different rates in different sites. Second, in the case of physician services, an expenditure cap implicitly presumes the same proportion of services continue to be delivered in the office, as opposed to the outpatient department or the ambulatory surgery center. One way to reduce the silo problem, which I favor, is to bundle payment for post-acute care with the payment for inpatient hospital care, but that does not appear politically possible now. A second is to abandon the cap on spending for physician services and update fees using methods similar to those used for hospitals and other institutional providers. How Medicare should pay for new procedures and products is another of the many important pricing problems within traditional Medicare, which constitutes 85 percent of the program.

The administered price methods for Medicare + Choice also face serious issues, especially the effort to bring more equality to rates across regions. This has unbalanced local markets between Medicare + Choice and traditional Medicare. Further, the availability of the private fee-for-service option in the floor counties potentially involves greater Medicare expenditure for little gain to beneficiaries.

The short-run pricing issues, however, should not obscure Medicare's long-run financing problem, assuming that historical rates of increase in health care spending resume. On the assumption that much of the historical increase in spending represents additional medical capabilities that are worth their costs, and that those capabilities will keep appearing, how to divide the burden of paying for them between future taxpayers and beneficiaries is a first-order political issue. Medicare now consumes more than 2 percent of GDP, a figure that will rise into the 4–6 percent range two to three decades hence. Perforce it will almost surely be on the agenda of every subsequent administration and Congress.

References

Aaron, Henry J., and Robert Reischauer. 1995. "The Medicare Reform Debate: What Is the Next Step?" *Health Affairs*, 14(4): 8–30.

Berndt, Ernst R. 2001. "The U.S. Pharmaceutical Industry: Why Major Growth in Times of Cost Containment?" *Health Affairs*, 20(2): 100–114.

Berndt, Ernst R., David M. Cutler, Richard G. Frank, et al. 2000. "Medical Care Prices and Output." In *Handbook of Health Economics*, ed. Anthony J. Culyer and Joseph P. Newhouse, 1A:120–180. Amsterdam: Elsevier.

Blendon, Robert J., Drew E. Altman, John Benson, et al. 1995. "The Public's View of the Future of Medicare." *Journal of the American Medical Association*, 274(20): 1645–1648.

Blendon, Robert J., John M. Benson, Mollyann Brodie, et al. 1997. "Voters and Health Care in the 1996 Election." *Journal of the American Medical Association*, 277(15): 1253–1260.

Board of Trustees, Federal Hospital Insurance Fund. 2001a. *2001 Annual Report of the Board of Trustees of the Federal Hospital Insurance Fund*. Washington, DC: Government Printing Office.

Board of Trustees, Federal Supplementary Insurance Fund. 2001b. *2001 Annual Report of the Board of Trustees of the Federal Supplemental Insurance Fund*. Washington, DC: Government Printing Office.

Brown, Randall S., Dolores Gurnick Clement, Jerrold W. Hill, et al. 1993. "Do Health Maintenance Organizations Work for Medicare?" *Health Care Financing Review*, 15(1): 7–23.

Butler, Stuart M., Patricia M. Danzon, Bill Gradison, et al. 1999. "Crisis Facing HCFA and Millions of Americans." *Health Affairs*, 18(1): 8–10.

Butler, Stuart M., and Robert E. Moffit. 1995. "The FEHBP as a Model for a New Medicare Program." *Health Affairs*, 14(4): 47–61.

Chassin, Mark, Robert H. Brook, Rolla Edward Park, et al. 1986. "Variations in the Use of Medical and Surgical Services by the Medicare Population." *New England Journal of Medicine*, 314(5): 285–290.

Congressional Budget Office. 1997. *Predicting How Changes in Medicare Payment Rates Would Affect Risk-Sector Enrollment and Costs*. Washington, DC: Congressional Budget Office.

Cowan, Cathy A., Helen C. Lazenby, Anne B. Martin, et al. 1999. "National Health Expenditures, 1998." *Health Care Financing Review*, 21(2): 165–210.

Cutler, David M. 1995. "Cutting Costs and Improving Health: Making Reform Work." *Health Affairs*, 14(1): 161–172.

Cutler, David M., and Sarah J. Reber. 1998. "Paying for Health Insurance: The Tradeoff between Competition and Adverse Selection." *Quarterly Journal of Economics*, 113(2): 433–466.

Ellis, Randall P., and Thomas G. McGuire. 1986. "Provider Behavior under Prospective Reimbursement." *Journal of Health Economics*, 5(2): 129–151.

———. 1993. "Supply-Side and Demand-Side Cost Sharing in Health Care." *Journal of Economic Perspectives*, 7(4): 135–151.

Ellis, Randall P., Gregory C. Pope, Lisa I. Iezzoni, et al. 1996. "Diagnosis-Based Risk Adjustment for Medicare Capitation Payments." *Health Care Financing Review*, 17(3): 101–128.

Epstein, Arnold M., Robert S. Stern, and Joel S. Weissman. 1990. "Do the Poor Cost More? A Multihospital Study of Patients' Socioeconomic Status and Use of Hospital Resources." *New England Journal of Medicine*, 322(16): 1122–1128.

Etheredge, Lynn. 2000. "Medicare's Governance and Structure." *Health Affairs*, 19(5): 60–71.

Fuchs, Victor R. 2001. "The Financial Problems of the Elderly: A Holistic Approach." Cambridge, MA: National Bureau of Economic Research.

Gluck, Michael E. 1999. "A Medicare Prescription Drug Benefit." Washington, DC: National Academy of Social Insurance.

Health Care Financing Administration. 1999. *Health Care Financing Review, Statistical Supplement.* Washington, DC: Government Printing Office.

Hsiao, William C., Peter Braun, Daniel L. Dunn, et al. 1988. "Resource Based Relative Values: An Overview." *Journal of the American Medical Association*, 260(16): 2347–2353.

Huskamp, Haiden A., Meredith Rosenthal, Richard G. Frank, et al. 2000. "The Medicare Prescription Drug Benefit: How Will the Game Be Played?" *Health Affairs*, 19(2): 8–23.

Institute of Medicine. 1996. *Improving the Medicare Market: Adding Choice and Protections.* Washington, DC: National Academy Press.

Kane, Nancy M., and Paul D. Manoukian. 1989. "The Effect of the Medicare Prospective Payment System on the Adoption of New Technology—The Case of Cochlear Implants." *New England Journal of Medicine*, 321(20): 1378–1383.

Kemper, Peter. 1988. "The Evaluation of the National Long Term Care Demonstration: Overview of the Findings." *Health Services Research*, 23(1): 161–174.

Kessel, Reuben A. 1958. "Price Discrimination in Medicine." *Journal of Law and Economics*, 1:20–53.

Kominski, Gerald F., and Stephen H. Long. 1997. "Medicare's Disproportionate Share Adjustment and the Cost of Low-Income Patients." *Journal of Health Economics*, 16(2): 177–190.

Laffont, Jean-Jacques, and Jean Tirole. 1993. *A Theory of Incentives in Procurement and Regulation.* Cambridge, MA: MIT Press.

McClellan, Mark. 1997. "Hospital Reimbursement Incentives: An Empirical Analysis." *Journal of Economics and Management Strategy*, 6(1): 91–128.

McClellan, Mark, Ian D. Spatz, and Stacie Carney. 2000. "Designing a Medicare Prescription Drug Benefit: Issues, Obstacles, and Opportunities." *Health Affairs*, 19(2): 26–41.

Medicare Payment Advisory Commission. 1998a. *Report to the Congress: Context for a Changing Medicare Program, June 1998.* Washington, DC: Medicare Payment Advisory Commission.

———. 1998b. *Report to the Congress: Medicare Payment Policy, March 1998.* Washington, DC: Medicare Payment Advisory Commission.

———. 1999a. *Report to the Congress: Medicare Payment Policy, March 1999.* Washington, DC: Medicare Payment Advisory Commission.

———. 1999b. *Report to the Congress: Selected Medicare Issues, June 1999.* Washington, DC: Medicare Payment Advisory Commission.

———. 2000a. *Report to the Congress: Medicare Payment Policy, March 2000.* Washington, DC: Medicare Payment Advisory Commission.

———. 2000b. *Report to the Congress: Selected Medicare Issues, June 2000.* Washington, DC: Medicare Payment Advisory Commission.

———. 2001a. *Report to the Congress: Medicare Payment Policy, March 2001.* Washington, DC: Medicare Payment Advisory Commission.

———. 2001b. *Report to the Congress: Selected Medicare Issues, June 2001.* Washington, DC: Medicare Payment Advisory Commission.

Newhouse, Joseph P. 1986. "Rate Adjusters for Medicare Under Capitation." *Health Care Financing Review*, 7 (Supplement): 45–55.

———. 1996. "Reimbursing Health Plans and Health Providers: Selection versus Efficiency in Production." *Journal of Economic Literature*, 34(3): 1236–1263.

———. 1998. "Risk Adjustment: Where Are We Now?" *Inquiry*, 35 (Summer): 122–131.

———. 2001. "Medical Care Price Indices: Problems and Opportunities." *Academia Economic Papers*, 29(1): 1–65.

———. 2002. *Pricing the Priceless: Medical Care, Insurance, and Capitation.* Cambridge, MA: MIT Press.

Newhouse, Joseph P., Melinda Beeuwkes Buntin, and John D. Chapman. 1997. "Risk Adjustment and Medicare: Taking a Closer Look." *Health Affairs*, 16(5): 26–43.

Newhouse, Joseph P., Willard G. Manning, Jr., Emmett B. Keeler, et al. 1989. "Adjusting Capitation Rates Using Objective Health Measures and Prior Utilization." *Health Care Financing Review*, 10(3): 41–54.

Newhouse, Joseph P., and Gail R. Wilensky. 2001. "Paying for Graduate Medical Education: The Debate Goes On." *Health Affairs*, 20(2): 136–147.

Physician Payment Review Commission. 1993. *Annual Report to Congress, 1993.* Washington, DC: Physician Payment Review Commission.

———. 1996. *Annual Report to Congress, 1996.* Washington, DC: Physician Payment Review Commission.

Prospective Payment Assessment Commission. 1996. *Medicare and the American Health Care System: Report to the Congress, June 1996.* Washington, DC: Prospective Payment Assessment Commission.

———. 1997. *Medicare and the American Health Care System: Report to the Congress, June 1997.* Washington, DC: Prospective Payment Assessment Commission.

Rice, Thomas H., and Jill Bernstein. 1999. "Supplemental Health Insurance for Medicare Beneficiaries." Washington, DC: National Academy of Social Insurance (http://www.nasi.org/Medicare/Briefs/medbr6.htm).

Riley, Gerald, Cynthia Tudor, Yen-Pin Chiang, et al. 1996. "Health Status of Medicare Enrollees in HMOs and Fee-for-Service in 1994." *Health Care Financing Review*, 17(4): 65–76.

Scherer, F. M. 2000. "The Pharmaceutical Industry." *Handbook of Health Economics*, ed. Anthony J. Culyer and Joseph P. Newhouse, 1b:1297–1336. Amsterdam: North-Holland.

Shleifer, Andrei. 1985. "Yardstick Competition." *RAND Journal of Economics*, 16(3): 319–327.

U.S. House of Representatives, Committee on Ways and Means. 1996. *1996 Green Book.* Washington, DC: Government Printing Office.

Wilensky, Gail R. 2001. "Regulatory Relief, HCFA Restructuring, and Medicare Reform." Subcommittee on Health of the Committee on Ways and Means, U.S. House of Representatives, Washington, DC.

Wilensky, Gail R., and Joseph P. Newhouse. 1999. "Medicare: What's Right? What's Wrong? What's Next?" *Health Affairs*, 18(1): 92–106.

Zuckerman, Stephen, Stephen A. Norton, and Diana Verrilli. 1998. "Price Controls and Medicare Spending." *Medical Care and Research Review*, 55(4): 457–478.

Comments

Nancy-Ann DeParle

Joe Newhouse's paper does a nice job of cataloging the many policy changes that occurred in the Medicare program over the past decade. Therefore, I will focus today on three things: first, I will attempt to fill in some of the context and color that Joe's paper does not cover; second, I will offer a preliminary assessment of how well the Clinton administration's Medicare policy worked, both as health policy and as economic policy; and finally, I will provide some thoughts on the unraveling of the Bipartisan Commission on the Future of Medicare, where my recollection differs from Joe's.

The Context

Strengthening Medicare became a defining policy goal for the Clinton administration, but it did not begin life as a campaign promise. Indeed, the 1992 campaign manifesto, *Putting People First*, contains exactly two references to Medicare in 232 pages: one claiming that a Clinton presidency would "increase Medicare-B costs for those with incomes of more than $125,000" as part of an effort to get spending under control and put the economy back on track, and the other suggesting that Medicare would be expanded to cover more long-term care services.

No, Medicare's problems hit with a thud in the middle of the famously frenetic activity surrounding President Clinton's efforts to provide health security for all Americans. Several members of the economic team got the bad news in room 252 of the Old Executive Office Building, in an early February 1993 briefing conducted by career staff of the Office of Management and Budget (OMB) for Leon Panetta, President Clinton's first budget director. The Medicare trust fund, we were told, was projected by the actuaries to run out of money in 1999. I recall this meeting as one of the rare occasions when Leon Panetta was not smiling. As we filed out of the room, one of the OMB old-timers leered: "If you're lucky and you get a second term, it will go bust on your watch."

Medicare's prospects were grim. The 25-year deficit had climbed to 2.10 percent of payroll. The Medicare trust fund was in about the worst shape it had ever been in, the result of the confluence of a number of factors. By the late 1980s and early 1990s, Medicare spending on hospitals, skilled nursing facilities, and home health and hospice services was increasing by as much as 40 to 50 percent annually. To make matters worse, the 1990–91 recession had reduced payroll tax income flowing into the Medicare trust fund.

Despite grumbling from many in Congress (and for that matter, within the administration), we resolved to shore up the Medicare trust fund in the president's first budget proposal, which became the Omnibus Budget Reconciliation Act of 1993 (OBRA 1993). The $54 billion in Medicare cuts over five years may not have been the *most* reviled items in the bill, but they ranked high on the list, somewhere between grazing fees and the so-called Btu tax. OBRA 1993's Medicare cuts—mostly "extenders" (i.e., proposals that extended existing policies that saved money relative to projected baseline spending)—represented the most significant spending reductions Medicare had ever seen. And notably, in addition to the spending cuts, OBRA 1993 eliminated the maximum wage base for the Hospital Insurance payroll tax so that it applied to all earnings without limit. Even so, the OBRA 1993 savings improved Medicare's outlook only slightly; the Medicare actuaries estimated that insolvency was pushed back another year or so, until 2001.

Then the world changed. President Clinton's health reform proposal went down in flames, never even making it to the Senate floor. The Democrats paid the price for health care reform and OBRA 1993 deficit reduction in the 1994 midterm congressional elections, losing control of both houses of Congress for the first time in four decades. Thus chastened by the experience of the Health Security Act, and mindful of the political price to be paid, President Clinton sent a budget to the Congress in January 1995 that contained exactly four Medicare policies—all extenders, nothing that could conceivably be characterized as any kind of health care reform. We were shocked when the Republican majority in Congress proposed $270 billion in Medicare cuts over five years as part of its "Contract with America" to eliminate the deficit by 2000. Among other things, the Republican plan proposed annual Medicare spending targets that were guaranteed by a "fail safe"—if the targets were missed, there would be across-the-board Medicare spending cuts to ensure that the reductions occurred.

The Contract with America forced the Clinton administration to return to the health care policy fray, but this time for a different purpose: we had to think hard about Medicare and decide how much it mattered and what we were going to do about it. We decided it mattered a lot, and that strengthening and improving Medicare had to be one of the president's chief legacies. Thus, when the administration countered with its own deficit elimination plan in June 1995, Medicare played a central role. In a bet-the-farm calculus, we proposed $124 billion in Medicare reductions over seven years, to be achieved by very different policies from those in the Republican plan. The $124 billion savings plan was based on essentially the same set of proposals the administration had put forward in the Health Security Act to help fund coverage for the uninsured and a prescription drug benefit for Medicare beneficiaries; no one had paid much attention because the Medicare cuts were buried in a much bigger and more objectionable plan.

Medicare was first among equals in the litany of "Medicare, Medicaid, education, and the environment" that became shorthand for why the president vetoed pieces of the Contract with America. The politics of Medicare played a major role in the resulting government shutdowns and two years of impasse on health policy. (The one notable exception was the Health Insurance Portability and Accountability Act, which passed right before the 1996 election.) When President Clinton was reelected resoundingly, the administration felt vindicated and pursued the twin goals of eliminating the deficit and strengthening Medicare "the right way" with considerably more conviction.

The president's FY1998 budget recycled most of his 1995 Medicare proposals; this time the scorekeepers said it added up to around $115 billion in savings over five years. Under the proposal, virtually every one of Medicare's payment systems was reformed, and the last vestiges of cost-based reimbursement were replaced by prospective or capitated payments; in all, more than a half dozen new payment systems were mandated, and every provider update was reduced. A portion of home health spending was transferred from Part A of Medicare, which is funded by the Medicare trust fund, to Part B, which is funded by beneficiary premiums and general revenues. Payments to Medicare HMOs were reformed to address longstanding concerns about risk selection and geographic disparities, and preventive benefits were expanded. As it emerged from negotiations with the Congress in the summer of 1997, the Balanced Budget Act of 1997 (BBA) followed the contours of the president's plan, with some important differences (such as the creation of the Medicare + Choice program and its payment methodology) that are detailed in the Newhouse paper.

An Assessment

So, how did we do? David Cutler asked me during the intermission if I had recovered from my eight years in the Clinton administration, and I told him that is at least a 12-step program, and I am only on about step 2. So with the caveat that I have been out of the government long enough to have some perspective, but not a wholly objective one, I would say that we did pretty well, on a macroeconomic policy level. Medicare is now projected to remain solvent until 2029, using the Medicare trustees' intermediate assumptions, and it now has the lowest projected 25- and 75-year actuarial deficits in more than two decades. The Medicare savings in the BBA—and I note that the BBA was a bipartisan achievement—helped drive the deficit reduction and the lower interest rates and economic expansion that ensued. Beyond the BBA, the Clinton administration's stewardship of Medicare included a crackdown on fraud, waste, and abuse in Medicare that played a major role in strengthening Medicare's intermediate-range financial prospects. We now have the luxury of talking seriously about how to add a much-needed prescription drug benefit to Medicare mainly because President Clinton and his economic and health policy team were committed to addressing Medicare's urgent solvency problems. Congress, to its credit, agreed.

Did we make all the hard choices? No, of course not. One could argue that we and the congressional leadership could have done more to educate beneficiaries and taxpayers about Medicare's looming demographic and financing challenges. And it has been suggested that the administration and Congress should have jumped off the high dive together to enact at least a few policies that would have required beneficiaries to pay a larger share of program costs (such as the so-called "income-related premium") in addition to, or instead of, the raft of provider cuts. There are probably many small things we could have done better, but I think we got the big things right and left Medicare much healthier than it was when we found it.

On a microeconomic level—from the narrower perspective of the health care sector and individual health care providers—my assessment of Medicare's policy impact over the past decade is more mixed. Implementation of the BBA, with its 300+ provisions affecting virtually every one of the millions of physicians, hospitals, home health agencies, nursing homes, and other Medicare providers, was a wrenching experience. One can argue that the BBA only reduced providers' payment updates, or increases, which were inflated. And there is some truth to this argument, at least on a macro level. But when spending for a given service has been increasing at an average of 40 to 50 percent a year, and suddenly it drops to 8.5 percent and then to −2.3 percent (as it did in the home health sector), there is no question that experiencing that reduction is devastating for the firm or provider experiencing it, regardless of the merits of the reduction from a Medicare policy perspective. And of course, all of this was going on at the same time that we were taking a harder look at billing abuses, and many private payors were reducing payments as well.

While many—I would argue most—of the individual policies embodied in the BBA were fully justified, it was very difficult to assess the cumulative impact of all of them together (much less in combination with the other external factors mentioned earlier). Members of the economic team—Alice Rivlin in particular—pressed for more analysis of the potential impacts on particular sectors of the health care industry, such as academic health centers or rural hospitals. But the experience of trying to provide this information was frustrating. The data are very lagged, and very aggregated, so it is almost impossible to say anything meaningful about the likely effects of various policies.

One lesson to be learned from this experience is that we should try not to do so many things in Medicare at the same time. The tendency to allow spending to get out of control and then clamp down with a vengeance is one of the unfortunate aspects of Medicare policy-making under the current statutory arrangement. Joe Newhouse's paper points out that the other major Medicare payment reforms occurred over a much longer period of time (the inpatient hospital prospective payment system was implemented 18 years after Medicare was enacted, and it was another 6 years before the resource-based relative value system, or RBRVS, for physician payments was slowly introduced). These new methodologies were shrewdly designed, with winks and nods, so that they did not really reduce spending for the first few years. In contrast, the BBA mandated dozens of new payment methodologies that were supposed to be implemented more or less at once and were intended to cut spending right away, with no pretense of transitions or glide paths to new behaviors on the part of providers. To be fair, Medicare's impending insolvency created an urgency that was not present before, but it would be good to avoid this roller-coaster ride of exponentially increasing spending and crashing reductions in the future.

A further lesson I hope future administrations and Congresses learn is to focus on the policy rather than the exercise of trying to hit a number. Another unfortunate side effect of the current statutory arrangement (in particular, the Budget Enforcement Act) is that it leads, at the margin, to Medicare policies designed to fill a budgetary hole rather than to achieve a policy goal. (That is not to say that reducing spending is not a legitimate policy goal, but it should not be the only goal.) We saw this problem in the final throes of negotiation of the BBA, when the Congressional Budget Office (CBO) "scored" the president's Medicare savings package as saving $89 billion over 5 years instead of the $115 billion the Medicare actuaries estimated. CBO's determination led to hasty efforts on the part of congressional and administration staff to "fill the gap" with policies that were sometimes less than thoughtful.

On the whole, my view is that Medicare was fortunate to have strong stewardship over the past decade, and that the groundwork has been laid to move forward in a positive way to secure it for the future. But let me mention two places where I think the administration and Congress came up short. First, we did not get as far as we should have in testing new, market-based models for determining how much Medicare should pay for services. Three major efforts at conducting a demonstration of competitive pricing for Medicare managed care plans were stopped by Congress. No matter how much people say they like market-based pricing, we were not able to test it in a meaningful way in *anyone's* backyard. That is unfortunate because all of the Medicare reform proposals now being debated rely on competitive pricing models that are untested in Medicare. We did manage to pull off two small demonstrations of competitive pricing for durable medical equipment in Lake County, Florida, and San Antonio, Texas; both produced evidence that Medicare could save money and beneficiaries could receive better service through this market-based pricing methodology.

Second, we could have made more progress in strengthening Medicare's administration. By the time I left in October 2000, the number of staff working at the Health Care Financing Administration (HCFA), the agency that administers Medicare, was at its highest level in a decade. Yet, with 4,400 full-time equivalents (FTEs), HCFA's staff was still well below 1980 levels, when it had 5,000 FTEs. By any measure, the agency has more responsibilities now than it did in 1980: Medicare alone had 39 million beneficiaries and $215 billion in spending in 2000. We continue to run one of the most important and popular programs the government operates with an administrative budget that hovers at around 1–2 percent of program dollars. No self-respecting private-sector insurance company would try to do so.

Medicare Reform

Finally, I want to comment on the difficulties of the Bipartisan Commission on the Future of Medicare. Joe's paper suggests that the administration may have been politically motivated in attacking the recommendation made by a majority of commission members that Medicare move to a defined-contribution framework. I read Joe's paper as implying that the 10-person majority on the commission came up with the right approach, and that with the president's endorsement it could have been enacted and we would now have the challenge of Medicare reform behind us.

My recollection is different, as is my assessment of the commission's work product. I acknowledge that the commission was operating in a politically charged atmosphere and there was plenty of polling and politicking going on from all sides. But the administration's objections to the defined-contribution approach as conceived by the commission were real and substantive, as were the objections of the members of the commission who declined, in the end, to support the proposal.

Both Laura Tyson and Stuart Altman have written about their experiences as the "swing votes" on the commission; Dr. Tyson will be here later in the week, and she can speak to this herself. What they have said is that they both agreed that Medicare should move away from administered pricing and toward a market-based approach. But they have also said—and they said at the time— that they identified three insurmountable problems with the commission's approach. First, the commission plan failed to guarantee that a prescription drug benefit would be available for beneficiaries who chose to remain in the traditional fee-for-service Medicare program as well as those who switched to managed care. Second, the commission plan included proposals that they were concerned would leave beneficiaries more vulnerable, such as the proposal to raise Medicare's eligibility age from 65 to 67 without any provision to help those people buy into Medicare or other health insurance. And finally, the commission plan failed to address Medicare's long-range solvency problems. The administration did not ask Dr. Tyson and Dr. Altman to oppose the commission plan. Rather, they have indicated that they could not support it because their concerns were never addressed.

The Newhouse paper characterizes President Clinton's Medicare reform plan, which he outlined a few months after the commission fell apart, as "something of an about-face." Again, my recollection is different. When the commission failed to reach consensus and disbanded, President Clinton expressed his disappointment, and the administration issued a statement outlining its concerns with the commission plan. The same day, the president instructed his health policy and economic team, myself included, to develop a plan that would accomplish his goals of strengthening Medicare and adding a prescription drug benefit. Some of us did not think that it was necessary or constructive to devote time to developing a plan, given that the commission had failed. But the president made clear that he believed he had an opportunity and a responsibility to see if we could work with Congress to get something done. So we worked for the next three months on the president's plan. Far from an "about-face" that mimicked the commission's proposal, the president's plan departed from it in significant ways. It is true that our competitive defined-benefit proposal was market oriented, and that it gave beneficiaries incentives to be more cost conscious and choose less expensive plans. In that sense, there was common ground with the commission proposal. But unlike the commission plan, it did not penalize beneficiaries who did not have access to a Medicare HMO by charging them higher premiums or denying them access to a plan that offered prescription drugs.

Most important, President Clinton's plan dedicated more than $300 billion over 10 years in additional revenues from the surplus to shoring up Medicare and extending its solvency. I do not understand why the provider trade associations did not support this proposal, particularly in the wake of the BBA. Here we had a popular second-term president explicitly acknowledging that Medicare needs additional revenues to meet the demographic and medical-care challenges of the future, not just another round of provider cuts, and offering to forgo a last hurrah of spending on his pet projects in order to save for Medicare's future. Unfortunately, we missed the opportunity to dedicate these revenues to Medicare; now, if they materialize, they will be devoted to tax cuts, which I would argue may be good politics but not good Medicare policy.

To borrow Kip Viscusi's litmus test from the first panel: yes, the world is a better place because of what the Clinton administration did to strengthen Medicare. So to my friend and fellow panelist Mark McClellan of the new Bush administration, I say, "We did the heavy lifting. Now you can finish up with the easy stuff." But of course, if the last 10 years proved anything, it is that nothing is easy where health care is concerned.

Comments

Mark McClellan

Much agreement exists among economists on important efficiency-improving reforms that could be undertaken in Medicare. For example, there is general agreement on the benefits of restructuring cost sharing in the Medicare benefit package to provide better insurance. Medicare doesn't provide an out-of-pocket limit, so beneficiaries are forced to choose between potentially unlimited financial risk or, as many of them do, supplemental Medigap policies that provide first-dollar coverage and introduce their own set of inefficiencies. Modest limits on that first-dollar coverage represent another area in which just about every economist would agree that we could do better. There is also some agreement about the benefits of price competition and a more effective competitive framework more generally in the Medicare program, with good risk adjustments and other steps to avoid problems of adverse selection between the different plans that might participate. As part of a modernized benefit package, Medicare also needs a drug benefit with subsidies to provide protection against very high expenses.

There is thus a lot of agreement among economists on what ought to be done, although there may be some differences on the details and also on the aggregate amount that should be spent on Medicare. The experience in the Clinton administration, however, proved that enacting these sorts of changes is politically difficult, to say the least.

One of the reasons that reform is difficult involves the political dynamics. The Medicare program is very complex. Any reform legislation necessarily will deal with more than one specific provision of the program, and that fact makes it easy to focus on the most controversial elements of the reform proposal—such as anything that can be portrayed in any way as a benefit cut. Thus a new copay or a higher deductible, or anything that could be portrayed as a mandatory new payment or tax on beneficiaries, is politically difficult. As a result, a lot of the rhetoric surrounding the major proposals on Medicare during the 1990s focused on finding some particular elements that were clearly unattractive when taken alone (and might even be unattractive in the whole package, but the debate often didn't get that far). Those elements were then used as a basis for undermining the whole plan.

One frustration in this type of debate is that it is very hard to focus on the desired economic perspective: the overall effects of a proposal on the expected value of Medicare as an insurance program over a beneficiary's lifetime. For tax programs and Social Security, budget scoring is at least somewhat meaningful. Perhaps the projections aren't done in the best way, but we can at least agree on the value of the benefits, since the value of a dollar is the value of a dollar. With Medicare, the situation is quite different. People are getting insurance. And there's little real measurement of the benefits that the insurance program brings. The program costs can be measured in dollars, and those can be forecast, but there isn't any serious effort to measure the benefits of those dollars, which might be quite different than the dollar values would suggest. For example, the value of Medicare might be higher than the dollar figures suggest, since insurance can be provided through Medicare that isn't available elsewhere. But they might be lower because of first-dollar coverage and because of inevitable distortions caused by a complex payment system.

Toss in the fact that this is an extraordinarily sensitive political issue, that it's one that people really remember during elections, and that both houses of Congress have been relatively closely divided over the past decade, and it is not surprising that we've made little substantial progress on modernizing Medicare in areas other than one: provider payments, which are relatively less controversial than other reforms.

During the 1990s there was thus only modest progress in modernizing Medicare benefits, with a little bit of preventive care added. But during the whole decade, no major reform effort made significant progress. Therefore, the main result of the 1990s in Medicare policy was to approach an extreme on the provider-side approach to limiting cost growth.

We now have prospective payments in Medicare for almost everything. It is possible to go further, to require prospective payments for items like outpatient and ambulatory services that don't have them now and then, going even further, to examine prospective payments for episodes of care that stretch across different types of providers. That's very difficult in a fee-for-service system, however, because it requires integrating new payments across different types of providers.

In the last two years, as the budget picture has improved, there has been a movement away from the prospective payment movement. There is thus a sense that we've taken that direction as far as we can, and we're now moving back toward reversing some of the reductions and changes that were implemented in the Balanced Budget Act.

Although these reforms in provider payments have probably increased efficiency on the whole, the program still relies intrinsically on an extraordinarily detailed and complex system of price regulation. I don't know how many prices there are now, but as a ballpark figure, there must be something like more than 10,000 prices in over 3,000 counties. It is hard to believe that kind of system produces efficient outcomes. If you add the associated congressional time on micromanaging these payments, as well as the huge lobbying expenses that go along with that, it is hard to think that this is all very efficient.

There is some consensus, even at a political level, on a way out of this situation. That involves improving options and making the system a bit more competitive. Indeed, if no one plan in the Medicare system had monopoly power, you could potentially rely on competition and choices to avoid this kind of microregulation. And there were some efforts in the 1990s to try to achieve that purpose; a big part of the BBA was meant to improve competition through the Medicare + Choice system. Unfortunately, the payment limits in the BBA and the new formulas for managed care plans took effect at about the same time that some other cost increases were affecting the private sector, so the result since then has been quite the opposite of what was intended from the Medicare + Choice provisions of the BBA.

I do want to take specific issue with one point that was raised in the paper: The difference between premium support–type competition in Medicare (the Medicare commission plan) and the competitive defined-benefit proposal (the Clinton administration plan) isn't a difference between defined-contribution and defined-benefit approaches. Both are price competition systems in which Medicare's payment to all of the plans in the program is tied to the cost of providing Medicare's defined set of benefits. The payment is not tied to some other extrinsic factor, like the rate of growth of the CPI or the rate of growth of medical costs more generally. In that sense, both systems are similar to the federal employees' plan. In the old days, the federal employees' program used a few reference plans for determining its contribution to all of the plans. Today that determination is based more on a weighted average across all of the plans. Relative to that level, beneficiaries pay more if they choose a more expensive plan. They pay less if they choose a less expensive plan. The differences between the Medicare commission proposal and the Clinton administration proposal came down to whether the premium in the fee-for-service plan was going to be protected in the new price competition system. The Clinton administration said the fee-for-service plan should never be any less affordable than it is under current law. The premium support plan proposal essentially said that we should not necessarily tie the level of support to the cost of the government plan. Rather, it tied the level of support to the average cost of providing Medicare's defined set of benefits.

It was very hard in the 1990s to make progress on making Medicare benefits better. They didn't get much worse during the 1990s, but they didn't get much better either. A drug benefit was not added, Medigap premiums continued to rise, and the options available for beneficiaries through alternatives to the government plan are headed in the wrong direction at this point.

To be sure, there was much progress on Medicare solvency as a result of the BBA and the strong economic growth in the last half of the 1990s. But there really weren't any steps—either as a result of the bipartisan commission or other Clinton administration policies—to address the long-term financial status of the Medicare program. In this year's Medicare trustees' report, the trustees took a step in the right direction for the long term by not presuming that the rate of growth in Medicare spending would automatically slow to the rate of growth of GDP. But they may still be a bit optimistic on their shorter-term cost projections, and a bit too optimistic between now and 2025 as well. Despite this optimism in the short run, the longer-term numbers are still very sobering.

One can evaluate Medicare policy during the 1990s as part of the ongoing effort to rationalize and strengthen the program that has provided health insurance to the nation's elderly and disabled Americans since 1966. Alternatively, one can analyze Medicare policy during this decade in the context of several efforts to pursue larger national objectives, namely a reduction in the budget deficit, an expansion of coverage for the uninsured, and a restructuring of the middle-class entitlement programs so that they might better cope with the fiscal challenges posed by the retirement of the baby boomers. Because Professor Newhouse's paper does such a thorough job providing a balanced evaluation of Medicare policy from the first of these perspectives, my comments will examine policy from the second.

From the mid-1980s through 1997, the energies of policy-makers in both the executive and legislative branches were directed first and foremost at reducing the federal government's large and seemingly intractable budget deficits. Medicare, quite correctly, was viewed as a significant part of the problem. In 1990, Medicare accounted for 10 percent of the federal government's non-debt-service outlays. It was the third-largest federal program, exceeded only by defense and Social Security. More importantly, Medicare expenditures were growing rapidly. The Congressional Budget Office's baseline projections during the 1990–95 period showed that Medicare would account for between one-quarter and almost one-half of the growth of non-debt-service spending (see Figure 13.5). Clearly if there was to be any hope of reducing the deficit, Medicare spending would have to be reigned in.

Whether this purpose could be accomplished without lawmakers committing political suicide was another matter. After all, the program provided an essential and very popular set of benefits to a large, politically powerful constituency whose needs were also a concern of other voters. The political risk associated with cutting Medicare spending was underscored during the decade's first attempt to reduce the deficit. On September 30, 1990, after months of acrimo-

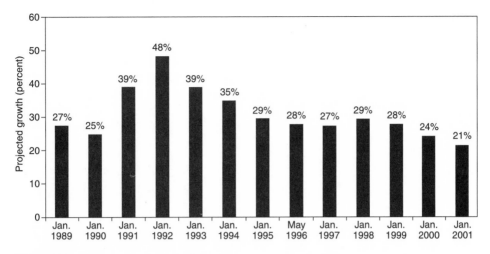

Figure 13.5
Percentage of Projected Five-Year Federal Spending Growth (Excluding Debt Service) Attributable to Medicare (Jan. 1989–Jan. 2001). (*Source:* CBO's The Budget and Economic Outlook, 1989–2001.)

nious wrangling and only hours before OMB was required to implement deep across-the-board spending cuts under the Gramm-Rudman-Hollings law, President George Bush and the Democratic leaders of Congress reached agreement on a five-year package of spending cuts and tax increases that included significant increases in Medicare Part B premiums, deductibles, and coinsurance. On October 5, this agreement was defeated on the House floor in large measure because members felt that the Medicare cuts were too severe.

Several weeks later, congressional Democrats fashioned a substitute multi-year deficit reduction package that was enacted into law as the Omnibus Budget Reconciliation Act of 1990. This legislation hit on a formula that allowed Medicare to play a major role in the effort to reduce the deficit without suicidal political consequences. The formula that was followed in the subsequent deficit reduction packages of 1993 and 1997 had three components. First, there would be some small, but popular, benefit expansions. These benefit expansions, which included coverage for certain preventive services like mammography screening, gave lawmakers something positive to mention when their constituents raised questions about the Medicare cuts.

The second component involved modest, not excessive, increases in the burdens imposed on beneficiaries and workers. Beneficiaries were faced with higher Part B deductibles and premiums. Even after these increases, the deductible and premium amounts remained far below the levels they would have reached had they been adjusted to reflect either rising per-participant Medicare expen-

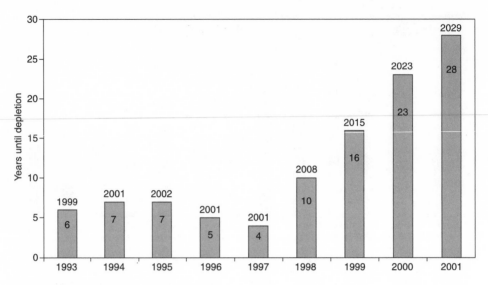

Figure 13.6
Projected Years until Depletion of Medicare HI Trust Fund. (*Source:* HI trust fund Board of Trustees' annual reports.)

ditures or beneficiary incomes since the program's inception. Payroll taxes were increased, but in a way that affected only a minority of workers. Rather than increasing the payroll tax rate, an action that would have hit all workers, lawmakers raised in 1990 and then eliminated in 1993 the maximum earning limit upon which the Hospital Insurance tax was levied, breaking, for the first time, the link between the tax bases of the Medicare and Social Security programs. Only the 6 percent of workers with earnings above the $51,300 Social Security cap were affected when the first change was implemented in 1991; when the new $125,000 wage cap was eliminated in 1994, only the top 1 percent of workers felt the hit.

While lawmakers might have faced an uphill battle if deficit reduction had been the sole justification for the modest added burdens they were imposing on Medicare beneficiaries and workers, these sacrifices could be, and were, rationalized on more compelling grounds, namely, that they were required to "save" the Medicare program. Through 1997, the annual reports of the Medicare trustees predicted that the Hospital Insurance trust fund would become insolvent within 10 years (see Figure 13.6). Politicians, therefore, could argue that the cuts were necessary to spare the program and its beneficiaries from an even worse, albeit somewhat ill-defined, fate.

Table 13.10
Medicare's Contributions to Estimated Five-Year Deficit Reduction in 1990, 1993, and 1997 Reconciliation Acts

Deficit Reduction Package	Percentage of Total	
	Spending Cuts	Revenue Increases
1990	16	17
1993	38	12
1997	57	N/A

Source: Congressional Budget Office.

Reductions in payments to providers constituted the third and, by far, the most significant component. For the most part these cuts involved freezes or reductions in the rates of growth of payments rather than declines in nominal payment rates. They also involved establishing prospective payment systems for some provider groups that were still being reimbursed on the basis of costs. Overall, these changes were not radical policy departures. They reflected proposals that academic, think-tank, and government-based analysts had developed during the preceding decade as they examined the appropriateness of Medicare's payment mechanisms and the possibility that certain classes of providers were being systematically overpaid.

Although historically providers have had considerable political influence on Medicare policy, the rapid increase in health care costs during the late 1980s and early 1990s weakened their clout and left them with little support among the public. Their willingness to negotiate sharply reduced payment rates from managed care plans and insurers during the 1994 through 1998 period left them in no position to object to Medicare's more modest discounts. It was not until the late 1990s, when it became clear that the discounts providers had granted to plans had undercut their financial viability, that some provider groups were able to make the case to lawmakers that further Medicare cuts could reduce Medicare beneficiaries' access to needed care.

Overall, Medicare contributed significantly to the successful effort to eliminate the deficit. Some 16 percent of the estimated outlay savings generated by the 1990 Omnibus Budget Reconciliation Act during the fiscal 1991–95 period was contributed by reduced payments to Medicare providers and increased Part B premiums and deductibles; 17 percent of the overall increase in revenues produced by this legislation was contributed by higher HI payroll taxes (see Table 13.10). Medicare contributed 38 percent of the outlay savings and 12 percent of the increased revenues generated by the Omnibus Budget Reconciliation Act of 1993.

Medicare played an even bigger role in the deficit reduction effort of 1997. The legislation enacted in that year had two objectives: balancing the budget by 2002 and providing Americans with their first tax cut in over a decade. To off-set the revenue loss of the tax cut, the spending cuts had to be much deeper than those that would have been needed to balance the budget by 2002. Law-makers called on Medicare for more than half—57 percent—of the required savings. Large as this figure is, even it understates the true depth of the Medi-care cuts because it nets the cost of Medicare benefit expansions against the spending cuts. And the benefit expansions were proportionately larger than they had been in the past, reflecting the desire of congressional Democrats and the Clinton administration to have the bill reflect their priorities as well as the Republican's desire to cut taxes. Congress's willingness to impose such deep cuts on Medicare reflected both the relative ease with which Medicare cuts had been accepted in 1990 and 1993, and the warning in the 1997 report of the Medicare trustees which indicated that the HI trust fund would be insolvent in four short years (2001) if measures weren't adopted to reduce spending or raise payroll taxes.

Not surprisingly, the deep reductions in provider payments called for by the Balanced Budget Act of 1997 proved to be unsustainable. The Balanced Budget Refinement Act of 1999 and the Benefit Improvement and Beneficiary Protec-tion Act of 2000 undid roughly one-third of cuts imposed by the Balanced Bud-get Act. Congress's willingness to reconsider its 1997 decisions was conditioned on the perceived sharp deterioration in the financial viability of certain health care providers, a rapid improvement in the budget situation, and the precipi-tous drop in the growth of Medicare spending which markedly improved the outlook for the HI trust fund.

The unified budget moved from deficit to surplus in fiscal 1998, four years ahead of the schedule laid out in the Balanced Budget Act, which had been viewed by most as highly optimistic. And a surplus was registered in the government's non–Social Security accounts in fiscal 1999, an achievement that most budget experts considered unattainable. By the time Congress began to debate proposals to relax some of the Balanced Budget Act's Medicare cuts, the program's spending growth had come to a halt. After a decade during which growth averaged 10 percent, Medicare spending grew by just 1.5 percent in 1998, then fell 1.3 percent in 1999, and rose by only 3.4 percent in 2000 (see Figure 13.7). While providers argued that the Balance Budget Act's "excessive" payment reductions were responsible for all of the slowdown, dispassionate analysts judged that most of the reduction was attributable to other factors such as the increased effort to root out fraud and inappropriate payments. No matter what the explanation, the spending slowdown led the trustees to push the date

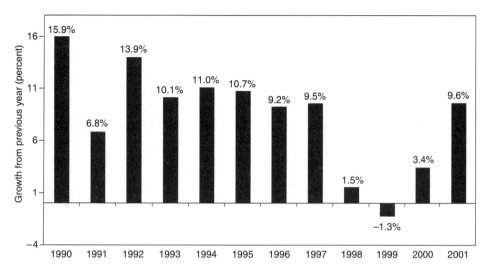

Figure 13.7
Growth in Medicare Spending from Previous Year* (1990–2001). (*Source:* CBO Budget Outlook, January 2001 (Table F-12); OMB Historical Tables [Table 8.5].)
*Includes Part B premium offset.

of HI insolvency off to 2015 in their 1999 report, to 2023 in their 2000 report, and to 2029 in their 2001 report (see Figure 13.6). With the Congressional Budget Office projecting growing on-budget surpluses in the foreseeable future and HI insolvency being several political lifetimes away, it was understandable that Congress would relax the provider cuts called for by the Balanced Budget Act.

In addition to playing a prominent role in the effort to balance the budget, the Clinton administration's Medicare policy attempted to move forward in two other areas of national priority. While these incursions were unsuccessful, they could prove consequential over the longer run if, as seems possible, they point the way for future legislative action.

Expanding coverage for the uninsured was the first of these areas. After the Clinton administration failed to enact fundamental health insurance reform during 1993–94, it began to push to expand coverage through incremental measures. First, the administration backed the efforts of Senators Nancy Kassebaum and Edward Kennedy to extend coverage among those of working age—those shifting jobs, small employer groups, and those seeking coverage in the individual insurance market after a period of coverage by an employer-sponsored plan. Their efforts culminated in the enactment of the Health Insurance Portability and Accountability Act of 1996 (HIPAA).

In 1997 the administration pushed the State Children's Health Insurance Program (S-CHIP) through Congress as part of the Balanced Budget Act. This initiative gave grants to states so that they could provide expanded coverage to low-income children who were above the income limits for Medicaid.

To expand coverage for uninsured near elderly, the administration proposed two initiatives involving Medicare in its fiscal 1999, 2000, and 2001 budgets. The first would have allowed individuals age 62 through 64 who lacked access to employer-sponsored coverage to buy into Medicare at an actuarially fair rate that was estimated to be about $300 per month. To ensure that there was no net long-term cost to the government, participants would also have been required to pay higher Part B premiums once they reached age 65 to compensate for the fact that participants would be less healthy than the average 62- to 64-year-old. The second would have let displaced workers—those affected by plant closings or slack work conditions—age 55 through 61 to buy into Medicare on the same terms.

Neither of these proposals was considered seriously by any committee of the Congress. The president's strained relations with Republicans who controlled Congress was one explanation for this failure. Another was concern some Democrats had that these options would be viable only for middle- and upper-income near elderly who could afford the $3,600 premium for Medicare coverage. Fiscal conservatives feared that, if the president's proposals were adopted, there would soon be pressure to provide subsidies to low-income near elderly so that they too could participate. Finally, there was the *Titanic* argument: why load more passengers on a ship that was predicted to sink in the foreseeable future? First, they reasoned, restructure Medicare so it can handle the retiring baby boomers and then expand the age groups eligible for its benefits.

And, during the 1990s, policy-makers did, for the first time, begin to seriously consider how the Medicare program might be restructured so as to deal with the long-term demographic challenge and the inexorable pressure from rising per-beneficiary health care costs. By the mid-1990s, the warnings in the trustees' reports of the impending insolvency of the HI trust fund had convinced many Republicans and some moderate Democrats that more was needed than repeated rounds of cuts in provider payments. Impressed by the apparent ability of managed care plans to hold down health insurance costs for employers, they argued that Medicare should be restructured to infuse it with more competition. When Congress rejected proposals to include such structural reforms among the Medicare provisions of the Balanced Budget Act, they inserted a requirement in that legislation that a commission with members appointed by the president and the leaders of Congress be established to recommend ways to strengthen Medicare financially for the long term.

The National Bipartisan Commission on the Future of Medicare, as it was called, developed a reform proposal that followed the premium support model and provided a high-option benefit package with a modest prescription drug benefit. The commission, however, was unable to muster the supermajority, 11 of the 17 commissioners, that the law required to make its proposal an official recommendation. President Clinton trashed the proposal before the commission had taken its final vote, arguing that under the proposal beneficiaries who wanted to remain in the traditional fee-for-service system could see their premiums rise substantially. In his statement about the commission's plan, the president promised to develop his own proposal for restructuring Medicare, a promise that was kept a few months later in June 1999.

While much was made of the differences between the commission's approach and that of the administration, what is noteworthy are the broad similarities between the two. Both called for structures in which beneficiaries could choose between receiving care through the traditional fee-for-service system or from an integrated health plan paid at a capitated rate. Both offered a standard benefit package and a high option with drug benefits. Under both, those choosing more efficient plans would pay lower premiums, although the administration's plan guaranteed that those remaining in the fee-for-service system would not have to pay more than they would under a continuation of current policy.

The administration's plan contained a number of significant innovations in fee-for-service Medicare and several important safeguards to ensure that comparable benefits were available to all beneficiaries. Notwithstanding these and other differences, over a few short years a significant consensus had developed concerning the general direction that Medicare restructuring should take to prepare the program for the 21st century. This accomplishment, which could well turn out to be the most significant Medicare policy development of the 1990s, stands in stark contrast to the situation facing Social Security.

Summary of Discussion

Bradford DeLong began the discussion by noting that he had hoped to hear answers to the questions (1) How large should medical spending on the elderly be 40 years from now? and (2) What share of this spending should be paid for by Medicare? DeLong argued that he could not understand how to even start thinking about what the future of the Medicare program should be without answers to those questions, yet no one seems to have set out a view on them.

Mark McClellan responded that the answer is part policy and part politics. He could not forecast what Medicare spending will be or should be in years to come, but was confident that it will be significantly higher than today. In his view, we should strive to set the program on an efficient course, with the result that spending will be lower and better targeted than it would otherwise be. McClellan acknowledged that major inefficiencies remain in the Medicare system, but he argued that progress has been made as well. On the normative question of how high Medicare spending should be, McClellan emphasized that it was a distributional and political question. For the foreseeable future, political factors will lead the government to continue to provide large transfers to the elderly.

Robert Reischauer added that the share of health care costs that should be borne by the elderly depends critically on the income distribution of the elderly as well as their level of health care costs. *David Cutler* has shown that the elderly's health care costs have risen faster over time than those of 30- to 45-year-olds, and Reischauer did not believe that the elderly would ever demand a lower quality or quantity of care.

Joseph Newhouse pointed out that, as *Victor Fuchs* has emphasized, it is not appropriate to consider this issue in isolation from Social Security. He also informed the conversation by noting that the elderly currently pay about 15 percent of Medicare-covered costs out of pocket. He believes this figure will likely rise. This does not include out-of-pocket payments for prescription drugs and long-term care.

Martin Feldstein asked the panelists why President Clinton had discredited the Medicare commission's report before its publication. Was it due to substantive objections or political motivations?

Nancy-Ann DeParle responded that the disagreement was over substance. She argued that the president would not have pushed his own staff so hard to come up with an alternative plan if the objections were purely political. The substantive issues of disagreement involved the effects of competition, the impact on long-term solvency, and access in rural areas.

McClellan further explained the president's action by suggesting that the commission could have come up with serious proposals, but unfortunately several of the core Democrats on the commission saw the outcome as precooked, and so they put little effort into crafting careful compromises.

Cutler responded to *DeLong's* initial question by arguing that the real question is "How do you pay for something that's expensive but worth it?" He then asked two pointed questions. First, according to Cutler, some have claimed that the main accomplishment of the Clinton administration with regard to Medicare was to avoid significant benefit cuts and to extend the life of the trust fund a bit. Despite the fact that people generally agreed that a benefit expansion and long-term care reform were needed, there was no progress on those issues. Was this an administration failure or the best that could be done? Second, Medicare depends heavily on administration rather than formal policy. *Cutler* specifically asked for *DeParle's* position on whether it has been administered well or whether it deserved the criticism it has often received.

DeParle, who had served as the administrator of HCFA (the Health Care Financing Administration), answered *Cutler's* second question first. Administration has been a problem, she acknowledged, largely because of lack of resources. The Clinton administration (and previous administrations) and Congress share the blame. She agreed with *Newhouse's* discussion of this problem in the paper. Administered pricing systems are expensive to operate, and HCFA's budget was limited: The staff level in the late 1990s was similar to that in the late 1970s even though the workload had expanded exponentially. As a result, there were things that were important but could not be done. She was embarrassed, for example, that there is no manual a doctor can turn to in order to learn how to participate in the Medicare program, and how that differs by state. She had tried to get such a manual written, but the people working on it had to be pulled off to work on the regulations for the Balanced Budget Act. Still, she felt, the agency did the best it could with what it was given.

DeParle continued that extending the life of the trust fund was a significant accomplishment. The cuts made for this purpose were not popular and were hard to pass. This is one place where the economic team and the administration played a central role in making sure the issue stayed on the table until it was dealt with. Incremental progress is the kind that works here.

Reischauer added that restructuring Medicare and obtaining short-run savings were politically inconsistent goals. Restructuring costs money because it is politically necessary to pay off the losers, and someone always loses in a cost-effective restructuring. Reischauer therefore argued that we should not have expected a restructured Medicare program when the immediate need, within an environment of deficit reduction, was to cut costs and not exhaust the trust fund.

McClellan argued that the changes made as part of the 1997 BBA were significant and had been discussed for an extended period prior to passage. He also argued that agreement is developing as to how the program should be restructured. Both President Bush and Vice President Gore ran on platforms that included substantial Medicare reform, and they were somewhat similar.

David Wessel asked to what extent public opinion is driven by unreasonable fears of "tapping the surplus" and "exhausting the trust fund." He observed that the government had been tapping the Social Security surplus for years and no one used to worry about it. Would there be serious economic consequences if the trust fund did run out?

Reischauer answered that depleting the trust fund had real and serious consequences. Legally, Medicare would have to stop paying benefits. So depleting the trust fund is not merely a chimera; the public concern is reasonable and appropriate. Furthermore, Reischauer's view was that if the depletion of the Medicare trust fund could be pinned on one party or the other, the political results would be catastrophic.

Jonathan Gruber observed that when prospective payments to HMOs were cut in 1997, they were only cut about 5 percent, whereas the HMOs were earning 15 percent profits on favorable selection. If those figures were correct, he asked the panelists, why did so many of the HMOs subsequently drop out of the market? Second, in reference to the defined-contribution proposals for Medicare, Gruber noted that increased competition could save money, but that unrestricted choice could also produce severe adverse selection into the defined-contribution component of the program. In that case, if the defined contribution amount matched the average cost of the defined-benefit program, overall costs could increase.

DeParle answered that proponents of such a defined-contribution plan believe the defined-contribution amount could be cut over time. She also suggested, as the lone non-Ph.D. economist on the panel, that to many people "choice" in health care means choosing a doctor, not choosing a health plan, so there may not be very much benefit to allowing lots of choice across health plans. This conclusion was underscored in focus groups HCFA conducted with current beneficiaries.

Reischauer responded to *Gruber* by agreeing that a competitive structure of this type would not generate large savings right away, but it would over time. If beneficiaries chose a cheaper plan, they would share the cost savings with the government, which would eventually produce a more efficient system.

As to *Gruber's* first question, *Reischauer* argued that in 1997 the HMOs were not in equilibrium. Some of them were being overpaid by the government, and some of them had expanded too quickly. Many of them would have left the Medicare market or at least some regional submarkets anyway, especially since some of them were only in Medicare for legal and technical reasons. Also, on average, the plans were not hurt by the Balanced Budget Act. If we had kept the law as it was before 1997, Reischauer said, these plans would be paid less than they are paid today. There are provisions in the law to make sure the plans do not suffer.

Newhouse agreed with *Reischauer* and said that even before the BBA not all the plans were making a profit. The smaller and less profitable plans were the ones that pulled out. A further explanation, he offered, was that HCFA interpreted the BBA as requiring a change in relevant policy. Before BBA, HMOs had offered different plans in different counties, but when HCFA subsequently required them to offer the same plans in all counties, they then stopped doing business in the low-rate counties. Finally, *Newhouse* said, if Medicare pays a rate such that no plans, however badly run, ever pull out, there's something wrong with the system.

McClellan argued that enrollment in private plans has not declined sharply. Furthermore, managed care has affected the whole industry and created spillovers of new ideas and technology, such as in disease management and integrated case management. McClellan argued that a single government plan is not likely to innovate in such areas.

Jeffrey Liebman, returning to the politics of the Medicare commission, felt that there was considerable ambivalence from the administration about an election-year Medicare deal. *DeParle* agreed that there was some ambivalence, but reiterated that the objections to the commission's plan were primarily substantive.

Liebman also brought out a difference between the portrayals of Social Security and Medicare's economic futures. Whenever Social Security actuaries received good news on the budget, he suggested, they tended to find some offsetting bad news to avoid significant changes in the long-term deficit and the projected date of exhaustion of the trust fund. The Medicare actuaries, however, seem to allow the trust fund exhaustion date to move back significantly in time. In his view, this approach made the Medicare problem seem less salient to politicians.

Robert Reischauer answered that Social Security and Medicare projections are really quite different things and subject to different kinds of "news." What caused the Medicare trust fund insolvency date to leap out into the future was that rather than a 7 percent annual increase in spending, there was, for example, a 1.3 percent decrease, so the base dropped. The projected rate of growth stayed the same, but when the base came in far below expectations for three years in a row, the exhaustion date moved back several years. That sort of thing does not happen to Social Security, he said, because the base is much more predictable.

Doug Elmendorf pointed out an irony of some of the comments about the projections of trust fund exhaustion. *Newhouse* had said earlier that fundamental Medicare reform was unlikely now because the exhaustion date is too far off, but later *Reischauer* and *DeParle* implied that an exhaustion date only a few years away was too close to get real restructuring because immediate cost savings were necessary. Elmendorf wondered whether a "politically optimal" exhaustion date existed for achieving structural reforms. He suggested 10 years as a horizon close enough to worry about but far enough to allow time for the reforms to take effect.

IV

Process

14 The Role of Institutions in the White House

The Process of Economic Policy-Making During the Clinton Administration

Jonathan M. Orszag, Peter R. Orszag, and Laura D. Tyson[1]

PANELISTS: *Gene B. Sperling, Sylvia Mathews, R. Glenn Hubbard, and Roger B. Porter*

By almost any standard, economic performance in the United States during the 1990s was impressive. Other chapters prepared for this volume explore the various policy contributions to that performance. But whatever the outcome of the debate over the underlying causes of the economic boom during the 1990s, the Clinton administration's economic policies clearly played some role. The overall effectiveness of the administration's economic policies, in turn, reflected in part the overall effectiveness of its internal policy process.

The economic policy process in the Clinton administration was coordinated by a new entity, the National Economic Council (NEC). The NEC coordinated the development and implementation of major economic policies in both the domestic and international spheres. The NEC also ensured that proposed policies were consistent with the administration's "message," vetted appointments to economic positions, and, as the 1990s progressed, increasingly developed and used its own in-house analytical capabilities in the policy-making process. Reflecting these myriad roles, President Clinton identified the creation of the National Economic Council as one of his most important innovations. As he recently stated, "I believe that no President will be able to have a White House

1. The authors thank Katherine Carman and Kevin Davis for excellent research assistance, and Lael Brainard, Paul Dimond, Jeff Frankel, Jeff Liebman, Roger Porter, Gene Sperling, and Diane Whitmore for helpful comments. The authors also thank the numerous former officials who agreed to be interviewed for this paper. Statements in the paper that are not referenced to published sources were derived either from these interviews or from the authors' personal experiences.

that doesn't have a National Economic Council that coordinates all the various parts that deal with economics."[2]

The NEC would thus appear both new and central to understanding the process of economic policy-making during the Clinton administration. Yet appearances may be deceiving. Recent administrations all had some mechanism akin to the NEC, albeit typically not as large, powerful, or effective. And the true impact of the NEC may not be as obvious as it initially appears. As Paul Samuelson once wrote,

The leaders of the world may seem to be led around through the nose by their economic advisers. But who is pulling and who is pushing? And note that he who picks his own doctor from an array of competing doctors is in a real sense his own doctor. The Prince often gets to hear what he wants to hear.[3]

The purpose of this paper is to examine the roles of the competing economic doctors during the Clinton years, and how the decision-making process reconciled their (sometimes contradictory) advice. The NEC is understandably an important component of the story, but the paper does not focus exclusively on the NEC. Instead, our focus includes the entire economic policy team, including powerful cabinet agencies (such as the Treasury Department), White House policy councils (such as the National Security Council), and Executive Office agencies (such as the Council of Economic Advisers and the U.S. Trade Representative), as well as forces outside the administration (including Congress, the media, and academic economists).

The paper is organized as follows. Section 14.1 discusses the National Economic Council, including its historical context and its organization. Section 14.2 examines a series of "case studies" in economic decision-making during the 1990s, including the 1993 budget process, the corporate responsibility debate, the HOPE Scholarship tax credit, fast-track trade negotiating authority, and Social Security reform. Section 14.3 explores the lessons from the case studies, such as the importance of a central coordinating body in the White House, the role of personality in policy-making, and the impossibility of separating "policy" from "politics." A final section offers conclusions.

14.1 Economic Policy Coordination

Recent administrations all had some mechanism for coordinating economic policy, but none achieved the longevity and few achieved the status of the NEC.

---

2. Paterniti (2000). Despite early suggestions that the NEC would be disbanded under the George W. Bush administration, it has survived without so much as a change in name or even offices.
3. Samuelson (1962), p. 17.

The NEC was located in the Executive Office of the President, had significant staff resources, and wielded sufficient power to coordinate cabinet-level decisions on both domestic and international economic policy. This section explores the NEC's predecessors, its creation, and its organizational structure.

14.1.1 Economic Policy Coordination Prior to the Clinton Administration

Modern presidencies have adopted various institutional mechanisms for exerting White House influence over policy.[4] Before the creation of the National Economic Council, previous administrations had experimented with different methods of coordinating economy policy-making.[5] This section briefly reviews the history of economic policy coordination since the Kennedy administration.

President John F. Kennedy's administration largely relied on ad hoc coordination to formulate economic policy.[6] Kennedy eliminated the Advisory Board on Economic Growth and Stability and the Council on Foreign Economic Policy, both of which had existed under President Dwight D. Eisenhower.[7] In their place, Kennedy created a series of ad hoc committees and relied on personal relationships among his top advisers to promote sound policy-making. As Carl Kaysen, one of President Kennedy's top international economic aides, recently put it: "President Kennedy was not a man with an organization chart in his head. He paid no attention to organization charts. He did have, I think, a sense of what people were good for, usually accurate, not always."[8] Kennedy created ad hoc committees in areas including housing credit, labor-management policy, and small business.[9] For guidance on international economic issues, Kennedy relied upon the Interdepartmental Committee of Undersecretaries on Foreign Economic Policy and upon Carl Kaysen, who directed a small NSC staff.[10] Kennedy also relied on the so-called *troika*—the chair of the Council of Economic Advisers, the director of the Office of Management and Budget, and the secretary of the Treasury—for guidance on economic policy issues.

---

4. Kelman (1987), pp. 79–83.
5. Roger Porter delineates three basic models for such policy-making: centralized, multiple advocacy, and ad hoc. Under the centralized approach, power is concentrated in the White House staff, and the executive branch departments are used largely to implement (rather than propose) decisions. Under the multiple advocacy approach, an interagency coordination process facilitates input by the departments on policy choices. Under the ad hoc model, responsibility for decision-making evolves on a case-by-case basis. The NEC combined all three models, with somewhat more emphasis on the first and second. See Porter (1980).
6. Juster and Lazarus (1997), p. 13.
7. Destler, (1980), p. 9.
8. Daalder and Destler (1999).
9. Juster and Lazarus (1997), p. 13.
10. Ibid.

President Lyndon B. Johnson adopted a more centralized approach to domestic economic policy coordination than President Kennedy. He largely eschewed cabinet involvement in economic policy-making and relied significantly on Joseph Califano, his top domestic policy aide.[11] He did, however, set up several ad hoc groups of advisers.[12] Johnson relied, as had Kennedy, on a deputy in the NSC to oversee international economic issues. (Francis Bator took over that role from Carl Kaysen.)

President Richard M. Nixon created the Cabinet Committee on Economic Policy in January 1969, which met regularly with him throughout his first year in office and less frequently thereafter.[13] Juster and Lazarus (1997) argue that international policy coordination was effectively nonexistent in the early Nixon years.[14] According to Destler (1980), the problem on the international side arose because NSC Director Henry Kissinger "did not designate an economic deputy and was both uninterested in economic matters and disinclined to delegate to his chief economic staff aide."[15] (That chief economic staff aide was Fred Bergsten, then in his late twenties.) Treasury Secretary David Kennedy had an interest in international economics, but did not have a mandate to coordinate a policy process.[16]

To address the institutional gap on international economic issues, President Nixon created the Council on International Economic Policy (CIEP) in 1971. The CIEP was designed as an economic analogue to the NSC, and Peter Peterson was named as its executive director.[17] But the CIEP was unwieldy and failed to live up to its promise.[18] At the beginning of his second term, Nixon therefore created the Council on Economic Policy (CEP).[19] He named the new secretary

---

11. Califano's role and the importance Johnson attached to the telephone are illustrated by the following story related by Jeff Shesol. "When his chief domestic advisor failed to pick up his POTUS (President of the United States) line, Johnson was told Califano was away from his desk. 'Well, where the hell is he?' the President barked at Califano's secretary. 'He's in the bathroom, Mr. President,' she answered, mortified. LBJ paused a moment. 'Isn't there a phone in there?' After a second presidential outburst, a red POTUS phone was hurriedly installed in the lavatory" (Shesol 1997, p. 153).

12. Juster and Lazarus (1997), p. 14.

13. Porter (1983), p. 410, and personal communication from Roger Porter, July 7, 2001.

14. Juster and Lazarus (1997), p. 15.

15. Destler (1980), p. 10.

16. Personal communication from Roger Porter, July 7, 2001.

17. Ibid.

18. Destler (1996), p. 6.

19. Near the end of his first term, Nixon also instituted the first White House review of environmental and other regulations. In 1971 he established the "Quality of Life" review program to examine how environmental regulations could be designed with minimal adverse impact on industrial activity. The program's activities were not particularly significant, but they did set the stage for later and more substantial White House participation in the regulatory process.

of the Treasury, George Shultz, as the chair of the CEP and the CIEP.[20] Kenneth Dam was ensconced in a West Wing office to coordinate the work of the CEP.[21] Shultz also instituted a morning meeting of the troika, which was central to the coordination process.[22]

After Shultz left government in the spring of 1974, a power struggle arose between Roy Ash (the OMB director) and William Simon (the new Treasury secretary). To resolve the issue, Nixon named Kenneth Rush, who had been deputy secretary of state, to a position as counselor to the president for economic policy. Rush continued to hold the morning meetings, but they were less effective than they had been under Shultz.

President Gerald Ford, concerned about the proliferation of interagency committees from previous administrations, followed up on an options memo from Chief of Staff Alexander Haig regarding ways of simplifying the coordination task. After some negotiations between William Seidman, the president's economic adviser, and Simon, who remained secretary of the Treasury, the Economic Policy Board (EPB) was created with Simon as its official chair and Seidman as its executive director.

The EPB included the secretaries of Agriculture; Commerce; Health, Education and Welfare; Housing and Urban Development; the Interior; Labor; State; Transportation; and the Treasury, along with the director of OMB, the chair of the CEA, and other officials. It had responsibility for both "national and international" issues, and its executive committee met every morning in the Roosevelt Room, following the White House senior staff meeting.[23] According to Roger Porter, the EPB met 520 times at the cabinet level, and the majority of principals attended more than 90 percent of the meetings.[24] The president

---

20. Shultz was also named an assistant to the president for economic affairs, in addition to secretary of the Treasury. Shultz played a particularly important role in Nixon's domestic economic policy. Even while OMB director during the first Nixon term, he had occupied an office in the West Wing, rather than the traditional Old Executive Office Building (Shultz, 1993, p. 29).

21. Dam has been nominated as the deputy secretary of the Treasury under President George W. Bush. (As of July 15, 2001, the Senate had not confirmed Dam's nomination.)

22. As Shultz and Dam note, "Despite the apparent complexity of the economic policymaking machinery (fortunately no one attempted to draw a formal organization chart), the new machinery was relatively simple. The heart of the coordinating process was a daily 8:00 am meeting attended by its Executive Office and Treasury members, representing all aspects of economic policy. These meetings were informal, but they were successful in permitting those who attended to grasp the interconnections between various economic issues and to form a common view of how to approach those issues" (Shultz and Dam, 1998, p. 176).

23. The executive committee originally comprised William Simon (Treasury), Roy Ash (OMB), Alan Greenspan (CEA), Bill Seidman (White House), and William Eberle (U.S. Trade Representative). Three additional members were subsequently added: John Dunlop (Labor), Elliot Richardson (Commerce), and Henry Kissinger (State).

24. Daalder and Destler (1999).

typically attended once a week.[25] By almost all accounts, the EPB was remarkably effective.[26] By 1976, media reports were calling it "perhaps the most important coordinating body in the Ford Administration."[27] Jules Katz, who held senior government positions in the Nixon, Ford, Carter, and Bush administrations, has noted that the EPB "was the best coordinating device of any administration that I ever served, and I've served in a few."[28]

Under President Jimmy Carter, the EPB was disbanded. Instead, Carter created the Economic Policy Group (EPG), initially cochaired by Secretary of the Treasury Michael Blumenthal and CEA chair Charles Schultze. The EPG was supposed to cover both domestic and international issues. Over time, however, President Carter relied increasingly on the policy staff directed by Stuart Eizenstat for domestic issues and the NSC policy staff under Henry Owen for international economic issues.[29] The EPG was weakened, in part, because it was not a senior official responsible for economic coordination: Charles Schultze had insisted that there be no formal White House economic adviser distinct from the CEA chair, and Schultze did not play a coordination (as opposed to substantive) role.[30]

President Ronald Reagan introduced a series of cabinet councils, which were in turn coordinated by Ed Meese. Secretary of the Treasury Don Regan directed the Cabinet Council on Economic Affairs, which was part of this system. Problems arose, however, because the distinction between that council and other related councils (for example, one on commerce and trade) was unclear.[31] Furthermore, the White House Legislative Strategy Group, led by Chief of Staff James Baker, often exercised substantial power in the policy-making process.[32] In the absence of an effective formal process for coordinating policy, Reagan

---

25. Destler (1980), p. 11.

26. Some have criticized the EPB for pushing too many issues up to the cabinet level and failing to handle some international issues effectively (see Destler, 1980, p. 221). Nonetheless, the general view is that the organization was remarkably effective.

27. Balz (1976), p. 426.

28. Daalder and Destler (1999).

29. Juster and Lazarus (1997), p. 17.

30. Porter (1983), p. 416. In regulatory matters, President Carter issued Executive Order 12044, which mandated cost-benefit analysis for proposals that "may have major economic consequences," in March 1978. To implement the executive order, Carter created the Regulatory Analysis Review Group, which was chaired by the CEA and included the OMB and other economic and regulatory agencies.

31. Daalder and Destler (1999).

32. OMB Director David Stockman realized that in this setting, with nebulous arrangements within the cabinet councils, OMB could be particularly powerful. As Stockman related to author Hedrick Smith, "Meese had a funny attitude. He thought that the Office of Management and Budget was where they did the technical auditing work to see if the motor pool had too many cars in it or something like that. They didn't understand that OMB is really the policy switchboard of the executive branch" (Smith, 1988, p. 352).

insiders note that an informal process developed: a small group of top officials would meet regularly to review decisions and make recommendations to the president.

At the beginning of the second Reagan term, the cabinet council system was consolidated into the Economic Policy Council (chaired by the secretary of the Treasury) and the Domestic Policy Council (chaired by the attorney general). Baker had become Treasury secretary, and many observers regard the EPC under Baker's leadership as having been quite effective in coordinating policy.[33] Some cabinet members complained, however, that Secretary Baker handled sensitive Treasury issues outside the EPC.

President George Bush perpetuated the EPC, but it became a shadow of what it had been under Secretary Baker. For example, the president often went outside the EPC process to obtain advice.[34] In general, according to some press reports, economic policy-making under President Bush was disorganized and ineffective. Reporter Bob Woodward wrote a devastating article on the lack of coordination among Bush's economic advisers in late 1992.[35] The article, for example, argued that CEA Chair Michael Boskin had difficulty obtaining a meeting with the president; Boskin finally had to threaten to resign before being granted the meeting. At least one former senior Bush official, however, argues that the Woodward article exaggerated the problems in the process, and that Woodward relied on only a limited number of inside sources in his reporting.

14.1.1.1 Motivations for the NEC

The NEC was thus not quite as new a concept as some Clinton officials have suggested.[36] Nonetheless, the economic policy coordination process before the Clinton administration, with a few possible exceptions, grappled with three significant problems. The NEC was designed to address these issues, and for the most part succeeded in doing so.

1. *Resolution of disagreements over economic policy.* Major cabinet agencies often disagree over crucial economic policy issues. If the process for resolving such

---

33. Destler (1996), p. 6.
34. Juster and Lazarus (1997), p. 18.
35. Woodward (1992), p. A1.
36. As one example of the misconceptions about past coordination efforts, a December 1993 NEC memorandum to the president noted, "Someone familiar with past White Houses told me that the NEC has lasted longer than either of the two previous efforts to provide similar White House coordination of economic policymaking." See Robert Rubin, "Year-End Thoughts on the NEC," Memorandum for the President, December 27, 1993. At that point, the NEC was less than a year old. The Economic Policy Board under President Ford, by contrast, operated for more than two years (it was created in September 1974 and met through December 1976). Similarly, the Council on Economic Policy under President Nixon existed for well over one year following its creation in February 1973, although its role was diminished after Shultz's resignation in May 1974.

disagreements is not perceived as fair, policy-makers will divert excessive resources into getting the last word with the president or devising creative ways of lobbying him.[37] The NEC was designed to minimize such wasteful activities while providing the president the full range of cabinet views. Many Clinton administration officials viewed this NEC role as particularly important because they believed that disagreements among the principal economic players had interfered with the substance and message of economic policy in the Bush administration.

2. *Interactions between domestic and international policy and between economics and national security.* The economic coordinating mechanisms adopted by previous administrations faced difficulty in issues that involved both domestic and international components. For example, trade adjustment assistance involves both domestic policies (coordination with other types of unemployment insurance and training programs) and international policies (international trade). Reducing greenhouse gas emissions involves domestic economic adjustments (including potential shifts in the sources of energy production and reductions in energy usage) as well as international negotiations. Over time, a growing number of presidential decisions on economic policy involved both domestic and international considerations, yet the policy apparatus imposed an awkward division between "domestic" issues and "international" issues. The international agencies had only limited economic expertise, and the domestic agencies had only limited international expertise. Observers of the decision-making process had long argued that the distinction between domestic and international economic issues was fading rapidly, if it had ever existed.[38] The NEC was designed to eliminate this increasingly arbitrary distinction.

3. *Political and communications issues.* In Washington, appearances can become self-fulfilling: Media leaks and other "communications" failures can undermine the effectiveness of an administration, ensnaring it in unnecessary public battles and providing ammunition to its enemies.[39] One of the NEC's purposes was to promote consistency between the "spin" and the substance of policy: The NEC ensured that cabinet officers had the most effective responses to criticisms of administration policies, tried to enforce adherence to administration "talking

---

37. As Roger Porter argues, "Such an organizational arrangement can help restrain the inevitable entrepreneurial advocates who will seek to shape the administration's policies to coincide with their own agendas or preferences." See Porter (1982), p. 359.

38. Destler (1980), pp. 1–18.

39. To take an extreme example, in the Woodward article mentioned earlier, OMB Director Darman was quoted as calling Secretary of the Treasury Brady a "dolt" and "probably the weakest treasury secretary in the history of the country." Such leaks could not have improved the working relationship between the two officials.

points," and reviewed documents that were to be released by administration agencies for inconsistencies with administration policy. As one of the coauthors of this paper noted when she directed the NEC, "We're really communicating the President's strategy as much as developing it. The NEC has increasingly become integrated, as I think it should be, with communications and the political and the legislative."[40] (Enforcement of the president's message can also, however, raise tensions with agencies: The CEA, for example, resented the pre-publication review of the *Economic Report of the President* that was undertaken each year by the NEC; many on the CEA believed that the NEC staff were too concerned about spin and not enough about substance.)

14.1.2 Economic Policy Coordination During the Clinton Administration

To address the shortcomings apparent in the Bush administration's approach to economic policy coordination, the Clinton administration created the National Economic Council. The idea for the NEC developed during the 1992 presidential campaign. Originally, the NEC was to focus only on international economic policy. Indeed, concerns over intensifying economic "competition" among the United States, Europe, and Japan, and a growing recognition of the links between economic security and national security in an increasingly interdependent global economy were a major impetus behind the original NEC proposal. *Putting People First*, the economic policy document that Bill Clinton and Al Gore issued during the campaign, called for the creation of an "Economic Security Council," which would be similar to the National Security Council and would be responsible for coordinating "international economic policy."[41] President Clinton mentioned the idea of the NEC only once during the campaign, in a speech given before the World Affairs Council in Los Angeles on August 13, 1992. That speech suggested that his intention was to create a body to coordinate international economic policy.

After the 1992 election, Clinton's advisers changed the name and focus of the proposed agency; some thought that the name "Economic Security Council" sounded too protectionist.[42] They also broadened the scope of the council to include all spheres of economic policy, not just international economics. (In 1983, Roger Porter proposed a "National Economic Council" staff.[43] Bruce Stokes of the Council on Foreign Relations subsequently proposed a similar concept in a 1992 article.[44])

---

40. Wildavsky (1996).
41. Clinton and Gore (1992), p. 13.
42. Jehl (1992), p. A1. See also Juster and Lazarus (1997), p. 3.
43. Porter (1983), p. 420.
44. Stokes (1992).

The NEC was promulgated in Executive Order 12835 and Presidential Decision Directive/NEC-2.[45] The executive order listed the functions of the NEC: (1) to coordinate the economic policy-making process with respect to domestic and international economic issues; (2) to coordinate economic policy advice to the president; (3) to ensure that economic policy decisions and programs are consistent with the president's stated goals; and (4) to monitor implementation of the president's economic policy agenda. It also stated, "All executive departments and agencies, whether or not represented on the Council, shall coordinate economic policy through the Council."[46]

The broad scope of the NEC caused concerns that it would supplant other agencies. The executive order and presidential decision directive reflect these various bureaucratic concerns. The executive order explicitly states that

the Secretary of the Treasury will continue to be the senior economic official in the executive branch and the President's chief economic spokesperson. The Director of the Office of Management and Budget, as the President's principal budget spokesperson, will continue to be the senior budget official in the executive branch. The Council of Economic Advisers will continue its traditional analytic, forecasting, and advisory functions.

14.1.2.1   NEC-CEA

The Council of Economic Advisers has historically served as the president's "in-house" team of economic advisers, with a chair and two members who are typically leading academics and a staff of talented economists often on leave from academic institutions and think tanks. The NEC-CEA relationship thus represented one challenge at the beginning of the Clinton administration. As one observer asked at the time, "What's left for the CEA if a National Economic Council becomes the top coordinating body for economic policy, integrating foreign and domestic economic issues?"[47] Nobel Laureate economists James

---

45. Officially, the "National Economic Council" included the president, the vice president, the secretary of state, the secretary of the Treasury, the secretary of agriculture, the secretary of commerce, the secretary of labor, the secretary of housing and urban development, the secretary of transportation, the secretary of energy, the administrator of the Environmental Protection Agency, the chair of the Council of Economic Advisers, the director of the Office of Management and Budget, the assistant to the president for economic policy, the assistant to the president for domestic policy, the national security adviser, and the assistant to the president for science and technology policy. The Small Business Administration and the Department of Defense were subsequently added, and other cabinet members or officials were to be included as necessary. The Department of Health and Human Services was included in the NEC in an early draft document, but was not included in the final executive order and presidential decision directive. In popular usage, the "National Economic Council" referred to the assistant to the president for economic policy and his or her staff, not this cabinet-level entity. (The nomenclature of the "National Security Council" is similar.)
46. The White House, "Establishment of the National Economic Council," Executive Order 12835, January 25, 1993.
47. Rowan (1992), p. A21.

Tobin and Robert Solow went so far as to oppose the NEC's creation publicly because "as alumni of the Council of Economic Advisers, we worry particularly about the duplication and subordination of its function.... If a national economic council supplants the current channels of advice to Presidents, the existing agency [CEA] will become a sideshow.... Even a distinguished economist as chairman would find his message distorted by a bureaucratic and political filter."[48]

During the administration's first months in office, Laura Tyson, chair of the Council of Economic Advisers, took steps to address these concerns. She negotiated a broad understanding with Robert Rubin, head of the NEC, that in addition to having a voice in all NEC decisions, the CEA would be responsible for providing economic analysis and advice to inform the NEC decision-making process. Rubin characterized this understanding as one in which the CEA would function as "the hand of economic analysis within the NEC glove"; the NEC was to serve primarily as a coordinating body and not as a source of policy development. Reflecting these different missions, Tyson and Rubin also agreed that professional economists in the White House would serve at the CEA rather than at the NEC.[49] The concentration of professional economists in the CEA helped to preserve its analytical role.

Tyson also spoke with the vice president about the need for the CEA to provide the president with analysis of national and international economic trends on a regular basis. In response to these conversations, the CEA worked with the Office of the Vice President (OVP) to develop a weekly economic briefing (WEB) document for the president. This document was not meant to supplant the memoranda developed by the NEC staff to summarize the recommendations of NEC participants on particular policy decisions, but rather was designed to present economic trends and analyses that would not generally be available elsewhere (such as in the press). The OVP, although it had no professional economists on staff, served in an advisory role, helping the CEA to choose relevant topics and frame the issues in an appropriate manner. After consulting with the OVP, the CEA decided what would be included in the so-called WEB document, although the CEA was also responsive to suggestions from other NEC participants.

Over time, the WEB grew to 10–15 pages and included both brief discussions of current economic news and the latest statistics, and a more in-depth analysis

---

48. Tobin and Solow (1992), p. A27.
49. One exception was David Cutler, who was both a senior economist on the CEA and a director on the NEC. Since Cutler held a joint appointment, his NEC position was not seen as inconsistent with the agreement. But the agreement was ultimately broken a few years later when several Ph.D. economists joined the NEC staff.

of broad economic trends, such as the determinants of productivity growth or national saving, relevant to policy. Preparation of the WEB quickly became a critical part of the weekly rhythm of the CEA. Anyone who served on the CEA staff during the Clinton administration will undoubtedly remember at least one late Thursday night striving to complete the WEB in time for delivery to the Naval Observatory before Mrs. Gore's nighttime deadline.[50]

The WEB was read by the president and the vice president, by some of their senior staff, and by the heads and senior staff of the NEC, the OMB, and the Treasury. Depending on the president's time, a meeting to discuss the document was scheduled each week and included the president, the vice president, the NEC chair, the CEA chair, OMB director, and the Treasury secretary. Such meetings occurred quite regularly during the first two and one-half years of Clinton's first term, but more sporadically thereafter as the president's attention was consumed by other matters. The reduced frequency of WEB meetings reflected the general tendency of the president to become somewhat less involved in the details of economic policy-making, and to rely on written rather than oral briefings, as his administration progressed.

During most of the first term of the Clinton administration, the existence of the NEC may well have bolstered the position of the CEA. The WEB, for example, provided the CEA with regular access to the president. More broadly, the establishment of an effective policy coordination process by the NEC enhanced the CEA's ability to bring disinterested economic analysis, as distinct from political considerations, to bear on policy decisions. In the words of one NEC staffer, the NEC brought the "CEA, with its professional economics expertise, back to the table, where it hadn't been since about 1976," especially on issues of regulatory reform and the environment.[51] As Krueger (2000) adds, "the National Economic Council elevated the Council of Economic Advisers, freeing it to advocate efficient economic programs and ensuring that the president had its input."[52] Roger Porter notes that the CEA was similarly bolstered by pre-NEC coordination processes:

What might appear on the surface as a competitive arrangement has rarely been viewed by the participants as a zero-sum game. To the contrary, both the CEA chairman and the White House economic-policy assistant have usually viewed the other as an ally and often as a trusted confidant.[53]

---

50. To ensure that it was included in the vice president's briefing book for Friday morning, the WEB had to be delivered to the vice president's residence at the Naval Observatory before a specific time set by Mrs. Gore. The deadline was often binding, at least during the first Clinton administration.

51. Ellen Seidman, "The NEC," Memorandum for Tom O'Donnell, October 7, 1996.

52. Krueger (2000).

53. Porter (1997), p. 106.

During Clinton's second term, however, some observers began to express concern that the NEC was indeed crowding out the CEA. By 1997, for example, *The Economist* was arguing that the CEA's advice had been "pushed to the fringes" by the NEC and a powerful Treasury Department, which at that time included a prominent economist (Lawrence Summers) as deputy secretary.[54] The relative standing of the two agencies may be reflected in the decisions of leading young academics. Early in the Clinton administration, top young economists were often found on the CEA staff. Later, some appeared more enthusiastic about joining the NEC or Treasury staff than the CEA staff.

14.1.2.2 NEC-NSC

The NSC was similarly concerned about the NEC. In response, the NSC quickly exerted its continued prerogatives in international policy. For example, the presidential decision directive establishing the NEC, issued in March, uses slightly different language than the executive order, issued in January. The presidential decision directive states that the NEC shall advise and assist the president "in integrating all aspects of national economic policy—macro-economics, micro-economics, domestic, international, and sectoral *(in conjunction with the National Security Council)*" [italics added].[55] The reference to the NSC was not included in the earlier executive order. It is also worth noting that the international economics staff on the NEC held joint appointments: They were staff on both the NEC and NSC.

At the end of 1993, Robert Rubin wrote to the president that "from the very beginning, the NEC and NSC have had an excellent working relationship, so that the merging of economic and foreign policy considerations has gone extremely well."[56] But over time, this relationship encountered a number of complications that, with the benefit of hindsight, make this early assessment appear overly sanguine. These complications took many forms. For example, during the first term, the NSC would regularly exclude the NEC director from phone calls made by the president to foreign leaders even if the planned topics of conversation included economic issues. Similarly, the NSC would often exclude the NEC from participating in the preparation of written briefing materials and in briefing meetings with the president in conjunction with visits by foreign leaders to the White House or foreign visits by the president, even when economic issues were on the agenda. More importantly, the NSC and NEC sometimes disagreed on how much time should be accorded to economic issues as

---

54. "Economic Policy Advice: Department of Debunkery," *The Economist*, January 18, 1997.

55. The White House, "Organization of the National Economic Council," Presidential Decision Directive/NEC-2, March 24, 1993.

56. Rubin, "Year-End Thoughts on the NEC."

opposed to other foreign policy issues during such visits. During the second term, some of these disagreements were ironed out. For example, the NEC and NSC agreed that the NEC would take the lead on international conferences or meetings that were primarily economic in nature (e.g., Asia-Pacific Economic Cooperation meetings, commonly known as APEC).

In addition, the NSC and NEC occasionally sparred over the preparation of decision-making memoranda for the president. By agreement, when such memoranda involved international economic issues, they were to be prepared and approved by both the NSC and the NEC. In recognition of its role as honest broker, the NEC believed that such memoranda should be circulated among NEC participants for their comments before final submission to the president. Reflecting its traditional emphasis on secrecy and security, the NSC strongly opposed this practice. Since the NSC had its own staff secretary who worked closely with the White House staff secretary, the body that processes all paper received by or sent from the president, the NSC was able to ensure that its staff controlled the submission of such memoranda.

Several factors may help to explain the tensions that developed in the NSC-NEC relationship. Although the NSC began as a small White House agency in the late 1940s to coordinate rather than make policy, over the years it evolved into a policy-making body with a sizable expert staff. In its interactions with the NEC, the NSC was understandably protective of its policy-making authority. Moreover, given the differences in background of NEC and NSC staff, it is not surprising that the two bodies sometimes differed on policy recommendations. For example, the NSC, along with the Department of Defense and the State Department, often favored the use of economic sanctions to influence the noneconomic behavior of other nations, while the economic agencies participating in the NEC believed that such sanctions were either ineffectual or counterproductive, as well as costly to U.S. businesses, in most cases. In dealing with nations like Russia, China, and Cuba, the NSC tended to give traditional security considerations much greater weight than economic ones in policy recommendations. On the most fundamental level, the NSC continued to accord traditional security concerns priority over economic concerns in foreign policy decisions, while the NEC was established in part to make sure that economic concerns played a more important role in such decisions. Tensions between the NEC and the NSC thus reflected not only differences in the backgrounds and training of their professional staff, but also differences in their missions.

14.1.2.3   Roles Played by the NEC

An internal review of the NEC completed in 1995 highlights the roles it played during the administration's first two years. The various roles are not mutually exclusive. They do, however, give some indication of the broad reach of the NEC:[57]

• *Interagency management.* The NEC played an "honest broker" role in delineating policy options and presenting the opinions of the various agencies. In this role, other agencies provided most of the staffing, but the NEC convened the players to examine (and perhaps revise) the options on a specific policy issue. The NEC would typically also write the decision memorandum to the president, including the views of all relevant agencies and perhaps an NEC view as well, as discussed in section 14.1.3. In particular, the NEC ensured that the views presented to the president on a variety of policy issues encompassed economic considerations. One supportive lobbyist went so far as to say that the NEC was "a conservative economic watchdog," although Robert Rubin responded to that charge by stating that "we're not a set of Milton Friedmans."[58] (Under Gene Sperling's leadership, the outlook of the NEC may have tilted somewhat more toward equity issues, although the NEC's overall emphasis on economic incentives and economic reasoning continued.)

• *Policy development.* On some presidential initiatives, NEC staff assumed more responsibility than policy coordination alone. For example, NEC staff played leading roles in developing the Community Development Financial Institutions initiative, a child labor initiative, planning the APEC meetings, the "New Markets" initiative, and designing the administration's defense conversion strategy.

• *Strategic planning.* At various times, the NEC also attempted to undertake strategic plans for future presidential initiatives. Given the pressures on the NEC to "fight fires" and solve more immediate problems, however, it was often difficult for the NEC to find adequate time for analysis and development of longer-term policies. (As one telling illustration, one of the authors of this paper was phoned by the NEC director late on a Sunday night. The NEC director suggested that the NEC needed to step back and focus on long-term issues, but the call was interrupted before the discussion became substantive by an urgent message from the Treasury secretary. The discussion never resumed.)

• *Policy implementation.* On some presidential initiatives, the NEC expanded its role into policy implementation, including negotiations with congressional staff regarding authorizations and appropriations for specific policy items. The Empowerment Community/Enterprise Zone (EC/EZ) initiative is one example of this implementation role.

---

57. Peter Yu, "Memorandum for NEC Policy Staff," January 12, 1995.
58. Starobin (1994).

- *Outreach to business community and others.* The NEC often served as a point of contact within the White House for the business community or other interested parties. On NAFTA, GATT, and telecommunications issues, for example, the NEC played a significant role in outreach to the business community. Industry officials in the technology sector, in particular, enjoyed an "easy access policy," although at least early in the first term the president thought that the NEC could do better at reaching out to a broader array of outsiders.[59]

- *Facilitation of private negotiations.* The NEC sometimes brokered agreements among private-sector agents, in addition to brokering agreements among government agencies. For example, the NEC spurred private-sector negotiations on Superfund reform and automotive technology advances.

- *Message.* The NEC played a significant role in promoting the administration's "message" to the press and the public. The NEC wrote and distributed talking points and briefed many administration officials before they appeared in public. (One manifestation of this role and the impact of the Internet is that, during the 1996 campaign, Gene Sperling, renowned for his late hours at the office, would have his staff read the next morning's news stories from the *New York Times* and *Washington Post* when they were posted on-line at about midnight. He would sometimes call the newspapers with corrections, hoping to change the version that appeared in print the next morning. The NEC staff also monitored the Sunday talk shows to facilitate an administration response if appropriate.)

Some of the NEC's roles, such as the facilitation of negotiations with the business community and management of the administration's economic "message," are not inherent to its original mission and may not even have been anticipated when the NEC was created. But the personalities present at the creation of the NEC affected the type of activities that it undertook. The next section therefore examines NEC staffing.

14.1.2.4   NEC Staffing

The NEC had roughly 20 professionals to carry out its functions (see Table 14.1).[60] It was a "deliberately flat" organization, with only four types of officials and with every member of the staff enjoying direct access to the director, who served as the assistant to the president for economic policy.[61] Below the director were two deputy directors, one of whom generally focused on international

---

59. For industry view, see Starobin (1994).
60. Technically, the NEC was located within the Office of Policy Development (OPD). OPD was the only significant White House unit protected from the staff reductions made to fulfill a campaign pledge by President Clinton in 1992. See Destler (1996), p. 24.
61. Starobin (1994).

Table 14.1
NEC Staff, 1993–2000

	Assistant/ Deputy Assistants to the President	Special Assistants to the President	Directors	Other professional staff	Support staff	Total
May 1993	3	7	9	3	9	31
November 1994	3	8	6	2	8	27
April 1995	3	8	5	2	6	24
April 1996	3	6	6	5	6	26
April 1997	3	5	10	3	5	26
April 1998	2	5	6	6	4	23
May 1999	4	7	5	5	5	26
March 2000	2	7	6	4	3	22

Source: White House staff directories, various years.

issues and regulatory issues, and the other of whom generally focused on budgetary and other nonregulatory domestic issues; these deputies also served as deputy assistants to the president.[62] Below the deputy directors were several "special assistants to the president." Finally, other staff on the NEC had a variety of titles—including, confusingly, "director," following the NSC precedent. The NEC also had a chief of staff, who would assist the NEC leadership in overseeing the staff and paper flow.

Strong personalities shaped the NEC in the early years. Robert Rubin, the former chairman of Goldman Sachs, served as the first director of the National Economic Council.[63] Rubin had two deputies: Bo Cutter, who had served as a senior official at OMB in the Carter administration, was responsible for international economic policies. Gene Sperling, who had been a senior member of the Clinton campaign economics team, became the other deputy, with responsibility for several domestic issues along with coordination of policy and "message." Sylvia Mathews served in a chief-of-staff role.

---

62. One exception to this model occurred in early 1997, when Dan Tarullo, who was the deputy for international affairs, became an assistant to the president for international economic policy.

63. Robert Reich suggests that President Clinton offered him the job, but that he recommended Rubin instead. Reich's rationale for rejecting the job is illuminating: "The job needs someone who isn't pushing any particular agenda or ideas—who can serve as an 'honest broker' among Treasury, Office of Management and Budget, Council of Economic Advisers, the Trade Representative, Commerce, and Labor. Otherwise, every player will try to do end runs around the process. The job also needs someone content to remain relatively invisible. Otherwise, the other players won't share information with him or her. On these two criteria, among all the registered Democrats in the United States, Bill couldn't find a *worse* candidate than me" (Reich, 1997, p. 22).

From the beginning, Rubin's personal style mitigated concerns that the NEC would dominate policy-making to the detriment of other agencies. For example, Rubin had a personal relationship with Treasury Secretary Lloyd Bentsen (Rubin had previously managed Bentsen's blind trust), and worked to minimize any conflict with the powerful Treasury Department by occasionally serving as Bensten's advocate within the White House.[64] Rubin also espoused the "no sharp elbows" principle—that NEC staff should not exert too much power or "elbow" other agencies out of the way—in both staff hiring and the daily operations of the NEC.[65] Indeed, one NEC appointment was delayed because of Rubin's concerns about the staffer's interpersonal skills. Rubin's personal prestige, combined with the caliber and interpersonal skills of the NEC staff, helped to establish the new institution with much less friction than might have been expected.

A significant step in the life of any new organization is its first transfer of leadership. In the case of the NEC, this step was necessitated by the resignation of Lloyd Bentsen as Treasury secretary and by the president's decision to replace him with Robert Rubin in early December 1994. Unfortunately, because of delays in the president's decision-making, aggravated by political uncertainties resulting from the Republican takeover of Congress in the 1994 elections, the NEC lacked a director from that time until the end of February 1995, when the president named Laura Tyson to succeed Robert Rubin. According to some observers, the resulting gap in leadership undermined the NEC's influence in early 1995, although it was reasserted later the same year.

Reflecting his satisfaction with the structure and performance of the NEC under Rubin's leadership, the president sought a successor who understood the economic policy process of his administration and would provide continuity. He chose Laura Tyson because he believed that she had the trust of her colleagues on the economic-policy team and shared Rubin's "honest broker" leadership style.

Even though Tyson was well positioned to maintain continuity in the NEC process, however, the challenges facing her and the NEC changed over time in response to a variety of forces, including changes in administration personnel, changes in the administration's relationship with Congress, and the growing political pressures of a presidential reelection campaign. By March 1995, the NEC was an established institution and "a force to be reckoned with on issues that range well beyond the traditional purview of economic policy makers."[66] But the former NEC director and arguably the most powerful member of the

---

64. Destler (1996), pp. 10–11.
65. Ibid, p. 10.
66. Starobin (1994).

president's economic team had become secretary of the Treasury (the most powerful economic agency in any administration), and the former OMB director, Leon Panetta, had become the White House chief of staff. Both Rubin and Panetta were in positions to weaken the NEC's authority if they chose to do so. Neither did, although under Panetta's leadership it became more difficult for White House staff (including the NEC staff) to claim regular time on the president's calendar.

In addition, the challenges facing the administration required changes in the focus of NEC activities. In 1993 and 1994, with the help of a Democratic-controlled Congress, the administration had the initiative in the formulation of economic policy. With the president actively engaged, the NEC coordinated the administration's policy-making efforts on the budget, on completion of NAFTA and the Uruguay Round, on trade policy with Japan and China, and on a host of microeconomic initiatives in such diverse areas as education, telecommunications, environmental policy, and science and technology policy. Health care reform was the only area of substantive economic policy development in which the NEC did not play the lead coordinating role during the first two years of the Clinton administration.

In 1995, after the Republican congressional victory, the administration had to adopt a defensive policy stance. The administration braced for a tough budgetary fight by announcing a budget plan that called for a "middle-class bill of rights," with an emphasis on tax cuts and lifelong learning. But in response to political considerations, the president backed away from additional deficit reduction in his new budget. Instead, he challenged Congress to work with him to reduce the remaining out-year deficits by finding ways to slow the growth of Medicare, Medicaid, and other health care costs.

Soon after its election, the new Congress, under the fiery leadership of Newt Gingrich, rebuffed this challenge and branded the Clinton budget as "dead on arrival." The congressional Republicans ultimately threatened to shut the federal government down if the administration failed to accept the budget developed by Congress. Not surprisingly, budgetary policy was the primary focus of NEC coordination in 1995. (Throughout the Clinton administration's years, the NEC and OMB worked closely together to coordinate budget policy. The NEC tended to focus on new initiatives and overall budget strategy, whereas the OMB focused on the budgetary details of the full array of existing programs.)

Early in 1995, over the objections of political advisers and many congressional Democrats, Gene Sperling and the CEA under Tyson's leadership led a successful NEC effort to convince the president to oppose a proposed constitutional balanced budget amendment on the grounds that it was "bad" economic policy. But later in the year, given the confrontational atmosphere in

Washington and growing concerns about the upcoming 1996 election, the president's inside and outside political advisers, including the newly arrived but still largely invisible Dick Morris, began to exercise greater influence on the administration's economic policy process. (See the HOPE Scholarship case study, section 14.2.3.) Despite these challenges, Tyson succeeded in keeping the NEC at the heart of this process, ensuring that substantive policy experts vetted politically popular ideas before they were embodied in policy proposals. In addition, she served as a more visible economic spokesperson for the administration than Rubin had during his tenure at the NEC. Some NEC staff believed that her role as spokesperson bolstered their influence.[67]

After the 1996 election, Tyson announced her decision to leave government to return to academic life, and the president chose Gene Sperling, who had served as NEC deputy for both her and Rubin, to head the NEC. (Daniel Tarullo, who had been serving as the NEC deputy for international policy, was simultaneously promoted to the title of assistant to the president for international economic policy. After Tarullo left government in 1998, the international position reverted to a deputy assistant level.) Sperling brought to the job a long institutional memory, having served on the 1992 campaign and the NEC, as well as a close bond with the president on policy matters and a keen political and policy mind. Under Sperling, the NEC sought to maintain its basic honest broker role, which became easier as officials became more comfortable with the policy process and cabinet departures narrowed the ideological divide within the administration. The NEC also bolstered its influence in the budgetary policy process, in part because of Sperling's strength on budget issues and a shift in the personnel and other duties of the chief of staff's office.

The NEC under Sperling expanded in some ways while contracting in others. For example, Sperling built a more self-sufficient NEC. He expanded the number of technical experts, as opposed to facilitators, on the NEC staff, and hired a press staffer who would later become the White House spokesman. The benefit of this centralized approach is that more of the analysis could be done directly in the White House, minimizing the likelihood of leaks, ensuring an integration of policies and politics, and permitting a broader view of the interactions among numerous policies. These benefits are highlighted most vividly in the Social Security case study (section 14.2.5). However, the more centralized approach often led to bottlenecks (as issues waited for Sperling's review).

---

67. For example, in a 1996 memorandum, one NEC staffer noted, "Laura defined a new, more visible role for the head of the NEC as an aggressive advocate for the President's budgetary and economic policies. That activity had the collateral effect of strengthening the staff's ability to manage agency interactions by reinforcing the view that the NEC was instrumental in serving the President's strategic as well as substantive agenda."

14.1.3   Stylized Policy Process

Despite its myriad and evolving roles, the fundamental mission of the NEC was the coordination of policy decisions. Furthermore, such coordination necessarily involved a broad array of administration players. Before moving on to the case studies, it may be helpful to review a stylized NEC policy process.

Let us assume for simplicity that the president noticed a newspaper article on some topic, say, the high school dropout rate among Hispanics. (President Clinton sent marked-up copies of press reports or other materials to his advisers for comments and response on an almost daily basis.) Alternatively, the CEA might have included such an article in the WEB. Regardless of the source of the article, the president might have written a short note on the side of the article, asking the NEC director to examine the phenomenon. The NEC director would then likely ask one of the NEC staff to follow up with various agencies.

Let us assume that the NEC staffer decided as a first step to convene a meeting of professional staff from the departments of Education, Commerce, Treasury, and Labor, along with staff from OMB and CEA, to discuss the issue. At the meeting, the Education staff would present evidence from the National Center for Education Statistics on the prevalence of the phenomenon, underscoring differences in dropout trends between Hispanic and other students, but also highlighting various ways in which the article that the president had read was misleading. (The NEC staff would likely *not* have shared a copy of the article with the president's notes, since doing so would unnecessarily expand the distribution of a presidential missive. Yet the NEC might have informed the other agencies that the president had read the article in question, and circulated the original article to them.) The Labor and Commerce departments, drawing on information from the Current Population Survey or other sources, would present their own perspectives on the issue. Other agencies might ask questions about the methodologies used, or request more information on other aspects of the trend under investigation.

Assuming that dropout rates among Hispanics were alarmingly high, staff would begin to evaluate whether policy changes were warranted. Eventually, the issue would be put on the agenda for an NEC deputies meeting. The "deputies" include the relevant deputy director of the NEC, who would chair the meeting, along with deputy secretaries or their designees from the relevant agencies, a member of the CEA, the deputy director of OMB, and a variety of White House staff serving at the level of deputy assistant to the president. The staff working group might have developed a background memorandum with the key facts and some of the proposed policies, to guide discussion during the deputies meeting.

If the deputies disagreed upon the appropriate course of action—and even in some cases when the deputies agreed upon the course of action—the issue could be revisited at a principals meeting. The NEC "principals" include the director of the NEC along with the relevant cabinet secretaries, the CEA chair, the OMB director, and White House staff at the level of assistant to the president. In some cases, the meeting would be chaired by the White House chief of staff; in other cases, the NEC director would chair the meeting. Regardless of who chaired the meeting, the NEC staff would have prepared a background memorandum for the meeting. Before the meeting, the NEC director and other principals might well have spoken to trusted advisers outside the government with insight into the issue. The meeting itself would generally be limited to "principals plus one": Each agency could send the principal (or a replacement) plus one other official to the meeting.

Following the principals meeting, the NEC director and the chief of staff's office would decide whether a meeting with the president was required. If the principals had significant disagreements, or if the issue were particularly important to the president's agenda, a meeting would be scheduled. The NEC would then prepare a background memorandum, the principals would meet with the president, and (in most cases) some decision would be reached about how to proceed. If the principals had largely reached agreement, if the issue were a relatively minor one, or if the president had a heavy travel schedule, a decision memorandum would substitute for a meeting. (After 1995, meetings with the president became less frequent as the president became increasingly comfortable with approving courses of action based on a decision memorandum rather than a meeting.)

The decision memorandum would embody the "honest broker" process. The NEC would draft the decision memorandum summarizing the policy question and the position of each agency. The memorandum would likely be circulated among the relevant policy officials inside the White House and in the agencies before being submitted to the president, to ensure that everyone's views and arguments were fairly represented. (As noted earlier, circulation of decision memoranda proved more problematic when the issue was international and involved the NSC.) The first section of the memorandum would describe the issue and the pros and cons of possible policy responses. The second section of the memorandum would present each agency's recommendation on a course of action; the NEC would typically include its own position in that section. In many cases, the agencies would be permitted to draft the language presenting their own position, to ensure that their case was presented fairly and accurately. Gene Sperling emphasized to the NEC staff that in a well-written decision memorandum, the president should not be able to detect the NEC's substantive recommendation before reaching the second section.

This policy process, although highly stylized, provides some insight into how economic policy was made during the Clinton administration. The next section moves beyond this stylized process to examine several actual policy issues.

14.2   Case Studies on Economic Policy-Making in the 1990s

14.2.1   1993 Budget

President Clinton had promised to "focus like a laser beam" on the economy. The centerpiece of the president's economic plan was his budget proposal. Soon after the election, the administration's economics team began detailed discussions on the budget plan. Indeed, Robert Rubin convened a budget meeting even before the Inauguration (the meeting was held on January 7). Over the course of that six-hour meeting, the major economic players in the incoming Clinton administration discussed deficit reduction, taxes on energy and gasoline, taxes on Social Security benefits, taxes on high earners, reductions in spending, and methods of encouraging investment in new technology and infrastructure. They agreed that because of the deterioration in the budgetary outlook, the president would probably have to postpone fulfillment of his campaign promise for a middle-class tax cut and to scale back his plans for increasing spending on education, the environment, and other investment initiatives. At the same time, the participants at the meeting agreed that the president's budgetary proposal should include both a long-run deficit-reduction package and a short-run economic stimulus package of tax cuts and spending increases to provide insurance against a possible downturn in the still-weak economic recovery under way. The distinction between long-term deficit reduction and short-term economic stimulus made economic sense, but proved to be a source of political difficulty in the administration's relations with Congress.

Over the next six weeks, leading up to President Clinton's address to Congress on February 17, the NEC convened a series of meetings to develop the administration's economic plan. President Clinton attended most of these meetings and went through the budget line by line, finding potential cuts to reach his goal of reducing the deficit by $500 billion over five years. A crucial issue was the balance between the degree of deficit reduction in the package relative to expansions in public spending and investments. Secretary of Labor Robert Reich, for example, supported substantial expansions in spending on training, education, and public infrastructure. OMB Director Leon Panetta, Secretary of the Treasury Lloyd Bentsen, and others supported more aggressive efforts to reduce the deficit.[68]

To inform these debates, the CEA provided analysis of how deficit-reduction packages of various sizes were likely to affect economic performance in both the short and long runs. In his best-selling book *The Agenda* (1994), Bob Woodward emphasizes the differences of opinion within the economics team on the trade-offs between deficit reduction and investment spending, maintaining that those who favored the former and represented the bond market prevailed over those who favored the latter and represented traditional Democratic values. Compared to the size of the economy, however, the policy differences separating these groups—on the order of only $50 billion to $100 billion over five years— were insignificant. In fact, the economics team was remarkably united in the view that a substantial amount of deficit reduction was essential to restoring the economy's long-run health. Deficit reduction came first—not spending increases or tax cuts.

Following Clinton's address to Congress on February 17, the focus shifted to congressional activity. Over the coming months, rifts in Congress would become painfully apparent to the administration. For example, Democrats from mining and oil-drilling states were opposed to the energy tax included in the administration's proposal. Others were concerned that there were too many new taxes and not enough spending cuts. Such concerns quickly killed the administration's economic stimulus package, which was separated from the long-term component of the proposal.

In August the budget legislation passed by the narrowest margin (218–216 in the House and 50–50 in the Senate, with Vice President Gore breaking the tie). The Republicans voted as a block against the proposal.

Most observers agree that the National Economic Council and the economics team in general were effective in developing the budget plan. Participants generally felt that they were treated fairly, and the process avoided damaging political leaks and missteps. The final budget agreement, which was largely taken from the administration's original plan, was perhaps the key contribution of the Clinton administration to the 1990s economic boom. Chapter 2, in this volume, by Elmendorf, Liebman, and Wilcox, discusses fiscal policy during the 1990s.

The 1993 budget deal, however, also highlighted some mistakes made by the new economics team. As already noted, the original package included both an energy tax and a modest stimulus package, neither of which was politically viable. In addition, the economics team did not play a significant role in the legislative strategy during the crucial early stages of the process. As Bob Wood-

---

68. See the discussion in Reich (1997), pp. 59–65.

ward has noted, "It had been more difficult to reach out to people than [Rubin] anticipated. He had to make the phone calls to people or invite them up. He was not involved in the legislative strategy which had overwhelmed the White House. . . . He was not comfortable or skilled at working with Congress."[69] One House aide added, "We don't know who's in charge. . . . All we know is we can't find the center of the operation."[70] This problem was, however, temporary. In July the White House created a budget "war room," under the leadership of Roger Altman, the deputy Treasury secretary. The administration's coordination of its legislative strategy quickly improved, and the NEC played an important role in the ensuing budgetary negotiations.

Overall, the 1993 budget deal represented a significant accomplishment for the economics team and the new National Economic Council.

14.2.2 Corporate Responsibility

The "corporate responsibility" debate in 1996 illustrates the fragility of interagency cooperation in the NEC. On January 4, 1996, Reich published an op-ed piece in the *New York Times*. He called for corporations to "take on more responsibility for Americans' economic well-being." Reich observed that the corporation had been transformed "into the agent of the shareholder." In order to balance the demands of shareholders against the interests of employees and communities, Reich believed that the government should provide corporations with incentives to do the right thing. He had several suggestions for achieving this goal. First, he suggested that the benefits of incorporation be reserved for responsible companies. Second, he suggested that the income tax liabilities of good corporate citizens be reduced.

In the weeks that followed, Senator Edward Kennedy formally drafted legislation embodying Reich's proposal. According to Reich, Clinton urged him to speak out about corporate responsibility, and Clinton encouraged his advisers to "come up with whatever [policy] ideas they could."[71] Clinton told the *Los Angeles Times*, "We have a capital gains tax differential now . . . to encourage the investment of money, so to look at other kinds of incentives to invest in labor like you invest in money . . . that's an entirely legitimate thing."[72]

Other members of the economic team, however, had considerable reservations about Reich's proposals. Both Rubin and Tyson were concerned that corporate responsibility was not a well-defined concept. What exactly was

---

69. Woodward (1994), pp. 237–238.
70. Cooper, Walsh, and Borger (1993), p. 24.
71. Swoboda (1996), and Chandler and Swoboda (1996).
72. McManus (1996).

responsible corporate behavior and what wasn't? Without an agreed-upon definition, how could tax policy be designed to encourage responsible corporate behavior? Furthermore, many companies, especially larger ones, already made significant investments in the training of their workforce and in such additional employee benefits as on-site child-care and health services. Therefore, Tyson was concerned that a large portion of new tax incentives to encourage such "responsible" behavior would be wasted on rewarding existing programs rather than encouraging new ones. She was also concerned about the feasibility of developing measures of corporate responsibility that could be used to assess whether a particular company qualified for the kinds of new tax relief proposed by Reich. Tyson told reporters that Reich's proposal was "not under active analysis or consideration."[73]

Rubin was also unhappy about the tone of Reich's public statements on corporate responsibility. The *National Journal* reported "that Rubin 'hates' the term 'corporate responsibility' ... because of the implication that companies ordinarily practice the opposite."[74] Second, Rubin believed that the initiative represented a violation of the policy process. A *Newsweek* article quoted Rubin as saying at a senior staff meeting, "I assume he [Reich] wouldn't want to read about my latest minimum-wage proposal in the *Wall Street Journal*."[75]

In late February, the NEC was assigned the task of resolving the policy dispute simmering between Reich and Rubin. The NEC convened meetings and sought to reach an agreement acceptable to both Labor and Treasury. Rubin, Reich, and Tyson ultimately signed a memo that called for a White House conference on corporate responsibility, along with a commitment that Reich would end his public statements criticizing irresponsible corporate behavior and proposed tax incentives to encourage responsible corporate behavior. (Despite that memo, Reich told reporters in early March that profitable companies were "resorting to laying off their workers to pump up their stock prices."[76] Tyson and White House Chief of Staff Leon Panetta discussed the policy problems caused by Reich's public statement with the president, and Panetta lectured Reich about violating the process.[77])

As part of the plan for resolving the internal conflict over the issue of corporate responsibility, the NEC organized a White House–sponsored conference on corporate responsibility. President Clinton praised specific companies for their worker-friendly activities, while maintaining that the "fundamental responsibility for any business is to make a profit, to create jobs and incomes by compet-

---

73. Pearlstein (1996).
74. Solomon (1996), p. 552. Also see Reich (1997), pp. 296–297.
75. Turque (1996).
76. Ibid.
77. For a description of the discussion between Reich and Panetta, see Reich (1997), pp. 302–303.

ing and growing."[78] The economic team agreed upon five areas in which the president could call upon corporations to be more responsible: family support, health and pension benefits, employee training, partnerships with employees, and workplace safety.

The White House conference on corporate responsibility was held on May 16, 1996. (It was delayed by the death of Secretary of Commerce Ron Brown.) As Tyson noted at the time, "The idea is to show that such programs don't necessarily lower profits, and in many cases raise them."[79] Featured companies included Starbucks, Patagonia, and Fel-Pro. In the end, the administration resorted to rhetorical powers and peer pressure to address the issue of corporate responsibility.

The corporate responsibility issue threatened but did not destroy the interagency process. When the president was willing to allow Reich to explore ideas outside of the normal process, Reich did. But ultimately, he was not allowed to continue proposing new policy initiatives that had not been vetted through the NEC process and approved by the president.

14.2.3 HOPE Scholarship Tax Credit

In June 1996, President Clinton proposed a $1,500 tax credit to help families pay for the first two years of a college education. The development of this proposal highlights the political pressures present during an election year and the economic team's response to such pressures.

Following the significant Republican gains in the 1994 midterm elections, President Clinton proposed a "middle-class bill of rights" in December 1994. The president's proposal included a number of tax cut provisions, including a $10,000 per year tax deduction for the costs of college or training. But while the president believed that the $10,000 college tuition tax deduction was "great," he thought it had "never penetrated" into the public arena because it "got lost in the debate about how large the tax cut should be."[80]

Late in 1995, as the administration began to put together its fiscal year 1997 budget, the Education and Treasury departments began to consider tax incentives to expand access to higher education. The focus on tax incentives rather than other approaches to expanding access to higher education reflected political realities regarding the attractiveness of tax incentives relative to spending increases: As Marshall S. Smith, the deputy education secretary, stated, proposing large increases in the Pell Grant program or other financial aid "wasn't

---

78. Purdum (1996).
79. Chandler (1996).
80. Morris (1997), pp. 223.

in the cards."[81] In November 1995 aides from these agencies traded memos suggesting that the 1997 budget plan include a $1,600-per-year tax credit for the first two years of college.

Senior White House officials, including George Stephanopoulos and Gene Sperling, raised political concerns about the tax credit proposal. In the final months of 1995, the White House and Congress were in the midst of a heated battle over the budget. The administration had launched an effective attack on the congressional budget proposal on the grounds that it involved substantial cuts in Medicare, Medicaid, education, and the environment to pay for tax cuts. In this context, the political wisdom of introducing a new administration tax credit proposal was questionable. In addition to these political concerns, several members of the NEC economic team expressed reservations about the effectiveness of a targeted tax cut to encourage college enrollment. As a result of both political and economic concerns, the education tax credit was not included in the president's fiscal year 1997 budget proposal.

In the spring of 1996, Bob Dole, the Republican presidential candidate, suggested he was considering a major tax cut as part of his campaign. Dick Morris, the president's chief political strategist, argued that the president had to respond to this political threat and that the education tax credit was the most effective response. Morris also argued that the tax credit should only be available to students with a B average or higher in high school, to emphasize the role of personal responsibility.

The economics team criticized the resuscitated tax credit proposal on several grounds. First, since the majority of children from middle-class families were already enrolling in college, the potential for the tax credit to raise their enrollment rates was limited. In addition, for lower-income families, increased funding for Pell grants was seen as a more effective way to encourage college enrollment. Second, the availability of a tax credit for college tuition could put upward pressure on tuition levels, mitigating any potential benefits for increased college enrollment. Third, the proposal to link eligibility for the tax credit to student performance in either high school or college would be difficult to enforce and would add to pressures for grade inflation among teachers and administrators. Finally, many members of the economics team feared that if the president proposed a college tax credit, he would start a bidding war on tax cuts in the 1996 presidential campaign—which would undermine continued progress on deficit reduction.

Despite the NEC's substantive and political reservations, the president decided to move ahead with the tax credit proposal, at least in part because of dramatic polling results. The president then turned to the NEC to develop a

81. Lederman (1997).

specific proposal that was "responsible." From early May until June 1996, the NEC therefore led an interagency group to develop a number of options from which the president finally chose. He announced the "HOPE" scholarship tax credit at a speech on economic policy at Princeton University in June 1996.

In a later comment on this episode, Secretary Rubin noted:

> I don't want to comment on other people's renditions of events, but this started as an idea that had a lot of problems associated with it, but within those problems was the nub, if you will, or a kernel of a very good idea. The President asked Gene ... to take this in its then existent form and see if we could work through to get the good idea out of it and not have all the problems that were associated with it.... we all worked with Gene and came up with what I think is a very good proposal."[82]

Other NEC members, including Tyson and CEA economists, remained much more negative about the president's proposal. In the end, the proposal was modified further before becoming law in 1997.[83]

The case study thus highlights the political environment in which policy-makers must operate, and the benefits of a team effort to improve the details of policies within that environment. In this case study, the NEC's fundamental substantive policy advice fell victim to the political exigencies of an election year. But the NEC process also arguably improved the details of the proposal once the president had made the decision to support a college tuition tax credit.

14.2.4 Fast-Track Trade Authority

In the fall of 1997 the White House sent a bill to Congress proposing the renewal of fast-track trading authority. Such authority, which allows presidents to negotiate trade agreements with the knowledge that Congress will not try to amend them after talks conclude, was first granted in 1974 and was renewed from time to time.

In 1994, U.S. Trade Representative (USTR) Mickey Kantor put together proposed legislation that included both the terms of the Uruguay Round of multilateral trade negotiations and continuation of fast-track authority. After months of negotiations, however, the final version of the legislation ratified the Uruguay Round but excluded fast-track authority.

Fast-track authority involved complicated political factions: Traditional free-trade advocates favored unconditional authority. "Fair traders" favored

---

82. The White House, Press Briefing on the President's Tax Plan, June 30, 1997.
83. For example, unlike the original administration proposal, the final version of the tax credit was not refundable. It is therefore of no benefit to lower-income families who, in the absence of the proposal, would have no income tax liability (before the application of the Earned Income Tax Credit).

fast-track authority, but only if it included provisions requiring labor and environmental standards as part of any trade deal. The inclusion of such provisions, however, threatened the support of the traditional free traders. The difficulty lay in finding strong enough language that satisfied the fair traders without alienating the free traders. Such language proved elusive in 1994.

Following the election of 1996, President Clinton vowed to regain fast-track authority. He placed particular emphasis on the issue in his 1997 State of the Union address. Republican leaders seemed prepared to negotiate. Senate Majority Leader Trent Lott said that fast-track action would take place "in the first six months of the year."[84] Acting USTR Charlene Barshefsky said, "The goal with respect to fast-track will be to find the compromise—that's what this entire exercise will be about."[85]

Despite the apparent readiness to compromise, fast-track authority was not pushed early in 1997 because of more pressing issues, such as the balanced budget negotiations. Destler (1997) argues that the NEC's internal structure was also at fault.[86] However, the real problem at that point was that other issues appropriately demanded the attention of senior policy-makers, not that the structure of the internal policy process was a barrier. Sperling stated "that moving on fast-track along with the budget and China would be more than Congress could handle."[87] The staff assigned to coordinate the fast-track effort lacked the clout to divert cabinet members from more pressing issues or to make decisions on behalf of the administration. As a result, the administration's effort stalled while opponents gathered strength.

After the balanced budget agreement of 1997, the administration turned its attention to other issues, including fast-track. The chief of staff assumed responsibility for coordinating the administration's fast-track effort. The economics team (the NEC principals) put together a fast-track proposal that included labor and environmental provisions and was submitted to Congress in September. By the time the proposal was submitted, however, it was doomed to failure.

Republican leaders told the administration that they would need to sway 70 Democrats to support fast track before any bill would be presented to the entire Congress. Between September and November, lobbying and negotiations continued. The AFL-CIO spent millions on advertising and lobbying to encourage undecided Democrats to oppose the legislation. Throughout this period, Chief of Staff Erskine Bowles held daily strategy sessions at the White House. Cabinet members were meeting with senators and representatives (both Democrats

---

84. Wildavsky (1997), p. 116.
85. Ibid.
86. Destler (1997), p. 24.
87. Simendinger (1997), p. 1338.

and Republicans) almost daily, trying to reach some compromise. In early November, negotiations reached a frenzy. Eventually, labor and environmental language was removed from the proposal. House Minority Whip David E. Bonior said, "They're 30 to 35 votes behind, and they have to make a decision whether they want to pull the bill or not."[88] On November 11, Clinton dropped his proposal for fast-track authority, although he said that he would try again later.

The administration's failure to obtain fast-track authority stemmed from an ideological divide between Democrats and Republicans. But it also reflected the other pressing demands on senior policy-makers, the initial assignment of responsibility to staffers without sufficient internal and external influence, and the resultant delay in bringing legislation to Congress despite the spirit of compromise at the beginning of the year.

14.2.5 Social Security

The looming retirement of the baby boomers placed Social Security reform high on the economic policy agenda in the mid-1990s. In 1994 the Quadrennial Advisory Council on Social Security (the so-called Gramlich Commission) was formed. Its members could not agree on a single approach to reform, and the commission therefore presented three different options when it issued its report in early 1997.[89] While the commission was deliberating, the administration had formed an interagency team on Social Security.[90] Consumed with pressing fiscal debates and faced with the split Gramlich Commission, however, the administration decided to place a balanced budget agreement ahead of addressing long-term challenges such as Social Security reform.[91]

In late 1997, following the budget agreement, policy-makers were faced with the new and unfamiliar prospect of large projected budget surpluses. Given the emergence of projected budget surpluses and the political debate surrounding tax reform, Social Security reform could not be addressed by itself. Furthermore, the emergence of significant projected budget surpluses dramatically changed the set of feasible options for Social Security reform. The Gramlich Commission recommendations, for example, were almost immediately irrelevant; given the history of budget deficits, the commission had not considered the possibility of revenue transfers from the general budget to Social Security.

---

88. Yang and Neal (1997).
89. *Report of the 1994–1996 Advisory Council on Social Security*, January 1997.
90. Laura Tyson and Gene Sperling, "Social Security Responses," Memorandum to the President, March 21, 1996.
91. Gene Sperling, "Long-Term Entitlement Reform," Memorandum to the President, July 3, 1997.

In the fall of 1997, Gene Sperling and Larry Summers therefore led an intensive effort to examine budget options and Social Security reform. These issues were so politically sensitive—Social Security reform had long been viewed as the "third rail" of politics—that the topic of the internal meetings was officially listed as "Special Issues," so that the daily calendars of the participants would not reveal the subject matter. In addition to Sperling and Summers, participants included Treasury Secretary Robert Rubin, OMB Director Frank Raines and Deputy Director Jack Lew, CEA Chair Janet Yellen, Social Security Commissioner Ken Apfel, and a limited number of Treasury and NEC staff.

In evaluating the new possibilities, NEC staff worked closely with Treasury staff and the Office of the Chief Actuary at the Social Security Administration. The early stages of the process highlighted a tension in the NEC: It was important to involve only a minimal number of people, but also important to have high-quality analysis on issues that had not been fully evaluated before.

In addition to the new analytical issues, the group focused on tactical considerations. For example, the principals evaluated the likely responses to different policy announcements, the timing of such announcements (the State of the Union in 1998, summer of 1998, or after the midterm elections), and how to coordinate Social Security reform with Medicare reform.[92]

Interestingly, the Lewinsky scandal may have allowed the substantive discussions to proceed further than they would have in the absence of a scandal: Put simply, the communications and political staff at the White House were enthusiastic about anything, including Social Security reform, that would divert attention from the scandal. (Several former officials with whom we spoke suggested a broader pattern to the effect of the scandals throughout the Clinton administration: At the beginning, the scandals diverted attention from policy issues and undermined serious debate over policy alternatives. As the scandals continued and as the Lewinsky matter came to light, however, the effect was reversed: The political staff realized that one of the best responses to the scandals was to show the president continuing "to do the people's work"; they were therefore enthusiastic about new policy proposals.)

Ultimately, the Special Issues team recommended a two-part strategy: reserve the budget surplus for entitlement reform and begin a "national dialogue" on Social Security reform during 1998. The president himself devised the slogan to capture this policy: "Save Social Security First," which was the key policy announcement during his 1998 State of the Union. The NEC continued to debate

---

92. Gene Sperling, "Laying Down a Marker on Social Security," Memorandum to the President, August 5, 1997; Gene Sperling, "Social Security Reform," Memorandum to the President, August 16, 1997; and Gene Sperling and Lawrence Summers, "Unified Budget Surplus and Social Security," Memorandum to the President, December 7, 1997.

various reform options through 1998 and organized a series of "town meetings" throughout the country that culminated in a White House conference in December.[93] Soon thereafter, the administration proposed allocating 62 percent of the projected unified surpluses over the next 15 years to the Social Security trust fund to extend its solvency. A limited portion (one-quarter) of the transferred surplus would be used to purchase corporate equities.[94] The plan was subsequently modified during the Midsession Review.[95]

By all accounts, the "Save Social Security First" policy was a brilliant political stroke, at least in the short run, staving off a large tax cut by using the political power of Social Security to defend the projected budget surpluses. As Waldman (2000) argues, as a result of the president's 1998 State of the Union, "a trillion dollars silently shifted on the budget ledger from the column marked 'tax cut' to the column marked 'Social Security.'"[96] In a longer-term sense, however, it is unclear how successful the policy was. On the one hand, the proposal represented sound fiscal policy. On the other hand, the year of dialogue and debate on Social Security produced no clear consensus for reform. The 1999 proposal induced charges of "double counting," and the proposal to invest part of the Social Security trust fund in corporate equities generated little support. (Indeed, Vice President Gore publicly renounced such investments during the 2000 presidential election.)

Social Security highlights the interagency process at its best: Options were thoroughly examined, both economic and political ramifications were considered, and most of what subsequently occurred had been predicted and discussed ahead of time. But the case study also highlights some shortcomings: Perhaps because it had spent so long examining the details of the issues, the interagency team failed to recognize the difficulties in explaining the administration's proposal to outsiders. In particular, the administration had difficulty addressing the confusion created by crediting Social Security surplus funds back to the Social Security trust fund—the so-called double-counting issue. The administration also apparently failed to brief Alan Greenspan ahead of time; his congressional

---

93. Agenda for Meeting with Economic Team on Social Security, November 4, 1998; Agenda for Meeting on Congressional and Think-Tank Social Security Reform Approaches, November 12, 1998; Agenda for Meeting on Congressional and Think-Tank Social Security Reform Approaches–Part II, November 24, 1998; and Agenda for Meeting on Social Security Opening Bid, December 22, 1998.
94. Agenda for Meeting on Social Security and State of the Union, January 14, 1999.
95. Agenda for Economic Team Meeting on Social Security, April 29, 1999; Agenda for Economic Team Meeting on Social Security, May 12, 1999; Gene Sperling and Chris Jennings, "Briefing Memorandum for Medicare Meeting," Memorandum to the President, May 29, 1999; and Sean Maloney and David Goodfriend, "Release of FY 2000 Midsession Review," Memorandum to the President, June 23, 1999.
96. Waldman (2000), p. 216.

testimony one day after the plan was announced undermined the viability of the proposed investments in equities.

14.3 Implications for Economic Policy-Making

Given the idiosyncratic nature of policy-making, it is difficult to draw general conclusions from any specific period. Nonetheless, the history of the Clinton administration suggests four lessons for effective economic policy-making: the importance of a unit in the White House tasked with an honest broker role; recurrent pressures that threaten to undermine that role; the impact of personalities and personal relationships on policy-making; and the difficulties of shielding good policy-making from political considerations.

14.3.1 *The Importance of a White House Unit to Coordinate Economic Policy*

Senior Clinton administration officials and others interviewed for this paper almost universally highlighted the importance of an honest broker located within the White House for the effective management of economic policy. Almost all observers believed that the NEC largely fulfilled this role.

The honest broker role entails ensuring that all relevant perspectives are brought to the table and that decisions are not made without the involvement of the most important internal players. The existence of such an entity produces several significant benefits:

• First, it ensures that proposals are "debugged" before decisions are made. As Juster and Lazarus (1997) emphasize, the "initiatives subjected to the coordination process generally fared well and those that were not vetted often failed." Illustrative examples of initiatives in which the NEC played a coordinating role in policy formulation are the 1993 budget package and the "Save Social Security First" policy, both of which were sound economic policy that strengthened the president's political standing. The most important example of a major policy initiative in which the NEC did not play the lead policy coordinating role was the 1994 health care proposal, which ultimately failed. Chapter 12 in this volume, by Cutler and Gruber, discusses that proposal. In the absence of a central coordinator, policies are often not properly vetted.

• Second, the existence of an honest broker role helps to minimize turf competition and "end runs." Cabinet secretaries who participate in the process are reassured that their perspective will be represented while they listen to the perspective of other agencies. They are thus less likely to attempt to go outside the process or to adopt intransigent positions within the process. The absence of an honest broker makes all agencies worried that their perspective will be neglected, encouraging them to engage in a variety of counterproductive internal squabbles to avoid such an outcome. As Robert Reich, who was willing to go outside the process if necessary (as demonstrated by the corporate responsibility debate), stated,

> The end runs are very few and far between. I have known the President for 25 years. I could easily call him up on the telephone and chew his ear. I don't think he'd appreciate that if I did that very often, but also there's no reason to do that as long as my views are fairly conveyed to him.[97]

• Third, the honest broker helps to utilize all the resources that are available within the government. For example, as Summers (1999) notes, "today first-rate economists staff departments from Treasury to Labor to Commerce to Justice to the Environmental Protection Agency, and they hold line as well as advisory positions."[98] An honest broker can help to ensure that the knowledge and resources of these economists, as well as other government staff, are injected into presidential decision-making. In our experience, the NEC sometimes drew upon available resources effectively, and sometimes not. In Social Security, for example, the policy-making process was substantially enhanced because of the technical assistance provided by Stephen Goss, then the deputy chief actuary at the Social Security Administration.

If an honest broker is important, where should the honest broker be located? We argue that the presumption should be the White House itself. Only a White House entity typically has the requisite access (in both appearance and reality) to the president and other senior officials (including the White House Chief of Staff) to enforce the rules of the game. Furthermore, only a White House entity can represent the interests of the president, rather than the parochial interests of a specific agency.[99] In the corporate responsibility case study, for example, the Treasury Department was one of the parties involved in an interagency dispute over policy. How could the Treasury Department have simultaneously brokered a deal and represented its own position?

In exceptional circumstances, the Treasury secretary may be able to play the role of coordinating economic policy-making, as George Shultz did under the Nixon administration's Council on Economic Policy and James Baker did under the Reagan administration's Economic Policy Council. But those excep-

---

97. Starobin (1994).
98. Summers (1999), p. 3.
99. Porter (1980), p. 13.

tions appear to prove the rule: Shultz had a White House position in addition to serving as Treasury secretary, he served during an unusual period, and in any case the system broke down after his departure.[100] Similarly, Baker had previously served as White House chief of staff, he had an exceptionally good relationship with the president, and the system again broke down after his departure.

The Office of Management and Budget could potentially coordinate economic policy, but we agree with Juster and Lazarus (1997) that

> many agency officials tend to view OMB less as a neutral honest broker than as a player preoccupied with trimming the federal budget.... A high priority for every agency involves its annual negotiation with OMB over its own budget.... if OMB is the interagency policy coordinator, either the agencies or OMB might be tempted to find ways to use the coordinating process to gain leverage in their budget negotiations.[101]

Similarly, a top NEC staffer noted in 1996 that "OMB is perceived as a player with a clear agenda, not an 'honest broker.' The NEC has provided a useful forum for development of policy on a broader basis, at a higher level" than an OMB-driven process.[102]

The experience of the Clinton administration supports the idea that to be effective, the body assigned to coordinate economic policy-making should reside in the White House. Other analysts have similarly concluded that the coordinating body should, in general, be located within the White House.[103]

14.3.2   Upholding the Honest Broker Role

Establishment of an honest broker in the White House is clearly not sufficient to ensure an effective policy-making process. Indeed, that power may be easily abused. Given the fragility of the trust that is the basis of the role, several key factors may help the honest broker remain both honest and a broker.

---

100. Shultz himself highlights the potential pitfalls in assigning a coordinating role to a cabinet member: As he noted in his book with Kenneth Dam, "A single cabinet officer may be made preeminent on a particular issue and be asked to serve as the coordinator for executive branch policy. If that cabinet officer is seen by all to have the confidence of the President, this solution works rather well. But ... this solution can create a variety of problems with Congress and with cabinet officers who find that they are in effect reporting to another cabinet officer" (Shultz and Dam, 1998, pp. 158–159). Destler (1980) adds: "But while his [Shultz's] approach might conceivably be replicated by a future treasury secretary with comparable style and substantive competence, he operated in a very unusual period, one in which a Watergate-enveloped president increasingly opted out of policy decisions, making Shultz a sort of deputy president for economic affairs" (Destler, 1980, pp. 220–221).

101. Juster and Lazarus (1997), p. 32.

102. Seidman, "The NEC."

103. Destler (1980), p. 227. See also Juster and Lazarus (1997), pp. 30–33.

14.3.2.1 President's Involvement

First, the president's involvement is essential to establishing the rules of the game for the policy process. Without the president's support, the honest broker is powerless. For example, the Economic Policy Group under President Carter was much less effective than the Economic Policy Board under President Ford or the National Economic Council under President Clinton in large part because the EPG lacked direct access to the president. As one official noted in an internal memorandum during the Carter administration, "The most telling criticism of the EPG until now is that there is little direct linkage between EPG activities and President Carter's heavy participation in economic matters." The result, according to Destler (1980), was that the EPG "could not establish itself as the primary decision channel and broker for economic policy, one that cabinet and subcabinet officials could depend on to get their views to the President."[104] Robert Rubin similarly emphasized in a memorandum to President Clinton at the end of 1993 that the "NEC's effectiveness depends on both the perception and reality of being the mechanism you use for dealing with economic issues, which has worked well during 1993."[105] Subsequent NEC directors similarly point to the president's support as critical to the NEC role. The president usually upheld the NEC process; the exceptions were rare.

14.3.2.2 Ethic of an Honest Broker

Second, those charged with leading the coordinating agency must uphold the ethic of honest broker. Rubin emphasized two important factors in creating that ethic: "inclusion of all appropriate members with respect to each matter being considered" and "full and fair reflection of all views in decision-making and, when decisions are referred to you [the NEC], in all memos and meetings."[106] The NEC was typically regarded as playing fair and not tilting the process toward one particular outcome.

To maintain its honest broker role, the White House body charged with coordinating economic policy formulation must not allow its own substantive policy recommendations to overshadow the recommendations of other participants in the process. The president must receive the recommendations of all participants in a policy process in an evenhanded and objective manner. Since these recommendations are usually conveyed to the president in decision memoranda, the preparation of these memoranda is an important task for the honest broker. NEC decision memoranda typically included a main body, which crystallized the arguments and the background, and a recommendation

---

104. Destler (1980), p. 224.
105. Rubin, "Year-End Thoughts on the NEC."
106. Ibid.

section, which summarized the position of each agency. The NEC tried to balance its honest broker role with the experience and insights of its director and staff by presenting the arguments in the main body of the memo and accurately depicting the position of the various agencies in the recommendation section (an honest broker role), but then adding its own recommendation as one of the agencies involved (an advocacy role). In most cases, this addition was not seen as undermining the honest broker role. Rubin argued, "I think you can do both as long as you are excruciatingly careful to make sure your own views do not taint the fairness of the process."[107]

14.3.2.3   Size of the Honest Broker Agency

Third, the honest broker must not become too large. A smaller staff provides flexibility and precludes taking on too much substantive responsibility, which could undermine the coordination function. By contrast, large staffs tend to "go into business for themselves," making it more difficult to serve as a coordinator.[108] Many observers, for example, believe that the NSC staff has become too large to serve as an effective honest broker in foreign policy.[109]

A relatively lean staff, however, raises the importance of filling each slot. At several points during the NEC's existence, its efficacy was undermined by a simple shortage of staff. The most dramatic gap was the transition between Rubin and Tyson, discussed earlier. Other staff gaps, although less dramatic, sometimes led to diminished effectiveness within the NEC.[110] One challenge in hiring staff is devoting sufficient time to that task; an unstable process can arise in which limited staff result in insufficient time to hire more staff.

14.3.3   Personality and Effectiveness in Government

The preceding sections focus on institutional design, but institutions alone cannot ensure the effective operation of economic policy. Economists and other academics often ignore the role played by specific personalities in policy-

---

107. Starobin (1994).

108. Destler (1980), p. 214.

109. Some observers argue that the NSC has become large because the State Department is dysfunctional. The Treasury Department, which is the principal economic agency and staffed with competent professionals, is not.

110. For example, Gene Sperling noted at the beginning of 1997 that the NEC lacked sufficient junior staffers to support the senior staff, and that one senior staff member was responsible for coordinating "Superfund policy, and economic aspects of our energy and environment policies, without any substantive staff backup" (Gene Sperling, "NEC Issues," Memorandum for Sylvia Mathews and John Podesta, January 9, 1997). Sperling also identified critical gaps in the international staff in June 1998 (Gene Sperling, "NEC Staffing on International Economics," Memorandum for Erskine Bowles, Sylvia Mathews, and John Podesta, June 3, 1998).

making. But in the practice, as opposed to the theory, of policy-making, personalities have a major effect on outcomes.

As Shultz and Dam (1998) write, "At any time in any administration there will be a few individuals who have a preeminence transcending their official post. This commanding position depends largely on their perceived influence with the President, though ability, ambition, stamina, and determination also play a role."[111] Larry Summers, for example, exerted more influence early in the Clinton administration than his official post as undersecretary for international finance at the Treasury Department would have suggested. Summers quickly dominated the Treasury Department; a CEA spoof on the Treasury Department's organizational chart had Summers occupying every position under the secretary (a position he later filled).

Summers' ascension illustrates one key aspect of an effective policy-maker: intelligence. But intelligence is generally not sufficient for effectiveness. In addition to intelligence, most effective economic policy-makers share three other characteristics: the ability to understand and communicate numerous economic concepts, especially to noneconomists such as the president; the ability to get along with other policy-makers; and the stamina to work long hours under demanding conditions. Shultz and Dam (1998) emphasize the importance of these factors:

For policy issues involving conceptual analysis, or for policy implementation where steadfastness of purpose and ability to compromise in the face of unforeseen obstacles are crucial, what counts more than the structure of the coordinating mechanism are the personal qualities of the key officials and their ability to work together. No substitute for individual ability can be found in organizational diagrams. Team spirit may be regarded by academics and pundits as a hackneyed concept, but nothing is more important for effective policy-making, especially in difficult periods.[112]

The NEC similarly recognized the role of some of these characteristics, putting a premium on collegiality and teamwork, analytic skills, and stamina in its hiring.[113]

14.3.3.1   Ability to Communicate Effectively
Effective economic policy-makers must be able to explain economic concepts to noneconomists, including key players in the White House and the president himself. Many academics ignore the importance of this skill in a top government job, especially at the CEA. The initial controversy surrounding the appointment of Laura Tyson to the chair of the CEA highlights this flawed view.

---

111. Shultz and Dam (1998), p. 11.
112. Ibid, p. 159.
113. Starobin (1994).

According to many outside observers, she proved to be a particularly effective CEA Chair, disproving her critics in part because of her communications skills and ability to deal with others.[114]

Indeed, an informal survey of opinions regarding the effectiveness of economists within the government suggests that teaching ability and perhaps applied research ability are better predictors than pure theoretical ability of a policy-maker's success. As Porter (1997) argues, "Successfully advising a president requires a careful gauging of one's audience. This is a skill that comes naturally to a good teacher."[115] Four factors explain this relationship. First, as Porter suggests, teaching involves some of the same communications skills required in the top levels of government: the ability to explain complicated issues, to "connect" to the audience, and to think on one's feet. Second, good teachers often rely on a broad understanding of and intuition for basic economic principles, which are essential in policy.[116] Third, applied research forces the analyst to confront the messy reality of limited data, imperfect assumptions, and the need to devise innovative approaches to new problems. Many of these skills are also important in government. Finally, theorists are often trained to examine the exceptional and unusual. That training could actually be counterproductive in a policy setting. As the economics folklore suggests: "Only a very clever man would discover that exceptional case; only a very foolish man would take it as the basis of a rule for general practice."

14.3.3.2 Ability to Get Along with Other Policy-Makers

Another crucial aspect of personality is the ability to get along with other policy-makers. Personal relationships are often essential to overcoming the tensions and bureaucratic infighting that are common at the top levels of government. Many effective policy-makers emphasize the role played by their personal relationships with other members of the team. For example, Carl Kaysen, one of Kennedy's top economics staffers, emphasizes the personal relationships among Kennedy's economics team, including Walter Heller, James Tobin, Kermit Gordon, George Ball, and Robert Roosa.[117] The fact that Robert Rubin, Bo Cutter, Gene Sperling, and Sylvia Mathews developed "easy and effective informal relationships" bolstered the role of the NEC in the early years.[118] Similarly, the

---

114. Destler (1996), p. 49.
115. Porter (1997), p. 105.
116. As one former chairman of the CEA has written, the economic adviser "must arrive at conclusions relevant to his local and temporal limits, and he gets little help in that from the body of economics in the journal mill. Generally, he must 'roll his own' conclusions from his observations and experience" (Stein, 1995, p. 77).
117. Daalder and Destler (1999).
118. See Destler (1996), p. 62, on the personal relationships within the NEC and between NEC officials and others.

international deputies grew to know one another during the first Clinton administration through regular meetings; "the resulting bilateral relationships also made it easy for individual deputies to 'pick up the phone' and settle lower-level disputes between agencies."[119] As Shultz and Dam (1998) emphasize, "Whoever the key individuals may be and whatever their talents, good personal relationships among them, though far from assuring desirable outcomes, certainly help to bring them about."[120] As Daniel Tarullo, the leading international official on the NEC for two years, stated, "You can't overestimate personal relationships, because you need to integrate personalities to integrate policies."[121]

14.3.3.3 Stamina

A final factor important to success within government is simply stamina. Inside the Executive Office and at the top levels of the agencies, policy-makers are often called upon to perform a wide variety of tasks. At the NEC, for example, Gene Sperling was renowned for working 100 hours or more per week. Sperling was an outlier, but senior policy-makers would have difficulty in fulfilling their professional obligations in less than 70 or so hours per week. The long hours take a toll on professional performance and personal lives. As Birnbaum (1996) argues, "Work in the White House is nonstop. It consumes almost every waking hour. Family life falls by the wayside.... A twelve-hour day is a short one. Fourteen and even eighteen hours are more common.... With little time to think, and barely enough time to act, mistakes are made often."[122] Since tight deadlines make those long weeks all the more stressful, many leave the government feeling burned out. It is said that in government, the urgent has a way of preempting the important. A more accurate statement is that urgent demands are a way of life. For example, in 1997 the economic team had to grapple with the budget agreement, climate change, Social Security reform, and Most Favored Nation status for China, all of which were major issues, along with numerous other less important issues. These competing demands may explain the delays in the administration's efforts to obtain fast-track authority that year.

14.3.4 Difficulty of Insulating Policy from Politics

Finally, the case studies of section 14.2 highlight the difficulties of separating politics from policy. Analysts sometimes propose such a dichotomy, but the case studies emphasize the complex ways in which politics and policy interact. As Robert Rubin recently wrote in a slightly different context, "One of the most

---

119. Ibid, p. 28.
120. Shultz and Dam (1998), p. 12.
121. Stokes (2001), p. 617.
122. Birnbaum (1996), p. 6.

important lessons I learned during my years in government is that, with economic change, the politics are as important as the policy. If you do not get the politics right, the policy will not happen."[123]

Policy-makers who attempt to ignore the political environment are likely to become irrelevant quickly. As Charles Schultze warned, "The CEA chairman and members cannot be effective if they are seen as political eunuchs, with little understanding of the political stakes involved."[124] A *New York Times* article noted that Laura Tyson was an effective CEA chair because "like most Presidential economic advisers," she "learned to read the political signals and then back off, or compromise, or enlist just the right political allies."[125]

To be sure, sometimes politics can be given undue weight. The college tax credit may be a case in point. For example, Joseph Stiglitz laments that in White House policy discussions,

It was not only that bad arguments seemed to drive out good, but good economists, responding to implicit incentives, adopted bad arguments to win their battles. In a process of cognitive dissonance reduction, possibly combined with some intellectual atrophy, sometimes good economists even seemed to come to believe their own specious arguments.[126]

It is important for economic policy-makers to recognize that the influence of politics and political advisers varies over time, mostly in response to the electoral cycle but often in response to other factors as well.

14.4   Conclusion

One reason for the Clinton administration's success in economic policy-making was the coordinated approach that characterized the economic team. Public disputes were rare, and policy-makers trusted the process to present their views fairly to the president. Trust encouraged collegiality and discouraged efforts by frustrated participants to appeal to the president or the press for policy validation. In our opinion, President Clinton was correct in arguing that no future president will be able to govern effectively without an NEC. As Krueger (2000) adds, "The National Economic Council provides a good model for future White Houses."[127] The future evolution of the NEC, however, also entails dangers: The institution could grow too large to fulfill its coordinating mission, and it could supplant other important sources of economic advice, especially the CEA.

---

123. Rubin (2001), p. 38.
124. Schultze (1996), p. 26.
125. Uchitelle (1998).
126. Stiglitz (1998), p. 5.
127. Krueger (2000).

After significant debate, President George W. Bush decided to perpetuate the NEC and appointed Larry Lindsey as director. That decision reflects some of the lessons presented here. A central organizing body located in the White House is often necessary for effective economic policy-making. It is not sufficient, however. For the Bush NEC to succeed, it must maintain the ethos of an honest broker, enjoy the support of the president, be staffed by people without sharp elbows, and be wary of the challenges of an evolving institution.

References

Balz, Daniel. 1976. "Juice and Coffee and the GNP—The Men Who Meet in the Morning." *National Journal*, April 3.

Birnbaum, Jeffrey. 1996. *Madhouse: The Private Turmoil of Working for the President*. New York: Random House.

Chandler, Clay. 1996. "Ambivalent about Business." *Washington Post*, May 12, p. H1.

Chandler, Clay, and Frank Swoboda. 1996. "Tax Break for 'Good' Employers; Clinton 'Encouraged' Consideration of Idea." *Washington Post*, March 2, p. H1.

Clinton, Bill, and Al Gore. 1992. *Putting People First: How We Can All Change America*. New York: Times Books.

Cooper, Matthew, Kenneth Walsh, and Gloria Borger. 1993. "Can Clinton Recover?" *U.S. News and World Report*, June 7, p. 24.

Daalder, Ivo, and I. M. Destler, moderators. 1999. *The National Security Council Project: Oral History Roundtables*. "International Economic Policymaking and the National Security Council," Center for International and Security Studies at Maryland and the Brookings Institution, February 11. Available at http://www.brook.edu.

Destler, I. M. 1980. *Making Foreign Economic Policy*. Washington, DC: Brookings Institution Press.

———. 1996. *The National Economic Council: A Work in Progress*. Washington, DC: Institute for International Economics.

———. 1997. *Renewing Fast-Track Legislation*. Washington, DC: Institute for International Economics.

Jehl, Douglas. 1992. "Clinton Names Bentsen, Panetta to Economic Team." *Los Angeles Times*, December 11, p. A1.

Juster, Kenneth, and Simon Lazarus. 1997. *Making Economic Policy: An Assessment of the National Economic Council*. Washington, DC: Brookings Institution Press.

Kelman, Steven. 1987. *Making Public Policy: A Hopeful View of American Government*. New York: Basic Books.

Krueger, Alan. 2000. "Honest Brokers Separate Policy from Sausage for the White House." *New York Times*, November 9, sec. C, p. 2.

Lederman, Douglas. 1997. "The Politicking and Policy Making Behind a $40 Billion Windfall: How Clinton, Congress, and Colleges Battled to Shape Hope Scholarships." *Chronicle of Higher Education*, November 28, p. A28.

McManus, Doyle. 1996. "Clinton to Nudge Enlightened Capitalism Along." *Los Angeles Times*, March 3, p. A1.

Morris, Dick. 1997. *Behind the Oval Office*. New York: Random House.

Paterniti, Michael. 2000. "Bill Clinton: The Exit Interview." *Esquire*, December. Available at http://www.esquire.com.

Pearlstein, Steven. 1996. "White House Upbeat in Economic Report: Minor Tinkering May Be Needed Advisers Say." *Washington Post*, February 15, p. D9.

Porter, Roger. 1980. *Presidential Decision Making: The Economic Policy Board*. Cambridge: Cambridge University Press.

———. 1982. "Organizing Economic Advice to the President: A Modest Proposal." *AEA Papers and Proceedings*, 72 (May): 356–360.

———. 1983. "Economic Advice to the President: From Eisenhower to Reagan." *Political Science Quarterly*, 98 (Fall): 302–426.

———. 1997. "Presidents and Economists: The Council of Economic Advisers." *AEA Papers and Proceedings*, 87 (May): 103–106.

Purdum, Todd. 1996. "Businesses Should Be Loyal to Employees, Clinton Says." *New York Times*, March 24, sec. 1, p. 32.

Reich, Robert. 1997. *Locked in the Cabinet*. New York: Random House.

Rowan, Hobart. 1992. "Economics Without Economists." *Washington Post*, December 10, p. A21.

Rubin, Robert. 2001. "Ex-Im Bank and International Economic Leadership." In *The Ex-Im Bank in the 21st Century: A New Approach*, ed. Gary Hufbauer and Rita Rodriguez. New York: Institute for International Economics.

Samuelson, Paul. 1962. "Economists and the History of Ideas." *American Economic Review*, 52 (March): 1–18.

Schultze, Charles. 1996. "The CEA: An Inside Voice for Mainstream Economics." *Journal of Economic Perspectives*, 10 (Summer): 23–39.

Shesol, Jeff. 1997. *Mutual Contempt: Lyndon Johnson, Robert Kennedy, and the Feud that Defined a Decade*. New York: W. W. Norton.

Shultz, George. 1993. *Turmoil and Triumph: My Years as Secretary of State*. New York: Scribners.

Shultz, George, and Kenneth Dam. 1998. *Economic Policy Beyond the Headlines*. Chicago: University of Chicago Press.

Simendinger, Alexis. 1997. "Slowpoke on Fast-Track." *National Journal*, June 28.

Smith, Hedrick. 1988. *The Power Game: How Washington Works*. New York: Random House.

Solomon, Burt. 1996. "Clinton Brags about the Economy and Bad-Mouths It at the Same Time." *National Journal*, March 9.

Starobin, Paul. 1994. "The Broker." *National Journal*, April 16.

Stein, Herbert. 1995. *On the Other Hand: Essays on Economics, Economists, and Politics*. Washington, DC: American Enterprise Institute Press.

Stiglitz, Joseph. 1998. "Private Uses of Public Interests." *Journal of Economic Perspectives*, 12 (Spring): 3–22.

Stokes, Bruce. 1992. "Trade Policy." In *Changing America: Blueprints for the New Administration*, ed. Mark Green. New York: Newmarket Press.

———. 2001. "Global Coordinator." *National Journal*, March 3.

Summers, Lawrence. 1999. "Distinguished Lecture on Economics in Government: Reflections on Managing Global Integration." *Journal of Economic Perspectives*, 13 (Spring): 3–18.

Swoboda, Frank. 1996. "Reich to Propose Tax Help for Firms Aiding Workers: Idea Could be Clinton Reelection Theme." *Washington Post*, February 6, p. C3.

Tobin, James, and Robert Solow. 1992. "Clintonomics Doesn't Need a Czar." *New York Times*, December 10, p. A27.

Turque, Bill. 1996. "The Battle of the Bobs." *Newsweek*, March 18, p. 28.

Uchitelle, Louis. 1998. "The Economics of Intervention," *New York Times*, May 31, sec. 3, p. 1.

Waldman, Michael. 2000. *POTUS Speaks*. New York: Simon & Schuster.

Wildavsky, Ben. 1996. "Under the Gun." *National Journal*, June 29.

———. 1997. "Trade Fatigue." *National Journal*, January 18.

Woodward, Bob. 1992. "The President's Key Men: Splintered Trio, Splintered Policy." *Washington Post*, October 7, p. A1.

———. 1994. *The Agenda: Inside the Clinton White House*. New York: Simon & Schuster.

Yang, John, and Terry Neal. 1997. "'Fast Track' Hits a 'Brick Wall': Clinton Appears Short on Democratic Support in Last-Minute Tallies." *Washington Post*, November 9, p. A1.

Comments

Gene B. Sperling

Peter and Jon Orszag and Laura Tyson have done an excellent job of trying to capture a very large topic in a very short amount of space. This is no surprise to me as Laura is among the very most talented and impressive people I have ever seen or worked with, and Peter and Jon are now universally regarded as two of the most brilliant young economists in the nation.

The chapter as well as my own comments—though both brief, preliminary pieces—are perhaps the first retrospective efforts to establish a clear factual record of how the Clinton National Economic Council actually operated. These efforts help us to determine what generalizable policy recommendations can be drawn from this eight-year experience. Unfortunately, such issues have been poorly or inadequately dealt with at times.

On the factual side, many articles have made assertions about the policy process which—however good or bad—are inaccurate descriptions of how our process worked. In newspaper articles on how the NEC and NSC would handle international economic policy issues in the new Bush administration, for example, the description of the coordination under the Clinton administration was often inaccurate.

On the recommendations side, it is too easy and simplistic to make recommendations based on situational circumstances. I've heard people cite my experience as evidence that an NEC director should be someone with a close personal bond to, and deep understanding of the views of, the president. I've also heard Bob Rubin used as an example of why an outside CEO with private-sector experience is a key credential for an NEC director. The true answer on many such "lessons" is that they depend on a wide variety of circumstances including the personality and background of the president, the particular period of time within an administration, the composition of the rest of the economic team, and a variety of variables. Therefore, in drawing lessons—both good and bad—from the past, it is important not to make assumptions based solely on situational or circumstantial issues, but rather to look for the generalizable lessons that will be true under a broader set of circumstances. In this comment I first give a brief overview of the composition and understandings behind the NEC, and then later a few generalizable rules of the road.

The NEC Is a Process—Commitment to Inclusion, Transparency, and Internal Vetting in Presenting Policy Recommendations to the President

At the core of the Clinton NEC was the commitment that policy recommendations should be undertaken through a unified team process in which all relevant perspectives would be included, considered, and debated before options were presented to the president. President Clinton called for this type of coordination based on his experience as governor of Arkansas, his belief that economic decision-making needed to be more integrated with other security and domestic issues, and his view that well-coordinated National Security Councils had been important to past presidents—including President Bush, Sr.—and that the same should be done on the economic side.

This effort required Cabinet members and senior White House policy-makers to give up being the sole adviser in their specific areas so that they could be part of a larger NEC team process—coordinated by a NEC director serving as an honest broker—on a wider range of economic policy issues. In the Clinton NEC, the NEC director, the OMB director, the CEA chair, the secretary of the Treasury—and usually all four deputies—were involved in all domestic economic issues, yet the rule of inclusion required that when any issue strayed into the jurisdiction or expertise of another agency, that agency would be included as well. For example, on any business, labor, or job-creation issue, the secretaries of labor and commerce would automatically be invited to the meetings.

On the international side, the core group included the U.S. Trade Representative (USTR), the secretary of commerce, and the NSC director, as well as the NEC, CEA, and Treasury. Divisions between the NEC and NSC were made on a case-by-case basis. If the meeting was fundamentally economic—a trade meeting—the NEC director would chair the meeting, but the national security adviser would always attend and present the foreign policy issues. Where there were major foreign policy implications—such as on the steel cases—the secretary of state would not only attend, but play a major role. When the issue was primarily an NSC one—for example, planning for a foreign policy trip to Russia—the NSC director would chair the meeting, but the NEC director would attend and help present the economic issues. On many issues, where there was too much overlap, the NEC director and NSC director would cochair the meeting. Examples of such issues included meetings on major financial crises or an economic issue in a country with significant foreign policy implications, such as Indonesia (under Suharto) or Russia.

Advantages of the NEC Team Process—Most Key Issues Are Complex with Multiple, Overlapping Impacts

A team process committed to inclusion of key policy members ensures that relevant and crucial perspectives are taken into account. A major trade initiative of the USTR has crucial effects on agriculture, labor, environment, and investment policy—and often has budget impacts—that require having the secretaries of labor, agriculture, and the Treasury, as well as members of the environmental and budget team, at the table. Economic decisions related to energy require the presence of the secretary of energy, but also the national security adviser and secretary of state (to assess the impact on OPEC and the Middle East). Therefore, the team process reflected a reality-driven need to have a variety of diverse, yet relevant, perspectives at the table.

1. *Creating trust and loyalty.* A fair and inclusive process is essential for building the trust necessary for an administration to function effectively. Bob Rubin, Laura Tyson, and I would all tell you that the most essential aspect of our job was building and maintaining that trust in the process on a day-by-day, issue-by-issue basis. All of us discovered that when people had a chance to be part of the policy process, to review the memos and the presentations of their opinions before they were submitted to the president, and to present their views directly to the president in a meeting, even the most disappointed losers in a policy process would instantly agree once the president made a decision and advocate it as if it had been their preferred view. Yet, when key policy-makers feel they were "cut out of the process," "excluded," or had their views misrepresented even on a small issue, they can stay bitter for months, even years to come. Roger Porter has expressed this same view when writing and discussing his experiences on domestic policy in President Bush, Sr.'s administration.

2. *Dealing with uncertainty and the law of unintended consequences.* To a certain degree, the benefits of a vigorous, analytical team process can be seen in the maxim "Several heads are better than one." Most major economic issues—especially the long-term ones—involve a wide number of variables, and therefore carry significant potential for unintended consequences. In addition to the importance of having people with various perspectives represented at the table, simply having a team of smart people knocking back and forth tough issues over time leads to more mistakes being caught and therefore better decision-making.

3. *Presidential efficiency.* One of the main reasons for an NEC team process is simply that it is a far more efficient way for a president to weigh competing considerations on tough policy issues. In many White Houses, the president would simply get different memos from competing cabinet officers. Each would sound good because he or she did not have to fairly represent the other's side. A process like this, which makes the president have to figure out which argument to believe with no disinterested party moderating the debate, is an enormous waste of presidential time and most likely will lead to flawed decision-making because a president will never be able to sort out the strong points and weak points adequately. In an NEC process, competing ideas are knocked back and forth among the NEC members. This forces people with competing views to listen to the other side, incorporate their concerns, and often narrow their differences. When the competing views are finally presented to the president, it is in a coordinated presentation with all competing pros and cons, and all the different cabinet perspectives right before him. He can then grill his advisers, cross-examine them, and get their ideas in one coordinated, efficient meeting or memo.

A Few Generalized Rules of the Road

1. *The NEC director must be first and foremost the coordinator and honest broker.* The NEC director certainly wears two hats in the job. He or she is the president's top personal staffer on economics in the White House, and he or she is also the one who must work with the rest of the White House on day-to-day operations, briefing the president, and overall strategy. However, when push comes to shove, the NEC director must always remember that his or her primary responsibility is to be the coordinator and honest broker among the president's economic cabinet. For example, whatever the political pressure within the White House to come out a certain way on an economic decision, it is essential that the NEC director be the protector of a sound and fair economic team decision-making process that empowers the economic team to get a full airing of their views with the president. Furthermore, while the NEC director should be able to give personal views to the president, he or she must first ensure that there is a fair, open process, and never allow personal views to interfere with this primary responsibility.

2. *The president must act to support the process.* The president himself must support the team, honest-broker process. If the president allows his policies to be influenced outside of the NEC process—by secret phone calls or pull-asides at events—every member of the economics team will feel that the real way to

have influence is just to find the right occasions to whisper in the president's ear. If, however, the president politely replies to such efforts, "Why don't you tell the NEC director about that idea, and make sure it is considered in our decision-making process?" the signal is then sent that it does no good to go around the process, and the fairness, inclusion, and transparency of the NEC process are protected. As the NEC was President Clinton's idea—and he firmly believed that bad process alienated team members and led to resentment and poor policy—he was particularly good at supporting and protecting the process.

3. *The NEC director cannot misuse his or her access.* The NEC director does not have the staff or perks of an official cabinet officer, but the one thing the NEC director does have over any cabinet officer is access to the president. The NEC director, NSC director, and DPC director each see the president far more times than any cabinet officer both because of their proximity—their offices are in the West Wing—and because they have to brief the president several times a week on day-to-day matters. If the key cabinet officers believe that the NEC director is using that access to push personal views on controversial matters, any and all trust in the NEC process will be defeated. Even if the president asks the NEC director for his or her opinion, it is essential that the director say that the matter is under dispute and that there are several different views—perhaps explaining them—but preferably simply to say that the economics team will respond to his inquiry quickly with a recommendation or options. Bob Rubin faithfully observed this practice when he started the NEC, and it was one that both Laura Tyson and I honored during our tenures.

4. *Coordinate but allow cabinet members to still be leads in their areas.* While the NEC director should coordinate the process, it is crucial that he or she still allow the relevant cabinet member to be the lead presenter in meetings with the president on specific issues. For example, in producing a budget every year, the NEC director and the OMB director would sit down and come up with a schedule for making decisions and meeting with the president. This was necessary because the budget must be coordinated with the State of the Union process for determining priorities and initiatives for the next year. In the actual budget meetings with the president, the NEC director would open the meeting by saying what the issues were that had to be decided, but then would always turn to the OMB director to present the paper and make the lead budget presentation to the president. After that, the NEC director could express his or her opinion or ensure that other competing voices were heard. In this way, the NEC director fulfilled the role of honest broker, coordinator, and adviser, but the OMB director's role as lead on the budget was still protected.

5. *White house coordinators who can work together.* It is simply impossible ex ante to figure out the precise divisions between the NEC, the DPC, and the NSC.

For example, at times health issues seemed to be purely a DPC issue, yet Medicare, which became such a major budget issue, at times fell more naturally into the NEC's jurisdiction. The issues related to international economics and foreign policy are even harder to predict. What is critical, therefore, is that the president pick policy coordinators who can get along and are committed to a fair process so that they have the capacity to work out these close jurisdictional matters on a case-by-case basis that is fair and best serves the president.

The same can be said of the White House chief of staff. It is important to have a logical division over who should run meetings. Simply put, when the meeting is about policy development, the NEC should run it, yet when the issue primarily involves legislative and tactical strategy, the chief of staff may be the more appropriate lead. For example, the NEC director should coordinate the budget process and the presentation of major budget issues. Yet it is more appropriate for the chief of staff to coordinate the appropriations strategy on the Hill—as this is more about legislative and tactical strategy. If a major policy revision is required, however, the chief of staff should kick the process back to the NEC.

6. *The NEC must deal with both the real and the ideal.* A good NEC process should start with the ideal economic strategy for the policy issue in question. This approach is essential, yet in the policy world it is not sufficient. In order to advise a president effectively, the NEC process has to engage in the tough work of considering all the legislative and political factors that a president has to deal with in determining what is often the least bad, or best possible, solution. This general rule should never mean, however, that the NEC should become simply an arm of the political advisers. On the one hand, the NEC must be willing to say when a policy idea is ill-advised regardless of the short-term politics, or when a compromise has been pushed so far that the measure in question would do more harm than good. On the other hand, simply staking out a pristine academic position will not help the president deal with the very real and tough decisions that any president must make, taking into account a variety of real-world considerations. The tough work of government consists of pushing toward the best ideal policy outcome in the face of considerable constraints and making the tough calls on whether the best you can possibly do still represents progress and should be undertaken, or whether it is harmful and should be rejected.

Comments

Sylvia Mathews

Thank you. The chapter was very well done and represented many, many things that I agree with based on my experience and the different vantage points from which I was able to participate in economic policy-making in the Clinton/ Gore White House. I want to touch briefly on three things that in my experience are relevant to the question of what is the best approach to economic policy-making and coordination in a White House and in an administration. The first issue I would like to focus on is, Where should the coordination occur? The second is the importance of the NEC's, or whatever body you choose, integration within the White House more broadly than just as a developer of economic policy. And finally I want to touch upon the issues of personality and style in economic coordination because I think they are very relevant to successful policy coordination.

On the question of where the coordination should occur, I have been fortunate to see economic policy-making from several different perspectives and in several different ways. I do believe that the White House and "an" NEC or "the" NEC, whichever way you want to think about it, is the right place for policy coordination for a number of reasons. First, the NEC as it was created did not have an institutional bias. Having been a part of the Treasury Department, it knows what it knows, what it does best, and what it thinks it knows better than others. Refundable tax credits are a good example of the institutional bias. Any time this issue came up, you knew where the Treasury Department would be. As the implementers of tax law, the Treasury is charged with writing the implementing regulations and enforcing the tax code. Refunding is difficult to implement, and the Treasury would therefore consistently oppose refundable tax credits. Treasury would come to the table with an institutional bias on a number of issues, and I do not think that is bad for economic policy-making, but in terms of a coordinating body, I think that can be troublesome.

Additionally, OMB, where I spent my last two years, had institutional biases as well. For example, when the economic policy team held the Social Security discussions that are mentioned in the chapter, OMB always came to the table with a point of view on the way we should think about the debt reduction, where it should be categorized, and how it should be done. That view comes from the institution and is present no matter which party is in power. I believe the issue of institutional bias is a relevant factor to consider in favor of having a nondepartmental body coordinate economic policy.

A second reason that I believe the NEC is a good home for coordination is that it does not have line responsibility. Therefore, NEC could potentially be more strategic and less in-box driven. The Treasury Department has to run a myriad of financially related issues as well as 40 percent of all federal law enforcement. OMB is acting on all the department's regulations, it is preparing a budget, and it is coordinating the department's management efforts. A separate entity in the White House is less likely to be stifled by the day to day, and it is able to operate more strategically. It provides an ability to focus only on presidential priorities. The Treasury and the OMB, and sometimes the CEA in terms of the economic report of the president, have responsibilities set in law that they must fulfill.

Additionally, not having line responsibility, the NEC can focus on a very wide range of activities. In preparation for our discussion today, I went back to my files and pulled out notes from a typical weekly meeting held by Gene Sperling, Bo Cutter, Bob Rubin, and me to make sure we were on top of the issues before the NEC. I'm not going to go through it all because, as you can see, it's a very long list. However, just to give you a sense of the breadth of what we were working on, I will read a few items from the agenda of the meeting on February 11, 1994: Japan, next steps; Balanced Budget Amendment; health care; trade; export promotion; the environment, subcategories: Ozone Transport Commission, EPA, and the federal implementation program; the California earthquake efforts; the Tourism Conference; China; urban policy; the Training and Education Group; African American unemployment; defense conversion; G-7 Jobs Conference.... The agenda goes on. These weekly meetings were an attempt to ensure that all the balls stayed in the air. As you can see, there were many issues that would be considered beyond the scope of the Treasury or OMB's responsibilities.

Another benefit of the NEC was proximity to the president. Immediacy increases the ability to give information to the president and receive decisions from him. Some might ask, Well, why not go to the office of the chief of staff to coordinate economic policy? Having spent time there as well, my answer to that question is, Yes, the proximity is there, but the office of the chief of staff does not have staff, nor should it. The other reason is that like the departments that I was speaking of, the office of the chief of staff has many, many other functions and many, many other things that it's focusing on, so it would not have a direct focus on economic policy.

Though the following points are not part of why I believe that the NEC is the best home for economic policy, I would like to mention a few things that I think are important to its functioning well. Having been on the receiving end of the NEC's economic coordination, I have found that there are some things that are important for the NEC to keep in mind as it works with departments. First, there's institutional bias for a reason. Implementation of refundable tax credits is hard. The NEC should recognize why that bias is there and is expressed, and should consider this difficulty when making policy. Second, it is very important that the NEC, which is entirely staffed by political appointees, recognize and appreciate the dedication of the career civil servants. And finally, I believe, the NEC should recognize the challenges of running a department and the fact that department heads have many other responsibilities besides participation in economic coordination.

The second point I wanted to touch on is integration of the NEC within the rest of the White House and why that's important to serving a president well. I think that in the Clinton/Gore administration the NEC added value beyond economic policy-making.

For example, the NEC reviewed all the president's speeches. It is a simple thing, but it contributed to consistency, clarity, and accuracy with regard to economic policy. The president was saying what the Treasury secretary was saying, what the head of the NEC was saying, what the head of the Council of Economic Advisers was saying. The NEC worked very closely with the CEA on this function. Speech review helped ensure that the administration had a consistent voice on economic policy and that economic policy would be expressed, no matter what the topic.

Second, with regard to integration, I think the NEC helped keep economic policy front and center, and gave life to the not so delicate phrase "It's the economy, stupid." The NEC participated in message and scheduling meetings, insuring that economic policy was a part of all the communication that the White House did. Another example of this economic focus is that the CEA, supported by the NEC, would report the economic statistics in the senior staff meetings.

For those of us who are policy wonks, and that category probably includes everyone in this room, the fact that CPI, PPI, and GNP were just as recognized and understood as DNC by the entire senior staff of the White House was a very important thing. Senior staff would go back to their own staff meetings and report economic statistics. They became an ingrained part of our measure of success. The number would come out, and then Gene Sperling would generally refer back to the promises we had made in the campaign in terms of certain economic goals. The easiest one was unemployment, for which we had set specific goals.

Finally, on the integration issue, I think it's equally important that others be integrated into the NEC process. It would be fair to say that the original NEC made some errors in our first month when we failed to involve the Office of Legislative Affairs and other parts of the non-policy-making organization. A specific example would be that we might not have done grazing fees had we had broader conversations about that topic in the initial budget. Later we would always invite John Hilley or Larry Stein or Chuck Brain, the heads of the Office of Legislative Affairs, to our Social Security meetings.

The final thing that I wanted to touch upon is the importance of personalities and work styles in making economic policy. As an undergraduate I took Professor Richard Neustadt's course on the presidency. I was an undergraduate, so I was affiliated with the government department here at Harvard. I took the course and could not really understand why there was all this talk of personalities. I wanted a more analytical framework. This talk of personalities . . . that really couldn't be the answer to how the White House "works"! I'd been through several years here at Harvard and was taught to be analytically rigorous. Then after two weeks at the White House I got out my Neustadt notes.

I think personalities are an important factor with regard to economic coordination for the basic reason that a big part of the policy-making ball game is trust. You have to trust the system; you have to believe that when you go to the NEC you'll get a fair hearing. I think that belief builds the confidence that when a decision is not made in your favor or your way, you will still articulate the administration's position, and not go off the record with reporters and say, "That's our decision, but. . . ." So I think that trust is very important, and that *is* related to personalities.

We did not start with a lot of formal organizational rules when we formed the NEC, in terms of what it would do. But the one thing that Rubin gave very clear instructions on as we were trying to put together the staff for the NEC was that the staff would not have "sharp elbows." And Rubin's guidance on the character of the NEC staff is reflected in the chapter. We didn't know if our different policy areas were the correct ones, but we knew that those choices were something we could fix if we got the other part right: hiring smart people with no sharp elbows. That tone came from the top and built trust in the organization very early on that was carried on throughout. The idea of the NEC was not to dominate economic process, but instead to lead it.

The final point on the questions of personalities and work style has to do with the president. I think the president's own style matters very much in making these entities or processes work. I think President Clinton's own style and personality were relevant to the success of the NEC. He is not a person who likes the pitting of people against each other. Instead he prefers tension created out of a collegial teamwork approach. That's how he likes to hear ideas and how he likes to work. He prefers a creative tension of ideas instead of people against each other. So a coordinated effort served him better in terms of the different approaches that have been mentioned as options for economic policy-making.

I think another reason the NEC worked for this president is that he also had a desire to move on many, many fronts at the same time, and even with all these different issues he could go to one place. The president would send out notes, and the notes would come in different forms, in the form of either questions or ideas. But he had one place to go—and a place to go where he knew, if he sent out an idea that was relevant to Secretary Reich, or Secretary Brown, or the CEA, that it would be shared with them, and that whatever response he received would be coordinated. So for this president, a person who was very interested in a broad range of things, having one place to go was an efficient approach to policy-making.

While I believe that the NEC during the Clinton administration had many successes and a number of failures as well, the NEC as it was constructed in the past administration was an essential part of President Clinton's implementation of his economic policy vision.

Comments

R. Glenn Hubbard

I would like to begin by thanking Jeff Frankel and Peter Orszag for organizing this conference. The project is a major undertaking, and the contributions are very interesting. When Jeff and I first started talking about my coming here some months ago, we started with one topic and then another, and he managed to find the one topic that I really know very little about in the conference, but I'll try to offer a few observations based on learning by doing. The chapter is very topical and well written. While I do not agree with the analysis of economic policy in the chapter, the chapter's introduction to policy management issues is excellent.

The chapter has four excellent approaches, the first two of which I think are its central contributions. First is a very good history of economic decision-making, an area that is underresearched relative to analysis of decision-making in the private sector. The second important contribution of the chapter is a thoughtful reflection on desirable characteristics of a National Economic Council. And I say "a" National Economic Council, not "the" National Economic Council because, as the paper points out, there have in modern times generally been coordinating bodies, though they have had different names. The question is really which characteristics lead to success or failure. The other two parts of the chapter, which are also interesting, are case studies of decision-making during the Clinton presidency and a discussion of the importance of multiple skill attributes for economic policy-makers.

The relative lack of attention paid, both in academic circles and in policy circles, to organizational structures in the White House or in government compared to the corporate sector is striking. For example, there are whole subfields in corporate finance and industrial organization that study the endogenous response of organizations to environments, with the premise that competition leads to a weeding out of weak organizational forms. While the White House structure lacks competition to weed out inefficient organizational forms in real time, the subject of organizational competition is still relevant, as I will argue shortly.

Another reason that relatively little attention is paid to White House organization is the tendency to believe "it's just the personality, stupid," or it's just the individuals involved that matter, as opposed to the organizational framework. I think that belief is incorrect, and the chapter makes that point well. We need to devote substantially more attention in this area to studying policy or management coordination, much as we do in the business world.

An important conclusion of the chapter is that any successful approach to economic policy-making requires three elements. One is the easy part, an understanding of economics and bringing good economics to bear. The other two are harder—paying attention to politics (not a natural thing for many professional economists) and the management of the policy process. How can one get better than two out of three of economics, politics, and management? To give an example, in the Clinton administration, the 1993 budget—and I'll, again, hold aside my negative views on the economic policy merits of that budget—stands as an advance (at least in the Clinton administration's view of the economics) with respect to both the politics of the time and management of the policy process. Likewise, enacting President George W. Bush's initial tax cut brought together economics, politics, and management.

It is possible to fail that triple test. In the Clinton years, for example, the Social Security debate fared better on economics plus management than on the current politics of the situation. Sometimes the process successfully incorporates politics and management, but not economics. In the Clinton administration, I would place climate change policy and the HOPE Scholarship tax credit in that category. The Clinton health care proposal, I would argue, fails all three. In general, the combination of economics, politics, and management is easy to say and hard to do. Although it is difficult to incorporate all three successfully, I will return later to factors most likely to lead to success.

What, then, is the "right" model for economic policy coordination? In my own thinking I am attracted to the idea that Roger Porter advanced some years ago of a distinction among three types of organizations. The first is "centralized decision-making," which I would think of loosely as the White House senior staff model. It's 7:30 a.m., the senior staff decides the positions to be taken by the agencies. Then the agencies ratify the staff's vision of the world. Under a second approach, which Porter termed "multiple advocacy," the agencies design policy approaches with much less guidance, giving rise to periodic consternation in senior staff meetings because the secretary of X or the secretary of Y has given a speech that seems contrary to administration policy. The third, or "ad hoc," approach represents a give and take between the agencies and the White

House senior staff; this practical approach is one in which a coordinating body like a National Economic Council can be successful.

The coordinating models that have struck me as most successful (in terms of economic policy management if not economic policy) in previous administrations were the late Nixon period and the Ford period. In the Nixon administration, for example, my colleague Ken Dam, who is currently deputy secretary designate at the Treasury, played the coordinating role. In that structure there were regular meetings, with a true coordinator—not an entrepreneur—bringing together the Treasury, the CEA, the OMB and the White House senior staff, and that model also worked with good personal relationships among the secretary of the Treasury, the CEA chairman, and the OMB director. In the Ford period, Bill Seidman and Roger Porter played the coordinating role.

The chapter helpfully highlights areas of organizational tension in a coordinator model, particularly if a coordinator lapses into being an entrepreneur. An obvious source, highlighted in the chapter, is the potential tension between the National Economic Council on the one hand and the Council of Economic Advisers (CEA) on the other. An idea behind an NEC-type organization would be that the NEC would be responsible for policy coordination and the CEA for economic analysis. That is indeed the division of labor in the current Bush administration, and I take it, it was much of the theme of the division of labor in the Clinton administration. Important questions remain, however. What is the division of issues? Is it simply by analytical content—that is, if you need to know elasticities, you ask the CEA; if it's policy coordination you don't? Is it by policy interest?

Another dividing issue is talent. Where do the particularly talented staff members want to be? I think both groups have done very well here. The biggest tension is probably policy development—that is, not just the division of providing advice, but who develops economic policies within the administration, and what is the process to communicate proposals to the president?

Two questions in this particular NEC-CEA potential tension are, first, How much "E" should there be in NEC? Currently the principal "E" in NEC is Larry Lindsey, the NEC director and a good economist, with the NEC staff almost entirely not economists. That staffing is appropriate for an NEC designed to facilitate coordination.

The second question is, What is the source of the CEA's survival over all these years? It has one seat at the table in senior staff meetings, and a seat with the president, but only a small staff and a small budget. I think there are several reasons for the CEA's longevity. First, the fact that the CEA has a small (though high-quality) staff, makes it a small target as well. The CEA has successfully been the Switzerland of the executive branch. Importantly, the CEA has maintained a good reputation for unbiased analysis that is important for the president and his political advisers. Finally, the CEA chairmen have generally avoided the temptation to reach for more than they can handle—that is, to try to grab too much operational turf, losing the CEA's analytical role.

Another area of organizational tension is that between the NEC and the National Security Council (NSC). Whether an issue is "economics" is increasingly hard to define. For example, is global climate change an NSC issue, or an economics issue? What about international finance? Who will place items in the in box of NSC and NEC?

I believe it is possible to identify key success factors in economic policy coordination. A critical factor is presidential involvement and interest. President Clinton's 1993 budget and President Bush's 2001 tax cut were obtained first and foremost because the president put himself and his credibility on the line. When that commitment is not there—as in President George H. W. Bush's 1992 health plan or Clinton's botched Social Security initiative—the outcome is less successful. In addition, personalities of senior economic policy-makers do matter.

Another success factor worthy of mention is that success is made easier when an area is neatly defined. A tax cut is an easy-to-define article of economic policy. International trade is a less well-defined area. Harder still is a topic such as global climate change, which is environmental policy, international security policy, and international economic policy at the same time. Another sense where "neatly defined" is a potential success factor in economic policy is analytical content. In the current administration the CEA has played a major role in the debate over the patients' bill of rights—in part because any attempt to defeat an unreasonable patients' bill of rights hinges on economic, analytical arguments. On an issue such as policy toward steel, the economics are so clear that it is a bit harder for an economist to have an influence.

To conclude, the chapter is a great contribution. The background history alone is something one should definitely read. The paper also suggests extensions. Business schools, for example, struggle with how to teach "leadership." What are the key "success factors" to communicate to M.B.A. students about leadership? The same issue arises in public management. More reflection on and study of the key success factors that make White House or presidential decision-making successful are likely to be at least as important as our analysis of corporate decision-making.

Comments

Roger B. Porter

Challenges and Functions

The development of an administration's economic policy partakes of two characteristics. It is at once highly personalized, reflecting the style and inclinations of the president, and at the same time it is the product of institutional arrangements adopted and shaped during the course of an administration.

Since the institutionalization of the White House reached a new level in the Nixon administration, the processes for coordinating economic policy have grown, and the staff capability to do so has increased. Presidents have come to appreciate the roles White House entities can play in performing four important functions.

First, the president needs help in determining which of the myriad of issues clamoring for his attention merit his time and the time of his senior advisers. This sifting and sorting function can play a crucial role in appropriately focusing the efforts of senior officials.

Second, the president needs expert policy advice designed to provide the basis for informed decisions. Most policy issues important enough to command the president's attention involve a large number of considerations that he should take into account. These considerations are usually represented by officials who hold strong institutional and personal views. Presidents benefit from competing advice, and the process by which they get it is anything but automatic. As government interaction with the economy has grown, managing the process by which presidents receive their advice has become more important and more challenging.

Third, the president needs help to resolve disputes and policy differences between departments and agencies. Not every issue merits the president's attention, but administrations must present a united front if they are to succeed. In resolving disputes, presidential staff entities have a powerful advantage in that the White House represents neutral ground for departments and agencies. The stronger the White House entity, the greater its utility. Success often depends on the perception that one speaks for the president. Skill in resolving disputes can do much to help produce coherent administration policies.

Fourth, the president needs help in communicating and persuasively articulating policy. Formulating policy is only part of the task. Persuading others (generally outside the administration) to support the president's policy preferences is also essential.

Assessing the National Economic Council

At various points and in various ways, the Nixon, Ford, Reagan, Bush, and Clinton administrations sought to institutionalize economic policy-making processes to perform these and other functions, often with considerable success. Nixon experimented, with only limited success, in establishing a White House–centered entity to address international economic policy issues. The Ford Economic Policy Board represented a sustained effort to coordinate domestic and international economic policy from the White House. The array of cabinet councils of the first Reagan term were streamlined into an Economic Policy Council and a Domestic Policy Council at the beginning of Reagan's second term, which continued during the first Bush administration.

The chapter by Peter and Jonathan Orszag and Laura Tyson based on their experience with the National Economic Council illuminates an eight-year-long effort by the Clinton administration to coordinate economic policy. As with all such efforts, including those of its predecessors, it included both successes and setbacks.

In assessing it, four themes are worth noting.

First, the National Economic Council seems to have enjoyed the president's support and earned the president's confidence. The formal NEC structure remained in place the entire eight years, and the inevitable informal processes that arise in every administration seem not to have undermined its basic effectiveness.

Second, the National Economic Council was clearly White House centered. In each of the past six administrations, the president has formally identified the secretary of the Treasury as the administration's principal economic spokesman. But chairmanship of the NEC and responsibility for its coordination efforts firmly rested in the White House. Previous councils sometimes split responsibility, with the secretary of the Treasury at least nominally chairing the entity while the staff was centered in the White House. As a White House–based operation, the NEC diligently sought to establish an excellent set of working relationships with other Executive Office of the President entities—the Office of Management and Budget, the National Security Council staff, and the Council of Economic Advisers. Competition between these entities appears to have been minimal and collaboration the norm.

Third, one is also struck by the collegiality that existed and the trust that developed among the four core elements in the economic policy making community—the Treasury, the Office of Management and Budget, the Council of Economic Advisers, and the NEC staff. Other departments and agencies— Labor, Commerce, Agriculture, State, Energy, Transportation, the Office of the U.S. Trade Representative, and so on—were engaged on particular issues, but the core of four formed the heart of the NEC.

Moreover, these four core agencies remained remarkably united in dealing with those outside their circle—whether in departments and agencies or within the White House in offices with other priorities. Political realities inevitably intrude, forcing adjustments in substantive policy proposals. The unity of the core economic agencies will not always prevail, but divisions among them make their task much more problematic.

Fourth, perhaps the feature that distinguished the NEC most from its predecessors was its attention to the task of articulating administration policy once the policy was developed. Over time, NEC officials sought higher public visibility as spokesmen and devoted considerable attention to the execution and defense of administration policy.

Differences of interest and viewpoints exist in every administration—differences of priorities and preferences, differences between idealists and realists, differences between economic and political imperatives. With a few notable exceptions, such as his early health care reform proposal, President Clinton pursued policies that relied on market-oriented arrangements—freer international trade and investment, restraining the rate of growth of federal spending, and incentives to reduce welfare rolls.

Many factors contributed to this policy pattern, not least budgetary circumstances. After the November 1994 elections, Republican majorities in Congress provided a powerful political reality encouraging the pursuit of such a policy path. A third factor, however, was the existence and the persistence of the core agencies of the National Economic Council. Having fought hard to promote fiscal discipline and free trade, these entities remained "the keepers of the flame." The stability of the National Economic Council and of the officials it convened played a substantial role in shaping the administration's economic policies, demonstrating that institutions and individuals matter.

Summary of Discussion

Martin Feldstein asked Roger Porter to compare the NEC as described by the panelists to the Cabinet Council on Economic Affairs (CCEA) in the Reagan administration. Specifically, Feldstein noted that prior to the session he felt the two entities were very similar. However, the discussion suggested to him some differences: While both entities provided policy analysis, the NEC also participated in outreach, marketing, and congressional relations.

Roger Porter responded that the discussion highlighted two differences. The first difference was the locus of coordination responsibility. In both the Reagan and Bush administrations, responsibility was not always clear, because the cabinet councils, and later the Economic Policy Council, were officially chaired by the secretary of the Treasury while the operating machinery was in the White House. The Clinton administration clarified and improved the situation by having the chairmanship of the coordinating entity in the White House.

The second difference, according to Porter, concerned the dual role of the entity in providing both substantive and political advice. Bringing these two together, not only in the process leading up to a decision, but ultimately in how that decision was packaged, sold, promoted, and ultimately negotiated with Congress was crucial. In the administrations he had served in, Porter noted, there were times when substantive and political reality were coordinated well, and other times when there was a fairly large disconnect.

On the issue of bringing together substantive and political reality, *Gene Sperling* added that the Clinton administration may have been a bit too guarded during the budget development process. Sperling highlighted the value in bringing together people of differing views. During the Asian financial crisis, for example, Sandy Berger and Madeleine Albright learned a lot about international financial currency movements, and Larry Summers and Bob Rubin gained a new understanding regarding what other countries might find diplomatically offensive. Sperling also noted that in the White House, you had to be concerned about larger dynamics and therefore needed different perspectives to see not just the first step, which might be obvious, but also to see how one step affected options six or seven steps down the road. An apparently poor decision at step 2 may actually lead to an overall better outcome at the end of all seven steps.

Lael Brainard commented that one of the chief original motivations for the creation of the NEC was the heightened importance of coordinating international economic policy. The decision to elevate this area and assign responsibility to the NEC remains quite contentious in the foreign policy community. Over time, the Clinton administration developed a regularized process, with a point person at the White House and a set of deputies whose primary concern was international economics. In previous administrations, international economics was one among a multitude of directorates at the NSC, with no one above the special assistant level having a deep interest in the issue. As a result, international economics often became an afterthought in the policy-making process. The Clinton administration, however, elevated international economics, developed a clear process around it, and evolved a fairly good division of labor between the NEC and NSC that ensured that the multiple dimensions of a particular policy were given due consideration. The elevation and coordination of international economic policy constitute a positive legacy that has been adopted by the new Bush administration.

Bill Hogan agreed with Gene Sperling's counsel to avoid perfection; seeking the best policy is bad politics. But he noted that in many situations bad policy is bad politics in the long run. The challenge internally is thus to decide when staff should voice their opposition. They risk being isolated if they do so too frequently.

Sperling agreed with Hogan, and reiterated his position that one should start with good policy and see how much of it can be accomplished politically. Many of the proudest moments of White House advisers, Sperling noted, are never seen. He pointed to the numerous times the administration resisted strong congressional, internal, and political pressure to use the Strategic Petroleum Reserve. Sperling also noted that good policy is often good politics. In 1993, Bob Rubin and Paul Begala argued about whether the president should criticize Alan Greenspan. Begala believed that he was concentrating on politics and Rubin was concentrating on economics. Rubin believed, however, that in this case good policy was good politics: respecting the independence of the Fed would help increase confidence, which was positive for the overall economy and therefore would ultimately help reelect Bill Clinton.

Rudolph Penner commented on staffing. He noted that the Economic Policy Board in the Ford administration had essentially no staff of its own, and instead relied on senior staff from other departments. That model had three positive effects: all the departments, having been intimately involved in the decisions, were fairly loyal to them; the expertise of the civil service was effectively tapped; and the coordinating body did not generate its own ideas. *Sperling* countered that without sufficient staff, the honest broker process would be jeopardized.

Martin Bailey commented on the evolving role of the CEA. In the early days of the CEA there were few economists in other agencies, but since then administrations have added economists to the OMB, Treasury, and other agencies. One sign of this trend is that when Congress changed hands in 1994, the CEA was initially zeroed out of the budget due to a belief that the CEA wasn't needed if the other agencies had their own economists. In addition, Baily argued, the CEA's practice of continuous rotation of staff is beneficial in that new perspectives are often voiced; however, this practice is also a disadvantage because it is difficult for people to be effective when they are only in government for a short period.

Murray Weidenbaum asked how the NEC could be a formal decision-making body if the council members do not automatically sit at the table but are invited on an issue-by-issue basis. That type of ad hoc approach, in his opinion, reflects informal decision-making.

Sperling agreed, but added that the formality existed in the sense of inclusion and transparency. There was a rigid process rule and people held to it. Without that formal dedication to inclusion and transparency, trust in the process would have been jeopardized.

David Wilcox suggested five characteristics of a good process: (1) exclusivity, in the sense that there is only one channel to the president; (2) inclusivity, in the sense that all relevant parties are included; (3) transparency, to ensure all parties are aware of others' views and are confident that their own opinions are heard; (4) conclusivity, so that there is closure to the issue; and (5) fairness.

Sylvia Mathews agreed that transparency is an important factor and offered the secretary of state's nightly notes to the president as an example of a nontransparent process. Because the notes were not transparent, they would often cause confusion and undermine trust.

Jeffrey Frankel questioned the panel on transparency with regard to the outside world, as opposed to within the government. He asked if there is a long-term trend away from the use of written memos through the hierarchy of government, toward the use of key decision meetings where all viewpoints are represented by persons who carry the information around in their head. If so, he worried about the costs imposed on the decision-making process and on historians from the lack of a detailed written record.

Glenn Hubbard noted that one cost of the trend away from written memos is that it taxes the time of people who must be in the meeting to contribute their perspective.

Sperling concluded the discussion by noting one reason for the reluctance to use written materials: they are too easily leaked. The Clinton administration increasingly relied on memos as the second term progressed, but also adopted a writing style that could convey politically salient details with little risk if the memos became public.

Contributors

Henry J. Aaron is currently a Bruce and Virginia MacLaury Senior Fellow in the Economic Studies Program at the Brookings Institution. From 1990 until 1996 he was the Director of the Economic Studies Program. His most recent book, which he coauthored with Robert D. Reischauer, is *Setting National Priorities: The 2000 Election and Beyond.*

Martin N. Baily joined the Institute for International Economics in Washington, DC, in March 2001. In August 1999, Dr. Baily was appointed by President Clinton as Chairman of the Council of Economic Advisers and a member of the Cabinet. Previously he was a Member of the Council and a Principal at McKinsey & Company.

Ambassador Charlene Barshefsky was sworn in as the 12th United States Trade Representative (USTR) on March 17, 1997, after serving as Deputy USTR beginning in 1993 and as Acting USTR since 1996. As USTR, she was a member of the Cabinet, the President's principal trade policy adviser and the Clinton administration's chief trade negotiator. She is currently Senior International Partner at the Washington, DC, law firm of Wilmer, Cutler, and Pickering.

Jagdish Bhagwati is the Arthur Lehman Professor of Economics and Professor of Political Science at Columbia University. His teaching and writings on trade theory and the politics and economics of free trade led him to an advisory role with the General Agreement on Tariffs and Trade in the early 1990s. Five volumes of his essays have been published by MIT Press, most recently *The Wind of the Hundred Days: How Washington Mismanaged Globalization* (2001).

Rebecca M. Blank is Dean of the Gerald R. Ford School of Public Policy at the University of Michigan. She is also Henry Carter Adams Collegiate Professor of Public Policy, and Professor of Economics. Prior to coming to Michigan, she served as a Member of the President's Council of Economic Advisers from 1997 to 1999. Previously she was on the economics faculty at Northwestern University.

Alan S. Blinder is the Gordon S. Rentschler Memorial Professor of Economics at Princeton University. Dr. Blinder was the Vice Chairman of the Board of Governors of the Federal Reserve System from June 1994 until January 1996. Dr. Blinder is the author of the textbook *Economics: Principles and Policy* (with William J. Baumol), from which well over a million college students have learned introductory economics.

Lael Brainard is a Senior Fellow at the Brookings Institution. She served as Deputy Assistant to the President for International Economics, Deputy National Economic Adviser, and the President's Representative to the G-8, all under President Clinton. She was responsible for coordinating the development and implementation of international financial, trade, and development policies. Previously, she was Associate Professor at MIT Sloan School.

Leonard Burman is a senior fellow at the Urban Institute and research professor at Georgetown University. He has held high-level positions in both the executive and legislative branches, serving as Deputy Assistant Secretary for Tax Analysis at the Treasury from 1998 to 2000, and as Senior Analyst at the Congressional Budget Office. He is the author of *The Labyrinth of Capital Gains Tax Policy: A Guide for the Perplexed*.

Richard N. Cooper is Maurits C. Boas Professor of International Economics at Harvard University. He has served the U.S. government on several occasions, as chairman of the National Intelligence Council (1995–97), chairman of the Federal Reserve Bank of Boston (1990–92), and Undersecretary of State for Economic Affairs (1977–81).

Charles B. Curtis is the President and Chief Operating Officer of the Nuclear Threat Initiative. Mr. Curtis served as Undersecretary and, later, Deputy Secretary of Energy from February 1994 to May 1997. He was the chief operating officer of the Department of Energy and, among other duties, had direct programmatic responsibility for all department science, technology, and national security programs.

David Cutler is Professor of Economics at Harvard University. During 1993 he was on leave as Senior Staff Economist at the Council of Economic Advisers and Director of the National Economic Council in the Clinton administration. Cutler's primary responsibilities were in helping to design the President's health reform plan.

J. Bradford DeLong is Professor of Economics at the University of California at Berkeley. He served in the U.S. government as Deputy Assistant Secretary of the Treasury for Economic Policy from 1993 to 1995. His major current project is *The Economic History of the Twentieth Century: Slouching Toward Utopia?*

Nancy-Ann DeParle is a Senior Adviser at J. P. Morgan Partners and an Adjunct Professor of Health Care Systems at the Wharton School. From 1993 to 2000 she served in the Clinton administration, first as Associate Director for Health and Personnel at the White House Office of Management and Budget, and then, from 1997 to 2000, as Administrator of the Health Care Financing Administration (HCFA), which runs the Medicare, Medicaid, and State Childrens' Health Insurance programs.

Peter Diamond is an Institute Professor at the Massachusetts Institute of Technology, where he has taught since 1966. He has been President and Chair of the Board of the National Academy of Social Insurance for whom he headed a panel, whose report, *Issues in Privatizing Social Security*, has been published by MIT Press. He has written on behavioral economics, public finance, social insurance, and uncertainty.

Esther Dyson as an investor/commentator focuses on emerging companies, emerging markets, and emerging technologies (peer-to-peer, artificial intelligence, the Internet, wireless applications). In 1997 she wrote *Release 2.0: A Design for Living in the Digital Age*. In November 2001 she finished a two-year term as founding chairman of ICANN, the Internet Corporation for Assigned Names and Numbers, the international agency charged with setting policy for the Internet's core infrastructure (technical standards and the Domain Name System) independent of government control.

Barry Eichengreen is the George C. Pardee and Helen N. Pardee Professor of Economics and Professor of Political Science at the University of California, Berkeley, where he has taught since 1987. His books include *Toward a New International Financial Architecture* (Institute for International Economics, 1999).

David T. Ellwood is Lucius N. Littauer Professor of Political Economy and former academic dean at Harvard University's Kennedy School of Government. He previously served as Assistant Secretary for Planning and Evaluation, Department of Health and Human Services, and was cochair of President Clinton's initial efforts on welfare reform.

Douglas W. Elmendorf is a senior economist at the Federal Reserve Board. He was previously a deputy assistant secretary for economic policy at the Treasury Department, a senior economist at the Council of Economic Advisers, and a principal analyst at the Congressional Budget Office.

Martin Feldstein is the George F. Baker Professor of Economics at Harvard University and President of the National Bureau of Economic Research. The NBER is a private, nonprofit research organization that has specialized for more than 75 years in producing nonpartisan studies. From 1982 through 1984, he was Chairman of the Council of Economic Advisers and President Reagan's chief economic adviser. In 1977 he received the John Bates Clark Medal of the American Economic Association, a prize awarded every two years to the economist under the age of 40 who is judged to have made the greatest contribution to economic science.

Stanley Fischer was, at the time of the conference, the First Deputy Managing Director of the International Monetary Fund, a post he assumed in September 1994. Prior to taking up his position at the fund, Mr. Fischer was the Killian Professor and the Head of the Department of Economics at the Massachusetts Institute of Technology. From January 1988 to August 1990 he served as Vice President, Development Economics and Chief Economist at the World Bank.

George T. Frampton became acting chair of the Council on Environmental Quality on November 7, 1998. From 1993 to 1997, Mr. Frampton served as Assistant Secretary of the Interior for Fish and Wildlife and Parks. Before assuming his position as Assistant Secretary of Interior in 1993, Mr. Frampton was president of the Wilderness Society from 1986 to 1993.

Jeffrey Frankel is James W. Harpel Professor of Capital Formation and Growth at Harvard University's Kennedy School of Government. He also directs the National Bureau of Economic Research program in International Finance and Macroeconomics. He worked in the White House, at the U.S. Council of Economic Advisers, during 1983–84 and 1996–99. In the Senate-confirmed position of Member on the Council during 1997–99, he had responsibility for international economics, macroeconomics, and the environment. He was previously Professor of Economics at the University of California, Berkeley. Books include *Regional Trading Blocs* (1997).

Victor R. Fuchs is the Henry J. Kaiser, Jr., Professor of Economics, Emeritus, at Stanford University. He is a member of the Institute of Medicine, President (1995) and Distinguished Fellow (1990) of the American Economic Association, and recipient of the Distinguished Investigator Award (1988) and the Distinguished Fellow Award (1996) of the Association for Health Services Research, and of the 1991 Baxter Foundation Health Services Research Prize.

Robert R. Glauber became the chief executive officer and president of the National Association of Securities Dealers, Inc. (NASD) in November 2000. Glauber served as Undersecretary of the Treasury for Finance from 1989 to 1992. In 1987, Glauber served as Executive Director of the Task Force on Market Mechanisms ("Brady Commission") appointed by President Reagan to study the October 1987 stock market crash.

Joshua Gotbaum is currently Executive Director of the September 11th Fund. He was, seriatim, Assistant Secretary of Defense for Economic Security, Assistant Secretary of the Treasury for Economic Policy, Executive Associate Director of OMB, and then also Controller at OMB in the Clinton administration. Prior to joining the administration, he was a partner in the investment banking firm of Lazard Frères & Company.

Robert Greenstein founded the Center on Budget and Policy Priorities in 1981 and has served since then as its Executive Director. In 1994 he was appointed by President Clinton to serve on the Bipartisan Commission on Entitlement and Tax Reform. From 1979 to 1980, he was Administrator of the Food and Nutrition Service at the U.S. Department of Agriculture, the agency that operates the nation's domestic food assistance programs.

Jonathan Gruber is a Professor of Economics at the Massachusetts Institute of Technology, where he has taught since 1992. He is also the Director of the Program on Children at the National Bureau of Economic Research. During the 1997–98 academic year, he was on leave as Deputy Assistant Secretary for Economic Policy at the Treasury Department.

Robert W. Hahn is director of the AEI-Brookings Joint Center for Regulatory Studies, a resident scholar at the American Enterprise Institute, and a research associate at Harvard University. Previously, he served as a senior staff member of the President's Council of Economic Advisers.

Ron Haskins is currently a Senior Fellow of the Economic Studies Program at the Brookings Institution, as well as a Codirector of the Welfare Reform and Beyond project. Before coming to Brookings, from 1995 to 2000, Haskins was the Majority Staff Director of the U.S. House of Representatives Subcommittee on Human Resources.

William W. Hogan is Lucius N. Littauer Professor of Public Policy and Administration and Faculty Chair of the Ph.D. programs at the Kennedy School of Government, Harvard University. He is also Research Director of the Harvard Electricity Policy Group, which is developing alternative strategies for the transition to a more competitive electricity market.

R. Glenn Hubbard is Chairman of President George W. Bush's Council of Economic Advisors. He is on leave as Russell L. Carson Professor of Economics and Finance and Codirector of the Entrepreneurship Program at Columbia University, where he has also served as Senior Vice Dean of the Graduate School of Business. From 1991 to 1993 he was Deputy Assistant Secretary (Tax Analysis) of the U.S. Treasury Department.

Ira A. Jackson is director and faculty chair of the Center for Business and Government. Jackson was previously executive vice president of BankBoston, where he was responsible for a variety of corporate activities, including economic analysis; regulatory affairs; philanthropy; community, press, and governmental relations; public affairs; community banking and CRA; global projects; and corporate communications. He has served as a top policy adviser to two mayors: Kenneth Gibson of Newark, New Jersey, and Kevin White of Boston; and served as Massachusetts Commissioner of Revenue.

Dale Jorgenson is the director of the Program on Technology and Economic Policy at CBG and Frederic Eaton Abbe Professor of Economics at Harvard University. He was awarded the John Bates Clark Medal of the American Economic Association and was president of the Econometric Society.

Paul L. Joskow is the Elizabeth and James Killian Professor of Economics and Management at MIT and Director of the MIT Center for Energy and Environmental Policy Research. Professor Joskow has been on the MIT faculty since 1972 and served as Head of the MIT Department of Economics from 1994 to 1998. He was a member of the EPA's Acid Rain Advisory Committee and currently serves on the Environmental Economics Committee of the EPA's Science Advisory Board.

Lawrence F. Katz is Professor of Economics at Harvard University. He served as the Chief Economist of the U.S. Department of Labor from January 1993 to August 1994.

Alan B. Krueger is the Bendheim Professor of Economics and Public Affairs at Princeton University. He is also Director of the Princeton Industrial Relations Section and editor of *The Journal of Economic Perspectives*. He writes a regular column on the economic scene for the *New York Times*. He served as the chief economist of the U.S. Department of Labor from August 1994 to August 1995.

Robert Z. Lawrence is the Albert L. Williams Professor of International Trade and Investment at the Kennedy School of Government, Harvard University, and a Senior Fellow, the Institute for International Economics. Dr. Lawrence served as a Member of President Clinton's Council of Economic Advisers from March 1999 to January 2001. He has held the New Century Chair at the Brookings Institution, and founded and edited the Brookings Trade Forum. His books include *Single World, Divided Nations* (1996) and *Regionalism, Multilateralism, and Deeper Integration* (1996).

Jeffrey B. Liebman is Associate Professor of Public Policy at the Kennedy School of Government, Harvard University. From 1998 to 1999, Liebman served as special assistant to the president for economic policy and coordinated the Clinton administration's Social Security reform technical working group.

Robert E. Litan is the Vice President and Director of the Economic Studies Program at the Brookings Institution. He also holds the Cabot Family Chair in Economics. Dr. Litan also has served as Associate Director of the Office of Management and Budget; as Deputy Assistant Attorney General, in charge of civil antitrust litigation and regulatory issues, at the Department of Justice; and as the regulatory and legal staff specialist at the President's Council of Economic Advisers.

N. Gregory Mankiw is Professor of Economics at Harvard University. His work has been published in academic journals, such as the *American Economic Review, Journal of Political Economy*, and *Quarterly Journal of Economics*, and in more popular forums, such as the *New York Times, Financial Times*, and *Wall Street Journal*. He is author of the best-selling textbooks *Macroeconomics* and *Principles of Economics*. He has served as director for the Monetary Economics Program at the National Bureau of Economic Research.

Sylvia Mathews is currently Executive Vice President of the Bill and Melinda Gates Foundation headquartered in Seattle, Washington. She was confirmed as Deputy Director of OMB by the Senate in 1998. Prior to OMB, Ms. Mathews was appointed Assistant to the President and Deputy Chief of Staff to the President in January 1997. Before that, she served as Chief of Staff to Secretary of the Treasury Robert Rubin from 1995 to 1997.

Mark McClellan has been nominated by President George W. Bush to be a member of his Council of Economic Advisers and confirmed by the Senate. He is on leave as Assistant Professor of Economics at Stanford University. McClellan has worked extensively with administrative data sets as a method to assess the impact of medical technology. He was also Deputy Assistant Secretary of the Treasury in the preceding administration.

Allan H. Meltzer, in addition to his position as Professor at Carnegie Mellon University, has also been a Visiting Scholar at the American Enterprise Institute in Washington, DC, since 1989. He has been a member of the President's Economic Policy Advisory Board, and during 1988–89 he was an acting member of the President's Council of Economic Advisers. From 1973 to 1996 he was coeditor of the Carnegie-Rochester Conference Series on Public Policy. He was Chairman of the congressionally created Commission on International Financial Institutions.

Lawrence Mishel is the Vice President of the Economic Policy Institute and was the research director from 1987 to 1999. He is the coauthor of *The State of Working America*, a biannual volume on trends in living standards.

Joseph P. Newhouse, John D. MacArthur Professor of Health Policy and Management, is head of the Interfaculty Initiative on Health Policy and directs the Division of Health Policy Research and Education, which administers the Ph.D. program in Health Policy at Harvard. He edits the *Journal of Health Economics*, has chaired the Prospective Payment Assessment Commission, and been the Vice Chair of the Medicare Payment Advisory Commission.

William A. Niskanen has served as chairman of the Cato Institute since 1985, having previously been member and then acting chairman of President Reagan's Council of Economic Advisers. Niskanen has taught economics at the University of California at Berkeley and Los Angeles. He has also served as director of economics at Ford Motor Company.

Joseph S. Nye, Jr., Don K. Price Professor of Public Policy, is Dean of the Kennedy School. He returned to Harvard in December 1995 after serving as Assistant Secretary of Defense for International Security Affairs, where he won two Distinguished Service medals, and as Chair of the National Intelligence Council. Nye joined the Harvard faculty in 1964, where he has served as Associate Dean of Arts and Sciences. From 1977 to 1979, Nye was Deputy to the Undersecretary of State for Security Assistance, Science, and Technology. He is the author of *Bound to Lead: The Changing Nature of American Power*.

Jonathan M. Orszag is the Managing Director of Sebago Associates, Inc. Prior to joining Sebago Associates, Mr. Orszag served as the Assistant to the U.S. Secretary of Commerce, as Director of the Office of Policy and Strategic Planning, on the Staff of the National Economic Council, and as an economic aide to the Secretary of Labor.

Peter R. Orszag is the Joseph A. Pechman Senior Fellow in Tax and Fiscal Policy at the Brookings Institution and President of Sebago Associates, Inc., a public policy consulting firm. He previously served as Special Assistant to the President for Economic Policy at the White House, and as a Senior Economist and Senior Adviser at the President's Council of Economic Advisers.

Rudolph G. Penner, an authority on government budgeting and public finance, holds the Arjay and Frances Miller Chair in Public Policy at the Urban Institute. He directed the United States Congressional Budget Office from 1983 to 1987, and has been a senior staff economist at the Council of Economic Advisers and chief economist at the Office of Management and Budget.

Robert Pitofsky was sworn in as Chairman of the Federal Trade Commission on April 12, 1995, and served until 2001. Previously Pitofsky was a Professor of Law at the Georgetown University Law Center and Of Counsel to the Washington, DC, law firm of Arnold and Porter. He also has held the positions of Commissioner (1978–81) and Director of the Bureau of Consumer Protection (1970–73) at the FTC.

William Poole took office as President of the Federal Reserve Bank of St. Louis in March 1998. Prior to assuming that position, Poole was the Herbert H. Goldberger Professor of Economics at Brown University, Providence, RI, whose faculty he joined in 1974. He was a member of the Council of Economic Advisers in the first Reagan administration.

Roger B. Porter is IBM Professor of Business and Government at the Kennedy School of Government, Harvard University. He served for more than a decade in senior economic policy positions in the White House, most recently as Assistant to the President for Economic and Domestic Policy from 1989 to 1993. He served as Director of the White House Office of Policy Development in the Reagan administration and as Executive Secretary of the President's Economic Policy Board during the Ford administration. He is the author of *Presidential Decision Making*.

Paul R. Portney has been President of Resources for the Future (RFF) since 1995. An economist by training, he joined the research staff of RFF in 1972. During 1979–80, Portney took leave from RFF to be the chief economist at the Council on Environmental Quality in the Executive Office of the President.

Bruce Reed is currently President of the Democratic Leadership Council in Washington, DC. He previously served in the White House, as the Assistant to the President for Domestic Policy and Director of the Domestic Policy Council. As the President's chief domestic policy adviser, he oversaw a variety of issues including education, crime, welfare reform, tobacco, family policy, health care, and philanthropy. Mr. Reed worked at the White House throughout the Clinton-Gore administration—first as Deputy Assistant to the President for Domestic Policy and later as Assistant to the President for Policy Planning.

Robert B. Reich is University Professor and Maurice B. Hexter Professor of Social and Economic Policy at Brandeis University. He served as the 22nd Secretary of Labor during President Clinton's first term. Previously, he was on the faculty of Harvard's Kennedy School of Government. He served as an Assistant to the Solicitor General in the Ford administration, and he headed the policy planning staff of the Federal Trade Commission in the Carter administration. He is author of eight books, including *The Work of Nations*, which has been translated into 17 languages, *Locked in the Cabinet,* his best-selling memoir of his years in the Clinton administration, and most recently, *The Future of Success.*

Robert D. Reischauer is President of the Urban Institute, Washington. Previously he was a Senior Fellow at the Brookings Institution. From March 1989 until March 1995, he served as the Director of the Congressional Budget Office (CBO). He is the Chair of the National Academy of Social Insurance's project "Restructuring Medicare for the Long-Term."

Alice M. Rivlin is a Senior Fellow in the Economic Studies program at the Brookings Institution and Chair of the District of Columbia Financial Management Assistance Authority. Ms. Rivlin served as Vice Chair of the Federal Reserve Board from 1996 to 1999. She was Director of the White House Office of Management and Budget from 1994 to 1996, and Deputy Director from 1993 to 1994. Ms. Rivlin was the founding Director of the Congressional Budget Office, a position she held from 1975 to 1983.

Paul M. Romer is the STANCO 25 Professor of Economics in the Graduate School of Business at Stanford University and a Senior Fellow of the Hoover Institution. He was the lead developer of new growth theory. Before coming to Stanford, he was a professor of economics at the University of California at Berkeley and the University of Chicago.

Cecilia E. Rouse is a Professor of Economics and Public Affairs at Princeton University. During 1998–99 she served in the White House at the National Economic Council.

Robert Rubin is currently the Chairman of the Executive Committee of the Board of Citigroup, Inc. Prior to Citigroup he served as the 70th Secretary of the Treasury from January 10, 1995, to July 2, 1999. Rubin also served in the White House as Assistant to the President for Economic Policy. In that capacity, he directed the activities of the National Economic Council. Prior to joining the administration, he spent 26 years at Goldman Sachs & Company in New York City and served as Co–Senior Partner and Cochairman from 1990 to 1992.

Pamela Samuelson is a Professor at the University of California at Berkeley with a joint appointment in the School of Information Management and Systems as well as in the School of Law, where she is a Director of the Berkeley Center for Law and Technology. In June 1997 she was named a Fellow of the John D. and Catherine T. MacArthur Foundation. Samuelson served on the National Research Council's Study Committee on Intellectual Property Rights and the National Information Infrastructure, which produced a report entitled "The Digital Dilemma: Intellectual Property Rights in an Information Age."

Richard Schmalensee is the John C. Head III Dean and Professor of Economics and Management at the MIT Sloan School of Management. He was a member of the Council of Economic Advisers in the first Bush administration.

Carl Shapiro is the Transamerica Professor of Business Strategy at the Haas School of Business at the University of California at Berkeley. He also is Director of the Institute of Business and Economic Research, and Professor of Economics in the Economics Department, at UC Berkeley. Professor Shapiro served as Deputy Assistant Attorney General for Economics in the Antitrust Division of the U.S. Department of Justice during 1995–96. Professor Shapiro is the author with Hal R. Varian of *Information Rules: A Strategic Guide to the Network Economy*.

Philip R. Sharp is a Lecturer in Public Policy at the Kennedy School of Government, Harvard University. He is Former Director of the Institute of Politics at Harvard University and an Associate of the Harvard Electricity Policy Group. He serves on the Secretary of Energy Advisory Board. He was a 10-term member of Congress from 1975 to 1995 from Indiana, and served as Chair of the Energy and Power Subcommittee of the House Committee on Energy and Commerce from 1981 to 1995.

Robert M. Solow is Institute Professor Emeritus at the Massachusetts Institute of Technology, where he has been a professor of economics since 1949. He received the Nobel Prize in Economics in 1987 for his theory of growth, and the National Medal of Science in 2000. He is past president of the American Economics Association and the Econometric Society. He is currently Foundation Scholar at the Russell Sage Foundation.

Gene B. Sperling, President Clinton's national economic adviser and director of the National Economic Council (NEC), joined the Brookings Institution as a guest scholar in January 2001. As director of the NEC, Sperling coordinated the administration's economic policy and played a key role in the 1993 and 1997 Deficit Reduction Acts, and the policy of saving the surplus for Social Security and debt reduction, among other things. Prior to joining the NEC, Mr. Sperling served as deputy director of economic policy for the 1992 presidential transition and economic policy director of the Clinton-Gore presidential campaign.

Robert N. Stavins is the Albert Pratt Professor of Business and Government, and Director of the Environmental Economics Program at Harvard's Kennedy School. He is also a University Fellow of Resources for the Future and Chair of the U.S. Environmental Protection Agency's Environmental Economics Advisory Committee. Stavins directed Project 88, a bipartisan effort cochaired by former Senator Timothy Wirth and the late Senator John Heinz, to develop market-based strategies for environmental protection. His recent books include

Public Policies for Environmental Protection, Economics of the Environment, and *Environmental Economics and Public Policy.*

Eugene Steuerle is a senior fellow at the Urban Institute and author of a weekly column for *Tax Notes Magazine.* Earlier in his career he served in various positions in the Treasury Department under four different presidents and was eventually appointed Deputy Assistant Secretary of the Treasury for Tax Analysis. Between 1984 and 1986 he served as Economic Coordinator and original organizer of the Treasury's tax reform effort.

Lawrence Summers is the former Nathaniel Ropes Professor of Political Economy at Harvard. In the past decade he has served in a series of senior public policy positions, most recently as Secretary of the Treasury of the United States from July 1998 to January 2001. Since July 1, 2001, he has been the 27th President of Harvard University. In 1993, Summers was awarded the John Bates Clark Medal, one of the signal honors of his profession, given every two years to the outstanding American economist under the age of 40. As Secretary, he engineered an historic paydown of U.S. debt, worked successfully to extend the life of the Social Security and Medicare trust funds, and led the effort to enact the most sweeping financial deregulation in 60 years.

Laura D'Andrea Tyson is currently Dean of the Haas School of Business at the University of California, Berkeley. She served as Chairman of the Council of Economic Advisers in the Clinton administration from January 1993 through December 1996 and as the President's National Economic Adviser between February 1995 and December 1996. Tyson was a key architect of President Clinton's domestic and international policy agenda during his first term in office. She managed economic policy-making as the administration's top economic adviser, serving as head of the White House National Economic Council. She published *Who's Bashing Whom? Trade Conflict in High-Technology Industries* (1992).

Hal R. Varian is the Dean of the School of Information Management and Systems at the University of California, Berkeley. He is also a Professor in the Haas School of Business, is a Professor in the Department of Economics, and holds the Class of 1944 Professorship. He is coauthor of a bestselling book on business strategy, *Information Rules: A Strategic Guide to the Network Economy,* and currently writes a monthly column for the *New York Times.*

W. Kip Viscusi is Professor of Law and Economics at the Harvard Law School. He has consulted to the U.S. Office of Management and Budget, the Environmental Protection Agency, the Occupational Safety and Health Administration, the Federal Aviation Administration, and the U.S. Department of Justice.

Murray Weidenbaum holds the Mallinckrodt Distinguished University Professorship at Washington University in St. Louis, where he also serves as Honorary Chairman of the University's Weidenbaum Center on the Economy, Government, and Public Policy. He served as chairman of the U.S. Trade Deficit Review Commission during 1999–2000. In 1981 and 1982 he was President Reagan's first chairman of the Council of Economic Advisers. During 1983–89 he was a member of the President's Economic Policy Advisory Board.

David W. Wilcox joined the official staff of the Federal Reserve Board as Deputy Director in the Division of Research and Statistics in January 2001. In his current capacity, Wilcox assists in the preparation of the economic forecast that is provided to the Federal Open Market Committee for each of its meetings. Immediately prior to joining the Federal Reserve, Wilcox served as Assistant Treasury Secretary for Economic Policy, from the middle of 1997 to the end of the Clinton administration in January 2001.

Robert Willig is Professor of Economics and Public Affairs at the Woodrow Wilson School at Princeton University. A former supervisor of economics research at Bell Laboratories, he is the coauthor of *Contestable Markets and the Theory of Industry Structure*. He served in the Antitrust Division of the U.S. Department of Justice as Deputy Assistant Attorney General for Economics, 1989–91.

Daniel Yergin is Chairman of Cambridge Energy Research Associates. He is coauthor of *The Commanding Heights: The Battle Between Government and the Marketplace That Is Remaking the Modern World*. Dr. Yergin received the Pulitzer Prize for General Nonfiction for his work *The Prize: The Epic Quest for Oil, Money, and Power*.

Richard J. Zeckhauser, Frank Plumpton Ramsey Professor of Political Economy at the Kennedy School of Government, Harvard University, pursues a mix of conceptual and applied research. The primary challenge facing society, he believes, is to allocate resources in accordance with the preferences of the citizenry.

Name Index

Subject Index